HENRY SMEATON:

A Jacobite Story

OF

THE REIGN OF GEORGE THE FIRST.

BY G. P. R. JAMES, ESQ.,

AUTHOR OF "THE OLD OAK CHEST," "THE WOODMAN," "THE FORGERY," "THE CONVICT,"
"RUSSELL," "RICHELIEU," "BEAUCHAMP," "GOWRIE,"
&c., &c., &c.

NEW YORK:
HARPER & BROTHERS, PUBLISHERS,
82 CLIFF STREET.

HENRY SMEATON.

CHAPTER I.

By the side of the large piece of water in the middle of St. James's Square—

"There is no large piece of water in St. James's Square. It is a very small one."

But there was at the time I speak of, namely, the year 1715; and if you will allow me to go on, you shall hear all about it.

By the side of the large piece of water in St. James's Square, looking at the playing of the fountain (which was afterward congealed into a great ugly statue), and watching the amusements of a gay boy and girl, who had come out of one of the houses—I think it was Lord Bathurst's—and were rowing about in the pleasure-boat on the water, stood a man of some six or seven-and-twenty years of age, dressed in a garb which did not very well indicate his profession, although the distinctions of costume were in those days somewhat closely attended to. His garments, of a sober color, were very plain, but very good. Especial care seemed to have been taken to avoid every thing in the least degree singular, or which could attract attention; and it was more easy to say what the wearer was not, than what he was. He was not a Presbyterian minister, although the cut and coloring of his clothing might have led one to believe that he was so; for he wore a sword. The same mark showed that he was not an artisan, but did not so precisely prove that he was not a trader; for more than one shop-keeper in those days assumed the distinctive mark of a higher class when he got from behind his counter and went into a part of the town where he was not known. Yet, had he been one of this butterfly tribe, the rest of his apparel would have seemed more in accordance with his assumed rank.

He was not a courtier; for where was the gold, and the lace, and the embroidery? He was not a physician; for there was no red roquelaure, no gold-headed cane; and who could pretend to call himself doctor without such appendages?

He seemed to have been riding too, for he had large boots on, and his hat and coat were somewhat dusty. In every other respect he was a very indefinite sort of personage; but yet, of three nursery-maids who passed him consecutively, taking out children for an airing, as it is called—as if there was any such thing as air in London—two turned their heads to have another look at his face, and one stopped by the posts which fenced the water, and, while affecting to contemplate the same objects as himself, gave a simpering look toward him, as if to intimate that she had no objection to a little pleasant conversation.

The hard-hearted young man, however, took no notice of her; and she walked on, thinking him a fool, in which she was mistaken.

The Square was now vacant for several minutes, longer, perhaps, than it ever is in the present day, or than it usually was then; but the fact is, that almost all the possessors of houses in the Square, the elder members of their families, and a considerable number of their servants, had gone down to Westminster, to hear the impeachment of Lord Bolingbroke and the Earl of Oxford. It is true, a footman would occasionally pass from one door to another; and a cook, with a night-cap on his head, an apron before him, and a knife at his side, was seen to ascend the area-steps of a house in the corner, and look out with an impatient expression of countenance, as if the fish had not arrived, or the butcher had failed in punctuality. The only other persons who appeared in the Square were, the stranger gazing at the children, the children in the boat, and an elderly gentleman who, under the name of tutor, had come out to watch them, but who, seated on a garden chair, had forgotten them, and Bolingbroke and Oxford, and every thing else on earth, in the pages of a book containing select fragments of Hesiod and Pindar.

The sun was shining brightly and warmly into the Square; the smoky fluid which Londoners mistake for air, tempered the light, and gave a misty softness to the surrounding objects; and altogether St. James's Square seemed a very pleasant sort of place, considering that it formed part of the suburbs of a great city.

There was nothing remarkable in any man staying there for a few minutes to look about him and enjoy himself, especially if he came through any of the dark dens in which commerce carries on her busy warfare in the heart of London; for the contrast was very great. But the stranger stayed more than a few minutes. A whole quarter of an hour elapsed without his changing his position, till at length a curious, fantastic-looking man, with a great quantity of ribbon at his knees and clothing of very gaudy colors, came up to his side, and spoke to him in a low tone.

The new-comer had some excuse for attempting to ornament his person; which, to say truth, greatly needed it. He was short, probably not more than five feet four inches in height; but he made up in width, especially across the hips, which would have required the full extent of a Dutchman's nether garment to cover them decently; and the late King William III., of blessed memory, might well have looked upon him with that favor which he is supposed to have bestowed very liberally upon his countrymen; not, indeed, that our friend came actually and personally from the shores of Holland, though he certainly looked very like a Dutchman. His features were large and by no means of the most delicate symmetry, the nose having been originally set somewhat awry on the face, and its obliquity being rendered more conspicuous by sundry warts, knots, and excrescences, with which, indeed, the whole of his countenance was amply provided. The eyes, however, were good, large, open, merry blue eyes; and, though certainly as ugly a personage as one could hope to see, there was yet something—strange to say—very winning in his look, notwithstanding the vast Ramillies wig by which he had contrived to add to his native ugliness.

Approaching from the side of Charing Cross, with a rolling, somewhat consequential step, this personage advanced to the stranger who had been standing in the Square, and accosted him in a familiar tone.

"It is settled, Master Smeaton," he said, speaking in a low voice. "They have carried it by a large majority. It would have done you good to be present. I never saw such attitudes."

"It would have been madness in me to go," replied the other. "Who moved the impeachment?"

"Why that depends upon which impeachment you mean," answered his companion. "Walpole moved against Bolingbroke, with one hand clapped in his coat pocket and the other stretched out for full five minutes, just like that of my nymph with the flower-basket. I could have sworn it had been cast in lead."

"Little use of impeaching Bolingbroke," observed the young man addressed as Smeaton. "He is safe enough, depend upon it; but it was not of him I thought. Bolingbroke, with all his abilities, is useless to any party, and would be detrimental to most. He has contrived to obtain a character for want of principle, which makes most men doubt and fear him."

"Principle, my dear sir!" said the other, with a low laugh, "what is the good of principle? 'Tis but an obstinate adherence to notions once acquired, after the circumstances have changed that rendered them worth having. Principle is a lane with a stone wall on each side and no room to turn the carriage. Principle is one of those cold, hard, stone statues which, when once broken, there's an end of; not like my dear divinities of lead, which, should any thing go wrong with them, I can throw into the melting-pot again and bring out in a new shape. No, no; give me, in ethics and in art, pliable materials which will make a Jupiter one day and a dancing faun the next; a Juno now, and then the Queen of Love. Principle, forsooth! Who has ever heard of principle since the blessed Restoration?"

The young man smiled and mused, and then asked abruptly: "But what of Oxford? Did *that* pass as easily?"

"O yes," replied his companion, "more so, if possible. The hounds are always more eager when the game is in sight. Lord Coningsby did it very well, with grave emphasis and a grand air. Ye gods and goddesses, how he did bespatter the noble earl! He must declare himself now, if ever."

"Is there any good in his declaring himself?" demanded Smeaton. "Many a man declares himself when it is too late. Twelve months ago, he might have done something; now, golden opportunity has slipped through his fingers, and he is powerless. Yet I do believe he is a profound, wise man, if it were not for that vacillating spirit, so often the stumbling-block of great abilities. I have a great mind to go back to France, Van Noost. I do not like my errand."

"Stay a while, stay a while," replied the other. "Just come with me, and you shall soon see whether Oxford is as powerless as you think. You shall have proof positive with your own eyes and ears. If he can but be got to speak and act, the power will not be wanting. I tell you," he added, in a lower tone, "fully three fifths of all England are firm Loyalists; and every third man among the Whigs, from Marlborough and Sunderland down to Townley and Chudleigh, would throw up their hats and cry, 'Long live King James!' if they did but see him in the way of prospering. All the common people, too, are of one mind."

"Ah, the fickle commons!" said Smeaton, thoughtfully putting his arm through that of his companion. "Where are you going to take me?"

"Only down to the cock-pit," replied Van Noost, "to see Oxford return from the House."

"Was he there?" asked Smeaton, in a tone of some surprise.

"Yes," answered his companion. "He came down early to the House in case the bill should be brought up at once; and there he sat as cool as a watering-pot. But he must be coming away now, since his impeachment is voted, and a committee appointed to draw up the articles."

"He shows firmness in these dangerous circumstances, at least," remarked Smeaton. "Perhaps he may be inclined to show vigor also."

While thus speaking, they had entered Pall Mall, which presented a very different appearance from that which it displays in the present day, as well as from that which it had borne half a century before. There were no longer double rows of trees on the one side, and detached houses, with scattered gardens, on the other; but the buildings were still very irregular, and occasionally an open piece of ground, with a tall poplar or two, intervened between a princely mansion—such as Marlborough House or Schomberg House—and a common inn, such as the Sugar-loaf or Richards's Tavern.

As Pall Mall was at this time a favorite place of residence for strangers visiting the metropolis, the thoroughfare was somewhat crowded, and numerous sedan-chairs were passing along, carrying gentlemen to visits or to chocolate-houses. The foot-path, though famous for its mud in wet weather, was now quite dry, and the feet of the chairmen, as they trotted along in the middle of the road, raised clouds of dust very inconvenient to the eyes.

It might be this circumstance which caused Van Noost's companion to press his hat further over his brows as he entered this street, and quicken his pace, to the discomposure of the other's somewhat jaunty steps. A distant shout, however, seemed to give wings to good Van Noost's feet; for, whispering, "Come on—come on here, across, or we shall be too late. He is issuing out of the House. I know the bark of those dirty muzzles well," he darted to the other side of the way, and, to the surprise of his companion, entered a dingy apothecary's shop, indicated by the sign of a golden pestle and mortar over the door.

"Good morning, Mr. Gingle," he said, to a man who was pounding something in a very large mortar, and raising an inconceivable smell. "Will you just let us pass by your back way into the park? My friend and I want to see the Earl of Oxford come up from the House."

"Go on, go on, Van Noost," replied the shop-keeper, sneezing into the mortar, and hardly raising his eyes. "You know the way; but don't leave the door open."

With this permission, the two companions hurried on through a little back parlor into a small yard behind the house, and thence by a door-way in the wall into a narrow passage which led them by some steps into the mall of the park.

As soon as they issued from between the brick walls, the roaring voice of the multitude was again heard, louder and nearer; and, hurrying forward, they passed up a narrow passage out of the park, the door of which, in the two former reigns, had been kept closed, but which was now generally left open as an entrance from the Spring Gardens. Thence, thridding numerous narrow passages among low pot-houses, mingled in a strange way with finer buildings, and crossing what was called Cromwell's Yard, they entered the world of coffee-houses and taverns which at that time occupied the space known by the name of Charing Cross. Carriages now roll over ground which, in those days, was covered with numerous dwellings; but the thoroughfare was not less crowded then than now; for the multitude, ever thronging to and fro, was compressed into a narrower space, and on that day especially the numbers were so great that it was hardly possible for any one to make his way along the street.

At the moment when the two whom we have mentioned more particularly were added to the rest of the human beings there assembled, a sort of compulsory motion was given to the crowd, some being driven forward in the direction of the Hay-market, and others pushed back against the houses behind them, by the advance of an enormous mob up the center or carriage-way of the street, in the midst of which might be seen, towering above the ocean of heads, a large, clumsy, but highly-ornamented carriage, drawn by four powerful horses. Hats were waving in the air, handkerchiefs fluttering from many a window, and several thousand voices were heard shouting all at once, and "making the welkin ring." Some cried one thing and some another, but the general meaning was alike.

One roared forth, "Oxford forever!" another, "High Church, High Church and Sacheverel!" another, "Down with the Whigs!" and then again might be heard "Ormond, the Duke of Ormond forever, and away with the Hanover rats!"

Not contented with thus asserting their own temporary opinions, the sturdy ruffians of the mob insisted that all persons whom they passed should give some sign of consenting to the same; and any one who hesitated seemed likely to be roughly handled.

"Off with your hat, and cry 'Oxford forever!'" roared one fellow in the garb of a sailor, approaching the spot where Van Noost and Smeaton stood.

The latter did not obey the injunction, but remained covered and silent. Van Noost, however, raised his hat and shouted readily, and the man passed on, swaggering and bawling with his companions, and following the carriage of the Earl of Oxford as it moved slowly forward.

The crowd of more respectable persons collected at both sides of the street began then to disperse, and Van Noost was turning round to walk away with Smeaton, when a sharp tap upon his shoulder made him suddenly pause and look behind him. At the same moment, a calm, clear voice, with a somewhat sarcastic tone, addressed him by name, saying,

"Well, my good friend Van Noost, you have shouted loudly for Harley to-day, which is generous, seeing that he has little chance of paying the obligation."

"Paid already, my good lord," replied Van Noost, turning round, not in the least discomposed, and addressing a thin, plainly-dressed man of the middle age. "He bought two nymphs and two dairy-maids of me no longer ago than this time twelve-month—size of life—dairy-maids with pails on their heads, nymphs with cornucopias in their hands, to say nothing of a little black boy with a dolphin to be put in the middle of a fountain. Surely I am bound to cry 'Long live the Earl of Oxford!' If your lordship will patronize me in the like manner—and should you chance to get into a scrape so as to win the applause of the mob, I will throw up my hat and roar, 'Long live the Earl of Stair!' with the best of them."

"Well, well," replied the earl, with a smile, "only take care what you are doing, my good friend; for, though being whipped for a libel has often made a bookseller's fortune, yet the being sent to Newgate for sedition would not greatly benefit a leaden figure-maker, I imagine."

"I did it on compulsion, noble lord," replied Van Noost, in an indifferent tone. "I make it a point never to quarrel with a mob; for I am a curious piece of statuary, not so easily mended as one of my own figures; and I don't believe any king on earth would help to mend me if I chanced to get head or bone broken by resisting the rabble. Would you not have done the same in my place?"

"No," replied the earl, who seemed for some reason willing to prolong the conversation. "I should have done just as this worthy gentleman who is with you did; kept my hat on, and remained silent. Besides, my good friend, your leanings are well known, although one would have thought that the son of jolly old Van Noost, who came over with King William, would not have inherited a vast store of Jacobitism."

"It was my mother's property I came into," replied Van Noost, with a laugh; "for, though my father was a Dutchman, my mother was a thorough Englishwoman, Betsy Hall by name. My father never meddled with politics, good man; but my mother was a stanch Tory, and a wise one; for she always cried when there was any thing to be got, and held her tongue when there was no use in crying. But how happens your lordship to be on foot among the rabble?" he continued, moving as if to pass the earl, who was right in his way. "Have you not been down to the House to see these gay doings?"

"Not I," replied the Earl of Stair. "My business is to stop intrigues, and not to mix with them."

"A hard cut, that, at your friends, my lord," said Van Noost, bowing low, and taking off his hat. "Bob Walpole wouldn't thank you, I think."

While this short conversation had been going on, the Earl of Stair had more than once directed his eyes, with a quiet, inquiring glance, toward Van Noost's companion. That personage, however, had, in an easy manner, without the slightest appearance of effort, contrived to keep his face averted, till the movement of Van Noost in advance obliged him to pass the earl, who then got a full but momentary view of his countenance. The two then walked on; and as soon as they were five or six steps distant, Lord Stair beckoned to a man who was standing at the door of the Rummer tavern, and on his running up, whispered to him,

"Follow the two persons with whom I have been speaking; see whither they go, and watch, for a little, if they soon separate. Then come and tell me."

Without a word of reply, the man glided away, and soon gained sight of Van Noost and Smeaton as they walked on. He kept at a certain distance behind them, dogged them round the corners of streets, sometimes crossed over the way, and watched them from the opposite side, sometimes even passed them, and then stopped to look at something that seemed to attract his attention. As the crowd in the streets diminished, however, his office became more difficult of execution; and his maneuvers were speedily detected by a quick eye that was upon him.

"There is a man following us, Van Noost," said Smeaton, in a low tone, just as they were entering Piccadilly. "He has dogged us ever since we left Charing Cross."

"He is watching you, not me," answered Van Noost, with a laugh. "My character and domicil are too well known to need watching. See what it is to have an established reputation. But you must not go home, for that might be dangerous. Come on to my little place: I will provide you such dinner as I can give, and will get you out the back way after dark. In the mean time, we can talk over what is next to be done with Oxford."

The other did not reply, but walked on with his companion. They took their way straight up Piccadilly, which was then still frequently called the Reading Road. Toward the top of the Hay-market, Piccadilly bore somewhat the appearance of a street, although a great number of the first houses were inns for the accommodation of strangers coming to London; but as one proceeded in a westerly direction, the country gained the day over the town, and Piccadilly wore much the appearance of that suburb called Kensington Gore. On the right hand especially were many splendid mansions, surrounded by large gardens, affecting a rural air, commencing, I believe, with the houses of Sir John Clarges and Lady Stanhope, and going on with Queensbury House, Burlington House, Sir Thomas Bond's house (through part of which has been carried the well-known Bond-street), Berkeley House, with its splendid garden, and several others, built and decorated at an expense and with a degree of luxury far beyond the means of any but a very few of our wealthiest countrymen of the present day.

Beyond these splendid mansions, as the two walked on toward Hyde Park, came a very different class of houses, not in continuous rows, though here and there two or three were even then beginning to lean their shoulders together as if for mutual support. Between the buildings were still gardens, and even fields; and the houses themselves seldom soared above the rank of the dwelling of some inferior artist, or some low public house or wagoner's inn, of which last there was an immense number, under signs which are still perpetuated in the names of streets: the Half Moon, the Black Horse, the White Horse, the Crown, the Dog and Duck, etc. Round the doors of these, and on the benches before them, a number of people were congregated, all talking and debating, and generally discussing politics; for the Englishman has been, during many ages, rather a political than a politic animal, easily led in any course, it is true, by one who knows his weak points, but having a wonderfully good opinion of his own capacity notwithstanding, and firmly convinced that he is fit for the rule and governance of states. The names of Harley, Ormond, Bolingbroke, Walpole, Coningsby, Cowper, met the ear at every step; but, without apparently taking any notice, Smeaton and his companion walked on, still dogged by the man who had been set to watch their proceedings, and who kept on the other side of the way, under shadow of the trees.

About a hundred yards beyond the grove of trees surrounding the reservoir, but on the other side of the Reading Road, they came to a house, standing a little back, with a paved court before it, and of which the upper half of the lower and the lower half of the upper windows were covered by an immense sheet of painted canvas, representing a variety of curious looking utensils mingled with figures of men and women, some in a state of nudity, and some clothed in the quaint and starched fashion of the day, while an inscription underneath announced that Jacob Harris constructed, repaired, and kept in order fountains of every kind, size, and description, and made chairs and garden-seats, ruined temples and summer-houses, with various other devices for the ornamenting of parks, pleasure-grounds, and gardens. The description of his talents was long and minute; but Van Noost seemed to hold them in but small esteem; for, as he passed by, and cast his eyes upon the inscription, he said, with a sort of grunt,

"Ha! he's forced to come to me for all his statuary. He can't do that."

Some three or four hundred yards further on, every step giving the country greater predominance over the town, and a little on this side of the spot where Apsley House now stands, was a small dwelling of two low stories, retreating from the high road, and having a garden before it of about a quarter of an acre in extent. This garden was ornamented with various fruit-trees, the medlar, the mulberry, and the ditch-loving elder-tree, notorious for its wine; but the principal decoration consisted in a whole host of figures, as large as life, cast in lead, and by no means ill executed. One might have thought that a living mob had taken possession of the garden, had not the heterogeneous costume of the figures themselves denoted their real nature. Almost all of them were painted "to the life." Here were soldiers presenting their firelocks as if in the act of shooting at you; dairy maids and country lasses with baskets on their heads, long boddices, and gowns tucked through the pocket-holes; mowers whetting their scythes—old Time among the rest; negroes kneeling and supporting sun-dials; "very black and beautiful," as dear Washington Irving says in his negro cosmogony; to say nothing of fair-skinned nymphs as naked as they were born. The garden was shut in from the road by a rustic fence, with a small gate in the center; and before that gate Van Noost stopped, and opened it for his companion to pass in.

As soon as Smeaton had entered the garden, the statuary (for so I suppose we must call him) paused and looked round. He instantly perceived the man who had followed them planted on the opposite side of the way; and, carefully locking the gate, he followed his companion through his grove of leaden figures, pointing out to him, with the mingled affection of a parent and an artist, the various excellences of his own productions. He had no modesty upon the subject—it was a quality, indeed, which did not greatly embarrass him on any subject, and probably Praxiteles did not value the immortal works of his hand, whether in marble or ivory, so highly as Jacob Van Noost estimated his own productions.

"See that Apollo," he exclaimed, pointing to a figure of the Belvidere God. "I have caught the fire and the spirit, you see; and as for the grace, I think I may venture to say that the little elevation which I have given to the left arm greatly increases it, as well as the dignity."

Smeaton walked on with more speed than was quite flattering to his companion. He was a good-natured creature, however, Van Noost; and he merely gave his shoulders a slight shrug, hurried his own pace, and, arriving before the other at the little old green blistered door, threw it open to give him admission, pointing with his hand, at the same time, to the entrance of a small parlor, the clean-washed and neatly-sanded floor of which you reached by descending a single step. He then shut and locked the house door, hung up his hat upon a peg behind it, and, entering the parlor, placed a chair for his guest with a low bow, saying,

"Here you are safe, my lord, and here you had better remain till the gray of the evening. Ay, your noble father often sat in that chair, speaking bad Dutch against my father's bad English, examining his beautiful models, and choosing out such as he wished to possess."

CHAPTER II.

We will now move, for a while, to a far-distant scene, and go back to a somewhat earlier period of the year; for, having a violent objection to all stiff rules, I can not even consent to bind myself by the very good advice of Count Antoine Hamilton: "*Mon ami, toujours commencez par le commencement;*" in which he differed from Horace, and a great many wonderful men of old.

On the western coast of England, and in one of the most beautiful parts of that beautiful coast, is a spot which I must describe, not only for the benefit of those who may profit by it, or of those who may love to identify any place they read of with some place which they remember or imagine, but because many of the principal events of my tale occurred in the midst of that precise scene. Those who know the sea-board of Devonshire will, I think, have no difficulty in recognizing the locality from certain distinctive marks.

The place to which I allude is a little bay, taking somewhat the form of a horse-shoe, and indenting the land deeply. It is formed by a high headland, on the southwestern side, which shelters it from the prevailing winds. The face of this promontory, to its very extreme point, is one precipitous cliff of cold gray stone, varying from six to nine hundred feet in height, rugged and broken indeed, but apparently pathless; and bold would be the man who should attempt to scale it, still bolder he who should seek to descend from the height above. This is called Ale Head; and the opposite limb of the bay consists of another promontory, not so steep or precipitous indeed, but still lofty and scarped enough, which bears the name of Ale Down. Neither does it project so far into the sea from the general line of coast, which trends away to the eastward at no very abrupt angle. Protected thus on three sides by very high ground, and with only a somewhat narrow opening in one direction, the waters of that bay, during the greater part of the year, are as soft and tranquil as a dream of Heaven; but they are very deep also, for the cliffs run down far below the low-water mark. Standing on the heights above, I have looked down, and beheld the sea lying beneath my feet as smooth as a mirror and as blue as a sapphire. A hundred-gun ship could anchor in that bay, within pistol-shot of the cliffs of Ale Head.

Between the higher promontory and the lower, however, is a deep dell. I must not call it a valley, for the sides are too steep, and the concavity too narrow to admit of that name. Down this dell flows a strong deep stream of beautifully clear water, over a rocky bed, from which a large quantity of sand is carried down, forming a soft, dry landing-place where the dell opens upon the bay. This little beach is not at all extensive, being, from the foot of the rock on the one side to the base of the hill on the other, not more than two hundred yards wide, and perhaps forty in depth. Through the center of it flows the stream into the sea, and twice a day ocean comes up to meet its tributary, covering by far the greater part of the sands.

There were then, and are now—at least I have never seen it without—some five or six boats hauled up on the shore, giving the first intimation which one receives on entering Ale Bay from the seaward that that wild and lonely scene has human habitations near. But so it is; and on each side of the little river, commencing at about a hundred yards from the mouth, and ending about a quarter of a mile further up the dell, are built a number of fishermen's cottages, pressed between the steep hill side on the one hand and the deep banks of the stream on the other. At various places down the dell, too, little bridges are built across from bank to bank—sometimes merely the trunk of a tree flattened on the side that lies uppermost, sometimes an ill-turned arch of roughly-hewn stone. These are all foot-bridges, I need hardly say; for horse, cart, or carriage never, I believe, ventured so far down the valley.

The next object, speaking of human life, which you see after the boats, on entering the bay, is the end of the lowest fisherman's hut peeping out through the opening of the valley; but a moment or two afterward, as you pull on, you will perceive upon the side of the hill to the southwest, if you raise your eyes in that direction, the gables and chimneys of a large old mansion, rising above a wood of considerable extent and luxuriance, which clothes the valley nearly to the shore, for in that favored climate vegetation does not shrink from the sea air, and at no great distance may be seen the trees actually dipping their branches in the waves.

They wisely eschew, however, the cutting winds upon the hill top; and the high summit of Ale Head is as bare as the back of a tortoise, and well-nigh as brown.

We must look a little more closely at the mansion, however. Let us suppose, then, that we have landed by the side of the stream, crossed the dry sands, and entered the little dell, with light clouds floating rapidly overhead, and making the blue bay, and the gray cliffs, and the brown downs above, sparkle with gleams like the sweet transitory hopes that brighten, as they pass, the hard, stern features of this earthly life. Oh ye bright visions of imagination, could one but grasp and arrest ye for an hour, how much happier, how much better might man be! what a different thing were life! But ye are of air, and only given us, in this stormy scene, to assure the sad and tempest-beaten heart that there is still sunshine above the clouds.

Walking on before the fishermen's cottages, along the very, very narrow path, we come to a spot where the road extends, but is no longer carried on upon both sides of the stream. It mounts, too; the valley becomes less deep, more wide. The left, or southwestern side, is covered with wood; the right slopes up sharply, clothed with short, green sward. Suddenly, at about half a mile from the bay, a road branches off to the left, while that which you have been pursuing by the bank of the stream widens out and becomes a good, sound carriage-road. We must take the left-hand road, however, which, forming an acute angle with the path by which we have arrived, seems as if its ultimate point, or terminus, as we should now corruptly call it, was destined to be the very highest and furthest part of the promontory of Ale Head. But it has no such ambitious notions; and, after rising somewhat abruptly for a little way, it runs on toward the sea, with a very slight inclination upward, winding through the wood till, with a sharp turn to the right, it passes between two gates of hammered iron-work, supported upon stone columns, with large, round globes on the top. Then come two or three little glades in a slight hollow of the hill, and then the old mansion, standing on a somewhat higher point. How can one describe it? It is but a collection of innumerable gables, and walls, and windows, built in the reign of Elizabeth, added to in the reign of James, left to go to decay during the Commonwealth, repaired and re-decorated under Charles II. It is all of the gray stone of the country; but the sea air, and the proximity of the woods, have tinged it with many colors, so that its aspect is not that of a venerable old man who has passed his life in peace and tranquillity, but rather like the weather-beaten face of an old sailor, bronzed and tinted by the wind and tempests.

Within are many rooms and many passages; flights of steps go down, apparently, merely for the purpose of going up again; and you are continually meeting doors and new rooms where nobody expected them. But many of these rooms are very handsome—spacious, lofty, and well formed; and though, to say the truth, they would be more lightsome and cheerful were they not generally paneled with walnut or black oak, yet there is something fine and impressive in that dark, carved wainscoting; and when the sunshine steals in and brightens it, it is like a sweet smile upon the face of age.

In one of these large, handsome rooms upon the first floor above the ground, on a spring day in 1715, sat a girl of about eighteen years of age, in the dress of a high-born lady of that time. I need not, and had better not, describe it; for it was as stiff and ugly a costume as ever was invented by the capricious taste of man. The character of an epoch is always displayed in the dress of the generation; and what could be expected from the dry gallantry of Louis the Fourteenth's latter days, and the stiff decorum of George the First's? Nevertheless, the most hard and unbending garments in which that fair form could be encased could never have repressed its wild grace, or shackled its free, light movements. Her maid complained that she burst more boddice laces than any lady in the country; and it is a certain fact, that her hair contrived to disentangle itself from combs and fillets, and sport in the wind like wreaths of smoke, more frequently than she herself wished or even knew. How it happened she could not tell, and she gave herself no great trouble to inquire; for her mind was often wandering after other things, sometimes with the eager sportiveness of a child after a butterfly, sometimes with steady and untiring thought, like a wayfarer on a long journey.

It must be said, too, in justice to her good taste, that she abhorred the vile fashions of the day in which she lived, and would often stand and contemplate the portraits of Vandyke, of which there were several in the house, or other older pictures still, and wonder by what curious process the mind of man had been led to abandon what is flowing and beautiful for that which is rigid and ugly. There was a refuge, however, even in the costume of those times, which saved part of the day from being spent in durance vile, and this was in what ladies called their night-clothes. The term, it is true, was a deceit; and the words "night-clothes" meant merely a light and easy morning-dress, in which they often spent the early hours of the day before they dressed for parks and promenades. It was put on as soon as they rose in the morning, in exchange for the garments in which they had really passed the night. Sometimes they even went out in those wrongly called "night-clothes" before the conventional hour for appearing in public had arrived.

The young lady I have brought before the reader sat a little out of the sunbeams, which, pouring in, and painting the floor with moving tracery, fell also over the table before her; but her eyes could reach the blue sky, and catch the clouds wafted over it, as with silent speed they hurried along upon the wings of the wind. It was very still and quiet, in that wide, high room. The birds could be heard singing without; the busy little flies, those most wonderful pieces of mechanism, buzzed about the windows; and a clock at the top of the stairs ticked faintly. But these were all the sounds, and they seemed only to soothe the silence.

The lady stirred not, spoke not, but sat with her elbow leaning on the table, her cheek, warmly tinged with the rose, resting upon her white hand, the "fringed curtains of her eyes" raised up, and the bright, soft hazel orbs themselves elevated toward the deep sunshiny heavens. A book was on the table, but she read it not. There was a mandolin in the corner, but she touched it not. Her thoughts were very busy, and her heart was with her thoughts. Yet the images, the questions, the answers which were presented to her mind touched not upon those topics which any one who did not know her would suppose. She was in the bright expanding time of life, the spring of existence, when the opening bosom of the rose courts the bee. But yet she thought not of love. She knew it not—hardly by name, not at all by sensation, although the young heart will yearn for that which was the only want in Eden's garden when Adam was first formed. It was not of the gay ball, the play, the promenade, or any of the fashionable amusements of the day, for of them she was as ignorant as of love; but problems which have puzzled many an aged philosopher were present to her mind, though not stated in the most philosophical manner. Wildly and strangely they rose, like the fantastic forms of clouds; and she chased them eagerly in thought, as a child chases the fleeting shadows that mock his speed.

"What am I?" she asked herself. "Of what strange elements composed? Body and spirit, soul and mind! What are these things? Is the body the spirit's slave, or the spirit's jailer —servant or master? I can perceive nothing but what it will permit me to perceive. Through its means must be all my communications with things animate or inanimate. There it rules and triumphs. There it is the tyrant, the jailer; and yet I can close my eyes, and the spirit, as if free from its hard bondage, can wing its flight afar into that bright blue sky, and question the heavens as to what is between myself and them. Can it be that the human race is the great pausing point of God's creation, and that between us and Him there is one vast void, untenanted, inanimate? Or is yonder wide expanse of air, the stars, the heavens, the universe, peopled with beings that I see not? Are there spirits in those clouds that skim like ivory chariots through the sky? Are there creatures of light and joy, now sporting with the sun-beams, or resting under the green leaves of the wood? If so, is it possible that there is no means of communication between me and them, that this body is a barrier between the spirit that I feel within it, and the host of spirits thronging around me? Strange, strange existence! what art thou, what am I?"

On went the mind in the same course, inquiring, eager, keen, but untutored and unsatisfied. All the great problems of human existence seemed to crowd upon imagination, and demand an answer from that which can not give it.

These were strange thoughts for a girl of eighteen; but yet, perhaps, not unnatural for a quick and active spirit in the circumstances which surround her. The heart had no occupation to give, and it was impossible that imagination could rest idle. They were strange thoughts certainly, but such were the thoughts of Emmeline.

She was without companionship. She had none whom she could call friends around her. The poor fishermen of the village of Ale were her nearest neighbors. There was none in the house with her with whom she could exchange thought. It had been so during many years; and her mind carried her back to little else than the same state. Far, far away, in the distant past, images like phantoms were seen by the eye of memory—sweet and pleasant images too, but faint and ill defined: beings that she loved, forms that hung over her with affection, voices that sounded musical even in remembrance; but she saw them as through a glass: she could not approach nearer; she could not trace them more distinctly. It was like the sight of a distant land beheld across the sea, pleasant to view, but not to be reached, with the waves flowing between the beholder and it.

After that, and after a succeeding period of darkness, in which she perceived nothing, the figure of a venerable old man, the poor curate of the parish, came on her memory. She remembered him well. He had taught her much, and had seemed to regard her with peculiar tenderness and affection. He had instructed her to think, and to delight in thought; to read, and to ponder on what she read; for she had never received what may be called the trifling parts of a woman's education. Masters, it is true, had been procured for her from neighboring towns; but they were dull, heavy, material teachers. The only one who had really instructed her was that old clergyman. But now he was gone, and she was without a guide; for the man who had succeeded was a fat and jovial priest, who loved the material much more than the mental, and whose weekly sermon laid a heavier burden on the shoulders of his spirit than it was well able to bear. He sought not to acquire or to communicate knowledge, except as to where good wine was given or good punch brewed, or where and at what hour the savory haunch was roasted.

I have said that the old clergyman had taught her much; but there was one subject on which he had taught her nothing—her own fate and history. He had studiously avoided it, suffering—perhaps unwillingly, but still intentionally —the facts of the past to drop from memory. She had sometimes inquired, it is true, but he had always stopped her gravely; and circumstances had occurred to make her think, even at the early age of fourteen, which she had reached when he died, that he had been bound by some promise to forbear all such information. She even sometimes suspected that his silence as to her history was part of a compact—the condition on which he was permitted to visit and instruct her.

But with whom was the compact? Probably with that swarthy man who is now walking on the terrace below, booted and spurred as for a journey, and waiting for his horses to be brought round. There is nothing very remarkable in his appearance. His face is not forbidding, his features not ill formed, though the eyes are perhaps somewhat too near together, and the pupils too small, as if they were always in excess of light. He is about the middle height, stout, but not corpulent, and perhaps fifty years of age. His air and manner are those of a gentleman, his dress rich and costly. He is altogether a good-looking middle-aged man, but with a certain look of overshrewdness that might perhaps warn men to be careful in their dealings with him. This is Sir John Newark, the possessor of Ale Manor-House and estates.

Emmeline could not remember when she had first seen him. It was too far back for memory; but she knew that she was not his child. She *felt* it too; and he always called himself her guardian. By that term he did not mean her tyrant, for he was kind to her, as kind as a man of a cold, calculating, selfish nature could be. Nor was he altogether an unpleasant companion; for, though he had not the slightest spark of imagination, and fancy with him was a bird without wings—though he could not even comprehend the existence of imagination in others, and still less any of the generous and thoughtless impulses of the heart—yet he had a good stock of information upon many subjects, conversed well, and had seen a great deal of the world.

He did not in the least understand the character of Emmeline; but yet, as I have said, he was kind to her, and even indulgent. She had her horses to ride, her servants to attend upon her. She was allowed to roam about, through the woods, over the hills, down to the fishermen's cottages, and even to the neighboring towns. All the restraints he placed upon her were such as the customs of society in that day justified, if they did not require. She was not permitted to visit any house unless accompanied by an elderly woman, whom he had placed about her, and who acted the part of duenna with much skill and discretion. When she went to the small town of Seaford, she was always well accompanied, and was never out of sight of some one, except while in Ale Manor-House or Park. There she was at full liberty, and she enjoyed it.

It must not be supposed that she thought Sir John's restraints very hard: she knew that they were in some degree customary, and he had always good reasons to give for every regulation. He would often talk with her on such subjects in the evening, when they sat alone; but there were two or three points which he strove to impress strongly upon her mind, and which created doubts and inquiries, for I must not call them suspicions. He had a great dislike to foreigners, no matter what their class; and when any even of the fishermen or smugglers from the coast of France visited the little village of Ale, as was sometimes the case, he enjoined Emmeline strictly to hold no communication with them, but to keep herself within the walls of the Park, and to receive nothing from their hands, even though sent as a present.

"You are not fond of gauds or laces, Emmeline," he would say, "that I know right well; but you might think it discourteous to refuse any little gift, presented with the grace which all these men have. Remember, however, these things are never offered without an object, and that generally an evil one."

At first, when she was very young, she listened to these injunctions with unquestioning reverence; but as she grew older and read much, she began first to doubt whether he was not prejudiced, and then, from his constant recurrence to the same theme, to imagine that he had some motive which he did not utter; for she had already discovered, by his dealings with others, that he seldom acted or spoke without a personal object. We too often forget that we teach children our own characters, as well as other things, and that each day is a lesson.

One evening, when perhaps such thoughts were in her mind, she said, in a musing sort of way, that she should like to see foreign lands and foreigners in their own country. The start that he gave alarmed her; but he answered nothing at the time, remaining, during the whole of the rest of the evening, in deep and somewhat gloomy reverie.

The night following, however, he returned to the subject himself, speaking in a grave but kindly tone, and evidently upon a plan. It seemed as if he had made up his mind to enter upon a subject which he would rather have avoided, and had weighed every word he was to utter.

"You told me last night, Emmeline," he said, "that you should like to visit foreign countries. You know not what you wish, my child. To do so would be your destruction."

"Then I will wish it no longer," she answered, with a bright look, followed by a momentary shade as she added, "But I did not know, I had not heard, that foreigners were so wicked, or their lands so evil. Indeed, I had read of many a high and noble act among them, and fancied they were much like Englishmen, only speaking another tongue."

"Far different, Emmeline, and far inferior," answered Sir John Newark; "but if that were all, I should little care, and would take you readily to some gay foreign court to let you judge of the difference."

"I have seen no courts as yet," replied Emmeline, "and little wish to see them."

"You shall soon," said her guardian; "for it is needful that every woman should see courts who is destined to move in the higher sphere of life. But to return to what I was saying: to visit foreign lands might be—nay, inevitably would be—your destruction. Some time ere long, and certainly when you marry, I will tell you the whole history of your family. It would be improper now to do so; but this much I may tell you, that there are pertinacious enemies of your race living beyond the seas, whose anxious, dearest wishes would be gratified if they could but get you into their power."

"What would they do with me?" asked Emmeline, simply.

The question seemed to puzzle him, and he paused for an instant in dark meditation.

"I can not tell," he said; "but all I know is, that they have ruined many by their schemes. You are the last that remains to destroy. They might indeed," he added, in a thoughtful, considering tone, "they might indeed, in consideration of your youth and innocence, restrain themselves to shutting you up in a convent, never to come forth again."

"That would be worse than death," replied Emmeline.

But he went on, not seeming to listen to her.

"Their object might be attained by that means as well as by others, and it is probably the course they would take, if they could make all so sure and irrevocable that no chance of your ever appearing again in the world would be left. If they could put you to this living death, they might be content."

Emmeline shuddered, and gazed at him with a look of fear.

"My only care is for you, dear child," he went on to say. "So long as I live, I will defend and protect you. When you are married, your husband, whoever he may be, will do the same; but till then, be warned, my Emmeline. Avoid, as you would a person with the plague, all persons from beyond the seas; for there is no art nor violence to which your enemies would not have recourse, if they saw even a chance of success. Hitherto *I* have guarded you, and will continue to do so; but you are old enough now to take precautions on your own behalf. I have warned you of the danger: keep it ever in mind, and strive to avoid it by every means in your power."

Emmeline answered not, but remained with her eyes cast down and her fair brow bent, as if in earnest thought, till he asked, somewhat sharply,

"Do you hear me, Emmeline? I said, 'Strive to avoid this danger by every means.'"

"I will—I will indeed," exclaimed Emmeline, clasping her hands together; but the next instant she burst into tears and ran out of the room.

Her guardian's only observation to himself was,

"It has had more effect than I expected; but it is quite as well."

Great indeed was the effect, for it produced the first fear her mind had ever known. She was not aware till then that she had an enemy upon earth. Every human being seemed to love her; all had been kind to her; even the rude, dull, obtuse son of her guardian, a lad about seventeen years of age, somewhat deficient in intellect, was fond of, and gentle with her; when at home (which was seldom, for he was kept at a school in London in the hope of strengthening and brightening his dull and feeble mind), Emmeline could do any thing with him. He would sit beside her, choosing by preference a footstool near her feet, listening to all she said, talking to her in return, and seeming to gain some brightness from her light. All had seemed friendly to her, all had seemed kind. But now she found she had an enemy—an enemy of the most dark and irreconcilable kind—an enemy without a cause. It was very terrible to her; and even the vagueness of the information she had received—the dark, obscure hints, which merely shadowed forth the passions, and the danger, and the person, added to the horror. It was in vain she attempted to nerve her heart against all fears, or to scan the things which surrounded her in order to discover where any real peril lay, and of what nature it was: her mind was like a timid person wandering in the dark, and casting his eyes round only to find objects of terror for the sight of fancy. All she knew was that she had an enemy, dark, mysterious, malignant; but that was quite enough to depress, and agitate, and terrify her.

The heart of youth, however, has a restorative power which does not easily fail, and the effect of the words which had been spoken to her, though permanent, was greatly softened during the two or three months which had passed since their utterance. She had taken refuge in thoughts and fancies; she had read more than before, dreamed more—waking, I mean—and had found solace in such occupations. She confined herself more to the park, however; seemed anxious to have more people with her when she went beyond its precincts; and kept altogether to the house, unbidden, for two whole days, when she was told that a foreign cutter was in Ale Bay. Her guardian remarked this conduct, and was well pleased; and now, when he was setting out for London upon business which seemed of importance, from the thoughtful brow which he bore for two days before his departure, he left her, convinced that the apprehensions which he had instilled would act as perfect safeguards during his absence. As she sat there, gazing up toward the sky, Emmeline did not know that he was actually about to depart, for he was not fond of leave-takings, and seldom said farewell when he went away. A minute or two after, however, she heard the sound of the feet of several horses, and, running to the window, saw Sir John Newark in the act of mounting, with two or three servants around him, and a pack-horse held by a man on foot. Her guardian raised his eyes to the window as soon as he was in the saddle, and Emmeline waved her hand, saying "Adieu!" He merely nodded his head, however, and rode away, leaving her the mistress of the house, and *apparently* of her own actions.

CHAPTER III.

WE must now return to the little parlor of Van Noost, the leaden-statue maker, and suppose that an hour or two has passed since we left him and his companion there together. We have but paused, indeed, to tell a story by the way. In the mean time, Van Noost had rolled about from one part of his house to the other, eager to show every sort of hospitality and attention to his guest. He had called a somewhat buxom cook to conference in his workshop, and had whispered instructions and directions to a man and two or three boys who aided him in his labors, and who instantly issued forth, by the back door of the house, upon what may justly be termed a foraging expedition, taking their way toward Mayfair and Shepherd's market; though be it understood that Mayfair then actually consisted of fields, on which the fair, till within late years, had been held. In the immediate neighborhood were a number of public houses, taverns, and eating-shops, of which one was the notorious Dog and Duck.

Notwithstanding all the precautions he had taken, good Van Noost thought fit to apologize beforehand for the scantiness and meanness of the only fare which he should have to set before his distinguished guest; but Smeaton laughed lightly, laying his hand upon Van Noost's shoulder, and saying,

"I should be little worthy of the name of a soldier, my good friend, if I could not appreciate the excellence of horse-flesh and dead cat in a besieged fortress, in which light I suppose we may look upon your house, as you have taken the pains to lock the door. Whatever you can give me will be very acceptable; for, to say sooth, I had so much to do this morning that I have not broken my fast."

The meal, when it was set upon the table, however, belied Van Noost's disparaging excuses. It was not only abundant, but very savory, although there was an hereditary smack of Dutch cookery in the dishes which might not have recommended them in general to English palates. Wine Van Noost had none, but the beer was very good; and after dinner, the worthy entertainer produced from a cupboard in the corner a large black bottle, with a neck like a crane and a body like a goose, which he pressed upon his companion, assuring him that it was filled with genuine old Dutch cinnamon, the like of which was not to be found in England. As the liquor was potent, however, and Smeaton thought he might as well keep his head cool, he declined the spirit, and left Van Noost to enjoy it himself.

Looking out through the low window after the meal was over, Smeaton cast his eyes up and down the road before the house, and then, turning to Van Noost, remarked,

"That man is no longer there, and I think I might as well take my departure."

"Oh, he is hanging about somewhere near, depend upon it, my lord," replied Van Noost. "I beseech you not to hazard yourself in the street till after dark. They will track you home, to a certainty; and then the first thing that greets you to-morrow may be a warrant for the Tower."

Smeaton seemed to entertain no great apprehension of such a result, remarking that with him there was no pretense for so violent a step.

"I would not willingly have them discover my abode, however," he remarked, "for they might hamper my movements. I think I shall return to France at once, Van Noost," he added, thoughtfully.

"Not surely before you have seen Lord Oxford?" said the other, with a look of surprise.

"Perhaps not," answered Smeaton; "but that can be done to-night. The letter I bear will gain me admission at any hour, without raising suspicion in him or any other person as to my real business."

"And even then, my good lord," observed Van Noost, "if I might humbly be permitted to advise, you would still wait a while—not in London, not in London, but in some quiet country place, where you would not be known, and yet could receive intelligence of all that passes, and be ready for any occasion. I am but a poor statuary, it is true, better acquainted with the arms of Apollo and the ankles of Venus than with the limbs of policy; but still I think it is better to be on the spot, especially when there is no real danger. At all events, you would be able to judge more of the temper of the people and the chances of success."

"I have judged of the temper of the people already," replied Smeaton, with a significant smile; "I mean, of the people of London. I might, indeed, see something more of the country gentlemen, though I much doubt their wit if not their wishes, their discretion rather than their devotion. As to the population of this city, the mob that we saw shouting 'Long live Oxford!' would in three months shout as gayly at his execution."

"Ay, ay," remarked Van Noost; "the people are always fickle, I know well. The time may come when even leaden statues may be out of fashion." And he sighed deeply at the very thought of such a catastrophe.

At that moment something seemed to catch Smeaton's eye, as he still stood near the window looking out into the road. His face became eager, his brow knitted, his eyes flashed, his lips curled, and his nostrils expanded. The next instant he threw up the sash, leaped out into the garden, crossed it at a run (knocking down two leaden soldiers and a wood-nymph), vaulted over the rustic fence, and exclaiming vehemently, "How dare you strike that boy so cruelly, sir?" caught by the collar a man who had just knocked down, with a tremendous blow, a young lad in gentlemanly attire, who still lay upon the ground as if stunned. Smeaton shook the man violently; and the latter replied, in a sharp and insolent tone, struggling to get free,

"Why did he switch my leg, then, and dirt all my stockings?"

"A mere accident," answered Smeaton. "He came up the road, swinging his cane about, and merely touched you by accident. Stand still! You shall not go till I know who is your master. The boy is bleeding."

"I sha'n't stand still," answered the man. "Take off your hand, or I'll serve you as I did him." At the same moment, he, in his turn, grasped Smeaton by the collar, and made an effort to trip him up.

His opponent, however, was younger, more active, and not a whit less strong, though his figure appeared a good deal slighter to the eye, from the symmetry with which it was formed. A struggle ensued, but it lasted not a minute; and at the end, the running footman—for such was Smeaton's opponent—was lying on his back in the dust.

The boy had by this time partly raised himself, and, clapping his hands with child-like satisfaction, exclaimed,

"Well done, well done!"

A little crowd had now collected, but Smeaton noticed nothing at the moment except his adversary; and he once more demanded in a stern tone,

"Who is your master?"

The man was silent; but one of the bystanders exclaimed,

"He's one of the Earl of Stair's men. Don't you see his colors?"

"Ay, I am one of the Earl of Stair's men," growled the footman, rising, "and he will make you pay for what you have done. There are eyes upon you, master."

"He shall punish *you*, or take the act upon himself," answered Smeaton. At the same moment Van Noost pulled his sleeve, whispering,

"You had better come in, sir, you had better come in. This is a bad business."

"Come, young gentleman," said Smeaton, laying his hand kindly on the boy's arm, "come in here with us, and let us see if he has hurt you much."

The boy followed mechanically; Van Noost locked the gate which he had opened; the footman went away grumbling, with two or three children running after him to look at him, keeping, however, at a wary distance; and the little crowd which had collected gradually dispersed.

Once in the house, Smeaton and Van Noost applied themselves to stop the bleeding of a wound of no great extent or consequence which the boy had received on his head in falling, and the former asked him a number of questions, to which he received answers neither nonsensical nor without pertinence, but somewhat strange and uncommon. Shakspeare would probably have called them "simple answers," for the meaning of that word simple was not so limited in his day as in ours; yet there was an occasional touch of shrewdness in his replies which savored not at all of the simpleton. He used, it is true, expressions sometimes child-like, sometimes not altogether intelligible to those unaccustomed to his way of talking, but often poetical, or perhaps I should rather say figurative. His head he invariably called "his noddle." The ground on which he had fallen he spoke of as "mother earth." The fist of the man who had struck him he denominated "his poulter," and the blow "a dunder." He bore the pain well, and seemed to care little for the accident, but, at the same time, exhibited a degree of enthusiastic gratitude toward Smeaton (more than commensurate with the service which had been rendered) for interfering on his behalf, and especially for avenging him on the bully who had struck him.

"Ay, ay," he said, looking eagerly in Smeaton's face, "it was good to teach the coulter-head that he's not too long to lie on mother earth."

In a few minutes he seemed quite recovered; and Van Noost poured him out a little of his Dutch cinnamon, which, though Smeaton rather disapproved of the remedy, had a marvelous effect in restoring the boy's spirits.

Nevertheless, he appeared somewhat eager to be gone, and his companions were not particularly disposed to detain him when they found that he was not seriously injured. Van Noost saw him to the garden gate, and, on his return, perceived that his companion had fallen into a fit of thought, in which he continued for a moment or two after his host entered.

"I have made up my mind, Van Noost," said Smeaton, at length. "There are circumstances in which it is as well to take the bull by the horns. It is evident that your good friend, the Earl of Stair, has recognized me. Although we never interchanged a word in our lives, he has seen me more than once. I will not play at hide-and-seek with him. I will go to him to-night, and demand that this man shall be discharged for the outrage he has committed."

Van Noost looked astonished—nay, aghast. "But, my dear lord," he exclaimed, "think, for Heaven's sake, of what you are doing. Were it to take a city or to save an empire, it might be worth while to get into the inside of a wooden horse and be wheeled into the lion's den, like the Greek gentlemen in days of old; but to punish a running footman, I can not say that the object is worthy of the risk. Bethink you of your policy, noble lord."

"It is the most politic course, Van Noost," replied Smeaton. "I have nothing to fear but a little inconvenience consequent upon discovery. The discovery being already made, all the danger that can be incurred is incurred already. A part of it may be obviated by boldness. But see who that is ringing at your bell."

Van Noost instantly ran to the window and looked toward the little gate, a large bell hanging at its side having been just rung violently.

"It is the boy again," he said, "and a gentleman with two servants. What shall I do?"

"Oh, let them in, let them in," cried Smeaton, in a gay and indifferent tone. "Now that I have resolved to throw off disguise, I may as well hold a levee."

Not without very apparent unwillingness, the worthy statuary called one of his workmen, and bade him open the garden gate and give admission to the strangers. He did not perform the office himself, for he would be seized with sudden fits of self-importance when he thought it necessary to keep up his dignity. The boy and the gentleman who accompanied him were speedily admitted to the garden, and, leaving the two servants at the gate, walked on to the house, and were introduced unannounced into Van Noost's little parlor.

"That is he, that is he," cried the boy, pointing to Smeaton, who had remained seated till they entered; and the gentleman by whom the lad was accompanied, a well-dressed, middle-aged man, advanced, holding out his hand, and saying, "I have to thank you, sir, for your generous interference on behalf of my son."

Taking his offered hand, Smeaton replied with a smile,

"I am sorry that it was not called into activity sooner, or I might have spared him a very heavy blow; but I had not the slightest idea that a great, powerful man like that would think of striking a young gentleman of your son's age for an offense which was, evidently, merely accidental."

"It is too much the habit with our great men, sir," observed the other, "to keep bullies and bruisers in their service. But the Earl of Stair shall hear of this, and learn that, though we are under a foreign king, his creatures must be a little more considerate of the feelings and rights of Englishmen."

"I know nothing of Lord Stair except by report," said Smeaton; "but, from all I have heard, I should not suppose he was one to countenance such outrageous conduct in his servants, and I shall certainly request him to dismiss this man on account of his insolence to myself."

"I shall insist upon it," replied the other. "Although he may never have heard the name of Sir John Newark, yet my possessions and my station in the country will not permit of my being insulted in the person of my son with impunity."

Smeaton smiled slightly as he rejoined,

"I shall hold out no threat, Sir John, but, dealing with Lord Stair as one gentleman with another, shall make it my request that he dismisses that man as one who disgraces his service. I do not think he will refuse; but, of course, in your own case, you will act as you think fit. Now, to speak of pleasanter subjects," he continued, holding out his hand to the boy, "I did not know, my young friend, when I interfered in your behalf, that I was serving the son of a gentleman to whom I bear a letter from one of his intimate friends."

The boy caught his hand, and shook it eagerly, exclaiming,

"I'm glad of that—I'm glad of that: I was sure my father would like you. You gave the coulter-head a fine fall. I heard all his bones crack and rattle as he tumbled. I should have liked to give him a kick; but that would not have been fair when he was down, you know."

"May I ask, then, to whom I have the pleasure of speaking?" inquired Sir John Newark, who had been eyeing his companion with some curiosity.

"I am called Colonel Henry Smeaton," replied that gentleman; "though my military rank, I suppose, will not be acknowledged in this country, as it has been gained in the service of the house of Austria."

Sir John Newark shook him heartily by the hand with the air and warmth of an old friend.

"I am most happy to see you, Colonel Smeaton," he said. "I have already received a letter, giving me information that you would probably come to see me at my poor house." Then, dropping his voice to a whisper, he added, "from Lord Bolingbroke."

"The letter I bear is from the Duke of Ormond," said Smeaton, in a colder tone, the name of Bolingbroke appearing to have no great charms for him. "Will you say where I shall have the honor of delivering it, for at this moment it is not about me?"

"Nowhere, I trust, but at my poor manor-house at Ale," replied Sir John. "It is a pleasure that I have promised myself; and I was even now on the eve of hastening back thither for the purpose of meeting you on your arrival. My son was walking from his school to meet me, in order to go down with me to-morrow, when he was assaulted. But I think you told me, my dear Richard," he continued, "that this other gentleman had been very kind to you also."

And he looked toward Van Noost, who had been standing near the window while the conversation took place.

"O yes," answered the boy. "He gave me some nice stuff, and cockered me up famously; but it was the other that made the big bully take measure of the paving-stones."

"Will you not be seated, Sir John," said Van Noost, putting a chair for the knight, "and allow me to give you a glass of the nice stuff, as your son calls it, which did so much good?"

"Well, I don't know what its name is," retorted the boy, "but I know it tasted like drinking gingerbread—hot and sweet—and a very nice taste besides."

"Dutch cinnamon, I'll warrant," said Sir John Newark, laughing, and seating himself. "We are not very much accustomed to such things in my house, so he might well not know what it was. I have almost forgotten the taste of it; but I know it is very good, and do not at all object, sir, to try your store."

Now be it known to the reader that at that period of history the greater part of the English nation had become afflicted with a disease from which they are not altogether free even yet, although a great physician has lately been among them undertaking its especial cure. The disease I mean is dram-drinking, which for some time affected not only the lower, but many of the higher classes, so that there was nothing at all extraordinary in Sir John Newark consenting to drink a glass of very strong spirit even before he had dined. But that worthy gentleman was not without his own particular motives in any thing he did, and frequently covered, or attempted to cover them by an air of frank and straightforward affability. At present, indeed, he seemed to have no thought but of Van Noost's good liquor, watching him as he brought from the corner cupboard both the long-necked bottle I have before mentioned and an exceedingly thin wine-glass, with a tall stalk lightly cut and gilt.

"It pours out like cream," observed Sir John, as his host held the neck of the bottle over the glass.

"Ay, this is none of your poisonous drugs such as they sell at the chandlers' shops and the barbers', made out of the lees of old wine or damaged sugar," replied Van Noost, still pouring; "none of your aqua mirabilis, or aqua salis, or plague-water, or colic-water, but genuine Dutch cinnamon, imported by my good father in his own sea-stock. Take it, Sir John: it will do your heart good."

Sir John drank, and praised, and drank again; and then turning to Smeaton, who was speaking with his son, he said,

"You are hard drinkers on the Continent, I believe, Colonel Smeaton, and would beat us Englishmen at a match any day."

"Not in the countries where I have principally resided," returned Smeaton. "I mean Spain, and some of the Austrian states. I have heard, indeed, of certain fearful orgies among the French officers in Spain; but I know little of France or Frenchmen, having merely passed through the country once or twice, and that very rapidly."

"Did you ever chance in your travels to meet with a gentleman named Somerville—Richard Somerville?" asked Sir John Newark, in a careless tone.

Smeaton shook his head, replying,

"No, I never did. In what country is he residing?"

"I really can hardly tell," returned Sir John Newark; "for, though he is a distant relation of mine, we have not held much communication together for many years. France or Lorraine, I believe, was the last country in which he was heard of."

"I think I do remember," remarked Smeaton, in a musing tone, "having heard the name mentioned at Nancy. But they said he had gone to seek his fortunes among the Spaniards in the New World. Somerville—yes, that was the name surely."

"Ay, very probable," said Sir John Newark. "I think a rumor of his intention reached me. You never were in those golden countries yourself, were you?"

"Never," replied Smeaton. "The journey is somewhat far; and, as I am well contented with what I have, I feel no inclination to banish myself from civilization in pursuit of wealth."

"I should like to see the country where gold grows," observed Sir John Newark's son, looking earnestly at Smeaton. "If I were a lord in golden land, I would give you a whole tree."

"Thank you, my dear lad," said Smeaton,

laughing. "I fear, however, I should have some difficulty in eating the fruit of that tree."

"Why, golden pippins—they would be golden pippins!" cried the boy, clapping his hands at the thought. "I wish I had some now; but they are not ripe yet."

The conversation then took another turn. Sir John Newark became actually gay and jocular, pressed upon Smeaton his invitation to his house at Ale, and did not depart till he had obtained from him a conditional promise to go down and spend a fortnight with him, if he determined to remain any time in England. He shook his new friend by the hand, at parting, with considerable warmth; but there was a degree of hearty cordiality in the boy's grasp of Smeaton's hand which pleased him better.

"You must and shall come down," said the boy, in a whisper; "and I'll show you all the coves, and the paths among the rocks and over the cliffs, where nobody ever perches but I, and the sea-mews, and the fishing-hawks. Old Jones Skinner, the smuggler, broke his neck there, and people are afraid ever since; but you are not afraid of any thing, I am sure."

"I trust not," answered Smeaton; and thus they parted.

When they were gone, Van Noost, who had been, for him, remarkably silent and reserved, broke forth upon the character of Sir John Newark.

"Take care what you do with him, my lord," he said. "He is not much to be trusted; and, for Heaven's sake, do not let him know your real name. First he has been one thing, then he has been another, just as he thought it served his own interest. He was once very great with Sunderland, in the old king's reign, and with the Duke of Shrewsbury too. Then he paid court to the Duke of Marlborough; and then he was one of Bolingbroke's men. I don't know whether he is a good enemy or not, but I am certain he is not a good friend. He is shrewd, mighty shrewd too, and has contrived to amass great wealth, and gain large estates, by not the fairest means, they say."

"I will be careful, Van Noost," replied Smeaton, quietly; "but yet I think I shall go. Much, however, will depend upon my interview with Lord Stair. He has recognized me, I am sure—nothing escapes his keen eyes—and I will soon see whether that recognition is likely to prove dangerous. If so, I will stay and confront the danger here. If not, I will go down to this Ale-Manor for a time, and watch quietly the course of events."

Van Noost shrugged his shoulders and shook his head, saying,

"Well, my good lord, well. You must have your own way, and put your head into the lion's mouth if you think fit; but it is an unpleasant place to rest one's noddle in, and, were I you, I certainly would not try it."

Smeaton laughed, replying,

"I do not think the beast is dangerous; but we shall see. And now, my good friend, I think I shall set out, for the shades of evening are beginning to fall."

"Not yet, my lord, not yet," cried Van Noost, who was evidently much alarmed at his companion's determination. "It is but a cloud come over the sky, and I would fain have you take a little more time to consider. It is well enough for me to brave Lord Stair, and talk as impudently to him as if I were his equal; first, because he can show nothing against me, except that I love one king better than another, and, secondly, because I am too powerless and humble to be dangerous: the man who will fight a boar, or a wolf, or even a lion (saving your presence), will often turn aside not to tread on a beetle or a worm; but with your lordship the case might be very different. You would make a fine cast of the net; and they seem fond of taking great fish just now."

"And very wise they are too," answered Smeaton, with a smile. "A large fish is always better than a small one."

"Wrong, wrong, my dear lord," exclaimed Van Noost. "Smelts for my money; only they are so dear—a shilling a score—that I can't afford them."

"But, my good friend," replied Smeaton, "you are much mistaken as to my objects and my position, though I strove hard to explain to you what they really are."

"Ah! some of my lead gets into my pate," said Van Noost with a sigh; "and when an idea is fixed there, it is as stiff as a river-god in a fountain, and requires to be melted and recast before it will take another shape. But your lordship was going to say—"

"Merely, my good friend," rejoined Smeaton, more gravely, "that I do not come over here to stir up any rebellion in the land, but simply, at the request of a very dear friend, to ascertain what are the real feelings of the country, and especially of the leading men therein. I have no dangerous papers about me, for I refused to be the bearer of any such. As yet I have communicated with no one but yourself, my object being simply to see with my own eyes, hear with my own ears, and communicate to some who are dear to me the result of my observations. Thus, although avowedly, as all my family have been, a friend of my legitimate prince, I have given no excuse for treating me as a rebel to existing authority. The faction that now rules the land can take hold of no word or act of mine. My father, it is true, was banished and proclaimed, but such is not the case with me, and I have a right to walk my native country at liberty."

Van Noost was evidently not convinced, and he contrived to detain his companion with arguments till the sun had actually set. Then, however, Smeaton rose, saying,

"Now, Van Noost, I must really go; but I shall see you to-morrow early, and we will talk further."

"I will open the back door," said Van Noost, somewhat ruefully, "and let your lordship out through the garden into the fields. The first turning on the right will take you straight up to the Dog and Duck, and then you can not miss your way."

"No, no, Van Noost," replied Smeaton. "The open way and the straight, if you please, my good friend, unless you are afraid to have me seen coming out of your house. I am tired of these maskings."

"Heaven forbid that I should be afraid, noble lord," cried Van Noost, eagerly. "I would walk with your lordship to the Council Office itself, if you liked; and, indeed, I think I had better go part of the way with you."

Smeaton, however, declined all company; and the door of the house and gate of the garden having been opened, he issued forth into Piccadilly, and took his way back toward St. James's Street.

Van Noost looked after him for a moment or two, shook his head gravely, and then, once more locking the garden gate, set to work in the twilight to put the leaden figures which Smeaton had knocked down upon their legs again.

CHAPTER IV.

It is curious what mighty business is transacted in mean places. The destinies of the world, and the widest-spread enlightenment of the human mind, have gone forth from two of the smallest, dirtiest, and most pitiful streets in London, Downing Street and Paternoster Row. John Dalrymple, Earl of Stair, one of the most remarkable men of the age in which he lived, and afterward celebrated for the extraordinary splendor both of his equipage and his table when embassador at the court of France, was at this time dwelling in a small hired house in Golden Square. Nevertheless, he had been already marked out for high employments by the clear-sighted eyes of the Whig ministry of that day, and it was without difficulty, though not until after two inquiries, that Smeaton discovered the house in which he lived. He paused before the door, and looked up in doubt; for the name of the Earl of Stair was so frequently in men's mouths, and his liveries were so well known in the neighborhood, that the young traveler had expected to find a magnificent mansion, fitted to contain a numerous train of servants.

But let us pass over his surprise and his inquiries, and enter the room of the noble earl at the moment when Smeaton approached his dwelling. He was seated in a large, straight-backed arm-chair, with a round, carved oak table on his left hand, having a thick, solitary candle close to his elbow, shaded by a fan-shaped piece of green silk fixed in the candlestick. Thus that keen, penetrating, but noble countenance was completely in shadow, while the bright light streamed upon a large packet of old papers on the table and upon one which he held in his hand. Better known to the English historian as a diplomatist and statesman of consummate sagacity than as a general, it may excite some surprise when I state that the paper which he was examining, with a pleasant smile upon his face, contained a rough plan of the battle of Oudenard, with a number of remarks, minute dates, and numbers written underneath in his own hand. He had drawn it up while hurrying over to England with dispatches announcing that great victory, in obtaining which he had borne a considerable share, that he might be ready with all the details in case of being questioned by the ministry. It had been of no service to him at the time, but now the sight of it occasioned pleasant sensations—the memory of triumph and success, the recollection, perhaps, of young, bright hopes and great aspirations—at all events, the thoughts and feelings of earlier and happier years. A refreshing breeze is ever blowing from the fields of youth, and when we read any record of those former days, we do but open a window to let it in. Melancholy may be mingled with it, and it may bring upon its wings the tolling of the church-bell for all that have departed; but still it is sweet and fresh, and beneficial to the health of the heart.

He laid down that paper and took up another, examined it for a moment and put it aside. In doing so, he touched the pile of old letters; they fell over, and he laid his hand upon another document at random. The instant he looked at it, however, he laid it gently on the table with a sort of shudder, and fell into deep thought.

While he thus remained, an old, staid serving-man opened the door and entered the room without the earl perceiving him.

"There's a gentleman below, my lord," said the man, with a strong Scottish accent.

The earl took no notice, but remained exactly in the same position, with his eyes fixed on the floor.

"I beg your lordship's pardon," said the servant, "but there's a gentleman below seeking to see you, and will indeed take no denial."

Lord Stair started from his reverie, and told the man to repeat what he had said; which he did, with the addition of the words, "He bade me give this card to your lordship."

The earl took it, and looked at the name before he answered; then a slight, very slight look of surprise came upon his face; but, bowing his head quietly, he said,

"Put a seat there opposite to me, and show him up."

The man did as he was commanded, and in a minute after Smeaton entered the room. Lord Stair rose, bowed, and pointed to the chair opposite, saying,

"Pray be seated, Colonel Smeaton."

His visitor placed himself in the chair in an attitude of easy grace, with his sword drawn up by his side, and the hilt resting on his knee. The old servant departed, and the door closed.

"I have intruded upon you, my lord," said Smeaton, at once, "to speak upon a somewhat unpleasant subject. I will therefore beg your patience for a moment till I have mentioned all the circumstances."

Lord Stair listened in silence, merely bowing his head, and Smeaton went on to detail the violent conduct of the earl's running footman toward young Richard Newark, and his after insolence toward himself, assuring him that he had witnessed the whole transaction from the beginning, and that the lad had given no offense but by accidentally touching the man's leg in swinging about his cane as he walked along.

Still Lord Stair listened in profound silence, interrupting the detail neither by comment nor question. When Smeaton had completely done, however, and paused as if for a reply, he inquired, in a somewhat dry tone,

"What is it you wish me to do in this case, Colonel Smeaton?"

"I have trusted, my lord, from your character," replied Smeaton, "that a simple statement of the facts would be sufficient to guide you as to what was requisite. But as you inquire what I could wish you to do, I must reply: to dismiss the man from your service."

"He is a useful fellow," said Lord Stair, with a slight smile. "Pray, what is the alternative, Colonel Smeaton?"

"Nay, my good lord," replied Smeaton, smiling in return, "I am not quite so pugnacious a person as to come ready armed with a hard alternative. I trust and doubt not that your lordship will do that which is right without considering any alternative at all."

"Very well," said Lord Stair, more frankly. "I will consider of it for a few minutes. But now let us speak of more important things than appertain to the fate of a footman. You seem surprised; but I mean the fate of a young nobleman, who has, I fear, placed himself in a dangerous situation."

Smeaton paused for a moment, for there was a kindness of tone, as well as of look and manner, in Lord Stair, as he introduced the expected subject, which he had not been prepared for. After very short consideration, however, he answered ingenuously,

"If your lordship alludes to myself, I do not imagine that my situation is dangerous at all."

"Then why appear in England under a feigned name?" demanded the earl.

"There may be many sufficient causes, my noble lord," replied Smeaton, "without apprehension having any share in the motives. I may be poor and proud, as is generally said of your ancestors and mine; and, to say truth, poverty was one of the causes of my determination not to assume any rank in this country. An unknown stranger, without any pretensions to dignity, can act as he likes; but it would not do for an English nobleman to take up his abode in a little lodging up two flights of stairs."

"In Gerard Street, Soho," added the earl, with a smile. "It is a very good street, notwithstanding. Great men have lived there before now." He paused for an instant in thought, as if considering how he should proceed, and then said, somewhat abruptly, "Are you aware that your father and myself were once intimate friends, and that, although unfortunately differing in our political views, nothing has ever occurred to diminish my regard for him, or, that I know of, his regard for me?"

"I have always heard my late father speak of your lordship with great respect and esteem," replied Smeaton, "but he never mentioned any intimacy. Indeed, I was not aware that you were personally acquainted."

"Oh yes," replied Lord Stair, in a very marked and peculiar tone of voice. "We were very intimate in the darker days of my life. There are circumstances, my lord, circumstances of deep pain and grief, which occasionally bind men together by stronger ties than any which can be formed amid joys and pleasures. But I see you do not know my history."

He paused, and fell into a gloomy reverie, which Smeaton suffered him to follow, uninterrupted, for a few minutes, and then, perhaps in order to draw his mind away from thoughts which seemed very painful, the young colonel recurred to a previous topic, saying, "I can assure your lordship most sincerely that I myself know no danger which I run in coming to England, or even in presenting myself at the house of Lord Stair. I mean that I am not the bearer of any letters, papers, or messages which can fairly give umbrage to the existing government."

Lord Stair roused himself from his reverie, and replied in an altered tone,

"Letters, papers, and messages may all be absent, and yet your intentions and your acts might place you in a dangerous position. I seek not, my lord, to pry into your secrets, if you have any, but I only wish to warn you, for your own good, that England is, at this present moment, a very perilous place for persons entertaining the views which your family have always entertained, and which, doubtless, you yourself entertain. Let me explain myself in what respects I think it perilous. Not alone are the eyes of government keenly fixed upon every suspected person: not alone are ministers prepared at all points to put down any attempt at insurrection: not alone are they ready to take the responsibility upon themselves of adopting measures, somewhat beyond the law, to meet circumstances not contemplated by the law—though all this might render your circumstances perilous enough, but there are other persons and other designs which may be more dangerous to you. I speak of those blind and infatuated men who entertain vain hopes of being able to overthrow the established government of the country, and alter, by force, the succession to the crown as settled by Act of Parliament."

He had spoken calmly, but somewhat sternly. He now again resumed a milder tone, and went on to say, "These men, deceiving themselves, are ever ready to deceive others; nay, more, are endeavoring, by every sort of artifice, by specious arguments, by false representations, by cunningly devised displays of an unreal power, and by maneuvers too numerous to detail, to lead the unwary or the ill informed into a belief that schemes perfectly impracticable are certain of success. I warn you, my dear lord, of these things, as an old friend of your father; and, to say the truth, nothing would give me greater satisfaction than to hear to-morrow that you had embarked for the Continent."

"That, I fear, is impossible," replied Smeaton; "for I have business to transact which must detain me some little time—business," he added, seeing a peculiar expression come over Lord Stair's face, "totally unconnected with politics or party."

"I think you would not say so with any reservation," replied the earl, and then fell into a fit of musing, which his companion did not interrupt. "I wish," he continued, in a kindly tone, after he had brought his rumination to an end, "I wish you would allow me to deal with you as a friend, and ask you a few questions in that character which might be impertinent in a stranger."

"Pray do, my lord," replied Smeaton. "Any thing concerning myself alone I will not refuse to answer; but I must beg you not to touch upon the business to which I have alluded, which I have undertaken for a friend, but which is, I give you my honor, merely of a private and domestic nature."

"I shall not meddle with it," replied Lord Stair; "and my questions shall be very simple ones. How long do you intend to remain?"

"Probably not more than three months," replied Smeaton.

"Somewhat long," said the earl, thoughtfully. "However, if it must be so, we can not help it. Do you intend to pass that time in London?"

"Certainly not," replied Smeaton. "I shall probably leave London in two or three days, having accepted an invitation to visit Sir John Newark at Ale-Manor, in ——shire."

"With a letter from Bolingbroke," said Lord Stair, dryly. "We have heard of that."

"For once you have been misinformed," replied Smeaton, smiling slightly. "I have no letter from Bolingbroke, and am barely personally known to him. It seems he did me the honor of writing to Sir John Newark; but I can not be responsible for any thing he may have thought fit to say in that letter. The only introduction I bear to Sir John is a friendly letter from the Duke of Ormond, who gave it to me, knowing that I had inquiries to make in that part of the country, and thinking that it might be of service to me; but it has no reference to politics, direct or indirect."

"It is in the hands of government," said Lord Stair, in a quiet tone, "but it will be restored to you. You seem surprised; but your arrival at Dover was known three days ago, and created some suspicion. Your assumption of another name, and your conferences with Van Noost—poor foolish fellow—increased those suspicions; and when I saw you with that person in the street, I sent a man after you to see where you went, in order that I might have some conversation with you, and save you from pain and annoyance, if not from difficulty. You stayed so long, however, with the leaden-figure man, that measures have been taken by other parties in regard to you which I could have wished avoided."

"Do you mean as affecting my personal liberty?" demanded Smeaton.

"No, not that," replied Lord Stair, "but examinations have been made at your lodging. Do you know much of this Sir John Newark?"

"Little or nothing," replied Smeaton. "I hear he is a waverer in politics, and that is all I know."

The earl mused again.

"I believe," he said, after a short interval of thought, "that the house of Sir John Newark is as safe a place as any for a gentleman in your position. He is one of those who, to use a vulgar term, do not readily quarrel with their bread and butter. He is more bold in words than in deeds, it is true; but he is not much suspected by government, as there are so many holds upon him. He may always be bound by self-interest. He may always be restrained by fear. I do not mean cowardice—for, personally, he is brave enough; but fear of losing an acre of land or a hundred guineas would make him swear allegiance to the devil or the Grand Turk. It is as safe a place for you as any that I know; but still, be on your guard against temptation; for a great number of unruly spirits are in the West, who will, before long, bring a heavy hand upon their own heads, if I am not mistaken. I had fancied, indeed, that you were going northward; and that might have been more dangerous."

"I have but little temptation to go to the North, my good lord," replied the younger gentleman. "It would be a painful sight to see my family estates in the hands of others, and our once splendid property enriching those whom even your lordship will permit me to call traitors."

"I will not find fault with your doing so," replied Lord Stair, with a smile, "for your father was certainly much wronged by near and dear friends, as they professed themselves. If I remember rightly," he continued, "your mother had lands in the West. Supposing they were not confiscated, I can conceive the motives of your journey."

"They were forgotten in the general sweep," replied Smeaton; "and, happily, we had faithful and honest tenants, who would not take advantage of their lord's calamities. They are all that is left us. But I will not, even in so small a point, deceive your lordship," he continued, abruptly, "nor willingly suffer you to deceive yourself. I am not going to the West to visit that small estate, and probably may never set my foot on it. I go simply to transact some business for a friend."

"Is he a *royal* one?" asked Lord Stair, with a keen look.

"No," answered Smeaton, laughing, "nor now at all connected with royalty. My friend is a merchant; but one," he added, gayly, "who does not traffic in any contraband commodities—not even in the delicate lace of treason. I have assured your lordship that this has nothing to do with any matters of state or policy whatever. I have to thank you for many acts of kindness to-night. I must beg you to add one more—to believe me."

"I do, I do," exclaimed the earl, warmly. "One accustomed to deal largely with men, judges them fully as much by the countenance as by the words. I remember well when your father and I were studying together, in deep seclusion, with a good minister in Ayrshire, and were told to read the historian Thucydides, we could make nothing of him, though we knew a little of Greek, till your father got from Edinburgh a copy of the work with copious notes in Latin at the bottom of the page. In a moment it became all clear, and we found how often we had been mistaken in our supposed interpretations. Thus one foreign language served to elucidate another; and I have often since had occasion to think that the expressions of a man's face are the notes which the grand commentator, Nature, has given us for the right understanding of his words. I do believe you, sincerely, and think I can insure that you shall not be molested during the three months you propose to stay, provided you pledge yourself to avoid all meddling with the politics of the country."

"I thank your lordship heartily," replied Smeaton, "and fully accept the terms." Then, changing the subject suddenly, he added, "I was not aware that your lordship had studied with my father. He, being a second son, was intended at first, to be educated for the bar."

"I also was a second son," said Lord Stair, in a low voice, with the expression of his face changing to a look of the deepest melancholy, "*I* was a second son; but not then—not then. This fatal hand had by that time done the deed."

The surprise which Smeaton felt at the sudden change in manner, tone, and look, and at the strange words of Lord Stair, could not be prevented from appearing on his countenance; and the earl, whose eyes were fixed upon him, said, "You do not know the story: it is a sad one; but I often force myself to tell it; and there is something strange in your coming here to-night. The moment before you entered, I had the letter now before me in my hand—the letter of recall out of a long and unjust banishment from the bosom of my family. To your father's kindness and support during those long dark years I owe much; and I may as well tell you how it all happened."

Smeaton replied in a few common-place words of interest, for there are times when nothing is appropriate but a common-place. The earl heard him not, however, but kept gazing into vacancy with a contracted brow and somewhat haggard eye.

"I have it all before me even now," he said, at length, in a low and tremulous tone, "that dark and horrible scene, and its terrible consequences. There are some things which brand themselves upon the mind even of childhood with marks never to be effaced; and though long years and busy scenes, passions, desires, hopes, joys, acts, feelings, have thronged so thickly into the intervening space that one would think they raised up a cloud between the present and the past which no eye could penetrate, yet there it is, that one terrible hour, as vivid and distinct as when it burst upon me like a blaze of lightning. This hand, young man, took my elder brother's life—not willingly, mark me—not with forethought, nor under the rash impulse of any sudden passion. We were boys together, and loved each other well. I envied him not his elder birth, God knows; I hardly even knew or felt its advantages. It was all in sport: I knew not that the gun was charged. He had presented it at me himself the moment before. God only knows how it was that I was not the victim, and that *he* was not left to mourn *me*. Think, then, of my horror when the musquetoon went off, and my brother fell at my feet a bleeding corpse! That was the first sickening taste of the bitterness with which my cup was to be filled; but when, instead of comfort in my agony, and support under the dreadful weight cast upon me, I found the awful misfortune imputed to me as a crime—when, in spite of its being shown and proved, by those who witnessed it, that all was accidental, and my horror and grief were apparent to all eyes, I was cast out from the bosom of my family like an exile, banished to a distance, and treated like a criminal who has only escaped condign punishment by some quirk of law, and who lives with the shame, and the reproach, and the stigma clinging to him forever—to describe my sensations then is impossible. At first it was all a chaos of sorrow; but gradually the sense of injustice raised up a spirit of resistance, hard, dogged, malevolent, but still serviceable, for it enabled me to bear up. And then, for my blessing and my safety, I found two friends, who gave a better direction to my thoughts—who raised up hope again in my bosom, and softened even the memory of the past. The first was the minister under whose tuition I was placed: a wise and good man, who moved in his humble sphere untainted by the vices or the follies of the day. The other was your noble father: a lad some years older than myself, who was pursuing his studies under the same tutor. Oh, how sweetly those days come back to memory, when first my heart opened to his kindness, and when, loaded with anguish, such as is rarely known but in manhood, I told him all my thoughts, and wept upon his bosom like a child! How sweetly, too, come back his counsels and exhortations! how gently, how kindly he soothed my angry feelings! how wisely he taught me to rely on higher and nobler principles for support under my affliction than the mere stern sense of being wronged! how he soothed my irritation, and won me away from my sorrows! My young friend, it is not to be forgotten; and if there was bitterness in the cup pressed hard to my boyish lips, there was sweetness to be remembered too. 'Tis well-nigh thirty years ago, I think—perhaps more, for your father married very early—and I have never seen him since; but I forget not one lineament of his face, one tone of his voice, one expression of his countenance; and you are very like him."

As he spoke, the earl extended his hand to Smeaton, and then added,

"You now can see the causes of the interest I take in your fate. That interest will never diminish, and will always be active in your favor, whenever my duty to the land of my birth and the sovereign whom I serve will give it scope. I am obliged to make this reservation, for it is a rule that I have always acted upon, to suffer no personal feeling whatever to interfere with my actions as a public man. But I trust to your own good sense, to your own good feeling, to preserve you from any position in which your interests would be opposed to my duties."

Smeaton replied not to the earl's last words, but inquired, in a tone of real feeling,

"How did this sad story end?"

"Perhaps to my advantage," replied Lord Stair. "I recovered my calmness and composure of mind—never my light gayety of heart. My own conscience acquitted me of any fault but boyish indiscretion, though the memory of having taken a brother's life remained as a dark cloud shading the too fervid heat of youth. I applied myself to intense study. I learned to think when others are dreaming. I sought abstraction from myself in the study of other men. I acquired in boyhood the mind of a man. The stream might be small indeed, for it was not yet flooded by experience, but it was diverted from its natural channel by the rocks and precipices which surrounded it. At length, representations from my good tutor of the forced progress I had made, his over-praise of my character, disposition, and abilities, and his mild, Christian expostulations against the injustice that was shown me, had their effect, and at the end of several years I was called back to my family. I returned with a feeling of dread and anxiety, which was not without cause; for, though I was nominally forgiven, I could see in all faces, I could hear in all tones, that what I had done was not forgotten—that a chilling memory existed of that dark accident, which extinguished all warm affection toward me. An opportunity of escape from such an icy dwelling soon presented itself, and I gladly seized it by entering the army. Life was of little value to me—less so than to most of my companions; my previous studies gave me some advantages over them; and I became what I now am, succeeding to my father's honors and estates on his sudden and somewhat mysterious death years ago. Wealth, power, and some share of fame have all been mine; but I can tell you, my lord, that I would sacrifice them all, fall back into obscurity, or even poverty, and pursue a humble course of laborious and unknown exertion, in any drudging profession, without a murmur, could I but blot out the past, could I but find some breeze to waft away the one dark cloud that hangs upon memory, could I but wash from my hand the stain of a brother's blood, however innocently shed."

As he spoke, Lord Stair covered his eyes with his hands, and then came a long, silent pause. Smeaton knew not how to break it except by rising to depart; but the movement instantly called the earl's attention.

"Do not go," he said, "do not go. You must stay and sup with me. We have other things to think of. I should wish to do something that would be of service to you, or might be useful, in case of need, for my mind foreshadows troublous times coming. But I must think of what can be effected."

"I thank you most sincerely, my dear lord," replied Smeaton, "but assure you as sincerely that I do not propose to meddle with troublous times, nor take part in troublous scenes."

"Propose!" echoed the earl, with a faint smile. "How many things affect the whole course of our existence in ways which we never proposed to our minds! Circumstances make man more often than man makes circumstances. Let no one answer for his actions even of to-morrow, for we may fearlessly affirm that he knows not what they will be. It is well to be prepared for all."

He rose and rang the bell, saying, when the servant appeared,

"Supper at the usual hour. This gentleman sups with me."

Then, resuming the conversation, he led it in a different course, talking of many general subjects, and gradually regaining his ordinary tone and manner.

"And now, my young friend," he said, at length, "to return to the object of your coming: what of this business between my running footman, Thomas Hardy, and young Newark, thrifty Sir John Newark's son?"

"I do sincerely hope that your lordship will dismiss him," replied Smeaton, in an earnest tone; "not to satisfy or gratify me—no, nor even to punish the ruffianly fellow himself, but for the repute and honor of my noble friend, the Earl of Stair. If your lordship had but heard the comments of the crowd upon the insolence of noblemen's servants, and especially of this man, who was recognized as yours, you would see that this is no specious motive put forth to cover personal anger. I punished the fellow on the spot for what he did to me; but the crowd handled your lordship's name rather roughly on the provocation given by him."

"I could swallow that easily," replied Lord Stair, with a somewhat haughty curl of the lip; "but he is, as you have said, a ruffianly fellow. He has broad shoulders, though, and stout limbs, makes his way well through a crowd, and has no more fear than decency. Nevertheless, you have justice on your side. I need hardly say he told his own story before you came; but I detected its falsehood, even in his own showing, reproved him for what he had done, and informed him I should wait till I heard further before I decided on my conduct. He has had much practice in lying, but does not do it dexterously. He shall be dismissed. Let us say no more on the subject. Look upon it as done; and now, here is supper announced. We will forget all unpleasant things, and I will endeavor to have one peaceful evening before I set out. You have heard, of course, that I am going to take the chief command in Scotland till Argyle can be made available. Then, I suppose, my destination will be France."

Thus saying, he led the way to a room on the ground floor, where supper was prepared, and Smeaton's evening was passed in a very different manner from that which he had anticipated in the morning. The topics on which they had touched recurred no more. General subjects were alone spoken of; and the only allusion to the fate or fortunes of either was made by Lord Stair, when he promised to send his guest, on the following day, a letter for a gentleman in the West, who might be serviceable to him in case of need.

"You can present it or not, as you think fit," said the earl; "but, at all events, it will show that I look upon you as my friend, which, I believe I am not too bold in supposing, may prove a protection for you against annoyance and suspicion in case of any troubles arising in the land."

Smeaton thanked him heartily, and thus they parted.

The colonel remained for three days more in London; but I will not here dwell upon his further proceedings in the great city, because I may have to speak of them hereafter as fully as their little importance deserves.

CHAPTER V.

It was a bright and cheerful morning, and the scenery round Ale would have been in its greatest beauty had but one cloud floated in the sky to checker the landscape with moving light and shadow. But there was not the slightest stain upon the heaven; and the sun, in his hot noon, was shining over the flat, waveless sea, and over the brown, high-topped hills and deep dells round about. The trees were in their rich foliage, green and full; no speck of road-side dust—no particle of soot—smirched the pure leaves; and underneath their branches might be found cool shade, and pure, refreshing air, breathing lightly from the sea.

There was a clump of ten or twelve beeches perched upon a little knoll overhanging the road which led to the nearest town from Ale-Manor and village. A few were decayed and hollowed out, leaving little but the bark standing, with two or three long branches stretching forth, and still bearing the verdant livery of youth, even in their extreme old age. Others were in their vigorous prime, too regular and rounded to be very picturesque; while one or two were in that state of half-decay which casts this peculiar tree into the most fantastic forms.

Sitting under one of those nearest to the road, from which it might be distant about fifty yards, was Emmeline Newark. She was shaded from the sun in the position which she had assumed, and, at the same time, caught any wind that was stirring; for, blowing, as I have said, very, very lightly from the sea, it came up the deep dell from Ale Bay and along the course of the stream, seeming to pause, as if in sport, among the beeches, and whirling round the wooded knoll. She had a book in her hand: I know not well what it was; it might have been Pope, or Addison, or any of those stars that were setting or rising about that time—never mind a mixed metaphor, dear critic. She was in one of her musing moods, however, and the book lay unnoticed on her knee, as, leaning slightly on one side, with her shoulder supported against the smooth bark of the beech, and her eyes peeping out from under the branches toward the opposite hill and the blue sky above it, she lay, rather than sat, in an attitude of exquisite grace.

The sun was very near the meridian, and his brightness would have been oppressive to the eye, had it not been that the cool coloring of the scene around, the green trees, the brown hills, and the gray rocks, seemed to drink up the rays, or return them softened and mellowed to the eye.

She had sat there some time, without seeing a living creature or a moving thing, except a large bird of prey, which kept whirling in immense circles far over head. But now a man on horseback, in the garb of a servant, leading another horse by the bridle, passed slowly along the road, without noticing her, and took his way up toward the old manor house. She gazed after him with that feeling of curiosity which is generated by a solitary state of life. She marked him along the road till it was lost in the wood, and as she did so, some one on foot was heard to pass along under the trees, as if coming up a very steep path from the little village.

"It is Richard," she thought, peeping under the branches. "Poor boy! he has not gained much during the last twelve months. He will be a child all his life, I fear."

She then turned to the pages of her book, and began to read. Suddenly the page grew somewhat dim, and she looked up, saying to herself, "There are clouds coming over." But, though she could not actually see the sun, the sky was bright and clear. She read on; but the page grew more and more dim, till at length she could with difficulty distinguish the words.

"A thunder storm must be coming," she thought, shutting the book and rising to take her way home; but, on stepping from beneath the branches of the old beech-tree, not a cloud was to be seen upon the sky. All was clear, though the light had diminished to the faintest gleam of twilight; yet it did not resemble either the morning or the evening light. There was no rosy glow, no golden tint, in east or west; a dim gray shadow had spread over earth and sky, and Emmeline could see here and there a star gleaming faintly in the deep concave above, as if night had just fallen, while a dark shadow occupied the place of the sun, with the exception of a narrow crescent of light still remaining at one edge. A sudden and instinctive feeling of terror seized her before reason had time to act. She knew not what she feared; and yet this sudden darkness, this unexpected extinction, as it were, of the great light of the heavens, seemed something very awful. Her heart beat, and her breath came thick. The next instant, however, she said to herself, "It is an eclipse. How strange and wonderful! It is not surprising that men in other days looked upon these things as portents. I could well-nigh be superstitious myself under that black sky at noonday. The sun is now taking the form of a ring of light, with a dark globe in the center."

She paused to gaze upon it; and strange wandering thoughts came through her mind, engrossing all her attention. She saw not that, from the edge of the wood behind and above her—where it stretched out with a sort of spur upon the hill side, leaving a space of about two hundred yards of clear soft turf, only broken by that knoll and clump of beech-trees between itself and the road—she saw not that there stole quietly forth first one figure and then another, and, with stealthy steps over the soft herbage, came creeping down toward her, keeping the beeches between her and them. The light, indeed, was hardly sufficient to show her their movements, even had not those trees formed a sort of leafy screen; but, as it was, they were completely hidden, and not till their steps were close to her was she aware that she was not alone on the hill side. She started at the sound of a footfall, and, turning round, beheld two strangers with their faces blackened. She would have run away toward the house; but, at the same moment, one man caught her by the arm, and the other seized her shoulder.

"*Pardie', nous l'avons!*" cried one of them.

The other said nothing, but strove to draw her away in a different direction from that of the house.

All the warnings she had received now flashed upon her memory; all the terrors which Sir John Newark had instilled took possession of her in full force; and, without pausing to question or remonstrate, she screamed aloud for help, while the two men, in spite of her resistance, forced her on in the path which they had chosen.

"They won't hear," said the one to the other, in French. "The wind blows the other way. This eclipse was a lucky chance."

Still, however, Emmeline screamed; and the one who had as yet said nothing, put his hand over her mouth to smother her cries, whispering, at the same time, but still in French, what seemed persuasions to come quietly, and promises which she neither heard nor understood.

Freeing her lips, she screamed again and again; and then—oh, blessed sound!—she heard the noise of a horse's feet upon the road.

"It is my guardian," she thought; and another long, piercing cry succeeded.

It caught the ear of the horseman on the road. He checked his horse, and beheld by the light, which was becoming now more strong, two men dragging a woman up the hill. There was a steep bank between the road and the turf above; but he struck his spurs fiercely into his horse's sides, and, with a straining effort, the fine, powerful beast overcame the obstacle, reached the turf, and sprang forward. Stretching out as if running a race, the horse, in a few seconds, brought him up to the spot where Emmeline was, and even a little beyond it, before his career could be checked. The latter circumstance, however, was favorable, for it placed the rider between the men and the wood, and also showed him in passing, that they were determined to resist his interference. As soon as they perceived that the intruder upon their enterprise was alone, the swords of both were drawn, and one of them said to the other, in a low voice, and in the French tongue,

"Keep him off while I take her on. Three hundred yards further, and we shall be within hail of the boat's crew."

But the stranger was not so easily to be disposed of. His horse was wheeled rapidly; his sword was out of the sheath in a moment; and in another instant he was upon the two men, from whom Emmeline was struggling hard to free herself. As if he at once divined their plan, he suffered the one who had let go his hold of the lady to advance, sword in hand, and aim a blow at him, unreturned, merely making his horse swerve to avoid it; and, pressing hard upon the other, who still held the poor girl in his strong grasp, he forced him to turn and defend himself. The rescuer was obliged to play a wary game, however, for the other man ran up behind, as if to strike him from his horse; but, practiced in every military exercise, although the animal he rode had never been trained in the *manège*, he governed his steed with perfect ease with the hand and heel, wheeling him now upon one, now upon the other, parrying a blow here, aiming a blow there, and, in the end, compelled the one who had still the young lady in his grasp to quit his hold in self-defense.

At the same moment, the loud, deep barking of a large dog was heard, and one glance showed the gentleman on horseback an enormous hound, followed quickly by a human figure, running over the hill toward them from the lower wood in which the road seemed to lose itself.

The same sight met Emmeline's eye also; and, finding herself free, she sprang forward toward the new comer; but, exhausted with struggling and with terror, she fell upon the green turf before she had gone twenty yards.

"Run, run, Matthew!" cried the man, who had last retained his grasp of Emmeline, still speaking in French; and then, with one of the blasphemous and horrid oaths of which that language has a copious vocabulary, he added, "She has escaped us! Through the wood, and by the path round at the back! I will show you the way down the cliff."

Thus saying, he turned to fly with his companion; but still he retired with a sort of sturdy cautiousness, stopping short every ten or twelve paces, and turning round ready for defense. The stranger, however, seemed in no degree disposed to follow him. His object was accomplished in freeing a lady from the hands of two ruffians: he had no knowledge of the circumstances; and, after pausing for an instant to make sure that the scoundrels had no intention of returning, he sprang from his horse and approached the poor girl, who was now raising herself upon her arm.

"I hope you are not hurt, madam," he said. "Do not be alarmed. The villains have fled, and will not return in a hurry, I think. At all events, I have marked one of them, so that we shall know him in time to come."

"Oh, thank you, thank you! How much I owe you, sir!" was all that Emmeline could utter. At the same time, the great deer-hound rushed forward as if to spring at the stranger; but, with that peculiar and marvelous instinct by which dogs of a noble race distinguish friends from foes, he suddenly checked himself in full career, dropped his tail and ears, and, turning from him with a shy and wary glance, as if yet not quite satisfied, approached the lady and licked her hand, fixing his large, bright eyes upon her face.

"Let me assist you to rise," said the stranger, offering Emmeline his hand; "here comes some one under whose protection, doubtless, you can be quite safe. Ha! my young friend, Richard Newark! You have made your appearance to help us just at the happy moment."

The young lad caught his hand and shook it heartily, exclaiming,

"What is the matter? What is the matter? I heard Emmeline screaming, and saw you fighting with two men, and just slashing one of them upon the forehead. Why, what a gay coat you've got on! You were dressed in brown in London."

"If it had not been for this gentleman's assistance," said Emmeline, rising slowly, "I should have been carried away, I know not whither—over the seas, I think, for they talked of a boat."

"Ay, he always comes up to help people when they are in need," replied the lad, gazing with a look of affectionate regard at Smeaton. "This is the gentleman, Emmeline, who came and made a jelly of the big footman who knocked me down. There are some people that have the luck of it. I should like to do such things too, but I am always too late. I came out to meet him, for his servant and baggage arrived a minute or two ago; but I thought he would come along the road, else I should have been upon the hill side in time. That brute, Brian, too, ran after a hare; and I sat down and reasoned with him, asking him if it were decent, in a gentleman of his high degree, to run after small game like that. He was too much ashamed of himself to make any answer; but he lifted up his great hairy nose, and wagged his tail, as much as to say, 'Don't talk any more about it.' Carried you away, Emmeline!" he continued, in his rambling manner. "Where could they want to carry you? They did not hurt you, did they?"

"They pinched my wrists till they will be black and blue, I am sure," replied Emmeline, simply. "But we had better make haste to the house," she continued, "for there may be more of them." Then turning, with a graceful inclination, to Smeaton, while she leaned upon Richard's arm, she added, "My guardian, Sir John Newark, will be most grateful to you, sir, as I am; for, had it not been for your courage and kindness, a scheme, against which he has often warned me, would probably have proved successful, notwithstanding all his precaution."

"I am more than sufficiently rewarded by having rendered you a service," replied Smeaton, in a very common-place tone; but the next instant he fell into a fit of musing, which was only interrupted by young Newark exclaiming, with a laugh,

"I would sooner do a day's work at digging, under a hot sun, than have to catch your horse on this hill side. He'll be at Exeter before tomorrow morning. Talking of the sun, Emmeline, did you ever see any thing look so funny as that great shining gentleman did just now—just as if he were sick of a surfeit. He's not much better yet, and looks black enough at the world, though he has now got a cocked-hat of light set on one side of his head. Old Barbara tells me it is an eclipse, and that it's all very curious. She saw one just like it in the reign of King William, of blessed memory, when all the birds went to roost, and the pigs hid their heads in the straw. I think it more disagreeable than curious. But look! he has caught his horse! He'll catch any thing, or any body—perhaps you, my pretty bird, before he has done."

A slight blush came upon Emmeline's face.

"Where are your wits rambling, Richard?" she said. "You should have helped him, Richard."

"Should I?" said the boy, with a start. "I am sorry I did not, then, for I would willingly help him in any thing. He is a fine fellow; but I never know what I ought to do, Emmeline, so you must tell me while he is here."

"Does your father expect him?" asked Emmeline. "He never mentioned it to me."

"Expects him as sure as he does Christmas," replied the lad; "but, like a wise man as he is, he held his tongue, knowing the quality of expectation, which, like a bad sword-blade, breaks through the middle when you most rely on it."

"That is not your own, Dick," observed Emmeline, smiling. "You have borrowed it from some one."

"Stole it, dear Emmy," returned Richard,

laughing; "pilfered it from a player in a lace jacket, who strutted about, perriwigged, in a barn at Putney last year, and called himself her majesty's servant. But here comes Colonel Smeaton again, with his horse in tow, as the fishermen say. How I should like to be a colonel! I wonder if I shall ever be a colonel, Emmy?"

Before the young lady could answer, Smeaton had rejoined them, and now walked by their side toward the house. He had cast off his fit of musing, and conversed with his two young companions gayly and easily, from time to time asking Emmeline questions in regard to the shameful attack which had been made on her, and endeavoring to ascertain if she had any knowledge of the persons concerned, or the motives by which they were actuated. She was obliged to confess her ignorance, however, merely telling him that her guardian had often warned her that such an attempt was likely, but had entered into no explanations.

It seemed now to have become Richard Newark's turn to muse, and they had very nearly reached the house before he opened his lips. Then looking up suddenly, he brought forth the fruit of his meditation.

"I've been thinking, Smeaton," he said, "whether we ought not to get all the servants together, and see if we can not catch these kidnappers."

"They are gone, I am afraid, beyond recall," answered Smeaton, gravely.

"Not they," cried the boy. "They can not get away except by the river, and we can stop them at the mouth. They took the path up to the top of Ale Head; and, unless they have got wings, they can not get down there. If I unchain the blood-hound and put him on the scent, he'll find them out for us in a minute."

"Nay, don't, don't, Richard," said Emmeline. "You must not leave the house without defense, for no one can tell how many there may be."

Neither did Smeaton give any encouragement to the boy's proposal. He looked grave and thoughtful, and the matter seemed to drop of itself. The three entered the house together, and Emmeline led the way into the smaller saloon, where Sir John Newark was accustomed to sit in the morning. While, with a timid grace, Emmeline was performing the various offices of hospitality toward Smeaton, Richard Newark slipped quietly out of the room, hurried to the great court-yard, and ran toward an immense blood-hound which was chained to a kennel near the stable door. The beast bounded up on his hind legs, tugging at his chain, to caress his young master, who, kneeling down unceremoniously in the dirt, threw one arm about the hound's thick throat, and, while the animal licked his face all over, struggled to unfasten the chain from the collar.

"Don't unchain the dog, Master Richard," said a groom from the stable. "He'll hurt some of you, if you don't mind."

"That is just what I want him to do, Bill," replied the lad. "You come along with me. Two men have been trying to carry off Emmeline; and Brian, who hunts by eye, was of no use."

"Have they got her, then?" cried the man, starting forward.

"No, no. Colonel Smeaton came up and broke their noddles," replied Richard; "but I want to catch them. So I have left the three—that is to say, the lady, the colonel, and the dog—in the house, and have come for old Bellmouth, here, to help me. You come along with me, Bill, and make haste. We'll put the hound upon their steps. Then, if he tears them to pieces, it's their affair and his, not mine."

As he spoke, he took his way out of the gates, the dog bounding on before. The groom caught up a stout stick and followed, asking his young master a number of questions, to which he got no satisfactory answer. By the shortest way, partly through the wood and partly over the hill side, young Richard Newark soon reached the spot where he had seen Emmeline on first being alarmed by her cries. Here, thrusting the dog's nose to the ground with both his hands, he cried,

"Seek, Bellmouth, seek!"

The enormous brute snuffed round and round for a moment without any other noise but the snorting of his nostrils as they were pressed upon the turf, and then the lad called him forward, a few paces higher up, still repeating the cry,

"Seek, Bellmouth, seek!"

The dog obeyed, moving hither and thither, still keeping its muzzle to the ground, and at length, with a loud yell, sprang forward in the exact direction which the men had taken. Richard Newark and the groom followed as fast as their feet would carry them, cheering on the dog with loud cries; but, dashing away without a fault, he soon outstripped them, giving tongue from time to time, as if to lead them on. He took his course straight through the spur of wood, over the brown hill beyond, and up in a direct line toward the top of Ale Head. The two pursuers caught sight of him again, as soon as they had passed the wood, rushing in a straight line toward the crags; and the groom remarked,

"We shall catch them now, Master Richard, or the dog will have them into the sea."

The moment after, however, the dog disappeared; for Ale Head, before it breaks off into the abrupt rocky promontory which actually beetles over the waters, is capped, as it were, with a rise in the ground, from which the turf slopes down to the edge of the cliff, so that what was beyond that highest point, and between it and the precipice, could not be seen. On reaching the top, the dog was not visible; but they heard a loud baying from some distance below, and Richard Newark ran forward to the edge of the cliff, while the groom exclaimed, "For God's sake, take care, Master Richard!" and followed with greater caution.

When they gained the edge, however, what had taken place became visible. On a point of rock close above the water, and reached by an exceedingly narrow path, broken, irregular, covered with loose stones, and interrupted by chasms, which, to an eye above or below, seemed impassable, stood the large blood-hound, baying with a furious disappointed bark, mingled with a sort of shrill whine; while, at the distance of about half a mile from the point, was seen a small boat rowing toward a cutter-rigged vessel lying-to about a couple of miles from the coast.

Richard Newark had paused suddenly at the edge of the cliff, and remained perfectly silent; but the groom, when he came up, exclaimed, "They have got off, sir! We are too late."

"Ay," said the lad, in a thoughtful tone; "they must have known the place well, Bill. I did not think there was a man in England knew that way down, except myself and young Jemmie Harrison, the fisherman's son. It is not the first time they have been here. Here, Bellmouth! Mind your footing, old boy. It's the first time you ever were down there, and you've got no map."

It was some time before he could induce the dog to quit his station on the rock below and begin the ascent. Perhaps the animal did not hear the voice from above at that great distance, but assuredly he saw his young master looking over, for from time to time he raised his head toward him with an angry howl, as if to intimate that the object of their chase had escaped. At length, however, he began to ascend; and with difficulty, and not, apparently, without fear, for his steps were slow and uncertain, he made his way up to the top of the precipice again, and then gave himself a great and satisfactory shake, and looked up in Richard's face. The boy patted his head, but said nothing, and took his way back to the house in silence.

CHAPTER VI.

From the groom to the stable-boy, from the stable-boy to the kitchen-maid, from maid to maid and man to man, by housekeeper and old butler, the tale proceeded, till every lad, and lass, and old blue-bottle in the family had heard that two men had seized upon Emmeline, and had only been prevented from carrying her off to a ship near the coast by the timely arrival and the gallant daring of Colonel Henry Smeaton, a gentleman well known to Sir John and Master Richard. True, the story suffered many variations in its course. It was embellished and improved, and gained at every stage, as the play-bills have it, "new scenery, dresses, and decorations." A great degree of confusion, too, prevailed as usual in the way in which it was told. One of the maids, in relating it to the housekeeper, either by the confusion of her own ideas or the inaccuracy of her language, made Brian, the stag-hound, act a very important and unusual part for a dog.

"Just at that moment, ma'am," she said, "Brian came rushing up, and, with his sword in his hand, he cut one of the men a great gash across the forehead."

"Good gracious!" cried the housekeeper, in considerable alarm and surprise at this phenomenon, "how came Brian by a sword?"

"Lawk, ma'am! I meant the gentleman," said the maid. "He cut the man upon the head just as the dog came up."

We can not, however, dwell upon all these variations. They were numerous and not uninteresting; but we have other things to do. Suffice it to say, all agreed in the general facts that Emmeline had been attacked and rescued; that Master Richard, and Bill, the under-groom, with Bellmouth, the blood-hound, had pursued the assailants to the very top of Ale Head, but that the latter had contrived to get into their boat and put to sea. One of the men, who had been long in the family, and knew Sir John Newark's propensity to gather as speedily as possible all the details of what took place in the house during his absence—a quiet, thoughtful, secret sort of man—walked out leisurely along the road as soon as he had collected all the facts, knowing well that his master would not be long ere he returned from the neighboring town, to which he had gone in the morning. He met him sooner than he expected, indeed—not more than a mile and a half from the house. Sir John was evidently anxious and in haste, for he was keeping his horse and his attendants, three or four in number, at a very quick trot, even against the breast of the hill. The man ventured to stop however, and the first words of the knight were,

"The lady--Emmeline? There has been a strange sail seen off the coast."

"Ay, Sir John," answered the man, "and they had very near carried her off. Two of the men got hold of her, your worship, not far from the house either; but just then a gentleman, coming to visit you—one Colonel Seaton, or Smeaton, or something of that kind—heard her screams as he was riding along the road, galloped up, and set her free. They say he cut one of the men terribly across the head—at least so Master Richard told me, for he was running to help her too, and saw the fight, as they did not give the matter up without a tough struggle."

"Thank God, she is safe!" said Sir John Newark; and, though the motives which produced this pious exclamation might have been of a somewhat mixed nature, he certainly did seem to rejoice sincerely.

Pushing his horse on even faster than before, he rode with great rapidity to the house, sprang from his horse's back like a young man, and hurried into the small saloon, where he heard voices speaking.

The whole party within were laughing and talking gayly; but the agitation and anxiety on Sir John's countenance at one showed them that he had heard of the events, which they themselves had nearly forgotten in pleasant conversation, and made Emmeline feel grateful for the deep and affectionate interest which he seemed to take in her safety. He shook Smeaton warmly by the hand, saying,

"You have rendered me an inestimable service, Colonel Smeaton, and added to all I owe you for the gallant defense of my son. I learn, too, from London, that Lord Stair has, at your demand, dismissed from his service the ruffian who struck the boy; so it seems you are not only our good angel, but a very powerful angel too."

"My dear sir, you overwhelm me," replied Smeaton, laughing. "I have no more merit in the matter than a man who, favored by good luck, picks up a purse and restores it to its right owner. As for Lord Stair, I made a point of seeing him immediately; and, upon due representation of the man's conduct, vouched for by my word of honor, his own sense of justice induced him to dismiss him, without any threat or means of compulsion whatsoever. It seems the earl was an intimate friend of my late father in early years, and that consideration, indeed, might in some degree have influenced him. I trust this fair lady will escape further danger, whatever may be the cause of the attack made upon her; and we were considering just now what would be the best means of protection for her, without subjecting her to the sort of captivity to which she seems inclined to condemn herself for the faults of others. Your son was proposing for her guards a brace of fierce mastiffs, to go with her wherever she goes; but I contend that he should be, at least, one of her guards himself; and I doubt not, now he has left school, you will arm him with a sword in so good a cause."

Smeaton spoke jokingly, but Sir John Newark looked somewhat grave.

"I am afraid," he remarked, "Richard would not know how to manage a sword. He has never learned to fence."

"Let me have the honor of teaching him," said Smeaton. "I will answer for it that in one week I will make him a very fair swordsman, whether it be with the small sword, the broad sword, or any other weapon of the kind. I have always been reckoned the most expert in my regiment at those exercises."

Sir John was evidently well pleased, and the boy delighted.

"I trust that he will have the benefit of your kind tuition for more than one week," said the former, "and it is certainly advisable that he should accompany his cousin whenever she goes any distance from the house. But surely, Colonel Smeaton, you have not come all this way from London to spend but a week in our rural scenes?"

"Oh no," replied Smeaton. "I shall remain in this part of the country, I dare say, for six weeks; but I can not intrude upon your hospitality for so long a period."

"If you quit our house one day before," exclaimed Sir John, warmly, "we shall conclude that you think our hospitality very cold, or our house very dull."

His manner was so sincere, and he pressed his invitation so heartily, that Smeaton accepted it without much hesitation, and again turned the conversation to young Richard Newark, pointing out the advantage it would be to him, especially in the somewhat unsettled state of the country, to learn various manly exercises early.

"They might be of great service," he said, "both to him and to you, Sir John. As I came through Dorchester, I saw two of the magistrates of the town taken to the pump in the market-place, and pumped upon till they were well-nigh drowned, because they would not cry 'High Church and Sacheverel forever!' Their cowardly lackeys ran away, and left them to their fate, and I did not feel myself called upon to interfere; but I am convinced that one man, with a little knowledge of horsemanship and the spadroon, would have dispersed the whole mob, and saved their worships a wetting."

"It served them right for their thick-headedness," said Sir John Newark, laughing; "and I can easily guess that you did not find yourself called upon to interfere. Your observations are none the less just, however, Colonel Smeaton, and I will send to Axminster to-morrow for a good light sword for Richard. My own are all too heavy."

"Pardon me," said Smeaton. "I will supply him with a very serviceable weapon, and as light as he could wish. It was manufactured for the late Duke of Burgundy, when about your son's age, and fell into my hands by accident. It is with the remainder of my baggage, which will be here to-night or to-morrow. You shall get him the less deadly weapons—a pair of fencing-foils, masks, and spadroons; for we must be mindful of the old proverb, and not jest with edged tools."

"There, Richard, you are at the height of your ambition," said Emmeline to the lad, while Sir John was pouring forth thanks upon Smeaton; "but I suppose, dear boy, with you, as with others, the ambition of to-day will not be the ambition of to-morrow, for that same steep ascent of ambition, the poets tell us, is like the mountains losing their heads in the sky, where we go on climbing, never thinking ourselves sufficiently high till we are above the earth. But what is the matter with you, Richard? You look sad!"

"I do not know why it is, Emmy, dear, but great kindness always seems to make me sad," replied Richard, in a low tone. "If I were with that man always, I believe I should soon be a man myself. But I fear that will never be," he added, with a sigh. "I feel myself so much younger than other boys of my own years; and I can not get things into my head as they do. This noddle must have some crack in it, Emmy, to let the thoughts fly out of it as fast as they fly in. It is no better than an old pigeon-house."

"Hush, hush! You must not think so," said Emmeline. "You will do very well, Richard, if you will but attend and be a little less heedless."

"I can not attend," said the boy. "I never could; and I am less heedless than you think, Emmeline."

Then leaving her, he went up to Smeaton's side, as he stood talking with Sir John near the window, and, laying his hand upon the colonel's arm, said, with all the eager impatience of a child, "When shall I have the sword?"

"To-night or to-morrow," replied Smeaton, with a smile; "but, before you wear it, you must learn how to use it. The first time that you can parry three lunges running, you will be fit to wear the sword."

The boy seemed satisfied, and left the room. The conversation between the master of the house, Smeaton, and Emmeline then turned for a few minutes to other subjects, such as the eclipse, the beauty of the scenery, the agitated state of the country, but gradually worked itself round to the strange attack which had been made upon Emmeline. Sir John asked both her and Smeaton a number of questions as to the appearance and height of the men, what they had said, and whether she had seen them long before they seized her. As to their appearance, Emmeline could give very little information; but Smeaton described them more accurately, saying,

"One was nearly as tall as myself; and it struck me I had seen him somewhere before—perhaps in France or Spain; but he was clearly disguised, his hair or a wig brought far over his face, and an enormous cravat tied in front. He will not be able to disguise himself so easily again, I think; for, though I only contrived to reach him with the point of my sword, it scored his forehead pretty deeply, as I felt it grate upon the bone."

Emmeline gave a slight shudder, and Smeaton added,

"Pardon me, dear lady, for speaking of such horrible subjects; but what I did, depend upon it, was necessary, for they seemed two desperate ruffians, determined not to give up their object without bloodshed. I trust they will never repeat the attempt."

"I think they will not," replied Sir John Newark, musing. "They have had a lesson. But they must have been well informed; for, if the fishermen had been at home, they would not have dared to land. All the men have gone round the point, however, and the wind would not serve to bring them back speedily, even if the appearance of a strange vessel had excited suspicion. I heard of her coming upon the coast this morning, when I was ten or twelve miles distant, and I hastened back with all speed."

"Then had you any cause for alarm?" asked Smeaton.

"Oh no, not particularly," replied Sir John, with a certain degree of embarrassment; and then immediately added, "But let me show you the apartments prepared for you, Colonel Smeaton. Every thing is ready, I know; though, fearful of any disappointment, I would not give my fair ward the hope of a great pleasure of which she might be deprived."

With this courteous speech, he led the way out of the room, leaving Emmeline musing, and not altogether satisfied.

There is a feature in insincerity which always betrays itself. I know not well in what it lies, this error of demeanor, which shows us that there is something very different flowing on under an apparently calm and clear stream of conversation. But so it has ever been; and it is hardly possible to deceive any one well practiced in the world's ways as to the ingenuousness or disingenuousness of the persons with whom he is brought into contact. The object may not be discerned; the thoughts, the passions, the motives, the wishes, the plans, may all remain hidden; but what we see is that the surface and the depth are different.

In the present instance, however, I must add, for the reader's information, that in many respects Sir John Newark's words and demeanor toward Smeaton were sincere. He was truly glad to see him at Ale-Manor; he was unaffectedly grateful to him both for delivering Emmeline and for defending his son; he was really anxious, also, that he should remain for some time at Ale-Manor. But yet a good deal was concealed; and Smeaton, perceiving this last fact, doubted, in some degree, all the rest. At all events, he said to himself,

"That is not a sincere man. It is clear that what the people in London told me of him is true."

Every care and attention had been bestowed upon the preparations for Smeaton's comfort; two rooms in Ale-Manor had been arranged for him, for the house had abundant space for its inmates; and the good, old-fashioned furniture, ponderous but convenient, had been freshly dusted and arranged, the windows thrown open, and free air and sunshine admitted, so that the whole bore a cheerful and pleasant look. The outer chamber had been arranged as a sort of sitting-room; the inner contained an enormous four-post bed, with blue velvet hangings; and the small quantity of baggage, which Smeaton had sent on with his servant, was already deposited in the first chamber, and spread out ready for his use. A hand-bell stood upon the table; and, on introducing him into his apartment, Sir John observed,

"I am sorry to say that, in this part of the house, there are no bells hung; but your servant has been placed on the opposite side of the court, so that, by just opening the casement at any time, you can summon him by that instrument on the table."

Thus saying, he left him, giving him notice of the hour of dinner, which was now approaching; and, even before proceeding to change his traveler's dress, Smeaton sat down in one of the large, easy chairs, to meditate over his situation and his prospects.

I shall not pause, however, to analyze his thoughts, but carry him at once to the dining-room. Nor will I dwell upon an English dinner of the olden time, though it had some curious features. Suffice it that it passed pleasantly, and that Smeaton's easy manners and varied conversation soon removed from the mind of Emmeline the feeling of restraint produced by freshness of acquaintance. As soon as dinner was over she rose and retired. Richard Newark did the same; for there were yet many hours of daylight left, and his rambling habits seldom suffered him to remain long in any one spot. Sir John Newark pressed the wine upon his guest, according to the fashion of the day; but Smeaton announced at once his very moderate habits, saying that he feared the school in which he had been brought up did not qualify him to compete with Englishmen in the use of the bottle. He had remarked, too, that during dinner, Sir John Newark, while conversing with the utmost apparent frankness, had dropped in questions with regard to foreign countries and to Smeaton's own adventures which he could not help thinking had a sinister object. He was, therefore, in some degree upon his guard; but he soon found that his companion knew more than he had imagined.

During the space of about five minutes after the dessert was set upon the table, one or other of the servants came in from time to time, to put more wine on the *beaufet*, to carry away this piece of plate or that; but when the last of them departed, and the door seemed finally closed, Sir John Newark stretched himself back in his chair, and said, with a very peculiar smile,

"Now, my dear lord, we shall be able to talk more at our ease, though I suppose it will be better for me to keep up the habit of treating you as Colonel Smeaton rather than as the Earl of Eskdale?"

Whatever he might feel, Smeaton did not suffer the slightest look of surprise to come upon his countenance. In truth, no sooner had he heard that Bolingbroke had named him to Sir John Newark, than he came to the conclusion that his present worthy host had acquired a great deal of true, and probably a great deal of false, information concerning him. He was not, however, very anxious to correct any false impressions that Sir John Newark might have received; for there were various reasons which induced him to wish that the notions of the knight regarding him should be as vague and undefined as possible, and he was well aware that nothing serves to puzzle and confuse the minds of very shrewd and cunning people so much as half knowledge. It is worse than ignorance, for it encumbers the ground. He was resolved, then, on his part, neither to tell nor explain any thing, but to let Sir John pursue his own course, and make any assumptions which he chose.

After a moment's seeming consideration, Smeaton said, "Perhaps, Sir John, it would be better to avoid my title both in public and in private. The name of Colonel Smeaton gives me quite as much dignity as I can well carry in this country, for the time being."

"Lord Bolingbroke informs me—and I was very sorry to hear it," continued Sir John Newark, after a pause to consider how he should pursue the attack, "that her ladyship was very unwell when he wrote."

"She was so when I left her," replied Smeaton, "but my last letters informed me she was much better; otherwise, I should not have ventured to protract my stay in this country."

Let it be remarked that Smeaton hesitated for

a moment at the very first word of the sentence which I have just reported. The original expression which first sprang to his lips was "My mother;" but, for some reason, he changed it to the word *she;* and, after pausing for an instant, he added;

"Pray what did Lord Bolingbroke say of her health?"

Sir John Newark took a letter from his pocket, and read as follows:

"The Countess of Eskdale has been very unwell, nearly at death's door; otherwise, she would have gone over to England too, I doubt not, for they have some lands to claim, and other matters to settle, which might require her presence also. However, she was too ill to go; and perhaps it is quite as well that she should not go, as it would only have embarrassed his proceedings."

Smeaton listened quietly while this was read, and then only observed, somewhat dryly, that the noble lord took more interest in his affairs than he had been aware of.

"I have had later letters," he added, "since then, and am happy to say that all danger is past."

"Then do you think," demanded Sir John Newark, "that her ladyship is likely to come over?"

"Assuredly not," replied Smeaton. "She would not venture upon such a journey without my company and protection."

Whatever there might be in this conversation of a satisfactory kind, and in whatever degree it might affect Sir John Newark personally, certain it is that it *had* considerable effect upon him. He seemed more frank and free in his whole demeanor from that moment; to put a greater degree of confidence and trust in his guest; and even to be more anxious for his prolonged stay. He had been every thing that was courteous before, but now he was warm and pressing.

I need not detail all that took place further that night. The potations of the host and his guest were neither deep nor strong, and the dinner closed with a walk through the park and neighborhood in the bright evening air, rather than with bottle upon bottle, as was too much the custom in those days.

Emmeline was not to be found at the moment they set out; Richard was rambling, no one knew where; and, during the course of their *tête-à-tête* walk, Sir John Newark tried hard, and not unsuccessfully, to converse agreeably on indifferent subjects with his young guest. He himself seemed delighted with the earl's whole demeanor and conversation; and, before the hour of repose, he had found a moment to tell Emmeline that Colonel Smeaton was one of the most charming and distinguished men in the world, laughingly adding,

"You must not fall in love with him, however, my dear child, for he is a married man."

Nothing could have been a greater relief to the mind of Emmeline than this announcement, for she was just at that age when an instinctive inclination to fly from those who are likely to pursue seizes upon the heart of woman; when a dread of the new and undeveloped sensations which are soon to take possession of her makes her shrink shyly and timidly from all that can give them birth. It is only when woman, in very early life at least, can say to herself, as Emmeline now thought she could say in regard to Smeaton, "There is no danger with him," that she is in peril of rushing rashly into love. Love is like all great things, affecting us with awe when we first see it from a distance, but soon growing familiar by habit and near approach.

Brought up in perfect seclusion, with few of her own sex to converse with, having none whom she could look upon as a companion, acquainted with no one near her own age, or with those feelings which produce harmony between mind and mind, often bewildered, as I have shown, by her own thoughts, and longing to pour them forth, she was ready—I must not say she longed, because there was no premeditation—to give her whole confidence, with the guileless heart of youth, to any one who seemed to seek it worthily.

Sir John Newark could be no companion for her. True, he was not without abilities and powers of conversation, but all his thoughts were different from hers. He was a complete man of realities; and, if he had any thing like imagination or fancy at all, the only purpose to which he could dream of applying such faculties was to the devising of schemes for the promotion of his own interest or ambition. There was something about him, too, she knew not well what—perhaps it might be this very difference of thought and character, this want of harmony between their two minds—but still there *was* something which forbade confidence. It was not so with Smeaton. Even in his look there seemed to her a very winning expression. His clear hazel eyes, not without fire nor even keenness, appeared to beam with high and generous soul; and in his whole demeanor and carriage was that sort of chivalrous aspect which had generally, in former days, distinguished the party called Cavaliers, with a slight touch of their free and careless gayety, but no appearance of their reckless licentiousness. There were moments, as we have shown, when he could be calm, thoughtful, and grave enough; but the general tone of his conversation was gay, and even playful, with no touch of satire or *persiflage*—one of the great vices of the day. Much dignity, at times, was evident, but never any haughtiness of demeanor. It gave one the idea that, confident in himself, satisfied with his own position, accustomed in all things to decide rapidly, and habituated from youth to act with ease and grace in any circumstances, he was never thinking at all of himself or his own manner, and that always gives an additional elegance. It was all evidently unstudied; and assuredly, when fair Emmeline lay down to sleep that night, she not only thought Smeaton one of the handsomest and most agreeable men she had ever seen, but lurking at her heart was a conviction that, of all beings on earth to whom she could pour out her thoughts freely, such a man would be the foremost.

Nevertheless, she slept soon and she slept well. Nothing in the slightest degree agitated her feelings. She was not even the least little bit in love with him; and though toward morning a dream visited her pillow which disturbed her much, and from which she awoke with a beating heart, it was only memory re-enacting, with very slight variations, the scene of the preceding day, in which she had been seized by strangers and rescued by Smeaton.

The same sensations, perhaps increasing a little in power, went on during the next three days. She became, of course, more intimate with her guardian's guest, lost the timidity and restraint of first acquaintance, laughed and talked with him easily, and saw, or thought she saw, more of his mind and character; and every thing she *did* see only tended to strengthen her first impressions. But during those three days she was never alone with him, even for a moment. Sir John Newark was always present, and his presence—it is a curious fact, but so it was—always checked any thing like free and confiding intercourse in whatever society he might happen to be. Man has his instincts as well as the brute creation, and it seemed to be by instinct that people felt Sir John Newark was not to be trusted.

On the day after Smeaton's arrival, the whole party rode over to a town in the neighborhood to purchase what was needed for the instruction which Smeaton had promised to give Richard Newark. The gay exercise, the free air, the little occupation of an hour, all made it a pleasant ride; and the morning passed over easily enough, although there was a little bustle and excitement in the town, caused by the apprehension of a man for drinking the health of King James the Third, which was construed into a treasonable act by the worthy magistrates of the place. Their reading of the law, indeed, did not seem much to please the people, who made more than one attempt to rescue the prisoner; but magistrates in other parts of the country went somewhat further, and were known to commit a man for refusing publicly to drink the health of King George. It is strange that some of the most tyrannical acts upon record have accompanied every movement in behalf of liberty.

On the return of the party to Ale-Manor, they found that the rest of Smeaton's baggage had arrived; and, reading the lad's eagerness in his eyes, Smeaton hastened to the room where it had been deposited, and took from a long coffer, which formed one of the packages, a very beautiful sword, light, and easily wielded, with a richly-chased hilt of silver and gold intermixed. Carrying it in his hand back to the little saloon in which Richard Newark was still waiting, as if anticipating his intention, the young earl presented him with the weapon, saying, in a jesting tone, but with some earnestness of words,

"Here, my young friend, I give you a sword which once belonged to a great prince; but I must exact from you a promise, such as was exacted from the knights of old, that you will never draw it except in the defense of a cause which you think just and righteous; for, depend upon it, if you do, though the blade is of the finest steel and of the highest temper, it will snap asunder in your grasp."

The boy caught his hand, and kissed it; and Smeaton went on, more lightly, saying,

"To-morrow you shall have your first lesson in the art of using it."

"Oh, let me come and see," cried Emmeline, eagerly.

"Nay, I must refuse you," answered Smeaton. "Every one is awkward in his first essays; and you must not see your young cousin exhibit till he is somewhat of a master in the art of fence. Am I not right, Sir John?"

"Perfectly, perfectly," replied Sir John Newark. "You must content yourself, Emmeline, with listening to the stamping, only thankful if it does not bring the old house down, for I can assure you an *assault d'armes* is no joke in a peaceable dwelling."

The lesson was given, and certainly Richard Newark was awkward enough, but he was proud and pleased, and the rest of that second day was spent in rides about the country. The third day passed much in the same manner, without any event of note; but as the proceedings of the fourth day will require somewhat more detail, I shall reserve them for the following chapter.

CHAPTER VII.

An old Norman church built in the earliest style of that fine but somewhat heavy architecture, stands about five miles from Ale Head and Bay, upon the slope of a gentle hill, with many other hills around it. It is a large structure for the present population of the adjacent country, if one may judge from the appearance of the land immediately round. The hill is part of a long range of downs, undivided by inclosures, and covered by short, dry sward, very much like that which spreads over Ale Head itself. No trees are to be seen as far as the eye can reach, except, indeed, two old yew-trees standing close to the church, and probably planted there by Saxon hands long before the first stone of the present edifice was laid. So close are they, indeed, that the long branches of one of them wave against the moldings of one of the deep, round-arched windows, and would, in stormy weather, break the lozenges of the casement were they not kept under by the pruning knife or shears. A piece of ground is taken in from the hill to form the burial-ground, and is surrounded by a low wall, with only one entrance, covered over with a pent-house raised upon high posts. By this gate pass in and out all who come to the consecrated ground: the child, to its baptism; the gay wedding party, to the altar; the congregation, to the worship of God; the corpse, to the grave.

About three or four hundred yards below the church, in the bottom of the little valley, through which runs a stream of the clearest and brightest water, are four or five small houses, or cottages, I should call them, built of the gray stone of the country, and most of them thatched. One, however, is of two stories, and has a tiled roof. They have all their little gardens attached, and are kept in tolerably neat order; yet, when one looks at this little hamlet from the downs above, and sees it lying gray upon the green and undivided turf, it has a desolate and neglected look, as if it had been left behind in the world's march to rest in the desert expanse around it. Except those two old yews, there is not a tree near bigger than a currant-bush.

Neither is there any other house to be seen, look which way you will; for the wide downs only serve for sheep-pasture, and have such a look of depopulation that, in some of the slopes of the ground, one might fancy one was standing alone upon the earth, just after the universal deluge had subsided. I know not whether it looks more lonely when all the heavens are covered with gray clouds, or when the bright sun shines upon it from the broad, undimmed sky.

Nevertheless, when the musical bell rings on the Sabbath morn from the old pale tower, the desert seems to waken into life, and people come streaming over the hills—now a solitary man or woman, now a group of two or three, now a family, young and old, age and boyhood, now a group of children, sporting as they run. The scene is all changed, and it is very pleasant to behold.

Within that church, too, are records of other days, which would seem to show that the neighborhood was not always so scantily peopled as at present. The grave-stones in the church-yard, indeed, are not thick or many, and you can walk at ease without stumbling over the little mounds where rest the mortal remains of the peasantry. But within, against the walls, and even let into the pillars, are many tablets of marble, black or white, recording virtues and good qualities, and affection and mourning, which have now left no other memorial behind them. In the aisles, too, and in the chancel (for the church is built somewhat in the form of a cathedral), are various very beautiful monuments of different ages: the mail-clad warrior, spurred and sworded, the pilgrim from the Holy Land, even a mitered abbot, judges, and statesmen, and soldiers of a later day—ay, and the tomb of an infant princess—are there; while on the pavement on which you tread, the old stained glass window at the east end, the only one remaining, sheds its gem-like colors upon slabs of marble bearing inscriptions and effigies in brass.

Various are the names which appear in different parts of the church; but, wherever the eye looks, more frequently than any other will be found that of Newark. Statues under which that name is written in old Gothic characters are among the Crusaders; and on one black marble figure, near the font, is a good representation of the heavy plate-armor of the days of Henry VIII., while above hangs a silken banner, of which neither the original color nor the emblems can be discovered through the dust and mold encumbering it. Nearer to the communion-table is the monument of another Newark, fresher than the rest, while an inscription below, in modern characters and in bad Latin, attests that the form above represents a gallant soldier of the name of Newark, who fell, bravely fighting for his king, on Naseby field. He is represented, certainly, not in the most classical costume, with a buff coat, large boots, and the end of a lace cravat finely sculptured on his chest. The features are not distinguishable; for, after the monument was raised—and it was a bold thing in those days to raise it—Cromwell's soldiers got possession of the church, and with hammers, or perhaps the pommels of their swords, sadly mutilated that statue and many others. It would seem that the family of Newark had been steady Loyalists, for on a tablet hard by is an inscription to the memory of that warrior's brother, erected during the reign of Charles II., and stating that he died while in exile with his king.

On the morning of the fourth day after Smeaton's arrival at Ale-Manor, a ladder was placed against the side of the church, and an old man, with something like a reaping-hook in his hand, was mounted upon one of the high rounds chopping away at the branches of the yew-tree, which approached too close, as I have said, to the window. He was far advanced in life; and his coat, thrown off, lay at the foot of the ladder. He had on, however, a waistcoat with woolen sleeves. His thin and shrunken nether man was warmly clothed, and, to judge from his dress, he was well to do in life. He had a fine bald head, with scanty white hair upon the temples; but his brow was knit as well as furrowed, and a sort of sarcastic expression played about his mouth, which was not altogether agreeable. Otherwise his features were good; and on looking at his face, one did not well know whether to think it pleasing or not.

While he was still hewing away, the solitude of the scene was somewhat disturbed by the trotting of a horse up to the door of one of the houses below, over which hung a large, straggling bush, with an inscription underneath to the following effect:

"THE NEWARKE ARMES. GUDE BEDS AND FUDE FOR HOSS AND MAN."

The animal which now trotted up to the door of this very rural inn was certainly what the worthy landlord might denominate a "*hoss*," but it looked much more like a barrel on four legs, and those not very long ones. It was, in fact, a little short, pursy galloway, as fat as it could be; and this fat must have been of a very perdurable kind, for, though the dust with which it was covered, and some splashes of mud upon its legs, seemed to indicate that it had come a long way, yet it had certainly lost none of its bulk by the process of perspiration. It was sleek and well to do, in short; and when its master stopped at the little public house, it stretched out its nose, as if prepared to ask the first person who appeared if it could have the dinner and bed which the inscription promised. The rider was a short, fattish man, somewhat resembling his beast, but rather more gaudily attired; for the pony contented himself with a coat of gray, while he who bestrid him was dressed, like Joseph, in a garment of many colors.

The old man upon the ladder heard the horse's feet on the road, and turned round to gaze, resting from his work the while. The sight of a stranger in the place seemed to give him no pleasure. He was callous to all such things; and he only set his jaws tight together, and mumbled something to himself. A boy, and then an old woman, came out from the house. The stranger dismounted, took his saddle-bags from the pony's back, and entered the little dwelling. The boy led the pony round to the rear of the house, and the old man assailed the yew-tree again.

If, however, he thought he was to go on uninterruptedly that morning, he was mistaken, for in about five minutes more the stranger walked up to the gate of the church-yard, advanced to the foot of the ladder, and looked up. The other took no notice of him whatever except by stretching forth his arm, and, with greater strength than one might have believed him to possess, striking off a somewhat thicker branch of yew than usual, which fell upon the visitor's head and knocked his hat off.

"Ay! ashes to ashes, dust to dust!" muttered the old man, with a slight smile curling the corner of his mouth.

The other picked up his hat, brushed off the dust with his coat sleeve, and then, without any observation on the accident, raised his voice, saying,

"I wish you would come down, sexton, and let me into the church."

"What makes you think I am sexton?" asked the old man, gruffly. "I never buried you or any of your kin."

"No, but you look like old Father Time," answered the other, laughing; "and *he* buries all men."

"Then you should take me by the forelock," answered the sexton, whom the joke seemed to mollify a little; "and I have no forelock to take. So you are out, master. I *am* the sexton, however. But what do you want in the church?"

"I hear you have some fine statues there," replied the other, "and I want to see them."

But the old man was not yet satisfied.

"Why, what do *you* know about statues?" he asked, running his eye over the round, fat, unstatue-like figure of the other with a somewhat contemptuous look.

"More than you do, old boy," replied the visitor, "though perhaps you have lived among them all your life; for I have made them all my life; and, depend upon it, there is no such way of knowing a thing as making it."

"That depends upon the workman," answered the sexton, beginning to descend the ladder. "I have made graves all my days, and yet don't know them as well as many who are lying underneath there. But I'll let you in," he added, in a more placable tone; "for they are fine monuments, finer than any for a hundred miles round; and, if you *do* know any thing about such things, you'll say so."

When he reached the ground, he picked up his coat, fumbled in his pocket till he got hold of a large bunch of keys, and then, walking round to the door, opened it. The stranger entered, and his guide followed, with his back bowed and his gait somewhat halting. He had the same sort of cynical expression on his countenance as before; but the visitor's first exclamation seemed to please him, for all the pride of his nature—and every man has some pride—centered in his church and its contents.

"Ay, this is something like!" exclaimed our good friend Van Noost; "I have not seen any thing like this in a ride of a hundred and fifty miles."

"Dare say not," observed the sexton. "Did you come all that way to see it?"

"No," replied Van Noost, who was somewhat skillful at evasions; "but I am very glad I *have* seen it." And, walking on, he began to scan the various monuments with critical eyes.

"Why, the barbarians have been knocking the noses off!" he exclaimed, after a momentary glance at one of the tombs. "Why did you let them do that?"

"Because I could not help it," answered the sexton, with a growling laugh, "seeing I was a baby and they strong men when that was done; and yet I am threescore and ten come Martinmas."

"Ay, Cromwell, that devil Cromwell and his sacrilegious fools!" cried Van Noost. "They had no more taste or judgment than pigs in Smithfield."

"That's true—that's true," cried the old sexton, chuckling. "I remember them well enough, for I was a school-boy when old Noll died, and heard him preach once. Those might understand him who could. To me he seemed to be talking nothing but nonsense; so I grinned; and one of his soldiers gave me a thump in the side with his fire-lock which nearly broke my ribs."

"Then you have cause to remember him," answered Van Noost, "and not to like him either. These are better times, Master Sexton."

"I don't know that," replied the man, gruffly. "We have got a foreigner for our king, and that's as bad as a Protector—at least I think so. But I don't know much of such matters," he added, with a look of shrewd caution coming upon his face. "King George may be a very good man, and Hanover rats as good as any other vermin, for aught I know."

Van Noost laughed aloud, and replied, with a significant nod of the head,

"They may have a rat-catcher among them some day soon, Master Sexton; but that is not my business either. Gracious goodness, how dirty these monuments are! And half the brasses are gone out of the marble!"

"Ay, they took the brass to make farthings of," said the sexton; "and as to the dirt, how can an old man like me keep such things clean? Besides, I don't know how to clean them properly, and I am afraid of spoiling them."

"I'll tell you what, old boy," replied Van Noost, "I am going to stay here for a day or two, and I'll help you. I know all about it; and if I have time, and can get a little clay, I'll cast you a leaden head and put it on that cherub at the corner. A cherub is nothing without a head, you know, Master Sexton, because it has got no body."

"Going to stay here for two or three days!" ejaculated the sexton. "Well, that's funny! I never knew any one stay here a minute after he could help it. Perhaps you have come down to these parts to make inquiries?"

"No," answered Van Noost, "no; I don't like inquiries, and always get out of their way."

The sexton put his finger to his bald forehead, and rubbed it slowly for a moment, repeating the word "Ha!" more than once; and then Van Noost added, in his usual *pococurante* tone,

"That is the very reason I came down here, Master Sexton. People were making important inquiries, which offended me, and I left London in a fit of indignation."

"Ha!" said the sexton again. "I understand. You'll be safe enough here, master. You'll see plenty of curlews, and a sea-mew from time to time. I've known a roe-deer too, in my day, down about the woody places; but men and women are the rarest birds of all in this country;" and, laying his old hand familiarly on Van Noost's shoulder, he added, with a laugh, "No bailiff has been seen in these parts for forty years—that I can certify."

"I fear not bailiffs!" exclaimed Van Noost, in a mock tragical tone. "Sexton, I am well to do in the world. I pay scot and lot, and owe no man any thing—though many owe me, by-the-way, who will never pay me. No, no, sexton, 'tis not for debt of vile and sordid gold that men, perhaps, may seek me, but for those thin ethereal essences called opinions, which suit not with the tyranny of the times."

The sexton chuckled, for he had a strong sense of the ludicrous, and Van Noost's bombast amused him.

"Ay, ay," he said, laughing and coughing, "how many a man there is who is obliged to make his heels save his head for the indiscretion of his tongue! Now I'll warrant you've been swaggering about London in praise of King James till you got frightened to death for fear King George should get hold of you. But you're safe enough here, man; you're safe enough here. Sergeants and pursuivants are as rare here as bailiffs; and it is not likely they'll be able to track you across the hills, even if a price should be set upon your head."

"There is no price upon my head," cried Van Noost, with a strong feeling of nervous apprehension at the very idea. "They could not hurt me even if they took me; but I love my liberty, Master Sexton, and should pine to death if I were cribbed up in a prison-cell."

"It would take a long time to pine you down even to a moderate size," replied the sexton, in a thoughtful sort of tone. "I've dug many a grave in my day, and there's only one I recollect that would have held you. You are so fat here behind."

"I have committed no crime," continued Van Noost, anxious to disabuse his companion's mind of the idea that he might be harboring a traitor. "I have committed no crime, I say; and the blessed English law admits that men may talk treason, though they may not do it."

"Ay, the tongue, the tongue!" exclaimed the sexton; "that's what has brought you into danger, I can see well enough. It is an unruly member, as the Bible says; but here you will be quite safe. If I have to bury you, I ought to have a crown more for the width of the grave. I had when the fat parson died, this time thirty years ago, though his heirs said they did not like to pay for his fat. But hark! More people on horseback all in one day! Master, I've a notion they've tracked you close."

Poor Van Noost lost his rosy color in a moment, for no man liked less the idea of martyrdom than he did.

"For Heaven's sake, my good friend," he cried, as the old sexton peeped through a chink of the church door, which had been left ajar, "for Heaven's sake, can not you put me somewhere where they will not find me? Let me go into the vestry!"

The sexton eyed him with his quiet old cynical smile. "How fond fat men are of life!" he said. "The vestry! They'd find you there in a minute. Here, you fool, go in there, down into the vaults. They'll not look there, I'll warrant."

As he spoke he unlocked a small door, which lay in a shady nook between two pilasters, and, under the impulse of fear, Van Noost hurried in, without a word, taking his chance of the old man recollecting to let him out again. He saw the head of a flight of steps before him, and was rushing down, when the sound of the key turning in the lock raised up new fears in his mind, and he paused for a moment to listen. The only sound he could hear at first was produced by the slow, irregular step of the old sexton upon the pavement of the church, as he again walked toward the great door, and then a loud manly voice from without was heard, as if saying to some one at a distance, "Walk them about till we come back. The air is keen upon these hills, even at midsummer."

The next instant another voice answered, "I like that free fresh air. It feels like liberty."

"Liberty!" said the other voice. "Have you ever felt the want of liberty?"

"They are marvelous sweet-tongued officers," thought Van Noost, listening. But no reply was made to the question, or, if any, it was drowned by the cough of the old sexton; and, when that had a little subsided, the second voice which had spoken was heard saying,

"We want to go all over the church, good Master Mattocks."

Van Noost trembled for the security of his hiding-place; but he was relieved in an instant, for the same voice went on, saying,

"So you must show us all the monuments, and tell us all about them, for this gentleman will not be satisfied with half information, I can assure you."

"That I will, my lady," answered the old man, "that is to say, all I know, for I never like to say things I only guess."

"My lady!" said Van Noost to himself. "Ho, ho! It is a party come to visit the church, and I am shut up here like a rat in a rat-trap, when I could have given them much more information than that old mummy, who has dealt so long with corpses that he has caught the look of them. I have a great mind to knock to get out. They'll be in sad want of a better *cicerone*."

Caution, however, got the better of vanity; and, after a little consideration, he began to feel his way down the steps, resolved to see what the vaults contained. At first the place seemed dark enough; but as he descended, he found that he had been admitted, not to funeral vaults in the usual acceptation of the word, but to a crypt or under-ground church, of a much earlier style of architecture than the structure above. Low, arched windows, earthed up for at least two thirds of their height, admitted sufficient light to render every object round dimly visible. Monuments and carvings were seen in various different directions; and, with true antiquarian enthusiasm, Van Noost soon forgot what was passing above in the examination of all that surrounded him.

CHAPTER VIII.

We must return here to an earlier hour in the day of which we have just been speaking. The breakfast at Ale-Manor was laid in the dining saloon, and presented a curious combination of the ancient and modern habits of the English people. Fish, meat, and various sweetmeats were spread upon the board; a large tankard of silver, which might have served up ale at the breakfast-table of Queen Elizabeth, was on the side-board; and good Bordeaux wine was there in another flagon, for those who adhered to the tastes of their remote ancestors; but, for delicate tastes, the more modern breakfast of coffee and chocolate was prepared. Sir John Newark was in a most gracious mood; his son Richard was all life and gayety; and last came in Emmeline, bright and blooming from her sweet sleep, like a blush rose refreshed by morning dew. Smeaton could willingly have gazed at her long, but he would not allow himself to do so; and the breakfast was proceeding gayly and cheerfully, when one of the servants entered to inform Sir John Newark that a messenger had brought a letter for him from Exeter. When the letter was delivered and opened, Sir John Newark read it with a look of grave and anxious thought. Then, nodding to the messenger, who had waited as if for a reply, he said,

"Get yourself some refreshment, and let his worship know that I will not fail to be there by two of the clock."

The man bowed and left the room; and Sir John, turning to Smeaton with the letter still in his hand, observed, with a somewhat affected laugh,

"Here is a strange affair!"

Then, turning his eye to the page, he read aloud:

"WORSHIPFUL SIR,—Whereas information has been received that various evil designing persons are traveling about the country for seditious purposes, some of whom are reported to be proclaimed traitors, and others persons lying under sentence of various offenses and fugitive from justice; and as it is matter of common notoriety that, in various parts of the land, and especially at several places in this county of Devon, serious disturbances have been stirred up contrary to the peace of our lord the king, and perilous to the state and constitution of this country as by law established: this is to give you notice, that a special meeting of the justices of the peace for this division of the county of Devon is summoned to assemble in this city of Exeter to-morrow, the —— day of July, in the year of our Lord 1715; and you are hereby invited and required, putting aside all other business, to attend the same, in order to consult as to the best means of preserving the peace of the said county, and frustrating the designs of seditious and disaffected persons.

"(Signed), &c."

He paused for a moment after reading the letter, and then added, with a smile,

"They must have got a fright from some circumstance or other. I hope no friends of ours have given them any cause of suspicion."

"If you allude to me," answered Smeaton, with a frank smile, "I have not, I can assure you, Sir John, and am under so little apprehension on the subject, that I have no objection, if you like, to ride with you to Exeter, if you feel yourself bound to go upon such a curious summons."

"Oh, I *must* go, assuredly," replied the knight; "but you had better remain here. I shall feel more satisfied in leaving my fair ward here under your good care and protection, for I must take several of the servants with me."

He did not speak without some consideration; but he was forced to decide quickly, for the ride before him was very long, and he was anxious to avoid all appearance of disaffection to the existing government, whatever he might feel. About three quarters of an hour were spent in busy preparation; but Sir John found an opportunity, in the midst of all his bustle, to caution his son more than once to watch carefully over Emmeline, and, if possible, not to quit her side for a moment. Richard promised, with every intention of performing; and the whole party stood on the terrace together to see Sir John depart. They watched him round the sweep till he disappeared into the woods, and then Richard, with a boyish leap over a bush, exclaimed, in a gay tone,

"Now, what shall we do?"

Smeaton smiled to see that, even with the simple boy, the petted and somewhat spoiled child, the presence of Sir John Newark was felt to be a restraint. He replied, however, turning toward Emmeline, and addressing her more than Richard,

"You promised to show me some day a fine old church in the neighborhood, with some beautiful monuments. Can we not make it the object of a morning's ride to-day?"

Emmeline consented willingly, and said she would get ready directly for the expedition; but Richard did not seem well pleased; and, as soon as she had gone to fulfill her intention, he thrust his hands into his pockets, and said,

"I sha'n't go. I hate old churches, and old monuments too. What the deuce is the use of going to see a pack of stones put on end? I'll go out fishing. You are quite old enough to take care of Emmeline, I should think; but you had better take some people with you, for my dad is always in a terrible fright for fear somebody should get his bird out of the cage. Poor Emmeline! I wonder she abides it so quietly. I could not, I know, if I were kept tight by a string round my leg like that."

Smeaton gave the boy no encouragement to come with them, merely answering,

"I will take care of the young lady, and warrant she shall come safely back. I will take my own servant with us; and one or two of your people would make our party quite sufficient, even if the country were more disturbed than I believe it really is."

"Then I'll run down and get a boat at once," exclaimed Richard Newark; and, before Smeaton could add another word, he was bounding down the hill like a great dog.

His companion betook himself to the stable-yard of the mansion, to give directions regarding the horses, and all the little preparations for the proposed expedition; and then, putting on the great riding-boots of the day, he returned to the terrace to wait for Emmeline. It was not long ere she joined him, gay, smiling, and happy at the thought of a pleasant excursion. She looked round for Richard, however, and asked where he was; and when Smeaton told her that he had declined being of the party, a grave look of anxiety and hesitation came over her face.

"Sir John Newark," she said, after a moment's pause, "does not like me to go far, or into any town, without the old housekeeper accompanying me."

Her companion smiled, answering gayly,

"But we are going to a church, not to a town; and, on this occasion, you must let me act the old woman."

A joke often prevails where an argument will not. The horses were brought round, Smeaton placed his fair companion in the saddle, and away they went, at a quiet and easy pace, with the three men following them. He was an excellent and graceful horseman, and not unwilling to enjoy, from time to time, the exhilarating sensations of a wild gallop over the green turf; but, for some reason or other, he did not seem, on this occasion, disposed to put the horses out of a quiet canter. Down the stony road he proceeded at a walk, and only quickened his pace a very little when, turning to the left at the end of the wood, they got upon the downs. But Smeaton was a good tactician, and he had his reasons for what he did. Emmeline did not know that such was the case, however, and she grew a little impatient.

"Shall we not have a gallop?" she asked, at length, after some broken conversation on indifferent subjects.

"Presently," answered Smeaton, in a quiet tone. "One can not gallop and think calmly too."

"Think!" echoed Emmeline, gayly. "Why should you think, Colonel Smeaton? Thinking is the most pernicious thing on earth; and what gentleman has any right to think with a lady by his side?"

"It is impossible to help thinking, and deeply too, with you by my side," answered Smeaton, in a low voice.

Emmeline almost started—it sounded so like a compliment; but Smeaton was not a complimentary person, as she had remarked with pleasure; and she replied, after turning an inquiring glance toward him, in the same light tone, "Why so? do you judge me such an enigma?"

"Not yourself," answered Smeaton, gravely, "but your fate and history are an enigma." He paused for a moment, and then added: "For yourself, dear lady, your character is as clear and pure as a diamond; which, if we do not see through it at once, it is because of its too much light; but your history, your circumstances, your fate, do constitute an enigma, which might well make any man of heart and feeling thoughtful."

He spoke very low; but every word fell clear and distinct upon Emmeline's ear, and instantly banished her gayety.

"It is an enigma I can not solve," she answered. "I have tried to do so a thousand times, but in vain. Whichever way my eyes turn, it is all darkness; and, weary with straining my sight upon the blank obscure, I have given it up, reduced to remain satisfied with knowing nothing but—which is perhaps as much as most persons know of themselves—that I am. But what is it puzzles *you* about me? What have you seen or remarked to make you believe that there is any mystery?"

"Much," he replied: "the very circumstances in which I first saw you—an attempt to carry you off forcibly from the midst of your family and friends—the constant, feverish sort of anxiety displayed by Sir John Newark in regard to you—his unwillingness to suffer you to hold communication of any kind with persons out of his own house."

"Is he unwilling?" exclaimed Emmeline, eagerly. "I do not think it—yet perhaps you are right," she added, gravely. "I remember—perhaps you are right. I do not recollect ever having been suffered to converse alone with any one except the people of the house, and good Doctor Boothe, who is dead. It is strange! I do not attempt to conceal from you that there *is* a mystery, even to myself."

"And you have tried to solve it unassisted?" inquired Smeaton.

"Often and often," she answered. "Oh, what would I give to know who were my parents—what I am—what are the causes of all this anxiety about me! I have tried, but tried in vain."

"Perhaps I can assist you," said Smeaton, in a lower tone than ever. "Nay, do not start, and look round at me. Those men behind must not see that there is any thing more than ordinary in our talk. Now let us have a gallop, if you will. I have ventured to open a subject with you, somewhat abruptly, which I have in vain sought an opportunity of touching upon from the first moment of my arrival. We must take opportunity when we find it. Now shake your rein, dear lady. Give your jennet her head, and let us cast these ideas from us for a moment or two. They will return before the end of our ride."

"They will not be shaken from me, let me gallop as I will," replied Emmeline. "However, let us forward;" and, touching her horse lightly with her riding-whip, she bounded away some paces before her companion.

Smeaton was at her side again in a moment, however; and when she turned her eyes toward him as he came up, sitting his horse with calm and quiet ease, motionless in the saddle, as if he were a part of the noble animal itself, she could not help thinking him the handsomest man she had ever beheld in her life, and so, indeed, he was.

To Smeaton she was an object of great interest—ay, and I must add, of great admiration also. The exquisite beauty of her face and form was at that moment heightened, not only by a dress which displayed it to the best advantage, but by the attitudes into which the exercise threw her, calling forth innumerable graces, and by the movements of the mind springing from the conversation just past, and filling her eyes with light and eagerness. Their looks met; and, with that sort of sudden sympathy which enables those of like character to read in an instant what is passing in the minds of others, each seemed to divine the feelings of the other. Emmeline's cheek glowed as if she had been detected in a fault; and Smeaton withdrew his eyes, with a thoughtful look, and made some common-place observation on the scene.

For a few minutes they rode on at the same rapid pace, leaving the servants still further behind them than they had previously been; and then Emmeline drew in her rein, saying,

"I have had enough of this. You will say I am a capricious girl, Colonel Smeaton. I wanted a gallop when you did not desire one, and I am tired of it as soon as I have got it. But, in truth," she added, "I am anxious that you should go on with what you were saying. I can not ride fast in a state of wonder and mystery. You say you can assist me in explaining all the many enigmas of my fate. You say that you have longed to talk with me on this subject ever since you have been at Ale. You must have very keen eyes, or Sir John Newark must have told you something about me when he saw you in London."

"Neither, dear lady," answered Smeaton, looking behind to see how far off the servants were. "I should have remarked nothing calling for much attention had I not had previous knowledge, and yet Sir John Newark would not have suffered me to enter his gates had he been aware that I possessed any information whatever regarding you."

"Then you *do* possess information?" exclaimed Emmeline, eagerly.

"You have been an object of interest to me, dear lady," answered her companion, "for some years. This seems strange to you; but it will seem stranger still when I tell you that, most likely, I should not have visited this part of England at all had you not been here. But, tell me, can you be very discreet? for much depends upon your prudence and your secrecy. If I tell you things which have been studiously concealed from you, you must put a guard upon your lips and upon your looks. You must seem as ignorant as ever of all that appertains to your own fate. That bright frankness—that free pouring forth of the heart must all be checked. You must learn the hard lesson which the world, sooner or later, teaches to all, to conceal the feelings and the thoughts—to hide the treasures of the heart and mind, in short, from the eyes of those who would wrong us. Can you do this?"

"I will try," answered Emmeline, gravely, "though I know not how I shall succeed, for I have never yet been proved. I have no experience in the art of concealment—and yet," she continued, "I fear I have not been altogether so frank as you imagine. I can not tell why, but there is something in my good guardian—kind and careful of me as he is—which prevents me from telling him all I think—from speaking my wishes or my thoughts upon important things. Any ordinary favor, any common gratification, I could ask without fear of refusal; but yet, the questions I most long to ask, I dare not put; the thoughts that are most strong and most busy in my brain, I do not venture to pour forth."

"It is an instinct," said Smeaton. "You must, however, try to attain the discretion to which I have alluded; and perhaps it may be better for me to say no more till you are more certain of yourself."

"Oh, no, no," said Emmeline. "Do not keep me in long suspense. I will be very prudent, indeed."

"Well, then, first let me ask you a few questions," said her companion; "but pray speak in a low voice, for the men are coming near, and no caution can be too great. Can you recollect any thing of your very early years?"

Emmeline shook her head.

"Very little," she replied, "and that little indistinct and vague. Things appear, indeed, to memory, but they look like the ships I have seen sailing over the sea in a thick mist. I catch a cloudy outline—a strange, ill-defined form—for one brief instant, flitting by, and then it passes into the fog again, and I see it no more."

"Let us try if we can not render these images more distinct," said Smeaton. "Do you recollect ever having lived in other places different from the scenes around you?"

"No," answered Emmeline, at once. "The old house, and the wood, and the hamlet, and the stream, and Ale Head, and the bright bay, are among the earliest things that I remember. I do not think I ever lived any where else, for I can recollect little things of no consequence happening at the Manor when I must have been quite a child. I remember well crying over a broken puppet in a room that was then called the nursery. I must have been very young then; and memory goes no further back."

Smeaton mused.

"I think it is very likely you are right," he said. "I do not know that you ever lived elsewhere; but you must have been surrounded in Ale-Manor by other people than those who now dwell in it."

"Oh, yes," cried Emmeline. "Of that I am quite sure; for memories come across me, and trouble me like figures in a dream."

"Do you recollect a lady," asked her companion, "tall and graceful, with a smile peculiarly sweet, and a silvery voice?"

Emmeline gazed down thoughtfully.

"Yes," she said, at length, "I think I do; and she was very fond of me, if I remember rightly. Stay! yes, I remember her quite well. You call her back to my mind. She led me out by the hand upon the terrace to see the soldiers go away. Oh, yes, I recollect it all quite well now."

"And who was at the head of the soldiers?" asked Smeaton.

"I do not recollect," replied the lady, gazing forward into the air.

"Was it a tall, dark, noble-looking man, with a broad hat, and a plume in it?" asked Smeaton.

"No, no," cried Emmeline. "He was standing by my side; and he took me up in his arms, and kissed me, before he mounted his horse. How strange it is that I should have forgotten all this until now!"

"No, perhaps not strange," replied Smeaton. "A single word will often wake up a long train of memories which have lain asleep for years. The association of ideas has wonderful power: like the wind touching one string of an Eolian harp, it sets all the harmonies of the heart vibrating. But do you recollect any thing more of those times."

"Not clearly," answered Emmeline; "but still you have awakened enough to lead memory on, I doubt not, through many another path of the past. I see, indeed, you must know much of me and mine. I beseech you, Colonel Smeaton, tell me more."

"I would rather, in the first instance," he said, "let your own memory do all that it can do, placing it in the right road, and letting it follow out the track, instead of prompting you by information which, after having rested in your mind for a certain time, will seem like memory. But there, if I mistake not, is the church before us. I did not seize so eagerly your offer to show it to me without a motive, dear lady. I wanted to point out to you certain monuments which it contains, and beg you to remark them particularly, for they may afford you much information."

"Oh, I have gazed at them for hours," answered Emmeline, "and could extract nothing from them."

"Perhaps you may be more successful now," replied Smeaton. "At all events, whenever I lay my hand upon a monument, remark it particularly. If we should be alone, I may, perhaps, read a comment on it at the time; but if there is any one with us—and we must not seem particularly anxious to carry on our observations in private—I will merely lay my hand upon the tomb I wish you to notice, and read the inscription upon it."

"But, then, do you know them already?" asked Emmeline. "Have you ever been here before?"

"Never," answered Smeaton, with a smile, "the words upon the tombs will be sufficient to guide me. But we are coming near. I had better call up the men to hold the horses."

Raising his hand, he beckoned to the servants behind, who rode up just as they reached the little gate at the church-yard.

Both Emmeline and he were very thoughtful when they dismounted, and they walked on toward the great door in silence. Just as they reached it, however, Smeaton turned, and called to the men who were holding the horses in a group, saying,

"Walk them about till we come back. The air is keen upon these hills, even at midsummer."

The rest of the conversation between himself, and Emmeline, and the old sexton, on their first entrance into the church, has been already detailed, as it was overheard by Van Noost; and Smeaton and the lady proceeded along the nave, listening with wonderful patience to the prolix details of the old man. He pointed out to them the tomb of Sir Reginald de Newark, who had gone to the Holy Land with Richard the First, and told them what gallant deeds he had done in battle, and how he had returned to his native country to die at home of wounds received in war against the Saracens. Many a blunder did he make, confounding kings, and countries, and events in a very disastrous manner. But Smeaton did not correct him, and laid not his hand upon that tomb. Then they came to a large slab of gray marble, with a figure in long robes sculptured on it, having a miter on the head, and crosier by the side, but with every feature of the face obliterated. This, the old man told them, was the effigy of William de Newark, Bishop of Exeter, who had chosen to be buried in that church because it stood upon the lands of the family. Still Smeaton passed on without question or comment. Another and another succeeded; and the old sexton was beginning to think the visitor exceedingly dull, when, approaching nearer to the communion-table, they stood opposite the monument of the gallant soldier who had fallen at Naseby.

This seemed to interest the visitor more, and, stretching out his hand, he laid it on the marble, saying,

"What a pity it is they have so brutally defaced this fine statue!"

The old sexton entered into his usual story about it, told how the church had been occupied by Cromwell's soldiers, and how they had made a stable of the nave. Many were the abominations with which he charged them; and Smeaton asked several questions, which helped him on wonderfully with his tale. The colonel then approached the wall of the church, and, pointing to the tablet which recorded the death of another member of the family in a foreign land, he asked the old man, after reading the inscription, whether the line had become there extinct.

"Oh, bless you, no, sir," replied the sexton. "After the happy Restoration, this good soldier's son returned with the king. He had been taken abroad by his uncle, who died at Breda. His monument stands there;" and, leading them across to a darker part of the church, he showed them a tomb with a kneeling figure, having a sword in its hand. The inscription on the marble tablet below was very brief. It simply said,

"To the memory of Algernon, Baron Newark, of Newark Castle and Ale-Manor, Knight, who died on the second day of July, 1690, this monument is erected, as a testimony of love and veneration, by his widow and his son."

"That was the day after the battle of the Boyne," observed Smeaton.

The old sexton nodded his head significantly. "Ay, sir, so it was. I recollect it well; and when they brought the body home from Ireland, these old hands dug the grave for as noble a lord and as good a man as ever lived. But it was all done very quietly, for people were in great fear of what might happen next; and the monument was not erected till two years after."

Smeaton laid his hand upon it, saying,

"It is fine in its simplicity. What became of the son who is mentioned here?"

"I don't know, sir," answered the man, shortly, and then walked on toward another part of the church, mumbling his jaws together as if he were muttering something to himself.

Emmeline looked up in Smeaton's face with an inquiring glance, but his only comment was by taking her hand and leading her away. He might press it gently as he did so, but he said nothing till they rejoined the old man, when he inquired, in a careless tone,

"Are there not vaults, or a crypt, to this church? From the height of the pavement, I should think so."

"Oh, yes," replied Emmeline, answering for the sexton. "There is a beautiful crypt."

"Ay, but I have not got the key, my lady," said the old man.

"Why, it is in the door, Mattocks," rejoined Emmeline. "I saw it as we passed."

The old sexton laughed aloud.

"That's true, my lady," he said; "but I've got a bird in there, and that's the truth, so that I would rather not open the door if I can help it; not that I think *you* would tell, or this gentleman either, for it could do you no good, and might do the poor fellow some harm."

"Oh, be assured we will not tell any thing," replied Smeaton. "But we must see the crypt, my good man. To me it is one of the most interesting parts of a church."

"Well, sir, must is must," answered the sexton, "and I can not stop you, if you like to go. Only mind, you've promised not to tell about seeing any one there."

"We'll be as secret as a father-confessor," answered Smeaton, gayly; "but first I should like to look at your register-books. Can not we see the inside of the vestry?"

The old man gazed earnestly in his face for an instant, and then replied, coldly and repulsively,

"You can see the inside of the vestry, sir, if you like, but the books are not there. They are always kept by the parson under lock and key."

"Are they at his house?" asked Smeaton.

"I think not," replied the old man; "but all I know is, that they are not at the church. If you want any certificates out, you must ask the parson."

"Well, let us down to the crypt, then," replied Smeaton. "Can we see down there, think you?"

"Your eyes are younger than mine, and *I* can," answered the sexton, gruffly; and he proceeded to open the door.

"I suppose you are clerk as well as sexton?" said Smeaton, as he passed him.

"I am not regularly appointed clerk," replied the man. "I hold both offices at the will and pleasure of Sir John Newark."

There was something very significant in his tone and manner as he said these words; but Smeaton merely smiled and passed on, holding out his hand to guide Emmeline in descending the steps. A few seconds brought them to the bottom, and both looked round, with not unnatural curiosity, to see whom the old sexton had shut up in the crypt. The next minute, however, Smeaton laughed gayly.

"Why, my good friend Van Noost," he exclaimed, "is that you? What, in Fortune's name, has brought you into this part of the country?"

"Ah, noble sir," cried Van Noost, in a lamentable tone, "what a fright you gave me a few minutes ago! It was not fortune, but misfortune, brought me. Have you not heard that the Earl of Oxford is committed to the Tower, and that they are seeking for all his friends and adherents to clap them up in Newgate?"

"No, indeed," replied Smeaton. "Not caring much about it, I have heard little about it; but I fancy you are frightened without much cause, my good friend; for, depend upon it, the falcons which are now on the wing are checking at higher-flying game than yourself. But what made you think of coming to this part of the world?"

"Why, I know it of old to be a lonely, desolate part of the country," said Van Noost. "Besides, I knew you were down here, and I thought you might give me a little help in case of need."

"How can I do that?" asked Smeaton. "I have no influence with these people. But come hither for a moment, and speak to me apart. If I can help you, I will."

As he spoke, he led the way to the other side of the crypt, where he conversed with the statuary for a few moments in a low voice, saying, in the end,

"Well, do as you like. If you find yourself safe here, stay; but in case of any danger, you can go to Keanton, where you will be quite safe. Tell the people the word I said, and they will take care of you."

"What a beautiful creature she is!" exclaimed Van Noost, whose eyes had been fixed on Emmeline for the last minute or two. "Dear me, what a delicious dairy-maid she would make, cast in lead!"

"More fitted for a Grace, I think," replied Smeaton, with a smile. "But, remember, go to Keanton if you like."

Thus saying, he rejoined Emmeline and the old sexton.

The last words were spoken aloud, and reached the ears both of the sexton and Emmeline. The old man muttered to himself the word "Keanton," and scratched his head. The young lady turned her eyes quickly toward Smeaton, but made no comment at the time. The party then, followed by Van Noost, commented on the various things they saw, and the worthy artist in lead enlightened them, from time to time, with opinions on the various monuments. No part of the conversation, however, would be very entertaining to the reader; and with regard to the monuments themselves, only one seemed, even to Smeaton, worthy of remark: this was a small tablet fixed in the lower part of a wall, bearing inscribed upon it the following words:

"To the memory of Edward and Henry Newark, sons of Henry Algernon, third Baron Newark. They died in infancy."

There was no date, but the monument was comparatively new. Dust, indeed, lay on the marble, somewhat obscuring the letters, with a softening effect, like that of Time on memory of sorrow; but the pure white stone had not yet acquired the yellow tint of age and decay.

"I suppose that tablet has not been long put up," said Smeaton, touching it with his hand.

"Sixteen years ago, sir, come the day after Michaelmas," replied the old sexton; and there he stopped, evidently not disposed to enter into any particulars regarding the later branches of the Newark family.

Smeaton, however, asked no more questions, but, shaking hands with Van Noost, and giving the old man a piece of money, which seemed more than he expected, left the church, and remounted with Emmeline.

The lady and her companion rode on for a few moments in silence; but at length Smeaton said, bending his head and speaking low,

"Do you comprehend what you have seen?"

She shook her head gravely, and then replied,

"It is like seeing the picture of a city we never visited. There are houses, and streets, and public places, but, unless we have a guide or a map, we know not what they are. The monuments I have already seen, the names upon them I have heard before, but know not to whom or by whom they were erected."

Smeaton paused, and gazed at her earnestly, as if he hesitated to proceed.

"Dear lady," he said at length, "I needs must trust you, or rather must trust to your own discretion, for it is yourself and your future fate which is to be influenced by your prudence or imprudence. Let me warn you, however, that your own happiness and the possibility of your obtaining further information depend upon your concealing from every one that you have received any information at all; but I believe you have a spirit of sufficient power, Emmeline, to govern your words, and even looks, when you know that so much is at stake."

He called her Emmeline for the first time—perhaps before the length of their acquaintance justified it; but it sounded very pleasant to her ear; and, indeed, that day's ride, and the matters of deep interest which had been discussed between them, had drawn them closer to each other than if they had been acquainted many months.

"I will be prudent and careful, indeed," she replied. "I should ill repay your kindness if I neglected your warning for a moment."

"Well, then," replied Smeaton, "you have seen just now the monument of your ancestor who fell at Naseby; that of his son, your grandfather, who died the day after the battle of the Boyne; and a tablet to the memory of your grandfather's brother, the father of Sir John Newark—"

"And my father?" interrupted Emmeline; "my father?"

"Of that hereafter," replied Smeaton. "This is enough for one day, surely; but I may add that the little tablet in the crypt which we last saw commemorates the death of your two brothers in infancy. They were older than yourself, but perished early. And now, dear lady, I have told you thus much in order to win your confidence, for I may yet have to ask you to trust me in many things; and, in the very first place, I must crave a great boon from you, which is this, to give me every opportunity—nay, to make opportunities—of conversing with you in private, for much yet remains to be said—nay, perhaps much to be done, and I can clearly see that Sir John Newark will not often let our conferences be unwatched, if he can help it. Can you trust me, Emmeline?"

"Oh, yes, I think I can—nay, I am *sure* I can," she answered. "Yet I do not know how I shall manage, for I am unaccustomed to such things. I thank you much for what you have told me, but I must—indeed I *must*—know more. I am not such an enigma to myself as I was; but still there is a cloud over one part of my history which must be cleared away, although I suppose I shall find to the end that there are enigmas in every thing in this world. Do you know that even you are beginning to be an enigma to me?"

"How so?" exclaimed Smeaton, looking at her frankly as she gazed, with a smile, in his face.

"I will tell you," she said. "You bade that man in the crypt go to Keanton, if he liked, as if you were its master. Now I always heard that Keanton was the property of the Countess of Eskdale—that countess who went to share her husband's exile."

"That enigma is soon explained," replied Smeaton. "I am her son. Heaven send that I be not soon the master of Keanton indeed! But I much fear it; for my mother has been very ill. As I ask you for much confidence, I must not withhold any part of mine from you, and therefore I tell you the fact at once. But this is a piece of knowledge, dear lady, that you must conceal from Sir John Newark, although he knows the fact; for, if he finds that I have revealed it to you, it may raise suspicion as to what more I have revealed, which it were well to avoid."

Emmeline mused for a moment or two with her eyes cast down, and then looking up again, she said,

"Then your name is not Smeaton really?"

"No, indeed," he replied. "My name is Eskdale. But let me explain to you. It is not at all an uncommon custom now, among the many who have been driven forth by the rebellions and revolutions in this land, to assume a name different from their own when entering the service of foreign states. Thus, while I have been in the Austrian army, warring in Spain and Italy, I took the name of Henry Smeaton, rose in the service under that name, and never dropped it until my father's death, somewhat more than a year ago. I have with me my commission, granted under that name, and many papers and letters, all addressed to me, or speaking of me, as Colonel Henry Smeaton, so that the title was not merely assumed for the present occasion. But here comes your young cousin, I think, to meet us. His fishing expedition, it would seem, is soon over."

"Poor boy!" replied Emmeline. "He is so volatile, he can pursue nothing long. I do not think he is so much without ability as he seems, for occasionally his thoughts are very bright and fanciful. But it is the power of fixing his attention that he wants. Of that he is utterly devoid, and it is the secret of his great deficiency."

A moment or two after, they were joined by Richard Newark, who exclaimed, in a joyful voice, "I am glad I have found you before my father comes back, for, after we had fished for an hour, I got in a fright, remembering what he had said about not leaving you, Emmy; so I got a horse, and galloped all the way here, thinking every minute I should see him riding back with you. So you must hold your tongue, Emmy, and not let him know that I have been away at all."

All conversation now ended for the time between Emmeline and Smeaton, for the boy's presence was of course a restraint, and the minds of both rested thoughtfully on the subjects of deeper interest of which they had been lately talking. This continued till they reached the mansion; but there they found Sir John Newark had not yet returned, and some time was destined to pass before he again appeared on the scene.

CHAPTER IX.

Emmeline had retired to change her dress. Richard had gone, Heaven knows whither; and Smeaton, after pausing for a few minutes in the hall, seemingly very busy in examining the suits of old armor which had hung there since the days of Elizabeth, but in reality seeing none of them with the mind's eye, though he moved round from one to the other merely like a piece of mechanism, at length walked up the stairs to the two rooms which, as I have said, had been appropriated to his use.

We must draw the curtain of the breast and look in; not, perhaps, tracing thought by thought—who can, even when he looks into his own heart?—but giving such glimpses as may show sufficiently what was passing within.

"This is unfortunate," he said to himself; "and I must resist such feelings—yet why? I can not answer why. She is very, very beautiful, graceful, gentle, bright, unsullied by this foul and dusty world in which we live. Why should I doubt or hesitate? Because my own sensations take me by surprise, and I feel myself led on by impulse rather than by reason. But what does boasted Reason do for us in such things as these? More frequently she misleads than directs us rightly. I will let things take their course. It is but my own happiness I peril; and, without periling it, I can not serve Emmeline as I could wish—nay, nor fully keep my promise. I will risk it. Perhaps these sensations will wear away. I remember when I thought myself desperately in love with the Spanish girl, the poor cura's niece at Valencia, and it ended in disgust: I do not think it will do so here. Then it was but sleepy black eyes, and a warm sunny cheek, and a neat boddice, and a pretty foot—with passion enough in all conscience, but neither soul nor mind. No, no! Emmeline is very different—yet it may wear off. If I have thought much of her—dreamed of her, I may say, by day and night, since I have known her—it is very natural, without love having any thing to do with it. Her strange fate; the wrong that has been done her; the greater wrong, I fear, intended her; the eager desire to free her from this thraldom, and to open her mind to her own history, and yet the difficulty of so doing, may all well have created an interest independent of love. Yet she is very beautiful and very charming. There is something winning in that smile, half tender, half playful; and certainly Nature, in its happiest leisure, never molded a form of more exquisite symmetry. It makes one's heart beat almost to gaze upon her, surpassing far the highest effort of the sculptor's art, and full of living graces which neither sculptor's chisel nor painter's brush could ever catch or portray. Hark! she is singing! Ay, a well-remembered song of my young days. Her chamber must be near this, from the distinctness of the sounds."

"Mellow year, mellow year,
The winter time is near
With its frost, and its snow, and its wind;
When the branches are all bare,
And tempests load the air,
And icy chains the dancing rivers bind."

The song ceased, and the light accompaniment of a lute or mandolin ceased likewise. It seemed but a little outburst of that spirit of music which is in almost every young heart; and Smeaton said to himself, "I will sing her the next stanza; perhaps she does not know it."

And with a rich, mellow tenor voice, he went on with the song thus:

"But the Spring, the bright Spring,
On his green-embroidered wing,
Is speeding from the South all the while;
Scatt'ring flowers on Winter's way,
And repairing all decay,
And teaching tearful eyes again to smile."

He listened for a moment, but all was silent; and then, opening the door of his room, he descended again to the saloon. He had hardly been there a moment when Emmeline joined him, with a bright, frank smile upon her face, saying, as she entered,

"You have been singing—and one of my dear old nursery songs."

"You left it incomplete," replied Smeaton; "and as it is one of *my* dear old nursery songs too, I felt myself called upon, for its honor, to add the last stanza—at least, the last that I remember, for I believe there are several more."

"Oh, yes," replied Emmeline. "I will sing them all to you some evening, though Sir John Newark is not very fond of music. Are you?"

"I do not know what life would be without it," replied Smeaton. "Mine, I know, would have lost many of its few happy hours."

"And does your wife like music? And does she sing often? And has she a good voice?" exclaimed Emmeline, putting question upon question before her companion could answer. But a gay smile upon Smeaton's lips stopped her at length.

"My wife, dear lady!" he said, half laughing. "My wife! I hope she will sing, if I am ever fortunate enough to have one; but up to the present hour, certainly, I have no wife."

Emmeline looked astonished, almost frightened; and for a moment she stood gazing in his face in silence, and then said, in a slow and hesitating manner,

"Sir John Newark told me you had a wife."

"Did he, indeed?" asked Smeaton, with a smile, not unmingled with a look of astonishment; but, the moment after, he added, "Now, I remember, there was conversation between us regarding Lady Eskdale. He must have changed my mother into my wife, it seems, which is contrary, dear lady, to the law of all lands. He pressed the subject upon me, I recollect, and I gave him very short answers, not thinking fit to enter upon my own or my mother's affairs with him. I imagined that he wished to discover what we intended to do with Keanton; but he has led himself into a great mistake, for I have no wife, I can assure you, dear lady."

Emmeline was agitated, she knew not why. Indeed, she did not ask herself. All that she felt was that her heart beat more quickly than usual; that a change seemed to have come over her thoughts and feelings in an instant; that all was altered in the relations between her and her companion. It seemed very strange to her: it confused her, even seemed to alarm her; and, with eager quickness, memory ran back over all that had passed between her and Smeaton, as though to ascertain if she had committed no fault toward him under the mistake into which she had been led. She remembered that he had twice called her Emmeline; and she recollected more than once that a look of admiration had come upon his face when his eyes were turned toward her, the very memory of which deepened the color in her cheek. She was very young and very inexperienced, and the discovery she had made filled her with many emotions which she strove not to disentangle or to scan, but which, though agitating, were certainly not painful. She remained so long silent, however, busied in these thoughts, that Smeaton himself was somewhat pained.

"She has been only thus bright and frank with me," he thought, "because she believed me to be a married man; and in all the signs of dawning regard which I fancied her looks and words betrayed, I have been mistaken."

Man's heart, however, is a very dark and intricate thing. Solomon and a great many other personages have affirmed this, and I believe it. There is nothing which spurs love on like a little difficulty; and Smeaton, who a few minute's before had been doubting whether he was really falling in love at all, and whether he ought to say or do any thing which might tend to win her affection, had no longer the least doubt on the subject. He did not pause long to consider, but, taking her hand in his, he said,

"Emmeline, you have been deceived by Sir John's representation; but does this make any difference in your confidence and regard? Will you not trust me—will you not rely upon me, though I be unmarried, as much as you would freely have done, had the tale you heard been true?"

She did not attempt to withdraw her hand from his, but raised her beautiful eyes to his face, asking simply,

"Ought I?"

"Why not?" he exclaimed. "Could my having a wife make me more a man of honor? Could it render me more anxious to serve you—to free you from a painful, a difficult, a dangerous situation? Could it make you more safe than in trusting to my word as a gentleman and a Christian to use all my efforts for your service, and for the promotion of your happiness alone?"

"No, oh no," answered Emmeline, in reply to his eager questions; but he still went on, saying,

"Would it not rather throw difficulties in our way? Might it not produce a thousand embarrassments, whereas, if any now occur, you can yourself remove them by a few short words?"

The meaning of the last part of the sentence seemed clear enough, and after a time it came back to her memory; but at the moment, confused by a variety of feelings, to her new and strange, and of thoughts which seemed only to become more entangled every moment, she replied,

"I have so little experience—I am so ignorant of how I ought to act, or even what I ought to think, that—"

She paused, unable to conclude the sentence; but, seeing a look of pain on his face, she laid her hand gently upon his, saying,

"Do not let me grieve you. I would not do so for the world. I have the utmost trust, the utmost confidence in you, and will show it frankly. But add this to all your other kindness: tell me truly and sincerely how I ought to act, what I ought to do, and I will do it. Guide me, guide me, noble friend, for I feel that I have none to whom I can look for guidance but you."

The tears rose in her eyes as she spoke; and Smeaton, with a look which could not alarm or agitate her, bent his head and pressed his lips upon her hand.

"I will be your guide, dear Emmeline," he said; "and so God help me as I seek, in guiding you, your own happiness, your own safety, before any other objects whatsoever."

Emmeline raised her eyes to his face, full of bright drops; and his words and that answering look formed a bond between them for life.

There are instincts far stronger, far clearer, far truer than any conclusion of reason or any deduction from experience. The shrewd, the cunning, the hackneyed in the world do well not to trust to them; for in the first two classes, Nature having endowed them with other qualities for their guidance and defense, in general denies them these instincts, just as she denies horns to a lion, and claws to an elephant: they are provided, and want not further help; and, with the hackneyed man of the world, if ever possessed of such instincts, they are soon worn out, and the traces of them obscured; but with the guileless and inexperienced, they are a sure, and often the only guide and defense.

The same instinctive feeling of dread and doubt which taught her to shrink from Sir John Newark, which barred all confidence and checked all affection, made her heart spring to meet the friendship—perhaps I might call it by a tenderer name—of Smeaton, and long to pour out all its feelings and thoughts before him. The agitation of new sensations, however, checked her for the time, and all she said was,

"Oh, how happy it is to have some one in whom we can wholly trust and rely!"

That was a blessed moment for Smeaton. It was to the affection which had sprung up, and was budding in his heart, like the soft beams of a bright morning sun upon an opening rose, teaching it to expand in all its full sweetness; and he gazed upon her with a look of love which could not be mistaken. Of words there was little need; yet words trembled on his lips which could never be unsaid. Suddenly Emmeline, with a start, withdrew her hand from his. They had thought themselves, throughout the whole scene, alone; but it was not so. The windows were partly open to admit the balmy air; and, though they did not descend to the ground, as modern windows do, yet they were not raised more than a foot or two above the level of the terrace without. For the last two or three minutes, a figure had been standing at the angle of the most westerly window, and looking in, half hidden by the stone-work. It now moved across toward the great door, and the shadow that it cast upon the floor of the room roused Emmeline from her dreams of happiness with a sensation of fear.

"What is the matter?" exclaimed Smeaton, surprised by her sudden start.

"Some one passed across the window," replied Emmeline, with the color mounting warmly into her cheek.

"Was it Sir John Newark?" asked Smeaton, while a cloud came over his brow. "If so, a full explanation must come before it is desirable."

"I think not," replied Emmeline. "The shadow first caught my eye, and, before I could see distinctly, the figure was gone. Nevertheless, I think it was that of Richard."

Smeaton mused for a moment, and then said,

"Of course he will tell his father what he may have seen and overheard, and we must take our determination accordingly, Emmeline."

"I do not think he will," said Emmeline, eagerly; but she paused at the next sentence, adding, more slowly, as if not knowing well how to express what she meant without some violation of propriety, "Very few persons here, I believe, are inclined to tell my guardian any thing unless he asks. Why it is I am sure I do not know, for he is very kind in most things; yet they seem to fear him, and do not like to say what they think lest they should make mischief. Some of the servants, indeed, but not many even of them, report to him all that passes under their eyes; but I have never dared to speak freely with him upon any thing, and I believe Richard feels the same. Hark! there is his foot coming through the great hall. It must have been he who was looking through the window. Poor boy! he would never think of repeating any thing which he thought could pain me; but I ought not to ask him to conceal any thing from his father."

"Certainly not," replied Smeaton, frankly. "Let things take their course; only ascertain as soon as possible what he really does do; and, in the mean time, dear Emmeline, let me beseech you to cast away all restraint toward me. It is needful to you and to your own future fate now; and I feel it is needful to me and my happiness that you should give me every opportunity of speaking to you, consulting with you, advising you in private. Though *I*, perhaps, must find the opportunities, you must aid me to take advantage of them. Much must be decided within the next two or three weeks; and upon what is decided, all the future course of your life will depend—and mine also," he added, in a lower voice: "ay, and of mine also."

Before she could reply, the latch of the door was raised, and Richard Newark entered the room with a slow and thoughtful pace, very different from his light, irregular walk. Emmeline drew a step back, but Smeaton remained exactly where he was, without the slightest change of look or manner, while the boy advanced into the room, humming to himself the snatch of some old song, as if wrapped up in his own thoughts, and hardly conscious that any body was there.

"Well, Richard," said Smeaton, "where have you been wandering?"

"I have been upon the terrace for the last five minutes," replied the lad, simply.

"That I know," rejoined Smeaton. "We saw your shadow on the floor."

"Indeed!" exclaimed Richard Newark, evidently with some surprise. "I thought you did not see me; but this preposterous knob between my two shoulders, filled with all sorts of things that never get into other people's heads, betrays me, I suppose, wherever I go. Well, never mind! What matters it to me if nightingales will sit and sing on the edge of a hawk's nest? It is no matter of mine; and I can keep things to myself as well as my elders and my betters. Only, 'ware the springe, noble colonel. Woodcocks have put their necks into a noose before now."

Emmeline and her lover, for so I think I may now venture to call him, looked at each other, as if uncertain how to act; but then, starting forward with her wild grace, the beautiful girl laid her hand upon her cousin's arm, saying,

"Do you not love me, Richard? Have you not said that, if you were my brother, you could not love me more?"

The boy's whole manner was changed in a moment.

"That I do, Emmeline," he cried, catching her hand in his, and holding out his other hand to Smeaton. "I love you both, and will do any thing I can to serve you. Trust to me, trust to me, and don't be a bit afraid. I will find means to help you at a pinch. I know that my brain is somewhat askew, but that is not my fault; and there is some wit within, though it lies in odd corners. For your sake, Emmeline, and for yours too, Smeaton, I will rummage it out, and try if I can not make it serviceable. I will do you no harm, if I can not do you good."

"Take care of that, Richard," said Smeaton, gravely.

The boy nodded his head significantly, and then added, with a loud laugh,

"And now I will be odder than ever, to cover what is going on within; but I can tell you, dear girl, that I have rendered you one service this morning already; for, if *I* had not been at the window, somebody else would."

"Who?" exclaimed Emmeline, with a look of apprehension.

"Old Mrs. Culpepper was going out for her evening airing," replied the boy, smiling, "with her stealthy tiptoe step, like a cat crossing the greensward on a dewy morning. She tended this way, Emmy; but when she saw me lolling against the window-frame, she crept off to prowl in another direction. She watches you, all the while she is purring around you, more closely than you know, and it is better to have me there than her, I can tell you."

"I am sure it is, Richard," answered Emmeline. "But what you say surprises and shocks me. I did not know that I required watching by any one. So Heaven help me, as I desire and seek no wrong, but only to be as rightly happy as it is God's will I should be."

"No more does a tit-lark, Emmy," replied the boy; "and yet they shut him up in an iron cage, and only give him a bit of turf to make him remember how joyful he would be if he could spread his freed wings, and soar away up into the sky."

There was something in the simile which touched Emmeline to the heart; her eyes filled with tears; and, darting away, she quitted the room, leaving Smeaton and Richard Newark together.

CHAPTER X.

Sir John Newark rode away toward Exeter. At first he went fast, for the thoughts with which he set out were not altogether devoid of uneasiness. He did not like leaving Emmeline, Richard, and Smeaton together; not that there was any definite cause in his mind for the unpleasant sensations that he felt, but, with most men of his character, there is throughout the whole of life a pervading feeling of insecurity, which is a hard price, taken at the full sum, and which by slow installments they pay sooner or later for any advantages obtained by cunning, duplicity, and deceit. They are never secure. They are always afraid of discovery and loss. The house they have built is based upon sand, and they know that it is so. There is an ever-present dread, a dark consciousness of the sword suspended by a hair over them. They may drown the thought in wine; they may outroar the small, still voice in revelry and merriment; by laughter and by song, they may strive to keep its sounds from their ears; but still it is speaking in the secret tribunal of the heart—ever, ever speaking, accusing, condemning, threatening.

There were times, of course, when this sensation of insecurity was more strong than at others: he never felt safe when Emmeline was left alone with any body but one of his own creatures; and there was something in the character and demeanor of Smeaton which made him feel that he might be very dangerous to dishonest purposes, if he had a knowledge of them. He quieted himself, however, in some degree, by a belief in his ignorance. He said to himself,

"It is evident he knows nothing of these people except by hearsay. Moreover, he can not suspect any thing from what he has seen here. He beholds nothing but kindness and affection. I treat her as a daughter—a beloved daughter. No, no, he can suspect nothing. Yet I have seen a light come up into his eyes when he looks upon her, a bland, fond smile upon his lip, which is strange for so short an acquaintance. It is natural, perhaps, for she is certainly very pretty; but he is married, so there can be no harm. Yet, suppose his wife were to die? Well, then I must shut my gates against him; that is all. He can not force his way in, unless I choose to let him. Perhaps I may make something of this Keanton property, if one could but get him to entangle himself a little more against the government. He would be glad enough to take a small sum from a friend for that which was likely to be forfeited to the crown. It is a fine estate, full three thousand a year, and carries, if I mistake not, the barony with it. These troubles must be productive of good, if one knew how to take advantage of them."

This train of thought carried him on further, and away from the subject of his apprehensions. He had been riding fast in order to return speedily; but now he slackened his pace, and proceeded to consider deliberately the condition of the times, the position of the existing government, and especially the state of that part of the country in which he dwelt. He was one of those men—and they are a somewhat numerous class—who are skillful at angling in troubled waters. He was well inclined to stir those waters, too, for the purpose of catching more fish, but he was very careful not to plunge into them too deeply himself. He knew, as well as any agitator of the present day, how to keep just on the right side of law, how to prompt without acting, how to suggest without proposing, how to make dissuasion act as a persuasive; how, in fact, to stir up rebellion without being a rebel, and to act a traitor's part without incurring the punishment of a traitor. He had, moreover, that great skill which consists in leading men, whom you are openly engaged in opposing, to believe that you may be induced by favors to support them; in fact, to put yourself up for sale at a high price, and to force it from the purchaser by annoyance; not to ticket or label the article with the sum demanded, but to let it be understood. This is the most useful of arts in the mercenary world we dwell in; and men do contrive to enact such tricks, and yet bear an unblushing front and a proud carriage, as if the honors and rewards they obtain were yielded to merit, not necessity. In his most vehement tirades against a minister or a government, Sir John could drop some few favorable words to show that he was not hopelessly adverse. He could praise one set of measures while he declaimed against others. He could affect uncertainty with regard to some of their lines of policy. He could pretend to believe the motives good, but the means mistaken. He could single out one man from a ministry, when he saw him falling, and pursue him with the most virulent rancor in order to attribute all the bad acts of his colleagues to him, if they choose to purchase his support after the other's fall.

He was not at all singular. We see such men every day, and all the time they are independent men. The very excess of their trimming, when managed skillfully, gains for them, among those who do not see deeply into the human heart, a reputation for conscientiousness. They are supposed to sacrifice their friends for their convictions, and to change their convictions from their judgment. Verily, they are wise in their generation.

"This dynasty will stand," said Sir John Newark to himself. "Yes, it will stand. It may not have the affections of the nation—doubtless it has not; but it has the passions and prejudices of Englishmen—ay, and their good, sober sense too. Love is a mad passion that will not be subservient. Prejudice is a sturdy beast, which will be guided any way, so that it get home at last. There is no lack of zeal among the Jacobites. Zeal! Heaven keep us from zeal. It is like a sky-rocket, which no one can direct. The Whigs have something better than zeal. They have firmness, consistence, unity, common sense, energy. Then they have the words that sooner or later rule the multitude: liberty — freedom — rights — privileges; and those not the rights and privileges of the few, but of the many. The others have nothing but zeal. Heaven help us! And courage—ay, and courage! There is no lack of courage; but with it, luckily, its usual adjuncts, wild rashness, pig-headed obstinacy, and a mighty host of all those brilliant qualities which, sooner or later, bring a party to destruction. Nevertheless, I must be somewhat of a Jacobite for the time—with caution—with caution. I must give a few hints to the people—some encouragement, also, to my Jacobite friends among the magistracy, for fear of the vigorous energy of the Whigs frightening them; but with many a saving clause, and much reservation."

With these thoughts, he rode on, and at the end of a few hours entered the good old town of Exeter, with dusty dress, and horses and attendants tired.

A good number of people were collected in the open space near the Cathedral, for the room in which the magistrates were called to assemble was not far distant, and a rumor of the meeting had spread through the city, that being market-day, and had caused some agitation in the place. Sir John Newark was well known in Exeter; and he was very popular — most rogues are. His name was soon pronounced among the people. They gathered round him, pressed upon his horse, cheered him, asked him questions. The sounds reached some of his fellow-magistrates, who had collected in the neighboring inns, and they came out to see what was the matter. The great body of people gathered together were decidedly Jacobite, and the magistrates, who had their eyes upon the knight, were of the opposite faction; but he managed skillfully between them. To those in the crowd near him, whom he knew, he spoke a few words of a very inflammatory nature; but when the people called upon him to speak to them aloud, he harangued them for a few minutes, from his horse's back, in language which suggested more than it expressed. He besought them to be peaceable, orderly, tranquil, and to make no disturbances; but he painted in glowing colors, and with much oratorical power, the disturbances which had taken place in other parts of the country; told them how the men of Dorchester had assaulted and pumped upon the magistrates when reading a proclamation from the government; how, in another place, they had burned in effigy "the great personage whom they very improperly called the Elector of Hanover;" how they had driven a party of the military out of one town, and forced the mayor in another to drink King James's health against his will. But all the time he besought them to abstain from such unseemly demonstrations of the popular feeling, and assured them that he doubted not, he trusted, he hoped they would ultimately obtain all they could rightly desire, without any recourse to violence or breach of the law.

His words were not many, but they were very well chosen, and at the end of his harangue a great number of the people escorted him to his inn with acclamations. The very inn he selected marked him out as one of the party to which, for the time, he chose to attach himself. It was called the Crown and Scepter, and was the Jacobite inn. There, however, he had but time to get some scanty refreshment for himself before the hour of meeting; and, leaving his horses and servants behind, he walked to the room where the magistrates were now fast assembling. It presented the usual aspect of such congregations in troublous times, where many persons of the most opposite views are collected to carry out measures in regard to which very few of them are agreed. The Jacobite party was here by far the least numerous; but they were weakened by want of unity in their plans more than by want of numerical strength. Some were for bold and vigorous demonstration; others were for firm and tranquil moderation: some were for temporizing and deceiving; others for throwing off disguise, and avowing their principles, if not their objects, clearly. Sir John Newark instantly ranged himself among them, with the most hearty contempt for every one of them; but he shook hands with them all warmly, lent an eager ear to what every man whispered to him, and said a few words in reply which signified nothing.

The Whig party, on the contrary, were united in object and in purpose. They felt their strength, and were confident in it; yet, at the same time, the entrance of Sir John Newark caused a little stir even among *them*. They had a sort of fear of him—not of his power, not of his real talents, not of his courage or energy, but of his subtlety, for subtlety can be carried to a point where it becomes awful. He had established a reputation of never forgiving, of never being turned from his object by any difficulty or opposition, and of seeking it by ways which could not be seen and by means which could not be combated. All that he said or did was a matter of doubt and mystery to those around. His frankness was as suspicious as his reserve; his boldest declarations in favor of a cause were known never to insure it his support; his most resolute opposition to a party gave no guarantee that he would not join it next day. It was known, moreover, that most of his enemies had been ruined by some means or other—and many of his friends.

Inimical critics will say, perhaps, that this character is overdrawn; friendly critics will declare that it is a portrait. To the latter, if there be guilt, I plead guilty; but it is the portrait of one who lived and died in the times of which I write, and not of any man now living.

If a meeting of country magistrates in the present day is irregular and desultory in all its proceedings—and I, as one of that worshipful body, can certify such is the case—if, in a time when artisans are competent to judge of legislation, and people who can neither read nor write rule or overrule the opinions of educated men—if, in such a time, we see that many public assemblies, called for the discussion of national and important questions, are very confused and sometimes violent in their discussions and conduct, what could be expected, in the beginning of the last century, when learning and information, if not wit and talent, were confined to the few? Strong native common sense occasionally, in individuals, did a great deal, and perhaps the cases were more frequent than now, for no one can look around him without admitting that, in the present day, common sense in certain quarters is the most uncommon of all things. It is more valuable than any other quality, and very valuable things are rare.

The course of proceedings on the present occasion was in somewhat the following order. The presiding magistrate, a verbose, pursy man, with that self-important air and voluminous stomach which carry great weight with the public, made a long speech about matters which he did not comprehend in the least, read some letters from the Secretary of State and other high personages, the sense of which he mangled and left nearly extinct in the reading, and then added comments in support of the course which he believed the minister to recommend, although, in truth, it was very different. Then got up a furious Jacobite, railed at the existing order of things, abused the government, spoke of the country being eaten up by foreigners, and asked how it could be expected that, in such circumstances, and devoured by Hanover rats, men should be at all energetic or active in defense of a state of things which the whole country only tolerated for a time. Another and another orator followed. Few of the saner Whigs spoke at all, but some of them showed a good deal of temper; one plan was proposed, and then another; nothing was decided, and nothing seemed likely to be decided. Then, when he saw that time was getting on, and that people would soon become anxious to return to their homes, Sir John Newark rose and addressed the meeting, presuming that no one was likely to speak after him. He said,

"Sir, I believe my loyalty is not at all suspected—"

A murmur ran among the Whigs, and he instantly took advantage of it.

"I do not in the least pretend to deny," he continued, "that I am, personally, strongly attached to the ancient royal line of this kingdom. I have always declared the fact, and I have suffered by it in many ways; but that surely can be no imputation upon my loyalty, when I always show myself ready to obey and to execute the laws. I stand in the same position as many others even on that side of the room, whose attachment to the house of Stuart is strong, but their attachment to the laws of the realm stronger. I gave what poor support I could to the government of King William and Queen Mary, because I thought that the rights and liberties of Englishmen required it of me; but I am not disposed, and I trust none here are disposed, to see those rights and liberties violated by one monarch more than by another. Now, as far as I can make out what is intended by the government—or rather, I should say, what is here proposed by some rash and misguided men, who arrogate to themselves, unauthorized, I am convinced, the task of declaring the views of government—it is intended to call upon the magistrates of the county of Devon to employ measures for quieting imaginary disturbances, and for apprehending persons who may be tranquilly passing from place to place on their own business, for aught that has been shown to the contrary, which would render us a nation of spies and bailiffs, be subversive of all personal as well as political liberty, and breed suspicion and distrust between man and man, so as inevitably to end in establishing within these realms a despotism as oppressive as can be found in any of the continental states. Against this I must and will protest, even if I stand alone; at the same time declaring my willingness and readiness to employ every constitutional means in my power to maintain the peace of the land, and the rule of order and law. Do not let us suffer ourselves to be agitated by idle rumors, and vain and groundless apprehensions. What proofs have we that any design is on foot for disturbing the peace of the realm, or attempting to overthrow the existing government? What signs of such things are even alleged? Why, no more than the shouting of a London mob round the carriage of the Earl of Oxford, whom, until he is tried and condemned by his peers, I may venture to call a very estimable and intelligent nobleman. Some drunken rioting of 'prentice-boys and coal-heavers, worthy of being repressed by parish beadles and chastised by flogging, rather than being opposed by regular soldiers and punished by military execution. The sousing in a horse-pond of some foolish and obnoxious magistrates, probably detested and scorned by the multitude rather for their stupidity and injustice than even for their hot-headed zeal upon the present occasion—zeal which we shall not do well to imitate, lest we incur the same contempt and share the same retribution."

"The *only* signs!" exclaimed one of the less discreet of the Whig gentlemen present. "What do you call arming ships on the coast of

France in favor of the Pretender, as stated in the Secretary of State's letter, which you have heard read?"

"That it is a case to be dealt with by our embassador at the court of France," replied Sir John Newark, adroitly, "and not by a body of country justices of the peace. Besides, what have we to do with Secretary of State's letters? Is a Secretary of State king, lords, and commons at once? and can his mandate supersede the law of the land? All that it is competent for him to do is to exhort us to diligence and activity in the exercise of those functions intrusted to us by the Constitution. Arming on the coast of France! What has that to do with gentlemen traveling peaceably from town to town in the county of Devon?"

"But the secretary says there are suspected persons," replied the same magistrate.

"By whom suspected?" demanded Sir John Newark. "Reasonable cause must be shown for suspicion before we can deal with the case. This Mr. Secretary may be of a naturally suspicious disposition. He may suspect me—you—any of us. But it would be a bold thing to apprehend a man merely upon a secretary's *suspicion.* I, for one, will issue no warrant against any man upon mere suspicion. I will have it shown what are the grounds of that suspicion."

"He did not deal with his own relations so tenderly," said one of the magistrates to another; and a third observed, aloud,

"All we know is, Sir John, that three or four persons, whom nobody knows, have lately passed through certain parts of the county, and taken their way toward Ale Head, if not toward Ale-Manor House. A foreign vessel also was seen upon the coast, and it is certain that she landed and took off some persons in the close vicinity of your dwelling."

"I should like to ask the worshipful knight whether there is not a suspected person in his house at the present moment," cried some one, in a loud tone.

Others were going on in the same strain; for, on all such occasions, when one person can be found to lead an attack against an individual, many more will follow. Perhaps Sir John Newark was a little staggered by this close questioning; but he saw that the allusion to the ship gave him an advantage, and, waving his hand, he exclaimed,

"One at a time, gentlemen, one at a time, if you please. You are becoming a little personal in matters which should be considered free from all personality; but I am ready to give every man his answer."

"The best answer to such insinuations is the sword," observed an old, hot-headed Cavalier, whose brains the snow of sixty years had not been able to cool.

"Pooh, pooh!" said Sir John Newark. "I repeat that I am ready to answer every question separately; but you must not overwhelm me with too many at once. First, then: if any suspected persons have journeyed toward Ale-Mano. by land, I know nothing about them, and have heard nothing of them."

"By land! by land!" retorted one of the opposite party, with a scornful laugh.

"Wait a minute," said Sir John Newark, sneeringly. "Next, I answer that I well know that a foreign vessel did appear upon the coast, and did land and take off again some men."

"Tell us if they were *all* taken off, Sir John," shouted one of his opponents from the other side of the room.

"If the gentleman who spoke can prove that one of them remained, and can bring him within my grasp, I will pay him down on the spot a hundred guineas, which is somewhat more than the reward of an ordinary thief-taker," replied the knight. "But what is the use of disputing with a thick-headed brawler who can not hear a sentence to the end? I say, sirs, I *do* know that such a ship appeared off the coast, landed men, and took them off again. I know it well, for I know it to my cost. She came, with what intentions I do not know. She landed men, whose only act, if not their only object, was to insult and endeavor to kidnap my young ward Emmeline; and they ran away as swift as they could, and re-embarked when frustrated, pursued by my son and servants, with dogs, as if they had been beasts of prey. I was myself from home at the town of Axminster; but, as soon as I heard that a strange sail had appeared upon the coast, I hurried back at full speed, and found that what I could have wished done had been well done in my absence. Now I will ask if any one of you, who ventures to call himself the most loyal in this room, can impugn my conduct in this affair? And I repeat that, if any of you will put into my hands one of those men who landed, so that I might bring him to justice for the insult he offered to my ward, and through her to myself, I will pay him a hundred guineas on the spot."

At this moment a dark, stern-looking elderly man, in a snuff-colored coat, who had hitherto sat quietly in a corner of the room, rose and said, just when Sir John Newark was congratulating himself on having avoided all mention of Smeaton's residence in his house,

"The worshipful knight has not answered the question whether there is or is not a suspected person at this very time staying at Ale-Manor."

"No one suspected in the least by me," replied Sir John Newark, who saw that he must grapple with the subject. "There *is* a gentleman staying at my house, but let me add that he it is who saved my young ward from the hands of those ruffians who landed, wounding one of them severely, and that his whole conduct, as far as I know any thing of it, is above suspicion. General, you are a brave man, as all the world knows; but I should like to see the bravest of you tell my guest, Colonel Henry Smeaton, that he suspected him of aught. Methinks he would soon have an answer that would satisfy him till the end of his life, even if he lived much longer."

"Perhaps so," replied the other, quite calmly; "but some questions are better decided by pens than by swords, Sir John. Although I have not given up fighting, and trust I may yet fight again in my country's cause, it certainly shall not be in a priva.e quarrel upon public matters. You say that this gentleman's name is Colonel Henry Smeaton. I should like much to know if he never bears any other name."

"By such only have I known him," replied Sir John Newark, with a slight inclination of the head, and without the least change in his complexion; for he never colored, though he sometimes turned pale.

"Then we have been misinformed, I suppose," replied the other, whose voice seemed to have quieted all the din going on around. "We were told that the Earl of Eskdale was staying at Ale-Manor, Sir John. Is it fair to ask you who first introduced this gentleman to you as Colonel Henry Smeaton?"

"I presume I am not under examination," replied Sir John Newark, a good deal annoyed, but determined to evade the question. "However, general, I have no objection to answer you; and, if you think fit, you may take down my reply, perhaps to be used against me on a future occasion."

He spoke with a sneering smile, which had not the slightest effect upon the gentleman whom he addressed, and who continued to look straight in his face till he went on, saying,

"You asked me, I think, who first introduced my visitor to me as Colonel Henry Smeaton. My reply shall be very simple, and more distinct even than your question. The first time I ever saw him, he introduced himself to me as Colonel Henry Smeaton. That was some weeks ago, in London; and I immediately, and on the spot, gave him an invitation to visit me at Ale-Manor. I intended to excite your surprise, and I see that I have done it, gentlemen; but I must now dispel that pleasant sensation. My first acquaintance with this gentleman occurred on his defending my son from a gross assault made upon him by one of the Earl of Stair's servants, and punishing the ruffian who had knocked the boy down. I was grateful to my son's preserver and avenger, and invited him to my house; but I have had more cause for gratitude since. Not content with punishing the man on the spot, Colonel Smeaton went that same night to the Earl of Stair, with whom he is well acquainted, and made it his request that the man should be immediately dismissed. Out of friendship for him, the earl readily acceded; and, behaving with that true honor and dignity which so well becomes him, he wrote me a letter, which I have here, to apologize for what his man had done, and inform me of the result. I think, general, you must be well acquainted with Lord Stair's writing. There is the letter."

He stretched forth his hand with the letter as he spoke, and the old officer, advancing a step, took it, and read it aloud. The following were the contents:

"SIR,—In answer to your note received this morning, I beg to inform you that the conduct which you complain of in Thomas Hardy, my late servant, was represented to me fully by my friend, Colonel Henry Smeaton, who called upon me last night. As he witnessed the whole transaction, and I have every reason to believe him, from my personal knowledge of his character, and old acquaintance with his family, to be a man of perfect probity and honor, I dismissed the footman at once, and beg to express my regret that a servant of mine should have committed so disgraceful an action. I trust the young gentleman whom he assaulted has not suffered any severe injury, and that, when my friend Colonel Smeaton returns from the visit which I find he intends to make to your country house, he will bear me a good report of your son's health.

"I have the honor to be, sir,

"Your most obedient humble servant,

"STAIR."

"Undoubtedly Lord Stair's handwriting," said the old officer, aloud; and, turning to another, who stood near, he added, "we must have been misinformed."

"Pray," cried one of the magistrates, "will you tell us, Sir John Newark, if this Colonel Henry Smeaton is the only visitor in your house at the present moment?"

"This is too bad!" exclaimed Sir John Newark, with well-affected indignation. "Do you suppose, sir, that I am likely to quibble in such a matter as this? There is no one whatsoever in my house but my own family and domestic servants, with Colonel Smeaton and his lackey—a rude, ordinary man, whom you might as well take for an archangel as a nobleman. It is by such injurious suspicions of loyal and tried men that you, and such persons as you, frequently produce disaffection. Such, however, shall not be the case with me; and, having expressed my opinion upon your proceeding, and repelled the insulting doubts which it seems you had thought fit to entertain of myself, I shall leave an objectless meeting, which can produce no good results, and can only tend to irritate the people and induce foolish magistrates to overstep the limits of their duty upon the shallow pretense of zeal. If I might advise, all those who think with me will follow me, for I believe the very fact of this meeting may do great harm in the county."

Thus saying, he left the room with some thirty or five-and-thirty other gentlemen.

A buzz of conversation succeeded among those who remained, the whole assembly seeming to conclude that the business of the day was over, and breaking up into little knots of five or six. In one or two of these groups the name of Sir John Newark was treated somewhat severely, and his general conduct censured with very little restraint. In most of them, however, the imprudence of those who had first commenced an attack upon him was pointedly blamed.

"Strange should not have been so violent," said one.

"Perry should not have insinuated what he did," remarked another.

"He is a very difficult personage to deal with," observed a third. "He is never to be caught, and is always ready to give back more than he receives in the way of sneers and bitterness."

"He often turns what was intended to annoy him to his own advantage," remarked a fourth. "The man must be a blockhead or a conceited fellow who attempts to meddle with him. The best way is to let him quietly say out what he has to say, and then to proceed without taking the least notice of him; but, as he has contrived to break up the business of the day, we had better betake us to our horses' backs."

One dropped away after another till the room was nearly vacant; but a little knot continued in low-toned but eager conversation for nearly three quarters of an hour after all the rest were gone, and in it were the old officer whom we have mentioned, the high sheriff of the county, and two or three gentlemen of importance and discretion.

"It will certainly be the best plan," said the high sheriff. "He is thrown off his guard for the time, and I am willing to take my share of the responsibility."

The general shook his head.

"He is seldom off his guard," he remarked; "but I do not fear the responsibility; and perhaps it is the best plan. Government will carry us through, even if we do stretch its authority a little in such a case."

With this observation the meeting broke up, and the little knot which had remained separated.

CHAPTER XI.

The events which I have narrated in the last chapter occupied nearly two hours, although, in their recapitulation, they fill so small a space. It was thus four o'clock, or somewhat more, before Sir John Newark reached the door of his inn, impatient to return as soon as possible to the Manor House. As we have seen, many of the party which he had now espoused followed him away from the place of meeting. Some mounted their horses and rode into the country; some strayed to the right or left as soon as they were in the street; some went one way, some another; and but few accompanied Sir John Newark, even a short distance. Sir John was not loved or trusted by any one. All readily availed themselves of his help; all admired the skill and dexterity with which he took advantage of an enemy's mistakes, and sometimes of a friend's, but they did not altogether feel safe in his private society.

There was one garrulous old knight, however—a Sir James Mount—who had no fears of any kind. Wrapped up in his talkative egotism, he thought little of the character and actions of his associates, chattered away gayly to any one who came near him, sometimes very sillily, sometimes well enough, and was ever ready with a smart repartee, at which he himself laughed, to lead the chorus right; and, being full of anecdote and a great gossip-monger, was tolerated and even courted by most of the gentlemen round, though he sadly wearied them till they had contrived to make him dead drunk. This worthy baronet adhered to the side of Sir John Newark all the way to the inn, at which, it would seem, he also had put up.

"You posed them, Sir John—you posed them," he said, as they issued from the door. "That smart Mr. Seely got a rap—a rap—a rap, I think. Puppy! his knuckles will ache. It is very droll that I am not good at public speaking—at public speaking—at public speaking, for I am fluent enough—fluent enough—fluent enough in conversation, I think."

Sir John Newark made no reply, nor, indeed, was any necessary. Sir James Mount paused for a moment to take breath, for he had been walking fast, with a peculiar dancing sort of step; but it was not long before he began again, saying, "Better times coming, Sir John, better times coming, I think, and the king shall have his own again. I dare say, now, you have got some news from over the water—over the water—over the water."

Sir John Newark replied this time, for a good number of people were in the street, and Sir James's conversation was getting somewhat dangerous.

"The last news I have heard of any kind, Sir James," he replied, "was that you had nearly pulled down the old house at Mount Place, and were building a very splendid mansion in its stead."

"Yes, yes, yes," answered the other, tripping along on the tips of his toes. "*Diruit—diruit—diruit, ædificat mutat quadrata rotundis—rotundis—rotundis.* Not exactly the whole house; only the wings—only the wings—only the wings."

"Getting yourself new wings, Sir James," said Newark, "will make the people say 'tis to fly with."

"Only to fly higher—to fly higher—to fly higher," replied Mount.

"Higher, higher, higher!" echoed Sir John Newark, with a cynical smile; "that is like the sky-lark. But you were born to *mount*, and so that is natural."

"True, true, true," answered his companion, laughing, and very much pleased at the exceedingly lame pun. "Like the sky-lark—born to mount—pretty, very pretty!" And he took out his tablets and wrote it down, talking all the time with marvelous perseverance. "Born to mount," he repeated three times, "like the sky-lark: must have wings, you know, Sir John—must have wings—must have wings. Shall we dine together? I have something very important—important—important to discharge my mind of."

"I fear that I can not stay to receive your fire," replied Sir John Newark. "You know I have a guest at Ale-Manor, and must be back to entertain him."

"Ay, that's just the thing—just the thing—just the thing," said the old knight. "Is he Lord Eskdale or not—or not—or not?"

They had at this moment just reached the great arched entrance of the inn, and, without answering the question, Sir John called aloud for his horses. He was doomed, however, to disappointment and the society of Sir James Mount, for one of his servants, coming forward, informed him that they had just discovered that one of the horses had lost a shoe, and that his own beast seemed very lame. Sir John Newark was angry, but he uttered none of the oaths and exclamations common in that day, and merely, in a thoughtful and moderate tone, directed the one horse to be shod and the other to be examined by a farrier. Sir James Mount instantly fixed upon the servant, commended his own farrier to him, gave him particular directions where to find him, volunteered an opinion upon the cause of the horse's lameness without having seen him, and recommended strongly a plaster of soap and boiled turnips, repeating one part of every sentence at least thrice, and sometimes more.

While this was going on, Sir John Newark was meditating what he should next do. It was very difficult, on all occasions, to get rid of Sir James Mount; and, taking into consideration the improbability of his succeeding in an attempt to do so, and the length of time he should probably be obliged to stay, he made up his mind to engage him to dine in a private room, saying to himself, "I shall, at all events, get from him every piece of news that is going about the country, and shall prevent him from doing mischief with his tongue for an hour and a half at least."

Sir James was delighted with the proposal; and, although the hour was somewhat late for the early habits of that period, the number of gentlemen who had visited the town in the course of the day had created great activity at the inn, and dinner was easily procurable.

As soon as it was upon the table in the little parlor to which they were shown, Sir John Newark, who had been kept in some uneasiness by the incessant loquacity of his companion, dismissed the man who brought in the dishes, saying, as soon as he was gone, with a meaning nod to worthy Sir James,

"It is better to be alone when we may have important subjects to talk of."

"True—true—true," returned the other. "In such things I am always discreet—discreet—discreet. I know how to be silent—silent—silent, Newark. No one can keep a secret better than I can, in case of need. I was just at that moment—at that moment—at that moment thinking of Lord Eskdale; but I was as mum as a mouse—mum as a mouse—mum as a mouse while the man was in the room."

Sir John Newark had by this time made up his mind as to the course he should pursue in case of the Earl of Eskdale's name being again mentioned, and he instantly caught at Sir James's words, saying,

"Ay, the Earl of Eskdale. Can you tell me any thing about him? He must now be advancing in life."

"Pooh, pooh! you are thinking of the father," replied Sir James. "He died last year, quite a young man: not fifty, I should think—I should think—I should think; married very early, you know, and left one son; know them all quite well: Lady Eskdale is an old friend of mine."

"Is that the young Lady Eskdale or the old Lady Eskdale?" asked Sir John Newark; and then, seeing that he had a little betrayed himself, he added, to cover the mistake, "I suppose the young lord is married?"

"Married—married—married! Oh dear, no. He is not married," said Sir James; "was not a month ago, at all events: I was over the water upon a little business—business—business. I could not see the old lady, because she was very ill in bed—in bed—in bed; but I inquired into all the particulars of the family, and found them better off than most over there, on account of the Keanton estate—estate—estate."

Sir John Newark was not a little puzzled and alarmed by his worshipful companion's words, and fell into deep thought; but, as the other paused, he said, mechanically, merely to fill up the gap, "Ay, about Keanton?"

"Why, you know," answered Sir James, in his usual rapid manner, "it was never forfeited, because it was settled upon *her*. People thought that she had dissuaded her husband from joining our friends. That was not true; but it saved her property, which was settled somehow—somehow—somehow, and they have taken care to keep it very quiet. The tenants pay their rents to an agent—an agent—an agent, and as little said as possible; for, although Shrewsbury spared them out of generosity, and Marlborough because he got something by it, I dare say, others might have made a snatch at Keanton, which is better than a penny loaf—a penny loaf—a penny loaf."

"But I suppose, if the old lady should die, the property would fall to the crown?" said Sir John Newark, becoming again interested.

"Oh no! oh dear, no!" replied Sir James. "The young man was a mere boy when the father was attainted, and as they had good interest with the late queen, they got a special act of grace in his favor. It is not generally known, but it is true—true—true, I can assure you. So he is right on both sides of the house. If King James comes and prospers, he'll get the Scotch estates and this too; and if the elector makes his hold good, and Eskdale keeps quiet, he'll get Keanton at all events."

"It is a fine property, and might be made better," said Sir John Newark.

"Yes—yes—yes," rejoined the other knight. "I know it well. It is not ten miles from me. Know every inch of it—very good ground—too much up and down—overrun with wood; but very good tenants—all of them strong Loyalists. We might call them all out in a moment of need. But so, this is not the young lord at your house, after all?"

"I only know him as Colonel Smeaton,' said Sir John Newark, thoughtfully, for the intelligence he had received produced some vacillation in his mind. "You heard, too, what Lord Stair said of him. Nevertheless, he has all the air and manner of a nobleman; however, Lord Stair would not, I should think—"

"That is nothing—nothing—nothing," interrupted Mount. "*Nom-de-guerre*, perhaps. I recollect he did take some name like that when serving with the Austrian troops in Spain and Italy. That is nothing. Lord Stair is a very shrewd, secret man—would not tell tales of his own friends, desperate Whig as he is. He knows better than that. I should like to see this young man. Tell you in a minute who he is—who he is—who he is."

As Sir John had not fully made up his mind, he took no notice of this broad hint, and Sir James did not receive an invitation to Ale-Manor. What he had heard, however, induced the former to hurry his departure at any cost; and after a few minutes more spent in conversation, eating and drinking, he called for his chief groom, and inquired for the report of the farrier. That report was unfavorable; the beast would not be in a condition to travel for two or three days; and, taking leave of Sir James Mount, Sir John Newark instantly proceeded to purchase a new horse, in order to set out for Ale-Manor at once.

Before all this could be accomplished, the saddles put on, and every preparation made, it was nearly seven o'clock, and the knight looked forward to being obliged to end his journey in darkness. He was well accompanied, however, for those were somewhat dangerous times; and, before he was quite out of the city of Exeter, he found that he was destined to have more companions. Coming at full speed down the street, Sir James Mount, followed by two servants, overtook him about a hundred yards beyond the old gates, much to the other's annoyance.

"I will ride with you as far as Aleton Church," said Sir James. "It is only five miles out of my way—out of my way—out of my way, and we can talk as we go. There is something I want to tell you in your ear. Come close—put down your head. Do you know," he con tinued, in a whisper, "a party of horse, under Captain Smallpiece, has just gone out of the town with Best, the justice, and they are right upon the road before us, as if they were going either to your house or mine—or mine—or mine! We had better reconnoiter them from the tops of the hills, and see which way they take. It would not be pleasant to be at home when such a visit happens."

"Certainly not," returned Sir John Newark; though, to speak truth, he did not exactly mean what he said. He had his own views, however, and he rode on by the side of his chattering companion, buried in thought.

"They are gone to Ale to seek for my young guest," he thought. "If he is apprehended, it will serve him right for deceiving me about his marriage. Ay, and it may drive him, though somewhat too fast, on the way I would have him go. If I could but find a means of giving him an intimation to keep out of the way for a time, before the military arrive at Ale, it would do very well. But the party will never let me pass them; and, if I traverse the hills with all these men, we shall be discovered. This babbling old ass, who is not contented with saying a foolish thing without repeating it thrice, would ruin any scheme he had to do with. It would be better to seem to humor him, and to follow his suggestion of reconnoitering. They must stop to water their horses somewhere, and perhaps we can pass them then."

Thus thinking, he rode on up the slope of a hill in front, and soon after caught sight of the party of horse winding through the valley below. Well acquainted with every step of the country, he was enabled to follow them unseen among the green lanes and hedgerows, keeping a wary eye upon them all the way, while Sir James Mount continued to pour a perpetual stream of idle prattle into his ear, which annoyed him without distracting his attention from the object in view. The troop went more slowly, indeed, than suited the wishes or purposes of Sir John Newark; but at length they began to ascend toward the steep, bare downs which ran along the sea-coast on the borders of Devonshire and Dorset. The maneuvers of the reconnoitering party now became more difficult; for, though the road was often cut between deep banks, it was often exposed upon the bare side of the hill, and worthy Sir James became very unruly. He had no diffidence of his own powers, and he would at once have taken the command of an army, although he had never seen a cannon fired in all his life; nor was he willing at all to submit to the cooler discretion of his companion, who sought to pass quietly through the hollow ways, while those whom they were following crossed the more open ground, and to gallop over the wide, exposed downs, while the soldiers were hidden by any cut or dip in the road. Struggling with these difficulties as best he might, Sir John Newark, with his companions, came in sight of the little church of Aleton, with the scattered hamlet below, just as the setting sun was spreading a thin veil of purple light over the broad, naked face of the hill. The soldiers had then reached the straggling houses of the village; and, to the surprise of all who watched them, they were seen, not only taking the bits out of their horses' mouths, but removing the saddles, as if they intended to remain there all night.

Sir James Mount was full of conjectures as to their purposes; but Sir John Newark's resolution was soon taken, and he exclaimed,

"Well, I can not remain watching them all night, and I do not intend to slink into my own house by a back way. If you will take my advice, Sir James, you will ride away by the short cut over the hills. I shall go on and talk with them."

He saw a little hesitation in his elderly companion's face, and, to put an end to it, he added,

"For my own part, I have nothing to fear. But I think that journey of yours 'over the water,' as you call it, may prove unpleasant in its results. We could not well spare you just at present."

"No, that must not be—must not be—must not be. I think—I think—I think I had better go. You keep them talking, Sir John, while I gallop over the hills. They can not chase me now, for their saddles are off. But, upon my life, I believe they are putting them on again. Good-by—good-by!"

And away Sir James went, as fast as he could go, while his companion slowly rode on toward the hamlet.

At some little distance from the houses, Sir John Newark beckoned up one of the servants, on whom he thought he could most rely, and said, in a low voice,

"It is probable that I may stay here some time. You contrive to get away as soon as it is quite dark. Ride on to the house, and tell Colonel Smeaton, in my name, that I think it will be better for him to be out of the way for a few hours. Tell old Mrs. Culpepper to put him where he can lie concealed; and if he is inquired for, let it be said that he is gone away for a few days."

The servant nodded his head quietly, and Sir John rode on.

Round the door of the little public house was gathered a group of five or six soldiers, already taking deep draughts of ale; and, dismounting, the knight exclaimed,

"Holloa, my men, what has brought you into this part of the world? We are seldom treated with such a sight here."

"I don't know, sir," answered one of the men, civilly; "but Captain Smallpiece is in-doors, taking a glass to comfort him, with the justice."

"Are you going to halt long?" asked Sir John Newark, in a careless tone. "I shall be glad of your escort, if you are going my way."

"An hour and a half, sir, to feed and rest the horses," replied the man. Having so far satisfied himself, Sir John Newark entered the inn, and walked straight into the only guest-chamber it possessed.

The justice and the captain, not being able to obtain wine, were discussing the contents of a small bowl of punch, apparently much to their satisfaction, when the unexpected appearance of Sir John Newark startled them in their potations.

"Why, Sir John!" exclaimed the magistrate, "we thought you were at Ale-Manor by this time."

"You made a mistake, gentlemen," said Sir John Newark, dryly. "I had business which detained me in Exeter. But may I ask what is the meaning of all this military display, which 'startles the land from its propriety?' Here, drawer, bring me some punch. My horses are so tired they can go no further just yet, and I may as well enjoy this worshipful society in the approved manner."

The justice looked at the captain, and the captain looked at the justice; but at length the latter replied,

"Why, the truth is, Sir John, we were going to pay *you* a visit at Ale-Manor; and, luckily, having met with you here, we trust that we shall have the pleasure of your company on the road."

"That depends upon circumstances, gentlemen," observed the other, quite calmly. "If you have business with me, it can probably be transacted here as well as at my house."

"Not exactly," answered Justice Best. "The fact is this: the high sheriff and several of our brother magistrates are not quite satisfied in regard to this servant of Colonel Henry Smeaton. They think you may have been deceived, Sir John. It is very easy, you know, to assume a rude and vulgar manner; and, having received very distinct information that the Earl of Eskdale, whom we all know to have been attainted in King William's reign, took his way toward your house, they imagine that this servant may be the man, and they wish him to be apprehended on suspicion."

Sir John Newark laughed aloud.

"What need of a troop of soldiers to arrest a single lackey?" he asked.

"Why, your fishermen in the village are said to be somewhat mutinous," replied the justice; "and in case of resistance, you know—"

"You do not suppose, sir, that I would resist or countenance resistance to lawful authority?" interrupted Sir John Newark. "But, if this mare's nest is so very important a one, I think you might have ridden on to find it, without stopping at this house to drink punch."

"We had another little business here besides," rejoined the justice, who stood in some awe of Newark; "but our doing so has procured us the advantage, I hope, of your company on the way."

"Nothing of the kind, sir," retorted Sir John, sharply. "I certainly shall not go with you to see a gentleman, my guest, and the intimate friend of my Lord Stair, insulted in my house, by the pretense that his servant is the Earl of Eskdale, forsooth! You may go on when you please. I shall stay here till this unpleasant business is over. But let me warn you that it be conducted legally, for it shall be strictly looked to, depend upon it."

As he spoke, a man entered with a leathern apron, a dirty face, a bowl of punch in one hand, and a tallow candle in the other, for by this time night was falling fast. Sir John Newark's eyes rested on him for an instant, and a confused, doubtful sort of sensation took possession of him, which we all of us feel when we see a face that we know, but to which we can not affix a name. Suddenly, however, the scene of the statuary's house in London came back upon his mind, and the round, odd-shaped, never-to-be-forgotten form of Van Noost was there before him, in a disguise partaking somewhat of the tapster and somewhat of the blacksmith. A single glance of intelligence passed from one face to the other, but not a word of recognition was uttered. Van Noost set down the candle and the bowl, went back to the tap for a fresh ladle and glass, and then, rolling out of the room, closed the door behind him.

CHAPTER XII.

From the turbulent scene among the magistrates at Exeter, and the somewhat annoying occurrences which Sir John Newark had met with on the road back, let us return to the quieter doings at Ale-Manor House.

Not long was Emmeline's absence from Smeaton and her young cousin. She came timidly, blushingly, in all the agitation of fresh and strong feelings; but she soon became more tranquil. Dinner, according to the directions of Sir John Newark when he left, was served at the usual hour, and when it was over, all three walked out to linger away the time in the summer eventide.

After two or three turns up and down the terrace, Richard Newark seated himself upon one of the large guard-stones which marked the separation of the gravel from the turf, from which he commanded a view of two faces of the house, and there he remained for more than an hour, whistling lightly, and apparently lost in thought. Emmeline and Smeaton continued to walk up and down side by side, and their conversation was carried on in tones too low to be heard from the windows of the house. Had any one been watching them, well skilled in the outward signs and symptoms of the sweet madness, he might have divined by the look of tenderness, by the sudden change of expression, by Smeaton's bended head, by Emmeline's faltering and agitated step, and by the frequent raising of a bright and sparkling look to her companion's face, that he talked of love, and that she listened to him well pleased.

So, indeed, it was. He led her on, step by by step, word by word, himself led on by the growing passion in his own heart. All was said between them which could be said; and, before that walk was half over, they were plighted to each other, not only in heart and affection, but by words and vows. It might be somewhat sudden; but—as I have endeavored often enough before to make the reader comprehend—there is no such thing as time. The flowing of events constitutes what we call time. The revolution of the earth round its axis—man's day—is the measure which we have capriciously adopted to mete the passing stream; but how inadequate is that measure to express the value of the thing measured! 'Tis just as if we should sell at the same price the yard of cloth of gold and the yard of dull serge. The events of one day are not more like the events of another than those two woofs. Thoughts and feelings are also events—the events of the mind and soul; and, measured by them, how long a space had Smeaton known Emmeline! The last four-and-twenty hours to both had been a lifetime. Cleared of the great mistake regarding time, they had not loved suddenly.

In the little scene which I have depicted—the two lovers walking to and fro within sight of the house, sometimes under the green trees, it is true, but more often upon the soft turf before the terrace; Richard Newark sitting whistling on the guard-stone; the sky putting on its evening raiment, and the purple draperies of the sun's couch being shaken down over the west—one thing was particularly worth remark, namely, the marvelous patience of the boy. He, so light, so volatile, so full of wild activity, sat quietly there the whole time. It is difficult to explain it; and I can but say, in explanation, that he did it without thought, in all simplicity. The mind might not be very bright or clear; it might be slightly warped from the right direction; but the heart went as straight as an arrow. He felt that Em meline would like to be alone with Smeaton, and he with her; and, loving them both right well, by an impulse—by an instinct with which thought had nothing to do, he not only left them by themselves, but watched that they were not interrupted; and with love like that of a faithful dog, he watched patiently.

At length, however, Richard Newark rose, and with a quick step joined the two lovers. He had seen some one coming round the other angle of the house; and he said, with a laugh,

"There is old Mrs. Culpepper upon the prowl again, Emmy. Take care, pretty bird, take care. That cat's steps are very stealthy."

Emmeline, brighter, but as simple as himself, replied,

"I do not fear her, Dick—I do not fear any thing now."

Oh, what a world of revelation was in that little word *now!* It spoke of feelings totally changed—of hope, and trust, and confidence sprung up—of the absorption, as it were, of her very being into the being of another—of the vast assurance with which woman's heart reposes upon love.

Richard Newark did not remark it, but Smeaton felt it, and was very happy, for it told him how completely she was his own. They continued their walk, and caught a glimpse of the old woman's figure moving quietly along at some little distance; but they heeded it not, and continued talking in a lighter strain, and of more indifferent things, but with the spirit that was in their hearts giving life and energy to their thoughts and words, and breathing tones which each understood as meaning more than the words expressed. There was no weariness for them. The sun sank gradually through the sky, touched the edge of the horizon, dropped below it, disappeared. Purple, and gold, and gray had each their moment in the western sky, then gave place, and darkness followed. The stars shone out bright and clear above, not large, but very lustrous; and then the moon began to throw her light upward from the east, preparing to sweep the diamond dust of heaven away from her path on high.

Still Emmeline and Smeaton walked on, and talked of every thing. Heaven! how their thoughts rambled, shooting up among those stars, flying on fairy wings after the setting sun, wreathing the purple and the gold into fantastic forms, and twining the evening clouds into rosy coronals. Aladdin's palace-builders, all spirits as they were, wrought not so fast or gorgeously as the spirit of love.

But hark! The sound is heard of a distant horse's feet coming at great speed along the road, and the three companions are retiring to the house quickly.

The lights had just been lighted, the windows closed, and they were seated calmly in the smaller saloon, though two of them were trying to banish from look and manner all trace of the emotions which had risen up in their hearts, when a step was heard in the marble hall without, the door opened, and a servant of Sir John Newark entered, followed by the old housekeeper. The man was dusty from the road, and eager haste was upon his face, as he advanced close to Smeaton to avoid being obliged to speak loud.

"Sir John has sent me, sir," he said, "to tell you there is danger abroad, and to say that he begs you to keep out of the way for a short time. Mrs. Culpepper will show you a place where no one can find you, and you had better seek it quickly."

Smeaton gazed at him with some surprise, but without much emotion.

"What is the matter, my good friend?" he said. "I have nothing to fear that I know of. I really do not see what can be the use of my concealing myself, for I have committed no offense, and know not that any one can wish me ill. What is it has alarmed Sir John?"

"I really do not know the whole, sir," replied the man, "but I heard they had a very stormy meeting at Exeter, and that a party of horse was sent out in the evening toward this place. We followed them close, and watched them all along as far as Aleton. There Sir John stopped, I dare say, to try and keep them as long as possible, while I came on to give you warning."

Smeaton laughed, notwithstanding the anxiety which he saw in the countenance of Emmeline.

"My good friend, Sir John," he said, "mistakes altogether my position. I have nothing to fear from troops of horse nor from bodies of magistrates. They may subject me to some little annoyance, perhaps, but that is all they can do; and I do not think it either needful or dignified to conceal myself. If discovered, as I probably should be, the very fact of my concealment would justify suspicion and look like guilt."

"Perhaps, sir," said the old housekeeper, in that quiet, plausible tone which is so very common to housekeepers, "Sir John may request you to do this for his own sake more than yours. He may have denied at Exeter, perhaps, that there is any such gentleman here."

Smeaton looked her full in the face, thinking that she was not paying any high compliment to her master's sincerity and truthfulness, and trying to discover from her countenance whether there was not some latent motive for the course suggested which she did not choose to explain. It was all blank, however; smooth, calm, and inexpressive; and, unable to make any thing of it, he replied,

"That alters the question greatly; for I suppose you do not speak without some knowledge, my good lady. However, my best course will be, in such circumstances, to mount my horse and ride away for a time. If I meet with any of these gentry, they must take me, if they please; but I should not like to be discovered lurking like a rat in a hole."

Emmeline looked at him sadly, almost reproachfully, as if she would fain have asked,

"Will you leave me so soon, and peril your own safety thereby?"

But the old housekeeper observed quietly,

"There is not the slightest chance of discovery, sir. I could place you in the priest's chamber, where they say that Henry Garnet, who was afterward hanged, drawn, and quartered, lay for six whole weeks without being found out, nearly a century ago. There is a way out from it, too, beyond the house; so that, if you heard the door above open, you could get down through the wood to Ale, and away for France in a fisherman's boat. Sir John, in case of need, would take good care to have a boat ready and the way clear."

Smeaton changed his mind in a moment, for the woman's words gave rise to considerations which she little anticipated or knew. He was still of the same opinion, indeed, that boldly to face inquiry and to meet those who were sent after him would be the best course for his own safety, for he was well aware that he had nothing to fear from straightforward conduct; but he reflected, at the same time, that by so doing he might curtail his stay in the same house with Emmeline, and he moreover foresaw that a time might come when the knowledge of such a secret entrance to Ale-Manor House might be serviceable in more ways than one.

These thoughts passed through his mind in a moment; but, before he answered, both Emmeline and Richard Newark had time to speak.

"I beseech you, be guided, Colonel Smeaton," said the young lady, trying to conceal, as far as possible, from the eyes of the housekeeper the feelings of her heart. "Depend upon it, my guardian has good cause for his advice."

"Oh, show it to me, show it to me, Mrs. Culpepper," exclaimed Richard Newark, alluding to the chamber and passage she spoke of.

"I must not, Master Richard," replied the old woman, in a familiar tone. "It is not a secret to be trusted to such a rattle-pate as yours. You and Miss Emmeline must both remain behind, if the gentleman consents to go, which I think he had better do."

"Well, fair lady," said Smeaton, addressing Emmeline, "as you wish it, I will consent, although against my own better judgment. Perhaps Sir John Newark may, after all, have more information than we know; and as I believe him to be a very shrewd and prudent man, and to wish me well, I will follow his counsel. I will leave a private message for him with you and Richard. I will follow you in an instant, Mrs. Culpepper;" and he then added, in a lower tone, "Send the man away, and wait for me a moment without. I will follow you directly."

She only replied by a low courtesy, and retired from the room, closing the door behind her.

"Now, Richard," continued Smeaton, in a whisper, "endeavor to see which way she takes me, and if you can discover, tell our dear Emmeline. Wherever the door of this chamber is, I will come to it from time to time, and if I hear a voice I know, I will give such intimation of where it is that you can easily find it."

"I will find it out, I will find it out," answered the boy, laughing. "I will watch the old cat every step that she takes for the next three days as cunningly as she ever watched any one. She must carry you food."

"I hope so," replied Smeaton, with a smile. "But be careful; and now farewell."

He found Mrs. Culpepper quite as near the door as was discreet; but, if she had been listening, she was disappointed, for the conversation within the saloon could not be heard.

"Now, sir," she said, in a low voice, "tread lightly, that they may not hear our steps. This way, if you please, sir."

She led him through the hall, up the large flight of steps to the floor above, past the doors of his own apartments and those of Emmeline, and then up a small stair-case of five or six steps to a large, old-fashioned room, fitted up in the style of Queen Elizabeth's days. On one side was an immense bed with green velvet draperies and canopy, having a plume of feathers like a hearse at each corner, and on the opposite side the deep-cut windows, with a sort of bench of black oak between them. A number of large pictures hung round the room, none of which, however, descended to the floor; and there was a huge fire-place on the left-hand side, which occupied so much space that it seemed impossible there could be any means of exit there. The door by which they entered was in the middle of another wall, and the paneling seemed heavy and solid.

"Now, sir," said the old lady, closing the door, "you would never find the way in, I think, if I did not show you."

"Perhaps a little examination would discover it," replied Smeaton. "I have been in countries, madam, where such secret places are very common."

"I think I might defy you, sir," she said.

"Perhaps it is here," said Smeaton, approaching the black oak bench, and pressing on various parts of the picture-frame above. "These walls are thick enough to contain a small chamber."

The old woman smiled, and he went on pressing more tightly upon the frame, and thinking that he felt it yield a little. At length he heard the click of a spring, and the frame, moving upon a hinge, came slowly forward at one side, showing a room or closet within of about five feet in width by ten or twelve in length, raised a foot or two from the floor.

"Well, that is strange!" cried Mrs. Culpepper. "I never saw that before. It must be done for a blind."

"Then, is this not the place?" asked Smeaton.

"Oh dear, no, sir," replied the housekeeper. "You would be stifled in there. The priest's room is as good a one as this; but that is a good hint to mislead searchers, any way. Shut it up, sir, and I will show you the other. Will you have the goodness to try and move back the bed, for it is very heavy?"

"I will try," said Smeaton; "but, though I am tolerably strong, I doubt that I shall be able to do it. We do not see such massive furniture nowadays."

As he spoke he grasped one of the large posts, and endeavored to stir the huge bedstead. It moved not in the least, however; and the old housekeeper stood near the head, holding the light and smiling at his ineffectual efforts. Smeaton remarked her countenance, and the peculiar expression which it bore. He saw, also, that she leaned her right hand against the post at the top of the bed. Approaching her then with a gay laugh, he said,

"I think I have your secret;" but, on pushing back the velvet hangings from the spot upon which her hand rested, he could only perceive one of two immense iron screws which fastened the bed, apparently immovably, to the wall behind it. He made one more effort, however, to move the bed, but in vain, and then laughingly gave it up, saying, "I must trust to your guidance, madam."

"Dear me," replied the old woman, "I thought you must be stronger than I am; but let me try;" and, putting her hand gently to the head-post, with hardly an effort, she made the huge bed roll round upon its casters like a heavy door, still remaining attached to the wall on one side, but quite free on the other. When it was thus removed, the fluted velvet back of the bed still remained fastened against the wall, but it might now be easily seen that this was a door which opened without difficulty.

Smeaton drew it back, and looked into a large and comfortable room. But he was not a man to shut himself up in a place from which he did not know the means of exit, and he was running his eye rapidly both over the wall and the back of the bed, when the old lady said,

"You see, sir, this thing, that looks like a great bed-screw, is, in fact, a catch, which runs into the post and fastens with a spring. To get into the room, you must press the plate upon the post through which it passes, and at the same time pull up the screw. Without that, no force on earth would move it. But the moment you do that, the bed of itself moves forward a little, the catch is thrown off, and you can easily roll it round."

"That is the way in," replied Smeaton, "but now, my good lady, tell me the way out. How am I to unfasten the bed when once you have rolled it back?"

"That is more easily done than the other," replied the old woman. "Look here. This iron bar, made like a screw, passes quite through the beam, with a long handle on the other side, and is fixed upon a pivot. You have nothing to do but to push down the handle, when the catch will be thrown off, and the bed will move an inch or two, so as to prevent it from fastening again. There is, somewhere in there, a block of wood—a sort of rest which you can put under the handle, and then nobody can undo it from the outside without pulling the whole to pieces. I come in here four times every year by myself to see that every thing is in order, and that all moves easily. But we must not wait talking. I will show you the way, sir;" and she stepped over the skirting board, which was left plain below the opening of the door. "You see, sir," she continued, pointing to a number of small loop-holes, both round and square, on one side of the room, "you will have plenty both of light and air; and there is no fear of any body seeing the light, even if you made a bonfire here, for those holes are hidden by the stone-work round Miss Emmeline's windows on the one side, and by the same round the windows of the room we have just left on the other. I will bring you some supper, and any thing you may want out of your room as soon as it is all safe, but you had better not come out yourself till I come and tell you, for I do not know how you would pull back the bed again if you were forced to retreat."

"Then show me the other way out which you mentioned," said Smeaton. "I am not very fond of rat-traps, and stories of these secret chambers get abroad about the country, so that people may know more of the way in hither than you believe."

A look of hesitation came upon good Mrs. Culpepper's face, which instantly gave way to her usual smooth expression, and she said, "There is no fear of that, sir. Nobody knows any thing of this room but myself and Sir John. I had better go now, and make all right below, and I can show you the other way out when I bring your supper."

"No, indeed, my good lady," replied Smeaton, in a determined tone; "you must show me now, or I certainly shall not stay. That piece of mechanism might get embarrassed. I might hear people breaking in. A thousand things might happen to make my discovery here inevitable, if I did not know the other way, and I will not be caught lurking here. If you please, you shall show me now."

"Oh, very well, sir, very well," replied the housekeeper. "It is very easily found. Be so good as to follow me."

Passing through a door to the left of the loop-holes, she led him through a passage curiously constructed in the wall between the upper and lower row of windows. As soon as it had passed beneath what Smeaton conceived to be the windows of Emmeline's room, came a very narrow flight of stairs, and then another passage. Again came a second descent, steep but broader than the first, which led to what seemed to have been originally a cellar, arched over in brick-work and of no great extent. Beyond it was a long passage, evidently under ground, and gently sloping downward till the whole was closed with a stone door in which was a key-hole.

"The key always lies there, sir," said Mrs. Culpepper, pointing to a little niche; "but I must tell you that, when you open the door, there is, just before you, the well, which you must step over to get out, or you might drown yourself. It is an old well with an arch over it, the water of which is thought good for sore eyes, so that the people come here often on a morning to get it; and, when you stand on this side of the door, you may hear all they say as they gossip round the well. The right-hand path leads away through the wood at the back of the village to the bay; the left takes round again to the terrace in front of the house; but that is well-nigh a quarter of a mile off, and no horses can come round here, for the hill is too steep."

Smeaton did not promise himself any great entertainment from overhearing the gossiping of the fishermen's wives and daughters, but quietly followed his guide back again to the room above. She there left her light with him, passed through the aperture, closed the door, and he could hear her roll back the bed, and the catch click upon the spring.

CHAPTER XIII.

There are moments in the life of every one, when some sudden and unexpected change hurries us rapidly through a bustling and exciting scene, where we are called upon to decide and act suddenly upon unforeseen conditions, and then leaves us to pause and reflect in solitude and silence upon what we have just done. The effect is strange, as all men arrived at mature life must have felt, when, left to our own thoughts, we scan the busy moments just passed, doubtful whether impulse or reason have guided us, and still more doubtful whether impulse or reason have guided us aright. Often the answer is "Yes," and often "No;" and when it is negative, man, with his great skill in covering his own faults and follies from his eyes, satisfies himself by shrugging up his shoulders and saying, "I acted for the best," forgetting too often how much of the fault he would thus palliate is attributable to the evil habit of not making reason his ever-present and ready guide. Exercise her daily, use her upon all occasions, and she will act at the first call. Neglect her for an hour: she falls asleep, and requires time to be roused. All very trite; but do any of us remember this as much as we ought?

When Smeaton stood alone, shut up in the

priest's chamber, he began to ask himself if he had done wisely in consenting to be hidden in that retreat, and he could not but acknowledge that love for Emmeline, and the thought of obtaining means of access to her under some remote and uncertain contingencies, had shared more in fixing his determination than the consideration either of his own safety, or of his own name and character. He saw that he had not acted in accordance with reason; but he too—for he was by no means perfect—treated the error lightly, saying to himself,

"Well, it is done, and can not be undone. Let us make the best of it. There is always a way out of this secret chamber, that is one comfort; but I had better examine it more closely. I saw the key lying there, it is true, but I did not satisfy myself that it would turn in the lock; and it seemed somewhat rusty."

Thus musing, he took the light from the table, and walked quickly through the passage along which the old woman had led him.

"She was foolish," he thought, "to hesitate about showing me the way. No one could miss it."

At the end of the lower passage, he found the key lying in the little niche, and taking it up, was about to apply it to the lock, when he thought he heard a step, without being able to distinguish at first whether it was in the passage behind him, or on the hill-side beyond the door. He turned round, and looked, and listened, and then clearly heard the step again, apparently close to him, but on the outside. The next instant a voice was heard speaking in a grumbling tone, and with a strong Devonshire accent:

"I don't see what is the use of sending us down here," it said. "Why, twenty people could pass us in this wood."

"Never you mind, Jim; do your duty, and obey orders," said another voice. "Let other people think what is *the use.* I am sure you would never find out for yourself, if it made you take ten steps off your horse's back. There, get on a little lower down. I'll mount guard here, where the path turns."

"Oh ho!" exclaimed Smeaton to himself, "the search has begun. I may as well wait here a little. Any one coming down the stairs, and along the passage, would soon be heard; and I think these two gentlemen outside would easily be dealt with."

He accordingly put the candle in the niche where the key had lain, brought the hilt of his sword a little round, and quietly placed the key in the lock. A few minutes passed in perfect silence, the men without either standing perfectly still, or sitting on the edge of the fountain; but then Smeaton's quick ear caught the sound of a distant footfall, which evidently came nearer and nearer, but not by the passage in which he was standing.

"Who may this new visitor be, I wonder!" he mentally ejaculated; and, bending down his head, he listened more attentively. The step came nearer and nearer, and approached the door close to which he had placed himself. Then a loud voice cried "Stand!" and Smeaton could hear the sound of what seemed a spring and a brief scuffle.

"Ugh, ugh! don't strangle me!" cried a good, round, jolly voice. "Man, I am apoplectic, by the blessing of God, and the assistance of capons and strong waters. If you twist my cravat in that way, you will get nothing but a dead statuary, which is as bad as a dead lion."

The last words confirmed what the tone of voice had intimated to Smeaton before, that his good friend Van Noost was the person who had fallen into the hands of the Philistines; and believing, from their conversation that morning, that the poor sculptor had more cause than himself to fear the pursuit of justice, he felt really sorry for him.

"Lion, or whatever else you may call yourself," replied the soldier's voice, "you must along with me. Come, come, no struggling, or I'll break your pate, master. By ——, they say, 'as fat as a lord;' and if this is a lord, it is a fat one of the sort."

"Ugh, ugh!" cried Van Noost. "I tell you, you will strangle me if you drag me in that way."

Smeaton could bear it no more. The impulse to help the poor caster of leaden figures was too strong to be resisted, and he gave way to it. In a moment the key was turned in the lock and the door drawn back, hiding completely the light in the niche. A slight gleam of the risen moon showed the waters of the well about three feet across, with a little path beyond, and a soldier pulling Van Noost along. In a moment Smeaton was across the well: the man, hearing a noise, turned his head; but before he could see whence it came or who was his assailant, a blow from Smeaton's clinched fist forced him to relax his grasp upon the sculptor, and a second, before he could use his sword, sent him rolling down the hill side among the trees and bushes.

"Quick! Come with me!" cried Smeaton, seizing Van Noost's hand, and pulling him on. "Jump! take a good spring."

The last words were uttered after he himself had cleared the well, and was standing in the passage, but still holding Van Noost's hand across the water. Some of the lead of the statuary's profession, however, seemed to have got into the poor man's hinder quarters; for, though he made a great effort to follow his conductor, he fell short by a few inches, and, had it not been for Smeaton's grasp, might probably have been drowned. The other, however, dragged him into the passage head foremost, and quietly closed and locked the door.

"Hush!" he whispered, seeing that Van Noost was about to speak. "Hush! be perfectly still."

"Jim, Jim," cried the voice of the soldier without, "look after them. They are coming your way; stop them—shoot them dead if they won't stand."

As he spoke, he scrambled up again toward the path, displacing a large stone, which rolled down into the valley. Whether the other soldier took it for a flying enemy or not, I can not tell, but instantly after he vociferated "Stand!" and the next moment the report of a pistol-shot was heard.

Smeaton smiled, and whispered to his companion, "All is safe; but keep perfectly silent."

The sound of many feet running from above was then heard, as some of the companions of the men below hurried down, alarmed by the shot; and great confusion, with much talking, ensued, of which only fragments reached the ears of those in the passage, somewhat after the following fashion.

"What is the matter—what is the matter?" "Here, come here. They have gone down here. I had got hold of him by the neck, but another came up and knocked me down." "Who did you get hold of?" "They have got a dark lantern with them, for the light flashed out and dazzled my eyes. If you don't make haste, they will be gone. They ran straight down for the bay."

Many other cries, questions, and answers were going on at once; but two or three of the soldiers, answering the call of the man who had fired the pistol below, hurried down the path, and, accompanied by him, ran on, some between the back of the houses and the steep hill side, and others along the verge of the little stream, thus sweeping the whole course of the valley till they reached the smooth white sand on the shore of the bay.

The scene was calm and beautiful, the moon shining brightly over the sheltered water of the bay, and changing it into rippling silver, while Ale Head, dark and shadowy, swept like a gigantic wall round the southwestern side, and the opposite point of Ale Down just caught the gleam of moonlight on its high head. It was a scene which might have led a lover of the picturesque, or one of the unhappy children of Imagination, to pause and dream. But the soldiers had no such thoughts; one single object attracted their whole attention. This was a fishing-boat, quietly rowing out of the little mouth of the bay, and darkening a diminutive space on the shining sea beyond.

They drew their own conclusions, which, like most hasty conclusions from insufficient premises, were altogether false. The boat was merely filled with fishermen; and, if the pursuers had paused to consider, they would have comprehended that sufficient time had not elapsed between the firing of the shot above, and the moment that they reached the beach, for any person to have pushed off the boat and rowed to the entrance of the bay. They determined in their own minds, however, that the persons of whom they came in search had made their escape by that means, and one said to the others,

"Well, they are off, that's clear, and there is no use of trying to follow; for, even if we were to get the boats off, I know no more about 'em than a jackass does of a powder-horn. Do you, Symes?"

"No more than you do, corporal," replied the other. "We had better go back to the house and tell the justice."

"Tell the captain, Symes—tell the captain," replied the corporal. "That is what we must do. We know nothing of justices. Justice has no more to do with us than my cap has with a bunch of keys. We act under our captain, Symes, and to him I shall go and report. Come along, my men."

In the mean time, while all these events had been passing on the side of the hill and in the passage near the well, other occurrences had taken place in Ale Manor-House itself which I must briefly notice.

Richard Newark had crept quietly after Smeaton and Mrs. Culpepper as far as he dared, and, at all events, had discovered the direction which they had taken. Emmeline had run out upon the terrace, and, watching the windows above, had gained some further knowledge from the way in which she saw the light travel. Indeed, she clearly perceived it through the windows next to her own, and it seemed to pause for some time there. A distant sound, however, caused her to return suddenly into the house and order the doors to be closed. This had hardly been done when the old housekeeper returned; and, going from servant to servant, in her quiet, smooth way, cautioned each to say, if Colonel Smeaton was asked for, that he had ridden away to Axminster for the day.

Then came a period of suspense, but it did not last very long, for at the end of five or six minutes the approach of the troopers was intimated by the noise of their horses upon the terrace. Sundry orders were given in a loud voice, and then the great bell at the door rang.

"Don't open the door," said Richard Newark to one of the servants who was crossing the hall. "Let me see who these folks are."

Then, partly opening one of the windows of the saloon, he called out,

"What do you want, my masters? Do you think we hold a horse-fair here, that you bring so many beasts for sale?"

"Open the door, in the king's name and to the king's troops," said the officer in command, who had imbibed as much punch as was compatible with the due exercise of his understanding. "We require to search this house."

"That you shall not do, were you twice as tall," replied the boy, boldly, "without a lawful right to do so. Do you know this is the house of Sir John Newark, a justice of peace for the county?"

"Oh, let them in, Richard," said Emmeline. "You can not keep them out."

At the same moment, Justice Best advanced on foot to the window, saying,

"Let your people open the door, Master Richard. My name is Best. You have seen me with your father, and must know that *I* am a justice of the peace too. Sir John is aware of our coming, and makes no opposition."

"Oh, that is another case, worshipful Master Best," replied the boy. "Open the door, my men, and let in the great magistrate."

Then, taking a light from the table, he went out into the hall and bowed low with mock reverence as the justice and two or three of the soldiers entered.

"Pray, what is your good will and pleasure, and whom do you seek, worshipful sir?" asked the boy, whose wits seemed to sharpen under exercise. "As for myself, I am quite harmless. I heard an old woman, one day, call me an innocent, and my nurse used to call me her lamb, so that, unless Justice be a wolf, I have nothing to fear from her fangs. Indeed, this knowledge-box of mine is so empty, that there are not materials within it sufficient to manufacture treason, even against a farmer's orchard; and as for robbery or murder, upon my life they never came into my noddle—always excepting birds' nests and mackerel in the bay."

"You are a merry boy, Master Richard," returned the justice; "but our purpose in coming hither is to seek a certain personage, passing for and reputed to be a servant of one Colonel Henry Smeaton. If he is produced at once, we shall give you no further trouble; but if not, we must search the house, for we are credibly informed that this man, in the disguise of a servant, is no other than the Earl of Eskdale, a known adherent of the Pretender. It is impossible for him to escape, as the house is surrounded, so you had better produce him at once. As I wish to do every thing with courtesy, however, you had better communicate what I say to Colonel Smeaton, who may escape injurious suspicions if he gives his companion up freely."

"Colonel Smeaton has gone over to Axminster this afternoon," said one of the servants, coming forward, "and won't be back to-night; but as for his man, your worship, he was in the hall not a minute ago, and making all the maids laugh with his funny stories."

"Ah, very likely," replied the justice. "We have heard he is a jocular person. This confirms our information. Be so good as to ask him to walk hither, and remember you have admitted that he was in the house not a minute ago."

"To be sure I did," retorted the man surlily; "and I don't doubt that he'll be in this hall in less than a minute more."

So saying, he walked away, murmuring something about a pack of fools, which the justice did not hear, or did not choose to hear.

Turning quietly to the door of the smaller saloon, his worship observed, in his usual soft and courteous accents, "Perhaps, Master Richard, you will allow me to examine my prisoner in this room. We have had a long ride, and a seat in a chair would be pleasanter to me than to remain in the saddle or to stand upon my legs."

"Ay, they seem weakly," answered the lad; "but you shall have right good leave and license to sit as long as a hen, if it pleases you, and see what you can hatch—a brood of nonsensicalities, doubtless!" he added to himself, as he followed the justice into the room. Then raising his voice again, he said, "Here is Justice Best, Emmy, come to look for Henry Smeaton's servant, accusing him of being attached to the three Kings of Brentford, and committing high treason against the wise men of Gotham. He is going to examine him in here, and we shall have rare fun, I don't doubt. Do stay and see the proverbs of Solomon put into action."

Emmeline, however, was fain to escape from the room, with an inclination of her head to the justice as she passed; for, although she was desirous enough to hear all that took place, she feared that her anxiety and alarm might be evidenced too strongly.

It was clear enough to Mr. Justice Best that Richard Newark was laughing at him; but, as the lad was generally considered in the county deficient in intellect, he contented himself with saying, "Poor boy!" and seated himself solemnly at the table.

"This fellow is not coming, it seems," said Captain Smallpiece, who had followed with some of the soldiers into the room. "I had better search the house, your worship."

"Nay, nay, nay!" exclaimed the justice; "have a little patience, Smallpiece. One of you have the goodness to call in my clerk."

"Here I am, sir," said a small man from behind; and, almost at the same moment, Smeaton's servant entered the room, with a curious and peculiar sort of leer upon his countenance, which seemed to show that he, at all events, entertained no apprehension of the result. He was followed by the servant who had spoken to the justice in the hall, and some other domestics; and, raising his eyes to his face, the justice asked, with an important air, "Pray who are *you*, sir?"

"I am Colonel Smeaton's servant," he answered, with a strong Cockney accent. "They told me you wanted me."

"Are you his *only* servant?" asked the justice, a good deal staggered by the man's appearance.

"He could not have a better," replied the man; "and, though I'm the only one, I'm as good as two, for I groom the horses and valet the master."

"Oh ho!" ejaculated the justice, "now we are coming to it. Methinks a common lackey, sir, would not put on such a demeanor to a magistrate of the county acting in the king's name. My lord, concealment is of no avail. We know all about you, and have full information."

"Lord! lord! *I* my lord!" cried the man; "to think of my turning out a lord!—I, who was born in a back garret at the corner of Fetter Lane, fattened upon the fumes of soap-suds—for my mother was a washer-woman, your worship—an honest woman, for all that—I to turn out a lord! Well, the transmogrifications of this 'varsal world are miraculous, I do declare. Has your worship got my certificate in that little book? for if you have, I'll be a lord for all the rest of my life—see if I don't—and get a pension from the king to keep up my dignity."

"Five foot eleven and a half," said the justice, reading from a paper he had taken out of his pocket-book, and then raising his eyes to the man's figure. "Deuse take it! he does not seem so tall as that."

"Five foot three quarters, without my shoes," replied the man, smartly; "but perhaps I shall grow, seeing that I am only one-and-thirty, and a peer of the realm. I don't see why I should not grow to any height, now I have right and title to hold my head higher than I ever thought to hold it. Humility has shortened me all this while."

"Come, come, sir," said the justice, thrown into a great state of doubt and indecision, "if you are the Earl of Eskdale, you had better acknowledge it at once; and, whether you are or are not, treat the court with respect."

"The Earl of Eskdale!" cried old Mrs. Culpepper, who had come into the room with the other servants. Then, seeing that surprise had done what few things ever did do, thrown her off her guard, she added, "No, I can answer for it he is none of that blood. Why, the Earl of Eskdale must be an old, white-headed man."

"Ay, ay, but that earl is dead," exclaimed the justice. "This is the young earl we talk of, my good lady—Mrs. Culpepper, I believe; I hope you are well, Mrs. Culpepper—but don't meddle with this business, for I don't think you can know any thing about it."

"How can *you* know, Goody?" cried the servant, turning sharply round to her, with a mock look of indignation. "Pray don't do me out of my dignity: I may be a peer or a prince for aught you know."

"I never saw such a one," said the old woman, sarcastically; "but I can answer for your being none of the Eskdale family, for they were all tall, handsome men and women, and you are no more like them than a beggar's cur is like a stag-hound."

"Civil, you see, civil!" said the man. "You perceive that high station is not without its inconveniences; but if your worship will only make me out a peer, I will take any title you please. I am quite indifferent as to names. Suppose you call me Lord Fetter Lane, or the Earl of Newgate."

"You may soon have a better right to either title than you expect," growled Captain Smallpiece, who was difficult to convince; but the justice, whose wits were somewhat clearer, though not very pellucid either, began to have marvelous doubts on the subject of the man's real condition.

"Pray, sir," he said, "if you are really Colonel Smeaton's servant, and nobody else, when did you enter that gentleman's service, and where?"

"In Lunnun town," replied the man, dryly, "on the fifth day of June last, at about half past three in the evening. Thank God, I have had a good edication, considering the mess I was brought up in; and I am very reg'lar in my habits—which I owe to my dear departed mother, who always kept her washing-books very correct, and wiped her hands whenever she took them out of the tub. She used to say she could always go into court with clean hands, poor woman, and so can I, for you see I always keep a little book here in my pocket, in which I put down when I enter and when I quit a service, and I get my kind masters to sign for me. Some of them don't speak as well as I deserve, it is true, but still they can not say much harm. There is the book. You may look at it."

"Let me see, let me see," said the justice; and, taking the book, he read some of the various characters which had been given to the man before him by the different masters whom he had served, one of which was as follows:

"This is to certify that Thomas Higham was in my service for eleven months and three days —a clever fellow, but a saucy rascal—passably honest, and not given to drink. I discharged him for his impudence.

"HENRY SACKVILLE,
"*Deputy Controller of Her Majesty's Household.*"

Such was the first certificate he read; but there were a number of others, all much to the same purpose, which fully accounted for the time of Master Thomas Higham from the age of sixteen up to the moment at which he stood before the magistrate.

"There must be some mistake here," said Mr. Best, beckoning up Captain Smallpiece and pointing to the papers before him. At that instant the report of fire-arms was heard through the window which Richard Newark had left open, and the justice exclaimed, "Hark! what is that?"

"Some of the fools let off a pistol by accident," answered the military officer. "Being fools, they are always committing some folly."

Having been thus oracular, he proceeded, with a somewhat unsteady gaze, to examine the certificates before him. He was one of those men who, even in their most sober moments (and he was not now sober), have a certain obscurity of mental vision, which prevents them from perceiving any thing but what is immediately before them. He stumbled and blundered through several of the testimonials, repeating from time to time, "Well, I don't see what that has to do with it. Well, I don't see—Tom Higham may be a good sort of saucy fellow, but who is Tom Higham, I should like to know? You can not tell that this is Tom Higham."

"But it is very clear that he can not be Lord Eskdale," replied the magistrate, "for his lordship is six foot high, and this man is five foot four. I am sure there has been some mistake. Our information is decided, it is true, that the earl was seen passing this way. But we have no proof that he came to this house."

"Well, we had better search, at all events," said the officer.

The magistrate, however, was of a different opinion. He thought he had gone quite far enough in offending Sir John Newark, of whom he stood in no little fear; he saw many means which the worthy knight might have of annoying, if not injuring him, and knew that he would not at all scruple to use them.

A somewhat sharp altercation ensued, which highly amused Richard Newark, and not less Smeaton's servant, who, after it had gone on for some minutes, interposed with his usual saucy leer, saying,

"Will your worships tell me whether I am to be a lord or not, after all? I am very willing to be a lord, if you wish it."

"Hold your tongue, fellow," said Justice Best. "You interrupt me in explaining to Captain Smallpiece that it would be wrong, discourteous, and perhaps illegal, to search Sir John Newark's house without information that an attainted person was actually here. All the suspicions were of yourself; and, if they turn out to be groundless, my functions in the case cease. If Captain Smallpiece, indeed, thinks fit to take upon himself—"

Before he could finish the sentence, one of the corporals of the regiment, followed by the men who had been down on the beach with him, pushed his way through the crowd round the door, and saluted in military fashion his commanding officer.

"Well, what the devil do you want, corporal? I told you to keep watch outside."

"I have come to report that they have got off, sir," said the man. "We could not overtake them before they got into a boat and away."

"Who, who, who?" shouted the magistrate. "Who do you mean by 'they?'"

"Why, the earl and his servant, I suppose, your worship," replied the corporal. "I got hold of one of them by the neck, but then up comes the other, flashed the light of a dark lantern in my eyes, and, before I could draw sword, knocked me head foremost down the hill. Good luck to the bush that stopped me. They ran away together down through the wood, and passed Jim, here, who fired his pistol at them."

"Ay, that I did," said a man behind him.

"They ran away down to the water, however," added the other, "and, before we could overtake them, had jumped into a boat and were rowing away out to sea."

"There, there, now," cried Mr. Best, "I told you how it would be." And he looked straight at Captain Smallpiece, as if the whole of this mischance had been of that officer's bringing about.

"No, you did not," rejoined the captain; "you did not say any thing of the kind. You were cock sure, like all the rest of them, that this lackey was the earl disguised, and that you would pounce upon him here like a hawk on a hedge-sparrow."

"But did you not wish to search the house without the slightest grounds of pretense?" demanded the magistrate. The officer, however, turned away from him with a look of half-drunken contempt, and, addressing himself to the corporal, asked,

"What sort of men were they, corporal?"

"One was short and fat," said the corporal, "with a great many ribbons about him. The other was a tall man, and seemed youngish, as far as I could see."

"The earl and his servant, without doubt," said the justice.

"I suppose so," grumbled Captain Smallpiece, in a disappointed tone. "What is to be done now? Shall we search?"

"Search! Search for what," demanded the justice, "when they have got off to sea? There is no proof they were ever in the house at all, and very probably have been, during the time, down in one of the huts. What is to be done! Why, march off your men as fast as possible, and let us see how we can patch up matters with Sir John Newark. He won't forget it in a hurry, depend upon it. I require you, sir, to march off your men."

"Oh, very well," cried the captain, indignantly. "That shall be done faster than you like, perhaps. There, sound boot and saddle;" and he walked away to the door.

"Could you favor me with a glass of wine, Master Richard?" said the justice, in an insinuating tone. "We have ridden far, and this is dry work."

"Not a drop," replied the boy, boldly. "You came on a fool's errand, and you may go dry away. I can tell you, Master Best," he added, with a laugh, "you'll want all the wit in your noddle to settle accounts with my father, and it would be unkind to take a jot out of the cannister by putting wine in. You have had quite enough to-night already, I should think; and, at all events, you'll get no more here."

The servants laughed; and, after trying hard for a look of dignity which would not come, Justice Best walked out of the room, with his clerk sneaking behind him like a beaten cur.

"There, there," cried Richard Newark, running out into the hall and to the foot of the stairs, "shut all the doors and windows. Emmy! Emmy! come down; all the fools are gone!"

CHAPTER XIV.

Having already changed the *venue* once in the same chapter, I have judged it best to finish one of those fragments into which the caprice of authorship induces men to divide romances before I return to Henry Smeaton and his companion in the passage. We must now, however, leave the party in the house, and once more place ourselves by the side of the well, where, soon after the last words spoken by Smeaton, the moving away of the soldiers toward the beach could plainly be distinguished, and the path without seemed to be left to solitude and silence.

"They are gone, my good friend," said Smeaton, at length, still speaking in a whisper, lest any lingerer should be remaining behind; "they are gone; but we must still be very cautious, if we would escape danger. In Fortune's name, what brought you over here, Van Noost? If I had not seen you in the morning, and recognized your voice to-night, you would still have been in the hands of the Philistines, my good friend."

"Thanks, great Samson, thanks!" cried Van Noost. "The very next figure that I cast—if I live to cast any more—shall be the Hebrew giant, with his friend's jawbone in his hand. I beg your lordship's pardon for joking, but it is an evil habit of mine from times of old, and I shall jest at my last gasp. You asked me why I came here. Odds life, I do not know where I am; but if you mean what brought me toward Ale-Manor, all I can tell you is, that it was zeal—zeal, which, like a bad huntsman, is always overrunning the good dog Discretion."

"Hush!" said Smeaton. "Do not speak so loud. But tell me in a whisper what road your zeal ran this time."

"Good faith," replied Van Noost, "it was in the road of your service, as I thought; but the truth is this: ever since you left me in the morning till toward the close of day, I have been helping the good old sexton, Mattocks, to clean the monuments in the church, breaking hard jests upon each other's jests all the time. I borrowed a blacksmith's apron, twisted myself up a paper cap, and stripped off my coat to keep it clean. Your lordship would not have known me, I looked so much like a journeyman. Just, however, as we were leaving off our work, what should I see, to my horror and consternation, but a troop of horse coming down the hill. There was no time to get my pony, or wash my hands and face, and escape. You know that side of the hill. It is as bare and as round as a baby's cheek. So there was nothing for it but to go down to the little ale-house, keep on the garb I had, which was disguise enough, and persuade the good people to pass me off for a tapster. Well, the soldiers came down, swept all the oats out of the hamlet for their horses, called for ale in the true dragoon style, and sat down to boose round the door, while their captain and a certain justice who was with them demanded punch in a magisterial tone. Didn't I make the punch strong for them! I paid for an additional bottle of rum out of my own pocket to fuddle their worships; and, if I had dared, I would have treated the whole regiment. A minute after, however, in came Sir John Newark, and he called for punch too. Sharp words enough passed between him and the others; and suddenly, as I brought him in his bowl, I found out from what was said that it was your lordship these people were going after, and not your poor humble servant. I argued the matter with myself for a minute. Zeal said, 'Go and warn the noble lord.' Discretion said, 'Take care you don't get caught yourself, Van Noost.' 'A fico for Discretion,' cried Zeal. 'It is quite dark; the soldiers are all drinking; the pony is at the back of the house; there is a good piece of green turf, which will do as well to silence his feet as felt to shoe a troop of horses; up into the saddle, Van Noost, and away. Do as you would be done by, man!' So I listened to the last speaker, and got off. To say sooth, though I had some directions, I was not quite clear of the road, and strongly suspect I trotted fifteen miles instead of five. However, I reached the place at last, tied my pony under a clump of trees some way off, and was walking round the house to find a private way in, when I began to perceive that other people had come straighter than myself. I heard horses and voices, and saw men and lights, and my wits got into such a tangle with fright that I could not make out where I was. I ran up one path and down another, and did not know which way to go, till at length a fellow got me hold by the throat, half strangled me, and was dragging me away, when all of a sudden I heard his cheeks give a squelch just like the sound of a lump of cold lead dropping into a furnace, then another tap, somewhat harder than one from a lady's fan, and away he went rolling down the hill. Somebody got me by the paw at the same moment, pulled me along, through a horse-pond I believe, for my feet are all wet, and here I am, your lordship's most devoted servant; but *where*, who can say?"

"In a safe place for the present, Van Noost," replied the young nobleman, "and I must care for your security as best I can. Hush! I think I hear them coming past again."

Advancing to the door, he put his ear close to it and listened. A moment or two after, the men returned from the beach, some of them, at least, passing along the same path, and talking as they went. Smeaton listened with deep attention; but Van Noost continued fidgeting about, notwithstanding an impatient gesture from his companion, who, as soon as the soldiers had passed by, turned sharply round, demanding, "What are you doing with the key? You are stopping up the wards."

"No, no," replied Van Noost, "only taking a model. I always carry some putty in my pocket for the express purpose."

"That is not right," said Smeaton, sharply. "Cease, sir, cease! You have no business with the key."

"Oh, very well, my lord," assented the sculptor, withdrawing the putty from the key, wrapping it up carefully in his handkerchief, and putting it in his breeches pocket. "It is a curious shaped key, too, and I should like to have a model of it—very old—Queen Elizabeth or King Edward, I should think."

Smeaton made no reply, but again turned his ear to the door. All remained silent for some minutes, and then came the blast of a trumpet above.

"I think they are gone or going," said the young nobleman. "I fancy I could distinguish the sound of the horses' feet marching away. Listen, Van Noost!"

"Oh, yes. Praised be God for all things!" ejaculated Van Noost, after he had listened for a moment. "The vagabonds are gone. Let us get out of this burrow."

"Stay a minute," said Smeaton; "we had better get more information first. Wait here for me a short time, and I will go above for intelligence. They will not leave me long without news if the men are really gone."

As he spoke he took up the light, somewhat, it would appear, to Van Noost's consternation. "But, my lord, my lord," he said, "I shall not be able to see if you take away the candle."

"What, are you afraid of the dark?" asked Smeaton, laughing. "Well, you shall keep it, only light me along to the foot of the first flight of stairs. And then, remember, whatever you hear, remain below. If need should be, and you should ascertain that any of these men have remained behind to search the place, you can take your chance of escape by that door; only remember it opens over a well on the hill-side, and, if you do not leap more lightly than you did just now, you will go down like one of your own leaden figures and be drowned, for the water is up to the brim, and it is deep."

"You forget, my lord," returned Van Noost, "that you were pulling me along head foremost, and I knew not where I was going. I can leap as well as any man with a clear space before me, but one feels some trepidation in jumping into a dark pit's mouth."

"Well, well, take the candle and light me," said the young nobleman.

Walking quickly on, he reached the foot of the first flight of steps. Then, leaving Van Noost below, he ascended to the priest's chamber, to wait in darkness for some intelligence. As he stood and listened—vainly, for some minutes—for any sound in the adjoining chamber, he had time to ask himself whether he had acted altogether rightly in bringing Van Noost into that secret part of Sir John Newark's house, and he concluded that he had no title to do so.

"And yet," he said to himself, "it is not, in reality, his house at all."

But that did not quite satisfy him; and he determined, if he found that the neighborhood was clear of the soldiery, to send the good sculptor forth by the same way he entered, so as to let him see as little of the secrets of the place as possible.

He was becoming somewhat impatient of the oppressive silence, and felt half inclined to open the door and look out, when he heard sounds not far off. A door was opened, closed, and locked, and then the large bed was rolled round upon its casters. The next instant the light shone in, and good Mrs. Culpepper appeared, with a candle in her hand. Her face bore greater traces of agitation than it displayed on any ordinary occasion, and Smeaton began to fear that he had considered himself safe too soon; but the old lady's first words dispelled alarm on that head.

"They are gone, sir," she said, entering the room, "they are gone;" and, with trembling hands, she set the candle on the table.

"I am sorry you have suffered such a fright on my account, Mrs. Culpepper," said Smeaton in a kindly tone; "but I can assure you now, as I did before, that there was nothing to fear on my account."

The old lady seemed hardly to attend to him and the state o agitation displayed by so very calm and demure a person set Smeaton's fancy busy with fears for Emmeline.

"I dare say not, sir—I dare say not," she said, with quick but faltering accents. "They came looking for the Earl of Eskdale, and your name is Smeaton. And yet," she continued, gazing in his face, "and yet—Will you be kind enough, sir, to let me look at your wrist?"

"I have no objection at all," returned Smeaton, a good deal surprised. "But what can my wrist have to do with the business?"

"I will tell you in a minute, sir—I will tell you in a minute," replied the old woman. "Your right wrist, if you please."

Smeaton drew up the sleeve of his coat as far as it would go, unfastened the studs which held it together just above the ruffles, and, baring his arm, held it out to her. The old woman took his hand in hers, and, holding his arm near to the candle, leaned her head over it. A large irregular scar appeared some two or three inches above the hand. The young nobleman had often remarked it, but had no recollection how it came there; and now, to his great surprise, he found warm drops falling upon it from the old woman's eyes. The next instant she kissed them away with an eagerness quite extraordinary, and then looking up in his face with the tears still upon her cheeks, she exclaimed,

"Oh yes, Henry, oh yes, my lord! I know you now. That mark cost me the bitterest hours that ever I knew in my life."

"Pray explain," said Smeaton. "I do not at all understand what you mean, nor know how the scar came there."

"I will—I will," she sobbed, wiping her eyes. "Often have you sat on these old knees—often have you clung with your arms round this old neck. I was your nurse, my lord, from the time you were taken from the breast till you were five years old. You were my nursling, my pet, my darling. It seemed as if God had sent you to me to console me for my own child I had lost; and I loved you as few mothers ever loved a child."

"I recollect my nurse Nanny very well," said Smeaton. "Can you be she?"

"Oh yes! Nanny Culpepper—poor Culpepper, the sergeant's wife, who was killed," she answered. "But let me tell you, Henry, about that scar. When you were just about four, you were a dear rash boy, and I left you only for a minute in a room where there was a fire. In playing about, you tripped over something, and fell with your arm upon the burning wood. I heard you cry, and ran back in haste, but I found you burned all across the wrist there. I dared not tell my lord or my lady, for I knew they would be very angry at my having left you; and I thought I should have a hard matter to quiet you. But the moment I told you that, if you made a noise, and they found out what had been done, Nanny would be sent away, and you would never see her again, you dried your eyes and ceased crying altogether. I never saw a child do the like; and, though the wound was very painful, and I had not much skill, you suffered me to go on dressing it for you, and doing my best to heal it, till it was well, without ever letting any one see that you were in pain. Fortune favored me, or I could not have concealed it so long, for those were troublous times. My lord was moving about, and a great deal in London. My lady was often away, too, anxious for his safety; and the wound got quite well before they ever remarked it. Then, however, my lord questioned me sharply. I made a sullen answer, and he would have discharged me on the spot, for he was a strong-spirited man, and had much to grieve him; but my lady interceded for me, and I was kept on till he was forced to fly beyond seas. Then, when she was about to join him, he wrote to tell her what servants should accompany her. I was pointedly left out; and I knew he had not forgotten me. But how you cried when you left me, I shall not forget. Oh, sir, you do not know what deep root is taken by the feelings of our hearts in those early years. Though you have not altogether forgotten your poor nurse, you *have* forgotten a great deal of what passed then; but there is not one thing—no, not one of your looks, or any of your little prattle—that I do not remember even now. I love Miss Emmeline very much too, though she does not know it; but I can never love any one again as I loved you."

"I am sure I loved you well too," replied Smeaton, "for the recollection of my poor nurse is the only thing referring to those days that still remains upon my mind."

"I am sure you did—I am sure you did," she repeated. "But oh, now, tell me, my lord, what do you mean by saying you are safe? Your father was what they call 'attainted,' I think, and that affected all his family, so how can *you* be safe? They are cruel laws to punish an infant for the fault of his father."

"Make yourself easy, Nanny," replied Smeaton, in a kindly tone. "The attainder was specially reversed as it affected my mother and myself. She had good friends at the courts both of William and Ann, and you know she is a wise, active, and prudent woman, so that she took every means to secure for her son both safety and competence. It is true, I might be put to much inconvenience by the suspicions of the government—nay, plans and purposes, greatly affecting my happiness, might be frustrated or rendered more difficult of execution than they are already, if I were discovered; but I have nothing else to fear."

"I think I understand," said the old woman. "Does Sir John Newark know who you are?"

"He does," replied Smeaton. "It was very imprudently revealed to him by one who had no business to meddle."

"That is strange—very strange," said the housekeeper, thoughtfully. "You are not married, are you, my lord?"

"No," answered Smeaton; "but I have much reason to believe he thinks I am."

"Ay, I see, I see," rejoined the housekeeper. "Now I understand it. But you must on no account let him know that I have recognized you. He is shrewd and keen. Beware of him, beware of him, for he pursues his objects without fear, or remorse, or hesitation, and few know what those objects are till it is too late to baffle him. He is a kind and good master to me, because I do every thing he tells me; and he does not fancy that he can be watched as closely as he watches others—no, nor that a poor creature like me can perhaps make all his schemes prove vain. Well, well, we shall see. But have a care of him."

"I will," replied Smeaton; "and, indeed, I am on my guard against him already. He is not aware that I know so much of his history and character as I do."

"He would not suffer you within these doors if he did," returned the old woman. "But now you can come out in safety, for these people are all gone; and they fancy, from some stupid blunder of their own, that you have got off to sea in a boat, and a fat man with you, whom one of the soldiers vows he got hold of by the neck."

Smeaton laughed.

"I think I can explain one part of their mistake," he said; "and, indeed, I was going to ask your advice upon a point of some difficulty."

He then related to her all that had occurred with Van Noost and the soldiers, as far as he knew it; but when he told her that the good statuary was even then waiting below, she shook her head gravely, saying,

"He must not be seen here on any account. Send him away, Henry, send him away, my lord—"

"Nay, nay," said Smeaton, "call me Henry still when we are alone, and at other times call me, and think of me, as Colonel Smeaton. But this matter puzzles me. I fear that the poor fellow may miss his way, and get into mischief, for I do not think I can describe the road to Keanton so that he can find it, not knowing it too well myself."

"You take him out by the door over the well," replied Mrs. Culpepper, "and I will send round a boy to the path, who shall guide him so far that he can make no mistake. Sir John must never know that he has been in there; and hearken! the moment Sir John comes back, he will make you pledge your honor not to tell the secret of this place to any one. Therefore, if you wish to tell it—and I think, perhaps, you may, if I judge right—do so before he returns."

Smeaton paused thoughtfully, and then said, as if speaking to himself,

"Is it wrong to meet a bad man with his own weapons?"

"No, no," cried the old woman, "quite right. I have been doing so for the last twelve years, and have beat him at them. You look doubtful. *I* have no doubt, and perhaps, if you knew as much as I do, you would have none either. But never mind. It shall be done for you. If you have scruples, keep them. Emmeline shall know without your telling. Indeed, I have often thought to let her know, as she has a right, but thought it might be dangerous; for, if he once saw that there was the least secret between her and me, I should not be here an hour after, and then all would be lost. But now get this man away, and then come back. Tell him to wait upon the path till a boy comes up to him, and says 'Keanton,' and then to follow him. I will wait here till you return, and will find means to talk to you longer to-morrow."

CHAPTER XV.

I AM not sure that the phlegmatic temperament, as it is called, is not the happiest for the possessor thereof. People are apt to exclaim,

"Give us great pleasures, even if they be accompanied by great pains."

Hopeful mankind! ye seldom estimate prospective pains at their real worth, and ye always over-estimate the pleasures—till they are gone. Two great races of philosophers, if not more, the Stoic and the Chinese Mandarins, judging more sanely—I am not quite sure that the Epicureans might not be included also, ay, and many more sects—have always sought for the less intense. Whether a respectable fat Bonze, having his toes tickled by his fourteenth or fifteenth wife, without the slightest expectation of any thing like high sentimental pleasure, but without the slightest fear of any thing like strong mental pain, is or is not in a more desirable condition than Galileo in his dungeon, I will not take upon myself to say; yet one thing is certain—that this world being full of miseries, so that when we open the door for one high enjoyment, thousands of pains rush in, there is some policy in having but few entrances to the house, and opening them as seldom as possible.

A phlegmatic temperament has assuredly the advantage of leaving few assailable points at the mercy of an enemy, and the Dutch are generally supposed to be as phlegmatic as any other nation; but such certainly was not the case with Van Noost. Whether, by transplanting, he had acquired more the character of a sensitive plant than of a cabbage, or whether the Norman or Saxon blood derived from his mother overbalanced the Frieslandish part of his composition given by his father, I can not tell; but certain it is, that he was of a very movable and excitable disposition, notwithstanding the national breadth of his nether man, and the firkin-like rotundity of his whole frame. His soul was a busy, fiery little soul as ever was put into a heavy body; and most intensely did he fret and fidget during Smeaton's long absence, although he had a candle to light him, and the coveted key to work upon. Three times he walked along the passage; thrice he measured the size of the key-hole; four times he took an impression of the key; and when, at length, he heard a step coming down from the rooms above, he was all in what is expressively called a twitter lest the person approaching should be any but the person he desired.

Whether he had calculated upon a comfortable sojourn at Ale-Manor House during the night, or whether his imagination suggested dangers which did not exist on the road before him, or whether his long evening ride, added to his morning ride, had somewhat bruised and fatigued the part that pressed upon the saddle, sure it is that he received the intimation that he must ride twelve miles further to Keanton with a somewhat rueful air, and sprang across the little well with less than his promised activity.

Smeaton went first to show him the way, and to help him out if he fell in, and his so doing gave some confidence to the poor statuary; but he still besought his noble companion, even after they had both safely reached the little path, to remain with him till his young guide came. When this was acceded to, he became much more composed, and hardly listened to the directions, repeated more than once, which Smeaton gave him regarding what he was to do at Keanton, so much was he occupied with the contemplation of the little well and the scene around. The moon had now risen higher—so high, indeed, as only just to catch the edge of the waters with a line of silver light; but she displayed beautifully in her pale beams the small Gothic arch of stone-work, let, as it were, into the face of the rock. The deep tank or well at the foot of this acclivity received the bright and healing fountain from some spot ten or twelve feet below the surface. The light through the half-opened door showed the interior of this little cell with its watery flooring and part of the passage beyond; and the eye could perceive upon the stone door itself how skillfully the workmen had marked out the freestone into divisions, so as to render it like a piece of solid masonry. The effect had been rendered perfect by the exhalations from the fountain, which had tinted it with many hues of green, and red, and yellow.

"I don't see how one could open it from without," said Van Noost, after gazing for a moment. "The well is so deusedly in the way, though I see the place where the key-hole must be well enough."

"I would advise you not to try, Van Noost," said Smeaton, with a smile. "Your legs are not long enough to stretch across. I think mine would do very well."

"Ay, noble lord, I did not cast myself," replied the statuary. "Gad's life! if we could do that, we might see strange changes, according to men's taste. Some of your stumpy, balustrade fellows would turn out Apollos, and many a long-legged Antinous would become a clumsy Vulcan. I am as lengthy in mind as you in limb, my lord, and could leap over mountains if—if—"

"If the body were not heavier than the soul," said the young earl, kindly, for he saw that the good man spoke somewhat warmly. "It is not your fault if Nature made you spread forth broad instead of running up tall. Some stones are made into a cupola, others into a column; but they have no choice in the matter, and each had better be satisfied with his condition. You have one advantage of me, however. You can make the figures of other men in a better mold than Fortune gave to yourself, and I can not."

"It would be difficult in your case, my lord," replied Van Noost, well pleased. "I only long for quiet times to take a statue of your lordship as a dancing faun."

"Spare me that! spare me that!" cried Smeaton, laughing. "The faun had not a good reputation in times of old, nor the dancers in the present day; and, good sooth! I would rather not appear in public in either character. But methinks this boy, who is to be your guide, is long in coming, and I am somewhat anxious to get back into the house again."

"Ay, I can fancy that," replied Van Noost, "if that pretty lady who was with you this morning be within. Do you know, my noble lord, you must set a guard upon your eyes, if you would not have all the villagers commenting upon your soft sentiments? Why here was the old sexton, Mattocks, saying what a handsome couple you would make, and only thinking of burying you both all the time, though he talked of nothing worse than marriage."

"It would be a pity to stop them," answered Smeaton. "I should imagine they have little to think of, and a marriage or a funeral must be a God-send to the gossips of the place. But now, my good Van Noost, remember, when you are at Keanton, you must be very discreet, or you may get into trouble. Keep the eyes of the people off you as much as possible, and mind not to exercise too much in dangerous places."

"But, bless your lordship, what am I to do?" exclaimed Van Noost. "You know mine is an active, bustling spirit, and if I am not to exercise my genius upon lead, I shall probably exercise it upon something else. Good faith, I must dabble a little in my old trade, even if it be but in casting little leaden figures of soldiers and dairy-maids, hand in hand, for the benefit of the children of the tenantry."

"I did not speak of that exercise of your genius," replied Smeaton. "Cast as many leaden figures as you will, my friend. They can find you a caldron as big as a witch's, I dare say, and you can set up a shop in the old court-yard; but eschew politics, Van Noost, and keep your hand from the treason-pot. You have put your fat in peril already, it would appear, my good friend, so keep quiet till the danger has passed away. Here comes the boy, I think."

It was as he supposed; and though the boy, with very limited instructions, had expected only to see one person to guide, so that he was somewhat puzzled on finding two, Van Noost was soon placed under his guidance; and while Smeaton returned to the house to enjoy for a short space longer sweet converse with Emmeline, the worthy statuary moved away to seek for the pony he had left tied under a tree. It was easily found; for, having been left at some distance, it had escaped all notice from the soldiery; but the beast was tired with its exertions during the day, and was very willing to go at such a pace as suited the convenience of the young guide.

The way seemed to Van Noost interminably long, as all new ways do in the dark; but the distance was in reality by no means very great; and at length the boy, who had chatted very freely with the statuary as they went, pointed to the entrance of a road between two deep hedgerows, telling Van Noost to follow it straight on, and it would lead him to Keanton House.

"There are seven gates to open," said the boy, "and about half a mile over the turf. You can not miss the road, for it is all straight."

Van Noost, however, did contrive to miss the road, for when he came upon the turf the moon had gone down, the tracks of the road had disappeared, and, instead of going on as his face was pointed, he turned a little to the left, which led him away from the object he had in view. The summer sun, however, soon befriended him, first by showing him, in the gray twilight of the early morning, that he had gone wrong, and then, by greater light, enabling him to get right. He had to turn back nearly a mile, however, the road lying all the way over smooth green turf, covering the gentle undulations of the country, with no indications of a path, but here and there the track of cart-wheels in the soft sward, or the prints of a horse's feet. Van Noost was led on, indeed, and in the right direction, by the sight of some fine old trees rising up over the edge of a hollow at the distance of about a mile, and some chimneys, and sharp-pointed gables and roofs, breaking the rounded lines of the foliage.

The sun was just up when the statuary, passing through the elms and oaks, came in sight of the whole building, a fine old irregular mass of brick-work, somewhat like an antique French chateau, with tall masses of no-styled architecture, small windows very irregularly disposed, and a somewhat superfluous number of doors. Gray and yellow lichens and green moss covered the walls and the eaves; the ivy ran up many of the square, tower-like masses; and the houseleek might be seen dropping over the edges of the lower roofs. Ten or twelve tall elms, loaded with rooks' nests, at one corner of the building, marked where the esplanade began which ran before the principal *façade;* but on the side next to Van Noost appeared a large farm-yard, surrounded by a low wall and thickly littered with straw, on which reposed a number of cows, promising a plentiful supply of milk, butter, and cheese. The early-rising and consequential cock was strutting about in his gaudy livery; the white, black, and gray ladies of his seraglio were wandering in quest of food. Numerous were ducks in a pond at one corner, and a troop of geese, waddling, and courtesying, and bending their heads, came forward to taste the morning air, and crop the green grass upon the downs. But no human being was to be seen: man was absent from the picture; and Van Noost raised his eye from window to window, to discover any signs of life within, but in vain.

"This must be Keanton," he said to himself. "It is just the sort of place; but they seem rather late risers here for country people. If they had been at the Ridotto last night, or at the Water theater, or at the Italians, they might well be lagging in bed; but here, where they have nothing to do but lie down and go to sleep when the sun sets, they might very well get up when he rises, methinks. Hark!"

The sounds which had called his attention increased, and round the corner by the rookery came a young peasant-lad in his broad hat and his yellow frock, whistling gayly. All Van Noost's weariness and wandering were forgotten in the joyful sight; and, whipping on his pony, he rode up to the lad, asking him if there was nobody up in the house.

"I can not tell," replied the youth, with a strong Devonshire accent. "Master Thompson at the farm is up."

As he spoke, he looked very earnestly at Van Noost, and there was a sly, quiet, inquiring glance of the eye, which did not at all harmonize with his gay, thoughtless aspect the moment before, as he came whistling along. It was not alone shrewd, but suspicious; and Van Noost said to himself,

"Ay, ay, these tenants are all well drilled not to endanger their master's interests by any indiscretion. Now, I will answer for it, there would be no slight difficulty in getting any straightforward answer from this good youth. I'll try."

"So the farmer's name is Master Thompson," he said, aloud. "A very good name, too. Pray what is your name, my lad?"

"What is yours?" said the young man, looking him point blank in the face.

"That is not the question," answered Van Noost. "I asked what yours is!"

"Then that is not the question either," replied the lad; "but if you be the gentleman come from Exeter, you ought to know my name."

"I have not been in Exeter," replied Van Noost; "and even if I had, I don't see how I should know your name, when I never saw your face before. If you carried it written upon your forehead like a certain old lady of Babylon, one might know something about it."

"To be sure," replied the lad, "and so should I know something about yours. I am not fond of answering questions, master; so, if you have come to speak to me from Exeter, you had better speak out. Ballimoree!"

"Ballimoree!" exclaimed Van Noost, with surprise. "What in the name of fortune does Ballimoree mean?"

"It means good morning to you, master," said the young man, with a knowing nod of the head; and he walked away, without waiting for any further question.

"Ballimoree! Ballimoree!" mentally ejaculated Van Noost. "What the deuse does he mean by Ballimoree?"

And when he had looked after the young man for a minute or two, he turned his pony's head to see if he could discover the farm-house which had been mentioned. It was by no means difficult to do so; for, as soon as he had passed the rookery, it became visible, with a number of small houses and cottages, in a little wild dell to the right.

At the door of the farm-house he found a stout, elderly man, of a very frank and open countenance, and having his hands in his pockets, according to the usually prescribed form of English farmers. Riding up straight toward him, Van Noost considered, as he went, how he should address him, and make his wishes known.

"The noble lord," he thought, "said I was to ask either for Master Jennings or Master Thompson; but then I was not told to say Ballimoree. I was to inform them that I came from the *River Head*, and to bid them give me shelter, food, and protection. It was to Jennings I was to say that; but perhaps the pass-word at Master Thompson's may be Ballimoree. I'll essay it;" and, riding up to the fence before the farm-house, he hallooed out,

"Your name is Thompson, sir, I believe—Ballimoree."

"My name is Thompson, sir," answered the farmer, "but not Ballimoree. What is Ballimoree?"

"Upon my life I don't know," answered Van Noost, frankly, "but a young lad I met up near the house said 'Ballimoree' to me, and told me that it meant good-morning."

"He was funning you, sir," replied the man. "He is a bit of an Exeter lad, is Dick Peerly, and they are all full of their jokes. Pray what is your business with me?"

"I was to tell you, Mr. Thompson, that I come from the *River Head*," replied Van Noost, laying particular emphasis on the last words; "and as I am anxious for some quiet and repose, you or Mr. Jennings are to give me shelter, protection, and food for a time."

The man's whole manner changed in a moment.

"You shall be right welcome, sir," he said. "It will be better that you should speak with Master Jennings; but, in the mean time, pray come in and have some refreshment. The cows will be milked in a minute; but if you like ale and bacon better, we have as good as any in the land. Ballimoree! what could he mean by Ballimoree? Pray come in, sir—pray come in. Give me your horse's bridle; I'll have him put up. A pretty pony, 'pon my life; but he seems to have had enough of it for once."

"Ay, poor beast, he is as tired as his master," returned Van Noost, walking toward the house. "He never calculated upon such a ride, nor I either."

The farmer pointed to a room on the left side of the entrance of his house, led the pony round to the back, and returned to his guest after a moment or two with a bouncing, rosy country maid-servant, bringing in the materials for a hearty breakfast; but that word "Ballimoree" seemed to puzzle him as much as, or more than it had done Van Noost, and he continued murmuring it to himself even while the woman was in the room. As soon as she was gone, however, and he had pressed his guest to take some food, he returned to the subject openly, asking,

"Pray, sir, what sort of a lad was this that said 'Ballimoree' to you? I saw nobody go up that way but Dick Peerly."

"Oh, he was a lad of nineteen or twenty, with flaxen curly hair and eyes rather close together," Van Noost replied. "He came up at first whistling like a merry innocent sort of noodle, but when he began to speak he looked 'cute enough."

"Ay, he is a dead hand at whistling," said the farmer. "It must be Dick Peerly; and 'cute enough he certainly is. I don't half like him; and, if it had not been to oblige my cousin Sam, I would not have had him on the farm at all. I'll ask him what he means by Ballimoree."

"Oh, I dare say it was only sauciness," observed Van Noost, and so the affair dropped for the time.

Shortly after, Master Jennings was sent for from the great house, where, it would appear, he acted as a sort of steward. He was a grave old man in a brown suit, and was very courteous and polite to Van Noost as soon as he was told the words which the other had been instructed to address to him. But he and Farmer Thompson made many inquiries after their young lord, and expressed great pleasure to hear that he was in their neighborhood.

"I think he might very well return and take possession openly, sir," said Master Jennings, "though things are looking rather bad just now. Yet, from those who know, I have heard that he is in no danger. However, that is not our affair; and, of course, we shall not say we know any thing of his being in the country. You had better come up with me to the great house, and we will soon get a bed ready for you, in case you would like to lie down after your long ride. Any thing we can do to make you comfortable, I am sure shall be done."

"I want nothing," replied the statuary, "but some clay, a great caldron, and as much lead as I can get, and I will show you one or two funny things."

"Any thing you want, sir, shall be got directly," said Master Jennings; "but the lead may be somewhat difficult, for I don't think there is much of it down about here. I will show you the way, if you please, sir."

"Have with you, good Mr. Jennings," exclaimed Van Noost, with a theatrical air, as far as the stiffness of his hind quarters would permit of his assuming one; and, after thanking his host of the farm-house for his courteous hospitality, he walked out toward the mansion above.

"Ballimoree!" said Farmer Thompson: "I wonder what the deuse he could mean by that. I'll find it out."

CHAPTER XVI.

The account given by Richard Newark to Emmeline and Smeaton, after the latter had returned, comprised nothing that the reader does not know; but he told his tale with great humor, and even some degree of wit, which called a laugh from Smeaton, and made Emmeline smile, although the former found matter in it for much consideration, and the latter for much alarm.

It was now apparent that, the moment he resumed his real name and station, Smeaton would be subject to annoyance and inconvenience, if not worse, from the zeal of the Devonshire magistrates; and, after some thought, he resolved to write to Lord Stair, explaining his position, and begging him to assist in removing the difficulties with which he was surrounded.

"I am determined," he said to himself, "to take no part in the foolish struggles which seem likely to take place in this land, and which I feel convinced can end in nothing but the destruction of those who promote them. Undoubtedly I look upon the Stuart race of kings as lawful sovereigns of the country, and did wish that the late queen had lived long enough to restore her brother quietly to the throne of his ancestors. But nations have rights as well as monarchs, and it is somewhat more than doubtful to me whether the great mass of the reasoning people of this country are not strongly opposed to the return of their ancient kings. I will take no share in this business."

Richard Newark himself had some questions to ask, as well as the tale to tell; and he put them, as usual, somewhat abruptly.

"Well, colonel," he said, after some conversation, "now tell us all about the priest's chamber."

"I am afraid I must not, my young friend," replied Smeaton. "That is another man's secret, communicated to me for my own good, and I must not betray it."

"Ah, you won't trust me," said Richard, in a sad tone. "I wonder why it is people will not trust me. I can be as faithful and true as any one."

"Indeed, I would trust you willingly," replied Smeaton, "with any thing that is merely my own; but this secret I ought not to divulge either to you or to this dear lady."

"Well, then, I'll try you," said Richard. "Are you, or are you not, the Earl of Eskdale?"

"I am," replied Smeaton, at once. "I tell you without the slightest hesitation, Richard, but I beg you not to divulge the fact till I have taken measures to effect my safety."

"I was sure of it," cried Richard, "I was quite sure of it. Poor colonels of horse don't have such beautiful swords to give away; and, besides, I suppose there is something in a lord that makes him different from other men. None of you have two heads, I think, nor four arms, nor eight legs; but yet, lack-a-day, there must be some difference, for I said to myself, soon after you came here, 'That man is different from the rest of them.'"

Emmeline looked up in Smeaton's face with a smile while her cousin spoke, as if she would fain have said, "I thought so too."

She spoke not, however, and Richard ran out of the room in his wild way to see what all the servants were "making of it," as he termed it. During his absence, which did not last many minutes, words of mutual tenderness were of course uttered by the lovers; but other matters were also to be spoken of besides their young affection, and Smeaton communicated to Emmeline all that had transpired between himself and old Mrs. Culpepper, expressing, at the same time his belief that she might be fully trusted

The evening then passed quietly for more than an hour, at the end of which time the trampling of horses and the voice of Sir John Newark were heard. He did not come into the small saloon for several minutes after he had entered the house, and, somewhat to Smeaton's surprise, neither Emmeline nor Richard Newark went out to greet him. But they knew him and his ways better than Smeaton did. The interval was occupied in speaking a few words to Mrs. Culpepper, which seemed to be rather those of inquiry than any thing else; but the replies he received were apparently satisfactory, and he entered the saloon with a pleasant and half-laughing air. The whole circumstances of the evening were discussed: he gave his own version of what had occurred, both at Exeter and at Aleton; he inquired minutely into the events which had taken place at the Manor House during his absence; and he ended by saying,

"Well, colonel, this is a fortunate escape from that which might have proved to be a somewhat unpleasant affair; and the mistake these men have fallen into regarding the flight of the Earl of Eskdale, who has never fled from them at all, will put you quite at your ease for some time, and save you, I trust, from further annoyance."

He glanced his eye toward Emmeline and Richard as he spoke, as if to indicate that it might be better to enter into no more particulars in their presence; and Smeaton very readily took the hint, for, to say truth, he had more confidence in Richard's kindness than in his discretion.

When the two younger members of the family had retired for the night, Smeaton remained, for a few minutes, to give Sir John an opportunity of explaining himself further; but Sir John Newark did not think it necessary to say much more upon the events of that day, merely observing, in a careless and somewhat light tone,

"I hear your lady-wife has quite recovered: I suppose she may soon be expected to join you."

"You are laboring under a mistake, my dear sir," replied Smeaton, at once. "I am quite wifeless."

"Why, I thought," exclaimed Sir John Newark, "that your wife was mentioned between us only the other day;" and he assumed, very tolerably, an air of incredulous surprise.

"I beg your pardon, Sir John," returned Smeaton. "You asked after Lady Eskdale, and I replied that she was better; but the name of wife was never mentioned between us. I spoke, indeed, fully with regard to my mother's illness; but she being the only Countess of Eskdale living, I might naturally assume that your words referred to her. I am a single man, I beg to assure you."

"Well, my lord, a happy condition," remarked Sir John. "Heaven forbid that I should attribute bigamy to you, or saddle you even with a single wife, when you have not got one. I would advise you, however, as you have no wife, to get rid of Keanton, for troublous times are coming, I can see very clearly; and, although you have contrived to keep possession of the estate so long, I fear very much you would not be able to hold it longer, if there should be any thing like a disturbance in the country."

"I trust that will not be the case," said Smeaton, "although I should not, of course, object to the sale of the place if it could be effected at a fair price. Yet there are memories which cling about our old ancestral homes, from the influence of which we can not well divest our hearts. I know nothing of this Keanton, though I was born there. I recollect not one stick or stone about it—have very rarely heard it spoken of, except for the purpose of giving me information which might be useful to me in any unexpected change of circumstances. Nevertheless, Sir John, so strongly is man's weak heart bound by the fine chain of association, that to put my hand to the deed which conveyed it to others would cost me a pang, severer, perhaps, than any other, except that of seeing it wrested from myself and my mother without that compensation which might secure comfort and happiness to her old age."

"I fear that the latter may be the case ere long," replied Sir John, shaking his head gravely. "From all I have heard this day, and all I have seen, I judge that many months will not pass before we witness convulsions which will be beneficial to the winning party, but utterly ruinous to the great body of the English gentry. For my part, I intend immediately to settle my whole estates absolutely on my son, in such a manner that he could not be deprived of them unless he were to take a part which his youth renders impossible. They shall, in short, be no longer mine, but his, so doubtful am I of the future. As to Keanton," he continued, with an easy and unconcerned air, "I have no doubt that many of the neighboring gentry would be found ready to pay a reasonable price for it. I myself should be most willing to come forward and offer you such a sum, but for the views I have expressed. I have always a certain amount of money in reserve; but that might be needful to me in case of any reverses, and it is not sufficient to pay a just price for such an estate as Keanton. Nevertheless, if at any time you or your lady-mother should wish by way of mortgage to raise a sum for any present purposes, command me, and you will find me delighted to testify my friendship for you by something better than mere words."

Smeaton made some courteous reply of no great value, and Sir John continued: "I speak, of course, merely in case you do not sell; but, as I have before observed, there are many wealthy country gentlemen around us here who would be right glad to purchase, I am sure; among the rest, Sir James Mount, an excellent old man, and generally considered a person of great ability. Of his genius I have my doubts, but of his high honor and good intentions, none. He was talking to me this very morning both of yourself and Keanton. As soon as it came out that the suspicions of the magistrates were directed toward you, and that they supposed you were dwelling in my house, he asked me privately if such were really the case. Of course I did not betray your secret even to him. He then went on to speak of Keanton, and it seemed to me that it was a possession he had always coveted."

"He knew my father and my mother in early years," replied Smeaton. "I have often heard him mentioned. Indeed, I have seen him, I think, but am not very sure."

"He is most anxious to see you," returned Sir John; "and, indeed, if you think fit to sell the place, I believe he would be found a ready purchaser. I was sorry to disappoint the good old man, for he expressed so eager a desire to greet his old friend's son, that I could have found it in my heart to bring him to my house to-night, had it not been that I look upon another man's secrets intrusted to me just as I should upon his purse if left in my care—a thing which I am bound to return to him untouched."

Now Sir John Newark was well aware that good Sir James Mount had not in reality a stiver at command, and that his passion for alteration and building had already compelled him to mortgage his estate. As Smeaton knew nothing of these circumstances, however, the suggestion would have excited no suspicion had it not been accompanied by profession of pure motives and honorable dealing, which he knew did not form the distinguishing characteristics of Sir John Newark's life.

"I will think of this, Sir John," he said; "and as to Sir James Mount's knowledge that I am your guest, I really do not see, so much as you seem to do, the great necessity for secrecy. I have explained to you that I have, substantially, nothing to fear, except, perhaps, a little inconvenience from zealous stupidity; but I think, in a few days, I shall have removed all danger even of that, for it is my intention to-morrow to write to Lord Stair, begging him to exert his influence in the proper course for enabling me to reside as long as I think fit in this country, upon the clear understanding that my residence here shall in no degree prove detrimental to the dynasty which he serves. At all events, Sir John, pray do not let my sojourn with you induce you for one moment to exclude any guests whom you might otherwise wish to receive, for I can not at all consent that your hospitality toward me should so embarrass you, and only regret that it has already produced so much disorder in your household. And now, with many thanks, good-night."

Sir John shook him warmly by the hand, and they parted, Smeaton retiring to his chamber, to think, if the truth must be told, more of Emmeline than of aught else, and Sir John to consider his plans further, under the aspect which they had now assumed.

Smeaton's carelessness as to discovery was not altogether pleasant to the knight, who would willingly have seen his young guest more embarrassed; and he liked not at all the prospect of difficulties being removed from the course of the latter.

"I must deal with this epistle to Lord Stair," he said to himself. "It will never do to let Eskdale clear his feet of the bird-lime altogether. But then again, in the mean time, I can work something, perhaps, out of the indiscretion of that foolish old man, Sir James Mount. It will be easy, as this my guest does not absolutely object to see him, to get them into such relations that some of the follies of Sir James may recoil upon the young earl. If the old knight snaps at the bait of Keanton, I can advance the money on mortgage of the two estates; if he do not, he may help to bring about embarrassments which may make my young bird eager to get rid of what can be but a clog upon him. And yet this bachelorism of his is an unfortunate affair. If Emmeline were out of the way, it would all go well. That, however, can not be; but I must make myself sure at home."

And, going to the hall door, he called one of the servants, and bade the man send the housekeeper to him.

CHAPTER XVII.

The events which immediately succeeded to those recorded in the last chapter I must pass over somewhat rapidly, for there was nothing that would much interest the reader in detail. Smeaton's letter to the Earl of Stair was written and dispatched, and it may be sufficient to say that it never reached its destination.

Sir John Newark, on the pretense of great courtesy and attention, hardly lost sight of his young guest for a moment, except during the times when he was giving Richard instruction in the use of the sword. Smeaton thus had no opportunity whatever of speaking in private with Emmeline; and the feelings of which the two were conscious, kept them more reserved when in the presence of others than they had been before those feelings became known to them. The restraint was very painful to both, and day by day it became more irksome, till, with the impatience natural to youth—impatience that can never bide its time—Smeaton felt inclined to do any thing rash to put an end to so oppressive a state of things. Richard, indeed, on the third day, afforded him some means of relief; for, when they were practicing in one of the old halls with the doors shut, the lad took advantage of a momentary pause for repose to say,

"Ay, colonel, you don't talk to me about it, but I know very well what is going on in your thumper."

"What do you call my thumper, Richard?" demanded Smeaton, with a smile.

"Oh, folks call it 'heart,'" answered Richard, "though there is no meaning in that word, and a great deal in 'thumper;' but what I mean is, that I know very well you are dreaming all this time about our dear little Emmeline. My father takes care that you shall not whisper sugar to her; so, if you have any thing to say, you had better tell me, and I will say it for you, because I am sent out with her every day to walk, like Shock, the lap-dog. I may as well talk to her about you as any thing else, for she is thinking about you all the time, and falling into such brown studies that if you ask her what o'clock it is, she looks up in your face and says, 'Tuesday, I believe.'"

"I wish to Heaven I could speak to her alone for about half an hour," observed Smeaton.

"Ay, you can not do that," returned Richard Newark, "and I must not help you, for, if my father were once to find out that I did, there would be a southwesterly gale and an end of all; but if you will only tell me any thing you want to say, I'll say it for you, word for word, upon my honor."

Smeaton had a great objection to confidants, though, in the countries which he had most inhabited, as well as in the plays and romances of the day, they were almost indispensable accessories to every love affair; but there was something in his love for Emmeline too pure, too delicate, to suffer the idea of intrusting his thoughts toward her to any one. There was no resource, however; and many a message to her did he send by her cousin, cautiously worded indeed, but expressive in some degree of the feelings in his heart.

On the same day that the above conversation occurred, a little after the hour of noon, a gay cavalcade appeared before the house. Sir John Newark affected surprise and some alarm at first; but then, suddenly perceiving that it was Sir James Mount, he left his young guest to say whether he would be present during that worthy gentleman's visit or not.

Smeaton consented to receive him without the slightest hesitation, and the moment Sir James entered the room, he recognized a person whom he had seen at the small court of the exiled Stuarts in Lorraine, though but for a few minutes. The worthy magistrate, however, advanced at once toward him, and, taking him respectfully by the hand, congratulated him on his return to England, not, indeed, addressing him by his real title, for Sir James piqued himself on his policy, but yet with marks of reverence which the old Tory courtier showed to nothing under the estate of a lord. His language, also, was so circumambulatory and reiterative, that it might have puzzled a very keen spy, unacquainted with his peculiar style, to make out what on earth he meant; and, indeed, he rather flattered himself that he spoke, on all occasions of difficulty, in such a way as to be utterly unintelligible to ears not initiated.

"I am truly delighted—delighted—delighted," he said, "to see you, sir, in what may be considered your native country—country—country; and although, habit being second nature, which is sometimes better—better—better than first—for why, if second thoughts are best, should not nature—nature—nature be in the same predicament?—you may consider other lands—other lands—other lands to be more your indigenous—indigenous—indigenous soil, nevertheless we may felicitate ourselves upon having restored to our country a distinguished personage—personage—personage, who, like a borrowed gem—borrowed gem, illuminated a foreign crown—crown—crown."

Smeaton, though somewhat surprised, replied courteously that he was exceedingly glad to see a gentleman whom he understood to be an old friend of his family, and the conversation went on for about half an hour as easily as it could do with the sort of hurdle-race talking of the worthy magistrate. In the course of that conversation, Sir John Newark took a small but not unimportant part, throwing in a few words here and there to guide Sir James Mount in the direction which he wished him to take. By his management, though that management was not very apparent, not only was the subject of Keanton introduced, but Sir James was led to expatiate upon the advantages of that estate, its close proximity to his own, its charming sites for building, and the great improvements which might be effected if it had the advantage of a resident proprietor. Smeaton thought, with a smile,

"The worthy knight seems really anxious to purchase it, and one knows not, in the state of affairs here, whether it might not be better to humor him."

Next came a cordial invitation to Mount Place, seconded by some such words as

"I trust you will not be under the least apprehension, sir, in doing me the honor—the honor—the honor of returning my visit; for I am very discreet—very discreet—very discreet. The place shall be kept quite solitary—solitary—solitary for the next three weeks—three weeks, to wait your convenience. Your excellent lady-mother—mother—mother would assure you of my discretion; and in case you should be desirous—desirous—desirous of taking a little—a little peep at Keanton, you can do so—do so—do so in half an hour, with great privacy. The road is quite lonely, through quiet lanes—quiet lanes. No Peeping Toms there; all still and comfortable; not a village or a hamlet on the way; and you can see what is going on—what is going on—what is going on without any risk."

Smeaton declared that his kind friends entertained more apprehensions for his safety than he did himself, feeling that he had, in fact, nothing to fear beyond a short temporary inconvenience.

"All danger even of that," he added, "will be over in a few days, and I shall therefore have the greatest pleasure in waiting upon Sir James Mount before my departure from Devonshire."

"Care and caution, noble sir—care and caution—care and caution," said the worshipful gentleman, "are always highly expedient under all circumstances — circumstances — circumstances. We can never tell what may turn up to-morrow—turn up to-morrow—turn up to-morrow, and therefore it is better to take care what we are about to-day."

"Very true, indeed," replied Smeaton, with a smile; and, with this aphorism fresh upon his lips, Sir James Mount took his leave, never doubting that he had made a very favorable impression.

Emmeline had been in the room during the above conversation, but had not received the slightest notice from Sir James Mount, who was too much taken up with the important secret intrusted to him to think of any thing else for the time. Sir John Newark, however, went out with his visitor to see him to his horse's back, according to the courtesies of those times, and Smeaton immediately advanced toward his fair companion with some laughing comment upon the peculiarities of the old man's manners. Emmeline, however, held up her finger, as if to call his attention to what she had to say, and then whispered,

"I wish I could speak with you! Oh! I wish I could speak with you! Good Mrs. Culpepper came to me for an hour this morning before I rose. She is a friend to me, not a spy upon me, as Richard thinks, and I have much to tell you. Hush! he is coming back!"

Smeaton drew a little further from her; but yet Emmeline could not altogether banish the eagerness from her look, and the eye of Sir John Newark rested on her fair face the instant he entered the room. He took no notice, however, if he observed any thing, but only said, in a gay tone,

"Come, Emmeline, let us ride out this breezy day. Colonel Smeaton, will you accompany us?"

"With all my heart!" replied the young nobleman; "but I must put on other apparel."

"So must I," said Emmeline.

"Well, then, to your toilet," cried Sir John. "I will order the horses in the mean while. It needs a good gallop to shake off the load of worthy Sir James Mount's words, he piles them upon us so rapidly. Quick, Colonel Smeaton! The horses will not be long."

The moment they were gone, Sir John Newark hurried toward that part of the house inhabited by the servants, and, ordering the horses as he passed, entered the room of the housekeeper. Mrs. Culpepper was busily engaged with an account-book; but she rose when her master entered, and laid down the pen.

For an instant Sir John Newark gazed at her in silence with a look not altogether placable; but the old lady bore it with perfect calmness, knowing very well the man she had to deal with.

"I have observed something I do not like," said Sir John, after he had seen that the door was completely closed; but there he paused, and turned his eyes to the ground, as if meditating what he should say next.

"Pray what may it be, sir?" asked the old lady, after waiting a moment. "Nothing in my conduct, I hope."

"No," said her master, "no. I think you would take care; and yet there was a look of consciousness on Emmeline's face just now, when I returned to her and this young man, which has awakened a doubt."

"Indeed!" said Mrs. Culpepper. "What could cause that? Had they been talking long?"

"Only for a moment," replied Sir John Newark; "and I heard him laughing just as I left the room."

"Then, depend upon it, there was nothing to be afraid of," rejoined Mrs. Culpepper. "People don't laugh when they are talking secrets. Do you think he was laughing at any thing you had said or done? for then very likely the lady might look conscious, thinking you might judge she had taken part in what was offensive to you."

It was happily turned; and, after a moment's thought, her master answered,

"It may be so. Not, indeed, that it was me he laughed at, but probably the old man, Sir James Mount."

"The old fool!" muttered Mrs. Culpepper, between her teeth. "I would have him as little as possible in my house, if I had one. He is sure to make mischief if he meddles with any one's affairs."

A dark smile came upon Sir John Newark's face; and he thought, though he did not say it, "That is what I desire."

There is no tool in a knave's hand so useful sometimes as the innocent mischief-maker who is dangerous to honest people; and although Sir James Mount's inquisitiveness and indiscretion were usually annoying and sometimes embarrassing to his more astute neighbor, yet he had often been rendered very serviceable to Sir John Newark's plans and purposes. Sir John was very confident in his own abilities, in his knowledge of the world and of the man, and he did not in the least fear to employ him as a tool in any work where it was necessary to lead others into difficulty. He seemed, however, to ponder on his good housekeeper's words; but his mind soon reverted to the former subject of his thoughts, and he said, with a sterner air,

"I hope you have relaxed none of the care which I enjoined upon you, Culpepper. People occasionally get negligent of such charges in the course of time; and, if I find that such is the case, I must have fresher service for the same purpose. So beware."

"I don't think you have cause to blame me, Sir John," replied Mrs. Culpepper, in her usual quiet tone. "I have performed exactly every thing that I promised to perform. I never undertook to watch when *you* were in the house; but when you were absent, or when I am with her at any distance from your own sight, I will undertake to say that there is not a step she takes, and hardly a word she utters, that is unknown to me. If there is any thing between her and this gentleman who is here, the fault is your own, not mine; first in bringing him hither, and secondly in not watching sufficiently what was passing under your own eyes."

"You are mistaken, woman," retorted Sir John, sharply. "I *do* watch with care that you little know. When did I ever neglect to watch?"

"During the four or five first days that he was here," answered Mrs. Culpepper, putting a pickling-pot on one of the shelves behind her, and not losing her composure in the slightest degree. "The second or third day he was alone with her for an hour in the saloon while you were talking with Martin, the horse-couper, about some horses you wanted to buy—"

"And other much more important things," added Sir John, significantly.

"I know nothing about that," replied the housekeeper. "All I know is, that they were there together; but I do not believe that any harm is done as yet; for, from words and actions which I have heard and remarked, I judge they have said little to each other. The conversation I speak of I contrived to break in upon three times, though I had no business to meddle with it, you being in the house. I wonder he is not smitten, indeed, for she is as pretty a creature as ever eye saw; but then I suppose it is that he has seen a great number of finer-dressed beauties in foreign lands where you say he has been, and, if he is poor himself, I suppose he will want money, which he is not likely to get here. Indeed, he can not tell that there ever was a chance of it. These foreign soldier-captains are not the people to fall in love with ladies without fortunes. No, no, that is not likely."

She shook her head gravely as she spoke these words in a moralizing tone, and Sir John smiled again as he felt his suspicions give way before the old woman's arguments.

"There is much truth in what you say, my good lady," he observed; "but be pleased to remember that no caution can be too great. I had my own reasons for bringing this gentleman here; but I have been deceived in one particular, ay, and helped to deceive myself. They told me he was married—at least, gave me to understand so. Now, however, I find that he is not; and although I do not think he is of a mind nor in a condition to do so foolish a thing as to wed a penniless girl, when he might do better, yet I will not have the slightest care neglected to insure that he has no opportunity whatever of filling her ear with lover's prattle. I have told you Emmeline must marry Richard. It is necessary to me and to both of them."

"Very well, Sir John," answered the housekeeper, dryly. "I have no interest in the matter."

"I will give you an interest," said Sir John, laying his finger on Mrs. Culpepper's arm. "Now mark me: I promise you, upon my honor, that the very day which sees Richard married to Emmeline, I will give you one hundred guineas."

"Ay, now you *do* give me an interest," answered the housekeeper, with a brighter face; "but you will have a hard matter to bring it about, Sir John, Master Richard is so very young—two years younger than the Lady Emmeline herself—and then you know, again, that he is really younger than his years. It is true, the young lady likes him well enough to marry him, I dare say; and, if he were but to fall in love with her, as I dare say he will by-and-by—for if you keep them always caged up together, what can they do?—she will like him better still. As to this gentleman here, I don't think there is any thing in it. I must have seen it, I must have known it. They can not hoodwink me, though they might blind you."

"How happens it your eyes are so much sharper than mine?" asked Sir John, with a sneer. "I should like to know your secret, if it is so."

"How happens it!" echoed the housekeeper. "First, because I am a woman, and next, because you have a great stake in the matter. Men never see these things; and, when suspicions come across them, always fix upon the wrong person; and then, when they have much at stake, they are sure to be blind altogether, or to see crooked. I have not lived sixty years in the world for nothing, Sir John, and I know men and women both well."

She shook her head oracularly as she spoke; and although in self-confidence there is something rather annoying to others, yet there is something very impressive too. If a person possessed of it have any talents, it is sure to double them in the estimation of others, while it may treble them in his own. Thus, at all events, something is gained. Even a fool does not suffer by that possession; for, if it does nothing else, it serves to cover his folly from the eyes of more modest fools than himself. Sir John Newark knew Mrs. Culpepper to be nearly as acute as she represented herself, and he took the rest for granted upon her own showing.

With renewed injunctions, then, to watch every thing that passed, not only during his absence, but when he was in the house, he left her, and the old lady took up her account-book again, murmuring to herself, "The knave! He thinks a hundred guineas will do every thing."

CHAPTER XVIII.

Several days passed, and the time elapsed which was requisite to bring an answer from London to Smeaton's letter addressed to Lord Stair, but none arrived. Rumors were thick and busy in the country of dangerous proceedings in the north of England and in Scotland. In the immediate neighborhood of Ale-Manor, however, the public mind seemed more quiet and tranquil. Some of the magistrates had relapsed into that careless indifference from which the intelligence of great dangers had aroused them; those, of a firmer and more consistent character, were tranquil from a sense of readiness and preparation for any event; and others, more keen, astute, and active, were vigorously carrying on the measures which they had previously resolved to take, but with as much quiet secrecy as decision.

In the interior of Ale-Manor House, the days passed almost without incident. Both Emmeline and Smeaton saw that they were watched, and put the greatest restraint upon their actions, words, and looks that was possible with a courteous and kindly demeanor to each other.

Mrs. Culpepper glided about as usual; was seen here and seen there when nobody expected her; and by her quiet and demure manner, satisfied even Sir John Newark that she was obeying his orders implicitly.

Richard Newark was the only one who enlivened the scene with little agitations. From time to time, in his rash, wild way, and with his figurative, but not very choice language, he would touch so close on the well-concealed feelings of the lovers as to alarm them both, and then, darting gayly away to some other theme, leave them scathless. He kept his father in some anxiety too, for a greater portion than ever of his careless, almost reckless spirit seemed to have entered into him. He contrived to tumble out of a boat into the water far out in the bay, and might have been drowned, as there was nobody in the skiff with him, had not swimming been acquired so early, and practiced so continually, that it was almost as natural to him as walking. He burst a fowling-piece, also, by putting in a double charge in a moment of forgetfulness. But he escaped without injury, and only mourned over his shattered gun.

It is not to be supposed, however, that the restraint to which they were obliged to submit was otherwise than very painful to Smeaton and Emmeline. They did not see where it was likely to terminate. It was natural that the male lover should bear this state of things with more impatience than the lady; for women, even in very early life, have a sort of prescience that their portion is to endure without murmuring. Smeaton was almost tempted to cast off all reserve, and follow what he felt to be a rash and even a dangerous course. None know, but those who have experienced it, how unbearable it is to be constantly in the presence of a beloved object without the opportunity, even by a whispered word or a glance of love, to tell the feelings that are busy in the heart.

How this might have ended, and whether he might or might not have been hurried into any rashness had this state continued much longer, I can not say; for, although he had been well drilled by adversity, by difficulties, and by dangers, and was competent to deal as calmly as any man with most of the ordinary things of life, yet he was impetuous by nature, and the sensations which he now experienced were so new and strange to him that he could not bring them under any rule obtained from experience of the past. That state, however, was not destined to last long; for, on the fourth day after Sir James Mount's visit, as he sat in his room very early in the morning, enjoying the splendid rising of the sun, and indulging the thoughts with which lovers vivify the morning beams, he heard a gentle tap at his door. No sound had previously disturbed the silence which had reigned throughout the house during the night; no housemaid's pail had been heard clattering; no ancient servingman of matutinal habits had unbarred windows and opened doors; and without venturing to say aloud "Come in," Smeaton rose to ascertain with his eyes who was his early visitor. He found good Mrs. Culpepper herself standing in the passage without; but as soon as she saw that he was up and dressed, she entered in silence with her noiseless step, and closed the door behind her.

"I have wanted to see you, sir, for some time," she said; "but Sir John Newark is all eyes, and I dare not let him perceive that I know any thing at all of you, for fear of spoiling every thing. But I thought that old Nanny might very well come to see her boy, even in his bed-room, and so I got myself up early. There are strange stories running about the country, sir. They say people are actually in arms in the North. Oh, Harry, have nothing to do with them, for this thing will never succeed, depend upon it. More than one half of the gentry, and most men of the middle station, are against it."

"I have not the slightest intention, my dear Nanny, to take any part in these rash movements," replied Smeaton. "I am quite as well aware of their hopelessness as you can be."

"But I fear Sir John," said the old woman. "I fear him very much. He is just the man to keep out of all perils himself, and to put other people in for the purpose of seeing what he can get out of the spoil. I wish to Heaven you were away, pleasant as it is to see you. I wish you were in France again. Can you not go, and keep yourself quiet there?"

Smeaton shook his head with a faint and somewhat melancholy smile.

"I can not go at present, Nanny," he said; "that is impossible. I have ties to this land now, more hard to break than those which bind me to any other."

"Can you not take her with you?" inquired the old woman, in a low tone. "Listen what I have devised for you. You love her. I know you love her, and she loves you. Take her with you; marry her under my lady's eye, and with her sanction; keep perfectly quiet, whatever takes place in England; and, when all is still again, demand to return and resume your rights, and I will so work here while you are gone that that dear child shall have *her* rights too, in spite of all the cunning of the cunningest man within the four seas."

"But how can it be managed?" asked Smeaton. "And will she go upon so sudden and unexpected a proposal?"

"Have you said nothing to her?" returned the housekeeper, with a look of surprise. "Have you not told her all your heart? I thought—I fancied—I felt sure, on that day that you were so long alone together, that you must have spoken all that need be said. Why, besides the ride in the morning, you were walking up and down the terrace in the evening for more than two hours, with Dick sitting whistling upon a stone at a distance."

"She knows that I love her," replied Smeaton, "and I trust that she loves me; but it is a very different thing to promise me her hand at some future period, and to agree to fly with me to a foreign land at a very short notice. The motives, the objects, her own state and condition here, the very necessity of her going, even if she did not go to be my wife, must all be explained to her, and I have no opportunity of explaining. I see her not for a single instant during the day without witnesses; and though I pass up and down the stairs more frequently, perhaps, than is prudent, for the purpose of catching one stray passing word, I have never met her."

"That is because it is another stair-case," observed the old woman. "You pass close by her every day; but there is no door open on this side. Let me see," she continued, pressing her hand upon her eyes. "I think I can manage it for you; but you must be very discreet. You know, I dare say, every corner of your sitting-room there beyond, and you must have remarked a door, like a closet-door, always locked. It is a closet—a mere slip. It leads out into the passage close by the state-room, behind which is the priest's chamber. The priest's chamber is close to that of Emmeline, and she can come out of her own room into the same passage. To-night, when you come to bed, you shall find somewhere or another—let me see where I will put it—yes, that will do—you will find, on the upper shelf of that cupboard there in the corner, the key of the closet which leads to the passage. To-morrow morning early, before any one else is up, rise and go through the closet to the state room. You shall find Emmeline there—or she will come very soon. But mind you do not linger long together, and do not make any noise. Speak low—tread softly—and on no account open the way into the priest's chamber, for that would be heard to a certainty by him who sleeps below. You must get her to decide speedily, for the clouds are gathering fast, and I would fain you were gone."

"If I am not to stay with her long," replied Smeaton, "it is very probable that I may not be able to explain all at once."

"Then you must get her to come back the next morning," said the old housekeeper; "for you must not stay long together—half an hour at the utmost—even if you rise at five. Remember, there are people up in the house always before six, and no one can tell where they may wander. This is a strange household, sir, where every servant is a spy upon the other, and the master a spy upon all. It needs skillful doings; but I so contrive that often, in reporting to him what I do, the other people do just what I desire. They tell him that I am prying here and prying there whenever he is absent, and am in all sorts of rooms and places, as if I was mistress of the house. That is just what he wants; and though, now and then, when he catches me creeping about, and any one is present, he speaks sharply as if he were angry—it is but a pretense, which no one knows better how to make. I *do* tell him almost every thing that happens, but that *almost* covers all I wish to hide. I do him no wrong, because he has no right in this house; and I always keep the means in my own hands of baffling him when I please. If he knew it, I dare say I should soon be found down the deep draw-well in the garden; but he shall not know it till I am safe beyond his reach."

"Then I may trust to find Emmeline there," said Smeaton, with a joyful heart.

"Yes, I think so," replied the housekeeper, in a more doubtful tone than he liked. "She will never refuse to go, surely. I will persuade her somehow, and love will take part with me. Oh, yes, she will come, I am sure. But now I will go; and before to-morrow morning I must contrive to have the locks well oiled and the key placed for you. Good-by, my dear boy. Be upon your guard against whatever Sir John proposes, for you can not tell what scheme may be at the bottom of any thing he says or does."

I must not pause to notice all the mingled feelings which occupied the heart of the young nobleman after the old housekeeper had left him. They were agitating enough; and though her words were well calculated to encourage hope of the speedy fulfillment of his warmest desires, yet they plunged him in thoughtful reveries during the day, which did not escape the keen eye of Sir John Newark. Smeaton saw, however, that his absent mood, and grave and thoughtful countenance, were remarked, and he turned suspicion from the course he feared it might take by expressing much surprise that he had received no answer from Lord Stair. Emmeline, too, marked the change in his demeanor, and was somewhat anxious, if the truth must be told; but for her an explanation was coming very soon.

I wish that I could, but fear that I can not, convey to the mind of the reader the feelings with which she listened to the words of the old housekeeper when Mrs. Culpepper visited her that night. I dread that I may suggest, even in the least degree, an idea that she was unwomanly, forward, or bold, when I say that the thought of seeing Smeaton on the following morning in private imparted no other emotion than joy; yet so it was. Emmeline's character, however, was eminently feminine, in the finest, noblest signification of that word. The idea of a clandestine interview with her betrothed made her whole heart thrill; it agitated, almost overpowered her; but it was all with joy. Her education had involved none of the conventional restraints of women in her class of society: restrained, tied down she had been, though in a different way. She knew not, she could not conceive, that any thing was wrong, any thing that could be even construed into wrong, in thus meeting him she loved. Her spirit sprang to meet his, to tell him all she felt, to pour into his bosom the pent-up thoughts of the last week. She could as much have fancied that a sky-lark could be blamed for trilling his glad song in air over the nest of his feathered mate, as she could be by the good and wise for that which she was about to do. The world is full of conventionalities, which have ever been accumulating since the creation; they are the fetters of the fallen. Adam and Eve found them out as soon as they had tasted the fruit of the tree of the knowledge of Good and Evil, and the green leaves which they twined to cover them formed the first sophistication. But dear Emmeline was in some sort like Eve before she suffered herself to be beguiled by the serpent. She had not tasted of that fruit. She knew little of evil, and had not a heart to imagine it; and, as I have said, the idea of meeting her lover, and enjoying one quiet hour of tranquil conversation with him, suggested nothing but thoughts of joy.

Some vague words, indeed, which the old housekeeper dropped, before she left her, in regard to the coming interview and the influence it was likely to have upon all her future fate, produced a certain feeling of timidity, though not great, and she was up and dressed before Mrs. Culpepper presented herself on the following morning. Her timidity, however, had by this time increased, and she besought the old lady to come with her and be present; but Mrs. Culpepper knew more of love and lover's feelings than Emmeline, and was quite well aware that she would be one too many at their meeting.

"No, my dear child, no," she said. "Young gentlemen, when they speak to young ladies whom they love, do not like to have old women listening. I will wait in the passage, however, and give you notice when it is time to part; but as to every thing else, you had better be alone."

In her heart perhaps Emmeline agreed with the old housekeeper; at all events, she submitted readily, and with a faltering step and somewhat agitated air, followed to the place of interview. Smeaton was there before her, and he took care to close the door.

I will not dwell upon what passed between them. Many important things were proposed, discussed, and settled; much was to be told, explained, and listened to; yet nothing was settled, and very little discussed. Marvelous how the time ran on in the words of love and the feeling of happiness! They forgot the future in the present; and they were just approaching the very object of their meeting, when the old housekeeper quietly opened the door and told them it was time to part. Then came the hurried and whispered engagement to meet again on the following morning, with a pledge to each other to act more wisely and providently, and use their time to better purposes.

Thus they parted; and Emmeline, agitated and confused with the inebriating taste of early love, returned to her chamber to dream dreams of happiness. Her head had rested on his bosom; his arms had clasped her to his heart; his lips had been placed on hers. It was all for the first time; and that first time works an eventful change in woman's heart.

They met again upon the following day; and, though strongly tempted as they had been before, they were wise, and remembered that much had to be determined. Neither upon this conversation will I dwell any more than upon that which preceded. The reader can easily imagine what were the feelings of a young, innocent, inexperienced girl, when a proposal was placed before her to quit the dwelling in which she had been brought up—to leave the protection to which she had been accustomed—and to go in silence and in secrecy to a distant land with one whom she loved dearly, but had not long known. She doubted him not; she trusted him entirely; she felt sure that he would take no base advantage of her confidence; she believed him fully when he told her that she should be to him as a sister till she became a bride; but yet her heart sank and her limbs trembled, and it was with difficulty that her lips could be brought to utter the promise.

Smeaton took every pains to reassure and comfort her. Perhaps the first might seem a strange way, but yet it was a very effectual one. According to a custom which he had seen in other lands, he bound her to himself, and himself to her, by a simple form of betrothal. With her hand in his, he pledged himself to her forever, and made her repeat the same promise toward him; then they mutually called upon God to bless them as they kept that vow; and then he placed a small jeweled ring upon her finger—an ancient gem of his house—and, after leaving it there for a moment, and pressing a kiss upon the hand that bore it, he told her to fasten it round her neck with a ribbon, and keep it always in her bosom.

Still, however, he found her agitated, perhaps I may say alarmed; but then he whispered a few words in her ear, and all irresolution was at an end. Emmeline's bright eyes grew brighter as they fixed upon his face with a look not fuller of surprise than of joy, and, clasping her hands together, she said,

"Then I go safely—rightly. It is a duty. I no longer fear."

"You shall have the paper to-morrow," said Smeaton; "but, as soon as you have read it, it had better be destroyed. I have kept it concealed where nobody could find it, even when my baggage was searched in London; but now, in justice to you, my beloved, I must show it, that you may feel yourself justified in all that you do."

Again they were forced to part. Little more remained to be settled, and that, they thought, would easily be done. The hour, the manner, the means of flight were to be arranged; but flight was determined, and they parted happily.

When Emmeline was in the solitude of her own chamber, however, and when all she had promised, all she was about to perform, came upon her mind like a dream, she was moved deeply. Dangers, difficulties, she thought of little; but the strange newness of all that was before her alarmed and agitated her. The very thought of leaving the wild, lonely scenes round Ale, leaving them perhaps forever, produced a very melancholy impression on her mind. There was not a rock or hill, a towering cliff, an indentation of the coast—hardly a tree all around—that she did not know as a familiar friend. They had been the companions of her youth and of her infancy: she had held more communings with them than with human beings; she had peopled them with her thoughts; they had linked themselves to her heart by the strong ties of association; they had been as brothers and sisters to her in the solitude of her own meditations; and, in the absence of other objects of affection, she had clung to them as if they had been living things. Love must be very powerful to break through all such bonds, and to make the heart yield up, with no other portion of regret than a passing melancholy, all that we have attached ourselves to for many years. Emmeline was going to leave them all, as she thought—to leave them all in a few days, and it was not to be expected that she should do so without some grief; but love had by this time the full mastery, and she did not and would not repent of the promise she had given. Its fulfillment, however, was far more distant than she anticipated; and, before nightfall of that same day, the relation of almost all things round her had been changed.

CHAPTER XIX.

Sir John Newark was in a peculiarly gay and lively mood when his noble guest descended to breakfast. He ventured upon a jest or two—a thing rare with him—and discoursed fluently upon matters of literature and affairs of state; not very profoundly, indeed, yet speciously and well. After the meal, he asked Smeaton when he would like to ride over to Mount Place, and the young nobleman replied,

"In a day or two."

Sir John seemed surprised and a little mortified.

"I understood your lordship," he said, in a cold tone, "that you would go to-day, when we were talking of this matter yesterday; and, judging that it might be as well that Mount Place should be free of any unpleasant guests, I sent intimation to Sir James this morning that such would be the case. True, I should not have meddled. Busy-bodies are always doing mischief."

"It matters not," rejoined Smeaton, good-humoredly, for his heart was opened by its own happiness. "I can ride over to-day as well as to-morrow; and, as you have sent, I will do so."

"Pray do not put yourself to any inconvenience," said Sir John Newark, with all his urbanity restored. "I only feared it might mortify the good old man."

"Nay, I will not do that," answered his guest. "I will set off immediately."

"Perhaps you had better wait an hour or two," remarked Sir John, "in case our friend should have any preparations to make."

"Oh no," returned Smeaton, "I will take the morning-tide. The less of ceremony on such occasions the better. Am I to have the pleasure of your company?"

Sir John Newark shook his head with a rueful countenance, saying,

"I shall spend the next two or three hours less agreeably. I have some persons coming to me upon matters of dull business; but, if they leave me in time, I will join you at Mount Place. And now, my dear lord, let me revert to a subject which has been mentioned between us before. Doubtless Sir James Mount will speak to you about the sale of Keanton. If so, you will hear what he says, and decide accordingly. His offer may meet your views, or it may not. Should you decline in his case, and yet wish to raise some money without parting with your property, I have forty thousand pounds quite at your service upon mortgage, if you choose to take it. The estate, I believe, is fully equal to such a burden, still leaving it your own."

They were alone on the terrace at this moment, and what might have come next I can not say, for their conversation was interrupted by Richard Newark running up and inquiring whether Smeaton was about to ride out, as he was wild for a gallop.

"You can not go with Colonel Smeaton to-day, Richard," replied his father, gravely. "He is going to Sir James Mount's, where your company may not be agreeable."

The lad gave a shy, sidelong glance at his father, and then, instantly resuming his light, reckless tone, answered,

"I'll ride with him part of the way, then. There can be no harm in that."

Sir John Newark frowned; but Richard pursued his point, and, catching Smeaton by the arm, exclaimed,

"Come, let us go and see the horses made ready."

Smeaton followed him to the stable; and,

though he returned for a few minutes to the house to make some change in his dress, he saw his entertainer no more that day.

In less than twenty minutes, he and Richard Newark were on horseback, and, followed by the young nobleman's own servant and another man, were riding away in the direction of Mount Place. They spurred on at a rapid rate, and every minute or two Smeaton could see the boy's eyes turned to his face with a sort of inquiring look; but he took no notice, leaving his young companion to explain himself if he thought fit.

"Don't stay long at Mount Place, colonel," said Richard, after they had gone about half a mile. "Mount Place is a rat-trap."

"I do not understand what you mean, Dick," replied Smeaton; "but I do not think I am likely to be caught."

"What I mean is plain enough," pursued the lad. "I have heard that in the year '92 a whole party of gentlemen were taken at Mount Place, and then again, later still, some more. The old man himself got off once, but the next time he was taken with the rest, and was eighteen months in prison. Either the lawyers found out that he was not a man, but a monkey, and did not hang him, or else they could prove nothing against him; but they hanged one or two of the others, or did something with them; so, if I were you, I would not stay long at Mount Place, for fear of being made to chew unlawful bacon."

Smeaton smiled, but at the same time demanded, in a grave tone,

"Have you any particular cause for your warning, Richard?"

"No—no," replied the lad, hesitating a little; "only two messengers went off from Ale this morning—one to Mount Place, and the other to Exeter. I have known harm happen after messengers went off, especially when they have gone so early."

Smeaton paused thoughtfully ere he replied.

"I will not stay long," he said at length; "it is but a visit of ceremony."

"Then now I will take some other road," rejoined Richard Newark; "but mind you are home before dinner, or I shall think they have kidnapped you."

"No fear of that," said his companion; "but, as your father evidently did not like your going at all, I think we had better, as you say, take separate paths."

"How goes it with you and Emmeline?" asked Richard, lowering his voice, and giving a gay look toward his companion. "Sad work, noble gentleman! The poor doves in their separate cages have been forced to silence their cooing. Ah! they will be obliged to come to me, in the end, to help them;" and, laughing lightly, he turned his horse's head and galloped away.

Smeaton pursued his onward course, directed from time to time by the servant of Sir John Newark who accompanied him, and at the end of little more than an hour came to a part of the country where trim hedge-rows and well-cultivated fields showed the neighborhood of some gentleman's seat. At length a long and beautiful avenue of tall elms was seen, with the road between the trees sloping gently upward, and terminating at what seemed a spacious lawn, with a handsome house raised upon a high terrace above.

"That is Mount Place, sir," said Sir John Newark's servant; and Smeaton, telling him that he should have no further occasion for his attendance, rode on with his own man.

His old military habits led him to mark every thing around him, in traveling, with greater attention than men usually bestow on small objects, and his eyes were soon withdrawn from the house and the scaffold-poles with which the two wings were disfigured to fresh marks of horses' hoofs deeply indented in the somewhat soft road. These traces were very numerous, and it seemed as if a large cavalcade had recently passed up toward the house. Without slackening his speed, the young nobleman looked to the right and left, in order to discover, if possible, whether this cavalcade had been a disciplined body or not; but the marks of the horses' hoofs were so irregular, that the suspicion which had first crossed his mind soon vanished. He easily perceived that some of the beasts had been going at a canter, others at a trot; some keeping the middle of the road, and some running upon the green turf under the trees.

Riding on at a good pace, however, the young nobleman soon approached what he had conceived to be a lawn, which now turned out to be a large grass court, or bowling-green, surrounded by dwarf walls, with the road sweeping round on either side to the terrace above. He could perceive servants in gaudy liveries standing at the principal door of the house, but there was no appearance of horses; and, trotting on, he dismounted and inquired for Sir James.

"He is within, sir, and expects you," replied the worthy old blue-bottle whom he addressed; and then, turning to Smeaton's servant, he added, "Take the horses round to the court at the back."

But Smeaton interfered promptly. "No, no," he said; "walk them up and down here upon the terrace. My stay can be but very short."

Thus saying, he turned and followed the servant into the house, passed through a great hall, and up a fine old oak stair-case. As he ascended, he heard many voices above; but, without hesitation, he went on. The moment after, the door of a large room was thrown open, and he found himself in the presence of eight or nine persons besides the master of the house.

Smeaton was greatly annoyed at the unexpected position in which he was placed; but his urbanity did not forsake him, and with good-humored cordiality he met the foolish old magistrate, who came forward and addressed him somewhat after the following fashion:

"Dear me, my noble friend—noble friend—noble friend, I did not expect you so soon—not so soon—not quite so soon; or I should have been at the door to receive you—receive you—receive you. Let me introduce you to Sir Harry Blake—Sir Harry, Colonel Smeaton—Lord Talboys, Colonel Smeaton." And so he went on round the whole room, repeating each name three or four times with vast volubility.

Smeaton bowed round, and then, drawing himself up somewhat stiffly to check any unpleasant communications which he apprehended might be made, commenced a conversation with Sir James Mount upon the weather and the beautiful scenery round his house. He could see looks of surprise and impatience upon the countenance of several of those present; but he went on in the same strain, giving little opportunity to his host for a change of topic. At length, however, a square-built, black-faced man, who was present, cut across the conversation, saying, "I beg your pardon for interrupting you, Sir James, but it is high time that we should consider the more important objects of our meeting. I suppose Colonel Smeaton, or by whatever name we are to know him, will take part in our deliberations."

Smeaton instantly caught at the opportunity afforded him. "Really, I have to apologize," he said, "for intruding at such a moment. I expected to find you, my dear sir, quite alone; and, had I known that any important business was to be transacted here to-day, I should not have presented myself. I will now immediately withdraw, and trust to have the pleasure of seeing you again before I leave England."

"But, my dear sir, you do not know--you do not know—you do not know," cried Sir James. "Our meeting was quite of a sudden--quite of a sudden—quite of a sudden. The intelligence that General Foster is in arms for the king--for the king—for the king, and the rumor that his majesty—his majesty has actually landed--"

"This is serious news indeed, Sir James," interrupted Smeaton, still drawing toward the door; "but, as I have no information myself upon these matters, and have no authority of any kind, I can not afford you advice or assistance. My visit was merely one of compliment in return for yours; and, as I have business at Keanton, I will take my leave."

With these words, and with a bow to the assembled gentlemen, who seemed a good deal disconcerted, he left the room and descended the stairs, followed to his horse's side by Sir James Mount, pouring forth apologies and explanations, to which Smeaton turned a deaf ear. He contented himself, as his only reply, with asking the nearest way to Keanton; and, having received information from one of the old servants of the house (Sir James himself being too much confused by all that had occurred to answer him distinctly), he rode away, somewhat indignant at the situation in which he had been placed. He judged, and judged rightly, that the persons whom he had seen at Mount Place had been gathered together in haste on the first intimation of his coming, with the view of committing him to participation in the rash schemes which were then beginning to develop themselves; and he clearly saw that, notwithstanding the studious manner in which the old magistrate had called him Colonel Smeaton, his real name and rank had been communicated to every one present.

But other and even more painful considerations than those which affected him personally now pressed upon his attention. The intelligence that a gallant but not very discreet officer was actually in arms in a desperate cause, and the rumor that an unfortunate prince, who, up to this time, had been suffering solely for the errors of his ancestors, had cast himself madly into the difficulties and dangers of an ill-considered insurrection against the existing government, grieved him deeply. By principle or by prejudice, as the reader may think fit to call it, he was attached to the exiled house of Stuart; his ancestors had shed their blood and lost their property in its defense; all the traditions of his family were in favor of its cause; and perhaps no man might have felt more ready to unsheath the sword for its re-establishment on the throne of England, had not many things occurred within the last five-and-twenty years to weaken in him that hereditary attachment which had brought ruin upon his father. His early life had been spent at the little court of St. Germain's; and all that he had witnessed of the mean intrigues of that court, and the shameless ingratitude of its princes toward some of their best and most faithful servants, together with the licentiousness, the weakness, the frivolity, and the baseness of the principal persons who surrounded them, if not of the princes themselves, had produced a feeling of disgust which, although it could not alter his view of the supposed justice of their cause, put an end to every thing like zeal in their favor. He felt with Addison's friend, the poet Tickell, in the, "Epistle to a Gentleman at Avignon:"

"From James and Rome I feel my heart decline,
And fear, O Brunswick, 'twill be wholly thine;
Yet still his share thy rival will contest,
And still the double claim divides my breast:
The fate of James with pitying eyes I view,
And wish my homage were not Brunswick's due;
To James, my *passions* and my *weakness* guide,
But *reason* sways me to the victor's side."

The progress of the human mind, and the development of more just notions of government and of the rights of people as well as of princes, had been great during the twenty-five years to which I have alluded. Smeaton had mingled with many classes in many countries, had heard opinions and arguments which were never uttered in the courts of kings, and it was impossible for him to feel in the cause of the house of Stuart that same devoted attachment which had led his father to submit to every loss without murmuring, and to bear ill usage without complaint Nevertheless, he felt much pain at the thought of all the disastrous results which might accrue from the enterprise which had now commenced, and his ride onward toward his mother's property was a melancholy one.

We must leave him, however, for a little, to inquire into what followed his somewhat abrupt withdrawal from the house of Sir James Mount That worthy magistrate -- shrugging his shoulders, confused and irritated, but thoroughly convinced that every thing he had done or could do was perfectly just, proper, and discreet--returned to his companions above, and found them in a state of great excitement. They all fell upon him at once, declaring that he had altogether misled them.

"Why, this man seems as cold a Whig," exclaimed one, "as any Hanover rat that ever swam over the sea from Bremen."

"You represented to me," said another, "that he came over expressly to ascertain what could be done for the good cause."

"You invited me this morning to meet and consult with him," said a third. "I have your note in my pocket at this moment."

"I doubt whether he is the Earl of Eskdale at all," said a fourth. "One of that family would not be so lukewarm."

Here Sir James Mount himself, who had hitherto only replied by shrugs and grimaces, found himself on more certain ground, and replied boldly,

"Why, I know him, Sir Harry. I have seen him myself at Nancy—at Nancy—at Nancy. There is not a doubt—there is not a doubt—there is not a doubt of who he is. As to his coldness, it may be all discretion—discretion. He came expecting to see and consult with me alone; and as to my inviting you here, gentlemen—inviting you here—inviting you here, I did it for the best, and on good advice. Look here what

Sir John Newark says;" and, drawing a note from his pocket, he read as follows:

"My worshipful and excellent friend,—I write you these few words to tell you that our friend the colonel will be over with you this morning, to speak upon the important business you wot of. He seems perfectly confident of his own safety, and to entertain no objection to meeting any one—in which I think he is rash; but I would have nobody at my house except discreet people, if I were in your case. Keanton is so near you, that most likely he will go over there before he fully decides upon what he will do. It is a very valuable property, and, I should think, ought to produce a good sum if sold."

"What he means about Keanton—about Keanton—about Keanton, I can not divine," said Sir James.

"He means it as a blind," replied one of the others; "and, in case his letter were to fall into any other hands, he would vow that it all referred to some matter of ordinary business. Ah! Sir John Newark, Sir John Newark! we all know him well. He is not to be trusted."

"Stay a minute," said Lord Talboys. "The letter may bear a different interpretation. Sir John distinctly says that the earl will decide upon nothing till he has been to Keanton, therefore we could not expect him to open himself to us now. Then, again, this matter as to the sale of Keanton may imply that he wishes first to see what funds he shall have at command in order to raise men. You say he is a very celebrated officer, Sir James?"

"Very distinguished — very distinguished — very distinguished indeed," replied the old gentleman.

"You had better burn the letter, at all events," said the black-faced man, who was at once the shrewdest and most determined of the party. "Here, I will strike a light with a pistol-flint."

"No, no, no," said Sir James Mount, "I may have to show it again—show it again. I expect several other friends; but he came so soon—he came so soon—he came so soon. Hark! I hear some of them coming."

Almost as he spoke, one of the servants entered the room abruptly, with a face in which the nose alone was rosy, and his aspect at once alarmed the master of the house.

"What is the matter?—what is the matter?—what is the matter?" he exclaimed.

"Why, your worship, there is a body of foot soldiers half way up the avenue," replied the man, "and some forty or fifty horses have just ridden up to the back. I am sure I don't know how they got into the park."

The confusion and disarray which now prevailed was extraordinary. Poor Sir James Mount was at what is commonly called his wit's end. Some were for running down and gaining their horses as fast as possible to escape; others were for attempting to defend the house; and others were actually at the door of the room to sneak away, when the voice of Sir Harry Blake was heard exclaiming,

"Stay! stay! Every one stay! There is no danger whatever, if we act like brave and prudent men. Should these soldiers come with any suspicion, we have only to say that we have met as a body of magistrates and gentlemen to concert means for the preservation of the peace of our district, very sinister rumors having reached us of risings in different parts of the country. No one can deny our right so to meet, or even say that it was not our duty to do so. Bring a light directly, Joseph," he continued, addressing the servant. "Offer no opposition whatever to whomsoever may be at the head of the soldiers. But the light—the first thing is the light."

As he spoke, he drew the note he had received from Sir James Mount from his pocket, and threw it and another paper into the fire-place. All who were present followed his example; and, as the light did not come as soon as they expected, the pile was set on fire by some gunpowder and a pistol-flint, and every scrap of paper was utterly destroyed. This was not done a moment too soon, for the sparks were still wandering about in the tinder when the high sheriff of the county entered, accompanied by the elderly general officer in the brown suit who had played a quiet but important part at the meeting of the magistrates in Exeter.

"I am sorry to disturb you, gentlemen," said the high sheriff, "but you have met here this morning in somewhat unusual numbers for purposes which require explanation."

"Methinks, to a magistrate of your prudence and experience," said Sir Harry Blake, "but little explanation would be required, if, as I take it for granted, the sinister rumors which have reached us of armed risings in various parts of the country have come to your ears also. But explanation is very easily given. We met in these perilous circumstances to devise means for preserving the peace of this district, and I think you will not deny, Mr. High Sheriff, that it was our duty to do so."

"I was not aware, Sir Harry," replied the gentleman whom he addressed, with a quiet sneer, "that your zeal for the peace of our lord the king was so warm."

"Warm enough to have left a strong smell of burned paper behind it," said the general, looking toward the fire-place. "Pray what may have been those papers just destroyed?"

"Some incendiary addresses," replied Sir Harry, readily, with a laugh. "We thought the flame that they have just made there might be less dangerous than any other they could light up in the country."

"Ha!" said the old general. "Nevertheless, Mr. High Sheriff, I must call upon you to do your duty."

The high sheriff looked round the group assembled, and then said,

"I think I know every face here present; but there is one gentleman whom we expected to have the pleasure of meeting, and who is not among you. Has the Earl of Eskdale been here? or is he expected?"

"No person of that name has been here," replied one of the gentlemen, boldly; and then, with a spice of malice, he added, "One Colonel Smeaton was here a short time ago, but, not liking our proceedings, he took his departure."

"Oh, Colonel Henry Smeaton," said the sheriff. "That will do." At the same moment, the general took a step toward the door.

"Then I suppose we may as well break up," said Sir Harry Blake; but the high sheriff waved his hand, while his military companion left the room.

"Pardon me, gentlemen," he said, "I must request the pleasure of the company of every one of you to Exeter. Informations have been sworn, of which you shall have copies. Here are warrants against five of you, which it will be my painful duty to see executed; and summonses have been issued against the rest to come in and surrender, which it will be well for them to obey at once."

As he spoke, the general put his head into the room, saying,

"I must away to Keanton, Mr. High Sheriff, and take a party of horse with me. I have got the information I wanted from the servants, and will overtake you on the road to Exeter."

"Join us at Silvercross, general," said the high sheriff. "I shall much need your counsel and assistance. We have four other friends to inquire after, remember, so you had better come on as soon as you have made sure of your man. Now, gentlemen, are you ready, and is it your intention to come peaceably?"

"Oh, certainly," replied Lord Talboys. "*We* met to preserve the peace. *You* apparently come to disturb it."

"It is all very good—very good—very good," said Sir James Mount, who had now a little recovered himself; "but I do not know what I have done to deserve this treatment, and I will have reason for it—reason for it when I get to Exeter."

"You shall have reason for it here, my dear sir," replied the high sheriff. "I think this is your handwriting—if not, it is an exceedingly good imitation; and in this letter, addressed to Sir William Wyndham, you tell him there is every reason to believe that King James is actually landed in Scotland. Now who King James is you best know; but that is a question government is determined to inquire into in conference with yourself, and therefore I am afraid you must take a journey to London. Now, gentlemen, I will show you the way, and I trust that you will follow, without obliging me to send up for you."

Thus saying, he descended the stairs, and one after another of the party above, with dejected looks and crushed expectations, walked down after him, passing between two files of soldiers in the hall. Few words were spoken by any of them; but Sir Harry Blake whispered to Lord Talboys,

"I would bet a guinea to a pinchbeck shoe-buckle that Newark is at the bottom of this."

CHAPTER XX.

Through quiet hedge-rows, and calm and solitary lanes, Smeaton pursued his way toward Keanton. As he advanced, he thought he recognized the objects around him. It might be fancy, or it might, indeed, be memory; but he had often heard the place described, and two well-executed views of the house and neighboring grounds always hung in his mother's chamber; so that a clear, brawling brook, which cut across the road, and a group of old oaks upon a knoll, seemed quite familiar to him, and showed him that he was approaching Keanton rapidly.

Before going to the family mansion, he thought it better to call at the house of Farmer Thompson, and inquire into the state of things in the neighborhood. He found nobody within, however, but the stout servant-maid, who looked at him apparently with some degree of suspicion, and gave very short answers to his questions. "She could not tell where Mr. Thompson was," she said. "She did not know whether Mr. Jennings was at the house or not. Her master might be home soon or he might not, just as it happened. He was very uncertain, 'specially just about harvest-time."

"Well, my good girl," said Smeaton, "there are two things I think you must do for me. Give me a draught of milk, if you have got any, and call somebody who can tell me more."

He spoke with soldier-like frankness, and the girl laughed, replying,

"Milk you shall have, sir, and welcome; and I'll call somebody else; but, whether they can tell you more or not, I can not say."

Leaving him in the passage where he stood, she went away toward the back of the house, discussing with herself, in half-uttered sentences, the question of whom she should call.

"Not Tom," she said, "for he would blurt out every thing in a minute, all about the fat man up at the great house, and all. I'll call Dick Peerly. There is no getting any thing out of him—at least *I* never could."

After getting a bowl of milk at the dairy, she mounted upon a stone step let into the wall of the yard, and screamed at the top of her voice to good Van Noost's first acquaintance at Keanton, who was working in the field behind.

"Here, Dick—Dick Peerly," she cried, "come hither. Here is somebody wishes to speak to thee, man." Having thus vociferated, she carried the bowl to the stranger.

Dick Peerly sauntered up to the house at her bidding, whistling as usual; but, as soon as he saw the visitor, he put his hand up to his forehead as a salutation with much greater signs of respect than he had shown to Van Noost.

"Can you tell me, my man, where Farmer Thompson is?" asked Smeaton.

"No, that I can not, sir," replied the lad "He may be gone to Ballimoree for aught I know."

"Ballimoree!" echoed Smeaton, gazing at him. "Where is that?"

"Why, you fool, Dick, can not you give the gentleman a reasonable answer?" exclaimed the girl. "It is all his nonsense, sir. There is no such place as Ballimoree."

"I only meant to say he might be any where in the world, sir, for aught I knew," replied the young man, eyeing Smeaton very attentively. "But here he comes up the road, if you want to see him."

Smeaton drank the milk, and then, leaving his horse with the servant, walked on to meet the good farmer, while the maid and the peasant-lad looked after him down the road. The meeting was too far off for them to hear any of the words spoken; but in an instant they saw the farmer uncover his head, and stand with his hat in his hand till Smeaton made him a sign to put it on again. Then, without returning to the farm-house, they walked away toward the mansion, making a sign to the servant to follow with the horses.

They reached the great iron gates and went in; the servant followed and disappeared also; and the girl was turning to her work again, when suddenly a clattering sound was heard upon the road near, and a small party of horse came down at full speed.

The moment the lad Dick Peerly beheld them,

he darted away to meet them, and laying his hand on the neck of the charger mounted by an elderly man in a plain brown suit, he uttered the word "Ballimoree."

"Ay, Ballimoree, to be sure," replied the general, ordering his troop to halt. "Are you Dick Peerly?"

The spy, for such he was, nodded his head, saying in a low tone, "He's up there at the house, or I am quite out. He came not ten minutes ago. But go carefully to work, sir, for there are so many ins and outs in that old place, that he'll get off if you make much noise."

"Come with me and guide us," said the general. "We will use all caution."

The whole party then rode quietly up the road toward the mansion; but their proceedings had not passed without notice. The servant-girl, startled and surprised by the suddenness of the lad's spring forward to meet the soldiers, ran into the front room of the farm-house, and watched them from the window. Whatever shape her suspicions might take, she resolved at once that her master should not be without help in need; and, casting her apron over her head, she ran out by the back way, from cottage to cottage, and from field to field, saying a few words to every man and boy she met. The effect of what she told was instantaneous. All her hearers seemed enraged and surprised. One got a thick stick, another a flail, another a scythe. One or two ran into the cottages and brought forth old guns used for frightening the birds from the corn; and some eighteen or nineteen men, together with a number of women and boys, were soon directing their steps toward Farmer Thompson's house, all muttering threats against some one, who was probably no other than treacherous Master Dick Peerly.

In the mean time, Smeaton and the farmer had, as we have seen, quietly pursued their way to the mansion, and had opened the great door, which was merely latched. A large old stone hall then presented itself; but it was vacant, as were also the rooms to the right and left. Voices, talking and laughing, however, were heard from a distance; and as the surest means of discovering where Master Jennings, the steward, was, Farmer Thompson led his young lord toward the great kitchen, in which a stout, rosy dame was bustling and scolding the maids. From her they learned that her husband Jennings was out in the little court with "the fat strange man, helping him in his tom-fooleries," as she chose to express it.

"They have spoiled my best ladle among them," she said, "that is all I know; and I think Jennings is as great a fool as the other, for he has let the two men be called off their work in the garden for his nonsensical lead-melting. But if my lord chooses all this to go on, there is no help for it, I suppose."

Smeaton smiled; and Farmer Thompson led the way toward the back court, through empty passages and a number of open doors. In the little stone-paved inclosure which they soon reached, an animated scene presented itself. Slung upon a tripod, such as that much in use among our friends of the gipsy race, was an immense large pot or caldron with a furious fire of brushwood beneath it. Two men in the garb of laborers were supplying fresh fagots to the flame; and the steward Jennings, a man upward of sixty years of age, was standing by looking on, while Van Noost himself, the presiding demon of the flame, bustled about, stripped to the waist, and thickly begrimed with smoke and dirt.

For an instant he did not seem to perceive the approach of the young nobleman and his companion, so busily was he engaged in looking into the great pot, and moving some substance in it with a long ladle which he held in his hand. When he saw Smeaton, however, he rolled toward him with a joyous laugh, exclaiming,

"Here I am, my lord—here I am, at my old trade, and in your lordship's service!"

At the same time, Farmer Thompson beckoned up the steward and introduced him to his young master. A few kindly words passed from the lips of Smeaton, and expressions of respect and attachment from those of Jennings; after which Smeaton turned to Van Noost, saying,

"Well, my good friend, what are you about now?"

"Casting balls, my lord—casting balls for pinnacles," replied Van Noost, turning back to his caldron. "There is not one left in the place. What is a pinnacle without a ball, more than a cannon without a shot? Halloo! halloo! who are these gentlemen?"

His exclamation immediately led Smeaton to turn in the direction which Van Noost's eyes had taken; and he beheld, at each of the three doors which led into the court, a small party of dismounted troopers, every man having his cocked pistol in his hand. At the head of one of these parties was the general officer, in his plain brown suit.

"Halt there!" said the old officer to the men; and he moved quietly, alone and unarmed, toward the scene around the caldron.

Without the slightest hesitation or embarrassment, Smeaton advanced a step or two to meet him, knowing that he himself was the person who must now speak and think for the rest.

"May I ask," said he, civilly, "to what we owe the pleasure of your company, sir?"

"To a somewhat unpleasant cause," replied the general, mildly. "One of the persons without is charged with a warrant for the apprehension of Henry, Earl of Eskdale. I do not know whether I have the honor of addressing that nobleman."

"The same, sir," returned Smeaton. "I shall of course submit, although this is a very inconvenient proceeding, which I was not led to expect. The Earl of Stair assured me that I should not be molested."

"I know not that he had any power to give such an assurance, my lord," remarked the old officer; "but the warrant runs in the name of the high sheriff of the county, and I have no choice but to see it executed, being directed to give him every aid and assistance. Nevertheless, I doubt not that, if you could prove such assurance had been given to you, it might have had great influence; but—"

He paused, and Smeaton instantly rejoined,

"I can easily prove the fact, sir. Among my baggage at Ale-Manor I have a letter from his lordship to General C——, which I was to deliver in case of obstruction."

"My name is General C——, my lord," said the old officer, "and I shall be most happy to receive his lordship's commands."

"Then, if you will take the trouble of riding with me to Ale," pursued Smeaton, "you shall have the letter immediately, by which you will see that not only is my presence in England well known to, and permitted by the government, but that my whole baggage and papers have passed under examination in London."

"This is somewhat strange," observed the old officer, "for no knowledge of such facts have reached this county. Nevertheless, I fear, my lord, it is my duty to take you to Exeter; and, indeed, I have not time to turn so far out of the way as Ale."

"I think you are a little hard," said Smeaton. "May I inquire whether I am apprehended on suspicion merely, or upon some positive charge, which might justify my being carried away—to jail, as I suppose—not only without the baggage necessary for my personal convenience, but without the very means of showing that such a suspicion can have no just foundation?"

"I do not wish to deal harshly, my lord," rejoined the other, taking out his watch; "and perhaps, as it is not yet two o'clock, I may make such arrangements as may tend to your convenience. I must now put you in the hands of the officer who bears the warrant; but I shall tell him, at the same time, that if he feels it consistent with his duty to take you round by Ale for the purpose of obtaining what baggage and papers you want, I have no objection. Your lordship demanded whether you are apprehended on suspicion. Such indeed is the case; but I am much afraid that what we have seen here this day must form the basis of a very grave charge."

As he spoke, he pointed with his hand toward the great caldron, by the side of which Van Noost was standing, an image of fat despair, and shaking in every limb, notwithstanding the heat.

Smeaton could not help laughing.

"Pray, general," he said, "what do you think they are about?"

"Casting bullets, beyond a doubt," replied the old officer. "We overheard the admission from that man's own lips as he came up. He talked of cannon, indeed, but we see none about the place. However, the object is perfectly clear, and he must accompany your lordship to Exeter."

Smeaton laughed somewhat bitterly.

"Prepossession induces strange mistakes," he said. "If you will ask the man what he was really about, he will tell you; and, if you please, I will tell you beforehand, so that you can compare the two accounts."

"I am not here to take examinations, my lord," returned the old officer. "Any explanations you have to give had better be reserved for another place. I heard some of the words I have alluded to, and the men heard others: that is all we have to testify to; and I presume there is no doubt of this being a caldron full of lead. At all events, I will see."

Thus saying, he walked up to the fire, and looked into the large pot, adding as he did so,

"The matter is very plain. This is boiling lead for casting bullets."

"For casting no such thing," exclaimed Van Noost, in a voice affected both by fear and indignation. "I have not got a bullet-mold in the world, and never cast a bullet in my life. The lead was melted to cast balls for the pinnacles and corners of the roof."

"A very good excuse," said the old officer, dryly, staring at the grotesque figure of the statuary. "Pray, sir, what may be your name?"

Van Noost hesitated to reply; and the old general added, with a smile,

"It does not much matter; for, under what ever name you go, we must have you in Exeter, my good friend."

"Well, then, my name is Van Noost," said the statuary, with the boldness of despair. Then, fancying he saw a better chance of obtaining credence for his story if he stated his profession, he added, "Van Noost, the statuary and founder of leaden figures, decorator of gardens, &c., &c. I have had the honor of doing many a piece of work for good Queen Anne; and I declare, so help me Heaven, I was doing nothing at all but going to cast round balls for the angles, where you may see the old ones have fallen off."

"I am afraid the balls might have been used for other purposes, good Master Van Noost," said General C——; "but I am very happy to have met with you, for you are wanted in London on a charge of holding seditious correspondence with his majesty's enemies."

"Upon my word, sir," interrupted Jennings, now speaking for the first time, "the poor man was doing nothing but what he says. You do not recollect me, I dare say; but my name is Jennings, and I believe I am well known to every body as a peaceful and quiet man, who never meddles with politics or any thing that does not concern him. At all events, my lord knew nothing of the casting, for he has not arrived two minutes, and this is the first time he has been here since he was a boy."

"You had better follow your rule of not meddling, on this occasion also," rejoined General C——. "You may say things that I would rather not hear. I am not at all disposed to act harshly, or put any one to the pain of imprisonment unnecessarily, although I am not sure that, in the strict line of duty, I should not send every one here to Exeter jail. However, I shall content myself with this noble lord and this worthy statuary, against whom charges exist, independent altogether of the present suspicious transaction. That also will have to be investigated; and then, Master Jennings, if you have any evidence to give, it will be received. Now, Corporal Miles, call in Captain Smallpiece."

Having said this, he crossed his arms upon his chest, and looked gravely down upon the ground till the person he sent for appeared; and then, pointing to Smeaton and the sculptor, he said,

"That gentleman's name is the Earl of Eskdale, and the other is Master Van Noost. I give them both into your custody, Captain Smallpiece, and you will have the goodness to conduct them to Exeter."

"I suppose I am to tie their arms?" said the insolent soldier, interrupting him.

"You are to show them no indignity whatever, sir," replied the general, "but to remember that, for your proper treatment of them, as well as for their safe custody, you will be held responsible. His lordship has expressed a wish to have part of his baggage, and some papers necessary to his defense, from Ale-Manor, and I have no objection to your riding round that way and permitting him to obtain what he wants. But you will, on no account, lose sight of him; and I think it will be better for you to seal up the rest of his lordship's baggage at Ale-Manor, and to mark, with your own hand, all the papers which he may think fit to bring away. These are precautions, my lord, which I am sorry to be obliged to take, but my duty requires them."

The young nobleman bowed stiffly; and Captain Smallpiece demanded, in a less bullying tone than ordinary,

"Are you not going with us, then, general?"

"No," replied the old officer, "I must ride after the high sheriff. Good-morning, my lord. I trust that you will be able to clear yourself of all charges; and, in the mean time, I shall be happy to receive my Lord of Stair's letter, for which I will give you an acknowledgment, and produce it upon the proper occasion."

Thus saying, he walked slowly out of the court, leaving Smeaton and Van Noost to the tender mercies of Captain Smallpiece, who beckoned up his troopers to assist in the removal of the prisoners.

At that period of English history, and for the greater part of that century, the constitution of the armies of England was very different from any thing we have seen in our time. Abuses, hardly credible to us, so rapid and complete have been the reforms of late years, existed in every branch of the service. When we hear of mere boys being made colonels and general officers, and receiving the pay and appointments due to active service, or when we read of *valet-de-chambres*, bullies, and more degraded persons still receiving commissions in the army by the influence of debauched and unscrupulous patrons, we are inclined to think that the tale is a romance; but such, alas! is not the fact. These things really did take place; and the mess-table of an English regiment presented a strange mixture, for which we have no parallel at present.

Now Captain Smallpiece was neither of the best nor of the worst of the classes which composed the British army. He was the son of a small hosier at Taunton; and having been found exceedingly difficult to manage or to instruct, given to swaggering, swearing, and drinking, his father took a quieter brother to his bosom and his shop, and contented himself with obtaining for his eldest son a commission in the army, through the interest of a nobleman who owed him money, and did not choose to pay it.

Placed under a very strict disciplinarian upon first entering the service, Captain Smallpiece decidedly improved. He lost some of his bad habits, or, at all events, he learned to control them; acquired a certain military tone and manner; and, as he was sharp and daring, though somewhat negligent, he gained the reputation of a smart officer. He had been in battle, too—had not run away, and had received a wound in the service, so that he easily contrived to get from an infantry into a cavalry regiment. Nevertheless, the old proverb in regard to the difficulty of making a silk purse out of a sow's ear was often brought to the mind of his military companions, and to those over whom he had dominion he certainly did not appear in the most favorable light. At the same time, he had certain notions with regard to the perquisites and privileges of his station which savored much more of the mercenary sworder of a former day, or of the thief-taker or jailer of his own times, than of the modern soldier. He had no idea of sparing any one the least pain, or yielding to any one the least convenience, without being paid for it; and he had a happy art of making his requirements known, without demanding money in formal terms, which might have subjected him to punishment.

Strange as it may seem, by no one would his hints have been more easily understandable than by Smeaton, for he had served too long in foreign armies not to have seen the same conduct even in greater excess. He appeared to enter into the character of the man at once; and, rapidly considering his own peculiar position, made up his mind to pay largely for any concession which might enable him to see Emmeline even for a moment before he was removed to Exeter, or perhaps to London.

"I presume," he said, as soon as the general was gone, "you will permit me to ride my own horse, which is waiting."

"If you pay for his keep and dressing, my lord," replied the captain.

"Oh, yes, I understand all that," said the young nobleman. "I have served many years myself, my good friend, and understand what is right and proper on these occasions. What is done for my own convenience must, of course, be done at my own expense."

Captain Smallpiece grinned graciously, for he at once perceived that he should be spared any embarrassing explanations. However, he thought it best to begin his exactions vigorously at once, for fear of any after resistance; and so, rubbing his head, he observed, in a sort of meditative tone,

"As to taking this round about by Ale, 'pon my life, I do not know what to do. Zounds, my lord, it makes nine miles difference, and that, upon a long march, is something. I don't believe we shall ever be able to reach Exeter to-night if we do, and then I shall have to feed the men and horses, and I doubt whether the magistrates will allow the money. The general did not *order* me to do it; he only said I *might*."

"Which was as good as an order," added the earl, who had heard him quietly to an end. "As to your expenses being allowed, whether the magistrates do that or not, I shall defray them. We can settle that, captain, at the first place where we stop for any time; but, if we do not go to Ale-Manor House, I shall have no means of defraying any thing, as, not expecting this adventure, I have not a guinea in my purse."

"Well, we must go, I suppose," grumbled the worthy officer. "That is to say, if you think what General C—— said was intended for an order."

"Oh, that it was, that it was," cried Van Noost, who was struggling, all begrimed as he was, into his smart coat and waistcoat.

"I should take it as such, were I in your place," observed Smeaton; "and I am a soldier, you must recollect, as well as yourself."

"Very well, then, come along, my lord," rejoined Captain Smallpiece, assigning two of his soldiers to guard each of the prisoners. "Stand back, fellows! No private talk with people in custody!"

This was addressed to Jennings and Farmer Thompson, who were pressing forward to take leave of their lord. The first bore it with much patience, and the second drew back and made no further attempt; but he had a hot and angry brow, and muttered something to himself with regard to basting Captain Smallpiece heartily before he had done with him.

"Halloo, what is all this?" cried Captain Smallpiece, when they entered the court before the house, and saw through the iron gates a great number of peasantry, armed and unarmed, and bearing a very threatening aspect. "Cock your pistols, my men, and mount your horses."

"Stay, stay a minute, my good friend," said

the young nobleman, not liking the appearance of things at all. "Thompson, Jennings, go and speak with those men, and get them away. Let there be no violence, I beg. It may do me harm, but no good; and I am not in the slightest danger."

"I won't have the king's troops insulted," exclaimed Captain Smallpiece, in a loud tone.

"I trust there is not the least chance of it," said the young nobleman. "Go forward, Thompson, and take them away into the hamlet."

The good farmer obeyed, but evidently unwillingly; and as he approached the iron gate to open it, the lad, Dick Peerly, who was within the court with the soldiers, sprang forward and caught hold of his sleeve, saying something to him which was not heard where Smeaton stood.

But the good farmer pushed him away violently, exclaiming,

"Get thee back, hound! Thou shalt have what thou deservest, if I catch thee in the place in five minutes. I have got other work to do just now."

Going to the gates, he was seen speaking to the people for a moment or two, evidently having some difficulty to persuade them.

At length, however, he walked down the road, with the little crowd following him, though some lingered a while longer, and many turned to look at the departure of the soldiers when they had got about a hundred and fifty yards from the gates. Smeaton's horse was then brought forward by his own servant, and, as he mounted, the man asked,

"Shall I come with you, sir?"

"Do as you like," replied Smeaton. "I shall not be long in captivity. Perhaps you had better ride with us to Ale-Manor, at all events."

"Ah, you impudent varlet!" cried Captain Smallpiece, "you are the rascal who made such fools of us at Ale."

"Heaven help me, noble sir!" replied the man, "I made no fool of you. That would have been trouble thrown away." At the same moment he loosed his lord's stirrup, and jumped out of the reach of the captain's arm.

After some questions and some trouble, good Van Noost was mounted upon his fat pony with a very rueful face, and, near the head of the troop, with a soldier on either side, he and the young nobleman rode out of the gates. Smeaton's servant, Thomas Higham, followed at the end of the file, a little indeed in the rear; and, before he left the village, he rode quickly down to the spot where Farmer Thompson was speaking to some people, said a few words to him, and then cantered off after his master.

CHAPTER XXI.

The life of man, like the life of society, goes in epochs. There are periods at which fair fortune or ill fortune seems to begin or end, and a long succession of bright or dark days follows, during which no folly seems capable of clouding the sunshine—no precaution sufficient to avert the storm.

The Earl of Eskdale was that day destined to disappointment when, after a long and tiresome ride, fatiguing from the slowness at which the troop moved, he reached Ale-Manor, and was admitted, strictly guarded, to the house and to his own rooms. He found that Sir John Newark had gone out about an hour before, and had taken Emmeline and Richard with him. There was no resource but to procure what letters, money, and apparel he required, and to accompany Captain Smallpiece on the road toward Exeter. The fine wild scenery round Ale looked more beautiful than ever, though the day was not so promising as many which had preceded it. The sky, indeed, was generally blue, and the air warmer than it had been in the month of July; but ever and anon came heavy masses of cloud, floating distinct, low, and heavy, and looking like the flying island of Laputa to the eyes of Gulliver. From time to time, too, they had let fall, in passing, a few large drops of rain, and among the mistiness which hung about the southwest might be seen strange forms of hardening vapors of a light reddish hue where they caught the rays of the sun.

When Smeaton descended from the room he had inhabited in order to remount, he found several of the servants in the hall, with old Mrs. Culpepper at their head. She seemed to witness his captivity with a stoical sort of apathy, which he knew to be far from her nature, and took no more notice of him than by dropping a formal courtesy as he passed. He easily understood her motives, and merely said,

"Be so good as to inform Sir John Newark, madam, that I trust to be back here in a few days. Do not let him make himself at all uneasy on my account, for, as he well knows, I have given no offense to the existing government, and can therefore be in no danger."

"I will tell him, sir," replied Mrs. Culpepper; and the young nobleman mounted and rode on.

The pace at which Captain Smallpiece thought fit to proceed was, as I have hinted, the very slowest possible, and it was evident to Smeaton that he did not intend to reach Exeter that night; but the clouds, which began to gather thick and lurid in the sky some way before they reached the hamlet and church of Aleton, induced him to quicken his movements a little. Rain was beginning to fall when they passed the small public house; and the sergeant of the troop, who seemed on very familiar terms with his commanding officer, ventured to hint that it might be as well to stop there, and refresh the men and horses.

"No, no, Jack," replied the captain; "we must get on a little further, till we come to Norton-Newchurch. There we'll halt at old Mother Gandy's. She brews the best, and I owe her a turn."

Perhaps he regretted, before long, that he had determined to proceed, for the menacing aspect of the clouds was soon changed into active operations. Thunder, lightning, and torrents of rain pursued the party for the next three miles, which was the distance between Aleton and Newchurch, and not a man but was drenched to the skin when the party dismounted at the door of the inn—if inn it could be properly called, being nothing more than a long, rambling public house, of two low stories, looking like half a dozen cottages put together.

As soon as he was under shelter, Captain Smallpiece drew forth his watch, and found that he had contrived to make it six o'clock before his arrival. This was just what he intended apparently, for he abruptly declared that, with wearied men and horses, it would be impossible to reach Exeter that night. He then made arrangements for the accommodation of his soldiers, and demanded a private room for himself and his prisoners, at the door of which he planted the trooper whom he most disliked in the party, to perform, in his dripping clothes, the wearisome office of sentry.

"Now, my lord," he said, as soon as the door was shut, "what will you please to treat the men with? Gadzooks! I shall be glad enough to put something warm into my own stomach, and I dare say they will too, poor devils!"

Smeaton smiled, and replied,

"If you will call the landlady—Mother Gandy, as you name her—I will order refreshment for ourselves. As to the men, you had better take these ten guineas to provide them with what you judge necessary."

The captain had no scruple; and, when the landlady appeared, the young nobleman gave an ample order for good cheer for himself and his companions, and the worthy officer ordered refreshments for the men to the value of about a fourth part of what he had received.

"Set a barrel of good strong ale abroach for them, madam, on my account," said the young earl; and, with a low courtesy, the good woman withdrew, while Smallpiece exclaimed, with a coarse laugh,

"D—n it, you must not make them drunk, my lord."

"I have no such intention, sir," replied Smeaton; "and if I had, they would get sober before morning."

In one respect, the young nobleman and Van Noost were better off than their captors, for they had dry clothes at hand, of which they did not neglect to avail themselves; and good Van Noost seemed to acquire fresh courage with a dry jerkin. A good supper—for in those old times seven o'clock might be considered as a supper hour—completely restored him to confidence; and Captain Smallpiece, gazing on his washed and rubicund face, and clean apparel, and listening to his flat jokes, and his discourses regarding all his leaden mythology on the Reading road, could hardly believe that he was the same man he had first seen at Keanton, and pronounced him a jolly good fellow. This impression was very greatly increased when Van Noost undertook to manufacture the punch for the whole party, and his brewing turned out to be the most delicious that had ever been tasted.

Fertile in resources whenever his first panics had subsided, the sculptor's brain was now entirely occupied with the thought of finding means for the escape of himself and his companion, never dreaming that Smeaton had no desire to escape at all. The first and simplest scheme that suggested itself to his mind was to make Captain Smallpiece drunk; and the worthy officer's propensity toward the bottle was written on his countenance in large letters. But insuperable obstacles intervened: the punch being made in the room, there was no deceiving Smallpiece as to the proportions of the rum and the water. Moreover, the worthy captain was upon his guard against himself; and though he drank fast and hard at first, he soon began to hold his hand. One bowl was emptied without doing harm to any one. Van Noost began to brew another; but Smeaton told him he should drink no more, and Captain Smallpiece said,

"Nor I either."

The sculptor went on, however, and took a ladlefull, saying,

"*I* am not afraid. My stomach is stout, and my brain too."

"Well, another glass," said the captain, in a resigned tone; and to that other glass he added a second, a third, and a fourth, sometimes making Van Noost drink with him, sometimes stretching forth his hand to the bowl and helping himself almost unconsciously. But his head was a well-seasoned cask, upon which the fresh liquor made little impression. He merely grew somewhat more loud and talkative, more domineering in his manner and his tone.

Then Van Noost thought that, if he could but get Smeaton's servant into the room and the sentry away from the door, they could soon overpower the worthy captain himself, and make their escape from the window which was on the ground floor; but the young nobleman would not take any hint. He did not want his servant, and would not send for him; and Captain Smallpiece continued with his long legs under the table, and his eyes turned toward the door, so as to see the sentry every time it opened. Some of Van Noost's maneuvers, too, seemed to excite his suspicion; for when, on one occasion, the statuary rose and went to the window, he exclaimed,

"Come, come, sit down, fat gentleman. What are you marauding about for?"

"I only wanted to see if it rained still," replied Van Noost; "but it is quite a fine night, and the moon is coming out between the white streaks."

Captain Smallpiece d—d the moon, and asked what he had to do with her.

"Perhaps she might light you to Exeter, if you like to ride," said the young nobleman, gravely. "Is such your intention or not, Captain Smallpiece? for I think I hear your men bringing out the horses."

"Not they!" cried the captain, without budging from his seat; "and if they do, they must take them in again. I gave my orders; if they choose to mistake, it is their own fault."

Van Noost kept quite silent, for the sounds which had reached Smeaton's ear reached his also, and there certainly was a noise as of many feet before the house. Then came a loud burst of talking and laughing, and a merry voice without tuned up some ribald song. A lull succeeded; then more loud talking; then, apparently, angry words; and at last a loud and confused din, as if twenty or thirty people were all shouting at once.

"Some of those blackguards of mine have got drunk, and are quarreling with the bumpkins," said Captain Smallpiece, in a growling tone. "Well, they must fight it out; but they had better make haste, or *I'll* be in among them."

The din increased instead of diminishing, and at the same moment a voice was heard speaking to the sentry at the door.

"What is the matter?" shouted Captain Smallpiece, without rising. But, almost as he spoke, there was the report of a pistol; the door was burst open; the sentry was thrown headlong into the room; and a number of men rushed in, with white shirts drawn over their garments, and their faces blackened.

Starting on his feet with a tremendous oath, Captain Smallpiece seized Van Noost by the collar, exclaiming,

"This is thy doing, and I will blow thy brains out." At the same time he pressed a large horse-pistol to the unhappy man's head, and the lock clicked as he cocked the weapon. The fury in his face and the fierceness of his gesture showed that he was prepared to execute his threat, and another moment would have sent the poor sculptor to an immortality somewhat different from that which his leaden figures were likely to procure for him. But a tremendous blow from Smeaton's strong arm saved Van Noost's life, and laid the doughty captain groveling on the ground. As he fell, the pistol went off, and the bullet struck the wall, while he shouted furiously, "Ah, my lord, you shall hang for this!"

What followed it is impossible to describe accurately, for the men from without, rushing in and throwing themselves both upon the officer and the sentry, contrived in the short struggle which ensued to bind them, to overturn the table, break the punch-bowl and glasses, and extinguish the lights. In the midst of this scene, Smeaton found his hand grasped by some one, and a voice said, "Come with me, come with me, and you are safe."

He hesitated for an instant, while a multitude of considerations passed through his mind, rendering it difficult to decide what to do. Another man, however, caught him likewise by the arm, and they hurried him on between them toward the door.

"This way, this way, my lord," said a voice, which he thought he knew.

All was darkness in the passage; and those who guided him did not take him through the room in which the soldiers had been regaling. The door of the kitchen was open, however, and the interior, as he passed, presented a somewhat strange sight. Two or three of the troopers were lying on the floor, apparently dead drunk; others were sitting upon benches or stools, with their arms tied tightly behind them; some were in a sleepy state of drunkenness, which rendered them nearly unconscious of what had happened; others were roaring forth a bacchanalian song in spite of their bondage, or sitting, gloomy and stern, meditating over the way in which they had suffered themselves to be surprised.

Among the latter was the sergeant Miles, who caught a glimpse of Smeaton, and exclaimed,

"Ah, my lord, I know you."

Smeaton paused as if to reply; but the two men hurried him forward forcibly, and the next moment he was standing upon the road before the inn.

"Here is your horse, sir," said the voice of his servant. "All the things are in the saddle-bag behind. Let us be off as fast as possible: then the good folks will separate. Quick, my lord! I will show you the way."

Smeaton mounted in silence among a number of horses, and with eight or ten men flitting round, but apparently taking not the least notice of him. They suffered him to ride away after his servant without even a word in answer to a question he addressed to one of them. Every thing was conducted in profound silence; and in a few minutes the young nobleman was over the brow of the hill, and out of sight of the house. The servant rode on before, leaving his master to follow, and soon left the high Exeter road on which the inn was situated for the downs, which extended nearly to Mount Place on the one side, and to Ale-Manor on the other.

It may be necessary, before I proceed, to take some brief notice of the various thoughts which had crossed Smeaton's mind during the last few minutes, as his conduct was greatly affected thereby. It must be recollected that in the whole transaction he was taken entirely by surprise. He was not, indeed, often found unprepared for any event, but all which had occurred had passed so rapidly, that impulse might well act in the place of reason. Though not without a thorough conviction that, if he did not interfere, another moment would terminate poor Van Noost's life, it was upon impulse that he knocked down Captain Smallpiece, and he much regretted the necessity of so doing to save the poor statuary. The consequences of that act presented themselves to his mind the moment after. He saw that it compromised him in a very serious manner, and that a little skillful torturing of evidence by an experienced lawyer would connect the fact of his taking part in the active struggle for his liberation with his having ordered the ale with which the soldiers besotted themselves, and that, again, with the well-organized plan for his rescue, which he doubted not had been executed by his own tenantry. To all this, moreover, would be joined the lead-melting at Keanton, and the words which Van Noost had spoken, and which General C—— and the soldiers had only partly heard.

The whole of the above incidents would indeed form a chain of evidence tending to the one conclusion, that, notwithstanding his promise to Lord Stair, he had taken active measures to promote the insurrection against the government. He knew well, too, that persons made prisoners in the first outbreak of a rebellion are sure to receive little mercy, and sometimes little justice. Party violence demands victims, and examples must be made to deter the wavering by fear, so that both passion and policy combine for their destruction. If he neglected the means of escape, there was no prospect before him but long imprisonment or death on a scaffold.

Then came another consideration; and I must leave it to the reader to settle, as he may be old or young, phlegmatic or ardent, how much this contributed to his decision. He thought of Emmeline—of how these events might affect *her*; nay, more, hopes and expectations flashed through his mind of being able, were he finally to succeed in escaping, to execute the scheme of carrying her away to another land, and uniting her fate to his. At the same time, he calculated, with the confidence of youth, upon easily clearing himself of all criminal share in the transactions which had occurred, if time were but allowed for him to prove the facts, and for men's minds to become composed and tranquilized.

Such were the motives on which he acted.

I do not mean to say they were altogether just, for I am not drawing a perfect character. They seemed sufficient to him at the time, however, and his next thought was how best to take advantage of the circumstances in which he was placed. Meditating in silence, he suffered his servant to ride on for about a mile; but then the latter dropped back, touching his hat and saying,

"That way leads to Aleton Church and Ale, my lord, and that to Keanton. Though I thought you would like to go to Ale, I took a round to avoid the people; but your lordship can do as you like. You are about half way between the two places, somewhat nearer to Keanton, perhaps; but I think Ale will be the safest."

"Why do you think so?" demanded Smeaton. "And what made you believe I should prefer going to Ale?"

"Why, my lord," replied the man, in his easy, *nonchalant* way, "at Ale you can have a boat always ready to carry you off to the coast of France for half a dozen guineas, and the valley is so narrow that you can get timely notice if people come down to take you. Then, as to your second question, I have always remarked that gentlemen about your age like better to live in houses where there are pretty young ladies, than in houses where there are nothing but ugly old women. Moths will fly in the candle, my lord, and young gentlemen are very courageous."

Smeaton smiled; and the man was falling back as if to let him lead the way, when his master stopped him, saying,

"Here, ride on beside me, Higham, and tell me how all this business has happened."

"On my life, I don't know, my lord," replied the man. "I had no hand in it but just getting out your horse and mine, and throwing the saddle-bags across them. All I did was, when they were carrying you out of Keanton, to ride down and tell the stout farmer, who was so busy, that he had better keep the people quiet for the time; but that, if he set people to look out for us from the top of the hills, he might find means of helping you out of the scrape before you got to Exeter."

"I am grieved at this," said Smeaton, somewhat sternly. "You should not have done so without orders. These poor people have now seriously compromised themselves with the government for an object which I did not at all desire, and I myself am thereby placed in very unpleasant circumstances. Do you think any of them were recognized by the soldiers?"

"Oh dear, no," replied the man. "I'll tell you how it all happened, my lord. When I heard you had ordered the men a whole barrel of humming ale, I naturally thought you intended to make them drunk. There were ten soldiers besides the sentry. A barrel holds six-and-thirty gallons. Now that is three gallons and a half a man. I say I could think nothing else, my lord, than that you meant to intoxicate the party, so I determined to help, and treated them all round to a glass of strong waters to begin with. Just about nine o'clock, when the ale had worked, and the strong waters had helped it, and the men were three parts tipsy, in came three country fellows, and called for a pint apiece. The soldiers began jeering them, and I thought they took it wonderfully quiet, for they only jeered them again, and there was a good deal of laughing and noise. Then came in two more country lads, strong, likely fellows enough, and they too sat down and talked. A minute or two after, some people on horseback came up to the front of the house, and had the landlady called out; and three of the soldiers went out after her, and we could hear a great roaring and noise about the door; and one of the half-tipsy soldiers said, drowsily, 'I dare say they are all smugglers from Ale.' This set one of the countrymen to pick a quarrel with him; and just when they were coming to blows, in rushed a whole set of tall, hearty fellows, with white shirts on, and their faces blackened. They pounced upon the soldiers like so many gosshawks, and, without much of a struggle, tied them, one and all, as tight as if they were going to Tyburn. There was some cracked crockery, indeed, and a stool or two upset; but it was all done very gingerly, for I was not away two minutes getting out the horses, and it was over before I came back."

"But what made you get out the horses at all?" demanded Smeaton.

"Why, just as the black-faced fellows were coming in, one of the countrymen whispered to me, 'Get out your lord's horse in a minute, and give him to the man who is holding the others at the door.' However, as I was saying, it was all done and over when I got back, the soldiers all tied, and as mute as mice; and one of the men said, in a feigned voice, 'Where is your lord? The old woman won't tell.'

"So I led them along up to the sentry, going first myself. He spoke a word or two, and asked what all the noise was about; and when I tried to get hold of him, he fired his pistol, and in the struggle we both tumbled into the room. Your lordship knows all the rest."

"But were all these men from Keanton, do you think?" his master inquired.

"I don't think it, my lord," replied Higham. "The black-faced fellows, at least, looked much more like Ale men, and they carried their hands inside out, like other marine animals. No, I think they came from Ale; but it is clear enough they were in league with the bumpkins; and I saw the jolly old farmer outside of the door. That I could swear to."

"Pray mention it to no one, then," said Smeaton, "for I should be very sorry that he suffered for this rash enterprise."

"The men might be smugglers, after all, my lord," observed the servant, "and might just get a hint when they came up. They are always ready enough to take part in a riot, and to thrash the soldiers. I can not say how it was, but I tell you all I know."

The information thus received did not induce Smeaton to take a better view of the aspect which the whole circumstances might present when brought into a court of justice. Here was his own servant acting with the mob who had rescued him, attempting to seize and disarm the sentry, and taking a prominent part in the whole affair. Nor did he at all feel sure that, though acting with the best intentions, the man had told him all. It seemed to him improbable that his horse should be so speedily saddled without some previous intimation of the attempt which was about to be made, but he thought it better not to question him any further, and pursued his way in silence toward Aleton Church.

The round they had taken made the distance fully six miles; but at length the building began to appear upon the side of the hill, and the Exeter road was perceived descending into the village. The moon, though occasional clouds still flitted over her, was shining with peculiar brightness after the storm, and by her light he perceived a number of persons, both on horseback and on foot, taking their way in the same direction as himself. They were going along in so leisurely and unconcerned a manner, that he could hardly fancy them the persons so lately engaged in a daring and hazardous act, although the white garments with which the greater number of them were covered seemed to mark them out as the same. He thought it better to avoid them, however, on all accounts; and, for that purpose, being higher up on the hill than the church, he so directed his course as to bring the building between himself and them. Before this was accomplished, however, he saw one figure separate from the rest in order to climb the hill, and in the short, round form, he recognized, with great satisfaction, a strong resemblance to good Van Noost.

"Those are some of the men, my lord," said the servant, "going back to Ale, you see. I should not wonder if they were smugglers, after all."

Smeaton was very much puzzled. A suspicion had more than once crossed his mind, from the words of young Richard Newark, from Sir John's eagerness to induce him to go that day to Mount Place, and from all which had occurred after, that his worthy host had led him into a trap. Yet who could have sent these people to rescue him except Sir John Newark?

"If that is Van Noost, I will know," he said to himself; and, turning again to the servant, he asked, "Is not that very like the stout man who was made prisoner with me? I hope so, for I was anxious about him."

"Oh yes, my lord, that is he," replied the man; "but there is no fear about him. He is too fat for any harm to happen to him. He'll roll like one of those things called buoys at sea, which are tumbled about in all sorts of ways, but always get right end uppermost."

"I must speak to him, however," said Smeaton. "Here, hold the horse, and I will go up to him on foot. If I ride after him, he will run."

"And burst himself," added Higham, taking his lord's horse.

Van Noost in the mean time had climbed the hill, approached the wall of the church-yard, and entered the gates; but when Smeaton, following with a quick step, approached them, he found them locked, to his great surprise, and Van Noost nowhere to be seen. Without hesitation, he vaulted over the low wall, and then ventured to call upon his stout friend's name. At first there was no reply; but upon his exclaiming again, "Van Noost, Van Noost, I want to speak with you," the head and shoulders of the statuary were protruded from behind a buttress, and he came forward as soon as he saw who it was that called.

"Ah, my dear lord," he said, "I am so glad to see you at liberty, and glad enough to find myself so too. You had better come in here where I am going. I am dead tired, I know, and I dare say you are too—those cursed saddle-bags have so fatigued me. But we shall be quite safe here; and I have got half a loaf and a long Oxford sausage with me."

"Where do you intend to hide?" asked Smeaton. "It will be better for you to come on with me to Ale, whence we can easily get to France."

"I would if I could, but I can not," replied the poor man. "I have been so bumped, and thumped, and knocked about, that I have not got a leg to stand upon. I am going down into the crypt. There is an end of my old candle left, just to keep away the ghosts, and I shall be quite safe there."

"But how will you get in?" asked Smeaton.

Van Noost laughed.

"Ah! my lord," he said, "I have a fondness for keys, you know. I don't keep keys long in my hands without having a model of them. I have got a key for the door of the hiding-place at Ale; for I thought, whatever your lordship might say, it might some day be of use to you, and I made one out of an old key at Keanton as soon as I got there."

Smeaton paused in thought for a minute, and then said,

"Give me that key, Van Noost. I should like to have it; and now, mark what I am about to say. *You* only know how far you have committed yourself with the government. I am going on to Ale, but not, in all probability, to the Manor House. I shall take up my abode in one of the cottages, if I can find a room. I shall have a boat kept ready to convey me to France in case of need, and, if you think it better for yourself to quit this country, you can come and join me at Ale before daylight to-morrow, resting here in the mean while. Some time will probably elapse before we are pursued, for the soldiers will doubtless go on to Exeter in the first place."

"I'll not fail, my dear lord, I'll not fail," replied Van Noost; "and yet, how can I go to France? It will almost break my heart. My statues! How can I leave all my statues? And yet, as I may say, the parting has already taken place. But let me get the key. It is in the saddle-bags by the little door. Would that I had never meddled with politics!"

As he spoke he turned back toward the church, accompanied by the young nobleman, who endeavored to learn from him, without much success, by whose orders the men from Ale had joined the rescue party. They had all been "monstrous silent," Van Noost said; but when the earl added some further questions as to whether they had ever mentioned Sir John Newark's name, the worthy sculptor exclaimed, somewhat vehemently,

"Ay, that they did, my lord—at least one of them; and I think you had a great deal better not go near Ale-Manor again. From what one of them said as two walked together, I made out that none of all this bad business would have happened if it had not been for Sir John. They say he has played the same trick to others before you, and always *peaches* and *plays booty* except in the matter of smuggling."

"Then he did not order the rescue?" asked Smeaton.

"Oh dear, no," answered Van Noost. "He sent messengers to Exeter in the middle of last night, with letters to the high sheriff. So you may judge of the rest."

"Give me the key, my good friend," said Smeaton, through whose brain were passing many rapid considerations regarding his future conduct. "Did you make acquaintance with the parson of this place when you were here?"

"Ay, that I did, and rose high in his favor too," replied the sculptor. "He is a good, fat, jolly priest as ever waddled."

"And thinks of the things of this life more than of the things of another, perhaps?" asked Smeaton.

"Ay, truly," responded the statuary. "He has more gods than one. A pipe of wine, a purse of guineas, a sucking-pig, or a haunch of venison, are better than any rubric for him, I wot."

"I must see to this," said Smeaton, in a musing tone; and, although the statuary could not divine whether he alluded to the parson or the pig, the purse or the pipe of wine, he did not venture to ask any questions, but got the key out of his saddle-bags.

Having given it to Smeaton, the latter bade him adieu and rode away.

CHAPTER XXII.

I trust the reader remembers well the description before given of the little village of fishermen's cottages at Ale, and of the way in which the road, after separating into two, in order to send off a branch to Ale-Manor House, proceeded to the entrance of the village, and there dwindled into a narrow path for want of room between the steep banks to reach the seaside in its original breadth. Smeaton passed the turning of the road toward the Manor, though evidently with some reluctance, for he paused an instant before he made up his mind, and then rode on more slowly. Five hundred yards onward brought him to the spot where it was necessary to dismount; but, before he had completely reached it, two men came out from under the shadow of the bank, and stood directly in his way. The moonlight enabled him to see, however, that they bore the ordinary garb of the fishermen of the place, which I need hardly tell the learned reader was very different from the fishermen's garb of the present day, and much more marked and picturesque. From these men he apprehended no opposition, even if they were not of the very party which had liberated him, and he was soon saluted in a civil tone with the words

"Good-night, sir. You know you can not ride down here. We thought it was some of the soldiers."

Smeaton dismounted, and gave his horse to his servant to hold; and, walking forward a little way with the two men, he explained to them his desire to obtain shelter in the village, and concealment from every body for a time.

At first there seemed some hesitation in their replies, and the young nobleman began to fancy that the danger in which he stood, and which might pursue him even there, made them look upon him as an unwelcome guest; but when he frankly put the question whether they were afraid to receive him, one of them replied with a laugh, "Lord bless you, no, sir. All the soldiers in Exeter should not take you out from among the men of Ale. Unless they brought cannon against us, they could do nothing in this village. We would beat them out with handspikes. It is not that at all. You are right welcome to all that we can do for you; but they say you are a lord, and you'll find the best house in the place but a poor hole for such a one as you."

"But, my good friend, I am a soldier," replied Smeaton; "and when I tell you that I have slept for a month together upon the bare ground, you will easily judge that one of your houses will be quite as good as a palace to me. All I want is shelter and concealment for a little time."

"That you shall have, sir," replied the other man, who was somewhat older; "and as for concealment, we have got plenty of places where the devil himself would not find you. We sometimes let the custom-house people come and search, just for the fun of the thing, and yet, somehow or another, we contrive to supply the whole country round with Bohea, which never paid toll to king or queen either."

"From what I saw to-night," said Smeaton, "you must have horses among you also; and my two beasts are in some degree an embarrassment to me, unless I can stable them somewhere."

"You will have to stable them on the Downs, sir," said the young man, "for there are no such things as stables in Ale. But stay a bit—I think I can manage it. Farmer Tupper will take them in, I dare say; he knows how to hold his tongue. As to horses for ourselves, Lord bless you, when we want them, which is not above once a month, we borrow them of our neighbors. Many a good farmer, and gentleman too, finds his horses not fit for much work on the day after the new moon. But then, what does he care? Every now and then he finds a pound of tea for his wife, or a bundle of Flemish hosiery for himself, lying at his door or on his window-sill, and he thinks himself well paid for his horses' night-work. Here, my man—Master Higham—you get down and go with your master. I'll lead the horses across the down to Tupper's farm; but take off the bags first. Grayling, you had better take the gentleman to your house, for you have more room, and my wife had a baby yesterday morning, so there is a fine squalling. Bless its little heart! it has got a pipe like a boatswain's whistle."

Thus saying, he led away the horses, leaving his companion with the young nobleman and his servant, the latter of whom seemed, during his stay at Ale-Manor, to have become very intimate with all the good fishermen of the village.

Before walking on, however, Smeaton judged it better to take immediate precautions for guarding against surprise, and inquired whether a lad could not be hired to watch the road, and give early notice of the approach of any party of soldiers. The old fisherman, Grayling, laughed.

"Lord bless you, sir, you don't know us," he said. "Don't you trouble yourself at all about it. No soldier or any thing else comes within three miles of us without our knowing it. 'Tother night, when they came to the Manor, we were all ready for them if they had come on. You were ready for them too, it seems, though how you got out of their way we do not know. I had a great mind to give the fellows who came down to the bay looking for you a drop of salt water to drink for poking their noses into Ale, and some of our men could scarcely be prevented from doing it; but it would only have made a noise, and so it was better let alone. However, you can rest quite as safe here as if you were a hundred miles out at sea. They sha'n't catch you in Ale, I'll answer for it; so come along, sir."

In a few minutes more, Smeaton and his servant were introduced into the fisherman's cottage, the lower story of which, consisting of a room on either side and a good wide passage between them, was encumbered with a variety of articles belonging to the man's craft or mystery, some of which were not of the most pleasant odor. Salted fish, sails, nets, fishing-lines, spars, oars, boat-hooks, barrels of tar, tallow candles, and a number of things which I can not describe, were huddled together in the rooms and in the passage, exhaling a smell, as I have said, more powerful than fragrant, which was considerably assisted by a quantity of smoke issuing forth from a room on the left-hand side. There, at the cheek of the fire, as they termed it, sat the old man's old wife, with two or three young dolphins, her grand-children, playing about as merrily as if it had been noon. To her the fisherman introduced his guest, and whispered a word in her ear, which instantly made her clamber up a steep little stair-case, which came down without guard or balustrade, not into the passage, but into the middle of the very room where she had been sitting. The floor above, I may mention, contained four rooms, and was nearly double the size of the floor below, which is only to be accounted for by the fact of the house being built against the steep side of the hill, which left not more than eight-and-twenty feet of flat ground between its base and the river.

The good lady not returning immediately, the fishermen himself went up after her, and found her, like all ladies when visited by an unexpected guest, in a great and setting-to-rights bustle.

"Pooh, pooh!" said the old man, "don't make such a piece of work, mother. He is quite a plain gentleman, and has been a soldier. He must have the back room too, for there he'll be snuggest."

"But suppose you want to get the tea out, Jack?" said the old lady. "Why, the bed is just over the hiding-hole."

"All the better," replied the man. "He may have to hide there before we have done with him. It is not the first time, I think, mother, that we have hid a man there, and so we must do now, if it is needful. Here, we'll put the chest for a seat at the foot of the bed. You bring the table out of t'other room. Then it will all look mighty comfortable. But we must get him some supper before he goes to bed, and I'll broach that little keg I brought in last time."

"I hope he'll pay for what he has," said the old lady, "for we can not afford to be giving away the things for nothing."

"There, there, don't be a fool," rejoined her husband. "Madam Culpepper will take care we are none the worse for it, and we all of us owe her more than that comes to."

When they descended the stairs they found Smeaton playing with the children, who were in high glee; but his servant was no longer with him.

"I have sent my man up to the house," he said. "He can stay there without danger to himself for to-night at least, and he may be of service to me."

The old man seemed startled and not well pleased.

"You know best, sir," he said, rather gruffly; "but—"

"But what, my good friend?" interrogated Smeaton. "You seem not to like my having done so."

"Why, sir, if he tells Sir John that you are down here, it may be a bad business," replied Grayling. "Mayhap you do not know Sir John as well as we do."

"I think I do," rejoined Smeaton, with a smile; "and, for that reason, I told the man not to say where I am, but merely to let them know I had been rescued and had ridden away. I have left him to tell his own tale; but I can trust him; and, depend upon it, Sir John will know nothing of the matter."

"Well, well, that is all right," responded the fisherman, his look brightening. "If he sees Mrs. Culpepper first, she'll tell him what to do."

A sudden light broke upon Smeaton's mind "Pray, was it Mrs. Culpepper," he said, "who directed you to come to my rescue?"

The old man laughed.

"You are quite under a mistake, sir," he said "None of us came to your rescue. We know nothing about it. Ask any man in the place, and he'll tell you the same. There has not been one of them a couple of hundred yards from the place to-night."

A sly smile contradicted his words; and Smeaton, comprehending the truth, answered laughingly,

"Nevertheless, Master Grayling, there is a great streak of soot, or some black stuff, all the way down your cheek."

"The devil there is!" cried the man, starting up, and walking with the candle to a little looking-glass that hung against the wall "Here, mother, give us a tuft of oakum;" and, having got what he demanded, he rubbed his weather-beaten cheek hard, and then threw the oakum into the fire.

"It is a rule here, sir," he said, "never to speak of any thing that we do beyond the cross-road; and it is a good rule too; so neither you nor any one else will get any thing out of us, ask what questions you will. Sir John is a keen hand, and he tried it more than once at first, but he could make nothing of it, for we all know that a man's greatest enemy is his own tongue. You could not make that little child there blab, I'll be bound. But I dare say you know that Mrs. Culpepper has a brother and two nephews living over at Keanton—good solid men they are, who know how to hold their tongues too; and that is all I shall say upon the subject. So now, sir, if you like to have a glass of Geneva and some broiled fish, we'll have our supper."

Smeaton explained that he had supped already; and the old man, lighting a fresh candle, conducted him up the stairs to his bed-room. When they were in it and the door shut, he put down the light and said,

"You won't be very comfortable here, sir, but you'll be very safe; and I'll tell you how to manage. But, mind you, I'm going to put myself a bit in your power, so you must keep my secret as well as I'll keep yours. That window there looks up the hill—but nobody can come down that way—and from it you can see all the way up the path by what they call the blind man's well. Then look here. Underneath that bed, three of the planks lift up altogether. They play upon a pivot; so you have nothing to do but put your knife under, and lift them as I do now. There, you see, is the top of a ladder, going down into our store-house, as we call it, though old Mother Grayling will call it my hiding-hole. If you get notice that any body is coming, you have nothing to do but to go down there, shut the trap after you, and push in the bolt. Light enough enters through the chinks for you to see in the daytime; but don't take a candle in, and mind you don't tumble over the bales and other things."

"Is it cut in the rock?" asked Smeaton.

"Oh, dear, no," replied the man. "You see it is the corner made by this floor sticking out above the other. It looks just like the rest of the house outside, and may be dug a bit down into the ground, for there are two steps up to get out below. But that was done before my time."

"Then one can get *out* from below?" asked Smeaton.

"To be sure," answered the man. "How could we get the goods *in* else? You'll soon see the door on the inside, though nobody can see it on the out; and, should any people come looking after you, and you want to get away to sea, that's the best way. You shall always find a boat ready, and men to jump into her too, and we'll take care that the way is clear for you. So now good-night, sir."

"Stay a minute," said Smeaton. "I might have to go in great haste, and not be able to pay you, at the moment, either for your services or my entertainment. I should like to do so now, therefore, and also for the hire of a boat to take me to France."

"No, no, sir. As to all that," returned the man, "you must speak to my old woman. She is ready enough to take money, so don't give her too much of it; and for the boat, you can pay the men who take you. That is all fair. What *I* have to do is to see that they are ready, if I don't go myself, which is likely. Good-night, sir. You'll see the old woman to-morrow, sure enough."

Thus saying, he went away and closed the door; and Smeaton, seating himself at the table, gave himself up to thought.

He was not long in determining his course; and what the result of his reflections was may be judged by some words which he spoke aloud, as one is apt to do when hesitation gives place to reflection.

"He is only to be fought with his own weapons," he said. "I owe it to her, to myself, and to others. Yet, if possible, she must be mine before we go. The occasion will justify the precipitancy."

After again pausing in thought for a minute or two, he approached the little window, opened it, and looked out. Finding that the distance from the sill to the ground was not above five or six feet, he quietly let himself down, and walked, though with much difficulty, owing to the steepness of the hill, to the little path which led up to the well. Opposite the well he paused, and striding across, so as to rest his right foot upon the opposite brim, he applied the key Van Noost had given him to that part of the chiseling in the rough stone-work which he fancied must conceal the key-hole. He had some difficulty in finding it, however, but at length succeeded. Van Noost was a clever artificer. The key turned even more easily than that from which it had been modeled; and Smeaton, satisfied that he could command access to Emmeline at any time he pleased, locked the door again, and returned to his chamber at the cottage. Then, exploring his saddle-bags, he brought forth from them a little round case, very generally used by notaries of that time, which contained some sheets of writing-paper, pens, and an ink bottle, and seating himself at the table, wrote a rapid letter to Lord Stair, explaining the circumstances in which he was placed.

"It is now more than a week, my lord," he said, "since I wrote to your lordship, requesting you to use your influence with the government in order to obtain my formal recognition as an English subject, and offering to comply with every proper form that may be required in such a case. I stated to you that I had inviolately adhered to the promise I gave you not to meddle in any shape with political matters, but that, nevertheless, I understood measures had been taken for arresting me, notwithstanding the assurances I had received from your lordship. Since I wrote the above letter, which, I fear, can never have reached you, I have every reason to believe that a scheme has been devised for driving me into the hands of parties opposed to the existing government.

"I was induced this morning by Sir John Newark to go over to a house called Mount Place to return the visit of its owner, and found a number of gentlemen with him, though I had been led to believe he would be alone. As I discovered at once that they were discussing questions of much political importance, I took my leave and retired, not having been, in the whole, two minutes in the house. I then rode on to my mother's property of Keanton, where I had previously sent the good man Van Noost, whom you know, in order to keep him out of danger. He was amusing himself, at the moment of my arrival, in casting leaden globes to replace some others which had been blown or knocked off the pinnacles of the house; but, before I had been ten minutes at Keanton, the place was taken possession of by a party of soldiers, and I and Van Noost were apprehended upon warrants previously issued, to which General C——, from a misapprehension of what the poor statuary was doing, added a charge of casting bullets for the purposes of civil war. Given into custody of one Captain Smallpiece and a party of horse, I and my fellow-prisoner were taken to an inn, where the officer determined to remain for the night, although I expressed my desire to proceed to Exeter. The peasantry had previously shown themselves inclined to resist my apprehension; and here a large body of men found means to introduce themselves into the inn, and to overpower the troopers, who were mostly drunk. In the affray, Captain Smallpiece was in the act of shooting Van Noost, who had taken no part whatever in the struggle, and, to save the poor man's life, I was obliged to knock the officer down. Feeling that such a chain of circumstances—some of which were evidently accidental, though some were brought about for the purpose of involving me in the rash schemes of others—would form a very dangerous kind of evidence against me, and knowing the peril of being one of the first persons proceeded against in troublous times, I took advantage of the opportunity of making my escape, with the resolution of writing immediately to your lordship—a resolution which I now execute. Every word of the statement here given is true, upon my honor as a gentleman and a soldier. Since I have been here, I have held no communication with any one on political affairs. I have taken no part in any disturbances or any schemes whatever; but the assurance given me by your lordship, that I should not be molested, has been grossly violated by the authorities here, as if it was their object and intention to drive me into the arms of the disaffected. Nothing shall do so, if I can by any means avoid it; and it is my intention immediately to return to France. If I am prevented from doing so, however, by any active pursuance of the sort of persecution to which I have been subjected, and I find my earnest desire to remain tranquil, and to take no part in any political affairs whatever, thus frustrated, I must, of course, follow those measures which I judge requisite for my own safety."

He added a few words more in regard to the general object of his letter, took a copy of it, and addressed it to the earl in London. After having done so, he retired to rest, and slept as tranquilly for some hours as if the course of the preceding day had been calm and smooth.

CHAPTER XXIII.

THERE were lights in many of the windows of Ale-Manor House when Thomas Higham approached by the back way. The gates of the great court behind, however, were bolted, and the blood-hound bayed loud and deep at the man's approach! but after he had rung the bell, and the animal had snuffed under the gates for a moment, his hoarse bark was silenced: he recognized a friend. Higham soon obtained admission, and found the household in much commotion from the rumors which had reached Ale during the evening. Various was the aspect of the different servants whom he encountered as he was led to the presence of Sir John Newark. Those who had been but a short time in the family were full of wonder and amazement at all the events which rumor had detailed and magnified, and did not scruple to show their surprise and curiosity. The elder servants, who knew their master and his affairs better, were calm and silent, and asked no questions whatsoever. They had observed that Sir John Newark, though he had affected much surprise at the news of his guest's apprehension, had been in reality but little affected thereby; and when a rumor of his escape had been carried to Sir John, a glance of angry disappointment had crossed the knight's countenance, which did not escape notice. They understood him pretty well, and read such slight indications aright. We seldom reflect that we are a constant object of study to our servants; that we are, as it were, a model set up for them to draw in their own minds, and that, walking round us in every position of life, they have full opportunity of completing the sketch.

Led on by the butler, Higham was conducted through the great stone hall to the room in which the knight usually sat. He found him alone, for he had sent both Emmeline and his son away, in order to reflect upon his course more at leisure. Something had gone wrong in his plans, and they required to be rectified. He had announced, on the very first intelligence of the young earl's capture, that he should ride in the early morning of the following day to Exeter, in order to see what could be done for him—in truth, to see what could be done for himself in regard to Keanton. In prison and in danger, Sir John thought Smeaton would not be very difficult to deal with; and if he were, it would be easy to tighten his bonds a little. Moreover, another object had been gained by his apprehension. The vague fears regarding Emmeline, which had taken possession of the knight's mind as soon as he discovered that his guest was unmarried, had been increasing lately with a sort of instinct, and he rejoiced to have his guest removed.

Though a bold man, as we have seen, Sir John Newark was also a timid one. It seems a paradox, yet it is true; and similar cases are not unfrequent. He was bold in devising, bold even in executing, schemes for his own aggrandizement; but he was timid in fruition. He never fancied himself safe. He was always taking precautions. The only imagination he had was for difficulties and dangers; and one bold scheme for the attainment of a particular object was continually succeeded by another for the purpose of securing what had been obtained. It is strange, but true, that most of the cruel acts and many of the rash ones found on the page of history had their source in cowardice.

Smeaton's escape was therefore doubly disagreeable to him; and when he heard the bell of the great court ring, and imagined that his noble guest might have returned to seek shelter in his house, he instantly set to work to hold a somewhat tumultuous counsel in his own breast as to how he should demean himself to attain his double object. The entrance of the servant instead of the master, however, put a stop to these considerations, and he asked impatiently,

"Well—well, where is your lord?"

"Really, sir, I don't know," replied the man, who, having received but vague directions from the young earl, thought himself privileged to lie at liberty. "I did not know that I should not find him here; but they say he has not come; and he took the road toward Keanton, sure enough. Perhaps I had better set out to seek him?"

Sir John thought before he replied.

"Then this rumor of his having been rescued is true?" he said, at length.

Higham nodded, and added to that mute mode of assent the words,

"A great pack of country fellows did it. Most of the soldiers were drunk, and were overpowered in a minute. I had no hand in it, however."

Sir John leaned his head upon his hand, and mused.

"Then you positively do not know where he is?" he inquired.

"No, really, I can not say, Sir John," answered Higham. "I dare say at Keanton, hiding among his tenants."

"Not unlikely," said the knight. "I think you had better not go just at present. Wait here to-night, and get some refreshments. To-morrow, perhaps, your lord may send for you; and if not, and you go to seek for him, you shall bear him a message from me."

"Would it not be better for him to come here, sir?" asked Higham, ever willing to probe the minds of those with whom he was brought in contact. "I think he would be safer in this out-of-the-way place than any where."

"On no account—on no account," exclaimed the knight, caught in the trap laid for him. "Of course," he added, after a moment's reflection, "suspicion will be directed toward this house from the fact of my intimacy with your lord. The place will be searched, probably more than once; and his own safety requires that he should avoid the neighborhood. His tenantry at Keanton, probably, can conceal him for the time; and, as soon as pursuit has somewhat abated, it will be well for him to get out of the country, if not out of the kingdom. I speak against my own wishes and my own views," he continued, seeing an expression on the man's face which he did not clearly understand. "Nothing would give me so much pleasure as to see your master, and to offer him every assistance in my power; but to persuade him to come here would be leading him to destruction. If I knew where to find him, I would go and visit him, for I have no personal fears in the matter, my good friend, whatever you may think."

"Oh dear, no, sir," answered Higham, "I don't think at all. I dare say, however, I shall very soon hear where my lord is to be found, for he told me, when last I saw him, to come to Ale-Manor, and whenever I hear I will let your worship know."

"Do so—do so," said Sir John Newark; "and now go and get yourself some supper. I dare say you are hungry after all this bad work."

"As a fox-hunter," rejoined Higham, and turned toward the door; but Sir John thought he might as well add a stroke or two to the picture of danger he had been drawing, and he called to the man just as he was quitting the room.

"Tell my people, if any party should come to search the house during the night, not to open the doors till they have my orders."

"I won't fail, sir," replied Higham; and then, closing the door, he thridded his way through the passages toward the servants' part of the house, saying to himself, "Now for the old housekeeper. I wonder my lord trusts that sly old hunks. But I must do as he has told me. She must be playing double somewhere, that is clear enough; but whether with my lord and the young lady, or with worshipful Sir John, I can not tell."

Quietly tapping at good Mrs. Culpepper's door, he went in, and the eagerness with which she looked toward him showed at once that his visit was not altogether unexpected. She made him a sign to shut the door, and then said abruptly,

"Have you any news from your master? And is he safe?"

"Yes, ma'am," replied the man. "He is quite safe, and told me to tell you—"

"Hush!" interrupted the old woman, putting her finger to her lips. "Not now! Go and get yourself some refreshment in the servants' hall. There are not more than two or three up. Pretend to fall asleep in your chair. They will soon leave you, and I will come when I am certain that all is quiet. Stay, I will order your supper." Then, approaching close to him, she asked, in a whisper, "Where is your lord?"

"Here, in Ale village," returned Higham, in the same low tone; and, opening the door, the old housekeeper passed out.

Crossing the end of the passage at the very moment, as if going toward his own bed-room, was Sir John Newark himself; and, raising her voice, without a moment's hesitation, Mrs. Culpepper said, in a somewhat sharp tone,

"Pray, Sir John, is this man to have supper at this time of night?"

"Certainly," replied her master. "He has had a very fatiguing day, and it is not *his* fault that he is late."

"Well, then, fellow, come with me," said the housekeeper, walking away with him to the servants' hall. There she ordered him some supper in a cold and commanding tone, and left him to enjoy it.

Higham played his part well. He ate and drank, nodded, took another cup of ale, and then seemed to fall fast asleep. The three servants who were still up dropped off one by one, and left him, with a kitchen lamp on the table, to follow when he thought fit to wake. He remained for half an hour longer, however, undisturbed, and had nearly fallen asleep in reality, when Mrs. Culpepper again appeared, and quietly closed the door behind her.

"Now, what says your lord?" she demanded, speaking very low.

"He bade me tell you, ma'am," replied the servant, "that he is quite well and in safety, and begs you to let those know who may be anxious."

The old housekeeper slowly nodded her head, to show that she comprehended, and then said,

"What more?"

"Why, only that he is here, in Ale, I was to say," answered the man, "at the house of a fisherman named Grayling, and that he hopes, in spite of all that has happened, to be able to carry out what was proposed, with your good help."

Again Mrs. Culpepper nodded her head, and merely asked, "Is that all?"

"He told me to ask you, ma'am," said Higham, "if it would be safe for him to venture here, for he much wishes to speak with you and somebody else, whose name he did not mention—perhaps he means Master Richard."

"Perfectly safe, if he could come in private," replied Mrs. Culpepper, "but most dangerous if he were to be seen. Yet stay. He is quite secure at Grayling's for two or three days. Now mark what you must do. Rise early to-morrow, before daylight; go quietly down to him at the cottage, and tell him what I say—he will understand you. Tell him the means of coming in, in private, he shall have by you to-morrow night. I can not get the key at present. As soon as you have delivered the message, come back here, and mind you close and lock the doors behind you just as you found them. Take care, likewise, to make no noise."

"If I am to go early in the morning," observed the man, "I had better stay where I am. I will put the edge of the tankard under my head, and then my nodding will wake me from time to time."

"Don't put it too often to your lips," retorted Mrs. Culpepper, gravely, "for your master's safety and happiness depend on your carefulness just now."

"Lord bless you, ma'am, I have been accustomed to these things," said Higham, "and could sit with a tankard of strong waters under my nose for a month without ever touching a drop, if there was any business to be done at the end of it."

"You will not lose your reward if you are faithful," said the old woman; "and so, good-night."

As soon as she was gone, Higham murmured to himself,

"She is on the right side, I *do* think. She must be a wonderful cunning old woman."

With this reflection, he folded his arms on the table, laid his head upon them, and in a few minutes was fast asleep. Every time the house clock struck, however, he looked up and counted, and at the hour of four shook off his drowsiness, took a tolerable draught from the flagon, and then crept quietly out of the servants' hall. He had the choice of three doors by which to make his exit. That of the great hall, however, had, to his knowledge, a very bad habit of creaking on its hinges. That which led into the court led also to the blood-hound; and, though he was not at all afraid of the animal's bite, he was afraid of his bark. There was a little door, however, which led into a lesser court, formed expressly, it would seem, for the entertainment of the men and maid servants of the family, and by this convenient passage Higham took his way out, with little difficulty and no noise.

Nothing interrupted him on his way to the village, and there, by the lights he saw in several of the cottages, he perceived that many of the inmates were up, preparing for some of their lawful or unlawful occupations. A light was in old Grayling's house also; and, looking through the window, which had no shutters, but plenty of bars, he saw the old man, with a short pipe in his mouth, lighting the fire in the kitchen.

Tapping at the window, Higham soon brought the fisherman to his door; and, with one accustomed to somewhat perilous enterprises, very little explanation was needful.

The young earl was soon wakened, and the message delivered. That message threw Smeaton into a fit of thought, which lasted, however, not long. Impulse, impulse! It is always getting the better of us till it is worn out and has lost its spring with years. It was very powerful, I fear, in Smeaton's case, when, rising, and dressing himself as rapidly as possible, he said to the man,

"You must go back. Get speech of Mrs. Culpepper as soon as possible, and tell her that she will find me in the priest's chamber. Say that I am sure I can get back unobserved by passing through the trees, and that, as speed is every thing, it will be better to form our plans quickly. If she can not come this morning, I will be there again at night. You must come with me, however, in the first instance. Now lock that door."

The man obeyed, with some surprise, but was more surprised still when he saw his master descend from the window as he had done on the preceding night. Being a great deal shorter, he had some difficulty, to say the truth, in following, but with Smeaton's assistance, succeeded at length, and reached the ground in safety.

"Now go on before me," said the earl, "and if you meet any persons coming down this way, say something to them in a loud tone. Keep straight on that path."

"Oh, sir, I know it very well," returned the man. "Many a time I have been down here since we came."

"Hush!" said Smeaton. "Go on, and keep silence."

Doing as he was bid, with the darkness rapidly giving way to twilight, the man walked up toward Ale-Manor, taking a quick, furtive glance behind him from time to time to see whither his master was going. Suddenly, however, when he turned round to look, the young nobleman had disappeared, and it is unnecessary to inform the reader which way he had bent his steps.

The moment the stone door beyond the wall closed, Smeaton found himself in utter darkness; but, feeling his way with his hands, he reached the steps upward, and soon after began to gain air and light. Nobody came near him for somewhat more than a quarter of an hour, and Smeaton's spirit grew impatient of the restraint. The moments were passing quickly on which so much depended, and yet no progress was made.

"The sun must have risen," he thought; "and perhaps Emmeline is already up. It is strange I hear nothing of my old nurse! Perhaps that foolish fellow has forgotten his errand, or missed his opportunity, or committed some other blunder. I must speak with her at once, if at all; and we shall soon have the whole household up."

As he thus thought, impatience overcame all other considerations, and he approached the door which led into the state bed-room beyond. No great difficulty presented itself in pushing back the panel, and, making as little noise as he could, he issued forth from the hiding-place. The room was vacant. After pausing a moment and listening for a step, he quietly opened the door and went out into the passage. Nobody was there; but the door of Emmeline's room was close beside him, and he thought he heard the sound of some one moving within. The temptation was too great to be resisted, and he tapped gently at the door. At first there was no reply: she did not hear the tap; but again a sound was audible within, like the quiet opening of a window, and he tapped once more.

The next instant he heard a light step near the door, and it opened. Surprise, which was the first expression on Emmeline's beautiful face, changed in a moment to joy; and, forgetting all things in the untutored wildness of her delight, she cast herself upon his bosom and wept. Smeaton held her to his heart and kissed her tenderly, drawing her in silence toward the state chamber; but Emmeline whispered,

"No. Come in here. It will be safer. This is my own sitting-room. No one will come hither;" and she led him into that large, airy chamber in which she was first introduced to the sight of the reader.

Impossible would it be to attempt any detailed account of the brief conversation which ensued—so much was to be told, so much to be spoken of, so many words of tenderness and affection to be uttered. Emmeline poured forth her whole heart. She knew not, she could not conceive, any motive, when once that heart was given and its love acknowledged, for concealing from him she loved any thing that passed within it. She spoke of all she had suffered since the moment when she heard of his arrest; of all the grief, of all the anxiety, of all the sleepless thought. She spoke, too, of her joy to see him safe and free. But the voice of happiness is still and low, and Smeaton had to read one half of her sensations in her eyes.

As but very little time could be spared, however, he told her as speedily as possible all that he proposed. He explained that his purpose of returning at once to France was unaltered, if she would still consent to go with him, but thought it would be far better that she should give him her hand before they took their departure; adding, he had but little doubt that he could so arrange that the ceremony should be duly and irrevocably performed.

She replied at once, without hesitation or reluctance,

"Whatever you tell me, Henry, I will do; and it will be much better that I should go as your wife. I am yours altogether; and if occasionally, since I promised to go with you, feelings of doubt—perhaps, I might almost say, of self-reproach—have come across me for so joyfully consenting to quit the protector of my childhood, those feelings have all passed. His conduct toward you, his betrayal of you, would remove all scruples. All was explained to me last night, and I never heard of darker baseness. To me, too, he has behaved very ill, and to my parents worse. What I looked upon as kindness and protection, have been, in reality, policy and imprisonment; and I have every right to leave him who has no right to detain me. Hark!"

Her exclamation was caused by a sound at the lock of the door. The next instant the door was opened, and Mrs. Culpepper appeared. She showed no surprise, but much agitation; and, without closing the door, she beckoned to Smeaton, saying, in a low tone,

"This is madness, Henry. Indeed, my lord, you must fly this instant. You can return at night; but do not come out of the priest's chamber till I knock for you. Come, my lord, come. Sir John is already moving in his room."

With one more embrace, Smeaton and Emmeline parted; and, holding up her finger to enjoin silence, Mrs. Culpepper led the young nobleman back to the priest's chamber, closing the aperture behind him. She then returned at once to Emmeline's apartment, and, having shut the door, said,

"Run into your bed-room, dear lady, and answer me aloud through the door."

Emmeline did as she was asked, and then the old housekeeper put several questions as to her night's rest, and several matters of ordinary interest, receiving somewhat wondering replies. But the old woman was politic; and she was still speaking, when Sir John Newark knocked at the door, saying,

"Who are you talking to, Emmeline?"

Mrs. Culpepper instantly opened the door, and replied,

"It is I, Sir John."

Her voice was as calm and quiet, her manner as unruffled and staid as usual; but Sir John Newark beckoned her out of the room, and then said, in a low tone,

"I heard a noise as if the entrance to the priest's room had been rolled backward and forward."

"Yes, Sir John," replied the old lady. "By your own orders, I go frequently to see that it opens and shuts easily. I always go early or late; but I thought I heard the young lady moving in her room, and I went to see what could have got her up so early."

Sir John Newark did not speak for a minute, but looked at the housekeeper quietly from under his eyebrows, and she saw at once that he doubted her. She was too much accustomed, however, to meet and frustrate his suspicions to be at all alarmed, though she felt some degree of apprehension, from various causes, when he said at length,

"I have not been in that priest's room for two or three years. I should like to look round it again."

"Very well, sir," replied Mrs. Culpepper; adding internally, "Pray God the dear boy be gone!"

Sir John Newark moved into the state-room with a certain quickness of step which showed how little satisfied he was; but the old proverb, "The more haste the worse speed," was verified in his case. He walked at once up to the head of the bed to move it back, but he had either forgotten the trick, or he mismanaged it in his hurry, so that after one or two efforts he was obliged to have recourse to Mrs. Culpepper, who, in order to avoid all suspicion, opened the entrance at once. Sir John Newark instantly stepped in, gave a quick glance round the room, and then advanced to the door leading to the passages below. Finding himself surrounded by darkness, however, he stopped at the end of the first two or three steps, and said, somewhat sharply, "Bring me a light."

The old housekeeper retired to obey; and, during her absence, which was as short as possible, her master remained with his head bent and his ear intently listening. When he had obtained the light, he walked quickly forward, followed by Mrs. Culpepper, and did not pause till he reached the stone door which led out upon the hill-side. He put his hand upon the lock, but it was fastened; and then, holding the candle to the little niche at the side, he looked in. The key was in its place, and he retired satisfied.

CHAPTER XXIV.

It was nine o'clock before Sir John Newark entered the room where preparations had been made for breakfast. He found his son Richard talking gayly to Emmeline in the window, while she replied with a bright and smiling face. Although, considering his designs respecting Emmeline and his son, it might be supposed that such a sight was pleasant to him, yet that poisoner of all peace, suspicion, would not have it so. Emmeline's excessive anxiety during the preceding day, after tidings had been received of Smeaton's capture, had not escaped his notice, although she had striven hard to conceal the emotions which were busy in her bosom; and now she seemed so bright and cheerful, that he said to himself, "She must have had some intelligence."

He resolved to watch her carefully; but, happily for Emmeline, emotions as strong, though very different from those of the day before, had still possession of her. They were more joyful, more hopeful, but perhaps even more thrilling, and several times during the meal she fell into deep fits of thought. Suspicion is always vacillating, and Sir John began to doubt whether he had been right or not. His son contributed, too, to remove the fancy which possessed him by saying, with one of his wild laughs, toward the middle of breakfast, "I was telling Emmy when you came in, father, that we should have this colonel lord back again here very soon. Great fish always lie on the same bank."

"I do not know, Dick," replied his father, gravely. "I think it is very improbable you will ever see him again. If he is wise, he will betake himself to France immediately; otherwise he may very well chance to leave his head on the scaffold some morning."

Richard laughed, exclaiming, "Well, then, he had a great deal better kick it before him across the sea. A precious foot-ball it would make."

Emmeline gave a slight shudder, and Sir John dropped the conversation till the meal was ended, when he said, "The earl's servant is here, as I dare say you know, Dick, but he has had no news of his master, and fancies he must be at Keanton."

"Oh, I know Higham is here," answered the lad, "for I had a long talk with him just before you sent for him. He told me all about the rescue. What fun it must have been to see those lubberly soldiers all tied, and lying heads and tails like herrings in a barrel! I wish I had been there. I should have liked to help poor Smeaton, and leather the jacket of that long captain. Higham says his master knocked him down just as he did the Earl of Stair's great bully, and vows that the punch-bowls jumped up a foot off the table with the shock of his fall."

"Well, Dick," observed his father, "the servant talks of riding over by the tops of the Downs to Keanton to see for his lord. Now, as you know there is nothing I would so willingly do as assist this noble gentleman, you and I will ride over with the man to within half a mile of Keanton. Then, if he finds his master, we can establish some communication with him, and perhaps assist him."

He paused a moment, and then turning to Emmeline, he added, "I fear you can not go with us, my dear child. Maiden modesty forbids your running about the country to inquire for a young cavalier. I think, too, it might be as well for you to remain within during our absence. There will be parties of soldiers, doubtless, scouring the country in various directions, and they are neither the most civil nor civilized."

"I have no inclination to go out," replied Emmeline, simply. "I am tired with all the anxiety of yesterday."

Sir John Newark, his son, and Smeaton's servant were soon on horseback, and, without any other attendant, they set out, turning sharp to the left after quitting the gates of the Manor House, and winding round the edge of the woods till they reached nearly the top of Ale Head. Thence pursuing their course across the Downs, with the high cliffs beetling over the sea at the distance of about a quarter of a mile on their left, they continued their course, alternately rising and descending up the brown hills and down into the green solitary hollows, which extend fifteen or sixteen miles along the coast.

At the distance of about seven miles from Ale-Manor, however, they came to one of those hollows, which assumed more the appearance of a regular valley, with a bright and beautiful little stream flowing down it toward the sea. Here they halted; Higham received instructions to ride on before, while the other two slowly followed; and Sir John added,

"We will wait at the distance of about half a mile from Keanton. Tell your lord that we are there, if he thinks it safe to come and speak with us. If not, bring us some tidings of him; but enter the village very cautiously, lest the good people of Keanton should have fallen into the hands of the Philistines."

Higham nodded his head and rode away. Sir John Newark, who had been very silent during the first part of the journey, now entered into an eager conversation with his son, which, as I must refer to it afterward, I need not notice more particularly here. Suffice it to say, that the father spoke earnestly and apparently impressively, and that the son, though at first he listened with eagerness and looks of surprise, and strove afterward to fix his wandering attention upon his father's words, soon resumed his usual manner, and laughed and talked gayly and wildly, flitting round the subject rather than resting upon it.

After they had reached the spot which had been fixed upon as their halting-place, Sir John and his young companion remained for about three quarters of an hour in expectation, Richard getting off and on his horse, throwing pebblos into the stream, and showing many signs of impatience. Sir John marked him with a slight smile; and at length Higham made his appearance again, trotting quietly and unconcernedly down toward them.

"He is not there, Sir John," said the man, riding up; "at least so all the people say; but they are mighty stingy of their words this morning. However, one thing is certain—they have heard nothing of the Exeter people; and I make out pretty surely that my lord is not very far off, and that they know it."

"Ah, how do you make that out?" asked Sir John Newark.

"Why, one man began talking about a stranger having come to Blacklands late last night; but his wife stopped his mouth in a minute; and when I asked where Blacklands was, and what it was, he gave a rambling sort of answer. But I believe it must be some farm near at hand."

"It is five miles off," replied Sir John, imme diately; "a wild and solitary place, shut out from the whole neighborhood, and a very likely spot indeed for a fugitive to take refuge in. We had better ride over there. You are sure there are no soldiers in the village?"

"Not a man, sir," answered Higham; "and, besides, they have got people on the top of the hill to look out."

"Well, then, we will take that way, as it is the shortest," said the knight. "Come, Richard."

"I think I shall go back," said Richard Newark. "I am tired of this work. I'll go back, and have a gossip with Emmy."

"Do not be rash, Dick," replied his father, holding up his finger, with a smile. "Remember, slow degrees at first! You do not scare birds that you want to drive into a net."

The lad laughed, and saying, "Oh, I'll not be

rash," turned his horse's head and cantered quietly away. When he had gone about a couple of miles, however, he fell into deep thought, took his feet out of the stirrups, let the reins drop on the horse's neck, and for more than half an hour proceeded at a walk. Then, as if suddenly rousing himself, he whistled a bit of a light air, put his horse into a quick pace again, and rode on to the Manor House.

It was very usual with Richard to stand in the stable-yard after a ride till he had seen saddle and bridle removed and the horse rubbed down; but now he left his beast immediately in the hands of the groom, and walked across the court till he came to a place where a large Irish eagle was chained to a heavy perch. The bird was fierce and untamable; but Richard approached it without fear, and took hold of the padlock on its leg. He had hardly done so when it struck him with its bill more than once; but he proceeded boldly till he had unfastened the chain from its leg, and given it a vehement push from the perch. The bird instantly took wing, and soared into the sky. Richard Newark laughed aloud, and, without looking after it, wiped some drops of blood from his forehead, and walked into the house. He pursued his way quietly through the passages, looked into the lesser and the greater saloon, and then, mounting the stairs, walked up to the door of Emmeline's sitting-room. There he paused a moment; and then murmuring, "What a fool I am! but I knew that long ago," he opened the door without knocking, and went in. Emmeline was seated near the window, gazing down upon the woods below; but she turned instantly at her cousin's step, and started up, exclaiming,

"What is the matter, Richard? What has happened? The blood is streaming down your face!"

"Nothing at all has happened, Emmy dear," replied Richard. "Only, as often occurs in this world, a friend took me for an enemy, and pecked my pate. Come here and sit down, and I will tell you all about it, though there is nothing worth hearing to tell. Sit down here, Emmy," he continued, again wiping away the blood. "There, put yourself in that chair, and I will sit on the stool at your feet, as I used to do before they sent me to school to see what part of my brain was sound."

"But what have you been doing, Richard?" said Emmeline, seating herself as he desired her.

"Nothing but giving liberty to an eagle," replied the boy, "and he pecked me while I was unchaining his foot."

"Oh, you should not have done that, Dickon," said his fair companion. "Your father will be angry."

"Why so?" demanded the lad. "The bird was mine. He was given to me, and I had a right to do what I liked with him. Well, Emmy," he continued, after a moment or two, "we have heard nothing of Smeaton, and a dull ride we have had of it; so I left my daddy to trot on his way, and came back."

Emmeline was silent, for she did not wish to speak upon the subject of her lover at all; but Richard went on in a rambling sort of tone, saying,

"Ay, dull enough it was; and while we were waiting for Tom Higham's coming back, my father had some serious conversation with me, as he calls it. I hate serious conversation, Emmy."

"But you should always attend to what your father says to you, Richard," observed Emmeline, "and do every thing that he tells you—*which is right.*"

The last words were uttered after a moment's pause, and in a lower tone.

"Very true," replied Richard, half laughing. "What you say is always true, Emmy; but the worst of it is—I suppose the soft place in my brain prevents it—my father and I can never agree upon what *is* quite right. The fact is, dear girl, I see one side, and he sees the other, as the old story-book has it; and if one side is black, and the other side is white, we can never agree in opinion. Do you know what he was telling me to-day?"

"No, indeed," answered Emmeline, "I can not conceive."

"Why, he was telling me," said Richard, looking down and speaking in an absent manner, "he was telling me that he intended me to marry you, and you to marry me; that it must be; that the fate and fortune of us both depended upon it."

Emmeline trembled violently; and as the shoulder of Richard Newark rested against her arm, he felt how much agitation his words produced. The moment after, Emmeline felt his hand laid gently upon hers, and she asked, in a low voice,

"What did you say to him, Richard?"

"Nothing much to the purpose," replied Richard, "for he set all my thoughts rambling and galloping like huntsmen at the field-halloo. I laughed and talked as if I had been very happy, but I was thinking all the time, Emmeline. First I thought (what I never thought of before) how very happy it would be to marry you—and how you might make any thing you liked of me—and what a changed being I should be if you were my wife—and how dearly I should love you—and how I *do* love you—and a great many other foolish things. Nay, don't shake, dear Emmy! there is no fear with your own poor Dick."

"I am not afraid, Dick," responded Emmeline, pressing the hand he had laid upon hers, "for I know right well that, whatever faults your head may have, your heart has none."

"That's a good girl," returned Richard Newark. "Well, I thought a great deal more still. After all these foolish things had had their gallop, I thought I would not marry you for the whole world, or if all the kings and queens in the world were to try to force us."

"Indeed, Richard?" said Emmeline, with a faint smile. "You had good reasons, doubtless."

"To be sure I had," replied the lad. "In the first place, I know that I am not worthy of you—that I am not fit for you. In the next place, I know that you would not like it; that you love another; and that, if you were driven to marry me, you would always be thinking of him, and loving him, and not me. I should be your jailer, and not your husband; and I should be wretched too, for I should be always flying after your thoughts, like a sparrow-hawk after a lark, to see if you were not thinking of your lover all the time. You know you love him, Emmy. You love him very well, very dearly, and I do not wonder at you."

The rosy color that spread over her face, and neck, and forehead would have been sufficient answer; but she said, in a low though distinct tone, "I do."

There was a pause of a moment or two, and then Richard said,

"What a fool I should be, Emmeline—a greater fool than I am, and that is bad enough—if I suffered my wits to be set wool-gathering by any nonsense about ever marrying you, or putting Smeaton out of your head. But still, Emmy," he continued, in a tender tone, "you will love me after a sort—as you always have—as a kind friend—as a sister."

"Indeed I will, Richard," exclaimed Emmeline, earnestly, "and love you all the better for your conduct this day. Now I know what you mean by setting the eagle free: you would fain set Smeaton free of all difficulties, if you could."

"No, dear Emmy," pursued Richard, "I did not exactly mean that. Indeed, I do not clearly know that I meant any thing; but as I rode homeward, and thought how happy you might be if people left you to do just what you liked, I wished to help you to do so—to make you quite free; and then, when I saw the poor eagle in the court, I thought how happy he would be if he could soar away in the skies again at his own pleasure; and then the thought came across me of what my father would say if I unchained the bird's leg; and I answered myself that I had a right—that the bird was mine—that he had been given to me, and so had you, and therefore I determined to set you both free. I do not know how it was, but somehow there seemed a likeness between your fate and his; though when he fluttered his wings, and struck at me as I unchained him, I said to myself, Emmeline will know better, and so she does."

"Indeed she does, Richard," replied Emmeline; "and she will never mistake you for an enemy."

"But do you know, Emmeline," continued her cousin, "that I have a strange notion it would be better for us both to dissemble a little? for I fancy my father has some suspicion about you and Smeaton."

"I fear I am a bad dissembler," returned Emmeline, incautiously. "I can not but dread that Sir John sees I have been dissembling with him lately."

Richard, however, did not ask in what respect, but rambled on as usual.

"Oh, we all dissemble more than we are aware," he said. "Here, I never thought to deceive my father in any thing; and yet, for some reason—either from something in himself or in me—I never can tell him all I think. I never can turn my heart inside out before him as I can with you. When I should most wish to say all, and make him understand every thing that is going on inside of me, some devil, I think it is, comes and stops me, and makes me go rambling away with vague answers about nothing at all, which he may take one way or another, just as he likes. But what I mean is, not that we should just exactly dissemble; for, as you love me well and I love you well, it is not dissembling to seem to do so. I would only have you look happy when I am with you, and I'll try to make you so too; for I'll talk to you of Smeaton, and we'll plan plans and plot plots about him, and all sorts of pleasant things."

"There can be no harm in that, Richard," replied Emmeline, in a graver tone than her young cousin had expected; for he was trying, though hardly knowing it, to win her mind away from all heavy thoughts. But, to say sooth, Emmeline was somewhat puzzled how to act toward him. There was so much candor, so much frank kindness in his whole conduct, that her heart smote her for not telling him all she knew and all she intended. She remembered, however, that the secrets in her heart were not altogether her own—that she had only a divided right over them; and, though it cost her some pain, she was silent.

Richard went on talking with her even after he heard the sounds which accompanied his father's return; and when he left her and went down the stairs, although he was inclined to be more thoughtful than perhaps he had ever felt in his life, he assumed a gay and joyous look.

"Well, Dick," said his father, when he met him, "where have you been all this time?"

"I have been sitting with Emmeline ever since I came back," replied the lad, "and we have been talking of all sorts of things. She is a dear girl indeed."

"But what is the matter with your forehead?" said his father. "Did your horse fall?"

"Oh no," cried Richard, "it was that brute of an eagle. I was tired of seeing him sitting moping on his perch, so I went to unchain him, and he pecked me on the head."

"Why, you foolish boy, you have not set him free?" exclaimed Sir John.

"Oh yes, I have," answered Richard, "and he pecked me for my pains. But Emmeline did not peck me, whatever I said to her, so I care not. No chance of my being hen-pecked, father;" and, with a gay laugh, he turned away.

Sir John Newark was well pleased with what he had done. "Women are strange beings," he said. "Who knows but what this boy's wild, dashing, light-hearted thoughtlessness—so like his weak mother—may not be metal more attractive in the girl's eyes than soberer, sounder reason? At all events, he will be a check and a guard upon her; and even supposing her fancy has kindled into thoughts of love in the society of this young earl, it can only render something for love to lean upon more needful to her when he is away. I have seen such things. It will do. I am glad I spoke to the boy, and told him my intentions."

Sir John Newark thought he had more reason to congratulate himself still, when, a few hours afterward, he received a peremptory summons to attend the authorities at Exeter on the following day. He mused for a minute or two before he returned an answer; but, in the end, he determined to assume a bold tone, and calling for the messenger, he told him to inform those who sent him that he (Sir John) would come right willingly, provided he was assured before noon that his house would be subject to no violence, and his family to no annoyance or insult, as on a former occasion.

"Hints are given in this letter," he said, "of a suspicion that the Earl of Eskdale is harboring in this house or neighborhood. Tell the high sheriff, who seems taking upon him the office of lord lieutenant, that after the proofs of loyalty which I have lately given, no such suspicion should be entertained; but before you go, and while your horse is feeding, I insist upon it that, by search or cross-examination of the servants, and by inquiry in the village, you ascertain whether there be any ground whatever for such a doubt. Satisfy yourself fully, and then report accordingly, first to me, and then to those who sent you. I shall set off at eleven to-morrow for Aleton, and will thence go on to Exeter, if I am met there by a full and proper assurance that, when I return, *I shall not find* my house has been visited by a party of soldiers while I have been allured to a distance."

The man, who was a person of somewhat superior station and intelligence, took advantage of the permission given to him, and made himself, as he thought, perfectly certain that no one, in Ale-Manor House at least, knew where the Earl of Eskdale was. The village, too, he visited; but there he got gruff and indifferent answers, and once or twice became somewhat afraid of pursuing his inquiries. Perhaps these fears tended to make him more easily satisfied than he otherwise would have been; but the conclusion he came to was, that the rough fishermen knew nothing of the matter, and did not like to be troubled with things that concerned them not. Before he departed, he saw Sir John Newark again, and told him the result of his inquiries. Sir John was very gracious, for the result was as satisfactory to him as it could be to any one.

"No," he said to himself, "no. He is at Blacklands, clear enough, though they would not own it. Or else this man, whom they spoke of going toward Exmouth, may have been he."

He dismissed the messenger, however, with a fee, as was not uncustomary in those venal times, and rested more tranquilly than he had done the night before, only wishing that he could hold some communication with the young earl for a day or two, to fix his meditated grasp upon Keanton.

CHAPTER XXV.

It was about nine o'clock at night when two persons on foot approached the little hamlet of Aleton. One of them advanced a little before the other, as if to reconnoiter; but all was still and quiet in the place; and even the small public house, unused, in that remote district, to late visitors, was closed. Light could be seen within, indeed, through the chinks of the rude window-shutters, and it is probable that the latch of the door would have yielded to the hand of any belated traveler; but there was no other sign of active life to be perceived without.

The two persons of whom I have spoken, however, passed by the door of the inn, and approached a house — the only other dwelling which deserved the name—a little further on the road to Exeter. Stepping up to the door, the shorter of the two travelers knocked with his hand; but the application producing no response from within, he was fain, though apparently very unwilling to make a noise, to take hold of an iron wire which hung at the side of the door with a bunch of hammered iron at the end of it, and give a gentle pull. A tinkling sound was immediately heard, and then the voice of a woman, saying aloud, to some one in an inner room, as she moved along the passage,

"I dare say it is nothing but old Drayton dead, and they have come to talk to you about the funeral."

The next instant the door was opened, and Van Noost (for he was the summoner) inquired if Parson Thickett were at home.

"Oh, dear, yes, Master Smith," replied the servant (for people even in those days called themselves Jack Smith when they sought concealment), "and he will be very glad to see you. He could not think what had become of you. Is this gentleman your friend?"

Van Noost nodded his head and entered the house, followed by Smeaton. The maid shut and bolted the door again, and then led them on into the parson's little parlor, where they found that reverend personage enjoying himself according to his evening wont. There was one lighted candle on the table; but the room, though small, was obscure, for a thick cloud of tobacco-smoke floated in it. On the hob of the vacant grate lay the pipe from which that smoke had proceeded, and close at the parson's elbow was a tall bottle containing some sort of spirits, a plate and knife with a lemon, and a pot of sugar. Between him and the candle-stick, however, was an open Greek book, in old and tattered binding; for Parson Thickett was an erudite man, notwithstanding some little failings. In person he was fatter than Van Noost, and of a very different sort of fatness. His limbs were large, but seemed almost disjointed, or at best held loosely together by the lax integuments that covered them. His stomach was large and prominent, betraying beneath his cossock—for he was generally in canonicals—a vast hemisphere of black. His face was somewhat coarse, it must be acknowledged. He had a large ear and a large lip, and, not contented with a large chin, he had two of them. There was a good deal of shrewdness, however, and a certain portion of fun about his gray, watery eye, and his whole face lighted up with jovial good humor as soon as he saw the statuary.

"Ha, my worthy friend!" he cried, starting up with greater agility than might have been expected, and grasping Van Noost's hand warmly, "where have you been so long? I thought the Philistines were upon you, by Jove. What of the brasses? What of the monuments? What of the inscriptions? By Jove, I thought you had left your work half done, and it might have remained long enough undone for me, for scrubbing brass and marble is no part of my calling. I love my flock well enough, but when once I've got them under ground I've done with them. Ha! who is this gentleman?"

"A friend of mine," replied Van Noost, "who has come to talk to your reverence about a little business."

"He is welcome," cried the jolly parson. "Sir, you are welcome. We will talk of business presently. Now, we'll have a bowl of punch and fresh pipes. Betty, Betty!"

Smeaton tried to persuade him that he was in haste and could not stay, but Parson Thickett would take no denial.

"I will have my way," he cried, laughing, "I will have my way, by Jove, for this time. You shall have your way the next time, upon my sacred word of honor."

"Indeed?" said Smeaton.

"Of a verity," returned the parson, "unless you ask me for the tithe pig that was brought in this morning. That is a reservation."

The glasses and pipes were brought in, fresh hot water procured, and the brewing commenced; but, as soon as the door was shut, Smeaton thought he might as well begin upon the subject of his visit.

"I will certainly hold the tithe pig reserved," he said, "for I trust to be able to increase your reverence's store of pigs instead of diminishing them."

"Ay, indeed!" ejaculated the parson, squeezing a lemon hard between a pair of pincers. "I think I know what you are come about. I heard all the news this morning from the packman—how they are up in Northumberland, and how the king has been proclaimed in Scotland, and all the rest of it. Well, well, I am no fighting man, but the king shall have my prayers; and Smith, here, can tell you that I have well indoctrinated my congregation. There is not one of them who does not say over his beer—or his cider, if he comes from the other side of the hills, 'Here's to him over the water!'"

"Nay, my reverend friend, you are making a mistake," replied Smeaton. "My business is altogether personal. I want you to perform the marriage ceremony for myself and a young lady."

"That I will, my lad, that I will," exclaimed the parson, joyously. "It is the function which I perform most willingly, for there is always something merry to be said at the beginning, and always something good to be eaten at the end."

"I fear there will not be in this instance," observed Smeaton, gravely, "for no wedding feast will be prepared."

"Never mind, never mind!" retorted the parson. "There is some fun in matrimony, at all events. I'll buckle you so fast that you shall neither of you get loose again in a hurry. Give me the names. I'll have the banns published next Sunday."

"But we do not intend to have any banns either," said Smeaton.

"Better and better!" cried Parson Thickett. "You *must* have a license, and that is a fee in my pocket."

"Then you are a surrogate?" said his companion. "That smoothes one great difficulty."

"No, not exactly a surrogate," returned the other, leaving off his punch-brewing, and growing somewhat interested in the conversation; "I am a 'peculiar:' that is to say, young gentleman, I have a peculiar jurisdiction ecclesiastical here, under the dean and chapter of Exeter. I can grant licenses, and prove wills, according to the canon, being a bachelor of laws as well as a doctor of divinity, let me tell you. Now, thank God for all good things!" he continued: "this is the first time I have had to exercise my peculiarity—to my own profit, at least."

The frame of mind which he was in seemed very favorable to Smeaton's object; but when the young nobleman, with some precaution, explained to him fully what that object was, the worthy parson looked somewhat aghast. The name of Sir John Newark, indeed, was not mentioned, but by some way he jumped at the conclusion that the lady referred to was Emmeline, and Smeaton did not contradict him. He shook his head gravely, rolled his fat thumbs round each other for a minute or two, and then shook his head again. Van Noost, however, came to the rescue, judging rightly that the first impression of fear would wear off under the influence of the glass.

"Come, parson," he said, "think of the punch a little. It is getting cold."

"So it is, by Jove!" cried the parson, ladling out the punch. "Here, take a glass, sir. It will keep up the spirits of both of us, for this is a bad business."

"Not at all," returned Smeaton, laughing. "It is perfectly right and proper. All that we require secrecy for is to prevent the intermeddling of persons who have no right to meddle."

"But Sir John Newark is her guardian," said the parson, drinking some of his punch.

"Not so," replied the young nobleman. "He is no more her guardian than you are."

"You must have some guardian's consent, said Parson Thickett. "That I know, because I've got the register of her birth in there—" and he pointed to a large box in one corner of the room.

"Indeed!" exclaimed Smeaton. "Will you have the kindness to give me a copy of it? I fancied that Sir John Newark kept the registers at Ale, and would not let you have them."

"Not he," replied his reverend companion. "A fico for Sir John Newark! The stingy hound has not asked me to dinner for three years, and, moreover, tries to defraud me of my dues. He'll pay no tithes of mint and cummin, not he. So, the last time I had my hand upon the registers, I took them away. He had had them then four years, and that was four years too many. You shall have a copy. He'll not much like that; and, if I marry you, there will be an awful explosion."

He finished his speech with a good draught of punch; and Smeaton remarked,

"I hope there is no 'if' in the case, my good sir. You promised, if I would let you have your way, you would let me have mine."

"So I did, so I did," cried the priest, with a jolly laugh; "but, upon my life, you must tell me something more: first about her being under age. That is the devil, as you have not got any guardian's consent."

"Nay," replied Smeaton. "There you are mistaken, my reverend friend. Have the goodness to look at that."

As he spoke, he put into the clergyman's hand a sheet of paper, on which were written two or three lines in a fine, bold style.

"Ha! what is here?" ejaculated the parson. "Then this is her lawful guardian, is it?"

"I am ready to swear it," replied Smeaton; "and our good friend here, whom you know, will testify—"

"Oh, I'll testify any thing you like," interrupted Van Noost, drinking off his punch and holding out his glass. "There, parson, give me some more, and don't let us have any further objections, there's a worthy divine. You know you will come to it in the end. We'll find means to melt you."

"But suppose I do *not* come to it," asked Doctor Thickett, looking at Smeaton, "what will you do then?"

"I have simply one alternative," replied Smeaton, gravely. "If you refuse, I shall go back to Ale, and, authorized as you see by this paper, take the lady to France with me this very night, as soon as the moon rises."

"What, unmarried!" exclaimed the priest, with an affected look of horror. "That can not be—that can not be. I *must* marry you, by Jove, to prevent scandal."

"Exactly," replied Smeaton, with a smile. "That is, in reality, my object. We can be married as soon as we reach Nancy; but I think, on every account, it would be better that the ceremony should be performed before we set out."

"Oh, certainly, certainly," replied Doctor

Thickett. "Let me look at that paper again. I want to see how the case stands."

Pushing the punch away from him, he examined the paper accurately, and at length, lifting his eyes, said,

"You are, then, the Earl of Eskdale?"

"He is none other, upon my say-so," chimed in Van Noost; "and as we can not cast many men out of one mold as we can statues, I will answer for it that there is not a copy of him extant."

The priest, however, was deeply cogitating the contents of the paper.

"This does not exactly say you are to marry her," he observed at length; "but as it tells the young lady that, in perfect confidence of your honor and integrity, she is to do whatever you direct, I suppose we must take the consent for implied. Well, that is got over. Now, then, the thing is, how to manage it. *I* don't care a rush for Sir John Newark, but I think *you* will find him difficult to manage. How will you ever smuggle her out of the house, and up here to the church, between the hours of eight and twelve?"

"I am afraid," replied Smeaton, "that the church must not be the place, and the hour somewhat different."

"But, my good lord, my good lord," said Parson Thickett, "the canon—you forget the canon—canon one hundred and four. Why, I should be punished; and *you* might be punished too, by the act affecting clandestine marriages."

"Which take place every day, notwithstanding," added Smeaton.

"Ay, ay, by Hedge parsons, May-fair parsons, and Fleet parsons, but not by a regular doctor of divinity. Why, I might be suspended for six months from the execution of my office; and I am not sure that they would not touch the temporalities. As for the office, deuse take it, I don't care much for that. I want a trip to London, and that would give me a holiday."

"Pray, how much might be the value in money of your loss, if suspended?" asked Smeaton.

"Why, the matter of well-nigh fifty good pounds," replied the parson, "and that is a great sum to risk."

"It is," assented the young nobleman; "but there is a way of insuring you against risk, my reverend friend. Suppose that, the moment you have concluded the marriage ceremony, I put into your hand this little rouleau, containing one hundred golden guineas of the late queen. You would be sure enough then. Moreover, the marriage need not be published immediately in this country; and, even if it were, I believe that none but the lady's lawful guardian could move in the business against you.

"That alters the affair very much," said Thickett, with a very comic twinkle of his eye. "I think it must be done."

"Good," replied Smeaton. "I see we understand each other. Perhaps you are not fully aware of all the privileges of your peculiar jurisdiction; but, at all events, in a case like this, now that the only real and substantial difficulty is removed—that respecting the consent of the lady's guardian—you must swallow any other little technical objections, which probably will never be taken notice of."

"Ah, my lord, you have a winning way with you," said Doctor Thickett; "but you have not drunk a drop of your punch;" and, with a resigned sigh, he filled himself another glass to the brim

The rest of the arrangements were soon made. It was agreed that on the following night, about the same hour, the worthy doctor should walk down to the village of Ale, and there put himself entirely at Smeaton's command. The register of Emmeline's birth was then produced and copied; and, rewarding him well for his small trouble, Smeaton took himself back to Ale with Van Noost.

CHAPTER XXVI.

Important business came thick and fast upon all the magistrates of the western counties of England; for, though parties were very nearly balanced, and the prompt, vigorous, and judicious measures of the Whigs—somewhat unconstitutional as perhaps they were at times—overawed the Tories or Jacobites, and kept down any open outbreak, yet positive information was received, if not of a thoroughly-organized and widely-extended plot, at least of an immense number of smaller and detached conspiracies, which only wanted time and opportunity to unite and co-operate. Exeter itself was but little tainted; but in nearly all other parts of Devonshire, in Dorsetshire, Somersetshire, and Gloucestershire, nightly meetings were held, at which some of the most influential persons in the county were present; and the very small body of troops quartered at Exeter were insufficient to perform the duties cast upon them in the neighboring portions of the country.

The arrival of Captain Smallpiece, and the account which he gave—not a very accurate one—of the surprise of his party and the rescue of his prisoners, called forth a burst of anger and disappointment from the more bustling and vehement magistrates, and somewhat alarmed even the more prudent. Nothing was talked of but sending a larger force to scour the country and recapture the young Earl of Eskdale and his companion, and proclamations were proposed, offering a great reward for his apprehension. In time, however, the counsels of the more prudent prevailed. They represented to their brethren that there was quite sufficient for the troops to do in several other directions; that if they sent a large force down into the comparatively wild and scantily-populated district round Ale and Keanton, more important parts of the county must be left open for the movements of the disaffected, and many gentlemen whom it was desirable to secure would have ample time to escape; while, if but a small force was sent, it would only provoke a collision with the adverse peasantry, who would probably gather in great numbers on the first signs of determined hostility toward them. Captain Smallpiece had stated positively that the inn had been invaded by between forty and fifty men; and though eager to go and take vengeance, he was desirous of having an effective force with him, and therefore laid great stress upon the probability of the number of opponents being increased.

General C—— made some allowance for exaggeration; but still he represented to the very zealous justices that it would be much better to let the effervescence in that quarter subside, and by securing every suspected person of influence who could be easily and rapidly laid hold of, crush rebellion in the bud without any bloodshed.

"Take my word for it," he said, "when these poor misguided fellows find there is no one to lead or to support them, they will resume their ordinary occupations, and then, if it be judged necessary, the leaders can be apprehended and punished. In the mean while, this young earl will either come in and make submission, or will fly beyond seas again, and the latter would be no bad thing. You must remember, gentlemen, you have proceeded somewhat sharply against him, upon authority the value of which you know best; and although government considered it necessary to make sure of all suspected persons, and render them impotent for evil, yet there is no desire on the part of his majesty or his minister either to cram the jails with prisoners, or to treat as traitors those not actually apprehended in arms."

These last words, which were taken as a rebuke, created a good deal of ill feeling, and roused a pettish spirit of resistance. None of the magistrates judged fit to interfere with the actual movements of the troops, but they insisted upon issuing a proclamation, offering a reward for the apprehension of the Earl of Eskdale, and some information which reached Exeter during that evening made them plume themselves mightily upon their sagacity. Four men were sent out, two in one direction and two in another, to paste up the proclamations on the doors of dwelling-houses and farms; and, in their tour round the country, they obtained intelligence of a strange messenger having passed across toward Exmouth, and of his having called at the farm of Blacklands, where he asked particularly if the Earl of Eskdale was at Keanton, and then inquired the way to Ale-Manor, but without going along the road pointed out. These tidings had scarcely been received in Exeter, when intelligence came from Exmouth of the appearance of this strange messenger in the town, of his having held communication with several disaffected persons, of his selling his horse, which was completely foundered by hard riding, and of his purchasing another, with which he rode away over the Downs toward Dorsetshire.

On hearing this, General C—— took a pinch of snuff, coolly remarking,

"Then we shall probably soon hear more. He won't get to Colyford uncaught."

Though he treated the matter lightly, to all appearance, the old general did not regard the journey of this messenger as at all unimportant. The persons and the places he visited proved sufficiently the object of his coming; and by his arrest, it was reasonably supposed that much information as to the feelings and intentions of many persons might be obtained. The old officer was as quiet as ever, but very active. He knew and understood well that the apprehension of a single stranger, a mere bearer of letters and messages, was a very different and much more simple affair than the arrest of a nobleman in the midst of a tenantry who bore a feudal, I might almost say, a clannish affection to his house. A number of couriers, armed, but in a civil garb, went forth from Exeter that evening. They were not unsuccessful. The stranger was met with, just crossing the border into Dorsetshire, by one of those sent to seek him. He was a stout fellow, and armed; and the courier bespoke him quietly. The stranger, however, was very uncommunicative, and showed himself desirous of getting rid of all company; but the other pursued him closely, and never left him till he could obtain assistance for his apprehension. He was then immediately seized and conveyed to Exeter, where, upon being searched, a great number of letters were found upon his person, many of them in hands well known in the county, and all of them bearing one peculiar address, namely, "To the General commanding-in-chief for his Majesty." They were all broken open and read without ceremony; and the man himself was then subjected to a long examination, which revealed a great deal more, and gave point to all the ambiguous expressions contained in the letters.

A change now took place in all the proceedings of the authorities at Exeter. Persons whose apprehension had been before a great object, were now left to escape, or to act as they pleased, and immediate measures were adopted against individuals who had been hitherto neglected or unsuspected. Troops were called in from different quarters, and marched in the most opposite directions; and many of the good quidnuncs of the capital, when they heard of these movements without understanding their causes, blamed severely the vacillating conduct of the people at Exeter, and prognosticated a general rising in the West.

For a dull chapter, this is long enough. The consequences of all these proceedings will be seen; and, in the mean time, we will go to matters of more individual interest.

CHAPTER XXVII.

It blew a gale of wind right up the long valley between Ale harbor and Aleton. The night was dark and cloudy. The sky, if not constantly covered with black vapors, was so frequently shrouded by them as only to allow the momentary gleam of a star. On, on, the clouds hurried confusedly over the firmament, like the thoughts of the human mind in a moment of sudden perplexity.

A stout man, well lined within and well cased without, battled sturdily with the blast as he walked down the valley. Many impediments did he meet with: his cravat was nearly torn from his neck; his long black garments fluttered like streamers in the wind; and more than once his three-cornered hat was blown off and sent hurrying away along the road. At length, after having caught it for the third time, with a somewhat ungodly oath, he tied it tightly upon his head with a pocket-handkerchief, and pursued his way in greater security. He was often half strangled, it is true; still he had not now, as before, to double the distance by the constant pursuit of his hat. Puffing and snorting, and venting many a malediction on those who had brought him such a journey on such a night, he made his way forward, supported by the thought of a hundred guineas as the reward of all his toils. About a mile from Aleton, he passed a man upon the road who seemed to know him, for he said, "Good-night, Master Parson," and walked on; but at the entrance of the hamlet he was encountered by our good friend Van Noost, who whispered,

"Is not this an unlucky night?"

"Ay, by Jove!" answered Parson Thickett. "I wonder what people are thinking of, to choose such nights for being married on."

"They must think less who go to sea on such a night," said Van Noost. "*I* would not, for all the world. I would rather stay on shore and have my head cut off."

The parson only laughed, and, walking on, they were soon at Grayling's cottage-door, which readily opened to admit them. The doctor was easily consoled for his long walk on that stormy night, for comforting appliances were within Grayling's cottage, and Smeaton took care that he should be well supplied. The old fisherman himself was in a somewhat grumbling and surly mood, and more than once went out, stayed a few minutes, and returned. Poor Van Noost sat by the fireside, with his eyes fixed upon the flame, unable to cheer himself even by the strong waters. From time to time he lifted his ear and listened, as the leaden casements of the cottage rattled and shook in the blast which came rushing up the stream; and though to the children he was good-humored and kindly as ever, it was evidently with a painful effort that the little statuary forced himself to notice them.

Smeaton, too, was grave and thoughtful. The idea of exposing Emmeline, in a night like that, to the fury of the stirred-up ocean in an open boat, was one that he could not entertain. Had he been alone, with any purpose to accomplish, he would not have hesitated for a moment; but we often feel fears for others which we know not for ourselves; and, even if he could have sheltered her from the cold blast and the dashing spray, he would not have risked a life so precious to him upon that tempestuous sea. Still, the thought of delaying their departure, even for a few hours, was very grievous to him. He knew right well how much may intervene between the cup and the lip. He had a sort of anxious dread about the morrow, and he hoped, and half persuaded himself, that the wind would go down as the night advanced.

Toward ten o'clock, however, old Grayling returned after a short absence, bringing his nephew and another man with him.

"It is no use, my lord," said the younger Grayling. "The ale is getting heavier every minute; and it is so dirty in the wind's eye, that there is no chance of a lull before noon to-morrow. As to getting off to-night, that you can not do. We might get a boat out of the bay, indeed, but she would not live five minutes off the head. I have seldom seen such a sea running as there is now on the Cobstone; for you see, my lord, the wind being southwestern by south—"

But Smeaton interrupted him, saying,

"I will take your opinion, my good friend. There is no use in explaining; *I* should not understand you if you did. For my own life I should not care, but where others are concerned I must be more cautious."

"We don't care much for our own lives either, my lord," said the fisherman, "but I think you would find it a hard matter to get any one to go off with you to-night, especially if there is to be a lady in the boat."

"Then I suppose I shall have to come down to-morrow?" whispered Parson Thickett to the young nobleman, near whom he was sitting.

"No, no, my reverend friend," replied Smeaton. "Your office can be performed in a hurricane as well as in the calmest weather, and in a few minutes we will go to the place where your assistance will be necessary. We must, however, have the cottage clear first, and obtain intelligence that all is safe."

"Ay, ay," added the parson. "Make sure of that."

After staying a few minutes, conversing with his uncle, the younger Grayling went away with the other man who had accompanied him, and soon after the children were sent to their beds. Smeaton looked anxiously at his watch, and then, gazing out at the door, he said,

"I think my servant is coming now."

But he was disappointed. A man arrived who was a bearer of what, to Smeaton, was bad news. The new-comer was a stout peasant, of a somewhat superior class, who looked round, shook hands with old Grayling and his wife, whom he called uncle and aunt, and then, doffing his hat, advanced to the young nobleman, and presented him a letter.

"That, my lord, is from Farmer Thompson—my cousin," he said. "I undertook to bring it over, for we find that some of our people are not to be trusted."

Smeaton broke open the letter, and read the contents with an anxious eye and a look of considerable emotion,

"What is all this?" he said, at length. "I do not understand it."

"Why, it is all true, my lord," replied the young man, bending down his head, and speaking in a whisper. "I saw it, and read it myself, posted upon the very walls of Keanton, setting a price upon your lordship's head, with the royal arms at the top, and 'God save the King' at the bottom. It made all the good men among us quite mad."

"It is not *that* I am speaking of at all, my good friend," returned Smeaton. "The proclamation here mentioned, perhaps, might be expected, though, I must say, such proceedings, after the assurances I have received, are by no means right and justifiable. But what I allude to are these latter words," and, holding the paper to the light, he read:

"According to your lordship's orders, I have sounded the tenantry, and find almost every man under forty ready to obey you in all things. Some of them, however, have not arms. But about twenty are fully prepared, and will be ready to mount at a moment's notice as soon as your lordship arrives. The rest can follow you by one or two at a time, in a day or so, as soon as the arms come from Exmouth."

He ceased reading, and looked in the young man's face as if for explanation.

"Well, my lord," said the other, "I don't understand you."

"Nor I this intelligence," added Smeaton. "I sent no orders to sound the tenantry or to levy men."

"Such orders certainly came, my lord," replied the young man; "not by your own servant, but by another person who seemed to know all about you."

"This is some base fraud," said Smeaton, musing. "However, my good friend, stop and refresh yourself for a little, while I write a letter to your cousin. Tell him that I thank him much for his zeal, but that nothing could be further from my thoughts than to authorize any raising or arming of the tenantry. I hope, however, this has been done so cautiously, as not to call the attention of the magistrates upon you."

"We all met on horseback," said the young man, with a laugh and a shrug of his shoulders, "upon the green before the great gates, but I don't know that any one saw us."

Smeaton thought gravely, and then replied,

"If it be possible, I will ride over before daybreak to-morrow. Stay, I will write."

Going hastily up to his room above, he wrote a few words in the same sense as those he had just uttered, and on descending, found the young man quite ready to depart. Parson Thickett, too, was becoming impatient to return to his own dwelling, for it was now past eleven o'clock, and with a long, bleak walk before him, he did not at all relish delay. Smeaton was evidently no less anxious, but still a quarter of an hour elapsed before the man Higham appeared. At the end of that time, however, he entered the cottage with his gay, saucy look, expecting, probably, to find no one except the old fisherman in the lower room; but, as soon as he saw his lord, he said respectfully,

"They are all gone to bed, my lord, and I dare say will soon be in a comfortable doze, for Sir John and half the servants have ridden hard to-day, and the rest have drank hard, which comes to much the same thing."

"Now, then, my reverend friend," said Smeaton, rising, "we will go, if you please. Van Noost, you must come with us. Higham, go on before to within a yard or two of the place where the small path quits the carriage road to the house. There stop, and make sure that no one comes that way without our having notice by some means."

"I understand," replied the man. "Wrangle, quarrel, talk loud, whistle, shout, or something! I understand. I'll manage it, my lord."

Thus saying, he walked out of the cottage, and Smeaton and the reverend doctor followed.

The young nobleman led his companion round between the two next cottages, desiring Van Noost to go a little in advance; and then said, in a low tone, "There is one question I wish to ask you, Doctor Thickett, which is this: The marriage you are about to celebrate will be a good and perfect marriage, notwithstanding some slight informalities—is it not so?"

"Just, just," replied the parson. "They may suspend *me*, but they can not unmarry *you*. They may punish you by the statute for a clandestine marriage, but they can not make the marriage of no effect. Marriage is like a good thrashing: when once inflicted, it can not be got rid of."

"And now, my good friend," pursued Smeaton, pausing, "you must suffer me, I believe, to tie a handkerchief over your eyes."

"Pooh, pooh! what is the use of that?" exclaimed the doctor, laughing. "I know where you are taking me, just as well as you do. I would not have gone so quietly if I had thought you were taking me into the lion's den except by a back way. Why, the priest's chamber, and the way in and out, has been a tradition at the rectory ever since those puritanical times when many an honest parson was forced to take refuge from skull-cap and Geneva, broadsword and bandolier. There used to be a key up at the church; but, by Jove! my predecessor was fool enough to give it to Sir John. How you got in I can not make out."

Smeaton did not think it necessary to explain, but led the parson on, and found Van Noost at the well with the door open. Doctor Thickett was with some difficulty got across the water; and then, when the door was closed, a match was kindled and a lamp lighted.

"Now tread cautiously," said Smeaton, leading the way, with the light in his hand.

When they entered the priest's room, however, it was still vacant; and, trusting to the promises he had received, the young nobleman did not venture to proceed any further.

"This has been a chapel once, I think," observed Doctor Thickett, looking round the room. "Some notice of it is in the books up at the church. There," added he, pointing to one of the sides, "is where the communion-table must have stood."

Smeaton held up his finger to enjoin silence, and in a minute or two after a slight sound was heard at the extremity of the room adjoining the next chamber. Cautiously, and as noiselessly as possible, the state bed in the other room was drawn back, and the door which it concealed was opened. All eyes were turned to that side, and there was certainly some emotion, if not some anxiety, in the breast of each. The light shone, however, upon the figure of the old housekeeper, who advanced quietly, holding Emmeline by the hand. The poor girl trembled a good deal with agitation rather than fear, and her face was very pale. But Smeaton advanced at once and took her hand, whispering some low, tender words, which instantly called her eyes to his face, and the warm glow into her cheek again.

Mrs. Culpepper had stopped the moment they were in the room; and now, looking anxiously in her foster-son's face, she whispered, "What an awful night it is, my lord! Every thing is ready; but—"

"It is quite impossible," interrupted Smeaton, "to expose this dear girl on the sea in such a tempest; still, as this worthy clergyman has come here to perform the ceremony, the marriage had better take place to-night, and before to-morrow I trust the wind will have gone down. What say you, dearest Emmeline?"

"Oh, certainly," replied Emmeline. "I shall feel more happy—more—more certain of what I am doing, and what is right to do, when I am your wife, than I do now. Besides, new difficulties might spring up."

"You are right, dear young lady, you are right," said Mrs. Culpepper. "Once wedded to him, wherever he may find you, he has a right to claim you, and against whatever wrong is done you he has a right to protect you. Besides, he is bound to take care of himself for your sake."

The young nobleman smiled with a glad and happy look at his beautiful bride, and then led her on toward the spot where Doctor Thickett and Van Noost were standing.

The stout priest would fain have said something jocose, but Emmeline's timid look and Smeaton's dignified bearing at the moment restrained him, and he contented himself with asking, "This is all with your consent and full consideration, Mistress Emmeline?"

"Entirely," she replied, without raising her eyes to the face of the clergyman, which she knew right well, and did not much like.

"Well, then, we have nothing to do but to begin," said Doctor Thickett; and, opening the book, he read the service for the celebration of marriage from beginning to end, without sparing them one word of it; and when he had finished, he added, "Well, that is done and tight. They can not untie that knot, let them tug as they will."

"Thank God!" exclaimed Smeaton, pressing Emmeline's hand in his own. "But we must each have some proof that this dear knot *is* tied, Doctor Thickett."

"Well, I will register it as soon as I get home," said the priest. "I could not bring the great lumbering book with me."

"Doubtless," assented the young earl; "but, if you please, we will each have a certificate under your hand, and those of the witnesses present, that the marriage has taken place. Van Noost, you have an ink-horn with you, I think."

"Every thing ready, every thing ready," cried Van Noost. "Here is ink, and pen, and paper, and a table; so, now, doctor, write away."

"Ah, well. I came to read, not to write; but I may as well do it," said the parson, sitting down to the table, and beginning to scrawl in a large but crabbed hand. "There, my lord, that is for you. There, my lady, that is for you. And now, this is my first fee and reward, by immemorial privilege," he added, pressing his great lips upon Emmeline's cheek.

She shrunk from him, unable to resist her sensation of dislike; but he only laughed, and, turning to Smeaton, received from him the full reward which had been promised.

"And now," he said, aloud, "I had better take myself home. My part of the affair is over."

"Show him the way, Van Noost," said Smeaton. "I will join you at Grayling's cottage very shortly."

The statuary was prompt to obey, and led the fat parson forth, taking Mrs. Culpepper's candle to light them.

Emmeline had borne up well: she had replied clearly and distinctly when taking upon her the irrevocable vows which bound her to the man she loved; but it must not be supposed she had undergone no deep emotions. Every thrilling sensation had been felt; every wide-extending association had presented itself; all the hopes, all the anxieties, all the bright dreams, all the shadowy forebodings, all the realities, all the imaginings, which attend the pledging of a young and innocent heart to the one loved and trusted, had hurried through her bosom and her brain in those few brief minutes. Yet she had borne up; she had seemed calm after her first entrance into the room. Love and strong resolution had given her power to conquer all agitation till the words were spoken, the vow was uttered, and she was his forever. Then, however, the mingled emotions rushed back upon her, together with the overpowering feeling that the great change was accomplished; that she was not her own, but his; that her fate was no longer lonely; that she was one with him she loved; and, had it not been for the arm which glided round her, she would have sunk to the ground where she stood.

The old housekeeper left them to watch in the passage, though she had little fear of any interruption; and to Emmeline and her young husband it seemed but a moment, though an hour had passed, when she again appeared, with a face of some anxiety and alarm.

"I hear horses' feet, my lord," she said. "Quick! You had better speed away. I know not what it may be; but it is strange at this hour of night. Some one will soon be up, for the sounds are on the road near the house. Quick, my lord, quick! Away!"

"Hark, hark!" cried Emmeline. "There are people speaking loud and angrily. Oh, Henry, go, go, for Heaven's sake!"

A brief moment given to thought—one more embrace—and Smeaton was gone. Emmeline followed the old housekeeper out of the room, and the secret entrance was closed as noiselessly as possible. The fair girl, the bride, the wife, retired to her own solitary chamber, while the lover and the husband took his way to his place of refuge. When were they to meet again? Who can ever say who asks himself that question when parting from another?

CHAPTER XXVIII.

Sleep was not destined that night to visit the eyes of the young Earl of Eskdale. He made his way through the passages to the stone door near the well, opened it cautiously, and looked around. Nobody was to be seen; and the sounds which had alarmed them above had ceased. Closing the door and locking it, he hastened back to the cottage of Grayling, seated himself with the old man, who was still up by the fire, and inquired whether he had heard any noise. But the sounds had not reached the hamlet; and, after waiting half an hour, the old man went out to seek intelligence. When he returned, he brought the servant, Thomas Higham, with him, whose explanation was so far satisfactory that it showed Smeaton, or, at least, led him to believe, that no fresh peril was to be apprehended for the time. The high words which had been heard by the lover and his fair bride had passed between the servant and a messenger from Exeter, and were provoked by Higham himself, in order to give early intimation to his master that the household was likely soon to be disturbed.

"You see, my lord," he said, "the truth is, Sir John rode a great part of the way to Exeter this morning, having been summoned thither, I dare say, upon your affairs. But he would not go the whole way, because he had required that assurance should be given him on the road that his house should not be taken possession of during his absence, and no messenger met him

The fellow says he was detained, and could not come on till to-night. I dare say he got drunk, and forgot all about it; but I picked a quarrel with him in order to let you hear."

"Then it was merely the messenger with whom you were speaking?" said Smeaton. "Do you know what reply he brought to Sir John?"

"Oh yes!" answered Higham. "I got that out of him in his passion. He said we were all insolent alike, Sir John and his servants (one of whom he took me to be), and that the magistrates at Exeter would give no such assurances to any body till Sir John had explained his conduct."

"Is he gone?" demanded his master.

"Oh yes, my lord," replied Higham. "I kept hiding in the wood till I heard him trotting back again, and then I was just coming hither, when I met old Stockfish here."

"Then I will ride over at once to Keanton," said Smeaton, "if you can get me your horse out of the stable."

"Why, it is only the pack-horse, my lord," replied Higham; "and though it is as strong as a lion, it is as slow as a bear."

"It matters not," replied his master. "It would take too long to get either of the others from the farm. Bring it down to the end of the hamlet as speedily as possible, and then remain here till I come back, in order that they may think you are riding it yourself."

The man sped away; the horse was soon brought; and, about two in the morning, Smeaton was on his road toward Keanton. On his arrival, he found that, though most persons in the little village were asleep, two or three of the principal farmers were congregated at the house of Thompson, waiting for his arrival. He was received with every sort of respect; but, nevertheless, there was a somewhat gloomy and dissatisfied look about the men, which gave him some key to their feelings. They said that the message they had received in his name had so completely misled them, that every preparation had been made for taking up arms, and without much secrecy or disguise.

"If we stand hesitating, my lord," said one of the men, boldly, "the people of Exeter, who have had spies among us, won't fail to be down upon us when we least expect them, and then we shall be marched away to prison. Nobody doubted, my lord, that the order came from you, for the only thing that surprised us was that you had not given it long before. We are, every one of us, willing to shed our blood for our right king, under the command of your lordship, whose good father was ever ready to draw the sword in a just cause; but we should not like to spend the rest of our lives in jail without striking a blow, right or wrong."

Smeaton was a good deal mortified, for there was but little time to give long explanations as to his motives, or to show the worthy men around him how hopeless was the course they were inclined to pursue. He told them, however, briefly but clearly, that he credited in no degree the assertion, so frequently made by the Jacobite party, that the majority of the people of England were anxious for the return of the Stuarts. He had convinced himself, he said, that such was not the case; and he added, what seemed to surprise them very much, that he thought the people of any country had a right to some voice in the disposal of the crown. It must be remembered that the divine right of kings had at that period been rarely questioned; that where, as in the case of England, it had not only been questioned, but set aside, the new doctrine of the people's rights had only made way with one party, and that that party had shown themselves so far doubtful of their own position as to choose for their sovereign a member of the same family whose head they had repudiated. The men to whom Smeaton spoke had been bred up under his ancestors, with the notion of this divine right inculcated upon them from infancy almost as a part of their religion, and it is not, therefore, to be wondered at that they marveled exceedingly to hear their young lord pronounce doctrines which to them seemed little less than treasonable. They could comprehend his arguments much better, however, when he went on to explain to them that the chances of an insurrection even in the north of Great Britain being successful were exceedingly small at that time, and that no chance whatever existed of a rising in the west of England prospering for above a day. He showed them that, from the information they themselves possessed, it was clear that all the principal leaders of the Jacobite party in Devonshire and Somersetshire had been secured by orders of the government, and that no force could be raised sufficient to resist the troops which were ready to act against the Pretender.

"Yes, my lord," replied the farmer who had before spoken; "but we might make our way across the country to help our friends in the North, and that *I* shall do, for one, now I have made up my mind."

The man spoke in a dogged and determined tone, and several others who were present, though they said little, seemed much inclined to follow his example. The time thus ran on for about an hour in fruitless discussion, and then it became necessary for the young nobleman to return to his place of refuge. He could, therefore, only entreat those by whom he was surrounded to pause and consider well before they acted upon a resolution which might hurry them into dangers they had not yet fully calculated.

With this advice he left them; and, according to custom on such occasions, his conduct became the subject of much comment after he was gone. Some blamed him as a waverer; some of the more rash affected to doubt his courage; and others marveled at what could possess him; when some one, in a jocular manner, alluded to the pretty lady at Ale-Manor as the probable cause of their lord's hesitation and reluctance. As usual, when any likely solution of a difficult question is suggested, every one seized on the idea thus started; poor Emmeline was looked upon as a sort of Cleopatra, who kept their Marc Antony in the toils of love; and the good farmers set themselves seriously to consider whether no means existed of forcibly withdrawing their young lord from this entanglement.

In the mean while, Smeaton rode back toward Ale; but, as always happens when speed is required, more than one impediment came in his way. It was still blowing hard, although the gale was somewhat more moderate, and the young nobleman's horse labored and panted up the hills as if his lungs were unsound. This, however, would only have produced a delay of about a quarter of an hour; but a much more serious obstacle soon presented itself. The beast cast a shoe; no means of replacing it were near at hand, and it was impossible to proceed with any thing like speed.

Embarrassed and annoyed, the young nobleman nevertheless pursued his way, though day dawned and the sun rose when he was fully six miles from the village of Ale. Two courses were before him: either to ride on boldly and risk a meeting with those whom he wished to avoid, or to hide in some of the hollows of the hills till night fell, taking his chance of obtaining food from the shepherds or herdsmen who fed their cattle on the Downs. But a feeling of recklessness had come over him, proceeding not alone from the conversation which had just passed, but also from a perception of the manifold dangers of his position, and of the difficult situation in which he was placed; and he had determined to go forward at all hazards, when he perceived some one on foot apparently watching him from the summit of one of the neighboring hills. As soon as the man got sight of Smeaton riding below, he ran down toward him as fast as possible, and the young earl conjectured that there was an intention of cutting him off on the road toward Ale.

"I can deal with one at least," he thought, and pushed on somewhat more rapidly, although his horse now went very lamely.

But the person on the hill ran fast, and cut him off at a turning in the path he was pursuing, when, to Smeaton's surprise, he beheld the face and figure of his servant Higham, who, holding up his hand to prevent his further advance, besought him not to ride on, on any account.

"You can not get to the village, my lord, but by passing round the Manor House, and it is in possession of the soldiers from Exeter. They have taken Sir John out of his bed this morning, and intend to carry him away to Exeter a prisoner. He talks very high, but looks low; and so I thought I might as well run on to tell you, and keep myself out of harm's way."

"Sir John Newark!" exclaimed Smeaton, in utter amazement; for the character of the knight was in no degree a secret to him, notwithstanding all the pains taken to conceal his real views and objects. "Are you sure, Higham, that *I* am not the real object of the search, and that Sir John is not arrested either from his having hidden me in his house so long, or as a sort of security for my discovery?"

"Lord bless you, no, my lord!" replied Higham. "Sir John Newark is lagged for Sir John Newark's own doings. He has played fast and loose with every government for many a long year, and has won a precious deal by the game—at least so the people here say. He has made people in London fancy he is much more powerful in Devonshire than he is, and so, whenever he wanted any thing, he made a show of going over to the other party, and got what he required. Now, if he wanted Keanton, for instance, and thought that the Whigs were likely to win the day, he would become very High Church indeed, and pretend to be plotting with your lordship just to be bribed to give it up and betray you. But such a man is caught out in the end. He can not carry on such a game without making some mistake, and the magistrates here are desperate sharp. I was in the house when the soldiers came, and it oozed out among them that Sir John was charged upon some letter found on a messenger in which he had gone a little too far. As to seeking for your lordship, they never asked for you at all; and though they got possession of the house quietly enough, they knew better than to go into the village to make any search. They would have been thrashed out soon enough. All they wanted was Sir John, and him they have caught and put in a bag. But, nevertheless, I think it would be better for you to keep out of the way till the men have gone and have taken their prisoner with them, for there is a great chance, if they found you, that they would bag you too As soon as they are gone, you have got the game in your own hands, for there will be nobody at Ale to stop your doing what you like; and I can go and watch from the top of Ale Head to see when they pass up the road."

The words of Higham were like the voice of Hope, promising bright things which might or might not be performed; but if a doubt previously existed in the mind of Smeaton as to whether he should or should not go forward, it was at once removed. To try to make his way into Ale, so long as the soldiery were at the Manor House, would have been madness; and, consequently, choosing his course at once, he determined to retreat a little way into the hollows, and to send the man up to the high ground above Ale Head, whence a considerable portion of the road the soldiers were obliged to travel was visible. He accordingly sought out a spot whence he could keep his eye upon his servant, while Higham watched the road, and arranged with his master a sort of code of signals for the purpose of communicating what his observations discovered from the height, without obliging the earl to descend. But the man had not been more than ten minutes at the highest point of the coast when, by stretching out his right arm in the same direction as the road to Exeter, he indicated that the guard and their prisoner had set out.

Waiting a few minutes to give time for their passing out of sight, the young nobleman moved his horse slowly forward, choosing the soft turf to ride over as the best for his horse's unshod feet; but, the moment he altered his position, Higham ran down again to meet him, and informed him that it would be better to wait a little, for, though the greater number of the soldiers were out of sight, yet two were far in the rear of the rest, and might recall the others in a moment.

"Sir John is determined to take it at his ease," added the man, "for he has got his great coach and six horses, with a servant on horseback at each wheel. It looks, for all the world, like the lord mayor's coach, and goes as slow; but, at all events, it will serve his purpose, and both make him comfortable in the inside, and delay the people who have him in custody."

"Then do you think he meditates escape?" asked the young earl.

"That is as it may be, my lord," replied Higham. "If he hopes for any one to help him, he is quite mistaken, for the fishermen would not stir a finger for him, and the peasantry do not like him much better, as far as I can hear. He is a sorry fellow, and a proud one, and won't find many friends in the world; but perhaps he thinks to get off by some trick; and then, if he does join the prince's army, he will have taken the first strong resolution he ever did in his life—but he won't do that. He will hold fast by the ruling power in the end, depend upon it, for Sir John is his own sovereign, and nobody is so despotic with him as his own interest."

Smeaton mused a while, and then moved slowly forward again, sending his servant a little in advance to see that the country was clear. No obstacle, however, presented itself. The cavalcade was out of sight; the grounds round Ale-Manor were perfectly solitary, and not even a herd or a laborer was to be seen. Dismounting from his horse where the road to the Manor House turned into the wood, the young earl descended on foot to the village, from which a sound of loud talking came up the side of the hill. He found the greater part of the people of the place —men, women, and even children—assembled in one of the little gardens, which, fenced with large flat stones, lay here and there between the cottages. All seemed in a state of great excitement, but it was evidently not excitement of an angry character, for some laughed, while others talked loud, though in no very sad tone.

As soon as Smeaton was seen advancing by those on the outside of the little crowd, one stout fellow waved his hat and cried "Hurrah!" and congratulations poured thick upon him as he advanced among them.

"Ay, my lord, we were in a bit of a fright about you," said old Grayling, grasping his hand unceremoniously in his great, broad, hard fist; "but not much either, for we sent out people to see that they did not get hold of you."

"Perhaps he does not know that the soldiers have been here, uncle," said the younger Grayling.

"No, not here, Dick, not here," said the stout old man. "They dared not put their noses in here, if they had been five times their number. Up at the house they might do what they liked. That was no business of ours. But they are gone now, and have a long march to Exeter, so that all is safe for a day or two."

"Then I suppose I can safely go up to the house," said the young nobleman. "I wish to hear the particulars of all this business."

"Ay, safe enough," replied the old man, with a meaning laugh; "safer, I fancy, than when you lived there quite at your ease, my lord. A bad friend is worse than a bad enemy."

"But won't you have something to eat, sir?" inquired Dame Grayling. "I'll get you something in a minute."

Smeaton, however, declined, and turned his steps by the shortest path toward the house, thinking, with joy, it must be acknowledged, of the removal of many obstacles in his way by the arrest of Sir John Newark. Bitterly was he destined to be disappointed, as is often the case when we suffer our hopes to be elated without a full knowledge of the circumstances. He found every thing quiet and tranquil about the house, though he could hear some of the servants, as he approached, talking together in the stable-court; and his eye ran over the windows, to see if Emmeline was at any of them. Nobody, however, was visible, and he lifted the great latch of the door to go in as usual; but the door was locked, and he had to ring the bell and wait several minutes before he gained admission. The servant, who appeared at length, was one of the younger men; and, putting on a rueful aspect, with perhaps a touch of hypocrisy, he was proceeding to inform the young nobleman of the sad event which had occurred, when Mrs. Culpepper herself glided into the hall, saying, with a low courtesy,

"If you will walk into the saloon, my lord, I will tell you all about it."

Smeaton followed her with some anxiety, for there was an ominous gloom upon her face which he did not think the mere arrest of Sir John Newark was likely to produce.

"You have heard what has happened?" she said, immediately the door was closed.

"That Sir John Newark has been made prisoner, and sent to Exeter," replied Smeaton.

"To London—to London," returned Mrs. Culpepper. "He will not even be examined at Exeter, they say, but be sent off to Newgate or the Tower at once. He has long been playing double with them, and now they have found upon a courier a letter of his to the Earl of Mar, which, by the explanations of the messenger, they make out to be full of treason. But that is not the worst of it, Henry—that is not the worst of it. He has taken the Lady Emmeline with him, whether she would or not. We knew not what to do—whether boldly to tell of her marriage, or still to keep it secret. To say that she was married to you would have been to make matters worse; and now, I will own, I am at my wits' end."

This was a terrible blow to Smeaton; one, indeed, on which he had never calculated; and difficulties presented themselves in all ways. If he lingered in that part of the country till tidings were obtained from London, he was sure to be taken, and probably kept a prisoner at Exeter; while, on the other hand, the intelligence he had received from the fishermen had shown him that every road between Devonshire and the capital was strictly watched and guarded, so that it was next to impossible for him to pass in that direction without discovery. Still, however, his mind was turned toward making the attempt at least, and the only consideration was how to do so in safety. He could devise no means; but good Mrs. Culpepper came to his aid with a plan which seemed feasible.

"To try and get over the whole distance by land," she said, "is hopeless; but the boatmen will easily take you round, and land you on some quiet part of the coast near Abbotsbury or Weymouth, whence you can easily get to London under another name; and I don't know that London is not as good a hiding-place as any in the land."

Smeaton's inclinations led him that way. Hope, too, unextinguishable Hope, was busy in his breast, telling him that in the capital much could be done which he would vainly attempt to do by letter. He would see Lord Stair, he thought; he would cast himself upon his honor, upon his generosity. He would explain his own conduct, and recall to that nobleman the assurances he had given him not long before. Then, when freed from the perils which now surrounded him, he could, with safety to her and to himself, claim his beautiful bride, and set at defiance the arts of open enemies or pretended friends.

"I will set out at once," he said, after having given a few minutes to thought. "Yours is the best plan, my dear Nanny, and I will lose no time in executing it. I have at least one good friend in London, who has the will and the power to see justice done me."

"Pray take some refreshment before you go," said the housekeeper, in the tone of old affection. "You have turned pale with all these bad news, and look harassed and grieved."

"Well indeed may I, Nanny," replied the young lord, laying his hand kindly on her arm

"Were there nothing else, surely the loss of my dear Emmeline, within ten short hours after she became mine, is enough both to grieve and agitate me. But I need no refreshment, and shall not be content till I am on my way."

"Nay, but stay a little," said the old housekeeper. "I can send down and order the boat directly, while you take some food; and besides, Richard, I am sure, will be glad to go with you as soon as he comes back."

"Has he not gone with his father?" exclaimed Smeaton, in great surprise.

"Oh no, my lord," replied the housekeeper, "he was not here at the time. He has not been in the house since five o'clock this morning, when he rode away on one of his wild expeditions. We all thought he had gone to seek you at Keanton."

"I did not meet with him," said Smeaton; "but doubtless he will be glad to follow his father; and, though his presence may be some embarrassment to me, yet, poor boy, it is well that he should go with me."

"Better tell him all, my lord," observed Mrs. Culpepper. "You may trust his word if he promises secrecy; for, though a little twisted by one thing or another, God gave him good wits at the first, and a good heart too. Hark! that must be his horse. Yes, he is calling for a groom. He must have heard what has happened, for that is not his usual way of speaking. Stay! I will get you both some food and wine. He will want it as much as you."

She had hardly left the room when Richard Newark entered: his manner of speech and bearing were wholly, almost miraculously changed, as, with a heated face and eyes full of wild light, he exclaimed, "Ah, you have heard the tidings, Eskdale! They have taken away my father, which was what I always expected, and Emmeline too, which I did *not* expect; for she meddled with nothing, and he meddled with every thing. Now, what do you intend to do? I know what *I* intend to do, if the chain and collar will let me."

"I propose," replied Smeaton, "to take boat at once, land somewhere near Weymouth where we are not known, and thence make our journey to London under fictitious names. I take it for granted that you are anxious to follow your father; and if you like to accompany me, I shall be glad, although there is no need of your doing so, for doubtless you would be permitted to pass unquestioned. As for me, the plan I propose offers the only chance of my being able to reach the capital except as a prisoner. But you must decide at once, Richard."

"What do you want in the capital?" asked Richard Newark. "What have you to do in that great ugly mixture of dirt, brick houses, and coal smoke?"

"I have much business, and important business there," answered Smeaton. "Lord Stair pledged his word to me that I should remain safe and unquestioned in this country for a time, if I meddled in no degree with politics. I have not done so, and yet you know how I have been treated."

Richard Newark laughed, and shook his head with a thoughtful and abstracted air. "I must not say what I would fain say," he remarked; "no, no, I must not. It is very odd that one's fate is so often managed for one! You have been played upon, Smeaton."

"At all events," replied Smeaton, "I have written two letters to Lord Stair, to neither of which I have received an answer. He is a man of honor and a gentleman, who will not deny his plighted word, and I must go to London to claim its fulfillment."

"There are two reasons why you must not," said Richard, "and good ones too, whatever you may think. First, you can't; and, secondly, there would be no good in going if you could. Listen to me, listen to me. A ship of war is lying off the mouth of the bay, sent down, as I learn, to watch the coast and search every boat. That is for the 'can't.' Now for the 'good of going.' Lord Stair is not in London. He is in command of the troops in Scotland; and, if you want him, noble lord, you must go North." Then opening the door, he shouted, "Where is the Flying Post? Where is the Flying Post that came yesterday? It was in this room last night."

In answer to his call, a servant brought him one of the newspapers of the day, where, among other brief and uncommented announcements, appeared a paragraph, stating that the Earl of Stair had set out on the morning preceding to take command of the troops in Scotland, and keep the rebels in check till a larger army could be assembled to chastise them.

Smeaton looked at the date of the paper, which, as it had come by an express courier, was very recent.

"If I set out at once," he said, "I may, by hard riding, catch him in Yorkshire or Northumberland. It states here that he will be in York on Monday next—somewhat slow traveling in a business of such importance; but doubtless he has re-enforcements with him. I will get my horses in, and ride off at once."

"I will be one with you," added Richard Newark, "for I am traveling North too."

"Will you not go to join your father?" asked the young earl, in much surprise.

"Not I," replied the lad. "I could give him no help, and he would not have it if I could. My father is quite sufficient for himself, noble lord—at least he thinks so, and he never thanks any one for meddling with his affairs, though he meddles with other people's often enough, whether they thank him or not. But now let us get ready. I do not know whether these people have carried off your baggage or not. Mine will be soon trussed. Heaven send me occasion to use the sword you gave me! But you had better go to Keanton first, and take people enough to force the way, in case Hanover and Pulteney should try to stop you. If you don't go there, your people, I can tell you, will set out by themselves, and perhaps do more than you like or think of. I was there half an hour after you this morning, and how I missed you I do not know."

For a minute or two Smeaton did not reply, but remained in deep thought.

"So be it," he said at length. "Come down, Richard, and join me at the end of the village as soon as you are ready. I must send for my horses, and, in the mean time, will bid my servant pack up the baggage which was left here."

"Be sure first that it has not been taken away," observed the lad.

"I trust it has not been," answered Smeaton, "for my stock of money is running low, and there are some jewels and other things of value in those large trunks, which are worth money at all events."

"Oh, the people at Keanton will furnish you

with money, I am sure," said Richard, "if you will lead them where they like."

"That is what I am least inclined to do, I fear," returned Smeaton. "Therefore I will go up and see, that I may be under obligations to no one."

He found his baggage where he had left it, returned to the saloon, partook of some of the refreshments which Mrs. Culpepper had provided, and then hastened away to make his arrangements in the village. More than once during his conversation with Richard Newark it had struck him that a strange transformation had come over the lad's manner. His tone was decided and quick, and his look grave, perhaps sad, even when he laughed. But Smeaton had too many things to think of to comment at length, even in his own mind, on this alteration, and the impression was swept away as soon as made.

The hurry and confusion of a rapid departure had many additions in Smeaton's case. What was to be done with good Van Noost was not the least consideration. When notice of the approach of troops toward Ale-Manor had been first received in the village, the statuary instantly hid himself, no one knew where; but now he had reappeared upon the scene, and the young nobleman could not bear the thought of leaving him behind for the consequences of his own indiscretion. The appearance of a ship before Ale Harbor, which had thrown the whole village into a state of commotion, prevented the possibility of Van Noost's escape by sea, and rendered the necessity the greater of all suspected persons hastening their departure without delay. The fishermen anticipated that the ship's boats would enter the harbor every moment, and they seemed to regard the landing of a number of seamen with much greater apprehension than an attack by a party of soldiers. They showed no inclination to abandon their friends, however, but, at the same time, eagerly assisted in all preparations which were necessary to put them beyond the reach of this new danger.

The horses were brought to the village with great rapidity; the baggage was packed and loaded without delay; and as Van Noost's fat pony was lost to his affectionate master forever, a stout farmer's nag was procured for him, on whose broad back the little round man was placed like a plum-pudding on a trencher. Still, the man who had been set to watch on the beach of the bay and at the top of Ale Head brought no intelligence of any movement on board the ship to create alarm, and all was quiet when the party of fugitives, consisting of Smeaton and Richard Newark, with Van Noost and two servants, rode away toward Keanton, where they arrived without interruption. There, for a time, I must leave them, to take up their history at an after period.

CHAPTER XXIX.

Considering the period of the year, which was only the end of September, the day was cold and wintery, when a party, consisting of some sixteen horse, took their way through one of the remote districts of Northumberland. The sky was covered with a film of gray cloud, and the wind, keen and chilling, as if loaded with hail or snow, swept over the bleak hills and moors.

Northumberland was at that time, from many local causes, far behind the rest of England in point of cultivation and numbers. Remote from the capital either of England or Scotland, and holding but very scanty communication with the rest of Europe, the power and authority of government was less felt and acknowledged in the great northern county than elsewhere; old thoughts and habits clung to the inhabitants with greater tenacity; news circulated less freely, and men were more under the influence of the great proprietors than perhaps in any other English shire. The party of horse, therefore, which I have mentioned, and which was headed, as the reader may suppose, by the young Earl of Eskdale and Richard Newark, not only passed unquestioned through a district where a great majority of the people were attached to the Stuart cause, but were received in the small towns and villages with much cordiality, as soon as it was perceived that they were not soldiers of the house of Hanover. The Northumberland man has a certain degree of Northern cautiousness about him, but he is by no means without the merry English spirit, and a good portion of wit. Few inquiries were made of the travelers as to the end and object of their journey, but a sly and jesting allusion was often ventured to the cause of the exiled king, and every information was given voluntarily regarding the insurrectionary movements in Scotland, and the general feelings of the people of the county itself.

The report which had reached the West of Forster and others being in arms in Northumberland proved to have been greatly premature, and Smeaton now found that nothing was certain as to the proceedings of the malcontents and the government except that warrants were out for the arrest of the Earl of Derwentwater, and Forster of Bamborough, member for the county, together with several other persons of less note, and that the earl and his companion, with several of their friends, were closely concealed.

The situation of the young Earl of Eskdale was peculiar, but his being placed in it had been brought about by circumstances which affected many at that period, and led them unwillingly to actions which they did not at first contemplate, and into a position which they had anxiously striven to avoid. A hundred instances of noblemen and gentlemen could be cited, who were led on, little by little, from a mere abstract feeling of loyalty and attachment toward the exiled house of Stuart, to a complete and sometimes furious enthusiasm in their cause, to an active part in insurrection, and to their own utter destruction. Such was not altogether the case with Smeaton; but it must be acknowledged that, before he reached Northumberland, his feelings and views were very greatly altered. The zeal and eagerness of all those by whom he was surrounded of course had their effect.

Few men—perhaps no young man—can prevent himself from being altogether infected by the enthusiasm of others, especially if no antidote be at hand; and certain it is that the young nobleman was inclined to look more favorably upon the conduct of the exiled princes, to make more allowance for their faults, and to regard their cause more hopefully than he had been when we first saw him in London. Moreover the treatment which he had received in Devonshire, the evident determination of the local authorities, if not of the government, to molest and persecute him, notwithstanding the strong assur ances he had received from Lord Stair, and the contemptuous silence with which, as it appeared, that nobleman had treated his letters, irritated him greatly against the house of Hanover. It was certain, he thought, that one at least of those letters must have reached the hands for which both were intended, although the second, perhaps, might not have arrived in London before the earl had taken his departure from the capital. Why had he neglected to reply? Was he inclined to violate his plighted word, or to connive at its violation by others? Or had he suffered his mind to be warped by false reports? and if he had, was he justified in so doing before stronger proof was adduced than any which Smeaton imagined could have been furnished by his enemies?

"I have kept my word to the letter," said the young nobleman to himself; "but I can not bear this much longer. If they will drive me into insurrection, it is not my fault. But I will yet make one more effort for an explanation, and if that fails, I and they must abide the consequence."

A sigh followed the conclusion of this train of thought, for a moment's reflection showed him, notwithstanding some new-lighted hopes, where the evil consequences of the course along which he was being hurried were most likely to fall. It is true, he had not committed himself in any degree either with Richard Newark or with the farmers and stout yeomen who had accompanied or followed him from Keanton. Although he suffered them to join his party—for he could hardly refuse to do so after they had placed themselves in a dangerous situation on his account—he told them from the first that he had pledged himself to the Earl of Stair to take no part in any of the political movements that were going on, if suffered to remain quietly in England for a short period.

"I have kept my part of the compact," repeated he, "and I have been treated ill; but, before I actually violate it, I must learn from the earl what is the meaning of the conduct pursued toward me. Perhaps all may be explained on both sides; and if so, I will keep my word to the letter, leaving you, my good friends, to follow what course you think fit."

Some of the men received the announcement rather sullenly, but others smiled with light-hearted shrewdness, thinking that their young lord's scruples would soon be overcome when once he found himself in the focus of the insurrection.

During the last day's march, many a wild and exaggerated report had reached the little party of the progress of the insurgent force under the Earl of Mar, and of risings in various other parts of England. Mar's army was swelled to the number of thirty thousand men, according to these rumors; he had been joined by all the principal noblemen in Scotland; the Highland clans were universally flocking to him; the Lowlanders were rising in every direction; the town of Perth had been taken by a *coup-de-main;* and a large magazine of arms and ammunition on the coast of Fife was said to have fallen into the hands of the insurgents. King James himself was reported to have landed on the western coast with an auxiliary army, commanded by the gallant Duke of Berwick; and the forces of the house of Hanover were stated to be a mere handful, collected in Stirling, and surrounded on every side by the legions of King James. In short, tens were magnified into hundreds, and hundreds into thousands on the Jacobite side, and every small advantage was reported as a great victory, while the numbers of the opposite party were diminished in proportion, and the great abilities of those who commanded them overlooked or unknown.

Smeaton himself received these rumors for no more than they were worth, and, perhaps, did not yield them even sufficient credit. Mar had, it is true, taken possession of Perth; his forces had certainly greatly increased; and the Master of Sinclair, one of his officers, had seized a small store of arms at Burnt Island. The forces of the government, too, at Stirling, were quite inadequate, in point of numbers, to cope with a regular army, commanded by a man of skill and experience; but Mar was totally deficient in both these points, and his army consisted of a mere mob of brave men, with little discipline and small cohesion among them. True was it, also, that General Whetham, who remained in command at Stirling till the middle of September had shown but little ability to encounter the grave and dangerous circumstances in which he was placed; but on the side of the Jacobites, all the advantages of number, zeal, and fiery courage were more than counterbalanced by the incapacity of the commander and the insubordination of the troops, while, on the part of the government, numerous bodies of disciplined soldiers, and officers of decision, experience, and courage, were hurrying to the scene of action, and preparing to crush the insurrection, which had been already suffered to proceed too far.

Vainly did Smeaton ask for tidings of the Earl of Stair, till, on the day which I have mentioned, a farmer told him, somewhat sullenly, that two regiments of dragoons belonging to the Earl of Stair had passed the border that morning, and that there was an ill-looking fellow at their head, with a number of lackeys in the rear, whom he doubted not was the earl himself and his servants. This news seemed sufficient; and, without delay, he hurried on till nightfall, gaining information of the march of these troops as he proceeded, till, on the best opinion he could form, he judged that they could not be much more than one march in advance. The place where he was obliged to halt could hardly be called a hamlet, but rather a group of small farm houses gathered together in a rich valley among the hills. No inn, no place of public entertainment whatever, was to be found; but the good farmers of the place not only willingly took in the travelers in separate parties, but seemed almost to expect some such visitation. Nods and hints were not wanting to signify that the cause of their guest's movements was known; and the worthy Northumbrian, at whose house Smeaton and Richard Newark were lodged, with their two servants, whispered in the ear of the young nobleman that it would be better for him to keep quiet where he was the whole of the next day, as Lord Stair's dragoons were at Wooler, and there was some talk of their halting there to refresh before they proceeded North.

The news was less unsatisfactory to the young earl than the farmer imagined; and his first act was to write a letter to Lord Stair, and to direct his servant to take it early on the following morning. He then returned to the room where he had left Richard Newark, and informed him of what he had done.

The lad laughed.

"Then, most likely, we shall all soon be in the hands of the Philistines," he said. "Your noddle, Eskdale, is doubtless much better than mine, but I don't think mine would have concocted a scheme for giving this good lord an opportunity of sending back a party to pick us up, just as if we were something he had dropped on the road. Twenty Tories, and an earl at their head, would make a good cast of the net for any Hanover fisherman."

"I have not been so imprudent as you think, Richard," rejoined his friend. "I can be careful for my friends as well as for myself. I have not mentioned to Lord Stair that there is any one with me, and have told him that I shall follow the messenger ten miles on the road to-morrow, to meet the man on his return, and that, if he assures me that I shall be safe to come and go, I would present myself at his head-quarters, in order that our conduct may be mutually explained. I will send you intimation by the messenger if I do not return to join you myself."

"And what am I to do?" asked Richard Newark, with a somewhat gloomy and desponding look. "Here I am, like a boat turned off to sea without sail, or oar, or compass."

"If you would take my advice, Richard," replied his friend, "it would be exactly what I have given you more than once before, namely, to make the best of your way to London, and join your father. That advice I give to you because I think the course of your duty is clear, and because I believe your single arm would be of very little service to the cause you are so anxious to serve, although I have not thought it fit or right to dissuade these good men of Keanton, who are with us, from following the course they have chosen for themselves. But the case is very different with you. You are young and inexperienced, and may hereafter bitterly regret the step you are now taking. They are older, know and see the consequences of all they are doing, and are only acting in consonance with principles long entertained. Were I to follow my own inclinations—my habitual prejudices, as I may call them—I should undoubtedly lead them on the way they are going; but still I should give you the same advice as I give now."

"Then why do you not follow your own inclinations?" asked Richard, sharply. "I won't believe that you are a man to hesitate at doing any thing merely because you think it is dangerous. All these men suppose it is because you have no great hope of success that you will not join the king's army."

"They do me wrong," said Smeaton. "I put before them what I thought a just view of the probabilities, because I would not have them act blindly; but I have used no other means of dissuasion. You ask me why I do not follow my own inclination," he continued, thoughtfully, "and I do not know that I shall be able to make you comprehend the reason."

"Try, try," said Richard Newark. "My skull is thick, I know, but if you tap at the right place you will get in."

"It is a very painful situation, Richard," said Smeaton, "when a man's reason, in points of such importance as those which are now agitated in England, takes part against the prejudices in which he has been brought up. My father was happier. He never entertained a doubt that kings possess their power by divine appointment, or imagined that the people had justly any voice in the choice of their rulers. To this principle he sacrificed all his earthly possessions, and would have sacrificed life itself. Neglect, ill treatment, duplicity on the part of the princes whom he served, made no difference in his opinions. He lived and died in them; and, during all my early life, I heard of none other. Ten years ago I should have thought exactly the same as my father, though I felt more than he did the wrongs that were done him, and the insolent indifference with which he was treated. Although I despised our rightful sovereign as a man, I should have been ready to shed my blood for him as a king. Since that time I have mingled much with the world, have been out of the atmosphere of such prejudices, have learned to think and reason for myself, and have come to the conclusion that, as kings rule for the benefit of the people, the people have a voice in their selection; that, in fact, kings have no rights but what they derive from their subjects. Now, if I could convince myself that the majority of the people of England did really desire King James for their sovereign, or even that parties were equally divided for and against him, I should not hesitate to draw my sword in his cause; for my prejudices are still strong, though they are weakened. But I am not convinced that such is the case, and all I have seen hitherto tends to an opposite conclusion. This is one view of the case; but there is another, which is even still more powerful with me. I pledged myself to Lord Stair that I would meddle in no way in this struggle for three months."

"But he has not kept his word with you," cried Richard, vehemently. "You can not be bound by a compact which he has broken."

"It is that which I am anxious to ascertain," replied his friend, "and that I will ascertain to-morrow. If I find he has really violated his word with me, or suffered it to be violated by others, of course I shall hold myself entitled to act as I please. But I can hardly suppose that this is the case, for I have always believed that his character as a man of honor is above suspicion, and I would not, for life itself, by any rash act of mine, justify him in saying that I took advantage of the unauthorized conduct of those Western magistrates to violate my plighted word."

Richard Newark fell into a fit of thought; but he never long retained any very somber impressions, and after the pause of a moment or two he broke into a laugh, inquiring,

"Do you not think that our dear Emmeline may have something to do with your great discretion?"

"Nothing," replied Smeaton, thoughtfully, "nothing. I trust and hope, though I do not scruple at once to say, Richard, that for her sake I would do any thing that did not affect my honor. Nay, more—"

He paused for an answer, for he was strongly tempted to tell his young companion how indissolubly his own fate and that of Emmeline were now bound together, but he hesitated on the very point of uttering the words. Richard was so wild, so rash—there might occur so many events to render the safe keeping of that secret important, and there seemed so many chances of his letting it escape him in one of his thoughtless moods, that a moment's reflection decided the earl to be silent on the subject, at least for the time.

"Well, what more?" cried Richard, impatiently.

"I have tried the question with myself times a dozen," replied the earl, "and though I need not tell you I love her dearly, I do not believe that that love has been suffered to interfere at all in the decision I have come to."

"Well, well," said Richard Newark, shrugging his shoulders, "when we march into London and proclaim King James, you shall have her, and I will give away the bride. A pretty father I shall make! I suppose I must hire a white beard for the occasion. You act as you like; and I must take my chance, as you will not lead me to draw the sword which you have taught me to use. I will take our king's side, and stay by it. I am sick of seeing people wavering between two parties—my father from policy, and you from scruples. There, I don't mean to offend you, noble friend. I doubt not you are quite right, and that your head was made for something better than being run against a wall, which was evidently Nature's intention when she furnished me with this noddle of mine; but you will own that, having seen all I have seen, I may well say, 'No time-serving for me.' I have heard people tell that my father has got together a great estate by now running with one party and now with another; it is but right that his son should break it to pieces again by sticking tight to one, be it fortunate or unlucky. And now I shall go to bed. Don't you dream of Emmeline, or you'll go over to Lord Stair to a certainty."

Thus saying, he rose and left the room, and Smeaton remained some time longer in thought.

CHAPTER XXX.

The morning was bright and beautiful; the clouds of the preceding day, although they had not passed off entirely, had broken into detached masses, soft, white, and buoyant, but low down, moving slowly across the blue sky, and leaving large intervals for the rays of the sun to stream through, and paint the brown moors in all the magic coloring of autumn. A faint aërial mist was seen softening the distant parts of the landscape as Smeaton rode slowly over the solitary hills, which lay tumbled about in large rounded masses, marking the frontier line of England and Scotland. The alternation of shadow and of gleam brought forth as varied and as beautiful colors as those which paint the dolphin at his death. The free, pure air, the rich, changing prospect, the wide expanse of view, all seemed to breathe hope, if not happiness; and that strange, mysterious sensation, that elevated and expansive feeling, to which I can give no name, but which takes possession of the heart when first we leave the busy haunts of men to plunge into a wide solitude, came strongly upon the young earl as he strained his sight along the distant hills and valleys. Not a soul was to be seen, not a living creature but a large bird of prey floating slowly in vast circles over his head. It was the early morning.

His servant had gone forward about half an hour before; the road which they had both to follow had been clearly pointed out; and Smeaton expected a ride of some twelve or thirteen miles before he could meet the messenger on his return. He gave himself up to thought, but not to that train of thought which perhaps might seem the most natural in his circumstances. He entered into no vain speculations as to the reply he should receive from the Earl of Stair. He suffered not his mind to rest upon the state of parties in the country, or upon the probabilities of the success or failure of the insurrection. He did not even dwell for a moment upon the various rumors of the day before, nor try to free himself, by reason, from any of those impressions—not exactly new, but revived—which had been produced in him by the zeal and enthusiasm of all those by whom he had been lately surrounded. His thoughts were of Emmeline, and Emmeline alone. That wonderful thing, association, had called up her image almost as strongly, as distinctly, as if her beautiful face and fair form had been before his eyes. The brown heath, the rounded hills, the gleams of sunshine, the floating clouds, the free elastic air, all brought back to memory the morning of his ride to the old church at Aleton, and Emmeline was the principal object in all that remembrance painted.

His thoughts and feelings, however, were his own, and peculiar. I do not believe that there are any two moments in a man's life in which he is exactly the same being, however well the general harmony of the character may be maintained. Years make a difference; months, days, events, circumstances, experience. The changes may be very sudden, or they may be so gradual as to be imperceptible at the time they are taking place; yet, fix any lengthened period, and we find them marked and distinct in the mind as well as in the body. There is as much difference between the sensations of forty and of twenty as between the face or form of the man and of the boy. Whether for better or for worse, we change them. They are things of the day, which pass from us and return no more.

Smeaton's love for Emmeline was intense, powerful, enthusiastic, but it was the love of a man, not of a boy. Ten years before, his thoughts would have been very different when turned toward her; more agitating, perhaps, but not so deep and strong. He dwelt, as a lover might dwell, on the beautiful memory of her look, the symmetry of her person, the music of her voice, the wild, untutored graces of her mind, the heart-breathing spirit which pervaded every thing she said and did; and the longing to hold her to his bosom again came upon him very strongly. He thought, too, with pain, of what must be her sensations, what her distress of mind, to be torn from him and carried away against her will, at the very moment when their happiness seemed almost secure; but it was not with that impulsive rashness which, a few years before, might have led him to fly to her in spite of obstacles, and without taking means to remove any of the difficulties which beset their path. He was old enough to struggle with his impulses, and generally to overcome them when he felt them to be rash.

Thus, in mingled meditation, he rode on, with sweet and pleasant images presented by memory, and painful reflections checkering the too bright vision.

He had not gone more than eight miles when he saw a man rapidly approaching him, down the slope of the opposite hill. He could hardly believe that his servant had returned so soon; yet the figure was so much the same—a diminutive man on a tall horse—that, though some distance intervened, he recognized him. They met at the bottom of the valley, and Smeaton asked eagerly,

"Well, what news? Have you brought me a letter?"

"I have brought your own back again, my lord," replied Higham, holding it out to his master as he rode up, "and no other answer could I get."

"No answer!" echoed Smeaton, taking the letter and seeing that it had been opened. "What did he say, or cause to be said to you?"

"Oh, he said very little," replied the man, "and caused nothing to be said at all, for he seemed quite capable of speaking for himself, and that pretty sharply. He broke open the letter, read it through from beginning to end, and then thrust it into my hand, saying, 'You had better ride back again.' I asked if he would not send an answer by me, or if he would send one afterward. But he said no answer was needed, and called out, 'Take it back to him who sent you. That is the only answer.'"

Smeaton's cheek burned, and his heart beat angrily.

"This is insult," he muttered. "This is insult as well as injury. Some day I may call him to account for it."

"I must say for him, my lord," added the man, "that it was not a lucky moment to fall upon, for he was at the head of the men drawn up on the little green, and just ready to march."

"That is no excuse," said Smeaton. "The same number of words, the same amount of breath, the same space of time, would have conveyed an honorable as a dishonorable reply. He might have said that he would write when he was at leisure, that he would see me if I would follow him, and that I might do so in safety. It would have cost no more time." Then, turning round his horse, with his heart all on fire, he asked himself, "Shall I stoop to be a beggar for simple justice? No, no. The case is very clear. They have made up their mind to drive every one they doubt into insurrection. They say, 'Those who are not for us are against us.' They have chosen their part with regard to me, it is time that I should choose mine with regard to them."

He had ridden slowly as he went, but he returned at a gallop, though the rapid motion did not tend to calm his feelings. The farm-house where he had slept was vacant of its guests. Richard Newark, his servant, and all the Keanton men were gone; but they had left word that, if Smeaton returned and sought them, he would find them at a place called the Waterfalls. The earl ordered the baggage-horse to be prepared directly, and in the mean time applied to the farmer for directions on the way after his party.

"I'll guide you, sir," replied the man. "There is something going on that I have an itching to have a hand in, and I think I'll pay some of the Newcastle keel-men for throwing me into the Tyne in one of their brute frolics."

Smeaton gladly accepted his guidance, and in about half an hour they set out, the earl riding a little in advance and alone, while the stout farmer jogged on conversing with the servant Higham. They took their way through a more cultivated part of the country than that which Smeaton had passed in the morning, but soon turned toward the hills again, and the farmer pointed out a piece of ground on the right, saying,

"That is Plainfield, my lord."

Smeaton, however, was busy with his own thoughts, and made no inquiry, not knowing any thing which should make Plainfield remarkable.* A few minutes afterward they began to ascend a somewhat steep hill, riding over the green turf, and as they wound round it to lessen the sharpness of the ascent, the young nobleman caught sight of a small party of horse gathered together at the distance of about a mile. "There are our friends, I think," he said.

"Ay, my lord, I dare say they are," replied the farmer.

The words seemed insignificant enough, but they were spoken in a significant tone, and the servant, Tom Higham, gave a low laugh.

A rise in the ground in another moment hid the party they had seen, and spurring quickly on, Smeaton soon came to the top of the height, whence a view of the country could be commanded for several miles. The prospect was very picturesque. The brown hill-side descended somewhat abruptly toward the more even country below, and was channeled by a sort of glen or ravine, through which leaped and tumbled a small mountain stream, fringed here and there with low trees and shrubs, but ever and anon glancing out under the eye, and catching the sunlight on its foam and spray.

Half way between the top of the hill and the head of this ravine was gathered together a party of men on horseback; not more than, if so many as, very frequently assembled on the most innocent occasions. In ordinary times, one would naturally have supposed that the little meeting consisted of a hunting party, or perhaps two or three dozen of gentlemen assembled to run their greyhounds. Besides those in this central situation, two or three small groups of horsemen were seen coming up from below at different degrees of speed, according to the steepness of the ascent; but still the whole number together might very well have formed a sporting party, only no dogs were to be seen. In the midst of the principal group, Smeaton's eye instantly picked out Richard Newark, who was mounted on a tall and remarkable white horse, and, riding quickly down toward him, he was soon by his side. The Keanton farmers, who were there assembled, greeted the approach of their young lord with a sort of half cheer, and one of them exclaimed aloud, "God bless your lordship! I thought you would not abandon us in time of need."

"What news from Lord Stair?" asked Richard, in a whisper.

"None," replied Smeaton, bitterly. "He sent back my letter, opened, but without reply."

"Then I must have been mistaken," said Richard Newark. "I thought that other hands must have been stirring your pottage for you, noble friend. Now the case is clear enough. Old Hanover won't have you for the giving."

* It was the place where the Earl of Derwentwater first openly took part in the insurrection.

"I never intended to give myself to *him*," replied Smeaton. "Nothing should ever induce me to draw my sword *against* a prince who has been pushed from the succession to the throne on a false and ridiculous pretense. But if they will force me to draw the sword *in his favor*, I can not help it: they must be gratified. Who are all these?" And as he spoke, he ran his eye over the rest of the persons present, who, gathered together in various knots, were regarding him with inquiring looks.

"Oh, you shall soon know them," returned Richard. "Common cause makes quick acquaintance. General Forster, here is my friend, the Earl of Eskdale—Lord Derwentwater, the Earl of Eskdale—Lord Widrington, the Earl of Eskdale."

"By my faith, we have more lords than soldiers," said the latter nobleman, with a laugh, "and more stout hearts and strong arms than weapons of war. It is to be hoped that supplies will flow in upon us somewhat rapidly."

"Come, come, my lord," said Forster, "you ought not to be the first to cry out, seeing that you have brought us the fewest men and the scantiest supply."

"Why, I only heard of the business last night," replied Lord Widrington, "and thought that this was but a preliminary meeting. Doubtless we shall have men enough, and weapons enough too, when once it is known we are in arms."

"Doubtless, doubtless," said the Earl of Derwentwater, a young and handsome man with a peculiarly prepossessing expression of countenance. "I am glad to see your lordship here," he continued, addressing Smeaton. "Your family have suffered much in the cause we all advocate; and I hope, by the success of our enterprise, you will recover what it lost—a success which, from the news we have just received, seems to be beyond doubt."

"Indeed!" said Smeaton. "May I ask what news that is?"

Derwentwater replied by detailing, in somewhat glowing language, and with a slight coloring from his own enthusiasm, all the first partial successes of the insurgents in Scotland. The greater part of the intelligence was merely confirmatory of the rumors which had reached Smeaton during the preceding day, that the Earl of Mar had taken Perth, that arms and ammunition had been seized at Burnt Island, that the army of King James III. was daily increasing in numbers, that money was flowing in rapidly, and that, while the troops of the house of Hanover were in a very critical position at Stirling, Mar was preparing to force the passage of the Forth, and that the Western clans were menacing the rear of King George's army. It was added that a great number of towns and districts of much importance had openly declared for the house of Stuart, and that King James had been proclaimed at Aberdeen, at Dunkeld, at Castle Gordon, at Brechin, at Montrose, at Dundee, and at Inverness, while the whole of Galloway and Dumfrieshire was stated to be flaming in insurrection.

Broad, general facts, without the small circumstances which modify them, and sometimes affect their whole bearings, are very apt to produce the most erroneous conclusions; and as Lord Derwentwater stated not, and probably knew not, the multitude of counterbalancing disadvantages under which the insurrectionary leaders lay, Smeaton naturally was led to look with a much more hopeful eye on the cause he had now determined to espouse.

His new acquaintance mentioned one important fact, namely, that the Duke of Argyle had taken command of the troops at Stirling. "But," added he, "with all his skill, he will have no easy task to prevent defeat, and probably surrender." He was not mistaken; for, had Mar possessed ordinary military knowledge and experience, there can be little doubt that the gallant nobleman opposed to him would have been forced to retreat, if retreat had been possible; but neither Derwentwater nor Lord Eskdale were at all personally aware that Mar was not a soldier, and the inconceivable folly of appointing a man totally destitute of military science to command an ill-disciplined army, in circumstances of the greatest delicacy and danger, did not once enter their imaginations. Nevertheless, the well-known skill, courage, and determination of Argyle, and the strong resolution he had shown in taking command in person of the small force at Stirling, led Smeaton to suspect that he either knew of circumstances or calculated upon events of which the Jacobite party in England were not at all aware.

It was too late now, however, he thought, to hesitate, even if his decision had depended upon the probabilities of success; and he joined the rest of the party in a hasty consultation, in which, from his want of all knowledge of the country round, he could give very little advice, except in regard to military matters, where he possessed more experience than any one present. Glad to have among them an officer of some skill, the noblemen and gentlemen present proceeded to an inspection of their little force, amounting in all, at this time, to only sixty or seventy horse. Arms they literally had none, except the ordinary riding swords used at that period in England (which were of little, if any use in the field), and here and there a brace of pistols at the saddle-bow. It was evidently an insurrection hurried forward without thought or preparation.

Every man, however, knew of some place where people would come in, in numbers great, to the standard of King James; but Smeaton pointed out that the most pressing necessity was to arm those who were already collected. The first blow, he said, should be struck at any place where their local knowledge showed them that a store of the necessary weapons was to be procured; but no one knew where any such supply existed except at Newcastle, which they were manifestly too feeble to attack. It was judged, therefore, needful to recruit their numbers even before they sought for arms; and those who were best acquainted with the district proposed that they should proceed to Rothbury and Warkworth, as the line in which recruits were most likely to come in.

Smeaton had nothing to object; and, forming into something like regular array, they rode from the place of meeting after a discussion which, though hurried and desultory, occupied several hours. The Northumbrian noblemen and gentlemen were full of hope and enthusiasm; but the young earl who had so unwillingly joined them viewed the matter with less sanguine anticipations, and, from the expressions of his new companions, derived no very favorable idea of their capability of conducting a great enterprise to a successful conclusion.

CHAPTER XXXI.

What need I tell of the first proceedings of the small body of gentlemen whom we have seen set out on the path of insurrection? How they marched to Rothbury, and thence to hermit-loving Warkworth; how they received small re-enforcements as they went along, and proclaimed King James the Third wherever they came; and how at Morpeth their numbers were increased to three hundred horse—are all facts well known to every body. Neither need I pause to describe the disappointment and apprehension occasioned by the scantiness of the numbers which came in on each day's march, nor dwell upon the anxious consultations which took place night after night, when they still found themselves unprepared for any enterprise of importance.

All hope of successfully attacking Newcastle soon passed away, and only one event occurred to brighten the dark prospect before them, namely, the capture of Holy Island by one of their number, Lancelot Errington, a gentleman of ancient family long resident near Hexham. The very next tidings received, however, were to the effect that the small fort had been re-taken by the troops from Berwick, and that Errington was wounded and a prisoner.

This was a bitter disappointment, for the least success in such perilous enterprises raises hope high, and often paves the way for other advantages. They flattered themselves that they only wanted some happy exploit to rouse the neighboring gentry in their favor; to encourage the timid and confirm the wavering. But the disaster which followed this first gleam extinguished all such vain hopes, and the principal leaders met, the evening after the intelligence was received, to consult as to what was to be done.

They were bold and high-hearted men, though few of them brought skill, experience, or wisdom to the cause, and not one of them would listen to the course which, probably, some inward conviction told each of them was the only path of safety, namely, dispersing their followers, abandoning the enterprise, and making their submission. Yet what was to be done? All their expectations of a general rising were at an end; they had no infantry, nor weapons wherewith to arm infantry; troops were reported to be marching toward them from various quarters, and all they had to oppose to them was only three hundred horse!

Many a plan was proposed—many a course suggested—at their sad conference, till at length Smeaton, who had sat silent and thoughtful, with his head resting on his hand, looked up, saying,

"It seems to me, my lords and gentlemen, that there is but one thing to be done. With such scanty means as we can command, no great purpose can be effected. We can not even undertake one of those trifling enterprises which, when successful, often change altogether the fortunes of such movements as these. We must have more men before we can do any thing."

"Ay, but where are we to get them, my good lord?" asked Lord Widrington. "That is the question which puzzles us all."

"Thus," replied Smeaton, boldly. "We have certain intelligence that Lord Kenmure, the Earl of Nithsdale, and other noblemen and gentlemen, are in arms just across the border, to the number, we are assured, of four or five hundred men. They have already undertaken several movements of importance, and, when joined by our small force, will be able to effect much more. The object of our own body, and of that under the noblemen I have mentioned, should be to unite as soon as possible, which can easily be done, either by our withdrawing at once from Northumberland and joining Kenmure, or by that nobleman advancing to our support and enabling us to undertake some enterprise of importance. Much can be done either in the north of England or in the south of Scotland by eight hundred men, which can not even be thought of by three hundred; and my own opinion is, that we should march at daybreak to-morrow to effect our junction with Viscount Kenmure, and, by giving force and vigor to the insurrection in the Lowlands, occupy the troops of the house of Hanover, and enable the Earl of Mar to profit fully by his advantageous position and the number of his forces."

This proposal, like every other proposal in a meeting where there is no real subordination, called forth a long and rambling discussion, and a great variety of opinions. Every one saw the wisdom of joining the two streams of insurrection in one, but none agreed as to the mode in which it was to be effected. National prejudices and antipathies, engendered by long border warfare, were by no means extinct; and although some few saw the prudence of Smeaton's suggestion of withdrawing from Northumberland, and confining their operations for the time to the south of Scotland, others declared that many of their followers would abandon the cause if such a retreat were attempted; and one gentleman boldly announced his belief that, in that case, they should not take fifty men across the border with them. This opinion prevailed, and it was determined to negotiate with Lord Kenmure for the advance of his forces into England.

The next question was, who was to be the negotiator? No one present was personally acquainted with the Scottish nobleman; and, to say truth, few liked to undertake a task in which they might very naturally expect to meet with a repulse, for every one felt it to be but little likely that Kenmure would cross the border with his men, without some better inducements than they had in their power to hold out. At length, after a number of excuses had been given by various gentlemen in the room for not undertaking the task, the Earl of Eskdale volunteered to be the person.

"I will endeavor," he said, "if you intrust me with the commission, to induce Lord Kenmure to join you, and will, of course, refrain from pointing out to him, whatever may be my own opinion, that it would be wiser for you to join him. However, I can not use any arguments in opposition if he should urge the latter course, but it will be better for General Forster to write to him by my hands, employing all those arguments which have been conclusive in his own mind."

Forster, however, was very unwilling to write, and only in the end consented to give such credentials to the young earl as would show that he was authorized to treat by the whole party. Even these he would have postponed till the following morning, alleging various motives for delay; but Smeaton interrupted him somewhat impatiently, saying,

"There is no time to be lost, sir. The distance is considerable, if the forces of Lord Kenmure are at Moffat, as we have been informed. We are more than thirty miles from Wooler; and, whether I take the road by Coldstream or direct to Kelso, nearly two days must be consumed in my journey alone. Then will come the negotiation, which may be more tedious than we imagine, as well as the march of the troops hither. I shall therefore most decidedly set out to-night; and if I might advise, you would, at all events, retire upon Rothbury, which is so far on the way to meet our friends from the North. If there is any delay, you may all be cut to pieces before they arrive to your support."

"Oh, we shall retire to Rothbury, of course," said Lord Derwentwater; "and the credentials can soon be prepared, without much trouble to any one. If you are willing to set out so speedily, it must not be any act of ours that delays you."

"In half an hour I shall be ready," replied Smeaton, rising, "and in the mean time I trust that the paper will be drawn up."

It was a full hour, however, before he set out, and then, notwithstanding the entreaties of Van Noost to be allowed to accompany him, the young earl departed only attended by his servant.

The light was already failing rapidly, and before many minutes had passed night fell over his road. A little more than three hours brought him to Wooler, with tired horses and a somewhat anxious mind, for he felt all the importance of the mission he had undertaken, and the movement of troops in the neighborhood of Berwick rendered it not at all improbable that he might be stopped upon the way. He found the little town of Wooler quiet and soldierless, however, and, as the hour was not late, he had no difficulty in procuring refreshment at the little inn for himself, his servant, and his horses.

Anxious to cross the border, beyond which the general feelings of the country people rendered the roads more safe to persons engaged in the Jacobite cause, he only gave himself an hour and a half's rest, and then set out again, taking the direct road to Kelso, which, though at that time steep and rugged enough, had great advantages over that by Coldstream, both in point of distance and of security, for he had learned at Wooler that a small party of horse had occupied the latter town during the morning. He was forced to proceed somewhat slowly, indeed, for his horses had been in exercise already during the early part of the day, and the wearisome twenty miles to Kelso occupied several hours.

The whole town, when he entered it, was profoundly still, and the inhabitants plunged in sleep. Not a solitary light was to be seen in any window, and the young nobleman had no means of knowing whether he might not rouse a lion instead of a lamb if he attempted to wake any of the good citizens from their slumbers. In these circumstances, he resolved to push forward, notwithstanding the weariness of his horse, and trust for hospitality to the first small hamlet or cottage he could meet with. He reckoned without his host, however, for at that time the country between Kelso and Hawick was much less thickly peopled than at present, and after going some two miles further, he was fain to turn the horses into a green meadow at the bottom of a valley, and seek shelter for himself and his servant beneath a loose stone wall.

The autumnal wind was blowing bleak and cold, but the beasts were better off than the men, for they soon found provender sufficient in the meadow, while their riders were left without food. Tom Higham groaned in the spirit as he sat, wrapped up in his cloak, shivering behind the wall, and Smeaton could hear him more than once muttering to himself,

"I am a mighty great fool—that is as clear as moonshine."

Perhaps the young nobleman thought the same of himself; but he bore his situation more patiently, and, shrouding himself from the cutting blast as well as he could, tried to obtain some sleep, as he had often done in other lands under similar circumstances.

It was in such lonely and darksome hours, when the mind was the most depressed and action impossible, that the thought of Emmeline frequently presented itself to Smeaton. The remembrance was like an angel visit; for, although many a melancholy and many an anxious train of ideas was awakened by the recollection of her and of her fate, yet there was something in the images then called up which left his mind calmed and even cheered. I believe it is a quality of high, pure love to strengthen and to elevate, however adverse may be the circumstances. The images which now arose in his mind effectually banished sleep; and when the gray daylight at length began to appear in the east, he was still waking, though his servant had been long buried in deep slumber. Smeaton rose at once, and, rousing the man, told him to catch the horses, and replace the saddles and bridles.

"Ay," cried Tom Higham, "we had better do that before any one comes and catches *us*; for the beasts have had a good feed at Sawney's expense, and a canny Scot is not a man to let us off scot free if he catches us."

"He shall not need," replied Smeaton, taking out his purse and putting down a couple of shillings on the top of the stone wall. "I trust he will find them; but, if not, my conscience is free."

The horses gave them some trouble, for they were not at all willing to leave their comfortable pasture for the hard, stony road; and just when the young nobleman had got his own beast by the forelock, he heard the voice of his man calling for help in lamentable accents. Turning round, he beheld good Master Higham in the grasp of a very tall, stout man, in an ordinary farming dress, and, leading his horse up, he inquired what was the matter.

"I can not understand what he means," cried Tom Higham; "but I know that he talks something about spearing me, or my spearing at him, though devil a spear there is among us."

Smeaton, however, more conversant, from his family connections, with the language of the country, was soon made to comprehend that the farmer, having seen two horses in his field from the window of his house, which lay hard by, though the darkness had previously concealed it, had come down in high wrath to repel an intrusion which, to say truth, was somewhat common at that time and in that part of the country.

"My good friend," replied the young nobleman, "we took refuge here in the night, neither very well knowing the way nor where to find shelter, and I certainly did not intend to go away without paying for the grass which the horses have taken."

"No that likely," replied the man, doggedly. "If ye wanted shelter, why did na ye joost tirl at the pin up by, or gie a halloo under the window?"

"Because I did not know there was a window near," replied Smeaton, with a smile. "As to my intention of paying you, you can satisfy yourself; for, before I went to help my servant in catching the horses, I put a couple of shillings down on the top of the wall, which I thought must be sufficient for the grass they had eaten."

The cautious farmer let go his hold of Higham's neck; but, before he expressed himself satisfied or otherwise, walked straight to the wall and took up the money, which he speedily found. His countenance brightened at once; and the young earl said to himself, with a somewhat cynical smile, "I wish my poor father's countrymen would not give so much cause for the imputation of greediness which their Southern neighbors are so ready to throw upon them."

He was mistaken, however, in the present instance; for, as soon as he approached, the good farmer held out the money to him, saying, "Here, tak' the siller. It was no for that I was a bit cankered wi' the wee body;" and he went on to explain that it was the fact of the horses being put into the field without his leave which had roused his ire. "There's na that man leeving," he continued, "wha can say I ever grudged him a bit for himself or his beastie; but ye might hae found a better beild up by, if ye had just trotted on a bit."

Nothing would serve him now, but he must give the two travelers some breakfast at what he called "his wee thack housie," which proved a very comfortable farm dwelling.

As information was one of the earl's greatest wants, he readily accepted the invitation, much to the joy and satisfaction of Tom Higham, who soon contrived to catch his horse and follow his master and the farmer as they walked away out of the field and up the road. It was not easy to induce the latter to speak upon any dangerous subject. The moment that politics, or the state of the parties then existing was mentioned, he curled himself like a hedge-hog, to use Tom Higham's expression, and it was not till he had discovered that his less weary guest was going to Moffat for the purpose of seeing the Viscount Kenmure that he at all unfolded himself. Then, indeed, he spoke more freely, but with a certain degree of caution still, as if not yet quite convinced that the English traveler was not trying to worm the secret of his political propensities out of him. He cared not for one king or the other, he said—no, not a bodle. He was a peaceable man, and they might fight it out among them; but as for the Viscount Kenmure and "his handfu' of men," he had heard tell, but he would not warrant it, for he knew nothing of his own knowledge, that he was not at Moffat at all, but at the town of Hawick.

At the same time, as far as slight indications went, he seemed not to be ill disposed to the cause of the house of Stuart. He took particular pains to direct Smeaton right on the road to Hawick, and insisted upon feeding both the horses with something more solid than the grass which they had cropped during the night. Gradually, too, he relaxed a little in regard to intelligence, and informed the young nobleman that there was no force capable of opposing the march of the Jacobite forces within many miles. He added that he had heard at Kelso market that Kenmure had given the good folks of Dumfries a fright some days before, but that, finding the citizens better prepared than he had expected, he had retreated to Langholm and thence to Hawick. As to the number of Kenmure's forces, he either could not or would not give any information; but it was, at all events, satisfactory to the young nobleman to find that his journey was greatly shortened; and, after having partaken of the worthy man's good cheer, he remounted and set out upon his way.

A ride of a few hours brought him to Hawick; but he found that Kenmure had not thought fit to take up his quarters in the town itself, but had occupied a village at a few miles' distance, where his cavalry was less likely to be embarrassed in case of attack. Thither, then, the young nobleman pursued his journey, guided by a country lad on foot, for the directions he received were far too elaborate and confused to be easily comprehended.

In consequence of various delays, he did not come in sight of the village till toward three o'clock, and then but very few symptoms of any thing like a numerous body of men were to be perceived. A sentry, if so he could be called, with a broadsword at his side and a pistol in his hand, was seen at the end of the long street of straggling, irregular houses which constituted the village, and here and there a person in the garb of a gentleman, booted and spurred, but with no other arms than his sword, was observed loitering about the doors. No precaution was taken on his entering the village, the sentry merely directing him, when he asked for the Lord Kenmure, to the minister's house near the kirk; and, wending his way through heaps of filth and cabbage stalks, which occupied a certain space before every house, and rendered the road well-nigh impassable for any vehicle on wheels, he at length reached the entrance of the manse, before which stood a similar figure to that which kept sentry at the commencement of the village. The approach of a couple of horsemen had caused a little commotion in the place, and two or three heads were thrust from the windows as Smeaton rode up; but he was admitted to the room in which the viscount sat without any delay, and presented to him the brief note he bore from Mr. Forster.

A long deliberation ensued, in the course of which many questions were asked by the Scottish nobleman. Smeaton told him the exact truth in regard to the numbers and position of the little insurgent force in Northumberland, adding that they had heard that the Lord Kenmure's troop amounted to five hundred men.

"I wish it did," replied the viscount, with a somewhat cold laugh. "I think, if that had been the case, my lord, you would have had to come on to Dumfries. No, no. I will deal honestly by you, as you have dealt by me. If you are a handful, we are less. We do not number more than one half the force you say General Forster has with him."

"Then the more need of your immediate union," observed the young earl.

"Ay, but it would have been better for him to come to me than for me to go to him," responded Kenmure. "Something might have been done here; but I gather from what you say, my noble friend, that little is to be done on the other side of the border, and every step I take in that direction draws me further from my resources and from all chance of support, of which we have good hope from the North."

"It is too late now, I fear, my lord," said Smeaton, "to consider such objections. Perhaps the course you mention might have been wisest. Here are two small parties, engaged in the same cause, but separate from each other, with considerable bodies of the enemy's troops hovering round them. If you continue in this state of isolation, at fifty or sixty miles' distance, you are liable at any moment to be cut up in detail, without the power of aiding each other, and probably before your succor from the North can arrive. Allow me to urge that it would be very much better for you to march without delay to join the gentlemen in Northumberland. You will then have a force of about five hundred men united, with which you can show a firm face to the enemy, even if you can not undertake any great enterprise; and should it be judged necessary, after consultation with General Forster, you can fall back upon your resources here, and make good any well-chosen position till you are re-enforced."

"Well, well," replied Lord Kenmure, "I must consult with my friends here before we can decide; but, in the mean time, I must care for your accommodation during the night. We have crammed the manse as full as it can hold already, and I fear you will have but poor accommodation. Some one be good enough to call Quarter-master Calderwood."

This was accordingly done; and, after a short consultation between that personage and Lord Kenmure, the young earl was placed in his hands, to be conducted to the only quarters which could be assigned to him, and left the manse somewhat doubtful as to the result of the consultation which was about to commence.

CHAPTER XXXII

Darkness was rapidly descending when the Earl of Eskdale, guided by Quarter-master Calderwood, entered the little street of the hamlet. They found Tom Higham amusing himself with talking nonsense in a strong London jargon to some Scotch lads assembled round the door, who hardly understood what he said, and whose own language was well-nigh incomprehensible to him. His master beckoned him to follow with the horses, and was led to the very outskirts of the village, where a small cottage appeared, in no very good state of preservation, and quite separated from the rest of the hamlet, being situated in the midst of its own garden or kail-yard.

"This is the only place I can assign to your lordship," said Calderwood, as they approached, "and I fear you must share it with another gentleman who joined us this afternoon from France. There is room, however, for two, and I must dispose of the servants elsewhere."

"I am in no way nice, quarter-master," replied Smeaton. "I have been too much accustomed to a life in arms to mind sleeping under that wall, should it be necessary."

"Ah, my lord, I am glad to hear it," replied Calderwood. "We are sadly in want of a few men of experience among us."

The ordinary reflection passed through Smeaton's mind, that the more men are wanting in experience themselves, the less are they inclined to profit by the experience of others; but he forbore reply, and Calderwood opened the door. No passage, no internal door, shut the single room in the lower part of the house from the external air; and on entering, Smeaton found himself at once in a large apartment, tenanted by four persons. One was in the garb of a servant; two others seemed to be the master of the tenement and his wife, a sandy-haired man and a black-haired woman of about forty years of age, and these three were bustling about, apparently preparing for the evening meal. The fourth person was seated before a blazing fire on the north side of the cottage. He was tall, stout, and apparently well dressed; but the last gleam of day being on the point of extinction, no candles lighted, and a considerable quantity of smoke in the room, not much could be discerned of his figure by the flickering flame of the fire.

Mr. Calderwood spoke a few words to him, explaining the necessity under which Lord Kenmure lay of quartering another gentleman in the same tenement. The stranger immediately rose, with some polite expression of pleasure, and, while the good woman of the house lighted a solitary candle, advanced to meet the new comer.

The presence of the stranger was dignified and easy, his figure fine, and his face, if not altogether handsome or pleasing, striking and remarkable. He had much the air of a military man, and his profession or his propensities seemed indicated by a deep and somewhat recent scar upon his brow.

The moment he saw Smeaton, his face flushed either with pleasure or some other emotion; and the young nobleman, after gazing at him for a moment, as if partly recognizing him and partly doubting his own eyes, held out his hand, saying,

"This is an unexpected pleasure."

The stranger took his offered hand and shook it hard, but with a peculiar look, not the most cordial. Putting his face close to Smeaton's ear, he said,

"Call me Somerville—my name is Somerville here."

Smeaton quietly inclined his head, saying,

"I believed you were in very distant lands,

Mr. Somerville. When did you return to Europe?"

"Three or four months ago," replied his companion. "I have been wandering about in France since. Now, my good woman, will my supper never be ready? Come, bestir yourself, and add something to it for this gentleman, who is doubtless as hungry as I am."

There was evidently a feeling of restraint upon him as he spoke, which he endeavored in vain to cover by an affectation of ease and carelessness; and the moment he had addressed this adjuration to the woman of the house, he fell into a fit of thought, without at all attending to her grumbling reply.

Smeaton was also thoughtful, but he did not lose his ease and calmness; and, by a few good-humored words, soon induced their hostess to hurry herself somewhat more than she had been doing previously.

I might give a long detail of all the little events which took place during the next hour, and relate how Smeaton's servant, and the servant of the gentleman calling himself Somerville, were provided with quarters elsewhere; how a bare-legged damsel, with all the beauty of youth and health, a clear complexion, and large black eyes, came in to borrow a pot, and was not suffered to depart without many gallant compliments and a half-resisted kiss from Mr. Somerville; and how two pretty children, with very scanty clothing, from a neighboring cottage, stood leaning upon each other, and watched the strange gentlemen who had come, while they enjoyed the meal prepared for them. But I must pass over all such minute facts, and bring the reader at once to the moment when, after having concluded their supper, Smeaton and his companion were alone together, the host and hostess having retired to their early rest, leaving the two gentlemen with a large jug of whisky on the table and a kettle of hot water on the fire.

More than once during the earlier part of the meal Somerville had given a momentary glance at his companion's face from under his heavy eyebrows, but withdrawn it as soon as he perceived that Smeaton's eyes were directed toward him. He meditated much and often too; and, as I have said, there was an uneasy air about him which surprised his comrade for the time, for, when he had known him slightly some years before, he was famous for that easy, daring impudence which was much affected in all countries by the class called men of wit and pleasure.

When they were left alone together, however, Smeaton at once changed the tone of conversation, saying,

"Well, now we are without witnesses, we may speak of more interesting matters, Newark. When did you return from South America? I heard with great surprise, when I was at Nancy, that you had determined to turn merchant, and had taken some *nom-de-guerre*."

"Ay, a merchant *adventurer*," retorted the other, laying great stress upon the last word. "But it was more in the latter than the former character that I went, my good lord. I have been back, as I told you, about three months, after having gilded my purse with a few ducats in the New World, let the Dons' blood when they were in danger of calenture from too much heat, and basked in the sweet smiles of the olive-brown dames of Peru and Mexico. I got tired of that, as of every thing else in this wearisome world; and, hearing that stirring times were coming in this quarter, I thought I might as well return and stake a trifle—such as life and fortune—upon the game that is to be played, in the hope of recovering, somehow or another, a portion of what I and mine have lost."

"Did you see your uncle and aunt when you were in France?" asked Smeaton, fixing his eyes steadily upon him.

"No," replied the other, in a careless tone. "The good lord, my uncle, is somewhat worse than senile, having fallen into a decrepitude of temper as well as of mind and body. He has turned himself into a corn-merchant, too, which does not suit my notions of propriety; and as he never appreciated my high qualities and good points, I did not think it worth while to trouble him with my presence."

"I know you never agreed," remarked Smeaton; "and, of course, it is not for me to say which was in the right—"

"Meaning that I was in the wrong," said the other, with a laugh.

But Smeaton continued as if he had not been interrupted, saying,

"You do not do him justice when you talk of senility. His mind is as clear and strong as ever, and his bodily frame but little shaken by the passing of years. I have had every opportunity of judging, having passed some weeks with himself and Lady Newark before I came to England."

"Ah! is he so strong in virtue and in muscles?" exclaimed the other, with a bitter laugh. "Heaven receive him to the place of saints, and that right speedily!"

"Nay, nay," said Smeaton, "I am sure, Newark, that wish is more upon your lips than in your heart."

"It is not, by ——," cried the other, with a fierce oath. "I should then be Lord Newark, at all events; and as to ever getting back the lands as well as the lordship, that would be as the stars willed it, and they have always been kinder to me than he."

"I do not think you ever judged him fairly," said Smeaton, gravely. "He was certainly very kind to you in early life, and strained his small means to afford you a high education along with his two poor sons; but—"

"But I was what old women call wild, you would say," cried the other, who seemed to have a great habit of interrupting. "Well, I *was* wild, and scoffed a little at the doctrines and notions of elderly gentlewomen of both sexes, liking much better the doctrines of younger ladies, and occasionally quarreled with gentlemen and soldiers who entertained heretical notions as to my right and liberties in certain cases. But what of that? I was none the worse for that. No, no, Eskdale. The head and front of my offense was his own weakness, folly, or treachery, in suffering his daughter to remain in the hands of the knave John Newark."

"How could he help it?" asked Smeaton. "His life was not worth an hour's purchase if he ventured into England, and there was no one in this island on whom he could rely to take her from the sort of imprisonment in which she was kept, and replace her under her father's care. Doubt not, he would willingly have done it, had it been possible."

"Why did he not rely on me?" retorted the other, vehemently. "I would have released her, and brought her safely to France. I offered to do it—I had every thing prepared; but he would not hear of it."

He muttered something to himself which Smeaton did not clearly hear, and then went on aloud:

"He made me appear like a vain boaster in the eyes of a dozen people. I told sweet John Newark that I would take away the girl from him, and cut his throat in the house where he has ensconced himself so snugly. I will do it, too, before I have done with him."

"You must get him out of the Tower first," replied Smeaton, "for he is safely lodged there by this time."

"Ha!" exclaimed the other, laughing aloud. "A bagged fox! But come, now," he continued, in a gayer tone, "what report do you make of that fair west countrie, which I hear you have been visiting lately? Was Sir John flourishing when you were there? And what adventures did you meet with?"

"Sir John was quite well, and apparently prosperous," replied Smeaton; "that is to say, till the very day I came away, on the morning of which he was apprehended, and sent, I imagine, to the Tower. As to adventures, I met with few, and those not much worth relating."

He paused for a moment, asking himself if he should say more; but the other again went on, inquiring,

"What of the lady—what of the fair lady, sweet Mistress Emmeline? Is she as beautiful as I hear?"

"She is very beautiful and very amiable," replied Smeaton.

"And the son—Sir John Newark's son?" demanded the other. "They say his father intends to marry him to Emmeline, in the hope of securing his title to the estates under all circumstances, and obtaining the title of Baron Newark, whatever party is in power. Did you hear any thing of all this?"

"Nothing," replied Smeaton, thoughtfully. "From the character of the man, indeed," he continued, "such a scheme is not unlikely, but I do not think there could be any idea of carrying it immediately into execution. Richard Newark is a mere boy, some years younger than Emmeline herself. When first I saw him in London, he was rude, wild, and strange; but he has wonderfully improved, both in intellect and manners, in the troublous scenes we have gone through; and though he will ever be eccentric and very different from other persons, yet there are high and good qualities in him which make me love and esteem him much."

"Is he with his father in London?" asked the other, quietly.

"No," replied Smeaton. "He came with me into Northumberland to join the Northumbrian gentlemen now in arms; and if Lord Kenmure agrees to the proposal which I have brought him this evening for a union of the two forces, you will see him in a day or two. In that case," he continued, gravely, almost sternly, "I must request you to treat him with all kindness, remembering that his father's faults are not his, and that he is under my protection."

The other laughed, though the hint galled him a little.

"Oh, certainly," he replied. "Your high and mighty protection, Lord Eskdale, will not be needed against me. I am not going to quarrel with a boy, nor to cut his throat because his father's ought to have been cut long ago; so there was no need of any threat."

"I used no threat indeed, Newark," said the earl; "but, knowing you are of a quick and impetuous temper, merely suggested considerations which I thought would enable you to control it."

"Ay, right good," returned the other; "but there is no fear. I am not quarrelsome nowadays, Heaven knows, or there is many a man I might quarrel with, without seeking out a boy for the purpose. But what, in this rout and dispersion, has become of fair Emmeline herself? Have you brought her too with you into Northumberland?"

"No indeed," replied the young earl. "Sir John has taken her to London with him."

"Damnation!" muttered the other. "Why," he added, after an effort to control himself, "if he had left her behind at Ale, nothing would have been so easy as to get her off to France."

"But he did not so leave her," replied Smeaton, calmly. "And now, Newark, I will go and lie down in the room they showed me, for I have ridden hard and far, and passed last night under a stone wall. I must be up early, too, in the morning, for these noble lords here must come to a speedy decision, and that decision must be communicated at once to General Forster."

"Well, I shall stay here and make some way in the flagon," said the other. "Though this stuff, which is just the same as they call usquebagh in Ireland, is little better than molten fire, yet I feel my blood wants warming in this accursed cold country."

"Your blood was always hot enough," observed Smeaton, moving toward the end of the stairs, "and that spirit is too strong for me; so good-night, Newark;" and he retired to rest.

The other remained for two hours or more, till the candle had nearly burned into the socket. During that time, however, he drank little, but was absorbed in deep meditation, checkered apparently by many various feelings, for now he laughed, and now he looked stern and fierce.

"He did not recognize me," he muttered, "that is clear—no, not even by the mark he put upon my forehead. He shall pay that debt, but not just now. I can wait; and the interest will accumulate. We may make something of this," he again muttered, after a long pause, "we may make something of this. Let me see. John in prison on a charge of high treason; William marries the heiress; and then—what then? Why, services to the house of Hanover; one slight whirl of the weather-cock, and all is safe, especially if one could bring some intelligence with one. A Newark on the side of Hanover! That seems a strange figure of speech. One starts at it. Why should I care for whom I draw my sword? What have the Stuarts done for me? Ah! ha! ha! Doubtless there will be plenty to keep me in countenance."

Thus saying, he rose, and retired also to rest.

Before daybreak on the following morning the young earl was up and dressed, and the sky was still gray when a messenger from Lord Kenmure reached him, requesting his presence at that nobleman's head-quarters. He found every thing in bustle and activity, and he could see at once that a resolution was taken.

"We have just come to a sudden determination, my lord," said Kenmure, when Smeaton entered. "We find that Brigadier Macintosh, instead of advancing at once, after passing the Frith of Forth, has marched toward Edinburgh. He writes word, however, that he will join us shortly with his infantry, if we can maintain ourselves for a few days in the South, and gather together a body of cavalry. We have, therefore, resolved to advance as far as Rothbury to effect our junction with General Forster. It will then be necessary to retire across the border, and take measures for keeping up our communication with Macintosh. We shall consequently be your companions instead of your followers on the march."

In an hour from that time the troop was mounted and on its way: but when in full array, its numbers and its equipment were inferior even to the young earl's expectations.

CHAPTER XXXIII.

It was on the evening of the brightest day which had shone for the last fortnight when the Earl of Eskdale, accompanied by Mr. William Newark, under the name of Somerville, and followed by their two servants, rode into the small town of Rothbury. They found the place all gay and busy, the news of the advance of Lord Kenmure having reached it some hours before, and spread joy and expectation among the disheartened gentlemen of Northumberland. Half a dozen times, in riding through the little street, the young nobleman was stopped to inquire how far distant was the Scottish force, and his reply of "half a day's march" seemed to give universal satisfaction.

One of the readiest to accost him was Van Noost, who, after having received his answer to the first question, ran on by the side of the earl's horse, telling him, with great pride and satisfaction, that he had taken upon himself the duty of engineer and armorer—that he had repaired and polished innumerable guns and pistols, and cast some thousands of bullets for the service of the forces.

"Your lordship's quarters are quite ready for you, too," he cried. "I have taken care of that. All the Keanton men are lodged together in those two white houses; and in the one on this side is a capital apartment for you, next to the quarters of Master Richard. By-the-way," he continued, "a boy has arrived from Ale-Manor with a large packet for you, which should have come to hand six days ago; but the poor lad has had to hunt us all over the country; and it is wonderful how he has escaped the enemy, for he has been in the very heart of General Carpenter's dragoons at Newcastle, and brought us intelligence of all his doings."

A few steps more took them to the house which Van Noost had pointed out, and Richard Newark came down to the door to meet his noble friend. He greeted him with every mark of joy and satisfaction, but glanced his eye from time to time toward Smeaton's companion with a look of inquiry and distrust. He rambled on, indeed, in his usual way, saying, as the earl dismounted and gave directions regarding the horses and the servants,

"Well, Eskdale, so you have brought us the Scots. Now there is hope of doing something, for all this marching and countermarching is poor stuff, and I have felt like one out of a flock of sheep, driven hither and thither by the shepherd's dog. The man does not hear me. The Scotch wind has blown away his hearing. Eskdale, I say, there is a large packet come for you from Ale, addressed to you in Madame Culpepper's own peculiar cipher. I had a thousand minds to break it open, for I longed for news, and I am sure there must be some for me. But a seal—I don't like fingering a seal. Strange that a little bit of red resin, under the effect of our prejudices, should be stronger than an iron box!"

Smeaton shook him warmly by the hand, and, requesting his companion of the march to follow, entered the house with his young friend, who asked, in a low voice,

"Who have you got there? His face does not please me."

"It is, nevertheless, the face of a relation of yours," replied Smeaton. "I will introduce him to you as soon as we are alone; but let me see this packet. It may contain news of importance."

At the top of the first flight of steps were two good rooms, one of which, on the right hand, was retained for the use of the young nobleman, and here he found the packet which had been mentioned. Breaking it open at once, he perceived that it contained two letters for himself and two for Richard Newark. Giving the latter instantly to his young friend, he invited Somerville to seat himself before he opened the letters which bore his own address, although one of them, in a small, delicate hand—more like that of a lady in the present day than one of those times—seemed too precious to be long delayed. As soon as he had shown this piece of attention to his guest, he retreated into the window, and eagerly broke the seal of the letter addressed as I have mentioned. He was not deceived. Emmeline's name was at the bottom of the lines that were written upon the page; and with a beating heart he read words which might well have come from a more experienced mind, or a less tender and affectionate heart. Yet love and tenderness were evident throughout, as the contents may show.

"My beloved Husband,—I snatch a moment and an opportunity to write to you, knowing what you must feel, but not knowing what you are doing. Anxious as I am to hear where you are, and all that you can tell me of your proceedings, I fondly believe that you are more anxious still to hear of your Emmeline. I am in London, in a small lodging near the Tower, at number thirty-two in Tower Street, surrounded by the servants of my cousin, Sir John Newark, and, as he believes, cut off from all communication with other persons by their means. Among them, however, is one placed there by her who has befriended us at Ale-Manor, and who has found means to assure me that he is devoted alone to my service. He will contrive to convey this to Devonshire. The time allowed me is but short.

"And now, what shall I say to you, my dear husband? I need not speak of love and gratitude. I need not tell you how my whole heart is devoted to you. I need not say how earnestly I wish it were possible for you to come yourself, and either claim me as your own in the face of all the world, or take me home in secret to spend my life with you in quiet retirement and content. But I must beseech you on no account to venture near this city, unless you can do so in perfect safety; to sacrifice for Emmeline no security, to run no risk, and, above all, not to let affection for her—that eagerness to see her which I am sure you feel—nor the indignation which you must experience at the conduct you have met with, induce you to take any part in the struggle for the crown of these realms which your own calm and ever just judgment does not warrant. I am sure you will not; and yet I write these words because I feel that it will be a comfort to you to know that Emmeline has no selfish wish to be gratified at your expense. Consult your own honor, consult your own dignity. Think of her; love her forever, but do not let one thought of her, one feeling for her, influence you in circumstances where duty and honor are concerned, knowing that your honor is far dearer to her than her own happiness or her own life.

"Oh, how I long to see you! How I long to tell you, dear Henry, all I have suffered, all I have thought, all I have felt—to pour out my whole soul and heart to him who has alone seen and known them. But let not my longing have the least weight with you. Act as if I had never existed, or as if you had never known me; but let the memory of your Emmeline be as the miniature-portrait of one well loved, ever nearest to your heart, and think, whenever you think of her, that she is blessing you, and praying for you, and beseeching Heaven to guide, preserve, and prosper you in whatever course your own wisdom and God's grace shall lead you.

"I know not how to end my letter. The words seem so strange that I have to write; and yet I am—I feel—I know I am—

"Your affectionate and dutiful wife,

"Emmeline Eskdale."

Smeaton, with all his warm and strong enthusiasm, was not a man of that soft and melting character which tender feelings, and what was then called "sentiment," easily moved to tears. In those days, and for nearly a century afterward, there was what I may call a lachrymose school, which was weeping on every occasion where any thing touching presented itself or could be found. He was not of this school, and hardly knew of its existence; yet the words of his dear and beautiful Emmeline brought the moisture into his eyes, and he turned to the window that no one might mark what he considered a weakness.

The other letter contained merely a few lines from Mrs. Culpepper, but they were not of much significance, merely informing him that Sir John Newark was lodged in the Tower to await trial, that the accompanying epistle had come from the Lady Emmeline, together with the letters addressed to Mr. Richard Newark, and that she herself, Mrs. Culpepper, was most anxious to hear of his proceedings, pointing out at the same time the boy who brought the letters as one whose wit and conduct justified the fullest confidence.

In the mean while, Richard Newark had opened the two letters addressed to himself, which were both in his father's hand, and had been written evidently under the idea that they might be opened and read before they were forwarded. The first was dated Exeter, and contained but a few lines, which were to the following effect:

"My dear Son,—I beseech you, as soon as you receive these, to set out and join me without any delay. Should I be removed from Exeter before your arrival, you will easily gain intelligence of where I am, along the road. Follow quick, and delay not, as you value the love of

"Your affectionate father,

John Newark."

The second letter was more in detail, and in not so mild a tone. It told the young gentleman that his father was detained a prisoner in the Tower, that his cousin Emmeline was lodging in the neighborhood, desiring an opportunity of serving her uncle and guardian, and that she required protection and assistance in her desolate and solitary course. Sir John then went on to say, clearly with a view of conveying his complete submission and attachment to the government, that he had heard, with great pain, a rumor that his son had taken part with those who were attempting to subvert the existing government, and establish the sway of *the Pretender;* and he went on to command him, on his duty to his father, to separate himself from all such rash and disloyal persons, and immediately make the best of his way to London, taking up his abode in the house which had been engaged for his cousin Emmeline.

Richard Newark concluded the reading of his letters with one of his wild laughs, and then turned his look to Smeaton, who was still standing in the window, with his eyes fixed upon the lines he had received from Emmeline.

"Well, noble earl," said the lad, "what news have you?"

Smeaton beckoned him up, and, with a sudden determination, put Emmeline's letter in his hand.

Richard Newark started at the first words, and his cheek became somewhat pale. For the moment he went no further, but laid his finger on the line, "My beloved husband." He said nothing, but his look was a question, and Smeaton answered, "Even so, Richard." At the same time he slightly raised his finger and looked toward the other side of the room, where Somerville, or William Newark, was seated, fondling the hilt of his sword, and observing every thing while he affected to observe nothing. Richard caught Smeaton's hand in his own, and wrung it hard, saying, in a low voice,

"I am sorry I have dragged you into this thing. You should have gone after her. You can go even now."

"Impossible, Richard," replied Smeaton, in the same low tone; "but *you* can, and you must My station, my age, my name, my family, all forbid me to quit this cause when I have once embarked in it. Such is not the case with you. Emmeline requires protection, assistance, and support. To you I trust her in the fullest and most implicit confidence; and I beseech you to fly to her, and to give her that aid which I cannot—I must not—attempt to afford."

"No, no," cried Richard, aloud, with a laugh "no, no!" And then suddenly breaking off, he exclaimed, "But you promised to introduce me to a relation, noble earl. Confer the favor, I beseech you. I am poor in such things. I have but one father and a cousin in my purse, and I am avaricious of more wealth."

Smeaton put away his letters, and introduced his young companion to William Newark, begging Richard to get hold of their quarter-master and find good quarters for their visitor.

Richard suffered his cousin to shake him by the hand, but eyed him still like a shy, fiery horse, glancing askance at the approach of an unskillful rider. The other, however, was all ease and self-possession, rejoiced exceedingly, as he said, to see his young cousin, spoke with expressions of regret of Sir John's confinement in the Tower, and cursed the chance which deprived the cause of so strong an arm and so skillful a head.

He then began to talk of his quarters, and Richard led him away to seek them with an air which he seemed to think very satisfactory, but which Smeaton, who knew the lad better, judged to be any thing but an indication of amicable feelings toward his new-found friend. The young nobleman's thoughts, however, were soon engrossed in other matters, for Emmeline's letter re-awakened many a pleasant, many a painful train of reflections, and he gave himself up to memories for more than half an hour before he turned his steps toward the quarters of General Forster.

CHAPTER XXXIV.

It is wonderful how rapidly Somerville, as he called himself, gained to all appearance upon the good opinion of his young cousin. They became quite intimate. Richard found out for him a very comfortable room, sat and talked gayly with him for more than an hour, and then left him with a promise to come and sup with him *tête-à-tête* that night, that they might talk over matters of family interest.

Quarters had not been procured for William Newark too soon, for hardly an hour had passed ere a troop of some seventy men entered the town, headed by a person named Douglas, whom good old Mr. Robert Patten terms a gentleman, but who, nevertheless, followed the ancient and honorable occupation of horse-stealing upon the border. In the bustle and confusion which attended the congregation of a body of between three and four hundred men, most of them calling themselves gentlemen, in the small town of Rothbury, little further communication took place between Richard Newark and the Earl of Eskdale. They met once, and Smeaton thought fit to give his young friend a hint in regard to the character of his cousin.

"He was always wild, rash, and intemperate," he said, "yet with a great deal of shrewdness, which deprived him of one excuse for the commission of follies. He can not be said to have committed any from mere thoughtlessness; and I do not think that your father feels at all well disposed toward him."

"Doubtless," replied Richard, "nor do I. I don't like that cut upon his forehead. It is an ugly gash, resembling the one you gave the fellow at the back of Ale Head, when they were carrying away Emmy. It is quite as well to mark a friend that we may know him again. I don't think your handwriting on that fellow's head can be mistaken."

"You let in light upon me," said Smeaton, gravely; "and, if your suspicion is correct, I think him more than ever to be avoided."

"To be watched, noble friend, to be watched," returned Richard, with a laugh. "I am the best watchman in the world. I recollect waiting three hours without moving hand or foot—I don't think I winked an eye—watching with my cross-bow for a hare, till Miss Puss came out, hopping, on her hind legs, with her ears up and her whiskers wagging; and I hit my mark. People call me wild and foolish; but I can always watch and make something of it—and I *will* watch now."

The concluding words were said with peculiar emphasis; and the moment he had uttered them, he turned away and plunged into a little crowd which had gathered round the last comers.

It was night when the two cousins sat down to their supper together, which William Newark had taken care to make as good and plentiful as the circumstances would permit. He had even contrived—Heaven knows how—to get two or three flagons of tolerable wine; but he did not show, at first, any inclination to drink deep, and began the conversation with topics very different from those which chiefly occupied his thoughts.

"Our numbers are swelling," he said, as soon as the servants had put the food upon the table and retired. "That was a large troop which came in this morning; and I saw a whole crowd of foot mounting the white cockade."

"Oh yes," replied Richard Newark. "The horse were a goodly body: thieves, sheep-stealers, smugglers, cattle-lifters, all well to do in the world, and expert in their professions. Take care of your purse, cousin of mine, if you have got one, for transfer is easy among gentlemen of that class. As for the infantry, poor men, they only come in for disappointment. It is wonderful how much more zeal than discretion there is in infantry. If soldiers were only things to be fired at and not to fire again, we should have had one of the best-equipped armies of infantry in the world by this time. Thousands have come in with a sweet petition for arms; and, though they have been daily sent away with the assurance that we have no arms to give them, they still march in, offering their services."

"I should think arms would be easily procured from your western side of the country," observed Somerville. "You are so near the coast of France, and have such excellent places for landing them."

"Ale Bay, for instance," added Richard, with a sharp look, and then a laugh. "Ay; but the worst of it is, Cousin Bill, that the people at Ale are always watching for something or another, and he would be a cunning man who could land without being caught. My father knows that, or he would not have lived there so long."

"Ay, he can not choose where he lives now, poor fellow," responded William Newark; "but I should think he would be somewhat uneasy at leaving our fair cousin Emily there. Take some wine, Richard."

"Emmeline, Emmeline," cried Richard, pouring out for himself some wine, "not Emily; how ignorant you are! But he is not at all uneasy about leaving her there, because he has taken her with him." And he laughed quite like a fool.

"Taken her to the Tower!" exclaimed his cousin. "I did not know they would receive a prisoner's family with him."

"Nor I either," replied Richard; "but they have *not* received her: she lives near with the servants and people; and my father took her to keep her out of harm's way. I have often heard him say that, if he had any thing he wished to keep secret and snug, London was the place for the purpose. Now Emmeline is just in that case, and therefore you see he acts upon principle. Oh, he has a head, has he not? The Hanover people won't get it off so easily as they imagine, for he knows how to take care of it as well as how to use it."

"Ay, doubtless," said the other. "And so the lady lives near the Tower, does she?"

"In good sooth," answered Richard, in somewhat of a mocking tone. "But what matters that to you, cousin of mine? It is a long way from this place to London. If you had a telescope, you could not see her."

"That would depend upon its strength," replied William Newark, "although, as I know not rightly where she lives, I could not well point it. In what street does she dwell? I know London thoroughly."

He spoke in an easy, indifferent tone, judging that the lad would readily betray the place of Emmeline's abode, and making no allowance whatever for that shrewdness which is often joined to great simplicity.

"Oh, Heaven knows," replied Dick. "It is in some street, and the street has got a name, but what that name is has passed from my noddle these six hours; and the letters, as in duty bound, I put into the fire."

"Ha! you have had letters, have you?" exclaimed his cousin. "Who were they from, and what news did they give you?"

"They were from father," replied Richard, "and gave me no news whatever, but merely commanded me to leave off soldiering, and go to London directly."

William Newark paused and meditated for a moment or two, while Richard watched his countenance keenly and searchingly, but with no more appearance of interest than if he had been marking the progress of a shadow on the wall. He saw a variation in the expression of his cousin's face; and, in truth, a total change had come over his plans. But Richard said nothing, quietly leaving the other to develop his own purposes.

"Do you know, Richard," said William Newark, at length, "I think your father is very much in the right in ordering you to join him in London, both on your account and his own? Your staying here in arms might damage him very much, and even bring his head to the block."

"Indeed!" ejaculated Richard. "What! cut off the father's head for the son's fault? That is reversing the line of succession, I think, and is neither heraldry nor justice."

"It sometimes happens, however," answered his cousin; "and the people will naturally say that you would never have joined the insurrection, being so young, if your father had not prepared you to do so. Therefore, if you love your father and would save his life, you had better do as he bids you: I might say, indeed, if you love yourself, and would save your own life, you would do so."

"I don't much care about my life," replied Dick, "but I have some small notion of honor."

"There is no honor to be got here," replied the other. "I am a man of honor too, and would cut any man's throat who said I was not; but I intend to leave these people, and that very speedily. Between you and me, Dick, there is neither honor, profit, nor safety to be had here. This insurrection will not succeed. Here are two generals with mighty armies of three or four hundred men, and neither the Englishman nor the Scotchman has the slightest knowledge of military matters. Kenmure and Forster are two quiet country gentlemen, who never saw a shotted cannon fired in their lives. They will get all who follow them into some horrid scrape, where you will be able to do nothing but hold out your hands for the king's troops to come and tie them. There will be disgrace, and ruin, and punishment. If there was a chance—if their own folly in appointing incapable country gentlemen to command in military operations did not deprive the cause of all likelihood—if we were going to fight like men instead of being trapped like sparrows, which will certainly be the end of it, I would let no danger daunt me: but as it is, Dick, I fairly tell you I shall march for London. You may do as you like."

His cousin's words were evidently not palatable to Richard Newark, who sat, gloomy and silent for a minute or two, with his eyes bent upon the table, saying nothing till his cousin exclaimed, with a laugh, "Come, take some wine, Dick; it will cheer you."

"No," replied Richard, and pushed the flagon from him. At length he went on, setting his teeth hard, "Well, I will go. I can do them little good, and can be of more service to true-hearted folks there than here. I will go, cousin of mine. When do you set out?"

"Early to-morrow," replied William Newark. "I don't think it needful to tell Kenmure or Forster that, having been accustomed to serve under generals, I do not like to be commanded by bumpkins. I can write all those sweet things afterward."

"I must tell Eskdale, however," said Richard Newark. "I can not leave him without explanation."

"Take my advice, and do not say a word," answered his cousin. "He will only try to persuade you to remain by arguments you should not listen to."

"Not he," cried Richard Newark, with a scoff. "All his arguments go the other way. He has never ceased teasing me to go to London after my father, and to take care of Emmeline, and all that. However, I'll consider of it."

"Indeed!" exclaimed William Newark, in evident surprise at what he heard of the young earl's conduct; and then he bit his lips to prevent himself smiling while he thought, "What a set of fools these people are! Surely one good head would be a match for a thousand of them."

Conceit is always an adjunct to cunning, and indeed is that adjunct which most frequently renders fruitless the dexterity of its companion. William Newark was mistaken in his calculations of Richard Newark's character; and though every now and then he felt some misgivings from certain sharp turns of expression used by his young relation, he could not divest his mind of the idea that Richard was a mere pliable and eccentric boy, whom he could soon find means to twist into any shape he pleased. "I will use him as a tool," he thought, "to work my own purposes; but I must make haste. While his shrewd father remains in the Tower, the stage is clear for me to play what part I please. Once let him get out, and I may meet with more than my match."

Richard Newark would drink no more wine, and soon after rose to return to his own quarters. He promised his cousin, however, to be ready to ride with him early on the following morning, with the full resolution of keeping his word. When he got beyond the door, however, he laughed aloud and muttered, "Egad! what a fine thing it is to be called a fool! Men are always showing you their plans when they think you can not make any use of the knowledge

Master William, you want watching, and you shall have it. I will be your shadow till I see you safe beyond the seas again. Ha, ha! The fool thinks to get hold of Emmeline, not knowing she is another man's wife already. He shall find himself mistaken."

With these thoughts he walked slowly to his own quarters, debating with himself whether he should tell Smeaton of his intentions. It was more in accordance with his character to set out without communicating with any one; but still his heart was kind and affectionate, and when he reflected upon the pleasure it would give to Emmeline to receive a letter from her husband, he soon made up his mind. He found the young earl seated quietly in his room, and alone, and a long conversation took place between them which I need not dwell upon here. Richard, indeed, did not tell his friend all his motives for the step he was about to take. He did not even mention that William Newark was to be the companion of his journey. He had no skill in explanations, and very often found it difficult to explain the motives of his actions to himself, rarely if ever attempting it to others; and in this instance he would have been obliged to enter into long details from which he shrank.

For his part, the earl felt a sensation of relief and thankfulness, not easy to be described, when he heard Richard's resolution. To see the kind-hearted lad placed beyond the perils attending upon a desperate enterprise and a hopeless cause would have afforded in itself much matter for rejoicing; but to know that Emmeline, in the difficulties and discomforts which surrounded her, would have the support and assistance of one so affectionate, true, and honest, took a great part of the heavy load from his heart. The conversation naturally turned to his marriage with Emmeline, in regard to which Richard evidently entertained some curiosity; and Smeaton succinctly detailed to him the whole facts, sparing the name of his father as much as possible. He then applied himself to write to Emmeline in such a manner as to prevent the possibility of any evil result if the letter should fall into the hands of others, and, having done so, he committed it to the charge of his young companion, and bade him good-night, never doubting that he should see him on the following morning.

The fatigues which Smeaton had undergone during the four preceding days made him exceed his usual period of rest by a few minutes; but, on rising, he found, to his surprise, that Richard had been gone more than an hour.

CHAPTER XXXV.

Many men were in the Jacobite army, both in the South and in the North, who, judging of the future by the present, and by the appointment of the most incompetent persons to offices of high command, clearly foresaw that a catastrophe of a dark and terrible kind must await the insurrection. That catastrophe, however, as far as the little body collected in the South was concerned, was now approaching with great rapidity.

I shall not trust to my own pen for the details of all that occurred during the next few days, but will merely abridge, and render a little more clear, the account of an eye-witness who shared in all the perils of the time, but contrived in the end, by a timely recantation and abundant testimony against his companions, to slip his own neck out of the halter into which he aided to place theirs.

Up to the time indicated in the last chapter, General Forster, as he was somewhat ludicrously called, and the gentlemen who accompanied him, had entertained sanguine hopes of being able, after their junction with Lord Kenmure, to surprise the important town of Newcastle-upon-Tyne; but, before the evening of the eighteenth of October ended, all such expectations were dispelled by the intelligence that General Carpenter, a man of great experience and decision, had thrown himself into Newcastle with one regiment of foot and three regiments of dragoons. This was a force which they had no means of opposing successfully, and great anxiety was felt for the junction of the Scotch troops. That junction was effected on the morning of the nineteenth, in an open piece of heathy ground, broken by the remains of what was once an extensive wood, and known as Rothbury Forest.

With no slight eagerness, the two forces examined each other as they approached; and if the gentlemen of Northumberland felt some disappointment at the scantiness of Kenmure's numbers, the Scotch gentlemen experienced perhaps more at seeing their English friends so ill provided with horses and arms. Lord Kenmure's little force, consisting of four squadrons of horse, certainly displayed much more the appearance of a royal army on a miniature scale than the irregular body of the Northumbrians. Armed with good stout broadswords, and mounted on strong, sinewy horses, they advanced with trumpets sounding and colors displayed; and surrounded by a chosen body of gentlemen was borne what they called the standard of King James, formed of blue silk richly embroidered with the arms of Scotland on one side and the thistle on the other, while long streamers of white ribbon hung from the corners, likewise embroidered in gold with the words, "For our wronged king and oppressed country." "For our lives and liberties."

The whole force, when united, made at this period a body of about six hundred men; and, a hasty council being called, it was determined immediately to march toward Wooler as preparatory to a retreat into Scotland, which had now become inevitable. It was much to be feared, indeed, that General Carpenter would not suffer them to effect this object; but, happily for them, the intelligence that Brigadier Macintosh, with a large body of Highlanders, had crossed the Frith of Forth, and was in full march for the South, had reached that distinguished officer and Lord Kenmure simultaneously, and, unable to obtain exact information as to Mackintosh's strength or line of march, Carpenter judged it inexpedient to leave so important a place as Newcastle without other defense than the somewhat doubtful loyalty of the inhabitants. From Wooler the insurgent force marched straight toward Kelso, seizing arms wherever they could find them, and also appropriating to themselves any public money they could lay hands on.

About the middle of the day, however, they all halted on a wild moor a few miles from the town, having received information that it was occupied by Sir William Bennet of Grubbet with a considerable force—that the streets were barricaded, and several pieces of cannon placed in position. It was soon discovered, however, that Sir William Bennet, who was only supported by a body of militia, had taken fright at their approach and left the town, leaving some store of arms and ammunition behind him. Intelligence was also brought that Mackintosh and his Highlanders were advancing rapidly from Dunse; and it was accordingly determined to march to Kelso at once, both in order to join their friends, and to possess themselves of the arms which Bennet had left behind him.

The Scotch cavalry passed through the town without halting, in order to meet their Highland friends at Ednam Bridge; but the Northumbrian gentlemen remained in Kelso, which had been appointed as the general place of rendezvous. The expectation of finding any great store of the munitions of war were disappointed, for nothing appeared except some small pieces of cannon taken from Hume Castle, a trifling quantity of gunpowder, and a number of good, serviceable broadswords, which had been concealed in the church, and which proved a great relief to the half-armed Northumbrian troops. A short time after, Macintosh and the Highlanders entered the town, with their bagpipes playing, and the sturdy old veteran who commanded them marching at their head. The forces now assembled consisted of some fifteen hundred infantry and six hundred cavalry; and many a good citizen of Kelso, who had not yet dared to avow his attachment to the house of Stuart, now shouted loudly for King James, adding thereunto much outcry against the obnoxious measures of the house of Hanover.

"No malt tax! no Union! no salt tax!" was vociferated by several hundred voices; but the worthy citizens confined themselves to words, keeping cautiously clear of any overt acts.

The following day, being Sunday, was spent in religious observance; and on the Monday, the whole troops being drawn up in the market-place, King James III. was proclaimed with great solemnity, and a lengthy manifesto read, sufficient to tire the patience of the best disposed. Not content with dealing more in words than actions, the insurgent force continued idle in Kelso till the Thursday following, wasting the three most precious days which were granted to them in the whole course of the insurrection. The troops of General Carpenter were fatigued and discouraged; his numbers were inferior to their own; the whole south of Scotland was open to them; and every inducement combined with opportunity to lead them in an active and energetic course.

But division was in their councils. One proposed that they should cross the Tweed and boldly attack Carpenter's force before it had recovered from long and frequent marches; another strongly urged to march to the westward in order to join the western clans, and with their aid attack Dumfries and Glasgow, threatening the flank and rear of the Duke of Argyle's army, while Mar attacked him in the front. The English gentlemen, on the contrary, stronly advocated a sudden and rapid incursion into England, declaring their conviction that multitudes would rise and join them as they passed through Lancashire, while Carpenter, with his wearied and harassed forces, would be unable to follow, or might easily be defeated if he did. Every officer of any experience opposed this insane suggestion; but, nevertheless, it prevailed, and each day brought over fresh converts to that opinion from among the thoughtless and inexperienced.

It would seem that no decision had been arrived at when they marched for Jedburgh on Thursday, the twenty-seventh of October, and hesitation and some symptoms of panic were very evident on the way. Twice or thrice an alarm of the enemy being upon them created great confusion, ending in merriment when they discovered that parties of their own troops were the cause of all their apprehensions. At Jedburgh a halt of two days took place, and here the fatal resolution of entering England was adopted. An unexpected difficulty, however, arose. The Highlanders—at the suggestion, it is supposed, of the Earl of Wintoun, who was highly popular with them—piled their arms, and refused positively to march out of their own country.

After long discussions, they were persuaded to proceed as far as Hawick, when indecision again appeared in the councils of the leaders. The opinion of the wiser party had gained strength by the resolute opposition of the Highlanders, and so far prevailed that a considerable party of horse was detached toward Dumfries, with the promise of being followed by the whole of the army. Hardly had this body departed, however, when another change of resolution took place. The English gentlemen received, or pretended to have received, dispatches from Lancashire, assuring them of the support of twenty thousand men, and an immediate march into England was determined. Messengers were sent to recall the party which had been detached to Ecclesfechan; but the great difficulty still remained with the Highlanders, who once more positively refused to cross the border. Persuasions, entreaties, and even bribes, as it is said, were urged upon both leaders and men, and proved so far successful that a considerable body at length agreed to march. More than five hundred, however, adhered to their first resolution, and, separating into small parties, abandoned the army and took their way homeward by the West. The other diminished body of the insurgents marched on toward Carlisle by Langholm and Longtown, gaining here and there a few volunteers, and hearing rumors of parties of the enemy's cavalry hovering about them in different directions. Money, which was much wanted, was gained at several places by the confiscation of the public revenues; but the people in general looked upon the progress of the Jacobites with indifference, and no signs for some time appeared of any general movement in favor of the Stuart cause.

After crossing the border, Forster assumed the command of the whole army in virtue of a commission from the Earl of Mar; and wisely judging that Carlisle, though but poorly garrisoned, was too strong for his small force, he marched to Brampton, and thence advanced toward Penrith, where a bloodless triumph awaited him over a body of men collected to oppose his march. The Lord Lonsdale, strongly attached to the cause of the house of Hanover, and, though still very young, a man of courage and decision, had collected a considerable body of the horse-militia of Westmoreland and Lancashire, and added to it the *posse comitatus* of the shire. He was strenuously aided by the Bishop of Carlisle; and the numbers collected at a little distance to the northward of Penrith amounted to no less than fourteen thousand men.

This undisciplined mob was drawn up on a small moor across which the insurgent army was likely to pass, with some woody lanes and broken ground at a little distance in the front. Intelligence of their proceedings had reached the insurgent leaders, but they resolutely marched on, prepared and eager for battle. The Highlanders, it would seem, were the first who issued from the lanes; but they did so in good order, and immediately extended themselves in battle array. The cavalry followed; but the very sight of any thing like a disciplined army was sufficient to overthrow all confidence in the *posse comitatus;* the spirit of flight seized on them all; arms were thrown away in haste; and the whole country was speedily covered with the flying multitude. Lord Lonsdale, left with a few of his own servants, was forced to take refuge in Appleby Castle; and the Bishop of Carlisle was hotly pursued on his road to Rose Castle by a worthy belligerent clergyman, who had formerly been a curate in his diocese.

The flight and utter dispersion of the enemy gave great encouragement to the insurgents, and the spoils of the field supplied them with many articles of which they stood in great need. Arms, horses, and powder were taken in considerable quantities; and they entered Penrith the same day in good order, and flushed with success. They were very civilly received in the town, and further stores, as well as a considerable sum of money, were obtained. After refreshing themselves for a day at Penrith, the insurgents moved on to Appleby, without receiving any of the re-enforcements which they expected. On the contrary, indeed, it would seem that many desertions took place, for no great confidence was entertained by the men in their commanders, and little obedience shown except in moments of urgent danger.

From Appleby to Kendal, and thence to Kirby Lonsdale, they marched on unopposed; but neither from Westmoreland nor Cumberland did they receive any of the re-enforcements they expected till on their march from the latter place toward Lancaster. Here, however, they were joined by a number of the Roman Catholic gentry, and were further encouraged by the news from Lancashire, which represented the whole county as ready to rise and join them. Manchester, then comparatively an insignificant little town, but somewhat famous for the unruly disposition of its inhabitants, declared for King James with very little reserve, and began to raise and arm bodies of men for his service. Lancaster, however, had well-nigh proved a stumbling-block in their way; for Colonel Chartres, and some other officers attached to the house of Hanover, were anxious to take measures for its defense, and even proposed to blow up the bridge. The fears, however, and perhaps the disaffection of the majority of the inhabitants, frustrated all their designs, and, marching into the town, the insurgents possessed themselves not only of money, arms, and ammunition, but also of six pieces of cannon, which they found in a ship belonging to so peaceable a personage as a Quaker.

These cannon were speedily mounted upon wheels; and during the stay of the insurgent force, which was from the seventh to the ninth of November, small parties of gentlemen continually came in, unhappily for themselves, and joined in an enterprise which was now fast tending to a disastrous conclusion. It must be said, however, that they aided greatly to hurry the catastrophe. During the whole of the long march from Jedburgh to Lancaster, the leaders of the insurrection, as may well be supposed, had been anxious to obtain information of the movements of the enemy's troops. General Carpenter's small corps was that which they principally dreaded, and we are assured that Forster spared neither money nor exertion to gain intelligence. It was known that Carpenter had immediately pursued the insurgent force as soon as he learned their line of march, but he was reported to be at a considerable distance in their rear; and a certain Mr. Paul, another Jacobite clergyman, who had doffed the cassock to assume military costume, brought positive intelligence into Lancaster that General Carpenter was at Barnard's Castle in Durham, with men and horses sorely fatigued. The other Lancashire gentlemen, who came in from time to time, assured Forster and his companions that no body of King George's troops could approach within forty miles without their receiving intelligence of it; and, in an evil hour, it was determined to waste more time in Lancaster merely as a resting-place, even after the plan had been decided upon for advancing into a district where a great accession of force was to be expected.

That plan was generally as follows, viz., to march direct upon Manchester, where the cause of the house of Stuart had numerous partisans, to seize upon Warrington Bridge, and to extend their operations to Liverpool, of which they hoped easily to make themselves masters. Orders were even given, it is said, for advancing at once; but the acquisition of cannon and the rumors from the country rendered them somewhat apathetic, so that from Monday the 7th till Wednesday the 9th of November they remained refreshing themselves in Lancaster, while the forces of their adversaries were drawing closer and closer around them. The seventh proved a very wet and stormy day; but the march toward Preston was begun early in the morning, and it would seem that some misgivings began to be entertained regarding the intelligence which had been received from the country. Rumors spread through the small force that large bodies of King George's troops were being collected to oppose their advance; and the necessity of taking up a position which would enable all their friends in the midland and western counties to join them was felt, but too late.

The roads were bad, and rendered nearly impassable by torrents of rain; the infantry struggled on, fatigued and somewhat disheartened; and even the cavalry found it difficult to advance in any thing like order. Accordingly, at the small town of Garstang, it was determined that the foot soldiers should halt for the night, while the cavalry pushed on for Preston, and dislodged a small body of dragoons quartered in that place. The dragoons did not pause to be attacked, but marched out at the approach of the insurgents, who rejoiced as for a victory, and took up their quarters in the town. On the following day, Thursday, the 10th of November, the whole of General Forster's force was reunited in Preston, and the usual ceremonies of proclaiming King James III. and praying for him by name in the church took place.

At Preston another delay occurred. No intelligence of the enemy's proximity was received; and, instead of marching upon Manchester on the Friday morning, as had been first determined, a halt was resolved upon until Saturday. During the whole of Friday, the insurgents enjoyed themselves in Preston with a feeling of the utmost security, and it was not till the troops were under arms on Saturday that any intimation was received of the rapid advance of General Wills upon Preston.

CHAPTER XXXVI.

It was during the evening of the 9th of November, on which the cavalry of the insurgent army marched into Preston, that a party consisting of three mounted men followed the course of one of the small deep lanes, of which there are several in that part of the country. The cavalry was proceeding in the same direction by a wider road to the right; and one of the horsemen of whom I have spoken lost no opportunity of getting upon any elevated spot, in order either to descry their course of march, or to study the features of the country. Wherever the banks of the lane sloped down and showed a way to higher ground, wherever a gate gave exit to the right or left, that horseman passed through and gazed about him. The two others were less watchful, and seemed contented enough with the shelter of the lane. One of them was tall and not very well made, riding his horse in a slovenly and slouching manner; the other fat and short, not the most graceful cavalier in the world, but one who showed a very discreet adherence to the saddle.

The rain poured down in torrents; the mud was up to the horses' fetlocks; and a cold, cutting wind blew the half-congealed drops into the travelers' necks and ears, notwithstanding an ample garniture of cloaks, with collars raised high and fastened tight before. It was as miserable an evening for a journey as could well be conceived; nevertheless, the latter of the two who remained in the lane contrived to keep his companion in a merry humor, eliciting frequent peals of laughter from him, partly at the matter of his anecdotes, partly at the manner of the narrator.

"Ay," he observed, with a strong Scotch accent, "ay, Mr. Van Noost, you are doubtless a very clever man in your way, and pretty gods and goddesses, shepherds and shepherdesses, you can make out of cold lead, as you tell me. But I can do more than that."

"I don't doubt it, my lord," replied Van Noost, chuckling a little at the idea, notwithstanding. "You are a great man, and I am a very insignificant one; yet I should not mind working against your lordship for a wager as to who should cast the best Diana."

"Let her alone, man, let her alone," said Lord Wintoun, with a laugh. "Keep to Venus; you may beat me there. I should beat you at Dianas, for I should cast them in cold iron suited to such a hard-hearted goddess. Lead is the fitter stuff to make Venus of, for we all know that she was every now and then in the melting mood. Why, man, if these fellows, who call themselves generals, and have no more knowledge of war than my nag, would but give me a leathern apron and a sledge-hammer, I could do them more service than they'll ever let me do them at the head of a regiment. In the one case, I could make them pikes to arm the common people; but in the other, I have the command of a regiment, as it is called, which is to obey every body but me."

Van Noost's curiosity was excited, but not by the most important part of Lord Wintoun's reply.

"Why, my lord," he said, "how came your lordship to learn such a trade as making pike-heads?"

"It came by nature and a little observation," replied the earl. "You see, dearly beloved Van Noost, I thought it just as well at one time to travel, and I had a strong inclination to see more of the world than the lords and ladies in it, which, after all, are like a sheaf of arrows all cut to one length and tricked out in the same manner; so I put by my dignity for the time being, dressed myself up as a blacksmith's boy, got a place with one of the dingy craft, and engaged to blow the bellows."

Van Noost burst into a loud laugh, observing,

"You soon got tired of that, my lord, I dare say?"

"Not I," rejoined Lord Wintoun. "I blew bellows and hammered iron for two whole years; ate pumpkin soup, drank sour wine, and cooked my own omelette for a treat on Sundays."

Van Noost laughed again, thinking he would rather not have partaken his lordship's fare; but Lord Wintoun went on, saying,

"Nay, more, I took many a buffet from the blacksmith's daughter with a patience which might have lessoned Job; and one time his wife would have basted me with a broom, but I took up a red-hot horse-shoe and threatened to set fire to her petticoats, though they were too short in all conscience to suffer much curtailment decently. The good woman laughed like a merry soul as she was, and laid down the broom while I quenched the horse-shoe."

"Perhaps the daughter was the attraction," said Van Noost, slyly. "Did she give nothing but buffets, my noble lord?"

"Faith, nothing to me," replied Lord Wintoun; "and as to attractions, those which she had were more vast in extent than peculiar in power. She was well-nigh as big as her father; and, though she had two great black eyes, they were not much better than one, for they drew to a point so close toward her nose that it was like a cross fire from the angles of a fortress; and if she saw any thing at a distance, I am sure it must have been reversed. Then her mouth—heaven and earth, her mouth! The very memory is painful. When it was shut, even, it looked like what we Scotchmen call a slit in a haggis; and when it was open, it looked like the entrance of the bottomless pit. It could never have been borne, had not the nose counterbalanced it."

Again Van Noost laughed heartily, exclaiming, "The love! The joy! What happiness your lordship must have had in her dainty society!"

"Good faith, I have fared worse than I did there," said Lord Wintoun, "and, I fear me, shall fare worse still. A man without a head is of no use to himself or any one else, Master Van Noost; and I doubt that I shall long have one upon my shoulders. How does yours feel? Is it shaky?"

"Not very easy, my good lord," replied Van Noost, in a dolorous tone. "At times a certain sick qualm comes over my stomach, as if I had eaten half-cooked pork. But does your lordship really think the case so bad?"

"As bad as it can be," answered Lord Wintoun. "Take my word for it, Van, your fat will soon be as cold and hard as one of your own leaden figures, unless you contrive to be politic."

"But what would you have me do?" inquired the poor statuary. "I think things seem going well enough for my part."

"Poor man!" ejaculated Lord Wintoun. "You have eyes, doubtless, for the heads of your statues, but none, it seems, for your own. However, here comes your pet, Lord Eskdale. Ask him. What do you think he is galloping about the country for, up on the top of this knoll, and over that hill, and through the other gate, or leaping his weary horse over a fence like a cat through a window? You don't know? I'll tell you, then. He is looking out to see if he can perceive, through all this rain, the enemy's troops, which he knows will be upon us before three days are over. He is not to be fooled, like your Forster and Kenmure, with the fancy that we shall be allowed to march through the land at our leisure. Well, Eskdale, do you see them?"

"It is hardly possible to see at all," replied the young earl; "but I see nothing except our own men on the right, and the church of Preston, I suppose, a few miles off."

"What do you think Carpenter is doing?" asked Lord Wintoun.

"In truth, I do not know," returned Smeaton; "probably marching after us till he knows he has us in a net, ready to fall upon us the moment it is advisable. We shall make a good fight of it, though, I doubt not, for most of these gentlemen have strong hearts, if not strong heads."

"Ay, the garret story is very empty," said Lord Wintoun. "Do tell this good poor man, Eskdale, why you have refused all command in our great army."

"Simply because I would not have any responsibility," returned Smeaton, "in an enterprise which is destined to end in misfortune and disgrace. There is no officer of experience whom I would not have served under, in whatever capacity he chose to assign me; but Mr. Forster, though a very good country gentleman, I dare say, is no soldier; and it requires fully as much skill and experience, my noble friend, to command an army as to cut out a wooden spoon. Any one who may attempt either without some practice will cut his fingers and spoil his work."

"Then, my good lord, why do you not leave them?" interrogated Van Noost, with a very unpleasant choking sensation about the throat. "Here is this noble Earl of Wintoun trying hard to persuade me that it would be better for me to run."

"Faith, Van Noost, I think he is right," replied Smeaton, with a smile; adding, in a half-joking manner, "The difference is very great between you and us, Van Noost. You see, as you are fully as broad as both of us, you run a double risk of musket bullets. Besides, if we should be taken, great men can find friends to pray for them. Now who would pray for you, I know not, but your cook and your garden shepherdesses. Seriously, however, with all the zeal in the world, I don't think you can do much good here to the cause, and none to yourself; and, if you would take my advice, you would ride away, surrender yourself to some magistrate, submit to penance for your sins, and save your body from Carpenter's carving-knives or your neck from a hempen cravat. Our honor keeps us here; but you have not much honor to gain by staying with us, and, in the circumstances, can lose little by leaving us. I give you my word that, had I not been burdened with an earl's title, I would have left the force the moment that the mad determination of marching into England was taken. I am not bound to serve under lunatics; but it would give too severe a shock to the cause for two noblemen suddenly to abandon it."

"That is what brought me back to Langton," said Lord Wintoun; "for I had fully determined to go, rather than be led to slaughter like a sheep, and that without even the object of my fleece or my flesh. But I asked myself how many would follow my example if I went, and that thought brought me back."

The idea of being led to slaughter like a sheep did not seem at all palatable to poor Van Noost, and he continued silent and dismal during the remainder of the way. Smeaton took up his quarters with several other gentlemen, forming a part of the little force which they called the gentlemen volunteers who had no separate command, and who served under no particular leader. Some supper was hastily prepared, and all the usual resources of soldiers employed for whiling away anxious thought and making the present pass cheerfully. The claret-flagon—for, both at Lancaster and Preston, good wine was found—circulated freely among the higher classes of the insurgents, while the fiery aid of brandy, either plain, diluted, or made into punch, kept up the spirits of the rest.

Of his favorite beverage, punch, Van Noost, who sat at the same long table as the Earl of Eskdale, drank so much that the young nobleman felt some apprehension lest his salutary terror should pass away, and he should abandon his purpose of quitting the insurgent army and making his submission; but toward the close of the evening Van Noost came up to him and whispered,

"I shall depart early to-morrow, my good lord, and go as straight to London as they will let me. Has your lordship any thing to write that I can take charge of?"

Smeaton was inclined to seize the opportunity eagerly; but a moment's reflection showed him that, by giving his humble friend even a single letter, he might endanger the good man's safety if he should fall into the hands of the enemy. He therefore called him aside, and charged him with a few words to Emmeline. They were sad as well as few, for his own expectations were all dark and gloomy, and he did not wish to raise up hopes which he felt certain would be disappointed. He said little more to Van Noost, and that was by way of warning. He urged him strongly to give himself up voluntarily to any magistrate, if he found the least difficulty in making his escape through the country; to submit unconditionally, but at the same time to avoid making any statements which could either betray the condition of those with whom he had been in companionship, or deprive them of any advantages in the present or the future.

He then retired to his chamber, saying he was fatigued, and would seek rest; but the rest he took, though he might find bodily repose, was not that of the mind. He slept not at all for the next three hours, but remained seated motionless, near the window, in deep thought.

CHAPTER XXXVII.

At an early hour in the morning of Saturday, the 11th of November, a good deal of bustle and commotion filled the streets of Preston. Private gentlemen and military officers were seen running hither and thither, and all who had command of regiments or squadrons, as their little bodies of men were called, received a summons to attend a council at General Forster's quarters at the Miter Inn. The Earl of Eskdale was not one of these, however. He had refused all command, notwithstanding pressing importunities; for his military skill had been seen and appreciated, even by those who would not follow his advice in the time of action. Nor was he, to say the truth, even up at the hour when this bustle began; for, as I have shown in the preceding chapter, he had been watchful and sleepless during the greater part of the night, and when he did at length lie down to rest, fatigue brought on a deep and lasting slumber, from which all the noises of the awakening town were hardly sufficient to rouse him. He had, it is true, many bitter and painful thoughts to deal with in his waking hours, but those thoughts had little to do with the conduct of the expedition in which he was engaged; and over him, as over a great many others who had joined the ill-starred enterprise, had come a sort of hopeless indifference, which left him little care of what might be the next move in the game of folly and madness then being played.

About half past seven, however, his servant Higham entered the room where he slept with a white and anxious countenance. Smeaton was up and partly dressed; and, looking quietly in the man's face, he said,

"Well, Higham, give me my sword. I suppose the Hanover troops are upon us, by your chop-fallen look?"

"Ah, my lord, God forgive us our sins!" exclaimed the man. "It will come to fighting this time, for they say that General Wills, with ten thousand men, is marching upon Preston, and can already be seen from the top of the windmill."

"I suppose you do not object to the fighting, Higham?" said his lord. "You have always been foremost in brave words, my good friend, and I shall certainly expect that you now act up to them."

"I will do my best, my lord—I will do my best," replied the servant; "but I had rather not be killed just now, if I could help it. I have done a great many wrong things, I am afraid, and I should much like time to repent."

"It is not a very long operation," observed Smeaton, with a faint smile, continuing his dressing. "God's grace can give repentance at any time, and render it effectual. A short prayer, my good friend, and a strong resolution to do better for the future, is what I would advise you to make, and then come and fight like a man on the side you have espoused."

"Ah, but, my lord, I have wronged you too," said Higham, "and that is one of the things I would repent of and atone for."

"Well, well," responded Smeaton, "I have no time now to hear confession of sins. I must go and see what is the truth of all this you tell me. As for the rest, I freely forgive you, my good man, for any little offense, known or unknown by me, which you may have committed against me. It is very unlikely that both you and I should come alive out of this day's work, if matters are going as you say; and, whichever is taken, let us part in charity. I forgive you with all my heart, Higham, for any fault in your duty to me."

"Ah, my lord!" cried Higham, with a rueful look, "if you knew all—"

He did not conclude his sentence, however, for at that moment, without any application for admittance, Van Noost burst into the young nobleman's room, and Smeaton, anxious for the good man's safety, made a sign to the servant to leave them together alone.

"Have you heard the news, my lord, have you heard the news?" cried Van Noost, in a state of great excitement, but without any signs of fear. "General Wills will be here in a few hours, they say."

"So I have heard," rejoined Smeaton; "but, my good friend, I did hope that you were far away before this time."

"I am very glad I was not," said Van Noost, rubbing his hands, "for I have a plan—such a plan!—for the defense of the place, if your lordship will but propose it to General Forster. It can not fail. It is sure to succeed."

Smeaton had not always the best opinion of Van Noost's plans; but the man spoke very earnestly, and the young nobleman replied with a smile, "Well Van Noost, tell me what it is, and if it seem to me feasible, I will propose it to those in command."

"It is this, my noble lord," replied Van Noost; "and it must succeed. General Wills is advancing from the side of Wigan with an overwhelming force. In two hours, they tell me, he will be in the town. If we run away and leave it empty, he will pursue us with his cavalry without a minute's delay, so that we shall all be cut to pieces before we can make our escape. Now what I should propose is this: to make an appearance as if the town were defended, even after we are all gone; for, by seizing the bridge over the Ribble, we can delay them for a while."

"That bridge will, of course, be maintained at any cost," remarked Smeaton; "but if General Wills is marching from Wigan, we shall not be able to pass that way without fighting."

"No, my good lord, no," replied Van Noost. "I do not propose to escape that way. Of course it will take some time to reconnoiter the bridge; but let the men retreat from it into the town, and follow the main body, which, in the mean time, must be marching down Fishergate Street to the meadows. I have examined all the ground well. There are two good fords for horse or foot across the Ribble. Then the road to Lancaster is open before us, and we shall have a town which we can defend, or a port from which we can sail."

"I doubt much if you will find that road open now, Van Noost," replied the earl, "though undoubtedly the possession of those fords is a great object; but I do not yet see how you will make General Wills imagine the town is defended after we have left it."

"Give me but two hours," replied Van Noost, "and I will dress you up men of straw so like Highlanders that you would swear you saw their bare knees."

Smeaton began to laugh.

"Indeed, my good lord," continued Van Noost, somewhat warmly, "the plan is a good one. I could make fifty or sixty of these men, and dispose them in beautiful groups at the ends of the streets. The general would never think of making his attack upon a town apparently defended without long preparations and skillful dispositions. In the mean time we should be getting to Lancaster."

"No, no, Van Noost," replied Smeaton. "As stuffed men can not fire muskets, General Wills would not long be deceived. Your idea regarding the defense of Ribble Bridge, and your suggestion to seize the two fords, are both very good, and I will mention them to General Forster as coming from you; but spare me the straw Highlanders. And now, my good friend, let me urge you most strongly to take your departure from this place. Indeed, I was in hopes you were gone long ago. Depend upon it, Van Noost, all who remain here are destined either to die in Preston or to be made prisoners. Had we a man of experience and military skill to command us, we might fight successfully, or we might retreat successfully; but as it is, there is no hope of either. You are not a fighting man, Van Noost; you can gain no glory here; and, if you will take my advice, you will not delay a moment, but ride out of the town as long as the way is clear. And now farewell, my good friend. I can stay no longer, for I must go to ascertain what is the exact truth of the reports which have reached me."

As he spoke he shook his companion kindly by the hand, and poor Van Noost, with drooping head and tears in his eyes, walked down with him to the door of the house.

The young nobleman took his way along the street toward the Miter Inn, observing the faces of all the persons he met. The streets were very full, for the news of General Wills's approach had spread rapidly; and Highland clansmen and night-riding borderers, Lancashire Roman Catholics, and Northumbrian gentlemen, were all hurrying out to gain further intelligence of the enemy, or to ascertain the plans of their own leaders. Those whom Smeaton actually met were generally of the inferior class—the common men, as they were called—and he remarked an expression of dogged resolution in their countenances, from which he argued well. I mean to say, he inferred that their resistance would be obstinate and vigorous, if not successful, so that perhaps good terms might be made, even if a victory could not be won On entering the Miter Inn, however, he found a number of gentlemen in the passage, and many more in a front room on the ground floor, who were waiting to hear the result of deliberations which were going on in an upper chamber. Among these he perceived any thing but the same looks which he had remarked in the men of inferior station. There was an appearance of discouragement, of doubt, in some instances of apprehension, which was very painful to witness; and the only one who seemed perfectly at his ease was the Earl of Wintoun, who now took no part in the councils of General Forster. The silence among such a multitude of persons was very remarkable; few spoke at all, and those who did speak raised not their voice above a whisper. The Earl of Wintoun himself sat on an old mahogany stool, playing with his sword, which he held between his knees, and humming a Scotch air with the most perfect appearance of indifference.

"Well, Eskdale," he said, as the other approached him, "have you heard the news? The elector's people are marching from Wigan to attack us, they say."

"Then we shall have what might have been expected long before," replied Smeaton, in a cheerful tone: "some good, hard blows; and God defend the right!"

"Amen!" ejaculated the earl. "I wonder what they intend to do. They are a long time in deliberation. But, after all, that may well be; for, while men of science would see that only one thing is to be done, our good friend Forster has the whole world of imagination to go through before he can fix upon a plan. Doubtless it will be something very extraordinary when he does draw the lot by chance."

"Nay, nay, I dare say we shall do very well," replied the young nobleman. "Forster is a brave man; and I strongly suspect that unconquerable resolution is what will be more serviceable here than any thing. Of course, ordinary precautions will be taken; and it seems to me that much generalship will not be required."

"The men will fight to the death," said a young gentleman of the house of Athol, who was standing near. "If we had but heads among us, we have plenty of hearts." And then, with a knitted brow, and a sharp glance of his eye round the chamber, he added, sternly, "But we will have no trifling—no cowardice."

"Of that I imagine there is little chance," replied Smeaton, coolly. "But here, I think, are the officers coming down, Captain Murray."

A noise was heard of many feet upon the stairs, and the next moment Forster himself looked into the room, and, when he saw Lord Wintoun and the young Earl of Eskdale, he advanced toward them, followed by several others. His look was cheerful and assured, and his manner composed and courteous.

"We have much needed your advice, my lords," he said, "and I truly wish you would sometimes join our councils. You have doubtless heard the rumor that General Wills is advancing from Wigan. I can hardly believe the fact, and am now going out with a small party to ascertain if it be so or not. If it be, I trust we shall give a good account of this general."

"Doubtless," replied Smeaton, calmly. "Is it fair to ask if you have determined upon any plan of resistance?"

"Not fully," replied Forster; "and I shall be glad of any suggestion from your experience, my lord."

"I doubt not, sir," replied Smeaton, "that you will take all requisite precautions, such as securing the fords over the Ribble, and taking possession of Ribble Bridge, which, when I examined it, seemed to me very capable of being converted rapidly into a strong point of defense."

"Ay, indeed!" said Forster. "Does not it lie somewhat distant from the town for that purpose?"

"Assuredly," replied the young nobleman, "if you are determined upon making your defense in the town; but the high ground about it, the number of hedges and lanes in the neighborhood, and many other advantages, afford an excellent position behind the bridge for a small army furnished with cannon, and principally consisting of infantry opposed to a larger force, strong in cavalry alone. At all events, there can be no harm in seizing the bridge at once, for it could be well defended for several hours by a mere handful of men."

"True—that is very true," replied Forster; "and it shall be done immediately. Colonel Farquharson of Invercauld, may I ask you to undertake this task, and seize upon Ribble Bridge with one or two companies of foot?"

The gallant soldier whom he addressed, with hardly a word of reply, left the room to obey the order he had received; and Forster, after having mused a moment, said, in a loud tone,

"To delay the enemy's advance for a few hours is as good as a victory; for, beyond all doubt, the greater part of the elector's troops will come over to the army of their real sovereign unless they are led into battle immediately before they have time for consideration."

This was evidently said for effect; and it is wonderful at what delusive hopes men will catch in desperate situations. The expectation spread of great desertion from King George's troops as soon as the two forces should be in presence; and, after pausing for a minute or two more, Forster proceeded to the door of the inn, where his horses were already waiting for him. He took but very few men with him; and, from among all the gentlemen present, his strange choice of a companion fell upon Robert Patten, the clergyman, who, in the military spirit which had seized upon him, acted the part of aid-de-camp throughout that eventful day. The assembly at the Miter did not altogether break up on his departure, but to the silence which had pervaded the lower part of the house succeeded a confused and buzzing clamor of many voices, in the midst of which Smeaton and the Earl of Wintoun quietly walked away together.

"We seem to be in a very active but not very industrious state," said Lord Wintoun to his companion, in a quiet, sarcastic tone. "What do you intend to do, Eskdale?"

"I shall order my horse and ride out of the town, to see the state of things with my own eyes," replied the young earl. "Not very *industrious* indeed! Why, the people are all sauntering about, as if we were waiting for the opening of a fair, and not of a battle."

"A sheep has its throat cut," said Lord Wintoun, "whether it struggles and kicks or not; so perhaps it is best to undergo the operation quietly. You are not going to leave us, I suppose, Eskdale?"

"No, my good lord, no," replied Smeaton. "I will be back in Preston before a shot is fired; but I must say, King James has treated us rather hardly in placing us under the command of so incapable a man."

Thus saying, he turned up the little street which led to the inn where he lodged, and, calling aloud for his servant, ordered him to bring round his horse at once.

"I wish, my lord," said Higham, in a very subdued tone, "you would let me speak with you for a few minutes. I have a good deal to say."

"By-and-by, Higham, by-and-by," replied Smeaton. "At present I am in haste, for I would fain see into this matter with my own eyes."

The man seemed about to speak again; but his lord made an impatient gesture with his hand, and, as soon as the horse was brought up, mounted and rode away. As he went through the narrow streets and lanes which then led out into the country, he heard more than one unpleasant observation from the groups which were collected every where.

"There goes another," said one man.

"I wonder any one stays who can get away," said a second.

"Ay, ay, these high Tory gentry take care of themselves," observed a third.

But no one attempted to stop the young nobleman's progress, and to all idle comments he was very indifferent. Beyond the immediate neighborhood of the town he found the country nearly deserted; the distance to Ribble Bridge, in which direction he first turned his steps, was somewhat longer than he expected; but, from the summit of a little elevation upon the right, he perceived the small body of Highlanders marching toward the spot which he had advised Forster to occupy; and, still gazing round, a cloud of dust, rising, at the distance of several miles, in the direction of Wigan of Lane, seemed to show him that the advance of General Wills's army was something more serious and substantial than mere rumor. A minute or two after, a single horseman, dressed entirely in black, was seen galloping along the road in the direction of the bridge over the Ribble. Smeaton spurred forward toward him, instantly recognizing Mr. Patten, and saluted him with the inquiry of "What news?"

"Oh, they are coming, they are coming," replied the clergyman, with a bold and assured face, "and I am just going to tell Lieutenant-colonel Farquharson to withdraw his men from the bridge and retire into the town."

"In Heaven's name, upon what motive?" demanded Smeaton. "Has General Forster formed any plan or not?"

"Oh, he has formed a very excellent plan," replied the clergyman, with a conceited air. "It can not be put in execution, however, for the ford above is not to be found. The general, my lord, had determined to pass the river and get into the rear of the enemy, or, at all events, attack them on the flank. But as this has now become impossible, he wishes Colonel Farquharson to retire, and to confine the whole defense to the town."

Smeaton looked at him with an expression of scorn and surprise, and then, without any further notice, turned his horse sharply, and rode toward the banks of the river.

CHAPTER XXXVIII.

Smeaton struck the banks of the stream some little distance above the bridge, and with a keen and rapid eye traced the whole distance within the range of sight. He instantly marked a spot where there was a gentle undulation of the ground, and where the river spread out wide. "There must be one ford," he thought; but, not satisfied without positive proof, he rode quickly on till he reached the place, and pushed his horse through the water and back again. Then turning round, he was tracing the stream toward the bridge, when he perceived Van Noost mounted on a tall horse, and pursuing a course at an acute angle with his own, as if tending toward Preston. The statuary rode on at a rapid rate, and his short, broad frame was agitated terribly by the quick pace of his rough-trotting horse. The legs flew out; the shoulders heaved at every stretch; and the bent back and head leaning far over the saddle-bow showed how he labored in the effort. The voice of Smeaton, raised loud to call his attention, made him give a sudden start in the saddle which had nearly overset his equilibrium—for he was no very skillful cavalier; but, as soon as he perceived what it was, he pulled hard at the right rein, and rushed across the little piece of open ground toward his noble friend.

"They are coming, my lord, they are coming!" he cried, in a voice full of excitement, evidently not of the most pleasant kind. "I have seen their advance guard myself. It is impossible to pass them, and I don't know what to do. I must back to Preston, I suppose, even though they catch me and cut my head off, leaving my body like a collar of brawn."

"Come here with me," cried Smeaton. "I will show you a way;" and, without waiting for a reply, he rode on to the ford he had discovered, and pointed to it with his hand. "Over there, Van Noost," he said. "Take the left-hand road, and then make a circuit, keeping to the westward, till—"

"But, my lord, my lord," interrupted Van Noost, "they say General Carpenter is at Clitheroe, or very near it."

"If you keep well to the west," remarked Smeaton, "you will come to Garstang and Lancaster; but speed on, my good friend. No time is to be lost."

"I shall never find it," replied Van Noost, with a rueful shake of the head. "Can not you come, my lord, and show me the way?"

The young earl smiled at the little kindly cunning of his poor friend, but shook his head, saying,

"No, no, Van Noost, I must back to Preston. Remember my message to my dear lady, and tell her, if she sees me no more, that I loved her with my whole heart to my last hour. Away, away, my good friend! No more words."

Seeing the good man pass safely through the ford, he once more turned his horse toward the bridge. When he reached it, he found that, according to the orders which had been sent, Farquharson and his Highlanders had abandoned its defense. He could just catch a sight of the tartans winding up the narrow lane; but he paused for a moment to gaze at the bridge before he rode after them. It was long, narrow, flanked with stout stone walls, and every foot of the ground on the Preston side was defensible. The young nobleman felt that a great mistake had been committed; that *there* was the place to fight, and that upon such a spot a small and irregular army like that of the insurgents, aided by cannon and sheltered by the hedges and high banks, might have won a victory even against a superior force of regular troops. He sighed as he turned away to ride after the withdrawing party. When he reached its head, he bowed to the commander, with whom he had a slight acquaintance, saying,

"So you have been withdrawn from the bridge, Colonel Farquharson?"

"Even so, my good lord; and now for the rat-trap," replied Farquharson, with a light, indifferent laugh, adding, the moment after, "We shall bite our catcher's fingers, however, I dare say, and that is some satisfaction."

"But a poor one," rejoined Smeaton. "I would rather have flown at their throats by the side of the Ribble."

So saying, he rode on.

All was bustle and activity when he entered Preston; the scene was completely changed from the morning; the excitement of preparation, the prospect of speedy battle, the very occupation of mind and body, had restored spirit and energy every where except among the superior officers, who, conscious by this time of their general's incapacity, entertained no very sanguine expectation of the result. Some, sullen and gloomy, watched all that was taking place, giving a few directions, but sharing little in the toil; others remained in the inns and private houses in melancholy despondency; but others, among whom was the young Earl of Derwentwater, labored cheerfully and zealously in the construction of the barricades, which were already in rapid progress. Their example cheered and their looks inspirited the men, and Smeaton was soon in the midst of them, laboring with the best.

But little time was allowed for the construction of the defenses, and that little was only obtained in consequence of General Wills being unable to conceive it possible that Forster had abandoned so important a point as the bridge over the Ribble. He hesitated in attempting to pass it; he caused the whole ground in the neighborhood to be carefully reconnoitered, fully believing that the hedges would be found lined with musketry, and his march was thus retarded nearly an hour. At length, however, the first men of his small army were seen from the tall house of Sir Henry Haughton, but by that time all was prepared to receive them. Four main barricades had been erected, with a number of smaller ones in different streets; the windows of the houses on each side, together with the lanes and inclosures, had been garnished with infantry as far as the smallness of the force would permit, and every thing showed the determination of making a resolute defense. But the leaders of the insurrection had, strangely enough, determined to defend only what may be called the heart of the town, so that the barricades had not been pushed to the entrance of any one of the streets, and several narrow lanes gave the enemy an opportunity of penetrating some way, at least, into the place completely unmolested.

Smeaton found the barricades nearly half completed when he re-entered the town. Following the example of the Earl of Derwentwater, he cast off his coat and labored with the best to complete the defense which was being constructed in the main street, a little below the church. He could not refrain, however, while pausing for a moment to take rest, from expressing his surprise to old Brigadier Macintosh, who stood near, that the barricade had not been placed at the extreme end of the street, toward Wigan.

"If the enemy push forward," he said, "with any thing like vigor, a third of the town will be in their hands in five minutes."

"My good lord," replied the old officer, somewhat sullenly, "even if you were right—which I think you are not—it is too late to mend the matter now. To defend the extreme ends of the streets, where there are so many narrow lanes and avenues, would require three times the force of foot I have at command."

"This barricade, at all events," observed Smeaton, "might have been placed near the corner of that other street, a hundred yards below—I mean just near the sign of the Ram, there. It would then command both the approaches, and the flank could no more be turned there than here. If the enemy get possession of that tall house, they will gall us sorely."

"Ah!" retorted the old officer, "young men are always wiser than their elders;" and, turning away, he walked to the other end of the barricade.

"Let him alone Eskdale," said Lord Derwentwater. "He is as obstinate as an old pig, and gets perverse and sullen in proportion to difficulties and dangers."

"I *will* let him alone, my good lord," replied the young nobleman, "but I think it a duty to myself and to all to do what I can to remedy the mistake which has been committed. You keep the men to their work, and I will be back in a minute or two. That great cart, if it could be brought down, turned over, and filled with stones and earth, would make a very good defense at the corner there."

"What are you going to do?" asked Lord Derwentwater, seeing Smeaton resume his coat and turn away.

"I am going to seek for Captain Hunter," replied Smeaton. "He is a man of activity, resource, and shrewdness, and will, I doubt not, lend me a few of his marksmen, if he can spare them, to occupy those houses down below, so as both to keep them for ourselves, and to gall the enemy in their advance up the street. Where do you think I shall find him?"

"He is up with Miller and Douglas on the Liverpool road," answered Lord Derwentwater. "Add my request to your own: the idea is a very good one." And, while Smeaton remounted his horse and hurried away, the other nobleman continued to animate the men, not only by his own personal exertions, but by distributing among them all the money he had about him.

In ten minutes Smeaton returned with a body of some fifty men and Captain Hunter, the borderer, whose moss-trooping propensities and experience had rendered him a very serviceable man of action in any great emergency. Passing the barricade without speaking to any one, they hurried on down the street till they reached the first turning out of it, where, dividing into two bodies, the one dispersed through the neighboring houses on either hand, taking post at the windows, while the other body, consisting of about twenty men, advanced some way down the narrow lanes which led out into the fields near the entrance of the high road to Wigan.

In the mean time Brigadier Macintosh had remained watching the operation with his arms crossed on his chest; but the moment he saw the men enter the mouth of the lane, he dispatched a messenger after them to order them instantly back. They returned unwillingly, with Hunter at their head; but those in the houses were suffered to remain, and did good service throughout the day.

At some period during the morning, and before the attack actually commenced, Captain Innes, with a body of about fifty Highlanders, was thrown into the tall house belonging to Sir Henry Haughton which the young Earl of Eskdale had pointed out; but they were recalled almost immediately, and the house left to its fate. In the confusion and hurry of that fatal day, it was not known who gave the order for their advance or that for their recall.

The cannon of which the insurgents had possessed themselves was divided among the different barricades; but the difficulty was to find gunners, for only one man in the whole army even pretended ever to have fired a cannon in his life, and he, by the time the guns were planted, had imbibed a sufficient quantity of brandy to render the accuracy of his aim rather doubtful. A small powder-magazine was established near the center of the town, and a lame man, incapable of any great exertion on foot, but zealous, active, and determined, was appointed to carry supplies on horseback to the several barricades.

As soon as all the arrangements were completed, and the foot soldiers stationed behind the hasty works which had been constructed, the gentlemen volunteers, as they were called, retired to the church-yard, with their horses at hand, ready to sally out upon the enemy whenever a favorable occasion occurred. General Forster established his head-quarters at the Miter Inn, with his horses at the door, ready to carry him wherever his presence might be needed; and it is now admitted on all hands that he showed no lack of courage or activity during the day.

When all was ready, a sort of solemn pause succeeded to the bustle; the noise and confusion died away in the town; and the occasional subdued talking of people in knots, with, from time to time, a loud-spoken word of command, or a call from one officer to another at a distance, were the only sounds that arose in the streets of Preston. From the fields and lanes beyond, however, came the beat of the drum and the blast of the trumpet, nearer, nearer, nearer yet; first in one spot, then from two or three different points around, showing that the forces of King George had reached the outskirts of the city, and were spreading themselves round it preparatory to a general attack. In silent and awful expectation, the insurgents awaited the appearance of the heads of the enemy's columns. Sternly and steadfastly they gazed over the barricades, and no sign of fear or wavering was visible; yet it was a terrible situation, to be thus waiting inactive for the commencement of a struggle which all well knew was for life or death.

At length, some boys, and a woman with a

child in her arms, came running up into the main street out of the lane in which Smeaton had posted the party of Hunter's troop, afterward withdrawn, and fled at full speed toward Macintosh's barricade. They were suffered to pass, and entered, exclaiming breathlessly,

"They are coming up the lane, they are coming up the lane!"

No body of soldiers appeared, however, for several minutes, and neither drum nor fife was heard. At length, however, a young officer, in his full uniform and with his sword drawn, entered the street from the head of the lane, paused calmly in the midst, and gazed up and down. In an instant the word was given at the barricade, the muskets were leveled, and the shot poured down the street. But there the young officer still stood, now examining the barricade, now raising his eyes to the houses on either side, amid the rattle of musketry and the whizzing of balls, as calmly as if he had been in a drawing-room.

"Upon my life, that is a gallant fellow," said Smeaton to the Earl of Carnwath, who was standing near. "I wonder who he is."

"That is Lord Forester," replied the other nobleman. "I know him well by sight. He is lieutenant colonel of Preston's regiment, the old Cameronians. I did not know they would be brought against us. If he does not mind, he will be shot down, poor fellow."

As he spoke, however, the young officer retired into the lane, but it was only to return at the head of his regiment, and to charge up the street. A small body of dragoons appeared at the same time to support the infantry; but a tremendous fire was opened upon the whole force, both from the barricade and the houses around, which instantly checked their advance; a number of the Cameronians and several of the dragoons were seen to fall; and, drawing up his men across the street, Lord Forester restored order, which had been lost for a moment or two, directing the men to keep up a sharp fire upon the barricade, while detached parties from the rear and flanks stormed some of the houses, and took possession of the mansion of Sir Henry Haughton, which had so imprudently been left undefended.

Though the troops of the government made no progress up the street, they still remained firm in face of the barricade, and the drunken gunner was ordered to point and fire the cannon upon them. He adjusted both guns before he fired either; but, from haste, stupidity, or drunkenness, the elevation of the first he discharged was so high that the ball, passing far over the heads of the soldiers, struck the chimney of a low house at the side of the street, and brought it thundering down upon the heads of some of Honywood's dragoons behind. The other gun was more accurately adjusted, and the ball went straight through the attacking force, killing and wounding several men in its passage. All haste was made to reload the two cannons, and, in the mean time, a continual sharp fire was kept up on the Cameronians from the barricade and the houses round. Nevertheless, Lord Forester maintained his ground; Haughton's house was filled with musketeers; several other houses were taken after a severe struggle; and a constant fire was kept up from the front upon the insurgents of the barricade. At length, however, the young officer was seen to fall; but he rose again immediately, and continued to give his orders, pointing here and there with his sword, while one of the men tied a handkerchief round his leg.

"A charge of cavalry," observed Smeaton to Lord Kenmure, "would drive them out of the town."

"Well, try it gentlemen, try it," said General Forster, who had just ridden up, and was speaking to Lord Derwentwater. "Mount your horses and follow me. We will get the brigadier to open a way for us."

Every one was in the saddle in a moment, and moved in good order down the street, while Forster rode on before; and the fire of the king's troops passing over the barricade, struck down one or two of the volunteers and several of their horses. As they approached the barricade, no movement was made to let them pass out; and Forster was seen speaking vehemently to Brigadier Macintosh, who, with a dogged look of defiance, turned sullenly away just as Smeaton arrived upon the ground. What had passed before, none of the other gentlemen heard; but Forster now exclaimed, in a loud and angry tone, "Very well, sir, very well. Please God, if we are successful, and your master and mine ever obtains his rights, I will bring you to a court-martial for your conduct."

Then turning to the noblemen and gentlemen who had come up on horseback, he said, "Brigadier Macintosh objects to our making this sally, my lords. We had better, therefore, retire again to the church-yard, as there is no need of our exposing ourselves here when we can not be of service. My Lord Derwentwater, I will ride up to one of the other barricades, and see if there is nothing to be done there, for I feel that this inactivity must be painful to a body of zealous and brave men, all burning for his majesty's service."

Thus saying, he rode away, and the other gentlemen retired slowly up the street, with the bullets still flying among them, conversing, even in a laughing tone, upon what had taken place, and the conduct of those with whom they were engaged.

"I hope Macintosh will not let them gain the barricade," said Lord Derwentwater, looking toward Smeaton as the most experienced among them.

"No fear at present, my lord," rejoined the young earl. "He has stout men enough with him to keep out any force they can bring against him without cannon. He is a dogged, resolute fellow too, and his honor is now staked upon the result, as he refuses counsel and assistance. Do you know where Colonel Oxburgh is, my lord? I have not seen him all day?"

"In an ale-house, at his prayers," replied Lord Derwentwater, with a laugh. "So I am told, at least. When I saw him this morning, he was telling his beads with great devotion. And my good Lord Widrington, too, is absent from among us; but he has the gout, you know."

Just as he spoke, a foot soldier ran up, saying, "They want more powder, my lord, at the barricade. Have you any in the church-yard?"

"Not a spoonful," replied Lord Derwentwater, turning in at the gates of the cemetery, while the bullets whistled thicker and more fiercely up the street, as if the troops below had been re-enforced, and a gentleman of the name of Ferguson was struck from his horse, with his leg shattered in a fearful manner.

"I will ride up and send some down directly," said Smeaton, galloping on.

The firing still increased; and the street, rising with a considerable slope, exposed any one passing along it near the top more than even at the barricade. But the young earl passed unscathed, and, reaching a narrow little court where the powder was piled up in bags, he found the lame man, waiting on horseback with a considerable load behind him, ready to set out in whatever direction he might be wanted.

"They are in great need of powder, my good friend," said Smeaton, "at the brigadier's barricade; but pause a moment till the fire slackens a little."

The man, however, put his horse in motion; and one of his companions, who stood near, exclaimed, "You will be killed, Rob, to a certainty, if you attempt to carry it up to the barricade now."

"I know that," replied the other, calmly. "That I can not avoid; but, as they want it, although I can not carry it quite up to them, I will carry it as far as I can;" and, so saying, he rode on.

Smeaton turned out of the little court, and looked after him down the street. He saw him pass the church-yard, and get nearer and nearer to the barricade; but, while he was still at about fifty yards' distance, he beheld the poor fellow fall forward on the horse's neck, clutching convulsively at the mane. In another instant he would have fallen from the saddle, but, before he did so, a ball struck the horse also, and both went down together. Some men ran out of one of the neighboring houses and took the poor fellow up, while the powder was carried forward to the barricade by others on foot.

But Smeaton's attention was now drawn another way by sounds which came from a different part of the town. A loud shout like a cheer, mingled with the report of musketry and artillery, showed that the battle was raging fiercely there also; and, turning his horse, he rode quickly in the direction whence the sounds proceeded, to see if any thing was wanted or could be done. Guided by the ear, he made his way down a long, narrow lane, which led out into the fields, and soon came in sight of another barricade, at which Lord Charles Murray, a son of the Duke of Athol, commanded. This young nobleman had seen some service as a cornet of horse in the reign of Queen Anne; but he had thrown up his commission at the commencement of the insurrection, and now appeared at the head of a body of his clan, dressed in the Highland garb, and covered with smoke and blood. The firing had ceased for the time; but a good many dead and wounded men lay both before and behind the barricade; and the young officer was leaning on his sword, speaking to Patten, the clergyman, who was beside him on horseback.

"Ah, my good lord," said the young nobleman, as soon as he perceived the Earl of Eskdale, "I am sending Patten here for some aid from the church-yard. We have had a sharp affair, as it seems you have had down below; but we have beaten the Hanover people back for the present, and, with a little aid, can maintain our ground till nightfall, which is not far off, I see. You are welcome to share in our work. If you will take a musket, there lies one in the hands of poor Jock Murray, who had just killed a stout Londoner with it before he was shot down himself. I hope it will be as fortunate in your hands."

"I hope so," replied Smeaton, laughing, and springing to the ground. "Mr. Patten, if you send up men, send up my servant with them to hold my horse."

The pugnacious clergyman promised not to forget; and in a few minutes Higham came running up, long before the appearance of the expected succor. The attack upon the barricade had been in the mean time renewed, and a furious fire was kept up by both parties. Lord Charles Murray was mounted on a pile of stones, giving his orders as coolly as if out of all danger, and the Earl of Eskdale, at a part of the barricade which had by some means been destroyed, was supplying by his own skill and experience the inefficiency of the only gunner who had been found to serve the two cannon which had been allotted to this position.

The servant ran up with a boldness and activity which a little surprised his lord; and when he received orders to look after the horse, which had been left in charge of a Highland soldier, he contented himself with tying the beast to a hook on a neighboring barn, and then, mounting the barricade close to where his master stood, discharged a musket at the advancing enemy.

"What have you done with the horse, Higham?" asked Smeaton, somewhat sharply. "I ordered you to take care of him."

"He is quite safe, my lord," replied the man, "and out of reach of the fire. I do beseech you, let me have a shot or two at these men. They killed my father when I was but a child—shot him at the back of his own cottage door."

"None of these before you, Higham," said the earl; "these seem all mere lads. But do as you please, if the horse be safe. Only come down from the top of the barricade. You can fire as effectually from behind it."

"Oh, my good lord, if you would but let me speak a few words with you!" said the man, in an earnest tone. "When we have beat them back, pray let me speak with you!"

"Well, so be it," replied his master, struck by the man's eagerness. "But come down at once, my good fellow. Come down, I say!"

Almost as he spoke, Higham turned to obey; but he either missed his footing, or some of the heterogeneous material of the barricade gave way under his feet, for he suddenly fell headlong down behind the defense.

The young earl had not time to ascertain if he were hurt or not, for, led on by their gallant officers with a loud cheer, the party of assailants rushed forward to the charge, determined, apparently, to storm the barricade. A well-directed and sustained fire from the Highlanders, and from both pieces of cannon, however, checked them before they were within a hundred yards of the defense, and they were once more driven back in confusion.

A few minutes after, a party of fifty gentlemen volunteers came up to support the weary defenders of the barricade, and when Smeaton turned to look for his servant, the poor fellow was nowhere to be seen.

A very short space of time was allowed for inquiry or repose. The troops of the government were speedily rallied, and again brought forward; but the effect of the re-enforcement, both upon the energy of the defenders and the heaviness of the fire, was soon perceptible to the officers of the attacking body. Their men were repulsed more rapidly than before, and fled in greater confusion from the hail of shot that was poured upon them. Night was approaching: it was evident that the barricade could not be carried by the force then before it; and slowly and reluctantly the commander of the assailants withdrew his force, just as the sky was growing dark. An angle of the road concealed, in a great degree, their movements, and some men were sent out over the barricade to ascertain whether the attack was actually abandoned. But even after they returned, announcing that the government troops were in full retreat, a hurried and desultory conversation was carried on among the officers and gentlemen within the barricade in regard to the events of the day.

Lord Charles Murray was almost ignorant of what had taken place at the other points of defense; but the gratifying news was brought in that the enemy had been repulsed at all points, except in front of Brigadier Macintosh's barricade, where they still maintained possession of some houses, and kept up a severe fire on all who attempted to pass. There were many words, and even some laughter rejoicing on the bloody spot where they stood, but little of what could be called either conversation or counsel. Yet some ventured to suggest one thing as advisable to be done, and some another; and Lord Charles Murray, without expressing an opinion, gave some directions for guarding the defense. Taking Smeaton's arm, he turned away, saying,

"By my soul, I must have some food and drink, Eskdale. I have been fighting here since two o'clock, and though the men have had brandy and beer enough, *I* have tasted nothing."

Smeaton walked away with him, unfastening his horse, and leading him as he went. As soon as they were out of ear-shot of the rest, his gallant companion asked, in a low voice,

"And what do you think had better be done in this affair?"

"Give the men three hours' rest, and then either retreat upon Lancaster, through the meadows, or attack General Wills in his camp," replied the young earl. "He is evidently but little of a commander, and I think we might have an easy victory before he is re-enforced, or effect a quiet retreat to a more defensible place, for the town is not one half invested."

"We must abide the commands of our elders and betters, I suppose," replied Lord Charles, "though it is certain that, if Wills is a bad general, Forster is a worse. However, here I stop to feed like a tired horse, if I can. Will you come in and sup?"

"Thank you, no," replied the young earl, "I must go to look for my servant, who, I fear, is wounded, poor fellow!"

Thus saying, he and Lord Charles parted.

As Smeaton walked back to the upper part of the town, Preston presented a strange and gloomy scene. The firing at the other barricades had ceased; but still, from time to time, a single shot or a whole volley was heard from the houses near Macintosh's barrier, where either party had lodged itself, and there, it must be remarked, the struggle continued throughout the night. The shops and dwellings were all closed along the streets; the inhabitants kept carefully within doors; and few people were met, except here and there a soldier hastening from one point to another, a wounded man plodding painfully to seek for relief, or a dead or dying man borne along by three or four others. From different parts on the outskirts of the town rose up a lurid glare, which lightened the vacant streets, showing that one party or the other had fired some of the houses in the suburbs, and the distant drum and trumpet-call from without mingled wildly with the sound of the bagpipe which was heard from two of the barricades.

The only groups of any size were collected round the doors of different public houses, which were kept open for the entertainment of the men, and at these Smeaton received full confirmation of the fact that the troops of the government had, as he supposed, been repulsed at all points. A feeling of triumph animated all with whom he spoke, in which he was far from sharing; but it is not impossible that, had the commanders been capable of taking advantage of the spirit of the hour, a different result might have attended the defense of Preston.

Nowhere, however, could Smeaton hear of his servant; and, after a long and fruitless search, he retired to his quarters, and threw himself down to rest after his fatigues.

CHAPTER XXXIX.

THE morning of Sunday the 13th dawned dull and heavily. The flames of the burning houses had been extinguished without doing much damage, although, had there been any wind, it is probable that Preston would have been reduced to a heap of ashes. The firing from the houses continued at intervals, and once or twice parties of King George's troops appeared in the streets, but instantly retreated under a sharp fire, by which several of the soldiers and officers were killed or wounded. A small number of prisoners, too, were made by the insurgents, and among the common men, high spirit and resolution were displayed, though the officers shared little in their anticipations of success. It is true, the latter had better means of judging, for the first prisoners that were made on that morning brought them intelligence that forces were pouring in upon Preston from different quarters, and that General Carpenter, with three regiments of cavalry, had passed the night at the small town of Clitheroe, about twelve miles distant. The next who came in informed them that General Carpenter was within sight; and, a few minutes after, some of their own men, from the higher buildings of the town, discovered his force advancing at a quick trot.

The soldiery were eager for action, and murmured loudly at the inactivity of their commanders. But no movement of any kind was made.

Forster, Lord Widrington, Colonel Oxburgh, and some others, continued in close consultation at the Miter; and Smeaton, after having obtained all the information he could from the gentlemen who thronged the lower story of that inn, walked away by himself, and, entering the church, mounted as high as he could in the tower, to observe the motions of the enemy without. Two or three gentlemen were there before him; and they pointed out the newly-arrived regiments of cavalry, which were drawn up in fine order on the right of General Wills's army. Smeaton said nothing except "They have no cannon, I see," and continued to gaze from the tower with very little satisfaction at the sight presented. Two officers, followed by a small party of dragoons, were seen to ride away at a slow pace from the main body of the army, and to direct their course completely round the town, sometimes exposed to view as they crossed the open fields and meadows, sometimes hidden by the trees and hedgerows. From time to time they stopped, and more than once a trooper was suddenly detached from the escort, and galloped away to one of the regiments which were in position. Immediately a small body would advance, and, riding quietly on, station themselves opposite to one or other of the many entrances to the town.

To the experienced eye of Smeaton, the proceedings which were taking place were very clear. He saw that a mind of greater intelligence than that of General Wills was now brought to act against the insurgents in Preston; that General Carpenter was changing all his predecessor's arrangements, and that, in a very short time, the town would be completely invested, and all chance of escape cut off. The thought of abandoning the cause individually had never crossed his mind. He had taken part in the insurrection most unwillingly, but, having done so, he considered himself entirely identified with it. Nevertheless, he could not see without a sigh the chance of the whole army effecting a retreat pass away. But despair begets indifference, and from the moment he beheld the movements of General Carpenter, he felt that all was lost. He hummed a gay French air as he descended the narrow stair-case from the tower, and though his face was thoughtful, it bore no trace of despondency.

Some gentlemen were gathering round the great gate of the church-yard, and about to take up their old position within its walls, but the young earl turned toward the little door on the left, near which was passing at the moment, on horseback, a merry Northumbrian physician, named Alcock or Walker (for he had an alias), who had acted as principal surgeon to the army during the preceding day. Anxious to obtain some intelligence of his servant, Smeaton hurried after him and laid his hand upon the bridle. The doctor seemed somewhat in haste; but, as soon as the young nobleman mentioned the subject of his anxiety, he replied,

"Oh yes, my lord, yes, the poor devil is shot in the stomach, and, if he have not the strength of an ostrich, he will not easily digest his yesterday's supper. By-the-way, I recollect he was exceedingly anxious to see you, but I did not know where you were."

The doctor seemed very desirous to move forward, but Smeaton still detained him, asking where poor Higham was to be found, and learned that the man had been carried into a private house near the barricade where he had fallen. The young nobleman then proceeded to ask some further questions regarding the man's state, but the worthy doctor's impatience could be restrained no longer, and, leaning down his head, he whispered in Smeaton's ear,

"I beseech you, my noble lord, let me go. I have made up my mind that we can not do any service here, now that Carpenter and his bullies have arrived; and, as I reconnoitered the ground pretty strictly yesterday, I know that I can get out by Fishergate Street, across the meadows and the ford, and away. If you will take my advice, you will do the same."

Smeaton shook his head, saying with a smile,

"Make haste, doctor, make haste! Carpenter is altering all the posts, and in five minutes he will be in those same meadows, across which lies your way."

Thus saying, he let go the bridle, and Doctor Alcock trotted off. I may add that he was just in time, for he and two or three others contrived to get out of the town and across the ford under the very eyes of General Carpenter, who probably did not think it worth while to detach any of his escort in pursuit.

Smeaton, in the mean time, with a quick step, took his way toward the other end of the town, in order to visit the poor wounded man; but to reach the place, he had to pass the door of the Miter Inn, and he soon saw symptoms of confusion and turbulence which caused him to pause for a moment. The common soldiers were by this time all stationed once more at the barricades, and a good number of the gentlemen volunteers were collected in the church-yard; but some thirty or forty gentlemen, not of the highest rank, were either standing round the door or crowding the passage of the inn. All were talking together eagerly; some were gesticulating vehemently; and one young man, of the name of Murray (not Lord Charles Murray), between whom and Smeaton a certain degree of intimacy had sprung up, as soon as he perceived the latter, ran up to him and caught him by the arm, saying in a low, but stern and eager voice,

"My lord, I pray you come with me for five minutes. These men within are betraying us; they are for giving us up into the hands of the enemy—the enemy we conquered yesterday at every point. Come with me, I beseech you. You are a man of rank, and also of experience—a soldier—a brave man. They *must* listen to you."

"They have listened to me very little," returned Smeaton, "otherwise we should not have been in our present situation. But go on; I will follow you."

Murray, whose eyes were flashing fire, and whose whole face was working with excitement, instantly darted back to the crowd, pushing his way fiercely through it and along the passage. Smeaton followed with a calm, grave air, more to learn what was taking place than with any hope of his voice being attended to. His young acquaintance reached the stairs, and mounted, taking three steps at a time, till he reached the door of a room, at which stood a man with a drawn sword in his hand.

"You can not pass, sir," said the man. "The officers are at council."

"We must be of their council too," responded Murray; and, without hesitation, he threw open the door and entered, followed by Smeaton, the sentinel making no effort to oppose them.

The scene within was already turbulent enough,

for the whole party, consisting of some ten or twelve, were talking together loudly and vehemently. Colonel Oxburgh, Lord Widrington, a Jesuit named Pierce, Sir James Anderton, and one or two others, were standing round General Forster, with a small table between them and another party, who seemed arguing some question with them very fiercely.

"Sir," said Forster, with a flushed face, in answer to something which had just been said, "you are insulting. I place before you the plain, straightforward facts of the case. There is no chance for us whatever, except in taking advantage of the successes of yesterday to obtain a favorable capitulation."

"Capitulation! Who talks of capitulation?" exclaimed young Murray, pushing forward quickly.

"*I* do, sir," replied Forster: "I, the general of this army, by the commission of King James. We are completely surrounded, outnumbered, and our store of powder is failing fast. I have not spared my person. I have not shrunk from the fire of the enemy; but I can see and judge of what is necessary as well as any rash boy in England! and I say, the only chance of our not being slaughtered to a man is to endeavor to make terms."

"What, with fifteen hundred gallant men, who would cut their way through a rock of stone rather than surrender!" exclaimed Murray, violently. "I will tell you what, General Forster, the soldiers—the brave common soldiers—will not hear of surrender. There are some gentlemen and noblemen among us, too, who are men of heart, and will not permit this. Here stands the Earl of Eskdale, a man of great experience, and as unprejudiced as any one. His voice, I am sure, is not for surrender."

"Certainly not," replied Smeaton; "for I would rather die with my sword in my hand, face to face with the enemy, than lay my head down on a block on Tower Hill, and I believe that is the only choice."

"My lord, you are in no command here," said Forster. "I am the general in command of these troops, by the king's authority; and, so long as I live, no one else shall command them."

"I do not in the least seek to do so," rejoined Smeaton. "I only give an opinion."

Before he could conclude the sentence, however, Captain Murray interrupted, exclaiming, in a loud voice,

"This shall annul a traitor's commission which he is unworthy to hold!" and, drawing a pistol out of his belt, he leveled it at Forster's head, and pulled the trigger. Some one,* however, struck up the muzzle just as he was in the act of firing, and the ball lodged in the wainscot, about two feet above the mark.

A scene of indescribable confusion ensued, in the midst of which the vehement young officer was arrested and removed from the room. It was not for several minutes that any thing like tranquillity was restored, and then Smeaton turned toward General Forster, saying,

"I regret this event exceedingly, General Forster, but I trust that the young man's intemperance and criminal conduct will not divert your attention from the truth of what he said. My belief is, that you will find it impossible to persuade the common soldiers to surrender, though they would risk less by it than we should; and I do not think any man would be safe who would propose such a thing to them."

"Nobody proposes to surrender, my lord, except upon favorable terms," retorted Forster, sharply; "and, if those could be obtained, I suppose nobody would be fool enough to refuse them. However, permit me to say that the advice which you have withheld from us during the whole campaign is not now desired."

"My advice was freely offered in the beginning," returned Smeaton, coolly, "but was treated, as all reasonable advice has been treated, with contempt, and was therefore never volunteered again till my own honor and life were concerned. I now not only give my advice, but protest, in the face of these gentlemen, against surrender upon any terms but those which shall secure our honor; and, having said thus much, I wish you good-morning."

"Depend upon it, my lord," said Forster, in a milder tone, "if we do treat for surrender at all, which is not yet determined, it shall be only on such terms as shall be satisfactory to all."

Every one knows what it is to begin to parley with an enemy superior in force to ourselves, and it would be tedious, even to the few readers who may be unacquainted with the events of that fatal day, to enter into details of all that occurred during the next four-and-twenty hours. Confusion, hurry, discontent, dismay, pervaded the whole town. Rumors spread of the intention to surrender, and the troops were more than once ready to fall upon their officers and put them to the sword, but were kept quiet by means of gross and shameful falsehoods. They were told that General Wills had sent in to offer honorable terms, promising that the lives and liberties of all would be guaranteed, and were assured that the coming and going of Colonel Oxburgh, and several of the royal officers, between the camp and the town, solely had reference to minute points in the capitulation. In the mean while, however, the messages which went out commenced with bold and somewhat excessive demands, but gradually firmness and courage oozed away. General Carpenter and General Wills sternly refused all terms, and only promised that, if the insurgent force surrendered at discretion, it should not at once be put to the sword. "No other terms," they said, "would be granted to rebels with arms in their hands." One small concession, however, was made, namely, that a cessation of arms should be granted till seven the next morning, in order to allow time to persuade the common soldiers to submit; but hostages were exacted to insure that no further defenses were thrown up in the town, and that no persons should be permitted to escape.

A night of intense anxiety, discussion, persuasion, turbulence, and confusion succeeded; but, before the appointed hour, despair had taken possession of almost all hearts, though there is some doubt as to whether the Highland troops were not deceived to the very last, and induced to believe that they laid down their arms upon favorable conditions. Before seven o'clock, the noise and confusion had subsided into sullen and discontented submission; the Highlanders were drawn up in the market-place; the noblemen and gentlemen who had joined in the insurrection remained at their various quarters; and, with drums beating and trumpets sounding, Generals Carpenter and Wills entered the town at the head of their troops, from the Manchester

* Mr. Patten declares that he was the man who saved Forster's life, but this is somewhat doubtful

road on the one side and the Lancaster road on the other.

It was a moment of some anxiety, for there was no certainty, even to the last minute, whether the troops of the insurrection would not make use of their arms in one last desperate effort in the market-place. But they had no confidence in their officers, no plan arranged among themselves; and, surrounded by a large body of cavalry and infantry, any attempt at resistance would have brought on a massacre rather than a fight. They laid down their arms, therefore, at the word of command, and were marched off by companies to the church, where they were kept pent up for many days under a strict guard. Some of the royal officers were then sent to receive the arms of the officers and gentlemen volunteers, who were put under arrest in various inns and private houses, and thus ended an insurrection which had begun rashly, and been carried on without skill or even ordinary discretion.

In the transactions which preceded the surrender, Smeaton had taken no part except that which I have mentioned. From the Miter he had proceeded to the house where his servant, Thomas Higham, lay, and found the poor fellow in a weak and apparently sinking state. The surgeon, who was with him at the time, and who had just extracted the ball, would not suffer any conversation, but expressed some hope of his recovery if he were kept quite quiet; and Smeaton, leaving a small sum of money with him to provide any comforts he might require, departed with a promise to visit him again if possible.

When, about half past eight o'clock, one of the royal officers entered the young nobleman's quarters, he found him calmly writing letters, with his sword and pistols on the table before him. He treated his prisoner with perfect courtesy; received his arms, and handed them to an orderly behind; and then, pointing to the letters, said, "I fear these can not be permitted to pass, my lord, without being submitted to the generals in command."

"I do not expect it," replied Smeaton; "but I think they will find nothing to object to. One is to my mother, which I should much wish forwarded to her as soon as possible, if she be still living. The other is to the Earl of Stair; and I should wish you to place it in the hands of General Carpenter, who will perceive that it refers to matters which have been already in discussion between us, and in regard to which I think I have been hardly treated. I know not, indeed, that it can have any influence on my ultimate fate, and that fate I trust I am prepared to meet as a man of courage and a man of honor; but I write it as a full explanation of my whole conduct, that no stain may be upon my character, and that it may be apparent that I have not in the slightest degree, or in any way, forfeited my given word. I trust that the Earl of Stair will be able to explain his conduct as satisfactorily. I do not accuse him, but there has been a fatal mistake somewhere."

The officer took the letters and promised to give them into the hands of General Carpenter, adding, in a kindly tone,

"If there is any thing I can do for your convenience, my lord, consistent with my duty, you have merely to command me."

"Nothing that I know of," replied Smeaton, "except, indeed, if you would exert your influence to have kind treatment shown to a poor servant of mine, who was severely wounded on Saturday at Lord Charles Murray's barricade."

"I will see to his comfort myself," said the officer; and then, putting down his name and the house where he was to be found, he added, "I will see to this directly. I fear I must put a sentinel at your door, my lord, till you are otherwise disposed of, but he will have directions to consult your convenience as far as possible."

Thus saying, he withdrew, and Smeaton was left alone in his room, a prisoner.

CHAPTER XL.

I MUST now turn to different scenes and to people whom I have long left, in order not to break the chain of events immediately affecting the young Earl of Eskdale.

In one of the narrow streets leading away from Tower Hill, there is a house rather better than the others, but still small and inconvenient. Centuries ago, that street was the resort of many a gay and gallant attender upon the court, and, even at the time I speak of, was inhabited by a respectable though poor class of the population. It was the place where captains of ships trading between London and foreign ports usually found lodging during their stay on shore. The house I have mentioned was the best of these lodging-houses, and, through the kindness of the governor of the Tower—who was an easy, kind-hearted man, as all his conduct to his prisoners showed—it had been hired for the family of Sir John Newark immediately upon his arrival in custody of the messengers from Exeter. Let it be remarked, the whole house had been hired; and the good woman to whom it belonged, who had not had the good luck before to let the whole of her apartments at once, went joyfully into a garret at a neighbor's to make way for Emmeline and the servants.

How the fair young Countess of Eskdale had passed her time in that small, dingy house; how sad had been her thoughts as, day by day, she received news from the North, and heard of her husband's part in the insurrection; how, at the end of about six weeks, she was joined by old Mistress Culpepper, and how, with marvelous fortitude and strength of mind, the good old servant supported the young lady in the sore trial which she underwent, I must not stop here to detail.

Emmeline sat alone in a little room on the ground floor, with small and narrow windows, parted by mullions and transoms, and affording but little light. She had paid her daily visit to Sir John Newark in the Tower, and had returned from a very unsatisfactory interview. The political prisoners, made at various times during the insurrections of 1715 and 1716, were treated, as all the world knows, with a degree of lenity—not to say laxity—during the time of their imprisonment, which contrasted strangely with the unrelenting severity shown to many of them in the end; and men waiting for trial, and destined to a bloody death, were suffered to enjoy the society of their friends almost without restriction—nay, more, were suffered to revel, to gamble, to drink within the dark walls which were only to be succeeded by the walls of the tomb, and to employ any means they might think fit, innocent or vicious, to while away the time and banish the grim thoughts of approaching doom.

All these facilities were given to Sir John Newark, and, indeed, nothing was wanting to his comfort except liberty; but yet the imprisonment weighed upon him, and rendered him irritable and suspicious. To be deprived of all power of scheming—to be obliged to sit idle when he fancied that great opportunities for playing the game in which he was well practiced were constantly occurring—to find the government maintain a cold and ominous silence in return for all the advances which he made, and to know that they had proofs against him of very dangerous intrigues, though not, perhaps, of high treason itself, all tended to depress and to annoy him more than the mere loss of his personal freedom.

During the last week he had, for the first time of his life, showed himself irascible and harsh toward Emmeline. He insisted that whenever she stirred out of the house, even to the gates of the Tower, she should be attended by two of his men-servants; and she discovered that one or the other of these men was sent for daily, and examined strictly by his master as to where she had been, whom she had spoken with, and what she had done—in fact, that she was watched in London as she had been at Ale-Manor. It is not, perhaps, wonderful that she felt more annoyed now than she had ever before felt at this *espionnage*, for, until the arrival of the old housekeeper, it was carried on so strictly that she could hardly obtain any information regarding those events in the North, on the turn of which depended her whole happiness for life.

The good woman's appearance at the house, which was sudden and unexpected, was a great comfort to the poor girl. She no longer sat and wept by herself, or, with her eyes fixed upon the embers of the fire, gave herself up to thoughts which passed in rapid succession, like dark and terrible shadows of approaching misfortunes. Good Mrs. Culpepper sat with her now the greater part of each day, obtained information of her, talked of him she loved; and there was consolation in the very companionship, though the housekeeper was in no way cheerful, for her own anticipations regarding Smeaton were gloomy and sinister. She did not suffer them to find voice, indeed, yet her whole manner and words were tinged with sadness. Even that which afforded poor Emmeline the greatest delight, gave her no comfort.

About three weeks before the period of which I speak, a letter had reached the lady, delivered by an unknown hand, but bearing the signature of her husband. It was the letter which Smeaton had written to her at Rothbury, and committed to the charge of Richard Newark. As her cousin's name was not mentioned, however, and he had never himself appeared, Emmeline knew not who had brought it, and she pored over it day after day as the only comfort of her solitary life; but the confirmation which that letter gave of the rumor that Smeaton was actually engaged with the insurgents in the North only excited darker apprehensions for his fate in the mind of his old nurse. It was in vain that tidings arrived, which produced some consternation in the minds of the good Londoners, by showing that the rebels were making a bold and, apparently, successful irruption into England: it was in vain that she heard of their advance toward Carlisle, or of the dispersion of the great body of militia in Penrith Moor, of the insurgents having seized upon Lancaster, and of the arming of Manchester in their favor: Mrs. Culpepper shook her head with a sigh. She had seen insurrection and civil war before, and her expectations were all sad.

On the morning of which I speak, a rumor reached her of the fatal events of Preston; and, after Emmeline's visit to Sir John Newark, on which occasion Mrs. Culpepper accompanied her, the old lady went out into the town to see if she could obtain further intelligence. Emmeline sat alone then in that small, gloomy room, and her thoughts were very dark and sorrowful. She reasoned with herself, as was her wont, upon human life, and the strange turns of fate. She asked herself what was the ruler of this world, and what was his decree? Were the good, and the wise, and the kind-hearted fated to sorrow and misfortune; the cunning, the remorseless, the unfeeling, to prosperity, and triumph, and success? Was hope only given for disappointment? Was imagination but the heightening curse to make all the bitterness of earth more bitter? Were the susceptibilities of every thing that is beautiful and excellent in life only given to sharpen the sting of adversity, and make the edge of sorrow cut more deeply? She could hardly believe it; and yet, when she turned her eye to history, or even pondered what her own small experience taught her, she could hardly doubt that such was the case; and the only moral she could derive from the consideration was, that "the reward of the good is not here."

Yet that is an oppressive and chilling conviction to the ardent heart of youth. It is a hard discouragement at the commencement of life's weary way. It requires an amount of faith and hope as its antidote which few of the young possess. It is one of the bars of the sieve through which the wheat is sifted from the chaff. Emmeline might and did turn her thoughts to God and to another world. She might and did feel that there was the rewarder and the reward; but yet her heart felt very sad to see the blight upon all the flowers of earth, and to fear that none would ever be matured into fruit.

While she was thus pondering sadly, she saw a man pass up the street whose figure had something in it familiar to her eyes. In an instant after he repassed, and looked up toward the house. She instantly remembered his face. It was connected in her mind with a scene and a moment never to be forgotten. It was connected indissolubly with the memory of him she loved; and, by a sudden impulse, she sprang forward and opened the window.

"He must have seen my husband," she thought. "He must bear me some tidings, some message —a letter, perhaps."

Van Noost (for he it was) stopped the moment he heard the window open, looked up and down the street, which was vacant at the moment, and then approached.

"Lady, lady," he said, "I wish to speak with you. I bear you a message from one you know and love."

"Speak it now—speak it quickly," said Emmeline, clasping her hands together in her eagerness.

"Ay, lady, it is a sad message and a sad tale," rejoined the good statuary, with tears rising in his eyes, "and you will hear it soon enough."

"Speak, sir, speak!" cried Emmeline. "What did my lord say?"

"He said, dear lady," answered Van Noost, "that he feared there was little hope of himself and the others escaping from the position in which they had placed themselves, much against his wishes and advice. He besought you, however, to take comfort, whatever might happen to him, and to place your trust in God. He would not write, he said, for fear of his letter falling into other hands; for I myself escaped with difficulty; but he bade me assure you that, whatever occurred, he loved you with his whole heart till his last hour."

"Then where is he? What has become of him?" asked Emmeline. "Tell me—tell me."

"I left him at Preston, madam," replied Van Noost, "but surrounded by the king's forces, and ready every moment to be overwhelmed by numbers. He insisted upon my leaving the army and making my peace with the government; but he himself remained, though fully aware of all the danger."

"At Preston!" said Emmeline, thoughtfully. "How long is it since you left him?"

"This is the ninth morning," replied Van Noost. "I reached London three days ago, and gave myself up to government. I looked honest, I suppose, or else they could not do without my statues any longer; for, after keeping me in prison two days, and examining me strictly, they let me go back to my own house upon the sole condition of showing myself to a messenger twice in every four-and-twenty hours."

"Nine days!" exclaimed Emmeline. "That is a long time. Has no news arrived from Preston since?"

Van Noost looked down upon the ground, and his good rosy countenance turned white with emotion.

"You have some tidings," said Emmeline, in a low tone. "Tell me what they are, I beseech you, sir. I can bear them, whatever they be. Speak quickly, or my heart will break."

"Alas, lady!" ejaculated Van Noost.

"He is dead," said Emmeline, in a tone wonderfully calm. "He has been killed in the battle!"

"No, no! Not so, indeed," replied Van Noost. "He is a prisoner, lady, but not dead. All the rest are prisoners too."

Before he ended, Emmeline's ear was deaf to his words. Fancy had so fully possessed her, only the moment before, with the idea of her husband's death, that when she heard he was still living, though a captive, the change from despair to hope was too sudden; her heart beat for a moment violently, then became still as if in death, and she sank upon the floor.

Poor Van Noost was shocked and terrified; he thought he had killed her, and he would fain have made his way through the window to give her help; but just at that moment the tall and stately form of Mrs. Culpepper appeared coming up the street, and, as soon as she saw him looking in at the window, she hurried her pace, asking him sharply,

"What are you doing here, sir, staring in at the window of this house? Are you a thief, who would fain break in and steal? Ah," she continued, as he turned more fully toward her, "I think I have seen your face before. Yes, I recollect you now. What are your tidings? Where did you leave my lord? Is he among the prisoners?"

"He is, madam," replied Van Noost, who stood in great awe of the stately presence of the housekeeper. "He is among the prisoners, if by 'my lord' you mean the Earl of Eskdale. But, I beseech you, look to the lady within, for a message I have just borne her has, I fear, well-nigh broke her heart."

"Or the rash telling it," said Mrs. Culpepper, somewhat sternly; but she added the next moment, "You did not intend it, I dare say. Come in with me;" and she knocked sharply at the door. It was opened by one of the men, who seemed somewhat surprised to see her accompanied by a stranger. But no one in the household ventured to question the proceedings of Mrs. Culpepper; and, telling Van Noost to follow, she entered the room on the right hand. They found Emmeline lying where she had fallen, with her cheek as pale as the lily, and her eyelids closed. It was long before she could be brought to herself; but the old housekeeper sent away the servants, told Van Noost to wait without and she would speak with him, and then whispered comfort in the poor girl's ear.

"All will go well, dear lady," she said. "All will go well, sweet Emmeline. He is a prisoner, but he is still living, and there are a thousand chances in his favor. They may try him, but not condemn him. They may condemn him, and yet pardon him. They may be obdurate, yet he may escape. He *shall* escape, too, if there be wit in woman's head, such as men say. Take heart, take heart; every thing is to be gained, so long as his life is safe."

It is wonderful how readily an old proverb springs before all other expressions in moments of haste or grief.

"Oh yes, while there is life there is hope," responded Emmeline, sobbing. "It was the joy of finding he was living, when Van Noost's first words had made me believe him dead, that overcame me. But where is Van Noost? Let him tell me more;" and she looked toward the window wistfully.

"The man is in the hall," replied Mrs. Culpepper. "I will call him in."

She accordingly summoned Van Noost, and ordered one of the servants who was still with him in the hall to go below and mind his work in a tone that admitted no reply. Van Noost was then questioned eagerly, and told the whole tale of his escape and the circumstances in which he had left the Earl of Eskdale. The good man was going on to disburden himself of all the news which he had gathered in London of the surrender of the insurgent army at Preston; but Mrs. Culpepper cut him short, saying, "What is your name, good sir, and where do you live?"

"My name is Van Noost," replied the statuary. "It is a well-known name. I am the famous artist in lead; and I live on the Reading Road, nearly opposite the end of Constitution Hill."

A grim smile came upon Mrs. Culpepper's face, and she said, "Very well. Perhaps we may want you. I doubt not you are willing to serve this young nobleman who so befriended you in getting you out of Preston."

"I would serve him with my life's blood," replied Van Noost; "but, gadzooks! I must take care not to burn my fingers in the business again."

"You are more likely to burn your fingers with your lead than with any business we shall give you," observed Mrs. Culpepper, dryly; "but, for the present, good-by, sir; and if you get any news or hints worth hearing, pray let us have them.

But be discreet; ask for me—Culpepper, the housekeeper; and, if I be not within, wait till I come."

"By my life, an imperious dame," said Van Noost to himself as he retired; and the housekeeper, after remaining for a moment or two in silent thought, turned to Emmeline, saying,

"Comfort yourself, dear lady. I will away to Sir John, and carry him the intelligence I have got, which probably has not yet reached the Tower. I must contrive to get rid of some of these men who are here, for they will hamper our movements; and I think, in this Preston business, I can find an excuse for sending one at least, if not more, down to Ale. He has not forgotten the bait of Keanton yet, and will rise at it as readily as ever."

CHAPTER XLI.

Slowly, and for him very soberly, with his eyes bent upon the ground, and his thoughts heavier than his own statues, Van Noost took his way across the little street toward a turning which led away to the westward some small distance higher up. He had not passed the doors of three houses, however, when suddenly a voice called him by name, and, turning round, he saw the outline of a man's figure standing some way down a narrow entrance passage, and beckoning to him with his hand.

"Van Noost," said the voice again, "come hither. I want you. Come hither, man of flesh and lead. There is no danger to your carcass. A dagger would lose itself before it found your ribs. Don't you know me, man?"

"I can't see your face," replied Van Noost, "but, odds wounds! your voice is very like that of Master Richard Newark, who left us at Rothbury."

"Come in, come!" cried the other. "Do not stand chattering there like a pie on an elm-tree, calling all the other birds to wonder what the fool is prating of. If you know my tongue, that is enough. Sound is as good as sight, and sometimes better. Come in, I say, thou man of molten images."

Without further question, Van Noost entered the door-way, although with some degree of trepidation, for the poor man had been sadly shaken by all that he had lately undergone, fat being no case-hardening of the nerves, as many of us must very well know. No sooner was he within the door, however, than Richard Newark threw it sharply to, caught him by the arm, and drew him along toward a small room on the left, where the stronger light showed the statuary that he had not been mistaken. The small chamber was a fair specimen of an ordinary lodging house of the day—dingy with ages of uncleaned walls and unwhitened ceilings. Wooden chairs of an indescribable brown; a table of the same hue and material; a corner-cupboard garnished with broken cups and saucers—a piece of sealing-wax—a tallow candle in a brass candlestick, and a bottle with two or three glasses; a looking-glass of the breadth of one's hand; an old cracked punch-bowl, and two apostle spoons, made up the furniture. To these were added a pair of tobacco pipes on the table, with a pile of shag tobacco in an open box, and several other articles, the peculiar property of the young tenant.

But if to find Richard Newark, the son of the wealthy and somewhat ostentatious Sir John, in so lowly a dwelling, excited the wonder of the statuary, what was his surprise at the appearance of the young man himself! The gay apparel which Richard, with youthful vanity, had ever affected, was partly cast aside, and he stood before Van Noost in the garb of a seaman, with large breeches tied with enormous bunches of ribbon at the knees, gray stockings, and half a foot of clean shirt shown at his waist. The upper man displayed the marks of a rather superior station. The long-waisted, broad-flapped coat, with a small silver lace, seemed to indicate an aspirant to future command, and, at the same time, gave him the appearance of a man five or six years older than he really was; while the waistcoat of embroidered silk, and the laced cravat, showed the remnant of still higher pretensions.

"Will Van Noost sit down and take a pipe?" said Richard Newark. "We will soon have a glass of grog and a good gossip. Ay, do not stare till your eyes leap into the tobacco-box. Here I am, a sailor for the nonce; and, on my life and soul, I have a great mind to remain one till my dying day. Why, man, I never knew what freedom was before. Here I can go where I like, do what I like, say any thing I please, to man, woman, or child, and no one takes offense or calls me a fool for my pains. 'Tis but a mad trick of the sailor-lad, do what I will; and I have learned more man's knowledge in this garb, during the month I have been in London, than I should have learned during ten years at Ale."

"Pray God, Master Richard, you have not learned more than is good for you!" ejaculated Van Noost. "I had an apprentice from the country who was quite spoiled with three months' residence in London."

"But I am no apprentice, noble lead-boiler," retorted Richard. "What makes you think there is any thing spoilable in me? I am not a haunch of venison, nor a new-caught trout, a cream tart, nor a jelly, to grow moldy on a moist day, or stink in the nose when the wind is southerly. What makes you think I may, can, might, could, should, or ought to be spoiled?"

"Why, because I find you here, sir, masquerading in a low house," replied Van Noost, "while your beautiful cousin is pining in solitude in a house hard by, your father a prisoner in the Tower, and your best friend in bonds at Preston."

Richard Newark was instantly serious, and he leaned his head on his hand for a moment in deep thought.

"You are wise," he said at length; "very wise, as this world's wisdom goes. So all men would judge me, seeing only what you see. But you are mistaken, nymph-maker. As to my father, his life is saved, if it ever was in danger, which I do not think. The son's virtue in abandoning rebels has been taken for an equipoise to the father's guilt in encouraging them underhand. That I have made sure of. Deserters and recreants are prime favorites now at court, and as I was one of the first, I was abundantly well received."

He paused, with a bitter and sarcastic expression of countenance, and then went on,

"As to Emmeline, do not think, Master Leadmelter, that I forget her. What am I here for? What am I in this garb for? Is it not to watch over her in secret, and turn the danger from her when it may come? Do I not know every step she takes through the streets? Do I not know when she goes out and when she returns? Do I not see every one who approaches her door? Poor Smeaton!" he continued, in a sadder tone; "what help can be given to him, Heaven knows! I do not. I wonder if it be true that he is one of the prisoners at Preston. Methinks he is not a man to be taken in the same sweep of the net with less fishes."

"Ay, sir, but he would not leave the less fish in the net and break through it himself, as he might have done," replied Van Noost.

"And as you did," said Richard Newark; and then, after a moment's silence, he added, "And so did I. Pshaw! man, do not look red in the gills about it! We are the wise men, and Smeaton the fool; but there are wiser men even than ourselves. For instance: the man who not only turns his back upon his friends, but sells them; the man who makes a merit of his treason, and bargains for something better than forgiveness. Do you understand me?"

"Faith, but darkly, Master Richard," answered Van Noost. "If you know any such, you know more than I do."

"I know one at least," replied Richard; and then, in his usual rambling way, he returned to the subject of his friend, saying, "Poor Smeaton! his has been a hard fate, to be lured into the fatal trap—cheated into the net at the very moment of his happiness. He has had foul play, Van Noost."

"Ay, he complained much of Lord Stair," observed Van Noost. "That man did not behave well to him."

"Lord Stair!" cried Richard Newark, with a laugh. "There were others who behaved worse than Lord Stair. Indeed, I know not that Lord Stair behaved ill at all—but others did. Lord Stair did not intercept his letters; Lord Stair did not lure him to meetings of conspirators upon false pretenses; Lord Stair did not give information secretly against him, pretending to be his friend—but others did. Lord Stair did not take every means to drive him into rebellion, in order to get his estate—but others did."

"Who—who?" asked Van Noost, eagerly.

"My father," answered Richard Newark; and a dead silence followed for several minutes.

At length Van Noost said, in a low, quiet tone,

"I think, Master Richard, if all this can be proved, the government would deal with the Earl of Eskdale's case favorably."

"And who is to prove it?" exclaimed Richard, vehemently. "Am I to go and denounce my own father to the government? Am I to expose all these turnings and windings of his to grave officials in flowing wigs?"

"No; but you might tell Lord Stair himself," replied Van Noost. "You might show him how this noble lord has been wronged; and, if he really have any regard for him, and be the man that people say he is, he will intercede for him with the king."

Richard Newark leaned his head upon his hand and mused.

"Lord Stair is in Paris," he said, at length, "and I can not—I must not—quit this spot. Besides, how do we know that Smeaton is living even now? They have shot some forty of their prisoners at Preston."

"Those were only officers who had served in King George's forces," replied Van Noost, "and, being found in rebellion, were tried by a court-martial and executed on the spot; but the noble lord was not among them. I have seen the list this very day. He is among those whom they are marching up to London."

"Well, we shall see, we shall see," said Richard. "We shall have time, at least. Time is every thing in this world, as the grasshopper says; and, if I dared stir from this place, perhaps I might do something; but I must see Smeaton first. They keep them somewhat loosely in their prisons, and I shall get in, I dare say."

"But what keeps you here, sir?" asked Van Noost. "You surely can not be tied down to this one little street."

"Very nearly," replied the young gentleman. "I am seldom absent for many minutes till that house opposite is shut up at night. Did you ever see a cat sitting before a mouse-hole, Van Noost, hour after hour, looking half asleep, yet ready to spring the moment the little brown gentleman with the long tail pops out, and nothing showing her impatience but by the convulsions of the tip of her tail? Well, I am just the cat, watching for I know what will follow, though I know not when. My scoundrel mouse is winding about in his secret holes and crannies, and thinking I know nothing of his doings. But let us talk of other things. I will think of all this, and you come and see me every day. There, drink some brandy and smoke your pipe—or will you have wine? We will get wine in a minute. Here, William—John! My two hounds, where are you?"

To Van Noost's surprise, two men, or rather lads, for neither of them certainly was two-and-twenty, appeared in answer to the young gentleman's summons, dressed both alike, yet not exactly in livery, though they evidently acted the part of Richard Newark's servants. One was sent one way for meat, and another for wine; and, changing his place, the young gentleman seated himself behind a blind near the window, whence he could see down the little street in which the house stood. When the men had returned and set down the things which had been ordered, with plates, glasses, and knives, Richard moved his place again, saying to the elder of the two,

"Mind the watch, for I shall be busy for an hour or so."

"A bird shall not fly past without our seeing him," replied the man, and left the room with his companion.

At all times and in all circumstances, Van Noost was well pleased to eat and drink. Care, fear, or anxiety never took away his appetite, and he did ample justice to the viands set before him.

A rambling, desultory conversation followed, but Richard Newark would not suffer it to fall back into the channels through which it had been previously flowing. He talked of all that had occurred during the insurrection, of his own escapade to the North, and of what he had seen and done while traveling about with the Northumbrian gentlemen; and, though his conversation and his manners were now more like his former self, yet Van Noost could not help being much struck with the great change which had come over him within the last few months. That short period of busy existence—the companionship of men, and the association with superior minds—had effected a remarkable transformation; but the manliness of manner and decision of thought which he had gained could only be attributed to the habit and necessity of acting for himself, and the development, under such necessity, of a character naturally decided, sharp, and fearless, though rather distorted and out of shape.

The time passed pleasantly enough, and on his departure Van Noost promised to return. He did not fail to keep his word, but went back more than once, gaining in some degree upon Richard Newark's confidence at each visit, and consulting with him upon what was to be done in the case of the Earl of Eskdale.

The result of these consultations we shall see hereafter; but one thing Van Noost could not comprehend in his companion, namely, the obstinacy with which he refrained from going to see his fair cousin, and from even letting her know that he was in her immediate neighborhood. The good statuary tried many circuitous ways of arriving at his motives; and when at length he asked him distinctly, Richard replied, with one of his wild laughs,

"Ay, you could not understand, Van Noost; and, to say truth, I myself do not understand. I have seen birds caught by perching on lime twigs. Things have been put into my head which I wish had never come into it. Besides, I am better where I am. I can do more, devise more, prevent more, when I am working unseen. No, no, it would never do; but I'll tell you what, good friend, I must have a little liberty and some fresh air. I must arrange, and trust to my two boys for a day now and then. I am getting ill in this close hole, and my brain begins to spin and whirl round as it used to do at school. Can you not contrive to hire us a couple of horses? for mine I sold when I came to London. We will have a ride, Van Noost—we will have a ride on the north road."

Van Noost readily consented; and it was agreed that the next day, at the hour of noon, he should be with a pair of horses in Smithfield, where Richard Newark was to join him.

The young gentleman was on the spot before him, and there was an eagerness and excitement in his look which the statuary did not understand. Springing on the horse's back, Richard Newark set off at a pace much too fast to be agreeable to his companion. They soon cleared the suburbs of London, however, passing a great number of people on the road, some on horseback and some on foot, who were all tending the same way, though at a more sober pace.

"I wonder what these people are all pouring out of London for," said Van Noost, as they rode along. "There must be some sport going forward."

"Ha! ha! don't you know!" exclaimed Richard, wildly. "They are going to meet the prisoners coming in, and so am I!"

This announcement was not altogether palatable to the good statuary, who felt certain that he should be recognized by some of the prisoners, and be placed in an awkward position. It was not, indeed, that he feared his acquaintance with those who had joined in the insurrection would in any degree endanger his personal safety—and, to do him justice, he would have risked that under any circumstances—but as it was, he had made a clean breast of it to the secretary of state, and obtained even more than he could expect, amounting, in fact, to a conditional pardon. The thought, however, of having fled from Preston; of not remaining with Roman courage (which he always had an ambition of displaying, if his constitution would but have let him) to fall with a falling cause; and of having sneaked away in much haste and trepidation at the approach of real danger, made him feel very awkward when he thought of encountering his former companions in rebellion. He explained his feelings to Richard Newark as well as he could, hinting, at the same time, that the young gentleman himself was in a similar situation.

But Richard only laughed aloud, saying, "Well, get out of the way, then, when we come near them. Pop into an inn, or hide your shame-faced noddle in some barn or shed. As for me, I shall go up and speak to any one I know. I am not the least ashamed of any thing I have done, and I will cut that man's throat who says I have cause to be."

They rode on as far as Highgate, leaving the crowd behind them as they went; and, a little beyond that place, they saw a cloud of dust upon the road before them, which seemed to announce the approach of the prisoners. There was a small public house near, in which Van Noost took refuge as speedily as possible. Richard Newark dismounted also, but he remained on the outside of the house, with his arms folded on his chest. Half an hour elapsed, however, before the procession which they expected appeared, for the dust which they had seen was raised merely by a large party of horse grenadiers and foot guards, sent out to meet the unfortunate prisoners from Preston and escort them into London.

After calling for something for the good of the house, Van Noost placed himself at the window of the little sanded parlor with a number of other persons, while the road before him was occupied by a small crowd from Highgate and the neighboring villages. At length the advance of a large body of men along the road was descried, and on they came at a slow pace, while a loyal shout of "Long live King George, and down with the Pretender!" burst from the crowd without.

Poor Van Noost's heart felt very big; and when he saw the whole indignity to which his poor friends had been subjected, it was too much for him. Noblemen and gentlemen of high and distinguished character, men of honor, and refinement, and unblemished reputation, were being marched into London with their arms pinioned with ropes, each of their horses led by one of the foot guards, often by a mere common halter, while a large party of cavalry preceded and followed, but did not flank them, as if for the express purpose of exposing them fully to the gaze of the multitude. Van Noost caught a momentary glance of many whom he knew, and especially of the Earl of Eskdale; but he saw little of what passed after, except that Richard Newark ran forward, laid his hand upon Smeaton's knee, and spoke to him eagerly, walking by the side of his horse till one of the soldiers put him rudely back.

The poor statuary's eyes filled with tears; and, retiring from the window, he made place for those who were struggling to get forward.

CHAPTER XLII.

The Tower, the Marshalsea, Newgate, and other London jails, were filled to overflowing. Prison regulations, which were few, and those not very strict, were all but entirely neglected; and scenes of revelry and merriment, the most discordant with the place and all its situations, occurred in the cells of the captives. It was not alone that the Tory or High-Church party, waking from the apathy in which they had indulged as long as activity could have been serviceable to the cause, now contributed large sums of money to make the fate of the captives as comfortable as a captive's fate can be; it was not alone that the numerous friends and relations of the prisoners flocked to give them consolation and support of every kind, but a revolution took place in that strange fickle thing, public opinion, and many of those who, had not their rank and station stood in the way, would have gone out with the hooting mob to witness the entrance of the rebel prisoners into London, now began to regard them as martyrs and laud them as heroes. Crowds hurried to see them and to testify their sympathy. No one who could find or frame even a specious pretext for admission was excluded; all hours and seasons were forgotten, and the gates of Newgate were often thrown open in the midst of the night to admit a visitor, a servant, or a friend. The jailers declared that they were worn to death with the continual turning of the keys; yet they did their work very willingly, from no great feeling of compassion, perhaps, but for the golden rewards which were sure to follow.

In the Tower, where the noblemen who had joined in the insurrection were confined, a greater degree of decency certainly prevailed; but even here very great laxity existed, and from ten o'clock in the morning till the same hour at night the doors were opened to almost any one who required admittance. In fact, the conduct of the authorities, from the day of the surrender at Preston till the termination of the whole tragedy, is perfectly unaccountable, so capricious and strange were the alternations of lenity and severity. During the march to London, it often happened that on one day the prisoners of note would be confined in separate chambers, and not permitted to see or speak with any one, while on the very next they were allowed to wander about any towns they passed through, each under the charge of a soldier, visiting their friends, or purchasing whatever articles they required in the shops. One day they would be compelled to sleep upon damp stone floors, with none of the comforts or conveniences of life, and the next they would dine with the officers of their escort, faring sumptuously on all that the place could afford. At one time the sick and the feeble were provided with coaches to carry them, with nothing but a trooper at the window, and then, at Barnet, they were pinioned on their horses, and led into London like condemned felons. Thus, too, after their arrival at the place of their destination, they were allowed to live in luxury, and, alas! in many cases in licentiousness, while all the time the terrible catastrophe was being prepared with stern, relentless determination.

In many instances the prisoners themselves, at least those of thoughtful and high-toned character, were obliged to entreat their jailers to exclude the mixed multitude which flocked in to see them, and even then they were often greatly annoyed, for the virtue of the turnkeys was not stout enough to resist the bribes which were frequently given for admission to the cells. The greater number, indeed, were well pleased with the attentions they received, and laughed, joked, and drank with the strangers who presented themselves; but it must be said that a general impression prevailed among them that the facts of their having surrendered at discretion, and of their being spared for the time, would secure them from the penalties of treason. Many were even ignorant of the terms on which the surrender had been made, and thoroughly believed that a promise of pardon had been given; and others felt quite confident that the exertions of influential friends would gain for them the lenity of a merciful sovereign.

But George the First was *not* merciful. Perhaps it would be too much to accuse him of a disposition naturally cruel; but his heart was as hard as that of any man who ever lived, and his conduct to the young Countess of Nithsdale would prove the truth, even if it were not witnessed by many another act.

Among those who took the least cheering view of his situation was Henry Earl of Eskdale, who flattered himself with no vain expectations. On entering the chamber assigned to him in the Tower, he looked round it as his last abode before he went to the scaffold; and, although the small sum of money he had remaining was sufficient to procure him comforts for the time, he counted it over with care, and assigned a certain portion for each day's wants, calculating, as well as he was able, the time likely to elapse before his death.

The morning after his arrival, a number of persons were admitted to see him; and at length he was glad to give the turnkey a guinea, as an inducement to exclude every one but those who could declare they were his personal friends.

"I have much need of thought and reflection, my good sir," he said; "but, if I am to be troubled with strangers all day long, however kindly their visits may be meant, I shall have no time to prepare to defend my life, or to meet my death as becomes me."

"If your lordship will give a list of those you wish to see," replied the man, "I will keep out all others."

Smeaton wrote down the names of the few whom he thought likely to visit him, but he had some difficulty when he came to the dearest name of all. It was too sacred a name to be lightly spoken of; and therefore, to meet all cases, he wrote down broadly, "Any one of the name of Newark, any one of the name of Eskdale;" and then thinking of poor Van Noost, he added his name to the paper, saying, as he gave it to the man,

"If any one should urge strongly that he is a personal friend, let him send in his name, and I will tell you whether to admit him or not."

The man had not even closed the door, however, when Van Noost presented himself, and his agitation on seeing his noble friend in captivity had something in it both touching and grotesque. He wept like a child; but the pathetic was greatly lessened by his attempts to conceal his emotion and speak through his tears. Smeaton treated him with great kindness, congratulated him upon his escape and his freedom, and listened patiently to his account of all he had undergone since they met. But he then turned the conversation to matters of deeper interest to himself by inquiring if his visitor had seen Emmeline as he promised.

Van Noost almost started from his chair, exclaiming,

"Good gracious! I had nearly forgotten. I saw her this very morning, my lord; and she charged me with a message to say that she would be here this evening as soon as it grew dark, if you would permit it; and, indeed, who would not permit it? It seemed as if she thought the time between this and night would never come to an end. I believe she would have run here at once, if the old lady, Madame Culpepper, had not dissuaded her."

Smeaton did not reply immediately, for many contending feelings were busy in his bosom. To hold her once again to his heart; to tell her how he had thought of her since they parted; to learn from her own lips her views, her wishes, her feelings; to consult with and to counsel her, were all motives which prompted him to say "Yes" without a moment's hesitation. But he feared risk, and embarrassment, and perhaps even misfortune, to her whom he loved better than himself. He knew not that she was accustomed to come daily to the Tower; that her person was known to the warders and many of the officers of the prison; and that she was always accompanied by sufficient men to protect her, as far as they were permitted to go. He thought of Emmeline only as the simple, inexperienced girl of the Manor House in Devonshire, timid even in her innocent boldness, utterly unlearned in the world and the world's ways. He knew not that she, as well as Richard, had been schooled in sorrow, and that her mind had put forth new powers, and her heart gained firmness since they parted.

Can he be blamed, however, if he yielded, in some degree, to his own wishes? He fancied that he considered all things fairly for her good, as well as for his own happiness; but perhaps he was not altogether unbiased when he said,

"Tell her, Van Noost, that I ardently long to see her, but yet I would not have her come, especially at night, unless she can do so in perfect safety, and in secrecy also; for, till we have well considered the next step, I do not wish our marriage to be made public; and I must have no spot rest upon her name, even for her love to me. If she can come safely, she knows what joy it will give me. If she can not, that joy would be dearly purchased by peril to her. So tell her, Van Noost. Go, my dear friend, go, and let her have my answer quickly."

"I will, my good lord, I will," replied the statuary, fumbling in the wide pocket of his coat; "but there is another matter I had well-nigh forgot too. Here is something I promised to deliver to your lordship."

And, as he spoke, he produced a little packet—in shape very much like a school-boy's ruler, wrapped up in paper, and sealed at both ends—which he laid upon the table.

"What is this, Van Noost?" said the young nobleman, taking it up and surprised at its weight. "This is money, my good friend. I can not accept of this."

"Indeed, my lord, you must," responded Van Noost, "or make a great many people very unhappy. It is your share of a purse made up among the loyal and true hearts of London for the support of all Preston prisoners, and for their aid in their imprisonment, their defense, or—" and he sunk his voice in a whisper—"or their escape. You have no more than your fair share; and I doubt not that, in a few days, a very much larger sum may be raised, of which your portion will be brought to you also, either by me or by somebody else."

"Their escape!" said Smeaton, thoughtfully. "Think you that escape is possible, Van Noost?"

"Nothing more possible, my lord," replied the statuary. "Why, never was such a scene known as there is now in the prisons. Money is abundant—all order is gone. The jailers think they do quite enough if they only lock the doors. They vie with each other in being corrupt; and, if we could but raise a few thousand pounds to bribe the scoundrels, and we managed the thing properly, your lordship might walk out of these gates in open day, without officer, turnkey, or warder seeing you. Such is the strange effect of a pair of gold spectacles."

"Would I could feel so certain," returned Smeaton. "The few thousand pounds you speak of could soon be raised. A word in my dear mother's ear would speedily procure it, if she be still living; and, if not, I could procure it myself."

"Think you so, my lord, think you so?" said the statuary. "Would you but trust me so much as to write down merely the words, 'Believe what the bearer shall tell you on my account,' sign your name, and address it to the dowager countess? I see they allow you paper, pens, and ink."

"With all my heart, Van Noost," replied Smeaton. "I am quite sure you would rather injure yourself than me."

And he wrote down on a sheet of paper the words which had been required.

When he had sanded the paper and was handing it to Van Noost, a sound of bolts being drawn was heard at the door. The statuary hurriedly concealed what he had received, and the next moment Richard Newark came in. He advanced toward the earl with a frank, bright look, and shook him warmly by the hand. Then turning to Van Noost, he said,

"Ha! idol maker! are you here? Get you gone—get you gone to Emmeline, and stay with her till I come. The dear *gouvernante* has gone forth questing like a spaniel dog upon a pheasant, from a hint I gave her last night. Do not leave her for a minute; and, if the man refuses you admittance, pull his nose boldly, and walk in. He is an arrant coward; so you may venture safely."

"I will—I will, sir," replied Van Noost. "He shall not stop me on such an errand."

"If there be two of them," continued Richard, "knock down one. That will be enough for the other."

Van Noost hurriedly took up his hat and left the room, and Richard Newark, taking Smeaton's hand in his, said, in a quieter tone than usual,

"Come, Eskdale, sit down and talk to me. I must try and keep my poor whirling brain steady for a minute or two, while you tell me all and every thing with regard to your transactions with Lord Stair. There is your only chance of safety. If you can show that you were driven into the insurrection against your own inclination by the conduct of others, as I know you were, a skillful lawyer tells me that you will certainly be pardoned. Now listen to what I know, then fill up the gaps, give me some proofs, and I will follow the scent as keenly as my blood-hound Bellmouth. You sent a letter long before the outbreak to Lord Stair. That letter never reached him. It was stopped by my father. You went over to Mount Place, led to believe that you would see nobody but one old fool, and you found twenty or thirty, young and old, assembled, on a hint from my father, to meet you and trap you into treason. The Exeter people sent down dragoons, who sought you at Mount Place, and thence tracked you to Keanton, for they had secret information from Ale-Manor."

"But what could be your father's motive?" asked Smeaton.

"Keanton for the first; to get you out of the way of Emmeline for the second," answered Richard. "But never mind motives; let us deal with facts. You afterward, in the North, sent your servant with a letter to Lord Stair, on receiving intelligence that he was on before us at Wooler. Now, Eskdale, I doubt that letter ever having been seen by him. Nay, I am quite sure it was not."

"Higham assured me," said the young earl, "that it was put into his hand, that he opened it, read it, and returned it with contempt. What can make you think that he never saw it?"

"Because Lord Stair was, on that very day and hour, more than seven hundred miles from Wooler as the crow flies," replied Richard. "His regiment was there, true enough, but *he* was in Paris. A man can not be in two places at once, noble friend. But come, do not pause and wonder. This is all I know. Fill up, fill up! Let me hear the whole, and I will try if my wits are not worth something, in spite of all folks may say against them."

Smeaton did as he was bidden; and, sitting down at the table with his young companion, he gave him a clear and complete narrative of every thing that had occurred after his arrival at Ale-Manor, and showed him the copies he had taken of his letters to Lord Stair. More than once Richard asked him to stop for a moment, while he wrote down the heads of what he had heard, and then, looking at the letters, he said,

"May I take these with me to copy? You shall have them to-morrow, for you may need them. Strange that a piece of paper should sometimes be the best armor for a man's neck!"

"Take them, take them," replied Smeaton. "They are but unauthenticated copies, and could not be given in evidence, if Lord Stair has not received them. Yet I can hardly believe that Higham would play me such a trick."

"Where did you hire him?" asked Richard.

"He was recommended to me by the man in whose house I lodged," replied the young earl: "a good, honest fellow, who had been a servant to the Earl of Oxford."

"Put about you by the Jacobites," replied Richard, with a laugh, "to keep you steady in the cause, and commit you to it if you wavered. The man must be found, and made to tell the truth."

"I fear you will have to seek him in the grave," said Smeaton, "for he was sorely wounded at Preston, where he fought as boldly as a lion."

"Never mind," replied Richard. "Some of these letters must have reached Lord Stair, I think; and, if I get at him, I will jump upon his back, and never take my spurs from his side till we have passed the winning-post. Good-by, Eskdale, good-by. Your trial will not come on for a month, they say, and you won't see me for a fortnight, perhaps; but I'll be working all the time. Tell Emmeline to mind well every step she takes, for the villain scoundrel, William Newark, alias Somerville, has made his peace with the court, pretends that he is the most loyal subject of King George, has betrayed all that he knew of Kenmure's and Forster's secrets, and is watching with all his eyes to pounce upon Emmeline. He can not rightly make out where she is, for I have puzzled him about it. But he thinks that if he could but get her into his hands, Ale-Manor—which is hers, you know—would be his, and he would be a great man in his generation. Once more, good-by, Eskdale; and if you hear that I am drowned, shot, stabbed, or otherwise disposed of, do not forget me. Say to yourself, 'I was kind to the boy, and he loved me well.'"

Thus speaking, he hurried to the door, and hallooed to the turnkey to let him out.

CHAPTER XLIII.

I WILL not dwell upon the first interview between Emmeline and her husband; I will not dwell upon many that took place, for many *did* take place between the time of his arrival as a prisoner in London and the day of his trial. There are sanctities in the deep emotions of the heart, the violation of which nothing but a holy cause can justify. I have no right to eat the shew-bread on the altar of their love. I have no right, be they real or be they ideal characters, to intrude into the secrets of their hearts, and place the thrilling nerves beneath a microscope for the public eye. Suffice it to say that they met often, daily, sometimes twice a day, by the skillful management of her who had been the young earl's nurse, and that no annoyance or inconvenience happened to the young Countess of Eskdale during nearly a month, although some circumstances of suspicion—a number of strange men hovering about the house, and the appearance of others dogging them in their walk to the Tower—caused some apprehension in the mind of the old housekeeper, and induced her to redouble her precautions.

Emmeline had seen her cousin more than once. Kind, affectionate, self-devoted, he showed himself during their short and scanty interviews, but those interviews were not very many. Suddenly he disappeared, telling his fair cousin that he was about to visit Paris, but without mentioning the business on which he went; for, although he was very sanguine in all things, he loved her too well to give her hopes which might be disappointed, or to shackle her exertions in other directions by expectations from the uncertain projects he had in view. She knew that he went for the purposes of her husband's defense, and she thanked him with her whole heart; but this was all she knew; and when he was gone, she felt anxious and eager for tidings which did not come.

Thus passed the days of a long imprisonment; but several steps had been gained, notwithstanding. The extreme laxity of those who had charge of the prisoners had become apparent, and Smeaton had established a certain sort of friendship with his jailers; but the principal fact was that they showed themselves accessible to bribes, so that the probability of escape was reasonably added to the probability of acquittal or of pardon. Nevertheless, with hope for their guide, they flattered themselves that the delay in bringing the prisoners to trial arose from the intention of sparing them; but they experienced a bitter disappointment in the end, when Smeaton and the rest were impeached of high treason by the House of Commons, and their trial came on with unusual rapidity.

As is well known, the greater part of the insurgent noblemen pleaded guilty. But Smeaton would not join in this plea. He acknowledged the whole share he had borne in the rebellion; he entered into minute details of all that had occurred; he showed, as well as he had the means of showing, that he was actually driven to join the insurgents; but he could bring no proof of the fact. Richard was still absent, although he had promised to return in a fortnight, and nothing had been heard of him when the trial took place. Smeaton's mere unsupported word had little weight with the peers; but, while most of the others were, upon their own plea, condemned at once, a space of time was taken to consider and to allow for the collection of evidence before his trial.

The lawyers labored hard to induce him to withdraw his plea of not guilty, and cast himself upon the royal mercy; but, although his mind, till the insurrection had actually begun, had been in that doubtful and undecided state which is most painful to men of a determined and resolute character, yet, once having joined in it, either the prejudices of early education resumed their sway, or the enthusiasm of his companions infected his own mind, and he could not bring himself to believe that there was guilt in supporting by arms the sovereign whom all his family had served, and whose claim to the throne of England they had never on any occasion renounced. He did not feel himself guilty, and he would not plead guilty. It was a dishonoring word—a word that he would not have attached to any part of his conduct by his own act, and he resolutely adhered to his former plea. He gave no unnecessary trouble, indeed; he admitted all the facts as they stood charged against him; but he contended that his acts were loyal and not treasonable; and it was only as an admission that he stated he had been willing to submit quietly to the existing state of things. To this, he added a detail of the transactions between himself and the Earl of Stair.

His defense was frequently interrupted, for the English law often decrees that the evidence which would clearly exculpate any man from all moral blame shall not be received in his justification. But he persevered in his course; and the very men who condemned him felt for him, and hardly believed their own words when they pronounced him guilty.

It is a strange thing, that law of treason, which affixes the most odious moral censure upon acts heroically mistaken and sometimes sublimely just; which compels men, by rigid rules and the admission of false premises, to pronounce that to be guilt which they know to be virtue; which places the same stain upon the lowest and most selfish crimes, and upon the most elevated and patriotic deeds. A great fault exists somewhere: it is true, order and respect for law must be maintained; the will of the majority must rule; it may be, even, that, for general security, men must be punished for bold attacks upon existing institutions; but let us not be called upon to denounce as guilt that which is mistake, or enthusiasm, or virtue.

The dark scene was over; the verdict was given, the sentence pronounced, the blade of the ax turned toward the prisoner; and one more of the gallant and the true was carried back from the bar to the Tower, to await the fate of a traitor.

In the anticipation of that moment, Smeaton had often felt how terrible it would be. He had doubted his own courage, his own fortitude; he had nerved his mind to resist all the impulses of his mortal nature, lest he should meanly and faint-heartedly supplicate for life, as others had done. He recollected that there were many endearing ties around him; that youth, and love, and hope, and high health, and all the bright amenities of being, attached him to the world in which he was; that it was full of delight and enjoyment to one so constituted mentally and bodily; and that the thought of parting with it in its hour of greatest excellence might well shake his resolution and undermine his firmness. But when each peer had pronounced his judgment, and when the frightful and barbarous sentence was passed, it was marvelous, even to his own mind, how calmly he bore himself, how firm and composed he felt. It seemed for the moment as if the tremulous, vibrating, anxious chord between hope and fear was snapped, and that his feet were firmly fixed upon the rock of fate. Take away hope, and there is no such thing as fear.

During a short space of time all hope was over in his bosom. But, in the mean while, others were preparing hope for him, and to two separate scenes we must turn, where busy love was eagerly exerting itself, in different ways and without concert, to avert the blow from his head. I know not which to depict first, for they both occurred on the same day and very nearly at the same hour; but perhaps I had better choose the one which, from presenting few if any characters already brought under notice, may have the least interest for the reader.

Into a gorgeous room of a palace, containing a number of distinguished persons—some marked out to the eye by the splendor of their apparel, some by their beauty or their grace—entered a middle-aged man, small in stature, insignificant in appearance, and with his somewhat large head rendered more ridiculously conspicuous by a huge Ramillies wig. He was dressed in tea-colored velvet, with his sword by his side and his hat on, and the door by which he entered was thrown open for him by one of the high noblemen of the court, while another, bearing a light in either hand, walked backward into the room before him. He was a very mean-looking person; cold, unlovable in aspect, looking like a small dancing-master in a holiday suit; but yet he was a king.

At one side of the room, supporting herself by the back of a chair, stood a tall and queenly woman of some sixty years of age. Her natural hair, as white as snow, appeared slightly from beneath the weeds of widowhood; and her striking and beautiful face—beautiful even in sorrow—was pale and worn with long and heavy sickness. The moment the king entered, she advanced toward him with a step firm and dignified; but she sank upon her knees as she came near, and stretch-out her hands toward him, holding what appeared to be a petition.

"Who are you, madam, who are you?" asked the king, in French.

"I am the unhappy Countess of Eskdale, sire," replied the lady, in the same language. "I do beseech you, hear me, and receive my petition for my poor son. Spare him, gracious monarch —spare him, and I pledge—"

She was not permitted to finish the sentence. The cold-hearted king drew back at her first words, and, with a sort of frightened and repulsive look, turned toward a different door from that by which he had entered. But the lady caught him by the skirt of his coat, pleading with all the earnestness of maternal love for her son's life, while he rudely endeavored to shake himself free, walking with a quick step toward the other side of the room, and literally dragging her after him as she still kept her hold, endeavoring to force the petition upon him.

A gentleman with a cut upon his brow, who had entered with the monarch, now whispered in his ear in French,

"Be firm, sire! be firm! Shall I remove her?"

The monarch made an eager motion of assent, and the other, casting his arms round Lady Eskdale, tore her away. The paper which she held in her hand dropped to the ground; and, instantly rising to her full height as the monarch passed the door, she turned a look of dignified anger on him who had interposed to prevent the reception of her petition, and exclaimed aloud, in English,

"Oh, William Newark, William Newark! Ever ready, like the viper, to sting the hand that has fostered you, and to aid in all that is hard and selfish!"

"Poor lady!" said the gentleman thus addressed, with a look of contemptuous pity; and he followed the king. But there was another who followed also—a grave-looking man of the middle age, with a calm and placid countenance, and a blue ribbon across his breast. With a quick but easy step, he hurried on and overtook King George just as he had crossed an ante-room and was about to enter a large drawing-room beyond, round which were grouped a great number of brilliant-looking people in a blaze of light. He ventured to stop the sovereign in his advance, saying something to him in a very low tone in the Latin language, for many of the first nobility of England at that period did not speak French or German, and the first George's stock of English was not very copious.

"Who is he—who is he?" asked the monarch, also speaking Latin, though not in its greatest purity. "What does he want at this hour?"

"He bears dispatches from Lord Stair, sire," the nobleman answered who had spoken to him, "and is charged to deliver them immediately into your majesty's own hands. He is the young gentleman whom your majesty declared to be more praiseworthy, on account of his speedy repentance and atonement, than others who had never joined the rebellion."

He spoke still in a low tone; but the monarch replied, aloud, "Admit him—admit him. He is a strange boy, but whatever comes from my Lord Stair is worthy of immediate attention."

"The dispatches were to be delivered in private, sire," observed the other; "but the bearer was detained for want of horses on the Dover road. Shall I—"

"So be it, so be it," replied the king. "Close the doors again. Make every body quit the room but you and Walpole, my lord, and then bring the young man in."

The personage to whom he spoke proceeded to fulfill his commands, and William Newark, in obedience to those commands, quitted the room with a scowling brow, which was not brightened by the passing of Richard Newark in the very door-way. He did not venture to say any thing, however, and the lad advanced with a small packet in his hand straight toward the king, without any other salutation than merely a low bow.

"Bend your knee, bend your knee," said the elderly nobleman, in a whisper; and the lad, after a moment's hesitation, did as he was directed.

"I am glad to see you again, young gentleman," said King George. "You have been to Paris, I suppose." And, at the same time he took the packet and broke it open. It contained two sheets; but, before he proceeded to examine either of them, the monarch added a question. "Do you know," he asked, "why Lord Stair happened to address me personally instead of the secretary?"

"Because the matter was for your majesty's own ear," replied Richard Newark, somewhat abruptly. "We do not give an apple to one boy to hand it to another, for fear he should eat it himself."

The king laughed good-humoredly, and proceeded to read the first sheet, which, beginning at the bottom of the first page, and ending at the top of the fourth page, did not seem to contain much matter. Whatever that matter was, it seemed to give the king great satisfaction. "That is good—that is very good," he said. "He is an invaluable man. We shall know how to honor him. All is safe in that quarter." He then turned to the other sheet, and his face instantly changed.

"Ha!" he said, with a curling lip and an irritable eye. "More about this Lord Eskdale! He joined the rebels wittingly, adhered to them till the last moment, was taken with arms in his hands, and he must die. I have signed the warrant."

"Then kill me first, sir," rejoined Richard Newark, bluffly, "for I first helped to engage him in the rebellion; and, had it not been for his advice, I should never have quitted it. He went against his own will, as your majesty will see if you read; and, if he dies, it will be as a bird that is caught in a trap because he was deceived by the baits set for him. Your majesty can not understand till you read, any more than I can see through that wall; for there is a great deal beyond your sight or mine, unless a door be opened for each of us to look through."

The king gazed at him for a moment in utter surprise, as if completely astounded by the lad's impudence; but gradually a sense of the justice of what he had heard seemed to overpower the slight sense of anger, and, without answering a syllable, he turned his eyes to the paper, and proceeded to read it to the very end. When he had done so, the expression of his countenance was again greatly changed: a hesitating and embarrassed look came upon his face. He put his finger under his large wig, rubbed his temple, and pulled up one of his stockings, which had somewhat slipped down the leg, and most likely tickled his shin; then turning to another gentleman present, he said, "Come with me, Mr. Walpole—come with me, my lord. I will go to my cabinet for a moment."

Thus saying, he took two steps toward the door by which he had entered, but then turned a sharp glance upon Richard Newark, who was standing by with a vacant air, looking down at the hilt of his sword. It was the same sword which Smeaton had given to him.

The monarch's look was certainly not very placable at first, but something seemed to touch the risible organs in his brain or heart—wherever they may lie; and we all know that in those organs a great deal of the milk of human kindness is secreted. He laughed, low but gayly, and said,

"Get away, sir, get away. Lord Stair has trusted his letters to a somewhat indiscreet messenger."

"The best in the world could not have done better, your majesty," replied Richard Newark, boldly, "for he has delivered them safely into the best hands in the realm."

If he meant it, nothing could have been more dexterous than his reply. It was a compliment, slightly veiled under a rudeness. But I very much doubt whether he did mean it. However, King George smiled most graciously, saying,

"Go, sir, go. We shall not forget you."

Richard Newark bowed and retired, while the king again took a step or two toward the door.

Before he passed out of the room, however, the king turned to a gentleman with a florid countenance, saying,

"We shall not meet that woman again, I hope, for I have not quite made up my mind. Keep that man, Sir William Newark, from me. I do not like him as I did."

So saying, and suffering Mr. Walpole and one of his attendants to precede him, he followed slowly and thoughtfully out of the room.

The adjoining chamber was by this time vacant; the unhappy Lady Eskdale had left it the moment after she had received so violent a rebuff; and the courtiers who had been present when she sought to force her petition upon the king, concluding that he had passed on into the drawing-room, had thronged thither by another way. But a full hour elapsed before the monarch joined his guests.

Now let us turn to the other scene which I have mentioned, in which strong affection was busily engaged for Smeaton's deliverance, but in a different manner. Let us break into the middle of it, however, for what is to follow will explain what is past.

"No, no, dearest lady," said old Mrs. Culpepper, in a low but eager tone, "it must not be. The boat is prepared, the ship ready to sail the moment his foot is on board. You must go with him, and all will be safe."

"Then who is to stay and personate him in the prison?" asked Emmeline. "Indeed it must be as I have said. Although you have bribed the people to shut their eyes, yet I do not believe they dare venture to let three people pass out when only two have passed in. In this I will have my way, indeed. I fear nothing. I do not believe there is any man so cruel as to punish a wife for saving her husband's life. I will wrap myself in his *roquelaure*, and sit brooding over the fire. My heart may beat, but no one will see it. My eyes may overflow, but I will cover them with my hands. The first plan was the best—far the best; and it is my bounden duty, as well as my earnest wish, to risk any thing to myself for his sake. Oh, Heaven! what happiness will it be hereafter, even if they should shut me in a prison and never let me see his face again, to think that I have saved him!"

"It is the same plan still, dear lady," replied Mrs. Culpepper, with her usual calm and quiet manner; "but you must not, can not execute it in the way you propose. Consider your height, the difference between your tiny figure and his. They would be blind indeed to mistake you; and we can not expect them to be so blind as that. I am shorter than he is, but still I am very tall, and the difference will not easily be seen. They will not mark very exactly, especially if he put his handkerchief to his face, and seem to weep. My clothes will nearly fit him, too, and—"

"And, will you—will you stay in his place?" asked Emmeline, gazing in her face with a look of wonder and gratitude. "What will you say when they find you there? You have no such excuse as I have."

"I will say, lady," replied the woman, earnestly, "that he drew the milk from this breast as an infant; that he was to me as a child when God had taken my own; that he was my nursling, my beloved, my only one, when I had lost all else on earth who loved me or whom I could love. Then, if they choose to shorten my days or make me pass them in a prison, it is but little they can take away and little they can inflict. It must be so indeed, lady; and now we are only losing time. They will not let us pass in or out after eleven. It is now past nine, and it will take some time to disguise him as we wish. Haste, then, to get on your hood. I am quite ready. With this *sacque* above my other clothes, and a large French *capote*, every thing is ready to hide his face and figure."

Emmeline looked down thoughtfully, but she said nothing, for her heart was too full to speak, and in a few minutes they set out upon their adventure, followed by two men-servants, whom the old housekeeper had already prepared for the task in hand.

The moment they were gone, however, one of Sir John Newark's men, who had lived at Ale for several years, and who had been accustomed to act as one of his spies upon all that took place in the house, crept silently out and pursued them with a stealthy step down the little street. He saw them cross Tower Hill, and obtain admission at the gates; and then turning to the right, he approached a house in a neighboring street, hurrying his walk as much as he could without converting it into a run. At the moment he reached the door, one of the ordinary hackney coaches of the day drew up, and a gentleman in somewhat brilliant attire descended with a slow step. The man waited till he had paid the fare, and then plucked him by the sleeve, whispering something in his ear. The gloomy and discontented face of the other instantly cleared up, and he exclaimed, with a mocking laugh, "Ha, ha! Then they have put themselves in the trap. I will away to the Tower. You stay and watch at the gates. But no—better let them be caught in the very act, just when they fancy themselves secure. It will be more meritorious to bring him back after he has actually escaped than to prevent him from doing so. You are sure—quite sure? It would never do to take an old raven instead of a young hawk."

"I am quite sure," replied the man, "for I overheard it all as I listened at the hole I have made in the wall. This morning I could not make out which of the two it is who is to play his part, but just now I heard, and I am quite certain. The old woman was his nurse, it seems, and is ready to sacrifice her life for him."

"Well, well, go to the gates and watch," rejoined William Newark. "Give instant information if they come forth. I will go and get a messenger. There is one lives hard by."

The servant did as the other bade him; but he had not remained many minutes near the gates of the Tower when some quick steps approached, and he turned round toward the new comers.

"Ha, ha, old Truepenny!" said Richard Newark, taking the man's arm in a firm grasp, "what are you on the watch for here?"

"Nothing, Master Richard," answered the man. "I am only just taking the air."

"You won't let your intentions take the air, at all events," retorted Richard Newark. "I know you, serviceable knave! This is the fellow," he continued, turning to the two young men who accompanied him, "this is the fellow who informed of the smuggled tea."

"Then I will baste him to a stock fish," cried one of the youths, brandishing his cudgel.

"No, no," interrupted Richard, with a laugh. "Wait till you get him back at Ale, and then tar and feather him. Hasten off, Argus, or we will leave you no eyes to see out of."

The man had no hesitation in obeying; and, as soon as the young gentleman had relaxed his grasp, ran across the open space as fast as his legs would carry him.

Richard Newark then turned toward the gates again; but, taking three steps in advance, paused, and, after a moment's thought, with his hand pressed upon his brow, quietly glided away to a little distance, followed by the two lads.

CHAPTER XLIV.

At the hour of half past ten, two persons issued forth from the room in the Tower in which the young Earl of Eskdale had been long confined. Both were dressed in female apparel; both were apparently much affected; and it appeared very natural that they should be so, as the following morning was appointed for the bloody spectacle of an execution on Tower Hill. The limbs of the younger and shorter lady trembled so much that they could hardly bear her up; but the other, though apparently weeping and holding a handkerchief to her eyes, seemed much more firm, and contrived to support the wavering steps of her companion as they passed out into the passage.

The jailer who opened the door to give them exit from the room looked in and saw a tall figure, wrapped in a red cloak laced with gold, seated by the fire, with the head leaning on the hand. "All is right," he cried, speaking to another man at the top of the stairs hard by. "Pass them out!"

Hastening onward through the passages and courts of the Tower, as fast as the agitation of the fair girl would permit, they came without obstruction to the outer gate, where the two men-servants were waiting in the little gate-house. The turnkey who accompanied them seemed to be a kind-hearted man for one in such an office, and, while the wicket was being opened, he said, "Don't take it so much to heart, lady. Perhaps he may be pardoned, after all."

One of the tall warders who stood near gave him a grim, contemptuous look, and uttered a short, cruel laugh; but the two visitors, without reply, passed unopposed through the wicket, and stood upon Tower Hill. The men-servants followed, and the gate was closed.

Still keeping profoundly silent, they all walked on with great speed, not toward the little street in which Emmeline had lived, but toward the end of another street. When they were half way across the open space, the taller of the two bent down, saying in a whisper, "Bear up, bear up, dear Emmeline. We are well-nigh safe now."

But hardly were the words uttered when two or three men came quickly across, and one of them caught hold of the apparently elder woman's arm, exclaiming, with a mocking laugh, "You are a tall lady, upon my soul, to walk upon Tower Hill of a night! Gadzooks, we must see more of your ladyship!"

Another man—who subsequently turned out to be a messenger sent in pursuit—at the same moment seized the young earl (for I need hardly say it was he) with a hard, strong grasp, exclaiming, "Henry, Earl of Eskdale, I charge you, in the king's name, to make no resistance."

With a faint, despairing cry, Emmeline sank to the ground, while they dragged Smeaton away from her side. The two servants, running up, demanded, "Who are you who dare to stop these ladies?" and angry words began to pass; but Smeaton interposed, saying, "It is in vain, it is in vain. Look to your lady, my good men. Convey her home safely. God bless you, my Emmeline!"

"What is the matter, what is the matter here?" cried Richard Newark, suddenly appearing with two or three more, while the man who had first seized upon Smeaton left him in the hands of the messenger, and raised Emmeline from the ground.

"Ah, Master Dick!" he exclaimed, "have *you* a finger in this pretty pie? Better put yourself out of harm's way, young man, as fast as possible."

"How dare you touch that lady, scoundrel?" demanded Richard, in a voice furious with passion, as he recognized the person of William Newark. "Take that for your pains!" and, holding the scabbard of his sword with his left hand, he struck his cousin a furious blow with the right.

William Newark started forward and drew his sword; Richard's was not long in the sheath; but the servants interposed, and parted them for the time, though not till words had been spoken —some in loud anger, some in the low tones of intense hate—which bore their fruit soon after. The last four of those words were uttered in a whisper.

"At seven, and alone," said Richard, in his cousin's ear.

The other nodded his head, and turned sullenly away, while Richard aided to raise the unhappy girl, whose last hope had been extinguished by her husband's recapture, and carried her, still insensible, to her dwelling.

In the mean time the messenger and two of his men conducted their prisoner back to the gates of the Tower with feelings in the bosom of Smeaton too dark, too painful for description. To his own fate his mind had long been made up, and the extinction of a brief hope of escape added little to the load he had to bear; but the thought of what might befall Emmeline in consequence of her effort to save him, and of the certain consequences to the devoted woman who had placed her liberty and even her life in peril for him, was too heavy to be borne with any thing like calmness.

Arrived at the gates of the Tower, they found the wicket, to their surprise, open, and a good deal of confusion under the arch-way of the gate-house. Some twelve or fourteen men were collected; a buzz of tongues was going on, and some loud and angry words were being spoken. The lieutenant governor himself, in a silk dressing-gown, was present, with a man beside him holding a lantern; and just as the messenger passed the wicket, still holding the prisoner fast by the arm, they heard that officer exclaim,

"Shut the gate—shut the gate! Every one keep silence! If you can be discreet, no harm may come of this. If not, some of your necks may pay for it. Ha! who have we here?"

"An escaped prisoner, Mr. Lieutenant," answered the messenger, who was willing to take all possible credit to himself. "I am sharp enough; and I got information of this fine plot."

The lieutenant governor stared at him coldly, with no great appearance of satisfaction in his countenance.

"Pray, Mr. Messenger," he said, after a moment's thought, "had you any warrant for what you have done?"

The man looked aghast at the question, but replied, in a somewhat insolent tone,

"I needed no warrant to apprehend a convicted traitor whom you have suffered one way or another to slip out of the Tower."

The lieutenant still gazed at him with a frowning brow and teeth tight shut, and then said,

"You may have to prove, Mr. Messenger, that you possess such a justification of your conduct. *I* tell you, you have not."

Then turning to one of the warders, he said, in a sharp tone,

"Shut the wicket, I say, and lock it. Let no one pass in or out till I return. Keep that man safe too," he continued, pointing to the messenger, "and be perfectly silent with him. Let no one exchange a word with him, as you value the king's favor. My Lord of Eskdale, will you do me the honor of accompanying me back to your chamber? I wish to speak a few words with you. Let go his arm, sir, this instant!"

The messenger instantly relaxed his grasp, and Smeaton, not less astonished than his captor, followed the lieutenant in silence back to the room where he had been confined. They found the door open, but within stood the turnkey, looking gloomy enough, with his arms crossed upon his chest, and old Mrs. Culpepper, with the young lord's *roquelaure* now cast off, seated in her usual attire before the fire. The moment she heard steps, however, she started up, and, gazing at Smeaton, clasped her hands together in silence with a look of unutterable anguish.

"Remove her to my lodging," said the lieutenant, speaking to the turnkey, "and keep her there under your guard till I come."

The young earl, however, started forward and took her by the hand.

"Thanks, excellent woman!" he exclaimed, "a thousand thanks! I pray God, as one of my last prayers, that he may defend you and my Emmeline, and shield you from all the ill consequences of this night."

Before she could reply—for her voice was choked with sobs—she was removed from the room, and the lieutenant, carefully closing the door, said, with a faint and rueful smile,

"That dress does not become you, my lord. Let me beg you to throw it off, for I hardly know whether I am speaking to the Earl of Eskdale or an old woman."

"That is easily done," replied Smeaton, casting off the loose garment called a *sacque*, which was, for three quarters of a century, a favorite habiliment of the ladies of France and England. "Now, sir, I am your prisoner again. I beseech you to leave me, for the last few hours of my life, to the thoughts which befit the occasion, and, if it be possible, to conceal the events which have taken place, so as to shield that excellent creature and all others from the consequences."

"This is a very awkward affair, my lord," observed the lieutenant, thoughtfully; "and, upon my life, I do not well know what is to be done. Will your lordship answer me this one question on your honor? Were any of the jailers—I do not wish you to specify the individual—were any of the jailers accessory to your escape?"

"Not in the least, to the best of my knowledge and belief," replied Lord Eskdale. "They have had from me the ordinary gratuities and nothing more; nor am I aware of their having connived in the least. They were deceived, as you yourself, perhaps, might have been, by the disguise."

"I thank your lordship for that assurance," said the lieutenant, "for it sets my mind greatly at ease; but yet I hardly know how to act."

"Methinks if you were simply to report that I had endeavored to escape, and had been prevented, that would be all that your duty requires."

"I do not know that," replied the lieutenant. "It is true, I never yet heard of a pardon being revoked; but certain it is, that an attempt to break prison—"

"A pardon!" exclaimed Smeaton, with his heart beating more vehemently than it would have done at the sight of the block and ax. "What do you mean, sir?"

"I mean, my lord, exactly what I say," replied the lieutenant governor. "Just at the time when your lordship must have been preparing to effect your escape, the secretary of state's messenger brought me a letter, authorizing me to announce to you his majesty's free pardon, and to say that, though it will not pass the seal till to-morrow, you may consider yourself from this moment at liberty. How the events of this night may be construed, and what I ought to do in these circumstances, I really can not tell. As a man of honor, my lord, what ought I to do?"

In a state of terrible agitation, Smeaton walked twice up and down the room, and then, turning to the lieutenant, he said,

"No consideration, sir, shall make me ask you to neglect your imperative duty. You must inform the king, however terrible the state of suspense must be to me, and however perilous may be the result. I could wish it, indeed, done immediately; but at this hour of the night—"

"My lord, you are, indeed, a noble man," replied the lieutenant, "and I do not think you will lose by your conduct. I had retired to bed, somewhat unwell, before the messenger arrived. He insisted upon my being awakened, and some delay consequently occurred, otherwise the pardon would have been announced to you before you made this attempt. When I came to your room with the information, as I was commanded, I found you gone. But I will tell you what I will do. His majesty is still up, for there is a court to-night; and I will immediately set out and lay before him or the secretary of state the facts as they are. Stay! Perhaps it may be better for you to write to the king yourself, and I will be your messenger. It is absolutely needful this step should be taken at once. You have writing materials here. Pray write as briefly as possible, while I put myself in a different dress to present myself at the palace."

Thus saying, he left him; and Smeaton proceeded, with a rapid hand, to write as follows:

"Sire,—Your majesty's gracious clemency has been this moment announced to me; and I beg to lay humbly the expression of my gratitude before you. I know not any thing but your own merciful consideration which can have induced you to spare me, though I assure you, on my honor, that the facts which I stated without proof at my trial, regarding the causes which, if I may use the term, had driven me or misled me to take arms, were strictly true. Let me also assure you that henceforth, neither directly nor indirectly, will I ever be found opposing your title to a crown which I am now thoroughly convinced you hold by the will of a great majority of the people, if you still condescend to extend your mercy toward me. But, at the same time, I feel it right you should be informed that, at the very moment your gracious pardon was notified at the Tower, I was engaged, without the participation of any one within these walls, in an attempt to effect my escape from prison, fully believing that in its success lay my only chance for life. That attempt was frustrated; and I will not even endeavor to persuade the royal officers of the Tower to conceal the facts from you, but willingly leave my life at the disposition of a monarch who has already shown himself more merciful toward me than I could have expected."

He had hardly concluded when the lieutenant returned; and, in a few minutes, the young nobleman was left once more alone, to wait with painful anxiety for the result.

But, in the mean while, we must follow the lieutenant to the palace. The secretary of state was called out to speak with him; and, after a brief conference, returned to the court. An hour passed, and a few minutes more, while the lieutenant remained in an ante-room, waiting the king's pleasure. At length the sound of many people passing out was heard, with the roll of carriages; and a page entering, bade the officer follow him to the king's closet. Unable to speak either French or Latin, he could simply lay the Earl of Eskdale's letter before the king, and trust to the secretary to translate it accurately, and give any further explanation. When the monarch had heard the whole, however, he laughed good-humoredly, saying,

"Escape! Of course he did try to escape. What could a gentleman in his situation do better? No, no: our sign-manual is to the pardon. It only wants the seal, and we will not revoke it. We could not revoke a pardon, gentlemen. Severity may be reconsidered—mercy never. Besides, it is clear, from the evidence of Lord Stair, and from that of Colonel Churchill, who took Thomas Higham's dying deposition, that this young nobleman had no will to the work they put him upon; that he was at heart our own, notwithstanding the prejudices of his family; and that the machinations of this Sir John Newark and others abused a somewhat rash and hasty disposition. Something must be done with that same knight. I fear we can not touch him for treason, but as to seditious practices, there must be some law which will affect him."

"I am not sure, sire," replied Mr. Stanhope, one of the secretaries of state, "that this gentleman's acts do not amount to treason. His letter to the Earl of Mar is undoubtedly treasonable."

"Well, well, see to it, see to it," said the king. "As to this young lord, let the pardon pass. He may be set free at once."

"His majesty says he will not revoke the pardon, Mr. Lieutenant," said the secretary. "You may set Lord Eskdale at liberty. But I think it would be better if he were to pass some time in France."

The lieutenant of the Tower bowed and withdrew. Much to his satisfaction, few questions had been asked; and, returning to the Tower as fast as a pair of slow horses would draw him, he entered once more that abode of gloom and sorrow. He found the messenger who had seized Smeaton on Tower Hill still in the gate-house, and ordered his liberation, saying,

"You have somewhat exceeded your duty, sir, but it was in ignorance. I find that the Earl of Eskdale's pardon was already signed. I have no orders with regard to you, so you may go free; but you had better be cautious."

He then proceeded straight to the room of his former prisoner, bearing him the joyful tidings that his pardon was confirmed.

"As to this old lady," he said, "who chose to personate a young gentleman, nothing whatever has been said with regard to her, and therefore I suppose I must take upon myself the responsibility of letting her go, having no warrant to detain her. With regard to yourself, my lord, you can either remain here for the night, or depart if you please. But I must not fail to inform you that Mr. Secretary Stanhope hinted it might be better for you to pass some time quietly in France. Will you pass out to-night or to-morrow?"

"To-night, assuredly," replied the young earl. "I would fain bear the comfortable tidings myself to those whose hearts are now full of mourning, and first to that good old woman who has risked so much for me."

"Come with me, then," said the lieutenant.

In about half an hour, Smeaton, holding his good old nurse by the hand, passed free through the gates of the Tower, with one of the governor's servants carrying his little stock of baggage after them.

They took their way straight toward the street in which Emmeline's abode had been fixed; and, though it was now nearly three o'clock in the morning, lights were still to be seen through the crevices of the shutters. It was with no slight anxiety that Smeaton waited for the opening of the door, and it seemed long before it was unfastened. At length, however, one of the men who had accompanied the Lady Emmeline that night to the Tower appeared with a light, and uttered an exclamation of joyful surprise when he saw the faces of those who had just knocked.

"Hush!" said Smeaton, in a low voice. "How is your lady?"

"Oh, my lord, she will be well enough now," replied the man.

"Hark!" said Richard Newark, from the little parlor. "Hark! Emmeline, look up. I told you so. There is hope—there is comfort still;" and, as he spoke, he threw open the door.

Emmeline had been sitting with her fair face, deluged in tears, covered by her hands, but at her young cousin's words she looked up, started forward, and in an instant was in her husband's arms.

I need not pause upon all the explanations that were given. I need not tell the joy that was felt; and, indeed, as to the further events of that night, it is only necessary to say that, after hearing but a very small portion of Smeaton's story, Richard Newark left the lovers to their own happiness.

On the following morning, about eight o'clock, a note, written in a crabbed, boy-like hand, was given to the Earl of Eskdale, who opened it hastily and read these words:

"Noble Friend,—I am going to try, this morning, whether you are a good fencing-master, and whether the blade you gave me is worth handling. Should I not join you and dear Emmy by eight o'clock, you will hear something of me in Mary-le-Bone fields. God bless you both for a pair of loving turtles. If you don't see him again, think, from time to time, of Poor Dick."

Emmeline had not yet risen; and Smeaton, calling some of the servants hastily together, set out with terrible feelings of apprehension for the spot which the note had indicated, and which, I may remark, was notorious at the time for the number of duels which it witnessed. Calling some people, who were better acquainted with the locality than themselves, to their aid, they searched the fields, which then extended where now stands Baker Street and the adjacent masses of houses, for some time without success; but at length they came upon the body of a man lying on his back, with his sword still clutched in his grasp, an old scar on his brow, and a sword-wound right through his chest. Life had evidently been extinct for some time; and Smeaton, who knew him well, bestowed little thought upon him.

Near the spot where he lay, which was one pool of gore, the ground was again dabbled with blood, and, tracking the drops which marked the frosty grass for nearly three hundred yards, they came to a place where, under some tall trees, and with his back leaning against one of them, sat Richard Newark, near a stile which he had apparently attempted, in vain, to reach. His face was ashy pale, and his hand rested languidly against the tree; but he still held a handkerchief, sopped in blood, to his right side, as if to stanch the bleeding of a severe wound. He could not speak, nor even lift his head at first; but Smeaton, while one of the men ran off for a surgeon and some restoratives, unbuttoned his waistcoat, and with remarkable skill soon contrived to stop the current which was draining away his life. He recovered a little in a few minutes; and after the arrival of the surgeon, who immediately gave him some of the essences then in vogue, looked up, with a light smile, in his friend's face, saying, "Ha, ha, Eskdale! I have paid our friend all debts; but that which vexed the scoundrel most was that he should be killed by the hand of a boy, as he called me. How he did curse when he was dying! Well, you may set up for a fencing-master when all other trades fail, though he did whip me his point over the arm, because I did not turn my wrist quick enough, as you taught me."

The surgeon insisted upon his keeping silence; and a door, taken off the hinges, being obtained, he was placed upon it and carried away to the nearest house where lodging could be procured. There the wound he had received was more fully examined, and proved to be, in reality, of no very dangerous character, except from the great loss of blood it had occasioned. Before evening he was better and stronger, and the sight of Emmeline and her husband by his bedside seemed to revive and cheer him greatly. But as the tidings of another fatal duel in Mary-le-Bone fields began to spread, inquiries and investigations were set on foot which, it was evident, could not long be baffled. The fact of the duel having taken place without seconds or witnesses rendered the youth's situation rather perilous, and a long consultation took place that night between the Earl of Eskdale and the surgeon.

On the following morning early, a ship in the Thames, bound for Dunkirk, received some five or six persons on board, and set sail immediately. Among them was Richard Newark, who was carried into the vessel on a mattress. There was also the young and beautiful Countess of Eskdale, somewhat pale and anxious of look, who sat upon the deck as they dropped down the river, with her hand resting on that of a tall, dignified lady, advanced in life and habited in deep mourning. The rest of the party consisted of Smeaton, two men-servants, the good old woman who had played such a conspicuous part in the events which have been narrated, and a maid-servant.

There can be no doubt that the government at that time connived at the escape of many persons from the rigor of the law, and certain it is that the vessel I have mentioned was suffered to set sail without any obstruction. The passage was smooth and easy, and the whole party landed safely on the shores of France.

CHAPTER XLV.

The darker scenes of the early part of the reign of George I. had passed away, and though there were troubles and contentions in many parts of Europe, and conspiracies and designs against the existing government in England, general tranquillity reigned in this island, and prosperity and happiness were following fast upon the steps of peace.

But I must lead the reader away from England to a small village in France, some eight or nine miles from the capital—a sufficient distance to retain all its rustic quietness, and yet near enough to allow the intelligence of the great world to penetrate before it had grown very stale. At the distance of half a mile from this village was placed a small French chateau, built in a little trim park on a rising ground. The chateau had nothing remarkable about it: it was just like all other chateaus at the same period; a congregation of oddly-shaped masses of building, with several little round towers, having conical slated roofs, like candles with extinguishers on their tops. It had a sunny and pleasant aspect, however, and an avenue of fine old walnut-trees ran up to it from the high road.

In a small room in this chateau, very quietly furnished, sat a group of people, with some of whom the reader is already acquainted, enjoying a pleasant dessert of wild strawberries and light Burgundy wine. Perfect contentment was upon all their countenances, and harmony in all their hearts. One young man, indeed, was pale and grave, though serene in aspect.

But I must begin with those of whom the reader as yet knows little. They consisted of two elderly people and one young lady. The first was a fine, dignified man, somewhat beyond the middle age, with hair very gray, but with eyes still bright and keen. The second was a lady younger, but not by many years; and though they were both advanced in life, as I have said, they continued to call each other by the names of early affection.

Passing from one part of the chain of life to another very distant, we must notice that bright-looking curly-headed boy, little more than two years old, seated on the knee of that very beautiful girl whom he calls "mother," in the good old Saxon tongue. It is Emmeline's boy; and I need not say who is that gentleman by her side. An old lady close by, now a little bowed with age, is the Dowager Countess of Eskdale.

But who are the two whom I have mentioned as rather beyond middle life? Emmeline calls them "father, mother;" and looks at them with love none the less because she was so long bereaved of their fostering care. The pale young man in a military dress, with signs of mourning, too, in his apparel, is Richard Newark; and that fat, round, rosy-pippin personage — Heaven! what a crowd of leaden figures rush upon the imagination as one looks at him!

"It is strange, Dick," said Lord Eskdale, "that you and good Van Noost should have arrived here this morning, after we have not met for so long a time! Do you know, Emmeline," he continued, turning to his wife, "that this is the anniversary of the day on which I first set eyes on that dear face?"

"Do you think I can ever forget it, Henry?" she answered. "It is the first of my days of brightness. It is like a sweet song remembered in a happy dream."

"And how can I ever thank you, my deat lord," continued her husband, addressing her father, "for giving me that commission to seek and regain for you your daughter, which has ended in bestowing such happiness on myself?"

"There are two things, my dear Harry, for which many sage friends have blamed me," replied Lord Newark, "which I can never regret, and of the wisdom of which even those who blamed me are now convinced: the one, my having trusted a young man, whom I knew to be the soul of real honor, with so delicate a task; the other, my having set at naught all ideas of imaginary dignity, and, as a merchant, having secured to my family that competence which I had lost by doing my duty as a soldier. I am proud of both these acts; and both have ended in happiness. Had my poor boys but lived to see this day, there would be little in the past even to bring one cloud of melancholy over my setting sun."

Richard Newark looked up in his face as he spoke, and asked,

"Would you never regret, my good lord and cousin, having lost in the cause of a bad prince those fair lands in Devonshire, to which I am sure, if you feel like me, you must cling even in memory?"

"Not a whit, Dick," replied the old nobleman. "The favors of Fortune, or, as some would call them better, the gifts of God, are loans, my dear boy, to be resumed when it is His pleasure; and—"

"Then I have borrowed them long enough," interrupted Richard Newark, in his abrupt way "and it is high time they should be restored."

"No, no, Dick," said Lord Newark. "They are yours since your father's death. I have naught to do with them, and could not enjoy them even if you gave them up."

"They are not mine at all," replied the young man, "never have been mine, never have been my father's."

"But the forfeiture — the forfeiture," exclaimed Lord Newark. "If they are not yours, whose are they?"

"Emmeline's," replied her cousin. "The forfeiture extended not to her. They were settled by deed upon your dear lady and her children, male and female, two years before the forfeiture. You lost them by drawing the sword against King William. She lost them, and your sons lost them, by accompanying you in the war and in your flight. You four are specially named in the act of attainder; and the lands fell to her at once as the next heir. The cunning lawyers, I believe, outwitted themselves by making the black and white parchment so particular; but the original act, always preserved by my father, was found by Van Noost when he went down to patch up an old monument in Aleton church, by putting a leaden hand on a stone figure. I was always sure there was something of the kind, or my father would not have kept such a sharp watch upon Emmy. He was not a man to keep pet birds in a cage for the sole purpose of feeding them and hearing them sing. God rest his soul! he did it all for me, and so I must say no more."

Lord Eskdale looked to Emmeline with a thoughtful inquiring glance, and she read his meaning in an instant.

"I will not take them, Dick," she said. "I can not, will not take them from you. Am I not right, Henry?"

"But you must, sweet lady," replied Richard. "With what is left I have enough, and more than enough, so that you do not make me pay back all that has been unjustly taken. The lands were conveyed to my father by gift of the crown, saving the appearance of any nearer heir not named in the act of forfeiture. The lands are yours, therefore, and ever have been yours. I will have nothing to do with them. I tell you, dear cousin, I have enough, and far more than enough, for a single man."

"But you may marry, Richard," said Emmeline. "You are very young to make vows of celibacy."

"Never, never, Emmy," he said; "I will not transmit to others an infirmity;" and he laid his finger significantly upon his forehead.

A moment of grave silence succeeded; and then, looking at her father, Emmeline said,

"Would that I could give them back to you, my father!"

"There is nothing to prevent you, Emmy," said Richard Newark. "Lord Stair tells me that your father can hop over the sea and perch upon Ale at once, if he will but promise to live peaceably under the government that exists. In a word, the attainder can be reversed in a moment upon such a promise. His not having joined in the last affair, where we all burned our fingers more or less, has won him high favor."

Lord Newark bent down his head upon his hand, and fell into deep thought.

"But come, let us talk of other things," said Richard Newark, after pausing for an instant. "Business is dull work, and that is settled. There is only one thing you must promise me, Eskdale and Emmeline. When you are Lord and Lady of Ale-Manor, you must let me have my little room up two flights o' stairs when I come to see you; and old Mrs. Culpepper, when she is housekeeper again, must not make the maids throw what she used to call my rubbish into the fire."

Emmeline held out her hand to him kindly; and her husband assured him that he should be as free as air in any house of his.

"I have already made free with this house, at all events," replied Richard Newark, "for I have asked Colonel Churchill to come down here to-morrow. He wants much to see you again, Eskdale; and, I can tell you, you owe him something more than a dinner and a bottle of wine."

"He was exceedingly courteous to me when I was a prisoner," said the young earl, "and I shall be very happy to see him."

"Ay, but you owe him more than that," answered Richard Newark.

"Let me tell him, let me tell him," cried Van Noost, who had sat marvelously silent after the allusion to the leaden hand upon the stone figure. "Let me tell him; for I first ferreted out the facts, and got Colonel Churchill to write them down for my Lord Stair. After he had received your surrender at Preston, my noble lord, he went to visit that rascal, Tom Higham, on his death-bed, and from his own lips heard that the fellow had deceived you; that, bribed to lead you on into the rebellion, he had given your letter into the hands of the colonel of Lord Stair's regiment, who tore it open, read it, and sent it back, bidding him tell you that Lord Stair was in Paris, and that, if you would send a messenger to him, doubtless every thing would be explained, as that noble lord had never failed in his word, not one syllable of which the rascal told you."

"Heaven forgive him!" said Smeaton. "He did much harm."

The conversation proceeded in the same tone. But enough of it has been given for all the purposes of this book. Were I to paint another scene, it would be that of Christmas eve at Ale-Manor House, where, round the wide fire-place of the great hall, might be seen the faces of the same persons as were seated round the table of that small *chateau*.

But the story is long enough, and the reader's fancy must supply the rest.

THE END.

SIR THEODORE BROUGHTON;

OR,

LAUREL WATER.

BY G. P. R. JAMES, ESQ.,

AUTHOR OF

"THE LAST OF THE FAIRIES," "THE CONVICT," "MARGARET GRAHAM," "RUSSELL," "BEAUCHAMP," "THE CASTLE OF EHRENSTEIN," "HEIDELBERG," ETC.

HARPER & BROTHERS, PUBLISHERS,

82 CLIFF STREET, NEW YORK.

1848.

PREFACE.

Though I am not, in general, fond of prefaces, yet a few words of explanation must necessarily be prefixed to this work, in order to guard against any misconception. The name which it has received will naturally lead the mind of the reader to conclude that the tale is founded upon the too-celebrated tragedy of "Lawford Hall," and such is certainly, in some degree, the case; but it must not be supposed that I have attempted to give any thing like a history of that lamentable transaction, or have even adhered closely to the facts. On the contrary, I have, in the course of the work, done every thing I could to mark that such was not my intention, upon the following considerations, and in the circumstances I am about to state. I had long known the general facts connected with the death of Sir Theodosius Boughton, and had dwelt upon them with much interest; but the minute details were more difficult to be obtained, and I was prepossessed with an idea, very generally entertained, that Captain Donellan, who was executed for the murder of the young baronet, was his guardian as well as his brother-in-law. In such circumstances, the relative position of the two parties seemed to me to open a fine field for the display of strong and dangerous passions, and no bad opportunity of drawing instructive lessons from their results. The work was about one third finished when, after considerable difficulty, I obtained a copy of the trial of Captain Donellan, as reported from Gurney's short-hand notes, and an impression of a very painful nature was produced upon my mind. I became convinced that Captain Donellan had been convicted upon insufficient evidence. I do not by any means intend to imply that I felt at all confident of his innocence; but merely that there was not sufficient proof to justify his conviction. Some doubts I had, indeed, previously entertained from traditions preserved at Rugby and its neighborhood; but when I read the evidence of the famous John Hunter, those doubts were changed into a strong and abiding impression that Donellan was condemned without fair legal proof.

It must be remarked that the father of Sir Theodosius, when by no means an old man, died as suddenly as his son; and although the evidence of John Hunter was given very cautiously, yet, in the following portion of his examination, he states a clear and decided opinion, which ought to have greatly damaged the case for the prosecution in the minds of the jury. I may premise that it had been attempted to prove, first, that the body of the young baronet displayed evident traces of poison; and, secondly, that the symptoms which immediately preceded his death could proceed from nothing but the effects of one particular poison, called laurel water. John Hunter was then asked, after hearing the whole details exactly as the other medical witnesses had heard them, what inference he would draw from the appearances presented by the corpse. He answered, "The whole appearances upon the dissection explain nothing but putrefaction;" and again, in reply to the question, "Are those appearances you have heard described, such, in your judgment, as are the results of putrefaction in dead subjects?" he said, "Entirely."

The examination then proceeds thus:

Counsel. "Are the symptoms that appeared after the medicine was given, such as necessarily conclude that the person had taken poison?"

Hunter. "Certainly not."

Counsel. "If an apoplexy had come on, would not the symptoms have been nearly or somewhat similar?"

Hunter. "Very much the same."

The last reply in his examination in chief is also very important. The counsel observed, "Then, in your judgment, upon the appearances the gentlemen have described, no inference can be drawn from thence that Sir Theodosius Boughton died of poison?"

He answered, "Certainly not. It does not give the least suspicion."

Now the judge, in summing up, remarks thus upon the evidence of John Hunter, such as I have stated it to have been: "I can hardly say what his opinion is, for he *does not* seem to have formed any opinion at all upon the matter."

It appears to me, on the contrary, that he had formed the most decided opinion that no inference of poison was to be drawn either from the symptoms that preceded death, or the appearance of the body after death, both main points in the case for the prosecution. Add to this, that no distillation of laurel leaves was traced to Captain Donellan; that it was never shown that he had ever possessed a laurel leaf; that he was never proved to have had access to the room in which the bottle stood, the contents of which were supposed to be poison, and you reduce the case to this, that Sir Theodosius Boughton died very suddenly, after having indulged for a considerable period in great excesses, and being at the time somewhat in bad health; and that the conduct of Captain Donellan after his death was extraordinary and somewhat suspicious.

It is to be remarked, however, that all the most suspicious circumstances rested upon the evidence of Lady Boughton, the mother of the dead man, who with her own hands gave him the liquid, as a medicine, which was afterward supposed to have been the poison, and whom Donellan indirectly charged with having poisoned her son. The suspicious circumstance of his having rinsed out the bottle even before the young man was dead, was stated by Lady Boughton to have taken place at a time when two maids must have been in the room, as she mentions the occupation of "one of the maids;" but one was dead at the time of the trial, and the other was not even asked if she had remarked the fact, or seen Captain Donellan do any thing with the bottles. It is, moreover, worthy of notice that Lady Boughton contradicted herself, as to whether Sir Theodosius spoke to her after taking the medicine; that she varied in her testimony before the coroner and at the trial, adding some circumstances on the latter occasion; and that, from the testimony of the coachman, it would appear that she had very soon endeavored to cast suspicion upon Donellan, which would account for some of the efforts made by him to prove his innocence before he was directly accused.

The counsel for prisoners charged with felony not being permitted in those days to address the jury in behalf of their client, none of these points were brought prominently forward at the trial, for the judge, in this case, certainly *did not act as counsel for the prisoner*. Doubtless, had he been permitted, Mr. Newnham, who cross-examined the witnesses on behalf of Donellan, with very great skill and acumen, would have called attention to the various facts I have mentioned, and would also have pointed out, that if the conduct of Captain Donellan, upon the death of Sir Theodosius Boughton, was extraordinary, so was that of Lady Boughton, who, while her son was yet living, though terribly convulsed, does not seem to have made the slightest effort to restore him. She sent a servant on horseback, it is true, for a medical man, but in that Captain Donellan joined, giving up his own horse for the purpose, as the swiftest. But she seems to have applied no

SIR THEODORE BROUGHTON;

OR,

LAUREL WATER.

CHAPTER I.

There was an old man sitting in an arm-chair—a very old man, and a very ugly one. It is an exceedingly unpleasant thing to be old and ugly, but as the one is brought about by time, and the other by fate, there is no use resisting, and still less use being cross about it. The remark is not impertinent, whatever the reader may think, for the old gentleman I have been speaking of had been cross all his life because he was ugly, and was still more cross now because he was old. He had labored hard at one period to cure the former defect by all the appliances which art can provide, and he had labored still harder, at a later period, to hide the traces of the latter state by somewhat similar means. But within the last three years he had given up the attempt as hopeless, for inexorable Time, creeping on with that stealthy pace which, sometimes so slow and sometimes so fast, catches us all at last, had got his claws so tight upon him, that he could only move from his bed to his chair, and from his chair to his bed, and then he thought it of no use to employ maréchal powder any more, or to lace up stays which would no longer support his shattered frame. He became a sloven where he had been a beau, and there he sat in his arm-chair, with his eyes bleared, his mouth fallen in, his knees, supported on a stool, nearly up to his chin, and his legs swathed in flannel.

There was a little table on his right hand, with a parchment upon it, by the side of which stood an inkstand; and on the opposite side of the fire sat a man of about five-and-thirty years of age, gentlemanly in appearance, rather good-looking than otherwise, tall and stout, and plainly dressed, although his garments had a sort of military cut about them. His feet were stretched out toward the fire—not too near the toes of the old gentleman, for he would not for the world have ventured a shoe within the limits of their territory—and he was skimming lightly over one of those little sheets of intelligence which were called newspapers in that day. From time to time, indeed, his eyes stole over the top of the paper toward the old man's face with a peculiar, inquiring, furtive expression, which was not very prepossessing.

"Can't you say something, Donovan?" said the old man, at length, in a querulous tone. "I am surely dull enough without your sitting there and making me duller by reading the newspaper all the while."

"I was in hopes, Sir Walter, you were going to take a nap," replied the person whom he called Donovan, "and so I would not disturb you."

"Disturb me!" echoed the other; "there is sometimes more disturbance in solemn silence than in loud-tongued loquacity. I could fall asleep, perhaps, while you were talking, but I can not while you are sitting before my eyes, like a great dark specter, or rather like the stone-hewn Memnon, emitting no sounds except about the break of morning."

"My dear Sir Walter," answered the other, in a most placable tone, though the sarcasm couched in his companion's speech was not lost upon him, "I can talk as glibly as most people when it is required; but your evening rest seemed of more importance to me than my idle conversation. I was reading matters of no great interest, I can assure you—only the details of that little disgusting affair of the Countess of Champarty, who has poisoned her husband, and half a dozen other people."

"Ah!" cried the old man, "let me hear about that. So she poisoned her husband, did she? That's just like them all. All the mischief that takes place in the world is sure to begin with a woman; I never knew it otherwise in all my life. If a man games, it is for the sake of a woman; if a man robs, it is for a woman; if a man murders, it is for a woman; if a man betrays his friend, cheats the revenue, defrauds his neighbor, or ruins his estate, it is all for the sake of a woman; and the worst of it is, men think it an excuse for every thing they do, as if woman, woman, woman, was the end and aim of man's existence."

"Well, thank God!" said Donovan, "I have no such end and aim. I can live within my means, however small they may be; I covet no man's wealth, however great it may be; I have not a debt in the world, thank Heaven! nor know a woman that I care two straws about."

"And do you mean really to say," demanded the old gentleman, "that you live upon your pay, and thirty pounds a year, Captain Donovan, and that you have not a debt in the world?" And there was a certain sort of roguish twinkle in his bleared eyes that might not altogether have satisfied Captain Donovan, had he been looking at him at that moment; but while the baronet had been speaking, Donovan's eyes had been fixed upon the fire, which was flickering and flashing rather in its decline, and he kept them there till Sir Walter had done.

The moment, however, the other had finished, he replied, boldly, "True, I can assure you, Sir Walter. I was early brought up, by my dear mother, your niece, to know how much I had to depend upon, and to limit my expenses accordingly. You may ask, when you like, any man in the regiment, and you will find that Tom Donovan does not owe a penny in the world."

"Why should I ask?" demanded the old man, cynically; for he knew right well what was the latent meaning of his worthy cousin's protestations; but the next moment he added, with a suppressed chuckle, "Well, Tom, well, the man who can so well manage a little is worthy of managing much, and some day or another you may have the opportunity of doing so. That I promise you, upon my honor."

Perhaps Captain Thomas Donovan had arrived at the exact point which he wished to arrive at, but he exclaimed warmly—not exactly *nolo episcopari*, but what was pronounced with as much sincerity—"Nay, nay, my dear Sir Walter, I know you are generous and liberal, but you must not quite overwhelm me. You know there is your grandson Theodore, although he is a silly, wild boy, wayward and somewhat weak, and not easily instructed, yet—"

"Never you mind, Donovan, never you mind," said the old baronet. "He shall be taken care of—he shall have as much as is right and proper; but, whatever you may say, this will shall be signed to-night, if that fellow Mullins comes, as he ought to have done three hours ago. This shall be signed to-night; for I feel I am failing, Tom—I am failing very fast," and he laid his hand upon the parchment by his side.

"Oh, don't say such a thing, my dear Sir Walter," answered Captain Donovan. "There's no need of such haste. I trust I may drink your health these ten years yet. Why, you are much better and stronger to-day."

"It shall be signed to-night, Tom," repeated the old man; "ay, that it shall. I'll take care of the boy, never you fear. He's a sad scapegrace, and weak, very weak, but he shall have enough, and it shall come back strictly, too. He sha'n't have the power to squander it—no, that he sha'n't. Whatever I leave him shall be tied up—tied up as tight as my fist;" and he clinched his thick and gouty fingers fast, as if he had got a purse within them.

As he spoke, a large bell rang in the house, echoing through many a solitary and long-disused suite of apartments, and giving notice that some unwonted visitor was at the gates, for Sir Walter Broughton had of late seen very little company, and it was seldom that any other persons visited the house but his relation, Captain Donovan, or the village doctor; and both preferred, from some peculiar idiosyncrasy, the back door to the front.

"That's Mullins," said the baronet; "that's Mullins, I am sure. Nobody else rings the front bell. He's an impudent fellow, Mullins. Now run away, Tom: you must not be a witness, you know. Go and talk to the boy, and see if you can do something with him. We must try and mend him. Why, he shot half a score of fowls the other day with a bow and arrow. He laughed when I told him I would disinherit him."

Captain Donovan shook his head, as if the case were quite hopeless; and a servant in rich livery, with a powdered head and black silk stockings, opened the door, saying, "Mr. Mullins, sir, is in the library."

"Show him in—show him in," said the baronet. "Away with you, Tom, or he'll think you have been persuading me."

With a bland smile, Captain Donovan withdrew, passed through a different door from that by which Mr. Mullins was about to enter, and then paused for a moment in the ill-lighted passage, saying to himself, "He is mightily good-humored this evening. I wonder what the deuse is the meaning of it; yet it did not seem affected either. However, I will have a chat with Mullins before he goes, and see what I can get out of him. He's an odd beast, but manner often tells as much as words."

In the mean time, Sir Walter Broughton sat in his chair with a degree of nervous irritability upon him, which made him shuffle his legs about upon the stool till the attorney entered; and, as soon as he heard his step, he exclaimed, without turning round his head, for he knew that he could not see over the chair, "You have been exceedingly long in coming down, Mr. Mullins. You might have been here three hours ago."

"If I had nobody else's business to attend to but yours," answered Mr. Mullins, snappishly; and then advanced to the table, producing a person and a look the most opposite in the world to that of Captain Donovan. He was a tall, thin man, of about fifty years of age, with a long, aquiline nose, exceedingly white hair (where his head could boast of any), eyebrows as black as jet, and large, fine dark eyes. There was every characteristic of decision about the mouth and jaw, and the broad, expansive forehead spoke no lack of intellect to guide his determinations aright.

"Good evening, Sir Walter," he said, as if what had passed before had been but a prologue to their conversation. "What do you want with me that you sent for me in such a hurry?"

"I want to sign this," said Sir Walter, pointing to the parchment. "It may do very well, but I want a little codicil."

"If you only wanted to sign it," said the lawyer, "you were a fool for bringing me down here. You could have signed it just as well without me; and as to the codicil, I think you are a greater fool still. When a man has made up his mind what to do with his property, he should not go fiddling and altering. But it is the age of fiddling; there is nothing left as it is once settled, and we never leave any thing alone when it is well."

It is strange what an influence force of character will have over the great mass of mankind, and especially over the capricious. Nobody on earth but Mr. Mullins could have said what had just been uttered to Sir Walter Broughton without producing a ringing of the bell and an order to the servants to turn the speaker out. But with Mr. Mullins Sir Walter was as calm and patient as a lamb; for, although in their interviews he would occasionally indulge his acerbity for the first two or three minutes, yet the strong spirit of the lawyer always cowed him before they had exchanged half a dozen sentences.

"You are cross, Mullins, you are cross," said the baronet; "I have made you get up from your dinner. You are a great gastronome, I know. What was it I made you lose, Mullins?

a *mayennoise à la soubise*, or a *pigeon en crapaudine?* But come now, be reasonable, and you shall have as delicious a *petit souper* with Donovan as my man Jerome Augier can produce, and you know he's a *cordon bleu.*"

"Donovan!" repeated Mullins; "have you got him in the house again? Then he has made you alter the will, that's clear enough. How old men will be such fools as to let a parcel of interested, mercenary toad-eaters get about them toward the close of their life, I can not conceive. However, my business is to draw the codicil, if you want it. What am I to write?" and, drawing the parchment toward him, he threw the several skins of which it was composed one after the other over his thumb, and seemed to examine the clauses rapidly, murmuring, "Devil take him! he might have been contented with what he's got here. The Ballinasloe estate and two farms in Dorsetshire, besides the funded property—why, it makes at least one half of the whole. You showed him the will, I suppose, and he was not contented."

"You are pleased to be very sarcastic, Mr. Mullins, but you are quite wrong," was the baronet's reply, as he saw that he had got a little advantage over the lawyer, and plucked up spirit accordingly. "I did not show him the will, and the codicil I have to propose is intended to revoke all those bequests. I shall leave the whole, with the exception of a few legacies to the servants, and two hundred a year for Tom, charged upon the Irish property, to my grandson Theodore. The estates must be strictly tied up, with remainder to Donovan if the boy should die without children; for I won't have my money squandered away after my death, and estates which have been so long in the family brought to the hammer. Tie it up tightly, I say."

"That's of very little use," answered the lawyer. "If Donovan is to have it in remainder, he'll squander it as soon or sooner than the other. You can't keep stuff of this kind from getting musty, Sir Walter, do what you will. Somebody will come to spend it at last; and, unless you put two or three dozen into the entail, the worms will scarcely have made their way into your coffin before the auctioneer will be knocking down your estate."

"But Donovan tells me he is no spendthrift," said the baronet, looking slyly up in the lawyer's face. "He lives upon his pay, and thirty pounds a year."

"Pooh, pooh!" answered Mr. Mullins; "you know better, baronet; he was trying to cheat you."

"For which very reason," replied Sir Walter, "I am determined to make the change. I will leave him the boy's guardian, however, and trustee, for then he will take care of the property on his own account; and, to prevent him spending it himself, I'll have another in the entail. Who shall it be, I wonder?"

"Your plow-boy," said Mullins, with a cynical smile. "I suppose any one will do."

"Ye-es," replied the old man, drawling out the word doubtfully; "ye-es, but not the plow-boy. I must have a gentleman."

"What do you say to Sir Charles Chevenix? He is as nearly related to you as Donovan."

"No, no, the scoundrel," answered the old man, with a look of bitter malice, "not a penny shall he ever have. I remember him, I remember him, and what he said of me one day."

"Oh! ay, ay, I forgot," answered the lawyer, with a bitter smile. "He called you a vain old fool, I remember, when you were going to marry Miss Birch. Well, you know, Sir Walter, I have no great love or respect for him, seeing that he grossly insulted my nephew, when Reginald entered the same regiment as a mere cornet, and the boy was forced to sell out immediately."

"What for—what for?" demanded Sir Walter; "why should he sell out because he was insulted?"

"Because Sir Charles was captain of his troop, and Reginald thought fit to call him out, which he could not do till he had left the regiment."

Sir Walter Broughton chuckled, rubbed his hands, then coughed violently, and laughed again, and when all this cachinnation was over, he demanded, in a quiet tone, "What's your nephew's name, Mullins?"

"Reginald," answered the solicitor; "Reginald Lisle. What has that to do with the matter?"

"Put him in as heir of entail," said the baronet; "put him in the entail;" and again he laughed, and coughed, and laughed. "So he called out our friend? put him in the entail. He'll do better than the plow-boy, Mullins;" and, after a moment or two more thought, he added, "I wish he had shot him!"

"He did," replied Mr. Mullins; "for, though only seventeen, the boy had a stout heart and a steady hand, and he wounded him in the hip, but not mortally. He limps a little, however, still, I believe, though it is nine months ago."

"Put him in the entail, then," once more repeated the baronet, who seemed quite pleased with the idea, "and set about it quick, Mullins. Let there be no delay."

"Why, it will nearly need a new will," rejoined the solicitor; and, once more taking up the parchment, he looked over it more accurately than before. "No, these first four sheets will do," he said, "and another will be enough for the rest. Where can one get a skin of parchment, I wonder?"

"Paper will do, paper will do quite well," said the old man; "why trouble yourself about parchment?"

"Well, well, we will see," said Mr. Mullins; "I shall sleep here, of course, Sir Walter, and will set up for an hour or two to do it. But I'll tell you what, I won't have that damp cold room in which you put me last time."

"Mr. Donovan's there," said the baronet, with one of his chuckles; "Donovan's there. Bless you, Mullins, he does not care where he sleeps, provided he is near me, dear young man!" and his ugly features assumed quite a diabolical look of triumph at having fathomed the character of his relation. "But get on with it as fast as you can; I long to have it signed. Can't you go into the library and get it ready at once?"

The lawyer said he would do as much as he could, but that it would take some hours. Sir Walter, however, said he would set up till it was done; and, as a bribe to make haste, he added, "Ring the bell, and I will tell Jerome to get the little supper ready for you when it is complete. But mind, not a word to Tom nor to Theodore either, if you meet with them. The boy keeps out of my way, because I was angry with him yesterday morning. Not a word to either of them;" and, promising obedience to the injunction Mr. Mullins withdrew.

CHAPTER II.

It is a curious thing to mark, among all the varieties in nature, and all the infinite combinations which are continually taking place, the different effects that external objects produce upon the minds of different men. To many a one, brought up even in the hardening practice of the law, a visit to an old man on the very verge of the grave—feeble, decrepit, decayed, and yet with many of the worst passions and weaknesses of our human nature escorting him, as it were, to the tomb—and then a walk through a somewhat long and gloomy passage, but dimly lighted, with a row of pointed, arched windows on one side, and some stone tracery and curious grotesque figures on the other, to a library filled with old books—those tombstones of the mind—would have suggested some grave and even melancholy reflections. But Mr. Mullins was a man of the world, who very seldom gave himself the trouble to moralize, and whose calls upon imagination were very few. He dealt with all things out of his own family sharply, acutely, decisively; bringing to bear upon them the powers of a strong intellect; acting among them with vigorous character and firm purpose; and judging of men very justly both by natural tact and long experience. He had a high sense of honor, and was by no means a cold-hearted or an unfeeling man; but intellect was always predominant. He was, in fact, judging every thing he saw, as he went through life, as if his bosom were a court, and he were the presiding magistrate. I do not mean to say that his decisions were always accurate—whose are?—but they were always well weighed, though the constant habit of judging rendered his decisions very rapid. He walked through that long passage, then, with no other feelings in the world than that he had just seen a disagreeable old man, whom he had known from his own boyhood, and understood from his own manhood, that the old man intended to make a whimsical, but not altogether an unjust will, and had commissioned him to put it into proper form, and that he should find pen and ink and paper in a large, old-fashioned, gloomy room called the library, where there were some ten or fifteen thousand very big books, the greater part of which were not worth reading. He gave not one moment's thought to the lamentable spectacle of vanity, malice, revenge, and hatred carried to the brink of the grave; he looked not at the curious chiseling of the Gothic windows on the one hand, nor to the grinning faces, and long, straight, stony limbs on the other; he thought not of the world of labor, research, imagination, genius, industry, hope, expectation, disappointment, and distress of which each of those books in the room before him might be a memento. He looked at the absolute, the tangible, the direct, and suffered not his mind to stray, even for an instant, to any thing collateral or remote.

On entering the library, he found it tenanted by two persons, different in age, appearance, and character. The one, Captain Donovan, needs no further description; the other, young Theodore Broughton, the grandson of the old baronet, requires but little. He was a good-looking boy of thirteen or fourteen years of age, well made and gentlemanly in appearance, with a pleasing face and good features, but a somewhat weak and restless expression. The boy was seated at one end of the room with some ten or twelve volumes of old-fashioned romances piled up round about him, which he was devouring eagerly, but changing often. At the other end of the room sat Captain Donovan, with his feet on a chair, and a large book in his hand, apparently enriched with plates, which he was studying intently, but yet, from time to time, raising his eyes and giving a grave glance toward the boy, his fellow-tenant of the library. The door by which Mr. Mullins entered was almost directly behind Captain Donovan's chair, and he was, to say the truth, not a little surprised to see that the object of that gentleman's study was a large work upon Botany.

"Nothing has so many caprices as idleness," thought Mr. Mullins. "If I had found him reading Mrs. Behn's novels, or Mrs. Centlivre's plays, it wouldn't have surprised me. Botany—what has he to do with Botany?"

"Ah! Mullins," said Captain Donovan, turning round, "is that you? I turned out of the little dining-room to let you have your confab with Sir Walter in private. Has he settled all his affairs?"

"He has arranged them all," replied Mr. Mullins, very well comprehending that the light and easy tone in which Captain Donovan spoke was not natural. "I have a paper to draw up, and then all will be done."

"Well, it is no great matter to me," said Captain Donovan, in a low tone, modulated to avoid the ears of the boy. "I have no great wishes for wealth, and still less expectations of it."

"That's lucky," said Mr. Mullins, dryly.

Donovan gave a start that was almost too perceptible. "What do you mean?" he said.

"Oh! I only mean," replied Mr. Mullins, "that it is always lucky to have no expectations, for I have always remarked that those who have the least are the nearest success."

"Indeed!" said Captain Donovan, looking up with a smile. "He said something, it is true, just as I was quitting the room to-night, about my one day having the command of large property, but I did not believe any thing of it."

There was a spice of that sort of generous malice at the bottom of Mr. Mullins's heart which honest men feel when witnessing the playing of a roguish game, and seeing the wiles of the trickster defeated; and, shaking his head gravely, he replied, "You might have believed him implicitly, captain. Sir Walter is not a man to say such a thing without meaning it; but, upon my life, I must sit down and finish the paper, for the old gentleman says he will remain up till it is done, and it will take two good hours at least. Ah! Master Theodore, how do you do?" he continued, as if he had not seen the boy before; and he held out his hand toward him in a kindly manner. Then, observing the eyes of Captain Donovan fixed upon him, he added, with a sigh—perfectly natural, whatever the reader may think—and in a low voice, "Ah! poor fellow!"

"He dislikes me, that Mullins," said Donovan to himself. "I'll turn him off when I come into the property. Well, I'll leave you, Mullins," he continued, aloud. "Theodore, my dear fellow, you had better come with me;" and the boy, after having timidly shaken hands with the lawyer, followed his cousin out of the room.

For about an hour and three quarters, Mr. Mullins continued to labor at what to him was an unusual task, that of copying with his own hand, upon a large sheet of paper, the words which had been previously written upon the parchment. He was a solicitor in London of large practice, and consequently, upon all ordinary occasions, had plenty of clerks about him to do the drudgery; and although at present there were several alterations to make as he went on, yet that did not relieve the dullness of the task so much as to prevent him from getting a little cross about it. As he was a very good lawyer, however, his crossness only seemed to make him the more scrupulously accurate; and Sir Walter having told him to tie the property up tightly, most tightly did he tie it up.

In the end, he paused for a minute or two in thought. "I don't half like putting Reginald's name in," he said, "and yet I have no business to keep it out. It's the old man's own doing, and as there's very little chance of his ever coming in for this good thing, here goes;" and he wrote down the words which entailed the property upon his nephew, failing the issue, lawfully begotten, of Theodore Broughton and Thomas Donovan. This done, he re-perused the will carefully, and seeing nothing therein that could be taken hold of by the most critical special pleader, he walked away with the paper to the small dining-room where he had left Sir Walter.

The baronet was dozing in the same position, and Captain Donovan, who had talked him to sleep, was sitting gazing at him with the newspaper on his knee, with his mind full of acres, roods, and perches, together with sundry considerations of three and five per cents. Without the slightest ceremony, Mr. Mullins woke the baronet, who, after a minute or two of that confusion of head which in old people often follows a short sleep, resumed his faculties as briskly as ever, and then with a sly smile, and a nod of the head, sent Captain Donovan once more out of the room, bidding him send in two or three of the inferior servants. In their presence, with spectacles on nose, and every now and then asking a question of the lawyer, he read over the will, and then, with a shaking hand, signed it, calling upon those present to witness his act and deed. He did it all with a gay and a jocular air, seeming right well pleased that it was accomplished; and when all was concluded, he bade one of the witnesses tell Lloyd to serve the supper there

"I have sat up so long," he said, "that I must have a bit of something before I go to bed, and a glass of wine. There's no use talking of it, Mullins. My old doctor, Starvington, says I should not taste any thing but bread or a cup of gruel after five o'clock, but I get quite exhausted, and so to-night—"

"You shall have a bit of the salmy," said Mullins, laughing.

"Ay, and a glass of that excellent Verzenay which you pronounced one day, Mullins, to be something between nectar and Champagne."

Mr. Mullins did not at all object to the Verzenay, and when Captain Donovan was called in, the will having been previously sealed up in a clean sheet of paper, and docketed by the baronet as "my last will and testament," with his signature added, the worthy captain, radiant in face, and full of quiet, inoffensive spirits, joined in the delicate little meal with a good zest, and then gave his arm to his uncle, as the old gentleman slowly moved toward his bed-chamber.

Sir Walter had not done amiss, considering the state of his health and the opinion of his physicians. He had dabbled with one or two little trifles very pleasantly, and the glass of Verzenay had deviated into five. But if he had done well, Mr. Mullins did better, for he remained at the table while Captain Donovan was absent, and amused the time as best he might with the things before him. When the captain returned, it was with the spirit of conviviality upon him. He was very gay; and as he sipped his first glass at the *tête-à-tête*, he said, "Well, he's a capital old fellow, after all."

"I am glad you think so," said Mr. Mullins.

"I do indeed," rejoined Donovan, on whom the wine had some effect, at least insomuch as opening the lips and untying the tongue. "He's a capital old fellow; here's to him!"

"Health and long life to him!" said Mr. Mullins, rather maliciously; but Donovan was a brave and determined man, and he swallowed the toast without hesitation. Indeed, it seemed as if he was inclined to make a night of it, and to carry his potations to the full extent of sobriety; but Mr. Mullins was rigid, though not abstemious. He drank a certain quantity of wine every day, but no more. He had drunk none that day, having abandoned his dinner to attend Sir Walter's summons, and, consequently, he took glass after glass till the number was complete, and then refused to taste another drop in spite of all persuasion. Moreover, when he had rested himself for a little after this exercise, he rose, took a candle from the side-board, and retired to rest.

How long Captain Donovan pursued the engagement of the table, Mr. Mullins did not know. As for himself, being a simple man in his habits, he produced from one pocket a night-cap, a razor, and a tooth-brush, and from the other a clean shirt, which he spread out upon the back of a chair. He then took off his wig, put on his night-cap, cleaned his teeth, and retired to bed.

A first sleep is certainly a very pleasant thing when a man has no great cares to fill his mind with the thoughts of this world, and no great imagination to trouble him with the dreams of any other. Comfortably, quietly, and well did

Mr. Mullins sleep for some two hours. Not a vision crossed the wide, dull plain of slumber. He was not even sufficiently awake to feel he was asleep; but suddenly something startled him, and sitting bolt upright in bed, he listened. A bell rang furiously, and then came a sound of hurrying feet, then a tap at a door not very far distant, and voices speaking, and then more hurrying to and fro, and then Mr. Mullins, getting up, sought for various portions of his habiliments, indued, as maiden authors would call it, his breeches, scrambled into his coat without his waistcoat, tied a towel round his neck because he could not find his cravat, and, unlocking his door, looked out. There was a light and a man moving along at the other end of the corridor, and Mr. Mullins exclaimed, "Lloyd! Lloyd! what's the matter?"

"Ah, Mr. Mullins, Sir Walter is very ill," said the butler. "His gentleman and the captain are with him, and Grub the helper is gone for Dr. Starvington. You had better go in and see him, sir, though I don't think he is much in the way to make a will."

"That is made, thank God!" said Mullins; and then he muttered in a low tone, "I may as well be in at the death;" and walked away to the baronet's room.

The attorney found Sir Walter Broughton lying in his bed, and, as some might have thought, in a very sound and heavy sleep. But yet there was a something—not to be described—that was not natural. He snored very loud, but there was a sort of gasp withal, and Mr. Mullins did not at all deceive himself, especially when he found that Sir Walter had woke ill, rung his bell twice violently, and after he had been joined by both Captain Donovan and the valet, had fallen into that heavy slumber.

"He'll not wake again," said Mr. Mullins to Captain Donovan, in a loud whisper. "How lucky the will was signed."

"Very lucky indeed," said Captain Donovan, in a lower tone. "I hope the doctor won't be long."

"Very little use of his coming," rejoined Mullins.

"Better have him — better have him," answered Donovan, with a significant nod; and then added, in the lowest possible whisper, "The will is all right, I suppose, Mullins?"

"Oh, quite right!" answered Mr. Mullins, with great internal satisfaction.

As he spoke, the baronet lifted his hand, which was lying on the bed-clothes, let it fall again, opened his eyes, and shut them.

"He is gone," said Mullins: and so it was.

The aspect of mourning spread over the house. Captain Donovan was very grave and sad. The servants all looked deplorable: the French cook alone maintained his constitutional and national cheerfulness, and laughed over his stew-pans while preparing dinner the next day for Mr. Mullins, Captain Donovan, and young Sir Theodore Broughton. But among them all, perhaps the only one who felt any thing like real sorrow was the boy whom we have seen reading romances in the library. His grandfather, it is true, had been cross and wayward with him, exacting, and at times severe; but at other times he had been kind, and he was the only one who ever had been kind. The boy mourned, therefore, naturally and unaffectedly, with more of the reality and less of the semblance than others. Mr. Mullins, it is true, did not affect to mourn: he was grave, indeed; for, though not a very impressible man, yet there is something in death, especially in the death of one with whom we have long been on habits of intimacy, which had its effect even upon him. He shook it off soon, however; for, though in reality a good-tempered man, yet the best natured of us feel, I believe, a little silent, secret satisfaction when we see the wily and the artful taken in their own net. Now, the thought of reading the will in the presence of Captain Donovan was a very great comfort to the solicitor.

The day at length came for that operation. A good number of the distant relations of Sir Walter Broughton were assembled to hear the last disposition the deceased had made of his property; and in the old library where the will had been drawn up, the party was received by Captain Donovan with an air of master of the house, while the young baronet, who seemed either to expect very little, to care very little, or to understand very little, sat at a table in the window, with his head leaning on his hand, speaking to nobody. When all had assembled who were expected, Mr. Mullins produced the will, the servants were called in, for such was the custom in those days, and the seals were broken.

In a loud, clear, dry manner, Mr. Mullins proceeded, but every now and then, with a malicious twinkle of the eyes, he looked over the top of the paper at the worthy captain's face, as he sat just opposite to him, expecting, beyond all doubt, some outbreak of wrath, for he knew the man's expectations and his disappointment.

The first glance of his eye, however, had been a warning to the object of his attention. It produced doubt, confusion, anxiety for a moment; but then Donovan exerted the whole powers of his mind, and they were not small, to subdue the passions within him, so far, at least, as to deprive them of all external expression.

The will was read out, conveying the whole property of the deceased, real and personal, to his grandson, entailing the estates strictly in the course I have previously stated; appointing Mr. Mullins and Captain Donovan executors of the will, and naming the latter as guardian of the young heir. Much to Mr. Mullins's surprise, not a muscle of Captain Donovan's face moved, though his cheek was somewhat paler than usual; and when the more distant relatives gathered round the young baronet to wish him joy of the large fortune he inherited, the captain was one of the first to offer his congratulations.

CHAPTER III.

There was a little blue bell growing at the edge of the road, by the side of a wild common, and a lad of about nineteen years of age, who was walking slowly along with the bridle of a horse over his arm, stopped to gather it. Few young men of nineteen ever think of stopping to gather blue bells—at least vegetable ones. They are past that stage; they have the dawn of passion in them, the seed of their first ambitions, the aspiration after things permitted and things forbidden. Ay, after both, for in nine hundred and ninety-nine cases out of a thousand, when the eyes of the youth of nineteen have been opened to the grand panorama of life, his bosom is one mass of aspirations, chaotic, vague, undefined, but still containing the germs of all the desires that animate and pervade the rest of his existence. He is burning to possess and to enjoy; and where is the youth who nowaday would stop to pluck a blue bell, with all the mighty world of untasted enjoyment open before him?

But that youth was peculiarly situated, and of a peculiar mind. His habits of thought, both from natural character—I am a believer in natural character—and from education, were different from those of most men, and he was still at that period of progress when the fresh heart can admire and enjoy the humblest flower that blossoms in the fields. His horse, though now following so calmly behind him, was covered with foam and sweat, and seemed quite exhausted with hard riding. But the youth was cool and quiet in demeanor, as if there had been no struggle and no exertion; and, as I have said, he walked on with a calm, deliberate, meditative step, looking thoughtfully upon the ground, till his eye fell upon the flower, and then he stooped to gather it. But suddenly he drew his hand back, saying aloud, "Nay, bloom on; why should I condemn you to wither before your time? It will come soon enough;" and, sitting down upon the little bank where the flower grew, he leaned his head upon his hand, and meditated deeply. He had no passion for the flower. Happy had it been for him had he so acted when passion moved him.

As he was there sitting, a young man, some five or six years older, with a portfolio under his arm, plainly dressed, and with eyes cast over the prospect around at every step he took, crossed the common toward him, and when at about sixty yards' distance, seated himself on a little piece of bank, and deliberately set to work to sketch the youth and his horse. Horses, like cows, have a consciousness of having their portraits painted, and, less vain than man, are not pleased with the commemoration. Dear reader, if you ever attempted to sketch a cow, you will know that, though her back be turned toward you, she will find out what you are about in a moment, and rise and walk away. The horse, tired as he was, began to fret and fidget within one minute after the stranger commenced his sketch, and as he tugged at the bridle over his master's arm, he naturally attracted the youth's attention to the artist. There is such a thing as being bold to dangers, and timid to the merest trifles. The young man, who had ridden that fierce and fiery horse straight across a difficult and dangerous country, priding himself in subduing his spirit and tiring out his vigorous strength, felt timid at the sight of a stranger sketching him. He felt a desire to go up and ask to see the portrait, and yet he could not summon courage to do it; neither did he like to sit still and undergo the process of being drawn. Perhaps there might be a little vanity in all this, and it is certain that he never imagined the horse was being sketched, and not himself; but when he at length got up to go away, the stranger raised his voice, saying, "If you would have the goodness to wait one moment, you would greatly oblige me. I want a horse for my foreground."

The animal, however, had moved a good deal, and it was necessary to put him right again. This led to a few words passing between the two young men; and when the sketch had been finished, looked at, and admired, they walked on together over the common, talking in a strain almost friendly.

Perhaps it is no wonder that they did so, for two reasons. In the first place, young Sir Theodore Broughton had hardly an acquaintance in the world, and the young sketcher was frank and easy in his manners, as well as perfectly gentlemanly and unpresuming. No one could doubt that he had mixed in good society—that he had been habituated to it, in fact, all his life. Every thing was done with ease, and it seemed as if he could not comprehend that there was such a thing as a feeling of awkwardness; but yet, what is strange, with his total want of morbid susceptibility, his conversation was full of fancy; occasionally, perhaps, a little too wild and volatile, but with a depth of thought pouring through the whole, like the deeper tones of a fine instrument, and harmonizing well with some of the characteristic traits of Theodore Broughton's mind.

"It must be a great pleasure to draw as you do," said the latter, as they walked on together. "Pray, may I ask, is it your profession?"

"Not exactly," replied the stranger. "There is, indeed, a great pleasure in being able to draw, even imperfectly as I do, and that pleasure has a thousand branches, each bearing fruit. Often, when I sit alone, I turn back to the sketches I made some years ago, and as I look at them, not only the scene rises again before me with all the soft, aerial perspective of memory, but the persons I have seen therein, the faces that smiled upon me, the voices that made my heart glad, come back as if time were annihilated, the fiat of fate revoked, and the grave gave up its dead. Then, again, if I wish to aid imagination in framing one of the gay day-dreams that we all indulge in, with the pencil or the brush, I can sit down and paint the scene of happiness I fancy, people it with beings that I love to look upon, and, better than all, can feel sure that they will neither deceive nor betray, nor malign nor destroy; that they are all truth—the truth of imagination, which, I am often inclined to think, is the only truth we find on earth."

His young companion thought for a moment or two. He had no great habit of expressing his feelings and ideas; and whether he possessed the power or not, he was timid even in trying to use it. At length he answered, "These seem to me more the pleasures of association than those of the act itself. I meant to say, I can not help thinking that it must be very delightful to be able to sit down and draw any beautiful thing we see."

"Oh, I understand," said the stranger; "to

analyze the beauty that charms us, to see and mark its elements, and admire and wonder at the means by which the Almighty, out of a few tints, and a few lines, and a few gradations and contrasts of light and shade, has produced such marvelous loveliness and effects so magnificent; and then to think of how infinitely beneficent it was to ordain such harmony between the soul of man and the wide creation, that every sight touches us with some different emotion, as if the whole were some grand instrument of music raising a hymn of praise unto the sky."

Theodore Broughton turned round and gazed at him with some surprise. He had never heard such words before; but they were a lesson to him: they taught him that from things plain, and of no apparent depth, were to be extracted thoughts and feelings high and profound. It gave him the first knowledge that there is a spirit in all things to be evoked by the earnest and the strong, and compelled to bring forth treasures from the rock. Happy had it been for him had he learned the lesson better; but as it was, it had its effect.

The stranger remarked his sudden look round, and the silence that followed, and he said, laughing, "You think I am an enthusiast; but it is not so. I only seek to derive the greatest amount of pleasure from all things; and I know that if we look only at the surface, we lose the most precious of the gifts of Heaven. The gold lies down deep in the mine; the diamond veils its well of light till it is cut; and the mind of man, if it would discover the richness or the brightness of any thing throughout the universe, must dig deep and labor hard. But this lesson I was taught by an insect. I was one day watching and admiring a quantity of wild flowers on a bank, when I saw a bee flying from blossom to blossom, pausing a moment upon each, diving down into the cup or into the bell, and flying onward with its load; and I said to myself, all flowers have their honey, but he must search who would find it."

The young baronet broke away from the subject somewhat abruptly, asking, "Do you stay long in this part of the country?" and his companion replied, "No, not long. I have been a great wanderer, hurrying from place to place; and, as soon as I get the least tired of any spot, I willingly quit it. Now, perhaps, I shall have to be more steady, both to one pursuit and to one position, for my wanderings have not hitherto been altogether voluntary; and when I go back to town, which will be in a few days, I suppose it will be to stay for some months."

"I should like to see London very much," said the young man, thoughtfully. "Are you usually a resident there?"

"I shall be for some time," answered the other, a slight shade coming over his face, which might or might not be from imagining that an invitation would be expected. "But have you never seen London?" he added, good-humoredly. "Oh! you should see it by all means. How strange that there should be any one on this side of the Atlantic who has never seen the capital of the whole world! Had you been one of my good friends, the Mohawks, I might have understood it; but, for a young gentleman of your figure, I can not conceive how it has happened."

"That is easily explained," said the young man, almost sadly: "my guardian does not choose it. He says it will be soon enough some time hence; that it is a vicious, corrupt place."

"Who is your guardian?" was the abrupt question of his companion; adding, the moment after, as if to soften the apparent rudeness, "He must be a very strange man!"

"Why so?" demanded Sir Theodore.

The other paused for an instant, and then replied with a smile, "I will tell you why I think so, as you ask. Here he sets you upon a fiery devil of a chestnut horse, as likely to break your neck and his own back as possible, when there can be no possible need of your ever mounting such an animal again, or of your being obliged to break the spirit of such animals at the risk of your life, unless you be destined, which I don't suppose, for a riding-master or a horse-breaker; and yet he will not let you go to London, when the risks to your mind are small in comparison, if he has given you a good education, and when they only imply lessons in life which you must one day receive. That was what made me say he must be a strange man, and ask his name."

"His name," answered the young man, "is Donovan—Captain Donovan."

A very grave, almost stern look came over his companion's countenance as that name was pronounced, and he was silent for several moments, but at length he replied, "You are Sir Theodore Broughton, then?"

"The same," replied the young man. "Do you know Captain Donovan?"

"I have seen him," said the stranger. "I have seen him, and may say that I have his acquaintance. I think he is absent from England now, is he not?"

"Yes," answered Sir Theodore. "He spends several months each year abroad. But, now that you know my name, perhaps there will be no impropriety in my asking yours."

The stranger smiled good-humoredly, and then replied, half laughing, "Certainly no impropriety, and yet, for particular reasons of my own, I will consider for a time before I give it to you. Will you come down to the little inn in the village, called the Hen and Chickens, and dine with me to-day, and then I will tell you more. I think I need not add," he continued, with a somewhat proud look, "that I am a gentleman by birth, education, and habits; and I do not think, from what you have seen of me, that you will suppose I am one of those men about town, of whose corrupting communication your guardian is so much afraid."

"Oh! I will come, with all my heart," replied the young man, cheerfully. "My tutor is away, so that I am quite my own master. What shall be the hour?"

"At four o'clock," replied the other, "I shall expect you. Good-by for the present;" and, while Sir Theodore put his foot in the stirrup to mount his horse, the other turned along a path to the right. The next moment, however, he heard the young baronet's voice exclaiming, "By what name shall I ask for you?"

"Oh! the captain—they call me the captain,

and know me by no other name," was the reply, and the two parted, I may say, mutually pleased with each other.

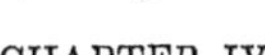

CHAPTER IV.

While Theodore Broughton pursued his way to the hall, the gentleman with whom he had made a casual acquaintance returned, with a quick, elastic pace, to the little village, which, it must be remarked, was an old-fashioned country village, such as was seen in England threescore years ago. Sadly, sadly are changed the villages of once-merry England. There are paintings enough of them remaining to show us what they were, and I will not pause to describe this one, for the contrast between what it was and what it is might be somewhat melancholy.

Past the church, which—with its church-yard, and its elms, and its iron railings, and its gravestones, and its monuments of old and high families, now long passed away—formed one side of an irregular green of perhaps a couple of acres in extent, the young stranger walked on, with his sketch-book under his arm, among several merry groups of children, not in their holiday attire, but clothed comfortably and decently, and having that ruddy hue of health, and that jocund sprightliness of aspect, which, from our rarely seeing any of them now, leads us to believe that the pictures of those times, either with pencil or with pen, savor of romance. Gayly and cheerfully the young gentleman went on, patted one curly urchin on the head, pinched another's cheek, said a kind word to a third; and with courtesies and nods, and sometimes a blush, and sometimes a smile, and sometimes a shy look of fun, was greeted by almost all, as if they knew him and liked him, and felt that he was a friend rather than a stranger in the place; yet he had not been there above four or five days in the whole course of his life.

At the further end of the green, where, gradually narrowing itself, it was degraded into a road—a good broad road, however, with a row of green trees and a foot-path on each side—stood the little inn of the Hen and Chickens, with a not ill-painted sign of the tender-plumed parent and her young brood. Whether the earth had arisen around the house—for it might be an axiom in natural philosophy as well as ethics that dirt has a tendency to rise, although contrary to generally received opinions—or whether the original founder of the house was a man of a lowly mind, certain it is that you approach the nest of the Hen and Chickens by two steps down from the foot-path. There was nothing cheerless, damp-looking, or unwholesome, however, about this sunken story. The windows were not large, it is true, and the panes were very small, for few windows were large, and all panes were small in England at that time. But still the sun contrived to shine cheerfully in, the floors were as clean as a new-mangled table-cloth, and the sand in the passage was as yellow as gold. The landlady, too (for landlord it had none), was, to use the terms of those days, "as clean and as neat as a carrot new-scraped," with an apron of snowy whiteness, a cap that vied with the apron, and a face that looked like a last year's rosy apple, tolerably well preserved, out of one's great grandmother's linen press. To her the young stranger first applied himself; but the good landlady, who had all an innkeeper's sagacity about her, having discovered one, at least, of her guest's favorite pursuits, and perceived that he was a little proud of his drawings, began upon him at once, without suffering him to order the dinner that he meditated, saying, "Ah, captain, you have been out sketching again. I dare say you have made some beautiful pictures of our poor place. Pray, let me look at them."

"Presently, presently, my good dame," said the stranger. "Just let me talk to you for one minute, and you shall see the drawings afterward. I have something for you to do; and you won't have much time to spare. I expect a gentleman to dine with me here to-day, and you must have as nice a little dinner for us as you can get, about four o'clock."

"Oh, dear, yes! captain," said the landlady. "Bless you, I am quite ready. I knew quite well you would ask him to dinner. It's not more than half an hour since he left the door, and a comical-looking gentleman he is."

"Who, in Heaven's name, do you mean, Mrs. Gillespie?" asked her guest. "You surely do not call Sir Theodore Broughton a comical-looking gentleman?"

"Ha, ha, ha!" cried the landlady, holding her well-lined sides. "Well, that is good, captain! Sir Theodore Broughton! Oh, dear! no. I mean the tall, thin-sided gentleman, with a nose like a crow's beak, and two small eyes, and a patch of hair on his chin. He was asking after you this morning, and all about you, and where you had gone, and then he said 'he'd take a stroll, and call back in the afternoon.'"

A look of some mortification came into the young gentleman's face, and he muttered, "That is unfortunate. The very last man I should like this youth to meet, for he is the last whom he would comprehend. How was he dressed, Mrs. Gillespie?"

"Oh! very funnily indeed," answered Mrs. Gillespie. "He had got on a long, blue-waisted frock, with a silver lace, and silver frognels on the pockets, and an embroidered waistcoat that was not half long enough to cover his stomach, and below that a pair of buckskins and jack-boots, just as much too large as the waistcoat was too short. But the oddest thing of all was, he had two great holes in his ears, and then he wore his hair in a club as thick as my arm."

"It might have been worse," said the young gentleman, dryly; "it might have been worse."

"Worse! Lord have mercy, captain!" exclaimed Mrs. Gillespie, as if the assertion far surpassed her faith. "What, worse than such funny clothes as that!"

"When I first saw him," replied her guest, "he had no clothes on at all."

"Oh dear, sir! fy for shame!" cried Mrs. Gillespie. "You don't mean to say he was naked, sir?"

"Indeed I do," replied the young gentleman, "unless you call having a bunch of feathers in his head being dressed, or think two human bones in those holes in his ears articles of wearing apparel."

"Goodness gracious!" cried the good dame, holding up her hands. "Why, the man must be stark staring mad. I thought so, I do declare."

"No, no," cried the young gentleman, who was very much amused at the astonishment of his hostess, but did not wish to injure the reputation of his friend's brains; "he is not and was not mad, but he was among the savages, Mrs. Gillespie."

"Ah, that may be, then," said the good woman; "and a very ugly savage he'd make; but I hope you won't have him here, captain, with any of his savage tricks. I should be afraid of his eating the little children."

"No fear of that, my good lady," was the answer; "he is as kind-hearted a man as ever lived; and, moreover, if he comes before Sir Theodore and I have done dinner, you must keep him down here, and make much of him, Mrs. Gillespie. Tell him I am engaged with a gentleman up stairs; give him plenty of good punch, and a nice dinner, and he will tell you of all sorts of strange things that he has seen in foreign countries. That gentleman once saved my life."

With this hint, and a significant nod, he turned away toward his own room, saying to himself, with a somewhat rueful smile, "And he has often made me pay for it by his oddities since. Upon my life! I must take the Ravenous Crow back to Canada, or the Sandwich Isles, or somewhere."

"The Ravenous Crow!" exclaimed Mrs. Gillespie, who was following him unperceived, and overheard the last words; "Lord have mercy, sir, do you call him a ravenous crow?"

"No, no, no," cried the young gentleman, laughing. "That was his name among the Cherokee Indians; they generally take themselves, and bestow upon their friends, the names of birds, and beasts, and other objects in Nature. His real name is Major Brandrum, a very gallant, honorable, excellent person, as you'll find when you chat with him a little."

"Well, sir, I will do any thing to please you," replied Mrs. Gillespie, "for I am sure you have always behaved very genteel in my house; but you are sure he is not carnivorous?"

Her young guest quieted her in regard to the propensities which he very well understood she was inclined to attribute to his friend by the term carnivorous; and, to his great relief, two hours passed away, and four o'clock came, without the appearance of Major Brandrum.

Sir Theodore Broughton was punctual to his time, and entered the little sitting-room of the traveler with that sort of depressed expression in his young face which is so painful to see in a countenance where time has left no wrinkles, and the only furrows are those of care. He had been thinking, ever since they parted, of the words of the stranger. They had opened to him new sources of thought—new questions to ask his own heart and his own spirit, and he longed, as the other had pointed out, to interrogate the vast universe, and gain replies which would raise up mightier questions still. He came prepared to follow the same strain of conversation; but, for some reason, the mood of his companion was changed; he would no longer rest upon deep things, but spoke lightly and gayly of what men are accustomed to call "the world," though neither altogether frivolously nor uninstructively.

Mrs. Gillespie and Mrs. Gillespie's cook had done their best to send up to one of the favorite guests of the house as nice a little dinner as the place would afford, and very successful had been their labors. The wine, too, was good, and, let a man be as intellectually constituted as he may, the spirits will rise, the heart will feel lightened, under the influence of the good things of this life, so long as matter is united to mind, and health cements the union. Sir Theodore Broughton soon shook off his grave and thoughtful air, talked and laughed joyously with his companion, and listened with keen zest to many a tale, and many an anecdote of London life with which the other enriched his conversation. It must not be denied that his host watched him, marked the effect his words produced, saw the changes of countenance which betrayed an eager spirit within when pleasures and pastimes were described, and in the end he said to himself, "Perhaps, after all, the guardian is right. Without some very safe companion, all that is good and noble in this youth might be lost among the fascinations of the metropolis."

In the mean time, the question of his name had been quite forgotten. In the charms of his society, Sir Theodore cared little what his name was, and, with a facility too frequent and too fatal, bent his thoughts to those of the companion of the hour, remembering nothing of his former ideas and feelings. The chameleon mind, which takes its color from that which is next to it, unlike the skin of the animal, is a peril, not a protection. Something, indeed, might be allowed for the fact that this was the first society deserving of the name which the young man had ever known. His guardian—often absent—was, when with him, grave and stern, indulging him, it is true, in many dangerous sports and over-fatiguing exercises, but repelling all confidence, and treating him as a mere boy. His tutor we shall see more of hereafter, and it will then be apparent that he was not fitted to be a friend or companion. All the rest of those admitted to him were persons upon business, a few masters of different sciences and arts, the parson of the parish—an old-fashioned parson, more frequently in the hunting-saddle than the pulpit—and servants. What a relief! what an enjoyment, when the imprisoned thoughts have long been shut up within the close cell of our own bosom, and every one who approaches seems but a jailer to force them back if they try to escape, to meet with a kindred spirit which gives them leave to wander, and encourages them to come forth, even if it be for but one short hour! No wonder the young man gave way to it.

In the midst of the most pleasant conversation which Sir Theodore Broughton had ever enjoyed, he was suddenly startled by sounds very different from those which he and his companion were uttering. First came a loud "whoop," which seemed to shake the floor under their feet, and then something which seemed intended for music; but the words of the song, whatever they were, though several articulate sounds rose up through the thin compartments, were quite unintelligible to Sir Theodore Broughton. His companion at first looked a little annoyed, but then smiled; and, upon the principle of taking the bull by the horns, he said, "That is a friend and fellow-soldier of mine, Sir Theodore—a most eccentric personage, but a highly worthy one in many respects, notwithstanding a few faults both real and apparent. He once saved my life in Canada, and, as often happens with men of warm hearts, he seems to think that act has bound him by a duty to look for occasions to serve me ever since."

"But why is he not dining with us?" asked the young baronet; "it would have given me great pleasure to have met such a person."

"He only called to inquire for me this morning," replied the other; "and, moreover, you would hardly have understood him in one short interview, and might, perhaps, have felt a good deal of surprise and little pleasure in the society and conversation of one who requires to be well known to be esteemed. But hark! I think he is coming up the stairs."

As he spoke, the tramp of a heavy foot was heard, which, from the sounds, might well be incased in such boots as Mrs. Gillespie had described; but when the door opened, a very different personage appeared from him whom Sir Theodore's entertainer expected to see: no other, in short, than Captain Donovan himself. A considerable change had taken place in that gentleman since last I presented him to the reader. The mortification which he had experienced in regard to Sir Walter Broughton's will, though deprived of all external expression, had not been without effect internally. He had become somewhat morose and stern in demeanor in all things where his young ward was concerned. He could be as gay, as dashing, and as light as ever in general society, but the very sight of Sir Theodore Broughton seemed to excite a sullen and a bad feeling, to which he gave way a little too much, perhaps, considering that he wished to establish a hold upon the young man's mind. His dress, also, was more rich and costly than it had formerly been, and—whether from the accessories of costume, or from any of those accidental causes which occasionally work changes in the human frame, independent of those wrought by the great destroyer Time—he looked altogether a younger man than at the period of his relation's death. On the present occasion, his brow, which was generally clouded when he was in that part of the country, was knit into a heavier frown than ever, and his eyes fixed instantly upon the young baronet, who seemed to cower beneath its influence.

"Well, Theodore," he said, "this is a strange vagary. I did not know, sir, you were in the habit of dining out during my absence. Who is your entertainer? Oh! Captain Lisle!" he continued, after he had gazed upon Sir Theodore's companion for an instant. "Sir, I am your most obedient humble servant. I did not know you at first. I feel particularly obliged by your kind attention to Sir Theodore Broughton; but you will pardon me for saying that I think it would be more prudent of him, when I am absent, to confine himself to acquaintances of my selecting; and, on your part—"

"Stop for a moment, Captain Donovan," said Reginald Lisle, calmly, but yet with a very meaning tone; "comment on the conduct of Sir Theodore Broughton, if you please. That you may be entitled to do; but do not comment upon mine without thinking twice of what you are going to say, for you seem somewhat heated just now; and, though I am not, I may not bear any unpleasant observations calmly."

Captain Donovan bit his lip, and paused for an instant ere he replied. He answered, however, at length, in a cold and somewhat sarcastic tone, "Do not suppose, sir, that I was going to say any thing which could excite your pugnacious propensities. You have had a good deal more fighting lately, of one kind and another, than I have had, or ever shall have again. For this young gentleman's sake, I have turned my sword into a plowshare, and have no particular inclination to bend it to another form again. The observation I was about to make was simply this, that on your part you will greatly oblige me if you will not attempt to thwart my views with regard to this young gentleman's education; for, although you are mentioned by some extraordinary accident in Sir Walter Broughton's will, yet you are not appointed his guardian."

"I am well aware of that fact, sir," answered Reginald Lisle, "and shall certainly not attempt to interfere with his education. But do not let us dispute, Captain Donovan," he continued, good-humoredly. "May I beg you to sit down and take some dinner, as you seem from your appearance to have ridden far and hard."

Captain Donovan seemed to hesitate for a moment, and then, with a mollified look, seated himself, saying, "Well, I have ridden far; for, as soon as I heard that Dr. Gamble had thought fit to go away and leave you alone, I set off to see what was the cause of such conduct."

His words were addressed to Theodore, although the invitation had come from Captain Lisle. The latter, however, rang the bell, and ordered a plate and knife and fork for Captain Donovan; but, though he remained, partook of the good cheer, and drank more than one glass of wine, his manner was still cold and stiff, and he seemed dissatisfied and ill at ease. There was a sort of absent, meditative air about him; and from time to time he fixed his eyes upon Reginald Lisle, as if that gentleman in some degree formed one of the elements of his calculations. "We see very little of you in London, Captain Donovan," said the entertainer at length, "though, to say truth, I can hardly know whether you are much there or not, for I have been so frequently absent. I wonder you do not bring Sir Theodore to London, to let him see a little of the capital."

A heavy frown gathered upon Captain Donovan's brows, and the young baronet seemed actually frightened at the probable effect which this hint might have upon his guardian. But, whatever was the reply which sprang to the worthy officer's lips, it was interrupted by a renewal of the sounds from below, which now seemed coming up the stairs:

> "Joliette, ma Joliette,
> Qu'elle est belle en chemisette!
> Je monterai ma charette,
> Irai voir ma Joliettè."

Such were the doggerel lines which, to a tune

then common among the *habitans* of Canada, were sung by a rich, full, but somewhat over-loud voice, upon the stairs of the little inn, the moment after Reginald Lisle's suggestion had passed his lips. Nobody could express wonder, or make any inquiry, before the strange figure which Mrs. Gillespie had very accurately described entered the room, and—in an attitude half theatrical, half military, with one leg advanced, and his hand, the palm turned outward, raised to his forehead—gazed round the company.

"Ah, Reginald, my boy!" he exclaimed, "found you at last. That charming old woman below, together with a capon and a bowl of punch, engaged me in deep conversation; nor did she admit that you were in the house, till I heard your well-known voice raised somewhat high just now. I always know a voice, sir," he continued, looking round to Captain Donovan; "the slightest tone of it is sufficient for me. Whether he be roaring through a speaking-trumpet, or whispering soft nonsense in a lady's ear, I know my man in a moment, if ever I heard his tongue before."

"Pray, is this gentleman a friend of yours, Captain Lisle?" asked Donovan, with a slight degree of sarcastic bitterness in his tone.

"Yes," replied Reginald, who had been leaning back in his chair a little mortified and a little amused, "yes, this is my friend, Captain Donovan; and a very good friend too. Let me introduce him to you. Major Brandrum—Captain Donovan; Sir Theodore Broughton—Major Brandrum;" and, shaking the major warmly by the hand, he placed a chair for him at the table.

"Ah, Captain Donovan!" said the worthy gentleman, taking his seat, and stretching his enormously long legs under the table till he kicked Theodore's shins on the other side; "that's not the name I am the best known by since the year seventy-two, nor the name I am most proud of either."

"Have you got an alias then, sir?" asked Captain Donovan, dryly. The major nodded his head, and Donovan proceeded: "May I ask what it is?"

"Assuredly," replied Major Brandrum. "In this barbarous and corrupt country—not the less barbarous for being corrupt, nor the less corrupt for being barbarous—I am called, as my friend Lisle has stated, Major Brandrum, but among the more civilized nations in North America I am known by the name of the Ravenous Crow."

"No doubt justly," said Captain Donovan.

"Of that you can tell nothing," said the major, "till you hear how I came by the appellation. You will then see that it is both significant and glorious; not the less glorious because it is significant, nor the less significant because it is glorious. You must know that when I was in command of a party of my tribe, the Cherokee Indians, we had gathered together some sixty baskets of maize. In whose fields it grew, far be it from me to say; but it was ours by right of war; when one day, while we were upon a hunting expedition, a party of Mohawks fell upon our wigwam, and carried off our maize and three young squaws, one of whom was my own especial property. On my return, I set off with twenty warriors of the tribe, and followed the marauders like a slot-hound. Not a twig they had broken, not a blade of grass their footstep had bent, but was marked as we went, and we discovered by the trail that there were full fifty men of them. However, we watched our opportunity, fell upon them unawares, and after a desperate conflict, in which I slew and scalped three of their most famous warriors—the Centipede, the Old Buzzard, and the Grizzly Bear—we recovered our maize and our squaws, and marched off in triumph. We well knew that the Mohawks would soon retaliate, and so we sent far and wide to all the families of the tribe, and all our allies; but every thing kept still for seven days, when one morning, as I was lying in wait for a moose in a cedar swamp, I saw an old gentleman painted like a Cherokee go creeping along through some sugar maples above. I knew what he was about the moment I beheld him; but I was blind to him, and a minute or two after he came creeping down till we stood face to face. Then he said 'Hum!' and I answered 'Hum!' So then, after five minutes more, we sat down together, resting our elbows on our knees, and he said to me, 'Brother, I am the Wappiti with the long horns, a friend of the Great Bison.' I knew he was lying all the time, and that he was the Rattlesnake. So I replied to him, 'Brother, I am the Bald Eagle. What does the Wappiti with the long horns want with the Bald Eagle?' Upon that he told me that he heard we had broken the stick with the Mohawks about sixty basketfuls of maize, and that if I would lead him to the wigwam, and give him three baskets, the Wappiti with the long horns and all his people would come down to fight with us against the Mohawks. Then I said, 'Brother, I can give no maize, for the Bald Eagle has devoured it all. He has no maize to give.' To which he replied, 'Then, brother, thou art no Bald Eagle, but a Ravenous Crow;' and thereupon he sprang upon his feet, brandished his tomahawk, and set up the war-hoop. But I was upon my legs as soon as he was, and to it we set, whirling round like the foaming of a waterfall, springing at each other like panthers, aiming here and aiming there; and all the time he kept shouting his war-hoop, till I cried, 'Is not the Rattlesnake known by his rattle?' and scarcely were the words out of my mouth, when down came ten or twelve men of his tribe, and I was overpowered and tied in a minute. I shall never forget the time when they got me to the wigwam, and were about to put me to the torture. The dry brush-wood was all piled round about me in the shape of a crow's nest, and they began singing a song of how they had caught the Ravenous Crow, and were going to pluck his feathers out. I answered by singing my war-song and laughing them to scorn; but still what they were about was not pleasant, and a glad sound it was to me to hear the war-hoop suddenly in all the woods round about, and see my own people—all beautifully painted—come rushing through the trees just at the nick of time. I was soon a free man again with a tomahawk in my hand, and I taught them that day that the Ravenous Crow could peck."

He had spoken hitherto in rather an exaggerated and pompous tone, but now he dropped his voice, and in an ordinary manner added, "They had burned off the calf of my left leg, but that mattered little; I did just as well without."

The reader must not suppose that this long story had proceeded uninterrupted, for Reginald Lisle had filled his comrade's glass more than once with wine, and Captain Donovan had sometimes asked a question in a peculiarly courteous tone. When the tale was finished, he assured Major Brandrum that he fully concurred in the appropriateness of his appellation of the Ravenous Crow; and then, turning to Captain Lisle, he said, "You were speaking of my going to London, and taking my young ward with me. Do you not think it is somewhat early for him to make acquaintance with the great metropolis?"

He spoke in so altered a tone that Reginald remarked it with surprise, and even suspicion; for he could not conceive that there was any thing in the entrance or conversation of the Ravenous Crow that could have so greatly modified Captain Donovan's feelings; but, before he could reply, Major Brandrum answered, "Too early! Not a bit. It can never be too early for a young man to be made acquainted with life. Life is a curious and exciting thing, Captain Donovan; not the less curious because it is exciting, nor the less exciting because it is curious. A man should gain a knowledge of it betimes. Then he sows his wild oats at a period when they are not likely to produce too large a harvest. Why, I started in the world at fourteen, with ten pounds in my pocket, three shirts, and two pairs of breeches, and I have never regretted it. Oh, take the young gentleman to London, by all means. Here's Reginald will soon make him acquainted with all the pretty sqaws—ladies, I mean—Heaven bless 'em! and I will show him every hole and corner in the old city, from the lowest blind alley at the back of the Tower, to Whitehall and St. James's; though, to say truth, I dare say it is greatly changed, for I did not see a tile of it for ten years, from the time I sailed away in the *Little Mary* of Boston, till about two months ago, when I walked along in my blanket and feathers, with all the women of Wapping following me, after my return from Canada."

"That must have been somewhat annoying," said Captain Donovan, laughing; "could you not contrive to get a coat and a pair of breeches on board the vessel?"

"No, sir, no," replied Major Brandrum. "I was resolved to make my triumphal entrance as the Ravenous Crow; and when the excellent brandy-faced ladies of the metropolis kept asking me impertinent questions as to the warmth of my naked legs, I replied to them in Cherokee, at which they set up a shout, just like a war-hoop. Oh, let him come to London, by all means. We'll show him a little of life."

"Well, we shall see, we shall see," replied Captain Donovan, good-humoredly. "I suppose, gentlemen, you are not going to leave this neighborhood just yet, and I trust that we shall have the pleasure of seeing you at dinner to-morrow at the hall." Thus saying, he rose: the invitation was accepted, the hour arranged, and guardian and ward took their departure, leaving Reginald Lisle in a brown study, and the Ravenous Crow humming "Joliette."

CHAPTER V.

"Why, what's the matter, Reginald?" exclaimed his friend Major Brandrum, when, after finishing his song, he perceived that his young companion still continued in meditation. "You are as deep in thought as a white bear in winter time."

"I'm puzzled, Crow," replied Reginald Lisle, "very much puzzled, and scarcely know how to explain myself even to you."

"That is strange," answered the major; "but come, tell me what's the matter. I'll follow the trail, depend upon it, let it be ever so intricate. Is it the young man that puzzles you or the old one? for with them is the mystery, I see."

"It is the old one," answered Reginald: "I do not know what to make of him. A moment before you entered, I was fully convinced that nothing could be so disagreeable to him as an intimate acquaintance between Sir Theodore Broughton and myself, and that if any thing on earth could render that acquaintance more to be avoided in his opinion, it would be to know that I was intimate with such a wild, harum-scarum fellow as yourself. He was as sulky as a bear with a sore head at Sir Theodore's having accepted my invitation to dinner, and was decidedly averse to his having even a sight of the capital, speaking like a Puritan on the subject, though every one knows he is quite the reverse of a Puritan in his morals; and yet, the moment you enter with your wild ways and wild stories, he changes all at once, invites us to dinner, half yields in regard to London, and is as civil as he possibly can be."

"I suppose," replied Major Brandrum, laughing, "he thought you were too good and too prudent, Reginald, and when he saw your friend, he was convinced that he had mistaken you."

"Upon my word, it looks something like it," replied Captain Lisle; "and yet, what good it can do him, I can not imagine."

"Well, let us reconnoiter the ground a little more before we come to any conclusion," answered the major; "and, in the first place, tell me what is the connection between you and this young baronet. I never heard of him before."

"No connection whatever, that I know of," answered Reginald Lisle, "except my having fought his cousin, Sir Charles Chevenix, and having been put into the entail of the estate, for that very cause, I believe, by his grandfather, Sir Walter Broughton. At least, so my worthy uncle Mullins always said."

"Upon my life!" cried the major, "that's an exceedingly philosophical plan. I wish it would get into vogue. I have more than once been tempted to shoot my own cousins, but I suppose that would not do as well. No man would put me into an entail for doing that."

"I am afraid not," answered Lisle; "nor would it be any great satisfaction if they did. Here, in this instance, there is just as much chance of my ever succeeding to the property as of your doing so."

"Why so—why so?" said his friend; "the lad might die without children."

"Heaven forbid!" cried Lisle; "he seems as amiable and fine a fellow as ever lived, if they do not break his spirit by a bad education. But, even if he were to die, there's still Donovan himself to come in."

"Oh ho!" cried the Ravenous Crow. "So he is the next heir, is he, and the guardian too? What, the lamb left under the kind protection of the wolf! Come, come, Lisle, you give me a new insight into the matter. Master Donovan may have his own views as to selecting the acquaintances of his ward. It might be no bad thing for him if I were to seduce the young man to go and join my friends the Cherokees, or undertake any other mad-headed expedition, which may suit very well with

'A soldier who lives on his pay,
And spends half a crown out of sixpence a day,'

but would never suit a young wealthy baronet, unless his guardian was heir to his property."

"I wish you would not put such things in my head, Brandrum," said Lisle. "Do you know any harm of this man Donovan? If not, why should you think so?"

"Because he is not Reginald Lisle," replied the major, "nor, for that matter, Jack Brandrum either. I declare I wouldn't hurt a hair of the head of a boy like that for all the estates in England, bating fair and open warfare, where a man may be called upon to scalp his enemy as a matter of course. But I'll tell you what, Reginald, we must look after this matter, my dear boy. It will become you, being the heir-presumptive as men call it, to see that the succession to the crown is not endangered. If I know you right, you'll be quite as willing to look after this lad for a year or two as if he were your own brother. Now, let you and I set about it, and the devil a Donovan of them all will be a match for us."

"I can not endure suspicion, Brandrum," answered the young officer; "we have really no cause for it on the present occasion. I almost feel ashamed of the thoughts that have come into my head; but yet it is very strange, Brandrum, that one so affectedly careful of the morals and character of his ward, should be so careless in regard to his life. The first thing I saw this morning, when I was sketching upon the common, was this young man riding a brute which the best horseman in Europe might have found trouble to sit. It was rearing, and plunging, and hogging its back, so that, although I am no very timid horseman, as you know—"

"You'd ride the devil red hot," interrupted Brandrum.

"I would not have mounted that beast for any thing less than to save another man's life, or to obey orders," continued Reginald.

"Pooh, pooh!" answered the Ravenous Crow. "Never talk to me of not being fond of suspicion. Where the devil should a man feel suspicion except in this world? It is the only place where it is likely to be useful. After the two sets of people are separated at the day of judgment, we shall all understand each other, and there will be no use of suspicion any more; but as long as we are all here, mingled together higgle-de-piggledy, each man concealing what he is, follow the Indian plan and suspect every body."

Reginald Lisle gazed at him for a moment, and then burst into a fit of laughter. "That is good!" he exclaimed, at length; "that is excellent, my friend the Crow! you who suspect nobody, except when you have got a blanket on and a belt of wampum. Was it not only the other day when I was in London, that you accepted two bills of exchange for a man whom I believe to be a great rascal, and I told you—"

"There, there, don't talk of that," exclaimed Major Brandrum; "that's a sore subject just now, Regy. You know, of course, that the villain didn't furnish the money as he promised. It's that which brings me down here just now. I found there was a writ out, and didn't know where to go to, so I came down here, knowing that I should find fun with you, if I found nothing else."

Captain Lisle's face became very grave. "Upon my life, Brandrum," he replied, "I have nothing else to give you. Why, this is a matter of four or five hundred pounds, and I have not got as much at my command in the world."

"There, don't talk of that," cried Major Brandrum. "Do you think I would take it if you had, lad? No, no: I'll keep out of the Fleet as long as I can, but when the time comes, I must go. It doesn't much matter where my old bones lie; but I'll give the bailiffs and their bums a run before they catch me. There, don't let us talk any more of it; it will be bad enough to think of the day I am taken, but till then I'll not think of it at all."

Nor could his young friend get him to speak upon the subject any more. With that light and happy humor which, like a cork, floats over the waves of circumstances that overwhelm heavier and more solid things, he seemed rather raised than depressed by the difficulties of his situation, and gayly and cheerfully chatted of every thing else, although Reginald Lisle remained grave and thoughtful, and ended the evening by saying, "I must talk to my uncle about this, Brandrum," evidently showing that the position in which his friend had placed himself had remained in his thoughts through their whole conversation.

On the following day, at the usual hour of dinner in those times, Reginald Lisle and Major Brandrum presented themselves in the large drawing-room at the hall, and were received with the greatest marks of kindness by Captain Donovan. His brow no longer wore a frown, his manner was no longer cold and distant; and not only to Captain Lisle, but to Sir Theodore Broughton also, he seemed a totally different man. The young baronet listened in silent surprise while he laughed and joked with Major Brandrum, and talked cheerfully with Captatn Lisle; and, in the end, after the bottle had circulated very freely, and the major had shown that he was competent and willing to drink any given quantity of wine, Captain Donovan turned gayly to his ward, saying, "Well, Theodore, what do you say to a trip to London? Would you like it?"

The young baronet did not affect to deny that it would be very agreeable to him; and Captain Donovan seemed to fall into a fit of thought, at the end of which he said, "I can not go myself for some time; but I feel quite sure I could trust your inexperience of London to the guidance of Captain Lisle, whose own character and reputation are the strongest of guarantees."

From particular circumstances connected with his own situation, Reginald colored a little at this speech, and perhaps the more so because he saw Donovan's eye fixed upon him. It can not be doubted that the captain perceived the deepening tint, but it seemed to make no difference as to his views, for he added immediately, "What say you, Lisle, will you undertake the task of showing our young friend here the lions of London for a day or two, till I can come up and join you!"

"I shall be most happy," replied Captain Lisle; "and am only sorry that I can not invite him to my house—not having one," he added, with a laugh, "to invite him to. I lodge at an inn, as you are probably aware."

"No, indeed," replied Captain Donovan; "I thought your mother was in town."

"No, I am sorry to say she is not," replied Lisle; "she went to live at a short distance from London while I was absent in America, and I am too poor to keep a house myself."

"Oh, that will make no difference!" cried Captain Donovan; "I could not have thought of burdening your mother's house with an uninvited guest, even had she been in town; but Theodore can easily take up his abode at a hotel, with his servant, if you will be with him as much as possible."

"With pleasure—with pleasure!" replied Reginald Lisle, his face brightening. "When do you propose he should come?"

"Oh, whenever you go yourself," replied Donovan. "When a thing is once decided, the sooner it is done the better: to-morrow, if you like."

"Oh, I am very willing," answered Reginald. "Will you come, Brandrum?"

"Part of the way," replied the Ravenous Crow, nodding his head significantly. "I have business which will detain me some distance from London for a short time; but I'll go part of the way with you."

Captain Donovan's face grew somewhat cloudy: whether he thought that the society of the eccentric major was absolutely necessary to the well-being of his ward in London or not, I can not divine; but he asked, in a very insinuating tone, "Is this a business that can not be put off, my dear major?"

"I wish it could," said Major Brandrum, with a sly smile; "but it is an important and troublesome affair, and not the less troublesome because it is important, nor the less important because it is troublesome."

"Well, it can not be helped," answered Captain Donovan; "and the only thing that now remains is to settle our plans."

A discussion then ensued, with which it may be unnecessary to trouble my readers, as it principally referred to modes of conveyance long disused, even before the flaming engine and the clattering rail whirled travelers through Europe at the rate of forty miles an hour. At one time it was proposed that the young baronet should go in the coach and four; at another, that he and his companions should take the stage-coach at Ludlow; but ultimately it was determined that as both Major Brandrum and Reginald Lisle had come thither on horseback, the whole party should return toward town in the same manner; and, if they found the journey tedious, should have recourse to post-chaises after they had proceeded a certain way on the road. An early hour was appointed for starting the next morning, and the party separated in great good-humor with each other. As they were going down the steps, however, Captain Donovan followed the two guests, exclaiming, "Major Brandrum, allow me to speak with you for a moment;" and, while the major paused at this summons, Reginald walked slowly on into the park.

"Thank you, my dear captain, thank you; I never borrow money. It is always unpleasant to borrow, and often inconvenient to pay; and not the less inconvenient because it is unpleasant, nor the less unpleasant because it is inconvenient."

Such were the words which, spoken in Major Brandrum's voice, reached the ears of Reginald as he walked on. A moment or two after he was joined by his friend, the Ravenous Crow, who said, laughing, "Hang the fellow! he wanted to lend me money. He is a quick guesser, that fellow. He seems to have found out what my important business was in a minute."

"Why did you not take it?" demanded Reginald. "I dare say he could afford to lend it you very well."

"Because, my dear Lisle," replied Brandrum, laying his hand good-humoredly upon his arm, "there are two sets of men whom you should never ask to lend you money—men you believe to be great rogues, and men you believe to be your most intimate friends."

"I can understand why the first should be proscribed, but not the latter, my dear Crow," replied Lisle.

"For the best reason in the world," answered Brandrum; "because they can not refuse you. It is, in fact, forcing a loan, which no man of honor or spirit would do. I'll seek some Jew or another, and borrow the money, and perhaps some time I may force the scoundrel who got me into the scrape to get me out again."

Lisle shook his head, with many doubts as to the probability of such a thing, and they walked onward to the inn to prepare for their journey of the following day.

In the mean while, Captain Donovan had been conversing with his young ward, and giving him a good number of hints as to his conduct. He had resumed, in a considerable degree, his somewhat stern and grave demeanor, perhaps imagining that if thrown off all at once the change would appear too strange and striking. His counsels were all very seemly and very proper; and, were they all written down here, it would be very difficult, even upon strict examination, to find fault with them; but yet the tone was not altogether what can be called moral. He told his ward particularly to avoid gambling, represented it as a horrible vice, which might lead to the most disastrous consequences; but he seemed to think that it was the only one against which any very serious warning was required. In other respects, his counsels were rather of the Chesterfield character; and he hinted very strongly that it would be necessary for Sir Theodore, in all other things, to do as other young men of his rank and station did; though he cautioned him, in rather a light tone, against excess of any kind. In a word, he said his tutor would soon join him, and he himself would follow in a few days. In the mean time, he placed the sum of six hundred pounds in his hands, that he might be enabled to make a figure in society, as he said; and, having concluded his advice, bade him good-night.

The worthy captain's proceedings, however, had not yet altogether come to a conclusion, and the step which was next to be taken seemed to require more attention than all the rest; for, seated by the table, with his head leaning on his hand, he gave it undivided attention for several minutes, speaking to himself as he did so, and commenting upon the characters of the various individuals whom he named. "Gerald won't do," he said to himself. "It was all very well here, and he has done his work well, as far as it goes; but we want another sort of tool to work with now. The fellow is too rigid. Then Martin's such a fool, and so indiscreet. Debauched enough, in all conscience, I believe. No, he would not do; he could not keep counsel for an hour, and would startle the lad at the first outset. Brown might do, but he's such a bear. Ay, Zachary Hargrave is the man. His sanctimonious face and canting expressions, and his loose life, will do very well. As the lad rides, too, he'll want somebody to take care of his horses;" and rising, he rang the bell, and directed the servant who appeared to send Zachary Hargrave to him.

"Well, Master Zachary," he said, as soon as the man appeared, "more of the old tricks, I find."

"Ah, sir," replied the groom, a long-faced, flat-haired, stout-made man of about forty, "we are all poor sinful creatures. The flesh will rebel against the spirit."

"I know it well," answered Captain Donovan, dryly; "but yours is peculiarly rebellious, Master Zachary, and therefore I think the best thing I can do for you is to send you out of the way."

The man, who was not ordinarily fond of looking people in the face, raised his eyes to Captain Donovan's countenance, as if to gather accurately what he meant, and then replied, in a quiet tone, "Ah, yes, sir, change of scene is a pleasant thing."

"And change of pretty faces too, I suppose you think," said Captain Donovan; "but, in a word, I intend to send you to London with Sir Theodore to-morrow morning early."

"Indeed, sir!" exclaimed the man, with unfeigned surprise in his tone; and then dropping his voice, he added, "It's a sad, wicked place, London."

"True," replied Captain Donovan; "but young people must get accustomed to these things sooner or later, Zachary, and Sir Theodore is old enough now to see a little of the world. People must sow their wild oats, Zachary, at some time of their life, and if they do not do it early, they will do it late, as you have done."

"Ah, very true, captain, very true," replied the man, with somewhat of a nasal twang; "the earlier they begin, the more time they will have for repentance. We can never tell at what time grace may come. I believe, if my dear respected parents had not been so strict with me when I was young, it might have gone better with me now."

"Perhaps so," replied Captain Donovan; "but, for various reasons, I shall send you to London with him, as I have said, and you will remember that you are to be useful to him in any way that he may require; but, at the same time, you will inform me, from time to time, either here or when I join you there, of every thing that has taken place, even to the most minute particular; for, in case he gets into any of the little scrapes or errors of youth, it will be, of course, my task to get him out of them again as easily as possible."

"I see, sir," answered Zachary Hargrave, with a low bow.

"That he will get into some of these adventures I do not pretend to doubt," continued Captain Donovan. "It is natural to youth, and he must, in some degree, buy his experience, like other young men. You will easily understand, therefore, that any thing you may tell me of him will not make me angry, so you need have no apprehension on the subject of any little *escapades* of his; only you must be perfectly frank and straightforward with me. If you are not, I shall discharge you; if you are, you may reckon upon my favor and protection through life. Now go away and prepare: there's a five-pound note for you."

The man expressed his gratitude, bowed low, and withdrew, murmuring, when he reached the back of the door, "What does he mean by escapades?" and then, after thinking deeply upon the subject, and traversing the whole of the long passage that led to the servant's hall, he muttered again, "Yes, he must mean that."

CHAPTER VI.

There are few counties in England which contain more beautiful spots than the county of Warwick; few that are more thoroughly English in scenery; few that possess so much of those landscape features which, without offering to the eye any thing peculiarly grand or striking, satisfy without tiring the mind. It was in the county of Warwick, then, that, about six o'clock in the evening of a fine spring day, three gentlemen on horseback might be seen riding along, with two servants behind them, one of whom led a strong, heavy horse, quite sufficiently loaded with portmanteau's and saddle-bags.

The era of traveling on horseback was rapidly passing away. People had become fond of post-chaises; and, to say sooth, I know few pleasanter modes of traveling when one has but a single trunk and no companion. There is a free and easy rattling independence about "the old yellow," as I believe it is technically called, which has something very delightful in it. The stage-coach has its fixed destination; on the rail you are bound in fetters of iron; if you travel in your own neat post-chariot, you have a world of cares upon your head—almost as many as if you had a wife and a small family of young children with you; but in the comfortable old careless post-chaise, you may cast away every heavy thought of where you are going, what you are doing, what the roads are like which you pass over, what the horses are that draw you. You can not hurt or offend it. It will go through every thing and over every thing, and any where you please; and if sometimes it lies quietly down upon its side, you have nothing to do but to get out and help the post-boy to put it right again, and on you go as friendly as before.

But this is a digression, and yet it is pardonable. It is like taking leave of an old friend for the last time. The old post-chaise will soon be defunct, and we shall never see it more.

To return, however: the era of traveling on horseback was rapidly passing away, like all other mundane things; but yet it was not actually gone, and a man who came with his saddle-bags behind him, if he had the aspect and manners of a gentleman, would still be received at the inn door with almost as much deference as if he came in a carriage and four.

The inn door, however, seemed somewhat far distant to our travelers; for at the little village of Ryton they had inquired how far it was to Dunchurch, and had been told, as is very usual in Warwickshire, that the distance was five miles, when, in reality, it was nearly seven. The evening, however, was beautiful; and as they skirted Dunsmoor, the scenery had all that picturesque beauty which is derived less from the forms than the coloring. The face of the country is now terribly changed; for, although much has been done for man's convenience, every act that tends to smooth the ways of life takes away from some of its enjoyments, even while it adds to its ease. Although Braunston Hill, with its steep descent, no longer makes the traveler fancy his neck in jeopardy, and though half the valley has been filled up to form a causeway for the high road, the beautiful view which used to extend from the brow of the steep—as the country lay beneath the eye in long lines of purple and gold, at dawning or at sunset—is now lost to the wayfarer, and he jogs on unconscious of half the beauty that is near. At the time I speak of, however, the road from Birmingham led straight through some of the most picturesque parts of the county, and Dunsmoor Heath well deserved its name. The sandy road upon which the three horsemen were riding now dipped down beneath deep banks, now rose up upon a level with the heath—and, as no space had been spared where ground was of very little value—it was here and there only marked out by its different coloring, and by the tracks of wheels, or by a solitary mile-stone.

After commenting more than once upon the deceit which had been put upon them with regard to the distance, the tired state of their horses, and their own hunger and thirst, which Major Brandrum pronounced to be intolerable and distressing—not the less distressing because it was intolerable, nor the less intolerable because it was distressing—Reginald Lisle, who was mounted upon a stronger and more enduring horse than either of his two companions, though one less fair to look upon than that of Sir Theodore Broughton, volunteered to ride on at a quick pace, and see if he could get a view of Dunchurch, all parties beginning strongly to suspect that they had lost their way. "If I can see nothing of it at the end of a mile," he continued, "I will return, and then we had better all go back to the Black Dog, near Stratton-upon-Dunsmoor. It's a villainous-looking hole enough, but we can put up there for the night, and that's better than roaming about in the dark, seeking what we very likely shall not find."

The rest agreed willingly, for the horse of the young baronet was dead beat, and that of Major Brandrum was exceedingly willing to go at a walk. Lisle accordingly rode forward with the shades of evening gradually gathering round, although the whole western sky was still yellow with the light of the setting orb. At the distance of about a quarter of a mile from his companions, the road, after surmounting a little rise, dipped down between some deep green trees, mingled with the yellower foliage of the late-leaved oak. There was a dense mass of wood on either side, and on the right a deep pool of water, so completely shaded by the boughs above that it was only distinguished in the obscurity by a single line of light where a water-hen dived down at his approach. On beyond, however, through a vista opening between the trees, the broad yellow road, slightly descending, might be seen in perspective, terminating with a deep purple line of distant country, and the golden edge of the sky above.

Cutting sharp upon the bright light were two female figures, linked arm in arm, and apparently walking slowly on. They were so far in advance, and the light beyond them was so strong, that it was impossible to judge of their costume, but yet there was something—indeed, there is something, and ever will be—in the air and carriage of a lady, which left no doubt in the mind of Reginald Lisle as to the rank in life of the persons before him.

"I think I may venture to ask them our way, and whereabouts we are," he said to himself; "but I must not ride too fast, or they may imagine I am a highwayman."

Now highwaymen were common in those days.

Hardly had the thought passed through his mind, when two objects struck him. One was some fifty or sixty yards of park paling appearing through the trees on the left; the other the figure of a horseman drawing out from among the trees on the right. Reginald Lisle was generally rapid in his combinations, sometimes rather too rapid in his deductions. "I am near some gentleman's park," he thought; "those are the two ladies of the house; that is a servant riding back from an errand."

For some short time he persisted in this view; for the horseman rode on at no very quick pace after the ladies, nor did they seem to hurry their pace at all. In a moment after, however, Reginald Lisle put his hand down to his saddle-bow, and into a holster that hung there, the cause of which proceeding was, that he perceived the horseman do something very much of the same kind. The next moment the man passed the two ladies, wheeled his beast right before them, and evidently brought them to a halt. At the same time a sound, not exactly a scream, for it was not loud enough, but rather an exclamation of surprise and fear, reached the ear of Reginald Lisle, and his spurs were in the horse's sides in a moment. On the beast went like lightning. The pistol was out of the holster, and throwing down the rein, the young gentleman crammed down the ramrod tight, to make sure that the ball had not slipped during a long day's ride. By this time, although it was a soft and sandy road, the sound of his horse's feet was heard by the two ladies, one of whom was evidently bestowing her purse upon the gentleman before her. The horseman, whose face was turned that way, must have become conscious some moments before that he was not the only mounted man upon the road; but, to say truth, he seemed to trouble himself very little about it, and made no movement whatever indicative of an intention of abandoning his object.

The lady with the purse, in her haste and terror, dropped it at the very moment when Reginald was within about thirty yards of her, while her companion, who was younger and slighter in form, turned round, and with a sort of joyful cry, ran toward the new-comer, as if certain at once that he brought deliverance.

"Be so good as to pick it up and give it to me, ma'am," exclaimed the deep voice of the man who had stopped them; and then, instantly turning the mouth of his pistol toward Reginald Lisle, he exclaimed, "Hold back, my man, or I'll shoot you as sure as you live!"

The reply of the young officer was a pistol-shot, and the man's hat flew off his head and rolled along the road.

"A devilish neat shot!" cried the latter, snatching from the lady's hand the purse which she had picked up. "Keep off! keep off!" and, as he saw the young gentleman still spurring on, he fired, not at him, but at the horse, and the poor beast, struck in the chest, instantly went down, crushing his rider's leg and thigh beneath him. A dying effort the animal made to rise, freed the young officer from his weight, and, regardless of the pain he suffered, Lisle started on his feet, snatched his second pistol from the holster, and ran forward. But, at the same moment, with a graceful bow and a wave of the hand, the highwayman wheeled his horse again, saying, "Good morning, ladies, with many thanks," and cantered lightly across the heath.

"Oh! sir, I hope you are not hurt," cried the lady who was nearest to Reginald. "He has killed your poor horse, I am afraid."

"He has, indeed!" said Reginald, gazing on the animal as it lay, with its feet beating the air faintly and convulsively; "he has, indeed!" and he pressed his lips together with a look of much grief. Then turning round abruptly, he continued, "I hope the scoundrel has not frightened you much. That lady—your mother, I suppose—seems very greatly agitated;" and so she was, indeed, for she was now supporting herself by a tree, with one hand clasped over her eyes.

"He is gone! dearest mother, he is gone!" cried the younger lady, running up to her, and laying her hand upon her arm.

"But he may come back again, Mary," cried the other. "How can we tell that he may not return?"

"Oh no!" said Reginald Lisle, approaching, "there is no fear of that. And if he did, he would only return to be taken, for I have two friends not half a mile behind, with a couple of servants. I wish they were here: he should not escape so easily. But he has killed my poor horse, so that I can neither follow him nor ride on my way."

"I am extremely grieved to hear you have met such loss in our service, sir," replied the elder lady, "and thank you a thousand times. If you are in haste, however, and vexed at being delayed, as I judge by your face, we can easily send you forward. There are plenty of very good horses in the stable, and I need not say they are quite at your disposal."

"Many thanks, madam," replied Captain Lisle. "I can not help grieving for my poor beast, for he has carried me through more than one bloody day without ever getting a wound. To say the truth, however, I fear I must decline your offer, for he has so crushed my knee in falling that I do not think I could bear the saddle."

Regret and sympathy were expressed by both the ladies when they heard this announcement; and—while Reginald limped forward, and took up the hat which his ball had knocked off the highwayman's head, in the hope that it might lead to his conviction—a hurried consultation seemed to go on between his two fair companions, the daughter seeming to urge something upon the mother, in regard to which the elder lady hesitated.

"But, my dear Mary, we are alone in the house," she said, "and we do not know this gentleman at all; I am afraid your father will think it strange."

"Not he, indeed, mamma," replied the other; "would he not do so directly himself? Well, then, ask Doctor Haviland to come up, if you hesitate only because we are alone. He is evidently a gentleman, and it would be cruel to let him go on when he is suffering so much. I am sure papa would not like it at all."

This last argument seemed successful; for, when Reginald turned back slowly with the hat in his hand, the elder lady, in courteous terms, begged that he would accompany them to the house, and send for the surgeon from Dunchurch. Reginald Lisle now hesitated, although he felt that he was hardly fit to pursue his journey; and, to tell the truth, perhaps he might have persisted in trying to go on, had not the younger lady said, with her deep blue eyes fixed earnestly upon him, and a very persuasive smile upon her lips, "Indeed, sir, you must not think of proceeding without some advice; and, as my mother will be frightened all the way home, you can not, in courtesy, refuse to escort us."

If Lisle could have resisted the words, he certainly could not resist the manner in which they were uttered, and the only difficulty that remained was, how to inform his two friends of what had occurred, and whither he had gone.

That, however, was removed the moment after, while he was consulting with his fair companions as to what was to be done, for spurring slowly along upon a jaded horse came Master Zachary Hargrave, bringing intelligence that Sir Theodore's chestnut had come down in descending the hill, and broken both its knees. "The major therefore thinks, captain," continued the servant, "that it will be better to go back to the Black Dog, at Stratton. If you will return, we can get a chaise there, or at Ryton, and go on to-morrow."

"Look there!" said Lisle, in return, pointing to his dead horse. "Tell them I have had a little affair with a highwayman here, and he has shot my poor bay. If they will go back to Stratton, however, I will join them to-night or to-morrow morning—"

"If he is able," added the young lady, who saw that Reginald's face was very pale. "The horse fell upon him and hurt him, and we must send to Dunchurch for a surgeon."

"Very well, miss, I will say so," replied Hargrave; and, turning his bridle, he rode back, while Reginald, putting the pistol in his breast, accompanied the ladies at a very slow and limping pace along the same sandy road. The younger, with the light and happy courage of youth, seemed to have forgotten all fear, and talked even gayly of their adventure; but her mother, holding fast by her arm, seemed by no means so easily reassured, spoke but little, and continued to gaze from time to time over the heath, as if she expected every moment to see the figure of the highwayman come cantering back again.

"Thank God!" she cried, at length, "we are at the park gates! It is really terrible this state of society, that one can not walk half a mile from one's own house without being exposed to robbery!"

"Well, dearest mother," said the young lady, "as far as we are concerned, it might have been worse; for I am sure you will admit that nobody could be more civil than he was, although he did take your purse; and, indeed, I believe there was very little in it."

"There were seven guineas," replied the lady; "but that I should care nothing about. It is the terror in which he put me that I mind. You know, my dear Mary, I shall not recover it for many weeks. Civil! I am sure I thought he was as brutal as he could be, frightful creature!"

"No, no, he was very handsome," cried the young lady; and laughing, "he made a thousand apologies for the trouble he gave in obliging you to hand out your purse. If one always met with such polite people, it would rather be a pleasure to be robbed than otherwise."

She spoke gayly and playfully, evidently with the intention of effacing from her mother's mind the impression left by terror; but the attempt was not successful; and although Reginald, understanding her object, endeavored, as far as he could, to treat the matter lightly also, the elder lady remained in a state of nervous agitation all the way, declaring that she had never heard any of the civil speeches of the highwayman; that she thought him the most frightful man she had ever seen, and that she was quite sure he would have murdered them both, if their gallant companion had not come up to their rescue.

Although Reginald did his best to be cheerful, it can not be denied that he suffered great pain at every step he took; and at length, after having passed through the gates, and walked some way through a very beautiful and apparently extensive park, he stopped, just as they got a view of an old Elizabethan mansion at the distance of about a quarter of a mile, saying, in a tone from which he could not banish the expression of suffering, "I am afraid I can not go any further. You can meet with no danger between this and the house, and I must, at all events, rest a little here, as I find it impossible to proceed."

Taken up with her own terrors, the elder lady had not perceived the pain which he endured, nor his efforts to master it; but neither one nor the other had escaped the eye of the daughter. "I saw how he was suffering," she said, in a tone of deep feeling; "but here is a nice mossy bank: if you will sit here for a few minutes, we will send up a carriage for you before it is quite dark."

No other plan could be proposed, and with a faint smile at his own weakness, Reginald seated himself while the two ladies went on. It was nearly half an hour, and quite dark, before the sound of carriage wheels met his ears; for servants are not always as charitably active as their masters, and the young lady's injunctions to make haste were not attended to with all the precision that she could have desired. At length, however, the carriage appeared, with a servant walking by the side, seeking for the spot where Reginald had been left; and in five minutes from that time he was stretched upon a sofa in a large and handsome drawing-room, with the two ladies by his side, making eager inquiries as to how he felt after his removal.

Every thing looked cheerful around him; the room was well lighted; there was a cheerful fire blazing in the wide, open grate; the furniture was rich and costly, and there was as beautiful a face as ever was seen, hanging over him with that sweet look of interest which is the greatest of all consolers. Reginald Lisle thought that the compensation was fully equal to the pain, and almost hoped that the surgeon's opinion might pin him to that sofa for many a day to come. The arrival of the man of healing was not long delayed; for the servant sent for him rode fast to Dunchurch, and he himself rode faster, for a patient at the great house was not an every-day occurrence, and well worthy of a gallop. His first injunctions, however, were by no means agreeable to Reginald Lisle; for they implied that he was to be immediately removed to bed, and there, as he was well aware, according to the ways of society, the beautiful face would be seen no more. However, he had no choice but to submit, and for half an hour or more he was kept under the torture of examination, fomentation, and all the other *ations* with which skillful surgeons make the process of cure as miserable as possible. The man of art had hardly taken his leave, promising an early visit on the following day, when a heavy military tread was heard along the corridor, and the next moment the tall, gaunt figure and hawk-like face of his friend the Ravenous Crow appeared at Reginald's bedside. "Well, my lad," he exclaimed, "so you have got into a very curious and uncomfortable mess; not the less curious because it is uncomfortable, nor the less uncomfortable because it is curious."

"Certainly not, Brandrum," replied Reginald Lisle; and, after having given him a more circumstantial account of all that had taken place, he explained to him how impossible it was for him to move, perhaps for more than one day to come: a conviction which had forced itself upon him, in despite of an eager and enthusiastic temperament, and a spirit not easily cowed.

"Well, then, we will wait for a day or two," said the good major. "The young spoiled child of fortune will not be at all the worse for a short drilling of a poor inn; and, for my own part, as London may be a little too hot to hold me just now, I shall do quite well in the country. I shall not go in to pay my compliments to the gay party below, for I came off in dusty garments as soon as I had housed Sir Theodore."

Thus saying, he took his leave, and left Reginald to seek such repose as aching bones would grant.

CHAPTER VII

Let the reader transport himself to the Black Dog. What an extraordinary verb that verb to transport is. It is a verb passive in most of its senses, and yet it implies the excess of human joy and the extreme of human suffering. "I am transported"—it may be a great lie or a simple truth—means that a man is carried out of himself; that his spirit is borne away from its natural, placid home of even, every-day life, to a state of joy indescribable. "He was transported," means that the man himself was carried from his native land, his kinsmen, his friends, the domestic hearth, the ties of dear affection, the long-accustomed objects of attachment, the scenes and things which had grown into his soul and mingled with his spirit, to a new world of pain and punishment, and worse than death—to degradation here, to long days of anguish, and labor, and privation—to the chain-gang and the oppressor's rod—to the contagion of example, to the corrupting influence of an atmosphere of vice, to crimes unheard of, and to moral death, where every feeling and principle of action, and thought, and habit, and sight, and sound, is all putrefaction, and horror, and decay. It is a strange thing, the English language, and stranger still to find that in almost every tongue under the sun, the terms which imply the highest, imply also the lowest; the words which signify perfect happiness, signify also extreme misery.

Let the reader transport himself to the Black Dog, and remember that an inn—a small country inn—in the years 1775–6–7, was a very different place from an inn in 1845–6–7. In general, in these small country inns, at the period of which I speak, there was one public room appropriated to the reception of company. At Harrowgate, at Bath, at the Hot Well, at Clifton, and at one or two other watering places, each suite of bed-rooms might have a sitting-room attached, for there persons came for a specific purpose, which implied a probable residence of some time; but in the country inn—the small country inn—a traveler might stop for a night; a family might stop for a night; a bagman might stop for two or three nights; and in the former or the latter case—as men in those days had not such a shuddering horror of the proximity of strangers as they have at present—the one public room was sufficient for all the purposes of the road. If there were two gentlemen with straight-cut coats and long pig-tails, talking of the price of leather, or the worth of calico, or the call for broad-cloth at one corner, there might be two gentlemen in buckskin, talking of policy, or horse-racing, or agriculture at the other, without interrupting each other in the least. Sometimes, indeed, an observation at one table or in one group, made in an over-loud tone, would produce a cross-fire from the other; and such events were known as bottles, or decanters, or pewter pots flying across the intervening space, as hostile messages to an opposite party; and swords would be drawn, and scuffles ensue, till the landlord and the constable interfered, and the landlord's wife, with shrill voice and excited countenance, scolded all round, with lungs peculiar to the fair part of the Licensed Victualers' Company.

But these things were of rare occurrence, and a man might say, "I will take mine ease at my inn" with less chance of disappointment than in almost any other human aspiration. There was a certain sort of code of politeness, too, which regulated, in a great degree, the intercourse of these places of public resort. It was supposed that a civil speech would produce a civil reply; that there was a certain sort of free-masonry about the place, which made all men, to a certain degree, brothers while they remained therein, without implying the slightest intimacy, or even acquaintance, from the moment that the foot passed to the outer side of the threshold, unless both parties, by mutual signs and indications, gave notice that they wished for closer and more permanent communication.

This premised, it will be hardly necessary to say that the small inn called the Black Dog, at Stratton-upon-Dunsmoor—I believe the sign has descended to the present day—contained but one room which deserved the name of a sitting-room, and that was open to all comers. If a family arrived and stayed the night, and wished to be very exclusive, they were under the necessity of converting a bed-room into a dining-room or drawing-room; but that was a case which very rarely occurred.

In that one sitting-room—it was upon the ground floor, with the windows looking out upon the high road, not over-large, and somewhat low in the roof—sat Sir Theodore Broughton and Major Brandrum, partaking of a very comfortable supper, which greatly refreshed the young baronet, who—though capable of violent, but not long-continued exertion—had been somewhat tired, as well as his horse, by riding the whole day long. The major had visited the bar before they had sat down to supper, and had, with nice discrimination, tasted the more ordinary wines, which, as was then not unfrequent, the landlord drew from the barrel for the benefit of his customers.

Now, to ask for claret in such an inn as that, in our own degenerate times, would be something worse than vain. You might insult the landlord, and get vinegar and water for your pains, but no claret; but the case was very different in those days, and the pure juice of the Bordeaux grape was as frequently to be found in a small road-side inn of England, as on the banks of the Garonne or the Dordogne. The Madeira did not please the major; the port was somewhat worse; but at the claret he raised his eyebrows with the air of a connoisseur, and ordered a magnum, informing Sir Theodore, in a whisper, that it was the most delicate and high-flavored wine he had ever drunk; not the less delicate because it was high-flavored, nor the less high-flavored because it was delicate.

The young baronet was much of the same opinion, although his own cellar — thanks to Captain Donovan's taste and discrimination— contained some of the choicest vintages of Guyenne; and there they sat, with the remains of the supper before them, slowly sipping their wine, the bouquet of which perfumed the whole room. Sir Theodore, who, during the greater part of his life—as is too often the case with happy youth under the rule of severe age—had lived in a state of awe, and who had been suffered to indulge but little (which, perhaps, would be better for all men) in that consoling juice of the grape, which was undoubtedly given for the comfort and support of declining years, grew cheerful and familiar under the influence of the claret. He conversed with his military friend, not without considerable powers of mind and stores of knowledge, but evidently rather anxious to gain from him some acquaintance with the wide world, in which, and in its wildest and most remote scenes, his companion had been so busy an actor, than to display his own information, limited to the stores of classic lore. Major Brandrum was inexhaustible; and, were this an episodical work, I might relate three or four very curious tales and anecdotes which he told during the evening, before the little party of two, which at first tenanted the chamber, was increased by the presence of a third. As it is my object, however, to tell one tale, and not many, I must leave the account of his adventures in North America, South America, the Falkland Islands, the Low Countries, Bengal, Spain, and Germany, for another opportunity, and merely say that as he was closing one of his narratives, the door of the room opened, and gave admission to a very well-dressed and good-looking man, of from thirty to five-and-thirty years of age. He was habited with great taste and neatness, and seemed to have a respect for the company he was about to join; for his dress—in which men were more particular at that time than at present—was perfectly well fitted for any evening party in London, perhaps more so than for a country inn. He wore a claret-colored coat, with cut steel buttons, silk breeches, and white silk stockings; and, although the buckles in his shoes were small, they were of the very last device, and exceedingly brilliant. The ruffles at his wrists were of the finest and most beautiful lace, and his hand, which was small and delicate, was ornamented with several very handsome rings. His countenance was frank and pleasing, though the under jaw was perhaps too large and massy; and his figure, though indicating great strength, was light and graceful. His whole bearing and appearance, in short, was that of a very distinguished personage; and there was that slightest possible touch of superciliousness in the curl of his lip, which is often to be found in the lowest mental rank of the worldly great.

With a slow and deliberate step, the newcomer took his way to the fire-place, glancing his eye for a moment at the two preoccupants of the room, and then leaning his elbows on the mantel-piece, and falling into a fit of meditation. The moment after, he rang the bell—for bells were common, even in England, at that time, though I can remember the day when they were unknown in many parts of Germany, except in church steeples—and when the landlord appeared, he asked if his supper was ready.

"In a minute, colonel—in a minute," replied the host; "it isn't quite your hour yet."

"Past, by five minutes," said the stranger, taking out a very handsome watch, with the numerous appendages which it was at that time customary to attach to the little curious contrivance by which man marks the passing of the hours he misuses; "past by five minutes," he repeated, after he had examined the dial. "You know I like to be punctual, Harrison."

"I know you do, colonel," replied the other. "Our clock must be behind."

"A bad habit for the clock," replied the stranger, dryly. "Correct it, Master Harrison, or some day it will be brought to a stand."

"It will only share the fate, then, of many a good neighbor of mine," replied the landlord, laughing. "Have you heard, colonel, that Lady Chevenix and the young lady have been stopped, just under their own park paling, and robbed of their watch, and money, and all sorts of things?"

"Good Heaven!" exclaimed the stranger, "this is too bad! Upon my life, if the gentlemen in London do not look after these things, it will be unsafe to travel without an escort. When did this happen?"

"Oh, three or four hours ago," answered the landlord; "those gentlemen brought the news, for a friend of theirs came up just as the highwayman was taking the ladies' purses, and got his horse shot for his pains, and himself very much hurt."

"Hurt!" exclaimed the colonel, again. "Did the villain shoot him?"

"Not exactly," replied Major Brandrum, chiming in, this conversation having gone on in a loud tone, "but he shot his horse, and the horse fell, as horses will do when they are shot, and, in falling, rolled upon our young friend, which was both painful and detrimental; and not the less detrimental because it was painful, nor the less painful because it was detrimental."

"A very just distinction," said the stranger, sententiously; "for it sometimes occurs that things which are painful to us are rather beneficial than detrimental."

"'True, O king!'" replied Major Brandrum. "In this case, however, it was the reverse, and our young friend is suffering severely."

"I regret it deeply," said the stranger, approaching the table, and presenting his snuff-box to Major Brandrum, who immediately took a pinch, and began to discuss the various kinds and qualities of snuffs. Thence he deviated to tobacco; described the cultivation of the weed in almost every country under the sun, and the differences between the leaf produced in different climates; and displayed an extent of information, not only upon that topic, but upon a hundred collateral subjects, which equally surprised Sir Theodore Broughton and the stranger.

"You seem to have been a very great traveler, sir," observed the last comer.

"I have had the honor of serving wherever the British arms have been carried during the last five-and-twenty years," replied Major Brandrum, "and in some other countries besides. I have been in Canada, North America, South America, the West Indies, the East Indies, the Falkland Islands, Germany, Hungary, and Transylvania, Spain, Portugal, and Italy, France, and the Low Countries, to say nothing of Norway, Sweden, Denmark, and Russia, with a short stay in Egypt and Nubia, and flying visits to Borneo, Sumatra, and Madagascar."

"May I ask, my dear sir," said the stranger, with the slightest possible smile, "if I have the honor of speaking to Captain Cook, Lord Anson, or Captain Dampier?"

"No, sir," answered Major Brandrum, laughing, and not at all offended by the jest. "I am called the Ravenous Crow, much at your service. May I ask your name in return?"

"My name is Colonel Lutwich," replied the stranger; and thus commenced a conversation which lasted for some hours, and in which jest and merriment soon predominated over the stiffer and more formal courtesies of early acquaintance. The colonel's supper was placed upon a table near that of the two other gentlemen, and during his meal he continued amusing himself with a strain of fine raillery, directed against our worthy friend, Major Brandrum, but in which he did not altogether get the better, for the major had all his wits about him, and was occasionally rather fond of that moderate approximation to the very vulgar kind of fun termed a hoax, which has been termed mystification. To say the truth, too, from particular circumstances, he was less scrupulous, perhaps, with the colonel than he might have been with other men, and he was soon in full tilt among his friends the Cherokees, relating exploits both of himself and others, which, though in the main perfectly true, sounded incredible from the manner in which he told them.

"Very formidable weapons, I have no doubt, those tomahawks," said the colonel; "but I should think a pass or two with a good small-sword would soon settle the affair with the most dexterous Mohawk of them all."

"Not all, colonel," replied Major Brandrum. "I would undertake now, old as I am, to disarm you in five minutes, though I have no doubt you are a perfect master of fence. What will you bet and stake down? Will you say a guinea? There is one now, the best miniature picture of King George that I am acquainted with."

"A wager we can not decide upon the spot," said Colonel Lutwich, who had by this time finished a considerable portion of claret likewise, "otherwise I should be very happy. We shall have to send to North America, or to some museum of curiosities, for the tomahawk."

"Ah! a good workman never fails for want of tools," said the major; "we'll soon find what will do as well. There must be a hatchet in the house. Come, stake down, colonel;" and, at the same time, he rang the bell sharply.

"Mr. Harrison," he said, as soon as the landlord appeared, "will you have the kindness to bring me a pair of slippers and a hatchet?"

Mr. Harrison stared. "I am going to perform for the amusement of the company," proceeded Major Brandrum, in explanation, "in what may be called my *native* character of the Ravenous Crow. It will all be in good humor, and therefore, if you have any women in the house, who would like to see the true Cherokee mode of defense against a European soldier, they may come and share in the entertainment. Now, colonel, stake down."

"Ah! with all my heart," answered the other, drawing an exceedingly delicate purse from his pocket, of blue silk, embroidered with gold, from which he produced a guinea, and laid it on the table, coloring a good deal as he did so under Major Brandrum's eye.

In the mean time the landlord had quitted the room to obey the orders he had received. Strange things were enacted in those days in the inns and taverns of England, and Mr. Harrison went upon the excellent rule of supplying every thing that his house could produce to those who demanded it, and could pay for it, and asking no questions as to the employment thereof. He accordingly returned in a minute or two with a pair of slippers, into which the major's feet, being unbooted, were speedily introduced, and a hatchet, which that gallant officer first poised in his hand, declaring that the handle was rather heavy, and then whirled round his head in a manner that startled, frightened, and delighted a small bevy of women, who, on Mr. Harrison's notification, had crowded to the door.

"Come in, ladies, come in," cried Major Brandrum; "I will scalp nobody, I promise you; and, although this tool is not so manageable as a real tomahawk, it will do, I've no doubt. You will excuse my taking off my coat and waistcoat, for the air is somewhat sultry;" and, divesting himself of his upper garments, with the hatchet in his hand, he stood forth in the midst, tall, lean, and sinewy, and certainly most portentously ugly and somewhat frightful; for he had contrived, by running his fingers through it, to make the long, narrow stripe of grizzled black hair upon the top of his skull to stand up like the crest of some strange bird. "Now, colonel," he said, "place yourself where you please, and we will begin the monomachia."

With easy grace, and a light, confident smile his adversary took his position at the other end of the room, drew his sword, and placed himself in the attitude of attack. It was evident, from the very first movements, that he was a master of his weapon; but while the landlady and her maidens exclaimed, "Why, surely, they are not going to fight really?" and

Sir Theodore Broughton ventured to remonstrate, in a low tone, against such dangerous pastime, Major Brandrum coolly placed his watch upon the table, saying, "Five minutes, you know, colonel. Now begin. Mark the watch, Sir Theodore."

Thus dared, Colonel Lutwich advanced cautiously upon his adversary, made a feint and then a lunge, but his blade was instantly met by the hatchet, and parried successfully. A little mortified and a little puzzled, for he did not apparently wish to hurt his opponent, the younger gentleman lunged again, and then again, but still the hatchet met him; till at length, both becoming more eager, their movements grew rapid; the hatchet and the sword flashed about in every direction; and, spinning round upon his heel like a dancer in the ballet, while his weapon whirled round and round him, dazzling the eyes that attempted to follow it, the Ravenous Crow seemed not alone animated with the spirit of the Cherokee, but actually to have eyes in the back of his head; for wherever the lunges, now become fierce and rapid, seemed likely to strike him, there the invariable hatchet met them, and turned them aside.

The landlord laughed, the women screamed, and Sir Theodore Broughton sat in wonder and terror, till at length, with a fiend-like whoop, the Indian sprang upon his adversary, seized his right hand, and both rolled over upon the floor together; but the sword was in Major Brandrum's grasp, and with another yell that shook the whole house, he waved the hatchet over his opponent's head.

The worthy major, however, cast off his Indian character more rapidly than might have been expected, perhaps, relaxed his fell gripe of the colonel, and, retiring to the other side of the room, laid the sword and the hatchet upon the table, and resumed his coat, his waistcoat, and his ordinary air.

The defeated swordsman rose from the ground confounded and ashamed. The color was very high in his cheek, and it was evident that a good deal of heat and anger followed his defeat; but his adversary, the moment he was dressed or redressed, advanced toward him with a frank and good-humored air, and presented him his sword, saying, "Upon my life, colonel, I never met a better fencer. I thought you would have pinked me several times, though I never yet saw a sword that could compete with a Cherokee tomahawk, rightly played. The French are very skillful at their weapons, but the best rapier of them all is no match for a tomahawk. It is scarcely fair to take your stake, for I knew that the game was unequal, and you did not."

"Oh, no! it is yours, it is yours, fairly enough," cried the other gentleman, recovering his good humor immediately; "I had no idea that a hatchet was such a manageable weapon. I think I must take some lessons."

"I will give you some, with all my heart," replied Major Brandrum; "and, as you are twice as young and as active as I am, you will soon excel me far. I will come and call upon you some day with a real tomahawk, and show you how to use it."

"Do you know where to find me?" asked the colonel, in a civil tone.

"Oh, yes!" answered the Ravenous Crow, "I can always find my friends when I want them," and, at the same time, he nodded his head significantly.

Colonel Lutwich seated himself at his table and fell into a fit of thought, and in a few minutes after, Sir Theodore Broughton, who had taken, to say the truth, more exercise, wine, and excitement than was altogether good for him, rose and retired to rest. Major Brandrum remained to finish what claret was left in the magnum, and for a few minutes a dead silence prevailed between him and his late opponent. "Come, come, colonel," he said at length, "I am sure you are too gallant a man to bear ill will. Let us drink a cheerful toast together."

"With all my heart!" cried the other, extending his hand frankly; "I was not thinking of our late bout at all, major. I was only trying to recollect where you and I could have met before."

The Ravenous Crow bent forward his head till his beak almost touched his companion's temple, and then whispered a word or two in his ear. The colonel started, turned a little pale, and gazed at Major Brandrum steadfastly.

"Upon honor?" he said, in a very peculiar tone.

"Upon honor!" replied the major; "although, perhaps, I might be justified in saying no; but come, let us have our toast. Here's success to all ways of life, and the honester the better."

"With all my heart!" said Colonel Lutwich, draining his glass; "but what brings you so far from London, Major Brandrum? I should have thought you were looking out for fresh service."

"Why, my dear fellow," answered the major, "you see I am in rather an awkward position. There's a man who was half drowned with me once, half burned with me once, of the name of Wilkinson—as great a rogue as ever lived, ten times as bad as a fellow who takes a purse on the highway. He got me to put my name to a couple of bills for him, swearing and vowing that though he had cheated half Europe before, he would never cheat an old friend and fellow-sufferer, but would have the money ready to a moment. I lent him a hundred guineas into the bargain, which he was to pay at the same time, but he has done neither the one nor the other, which is dishonorable and unfriendly; and not the less dishonorable because it is unfriendly, nor the less unfriendly because it is dishonorable. So there are now two writs out against me, information of which inspired me with a desire to travel. They shall be backed by all the sheriffs in England and Wales before they are served upon me; and, in the mean time, I may catch Master Wilkinson, and take part payment with a tough ash-stick."

"He is a great villain," answered the colonel; "for, to my certain knowledge, if the debt is not a very heavy one, he can pay it. I know the fellow well: he won two thousand pounds of Joe Benson the other day. When do you go?"

The question was rather abruptly put, and Major Brandrum found it not easy to answer. "Why, I don't exactly know," he replied. "My poor friend Lisle is a good deal hurt, and when he will be able to go on I don't know. I certainly sha'n't go on without him. When a man's knee is crushed by a horse falling, you know, colonel, there is no certainty of how far the mischief may go."

"Why, what Lisle is that?" asked the other; "not the Lisle who distinguished himself so much at Bunker's Hill?"

The major nodded his head, and Colonel Lutwich continued in a tone of much sympathy, "I am very sorry for that, indeed; but which way do you go, major, when you do go?"

"Oh! straight on," answered Major Brandrum, "by Daventry and Stony-Stratford, and either there or at Dunstable I shall leave them, for it might not be quite safe to get much nearer the great Maelstrom—which is a whirlpool or vortex in the sea, off the coast of Norway, colonel, as perhaps you know, and the best image of London I ever saw."

"Well, I shall go on before you," said Colonel Lutwich, thoughtfully; "and, perhaps, may be coming back again about the time you are on the road. If so, we shall have some further talk about your affairs."

"Take care what you are about, colonel," replied the Ravenous Crow, laughing; "remember there are highwaymen about."

"Oh! I am not afraid," replied Colonel Lutwich. "I have got my horses down here, but I think I shall post. Let us have another magnum, major."

"A bottle will do," replied Major Brandrum; and, after discussing that quantity, they shook hands with a good deal of warmth, and each retired to bed.

CHAPTER VIII.

We are a cold nation—there can be no doubt of the fact. In general, it takes a great deal to warm us, and then the fire is not very hot. We even wonder at the fiercer passions of more ardent nations, and we have to remember that the scene was Italy or Egypt, ere the burning words of Juliet, or the rapt self-abandonment of Antony, cease to excite surprise. Except in Shakspeare, who could conceive all things, and once in Herrick, there is hardly a piece of passionate love-poetry in the language.

Nevertheless, there are exceptions; and sometimes it happens that the eager love at first sight which made Juliet exclaim,

> "Go ask his name. If he be married,
> My grave is like to be my wedding bed,"

is found even in English men and women. Perhaps, too, as the hardest and the coldest fuel, when once lighted, burns with the most durable and warmest fire—the hearts that are least easily kindled by passion retain it longest and brightest when it is aroused. It is a curious fact, too—but no less a fact—that the warm, eager, impetuous love I have described is seldom without return, if it be excited by one with a free heart. It may startle, surprise, alarm even, at first; but, like a torrent, it carries all before it when the first resistance is vanquished.

Reginald Lisle thought all night of the deep blue eyes, and their jetty fringes, and the bright face full of soul and heart; and he remembered each look as the page of a student's book, which, when rightly translated, was replete of poetry.

The reader unlearned in untutored nature—the reader who has been bound in the conventional habits of a rigid society, will ask, "What! after one brief interview?" or perhaps he may fancy that Reginald Lisle's was one of those very volcanic hearts which are always in an eruption.

No such thing. He had never loved before, for his short life had been a very active one; but its course had been so shaped by circumstances that love had never lain in its way. He had met many beautiful girls, it is true, and many very amiable girls, doubtless; but his was a peculiar mind, which sought something more than mere beauty or mere gentleness, and he had never found, or fancied he had found it.

Take a sphere, reader, and try to put it in a hollow cube containing the same measure, or even something more. You can not do it, do what you will. In short, it does not fit. No other shape will do but a hollow sphere, and thus it is with human sympathies, more especially when they have place in a firm and steadfast heart.

I have said that Reginald Lisle thought of those sweet eyes all night—and from time to time throughout the night he certainly did so. Nor is it at all improbable that the very nature of his thoughts helped greatly to keep him waking, and to make him think at all. But still, it must be admitted that pain had something to do with his watchfulness. For four or five hours, all the applications of the surgeon seemed to have produced no effect, at least in mitigating the aching of his knee; and whenever weariness made him drop off into sleep, a new pang woke him again. At length, however, the pain diminished, and just as the first gray streaks were in the sky, slumber more calm and quiet than any he had yet known during the night fell upon him. It lasted not long, indeed; but when he woke again, the broad daylight stole into the room through the curtain chinks, and Reginald Lisle, forgetting the surgeon's injunctions, and saying, "I feel quite well—I will get up," rose from his bed, and proceeded to dress himself as well as he could, deprived as he was of all the usual appliances but mere soap and water.

It would have been difficult, however, to spoil his appearance, for there was the gentleman in every feature and every line; and though somewhat pale at the end of his hasty toilet, his face was still one that woman's eyes might look upon well pleased.

Perhaps Lisle felt, as he was dressing, that he was doing an imprudent thing, and that it would have been better to follow counsel and lie still; nevertheless, he went on dressing himself to the end, although he experienced much pain in doing so; and I am afraid the beautiful eyes had somewhat to do with his obstinacy. When he was dressed, he sat down for a moment or two to rest, but soon started up again, and opening his room door, went out. A voyage of discovery in a strange house is not always an uninteresting enterprise: there is so much of the character of the owner in the dwelling, that one might almost learn the natural history of the inhabitants by the various objects which a house displays.

Reginald found himself at once in a long and large corridor terminating in a stair-case, and lighted by a window at each end. On the wide landing at the head of the stairs were two rich china vases, of the size, and probably of the shape, of the oil-jars of Ali Baba's friend, the robber; and from thence proceeded an odor common in the houses of our grandmothers, and proceeding from what, I believe, was called *pot pourri:* not a very savory name, but yet the odor was extremely fragrant. The walls of the landing-place were hung with small pictures, some of them exceedingly good, and these the young officer paused to examine with an artist's eye. On a large ebony pedestal, too, there was a marble bust, very beautifully chiseled, and pure as snow. It was that of a gentleman of five or six-and-thirty years of age, and the features seemed familiar to the eye of Reginald Lisle; but the sculptor—whether in good taste or not, let those judge who are competent—had chosen to dress an English gentleman of the last century in the garb of an old Roman, and consequently the likeness, if not lost, was without any accessory help.

Descending the stairs, Reginald came to a hall decorated with more pictures, not so good as those above, and a great number of little objects of curiosity and art. He thought he knew the drawing-room door by a large and handsome japan cabinet which stood near it; and he accordingly applied his hand to the lock and went in. Fortune favored him. The sun was not shining directly on the windows, but its light poured free over the grassy lawn beyond, and there, at the open casement, stood the same light and graceful form which had occupied so much of his thoughts within the last eight hours, with the right arm resting upon the side of the window, and supporting the whole figure, one small foot crossed lightly over the other, and the head bent slightly to the side. The grace of the whole was perfect, and Reginald paused for a single instant to gaze, while she seemed lost in meditation.

Two steps more, and the sound of his footfall caught her ear, making her start and suddenly look round. An expression varying from surprise to pleasure, and then to grave apprehension, came over her face; but that which Reginald Lisle most marked, and which pleased him most, was the warm blush which fluttered over her cheek when she first saw him.

Could she have been thinking of him? It was a question he did not ask himself—for he was not vain—but which the reader, perhaps, may ask, and which, if he do, I will not take upon myself to answer. Certain it is that her demeanor corresponded with the changes of her looks; for she first paused as if in doubt how to act, then stretched out her hand to him, and then began to scold him kindly for rising. It was exceedingly imprudent, she said, and very wrong; but he assured her that he was much better, and that it would do him no harm.

Then began a conversation which could only take place between two people, one of whom, at the least, intended to fall in love with the other—wild, wandering, dreamy, roaming from the smallest things to the greatest, with the name of love never mentioned, but with the latent passion warming the ground, like the subterraneous fire near the crater of a volcano.

The reader has already had a specimen of Reginald Lisle's conversation, so that it would be unnecessary and indiscreet to repeat all that was said at present; for, though there was a great difference in the subjects and in the words from that which he had held with Sir Theodore Broughton, yet there was the same general character. It was, in short, full of imagination, but imagination always directed aright, ruled and guided by a fine mind, and high principles of thought as well as action.

There is many a man who will think a wrong thing, but will not do it. He only is happy who does neither the one nor the other. Thoughts are the mind's deeds, and if mind be immortal, these are recorded for immortality.

I have said that his conversation on the present occasion was, in several respects, very different from that which he had first held with Sir Theodore Broughton; but such was the case naturally enough. His present companion was a young and beautiful girl. The age as well as the sex made a difference: not that she was older than the young baronet in years, for such, perhaps, was not the case, but she was older in mind—in feelings. All women are older than their male cotemporaries. Her intellect was more expanded, more free, more active; perhaps it was naturally of a firmer character than the youth's; and she now followed Reginald on all the paths where he chose to lead her with a free, light step, and a face sometimes grave, sometimes smiling, but always intelligent and always pleased. Sometimes, too, when she had nearly lost him in one of his wild flights, and he came back within sight again, a timid, mantling blush of pleasure would spread over her bright face, and make it look a thousand-fold more lovely than ever. Her heart was free, her spirit unsoiled by the world; and when, at the end of three quarters of an hour, her mother opened the drawing-room door, she thought the minutes she had passed there the very pleasantest she had ever spent in life. That was going a great way, reader; but it is true, she went quite as far as that, and she was not wrong.

The elder lady reproached her daugher very gently for not having made breakfast, and reproved her guest for not having obeyed orders. The young lady colored, and excused herself as best she might, and Reginald repeated his assurance that he was much better; but the lady of the house still shook her head gravely, and led the way to the breakfast-table with a moral reflection upon the restless impatience of young men.

She was no great talker; a somewhat timid and retiring person, with strong feelings and strong affections hidden under a good deal of reserve; but there was something so winning in Reginald's manner, so buoyant, so irresistible (I must use a word I hate) in his conversation, that even she was carried away by it, and enjoyed his society nearly as much as her daughter. Nearly—not quite, reader, for there was a difference of four-and-twenty years between them.

Before breakfast was over the surgeon was

announced, and his air of consternation on perceiving his patient seated at table made Reginald smile. He suffered himself to be carried off, however, and for nearly half an hour mother and daughter waited to hear the report. At the end of that time the surgeon returned alone.

"Well, where is your patient, and how is he?" asked the elder lady; while her daughter sat silent, with some degree of apprehension at his non-appearance.

"He is in bed, your ladyship," was the reply, "and very much worse for having risen. There is a considerable degree of inflammation about the knee, which must absolutely be brought down. He must have on twelve leeches, and then, if he will but keep perfectly quiet, he may, perhaps, proceed on his journey the day after to-morrow. If he had obeyed my directions, he would have saved himself a whole day's confinement; and I must request your ladyship to enforce obedience at present, otherwise I will not be answerable for the consequences. The inflammation might affect the cartilages, and leave him with a stiff joint for life, or even require amputation."

"Good Heaven, how horrible!" cried the younger lady. "If he comes down again, I will drive him back myself."

"Pray do," replied the surgeon; and then, turning to her mother, he inquired, "Does your ladyship know who the young gentleman is? He seems a person of distinction."

"I should certainly judge so," replied the mistress of the house; "and, I must say, he is one of the most agreeable young men I ever met with; but I have no idea of his name. According to the old rules of hospitality, we have never asked his name."

"I fished a little for it," rejoined the surgeon, "but was not successful; and I thought your ladyship must know. But I will find out—I will find out. I hear there are two gentlemen—friends of his—waiting for him at the Black Dog, with a number of horses and servants. I will just drop in upon them as I go back, give them a report of the case, and then I can inquire his name."

Neither of the ladies said "Pray do," but they did not tell him not; and the surgeon cantered away upon his errand.

He was disappointed, however, for he found at the inn that Reginald's two companions had ridden out to see some sight at ten or twelve miles' distance, and all he learned was that one was called Major Brandrum, and the other Sir Theodore Broughton. That was something, however; and at night he rode back to pay his evening visit with that degree of increased importance which attaches to the possession of information. His first visit was, of course, to the two ladies, and to them he immediately communicated the fact that their guest must certainly be a gentleman of consequence, inasmuch as he was traveling with Major Brandrum and Sir Theodore Broughton.

The first name did not at all possess the ladies with an opinion that his conclusion was correct; for in those days commissions in the army were given away with very little discrimination, and the fact of being a major, or even a colonel, did not at all prove that the individual was not a valet-de-chambre, or an infant. The name of Sir Theodore Broughton, however, brought up a look of surprise in the face of the elder lady, and she exclaimed, "Sir Theodore is forbidden, I suppose, to visit us; but, at all events, this intelligence gives us an assurance of the station and character of our guest."

"He can not be that horrid Captain Donovan, I am sure," answered the younger lady.

"Oh, no, my dear child!" replied her mother; "Captain Donovan is twenty years older, and a very different man in appearance. I have seen him. As to this young gentleman I am quite satisfied. He is all that one would wish in manners and behavior, and he must be a man of honor and respectability, or Captain Donovan would never admit him into Sir Theodore's society. To do the man but justice, he is only too strict and severe as to his ward's companions."

"Oh, I will find out the young gentleman's name, my lady, depend upon it," answered the surgeon. "I know how to pump it out of him without seeming to do so."

"I beg you will not, on any account," replied the elder lady, in a somewhat cold tone; "we shall doubtless have his own name from his own lips before he goes; and, in the mean time, I think pumping at all, as you call it, sir, is quite unnecessary, and would be improper."

Not well pleased with the rebuke, the worthy surgeon took his leave, and proceeded to visit his patient, whom he found decidedly better; and, notwithstanding the warning he had received, he went on, for his own satisfaction, to angle for the young gentleman's name, resolving that the lady of the house should not have the advantage of any information he might obtain.

"I am happy I shall be able to give your friends at the inn so good an account," he said. "I think you may get down stairs to-morrow evening, and may travel, *in a chaise*, a day or two after. I dare say Sir Theodore and the major are very anxious about you."

"Oh, no, my dear sir," replied Reginald; "Sir Theodore is too young to attribute much importance to such accidents, and Major Brandrum has seen too many severe injuries produce no bad results to feel any alarm regarding this."

"Pray, can I give them any message for you, sir?" inquired the man of healing again. "I pass by the door, and shall just look in upon them."

"None, I thank you," replied Captain Lisle, "unless it were that I should be obliged to Brandrum if he would send over my small black portmanteau which was upon the brown horse. I am very much in want of my razors and other dressing things."

"But whose portmanteau am I to say, my dear sir?" asked the surgeon, with a peculiar air. "You must remember that, though I belong to a learned profession, I am among the ignorant as to your name—and so is Lady Chevenix, I find."

"Lady Chevenix!" said Reginald Lisle, in a thoughtful tone: "is the lady I had the pleasure of assisting Lady Chevenix?"

"Yes, sir, the wife of Colonel Sir Charles Chevenix," replied the surgeon. "A charming person she is, and so is Sir Charles too; one of the gayest, most light-hearted, friendly gentlemen I ever knew. He is, unfortunately, absent just now. But, as I was saying, Lady Chevenix is as ignorant of your name as your humble servant."

Reginald started as if from a fit of profound thought. "I will have the honor of informing her myself to-morrow," he replied. "In the mean time, I will write a note to Major Brandrum, if you will be good enough to present it. Could you give me those writing materials?"

The surgeon did as he was asked, and Reginald Lisle, sitting up in bed, wrote the following few lines:

"My dear Crow,—This will be given you by the surgeon who is attending me—a talkative fellow, full of curiosity, who is anxious to know my name. Do not give it to him, and prevent Sir Theodore from so doing. You may guess some of my reasons when I tell you I have just discovered that I am in the house of Sir Charles Chevenix. I shall certainly rejoin you the day after to-morrow. In the mean time, send me over, by some of the people of the inn, the small black portmanteau which was upon the brown horse. Yours ever,

"Reginald Lisle."

This written, he sealed and addressed his letter, and gave it into the hands of the surgeon, who retired, fully satisfied that, though frustrated at present, he should obtain the information he desired before the night was over.

Reginald Lisle, as soon as he was alone, plunged into thought again, and meditated bitterly

CHAPTER IX.

It wanted about twenty minutes to the dinner hour on the following day when Reginald Lisle appeared in the drawing-room. It was still untenanted, and he gazed round with a very sad and pensive air, marking the different objects which it contained with the degree of interest that we feel in even small and insignificant things which have connected themselves with any of the strong emotions of the heart. He was only left about five minutes alone, however, ere Mary Chevenix appeared, and greeted him with a joyful congratulation upon his recovery. But Reginald answered in so grave a tone that she could not help remarking it, and said, "You are suffering still, I am afraid, and I am foolishly taking it for granted that you are quite well, because old Doctor Haviland allows you to come down."

"Oh no, I am much better," replied Reginald; "and if I am suffering, it is not from the late accident, Miss Chevenix."

"Then you are suffering," she said; "I was sure of it; for yesterday, when the surgeon gave so grave an account of you, you were quite cheerful, and now you seem quite sad."

"There are sufferings of the mind as well as of the body," answered the young officer, "and I know none greater than unavailing regret for any act that we have ourselves done."

She gazed at him for a moment with a look of surprise and inquiry, and then replied, "I do not clearly understand you. I can not think that you are one to do any thing that you could bitterly regret."

"Oh yes," answered Reginald. "Once, in my mere youth, I did what I have regretted ever since, and now more than ever. I will not speak of it more at present, however, for my secret will be all explained to-morrow before I leave you."

"And do you really go to-morrow?" inquired Miss Chevenix. "Oh, are you fit?"

"Fit or not fit, I must go if it be possible," replied Reginald Lisle. "I must not stay longer in this house."

"Why? why?" demanded his beautiful companion, with her deep blue eyes raised eagerly to his face. "If traveling is likely to injure you, why should you not stay?"

Reginald Lisle took her hand for a single instant, saying, "Thank you, thank you for your kind interest; but it would be far more dangerous to my peace to stay, than to my health to go."

The warm blood came up into her face, then fled from it again, and left it pale as a moonlight night. Reginald saw that he was understood, and there was a struggle in his breast as to whether he should say more; but resolution triumphed, and while Mary Chevenix turned and walked with an uncertain step to the window, he remained silently gazing on the ground. After she had reached the window, however, and had seemed to gaze out for an instant, she suddenly turned, and with glowing cheek said, in a low tone, "I wish you would stay. I am sure you are not fit to travel. I see no cause why you should go; and my father, who will be home in three days, will be most happy to thank you for the service you rendered my mother and myself."

"He will only think I have stayed too long already," replied Reginald; "and so, perhaps, will you, and regret even your kind words and feelings toward me."

"No," she answered, firmly; "no, never! There seems to be some secret; but I shall never regret that I have been grateful, or that I have felt—" She paused, hesitating; for something rose up in her bosom to tell her that she hardly knew, as yet, what were the feelings she was about to speak of; and before she could finish the sentence, Lady Chevenix entered the room.

She had greatly warmed toward her young guest. The very habit of thinking about a person familiarizes us to him. We become intimate with him in thought; and Lady Chevenix had been thinking a great deal about Reginald Lisle. She had been somewhat uneasy as to what might be her husband's opinion of her conduct in asking him to the house; but upon that subject her mind had been relieved, not half an hour before, by a letter from Sir Charles. She had also thought of his gallant interposition in the rencounter with the highwayman, and of the injury he had sustained thereby, and the suffering he had undergone since, and of the loss of his horse, and of his graceful manners and pleasant conversation. In short, by the time she entered that drawing-room, she was quite friends with him in her own mind. She now congratulated him kindly upon his recovery, and her attention was so far engaged by her own words and his reply, that she did not observe his grave and somewhat embarrassed manner, nor her daughter's glowing cheek, which, as cheeks will do, had become more crimson than ever, just because she made an effort to banish all trace of emotion.

At dinner, however, Lady Chevenix remarked that her guest's demeanor was very different; that it had lost its light elasticity; that his conversation, though still striking and full of fancy, always sought grave subjects; that the images were all sad. He described several beautiful and strange scenes which he had beheld in the different parts of the world where he had served, but his descriptions now were like the landscapes of some painters, very true to nature, very powerful even, but one felt a want of sunshine. She, too, like her daughter, imagined he must be suffering, and questioned him upon it; nor need I tell the reader that his answer was very different to her.

I never knew in my life a man answer mother and daughter in the same way. He made an effort for cheerfulness, however, and so far succeeded as to cause Lady Chevenix to smile more than once, and sometimes even to laugh. Mary tried to be gay, and happy too; but still, beneath all ran a train of thought of which Reginald Lisle was the theme, and, perhaps, had he artfully contrived a scheme to win a heart, he could not have fallen upon a better one than that of his changeful demeanor. The first step in love is to interest, and that he contrived to do most completely. But as the Eleusinian mysteries were not more secret than are the feelings of a lady's heart when she is first in love—often even to herself—I must not go on, lest I profane the temple. And a very beautiful temple it was; for that pure, warm, kind, snowy bosom was a fit place for a noble spirit to raise its prayers to heaven.

Under the influence of her eyes, the effort by which Reginald had at first sought to shake off his gloom was gradually relaxed, and he became naturally cheerful. He felt it impossible to be long sad in her company, perhaps; or, what is still more likely, she engrossed his thoughts so much that they would not rest upon any other thing—no, not even upon separation. The hour of retiring came sooner than Reginald had expected. He had not, as yet, named to Lady Chevenix his approaching departure; and as they all three stood together about to part for the night, an anxious and grave expression in Mary's eyes first brought the subject back to his mind. His manner instantly changed; and, taking the elder lady's hand as she extended it to him when bidding him good-night, he said, in a tone of much feeling, "I have many thanks to offer you, Lady Chevenix, for all your kind care and hospitality."

"No, indeed," she answered, "it is we who have to thank you; and I know not how to compensate for the injury you have sustained in our service, and the fine creature you have lost."

"Nay, nay," replied Reginald, "that is more than compensated, my dear madam; but I will not detain you now to say more than to assure you that I feel deeply grateful. To-morrow, I shall still trespass upon your hospitality at breakfast, and soon after I must take my departure, having ordered a chaise over from Stratton. Before I go, I will trouble you with a word or two about myself, for I have reason to believe that you do not yet know who I am, or any thing about me."

"Not even your name," replied the lady, with a smile; "but, though very much of a recluse, I have not the curiosity of one, though good Doctor Haviland has, I can assure you."

"So I perceived," answered Reginald, "and I would not gratify it. To-morrow, however, I will tell you all about myself; and, though the tale in the abstract may have nothing very amusing in it, yet you may and will feel a personal interest in it of some kind."

"Oh, I certainly shall, in the history of one who came so gallantly to our rescue," replied the lady. "It is, indeed, somewhat tyrannical of you, to keep us in suspense till to-morrow; and I dare say Mary will lose her sleep all night in trying to divine the mystery. As you have so arranged it, however, it must be, for we have already sat up somewhat late. Good-night, then, for the present."

Lady Chevenix prophesied rightly as to her daughter's sleepless night, and Mary Chevenix was up and down very early on the ensuing morning. The words of Reginald Lisle were still sounding in her ears; his looks still were before her eyes, and she tried hard to read the book thus opened to her. She had thought but little of love before that night, and she dared hardly think of it then; but the heart still prompted the mind, and the mind asked strange questions. It was vain for her to tell herself that it was all nonsense; that what he had said was nothing more than a few words of overstrained gallantry; that he would soon forget her, and she him. She could not persuade herself of the fact. She felt sure, in short, that he loved her, and not very sure that it was unpleasant to her to be so beloved. That there was some mystery, and that it was a sad one—one, perhaps, which would render it difficult, if not impossible, for him to pursue his suit—she clearly perceived, and with the eager, anxious yearning of a young heart, she strove, as I have said, to imagine what it could be that threw such gloom over a lover's hopes.

Perhaps he might be poor, she thought, and know that she was wealthy; perhaps lowly born; but then his appearance and his manners, and some of his words, contradicted the supposition. Besides, he had spoken of some act committed in very early youth which had cast regret upon his after life, and especially upon his acquaintance with her. With a start, she asked herself, Could he be already married? and the feeling that passed through her heart like a pang, first taught how far that heart had yielded. The next moment, however, she cast away the idea with indignation. "No, no!" she said; "either all his words and looks belie him, or such is not the case; and all other difficulties may be removed."

Ah, Mary Chevenix, Mary Chevenix! I am afraid the matter was very nearly settled with that little heart of yours. "He will soon be down," she thought, after she had gazed out up a vista in the trees for a few minutes, "and I must not let him find me meditating in this way."

Alas! what a hard world it is that makes woman strive ever to veil some of the dearest emotions of the heart! If there were no robbers, what would be the use of locks and keys? but as there are plunderers, who spoil the weak and the confiding of all sorts of treasures, it is but too needful to hide the wealth that we are not able to defend.

Mary sat down to a table and took up some work, but it was soon laid down again, and her beautiful eyes fixed sightless upon air. She had better have remained at the window, for the next instant a shadow darkened the casement near her, and, turning her head, she saw Reginald Lisle looking in. The next window served the purpose of a door upon the lawn, and in a moment he was by her side. She was blushing a good deal, for she had been detected, she felt, in a deep reverie; and there was so much agitation in her manner, that Reginald Lisle was agitated too. In haste, or passion, or agitation, people do not well know what they are doing. It is a truism of the utmost platitude, but yet we very seldom take it into consideration in judging of the conduct of others. Now, Heaven knows what Reginald Lisle or Mary Chevenix said or did—I do not, and I much doubt whether they did themselves—but they were near an hour together quite alone; and when Lady Chevenix was heard speaking to one of the servants on the stairs, her daughter escaped out of the drawing-room by a side door. Reginald, with more agitation than he liked, stood his ground. The lady was delayed some minutes, however, before she appeared, and though her young guest was very pale when she entered, that was the only remaining trace of emotion.

"I suppose Mary is making breakfast," said Lady Chevenix, after the first salutation; "let us come and see." But breakfast was unmade; and when the young lady did appear, she was again gently reproved for her neglect. Lucky, perhaps, it was so, for the variation of her cheek had then an apparent cause. But it mattered little, for Lady Chevenix was one of those women who can not conceive it possible to fall in love in three days.

The breakfast was put all in order, the butler had left the room, and there seemed no earthly reason why every body should not be cheerful and conversible; but all were silent, abstracted, thoughtful. Every one tried to talk, indeed, just at the moment when nobody else was in a case to help them; and as conversation is an undertaking which can not be carried on by private enterprise, it very soon fell to the ground.

At length, when Reginald had more than three quarters finished his breakfast, he heard the sound of wheels rolling up to the other side of the house, and a moment after a footman came in to inform him that the chaise was there.

"Very well," he said, in an exceedingly grave tone; "put in my portmanteau, if you please: I will come in a few minutes. I promised, Lady Chevenix," he continued, as the man closed the door, "to tell you my short story, and I secure you against its being a long one by beginning when the chaise is at the door." He dared not give a glance to Mary, for he feared that even one look might deprive him of the courage which he had summoned up. "My father," he continued, "was of a very good family, being the third son of a peer. His portion, too, was good for a peer's younger son, and he early entered the army and served with some distinction. Having found it necessary to cane a man of high rank, and not being on the best terms with his elder brother, who might have given him protection,* he was prosecuted for an assault, and saved from serious consequences by the skill and zeal of the lawyer he employed. He became intimate with him, and finally married his daughter, who brought him a moderate fortune. He died on the field some ten or twelve years ago, leaving two children, myself and my sister. My inheritance was not very large, but it was sufficient; and at the age of seventeen, or a little before, indeed, I entered the army in a dragoon regiment. I had not, perhaps, misspent the years of youth, for I had acquired much which those with whom I was now called upon to associate were without. But that fact was in some degree unfortunate, for it taught me to look down upon the understanding of my companions, while they looked down upon me for want of knowledge of the world, and acquired the habit of calling me 'the book-worm.' I was irritated by their conduct; but, while it kept within certain limits, I contrived to master my anger, and to conceal it; till one day, the person for whom in the whole corps I felt inclined to entertain the most friendly feeling —a frank, gay, high-spirited man, and my superior officer—rallied me perhaps a little too severely at the mess table. I retorted petulantly, I am sure. He had drunk wine enough to heat, but not to intoxicate him, and he answered, I think, rashly. In short, words were spoken which are difficult to bear, and in an evil hour I threw up my commission and called out my superior officer. I had no sooner taken the irretrievable step than I regretted, but regrets were in vain. We met, and I am sorry to say I wounded him severely. He behaved to me with the utmost generosity; but, at the time when his life was despaired of, by the advice of my friends I embarked for America, entered an infantry regiment, and have risen by degrees in the service, without discredit. The unfortunate affair, however, with which my career commenced, has always left bitter sorrow behind. I need not tell you, Lady Chevenix," he continued, rising, "how much that regret is increased now, when I inform you that I am Reginald Lisle."

Lady Chevenix turned very pale, and started up from her chair, exclaiming, "Sir, sir, this is—"

She did not finish the sentence, and Reginald turned one imploring look to the face of Mary Chevenix. At first the blood fled from her cheek too; but the next instant it returned, and a smile—faint, indeed, but certainly a smile —met Reginald Lisle's sight.

He could not account for it; but it seemed to his eyes the smile of reviving hope; and, turning to Lady Chevenix, he took up the sentence which she had left unfinished, saying,

* Protection against the power of the law may seem strange to our ears, but there were cases in those days where such shelter was found.

"This is—what, my dear madam? You can not suppose that, had I known who you were, I would have ever intruded myself into a house where each member of the family must remember that I once raised my hand against a husband's or a father's life. I only became aware of the facts the night before last, and instantly resolved to relieve you of my presence as soon as it was possible to do so. Nevertheless, I must, ere I depart, call to your recollection that Sir Charles Chevenix himself declared publicly that I had conducted myself as a man of honor and a gentleman, and was pleased to take upon himself even a greater share of the fault than was his due."

"He does you justice still, Captain Lisle," said Mary, warmly; "and I am sure, were he here, he would be the first to hold out his hand, and thank you for the assistance you lately rendered us, and for all you have suffered from so doing."

"Be silent, Mary," said Lady Chevenix; "you do not understand these matters. Your father speaks, as becomes his character, of an adversary who did nothing dishonorable or actually wrong toward him; but he does not and can not forget that Captain Lisle is an adversary, nor I that he shed my husband's blood. I thank you sincerely, sir, for the assistance you rendered to my daughter and myself. It was given as a gallant gentleman, such as we all know you to be; but you yourself will feel that I could wish it had been rendered by another hand, and probably you could yourself desire that it had been afforded to other persons."

"Far from it, madam," replied Reginald, raising his head high with a look of bitter mortification; "if any thing could add to the pleasure of being of service to two ladies, it would be the fact that they are the wife and daughter of Sir Charles Chevenix. It gives me an honorable opportunity of assuring him that I bitterly regret, and have ever bitterly regretted, the results of my boyish impetuosity, and that I am well aware I merited more blame in the affair than he was pleased to assign to me. Pray, let that assurance be conveyed to him; and now, with many thanks for the hospitality I have received, I take my leave."

Lady Chevenix made him a formal inclination of the head; but her daughter exclaimed, "Oh, mother, this is unkind! Do not let him go thinking us so ungrateful."

"Ungrateful!" replied the elder lady, in a sharp tone; "for raising his hand against your father's life, and bringing him to the jaws of death!" and, passing her daughter, she quitted the room. Mary tarried for a moment, and held out her hand to Reginald Lisle: "Farewell," she said, "farewell. Do not carry away the belief that either my father or myself feel thus. It is her love for him that makes my mother so unjust; and, although I do not love him less than she does, it is from himself I have learned to judge of your conduct more fairly. I am sure you will hear from him soon. Let that console you till—"

"Mary! Mary!" cried the voice of Lady Chevenix from the next room; "I want you, my dear."

Reginald Lisle pressed his lips upon her hand, murmuring, "Thank you, thank you, dear, beautiful girl," and in two minutes more was in the chase rolling away toward Stratton.

CHAPTER X.

In former times there was an inn at Dunstable: I hope none of my readers recollect it, for their sake and my own, because it was seventy-two years ago, and I am going to describe it. The reader may say that perhaps it lasted long after that, so that men of moderate years may remember it without shame. If he will wait a little, I will show him that could not be.

However, in former times there was an inn at Dunstable, such as good old English inns frequently were. Now Dunstable, in those days, stood on the high road to Holyhead and Birmingham. It has removed since by rail-road; but, such being the case at the time I speak of, and the little town, which then did not contain above eleven hundred inhabitants, being at the distance of a good day's ride from London, on the way to the above-named places, it required, as the reader may imagine—at a time when many people traveled on horseback, and others in carriages drawn by their own horses—a good large inn to receive those who chose to stop there on their first day's journey out of, or their last day's journey into, London. A good large inn it had too, as well as three smaller ones, which swept up the crumbs that were left by their more voracious neighbor.

In those smaller inns put up peddlers, and stray carriers, and men with pack-horses; but the regular wagons, with their tilt and team, went to the great inn, a part of which was peculiarly appropriated to their conveniences. It was a large building, in the form of a parallelogram, built round a large court-yard, and having two wide, arched entrances on the main road, one exactly similar on the little road that crossed the highway, and two passages through the back part of the building into a garden, which supplied the cook with cabbages for her beef broth, a favorite dish with the drivers of, and passengers by, the wagons.

The front of the inn was gloomy-looking enough; the windows were exceedingly small, according to our present notions, and the archways enormously large. Over one was a painting representing something very like a deformed black cow with golden horns: that was the wagon entrance which lay beneath the picture. Over the other arch, or, rather, projecting from the top of it into the street, was a carved image of the animal which the painting was really intended to depict; but so much greater was the skill of the sculptor than that of the painter, that no one could have any difficulty in discovering that the image was meant for a black bull. Lest any one should mistake, however, on a large board, in gigantic letters, was written, along the front of the house, "The Black Bull—Matthew Spinner," with a list of all sorts of things which Matthew Spinner could and would supply, upon a consideration. The house was of four stories in height. The windows were not exactly above each other, but, either for convenience or from whim, those on the first floor had been placed over the piers of the ground floor, and those on the second floor over the piers of the first, and so on. Thus, if it had not been for those two great gaping archways, the front of the house would have looked just like a great chess-board.

So much for the external face; but now—although the description is somewhat long already—I must say a word of the internal, or court-yard face of the building. It also showed four stories, but not by the windows, for it was only on the upper and the lower story of all that any thing of the kind was visible. Between were two long wooden galleries, running all round, supported by stout squat pillars, and defended by a balustrade.

I can not say that the court was very clean or very well paved; for, although the boots and the hostler seemed to be eternally sweeping it out with everlasting birch brooms, nevertheless it was continually covered with wet straw; which, perhaps, may be accounted for by the fact that, besides the chaise horses, the wagon horses, and the riding horses, which were constantly going in and out, a whole herd of pigs had, from time immemorial, possessed a right of road through it.

On the left-hand side, as you entered from the street, was the portion of the yard appropriated to the wagons, and that flanking part of the building which overlooked them as they stood ranged in order below was very judiciously assigned to the wagoners, and the guests whom they brought to the Black Bull under their tilt, which, in those days, were not few; for people who had not much important business to transact, and but little money in their pocket, could be content to travel at the rate of two miles and a half an hour. Now they grumble at twenty. The *corps de logis*, or principal façade, was occupied by a large dining-hall on the ground floor, where an ordinary was served at one and at three o'clock; the host's own private apartments, including all kinds of offices and a small hall for private parties; various sitting-rooms, and one or two bed-rooms for "the quality" on the first floor; and the same over that again—only here were more bed-rooms and fewer sitting-rooms; while on the fourth story were rooms for servants. The whole right-hand building was devoted to bed-rooms, generally assigned to single travelers, except, indeed, the ground floor, which disposed itself into kitchens, pantries, larders, sculleries, wash-houses, and an inconceivable number of unnamed and unnamable holes and corners.

"Upon my life! here is a whole page devoted to a description of a very common, old-fashioned country inn!"

"Was there ever such a tiresome fellow in the world?"

"That is the worst of James's books: he is so fond of long descriptions."

"I always skip the descriptions in your books, papa."

"I always skip the love."

Very well, dear reader; very well, dear critic; very well, dear children. Whoever skips any thing, omits that which was not written without an object, loses an emotion or a fact, and will, in the end, perhaps, be obliged to turn back, because he does not find out the story which he has been running after so eagerly. Oh, rail-road, rail-road! you have got even into romances, and one must hurry on at forty-five miles an hour. No, I will not. I will stop for a night at Vantini's—or at the Black Bull at Dunstable, which will do quite as well, and be cheaper.

I hope the reader has remarked every particular of the description which has been lately given. If so, let him look into the inn yard, in the fine spring evening, with the yellow light of the sinking sun streaming into it, and making the whole, from the garret windows to the old, ill-painted wooden pillars—nay, even the stray straws on the pavement—look cheerful. He will see that, at one and the same moment, each arch-way is pouring into that court-yard a stream of living creatures. One gave admission to three gentlemen, two servants, and six horses. The other afforded entrance to a wagoner on foot, and six horses, drawing after them a long, heavy, clumsy, broad-wheeled wagon, covered with a new tilt, inscribed, in large letters, with the owner's name and the vehicle's starting-place and destination.

The mounted gentlemen were received by mine host, Matthew Spinner, the head waiter, and the head hostler, with assistants. The wagon had its own particular attendants; but the first-named party were encountered with bowings and scrapings, and the wagoner at least, if not the wagon, with shakings of hands. The golden calf has ever been the idol of the best repute: Baal, and Dagon, and Ashtaroth, and other gentlemen and ladies of stone, and brass, and wood, and ivory, have had their vogue; but the golden calf is the only perennial deity, and even Mammon's simular will bend the knees of men to worship, though the real demon be very far from present. Horses and servants, fine coats, and the mere appearance of wealth, with half the world, are the great claims to reverence; and no wonder, then, that the aristocracy of the Black Bull, the priests and senators of the temple of mercenary hospitality, were busy in doing honor to gentlemen who came well attended.

In the mean while, the democracy of the inn, consisting of a hostler of inferior grade, a horse-keeper, a boy, and two fat, greasy girls, were busy about the wagon. The end of the tilt was thrown back, and two or three words from the wagoner instantly brought forth a wooden chair, which was placed at the end of the vehicle furthest from the horses.

"Now, ma'am," said the driver, "step on this here. It will help you down easy. I hope the gentleman is none the worse."

"He *says* he is better," replied a very sweet female voice from within; and, the moment after, a young girl, with bended head and somewhat doubtful steps, picked her way to the end of the wagon, and, with the wagoner's assistance, descended, putting first one foot and then the other upon the chair, and then springing lightly upon the stones, as if the very first breath of the fresh air revived her. There was no room for any great display of grace; but yet she was very graceful. She seemed hardly sixteen years of age, and there was a child-like way about her, which made her appear younger than she really was; and yet there was womanly thought in her fair face, mingling with that youthful look somewhat strangely. I am not fond of any exaggeration—not even of an exaggerated simile. Many I could find—half a dozen at least—to illustrate that mingling of expression. But so it was, just as I have plainly said, a grave, thoughtful cast upon a very young and happy face. The look became almost sad as she turned again toward the wagon, after she had alighted, and held out her hand to some one within, saying, "Here, my dear father. It seems a very nice inn."

With a slow and feeble step, and a frame bent and emaciated by illness, a man of the middle age approached the end of the vehicle, and, with the aid of the wagoner and the girl together, with some stray assistance from the hostler, descended and looked about him with a wearied and anxious look. He then spoke a few words to one of the chamber-maids, and retired from sight, leaning on his daughter's arm.

In the mean while, the three gentlemen had dismounted much more rapidly from their horses, though one of them seemed a little lame; and, though the landlord, with obtrusive civility, repeated, more than once, "This way, gentlemen," the eyes of all three were turned to the little scene which was taking place at the further side of the yard. Sir Theodore Broughton gazed somewhat eagerly at the young girl; and it was evident to Reginald Lisle that he was in one of those dreams which seize upon the young fancy when a fair face crosses our path, and, disappearing before we have had any time for observations, seems lovelier than any that we ever beheld, often remaining so impressed upon memory for long years.

Reginald himself gazed with very different feelings, and with a higher, a brighter interest. His imagination was not less rapid and eager, but it was less selfish in its course; and the daughter's manner toward her father, the stretched forth hand, the anxious, thoughtful look at his face, and a something of high breeding in the air of both, conjured up a story in his fancy, which was only not a romance because it was too near the truth. Major Brandrum seemed, or was, the most moved of the whole party. He looked steadfastly at the pair for a moment, and then his lips moved, muttering sounds which were only distinct to himself; but the next instant, with a cloudy brow and thoughtful look, he turned upon his heel, saying, "Come, Lisle—come, Sir Theodore," and followed the landlord toward the part of the building containing the dining halls, with his spurs jingling over the pavement of the court even more than was their wont.

"The ordinary is over, gentlemen, I am sorry to say," quoth the landlord; "have you dined? or will you please to order any dinner?" As he spoke, he took a new survey of his guests, and more especially of Major Brandrum, whose strange costume seemed to strike him a good deal. But the major was absorbed in thought, and Reginald Lisle took upon him to order dinner, while Sir Theodore walked to the window and beat time upon his boot with his riding whip.

"Lisle, lend me ten guineas," said the major, approaching his young friend as soon as the landlord was out of the room, and speaking in a low voice.

"Certainly," replied Reginald, without the slightest hesitation, taking out his purse.

"I will pay you on the seventeenth of next month," said the major, taking the money, and hurrying out of the room. Reginald Lisle would not follow, though he murmured to himself, "Some good deed to be done, I am sure; perhaps that poor fellow we saw get out of the wagon."

The next moment the door opened, and Zachary Hargrave, Sir Theodore's servant, entered, with his demure look. "Please you, sir," he said, addressing his young master, "I wish you would just come to the stable and look at Roland's back. The saddle has galled him a bit."

"How is the horse I bought at Stratton-upon-Dunsmoor, Hargrave?" asked Reginald Lisle.

"Oh, he is quite well and fresh, captain," answered the man; "he's an impudent beast."

Lisle did not seem to notice this imputation upon his horse's modesty, but turned, musing, to the window, and Sir Theodore followed the man out of the room.

"Why did you call Captain Lisle's horse an impudent beast, Zachary?" asked the young baronet, as they walked along.

"Because they say, 'As impudent as a highwayman's horse,' Sir Theodore," replied the man, with a grin; "and I've a great notion that this here horse has been upon the road in more ways than one."

"Pooh! nonsense!" cried the young baronet; "it was Colonel Lutwich's horse."

"No matter for that," answered Zachary, dryly; "howsomdever, it's a fine piece of flesh and blood, that it is, but I can show you a finer, I think, Sir Theodore."

"Indeed!" exclaimed his master; "I should like to see it."

"This way, then, sir," said Hargrave; and, instead of leading the young baronet to the stables at the back, he kept to the left, passed round behind the wagon which had last come in, and entered that wing of the house. First came a door, which was open, and a passage, at the mouth of which three or four men were talking together, among whom was the wagoner, and then, on the right, was a swing door, which Hargrave pushed open, ushering Sir Theodore into a large, dingy room, furnished with two or three tables, several wooden benches, and four or five chairs of the same material. There was some fire in the grate, and a large tea-kettle hissing upon the embers.

Only three persons tenanted the room. The one nearest the door by which the young gentleman entered was the beautiful girl whom he had watched descending from the wagon. She was busily making tea at a table some distance from the fire; and now that her cloak and hat were thrown off, with her slight, budding figure displayed by neat and well made, though very plain apparel, she looked, to the eyes of Sir Theodore Broughton, far more beautiful and graceful than ever. Near the fire, and seated on a chair at one side of the chimney, was her father, with his pale and emaciated countenance, lighted up with a bright and cheerful look, while just opposite to him sat Major Brandrum, his body inclined to an angle of forty-five, in order to talk low to the other traveler, and his long legs, in their heavy riding boots, stretched out till they passed his companion's feet on the opposite side.

"Kate, my dear, come hither," said the sick man, raising his voice, which was peculiarly sweet in tone. "This is Major Brandrum, an old fellow-officer of mine, who remembers me well at the taking of Quebec, he says."

The girl put down the cup, and, advancing toward Major Brandrum, held out her hand to him frankly, saying, "I am very happy, sir, my father has met with a friend. He needs one."

"Have I not you, my child?" asked her father, "and have I not God? a friend on earth, and, I trust, a friend in heaven. It is enough for any man; but still I am most grateful for finding another, when I imagined that all I had were confined to those."

None of those who were now speaking seemed to notice Sir Theodore in the least, though the young lady had given him a casual glance as he entered. They were occupied with their own feelings, and those feelings were too profound to let the idle thoughts go wandering at the first call of the eye. After pausing an instant, the young baronet was drawing back toward the same door by which he had entered, but Zachary Hargrave led him to another at the opposite side of the room, which opened into the cross-road. When the door had swung to behind them, the man said, in a low tone, "It was better to come away: it would not do now."

"What would not do?" demanded Sir Theodore, in a tone of surprise.

"Oh, nothing particular, sir," replied the man; "I only thought you might like to have a talk with the young lady alone, for she is one of the prettiest girls I ever set eyes on, to my thinking."

"Talk to her alone!" exclaimed Sir Theodore; "why, what should I say to her?"

"Why, Lord bless you, sir, you'd say plenty of things to her soon enough, I dare say," replied Hargrave; "and I do not think there would be any great difficulty in the matter, for the wagoner says they are as poor as Job. It is not to be expected that you should do different from other young gentlemen just at present. If it be a sin, nobody can expect grace without sin, otherwise grace is unprofitable, which can't be, sir; and I do not know many young gentlemen of your years who would let such a prize as that escape."

Accursed be they who plant the first seeds of evil in the hot-bed of the youthful mind! When Sir Theodore Broughton first gazed upon that beautiful young girl, no taint of coarser passion sullied his thoughts. She was to him, as I have said before, as a fair vision, and he never even dreamed of the possibility of wronging her; but the voice of the tempter once heard—the corrupting influence of example brought to act upon his mind—thenceforth his thoughts hung round the idea placed before them—fluttering away—returning—hovering about it and above it—now scared and timid—now bolder and bolder, urged on by passion and the boiling blood of youth.

The tempter was still with him, and they walked on slowly toward the stables; but the man well understood his trade, and he left what he had said to work a while, before he added more.

Sir Theodore wished him to speak, but yet he was silent; and at length the young baronet asked, in a sharp tone, "Well, where is this marvelous horse that you were to show me?"

"Why, bless you, Sir Theodore!" replied the man, "it was no horse at all, but the girl we have just seen. I said I'd show you the finest piece of flesh and blood I ever saw, and so she is, upon my honor! I can see how it is, sir; you think that the captain would be angry, and make a great piece of work, but he knows better. He's been a young man himself, and knows, God help us! that we are all poor frail creatures, who must be tried in the fire, as it were. He has often said, for I've heard him, that young men must prove every thing. That is the reason why he let you ride such wild horses even from a boy; and now he sees that you are growing a man, he has sent you out to Lunnun without going with you, just to let you have your swing. He told me himself that I was not to try and stop any of your little *escapades*, as he called it, which I take to mean such affairs as those that are happening to young gentlemen every day."

"Did he say that?" asked the young baronet, musing; and, after the man had reiterated his assurances more than once, without seeming to receive much attention, Sir Theodore said, suddenly, "Come hither, Zachary—come hither into the stable;" and, going in, he looked through every stall to see there was nobody to overhear. Even then, he and the man spoke in a whisper, though occasionally a louder word was heard.

But I have no wish to listen to the lesson of iniquity. Suffice it that never was a better instructor known; and though the words of hypocritical cant which mingled in his discourse at first disgusted, Sir Theodore soon found that they might be useful in the deceit which he, like all men plunging into vice, was glad to put upon himself.

Let us return to purer things. Major Brandrum sat with the invalid and his daughter for more than half an hour, and the poor officer's heart opened to the frank old soldier. But Brandrum was a good tactician too, and he was resolved to make himself master of all the defenses before he opened his fire upon the place. He talked of scenes which were familiar to them both, and events in which they had both had a share; and he told his own story briefly as encouragement, and listened to that of his companion at large. He even took a cup of tea from Kate, because she offered it, although he had not dined; and putting his arm familiarly through hers, as she stood beside him, he said, "And so you have been his companion and his consolation in all these troubles, my dear? That's a good girl. Never you leave him; for the thought of what you have done for your father will be the best comfort to you when you are older, perhaps, and sicker than he is."

"It is so now," answered the girl, simply, and with a smile.

"Well, well," continued Brandrum; "and so, my good friend, you have been badly treated by the powers that be. Because you were sick, and not wounded, they would not allow you any pension, and now order you to join when you have neither strength nor money? That seems hard of them, and stingy; and not the less stingy because it is hard, nor the less hard because it is stingy; but I'll tell you how it is: these fellows are very shrewd, and they wish to keep up a good feeling in the service."

"That is what they say," replied the sick man; "but I do not see how their conduct tends to that. Here I became sick in the service and for the service. During my short leave I have spent a fortune upon doctors and—"

"Oh, it is not that at all," said Major Brandrum; "you see it is a rule, my dear friend, that every officer should help another. Now, if government were to do every thing, we should always look to government to do every thing, and we should grow as hard-hearted as a rock, instead of having our purses and our means almost in common, as it ought to be with all old comrades. I recollect quite well, when I was wounded in the shoulder and had a pike-hole in my hip, under Lord George Sackville, in Germany, they were obliged to leave me behind; and my baggage having been taken, I had not a sixpence nor a clean shirt, and was likely to die of dirt and starvation; but just as I was giving up spirit, old Honeywood came into the village with his dragoons—you recollect the old 'Chopping-block,' as we called him, I dare say?"

"Very well, very well," said the sick officer, with a sigh; "a braver officer or a better-hearted man never lived."

"Never!" repeated Brandrum, warmly; "but, as I was saying, as soon as I saw him in the market-place, I went up to him, and told him how I was left; and he swore at me very hard, as was his custom, and cried out, 'We can't give you a horse, for we have got none to spare; nor a dinner, for we have not enough for ourselves; but there is something that will get you both;' and he thrust a large roll of rix-dollars into my hand, which I paid him back again as soon as I could, and that was seven years after."

"It was very kind of him," said the sick man, feebly and sadly.

"Pooh! not a bit," answered Major Brandrum; "I'd have done the same for him; but now let us talk of other things. So you are going to Holyhead, are you? I can tell you what, you must not travel in the wagon. It is both slow and rumbling; and not the less rumbling because it is slow, nor the less slow because it is rumbling. All very well for a lift on a march, but not for a sickish man going to join."

The officer shook his head. "I have no other means," he said.

"But I tell you, you shall not," cried Major Brandrum, looking fierce; "I'll be —— if you shall," and he added an unnecessary oath. "There's a diligence goes down the greater part of the way, and you and your darling Kate here shall go in that, and you shall post the rest, or my name is not Jack Brandrum. There—no more about it," he continued, pulling out his purse. "I'm the senior officer, and I take the command. Kate, attention! Ground your tea-cup, and hold out your hand—as pretty a little hand as ever I saw, except that of my dear departed squaw, who was called the Sugar Maple; but it was blackish. Look, here are twelve guineas, of which you are to be a good housewife. Remember that your father's health is the first thing, and you are not to let him want comforts, but to take him safe and sound to Ireland, and then write me word how he is. There's a good girl—you understand me, my dear, I see."

"Oh yes, I understand you quite well," replied Kate, with the tears in her eyes; but her father interfered, saying, "Indeed, major, I can not. I never borrowed money of any one in my life, and it would be burdensome to me to think I was in debt."

"That is insulting," said Major Brandrum; "do you not think, my friend, that it must be equally burdensome to me to be in debt? Now, if you refuse to take that, you leave me so."

"How can that be?" exclaimed the sick officer; "you owe me nothing."

"I owe every thing to the manly spirit and kind feeling of the service to which I belong," replied Major Brandrum, gravely. "I owe it a thousand acts of kindness of this and many other kinds; and I am under a bond to pay this debt to any comrade I meet in sickness, sorrow, or distress. Now, sir, refuse me, if you have the heart to do me such great wrong."

"Well, I will not, I will not," cried the other, wringing his hand hard; and Kate turned away her head and sobbed.

Major Brandrum seized the moment to rise and retire; but, before he did so, he took the beautiful girl by the arm, saying, "Pooh, pooh! my dear child, do not be silly. Your father will be a general yet, never fear; and only remember, if ever you want help or protection, your friend the Ravenous Crow is ready to give it to the utmost of his power."

"The what?" exclaimed Kate, looking at him through her tears, in some surprise.

"Oh! that's an old story," said Major Brandrum; "I'll tell you how I got that name some other time. I shall see you in the morning before you go. Hark you, Malcolm!" and he turned back, saying in a whisper to the invalid, "I have seen my young friend, Sir Theodore's servant, Zachary Hargrave, put his head in twice during the last five minutes. He's a great blackguard, that fellow, and a hypocrite. Have an eye upon him;" and, with this caution, he left the room and returned to Reginald Lisle.

CHAPTER XI.

Reginald Lisle was leaning his head upon his hand in thought, and he had remained in thought ever since his friend had left him. Such had not been his custom; but Reginald Lisle was very much changed. He had always been a thinker, but he had been a rapid thinker, and not a meditative one. Now it is always passion of some kind which makes a meditative thinker.

The reader will instantly deny the proposition, and vow that he has seen a dozen or more meditative thinkers, whose greatest error was having no passion—no, not even an object. But that is a mistake; they were dreamers, not meditative thinkers. There is another marked distinction, too, to be kept in mind: meditative thinkers are very different from calculating thinkers. The lat•r have seldom any passion.

Reginald, however, had become very meditative. He was not dreamy, but he was really very thoughtful. He gave both memory and judgment way as well as imagination. He thought of Mary Chevenix, and of the position in which Fate and his own words had placed him in regard to her; and when Love looked to Hope and to Reason, and asked, in the mariner's tongue, "What cheer?" the reply of the first was faint and low, and the second said aloud, "Breakers ahead!"

Such was his frame of mind, and such the subject of his thoughts, when Major Brandrum rejoined him, with his heart running over with satisfaction. The table had been laid without Reginald knowing it, and supper, or dinner—be it called whichever any one will—was nearly ready; but Sir Theodore had not yet appeared, and, to say the truth, the young officer had not much noticed his absence.

"Well, my dear Crow," he said, raising his eyes, with an effort to look *not absent*, "what have you been about?"

"Nothing of much importance, Lisle," replied the major. "I fell in with an old brother officer, who fancies he is beginning one journey, when he is far on upon another, I fear. But it was some satisfaction to be able to give him a little comfort, poor fellow!"

"Which you did not fail to do," said Reginald, "I am sure."

"To be sure," answered Major Brandrum. "I am still anxious about the poor girl, however;" and so he truly was, for Major Brandrum, otherwise Jack Brandrum, otherwise the Ravenous Crow, was almost always anxious about somebody, though never about himself. He had a tender, affectionate, benevolent heart, which was full of very refined sensibilities. All this, pray recollect, dear reader, without the slightest touch of sentimentality. He could feel with the young, he could feel with the old, he could feel with the poor, he could feel with the sick, and though he was always ready to relieve, to comfort, to console, where he saw real need, or pain, or sorrow, yet he never tried to make miseries to grieve over, either in others or himself. He was at times a little ashamed of his sympathies; and in early days, being of a very gay, cheerful, dashing disposition, had endeavored to cover over kind actions and kind feelings with a rattling, thoughtless manner; but two or three people detected him, and his cue was now to persuade himself and others that what he did was only done because it was right and proper, and what every man ought to do, and most men would do.

"I am still anxious about the poor girl, however," said Major Brandrum; and Reginald Lisle asked "why"—not in an indifferent manner, but in a tone which his friend well understood to imply a desire of hearing the circumstances which caused his anxiety.

"It will be bad enough, you see, Lisle," replied the major, "to lose her father, whenever it happens. It is always a blow; but, under ordinary circumstances, men feel that it is in the course of nature, and religion, philosophy, and time dry the eyes which torn affections have moistened; but this girl, I can see, has devoted herself to her parent with that absorbing attention which concentrates all the feelings upon one object. It will be bad enough at any time and in any place for her to lose him; but what will it be to lose him perhaps on this very journey, or even after he has joined a regiment where he is unknown? Then, she is very beautiful, very poor, and quite defenseless."

"But surely she has some friends," said Reginald, becoming much interested.

"They did not appear, to support her father in his career, to comfort him in his sickness, or to help him in his need," was the sad reply. "What they have not done for the father, will they do for the child? Even if they do, will it not be too late, when she is left alone amid strangers, and perhaps profligates?"

The door opened while he was speaking, and the young baronet entered. His cheek turned somewhat red as he heard the last few words that Major Brandrum uttered; but, sitting down without speaking, he began playing with the knives and forks.

"If I can help in any way, you know you can command me," replied Reginald, warmly.

"I know it, my dear fellow—I know it well," answered his friend; "but you are far too young, and I not quite old enough, to act as the protector of a girl of sixteen or seventeen, without calling forth insinuations, unfounded but injurious; and not the less injurious because they are unfounded, nor the less unfounded because they are injurious. However, I will think about it till to-morrow, and then we can talk it over. If your dear good mother would countenance and protect her, indeed we might do something."

"I was just about to say," answered Reginald Lisle—but at that moment the landlord appeared carrying the first dish, which he set down with all care and gravity, and then turning to the gentlemen present before he took the cover off, said, "May I inquire if one of you gentlemen is Major Brandrum?"

"I am, sir," replied the major; "what are your commands with me?"

"There is a person in the court wishes to speak with you, sir," answered the host; and the officer, putting down his head to Lisle's ear—the latter having already taken his seat—said, in a whisper, "I suspect I shall not sup with you to-night. This is a bailiff, depend upon it. What sort of a person is he, my good friend?" he continued, aloud.

"Why, an odd-looking sort of man, sir," answered the other; "he looks like a beggarman with a patch over his eye."

"Is there only one?" asked Lisle.

"Only one, sir," said the landlord.

"Send him in, then, send him in," cried the major; adding, in a low tone, "we can deal with one; and, moreover, it is after sundown."

Mine host, upon the injunction he had received, opened the small dining-room door, beckoning to some one without, and immediately, with a slow step and limping gait, a very poor-looking object entered.

He was dressed in a large, dirty brown coat, worn to the threads, various parts of which showed the marks where the lace, which had once decorated it, had been picked off. The hat which he doffed as he came in was dented in every part, so as to leave no trace of its original shape; and the wig which was underneath, of the peculiar cut called *scratch*, had probably been picked out of some gutter into which it had been cast, when judged by a third or fourth wearer to be incapable of further service. It was much too large foi his head also, but the danger of its falling off was remedied by a large black ribbon nearly worn to shreds, which, passing over the apex of the head in a diagonal line, bound the patch mentioned by the landlord over his eye.

"My name is Brandrum, sir," said the major, after this unprepossessing personage had made sundry bows; "what do you want with me?"

"Why, sir, I have got something for you," replied the man, "and a message from your friend Colonel Lutwich, if you will just step a little aside."

The major eyed him very intently for a moment, and then, with a smile, walked toward the further side of the room, at which stood another table. The visitor hobbled after, and they were soon in eager conversation, which, however, was for some time carried on in so low a tone that nothing transpired. At length, however, Brandrum exclaimed aloud, "What, the whole! the hundred guineas too!"

"Every penny," answered the man; "with such scurvy fellows as that, depend upon it, a neat pistol well crammed is more efficacious in making them pay their debts of honor than a dozen writs of *ca. sa.* He had the impudence to say, that if you had won it at hazard he would have paid, but because you had only lent one part, and become bound for the other, he would not; and so, then, *the colonel* took to the *ultima ratio* with him. He knew his man too well to hesitate; and here is the money; but you must give me a receipt in the specified form. Here it is drawn up."

"With all my heart," cried Brandrum, rubbing his hands joyfully. "Here, landlord, pen and ink."

"Directly, sir—directly," said mine host, who was skilled in reading prosperity on men's faces, and was always deferential in proportion. The writing materials were soon produced, and a paper placed before the worthy major, which, after reading carefully over, he signed with a flourish, saying, "There! Give my best compliments and thanks to Colonel Lutwich, who is, I suppose, your master, though his livery is somewhat out of the common run."

"Oh, sir, that is policy," replied the man, producing a small bag and a little paper parcel not much bigger than a letter; "having such a sum as this about me, it was better to look as if I had nothing, for fear of highwaymen, you know; so I put off the clothes I usually wear."

"You did wisely," replied Major Brandrum, taking the bag, and counting a considerable number of guineas which it contained, and then running over the bank-notes with his finger and thumb. "Five hundred and thirty-two guineas, good tale," he cried; "well, I never knew such a rascal pay such a sum before—when he could help it."

"Ay, but he could not," replied the man, pocketing the receipt; and then, putting his lips close to the ear of the Ravenous Crow he added, in a whisper, "Take care of your money: you have counted it before the landlord and the waiter, and it is a prize which might tempt some one to your bed-room door. I had better send the bailiffs to you: they are both in the house at this moment, following you down to Warwickshire. Pay them in the gold, major, and keep the notes. They are easily carried, and not worth any one's risk to take. Good-by, sir," he continued, aloud: "I hope you'll remember the porter."

Major Brandrum took a crown out of his purse—it was well-nigh the last it contained—and gave it to the other, who, with an awkward bow to the rest of the company, quitted the room, thanking his honor a thousand times.

Major Brandrum then apologized to his two friends for keeping their meal so long waiting; and, sitting down to table with them, prepared to enjoy himself as was his wont. He had more business, however, to transact before he could satisfy himself with the "cates divine," or quaff the foaming bowl.

"Upon my life! here are roast fowls and ham once more," cried Reginald Lisle. "We have had them at every inn where we have stopped."

"Those two dishes are patent in England," replied the major; "they are just as much a staple commodity as roast beef. I remember being seated at dinner, two years ago, beside a Frenchman; and when, after grace, which was very long, the covers were removed and the contents of the dishes displayed, I saw my neighbor's face work lamentably, and he murmured to himself, but loud enough for half a dozen people to hear, 'Begar! dere be cock and bacon once again!' Sir Theodore, shall I send you a wing?"

The young baronet, laughing, had just answered in the affirmative, when two very suspicious-looking men entered the room; and, to the waiter's demand of what they wanted, and intimation that they had made a mistake, one of them replied, "We knows what we are wanting: no mistake in life. That's the gentleman, Bob."

"Pray, who are you, and what do you want?" demanded Major Brandrum, in a stern tone, very well understanding the nature of the intruders' calling.

"I am an officer of the sheriff of Middlesex," replied the man, boldly, touching the shoulder of the Ravenous Crow with his finger; "and I arrest you, John Brandrum, at the suit of Simon Cox and Hezekiah Skeingelt. You must come along with me, major."

"Show me the writ," said Major Brandrum, coolly.

"Oh! here it is," replied the officer, producing a slip of parchment, which Major Brandrum examined very carefully. "It's of no use, major: you must either come or pay."

"Now, if I served you as you deserve," replied the officer, bending his brows upon the man sternly, "I should take you by the neck and back, and throw you out of the window, while my friends did the same by your follower. In the first place, you know that you are executing this writ at an illegal hour; and, in the next place, that it is not backed by the sheriff of Bedfordshire."

The bailiff winked his eye to his companion, remarking, in a loud *aside*, "They told us he was a new 'un; but he's up to snuff, Bob. I beg your pardon, sir," he continued, in a more civil tone; "but the truth is, one Colonel Lutwich sent us word that you had got the money from Mr. Wilkinson as drew the bills, and we had nothing to do but ask for it."

"Then why did you not ask for it civilly?" demanded Major Brandrum. "I have a very great mind not to pay you one farthing, and to drub you for half an hour: first, because, as you know quite well, these Cox and Skeingelt are two Jew usurers, who never gave half the money to the wretched vagabond who drew the bills; and, next, because I hate all bailiffs and men who live by the miseries of their fellow-creatures."

"Lord bless you, major! you'll get accustomed to us in time," replied the man; "that is to say, if you go on accepting bills for other people that you can't pay yourself."

The look of anger passed away from Major Brandrum's face in a moment, and he hung his head with an expression of shame and mortification. "You are quite right," he said, at length, "you are quite right; and I acted not only foolishly, but wrongly. I will never do it again."

"Ay, sir, that's what many a boy says when he is being whipped," replied the bailiff.

"True again," replied the Ravenous Crow. "You are a philosopher, my good friend; but let us have as little of your company, as possible. Draw out a receipt, and I will pay you the money."

The rest of the affair was soon settled, and at length the worthy major was permitted to go on in peace with his supper.

"Pray, Major Brandrum," inquired Sir Theodore Broughton, in his usual timid and diffident tone, when the meal was nearly done, "who is Colonel Lutwich that the man mentioned?"

"The same whom we saw at Stratton-upon-Dunsmore," replied the major, dryly, going on with his meal.

"But who is he? of what family?" persisted the young baronet.

"Oh! there is a large family of them," answered the major. "I really do not know how to describe this gentleman more particularly. I saw him once in a very crowded assembly in London, where he played for very high stakes, and won the game. I never saw him afterward till we met at Stratton; but there, after you were gone to bed, we chatted over our last meeting, and I happened to tell him of this man Wilkinson's roguery. It seems that he generously found means to force the fellow to pay me, not only the amount of the bills, but a hundred pounds I had lent him likewise, for which I am very much obliged to the good colonel. That is all I know of him."

Perhaps the young baronet might have asked further questions; but at that moment the man Hargrave put his head into the room, saying, in a quick tone, "I want to speak a word to you, Sir Theodore, if you please;" and, springing up from the table, the youth left his two companions.

Major Brandrum gazed at Reginald Lisle, and shook his head gravely.

"That lad is going wrong," he said; "we shall have to look after him. Donovan has placed a scoundrel with him, if ever I saw one; and the result will be—perhaps what he expects."

"Going wrong!" exclaimed Reginald, starting. "In Heaven's name! what makes you think so? Surely you must mistake: his very timidity and shyness must have kept him from all temptation up to the present time at least. It will be lost but too soon, doubtless; but it will prove a safeguard at present, I do hope."

"Those shy and timid lads, who seem frightened at the very first step in our evil world," replied Major Brandrum, "always make the greatest start when the first step is taken; and as to his wanting temptation, he will never want that while Master Hargrave is with him. The scoundrel brought the lad into the room where my poor friend Malcolm was sitting with me and his daughter, and I remarked how the boy's eyes kindled at her beauty while we were dismounting. Twice after that the groom's ugly face was thrust in; but if I find he is prompting his young master to insult her, I will break every bone in his body."

"He shall not insult her, if I can prevent it," said Reginald Lisle, rising. "She is very beautiful; and I too remarked how much young Broughton's admiration was excited. But he is under my charge, and I will interfere to prevent him from doing any thing disgraceful to himself or injurious to her. I will go and see. You stay where you are, my dear Crow. You are too much excited: you would peck his eyes out." And, thus saying, he left the room.

CHAPTER XII.

"Sir, you insult me," said a very sweet voice, as Reginald Lisle, after seeking through several places, was walking along one of the many intricate passages of the inn; "let me pass, I insist, or I will soon bring those who will punish you. Your conduct is base and ungenerous—you think me unprotected and friendless; and I am sure that man has directed me wrong on purpose."

"Nay, I do not insult you," said the tongue of Sir Theodore Broughton; "surely, it is no insult to tell you how lovely I think you, and to—"

"Yes, sir, it is an insult from a mere stranger," answered the girl's voice; "and I insist upon your letting me pass."

Reginald Lisle hurried forward in the darkness, which was but faintly softened by a light in a cross passage which shed some stray beams upon the opposite wall. But Catharine Malcolm's voice was raised very loud, and just when the young officer reached the end of the cross passage, which was a very long one, some other ear seemed to have caught the sound, for a door was suddenly opened between the spot which Reginald had reached and that where the young baronet stood, and a good-looking and fashionably-dressed man issued forth, exclaiming, "What is the matter? Why, my young friend, Sir Theodore, what is all this? Fy, fy! Let the young lady pass. This is not a bar-maid to hear vows in an inn passage.

Madam, this is a mistake—the gentleman is very young and romantic. Come in here with me, Sir Theodore; you will have the whole inn upon you. Sir, there is some one coming already;" and, without ceremony, he took the young baronet's arm, and hurried him into the room from which he had himself just issued forth, so suddenly, that the latter did not see the advancing figure of Reginald Lisle.

The door was instantly shut, but the young officer continued his course up the passage, drawing to the side to allow Catharine Malcolm to pass. With a trembling step the poor girl came forward, with the light she carried shining upon her beautiful countenance, and showing how pale she had become with agitation. She looked somewhat wildly round her, too, as if not well knowing where she was; and judging from the words he had overheard, as well as her look, that she had been directed wrong, Reginald bowed gravely, saying, "You have lost your way: will you allow me to show you? Nay," he added, as she drew somewhat back, with a look of alarm, "you are quite safe with me, Miss Malcolm. I am the friend and fellow-soldier of your father's friend, Major Brandrum, and I will lead you to your parent's room at once. I inquired where it is just now."

"My father is in bed, and I trust asleep, sir," replied the poor girl. "I stayed with him till he was drowsy, and then went back to the hall for something I had left there. As I returned, a man I met on the stairs told me I was going wrong, and directed me here—one passage is so like another—I really do not know—"

"Well, I will show you," said Reginald; "but just let me look at the number on this door;" and, advancing a step, he gazed up, repeating "Twenty-three." "Now, Miss Malcolm, I will attend you. The best plan will be to ring for the chamber-maid. There is a bell in that next passage. She will go with you wherever you like. I know you have met with some annoyance just now, and was coming to your assistance. The young offender shall not go unreproved; but, as he is a mere boy, you must forget it."

"It was very wrong," replied Kate Malcolm, coloring; "I did nothing to deserve such treatment, I am sure."

"I am quite certain you did not," replied the young officer; "but here is the bell;" and he rang it sharply.

The girl who appeared in answer to this summons was a saucy English chamber-maid, and when Reginald informed her that the young lady had lost her way, and directed her to accompany Miss Malcolm to her room, which was next that of her father's, and numbered a hundred and three, she tossed her head, replying, that was not her floor: she had nothing to do with the wagon folks.

"You will be so good as to do as I direct you, whether it is your floor or not," replied Reginald Lisle, sternly; "this young lady, whose father is a fellow-officer of mine, has been already misdirected and insulted by some persons in this house, and I am now going to complaim to your master of their conduct. Take care that I have not to add yours to my report. See this young lady safely to her room, and do not leave her till she is there."

The girl gazed at him for a moment with an air of surprise and sauciness which had well-nigh made him laugh; but she was overawed, and with a look of flippant submission, she said, "Very well! Come along. This way, madam."

"Good-night," said Reginald, in a kindly tone; "tell your good father when he rises that Captain Lisle and Major Brandrum will both come to see him before you start to-morrow."

The tears rose in Kate Malcolm's eyes again, and though she murmured "Good-night, sir," it was all she could utter.

As she retired with the chamber-maid, Reginald found his way down to the bar of the inn, and, on second thoughts, judging it better to say nothing of what had occurred, merely asked, in an ordinary tone, who was in number twenty-three.

"Colonel Lutwich, sir—the Hon. Colonel Lutwich," replied the landlord, consequentially; "we have a great deal of fashionable company in the house to-night. John—William—Thomas—Peter—Harry," he continued, at the top of his voice, screaming to half a dozen different waiters and getting none of them, and then putting his mouth to the end of a long tube, which ran up to the story above, he shouted something which sounded like the gurgling in the long neck of a wine bottle when it is turned upside down, and the liquid contained has some difficulty in getting out.

Reginald Lisle walked slowly away, and found Major Brandrum finishing his wine, without a certain quantity of which—in default of active exertion—he had great difficulty in believing that any day was actually ended.

"What news, Lisle?" the major asked, as the other entered. "Have you found the lad? How was he demeaning himself?"

"Not very well," replied the young officer, "but yet not so badly as perhaps he might have done. Nevertheless, I fear for the future. Let him alone, however, my dear Brandrum; I will give him a sort of lecture when he returns."

"But where is he?" demanded the major. "What is he doing now?"

"He is in your friend Colonel Lutwich's room," replied Lisle. "That gentleman came upon him in the midst of his impertinence to the poor girl, and really behaved very well, representing to him the impropriety of his conduct, and dragging him into his room, to put a stop to what was likely to become a very painful and disgraceful scene."

"The stupid young fool!" exclaimed Brandrum. "But it is all that knave Hargrave's doing; and, please Heaven, I will beat him to a jelly before I part with him. Lutwich is a fine fellow, with all his faults, and, I am sure, would not see an innocent girl ill treated."

"It is very strange," said Reginald, musing: "I feel certain I have seen his face somewhere before."

"That is very possible, my dear lad," replied Major Brandrum, dryly; "but, if you will take my advice, Lisle, you will not ask him where. He is a man of good family, good education, and many good feelings, as he has shown in my case; but he has his oddities, of which the less said the better."

A look of sudden intelligence broke over

Reginald's face. "I understand it all now," he exclaimed: "it is the same countenance, I do believe; and yet there seems a difference too, so that I certainly could not swear to him."

"I hope you never will, Lisle," said the major, gravely; "a wig makes a great difference, and Lutwich has many, as you might see when he brought the money here this evening."

"Good Heaven! was that the same man?" exclaimed Reginald; "then it would certainly be as difficult to swear to him as to bind Proteus. But be assured, on your account, I never would, even if I could."

"The first time I ever saw him," said Brandrum, "he was, as I told this silly youth, playing for a great stake—for neither more nor less, in short, than his life. It was at the Old Bailey; but he got off, for he cross-examined the principal witness against him himself; and though the man was very much inclined to swear to his person, he asked him, in a stern tone, whether the highwayman had not a very black beard. 'So he had,' exclaimed the person who had been robbed; 'I did not think of that:' upon which the lawyer for the prosecution turned crossly round to Lutwich, saying, 'How came you to know that?' 'Because the same man tried to rob me at the very same spot,' replied Lutwich, 'only I would not let him. He had a black beard, as you have, Counselor Barrett; and, in fact, was very like you indeed. I could almost fancy you were the same man.' This set the whole court laughing, and the jury acquitted the prisoner without leaving the box. This little scene did not lose him his place in society; and, though he frequents a great number of gay and dangerous places, and associates with a good number of fashionable blackguards, he has never lost his reputation of a gentleman and a man of honor, wherever his means may come from."

"Perhaps he is not the best companion for Sir Theodore," replied Lisle; but the major instantly replied, "There might be worse—there might be worse;" and the conversation taking another turn, Reginald raised the gall of his gallant friend by detailing minutely all that had occurred between the young baronet and Catharine Malcolm, as far as he knew it himself.

An hour passed by without the return of Sir Theodore; and, at the end of that time, Reginald Lisle rose, saying, "I will to bed, Brandrum, for I am tired, and my knee is somewhat painful."

"So will I," rejoined the major, taking up his heavy riding-whip; and, having procured lights, they issued forth.

Reginald Lisle mounted the stairs first, while his friend paused for a moment to gaze out into the court of the inn, where the moonlight was sleeping quietly; and the younger officer had reached the middle of the long, open gallery which led to his bed-room, when he heard the voice of the Ravenous Crow exclaiming, in violent tones, "Why did you tread upon my toe, sir?"

"I did not intend it, major," said another voice.

"You did, sir! you intend every thing that is bad: I'll teach you to behave better;" and instantly followed a sound like that which is often heard at watering-places, produced by the repeated application of a cudgel to the tough, hairy skin and hollow sides of an unfortunate donkey. The report of these echoing blows was mingled with cries and almost screams and shouts for mercy, which soon brought a dozen people and a dozen lights into the court-yard; and Reginald, looking over the wooden balustrade, beheld his friend holding Master Zachary Hargrave by the collar with a tight grasp, and laying on repeated blows of his horsewhip upon his legs, shoulders, and back, with a force and vigor which had well-nigh flayed the unfortunate patient. Seeing people hurrying up to interfere, the major ceased for a moment—without letting go his hold, however—and, turning a fierce glance round, demanded, "Does any one want the same?"

No one seemed inclined to demand the privilege; and then, swinging his victim round so as nearly to throttle him, the major raised his foot and applied it to Hargrave with a force and unction which sent him through the crowd almost to the other side of the court. Then stooping down, Brandrum raised his candlestick from the ground, and in a calm and somewhat jocular voice—for he was well satisfied with what he had done—addressed the mistress of the house, saying, "Will you allow me to light my wick at yours, madam, for candles will go out when people are engaged in interesting occupations."

Every one gazed at the other while the worthy officer obtained a light, but no one ventured to say a word; and bowing round with mock courtesy, much amused at the consternation upon all faces, Major Brandrum walked quietly away and sought his bed-room.

CHAPTER XIII.

"Pray be seated, Sir Theodore," said Colonel Lutwich, when he had drawn the young baronet into his room and shut the door. "We must let the gentlemen and ladies, whom your somewhat too warm admiration of a very pretty girl may have collected in the passage, satisfy their curiosity, and go back to their supper and their beds, before the provider of this treat for their appetite for the marvelous makes his appearance again."

He spoke somewhat sarcastically; and, perhaps, no better tone could be taken to impress an inexperienced and shy lad with a sense of the impropriety of his conduct.

Pray let it be remarked, I say only, the impropriety; for Colonel Lutwich did not pretend to go further. He might feel, and probably he did feel, for his after conversation was a proof thereof, that there was much beyond mere impropriety to be censured in the young baronet's late behavior; but there are men who systematically act wrong themselves, and yet are so conscious and internally ashamed of their own misdeeds, that they do not venture boldly to condemn the misdeeds of others, though the faults and follies they see are not exactly in the course which they follow themselves. These are persons in whom the moral sense is not yet either quite depraved by habit or naturally obtuse, for in both those cases the vices that we do not cherish are the objects of our censure or our ridicule.

Sir Theodore Broughton cast himself down into a chair overwhelmed with confusion and mortification. He knew not what to reply, or which way to look. His pride, his vanity, his desires were all disappointed or wounded. His first step in the career of passion and vicious indulgence had ended in rebuke and ridicule; and, for the time, he cursed Hargrave, and himself, and all concerned.

Colonel Lutwich saw how bitterly he was mortified, and, being in reality a very good-natured man, was sorry for him, and hastened to his relief.

"Come, come, Sir Theodore," he said, "do not let this affect you so much. In all probability the young lady is not aware of who you are, and will think little more about it. Few women are very seriously averse to be the object of admiration, though it may hurry the admirer into somewhat rash actions. I do not, indeed, know the circumstances of the case, but I think you must have made a great mistake in the character of the person you addressed, and it is very necessary to learn to discriminate. Doubtless you have no great experience in these affairs, and—"

"None, none!" replied the young baronet, encouraged by his tone. "Doubtless I have been very wrong; but it is all that fool Hargrave—my servant's doing. I never saw so beautiful a creature in my life; and he told me —Why do you laugh?"

"Not at you, my young friend," replied his companion, "but because a servant—a low-minded, vulgar fellow like that, is not fit in any way to give you counsel or information. You must learn, as I was saying, to discriminate for yourself. This young lady is very beautiful—very beautiful indeed. That was evident, even at the casual glance I obtained of her; but still that casual glance was enough to show any man of the world that she is not accessible to the sort of means you seemed to be employing. There are some forts which can not be carried by storm, Sir Theodore, against which nothing will succeed but long and incessant siege, and not even then without bringing up the heavy artillery of matrimony. Even that will not always carry the place; and that man makes the greatest mistake in the world who thinks that with the heart of all women, rank, station, wealth, even accomplishments, *must* be successful. Women have their fancies as well as men, and the most captivating youth of the whole world will often meet with a bitter mortification if he thinks that his suit will prove equally acceptable to all."

"But do you think I have offended her beyond forgiveness?" asked the young baronet, in so dolorous a tone as to make his companion laugh again.

"No, no," said Lutwich; "as a first principle, no woman is offended at being loved—so far from it, that nine out of ten will forgive any errors that proceed from that love; and you seem somewhat deep in the mire, my dear baronet, considering that you have only known the young lady—at least so I imagine—a few hours."

"That matters not," said Sir Theodore, growing bolder as he went on; "sometimes a few hours are as much as a life-time. I have never seen—I am sure I never shall see, any thing half so lovely, and were I master of my own fortune, I would give one half—nay, the whole, to call her mine."

"Nay, that is a very serious affair," replied the other. "Do you mean to say that you would marry her?"

The young baronet paused and hesitated; and Lutwich resumed more seriously, but in a sort of contemplative, disquisitional manner, which took all appearance of rebuke from his observations. "It is, indeed, a very serious affair to think of marrying a girl one has only known a few hours. It is not only fortune and comfort that we stake upon our die, but often the happiness, the success, even the honor and conduct of a whole life. Marriage blends with our being the being of another, which mingles a certain dissimilar stream with the whole current of our existence, modifying not only our fortunes and our fate, but our thoughts, our feelings, our character. The person we wed may seem to possess no influence over us, may obtain no power of controlling our actions, or directing our course in any thing; but still, whether leading or opposing, going with us or against us, there will be constantly-recurring effects produced upon our minds and our deeds by that inseparable union with another, which will affect us in all our mortal life—nay, perhaps in eternity."

He paused long between the former and the latter words, and the last were uttered with an effort, as if in despite of himself. The next moment he resumed in a less serious tone, "Doubtless you did not think of marriage, my young friend; and now let us consider for one instant what you were about. In this world there are many women who, loose and vicious by habit, are ready to sell, give, grant, favor and encouragement to all who seek them; there are some, too, who by temperament, vanity, idleness, want of character or principle, though not actually fallen, are only waiting upon inclination, opportunity, or temptation. But there are others—and, if I judge rightly, this girl is one—who in purity of heart and feeling, though not without affections, which become passions when strongly excited, devote themselves to high and holy duties in the strength of innocence and truth. I can feel that it is so," he added, sadly, "though I am not, never have been, one of them. I will not blame the man who, in the hot blood of youth, sports with the wanton or the libertine, provided he debases not his own mind to the level of theirs. I have no right to blame him, alas! I will not even venture to censure the man who meets passion with passion, and rolls the falling pebble down the bank. These things are wrong, all very wrong; but it is not for me to condemn. But what must that man think of himself, who for an idle fancy, or a short-lived passion, would deliberately seek to sully a pure heart, to withdraw from a course of noble innocence and high devotion a being whose corporeal beauty is but an image, a type, a sign of the beautiful spirit within? No, no, Sir Theodore; as Shakspeare says, 'We have willing dames enough.' We may be sinful, we may be foolish to make them our companions, or to give them even an idle hour. A man may be tempted of the evil spirit, who is ever too near us all, to fall into wrong and wickedness himself, unwilling slave to his own passions; but to tempt others who are pure and innocent is the first great attribute of the evil spirit himself."

He paused, but Sir Theodore remained silent, with his head leaning on his hands, and his eyes averted; and Lutwich gazed on him with a keen and contemplative look, as if revolving several things in his mind, and striving to draw conclusions from them. The fine, delicate features of the young baronet, his look of extreme youth, and expression of almost melancholy thoughtfulness, joined with no indications, either to the physiognomist or the phrenologist, of strength and firmness of character, might, perhaps, have some share in the conclusion at which he seemed to arrive. "Come, Sir Theodore, to speak the truth," he said, "did not some one, to use our London slang, put you up to this? I am sure your own heart would not lead you to such a step."

It is a natural impulse of feeble minds, easily led by stronger ones, to throw the blame of all miscarriages upon others. Sir Theodore Broughton, although he had alluded slightly to the participation of his servant Hargrave in the fault he had committed, had not told the whole; but, since his conduct had been placed in so unfavorable a light by a man of the world, and evidently a man of pleasure, indignation at having been misled, and disappointed too, had been gradually rising up in his breast, and he replied aloud, "Yes, you are right. It was that scoundrel of mine, Zachary Hargrave. He saw how much I was struck with her, and led me to suppose that she might very easily be won. He would fain have had me believe, too," continued the young baronet, following the common course of endeavoring to create a prejudice against the person he accused, "he would fain have had me believe, too, that you were a common highwayman, Colonel Lutwich."

His companion smiled sarcastically. "If he had said an uncommon one, he might have been more correct," Lutwich replied. "I certainly do travel the highways a good deal, as much as, or more than any other gentleman in my position of life. I could almost say with the great Earl of Peterborough, that I have seen more kings and more postillions than any man in Europe. But this is all trash and nonsense, Sir Theodore. The man must be a fool, as well as knave, to try to make you believe such idle stuff. I am glad, however, to hear that it is such a low blackguard on whom the blame of misleading you lies. I felt sure that neither Major Brandrum nor Captain Lisle would have any share in such things. This man is not a fit counselor for you, my young friend. Lisle may be too high-flown in his notions—at least so I have heard—and Brandrum is too old to be a fit companion for youth; but all I can say is, if my advice and assistance can at any time be of service to you, you may command it. Before we part, I will give you an address where you will always find or hear of me. I will write it down now, and after that we will have a bottle of our landlord's Burgundy, of which, by-the-way, he has some of the best in England, and then to bed, and sleep, and forgetfulness."

From a small but very handsome writing-desk Lutwich took out a quire of perfumed paper, and wrote down a few lines, which he handed to his young companion, who, on his part, put them in his pocket without further thought. The bell was then rung, and the landlord himself appeared, with a look of the most deferential respect.

"Bring a bottle of Burgundy, Master Spinner," said Colonel Lutwich; "a bottle of that same wine which Lord St. Jermyn and I had here last Saturday twelvemonth."

"Lord, colonel, how well your honor recollects things!" said the landlord, fawning.

"I shall recollect the taste of the wine, too, Master Spinner," replied the other; "so, be sure that it is the same; and, do you hear? uncork it below, and see that it be not ropy."

"Certainly, sir, certainly," replied the landlord; and in five or ten minutes the wine was brought, and proved worthy of its reputation. However, whether it was that Sir Theodore had drunk more than ordinary at supper, or that his brain was in an excitable state from all that had lately passed, his eyes soon began to assume a vacant and unsteady look, and his utterance to become less clear, though more voluble. Still, however, he continued to sip slowly, glass after glass, though, to do Colonel Lutwich no more than justice, he did not press the bottle upon him, notwithstanding the custom of the times. Those were days of deep drinking, when no man was considered worthy of society who did not occasionally, if not frequently, make himself unfit for it. But still the young baronet's companion was unwilling to lead him to expose himself more on the same night than he had done already. By the time the bottle was finished, the elasticity had strangely gone out of Sir Theodore's knees, and he at length rose, saying, "I must go, colonel, and hunt out Lisle and the major. They won't know what has become of me;" but, as he spoke, the sort of oscillating motion of his body indicated sufficiently that he was in no very proper condition for hunting out any one.

"You had better go to bed, Sir Theodore," replied his companion; but, knowing well that there is not so great an offense to a drunken man as to perceive his condition, he added, "you and Lisle might quarrel; for, though you do not seem to be aware of it, he was the person who was hurrying to the young lady's rescue just now."

"I do not care," replied the young man; "he has no right to meddle with me, and I'll go and tell him so."

"No, no, let him sleep over it," said the other, "and you do the same. Come, I will show you the way, for I dare say you do not know whereabout you are. I am acquainted with all the turnings and windings of the place from times of old;" and, having ascertained the number of the young baronet's room, and obtained a light, he good-humoredly conducted him thither, and persuaded him to go to bed at once.

This accomplished, Lutwich returned to his own chamber, and sat down to meditate. "A pretty fellow I am," he thought, "to lecture others upon their conduct! But still, if he knew all, he might well think his behavior bad enough, when I condemn it. And Master Hargrave, too, I must settle accounts with him. Where can he have seen me? He must be silenced one way or another;" and, putting his hand in his pocket, he drew out a very beautifully-fashioned pistol, mounted with silver, examined the priming, and thrust the ramrod down once or twice into the barrel.

"Now for Master Hargrave," he said aloud, after about half an hour's further meditation, and rang the bell.

"Send up a man named Hargrave to me, Sir Theodore Broughton's servant," were his words to the waiter who appeared.

"Why, your honor, he is hardly in a condition to come yet," replied the waiter. "He has had as good a horsewhipping as e'er I see a fellow in my life, and so he is just now unstomaching himself to the people in the wagon-room, over a glass of brandy punch, upon free grace and predestination."

"Then he's just in the fit state of mind. Send him up," said Colonel Lutwich. "Who horsewhipped him?"

"Why, one Major Brandrum, they say, sir," answered the other; "but I hope you will not say I told you."

"Shall I say the house-bell will not ring when any one pulls the handle?" demanded Lutwich. "See that the man comes up directly, for I am going to bed."

Ten minutes elapsed—nay, perhaps a quarter of an hour—for it required some persuasion to induce Zachary Hargrave to trust himself within reach of any thing like an arm accustomed to wield a horsewhip; but the waiter assured him that the colonel was all honey and water, and that Sir Theodore had just left him, so that there was nothing to fear; and, in the end, the worthy head groom, or groom and valet, as he now termed himself, was coaxed into mounting the stairs, and entering No. 23, after knocking respectfully. After having been told to come in, he presented himself in the glare of two wax candles, but took care to keep the means of egress close behind him, standing with his hat in one hand, while he smoothed down the short flat hair on the top of his head with the other.

Without speaking a word, Colonel Lutwich eyed him from head to foot with a thoughtful look which is peculiarly unpleasant and discourteous in the eyes of small and rascally men. In the first place, they feel, from the very manner of the glance, that they are looked upon merely as things—a very disagreeable mode or state of objectiveness; and, in the next place, they are always more or less afraid of having something or other discovered under such a scrutiny.

"So your name is Hargrave?" said Lutwich, neither very warmly nor very coldly, but with the most indifferent tone in the world; "and you are Sir Theodore Broughton's servant? Look here! I have something I wish you to see."

The man took a couple of steps forward toward the table, not perceiving what it was the gentleman had in his hand, when, with a rapid movement, Lutwich placed himself between him and the door, which had been left partly open, closed it, and turned the key.

"Now march on, Master Zachary Hargrave!" he said, in a stern tone. "There—place yourself there; and neither stir hand nor foot, as you value your life!" At the same time, he displayed the very elegant little pistol which he had taken from his pocket a few minutes before, and coolly seated himself in such a position as to command both the door and the bell.

"Now answer me a few questions, Master Hargrave," he continued, in a contemptuous tone; "I find you have done two things, of which you must give me some account. In the first place, you have been leading your young master into mischief. What made you fix upon the young lady he was speaking to an hour or two ago in the passage, as the object of the honorable attentions you suggested?"

"Lord, sir! I did not know that you had any thing to do with her," replied the man.

"No evasion!" rejoined Lutwich, frowning. "What made you fix upon her, I say?"

"Because she was very poor, I heard, and her father was too sick to meddle," he replied.

"Scoundrel!" said Lutwich; "who set you on to such tricks?"

"No one, sir—not exactly," replied Hargrave, with his knees shaking; "the captain—that is, Captain Donovan, did say he did not care about Sir Theodore having a few escapades, and so I thought that was a hint to—to—"

"To pander," added Lutwich, finishing the sentence for him; "well, perhaps it was. I shall remember. Now for the second question. I find that you were wise enough to tell Sir Theodore that I was merely a highwayman. Now what induced you to venture on such an assertion? Out with it, for depend upon it you do not quit this room alive till you have spoken."

"No, sir, no; I did not say so, indeed," whimpered the man; "I only said the horse your servant sold to Captain Lisle was an impudent beast, and when my master asked me why I called him so, I said, because it was a proverb—as impudent 'as a highwayman's horse.'"

Colonel Lutwich laughed aloud; but the instant after, his fine and almost delicate features assumed a look which no one who saw them in their milder expression could have conceived them capable of putting on. Indeed, it was a peculiarity often noticed in that remarkable man, that his face, though the lines were all soft, and almost feminine, could, according to his will, display every kind of different expression, and, indeed, undergo so complete a change, that, without even an alteration of dress, he could deceive any one not well acquainted with him as to his identity. On the present occasion, after that gay and almost joyous laugh, the broad, clear brow became suddenly furrowed by deep wrinkles; a perpendicular line, in which one could have laid a finger, appeared between the eyebrows, which were drawn down together, and depressed over the eyes; the nostrils expanded wide; the corners of the mouth were drawn down; the muscles of the cheeks seemed to stand out, as if working under strong passion; and the countenance, so lately all radiant and soft, was changed to that of a menacing demon.

"Mark me, Zachary Hargrave!" he said, in a low, stern tone, speaking through his brilliant white teeth, "you see this pistol. In it there is a single ball. I will keep that ball for you; and if ever, in the whole course of your life, you venture to breathe such a word as that which you uttered to your master—be it to man, woman, or child—within twenty-four hours after, that bullet shall lie in the middle of your brains. You understand me. You may know me, or you may not; but those who do know me are sufficiently aware that no one ever offended me and lived. You are warned—Begone!"

The man, who, like all of his kind, was an infinite coward, made his way to the door with knees knocking together, and so great was his terror, that for nearly a minute he could not contrive to turn the key the right way in the lock.

As soon as he was gone, Lutwich laid the pistol on the table, and, casting himself back in his chair, gave way to thought. Once more the expression of his countenance changed; the fierce and vengeful look passed away; a cloud of deep—may I say tender—melancholy spread over his face. At the end of about half an hour he retired to bed, and, notwithstanding all that had passed, slept profoundly for some hours.

At length he seemed oppressed in his slumber—turned, and tossed, and breathed with difficulty; then murmured a few words, "Why, Hal, you have dropped the candle into the chest. Don't you see the flame? the smoke—the smoke?" and, suddenly starting up, he gazed round him, exclaiming, "By Heaven, it is no dream! The room is full of smoke! Some one has set the inn on fire!"

CHAPTER XIV.

"There, that's your room, miss," said the chamber-maid, pointing to a door on the second story of the wing of the hotel appropriated to inferior travelers; "I am sure you need not have missed it, for it is as plain as a pike-staff, just next to the old gentleman's."

"I should not have missed it," answered Kate Malcolm, "if a person I met below had not misled me by telling me I had taken the wrong stairs."

"Pooh, pooh!" said the chamber-maid, with a saucy air; "young ladies should not be so easily misled;" and away she whisked.

Kate Malcolm entered the poor chamber assigned to her, which had no advantage on earth, either in furniture or situation, except that it possessed a door at the side, and that door communicated with her father's room. She approached it, and listened. All was still within; and then she sat down by the little oaken table, and wept. The grief, smothered all the day from her father's eyes, because they were too kind; from the world's, because they were too cold, broke forth in the solitude of her own chamber, and her evening hymn was tears.

But she was weary as well as sorrowful; she had gone through much labor and fatigue during the day—fatigue of mind as well as body—and she knew that the same was to recommence very early on the day that followed. So, after having let the drops roll down her fair cheeks for a few moments, to clear away the sense of indignity, and sorrow, and hopelessness from the brain, she rose, wiped her eyes, went through the simple task of her nightly toilet, and, only partly undressing, lest her father should call, and tying up the money which Major Brandrum had so kindly bestowed in a corner of her handkerchief, she lay down to rest. She would not let her mind dwell upon miseries, and slept.

In the mean time, the chamber-maid went tripping along the passage, and pushed open a door which communicated with the other parts of the house. As she did so, she met the head waiter, with a decanter half emptied in one hand, and a candle in the other, and they stopped in that snug corner to talk. I will not trouble myself or the reader with their conversation. Suffice it that it was sufficient to show that a very intimate friendship existed between the two parties, for the waiter liberally offered the decanter to the lips of the fair, declaring it of the very best vintage in the cellar; and she, after having quaffed an inconvenient draught, snuffed the waiter's candle for him with the scissors which hung by her side, and threw the charred wick upon the ground. A step and a loud call from the landlord's own voice caused them to part suddenly, and the swing door banged to after Betty, while John took another way down.

I will pause behind that door, however, for a moment; and, as no one passed it for many hours after, I shall not be disturbed while watching a small spot upon the floor, just on the left hand, within six inches of the skirting-board. It was just where the sides of two of the planks ought to have met; but the house was old, and they had shrunk away from each other, leaving a crevice between of half a finger's breadth in width. At first, after the chamber-maid and waiter had separated and departed, nothing at all was to be seen, though a light from the court-yard found its way through the windows—a faint, feeble, lantern light indeed it was, for gas was not dreamed of. Steam, too, was in its infancy; and nobody was aware that one day we should gain the brightest light and the swiftest motion from the vapors which were blown up our chimneys or hissed out of our tea-kettles.

Presently the feeble ray gleamed up upon something, curling gracefully and slowly upward from that spot, like the spirit of the Arabian tale out of his copper vessel. It seemed too small in volume, indeed, ever to grow into a giant; but it did so, nevertheless, before it was done. For the time, it was only a pale, bluish, spiral column, writhing itself up into the rays that came through the windows, and only growing visible when it reached their light. Then it sank away again, and was not seen for some minutes; and then rose somewhat thicker, while a faint smell of charred wood was perceptible near the spot.

Nobody took any notice, however, for the odor penetrated no further, and the light, curling smoke was not perceived. Every body was very busy, too, till every body went to bed, and then chance conducted them all the other way. The wagoners and their parties had all gone to rest before the people appointed to attend upon them took their road to their several dormitories by the court-yard and the stable; the guests from the better part of the house had no business in that passage, and their servants found their way to their rooms by the open galleries.

Before one o'clock, all was quiet in the inn. At half past two, a stage-coach stopped on its road to London, and the coachman, guard, and passengers supped there. A solitary, sleepy-headed youth was usually left by the kitchen fire, to attend upon the passing guests on their arrival; and at about a quarter past two, the horse-keeper woke him, on his way to open the great gates. The youth walked along a passage which led just under the swing door I have mentioned, and, as he went out to the hall, where the coach supper was laid, he left an outer door open behind him, through which the night wind swept cold. There was, by this time, a good deal of smoke in the upper passage; but it is wonderful how it increased after that door was opened. Nevertheless, not a speck of fire was visible; and the coach arrived, the passengers supped, the fresh horses were put to, and on it went, leaving the weary hostler and sleepy waiter to seek their mews, without remarking either smell or smoke.

Half an hour elapsed, which brought the night to half past three, and then a faint, red, ill-defined glow might be seen upon the flooring, in extent not much bigger than a man's hand, and the smoke became thick, the smell overpowering toward the end of that passage. But there was no one sleeping in the rooms adjacent, and the wind blew the other way toward the swing door, underneath which, however, the smothering vapor was now creeping fast. The red patch extended slowly—more slowly and quietly than can be conceived; and about four o'clock, a faint, glimmering flash rose through the dense cloud, and passed away; but the moment after a red line began to creep along the skirting-board, at first very slowly, then more quickly, but was stopped by the frame-work of a door leading to an empty room. It crept round the molding, spotting it with patches of fire; and a crackling sound was heard. Another blaze then broke through the smoke, and, like one of the sudden illuminations which succeed a display of artificial fire-works, the whole wainscot, and part of the floor, displayed lines of flame. A roaring sound might now be heard; but every one was sound asleep, and the progress of the fire in the passage was more tardy than might have been supposed. The smoke seemed to choke it; for there was a door at either end, and the supply of air was not sufficient to hurry it on rapidly. At length, however, the swing door was burned completely through, about half past four; and then the advance of the conflagration was rapid indeed.

Three minutes after, a door was suddenly thrown open, and Colonel Lutwich rushed out, shouting loudly, "Fire! Fire!" while he made his way to a large bell-rope which he had seen hanging at the head of the stairs. The next instant the alarum was sounded loud and rapidly, and, careless of his own safety, Lutwich hurried along, knocking violently at different doors, and still shouting "Fire!"

First one appeared, and then another; the cry was taken up by fresh voices, men and women, in every state of dress and undress, appeared in the court-yard, without any one knowing how—nay, not even themselves. All the pranks of terror and confusion of mind were played which such scenes usually display. Some were overpowered with fear, and did nothing; some were more actively terrified, and did all the most absurd things in the world. A waiter was seen throwing pump water at the windows out of a slop-basin; a woman-servant was running back into the flames to fetch her garters; the landlord sat himself down on the shafts of a wagon, saying, "Well, there goes every thing I have in the world;" and the landlady ordered the bar-maid to throw the best china out of the window, to save it from being cracked with the heat.

There were two or three, however, who did not lose their presence of mind at all, and several more who retained sufficient of that very useful commodity to do what the others told them. Among the first were a middle-aged man, of very distinguished appearance and a somewhat jovial countenance, Colonel Lutwich, Major Brandrum, and Reginald Lisle. The first at once ordered the great gates to be opened, and the court to be cleared of the women; and he himself led a middle-aged lady, and a younger one who had come down with him, into the street, but returned immediately. At the moment of his reappearance, Lutwich was bringing forth from the stables, aided by two or three men, a long ladder; and Major Brandrum was exclaiming, "They will be too late!"

No sooner were the words spoken, than, darting through a little knot of stupefied servants, the major rushed up to a door on the left, and disappeared. The open gallery on that side of the house was on fire at both ends; but the instant after, Brandrum was seen at the angle, hurrying forward. He paused one instant as the fire met him. It needed a heart of steel, but he had one. Without setting foot on the burning beams, he sprang across, and darted down a passage near that in which the fire had first begun. At the same moment Reginald caught hold of the ladder which Colonel Lutwich was bringing forward, and aided to raise it. They seemed to understand each other without a word, for not one was spoken; but they joined their efforts to rear it and place it against the gallery; and while the end was still vibrating, Lisle was upon it, and half way up.

"Gallantly done!" cried the middle-aged gentleman I have mentioned; "but there may be more to be saved than one. Some of you men come with me! Stevens, follow quick! Let us ascertain, as far as possible, that all the rooms are clear before the fire reaches the main body of the building."

"Yes, Sir Charles, I'm coming!" cried a man in livery breeches, but without any coat.

But at that moment a sight was seen which made his master and himself both pause. Major Brandrum appeared at the end of the passage, bearing a young girl in his arms, only half clad, and hurried toward the ladder. Reginald was nearly at the top, and with a spring he reached it, and leaped over into the gallery. The major paused for an instant to say something; but his young comrade exclaimed, "Down, down, Brandrum! I will see to him," and instantly disappeared.

Major Brandrum strode on, reached the top of the ladder in safety, and descended cautiously, holding the girl in his long arms as one would hold an infant. It was somewhat perilous, that descent, for he could not relax his hold of the gentle burden he bore to steady his steps with his hand; and the people below watched him with breathless anxiety. But the habit of every kind of exercise gave him great advantages; and as he came near the bottom, Lutwich and another approached on either side to support him.

"All safe, all safe!" said the old officer, with a smile of conscious skill and power; and, taking the last three or four rounds more rapidly, he reached the court, and set down his fair burden on her feet.

Kate Malcolm's eyes had been closed; but now she opened them, and gazed with a terrified and bewildered look around. One glance was given to the burning building, and then her eyes ran over every face in the court. The next instant she put her hands to her head with an expression almost of distraction on her face, and exclaiming, "My father! my father!" rushed toward the ladder. Lutwich, however, caught her arm ere she could ascend, and stopped her, exclaiming, "Captain Lisle has gone for him! Stay, I will go too. Major, take care of her: do not let her follow!" Thus saying, he began the ascent, and soon reached the gallery.

"Oh, let me go!" cried the girl; "he will come with me—perhaps they will not find him."

"Yes, yes they will," replied Major Brandrum, detaining her kindly. "Lisle knows it is the next room to yours. There, there, don't you see they are bringing him in their arms? Now be calm, my dear child; turn away your head while they descend."

But Kate could not refrain; and, though motionless as a statue, she continued, with eager eyes and parted lips, to gaze, while—Lutwich supporting the feet and Reginald the shoulders of her father—they bore him to the top of the ladder; then, one above and the other below, carried him safely down.

Springing forward, Kate cast her arms round the sick man's neck, and wept. Captain Malcolm turned a faint glance upon her, and murmured, with a voice broken by gasps for breath, "Thank God! she is safe! Oh, my child! a dying father's blessing be upon you!"

"Come, cheer up, Malcolm, cheer up!" cried Major Brandrum; "all will go well. Let us carry him to some place of shelter," he added, in a whisper, to Reginald; "he is going, poor fellow! In Heaven's name, where is Sir Theodore? See for him—see for him. I will attend to Malcolm."

"He is safe," said Colonel Lutwich. "I saw him cross the end of the gallery just now, and reach the top of the stone stairs. His blackguard, Hargrave, was with him."

Placing the sick officer on one of the shutters of the hall, Major Brandrum, Lisle, Lutwich, and one of the men, carried him across to the house of an apothecary on the opposite side of the street, where a number of the women had already taken refuge; and, in the mean time, the middle-aged gentleman whom I have mentioned mounted the stairs, and searched through every room he could find, often venturing further into the fire than was safe or prudent. The servant to whom he had spoken in the court, and several other men, accompanied him, and after insuring, as far as possible, that no living being was left in any of the rooms, he and the rest applied themselves to save some of the property that was most easily carried.

As may be supposed, the scene was one of terrible confusion: many people had rushed in from the town; all the hangers-on of the inn, who were not stupefied by personal fear, busied themselves either with saving or appropriating; a fire-engine and manifold buckets were procured at length; and though the flames could not be stopped, their progress was delayed. With the greatest possible difficulty, a number of valuable horses were forced out of the stables at the moment the fire reached that part of the building. A pile of trunks, portmanteaus, and saddle-bags was raised up in the middle of the road, and a man stationed, with a pistol in his hand, to guard them from the over-fondness of those who might be partial to their neighbors' goods and chattels. The landlord was roused to some exertion, and the landlady made aware that porcelain will break when thrown out of a window; and, in the end, a good deal of property was collected and placed in safety.

Much was lost, much was stolen, much was consumed indeed; and still the obstinate element ran from room to room, and passage to passage, on both sides of the spot where it first broke out. The gallery on the left soon fell; the large wooden columns caught fire; and though, as I have before shown, the court was very wide and extensive, the heat and smoke within its area became intolerable. The fire-engine, badly constructed and worked by ignorant men, was of very little service, and it was soon evident that nothing could be hoped beyond the preservation of the adjacent buildings. To that object all attention was at length turned; and though some other houses suffered a little, yet the conflagration may be said to have been confined to that in which it first broke out.

Gradually every one had been driven out of the court, and at a little distance many small knots of men and women appeared watching the progress of the flames which they despaired of suppressing. The red light glared through the windows; a dense cloud of smoke rose high into the air; the clouds above were tinged with the reflection of the fire, which burned in the court as in a vast furnace; and gradually the lambent flames burst forth from the casements, catching the frames, and licking the thick walls. At length the roof of the main building fell in with a tremendous crash. It seemed for an instant to deaden the conflagration, and nothing was seen but a thick mass of heavy smoke; the moment after the fire regained its ascendency, and a tall column of flame rose like a burning steeple into the sky. The large board before the house, with its long inscription, caught the fire, and was soon in a blaze; and the iron crane on which swung the great sign became red hot. The wood-work below took light, and the broad sheet of painted canvas, bearing the black bull as large as life on both sides, crackled, shriveled, burst into a flame, and fell thundering into the road, scattering a group of urchins who had collected somewhat too near.

"There goes the black bully," cried one boy aloud, with all the delight that young and unchastised human nature takes in mischief of any kind.

"There goes the black bull, indeed!" said the melancholy landlord, in a very different tone; "and there will never be another Black Bull here as long as Dunstable is Dunstable."

Whether his vaticination was wrong or right, I leave the reader who has traveled that way to decide; and I only need add, that if there has been another inn of the same name in Dunstable since, or if there be one there now, it certainly is not the same Black Bull which I have described in the tenth chapter of this true history; for, ere the light of morning had shone for more than one hour upon the sad though busy scene presented by the streets of the little town, nothing remained of that building but a part of the four external walls, with the blackened and vacant windows gaping like the mouths of dead men upon a field of battle. It was for this reason, and inasmuch as nothing in this book is written without a reason, that I averred no one could remember the Black Bull inn which I was describing, unless he had lived, and memory had lived with him, some seventy-two years; and now I will turn to show what were the consequences of the events of that night to the various characters, for whom, I trust, I have created some degree of interest.

CHAPTER XV.

I HAVE mentioned a middle-aged gentleman, of distinguished appearance, who busied himself in searching for any persons who might have been left in the many bed-rooms of the inn, in that state of slumber which was likely to precede one still more profound, unless some means were taken to rouse them. He did much, also, to rescue a considerable part, at least, of the travelers' baggage from the flames, and by his wise precautions prevented more plunder than actually took place. When that was done, however, and he saw that the efforts of the people were directed aright to stop the progress of the fire toward other houses, he quietly turned upon his heel and approached the shop of the apothecary, to whose house he had previously conveyed two ladies, one of his own age and the other younger.

There be people who enjoy the sight of big bonfires, whoever may suffer by them—who find pleasure in that sort of excitement which is found in any grand or unusual act of destruction, just as some are fond of seeing a fellow-creature hanged, or as I myself am fond of watching a thunder-storm. I blame them not, for in them, probably, the sense of the sublime is superior to that of the benevolent. I suppose that is the only method of accounting for such tastes; and yet, what can be accounted for in that most unaccountable being—man? One of the most truly benevolent persons that I ever knew—for he was benevolent in small things as well as great—could never hear of an execution or a prize-fight, which is still worse, *without going to see it.* Yet he would admit the horror and the cruelty of the thing, and, like a wise man, never attempted to account for his own conduct on such occasions, merely saying that he acted upon an impulse which he could not resist.

The middle-aged gentleman whom I have mentioned was not fond of big bonfires of any kind; and as soon as he had done what he could to render service, he turned his back gladly on a spectacle that was painful to him, and entered the shop, which consisted of two separate rooms. In the first he found no one; for some of those who had sought refuge there had been taken up stairs, and some had gone to other places of shelter. In the back shop, however, which was called the surgery, he heard voices, and as the glass-door was ajar, he pushed it open and went in.

The pale morning light was streaming in from a window at the back, upon a group of eight persons disposed close together in the midst of the little chamber. A chair stood in the center, supporting the emaciated form of poor Captain Malcolm, with his face as pale as marble, and his head leaning back upon the arm of an elderly woman of the middle class. At his feet kneeled his daughter, with her eyes fixed earnestly, immovably upon his countenance, her head bent forward in her eagerness, and her hands upon his knees. On one side of the poor officer stood Major Brandrum, holding his hand; and on the other was the apothecary, supporting his shoulders with one arm, while he applied a bottle of hartshorn to his nostrils. By the side of Kate was Reginald Lisle, with his hand stretched out toward her shoulder, as if about to draw her gently away; and on the other was Lutwich, gazing down at her with that expression of tender pity which his changeful countenance could sometimes assume; and behind the apothecary stood his assistant, with a glass in his hand, the contents of which he stirred diligently from time to time.

"It's of no use," said the master of the house, turning his head toward the man: "you can't put it down. He could not swallow it."

Kate gave him a look of terror and inquiry. "Ah, my poor young lady," he said, with some feeling, "it is what we must all come to—you had better take her away up stairs. My wife is there with the ladies."

"Oh no, no, no!" cried Kate, starting up, and casting herself upon her father's bosom. "Not while there is life! not while there is life!" and she burst into a violent passion of tears.

Her sudden movement seemed to rouse the dying man from the cold lethargic doze into which he had fallen. He opened his eyes, and there was light in them: they fixed upon her for a moment with a look of intense love, then wandered round to Major Brandrum. He pressed his old comrade's hand with the feeble, clammy fingers of the dying, and the good old officer put his left upon the poor girl's head, saying, in a loud tone, as if he thought the ear he addressed must have become dull, "Henceforth, Malcolm, she is my child."

The words were hardly uttered when the poor father swayed for a moment on his chair, and then, without a sigh, his head fell forward on his daughter's neck. He was a corpse.

Lutwich turned round to one who had entered the room the moment after the gentleman I have mentioned, and said, in a whisper, laying his hand upon the arm of Sir Theodore Broughton, "Look there! You would have wronged her!"

His face was very stern; but the eyes of the young baronet were fixed upon the weeping child and the dead father, and he saw nothing else.

Reginald Lisle stooped down, and gently, tenderly, raised poor Kate Malcolm; and she, unconscious of what she did, suffered him to support her in his arms, and, turning her head, pressed her streaming eyes and forehead on his shoulder.

"Stay a moment," said the gentleman who had entered just before Sir Theodore, addressing Major Brandrum, who was advancing toward the child he had just adopted; "I will bring Lady Chevenix to comfort her. Let this poor girl be with her for a short time. She shall be safely restored to you shortly."

"Would to God she were with her altogether!" said Major Brandrum, in his frank way. "To be solely under the care of an old soldier, without a shred of a petticoat among any of his kith or kin, is both dangerous and disagreeable; and not the less disagreeable because it is dangerous, nor the less dangerous because it is disagreeable.

But, almost before this speech had commenced, Sir Charles Chevenix had turned away. He paused an instant, indeed, by Reginald Lisle, holding out his hand frankly, and saying, "Captain Lisle, I am glad to see you, and to see you, as ever, acting the part of a fine English soldier. I must find you out in London; for, gadsooks! I shall not have time to thank you half enough now for some late passages. I will bring a lady who knows how to be kind to the orphan, and we will do our best to console her."

Thus saying, he quitted the room, and returned in a few moments with Lady Chevenix, who gazed round inquiringly, turned a little pale as her eyes fell upon the dead body of poor Captain Malcolm, passed Reginald with a cold bow of recognition, and then, with her face assuming a more kindly and beaming expression, advanced to the chair in which Kate was now seated.

"Come with me, my poor child!" she said, in a low and gentle tone. "You are among friends, who, though new ones, will prove good ones. This is the hand of God, my child, and you must bow before it."

"His hand has pressed me sore," murmured Kate; "but His will be done!" and, rising slowly, she took a step toward the door—paused—gazed round at the figure of her parent, as he sat with the head now raised and leaning against one of the wings of the arm-chair; and then a shudder passed over her. The next moment, however, she walked rapidly toward him, knelt, and pressed her lips on his cold hand. She murmured a few words too, but nobody heard their import; and then, rising, she followed Lady Chevenix out of the room.

Hardly had they passed the threshold, when a servant came in from the street, exclaiming, "Sir Charles, your honor had better come and see to the things, for every body is insisting upon helping themselves to their own; and the constable says they can not lie there, for the coach from town will be down in a minute or two. They've smashed one of the windows of the carriage, too, in getting it out of the yard. I am sure it was Mildew, the coachman's fault, for he was in such a fright he did not know what he was doing. But the pokemantles is the things just now; for I shouldn't wonder an' half of them were gone before you can get there."

This elegant oration was powerfully seconded by a loud and authoritative voice exclaiming in the road, apparently with much ire, "Sir Charles this, and Sir Charles that, and Sir Theodore the other! I don't care a button for Sir Anything Anybody. I say the things sha'n't be there. It's bad enough to have a house burned down in the place, not to say the road blocked up with lumber."

Sir Charles Chevenix instantly issued forth, followed by all the rest of the party; and—as so frequently happens on this earth—a scene of wordly business and scramble succeeded quick upon the dark footsteps of death and sorrow. Each man sought his own amid the pile of infinitely varied articles which had been collected in the road, at a little distance from the inn, and Master Zachary Hargrave was well-nigh engaged in personal conflict with a smart-looking groom, who acknowledged the sway of Colonel Lutwich, in regard to a trunk-mail, which, after all, turned out to be the property of Sir Charles Chevenix.

The latter gentleman, casting off all thought of the darker things just past, looked on, amused at the scene of confusion that was going on, pointed out from time to time some article of his own, exclaiming, in a jocular tone, "That saddle-bag is mine, if any gentleman has a mind to it. When you have carried off that portmanteau, my good friend, will you tell me where you put it, for I shall want a pair of breeches out of it to-night? You will find the razors in that case, excellent sir; they were made expressly for my stiff beard, by Webb. Look at that man, Lisle; would you not swear that roquelaure was his own by his affection for it? Sir, I will thank you for my cloak; I find it cold after the cooking I have had in that great oven. In the name of Heaven, Mildew, get the horses to the coach, if they be in life, for if I do not make haste away, some one will steal myself."

"Please your honor, Sir Charles, I have neither coat nor hat," answered the man.

"Then drive in your waistcoat and wig," replied his master. "Now, Lisle, where shall I find you in London? We will deliver your pretty little sorrowful friend safely there, when Lady Chevenix has comforted her a little; but, by my honor! she shall pass a day or two with us at my old friend Jarvis's, where we are now going; and as he has as kind a heart as ever beat in an old bachelor's bosom, I should not wonder if he fell in love with her, and tried to cut you out."

"You are mistaken entirely, Sir Charles,"

replied Lisle, who was not at all willing to acquire the reputation of a lover of Kate Malcolm's. "I have no feeling toward the young lady but those of compassion for undeserved sorrow."

"Pooh, pooh!" replied the baronet; "no mistake at all. But where shall we bring her? Nay, the best way is, come and fetch her. You will find us in Grosvenor Square. Who is that young fellow looking so black?" he continued, in a familiar whisper; but, before Reginald could explain that it was Sir Theodore Broughton, Major Brandrum joined in the conversation, saying, "Sir Charles Chevenix, you are a rattle. So am I; but we always, or at least often, jump at conclusions which are wrong. Miss Malcolm falls to my lot to protect as a father, so soon as she quits the care of Lady Chevenix. I am an old comrade of her dead parent's, have promised him to be a second father to her, and God willing, will be so. I will have the honor of waiting upon you in Grosvenor Square as soon as I have ascertained where I can place the dear child in honor and security."

Sir Charles took his hand and shook it warmly, saying, "I shall be delighted to see you, and Lisle too. I was only joking, as you may suppose. It is a sad subject to joke upon, indeed; but the habit is bad and inveterate. When this lad here hit me in the hip, I made the surgeon laugh who was probing the wound by asking him if I should ever be able to dance the *minuet de la cour* again. Well, I shall expect you; and, in the mean time, rest satisfied that Lady Chevenix, who is the best of women, will do all for your young protégée that motherly kindness can do. I will not ask you up to the room where the ladies are, for, upon my life! I believe my wife has got no stays, and my daughter got no stockings."

"Who does this pack belong to?" cried a voice near. "Captain Malcolm, 19th regiment. Where is Captain Malcolm?"

"In heaven," answered Major Brandrum, gravely; "but whatever part of his property is found belongs to his daughter, at present under the charge of Sir Charles Chevenix."

"Bring it in here, Stevens," cried the baronet; "and do help that fool Mildew, and the greater fool Thomas, to put the horses to. We shall never reach our journey's end before dinner-time. Good-by for the present, gentlemen both. I trust our next merry meeting may not have so warm a commencement, and, pray Heaven! not such a sad conclusion as this has had."

He was turning away toward the house of the apothecary, when, suddenly appearing to have forgotten something, he came back—nearly run over on the way by two splendid horses brought up by Lutwich's servant—and said, addressing Major Brandrum, in a highly courteous and graceful tone, "There is one thing escaped my memory, sir. When I see a gentleman, especially when he belongs to the same profession as myself, whose conduct and demeanor does honor to his heart, his head, his position, and our common nature, I am always anxious to write his name on my remembrance, to be kept among the few precious recollections of a life. Of yours I am still ignorant. Curiosity might not be a good excuse for asking. I trust that esteem and respect may prove a better apology."

"None is necessary, Sir Charles," replied the old officer, in the same tone; "in war we hold it only a fair battle when the parties are tolerably equal. I have an advantage over you. All the world knows who and what Sir Charles Chevenix is, and I know you to be Sir Charles Chevenix. It is but fair that you should be aware of who I am, though perhaps you may be little the wiser when I tell you that I am called, in one hemisphere, 'The Ravenous Crow,' and in the other—"

"Major Brandrum," cried the baronet; "that is title to respect enough."

CHAPTER XVI.

A VERY celebrated author, who lived near the times of which I write, has given the following warning to his reader, which is a hint required every day by readers in the present age as well as in his. "First, then," says Henry Fielding, Esq., in the tenth book of his most celebrated work, "we warn thee not too hastily to condemn any of the incidents in this our history as unimportant and foreign to our main design, because thou dost not immediately conceive in what manner such incident may conduce to that design." He then goes on to speak of his own work in terms of commendation, and of the critics in terms of disparagement, which no human being who has not the courage of an old Roman, or the fortitude of a martyr, would venture to do in Anno Domini 1848. Heaven have mercy upon the poor man who would even dream of such a thing! Not a baker's cur with a tin kettle tied to his tail would be so hooted, pelted, kicked, beaten, and pursued as he would be.

The Hebrew sage declared there was nothing new under the sun; but since his days, and even since the days of the English sage whom I have mentioned, a new thing has arisen, and that a mighty and ever-increasing power.

The daily and weekly press, the mightiest engine for good or evil that ever was invented by the prolific brain of man, possesses—neither unreasonably nor unjustly do I mean to say—an amount of power which any individual might as well attempt to contend with as an infant to stop a locomotive with a straw. A power, I say, has risen up—an absolute power—over which there is no control, but in which there is no unity: a pure democracy of mind, the only counteracting influence is within itself, for it has all the vices and the virtues of a democracy. Let those who have elected themselves to authority, alone—let them write their articles, silly or wise, as senators and deputies make their speeches, foolish or profound, as the case may be, and you have at least a chance that the variety of opinions will elicit truth and award justice in the end—unless some president puts his veto against it. But if you attack the institution, refuse the judgment, impugn the motives, or deny the authority, you commit high treason at once, and will be executed accordingly. All will be against you, for you assail that which it is the interest of all to uphold.

I will therefore abstain from following Fielding any further. I will not, with him, call the critics reptiles, for there are some who soar as well as some who creep; but, pursuing the even tenor of my way, will only humbly and with bated breath beseech the reader, and especially the critic, to believe that there is an object in every page I write, that there is a link of connection between one incident and another, and that, if he has not perceived it when he gets to the end of the book, he had better turn back again, for he may depend upon it he has skipped it.

Now skipping, which is undoubtedly a mortal sin in a reader, is not only a mere venial one in a writer, but often a commendable virtue; for wherefore, on any occasion, should I detain the reader or myself, more especially at present, to tell who went on horseback, who went on foot, who rolled with one pair and a post-chaise, who traveled with four horses in a coach, who took the stage, or who were taken by the wagon? Suffice it that—though the road before the inn which had been burned down could not be said to be clear of idlers and spectators during the whole of the day—all who had been accidental tenants of the building on the night of the conflagration, were gone on their several roads before twelve o'clock. The landlord and landlady were left alone to bewail the destruction of their property, and waiters, chambermaids, ostlers, and all the race of boots to grieve that Othello's occupation and their own were gone.

Among others, two very jovial persons jogged on together toward London in a yellow post-chaise, with a pair of horses from the defunct Bull. The post-boy drove slowly, for he was both mournful and meditative. He thought over the snug stable at Dunstable, of the snug little room over the stable, and the three-cornered bit of broken looking-glass at which he and Jim used to shave by turns; and when he remembered that he should never see them more, the next bump upon the posting saddle produced a sigh of unusual depth and magnitude. Though the horses had all been saved, that was a poor compensation for a pair of leather breeches which had been curled up into a cinder by the fire; for the horses were his master's, the leather breeches were his own. Then he revolved in his sagacious head the chances as to whether Mr. Spinner would set up again and keep on the posting business; and if he did not, how he himself was to earn his daily bread.

In the mean time, not to proceed further with his slow meditations, in which his horses seemed to sympathize, let us turn to the two gentlemen within the chaise, who cared little about going quick, for they were in that happy frame of mind which made their journey a pleasant expedition. They had attained their object when there was every chance of failure. They had escaped cudgeling when there was the greatest probability of their being made acquainted with crab-tree. Their expenses were to be paid; they were to have a handsome bonus if they recovered, as they had recovered, an unjust and usurious debt; and, after the toils and dangers they had encountered, they proposed to enjoy themselves on their way back to London. In fact, the bailiff and his man, who had served a writ upon Major Brandrum the night before, and received payment of their claim in full, were in a very comfortable frame of mind, and laughed more than once at the folly of that officer in satisfying their demands.

Merrily went they through Markyate-street, and at Redburn they stopped to bait both the horses and themselves. They took a cheerful glass; they gave the post-boy another; they remained even longer than he thought necessary; and it was two o'clock when they crossed the little River Colne, on their way to St. Alban's. At the latter place they were doomed to change horses, and they doomed themselves to dine; but the landlord made them wait long, preparing for such reverend guests; and they prolonged the meal and the bottle till he was in hopes of keeping them through the night.

The sheriff's officer, however, at length observed that it was growing dark, and spoke of a chaise on; but the host, who was in the room, commended some exceedingly choice old port, such as was to be found nowhere but at the Woolpack at St. Alban's, and his soft seductions proved overpowering to men who had drunk quite enough already. A bottle was ordered, and the landlord invited to take a glass himself; but though, to do him bare justice, he very considerately prevented them from drinking more than half the bottle between them, by drinking the other half himself, yet the quantum left for each was quite sufficient to unsettle any little brains they had left.

A consciousness of there being such a thing as to-morrow, however, made the bailiff insist upon his bill and a chaise; and at length, he and his substitute, who was, moreover, his cousin, entered the crazy vehicle, each displaying his character and condition in his own peculiar way, the principal singing a ribald song, of which the words were very indistinct, and the inferior falling asleep in his corner, and snoring most potently.

Every reader is supposed to know every thing in the world except the tale he is perusing, which he ought to be unacquainted with, otherwise there would be very little use of reading it; but perhaps he may have forgotten that a well-known hill, called Ridge Hill, lying between Colney Bridge and South Mims, a little to the northwest of Barnet, was once a hill indeed. It has of late years been pared, and scooped, and avoided, till it hardly deserves the name of a hill, and still less of ridge; but then—that is to say, at the time I write of—from the bridge over the small River Colne to the top of the ridge, was a long and steep ascent, which took away the breath of many a well-winded horse, and which had a terrible effect upon the two sorry jades that were drawing chaise, bailiffs, and wine up the hill. On either side of this ascent were scattered woods, with an open space guarded by park paling here and there, and one or two narrow roads leading to the seats of lords and commoners, thickly sprinkled over that part of the country. In short, it was rather a cut-throat looking hill.

Moreover, had the bailiff and his follower not

been blind with wine, they would have seen that the post-boy who drove had a face not commended by physiognomists. I have called him a post-*boy*, out of compliment to an old dictionary I have, which defines the word postillion, "one who rides the first coach-horse *of four*;" *but boy* he was not, in the usual acceptation of the word, being three years on the century side of fifty. He had gone through the world hitherto with an uncommonly low forehead, a wide mouth, a swivel eye, as it is sometimes termed, and a crooked nose, somewhat oblique in its direction. How it happened, no one could tell; but he was particularly obnoxious to highwaymen, for he had himself recorded seven different occasions on which he had been stopped, four on which he had been fired at, and one on which a bullet had passed through his hat; so that, from a curious association of ideas, his friends and companions called him Hangingwood Billy.

Notwithstanding all these seven adventures on the highway, he was destined to go through an eighth. Hardly had he commenced the ascent, coming over the bridge at a quick trot to give the horses the advantage of an impetus, when a mounted cavalier passed him at an easy canter, saying "Good-night" as he went by.

Bill spurred his horses a little faster, and then, of necessity, relaxed his pace. The bailiff was still singing, his cousin was still snoring. Slowly the panting horses pulled up the hill, and when they reached the first little turn, Bill pulled up, dismounted, and put a large stone under the hind wheel.

"Go on, boy!" cried the bailiff, letting down the window.

"Bless your honor, the horses must get wind," replied Billy; and there he pertinaciously stood for at least five minutes. At the end of that time, however, he slowly swung himself up into the saddle again, and laid his whip quickly over the off horse's neck. The chaise and its contents were dragged at the same heavy pace some four or five hundred yards further, just up to a spot where a small road ran in between plantations to the right, and another to the left; and as the ground was there somewhat more level, the post-boy either did, or affected to commence driving faster. But that very next instant the dreaded word "Stop!" sounded both in his ears and that of the unhappy bailiff, and a man on foot, with a pistol in his hand, seized the heads of the horses, while another on horseback rode up to the window of the chaise. He seemed an exceedingly broad-made man, in a large, white horseman's coat, and was mounted on a powerful black horse.

"Sorry to interrupt you, gentlemen and ladies," he said, in a deep bass voice; "but you see there are highwaymen on the road between Barnet and St. Alban's, so you had better hand over to me your money, watches, rings, and trinkets for protection."

"I declare I have nothing to lose," cried the bailiff, restored to a great portion of his sobriety by fright; "I am a poor sheriff's officer, who have been hunting for a fellow down at Dunstable, who has given us the slip completely."

"Come, come! quick's the word, Master Bailiff," replied the man; "hand over, or take a shot. Your purse first," and he suddenly turned the light of a dark lantern full into the carriage.

With trembling hands the bailiff drew a dirty leathern purse from his pocket, containing some five or six guineas, and gave it to this unpleasant custos of the road. But the next instant he heard the lock of the pistol click, and the same voice said, "That won't do! In a word, will you deliver or not? Hand out that bag between you and the other fellow. Hell and fury! If you keep me one minute longer, I will blow your brains out!" and, stretching his arm into the carriage, he pressed the muzzle of the pistol to the unhappy bailiff's head, sending a cold shudder over his whole frame. The bag was instantly drawn from the side of the sleeping man, who merely grunted in swinish unconsciousness of all that was taking place, and, being delivered into the hands of the highwayman, was instantly examined by him with a very careful scrutiny. When he had satisfied himself that the contents were of gold, he gave a low laugh, saying, "That will do, Master Bailiff; and, as you may want to know what is the exact hour at which you delivered this little sum into my custody, I will spare your watch. I have not time to give you a formal receipt; but I dare say we shall meet again some night, and if I find you have been too exact in your description, I will then afford you a discharge in full which will settle all accounts between us. Hark you, post-boy! keep a quiet tongue in your head, for I am apt to deal roughly with talkative persons, and my ears reach to St. Alban's. Now drive on, and no chattering at Barnet."

Thus saying, he forced his horse back; the man who held the reins withdrew; and Hangingwood Billy, striking his spurs into his bearer's sides, while he laid his whip smartly over the shoulder of the other horse, produced something like a trot, while the bailiff punched the sides of his unfortunate kindred follower, and abused him as violently as if he had stolen the money.

It is wonderful how courage returns in the absence of danger. Notwithstanding the warning he had received and the terror he had undergone, the bailiff had not been rattled along more than half a mile on the road ere he resolved immediately to raise the country in pursuit of the man who had robbed him, and more than once he put out his head, ordering the post-boy to make more haste, and swearing at him in a very heathenish manner for his tardiness. Barnet was still some miles off, however, and a full hour passed ere the chaise drew up at the door of the house corresponding with the Woolpack at St. Alban's.

"Horses on, your honor?" asked the post-boy, in the coolest possible tone; but the bailiff replied, "No: d—n you, open the door;" and, descending, he soon engaged the attention of landlord, landlady, waiter, ostler, and chamber-maid to a full and particular account of the rape of the linen bag, ending with a demand for the address of the nearest magistrate.

"Why, Mr. Mansell is a magistrate," replied the host, contemplatively; "but then, you see, sir, he is away in the North; and the nearest is Sir Harry Jarvis; but he lives two miles off, on the Hertford road."

"Never mind, I will go to him directly," cried the bailiff; and out he rushed, intending to spring into the chaise again, and proceed at once upon his errand. By this time, however, the chaise was standing abandoned in the court-yard, with the horses out, and the bailiff's follower, with a bundle in his hand, was balancing himself disconsolately upon his unsteady heels at the inn door. Another chaise had to be ordered, the post-boy of the last had to be paid, which was effected out of the pocket of the follower, and twenty minutes elapsed ere the injured officer was upon his way to the house of the justice. The cousin was left behind to await his return; and, running along more lightly than in the preceding vehicle, our friend soon passed the gates of what seemed a handsome park, and rolled up to the door of a large, old-fashioned house, before which two horses were standing, with a groom in livery holding them.

To his inquiry for the magistrate, the servant who opened the door replied that Sir Harry had company with him, and, moreover, was engaged with a gentleman upon business.

"I am upon business too," answered the bailiff, "and very important business. I come to your master as a magistrate, and I must see him. I have been robbed, sir, and nearly murdered."

"John, tell Sir Harry," said the first over his shoulder to a second servant who stood behind; and, after waiting a minute or two, the sheriff's officer was conducted to a small, well-furnished room, where, at a table near the fire, sat an elderly gentleman, very well dressed and powdered. But by his side, with his hat in his hand, and his riding-whip lying on the table, appeared no other than Colonel Lutwich.

CHAPTER XVII.

"Well, sir," said Sir Harry Jarvis, somewhat impatient—less, perhaps, with the man's silent stare at his companion than with his general appearance, which was of a kind and character which the worthy justice did not altogether like—"well, sir, what is your important business with me?"

"Why, please your worship, I have been robbed," replied the bailiff, "upon the king's highway—robbed of all the money I received only last night, in satisfaction of a writ *ca. sa.*, with costs and expenses."

"Well, my good friend, you are not the only one who has been robbed," answered the baronet; "this gentleman is in the same plight, and has come to complain, perhaps, of the same person."

"Lord a' mercy, colonel! have they robbed you?" cried the officer, with very peculiar emphasis; "well, I'll tell you how they served me."

"As your case can not be more pressing than my own, my good sir," said Colonel Lutwich, in a somewhat foppish tone, "I will beg to proceed with mine (having precedence, at all events, in point of time), first informing you that they should not have robbed me, had I not previously been deprived of the weapons with which I usually travel, in tha thorrible fire at Dunstable. As I was telling you, Sir Harry," he continued, turning to the justice, "the man who caught my horse's head was a tall, raw-boned fellow on foot; but I was preparing to knock him down with the butt end of my whip and ride over him, when another scoundrel, mounted, rode up, and, presenting his pistol, ordered me, in the usual form, to stand and deliver. The latter was a very stout, broad-built, powerful man, in a white horseman's coat—"

"That's he! that's he to a tee!" cried the bailiff; "with a black beard."

"I did not remark his beard," answered Colonel Lutwich, "for it was very dark; but the general appearance of the man I saw quite well. As one had got hold of my horse's head, and the other had a pistol to my breast, while I had no arms but my whip, and my servant's courage was not much to be trusted, I made no resistance, but delivered over my watch and money. There was not much in my purse, indeed, and the scoundrel seemed dissatisfied; but just then the sound of carriage wheels coming up the hill seemed to scare him, and he let me go."

"Scare him! devil a bit!" cried the bailiff; "he only let you go that he might rob me more quietly. Now, sir, let me make my charge;" and he proceeded to relate all that had occurred to him on the hill with less exaggeration than might have been expected, for he well knew, from his professional habits, the necessity of accurate description where any person was an object of pursuit.

"And now, gentlemen both, what do you expect me to do?" asked Sir Harry Jarvis, after taking a few notes; a question which seemed somewhat to puzzle both the applicants, for they remained silent for a moment or two, and at length the bailiff replied, "Why, raise the hue and cry, and try to catch him."

"What, at eight miles' distance!" exclaimed the magistrate; "no, no, my good friend, that would be a very ridiculous proceeding. I am not fond of being made a laughing-stock. I will grant a warrant, if you like; but as to sending people at this time of night to catch a man who robbed you, nearly two hours ago, at Ridge Hill, and is now probably supping at Hertford or in London, that is out of the question."

"For my part," said Colonel Lutwich, "I would not propose such a thing; but I thought it my duty, Sir Harry, to give notice to the nearest magistrate, in order that the road where I was stopped may be strictly watched; for, as we are all aware, highwaymen have their favorite haunts, and no robbery comes single. I must now ride on to London, though my horses are very tired; for, in the first place, I have not a stiver of my own left in my pocket to pay an inn bill, and, in the next place, I am anxious to see a young lady for whose sorrows I entertain the most sincere sympathy, and a part of whose property I became accidentally possessed of in searching for my own during the fire at Dunstable."

"Stay one moment, colonel, stay one moment," said Sir Harry Jarvis, as Lutwich rose; "I will speak further with you in a moment. Now, my goad sir, do you wish for a warrant?

If so, we must have a more formal information."

"Oh, warrants be hanged!" replied the bailiff, rudely; "I can get a warrant in London, and them as knows how to execute it, which I dare say they don't down here. The hue and cry is the only thing, but that I am not to get, it seems."

"Not by my authority," answered the justice, gravely, "and therefore, if you have no further business, you can retire. Now, colonel, let me hear a little more of this business at Dunstable."

The bailiff took his departure, twisting his hat round and round in his hand, and muttering to himself, "Colonel! my eye!" and, in the mean time, the gentleman on whom he bestowed such contemptuous comments proceeded with the tale of Kate Malcolm's bereavement, which he related in a graceful and touching manner, and then added, "In searching through the rooms, I found, accidentally, a handkerchief belonging to this poor young lady, with twelve guineas wrapped in one corner of it, and a letter by which I discovered who was the owner. I could not discover where she was, after I had lost sight of her at the apothecary's, till she had set out for London with the family of Lady Chevenix; and I now wish to overtake them and restore her property, as I do not know whether they make any stay in the metropolis."

"I can save you a journey to-night, colonel," replied Sir Harry Jarvis, "and shall be delighted if you will be my guest till to-morrow. The poor girl is even now a tenant of my dwelling, as well as Charles Chevenix, who is here with his family. If you will follow me to the withdrawing-room, I will introduce you to the whole party. Miss Malcolm, indeed, is in a little room up stairs, as her severe loss makes society painful to her at present, but we trust to win her forth soon; and, in the mean time, I doubt not she will see you, in order to receive her property."

Colonel Lutwich made some excuses in regard to joining the larger party in the drawing-room, pointing to the dusty state of his apparel; but the old gentleman pressed his point, and, without any great resistance, his visitor suffered himself to be persuaded, stating, however, that he must nevertheless go on to London that night, as soon as he had executed his task to Miss Malcolm.

With an easy, self-confident, but graceful air, he followed the baronet across the hall to a very large and handsome room, in which Sir Charles Chevenix was seated with his family, and was there introduced to them separately. Lady Chevenix received him courteously, and Sir Charles, who recognized him as one of the party at Dunstable, shook hands with him frankly; but Mary Chevenix turned very pale, and gazed at him with a look of wonder and inquiry. It was to her, however, he principally addressed his conversation, taking a seat by her side with the most unembarrassed air, and talking over the incidents of the fire.

"It is strangely unfortunate," he said, after some observations, while Sir Harry Jarvis went to inform Miss Malcolm of his errand; "I have been detained in London for the last month, almost altogether, waiting for the pleasure of your friend the Marquis of Granby, Sir Charles, and had only got as far as Dunstable on my way to Wales, when I am driven back to replenish my wardrobe by this fire."

"I should think the tailors will not complain so loudly," replied Sir Charles Chevenix, looking with a smile at the rich dress which Colonel Lutwich did not abstain from soiling on the road. "I now remember, colonel, having had the pleasure of seeing you once at Lord Granby's house."

Of the latter part of this reply Colonel Lutwich took no notice. The recognition was enough for his purpose—for he, as well as other men, had a purpose—and he wisely let it rest; but, remarking the smile, and the glance at the gold lace upon his frock, he answered, with a laugh, "My poverty, and not my will, consents, Sir Charles. This is the suit I wore last night, and I had time to save little else. These ladies were, I see, more fortunate. I trust Miss Chevenix was not much alarmed, though such an event may well shake a stout heart."

"I was less frightened than I could have supposed possible," replied Mary Chevenix. "I fear, however, that it was not courage, for I was so taken by surprise that I was hardly aware of all that had occurred till I was out of the house and safe. It would have been unnecessary to be afraid then."

"Perfectly," answered Lutwich; "but I will hardly lay claim to so much courage as that. I am not very easily frightened in general; but on this occasion, what between the suddenness of the thing, and the danger, and the thought of so many human beings likely to perish in a moment, I lost my presence of mind for the first few minutes, ran out and rang the great bell quite undressed, and only returned to my own room to gather together some clothing, when the cold air had at once restored my senses and taught me that I needed covering."

"We have all to thank you much for ringing that bell so promptly," replied Sir Charles; "for, had it not been for that, these ladies would have had to go forth and brave the night air much in the same costume as that in which you first encountered it. As it was, colonel, I had timely warning, and stood at the door watching the progress of the fire, while Lady Chevenix and Mary learned for the first time what it was to dress in a hurry."

"I am sure, my dear Charles, I am never very long," replied Lady Chevenix; "and you would not be well pleased, on ordinary occasions, to see me come down as I did this morning."

"What, with a cotton petticoat over a silk gown?" exclaimed her gay husband, "and the pockets outside, as I well remember my poor mother. It is an ancient, respectable, and housewife-like dress, my dear, and only wanted a large bunch of keys to be complete. However, your maid took care of the keys, and the trunks too, or you would be rather bare of apparel even now. Doubtless she had an eye to future perquisites; but still we owe that wench a guinea or two for saving two or three hundred, and she shall have them. I never saw a cooler person in an emergency: even when the flame was walking up the bed-posts, and we were all out on the staircase, she cried, 'La! my lady, you have left the essence bottle on the toilet table,' and was running back to fetch it—but here comes Jarvis. Well, Sir Harry, how is our pretty little orphan?"

"She will be happy to see you, colonel," said Sir Harry, pausing at the door, "but you must speak to her very tenderly of her poor father, for the very name brings the tears again, and they have already flowed long and bitterly."

"I will be cautious, and brief also," replied Lutwich, in a tone of much feeling; "I could not be blind to that devoted love, Sir Harry, which, centering all in one object, leaves the rest of the world like earth without a sun when that object is taken from us. I have felt such things myself, and know how they affect us."

"Then you too were an orphan," said the old man, gazing on him with fresh interest.

"Left with my mother alone in adverse circumstances," replied Colonel Lutwich, "she, after twenty years, became to me, what I had been to her in infancy—the only one. Her happiness was my whole thought, sir; to please her my sole endeavor; and, with all my faults, which have been many; with all my cares, which have been not a few, I had this satisfaction, to make her latter days pass peacefully, and to lay her head in the grave with her blessing upon mine."

There was an elevation in his look and tone while he thus spoke which swept away prepossession, and made the mere man of fashion, pleasure, and display assume a higher character in the eyes of Sir Charles Chevenix and his wife. But Lutwich did not pause to mark the impression he had created, and, moving toward the door, followed Sir Harry Jarvis up the large old oaken stairs to a small room on the first floor, communicating apparently with a bed-room on the left.

Kate Malcolm was seated at a small table, with wax lights and several books upon it, in a plain dress very similar to that which she had worn on her arrival at the inn at Dunstable. It was somewhat better in quality, perhaps, for it was one which, reserved for extraordinary occasions, had been packed up in the portmanteau of her father, and saved from the fire, as we have seen, by having been left in the wagon. Her face was sad, but calm, and her beauty not the less striking under the expression of deep sorrow than it had been under that of strong devotion. A faint blush came into her cheek as Colonel Lutwich entered, and she recognized in him the person who had first interposed to deliver her from the importunities of Sir Theodore Broughton. But she received him with more lady-like grace and self-possession than might have been expected from one so young, and looked up to Sir Harry Jarvis with a look almost of affection as he introduced her visitor; for there is something in genuine kindness of heart which wins confidence almost at once. But the old baronet merely said, "I shall leave you with Miss Malcolm, colonel, and hope you will give me the opportunity, as you come down, to press you to stay the night," and then retiring, he closed the door.

"Perhaps, Miss Malcolm," said Lutwich, taking a seat, "it might have seemed more considerate if I had sent you the few articles of yours which I have in my possession by one of your friends here, instead of asking an interview to deliver them myself; but, believe me, I did not at all wish to intrude upon you, nor would have done so without a reason."

He paused for an instant after uttering these words in a low and kindly tone, and Kate replied, "I did not know you had any thing of mine, sir. Sir Harry Jarvis merely said you desired to speak with me on business."

"Hardly business," answered Lutwich: "in the midst of a scene which I am unwilling to recall to your memory, I found, in one of the rooms through which I searched, this handkerchief, and the sum which is tied up in it. Both belong to you, I think."

"They do," answered Kate, "and I am much obliged to you for restoring them, sir."

"Not at all," he replied: "pray see that the amount is correct. Had that been all I found, Miss Malcolm," he continued, when she had counted the money, and bowed her head in token that it was all there, "it would have hardly formed an excuse for asking to see you personally, nor should I have known to whom it belonged; but I also perceived this letter addressed to you, and thought it might be as well to place it in your own hands. I need not tell you that, as I am a man of honor, I have not looked at one word beyond the mere address."

Kate took it with a faint smile, replying, "I feel quite sure of that, Colonel Lutwich; but it would have mattered little if you had. There, take and read it now," she continued, from a feeling that he might think there was some mystery, and connect it with the conduct of Sir Theodore Broughton toward her. "It has afforded me one of the sad lessons I have had to learn very early, sir."

Lutwich took the letter, which bore a Yorkshire postmark, and paused a moment, hesitating whether he should or should not read it; but curiosity and much interest triumphed, and he opened it and ran his eye over a few lines written in a large hand-writing. "I can make nothing of it, Miss Malcolm," he said, at length: "it seems a very formal and somewhat cold epistle."

"Cold indeed," said Kate, casting down her eyes in sad meditation; "cold indeed. That gentleman, Mr. Eaton, is my first cousin—my poor mother's nephew. Many is the time, in the days when we were prosperous and he was poor, that he has dined at my father's table; but when he became rich and we poor—"

She paused, and seemed to struggle with rising tears; and Lutwich kindly took her hand, saying, "Do not distress yourself with explanations. I understand it all. It is one of the common things of this world. Nay, I do, indeed. He became cold and distant, or perhaps censorious; blamed him he had fed upon, or sought subject of dispute, and *broke off the connection*, as the world calls it."

Kate bowed her head upon her hands and wept; but then, raising it again with a slight touch of pride, she said, "But this is foolish and unworthy of me. The fact is, when, in dire distress, my beloved father was about to set out to join his regiment—ill, poor, and indeed dying—as a last resource, when all else failed, I secretly wrote to this gentleman. He is nearly of the same age as my mother, and in my infancy had often had me on his knees, and called me his darling Kate—his little pet. I asked nothing, but told him our fate and our prospects. That is the answer. I dared not show it to my father, for he knew not that I had written; and now I grieve that I wrote at all."

"That I would not do," replied Lutwich: "you did, in this as in all else, a duty to your parent. That is in itself a satisfaction; and he who should grieve and feel shame is the man who could write this letter;" and Lutwich struck it with the back of his hand. "He may yet live to repent it, Miss Malcolm; for, in the strange turns of Fate, there are things more improbable than that he should sue and you should reject."

"Oh no, I would not," exclaimed Kate. "He should never find that I forgot he was my mother's nephew. But that is out of all probability. He is now wealthy, and will be more so, I believe, for he is related to some people of great riches, of whom he is the heir. I have never seen any of them, but I have heard so, and believe it."

"Eaton!" said Lutwich, in a thoughtful tone; "Eaton! Well, I will inquire; but be sure, Miss Malcolm, no good to himself will spring of wealth so used. The vulgar have a proverb that evil comes of riches badly acquired, but I think that tenfold evil must follow riches badly employed. There is a curse upon them."

Kate did not reply, though his whole demeanor and conversation pleased her; but Lutwich seemed somewhat unwilling to end their conference; and, after having paused a moment, he spoke of Major Brandrum, and extolled him highly to ears that were willing listeners. Next he mentioned Reginald Lisle; and, as he did so, his eye fixed upon the fair girl's cheek, but not the slightest change of color betrayed emotion. That seemed to please him; and rising at length, he said, "And now, dear Miss Malcolm, I will take my leave; but let me hope that as Fate has brought us into many strange and some trying circumstances together, I may claim the privilege of a friend, and say, that if ever I can serve you in any way, you will not find me as you have found this man. Although there seems, indeed, but small chance of such being the case, yet it may happen, and then try me. Farewell."

He turned again to look at her as he closed the door, and paused thoughtfully on the stairs ere he descended.

In the mean while, his manner and appearance had been discussed in the room below, as usually happens upon such occasions. We all leave our characters behind us as well as Teazle, and if they are not brought upon the carpet by those whom we have just quitted, it is only when we are so well known that there is nothing new to be said.

"I think he is exceedingly handsome, and very distinguished in air and manner," said Lady Chevenix.

"I am glad to hear it, dear mamma," replied Mary, with an arch smile, "for he is the very image of one whom I thought very handsome, and you pronounced hideous."

"You do not mean Captain Lisle, Mary?" exclaimed her mother: "I thought him exceedingly good-looking till—"

"Oh no, no!" answered Mary, whose cheek had grown a good deal redder than before; "I meant the man who robbed us under the park paling."

"Good Heaven! you do not mean to say that this is the same?" cried her mother, turning pale.

Her husband and Sir Harry Jarvis both laughed, and Mary hastened to exclaim, "Oh no! So like, indeed, that at first I almost thought it was he; but that was a fair man, and Colonel Lutwich is dark. The other had light hair—almost sandy, it appeared, and blue eyes, I think; but this gentleman's hair is clearly black, and his eyes very dark."

"In pity, my dear Mary, do not let him know that you think him like a highwayman," exclaimed Sir Charles, still laughing.

"Or that you think him very handsome either, my dear young lady," said Sir Harry Jarvis: "that, in my mind, might be the more dangerous of the two."

"I think I have heard he is a very good officer," continued Sir Charles, while Mary colored again. "I know I saw him once at Lord Granby's. He is a fop, that is evident; but I have known a man who took exceeding great care of his person out of battle, expose it more fearlessly than any one under fire."

The conversation had exhausted itself upon Colonel Lutwich, and taken another turn before he returned; but when he did make his appearance again, Lady Chevenix gazed at him somewhat steadfastly, and then looked to her daughter, saying something with a smile, and in a low tone.

"Very like, nevertheless, my dear mamma," replied Mary, with no great caution, for the object of her mother's observation was apparently busy conversing with Sir Harry Jarvis; but Colonel Lutwich had remarked Lady Chevenix gaze at him, and caught her daughter's reply, and with that sort of well-bred self-possession which carries many a man through a great number of impudent things, he asked, with a smile, "Very like whom, Miss Chevenix?"

Mary's cheek burned at her own imprudence; but her father came to her aid, saying, "Oh, only a person she saw once, and only once."

"Nay, but I must know," cried Lutwich, laughing, and casting himself into the vacant chair by Mary's side. "I have a particular reason for wishing to hear, which I will tell you presently."

"Your reason first, Colonel Lutwich," replied Miss Chevenix. "I will explain my foolish remark afterward."

"My reason is a very strong one," answered the gentleman; "there is some one, in this good world and this good country, very like me. I never met any one who seemed so, to myself; but they tell me the resemblance is perfect in every thing but the hair and complexion. Indeed, so strong is it, that it once nearly cost me my life, and my reputation too. I have hunted him through half England, and some day or another I will find him."

"Then, perhaps," said Lady Chevenix, "Mary's fancy is not so far wrong as I imagined, colonel. Some days ago she and I were stopped and robbed by a highwayman under our own park palings, and she said that his features were exactly like yours, though the complexion was different."

"The same man, upon my life!" cried Colonel Lutwich, gravely. "So he is performing his old feats again. This must be stopped, upon my honor! Pray, does he ape my dress too, Miss Chevenix?"

"Oh no," answered Mary; "he is much less carefully habited. He had on a loose horseman's coat, and large boots over his knees."

"To conceal his figure," said Lutwich; "it has been my fate twice to be stopped, and once, probably, by this very person. My vanity, I suppose, prevented me from seeing the slightest resemblance; but yet, a good fellow who was robbed an hour or two after swore that his friend and myself were identical, till I asked him in regard to the beard and complexion, and then his evidence broke down, and he was obliged to admit that there was a great difference. However, I must now take my leave, Sir Harry; and if any of these collectors of highway-rates meet me on my road to London, I must tell them that some of their comrades have been beforehand with them, for they did not leave me a crown at Ridge Hill. It was lucky that I had Miss Malcolm's money apart."

"Will you allow me to replenish your purse in case of need?" asked Sir Harry Jarvis; but his visitor declined with thanks, saying that he should want nothing till he reached London, as he had fed his horses at St. Alban's, and with a graceful adieu to all, he withdrew.

There was a smile upon his countenance as he mounted his horse; and, followed by his servant, he rode at a quick canter through the park, passed the gates, and then along the Barnet road till they reached the first turning to the right. Then, however, the servant rode up to him, saying familiarly, but not disrespectfully, "Hang it, sir, you were so long, I thought they had found you out."

"Pooh, pooh!" said Lutwich, "I always know what I am doing, Hal. The scoundrel bailiff came in while I was there, to lodge an information against a great broad-made man in a white horseman's coat; but I had been before him, and done the same. Our descriptions tallied exactly; and if Sir Harry had raised the hue and cry, as he wanted, why, I would have joined the rest, and led them half over the country in pursuit of myself—ha, ha, ha! Now let us get to the cottage and take some rest, for we must both be at my lodgings in London early to-morrow."

As the reader well knows, in that part of Hertfordshire there are many very wild and heathy spots, of no very great extent indeed, but having a more solitary and unpeopled look, from being surrounded by a number of gentlemen's parks and plantations, which, of course, render the population thin. In the midst of the most unfrequented and lonely part of the country between Barnet and St. Alban's, but a good deal to the west of the high road, lay a pretty small cottage, sheltered by many tall trees, and reached only by a cross road, along which Colonel Lutwich and his servant now pursued their way with great speed. They were within half a mile of the gate which opened into the little inclosure round the house, when a loud halloo was heard behind them, and then the quick galloping of many horses' feet. Lutwich only spurred the faster, as the reader may suppose; and, quitting the road, which ran along with a tall hedgerow on one side, he cantered over the heath which flanked it on the other, reached the paling of his own gardens, and, without waiting to ring bells or raise latches, leaped his horse over, and was followed in the same manner by his servant Hal.

CHAPTER XVIII.

Sir Theodore Broughton was sad, shy, and silent. He was evidently ashamed of himself; but Reginald Lisle let it work. Forced by circumstances into active life at an early period, it is not wonderful that the young officer had acquired a considerable knowledge of human nature, both general and individual. No man, but one who shuts his eyes, or is morally or physically blind, can do otherwise, if he mingles much with fellow-men. Peers and members of Parliament, of course, know nothing of human nature. There are exceptions, but they are rare; for as there are smoked glasses for looking at the sun, by the aid of which the glorious orb of day is transformed into a small, hazy, yellow disk, very like a new farthing, so are there parliamentary spectacles for looking at human nature, through which a rigid external form is seen, but no more like what the real thing is than a new farthing is to the great light-bearer; otherwise we should have had different laws for our poor, our criminal, our industrious, our idle, and our convict population long ago.

However, Reginald Lisle had, from the age of sixteen, gone through the world, or at least a great part of it, with his eyes open and his senses alive, and he had seen man on many sides. He was not a lawyer, and therefore he had not seen only the basest side; he was not a physician, and therefore he had seen more than the weakest side; he was not a clergyman, and therefore had seen men on others than the most selfish side. I could go through a great many more sides, for it is my opinion that human nature is an octagon; but perhaps these are enough; and although Reginald knew that the curious thing we are speaking of has many faces, he knew that underneath them all there was one particular substance, which required dealing with in a particular way. He was aware, therefore, that if, when a man's own heart reproaches him, any one attempts to take part with heart too openly against self, vanity—the devil take it for a troublesome commodity—is sure to come in aid of self, and vanquish both the counselor within the bosom and the counselor without.

As he saw, then, that Sir Theodore was ashamed of himself, he took care not to say a word in regard to what had passed at the inn; and Major Brandrum, upon somewhat different grounds, did not allude to it either. He felt very much inclined to horsewhip the young baronet, and yet his better sense told him that it would be unwise, and not altogether benevolent to do so; and therefore he spoke to him as little as possible, lest Sir Theodore should say something which might give inclination an advantage over reason.

As they rode along, too, he perceived, what Lisle had perceived long before, that their young companion was ill at ease in himself; that his heart smote him; that he was sorry for what he had done; and he was not one to be severe upon repentance, or to crush by harshness, as is so frequently the case, the first, ingenuous sense of wrong.

Lisle was grave, the old officer was grave, the young baronet was grave, for the first ten miles of the ride; but even the passions are lessons which teach us while we feel them: lessons of good or of evil they may be, but they instruct the heart of that which is within itself; they prepare us for after things; they make us men.

Sir Theodore Broughton, during that night's turbulent emotion, had taken a great stride on the road to manhood.

Gradually the gravity of the two elder gentlemen relaxed, and they talked over all the events which had lately passed (with the exception of one group) freely and discursively. The fire, and the scenes it had presented, were mentioned; and sometimes they even laughed at the whimsicalities which fear had produced; but still the general tone was not cheerful, for both felt that the event itself was a sad and serious one, which plunged many in distress and difficulties, and was shadowy, not light.

Reginald, also, had other thoughts and feelings in his bosom, which, if they were more hopeful than those which he had entertained during the last few days, were still too intense, too deep-seated for gayety. His meeting with Sir Charles Chevenix, the frank and even kind recognition which had passed between them, the invitation to the house of her he loved, all was joyful and fruitful of bright expectation; but he had only caught one brief glance of Mary herself, and there was disappointment. Even in the brighter part, too, there was matter for much meditation—ay, and on subjects which Reginald was unwilling to look steadfastly in the face. He was not accustomed to fly from such considerations, for he was morally a bold man; but perhaps he had never before seen dangers and difficulties threatening where his feelings were so deeply engaged: and thus he was weak, and would fain have turned away his eyes. Still, however, like a thunder cloud in harvest, the shadow of a storm spread over the scene, while he turned away his eyes from the tempestuous horizon; and he could not but feel that the air was growing dark even while he looked at the golden promise of the field. With but a very moderate fortune, with no high rank or distinction to support him, he had aspired to the love and the hand of one, the heiress of great wealth, and the representative of an old and widely-connected family. Her father might be kind and generous, but her mother was evidently full of prejudices against him, and he had naught to trust to but the love of a heart, the sentiments of which he might fancy, but he could not know. He was young, however; and hope is the constant companion of youth. It is only in maturer years, when we view the perils before us as they really are, that the heart sinks at the chances of the winning game which Fate is playing against us. Thus he remained grave after his elder companion had resumed all his cheerfulness; for strong feelings, even of joy, are always thoughtful, and his bosom was full of emotions to which that of Brandrum was a stranger.

Sir Theodore Broughton marked the serious aspect of the young officer, and with that sort of sensitiveness which the consciousness of having done wrong not unfrequently produces in a fresh mind, looked upon Reginald's demeanor as a tacit reproach to himself. He drew, therefore, more toward Major Brandrum than to his other companion; and, in the course of their ride to St. Alban's, had contrived to get the elder, but lighter-hearted man between him and Lisle.

Now, in those days, the distance between Dunstable and St. Alban's was somewhat more than fourteen miles by the high road. The party whom we are now following had not set out till nearly noon, and they rode slowly, for their horses had traveled a long distance the day before, and had been not a little disturbed during the preceding night. Thus it was about three o'clock when they reached the small town; and as those were days when men dined early, they paused there for that purpose, but not at the Woolpack. While their meal was preparing, they sauntered, naturally, to the abbey; and as Reginald Lisle viewed it with an artist's eye, he lingered about the precincts, pointing out beauties to his two companions, and commenting with his peculiar discursive sort of fancies, extracting thoughts and histories from the decaying stones, and carrying the mind of his hearers now back to ages long past, now forward to generations yet unborn; and, in the diorama of his imagination, now clouding the scene with dark shadows, now bringing every excellence out in bright light.

"You are a strange, fanciful fellow, Lisle," said his friend, the Ravenous Crow; "but your dreams are very pleasant ones."

Sir Theodore thought them delightful too, and was almost inclined to forgive Reginald for censuring him in his heart—an offense not easily forgiven in general. But the landlord of the inn was exceedingly angry that they stayed so long at the abbey, for he looked upon the goose which he had prepared for them as much more worthy of their attention (till it was roasted too much) than all the abbeys in the world.

At length, however, they returned, and the first course of their dinner was over, when—after some little bustle without, such as that which in most inns announces the arrival of new guests—the door of the ordinary dining hall, in which they were taking their food, was thrown briskly open, and a personage entered whose name has been mentioned before in this book, but whom, for many reasons, I have refrained from bringing into the more active scenes till the present moment. He was a middle-aged man, dressed in black, with a large cravat tied somewhat tightly round his neck, and the ends fringed with lace, hanging down upon his coat. He could not be called corpulent, but the period when the human frame begins to spread laterally had clearly commenced; and if an abhorrence of the good things of this life had at all retarded the growth of fat, his countenance belied him. He was tall, and had certainly, at one time, been good looking, as far as mere features were concerned; but the expression could never have been prepossessing, and now it was quite the reverse. There was a great deal of moisture swimming between the eyelids, one of which dropped occasionally half over the eye, giving involuntarily a curious meaning look to his face, in good keeping with the general expression. His mouth was large and sensual, but yet there was a merry turn about the corners, which seemed to speak it as well fitted for jest as eating; and the protuberant chin, rounded and somewhat turned up, had a bold and impudent air, as if conscious that there was a spirit within ready to defend whatever the lips uttered. The worst feature, however, of the whole, was the forehead, which, though broad, was "villainous low." I may as well mention the foot and leg, though on the present occasion they were concealed by large riding-boots, but upon all ordinary occasions the former might be seen covered with an exceedingly neat shoe, displaying its small size and fine proportions to the best advantage, while a black silk stocking set off the ankle, surmounted by an exuberance of stout and symmetrical calf shaking underneath at every well-planted step the owner took.

Not knowing whom he was about to meet with, this worthy personage entered the public room of the inn with a gay, dashing, reckless sort of air, and, taking no notice of the party assembled at the further end of the room, kept his head turned toward the landlord, who was following obsequiously, continuing to give directions which he had commenced at the door. "And, harkee, mine host," he said, "after that, a broiled chicken and mushroom sauce: mind, I say a chicken—not the old cock I just now saw upon the dunghill—a chicken, young and tender as Hero just after she had first seen Leander: do you understand me? The cut of salmon, not boiled till it is as dry as your or my grandmother, but just till the red has changed to pink all through, and the flakes acknowledge the cream between. 'Tis a pity you have no lobster; but let the cook beat up the flesh of two anchovies in the sauce, eschewing the bones and scales, then add ten drops of vinegar, and as much onion as would lie upon a sixpence. As to the wine, it must be Madeira; and I shall not object to an apricot tart, wound up with old Cheshire and a bottle of Port; not black strap, but real, genuine, crusted old Port, of the best vintage in your cellar. See to it, mine host, see to it; and, in the mean time, let me have the *Advertiser* to doze over and preserve my appetite."

The back of Sir Theodore Broughton was turned toward the new comer, but at the first sound of his voice he turned somewhat white, and then red; and then he knitted his brows, and an expression of somewhat dogged resolution came upon his young face, while he turned an attentive ear to the eloquent words of the guest. At length a smile, almost sarcastic, came upon his lip, and those changes might have shown any one who knew him well, and had watched the history of his mind—for minds have histories—that Sir Theodore Broughton was an older man than when he set out upon that journey.

The stout, dashing gentleman in black, however, as soon as all his directions were given, sauntered up the room, making his boots creak importantly, till he came within sight of Sir Theodore's profile, while the youth kept looking steadily before him, taking not the slightest notice of any thing, with the eye at least, but the viands on his plate. As soon as the stranger saw him, he exclaimed, in a tone of much wonder, "Good Heavens!, Sir Theodore, you here? Why, I expected to overtake you in London. Do you not know me?"

"Oh yes," answered the young man, laconically, "I know you, doctor. I knew you ten minutes ago, by your tongue."

"Nay, I have not been ten minutes in the room," replied the other, with some confusion of manner.

"I beg your pardon, doctor," said the baronet; "three minutes describing the chicken and mushroom sauce; four minutes ordering the salmon and lamenting the want of lobsters; two minutes given to the anchovies and onion, with the ten drops of vinegar, and the rest spent upon the Port and the Madeira."

The gentleman whom he called doctor looked utterly confounded, and Reginald Lisle and Major Brandrum gave each other a meaning glance. It is probable that, had the expression upon each of their faces been interpreted into the vernacular, it would have been the same in all, and might have been rendered, "He is getting on!" Nor is it unlikely that such was the impression which Sir Theodore intended to produce, at least upon the mind of the new comer, for from that moment he had chosen his part. Whether he would have had firmness to carry it through in the face of opposition, is another question; but he was not put to the proof; for, after a very brief period of consternation, the other accommodated himself to the circumstances with wonderful facility.

"It is very necessary, my dear sir," he said, laughing, "to be quite precise in one's directions on such important subjects, especially at an inn. I have, within the last ten days, eaten enough smoked mutton chops, tough beef steaks, and under-done veal cutlets to choke an elephant, or give an ostrich the nightmare. But pray, introduce me to your friends."

"Captain Lisle, Doctor Gamble," said Sir Theodore, "the gentleman who *was* my tutor. Major Brandrum, Doctor Gamble," and there Sir Theodore paused, hardly looking at one for whom, not many weeks before, he had felt great awe.

The worthy doctor, however, made himself quite at his ease, drew a seat to the table, entered into conversation with the two officers, rattled on upon a thousand different subjects, and played the complete man of the world. The major talked to him more than Reginald; for the old soldier, accustomed for thirty years to camps and armies, was—notwithstanding his high sense of honor, and very scrupulous delicacy upon subjects of much importance—a far less keen observer than his young companion of small traits; and though Reginald thought the doctor's conversation not very edifying, especially for young ears, his friend took it all as a matter of course.

Doctor Gamble's dinner was brought in just as that of the other gentlemen was concluding, and Reginald rose, saying, "I will go and look to the horses." The major accompanied him to the bar to make sure of a good bottle of wine, and Sir Theodore was left alone with his tutor. A momentary hesitation seemed to possess him, for he sat for one instant silent, looking at the table-cloth; but then, setting his fine white teeth together, he rose, walked to the table at which Gamble was devouring some fish, and drew a chair right opposite to him.

"We must have a word or two, doctor," he said, leaning across and speaking low.

"A dozen or more, my dear young friend," answered Gamble; "what do you wish to say?"

"Simply what is necessary to insure that we begin as we are to go on, and go on easily," replied Sir Theodore; "the case is this, Doctor Gamble: I have been for some little time my own master, and I intend to continue so. Now, if you are come with the intention of assuming the same authority over me which you exercised at Ashton Hall, you will be disappointed. No, no, hear me out. I have seen already enough of the world, and heard enough of your conversation just now to understand things better than I did. Your manner is much changed, doctor."

"And so is yours, Sir Theodore," replied the tutor, in the most unabashed manner in the world; "the only plan left for us is to accommodate our ways to each other."

"I am afraid you must accommodate yours to mine," said the young baronet.

"Exactly so," answered Doctor Gamble; "'*tempora mutantur et nos mutamur.*' But make your mind easy. I came with no such views and purposes as you suppose, but simply to act as your humble friend and adviser in any course you may think fit to pursue, to give you all the information that my somewhat extensive knowledge of the world can supply, and render you every assistance that zeal, a good deal of habitual skill, and some experience can afford. I had a long chat with your guardian before I came away from Ashton Hall, and we perfectly understand each other. You are launched in life as a man; and on my part, though still retaining my functions in name, the pedagogue is to be laid aside."

"And where is Donovan himself?" asked Sir Theodore. "If he comes to London after me, he may find it difficult to deal with me as he did before, for I am determined—"

He paused, while the landlord brought in the next dish with his own hands; and Doctor Gamble took up the conversation as soon as the host was gone, saying, "The captain is about to go back to the Continent for a month or two; but be under no uneasiness. He has made up his mind, like a wise man, to the changes that must come, and to part with authority as nonchalantly as I do. But how happen you to be here at St. Alban's? I thought you had been in London four or five days, and expected to find you at the theater, the masquerade, or the tavern. I should certainly have sought you out at some of those gay places; for, being only an LL.D., and not a D.D., my cloth would not have stood in the way."

A smile came upon Sir Theodore's lips, somewhat cynical for one so young, indeed, but yet well satisfied. He understood Doctor Gamble from that hour, and Doctor Gamble him; and he felt that an explanation was over which left nothing more to be said. He then detailed to his companion all that had passed to detain them on their journey, keeping other matters for a more private conference; and the tutor was in the act of inquiring how he liked his two companions, when Major Brandrum returned.

To him and Reginald Lise, when he appeared, the doctor communicated his intention of riding on with his young pupil and themselves, adding, "So let me know when you will be prepared to start, and I will gobble my chicken and swallow my Port accordingly."

"I have a bottle to finish too, doctor," replied Major Brandrum, "and so we can drink glass for glass; but order your horse to be got ready in the mean time, as we have done, for day is already down, and we shall have to start by starlight."

"Oh, never mind," replied the worthy doctor. "What road do you take? By Barnet, eh? I will take you a shorter, by a couple of miles at least. I know every inch of every road within twenty miles of London; and it will save you full two miles, as I have said, to go by Edgeware. Hilly—hilly it is, to be sure; but so is the other road—worse than this, indeed; and two miles gained are two miles gained, which is something when one has ridden far. Come, Theodore, join me in my bottle. That Madeira has gone wonderfully fast."

The young baronet, however, wisely declined; and Major Brandrum, dispatching his wine with great celerity, kept the powers of the good tutor at the full stretch till the last glass was drained. Shortly before this happy enterprise was achieved, a waiter announced that the horses were ready, and then came the paying of bills and the adjustment of reckonings; but the mind of good Doctor Gamble seemed a little hazy. It would seem either that the Port had been stronger than he had anticipated, or that the doses had been too rapidly repeated, or, which is perhaps more probable, that where he had last watered his horse he had wined himself; for it is impossible to conceive that merely two bottles of wine, mitigated and alloyed by a good dinner, could have the least effect in those days upon a well-seasoned head like his. He was not drunk, by any means; but it was with some difficulty he made out his bill. He talked a good deal over it; and when he came to mount, he held one foot in the stirrup till the other was tired, and talked a good deal again, praised the landlord's wine, commended his fish, declared the broiled chicken was excellent; for he was exceedingly good-humored, and by no means censorious under this first faint influence of the liquor; and Heaven knows how long he might have gone on, had he not suddenly perceived that the whole of his party had ridden away before him.

Now I can not, for the life of me, tell whether the reader is well and thoroughly acquainted with the road from St. Alban's to London or not; but if he recollects accurately every step of the way, he will remember that about the same spot—or not very far from it—where the highway by Barnet and the other way by Edgeware divide, or used to divide, there is a third road leading to Watford, Rickmansworth, Amersham, and the deuse knows where besides. It was not two hundred yards on the St. Alban's side of the separation of the roads that Doctor Gamble overtook the three gentlemen and their servants, and he immediately took upon himself the office of pilot. To say truth, both Reginald Lisle and Major Brandrum had been so much absent from their native land, that their topography might well be at fault; and as for Sir Theodore Broughton, he had no topography at all. They therefore gave themselves up, like most other men, to the guidance of one who assumed knowledge. There was no lack of finger-posts, it is true; but the night, as we have shown, had fallen, and that night was dark, so that whatever indications the finger-posts might have given, nobody could make them out.

Is it surprising, then, that in ten minutes they were riding along at an easy pace upon the road to Watford? They were six bold men and stout, and therefore they had no fears of robbers and highwaymen, the great terror of travelers in those days. Thus their conversation was cheerful and entertaining; for Doctor Gamble had a good deal of learning, a great deal of knowledge of the world, and two —if not more—bottles of wine under his waistcoat. It is true, the first effervescence of the balmy juice—that hazy fume which somewhat obscures the perceptions—soon wore off, leaving nothing behind but a little bright hilarity. The learning and the knowledge of the world remained, however; and he made himself so agreeable, that even Reginald Lisle, though holding still the same opinion of the man which he had first formed, unbent in manner, and listened and conversed, amused.

In this sort they rode on, and passed a toll-gate at the distance of about four miles from St. Alban's; and, as Doctor Gamble had a shrewd memory for toll-gates, inasmuch as he made it a point of avoiding them, the sight of one here, where he did not at all recollect one, gave him the first suspicion that he was not quite in the right road. He was not fond of confessing himself wrong either; and as his companions jogged along by his side in the utmost confidence, talking of any thing else in the world but the road, he had no encouragement to make an avowal. He looked about him anxiously and in silence, then, for some time, thinking that he must soon come to the few houses which then constituted Colney-street; but he was disappointed, and at the end of about a mile and a half he saw a solitary public house. He was now quite sure that he had made a mistake; but he was a man of enterprise and resources, and he thought, "We can not have got far from the road by Edgeware. The first turning to the left must bring us into it."

The first turning to the left soon presented itself, and Doctor Gamble, in a confident tone, exclaimed, "This way, gentlemen, if you please."

They followed, but not exactly like sheep; for Reginald Lisle said, as he wheeled his horse, "Why, this must bring us back into the Barnet road. It seems very muddy and cut up, too."

"It is a short cut," replied Doctor Gamble; and, with a suppressed chuckle, he added, mentally, "Heaven knows whither."

After riding for somewhat more than a mile, they came to a place where the short cut divided into two; and as the left-hand path would too evidently have led them either back to St. Alban's or away to Barnet, Gamble boldly took the right at once, which soon entangled them in such a labyrinth of lanes and hedges, that the poor doctor began to fancy they would never get out of them. For one mortal hour, however, with Spartan fortitude, did he continue to ride on, without giving the slightest indication of the pangs of doubt which consumed him internally, till at length Major Brandrum exclaimed, "Why, doctor, I think your short cut is a very long one. It seems to me that we have been going round and round for the last half hour. Are you sure you are right?"

"Why, I begin to doubt," replied the doctor, in a grave tone. "I do not see the Seven Magpies."

"Nor I either," answered Brandrum, dryly.

"I think I must have mistaken the fourteenth turning," continued Doctor Gamble.

"Come, come, this will not do," said the major. "We must try the Indian way, Lisle. You've got a repeater: we will set a star, and ride straight on. London must be very nearly southeast. You keep the time. I'll fix the star, and we'll calculate its progress westward between us."

But the plan of the Ravenous Crow did not succeed well in England; for, after riding straight forward for twenty minutes, they found they had got into a *cul de sac*, and had nothing to do but turn back and choose another road. This was accordingly done; but horses and men were by this time heartily tired, and it was agreed on all hands that the best plan to follow would be to ask their way at the very first house they could find, and then rest for the night at the nearest tolerable inn. A house, however, was nearly as difficult to be found as the right road. There was many a tall hedgerow, and here and there a pond, with some ghastly weeping willows bending over it, like stone women upon tomb-stones; but houses seemed a scarce commodity, and Reginald Lisle had just struck his repeater, and told his companions that it was ten o'clock, when they issued forth from the lanes upon a small heath or common, and heard on their right the sound of horses' feet at a quick trot. A shout was instantly raised to call the attention of the traveler to their distressed situation, and the whole party set off at full gallop to overtake him, as he was evidently riding in an opposite direction. An instant after, they saw, first the figure of one mounted man, and then that of another, cross the common, like two dark shadows, and canter away toward a group of large trees standing alone. To follow was the general impulse; but in two minutes both figures disappeared beneath the trees; and, riding more slowly, the pursuers came to a very neat and well-kept paling, evidently inclosing a gentleman's grounds. As they had left the road, they had to ride round some way before they could find a gate; but at length they were successful, and saw with pleasure close to it a small lodge or gardener's cottage, with a light burning within.

A stout pull at the bell soon brought an old man to the gate, who told them, in answer to their inquiries, that they were five miles from Barnet, and that it was the nearest place at which they could procure accommodation.

As they were turning away with no slight disappointment, it struck Reginald that he might as well inquire the name of the owner of this solitary dwelling.

"Colonel Lutwich, sir," replied the gardener; and immediately a joyful exclamation broke from two or three of the party.

"Pray tell Colonel Lutwich—" said Major Brandrum.

"He is not at home, sir," replied the man; "he has not been here for ten days or more."

"I wish you would go and see," rejoined Reginald; "we saw two persons on horseback, very like him and his servant, cross the common a minute ago, and go to the opposite side of the house."

"Well, he may have come in t'other way," replied the gardener, with a shrewd look; "I can go and see."

"Tell him that here are Captain Lisle, Sir Theodore Broughton, the Ravenous Crow, and Doctor Gamble, dying at his gate for want of a night's lodging," said the major, in a gay tone; and with this collection of names to deliver as best he might, the gardener stumped away down a short avenue overhung with broad chestnuts.

The party of travelers remained gazing over the gate, which had been kept carefully shut by the old man during the whole of the above-written interesting dialogue, and they could see his lantern move down about a hundred yards, when the faint light began to display something like a white building, with various dark windows and doors. A moment after, the lantern disappeared, and they had to wait some three or four minutes in expectation, after which a door was suddenly thrown open in front of the house, a blaze of light broke forth, and the voice of Lutwich was heard in a gay tone giving them a sort of hunter's halloo. At a quick pace, he came up the avenue without hat or boots, and welcomed them cordially. Some excuses were made for visiting him so late and in so numerous a body; but he only laughed, saying, "Come in, come in. You shall have bachelor's fare and a good bottle, a blazing fire and a hearty welcome."

"I fear," said Reginald Lisle, as they approached the house, and he saw how small was the promise of accommodation, "that we shall put you to much inconvenience, colonel. Nor is it indeed necessary. If you will afford us and our horses some rest and refreshment, and then direct us to Barnet, the major and I, at least, can ride on."

"Pooh, pooh, Captain Lisle," said Lutwich, "you shall not stir to-night. You do not know how many I can accommodate even in this small place. Why, I have lodged twelve friends here before now, some of them great men, and several of them big men; and if your rooms be not very large, and not exceedingly well furnished, you have slept in a barrack before now. Barnet! why, you have been coming away from it for the last mile, if you are the people who chased me across the common, and whom I took for highwaymen. Your servants must sleep over the stables, however."

By this time they had reached the door of the house, and the next moment they were in a very handsome saloon, fitted up with books, and a thousand little objects of virtu. A large fire was blazing in the grate; comfortable arm-chairs were all around; and, begging them to make themselves at home, Colonel Lutwich left them—to give some orders, he said, for the accommodation of their servants and horses. Two very tidy maid-servants in mob caps, and a respectable-looking footman, were set to work to get ready beds and supper; and then going out to the door, the master of the house put one of the two servants under the charge of his groom Hal. As Zachary Hargrave was about to follow, however, Lutwich said, "Stay a moment, my good fellow; I have something to say to you."

Hargrave turned as white as a sheet; but the colonel let the other servant wend slowly away to the stable, with Hal and several of the horses, before he uttered a word more. Then approaching close to Hargrave, he asked, "Do you know, my good friend, that I could hang you to-morrow?"

"What for?" cried the man, with a start.

"For stealing a pearl necklace with a diamond clasp, belonging to Lady Chevenix, during the fire," said Lutwich, fixing his eye steadily upon him. "I can prove it whenever I please; but I have the secret under my own command; and if you do exactly as I direct you, you are safe. Now put off that hang-dog look! Take the rest of the horses to the stable, and then come in and get some supper. Your life depends altogether upon your own conduct."

Thus saying, he shut the door, and returned to his unexpected guests.

CHAPTER XIX.

I must have a bit more of Fielding; for the faults he complains of in the readers of his day are even more to be observed at the present time; and I have remarked, on a thousand occasions, in reading criticisms upon the works of others, that the nice discrimination of the delicate shades of character which he requires is entirely lost sight of, while nothing but broad and strong-marked distinctions are even noticed. Perhaps this is less a fault than a taste. There are many who prefer Ribiera to Murillo, Salvator to Claude, Sebastian del Piombo to Correggio; but certain it is that broad lights and shades, exaggeration of outline and strong contrast of coloring, are what is more remarked and sought after in the present day—in the world of letters at least—than accuracy of delineation and delicacy of handling.

"Another caution we would give thee," says Fielding, "is, that thou dost not find out too near a resemblance between certain characters here introduced; as, for instance, between the landlady who appears in the seventh book and her in the ninth. Thou art to know, friend, that there are certain characteristics in which most individuals of every profession and occupation agree. To be able to preserve these characteristics, and, at the same time, to diversify their operations, is one talent of a good writer. Again, to mark the nice distinction between two persons actuated by the same vice or folly, is another; and as this last talent is found in very few writers, so is the true discernment of it found in very few readers, though I believe the observation of this forms a very principal pleasure in those who are capable of the discovery."

Now, in the present work under my hands, I wish to guard the reader against the supposition that the character of Doctor Gamble and that of Zachary Hargrave are too nearly alike to be admitted into the same book. They were, in reality, widely apart; for in the natural history of the scoundrel, as great a variety will be found as in the feline, the accipitrine, the psittacine, or any other genus of animals. Hargrave was a cold-blooded reptile, a snake who crept quietly on through the grass, while Doctor Gamble had much more of the insect in him. He fluttered as well as stung. Loose in morals, needy of means, expensive in habits, daring in character, careless of consequences, loving adventure, he was ready to be to any one both an example and a guide in any course they might like to follow—except that of virtue. Habit had rendered him very indifferent of appearances, but necessity had taught him, after he had been engaged as the tutor of Sir Theodore Broughton, to comply with the rigid injunctions of his guardian, and assume the severe and domineering pedagogue. He had escaped from time to time, indeed, as we have seen, to enjoy himself in pursuits better suited to his tastes, otherwise he could not have sustained the character he was required to adopt; but it was an infinite delight and relief to him when Captain Donovan announced, on his return from his last truant expedition, that it was high time to give Sir Theodore the reins, and let him see the world and taste its pleasures.

Donovan used guarded language, it is true; he was not so open with him even as with Hargrave; but he was well aware that Doctor Gamble would understand him more readily; and thus the worthy tutor set out to join his pupil in London with much of the feeling of a schoolboy just emancipated from his task, wild with permission to play at liberty, and ready for any mischief that might offer. He was a little surprised, indeed, at the change he found in Sir Theodore himself; nor had he been altogether pleased at first, for he had calculated upon retaining great influence over the mind of the young baronet. But he soon saw that his power must be established upon a very different basis from their former relations of master and scholar; and, as the reader has seen, he changed his plan of operations with admirable facility. He required further information, however, to guide him—explanations as to what had already taken place; and, although he could not extract from Hargrave the whole facts, notwithstanding a strenuous effort to do so before he retired to bed, yet he obtained so much intelligence of scattered incidents that he was able, by shrewdly combining them, to form a net, in which he doubted not he should be able to catch the truth in conversation with the young baronet himself.

Let us pass over all the other events of that night, for there were none of great importance. On all ordinary occasions, men go to bed and to sleep in the same manner. Heads were placed upon pillows, the drowsy god came sooner or later to all, and the whole of Colonel Lutwich's house might have well been ridden through by Queen Mab before one o'clock.

It so happened that the bed-room assigned to Sir Theodore Broughton was next to that of Colonel Lutwich himself, and that in his cottage the partitions were thin. The young gentleman retired to rest first, for his host had household matters to attend to.

In a small room on the ground floor, which had no window apparent on the outside of the house, though somehow or another light found its way in—perhaps through a very thin marble slab with an inscription upon it—and which had no door apparent within, although Colonel Lutwich contrived to effect an entrance—perhaps by sliding away the back of a large, old-fashioned commode, which presented nothing but stands for fowling-pieces and fishing-rods to the eye—in this room, the master of the house spent full half an hour counting money and putting away sundry curious pieces of apparel, among which, be it remarked, was a large, white horseman's coat, so thickly padded in every part that it stood alone. When all this was done, and he had spoken a few words to his groom Hal, the colonel also retired to his bed-chamber, passed three quarters of an hour in care of his person, and then went to bed. While he was undressing, and after he had lain down, he could hear Sir Theodore tossing upon what seemed a very restless couch, and Lutwich said to himself, "He is thinking of Kate Malcolm. I do not wonder at it."

It would seem, however, that he himself was thinking of her too, for a moment or two after he murmured, "He shall never have her, by ——!" and Lutwich lay awake for more than an hour, as well as Sir Theodore Broughton.

What is that strange fascination which is about some women, and which captivates, in a moment, men of the most opposite characters, unless their bosoms be armored with a previous passion, or shielded by a cold buckler of egotism? I have seen the old and the young alike charmed, the hackneyed man of the world, the purse-proud man of wealth, the haughty man of ancient race, the mere unpracticed boy. It could not be mere beauty, for there were others, perhaps fairer, there; nor wit, for she was quiet and reserved; nor art, for she was all simplicity. Was it not that simplicity, that easy, unaffected, quiet grace—the grace of all the graces, unconscious simplicity! Perhaps this was the case with Catharine Malcolm; but certain it is, there were two within those walls who loved her.

At length Lutwich slept, and the first thing which woke him was a voice in the adjoining room. He heard not what it said, for somehow he was often up late at night, and accustomed to sleep long in the morning; but he was sufficiently roused to hear and mark the reply which was given in the voice of Sir Theodore.

"Well enough, doctor," said the youth; "I do not sleep as well altogether as I used."

"I dare say not," answered Doctor Gamble, in a meaning tone.

"Why should I not?" asked the young baronet; and the moment after, he added, "what makes you look so shrewd?"

"Because I can easily conceive many of the sights and scenes of the great world have given you thoughts fit to banish sleep," replied the tutor; "this earth is full of emotions for the young—alas! that the time for enjoying them should pass so soon—for instance, love, my young friend. That is a strong spell to charm away slumber."

Sir Theodore was silent; for, though he had half made up his mind to tell his old tutor all, and seek aid at his hands—to do he knew not what—yet he still hesitated, and Doctor Gamble went on: "Come, come, my young friend, remember the convention entered into between us. Speak out to a friend anxious to serve you, and the next book we read together shall be Ovid's Art of Love."

Sir Theodore laughed, but replied, "Who should I fall in love with, doctor, in five or six days?"

"What think you of the pretty girl at the Black Bull at Dunstable?" said the tutor.

There was a dead silence for a moment after Doctor Gamble had given this home-thrust, and then the young baronet was heard to ask, in almost a stern tone, "How much has that scoundrel Hargrave told you? I insist upon knowing."

"Nay, he has not betrayed much *to me*," replied the tutor, laying strong emphasis upon the last two words; "he merely told me you had been much smitten with a young lady whom you saw at Dunstable, and whose father died there in consequence of the fire. That is all he said; but, seeing that you were evidently thoughtful and uneasy, and understanding such signs right well, I resolved to speak to you on the subject first, lest you should feel any hesitation in seeking my counsel and assistance. But, while we are on the subject, let me warn you at once against putting confidence in that man Hargrave. First, he is unfit to advise you in such circumstances; and, next, he will betray you to another whom you might not like to know all your secrets."

"Unfit to advise me, indeed!" said Sir Theodore; "and betray me he would, doubtless, for it seems he has done so already."

"Pooh, pooh! do not speak in so sad a tone," said Doctor Gamble, gayly; "you seem to regard this little affair as the most serious thing in life. There, now, do not look angry. I dare say you are very much in love—all the better. We will find out the young lady, and see what can be done."

"I do not see that any thing can," replied Sir Theodore, cheered a good deal by the doctor's tone; "by that rascal's advice, I offended her greatly."

"You would have done better to trust your own unaided judgment than that of a low-bred fellow like that," said Doctor Gamble; "but let me hear all about it, and I will undertake to set it all to rights."

The young baronet had some difficulty in telling his own story; but, when once it was commenced, a long detail followed of all that had occurred, and to this Sir Theodore added an account of the feelings which he attributed to Reginald Lisle and Major Brandrum, from their demeanor toward him during the preceding day.

"A couple of prigs!" exclaimed Doctor Gamble, with a laugh; "we must get rid of them as soon as possible. As if a young man like yourself might not fall in love with a pretty girl, and say a civil word or two in a passage, without calling down their high indignation! The man's scheme was a clumsy one, certainly, and we would have managed the matter very differently had I been with you. We would have befriended the father, and all that; but now we must think of what is to be done."

"We shall have no opportunity of doing much now," replied Sir Theodore, in a desponding tone; "she is under the care of Lady Chevenix, who has taken her to the house of a Sir Harry Jarvis, not far from Barnet, Hargrave tells me. She is then to be given over to this Major Brandrum, who has adopted her, and to be placed with Lisle's mother, if she will receive her. That I heard myself."

"Ho, ho!" said Doctor Gamble, thoughtfully; "this seems a golden fleece indeed, when there are so many dragons watching it!"

"She is very beautiful," replied Sir Theodore.

"Then we must lull the dragons, my young Jason," answered his tutor.

"But how?" exclaimed his companion, impatiently. "What is to be done? I do not see."

"Carry her off," said his excellent and virtuous tutor; and then all was silent again for a minute or two.

At length Sir Theodore answered in a tone of doubt and hesitation, "Would not that only tend to offend her still more deeply than I have done already?"

"Pooh, pooh!" said Doctor Gamble, "women are never offended with a little ardent love. It will give you, at all events, time and opportunity, and I think the little god will teach you how to make use of them to win your way into her good graces. But, moreover, we may so contrive it as to turn an action that you think will offend her, into an occasion of gaining her esteem and gratitude—a great step with every young girl. You shall not appear in the affair at all—nor I either, for that matter—or, rather, you shall appear only as a deliverer, and I will be your humble squire—the Sancho Panza of the knight-errant. We can then very well keep her under our respectable protection for two or three days, till we give her up to her friends; and, in the mean time, if you can not find persuasions to induce her to stay altogether, it will be your own fault. Oh, give a young man solitary converse with a girl who thinks she is indebted to him for three whole days, and if he do not make her do all he pleases, his love or his eloquence must be very cold."

"The scoundrel!" muttered Lutwich to himself.

"We shall be obliged to employ Hargrave in part of the affair," continued Doctor Gamble; "but we must have others to help. So now, as you look more cheerful, get up, and let us to London, where there are plenty of men who will do any thing in life for a guinea and a bottle of wine. Leave all the arrangements to me. You shall know nothing of them, though we can talk of some of the minor facts, that I may be well aware of all that is needful. Where does this Sir Harry Jarvis live? What is the name of his place? I must go and reconnoiter the roads."

"They shall be well reconnoitered for you," murmured Lutwich, sufficiently loud to call the admirable tutor's attention, though he could not distinguish the words.

"Who sleeps in there?" he asked.

"I do not know," replied Sir Theodore; "I could hear him, whoever he is, moving about very long last night."

"Let us speak low," said the tutor. It was too late, Doctor Gamble. Your plot was in possession of another, not likely to lose the clew.

CHAPTER XX.

I MUST now return to a period somewhat antecedent, in order to unite the two broken ends of the history of the Chevenix family, and to give some account of what had taken place in the interval which occurred between the moment when Reginald Lisle left Mary and her mother near Dunsmore, and that of their reappearance at the Black Bull at Dunstable.

Mary Chevenix had been very bold in anticipation. She had resolved to tell her father all and every thing about Reginald Lisle, except a few looks and tones which she knew she could not describe. She might tell him very well, she thought, every thing that Reginald had done and said—how he had come to rescue them—how he had suffered from so doing—how charming was his conversation, how winning his manner. She had never had a concealment from her father in her life. Sir Charles's gay frankness, and his kind tenderness for her, had made her share every thought with him, from the earliest days when she ran up to prattle at his knee, till the hour when he last departed for London on business; and she thought she should not be the least afraid if he could see every thing her heart contained.

In short, Mary Chevenix had been very bold in anticipation. Performance, however, was quite another thing. When her maid brought her word that her father had suddenly arrived two days before he was expected, Mary began to feel somewhat nervous; and when she went down and found Lady Chevenix in full career, giving her own version of their history, Mary, of course, could say little. She resolved to wait for an opportunity. It was a bad sign. Nobody waits for an opportunity without feeling that what they are going to do requires some favor.

I have said Lady Chevenix gave "her own version;" but I must not do that excellent lady injustice, for she did not do so by Reginald Lisle, though she certainly did by the highwayman. The latter she described as a very terrible, rude, furious-looking personage, when he was, in fact, quite the reverse; but the gentleman who came to their aid she spoke of as a very handsome and distinguished person, graceful and polished in his manners, and entertaining in his conversation.

"Mary thought, and I thought," continued Lady Chevenix, "that as he had lost his fine horse, and had been severely hurt in our service, we could not do less than receive him as a guest, and see that his injuries were well attended to"

"To be sure, to be sure!" cried Sir Charles, warmly; "I should not easily have forgiven you if you had not, my dear."

"Well, Charles, I am exceedingly glad you do approve," replied his wife, "for when we made the discovery, which we did afterward, I was vexed at myself for having asked him at all."

"A discovery!" exclaimed Sir Charles. "Why, who the deuse was he—a merchant's clerk, or a traveler for a manufacturer?"

"Oh dear, no," answered the lady; "no other than Captain Lisle, your old enemy, who wounded you so severely seven years ago; and I must say I was highly surprised and mortified to find that we had received any service from such a person."

"Pooh, pooh!" cried Sir Charles Chevenix; "Lisle is an excellent fellow—one of the ornaments of the service—gallant and chivalrous, polished, humane, and generous. His name is in the mouth of every one who has been in these Canadian and American affairs. Then, as to the matter between him and me, I have told you, my dear, a dozen times, that he was very little in fault. I ran him too hard, in my foolish, jesting way, when a great number of others were all at him. He was a little impetuous, perhaps, but I was a great deal more in the wrong than he was."

"But he owns he was in fault," said Lady Chevenix.

"The more generous he!" exclaimed Sir Charles.

Dear Mary's little heart beat joyfully, as the reader may suppose.

"I hope," continued her father, "you did not treat him with any coldness after you made this notable discovery, Louisa?"

Mary looked down upon the carpet somewhat pained for her mother; but Lady Chevenix answered, "We did not know any thing of the fact till within a few minutes of his departure, Charles, so there was very little time to show coldness or any thing else; but I will not deny that I could not feel, or appear to feel, toward a man who had nearly killed my husband, as I should have done toward one who had not so acted."

"Louisa! Louisa!" cried her husband with a mortified look, "will you never get rid of such prejudices! Upon my life!" he added, in a low murmur to himself, "when a woman once gets a thing into her head, there is no getting it out again, especially if it be a bit of vindictiveness. Now, my dear wife, if, after all I have often said, you have treated a young officer, of so high a character, who, at the risk of his own life, and with serious detriment to himself, had rendered you so importrnt a service, with any want of kindness and good feeling, simply because, when he was a mere boy, he behaved like a brave fellow and a man of honor against your husband, you could not have mortified me more. I must find out Lisle in London, and try to make up for this by some means."

Lady Chevenix looked very much vexed, but, of course, did not feel any more warmly toward Reginald Lisle because her husband blamed her conduct; and Mary, who knew her mother well—she could not help knowing her—felt perfectly well aware of the impression which would be produced, and that it would require months to obliterate it. She was very glad, therefore, to change the subject, and talk to her father of any thing else on earth than the topic she would have been well pleased to speak of in other circumstances.

Moreover, she was afraid Sir Charles might ask her for a more detailed and impartial account of what had taken place with Reginald Lisle after he had informed them of his name, than, for her mother's sake, she was willing to give. Sir Charles was, it is true, the most easy man to manage in the world, when any one knew how, and his character was the most easily understood; but there are some people who always, in every thing they have to do, set out with prepossessions, and Lady Chevenix was one of them. Thus she had contrived to live with a husband, whom she loved almost to idolatry, for nearly twenty years, without understanding him in the least, and constantly giving him pain when she thought she must be giving him pleasure.

Mary had very little of what the French call *ruse* about her; but on this occasion she certainly did strive to turn the conversation, by asking, with a greater appearance of curiosity than she really felt, what it could be that had brought her father back before the time he had fixed.

"Not because I have concluded my business, my dear little girl," replied Sir Charles, "but, strange to say, because I have not. I find that it will take a fortnight more, love; and as, during the next three or four days, nothing was to be done, I first ran down to see Jarvis at Barnet, told him I should bring you all to cheer him for a day or two on your way to town, and then came on to fetch you."

"Oh, that is delightful!" cried Mary. "When are we to go, papa?"

"As soon as possible," replied Sir Charles; "to-morrow, if you can all get ready."

Why did Mary think it so delightful? In what little secret train of emotions or ideas was the pleasure found of visiting a place which she had never particularly liked? Was it that Reginald Lisle was going on to London, and that her father had threatened to find him out there?

Well, if it was, there was no great harm in it. If one could knock down half the houses, and clear away the coal smoke, and lay out one half of the area with trees, and walks, and shrubberies, and beautiful lawns, and make all the people honest and good, and get a peep of the sky, and stop boys, women, and men from crying old clothes, and mackerel, and muffins, and chairs to mend, and put a total end to the second edition of the *Evening Courier*, and to men with cigars in their mouths, would not London be very delightful indeed? Depend upon it, dear reader, love—or, rather, the society of him or her we love—does all this, and more too.

Lady Chevenix was quite as willing to go as her daughter. She was rather tired of elms and oaks, highwaymen, and flannel petticoats for laborer's babies. She had a great regard for old Sir Harry Jarvis too, and therefore she willingly acceded to her husband's plan, which is somewhat rare in domestic economy. It was agreed that their own four fat horses should draw them to London; and the male servants were carefully selected, with due attention to weight, while the maids, as if they had been first-class travelers on a rail-road, were allowed to carry what weight they liked.

The only adventure, as the reader knows, which the party met with on their road to Barnet, was one sufficient to serve them for a long time; but Mary Chevenix was not quite contented with the fire, for, although it had brought Reginald Lisle within sight, it had not brought him within speech. She saw him, however, out of the apothecary's window talking to her father, and she remarked them shake hands with each other, which was a great comfort, although she would have given the world to hear what they said. But no information was afforded her till they reached the house of Sir Harry Jarvis, and Mary had enough occupation for her time and her thoughts in consoling poor Kate Malcolm by the way.

With his usual kindness and liberality, Sir Charles had given orders, before he left Dunstable, for the funeral of the poor girl's father, and it only need be said that nothing was left undone by any of Kate's new friends which could tend to soothe her under undeserved misfortune. Lady Chevenix, with all her little faults, was a really kind-hearted person, and Mary and her father, as the reader well knows, were ready to do any thing which a human being could do to comfort the sad-hearted.

As soon as the brief visit of Colonel Lutwich was over, Mary left the party in the drawing-room and went up to poor Kate. We all know what an open-hearted thing girlhood is, and the two were very soon upon the footing of sisters; but during the whole of this time it must be remarked, that the opportunity which Mary had promised herself of telling her father about Reginald Lisle had, like every desired opportunity, been always delayed, and the evening passed by without its presenting itself.

There, that part of my history is brought up to the same period with the rest; but, as we are already at Sir Harry Javis's house, we may as well forward the characters it contained another short stage upon the road of life.

The morning of the succeeding day broke fair and bright, and Mary Chevenix was up and dressed betimes. It was her habit; but yet that day she was awake earlier than usual. There is something in a new house or a new bed which certainly gives one—especially in youth—an inclination to get up early and look about one. She went down to the drawing-room then, gazing for a minute, as she went, out of the stair window into the park, and admiring a fine buck, who, with head erect, was snuffing the morning air, unconscious of the fate of venison. Whatever she expected to find in the drawing-room, she found her father with his hat on, just going out of a door which led to the lawns; and calling to him, she put her handkerchief over her head, as ladies will do, and went out with him. Mary thought this would be an excellent opportunity to talk to him about Reginald Lisle; but, as she thought, her heart beat a great deal too fast to permit her to talk of any thing.

Sir Charles soon settled the subject of conversation, however, for he began to speak of Reginald himself. "I am afraid, my dear Mary," he said, "that your mamma was not very kind to him."

"Oh yes, indeed she was," replied Mary, "till she found out his name, and as that was only five minutes before he went, she had not time to undo all she had done; and besides," she added, in a half-laughing tone, but with a blush upon her cheek, "I was very kind to him throughout, for I liked him very much indeed, and I was sure you would wish me to be so."

"Assuredly," replied Sir Charles; "but nevertheless, my dear girl, we must find some means of showing our gratitude to him, and compensating him for the loss he sustained in rendering you and your mamma a service."

Mary thought she knew a way that would do very well, but she dared not say so, and her father went on. "I have asked him to our house in town, to deliver our fair little friend, Miss Malcolm, into his safe custody."

"Into his!" exclaimed Mary, with her cheek growing suddenly pale; "what has he to do with her?"

"Oh ho! Mistress Curiosity," said Sir Charles, laughing, "I am not going to let you into the secret."

"But Kate told me last night," said Mary Chevenix, "that a Major Brandrum had nobly and kindly promised her poor father to adopt her."

"Ay, till she marries, you know, Mary," replied her father; "and, in the mean time, she is to live with Lisle's mother: so, you see, it is all comfortably arranged; but I dare say her marriage will be soon."

"Not with Captain Lisle, I should think," said Mary, almost bitterly.

"Why not, my dear? why not?" asked her gay father; "she is an exceedingly pretty girl, and he a very handsome young man."

"Simply because she tells me she never saw him more than twice in her life," answered Mary.

"Oh, but you know, Mary, a great deal of mischief can be done in a short time," said Sir Charles, maliciously. "All I know is, that, the night before the fire, I saw them standing in one of the passages talking together very confidentially; and the first person who took her in his arms after her poor father's death was our young friend Lisle. She seemed to find those arms her natural resting-place too, for his bosom was soon wet with her tears."

Sir Charles spoke partly in jest, but partly with a belief in what he said. He knew not how cold he made his poor daughter's heart feel by his light words; he knew not that he was sowing the seeds of that fell poisonous weed, suspicion, in a bosom that had never felt it before. Whether it was that he wondered she did not answer, or that he felt her hand tremble on his arm, or what, I know not; but, after taking two or three steps further, he turned his head and looked at her. She was as pale as a corpse; and, in much alarm, her father exclaimed, "What is the matter, my dear Mary? you look very ill."

"I do not feel quite well," answered Mary, in a low voice; "a sudden faintness has come upon me; perhaps I had better go back."

Supporting her tenderly, Sir Charles led her to the house, but without uttering another word upon the subject of which they had been speaking; and, before they reached the door, the color was returning into his daughter's cheek.

"I will go and lie down again till breakfast," said Mary, in a more cheerful tone. "I shall soon be better. Do not tell mamma, or she will be frightened, and it is nothing indeed."

She left Sir Charles Chevenix to a deep fit of hought. "I must see to this," he murmured, "I must see to this. Lisle is not a man to sport with woman's heart, I should think. But I must inquire further, and take some resolution upon this matter."

In the mean time, Mary sought her own room, and found relief in a violent burst of tears. They were almost the first she had ever shed, for her life hitherto had been a sunny day without a cloud. The tears were wiped away, however, almost as soon as they came. "No, no," she said, "my father must be mistaken; Reginald is not such a being. I could not be mistaken in his words. Oh no, no: nor would he try to deceive me—he could have no object; nor if he had, would he, whose every thought was honor, so basely treat a heart that trusted him! No, no, my father is mistaken. If he did take her in his arms, it was but compassion prompted it. I will speak to this poor girl: she is simplicity and candor itself, and I shall see in a moment what are her feelings toward him, and his toward her."

With this resolution, Mary set to work to remove the traces of the tears from her eyes, and bathed them till they looked as bright and beautiful as ever. She then went to the room which had been assigned to Kate Malcolm; but by that time she had quitted it, and when Mary turned away to seek her below, she met Lady Chevenix, and her opportunity was lost.

CHAPTER XXI.

Man's virtue, honor, and honesty are often, I am afraid, but very frail commodities; and when they travel, Fate kindly packs them up in a crate of circumstances which very frequently keeps them from cracking. Sometimes, however, that most dangerous sort of animal, a serviceable friend, cuts open the crate, and lets them all tumble out and dash themselves to pieces.

Such was the case with Sir Theodore Broughton. Had he been let alone till his newly-excited passion for Kate Malcolm had subsided, the obstacles in his way, the demeanor and example of Lisle and Major Brandrum, and some feeling of right—a natural feeling—for it had neither been implanted nor cultivated, might, and probably would, have acted as the osiers and withes of the crate, and prevented his crockery kind of virtue from getting damaged; but then comes Doctor Gamble to relieve him from all difficulty or opposition, and passion has its own way altogether.

In this chapter, however, neither Sir Theodore himself nor Doctor Gamble are destined to appear, and the reader may therefore marvel that they should be mentioned at all. Nevertheless, there was a reason; for very often the things that appear have much less to do with the results produced, than unseen causes which are acting powerfully all the time.

The day which had just begun at the end of the last chapter, went on to its close without enabling Mary to obtain even five minutes' private conversation with Kate Malcolm. These things will happen in the very simplest manner, and I could state a dozen different obstacles which presented themselves, only that it is not worth while, for they were all utterly insignificant, though sufficient for their purpose.

On the following day, the morning passed in the same manner; but toward noon, when her father had gone to the stables, and Sir Harry was busy, and Lady Chevenix was writing letters, Mary walked up quietly to the little boudoir where her fair young friend sat—*nota bene*, it was not called a boudoir in those days—and seated herself beside her. But Mary had something to conceal as well as to discover—the state of her own heart, while she inquired into that of her companion's—and, of course, she did not go directly to the point. Woman's love is like the timid hare; though to a proverb it may return always to the place whence it set out, it turns and doubles often by the way. She went on for some five minutes, then, preparing for those questions which were to be decisive, but in the midst of one of her circuits the door opened, and Sir Harry Jarvis entered with an open letter in his hand. He paused on seeing Mary, but then immediately, with the air peculiar to him, mingling courtliness with kindness, he advanced, and taking the hand of Miss Malcolm, whom he had not yet seen that day, he asked after her health, and sat down beside her with the look of one who intended to stay a long time.

Mary, not judging that he had any particular business, resolved to stay him out, let his visit be long as it would; but, ten minutes after, a servant came to tell her that her father desired her company in a drive, and her resolution went for naught.

She had now to get ready, which, as she was in a very thoughtful mood, took somewhat longer than usual; and as she descended the stairs after dressing, she heard Sir Harry Jarvis ordering his horse and groom to come round immediately.

"I am going to London for an hour or two, my bright one," he said, using a term he often applied to his friend's daughter; "have you any commands for the giddy capital?"

But Mary had none; and while the old baronet retired to pull on his boots, she accompanied her father in the carriage toward [illegible], whence they proceeded to the house of an acquaintance some miles distant.

They were absent nearly till dinner time; but Mary, on her return, hurried the act of dressing, and then once more sought her young friend; but Kate was neither in the room where she usually sat during the first period of her mourning, nor in her bed-room, and Mary Chevenix rang and inquired for her. The butler, in reply to her questions, informed her that Miss Malcolm had gone out about two hours before in a post-chaise, which had come for her from London.

"There was a servant with it, madam, in livery, who brought her a note," added the man, "and she dressed and went away directly."

Mary was somewhat surprised, and a little agitated, she knew not why; but she did what was perhaps the best thing she could do: she went to her mother's dressing-room, and told her what had occurred.

Lady Chevenix was dressing for dinner. "Has she not come back?" she inquired, without the slightest expression of wonder. "She will return with Sir Harry, Mary. She came and told me that she had been sent for to London; and I conclude that it was he who sent, as she said he had gone most kindly to inquire into some affairs of her poor father's at his agent's in town. He certainly is one of the best and kindest old men in the world."

This answer satisfied Mary Chevenix for two minutes and a half, but no more; for, while descending the stairs, after having sought her gloves in her own room, she met Sir Harry Jarvis just alighted from his horse, and apparently in a great hurry to dress.

"But ten minutes, bright one," he said, "but ten minutes to wash, and powder, and change dusty garments for clean ones; but I will do it, and neither spoil fish nor keep soup waiting."

"But where is Kate Malcolm?" asked Mary; "have you not brought her back with you, Sir Harry?"

The old baronet looked astonished. "Where is Kate Malcolm?" he said; "is she not here?"

Mary and the butler, who was standing near, told him, almost together, what had occurred, and then Miss Chevenix stated what her mother had said to her. All was now surprise and inquiry; and, without minding either fish or soup, Sir Harry stayed to ask a dozen questions, with more anxiety than seemed natural, considering his short acquaintance with Kate.

"I think there was a note lying on the table in the little room," said Mary; "but I had better go and inquire if mamma knows any thing more, as Kate went to consult her about going."

Lady Chevenix, however, had told all she knew, and was as much astonished as any one when she found that Kate had not gone to join Sir Harry. "She came in with a note in her hand, while I was busy writing," said that lady, "telling me that she had been summoned to London, as supposed by Sir Harry, as, upon some inquiries he had made, she had informed him of various particulars concerning her father, and he had gone at once to town to see about the whole affair. I did not pay much attention, for, as I said, I was busy. Good gracious! what can have become of the poor thing? I hope it is no foul trick."

Lady Chevenix rose while she spoke, as if to follow her daughter down stairs; but at that moment Sir Charles entered the dressing-room in much agitation. "There is something very wrong here!" he exclaimed, holding out an open note to his wife; "this poor girl has been decoyed away from our protection, when I pledged my honor to give her over safely, in a few days, to him who is to supply the place of a father to her. Read that, Louisa. Sir Harry says he knows nothing of it; and it seems to me evidently a trick."

Lady Chevenix took the letter, and read the few words which it contained, as follows:

"Miss Malcolm is requested to accompany the bearer immediately to London in the chaise which he will bring, as her signature is wanted directly to her father's papers. She can be easily back at Barnet by the usual dinner-hour of the family."

It was dated from Lincoln's Inn, but the hand-writing was unknown to every one; and a scene of bustle and confusion ensued which banished all thoughts of dinner. As soon as Lady Chevenix could go down, a consultation was held in the library, and the servants who had seen the bearer of the note and the chaise were strictly examined, but without being able to afford any satisfactory information. The man was quite a stranger, the old butler said, and seemed to know nothing of his errand; for, as soon as he had delivered the letter, he sat himself down on the steps, and remained whistling till the young lady appeared. He was in a brown and red livery, with worsted lace, and had a cockade in his hat; but that was all that could be discovered.

"Perhaps it may be no trick after all," said Lady Chevenix, anxious to soothe her husband. "Miss Malcolm may have many friends and relations in London of whom we know nothing, and it is not at all improbable that some one of them should require her presence and write to her."

"Quite out of the question, my dear lady," replied Sir Harry Jarvis, who seemed even more excited than Sir Charles. "A curious circumstance, which I can not pause now to explain, led her this morning to give me an account of her family; and I will take upon me to say that she has no friend in London who would so write. Besides, who could know that she was here?"

That question threw Sir Charles Chevenix into a fit of meditation. The only persons to whom he had mentioned whither he was going, when he placed Kate under the care of his wife, were Major Brandrum and Reginald Lisle; and, for an instant, a doubt of the latter crossed his mind. It was banished the next moment, however, not only by the remembrance of Reginald's high and honorable character, but by the recollection that Kate was to be put under the protection of his own mother, and therefore he could have no possible object in luring her away from the house of Sir Harry Jarvis. The next instant his mind turned to Lutwich; and, in a low voice, he asked Sir Harry what he thought on that point. Nothing, however, but conjecture was to be had, although the old baronet did not at all seem to imagine that his friend's suspicion was directed aright.

At length, Sir Charles, starting up, exclaimed, "We are wasting time. Lend me a good horse, Jarvis. I will take two of my men with me on two of the coach horses. We shall learn at the lodge which way the chaise turned, and doubtless track it for a considerable distance, at least. If it did go to London, we will set the Bow-street officers on the track, and I will ride straight to the Hummums, where, I find, my good friend Major Brandrum is to put up. His long experience of Indian warfare must have taught him to follow a trail better than any of us, and, I will answer for it, his whole heart and soul will be in the pursuit."

"Oh, stay and take some dinner, Charles," cried Lady Chevenix; "and do promise me that, if you overtake the man, you will do nothing violent."

"I will not leave a whole bone in his body," answered her husband, hotly. "Dinner, Louisa! Do you think I would stay to eat dinner when very likely this poor girl is in the hands of a villain?"

"I will go with you, Chevenix," said Sir Harry, ringing the bell.

His friend endeavored to dissuade him, saying, "No, no; you stay and amuse the ladies, Jarvis. You are not so deeply interested in this matter."

"I am more interested than you know," replied the old baronet; and, turning to the servant who entered, he ordered a fresh horse for himself, and another for Sir Charles.

In about twenty minutes the two gentlemen set out, followed by four servants, and as both, notwithstanding the age of the one, were stout riders, they were soon at the lodge of the park. There they received the first information of the way the chaise had taken, the woman who opened the gate informing them that, though it came from the Barnet side, it had gone on the road to Hertford.

"Stay," said Sir Charles, as they received these tidings; "it will be better to send my man Stevens to Barnet to make inquiries at all the inns; most likely they watered the horses there. Did you remark any name on the chaise, my good lady?"

"No, I did not think to do that, sir," replied the woman; "but it was a yellow chaise, any how."

"They are all yellow!" said Sir Charles, with a sigh; "that is the devil; one can not distinguish them by head-mark;" and, calling up his servant, he gave him directions in regard to the inquiries he was to make, and bade him afterward ride on to London and seek him at the Hummums.

This done, the Hertford road was pursued to the first toll-gate; but there they learned from the keeper that no such vehicle had passed within the time he named.

"Then they must have taken the by-road to the left," said Sir Harry Jarvis, "for the other on the right only leads to my neighbor General Hinds's."

Back, therefore, they turned, and pursued a narrow lane till they came to some cottages, where they again got intelligence of the object of their pursuit, and thus traced it on to the highway to St. Alban's. At the junction of the two roads there was a small public house, the landlord of which puzzled them sorely by replying to their inquiries, "Yes, yes, sir, it came along here, sure enough; but, just at the corner there, two men on horseback, who had been hanging about all the day, met it and turned it t'other way. I could hear one on 'em say to the fellow on the box, 'You sha'n't pass here,' and so round they went toward Lunnun; but I don't think they got far that way either, for I saw two others—just such as were standing here—waiting a mile further up, as I went by about an hour afore."

"What other road is there between this and the place where you saw them?" demanded Sir Charles; but his friend replied instead of the landlord, "Nothing but a cross country road toward Watford."

"There, sir, you can see where the chaise turned," said the master of the ale-house, "for she made a mighty great scrape upon the road."

"That may be some guide," said Sir Harry; "let us track the wheels from that point till we get further information."

This was accordingly done, and the chaise was thus distinctly traced to the corner of the by-road toward Watford, and for some way along it. But night began to fall; there were no cottages near to afford information; and at length Sir Charles and his companions were left completely at fault, among the narrow lanes which had puzzled Doctor Gamble and our other friends two nights before.

CHAPTER XXI.

Colonel Lutwich was writing a note in the saloon where he had received his guests so hospitably, and had just sealed it and written the address, when the stiff old man-servant, who walked about the house with a very dignified air, came in and stood before his master, like a captive Hebrew before one of the kings of the Medes and Persians. The guests had departed at an early hour on the preceding day, and Lutwich, notwithstanding all his schemes of going to his lodgings in London, had remained at his cottage in a somewhat troubled and restless state. Several letters had he sent off in different directions the evening before, and now, as I have just said, he seemed about to dispatch another.

"What is it?" he asked, as he finished the address, looking up to the old man's face.

"Hal is mounted, sir," replied the butler, for so I suppose we must term him, "and the servant who was with the gentleman the other night has just ridden in—Hargrave, I think they call him."

"Send him in, send him in," exclaimed Lutwich, eagerly. "Tell Hal to wait, but keep in the saddle."

With slow and ceremonious step, the grave domestic went out, and soon ushered Zachary Hargrave into his master's presence. He then retired, closing the door behind him. Moreover—and I mention it as one of the most curious exceptions to a general rule—he did not linger near the door, nor put his ear down, but walked away, as if he had no curiosity whatsoever. It was not, indeed, that he did not suspect Colonel Lutwich of having secrets, for he knew he had many—perhaps too many; but he knew, likewise, that some of his secrets were very dangerous ones, and he eschewed them, being a man of extreme caution, a quality which he had obtained many years before as a marker at a billiard-table.

What passed between Colonel Lutwich and Zachary Hargrave I do not know; but their conference lasted some ten minutes, and then the latter came forth and left the cottage. No sooner was he gone, than, tearing a sheet of paper in scraps, Lutwich wrote a Christian and surname upon each, and then, just beneath, inscribed the cabalistic words, "Barrow Hill, noon." Having done this, and seen that the writing was dry, he went forth to the little ride before the cottage door, and, advancing to the side of his servant's horse, he placed the note in his hands, saying, "That to Sir Harry Jarvis: deliver, and come away. But give these as you go: they are all in order. Then join me at Swivel End as fast as possible."

The man made no reply but a nod, and rode off.

"Have a nice little supper ready at nine," said Lutwich, speaking to the old servant as he returned into the house; "and see that every thing is in order, Joseph."

"For how many, colonel?" asked the man.

"Oh, not many," replied his master, looking a little puzzled; "one or two. See if Hal saddled the bay for me before he went. If not, tell the boy to do it. And, stay! put these into the holsters."

"Ah, colonel!" said the old man, shaking his head ruefully as he took a beautiful pair of pistols which his master handed him, "Ah, colonel!" and he heaved a deep sigh.

"Pooh, pooh! you old fool," said Lutwich, "there is nothing going on to-night. You think yourself mighty wise, and fancy all kinds of foolish things; but you know nothing about it."

"Thank Heaven for that!" said the old man. "I'm only sorry, colonel, to see you out about such matters, and with such things as these."

"About what matters, Master Joseph?" replied his master, sternly; but then, relaxing his frown, he added, in a good-humored tone, "those things you seem so much afraid of are only destined to deliver an excellent and amiable young lady from the hands of a villain. Now, old man, are you satisfied?"

"Yes, sir, for to-night," replied Joseph; "I wish they may never be worse employed;" and he withdrew.

When he was gone, Lutwich sat down, leaned his head upon his hand, and meditated deeply for a moment or two. There are sometimes a few plain words, spoken even by a person for whom we have little respect, which strike home to the heart more closely than the most powerful oratory. I believe, indeed, that, under some circumstances, the less respect we have for the speaker, the more is the force of the remonstrance. When we place ourselves in such a position that a man for whom we have no reverence feels himself elevated to the superiority of admonition, the warning derives point from the fact.

At length Lutwich started up, hurried out to the stables, examined his horse's girths, leaped lightly into the saddle, and galloped away. Ten minutes after, he might be seen, with his beast reined in, upon the top of a little mound-like hill, which, I am inclined to believe, was originally the rude monument of the savage dead, from the name of "the Barrow Hill," which it still retained. He was no longer alone, however, for two well-mounted men were there before him. Another followed, cantering gayly up three or four minutes after, and another and another at short intervals, so that one might have imagined that it was "the meet" of a hunting party. Lutwich spoke little to any one, but what he did say seemed to receive respectful attention; not that there was any very solemn reverence in the aspect of his companions, for they laughed and talked when he was addressing them; but when he did, it was "Yes, sir"—"Certainly, colonel"—"I understand quite well, sir."

At length the party, including Lutwich himself and his servant, amounted to no less than ten; and then, in a few brief sentences, he distributed to them their several posts and duties. "You, Wilcox, ride forward alone on the Hertford road, within sight of the toll-bar. I do not think they will attempt to go straight on; if they do, stop them. Tell Tom, the turnpike man, to let them pass at his peril. Mind, the man has brown and red livery for his disguise. If they go down the lane—when you are quite sure of them—come round by Barnet on to the high road, and join our friends there. You, Captain Swan, with Browne, go on St. Alban's way—about a hundred yards beyond The Skittles will do. They must come out of the lane there, if Wilcox turns them at the toll. Just say, 'You can't pass here.' He will understand you in a minute. But you must know him, I think. He is the man they call Ben Plowshare, who was kicked out of the chocolate house."

"Oh, I know him, colonel," replied Captain Swan, "and he knows me. He won't try to go on when I tell him to go back."

"Then you, Martin, Jones, and Dick, keep together a mile on this side of Barnet, and stop them there. The other three must watch the corner of Mim's Lane, and the little road by the church, and the turning by the Three Horse Shoes. Divide them among you as you like, but, mind! do not let them break through. Sooner send a bullet into the fellow's head; and remember, the object is to turn them at every corner till they are driven up toward the cottage. I do not mind if they have a long round of it—all the better, indeed. I and Hal will be near most of you some time in the afternoon. Now away! Who'll be over that fence first?" and, cantering down, he took the hedge and ditch with grace and ease.

In less than a minute after, there were not three of the horsemen any where together. But it may be as well to leave them now to their own arrangements, and to follow the chaise which carried poor Kate Malcolm away from the house of Sir Harry Jarvis. She had obeyed the summons she received without much hesitation—not exactly without a doubt crossing her mind, for she thought it somewhat strange that the note she had received gave no indication whatsoever of the writer's name; but the common-place way in which Lady Chevenix had heard what she said, made her think the doubt silly, and she banished it.

When the chaise passed the lodge gate, had she been acquainted with the country in the neighborhood, she would have seen at once that she was not going toward London; but she knew nothing of the way, and the vehicle went on upon a good broad road for some distance, till suddenly the man upon the driving-seat called out, "Boy, to the left!" and the horses were turned down a narrow lane. Kate thought it strange that the driver should require to be told the road; but still she did not take much notice, and at the end of about a quarter of an hour they issued out into the wide highway again.

Suddenly a loud voice shouted out, "You can't pass here!" and with a sharp whirl the chaise wheeled round in the opposite direction. Kate now put down the front window, and inquired what was the matter in a tone of some alarm; but that was soon quieted; for, turning round and touching his hat, the man said, "They've got the road up there, ma'am, laying down new water pipes, so we must go round by the lanes—that's all."

On they went again for about two miles more; and then, suddenly, Kate saw two men on horseback draw out from the side of the road, and plant themselves directly in the way. The post-boy looked back to the servant, and the latter pointed sharply with his thumb to the right, when the chaise was turned at once up a narrow by-road, and Kate began to feel a good deal of alarm. What could she do? she asked herself; how should she act? but there was no reply at hand, and she sat still while the vehicle rolled on.

"If I see a house or cottage," she thought, "I will stop the chaise and make inquiry, or apply to the first person of gentlemanly appearance we meet."

Just as this resolution was taken, she perceived a gentleman on horseback, with a servant behind him, riding apparently through the fields, at the distance of two or three hundred yards, on a line parallel to the course of the chaise. She could not, indeed, see distinctly, on account of the hedge, whether he was in another road or on the meadow; but a moment or two after his horse rose to a gate, and he went gracefully over, followed by the servant. The next instant he disappeared, and no cottage came in sight, while still the chaise rolled on, and turned and returned, in what seemed to poor Kate a very strange and somewhat alarming fashion. She fancied, too, that she saw signals passing between the post-boy and the servant. She had no watch to tell the hour; but a shade came over the sky, and it seemed so long since she had quitted the house of Sir Harry Jarvis, that she felt sure, if they had directed their course toward London, they must have reached at last the suburbs.

At length, terror overcoming timidity, she let down the front glass again, and asked the man if he was sure they were going right.

"Oh yes, ma'am," he replied, "quite right, only they are so mending the high road, they have torn it all to pieces. That makes it a little round, but it is all right."

She was less easily satisfied now, however, for she felt sure that she perceived a meaning grin upon the fellow's lips as he half turned his face toward her, and she looked to the right and left to see if there was any one near to whom she could apply. Again, but this time on the right, she saw a gentleman on horseback and a servant, and though they were still at a distance, she felt sure that they were the same. The sight puzzled her; and though her simple heart was not suspicious, yet she thought it strange that the two should thus apparently follow the chaise. While she paused to consider, again the figures disappeared, and the carriage took another sudden turn. At the distance of about half a mile, the trees and hedge on the left ceased, and an open common presented itself on that side. It was now evidently growing dark, and Kate felt extremely terrified. At a distance there was a clump of tall trees, with smoke rising up from among them, but no sign of the city, nor, indeed, of any other habitation; and yet the post-boy spurred on hard, coming nearer to the clump of trees, but apparently intending to turn in on the left. Suddenly, however, through the darkening twilight, the horseman and his servant again appeared, and Kate's doubts of them, for a moment, returned in full force. They were instantly changed to the most opposite feelings, however; for the man on the box, leaning forward, exclaimed with an oath, "There are those fellows again, d— me! Turn sharp away across the common, and back into the Barnet road."

The poor girl's resolution was instantly taken; and, putting out her head, she called loudly to the gentleman on horseback, while the driver turned his horses as he had been directed, and flogged them almost into a gallop.

The man's manœuver was in vain: the beautiful hunter which the gentleman she had seen was riding, stretched out fiercely, cleared the ground in a moment, was wheeled in front of the chaise; and a voice of thunder cried "Stop, or you are a dead man!" and at the same moment Kate saw a pistol drawn from the horseman's holsters.

The post-boy reined back the horses so suddenly as almost to overturn the chaise in the ditch, and wellnigh throw himself out of the saddle, and the worthy gentleman on the box jumped down, leaped the hedge on the other side of the road, and ran away.

"Stand at the horses' heads," said Kate's deliverer, speaking to his groom; and at the same time dismounting, he came round to the side of the carriage and opened the door, adding sternly to the driver, "Keep your horses still, sir!"

But the horses, probably rather under the secret application of the spur than from any great restiveness after so long a drive, continued to rear and plunge, and the gentleman, holding out his hand to the poor girl within, said, in a kindly tone, "You had better get out for a moment. I have been watching this chaise for more than half an hour. I think you will be safer out."

Kate Malcolm eagerly took his hand, and sprang out, saying, "Oh, thank you, Colonel Lutwich, a thousand times: I do not know where they were taking me."

"Keep the horses still, sir!" exclaimed Lutwich, fiercely, "or *I will find* means to make them and you quiet;" but at that moment, as the groom relaxed his hold of the bridle for an instant, the post-boy drove his spurs into his bearer's sides, the animal sprang forward, striking the servant's horse with the pole, and the chaise went rattling down the road at full gallop.

"Shall I go after him and give him a shot, colonel?" cried Hal; but Lutwich answered, "No, no. Let him go. We must find other means of getting the lady safely home. Take my arm, dear Miss Malcolm," he continued; "you have been alarmed, I am afraid. Be under no fear now. Look upon me, for the moment, as a brother; and be assured that all a brother's affection and regard can do for you shall be done, till you are again placed with those who have a better title to protect you."

"Oh, I am so much obliged to you, sir," she said; "I do not know where those people were taking me, or what was their object; but I am now sure that they have deceived me, for they could not be going toward London."

"Quite in an opposite direction," answered Lutwich; "but we will have explanations hereafter. In the mean time, you shall rest at my house, which you see there, till we can find means of sending you back."

"Can not I walk back?" asked Kate, eagerly.

"Impossible, dear young lady; the distance is far greater than you think," replied Lutwich. "No, no. Come in and rest, and take some refreshment. We will then talk over what is to be done. Believe me, you are with a man of honor, who would not, for life, say or do any thing that could give you pain. Come, dear Miss Malcolm;" and, drawing her arm through his own, he gave his horse to the servant, and led her across the common toward the cottage.

His words and his manner were all calculated to disarm apprehension. He was kind and even tender, but without the least appearance of gallantry; and though once or twice, as they went, the subject of Kate's adventure was referred to, he neither asked nor gave explanations, touching upon the topic with a degree of reserve which excited some curiosity.

Kate told him, indeed, how she had been inveigled away from the house of Sir Harry Jarvis, and asked, "What could be their motive?"

"A bad one, my dear young lady," replied Lutwich, dryly; "we will talk more about it presently, for there are some things to be considered which perhaps may puzzle you a little. Suffice it, I have been watching the chaise for some time, as I said just now, anxious to see if any of the principal actors in the affair would appear, but fully resolved to prevent your being taken much further."

"Then did you know I was in it?" asked Kate, in surprise.

Lutwich turned toward her, and she could see a faint smile upon his lip. "I guessed it," he answered, "from some information which reached me this morning; but let us just now talk of other things. I will very soon give you every information you can wish. You are safe, and that is enough for the present."

In about a quarter of an hour they reached the gate of the cottage gardens, the groom following with the horses close behind. The old gardener opened the gates; and, leading his fair companion down the avenue, Lutwich rang the bell at the door, which was opened by the butler, whose face exhibited a little surprise to see a young and very beautiful girl upon his master's arm.

"Lights!" said Lutwich, leading the way into his saloon. "Now sit down, dear Miss Malcolm, and rest for a little," he continued, conducting her to a seat near the fire; and then, while the old servant, after having lighted the tapers on the table, closed the door and retired, the master of the house leaned thoughtfully for a moment on the back of a chair, his handsome figure falling naturally into an attitude of great grace. Then taking out his watch, he said, "It is past seven, my dear Miss Malcolm. Before we could get a chaise from Barnet, and you could reach Sir Harry Jarvis's, it would be about one o'clock in the morning, and Barnet is the nearest place where we can get post-horses. I see no course to be pursued but for you to write a note at once to Lady Chevenix, telling her briefly what has occurred, in order to relieve the mind of your friends. I will send it over by a servant, and they then can either come to-night or to-morrow morning for you, as they judge best; but I trust you will tell them, also, that I will do all that I can in my humble dwelling to put you at your ease and make you comfortable."

Kate Malcolm gazed in his face anxiously. The circumstances were new and strange to her. She had struggled with poverty—borne deep sorrow—fulfilled many a difficult duty well and unhesitatingly; but the thought of remaining alone in the house of a man nearly a stranger to her, and that man a young, gay man of the world, alarmed her—not, indeed, from any dread of what might be his conduct, for his whole demeanor from the time they had first met—his tone, his look, as well as his words—had won upon her confidence wonderfully. She thought—nay, she felt sure that she could trust herself with him in any circumstances with perfect safety; and perhaps, of all the men she had ever seen, he was the one in whom she would have felt most inclined to trust; but her mind had been somewhat strictly tutored in very early days to proprieties, and she shrank from the very thought of what might be construed into wrong.

"I know not what I ought to do," she said, at length.

"Do as I advise you," he answered, gravely; and then added, in almost a reproachful tone, "Miss Malcolm, do you doubt me?"

"Oh no!" exclaimed Kate, holding out her hand to him frankly. "I am obliged to you, Colonel Lutwich, for so many acts of kindness. I could not doubt you if I were willing—and, indeed, I am not. I only fear they may think it strange that I do not go back directly instead of writing. But I do not think you would advise me to do what may even seem improper."

"Not on any account, upon my honor," replied Lutwich, warmly, taking her hand and releasing it again immediately. "But consider, my fair young friend, it is very easy for me to send a letter by a man on horseback, who will speedily reach Jarworth Park; but that you can not go without sending to Barnet for a chaise, without waiting for its coming, and then traveling at midnight all the way back again. Had I my own carriage here, I would immediately put it at your disposal; but I have only saddle horses, and not even a lady's saddle, should you be inclined to act the dame of romance."

"Well, I will write, then," said Kate, with a faint smile; "I see no other course."

"There is none, indeed," replied Lutwich; "but, to make your mind easy as to what your friends may think, I will, at the same time, dispatch a note to Sir Charles Chevenix, expressing my regret that, having no carriage here, I can not send you back at once. This will account for all, and I will answer for it, Lady Chevenix will blame neither you nor me for the course we are pursuing."

"Thank you a thousand times for all your kindness, and for all the trouble you are taking," replied Kate.

The two notes were written at once; and, ringing the bell, Colonel Lutwich gave them to old Joseph, saying, "Let the boy mount the freshest horse, and carry these over at once to Jarworth Park. Tell him, should the family be up, to wait and see if there be any answer. Then, when you have given these orders, return here yourself. I must endeavor to make you as comfortable as possible, my dear Miss Malcolm," he continued, as the old man retired; "but I am afraid you will find my cottage but a poor place."

Kate shook her head sorrowfully, saying, "I have been accustomed to far poorer of late years, as you may divine."

"I trust those fortunes are changed," said her companion. "Would it were my lot—" The conclusion of the sentence seemed to hang suspended on his lips for a moment, and then he abruptly turned away, and moved some of the books from one side of the table to the other.

In a moment after, the old servant came in again, and his master said, "Tell the maids to prepare the room in which Major Brandrum slept the other night for Miss Malcolm. Let them move the little bed in from the closet, and tell your wife, Joseph, that I should be obliged to her to sleep there for to-night, as I dare say this lady will be well pleased to have a companion in a strange house."

Kate bent down her head. She felt very grateful, and her heart swelled to express her sense of his delicacy and kindness, but she could not find words to do so. "And now, Joseph, let us have tea in the next room," continued Lutwich; adding, when the man was gone, "His wife is a very respectable old lady—indeed, a superior person—and she has done much to make him better than he once was. We are all molded more or less, my dear young lady, by those whom Fate assigns us for our yoke-fellow in life. Many a man has been saved from perdition by the calm, gradual influence of a good and amiable wife."

A short silence succeeded, and indeed Colonel Lutwich seemed very thoughtful that evening; but at length Kate raised her eyes and said, with a slight glow upon her cheek, "You promised that you would give me some explanation of all this strange affair, in regard to which, though I have been made a principal actor therein against my will, I am more ignorant, it would seem, than any one."

"And now," said Lutwich, with a laugh, "I am half sorry that I made the promise, for I find it somewhat difficult to perform, without risking consequences which I know would be painful to you. Have you no idea whatsoever how and why this has occurred?"

"None, I can assure you," replied Kate, looking him full in the face with an ingenuous blush. "I can not even imagine why any one should treat me in such a manner."

Lutwich sat down near her, and gazed at her almost sadly for a moment, but then withdrew his eyes and said, "I believe you, from my heart. You do not know how beautiful you are, my dear Miss Malcolm; nor perhaps, even if you did, would you be able to imagine the baseness to which that beauty may subject you."

Kate Malcolm's face was now crimson; and her companion proceeded rapidly, laying his hand gently upon hers and withdrawing it again immediately. "But why should we talk of such things? why should I alarm a young and confiding heart with even a knowledge of all the evil that is in the world? Go on, go on in your innocence and truth; and trust to them for defense in yourself, or for friends to defend you. Suffice it, that when first I ever beheld you, I found you, as you must but too well remember, insulted by a mere boy, who I thought knew no better. That may give you some indication of the causes of an event which has been a mystery to you. Accidental circumstances brought to my knowledge that a deceit was likely to be practiced upon you; and I not only cautioned Sir Harry Jarvis, anonymously, to be careful of you, but gave him reasons for so being. Not satisfied, I took means to gain further information, and then watched to serve you. Luckily, I did not watch in vain—But here is tea; let us go into the other room, and think no more of these things at present."

Kate Malcolm rose thoughtfully to accompany him, but paused ere she reached the door, saying, "How can I ever thank you sufficiently?"

"More than sufficiently," he answered, "by never mentioning the subject again."

When in the dining-room, where the service had been laid, Lutwich led her to the end of the table, and gazed at her, while she made tea, with a look of admiration that he could not restrain. Busy with her occupation, to which she had been accustomed, she did not observe the expression of his face for some time; but at length, raising her eyes, read there a history which made her heart beat quick. Lutwich instantly withdrew his glance, and attempted to explain the eagerness with which he had been gazing by saying, "You are the first lady, my dear Miss Malcolm, who has ever made tea for me in this house, and it looks strange—but very pleasant."

Kate was not deceived, however; but even the attempt to conceal his feelings under the circumstances in which she was placed, tended to win gratitude still more, and something like a tear of admiration and thankfulness for such conduct swam for an instant in her eyes, and then seemed to be absorbed in their light. She was silent, however, and Lutwich a moment or two after returned in some degree to the subject on which they had been previously conversing.

"Do you know, fair lady," he said, in a gayer tone, "you and I have to consider what our conduct must be when Sir Harry Jarvis or your other friends come or send for you?—nay, do not look astonished or alarmed. This I *must* explain to you, for we shall have to come to some resolution."

Kate's heart beat again very fast, for she knew not what was coming next, and her feelings were already such toward her companion as to render even that doubt very agitating.

"The case is this," continued Lutwich. "The trick which has been played upon you may, and indeed must be, considered as insulting by those who have you under their protection. Sir Charles Chevenix is, I have always heard, as generous and noble-minded a man as any in the world; but he is hot and hasty, and I think would undoubtedly resent this business in a manner likely to lead to very serious consequences if he should be made acquainted with the name of the person who attempted to lure you away from his care."

"Oh, then, do not tell him, if you know," cried Kate Malcolm.

"I do know certainly," replied Lutwich; "but there is also another view of the case, my dear young lady, which you, in your simplicity and innocence, do not think of. If I do not tell Sir Charles the whole facts, he may, and probably will, suspect that I have had some share in the business."

"Oh, he will never think of such a thing," cried Kate; "you could have no motive."

But Lutwich shook his head. "You are mistaken in your conclusion," he replied. "Sir Charles will easily divine that to have you thus for one day in my house, I would do any thing short of a breach of honor; and, besides," he continued, rapidly glancing away again from the avowal of his feelings, "besides, he will hear that I watched the chaise for several miles. He will think it strange that I did not stop the post-boy, and force him to drive you back. He will not understand that, in the hurry of the moment and by an instant's hesitation—" He paused very gravely, and then added, "Ay, by an instant's hesitation, I let the opportunity escape of doing that which was right. I blame myself—will he not blame me still more?"

"Oh, do not blame yourself," cried Kate, warmly; "it was not your fault."

"Yes it was," answered Lutwich, almost bitterly; and, drawing his chair somewhat nearer, he added, in a low voice, "I hesitated between the pleasure of having you here—of seeing you, and being with you for one whole day, and taking you back in the chaise at once. It was but an instant; but that instant, and the eagerness of the scoundrel driver to escape, made it too late to act right. Now I have confessed my fault. I repent it—I grieve for it. Only say that you forgive me, and I will utter not one other word upon this subject till I can do so boldly and openly. Tell me, do you forgive me?" and he held out his hand toward her with a look of sorrowful doubt.

"Oh yes," replied Kate, giving him her hand; "but what is to be done?"

"I know not," replied Lutwich; "but such are the consequences of even hesitating to do right. I am not one," he added, with a melancholy smile, "to moralize too deeply upon such subjects. I have done many a thing in life very, very wrong; but I could have wished my every action—ay, even my every thought toward you to have been free from the least shade of selfishness; and now I have placed myself in a position where I risk the chance of incurring suspicion unjustly, or of bringing about serious mischief if I place the responsibility upon the real culprit."

Kate had been thinking deeply while he spoke; but when the sound of his voice ceased, she looked up with a smile, as if her mind had come to some satisfactory conclusion, and she said, "Tell him—tell Sir Charles Chevenix. I have always found it best to be frank and straightforward. I never concealed any thing I did in my life, except that letter to Mr. Eaton, which I showed you. I knew that my poor father's pride would make him prevent me from sending it, if I told him, and when the cold answer came there was no use of speaking; but I have always regretted even that. Tell Sir Charles, then; but you may make it a condition that he takes no vengeance for what I believe, as you do, he will look upon as a personal insult to himself. He has been very, very kind to me, and so has his dear daughter—ay, and Lady Chevenix too, though more cold and stately."

"You are right," said Colonel Lutwich; "I will tell Sir Charles; and I have a good excuse for binding him to refrain from all chastisement in this person's case, although, had I met him to-night, I had resolved to horsewhip him upon the spot. That would have done him good."

"Then you are quite sure you know who it is?" asked Kate.

"Oh yes! Sir Theodore Broughton, beyond all doubt," replied Lutwich.

"Who is he?" demanded Kate Malcolm, with a look of some surprise; "did I ever see him?"

"Certainly," answered her companion; "the same whom I found insulting you in the passage of the inn at Dunstable. I heard the whole scheme sketched out through the thin partition of a room very near that in which you will sleep to-night, and received further information this morning. So now that is off my mind. I will tell Sir Charles; and now we will think of other things."

"What can make him persecute me so?" said Kate, in a meditative tone.

Lutwich smiled. "All men are beasts of prey," he replied; "but there is this distinction between them, dear Miss Malcolm. Some, of a bolder and stronger nature, attack those who are prepared to resist and to prey upon them in return, and scorn to assail the weak and unresisting. The lion does not pursue the hare. Others, however, chase the unprotected and defenseless; and, though they be pitiful beasts, depend upon it they are very dangerous to those who have no power of resistance."

His mind seemed to rise as from under a load now that his resolution was taken, and he spoke cheerfully, though thoughtfully, of many things during the next two or three hours, without, however, even approaching again the subject of his heart's feelings toward her beside him. He lured her from her thoughtfulness, too, although with a strange, new sensation, almost approaching fear, Kate felt that she was loved, and, perhaps, that she could love in return. She was no way versed in such sensations, it is true, and she was eager to question her own heart; but she was sure that her gratitude was very, very strong, or that there was something warmer still within her bosom.

CHAPTER XXIII.

We are informed, in one of the truest histories which has ever been produced since the deluge—I know not very accurately what went before—that when Beder, king of Persia, had been carried, in the form of a white bird with a red bill and feet, by the waiting-maid of Giauhara, princess of Samandal, to a beautiful plain in a well-frequented island, he was for some time at a loss how to get his daily bread; but, having no other resource, and being likely to die of hunger, he was obliged "to live upon such nourishment as birds of his kind were wont to have." Such was exactly the case with Sir Theodore Broughton. He had worked himself up, as lads of his age are accustomed to do when they have a strong imagination and not very strong judgment, to a belief that he could not live without Kate Malcolm; but, finding that some time would be necessary for the completion of Doctor Gamble's arrangements, he was forced to content himself with expectation, which is exactly such nourishment as "birds of his kind are wont to have." Gamble, it is true, did his best to gratify him as soon as possible; and, indeed, in a piece of somewhat romantic intrigue, the doctor was quite in his element. He ran hither, he ran thither, from Bow-street to the Dog and Duck; he conversed with rogues and vagabonds of various classes and various grades; he inquired for old acquaintances, and made new; and, though some of those old acquaintances had been raised higher than their wishes ever reached, by an unpleasant process, which kept them in suspense to the end of life, and others had gone to visit foreign countries in the least expensive manner, and though his very critical taste was not easily satisfied as to the perfections of new professors in the art he was about to practice, he at length found two or three to his mind, to whom, after long consultations, he intrusted the execution of the scheme he had conceived.

Sir Theodore Broughton was, in truth, very much astonished, not only at the activity of his respected tutor in his new capacity, but in the thorough knowledge which he seemed to possess of all the means and appliances for arriving at any ends, however flagitious, in a great capital like London; and the young baronet became convinced that all the severity and bursts of pomposity which had been displayed by Doctor Gamble as his preceptor in the early part of his engagement, had been merely a robe put on for the time to cover the real character below. Nevertheless, he had an internal consciousness that such a man as the tutor now appeared might be very useful to him, and he listened eagerly to all the varied reports which were brought in of the failure of this part of the negotiation, and the success of another; but at length Ben Plowshare was found, whose wit was notorious, though the greatest exercise of that quality which he had practiced was to keep his own neck out of a halter, a feat which much more honest men than he was have not always succeeded in effecting. His stipulations were somewhat hard, but they were complied with; and, in return, he undertook to find two assistants, one of whom was to personate a post-boy and drive a hired carriage, while the other was to ride off to inform Doctor Gamble and his pupil of the success of the scheme, as soon as poor Kate Malcolm was once beyond the gates of Sir Harry Jarvis's park. These arrangements occupied the whole of the first day after the arrival of the young baronet in London; and the chief remaining difficulty at its close seemed to be, how to separate decently from Major Brandrum and Reginald Lisle, with whom Sir Theodore had taken up his residence at the Old Hummums.

"Leave it to me," said Doctor Gamble, as he sat for a few moments in Sir Theodore's room, previous to the whole party setting out to see Garrick; and choosing his moment in the theater when the business of the stage was suspended, he saw, or affected to see, an old acquaintance on the opposite side of the house, crossed over, was seen speaking to a distinguished-looking man almost alone in a box opposite, and then returning, called Sir Theodore away from his two companions, saying aloud, "Lord Milson tells me he is an old friend of your grandfather's, and particularly wishes me to bring you over and introduce you to him."

Sir Theodore rose and followed, and Reginald Lisle and his friend saw all the ceremonies of introduction take place, and the young baronet assume a seat by the old nobleman. After remaining a few minutes, Doctor Gamble retired into the adjoining box, and Sir Theodore remained till the play was concluded.

"Not very courteous to leave his party," said Major Brandrum, as they were preparing to depart; "but he's a mere boy, and it is that sensual sycophant's doing."

"I have a strong notion," said Reginald, "that he is something worse than you call him. I believe that man Gamble to be a base scoundrel, who will end by completely corrupting the youth's mind."

The words were hardly out of his lips when they were rejoined by the two of whom they had been speaking, and Sir Theodore said at once, "I must put off my trip to Ranelagh, Lisle, for I have accepted an invitation to spend a few days in the country."

The color came into his cheek as he spoke, and Reginald evidently remarked it, which made it turn deeper still. Nothing more was said, however; and on the following morning, by gray daylight, Sir Theodore and his tutor left the Hummums.

The busy, cheerful satisfaction of Doctor Gamble was quite edifying. He evidently looked upon himself as a good man doing a benevolent action; he was delighted, he was quite happy, for no boy naturally delights in a piece of mischief more than Doctor Gamble delighted in an enterprise, of whatever kind and character it might be. It was not alone that he saw profit, and pleasure, and power in aiding the passions of his pupil, and entangling him in difficulties from which he could not extricate himself without his assistance, but there was in his very constitution a love of, and desire for, adventure and intrigue, quite separate from his interested views. He had enjoyed few opportunities of indulging this propensity since he had held his appointment of preceptor to the young baronet, although, whenever Captain Donovan was absent for any length of time, Doctor Gamble had taken care that his skill in such affairs should not get rusty; and now he was like a fish which, after having lain in an angler's basket for some minutes, suddenly finds itself, by the upsetting of its wicker prison, restored to its own free element again.

Very different were the feelings of Sir Theodore Broughton. He went on, it is true. He resolved that he would not pause or hesitate. He felt more manly in the very undertaking; and that sensation would have gratified his timid vanity and hurried him forward, even had there not been passion in his heart. But yet his bosom was not free from remorse, nor his mind from apprehension. He was agitated, he was nervous, he was by no means confident. He asked himself, "What if Kate should discover that, instead of being really her deliverer, he was, in fact, her persecutor, and that the whole scheme, which he was to appear as frustrating, was of his own devising? What would she think of him? How should he act if she reproached him with it? What would be the shame of exposure?"

Be it remarked, he never paused upon the idea of the vengeance which Sir Charles Chevenix and Major Brandrum were likely to take for an insult offered to the poor girl under their protection. The youth was only mentally, not corporeally timid; and in answer to these questions to his own heart, his reply was, "If she does discover all, I can but cast myself at her feet, and tell her that it was love which drove me to madness."

Then, again, the easy, jaunty, confident air of Doctor Gamble, and his constant assurances that every thing was going right, that the scheme could not fail, kept up his spirits, and taught him to crush his fears as they arose.

Now, although I have called this work an old-fashioned romance, do not let the reader say that the events are improbable—altogether unlikely; but let him be assured, on the contrary, that such a scheme was actually conceived and executed not many years ago, that the facts are given as nearly as possible with accuracy, and that nothing but the names are changed. Perhaps the most difficult period of English history is that in which the scene of the present work is laid. It is so near our own days that we naturally fancy that the customs and manners must have been very much like our own—they have not become traditionally different—and yet in no country has there been so great and extraordinary a change as in this, within the same space of time. Where are the banded highwaymen, the conniving justices, the art-and-part constables, the mock parsons, the Fleet marriages, the capital punishments remitted at the solicitation of peers, the hired bullies? Yet we know that all these things existed, though they have passed away with swords, queues, hair-powder, and laced coats.

At that time all these things not only existed in reality, but were daily described in books, spoken of in journals, and represented upon the stage, so that acts which would seem, if proposed to any young man of the present times, so rash and dangerous as to savor of madness, did not appear to the eyes of Sir Theodore Broughton as any thing very extraordinary; and what he felt was only that timid hesitation, and fear of discovery and shame, which affects naturally every young and not wholly corrupted mind in the execution of any evil device.

He showed no want of resolution, however; and Doctor Gamble, though he saw that his pupil was somewhat nervous and agitated, did not at all see how much. He tried to encourage him by all means in his power, indeed, and knowing that active exertion was the best means of banishing such sensations, he at once led the young baronet on the road to St. Alban's, leaving Zachary Hargrave with directions to watch the gates of Sir Harry Jarvis's house near Barnet. When a favorable opportunity for carrying out their scheme against poor Kate was presented by the family with whom she was staying going out, Hargrave was ordered to ride at once to Ben Plowshare, at Barnet, and inform him of the fact.

Doctor Gamble calculated most things very nicely. He said, "Of course the young lady will not go out herself till her mourning is ready and her father's funeral over; but that will be no reason for the rest staying at home." But he did not calculate one point, which was, that a man of the character of Hargrave might not like half confidence, and be somewhat displeased to see a person whom he had always believed his young master hated very energetically, suddenly supplant him in the agreeable task of misleading Sir Theodore at his outset in life. It is true, Hargrave had other and very cogent motives for paying a visit to Colonel Lutwich, and giving him information of all that was going on; but still, spite had a good deal to do with it.

The next task of the tutor was to seek some place to which poor Kate Malcolm might be carried; but there is no use of inflicting the details upon the reader. Suffice it, that after a good deal of difficulty, a cottage not far from St. Alban's was found, with a good lady for its owner, who was willing, upon certain considerations, to be very discreet; and this being accomplished, and the resolution of Doctor Gamble and Sir Theodore having been strengthened by dinner and wine, they waited with some impatience for the appearance of their messenger. He was so late that even Doctor Gamble began to fancy something must have gone wrong, or, at the best, that a part of the scheme would be frustrated by enveloping its execution in darkness.

At length, however, Ben Plowshare's friend entered the room where they were sitting, hot and dusty with hard riding, and exclaimed, "They are off, gentlemen. Mount directly, and you will meet them about three miles before they reach the town."

"That is just the thing," cried Doctor Gamble; and, running down to the stable-yard, where their horses were already saddled, followed by Sir Theodore with a face pale from agitation, he mounted and set out.

"Now remember, my dear young friend," said the tutor, "you are to look full into the chaise, and when you see your fair Dorinda, pull off your hat, stop the post-boy, and speak to her in a common-place way, asking if she is returning to Dunstable. She will of course say 'No, she is going to London;' and then you must tell her she is deceived, and we will undertake to see her right, and punish the wicked men who have misled her—ha, ha, ha! Do you understand?"

In such conversation they rode on at a quick rate, till three, four, five miles of the Barnet road were passed, and they began to entertain serious alarm. Barnet itself at length was seen, and Doctor Gamble, with a look of considerable astonishment and consternation, exclaimed, "Let us ride to the inn and make inquiries." But there, no information was to be obtained except that the carriage they inquired for had been gone more than two hours, and they set out to retread their steps just as a servant on horseback rode into the yard, inquiring about the very same vehicle.

CHAPTER XXIV.

Reginald Lisle, after having passed the morning of that day, the events of which have occupied the last two or three chapters, at his mother's cottage, rejoined his friend, Major Brandrum, at their inn, and set out in the afternoon for Ranelagh. The conduct of their young companion, Sir Theodore, did not altogether pass without notice between them, and Reginald at once expressed an opinion that the pretended invitation to the country was merely an excuse for separating himself from persons whose presence might be a restraint.

"I can easily see," he said, "that this tutor, whose conduct in leaving the youth entirely alone during his guardian's absence was sufficiently reproachable to justify his dismissal, has been retained for some object or another, which it is not worth while to inquire into; and he is evidently not at all well pleased that any one should be at hand to give counsels opposed to what I am afraid his own will be."

"My dear Lisle," replied the other, "if he were among our friends the Indians, Master Gamble would soon acquire the name of the 'Slimy Snake.' I happened, accidentally, to overhear yesterday a part of his conversation with his pupil, and from that moment I clearly saw that, if he were to remain with Sir Theodore, our society would serve the lad but little. Donovan is a scoundrel, that is clear; and, whatever be his ends, he is working that youth's moral destruction. I shall trouble my head no more about the matter, but sing Jolette as usual; and, if you will take my advice, you will do the same. Heaven help me! I shall have enough to do with what I undertook for poor Malcolm. I never thought the Ravenous Crow would have to take such a pretty little bird under his wing; but, at all events, he must contrive to provide for her, and fight for her too, if there should be occasion."

"I trust there will be no occasion for any thing of the latter kind," replied Lisle; "I have spoken to my dear mother to-day about her, and she will receive her, and treat her as a child of her own. There she will be quite safe, whatever happens to you or me, Brandrum. My sister Lucy laughed at me about the matter, and would fain make out that my mother will soon have a legal title to call the poor girl by the name of daughter. There was no convincing her; so I must take you to dine at the cottage to-morrow, to give her a truer account of the business."

"Perhaps Lucy may be right," answered Brandrum, with a laugh.

"No, my dear Crow, no!" answered Reginald, warmly.

"But why not?" asked Major Brandrum. "I think she is as beautiful a little creature as ever I beheld."

"Doubtless," answered Captain Lisle; "but if you ask why not, I will tell you in a word, Brandrum—my whole heart and affections are engaged to another."

Major Brandrum meditated thoughtfully for a few moments, and then said, in a grave tone, "Miss Chevenix! Lisle, Lisle! I am afraid you are cutting out unhappiness for yourself. She is an heiress of great wealth, and her family are proud. You have yourself some six hundred a year, I believe, and your mother and sister, between them, about the same. What will Sir Charles say?"

"Nay, I know not," answered Lisle; "indeed, I believe it is a piece of madness; but I never yet heard that love was governable by reason. Sir Charles himself is not haughty in the least; but Lady Chevenix is proud, as you say—I can see that clearly. However, my family is as good, or better, than their own; and in regard to fortune, though I never till now cared about it, or calculated upon future contingencies, yet one day I may be wealthy. My uncle Mullins is very rich, and without a child. I am his nearest, and, indeed, his only male relation, and I have ever been a great favorite with him. Were he a father, he could not be more kind and affectionate, in his blunt way."

"Well, well," said Brandrum, with a sigh, "you may have many years to wait, and yet succeed at last."

Here dropped the conversation, and shortly after the two officers reached that place which was then the resort of all the fashionable company of London. It has been too often described for any account of its tinsel splendors to be needed here, and therefore I will pass over all smaller events, merely remarking that Reginald Lisle and his companion met with a number of acquaintances, talked with them gayly in turn, drank tea according to the prescribed mode of the place, and were thinking of returning home, when one of the waiters, who knew them, approached, and handed a card to the elder officer, saying, "That gentleman, sir, is waiting at the foot of the stairs to speak with you. He is in a riding dress, and can not come up."

"Sir Charles Chevenix!" exclaimed Brandrum: "what can he want at this hour? Come, Lisle, let us go and see."

The two gentlemen hurried down, and the cause of Sir Charles Chevenix's coming was soon explained. "I went at once to the Hummums," he said, "and there being informed you had come hither, I hastened after, while my friend Sir Harry Jarvis remained to catch you if you returned; for Ranelagh, unlike a rat-trap, has as many ways out as it has in. Besides, we sent a servant to Barnet to inquire at all the inns as to where the chaise came from, and gave him directions to follow us to your inn."

Reginald's face turned red with indignation, and his brow gathered into a heavy frown. "This is too bad," he cried; "I will horsewhip the scoundrel as long as I can stand over him."

"We must find him first," replied Sir Charles Chevenix, who had watched the young officer's countenance very attentively, and drawn his own conclusions. "Let us return to the Hummums, and consult. This is too public a place. What say you, major?"

"With all my heart," answered Major Brandrum, much more coolly; "we will soon find our young friend; but, by Lisle's leave, I claim the horsewhipping business to my own share, by right of seniority both in years and servitude, and also of my guardianship of poor Kate. I must not scalp him, I am afraid, living in this cold, phlegmatic country, otherwise it would be a satisfaction; but I may skin him alive, which is the next best thing. There, boy, call a hackney coach." And, as soon as one of those rumbling vehicles was procured, the three got in, and gave orders to drive with all speed to Covent Garden.

"And now, gentlemen, can you give me any clew to where the young lady is?" asked Sir Charles, as soon as they were seated; "for, between you and me, I look upon the insult to be personal to myself, and I shall certainly treat it accordingly."

"Oh no, Sir Charles," said Lisle, "leave that part of the matter to us. You have a family—we have none, either of us. I can form no notion where he has taken her, but doubtless we shall soon discover, and will take the necessary steps to bring back poor Miss Malcolm, and punish the offender."

"Then you know, or at least suspect, who is the culprit," said Sir Charles Chevenix, in a tone partly of inquiry and partly of affirmation.

Reginald Lisle was silent, but Major Brandrum answered, "Yes, Sir Charles, we suspect, with that degree of suspicion which amounts very nearly to conviction. But as doubts are unpleasant and dangerous things—not the less dangerous because they are unpleasant, nor the less unpleasant because they are dangerous—we will soon find means to change them into certainties. Let us hear what your servant has to say, and then leave Lisle and me to find out the rest. We have been accustomed to follow trail, and you need not have any fear lest we should miss our mark."

"We will talk of all that by-and-by, major," replied Sir Charles Chevenix, not at all disposed to leave a matter altogether in other hands which he looked upon as affecting his own honor and character; and the coach rolled on in silence toward the Hummums.

From time to time—as they passed one of

those dim and dingy globes of ill-cleaned glass, with a few drops of oil at the bottom, and a dull wick burning in the center, with which the streets of London were then illuminated, and which have been long forgotten by all but those whose dwelling-place of memory is in the past —Sir Charles gave a glance to the face of Reginald Lisle. It was stern and anxious, and again the baronet drew his own conclusions. At length the Hummums, as the inn was called, was reached, and, alighting in haste, the three gentlemen ascended to the room of Major Brandrum, where they found Sir Harry Jarvis, waiting with some anxiety, and Sir Charles Chevenix's servant, Stevens, standing before him, hat in hand.

Brief introduction sufficed, and, as soon as that ceremony was over, Sir Charles exclaimed, eagerly, "Well, Stevens, what news? Have your discovered any thing? Is there not a mare's-nest in all Barnet to give us some occupation, at least?"

"Not that I know of, Sir Charles," replied the man, dryly; "and I have been able to find out little. I went to one inn and another, till at length I rode into the yard of the Swan; and just as I was going in, I saw two gentlemen a' horseback ride out; and when I asked for the chaise, the hostler could tell me little enough about it. He said, your honor, that there had been a hired carriage—a yellow one —standing there for an hour or two, with a servant in red and brown livery; but the postboy was a stranger, not at all known on the road, who would neither talk nor drink. The hostler said, however, winking his eye, that the two gentlemen who had just gone off had been inquiring after the same, and he had told them just what he told me, which was little enough."

"What like were the two men?" demanded Reginald, abruptly.

"Why one, sir, was fattish," answered the servant; "not to say very fat, either, but an elderly gentleman in black, some forty-five years old or so."

"Hang the fellow!" cried Sir Charles; "does he call forty-five elderly?"

"Beg pardon, your honor; no offense, I hope; but he was past the middle age, I mean," rejoined Stevens. "However, he was dressed in black, and t'other was quite a young gentleman like—not over nineteen or twenty, I should say. I've seed him before, too, I think, and I've a notion it was at that there fire at Dunstable."

"Exactly so," replied Reginald Lisle, looking toward Major Brandrum.

"Then you know him?" said Sir Charles Chevenix, once more. "Now, my dear Lisle, be so good as to favor me with his name."

Reginald took his hand with a frank but meaning smile. "No, Sir Charles," he said, "I will not. Lady Chevenix shall not have it to say that I have brought you into two affairs of the same kind. You must leave this affair to me and Major Brandrum. We have a knowledge of the culprit, and the means, I doubt not, of finding him speedily. It is more our business a great deal than yours, for this young lady is the adopted daughter of my friend, and was going to take up her abode under my mother's roof. Am I not right, Sir Harry Jarvis?"

"So far right, my dear sir," replied the old gentleman, "as keeping pepper away from a fiery spirit goes. But still, it will be a satisfaction to Sir Charles and myself if immediate means are taken to set free our fair young friend, for I can hardly suppose that she is at liberty; and I take a deep—a very deep interest in her."

"She is certainly not at liberty, or she would be in your house, Sir Harry," replied Major Brandrum; "for I do not scruple to assert, judging from her devoted conduct to her poor father, that she would judge it both improper and unpleasant to absent herself from the protection of Lady Chevenix, and not the less unpleasant because it was improper, nor the less improper because it was unpleasant."

"I will go and make instant inquiries into the matter," said Reginald Lisle; and, without more ado, he quitted the room and sought out the stables where the horses of Sir Theodore Broughton had been put up. There, by dexterous interrogatory, and the influence of that facile opener of the hearts of grooms, hostlers, and stable-boys—money, he speedily obtained sufficient information to lead him aright in pursuit of the young baronet; but, not contented with this, he questioned the waiters and servants of the hotel till he had elicited that a well-known and suspicious character, of the name of Benjamin Lee, otherwise Ben Plowshare, had been with Doctor Gamble and Sir Theodore Broughton several times during the preceding day.

With this clew, he returned immediately to his friends above; but, acting upon the plan he had laid down for himself, he did not communicate the intelligence he had received. He found Sir Charles Chevenix, indeed, in eager discussion with Major Brandrum in regard to the necessity of perfectly open dealing in a matter where the honor and reputation of several parties were concerned; but the worthy officer had at once conceived his young friend's views, and defended stoutly the position he had been left to maintain.

"It is all very true, Sir Charles," he said, just as Lisle was entering the room; "you are naturally anxious to have a matter of this kind in your own hands, but equally natural that Lisle and I should desire to keep it in ours; and as you have retired from active service and we have not, we take the liberty of holding our own right to act, notwithstanding your being our superior officer. He and I must settle our share of the affair as we can; but that will be easily managed, for he is always reasonable, though sometimes a little hot, and is quite ready to fight or let it alone, according as circumstances may require. Indeed, I have seldom seen a man so indifferent as to which he does, which I believe to be more consonant with the character of a true soldier than the most impetuous daring."

"He is ready enough to fight, that I can answer for," replied Sir Charles; "perhaps a little too ready, Lisle," he continued, turning his head; "but now, Jarvis, what do you say? Ought not these gentlemen to let me know who it is they suspect?"

Sir Harry Jarvis, however, took the side of Major Brandrum and Reginald Lisle, who cut the matter short by exclaiming, almost in a gay tone, "Boot and saddle, major! boot and saddle! I have ordered the saddles to be put on, you have naught to do but to put on the boots. I must run and do *the same, for I am resolved I will not sleep till I* have ascertained that poor Miss Malcolm is in safety. Your pardon for leaving you, gentlemen."

"But whither wend you?" demanded Sir Charles Chevenix; "that, at least, may be communicated."

"Toward St. Alban's," answered Reginald Lisle: "rest quiet, Sir Charles; we will soon find your fair protégée."

"If toward St. Alban's," said the baronet, "we may as well ride with you; for we must be back to Barnet, or my fair lady will expect to have me brought home with a wound in my hip, Mr. Lisle."

"My dear Sir Charles," said Reginald, taking his hand, "do not, I beseech you, mention that painful subject to me any more. Believe me, it has ever been to me a matter of shame and remorse since the ill-fated hour in which I raised my hand against you. That you have long since forgiven me, I am sure. I wish that both you and I could forget it: for my own part, I can not forgive myself."

"Pooh, pooh! there is nothing to forgive," replied Sir Charles; "I ran you too hard; you were a little too hot; and, after having been both a little wrong, we had not sense enough to get right again, and friends did their best to make bad worse. Now, away with you, Lisle; get ready for your ride; and, in the mean while, Sir Harry and I will have something to eat and a bottle of wine."

The town was passed through at a somewhat slow pace, for the streets of London were in those days not what they are now, dear reader. Large, slippery paving stones carpeted every path, and a horse's knees and his rider's head ran a great chance of being broken, if any thing like rapidity of progression was attempted. As soon, however, as the open road to Islington was reached, each gentleman applied the spur, and on they went at a quick trot. Little conversation took place, except a few low-spoken words between Reginald Lisle and Major Brandrum; and the whole party had just reached Finchley Common, which was then a common indeed, when a man was seen coming on horseback through the mist; for, though there was a pale moon in the sky, the night was somewhat foggy. Too formidable in numbers to fear attack, they were riding on, when a voice exclaimed, "Sir Harry! here is a note from Lady Chevenix, sir, and another for Sir Charles from Colonel Lutwich."

"We must stop at the Dragon, at Whetstone, to read them," said Sir Harry.

"You will have to knock the people up, then," replied his friend, taking the note from the servant; "the people will be all snoring. It is near one o'clock. You know the contents, I dare say, my good fellow."

"No, Sir Charles, I don't," replied Sir Harry Jarvis's servant; "but I believe the young lady is found, your honor, and that her ladyship wrote to save you the trouble of hunting any more to-night—so the butler said when he gave me the notes, and told me to take them to the Hummums, and if I did not find you there, to return directly."

"Well, well, but are you quite sure Miss Malcolm is found, and safe?" asked his master, impatiently.

"Oh yes, your worship," replied the man, "for Colonel Lutwich's groom said so—I heard him with my own ears—and how, when she called for help out of the chaise, the colonel had galloped up, and threatened to blow the post boy's brains out if he did not stop. I dare say she is at the park by this time."

This dare say, as many another dare say has done, gave a new turn to all proceedings, and one which, probably, they would not have taken, had the parties concerned been aware that it was put forth without just cause.

"Well, Major Brandrum and Captain Lisle," said Sir Harry Jarvis, in his courteous tone, "your minds are now, I trust, relieved as mine is; and that, after hearing all the particulars, you will be able to sleep quietly upon such hard beds as Jarworth Park can afford. So, if you please, we will all on to Barnet, without further question."

The proposal was agreed to readily, and in about three quarters of an hour more Reginald Lisle was seated at a well-covered supper-table by the side of Mary Chevenix.

CHAPTER XXV.

Some hours, I have said, went by in Colonel Lutwich's cottage, passed in pleasant conversation between him and Kate Malcolm. He avoided all subjects that would agitate her; he controlled his feelings; he guarded his looks; he put a watch upon his tongue; he said and did nothing which to any but a very keen and practiced observer of human nature would have shown that there were warm and powerful emotions raised up in his breast by the presence of that fair young creature. A very practiced observer, indeed, might have seen that the suppressed fire gave a glow and warmth to every word he uttered; that the vigor of powerful sensations was communicated to his language and his tone, however indifferent might be the subjects on which he spoke.

His conversation was, indeed, very different from that of Reginald Lisle. He had not the younger gentleman's eloquence or fancy, but every sentence was terse and powerful, and almost fiery, and on the mind of one so young as Kate Malcolm the whole had great effect. Force of character is one of the master secrets of all rule; and Kate felt that she was beside one whose resolute nature and strong decision afforded—though widely different from her own passive powers—a potent spell that she could not resist. His varying countenance, the innumerable shades of expression that flitted over it, from the tender and gentle look of affectionate concern with which he spoke of the anxiety and distress she had suffered, to the stern, angry frown his face assumed when commenting on the wrong-doers, excited admiration, almost wonder. She had not believed that any countenance could so change; and she compared it in her young fancy to a beautiful country swept by clouds and sunshine. Then, again, he would be the light man of the world, and speak gayly and sportingly of pleasures, and pastimes, and enjoyments, with a dash of harmless satire indeed, but still merry and not bitter. That mood, however, lasted never long, for the stronger emotions were too much for it; and it was generally followed by a melancholy train of thought, during which the expression of his countenance was so sad, and his words so touching, that all her own sorrows during the last six years seemed raised up by the plaintive music of his voice, and she had well-nigh wept.

The time seemed to fly very fast, for, ere she imagined more than an hour had passed, the clock on the sideboard, during a silent pause, struck ten, and Lutwich rose and rang for supper.

"I do not need any, indeed," said Kate—and truly too; for she had fed upon his words for the last two hours.

"It will do you good," replied Lutwich, with a smile; "and besides, dear lady, let me tell you, that except that cup of tea from your fair hands just now, I have not tasted food or drink to-day."

"And all on my account," cried Kate, feeling really much distressed. "I am shocked that such should have been the case. You must, I am sure, feel quite exhausted."

"Oh dear, no," answered Lutwich, gayly. "I could go on for many an hour yet. A soldier's life requires him to care little about any food but that of the mind, which I have surely had abundantly to-night. But the truth is, I think some refreshment is very necessary for you; and though tea may be very well, rousing the faculties and quickening the mind, yet it gives no strength to the muscles, and supplies not to this mortal frame the materials wasted in the wear and tear of life. Stimulating the mental powers, it rather tends to overtask the body, and sometimes makes the mind's slave work himself to death. Besides, I love a supper-table. It is the only meal beyond which there is a lapse of peace. Breakfast is a farewell to repose; dinner an interruption to business; but supper has fruition for its memory, and repose for its hope. Yes. yes, we will have supper, dear Miss Malcolm; then sit for a while, with the sleepy world of darkness before us, till my servant returns from your friend's house. Then you shall to your pillow, and in peaceful slumber forget all the strange sensations which I see you feel at finding yourself here the guest of Henry Lutwich, and spending a long evening in rambling chat with him alone."

"They *are* strange sensations," said Kate, simply.

"Doubtless, doubtless," said her companion; "and I will tell you what, my sweet friend; the years will come when you will look back to this night as to a curious and even interesting dream—an episode of life, not without its emotions at the time, or its clinging memories beyond; and I do trust that it will be a binding tie to attach me to your remembrance; and when you think of me, with all my faults, and perhaps hear others comment on them harshly, you may be able to say, 'He had none for me—'"

Here the old butler entered, and Lutwich stopped abruptly; nor was Kate sorry. It was a relief to her. There are times when emotions, however sweet, become painful in their intensity.

Though the minutes glided quickly for those over whose heads they there passed, yet the supper was really slow. They lingered over the meal, which was light and graceful, and old Joseph thought them very tardy indeed. He remained in the room all the time; and it is a somewhat tedious process, no doubt, to stand behind a chair in silence, while others eat and talk. I am not sure, however, that the presence of another was not, on the whole, agreeable to Lutwich as well as to Kate. The one dreaded his own impulses. He feared that he should go beyond the line he had fixed for himself—that he should say more than in Kate's unprotected situation in his house he thought would be right and delicate toward her. The other feared her own emotions, and that, if much more were said, they would be too strong for her, and she should weep.

At length, before the table was cleared, there came a tap at the door, and a woman's voice said, "Hal has returned, Mr. Joseph, and brought this note for the young lady."

It was instantly placed upon a salver and handed to Kate, who opened it with some anxiety; but, before she did so, she raised her eyes timidly to her companion's face as he sat opposite. It was very radiant, for he augured that no one would carry her thence that night; that she was with him, at all events, till the next morning. It was very strange! He knew that she would soon leave him to take rest; and yet there was something in the thought that the same roof would cover them, which was very pleasant to him. He had never felt such sensations toward any one before. He was a man of the world, gay, bad, reckless, full of manifold experiences; and she, simple as a child, pure, devoted, unread in the dark page of universal history—human nature. Was it the very contrast of her character with his own that formed the charm which he felt might, if long exercised, transmute his character into hers?

These things are very strange, but yet they are in nature.

Kate read the note. It was kinder, warmer than she had expected. It spoke with full confidence of Colonel Lutwich, and explained that the writer, Lady Chevenix, could not send over the carriage that night for her young friend, as both Sir Charles and Sir Harry had set out in search of her, and she, Lady Chevenix, did not know how to act in their absence. She never knew how to act. There are many people who never do; and they may be sure that there is something wrong at the bottom of their indecision. Is it that their vanity is so afraid of censure, they will not act right for fear of being blamed for acting wrong? I am afraid it is. At least there is much more of vanity than true diffidence in it. It is not of acting wrong they fear, but of being found fault with; and that such is the case is proved by the fact that, when on rare occasions they do act, it is always under the influence of some one passion or another.

However, Lady Chevenix went on to express her thanks, and those of her husband by forestalment, for the kindness which Colonel Lutwich had shown their protégée; and she added an assurance that she felt Kate would be as safe and as comfortable under his roof as at Jarworth Park.

Kate Malcolm gave him the note across the table, for it was evidently intended for his eye; and as she did so, she smiled sweetly, affording him a pleasant conviction that she herself did not regret being compelled to remain with him for some time longer. To speak the truth, the smile merely arose from a relieved mind. Her conduct was not disapproved; no blame had attached to her; and the course before her was decided.

When Lutwich had read the note, she rose, saying, "Now I think I will go to bed, for, to say truth, I am somewhat tired."

He would not try to detain her; but he asked, somewhat eagerly, if she usually rose early, and, having found that it was her invariable custom, seemed well satisfied. Joseph was sent for his wife to show Miss Malcolm to her bed-room, and Lutwich took his young companion's hand to bid her good-night. He held it for some time, having always some little thing more to say; and three several times the parting words were repeated between them.

Kate lay down then to rest; but sleep was very coy, and did not visit her pillow very soon. It was not the agitation she had suffered from the trick which had been played her that kept her waking; it was no curious inquiry into the circumstances: she thought of Lutwich, and if not of Lutwich alone, the only other image which had a share in her reveries was that of her dead father. She thought of what he would have felt, of how he would have rejoiced to know—for she knew it—that she had won the love not only of a man of fortune and station, who could support, protect, defend her, but whom she herself felt she could love in return. Love is ever confiding; but Kate Malcolm was very young and very simple in mind. She had met misfortunes; she had seen somewhat of the world's ingratitude; but she knew little of any other of all the many traits which strip off the gilding wherewith the foul things of society are covered. She had learned, mayhap, that, according to the old adage, "all is not gold that glitters," but she had not learned how very little of all that glitters is gold.

In one point, indeed, she was right; Lutwich did love—ay, with the sort of love which she could have desired. The sight of her at her dying father's feet—what he had seen—what he had heard—what he had taken part in, regarding herself, had roused in him all that was noble and generous in his nature; and there was much. It had done even more: it had made him regret most bitterly all that was evil, all that was rash, all that was criminal in his conduct and character; and, alas! there was much of that also.

After she had left him, he sat for more than an hour with his head resting on his hand in deep thought. He was reviewing life; he was criticizing the past with a severe eye; he was making resolutions for the future. A ray of innocence, and purity, and love had streamed in upon him, like a beam of summer sunshine into a dark room; and it gave him light to see things he had never seen before. He took his heart and cast it to remorse, to gnaw as it would; and there he sat in deep and bitter meditation.

At length, springing up, he said aloud, "I will change—I will be a new man: for what vanities have I sacrificed peace! It may not yet be too late;" and he retired to rest.

He slept not the later the next morning on account of the hour at which he sought his bed, for the morning was still rosy with its first light when he rose. Kate was longer; and as time went by, he grew uneasy, lest people should come to snatch her from him before he had passed some moments more with her alone. He thought that every body must be as anxious to have her near as himself. He could not conceive that Sir Charles Chevenix would sleep till nearly eight, and that Lady Chevenix would pass an hour at her toilet, and that breakfast would occupy nearly another, when Kate Malcolm was absent and had to be brought back. But so it was; six—seven o'clock struck: nobody had arrived. There was a light foot on the stairs. It paused between the two doors, as if she had forgotten which was the right one; and then she entered, looking more beautiful than ever in his eyes, not alone from the freshness of repose, but from a sort of conscious spirit in her eyes—a look of soul—of love, perhaps. He met her as she advanced, and took her hand, and inquired tenderly after her rest, and led her to a seat, and placed himself beside her, and gazed at her as if he would fain engrave every line of her features deep on memory, so that they might never—even for an instant—be effaced or obscured.

She was agitated, and he saw it; but so was he; and he could hardly find words to speak what he desired to say: yes, he—bold, rash, resolute as he was—felt agitation in speaking to a young, timid, inexperienced girl. He conquered it, however; and in a gentle tone, that he might not frighten her, he said, "Sir Charles Chevenix will soon be here to take you away from me. My little dream of happiness is well-nigh over."

"He will not be here very soon," replied Kate, in a very low voice; "he is not generally an early riser."

"He will be here too soon, whenever he comes," said Lutwich; "and I must not waste our precious moments. I would not speak last night lest I should agitate—perhaps alarm you; but now—now, when I am so soon to lose you, it is no longer wrong. I must speak all that is in my heart. You are soon going from me—say, Kate, is it to be forever? Will you not return some day to be the light of my dwelling, the mistress of my house, the wife of one who loves you as he never thought to love any human being? But stay! do not answer me yet. There is much to be atoned for, much to be remedied. With your love, if I can gain it—if I do possess it," and he drew a little closer to her side as he marked the varying color in her cheek and the diamond dew gathering between her long-fringed eyes—"with your love for my guide, my support, my reward, I can accomplish all—any thing. I can conquer my own self; I can wipe out my past acts; I can renew life, and have to thank you for self-respect, for honor, and for virtue, as well as happiness. Before I ask you to give me this dear hand, before I desire you to trust your peace to me, you shall have proofs that I am altogether changed, and that I have already begun the work which love for you shall finish—only tell me, Kate, that I may hope for love in return."

She answered him not—she could not answer. The words were spoken which she had almost dreaded to hear, and they were very, very sweet—but overpowering too. She leaned her forehead on her hands, with the small, delicate fingers covering her eyes; but the tears dropped through and fell upon her lap. The next moment she stretched forth one hand and grasped the arm of the sofa, as if for support.

Lutwich drew her gently toward him; she resisted not, but her head fell gently on his shoulder. Her face was very pale. She had fainted. Laying her softly on the sofa, he ran out for water. He would not call the servants, for he feared long interruption; and some time passed ere he could find what he wanted and return. When he re-entered the room, Kate had raised herself a little on her arm, and she murmured, "Do not call any one: I am better —I shall be well soon: this is very foolish."

He approached her gently, and gave her some water to drink, kneeling by her side; and then he bathed her temples, and then he kissed her hand. "I was thinking," she said, at length, with a faint smile, "how happy my poor father would have been if he could have seen this hour. It was too much for me."

"Then can you—do you—will you love me?" said Lutwich, eagerly.

Kate left her hand in his, and her cheek glowed again; but she was silent. He gazed at her still eagerly, and said, "Oh, speak!"

"Do you not see?" she murmured, at length, turning away her head; but Lutwich's lips found hers, and sealed there the promises they had made.

"Forbear—oh, forbear!" she said: "remember how I am situated, and act generously, kindly, as you did last night. Oh, believe me, that such conduct as that is the way to win every thought and feeling of a pure and honest heart."

"Nay, nay, one kiss is but a ratification of our pledge," replied Lutwich; "but I will not distress you, dear girl. I will ask—I will take no more. Look up, dear Kate, and listen to me, for I have yet much to say."

And much did he say, during a conversation of more than an hour, before breakfast was ready. In general terms, he acknowledged again and again many faults, though he entered into no details. He told her, too, what was true, that he was of a high and honorable family; that he had won some distinction in arms; that he had set out in life with more than competence; but that expensive habits, gay associates, and a careless disposition, had greatly impaired his original fortune.

"I have been hard pressed," he said, "and driven to many things to keep up the same style of living, the same show, the same vain profusion; but I have now higher objects and better motives for a line of conduct the complete reverse. Enough will be left, my Kate, of the wreck, I do believe, to leave us our peaceful cottage, and all the necessaries of life—nay, many of its superfluities; and if the lot be not very brilliant I offer you, still I think Kate will not repine."

"Oh no," she answered; "I have felt before now, that with one we love, even the stings of poverty can be cheerfully borne; but competence—bare competence is happiness, so there be affection and content. But will you never regret, Lutwich?"

"Call me Henry," he said. "No, I will never regret aught but the past; and my first step shall be, dear Kate, to go at once to London, and sell off all the superfluities there—horses, carriages, rich furniture, every thing; to pay off all I owe, discharge a host of servants who have eaten me up, and reduce my whole expenditure to the most humble scale."

"Then you have two establishments," she said, with a look of some surprise.

"I have, indeed," he answered, smiling; "and not long since I had three—one at Newmarket likewise. That I gave up some six months ago. Why, this cottage, dear girl, I once thought but a poor shed, fit only to shelter me and a friend or two for a night. Now it shall be a home, for it is hallowed to me. You have slept under its roof, you have brightened it with your presence: here our vows of love have been plighted; here the first real joys have been experienced that I have known for years; henceforth it is for me a palace built up of hopes, and decorated with memories."

Oh, how the sweet girl's heart beat at his words; how the dark and fearful period lately passed threw out—like a black back-ground—the brilliant present, and the soft, glowing future. And he led her on, too, to pledge herself deeply, deeply, deeply to him, in the full confidence of youthful love. Breakfast came, and was a meal of joy; an hour more passed by—a waking dream of happiness; and then a grating sound of distant wheels came with the soft air through the open windows, and a bell rang at the garden gate.

"It is Sir Charles," cried Kate, starting up. "Oh, let me run to my room, Henry, to compose myself for a moment. What shall I say to him? Shall I tell him?"

"As you please, love," answered Lutwich; "perhaps better not at present. I will tell him soon myself. Nevertheless, I lay you under no restraint toward him. Should need be, tell him; but choose some moment when he is alone."

She had hardly left him when the wheels rolled up to the door; but Lutwich was by that time grave and firm enough. He was parting with Kate Malcolm; the episode in his strange life was at an end; and the cloud seemed falling over him again. He took one turn in the room, and his brow was heavy with gloom when Sir Charles Chevenix entered.

"Ah, Lutwich," cried the gay baronet, shaking him by the hand, "a thousand thanks for your care of Lady Chevenix's sweet little protégée. I am sure you have done your best to make her happy and at her ease, though doubtless the poor bird was a little fluttered to find herself caged here alone with such a falcon as yourself."

"She was a good deal agitated and alarmed,

indeed," replied Lutwich, gravely; "nor did she know well how to act—whether to trust herself here for a night, or to send for a chaise to Barnet, as I have not my carriage or carriage horses here. I took upon myself to give her my advice; and, as she followed it, I was bound, you know, Sir Charles, to make it prove the best. I have done what I could to put her mind at rest; and, though falcon enough to strike a heron now and then, I trust I am too noble a bird to check at a dove."

"But let me hear the particulars of all this affair, Lutwich," said Sir Charles. "Who planned the rape of the Sabines—how you happened to come so fortunately to the rescue, &c., &c., &c. My two good friends, Major Brandrum and Reginald Lisle, have set out early this morning for St. Alban's, fancying they have got a clew to the whole, and intent upon punishing the culprit; but it would be amusing if they were all mistaken, and that I should find him out and horsewhip him before them, for you must know they were marvelously stingy of their secret, and would tell me nothing."

"For fear of your taking out of their hands that which they were resolved to do themselves," said Lutwich, with a laugh. "And now, do you know, Sir Charles, I have a great mind to deal with you after their fashion. You are reputed somewhat hot; I have no mind, by any indiscretion of mine, to make Lady Chevenix a widow, and therefore, methinks, the best way would be for me to hold my tongue too, and leave Major Brandrum to settle the affair as his wit and experience shall suggest."

"Pooh, pooh!" cried Sir Charles, "that is all nonsense. I will be as calm as a judge, upon my word! But do you really know who it is? Can you tell, if you would?"

"Undoubtedly," replied his companion; "I can and will tell you all about it, provided you promise me, upon your honor, to wreak no vengeance whatsoever, except mere scorn, upon the person whom I am going to mention. He is less in fault than another, though he is, of course, responsible. Will you promise?"

"It's bitter," said the baronet. "Come, come, Lutwich, be frank, and speak out."

"I will be perfectly frank, upon that one condition," answered Lutwich.

"Upon my life, I think my dear wife must have sent off carrier pigeons to you all!" exclaimed Sir Charles. "I will tell her, when I get back, that she has contrived to turn three gallant officers into as many tender-hearted old women, who are afraid of a young boy like me getting himself into a scrape if they give him too much tether. Well, Lutwich, I promise, if it may be no better. Curiosity wins the day. Who is the man?"

"Sir Theodore Broughton," replied Lutwich, still gravely.

"What, that whey-faced boy?" exclaimed Sir Charles; "that mere lad whom I saw staring gloomily at us, while Lisle and I were talking together by the pyramid of portmantles at Dunstable?"

"No other," said Lutwich; "and, moreover, it was at Dunstable, Sir Charles, that he thought fit—urged on by one of the two evil genii who have been placed about him for his guidance—to insult Miss Malcolm with very unmistakable civilities."

"A birch rod for him," cried Sir Charles Chevenix; "but let me hear all about it. How did you find it out?"

Lutwich informed him succinctly of the facts as they have already been stated, only speaking generally and in vague terms of the steps he had taken after overhearing the conversation between Doctor Gamble and his pupil. "I determined," he said, "to have them well watched, and it was lucky, as it turned out, that I did so, my good friend. At the same time, however, I gave Sir Harry Jarvis an intimation that he had better take care of Miss Malcolm, in a letter which I wrote to him concerning some particulars of her family with which he was unacquainted."

"And which letter, unfortunately, carried him straight to town," said Sir Charles; "he did not understand your hint, Lutwich, but told me he was going to inquire about some Mr. Eaton, who is related to her, one way or another. As for Gamble, I'll kick him wherever I meet him—I'm under no bonds as to him—and if he asks me why, I'll tell him, for not whipping a prurient schoolboy enough to teach him that the daughter of a gallant officer is not to be insulted."

"That will be hardly a fair reading of our compact," said Lutwich; "but here comes Miss Malcolm herself; and, though I can not flatter myself she will give any favorable account of her host's abilities to make her comfortable, yet I trust she will allow he had every wish to do so."

Sir Charles Chevenix met her with frank and fatherly kindness, remarked laughingly upon the traces of tears on her eyelids, which he ascribed to agitation and anxiety about her situation, and, thanking Lutwich again for the care and kindness he had shown her, prepared to depart. Kate Malcolm gave her lover her hand. Her heart was almost too full for words; but she contrived to murmur some expressions of deep gratitude, and, without reply, he led her to the side of the carriage, with his face very sad.

"By-the-way, I had forgot," said Sir Charles, just as he was about to follow her into the vehicle. "Jarvis told me to ask if you could dine with him to-morrow or the next day, Lutwich? To-day he is going to London again."

"To-morrow, with pleasure," replied Colonel Lutwich. "This morning I have business of importance in town myself;" and the hour being settled, Sir Charles got into the carriage. As they drove homeward, he listened both with surprise and pleasure to some scattered details of the delicate kindness which his young companion had met with at the hands of her deliverer during the preceding evening.

"He is a fine, gallant, honorable fellow," said the baronet, when she had done; "a little wild, my fair young friend, and lives a stage or two beyond his means, they say; but true metal at bottom, and one who would not injure or offend an innocent and unprotected girl for the world, I do believe."

CHAPTER XXVI.

Captain Donovan was seated in an inn at Dover waiting for the sailing of the ship or packet-boat which was to convey him to the quaint old town of Calais. The relations between England and France were at that time in what is called a very ticklish state, and the traveler had encountered some difficulty in obtaining a passport, which had prevented his departure from the shores of England on the preceding day. He was somewhat impatient, indeed, to set out, for Captain Donovan had his own particular pleasures and amusements on the other side of the Channel, and he had been deprived of them for a longer period than usual; but still, his thoughts were at that moment turned to other things; and so intent was his mind upon them, too, that he heard not how the wind whistled and the sea roared.

"He's in good hands," said Donovan, mentally, "he's in good hands. Master Gamble knows his part, and he will play it out. If he does not reach one-and-twenty, I have no one to account to but myself. It is getting devilish near, however, and some progress must be made. I will give them three months, and then see what is to be done."

He paused, and, rising, walked to the window which looked out upon the port, murmuring, "I wonder when this cursed boat will sail. It is blowing very hard. Why, who the deuse is that passing?" he continued, as a figure hurried rapidly across the window. "Gamble, upon my life! The lad must be dead. He would not leave him, I am sure;" and, throwing up the sash, he called out, "Gamble—Doctor Gamble!"

The worthy doctor turned and looked at him, exclaiming, "Oh, captain, I am glad to see you, sir; I was looking for you, but could get no information as to where you had put up."

"Come in, come in," cried Donovan; and, while Gamble walked round to the door, which was on the other side of the house, a look of savage triumph came over Donovan's face. "It must be so," he said, in a low voice, "it must be so! Some accident, or perhaps a duel."

The next minute Doctor Gamble entered, looked round the room to see that there was no one in it except his pupil's guardian, and then advancing to Captain Donovan, said, with a grave and respectful look, "I have something serious to tell you sir, which will require you to put off your voyage."

"Oh, that is easily done, Gamble," replied Captain Donovan; "what is it? Has any thing happened to Sir Theodore?"

"I am sorry to say there has," answered the doctor; "a very serious affair, indeed."

"Well, well, out with it! Don't keep me in suspense," cried Donovan; "what has happened?"

"Why, you must know, captain," replied the tutor, "that he thought fit to fall in love with a young girl, the daughter of a Captain Malcolm—who is dead, by-the-way—but that does not matter, for she is under the guardianship of that fire-eating devil, with whom you sent him to town, Major Brandrum, or Major Ravenous Crow. Sir Theodore, as she was somewhat coy, made up a little scheme for carrying her off. I could not thwart him in his proceedings, you know, captain—and, indeed, you told me not—'lest the young horse should kick over the traces,' as you justly apprehended."

"There, there, never mind what you could do or what you could not do," exclaimed Captain Donovan, sharply; "on with your tale, man."

"Well, the scheme failed," continued Doctor Gamble; "the girl cried out when she found they were not taking her to London; a fellow was going by on horseback, and stopped the chaise; and somehow your two good friends, Messieurs Brandrum and Lisle, instantly fixed upon Sir Theodore and your humble servant as the parties concerned in 'the abduction,' as they called it. They tracked us down to St. Alban's with the fierceness and shrewdness of two bloodhounds, and, while we were quietly breakfasting in the coffee-room with another gentleman or two, in they came, horsewhip in hand. Two or three words to Sir Theodore, and an evasive answer on his part, was all that passed, and they set to. The major horsewhipped him, and the captain horsewhipped me; and, 'pon my life! I have not had such another flogging since I got from under old Burgess's rod."

"Well, well, what followed?" demanded Donovan; "did Sir Theodore call him out? Have they fought?"

"It might all have been avoided," replied Doctor Gamble; "but, unfortunately, there was a wild Irish fellow in the room who instantly took upon him to act as Sir Theodore's friend, doing things in the most gingerly manner, as if cold iron and hair triggers were mere matters of etiquette. He offered to do the same for me, but I begged to decline his friendship—d—n him—and finding that the meeting is to take place to-morrow, at the back of Montague House, I hurried down here to find you, knowing by your last letter that you must be crossing about this time."

"And so I must," replied Captain Donovan, sternly, putting his hands behind his back; "I have business of importance to transact which can not be delayed. The young fool must brew as he has baked: he has made his bed, let him lie upon it. I shall be off in half an hour."

"But, my dear sir!" exclaimed Doctor Gamble, whose interests it did not at all suit that Sir Theodore Broughton should be removed from his superintendence by a pistol-ball or a lunge of a small sword. But just as he spoke the door opened, and a rough-looking man approached, touching his hat to Captain Donovan, without taking it off.

"Please, sir," said the intruder, "Captain Butler sent me up to say there's no chance of the boat getting out to-day. The wind's dead against her, and blowing a gale."

"There! there!" cried Doctor Gamble; "now you have no excuse."

"I seek no excuse, sir," cried Donovan, turning on him fiercely; "take care what you say."

"But, my dear sir—my dear captain, you really must interfere," said the tutor. "You do not consider he is but nineteen."

"Lisle shot Sir Charles Chevenix when he was younger," answered Donovan, gloomily; "if the young man will get himself into such scrapes, he must abide the consequences."

"Well, then, I will stop it myself," said Gamble, in a determined tone. "The lad does not want to fight unless he is driven to it, and I will stop it."

"What will you do?" asked Captain Donovan, in a sharp tone.

"I will go back directly," replied the tutor, who saw he had got an advantage, "and give information at Bow-street, telling the magistrate that I have done all I can to persuade you to interfere; but that, being a military man, you will not, although you are his relation, guardian, and next heir to his property."

"Sir!" exclaimed Donovan, in a voice of thunder; and then he stood glaring at him for a full minute, with the look of a tiger ready to spring. But Doctor Gamble had gone too far to recede, and, after a brief pause, he asked, "Shall I, in so speaking, say any thing but the truth?"

"Truth!" said Donovan, with a bitter sneer curling his lip; "what do you care for truth?" and, turning away, he walked moodily to the window again.

The tutor paused for a few moments, and then taking up his hat, which he had lain down upon the table, he said, "Well, captain, as you will not go, I must."

"Stay, stay," said the other, in a milder tone, but still one of much vexation; "this is the greatest annoyance in the world. I promised to be at Amiens yesterday, but could not get my passport signed; and now I shall be kept till the day after to-morrow."

"Oh, never mind, never mind," said Doctor Gamble, with a sly leer; "she will wait for you."

Donovan laughed somewhat affectedly, saying, "You are a fool, Gamble; but, if I must go, I must. Only remember, this is the last time I will interfere in such a business. I may chance to get myself shot instead of him for meddling in such affairs, and I have a good deal to do in the world yet."

"I don't doubt it," answered Gamble, dryly; "but now, as you have taken your resolution, let us set out at once."

Captain Donovan, however, contrived to create a great number of delays. Had the packet-boat been about to sail at the hour which had been stated, he certainly would have been too late—if he really required so much time to pack up his portmanteau. Then he must needs dine before he went, trying to reconcile Doctor Gamble to his procrastination by the delicacy of the viands he ordered. The time for starting, however, at length arrived; and, though Captain Donovan would not afford four horses, away went he and the tutor at a very tolerable rate; but as they were in a hack post-chaise, which had to be changed at every stage, there were numerous opportunities of wasting time, which Donovan took advantage of. At other moments he lay back dozing in the chaise; or, putting out his head, told the post-boy not to break their necks by rattling down hill; or, meditating over the perfections and qualities of Doctor Gamble, wished that he were not quite so much in his secrets.

The morning was gray when they reached London; but Gamble, who understood the game only too well, called to the post-boy, without asking any permission, to drive straight to the back of Montague House, as fast as he could go; and away they went. As they came near, Donovan listened for the crack of a pistol; but all was still; and when they reached the road (which at that time ran at the back of what is now Portman Square), and looked over the hedge into the neighboring field, they saw a group of three persons, consisting of Major Brandrum, Reginald Lisle, and a gentleman in black, while coming over the stile appeared Sir Theodore Broughton and another young man seven or eight years older.

"There they are," cried Doctor Gamble; "now let us be quick. Pull up, boy! pull up!"

Donovan had by this time taken his resolution, and merely saying sternly, "Leave the whole to me, sir," he sprang out of the chaise, while Doctor Gamble followed at a considerable distance, having certain reminiscences of Reginald Lisle's handiwork, which rendered too near an approach to that gentleman unpleasant. In one minute, Captain Donovan was over the hedge and close to the would-be combatants; and to have seen him at that moment, one would have supposed that no one could be more eager to prevent his ward from suffering the consequences of his ill conduct.

"What is this, gentlemen?" he exclaimed, in a loud and stern tone; "what is this, sir?" and he bent his brows upon Sir Theodore with a frown which had often made the youth shrink into himself in terror. Nor was it without effect even now; for, although Sir Theodore had been able at once to assume a new character with a man whom he despised like Doctor Gamble, there was a sort of dark enthralling spell connected with his very earliest memories of the man now before him, which he could not shake off; and for a minute after Donovan's sudden and unexpected appearance, the young baronet stood silent, with his eyes turned to the ground.

His Irish companion, however, undertook to answer for him, saying, with a strong Irish accent, "The matter, sir, is a very simple one. Those gentlemen just coming near thought fit to horsewhip both our young friend here and a person I understand to be his tutor—that person there behind—which, indeed, any gentleman has a right to do to another, if he considers himself aggrieved. Our young friend here thought fit, in return, to call his assailant to account in the usual way, which any gentleman has a right to do also."

"If he have arrived at the years of discretion," said Donovan, sternly.

"That has nothing to do with the matter," said the other, who could not comprehend that the person newly arrived had any authority in the affair. "Now, you look very much like a gentleman, sir, so I will just beg you either to withdraw, or stand quiet and not meddle."

Captain Donovan laughed. "Very good," he said; "and see this boy, my ward, shot before my face. Sir, you are very much mistaken; and if you do not very speedily take your case away, and be off, you will be in the hands of the officers of Bow-street in five minutes. No blustering, sir, if you please. We know how to deal with gentlemen of your warlike propensities; and, I can tell you, you have not too much time to spare. Now, Major Brandrum, what apology do you demand of Sir Theodore Broughton? He shall make it immediately, for I am informed of what has occurred, and see that it is due."

"I will make none," murmured the young man, in a low but determined voice.

Major Brandrum, however, saved all contention on the subject by his reply. "I have no apology to require, Captain Donovan," he said; "Sir Theodore Broughton thought fit to behave to a young lady, whom I have adopted as my child, in a manner both rascally and ungentleman-like, and not the less ungentleman-like because it was rascally, nor the less rascally because it was ungentleman-like. Seeingt hat he is a mere lad—though he thinks himself a man—I punished him as a lad, and horsewhipped him soundly. I never, however, refuse to fight, when any body asks me; and, therefore, I came here by his appointment, though the morning is windy, and the hour somewhat early."

"It might have been better to treat him as a boy to the end, major," replied Donovan. "However, you are a soldier, and a gentleman of honor, and I, being in the same service, must make allowance for professional prejudices. I may trust, however, to your good feeling, I am sure, to promise me that you will not give him another meeting while I am absent from England, as business of importance calls me to France."

"I really can not tell, sir," replied Brandrum; "it entirely depends upon his own conduct. In reference to this affair, I certainly shall not meet him again, for once is enough, in all conscience; but if he still thinks fit to behave ill to any one under my protection, I shall most likely treat him as I did before, and then things must take their course according to circumstances. Come, Lisle, I think we have had enough of this, and we are likely to get blown away in this wind."

Thus saying, he walked away, followed by Reginald Lisle and the gentleman in black. They reached a hackney coach which was waiting for them in the other road, and when they were seated, Lisle, who bore a greatly puzzled look, said, in a low tone, "This is curious, Crow."

"Very!" said Major Brandrum, dryly; "and then added, "we have been doing the fellow injustice in our hearts. His conduct is certainly strange; but it is evident that he can entertain no sinister designs such as I had fancied."

In the mean time, Captain Donovan was somewhat at a loss how to deal with Sir Theodore Broughton, whose Irish friend having a much greater antipathy to incarceration than to a pistol bullet, had disappeared somewhat rapidly from the scene of action after the officers of Bow-street had been mentioned. To remonstrate with the youth was absolutely necessary, but to treat him altogether as a boy was not possible, and would not have been expedient, according to Donovan's views, even if it had been. He therefore determined to cut his sermon very short, on the pretense of anxiety to get back to Dover at once; and in a few short sentences, severe enough, though mingled with a sarcastic jest here and there, he pointed out all that a common-place view of dissipation and dueling could suggest—very well knowing that common-places never have the slightest effect in the way of warning or dissuasion. He looked three times at Doctor Gamble with an expression of countenance which the tutor did not at all like; but, whatever it was that fermented in his mind at the moment, it brought forth nothing; and, leaving his ward still under the guidance of his ill-chosen tutor, he quitted them, and took his way back at once toward the sea-coast.

When Donovan was seated in the chaise and rolling away from London, he ground his teeth bitterly, murmuring, "Ay, Master Gamble, your day will come. In the mean time, your vices and licentiousness will do my work for me, while you think you are doing your own."

CHAPTER XXVII.

Abon Hassan wished to be caliph for only one day, and I sincerely wish that I could be a woman for only one day. Let it be understood, I would not for the world be one for any longer space, as I look upon it that woman, like every other weak thing, is hardly used by man. If I could have my wish, I might, perhaps, be able afterward to give the reader some account of the feelings of Mary Chevenix, as Reginald Lisle sat beside her at supper, where we left him at the end of the twenty-third chapter. As a man, however, it is impossible to do so accurately. The general facts, indeed, I can state; but all those minute shades of emotion, those fine, soft lines of feeling, which display the principal difference between the mind of woman and that of man, I must pass over in silence. One must be, or have been, a woman, to know them, and, perhaps, something more than a woman, to tell them.

When Reginald first entered the room, where she and Lady Chevenix had been sitting up for the return of her father and Sir Harry Jarvis, her sensations were strangely mingled. The joy and surprise of seeing him, and her uncertainty as to what character he had come in, and what was his motive for coming, together with some apprehensions as to what might be her mother's conduct and demeanor toward him, were enough to agitate her greatly; but through all other emotions stole one small thread of doubt, which, however thin and filmy, checkered and dimmed the golden web of love and hope most sadly.

When she gave him her hand, it trembled, and her cheek varied through every hue of the rose, from nearly white to crimson. But when she looked up in his face, the expression with which he regarded her, the deep and intense love in his eyes, made her hand tremble still more, but made her heart flutter also with renewed trust. Had any one spoken for an hour, with the tongue of eloquence itself, upon the theme of Reginald Lisle's constancy, and truth, than the effect of that one look.
and affection, the result would have been less

Let us pass over all explanations and minor particulars—how Lady Chevenix told all that had occurred, and said she had not known how to act, and how she and Mary had had a very anxious dinner, and how she was sure her husband and Sir Harry would be half tired, half famished to death, and how she had taken the liberty of ordering the cook to exercise his best skill on the supper, and how it would be on the table directly, now that they were returned. Nor should I wish to detain the reader to describe how Reginald Lisle and Major Brandrum washed their hands, and brushed the dirt off their persons, and consulted together for a minute or two before supper. It was all very right at the time; but we have nothing to do with it. Let us seat Reginald once more beside her he loved, and tell what was Lady Chevenix's demeanor toward him, for that was a point in regard to which he and Mary too were not a little anxious.

She was civil enough; that is, perhaps, the only way to describe her conduct; but what a different thing that is from being cordial. She failed in no rule of politeness; she was not even cold and distant. Her husband's presence and his known wishes shielded Reginald from that negative kind of repulsion, for Lady Chevenix was a really good woman, and wished to please her husband very much; but still she was not cordial. She could not forget that Lisle had fought a duel with Sir Charles, and wounded him severely. She did not forget it; indeed, she did not try; and Reginald felt it. Nor was it without effect upon his own demeanor. He said to himself, "It is evident that Lady Chevenix is not well disposed toward me. I must contrive to win her esteem, to teach her to forget that unfortunate affair, before I venture to press my suit, or even to show my love openly. Although she is all submission to her husband, yet I know right well how much a mother's opinion must influence a father in such circumstances; how the private ear of affection will listen even to arguments unreasonable; how the whispered word will damage—the reiterated objection will have weight. She sees not that I love her daughter—they none of them see it but Mary herself, and I must not let them see it till I have won upon their regard as well as hers."

I know not whether the resolution was wise or foolish; but one effect it had, which was unfortunate. It put a restraint upon his manner toward Mary herself; it made it far less warm, far less tender than love might well have been, even under the restrictions of society. Mary thought his conduct strange; the thin thread of doubt appeared again, running throughout the web of hope, and she was very silent during the rest of the meal.

At length, the party rose to retire to rest, and Major Brandrum significantly informed Sir Harry Jarvis that he and his young companion should most probably ride on to St. Alban's before breakfast, on business of importance.

"I have half a mind to go with you, major," said Sir Charles Chevenix; but his wife instantly interposed, saying, "You forget, my dear Charles, you will have to go over to Colonel Lutwich's for Miss Malcolm, as Sir Harry has just told you he must be all day in London."

Sir Charles Chevenix thought that his wife could fulfill that task as well as himself; but he knew her habits, both of mind and body; he knew that there would be a hundred objections to overcome, which he did not choose to war with; and, therefore, he merely replied, "I *had* forgot."

"I trust, gentlemen, you will make Jarworth your half-way house on the way back," said Sir Harry Jarvis, addressing Major Brandrum and Lisle. "I shall be absent to-morrow myself; but Chevenix and her ladyship, and my fair young friend here, will entertain you. On the following day, if you will do me the honor of staying, I will endeavor to induce Colonel Lutwich to meet you at dinner."

Both Major Brandrum and Reginald Lisle promised to take Jarworth Park on their return from St. Alban's; and the major charged one of Sir Harry's servants with a note to London, requiring somewhat more suitable habiliments for a dinner-table than those in which they had ridden thither.

On the following morning, early, they set out for St. Alban's, and with a part of what was done there the reader is already acquainted. After the scene in the coffee-room of one inn, they returned exceedingly calmly to the other, the major laughing heartily at the contortions of Doctor Gamble under the lash of Reginald Lisle, which he had not failed to remark even while inflicting a similar but more moderate dose of the same medicine upon Sir Theodore Broughton.

"I wonder, my boy," he said, "how that fellow would bear a slow fire, with splinters of resinous pine stuck into the calves of his fat legs. Heavens! what a shout the Slippery Snake, and Bald Eagle, and all the rest of the tribe would have set up, to see him writhing so under such a puny thing as a horsewhip. They would have danced themselves mad with delight."

Reginald was somewhat graver; and, when they had reached their inn, and ordered their breakfast, he called for a newspaper, and one of the meager, yellow things, so denominated in that day, was brought him by the waiter, over which he cast his eyes, somewhat indifferently at first. After a while, however, a sudden eagerness seemed to seize him: his eye was fixed intently on the page; and, after reading a few lines more, he exclaimed, "Here is intelligence indeed, Crow! The enemy have landed on the west coast, and plundered a village. It is not well ascertained whether it was a party of Frenchmen, or the crew of the American squadron, which had been hanging about upon the coast. But the news is certain."

"A chance of active employment, Lisle," replied the major. "Well, I have nothing to do but provide for this girl, fight this boy, and then I am ready. To say truth, I am tired of inactivity, and should have to do some exceedingly extravagant thing very soon, just to relieve the monotony of existence. Well, here comes breakfast; and, as soon as that is over, let us march. Perhaps Sir Harry may bring back a budget of news from London to-night."

But neither Lisle nor his friend were destined to stay long at Jarworth Park. They rode thither rapidly, for Reginald was not without hopes of gaining Mary's ear for a few dear private moments; but the first words of Sir Harry's butler were, "Your servant, sir, has come down with your things from London, wishing to see you directly, and Major Brandrum too."

"What does he want?" asked Lisle, with the impatience of apprehended disappointment.

"He has got a letter for you, sir, from the commander-in-chief," replied the butler, "and one for the major too. I will call him up directly: he is in the servants' hall."

Without quitting the vestibule, Reginald received the letter where he stood. It was a mere formal epistle, requiring him to put all other things aside, and report himself at head-quarters without any delay. There was also a vague hint that his services might be wanted immediately in the field, for official brevity had not then reached its climax; but still the epistle was dry and impenetrable enough. The letter to Major Brandrum was precisely the same, written by the same clerk, in the same hand, and the same words, and signed by the same officer.

"We must take wing at once, Regy," said the Ravenous Crow; "the service bears no delay, and the order is peremptory."

"We must see if Lady Chevenix and Sir Charles are within, in order to make our excuses," said Reginald. The major smiled; but the butler, who had been standing by, put an end to Captain Lisle's hope, even of one more glimpse, by saying, "Sir Charles has not returned yet, sir, and her ladyship is out walking with Miss Chevenix."

"Well, then, we must trust you to bear our apology, my good friend," said Major Brandrum. "Pray inform Sir Harry how deeply we regret not being able to stay to dinner—and here, show him that letter; he will see by that what it is that hurries us away so fast." Thus saying, he passed out and remounted his horse, while Reginald only remained to give the necessary orders to his servant for following with his baggage.

When Mary Chevenix returned, about half an hour after her lover had departed, she had the disappointment of finding that he had been there, and gone again; and a bitter disappointment it was, for she had been dreaming a dream of spending half an hour with him before dinner, at some time, and in some spot, where they could speak all they felt, and where he, she hoped, might explain all that seemed strange. The letter was shown to her, however. She saw that Lisle had no choice but to obey; and as she was not in the least of a captious nature, she did not even fancy that he could have found an excuse if he had been very much in love.

Her father returned shortly after with Kate Malcolm; and perhaps Lady Chevenix received the fair truant more warmly than her daughter did, for there was still that little dark thread of doubt which Mary could not remove, do what she would.

"I will try before I sleep to tear it out, even if I tear my own heart too," she thought; and she listened to all Kate told her mother of the kindness and delicacy with which Colonel Lutwich had treated her, with much interest, even under her quiet demeanor. The three ladies were alone together, for Sir Charles went at once to write letters; and Lady Chevenix questioned Kate closely as to the person who had practiced so base a stratagem upon her, and his object. Even before two women, the subject embarrassed the poor girl; but her catechist wrung Sir Theodore Broughton's name from her, and then exclaimed, "Why, surely some one told me he was in the inn at Dunstable on the night of the fire."

"He was, indeed," answered Kate Malcolm; "he insulted me grossly there; but Captain Lisle came up, and—"

But the remembrance of that night oppressed her; and while her cheek turned crimson, her eyes were suffused with tears, and she stopped.

How strange a thing is jealousy! that most bitter preconception of the mind, which blinds the most clear-sighted, hardens the most just! There was not a person on all the earth better fitted by nature to comprehend and sympathize with the emotions which produced so much agitation in Kate Malcolm than Mary Chevenix, and yet now she attributed all to a wrong cause. The blush and the tears were close coupled with the name of Reginald Lisle; and she thought they must be given to him. The reader may ask, Why? and there is but one answer, "Because she loved him herself."

Still she was resolved to be further satisfied. She fancied herself very reasonable indeed. She said she would not judge without full proofs; she resolved that she would not let jealousy have the least dominion. Nevertheless, she was very grave and silent during dinner; and when the ladies had retired from the table, she took advantage of her mother's absence for a few minutes to put her own questions to Kate. Nor did she do so quite sincerely. No, reader, Mary did not act sincerely toward her young companion: no woman stung by jealousy ever does—perhaps no woman in love. However, it was the first time in her life, and it was the last likewise; for she found afterward that, had she been but as frank on this occasion as on others, she would have saved herself much misery. As soon as Lady Chevenix was gone, Mary went and sat down beside Kate upon a sofa, and putting her hand on hers, she said, "And so, Kate, this young officer came very opportunely to your assistance?" She would not mention Reginald's name, for fear her face should betray her own secrets while she was seeking those of another.

A glow instantly came up in Kate Malcolm's face, for she, on her part, had been thinking of Colonel Lutwich for the last half hour, and Mary's eyes were searching her countenance eagerly. "Very opportunely indeed," she answered; "I should not have known what to do had he not come up, for I did not know my way, or any thing."

"And he was very kind to you?" asked Mary.

"He was, indeed," replied Kate.

"A little in love, too, with that fair, glowing face, I've a notion?" said Mary.

Kate blushed still, but made no answer; and Mary went on. "Nay, tell me, Kate—tell a friend who can counsel, and perhaps help you. Did he not say he loved you?"

"Oh, do not ask me any more questions!" exclaimed Kate Malcolm; but her face made confession, and Mary's heart sank low—very low. She could not speak for a moment, though she longed to go on—to have the admission in words; and just as she was framing another question, and struggling with herself for voice, Lady Chevenix returned.

The impression, however, was made, the fears confirmed. They seemed to her no longer doubts, but realities; and Mary, pleading headache, but too truly, retired early, not to rest, but to weep.

On the following morning she was up, and dressed, and out, before any one else in the house was stirring. She felt that she needed the free air: rooms were too close and narrow for the feelings which struggled in her bosom. She wished to catechize her own heart; to ask herself if she was the person to blame; if, with foolish weakness or idle vanity, she had mistaken mere common compliment, and, perhaps, a somewhat too warm and winning manner, for the words of love and the looks of affection. But her heart absolved her. There could be no mistake. All she had to blame herself for was for listening too eagerly to one who was so little known to her. Yet she strove not to admit that either: he had seemed so frank, so true, so high principled; and, equally unwilling to blame him—strange as it may seem—she threw the fault upon the shoulders of his whole sex. "They are all deceitful," she said; "they are all fickle. I have heard a thousand instances of it. I must tear out this love from my heart. Willingly, I will never see him more. What is it makes me feel unkind and angry toward poor Kate? It is not her fault, dear girl, and I will not suffer my heart to be embittered. I will forget him—not think of him. He can be nothing more to me. Let her be happy with him; but I must not see it. I can not see! Well, well."

As she thus pondered, and while she was trying to nerve her mind for the course before her, she was walking up and down an avenue of old trees; and how long she had been there Heaven knows—for in such internal strife time flies fast—when she saw her father coming toward her. Mary had not been weeping: all her tears had been spent upon her pillow; otherwise she might have tried to avoid him. There is, however, a sort of recklessness in despair, which, perhaps, might have led her to go on, even had she known that her father would see her suffering, and divine its cause. She hardly cared now who knew it, except Kate Malcolm. That she could not have borne.

Sir Charles advanced toward her in his gay, good-humored manner, holding out his arms to clasp her for his morning's embrace; and, when held to his bosom, Mary felt, perhaps for the first time fully, what a blessed thing is a parent's love.

"You look pale, my girl," he said; "have you not slept well? Have all our adventures been too much for you? Fy, fy! I thought you were brimful of chivalry and romance, Mary; and let me tell you that many of our knights-errant in petticoats would give their ears for such luck as you have had. To be robbed and escape murder, to be burned out and escape singeing, to lose a little friend and find her again all safe, is not the chance of every one, Mistress Mary."

"I have not much luck of any kind," answered his daughter; "and in truth, dear papa, I should not covet luck of that sort. I would rather not be robbed, or burned out, or lose a friend at all."

"You ungrateful little toad!" cried Sir Charles, laughing. "No luck at all, did she say? What! with the best mother and the best father in the country, and the largest fortune to boot, at least within fifty miles of Dunsmore!"

"Nay, the fortune I care very little about," answered Mary Chevenix; "but for the best father and the best mother I am not ungrateful. That, indeed, is a blessing;" and she ended with a sigh.

Sir Charles Chevenix saw she was unhappy. He loved her dearly, too; and yet he resolved to make her more unhappy before he had done, for he thought it would be salutary. Almost all fathers are rough physicians, even in their love; but it were wise, when about to give a wholesome bitter to a child, to be sure that they have got hold of the right bottle. Sir Charles had got the wrong, and he proceeded to administer to his daughter more of the same poison which she had lately been tasting. He spoke of Kate Malcolm, and expressed sympathy with the disappointment she must have felt on the preceding day at "Captain Lisle being obliged to be absent." He then went on to say, "I thought of asking her to stay with us for a week or two in Grosvenor Square; but as Lisle is likely to be busy, if all this sharp work is to go on, it would be better, perhaps, to take her to his mother's at once. There they will have more opportunities of being together; for, of course, he must often go to see Mrs. Lisle, and can kill two birds with one stone. What do you say, Mary?"

"I think so, certainly, in such circumstances," replied his daughter, in a wavering voice, for her heart felt as if some giant were squeezing it in a cold hand. "I shall be sorry to part with her; but, of course, she will be more happy there."

Sir Charles was a little puzzled; for, though her manner was somewhat agitated, her words were calm. As she bore it well, however, he thought he might go on; and he proceeded to tell her how angry and indignant Reginald Lisle had appeared when first informed that Kate had been inveigled away. He dwelt upon all that he had observed; and as he was, in truth, convinced himself, he had no difficulty in convincing her. He tortured her terribly, however; and Mary saw and felt that he was saying more, far more than he otherwise would have done, because he thought it for her good. At length, she could bear it no more; and, suddenly stopping, she looked up in her father's face with those beautiful appealing eyes, and said, "Say no more, papa, say no more: I am quite satisfied. If I have indulged foolish fancies, they are gone forever;" and, turning away from him, she ran back to the house.

"Poor child!" said Sir Charles to himself, "I am afraid it has gone deeper than I thought;" and he continued to walk up and down for some time.

The party at breakfast was grave, but Mary showed herself peculiarly kind and gentle toward Kate Malcolm; and Sir Harry Jarvis, too, bestowed upon the poor orphan girl more attention than he would, perhaps, have shown to lordly guests. He often gazed at her, too, with a look of tender interest, as if scanning every line of her face, when her eyes were turned away from him. At dinner they were joined by Colonel Lutwich, and Sir Harry took an opportunity of saying to him, before Kate came down with Lady Chevenix, "You will find your fair guest of the other night, colonel, even somewhat more sad than before. To-morrow is the day appointed for her father's funeral; and, though we have not told her—not thinking it necessary for her to be present—and have persuaded her, both yesterday and to-day, to come down to dinner, yet she must feel that it is coming near."

Kate was sad, and even Lutwich's presence could not banish her gloom; for Lady Chevenix had accidentally let out the secret, which Sir Charles had wished to keep concealed till the dark ceremony was over. Lutwich, however, knew well how to feel for her, and his whole manner and demeanor spoke his sympathy. His tone might be tender, but it was always grave throughout the evening; and he made not the slightest effort to force upon her one cheerful thought, for he knew that it would jar with her feelings. Kate did not love him less when he went away.

The next day passed with her in mourning. Sir Charles and Sir Harry Jarvis posted early in the morning to Dunstable, and returned late at night, for the day following had been appointed for the Chevenix family to proceed to London. They did not set out early, however, and Colonel Lutwich was at the carriage door when they departed. He was able to gain a few moments with Kate while some arrangements were made, and Sir Harry Jarvis handed in Lady Chevenix; but the old baronet returned for his fair young guest; and, as he led her along with somewhat formal courtesy, he said, in a low voice, but full of feeling, "My dear young lady, I should much like to disappoint good Major Brandrum, and keep you all to myself here as a daughter; but I fear I can not make out a title to so fair a property. However, pray remember, should you at any time want assistance, support, counsel, you are to apply to none but me, and you will find a father in me."

Another step brought them to the carriage door, and Sir Harry shook hands with her and bade her farewell. The maids followed, the servants mounted their horses; and Colonel Lutwich, with a very thoughtful air, was turning toward his own steed, when the voice of the old baronet stopped him.

"Colonel—Colonel Lutwich!" said Sir Harry, "whither away so fast? Can you not spare half an hour for a solitary old man?"

"I have a journey before me, Sir Harry," replied Lutwich; "nevertheless, I must not refuse to stay at your bidding."

"Where are you going?" asked his companion.

"Into Yorkshire," replied Lutwich, significantly. "I am not satisfied."

"Well, well, then I will not stop you," said Sir Harry Jarvis; "let me see you when you come back. I seldom dine from home."

Lutwich promised, and rode away; and before night he was fifty miles on his way to York.

In the mean time, Sir Charles Chevenix and his party reached Grosvenor Square in safety, and the rest of the evening was passed in calm repose. On the following morning Sir Charles and Lady Chevenix drove out to convey Kate Malcolm to the cottage of Mrs. Lisle, having previously notified their intention to Major Brandrum by a note which received no answer.

Both Sir Charles and Lady Chevenix showed themselves very kind, the latter warming greatly to her young protégée on the eve of her departure. Sir Charles took care of her purse, although she would fain have refused. Lady Chevenix had before provided for her dress. Mary was sad and grave, though she strove hard to be kind too; and when Kate bade her good-by in the drawing-room, she kissed her tenderly, held her at a little distance from her to gaze at her, and then hung a little diamond cross round her neck, saying, "Wear that for my sake, Kate; and think of me when you are married."

Kate did not comprehend her; and as soon as she was gone, Mary ran up to her own room to weep. Hardly half an hour had elapsed when there was a loud knock at the door, and in about three minutes Mary's maid came to say that Captain Lisle was below. "He asked for Sir Charles and my lady, ma'am, and then for you," said the girl.

The name had made Mary Chevenix turn very red, and then very pale. "Tell him," she said, after a moment's terrible pause, "tell him I am—that I can not come down, as I am very busy at present;" and such, word for word, was the message which Reginald Lisle received.

CHAPTER XXVIII.

This work has very little to do with history—so little, indeed, that I do not half like to intrude even the smallest bit of history into it. Nevertheless, two facts must be recalled to the mind of the learned reader; for, unless he does happen to remember them, he will be somewhat puzzled with regard to certain incidents recorded in these pages. Shortly after the outbreak of the American war of independence—a multitude still living can recall those times—a number of privateers belonging to the revolted colonies hovered about the British Channel and the neighboring coasts, carrying off many of our merchant ships, daring our smaller vessels of war to action, and even, in one or two instances, making descents upon the coast, when they learned that no great force was ready to repel them, plundering villages, hamlets, and farm-houses, after a somewhat piratical fashion. Rumor, at the time, swelled these occurrences—in themselves of no great magnitude—into events of vast importance; terror and confusion spread among the sober citizens, and bustle and activity prevailed in the public offices. An event, which was hardly known or talked about within twenty miles of where it had occurred, was magnified in London into an invasion; and those, even, who obtained the most exact accounts in their official capacity, shared the panic of the multitude, and increased it by superfluous preparations for meeting dangers which did not exist. One of the most formidable dresses which Rumor assumed was afforded to the vagrant goddess by the fact of the French embassador having quitted London, and the English embassador having been recalled from Paris, while a secret treaty—as was well known, like all other secrets, almost from the beginning—had been entered into between the absolute monarch of France and the ruling powers of the new republic. It was reported, and believed for some time, even in high places, that the French and Americans combined had landed on the western coast of England, when, in truth, the origin of the whole story was the plunder of a farm-house by the well-known leader Paul Jones, famous in song and tale. Troops were instantly marched from various quarters to the part of the country supposed to be threatened or assailed; the militia was called out; and all officers of skill and experience were, like Major Brandrum and Reginald Lisle, commanded to hold themselves in readiness to afford their services in repelling the enemy from our shores.

Another fact—which has been taken too little notice of in history, though it affects one of the most important points in that of any nation—the history of opinion—rendered it the more imperative upon the government to call to their aid every military man willing to serve, and able to serve well. The American war was, throughout the country, one of the most unpopular that ever was undertaken. Whatever faults were imputable to the Americans themselves—and there were not a few, even among their greatest men—there could be no doubt that England had greater still toward them. A sense of the injustice, as well as the inexpediency of the war, was general, and in many cases so strong, that a very great number of distinguished officers resigned their commissions rather than take part in hostilities which they conceived iniquitous. They might be wrong, and perhaps they were in many points of view; but still, such was the fact; and, be it observed, that was a fact which never could occur in any country but England. These resignations greatly embarrassed the government, and made ministers only the more anxious to secure the immediate services of experienced soldiers who formed a different judgment of military duty.

Such were Major Brandrum and Reginald Lisle. Reginald, though he had his feelings as a citizen as well as a soldier, though he might disapprove of the war and condemn the measures which had produced it, would have as soon thought of flying from a field of battle as of refusing to serve the crown on any motive of private judgment. The major, who was much more the soldier than the citizen, never thought upon the subject at all, and only disliked fighting the "Provincials," as he called them, because they spoke the same language as the English. "One hardly knows one from the other," he said, "which makes it inconvenient as well as unnatural, and not the less unnatural because it is inconvenient, nor the less inconvenient because it is unnatural."

The morning of the frustrated duel passed over; and in the afternoon, the major and his young comrade presented themselves to the commander-in-chief for the second time since they had received his summons. They were very graciously received with nod and smile, and dismissed with a hint that they would hear from him that day or the next.

Lisle seemed a good deal disappointed, and as they walked home together through the busy streets, his companion remarked, "Ah, Lisle, you long to be at the old work as well as I, say what you will, though you have love and hope fettering your ankles, and I have nothing to stay me but age, and—thank God! not the rheumatism."

"I have neither love nor hope," answered Reginald, in a very gloomy tone; "those are among things departed, major—at least the one which gave brightness to the other is gone, and the love can be borne as heavily or as lightly in another land as here."

Brandrum looked at him with grave surprise; but he would make no effort to wring his confidence from him, well knowing it would come as soon as it was no longer painful for him to speak upon the subject at all; and, after having walked on through the streets for some way, Lisle proposed that they should dine, leave word at their inn where they were to be found, and go down to spend the evening with his mother.

"Poor Miss Malcolm is there, of course, as your note from Sir Charles Chevenix intimated," he continued; "and as you and I, my dear Crow, may be winging our way to distant lands ere long, I should wish to make her as much at home with my mother and sister as possible."

The plan thus proposed was speedily executed, and one entire peaceful night was spent by the two soldiers at Mrs. Lisle's cottage. It afforded no incident that would bear even the slightest detail, and therefore let it pass. The man of whom the world says nothing, is likely to have the happiest life; and so with those portions of time in which the author has nothing to chronicle. Alas! that it should be so; that the great efforts, the noble impulses, the generous actions, if not absolutely referable, in the catalogue of human cares and sufferings, to the same category as the pitiful strifes, the degrading vices, and the destroying crimes, seldom, very seldom meet with any reward except the radiant glow from the inner heart, which can have no expression, and which admits of no description.

Early on the morrow, Major Brandrum and Captain Lisle were summoned to the presence of the commander-in-chief, and each received a mission, which, if not strictly of a military description, might at any moment assume that character, according to the progress of events. In two hours after, the one was on his way to Dublin, the other traveling down into Cornwall; but both received a promise of promotion and active employment upon their return, if the business intrusted to them was conducted to the satisfaction of government.

With their proceedings during their absence—which lasted nineteen days—I will have nothing to do, as they do not come within the scope of this work. Suffice it to say, that Lisle found little, Major Brandrum much, to employ him, and that for the peace of the former—for that relief from corroding thought which active occupation affords—it would have been better for Reginald if they had changed places. Nor will I dwell upon his thoughts either, for the reader will well conceive what they were, while looking upon the cold refusal of Mary Chevenix to see him as an intimation that his hopes must end. Hope, indeed, with as persevering but more benignant fire than the famous naphtha of the Greeks, will not be extinguished; and a small light rose up in his heart upon reflection. "Perhaps," he said, "I have been too hasty; perhaps some unavoidable accident prevented her from coming down to see me. At all events, I will make another effort. I will call upon Sir Charles—if it be his commands, or those of Lady Chevenix, which place a barrier between Mary and me, I shall at least be able to learn the fact; and if she loves me, I may win her still."

With such thoughts he lay down to rest, and in his dreams Mary's beautiful eyes gazed on him, full of smiles, and her dear voice bade him trust. But when, on the very morning after his return, he called in Grosvenor Square, he found that the whole family had left London eight days before.

I heard a young lady once recommend a friend just about to be married always to have in her house a bag for "odds and ends." I have made such a sort of bag of this chapter, which I beg the reader to look upon as purely interpolated, and to be skipped or not, as he pleases. It might have seemed kinder, indeed, to insert the notice to that effect at the beginning instead of at the end; but it is a matter of principle with me to discourage all skipping: first, because the reader can never understand the story rightly if he does skip; secondly, because he may omit something that would do him good mentally or corporeally; and, thirdly, because it is a bad compliment to the writer. And, besides, what author can ever tell, at the beginning of a chapter, what that chapter will produce before it comes to an end?

CHAPTER XXIX.

I have left Sir Theodore Broughton so long, that it is absolutely necessary to return to him, even if it be for a very short time. Such a young man is not fit to be trusted in the midst of a city like London, even though he have a tutor of the learning, experience, and prudence of Doctor Gamble by his side. I must, therefore, go back to look after him, from the moment that he left the fields at the back of Montague House. For a time, Sir Theodore Broughton was very sullen and discontented: in the hackney coach, which conveyed them back to a well-known inn in London called the Turk's Head, Doctor Gamble endeavored in vain to engage him in agreeable conversation. He got no answer from him but a monosyllable, and that a rude one, uttered in a rude tone. Doctor Gamble then retired into himself, and asked of the counseler within what was to be done next. Captain Donovan was evidently greatly offended and annoyed; Sir Theodore seemed no less so; and the possible—nay, probable—result of their joint dissatisfaction was by no means a pleasant subject of contemplation to the worthy tutor. How it was to be avoided became the great question, and he revolved that point in his mind very seriously for the rest of the way. He had often seen self-confidence and a somewhat domineering air succeed with men of no great force of character, and he had always seen it succeed with Sir Theodore himself. Circumstances had changed, indeed; the young baronet had assumed the tone and air of manhood; but still there was something in the good doctor's heart which led him to judge that the native weakness had not been eradicated entirely; and, indeed, the youth's behavior during the short interval of Captain Donovan's presence proved that there was something he was prepared to reverence and obey.

"If I am to be dismissed," thought Doctor Gamble, "I may as well carry matters with a high hand. Perhaps that may put affairs right again, and I am no worse; but I must be tender, too—affectionate, d—d affectionate. I will let him begin; I'll not say another word. That will make him feel awkward at the outset, and then I will look for an advantage."

But Sir Theodore Broughton did not seem to feel at all awkward about the matter; and, as soon as Doctor Gamble and he were once more quietly introduced into his sitting-room at the Turk's Head, he gazed gloomily at the tutor for a moment, and then said, "Very pretty this, sir."

"Very pretty indeed, Sir Theodore," answered Doctor Gamble, with perfect coolness: "I never saw a very ugly affair more nicely settled. Of all the many very difficult transactions I have had to deal with in life, I shall always look back to this as the most delicately managed."

"Let me tell you, Doctor Gamble," exclaimed Sir Theodore, in a loud and angry tone—

"Pooh, pooh!" cried the tutor almost contemptuously; "you are heated, young gentleman. Wait till you are cool, and you will find reason to thank me most gratefully. Do you think, sir," he continued, with great volubility, "that I was going to see you shot before my face by one of the most notorious marksmen in Europe, who would knock any button off your coat at the first shot? Had he chosen small swords instead of pistols, I might not have interfered, inasmuch as you might be somewhat equally matched. You are a good swordsman, and what you wanted in practice you might make up in activity."

Sir Theodore thought not, for he recollected a certain scene between Major Brandrum and Colonel Lutwich, at Stratton-upon-Dunsmore, which showed no want of activity upon the part of the former. Doctor Gamble went on, however, without giving him time to comment. "To have you to fight him with pistols would have been to consent to your murder. I had only one of two courses to pursue: to give information at Bow-street, and have you all apprehended and conveyed to prison, or to fetch your guardian with all speed, by which your honor would remain intact, and your person be saved incarceration. You may think it a very fine thing to be killed for the sake of a pretty girl, but I know it is a much finer thing to live for half a dozen. Why should you go out of the world, at not much more than nineteen, like a drowned kitten, when you have every sort of enjoyment that the world—a very pleasant world it is, too—can afford you, only waiting to be tasted? It might suit you very well, Sir Theodore, to have a bullet sent through your young, hot brains, or into your warm, passionate heart, but it would not suit me at all."

"Who brought me so near it?" asked Sir Theodore, sternly; for, though the words of his tutor had not been without effect in raising up very unpleasant considerations, which had been smothered in the heat of passion and under a false sense of honor, yet his angry disappointment at all that had taken place was in but a small degree softened.

"Not I," answered Gamble, boldly; "the devil and ill luck brought you so near it. The best-laid scheme may fail, Sir Theodore, as ours did. I had nothing to do with its failure. It was accident or treachery upon some other part than mine. I did my best to please you and to assist you in your object; and, had not a very extraordinary chance intervened, the girl would most likely now be sitting beside you at St. Alban's, with her hand in yours. We must try what we can do to recover from our failure, but it is not grateful of you to reproach me when I have both labored and suffered in your cause."

He presented a pleasant picture to the young man's mind, which he calculated it would seize upon at once—for he was a great calculator: nor was he deceived in this instance; for Sir Theodore Broughton, though by no means a peculiar character, had, amid much weakness, certain points—I will not say of strength, but of stiffness. In many things he was pertinacious to a degree beyond obstinacy. This disposition had shown itself in very capricious fashions from his infancy, sometimes in the books he would read, sometimes in the amusements he would seek; and even Captain Donovan, although he never knew beforehand in what his ward's pertinacity would display itself, had been fain to yield when the first symptoms appeared, for he soon learned that to oppose or thwart only rendered him more determined. I do not know that I have used the right word, for perhaps determination had nothing to do with it. No operation of the mind seemed to take place: it was a sort of instinct of the flesh to seek more earnestly, to pursue more eagerly, that which he had set his mind upon, as soon as impediments presented themselves.

Doctor Gamble was aware of all this, and he was quite sure that, instead of being discouraged by the failure of his evil schemes, the young man would only go on more vehemently, and that every thing which presented to him an image of success would be pleasant to him, and soften the asperity of disappointment and disgrace.

There were two points in the doctor's reply which Sir Theodore seized upon: the one, to feast his imagination, without comment; the other, to consult upon at once. The idea of sitting beside Kate Malcolm, with her hand in his, only stayed him for a moment, however, and then he remarked, in a more placable tone than he had hitherto used, "You say we must try what we can do to recover from our failure. Something we must do, certainly; but what it is I do not see. Can your wit help now, doctor?"

Gamble was inclined to be a little coy. "I will try, upon certain conditions, Sir Theodore," he said: "I will not any more take the responsibility upon myself. I will do every thing I can to serve you, my young friend, but first I will lay the whole matter before you fairly and clearly. Then you shall say, go on, or stop; and whether what we do attempt fails or not, I will not be blamed."

"You will expect to be praised if it succeeds, I dare say," replied the young baronet, with a laugh; "but go on; that is agreed. What step can we take now?"

"I would first ascertain how we have been frustrated," replied the doctor; "we must know what engines are at work against us, before we can determine how to meet them."

"Oh, that is plain enough," replied Sir Theodore, impatiently: "Major Brandrum and Captain Lisle are the engines—and strong enough engines to encounter, too," he added, bitterly.

"I think you are mistaken, my young friend," answered Gamble. "I saw the man, Ben Plowshare, for a minute before I went out of town, and a word or two which he let fall makes me think that neither Lisle nor Brandrum had any thing to do with snatching your pretty little pigeon out of the net. We shall learn more from him when we can talk with him."

"The vagabond was here yesterday," replied Sir Theodore, "wanting money; but I was busy with Fitzgerald, and told him to apply to you."

"He will soon find us out again, depend upon it," answered the doctor; and now, having brought the business to this point, and contrived to efface all traces of anger from his pupil's mind, Gamble turned to another very frequent topic of thought, which, indeed, he never entirely forgot, and added, "But now, Sir Theodore, I must crave some breakfast. I have not touched meat or drink for fifteen hours."

"Poor Doctor Gamble," cried Sir Theodore, sarcastically, "I wonder he is living after such a fast. You would not do for a popish priest, doctor, I suspect."

"I do not know," replied the tutor. "I fancy I fast and pray as much as most of them; and as for celibacy, search all the parish registers through England, and I will defy you to find the name of Stephen Gamble coupled with that of any thing in woman's shape."

Thus saying, he rang the bell and ordered breakfast, of a kind to make ample amends for his long abstinence.

The meal was barely over, and Gamble was lolling in his chair, according to an invariable custom of his, to chew the cud, as it were, for a quarter of an hour after every operation of the jaws, when the personage of whom they had been lately speaking made his appearance, and was soon in familiar chat with the baronet and his tutor. He was a keen, vivacious fellow, always cheerful, though laughing little, with a sharp, hawk-like bill, and a roving, unsatisfied eye. As if he had been an honest tradesman, he began the conversation, after the first salutations, by asking for the settlement of his little account.

"Why, you rascal," answered Gamble, who knew well how to deal with him, "you did not succeed, you know. You had enough in hand to pay you well. If you had not spoiled the job, you would have had more."

"Not my fault, 'pon honor, gentlemen," answered Ben, with perfect composure. "I told you all about it, doctor, and you must see—"

"Stop, stop, Master Ben," replied Doctor Gamble, "you did not tell me *all* about it: I was in too great a hurry to stay. So you must tell us now, and if we find you really could not help it, of course Sir Theodore will consider your services."

"Well, sir, you see the case was this," replied Ben, "though I can't make a long story of it, for I was never good at a long story in my life; and I recollect once when an old beak said, 'Give an account of yourself, sir,' I had nothing to say but, 'Please your worship, I can't.' However, I got the young lady safely out of the park, and down the lane, and into the road; but just at the corner by the Skittles —I dare say you know the Skittles, doctor: it is a noted house—I saw two men a' horseback. There had been one on the Hertford road, just by the bar—but as soon as they saw me, they drew out, and one of them said, 'You can't pass here!' so I wheeled, round and—"

"Did you know either of the two men, that you turned so fast?" asked Doctor Gamble. "I should have thought you and your friend upon the horse might have forced your way against only two."

"Did I know them?" said Ben, with a laugh; "to be sure, I knew them fast enough. One was Captain Swan, and t'other was Dick Bromer; and if we'd tried to go on, they'd have shot us like cattle. So, as I was saying, I wheeled round and took to the lanes; but, whichever way I turned, there were folks to head us, and I soon saw it was a regular thing, and that they must have nosed the job, for all along, here and there—sometimes to the right, sometimes to the left—I saw Lutwich himself—that is, the colonel—and his lad Hal. Over hedges and ditches they went, as if it were nothing. He's a capital rider, to be sure; and then, when at last I thought we had cut away from him clean, up he comes again, and the young woman puts her head out and holloas, and he's afore the pole in a minute, and that there pistol in his hand that's not like to miss."

The start which Sir Theodore Broughton gave at the name of Lutwich had not stopped the narrator, though he remarked it; but when he came to this part of his tale, he looked in the young baronet's face with one eye half closed, and added, "You know the colonel, I should reckon, sir; and if you do, you know he's one not to be meddled with more than a bulldog."

"He must not meddle with me much more," said Sir Theodore; and he was going on to give further vent to his anger, when Gamble interposed, saying, "Stay, stay; how can he have got scent of this? You say you are sure it was a regular plan of his to stop you, wherever you turned?"

"Quite sure," replied Ben, in a most decided tone.

"How could he find it out?" said Gamble, musing; "some one must have betrayed us."

"Lord bless you, sir!" cried the serviceable scoundrel, with a look of contemptuous pity, "you don't half know your man, that's clear. Why, there's nothing takes place from Charing Cross to the pump at Aldgate that he does not know of before it is done. Not a gentleman can go out of town in a moonlight night, whether it be on the outside of a horse, or the inside of a shay, but he contrives to get information of it somehow."

"But what for?" exclaimed Sir Theodore; "he must have some motive."

Ben Plowshare now laughed aloud. "Well," he exclaimed, "I thought every body knew who Colonel Lutwich is."

"I do. I have the pleasure of his acquaintance," answered the young baronet, somewhat haughtily.

"Well, if it's a pleasure, that's more than many can say," answered the other; "but I'll tell you as much of it as I dare, sir. Who's in that room there?"

"No one," answered Gamble. "Go on, and don't be afraid."

"You must know, then, sir," continued Ben, lowering his voice, "the colonel is, or was, a real colonel; and he was rich, too, and his relations high people; but he was very extravagant, and used to play high, though they say he did not care much about it; and he used to bet high too; and one night, about three years ago, he lost more than he had in his pocket—people do say more than he had in his house; and the fellow he lost it to jeered him about it, and pretended to be afraid of not getting his money. So Lutwich said, 'Wait here for one hour, and you shall have it;' and, sure enough, he brought it; but that night the store-keeper of Portsmouth yard was robbed of a thousand pounds hard cash upon Wimbledon. Since then there have been plenty of stories, and they say he quite weighs his weight. I dare not say much more, for he's a terrible hand when he's angry; but all I know is, whether he does such tricks or not, nobody has ever been able to prove it against him, though he was once tried for his life, and has never been employed in the army since. He is so desperate 'cute. I've heard say, however, that there is one could hang him if he liked, and I believe it."

"Who is that?" demanded Gamble, quickly.

"Why, Hangingwood Billy, the swivel-eyed post-boy, who's been so long at the Woolpack at St. Alban's," said Ben; "he knows more of his ways than any one."

Sir Theodore Broughton rose, and walked up and down the room for a minute, in thought. Doctor Gamble eyed him attentively, and then went and spoke to him in a whisper. "Yes, yes, if it can be managed," replied the young baronet, with his face lighting up with not the most pleasant fire.

"Here, Ben, there are two guineas for you," said the doctor; "and now, if you can bring Hangingwood Billy here to speak with us for an hour, we will give five pounds to share between you."

The man nodded his head, pouched the money, and then, after a very few pithy inquiries as to convenient hours, &c., left the room.

CHAPTER XXX.

The cottage was a very pretty one. England has always been famous for pretty cottages; indeed, it is the only country in the world which has such a thing, except, perhaps, Switzerland and some parts of the Tyrol. The French *chaumière* is as different from an English cottage as a French woman is from an English woman. An Italian *capanna* does not give you the least idea of the thing, nor a *casarellina* either, nor any of the *inas* nor *ellas*. The Spanish *casilla, casita*, or *casica*, are all as far off, and the German *hütte* is as bad. A pretty cottage is only to be found in England.

There is no doubt of it: we are naturally a democratic people in our tastes. Our kings have palaces built for them, and then they build cottages for themselves. However, the cottage of Mrs. Lisle was a very pretty cottage indeed, in that peculiar style which covers a very convenient house, intended for the residence of the wealthy and the luxurious, with the thatch of the peasant. The rooms were not very large and not very lofty, neither were they very small nor very low; and they were all beautifully proportioned, and exceedingly neatly furnished. In fact, externally and internally, it had every thing for comfort and nothing for ostentation; though Reginald, in moments of temporary repose, had taken care to do, externally at least, a great deal for ornament, and had done it with a painter's eye. But I will not pause upon the pretty little lawn in front, separated from the smooth green fields beyond by a hawhaw; nor speak of the groups of old elms upon that lawn, so arranged, by lopping a branch here and there, as to frame a view of the hills; nor rest in the little veranda, with its rich climbing plants, keeping the eyes from the glare without excluding the sunshine; but, on the contrary, I will proceed at once to the group within, consisting of five persons: three of them are already known to the reader, and therefore I will only deal with two.

That elderly lady in the widow's cap shall be the first: she has worn those weeds ever since a gallant husband's death, now fourteen or fifteen years ago. The hair, indeed, is not all concealed; but, gray nearly to silver, without powder, it is plainly braided upon the forehead. She seems fifty-three or four; but she is in reality less, not more than forty-eight; but cares and sorrows, strongly felt, have made years for her. She is tall—taller for a woman than her son for a man, and probably was once very graceful, for her form is still fine; and, though her movements are somewhat slow, yet there is a dignity in them, such as young graces, when they die, sometimes bequeath to age. Her brow is ever grave, but gentle, and the smile that comes upon her lip, even in her happiest moments, is faint, though very sweet. Such is the Honorable Mrs. Lisle.

The pale girl of two or three-and-twenty, seated at a little distance from Mrs. Lisle, with Kate Malcolm between them, is her daughter; but—oh! what a contrast between that slight, delicate creature and her brother! He, browned and hardened by years of campaigning, powerful, though graceful in form, and upright, though not stiff; she, light, slender, bending like a flower, and colorless as a snow-drop.

As nothing more than a glimpse of Mrs. Lisle will ever be given to the reader, I may as well say a few words of her character here, there being no opportunity of displaying it in her actions. Though gentle and kind, and enthusiastic by nature, she had a great deal of that firm and quick decision of character which characterized her brother, and which had given him so much power over old Sir Walter Broughton, whom no one had ever been able to manage but himself. Though plain and simple in her words, there was a great deal of imagination and rich fancy in her conversation, and the images by which she would illustrate her meaning seemed only the more striking from the simple language in which they were conveyed. She had long been in very delicate health, however, and the feebleness of the body was, in her case, a shackle upon her fancy.

She was now looking extremely grave, perhaps I might say sad; and, indeed, she had some cause, for her son and Major Brandrum were just at the close of a parting visit, before they once more sailed for the Far West. Only on the preceding day they had received their promotion and orders; but those orders were peremptory to proceed to the St. Lawrence by a ship just about to sail, and the chaise was now expected at the door every moment.

For the last ten minutes, Major—or, as he should now be called, Colonel—Brandrum had been talking eagerly to his adopted child; and then, turning to Mrs. Lisle, he said, "To your charge, my dear lady, I leave her; and I know she will be well and happy with you; but, at the same time, as life is uncertain, and I may never see these shores again, I have been telling her that she will find in my agent's hands, whose address I have given her, all that is necessary to entitle her, in case I am shot, bayoneted, or scalped, to all the fragments which the service of my country and a reckless disposition have left me. Had I known I should ever have a daughter, Kate, I might have been more careful."

"But not less generous, colonel," replied Mrs. Lisle. "Can you take away its smell from the rose, or its luster from the diamond? But leave her with me in all security. Poor dove! she has found a cot at last, and under my wing she will be safe as long as God spares me."

"We will be sisters, Colonel Brandrum," said Louisa Lisle, in a low voice.

Kate was troubled about something. Either gratitude for the kindness she received, or pain at seeing her kind protector about to leave her so soon, or some other emotion, made her turn pale and red by turns; and at length, rising as if with a great effort, she said, addressing Major Brandrum, "May I speak with you in the other room for a moment? I have something I wish to say."

But, even as she spoke, the grating sound of carriage wheels was heard, and a chaise, well loaded, with two servants on horseback behind, passed along the little drive before the windows, and drew up at the door.

"Good faith! my dear girl, if you have any thing to tell, you must write it," replied Major Brandrum, pointing to the vehicle: "I would rather risk scalping than miss the vessel, and the fellow is now somewhat late. Farewell, Mrs. Lisle. Louisa, little darling, fare you well."

"Colonel Lutwich, madam," said a servant, throwing open the door, and Kate's cheek instantly glowed warmly.

"Who?" asked Mrs. Lisle.

"Lutwich," answered Major Brandrum: "an exceedingly good fellow, to whom Kate is under great obligations."

"Oh! I know—I have heard," said Mrs. Lisle. "I wish, however, it had been at another time. A stranger's presence, at a moment like this, is like frost chilling the last flowers of autumn."

The words were hardly uttered ere Lutwich was in the room. His first look, his first words, were for Kate Malcolm; but then he turned to Lisle and Brandrum.

"I have heard of your good fortune," he said, shaking them warmly by the hand. "Are you away at once? Well, God speed you! Perhaps, Brandrum, it may not be long ere I follow. I have good hopes."

"Indeed!" exclaimed Brandrum; "then I do wish you joy."

"Yes, indeed," said Lutwich; "I have seen the commander-in-chief, besought pardon for past offenses, promised order and obedience for the future; sold off my stud, my house in town, my wines, my carriages, as the first mark of sincerity; and henceforth I am a different man."

"That is good news indeed," answered Brandrum, grasping his hand. "Take my advice, Lutwich: get on foreign service at once. It will break through bad acquaintances."

"I have good hope of doing so," replied Lutwich; "and, as I said, I may come out and join you soon. But," he added, as his eyes turned to Kate's face again, and he saw that the color had left her cheek, "I must not come alone, my good friend. I must have some one to take care of me, and to keep me in the right path."

"Now, colonel," said Reginald Lisle, who had been standing with his mother's hand in his, "we must go indeed."

Another minute, the parting embrace was given, the farewell spoken, and the two officers were gone. Louisa went to the window, and watched the carriage roll away with streaming eyes. The dew was in Kate's also, and one tear trickled down Mrs. Lisle's cheek.

Colonel Lutwich felt a little embarrassed; but his impulses were graceful always; and, approaching the lady of the house, he said, "I really beg pardon, madam, for intruding upon you at this moment; and I would not protract my visit now, but that I have a few questions to ask Miss Malcolm, which I must not defer, as I dine to-morrow with one to whom her answers will be of much interest. But I can speak with her in another room, if my presence is oppressive to you, as I am sure it must be."

"No, no, Colonel Lutwich," answered Mrs. Lisle, holding out her hand to him; "a mother must feel in parting with her son for the last time; but do not suppose I would keep my young falcon to the nest when nature teaches him to soar. I am a soldier's widow, my dear sir, and know what are a soldier's duties."

"And appreciate what may be a soldier's renown," said Lutwich, sitting down beside her; "and believe me, my dear madam, all affectionate hearts, when they part with those they love, feel those sad pictures of what may be, rise before them, which they are inclined to look upon as dark presentiments. Lisle goes to gain glory and honor as he has done before, and doubt not that Heaven in its goodness will send him back to your arms safe, happy, and prosperous. But I will not intrude upon you long."

"Nay," said Mrs. Lisle, "I must not let you think me inhospitable. We shall soon have tea, and, as Reginald's friend, it will give me sincere pleasure if you will stay and partake of it; indeed, it will be better for me—better for us all, for your society will keep us from gloomy thoughts. When there are black clouds overhead, we naturally think there will be a storm."

"Which the wind often wafts far away," said Lutwich; and for a few minutes more he continued to converse cheerfully, but not gayly, with the elder lady, who was evidently pleased with his conversation and demeanor. Kate and Louisa Lisle soon joined in; and in pleasant, easy talk, if they did not forget the pain they had just experienced, the most poignant sting was lost.

Tea was brought, evening began to fall, and yet Colonel Lutwich's questions had not been propounded. At length, however, Mrs. Lisle reminded him of them, and he asked, with a smile, "Are you ready for a cross-examination, dear Miss Malcolm?"

"If it be not a very severe one," answered Kate, timidly.

"You may stay it when you please," said her lover; "first, then, I think you told me that you had a relation in Yorkshire of the name of Eaton."

Kate bowed her head, and he went on. "Is his name Charles or William Eaton?"

"William," she answered.

"It is very strange!" said Lutwich, in a thoughtful tone; "did you not say he was your mother's nephew?"

"Yes," replied Kate, in some surprise; "he was her sister's son. But what is it that is strange?"

"That he should deny the relationship," replied Lutwich; "he must be a gross liar."

Kate's cheek was glowing very warmly. "Stay, stay," she said, "I have his letter: I look at it often to see the contrast between his cold selfishness and the noble generosity of others: I will bring it this moment. He signs himself my cousin;" and, rising, she ran hastily to her room, and returned in a few minutes with the letter.

"There," she said, putting it into Colonel Lutwich's hands.

He read it through with a frowning brow, and then said, "I wish I had had it with me. This man had the impudence to deny, in the most distinct manner, that he ever had an aunt of the name of Malcolm."

For an instant Kate seemed confounded; but then a look of sudden intelligence spread over her face, succeeded by an expression of scorn. "He has not lied with you," she said, "but only equivocated. I now remember, my mother never took the name of Malcolm. She was dead before the small property was left to my father, upon condition of taking that name, which, in the end, by the lawsuit it entailed, proved his complete ruin. My mother always bore the name of Marsham, which was my father's at the time of their marriage; but that can not excuse Mr. Eaton, for he must have known as well as I do whom you meant."

"It is all right," said Lutwich, with a look of grave joy, "it is all right: Marsham was your mother's name first."

"No," said Kate; "her unmarried name was Carr. Marsham was my father's name before he took that of Malcolm."

"Carr—that is right too," exclaimed Lutwich; and then he fell into thought, and fixed his eyes vacantly upon a spot in the carpet.

"*But* now tell me," said Kate, after giving him time enough to meditate—for there is no view from which a man likes so little to be recalled as that which presents itself when his eyes are upon his own thoughts—"but now tell me what has made you ask me all these questions? Is it merely because Mr. Eaton disowned his poor cousin?"

"No, no, dear Kate," said Lutwich, forgetting the presence of others; "I had a strong motive. I will not tell you now, but you may hear hereafter—perhaps to-morrow. You shall hear, at all events, from me, if not from another. I know not," he continued, rising and taking her hand, while he gazed into her eyes, "I know not whether what I am doing—what I have been doing—what I shall do—may not be directly opposed to my own interests; but I have not forgotten a lesson you gave me one night in regard to candor and frankness, and I will act up to it—to the very letter, my dear instructress. I think another has a first right to the information I have obtained; but yours is the next, and you shall have it. I must now, however, leave you, for it is growing late, and—"

"Good Heaven! there is a man looking in at the window," cried Louisa Lisle.

Lutwich instantly turned his eyes in the direction of the casement, and clearly saw a figure retreating through the darkness without. "You had better ring and order the shutters to be closed," he said; "I will stay till it is done."

Mrs. Lisle, who had been gazing toward the window too, put out her hand to ring the bell; but, before she had pulled the rope, another bell was heard, and then a considerable noise in the little vestibule. The next instant the door burst open, and two men entered the room. Lutwich turned deadly pale.

The first who appeared was a powerful fellow of about five foot eleven, well dressed, as a man of the middle station. The second was shorter, and amazingly broad over the shoulders; but it was the first who spoke, and that in a civil though somewhat stern tone. "Sorry to trouble you just now, colonel," he said, "but we want you."

Lutwich bowed his head significantly, calm and composed, though very grave, and with a face still pale. "I will come with you at once," he said. "Good-by, Mrs. Lisle, Kate—"

But, while he was speaking, the second man, who had been diving with his hand into his large pockets, produced a pair of thick, shining iron rings, screwed together in the midst, and said aloud, "I suppose you'll have the 'cuffs on him, Master Williams?"

"Good Heaven!" cried Mrs. Lisle, "they are handcuffs!"

Lutwich's face turned now as red as fire, and he seemed as if he were about to start forward and knock the man down; but Kate sprang to his side, and caught his arm, exclaiming, "Oh! what is it—what is the matter, Henry?"

"Why, the matter is, ma'am, that we have a warrant against the colonel for robbery on the king's highway," said the first officer; "but, as he is quite a gentleman, and seems likely to come without giving any trouble, I'm not inclinable to put the darbies on him, or the 'cuffs either, till I'm told."

Kate put her hand to her head, and then burst into a violent flood of tears.

"This must surely be some mistake!" cried Mrs. Lisle, greatly agitated. "Colonel Lutwich, explain to the men who you are!"

"It is of no use, my dear madam," said Lutwich. "They know who I am quite well. This charge has been brought once before."

"No, not just the same, colonel," replied the officer: "this is for stopping Ned Warwick, the sheriff's officer, and his bum; t'other was for robbing Mr. Sheepshanks, the broker. You're over weight now, colonel, I am afeerd. But, come, you had better jog at once. The women will blubber a bit, you know."

"Go on, sir," said Lutwich; "I come with you;" and he seemed about to follow; but Kate caught his hand, exclaiming, "Oh, Henry, where are they going to take you? Write to me—tell me all. It must be false—say it is false."

Lutwich bent his head, and kissed her cheek; but the only words he uttered were, "I will write, dear Kate—I will write to-morrow;" and he hurried out of the room with the two officers.

Louisa took Kate's hand, and led her back to the sofa; but the poor girl was utterly overwhelmed and bewildered with grief. She felt now, for the first time, how deeply she could love, and how love could triumph over every other sensation. She longed to follow Lutwich, to share his prison, to soothe, to comfort him; to assure him that she believed not a word of the accusation brought against him; that she was sure it was false; that it could not be true; that he who could act so nobly, so generously by her, could be guilty of no crime. But strength of body and of mind had failed her for the moment, and she sat, with the tears running rapidly down her cheeks, and her lips murmuring, "It is impossible! it is impossible!"

Mrs. Lisle, too, was greatly agitated and shocked; and she remained silent, with her hands pressed upon her eyes. But at length she made an effort; and, sitting down by her young guest, she said, in a gentle and kindly tone, "Be comforted, Kate; I, too, think it impossible—quite impossible, that the friend of my son should be guilty of any crime. Compose yourself, my love. Let us wait till to-morrow, and hear what comes of this. It is, perhaps, a charge to extort money."

But while she was proceeding thus, and while Kate was still weeping bitterly, Louisa Lisle approached her mother's side, saying softly, "You, too, mamma, be calm. You are too much agitated. Your face is pale—your lips are blue. You know what Doctor Grant said: you will make yourself ill. Let me bring you some of the drops."

But Mrs. Lisle waved her hand; and Kate instantly lifted her head, and wiped her eyes, saying, while she gazed in her kind hostess's face, "I will weep no more; I will be calm. Forgive me, dear Mrs. Lisle. I was selfish in my sorrow; I will be quite calm."

She might be so externally; and, indeed, to a certain degree, she was so during the rest of the short summer evening; but no one could tell how fearfully she was agitated within.

The afternoon came to an end, and Mrs. Lisle rose early to retire to rest. Kate and Louisa followed her closely. When she had reached the top of the steps, something seemed suddenly to strike her; and, turning to Louisa, she said, quickly, and in an eager manner, "Louisa, my love, I for—"

But the sentence remained unconcluded, and will do so forever. As she spoke, Mrs. Lisle fell back, and was caught, partly by her daughter, partly by Kate Malcolm.

Louisa called aloud for help; the man-servant, who was in the vestibule below, ran up, and, with his assistance, Mrs. Lisle was carried into her own room, and laid upon her bed.

"Run—run for Doctor Slater!" cried Louisa Lisle; "quick as lightning, Groves."

Kate brought water, and sprinkled the cold face. There was a slight movement of the muscles round the lips, and then all was still. The maids were summoned, and various remedies tried, till the surgeon came; but none were the least effectual in breaking that heavy sleep. When he did come, he tried none, but put his hand upon the wrist, watched the face for a moment, and then took Louisa's hand, saying, solemnly, "She is at peace!"

CHAPTER XXXI.

When the United States of America have accomplished the great destiny that is before them—when civilization and prosperity in its train have emigrated completely to the West—when the seeds of inevitable decay, which are planted in the foundation of all states and empires, have spread, like the lichen and the moss, over all that we are proud of in this land, and when the citizens of the greatest republic, or the subjects of the greatest empire (as the case may then be) that the world ever saw, cross the Atlantic to view, as travelers, the half-desolate country from which their fathers sprang, how many objects of interest and inquiry will present themselves to their eyes!

I see some readers smile, and others laugh, and both in proud scorn. They will find a thousand reasons why the vain anticipation of permanent power and pre-eminence should not be disappointed in the English people, though it has been so with every other nation. They will say, "We are Christians, free, orderly, ingenious, energetic: there are a thousand qualities in us, a thousand accidents in our condition, a thousand opportunities in our position, which none of the fallen nations have ever possessed."

True: but the march of events is sure, the law of nature invariable; there is nothing which it does not affect, nothing which can do more than delay its progress for a few short years. Decay is in every thing, and as certainly follows complete development as old age follows manhood. The walls of Babylon, the towers of Nineveh, the monuments of Rome, the temples and the citadels of Greece, are witnesses against us; and neither freedom, nor arts, nor arms, nor energies, can save us from the fate of all earthly things. The follies or wisdom of princes and people—the faults or the excellence of statesmen and legislators, may retard or hasten, by a century or two, the period of the fall; but nations shall die as individuals, and the land they inhabited become their tomb.

When such is the case with England, there may, perhaps, be for future generations more important and more interesting fragments left than have been bequeathed to posterity by any other nation. France will leave little or nothing but a history of blood or tyranny, the shocks of alternate anarchy and servitude.

Nevertheless, in many of her social relations, how poor and pitiful will England appear! how narrow, how material will the notions of her people seem! how little expansion of soul and feeling will be found among the records of her society! Her great and her good men maltreated or neglected; powers of mind and nobility of heart considered the lowest of claims upon public estimation or gratitude; the recompense of merit dependent upon party spirit, and the road to success only open to material exertion. The splendid exceptions to the general tone of the whole nation will only prove more painfully the general rule.

One point in the history of the people which will probably excite great attention hereafter, is the enormous and extraordinary advance in civilization, if not in elevation, made in the society of England during the last fifty or sixty years. The wonderful progress during that period—to a part of which, at least, we have ourselves been witnesses—is without parallel in the history of nations; and if we take up a book of the times immediately antecedent—whether it be the private diary of an individual, or his collected letters, or one of those works which, though the narrative be fictitious, profess to paint the manners of the day—we shall be more startled by the contrast between our days and those, than between the present and some centuries ago.

Among the abominations which have been swept away, a mass of the most foul and loathsome existed in our prisons, the miseries of which, and some of the crimes of those under whose rule they were, have been exposed by the immortal Howard. But the vices practiced within those gloomy walls, the revelry, the debauchery, the iniquity which reigned side by side with famine, pestilence, and death, can only be gleaned by scattered anecdotes, or by the glimpses given of those mansions of sin and despair, by those who had known and escaped from their baneful atmosphere.

Let the reader picture to himself one ward crammed to suffocation with wretches dying of a fever so pestilential, that when a few of them, just able to stand in the dock, have been brought into court for trial, the disease has spread to every one around—judge, jurors, officers, spectators—and in the next ward, the ringing shouts of wild and drunken revelry, or the more secret orgies of a darker licentiousness. Then let him look at the miserable man committed for some unprofitable crime, without money to fee a mercenary jailer, or to procure necessary food, pining and wasting upon bread and water, and then turn his eyes to the wealthy prisoner lodged in the governor's house, treated with all reverence, living on delicacies, and freely tippling his Champagne. Or take them altogether, meeting in promiscuous groups, men and women, boys and young girls, the hardened felon, the repentant novice, the man to whom the load of crime has become easy by habit, and the bewildered innocent overwhelmed by a false accusation. No limit but a jailer's caprice was placed upon the persons admitted to see the prisoners. Rules and regulations might exist, but were totally neglected. Every thing for which they might please to pay toll was admitted, whether the strong stimulant to drive away thought in drunkenness, or the means of effecting an escape, or those of perverting the course of justice. The turnkeys themselves were in league with the "Old Bailey witnesses," and many a successful defense has been made up, for a criminal who could afford to pay, between the jailer who had him in charge and the "man with the straw in his shoe," who saved him from the gallows by direct perjury.

Such things have passed away; but such things have been, and they existed in full force at the time when Colonel Lutwich was carried as a prisoner to one of the many jails which then existed in or near London. It was dark, as I have said, when he was apprehended, and as the distance was considerable, it was nearly twelve o'clock before he had passed the gloomy gates where he was to await examination and trial; but the governor of the prison was himself up, and the sounds of laughter and singing announced that some of the prisoners were likewise awake.

With profound respect and attention, the governor received so distinguished a captive, and lighted him into his own parlor with a candle, which he had brought out when the great bell rang.

"How do you do, colonel?" he said; "I hope your honor is quite well. It is two years since I have had the pleasure of seeing you—you will, of course, like a room to yourself? We have got one quite ready for you."

"Did you expect me?" asked Lutwich, gazing in his face.

"Oh dear, yes, sir," replied the governor; "we have been expecting you all the morning."

"Then I think the officers might have been civil enough," said Lutwich, "to execute their warrant more privately. I have been at my own house, and in that neighborhood, all the afternoon—I shall, of course, like to have a room to myself, sir; but I require nothing extraordinary or extravagant."

The jailer's face fell a little, for in those days the custody of an extravagant prisoner was a privilege of some value, and he began to think that Lutwich must have exhausted his means. It was not an unreasonable supposition either; for in days of "trading justices," it was rarely a culprit found his way to the gallows till the greater part of his funds had been expended in purchasing immunity. He murmured something then about "persons paying for accommodation," but the prisoner took him up sharply, saying, "There, there! do not make yourself uneasy, my good sir. I know your customs, and have plenty of means to agree with them all. I am richer, perhaps, than ever I have been, and shall, as before, require the best of every thing. There," he continued, taking out his purse, "there are five guineas for my garnish, as you call it. Now, show me my room—I would rather have two, if possible, for I do not like to sit where I sleep."

"Certainly, colonel, certainly," replied the jailer, with his mind relieved. "You can have two. One we will make into a sitting-room for you to-morrow. It has a bed in it just now, but that will soon be taken out. This way, sir. I suppose you will like to have a servant, too? there's a nice room for him at the lodge."

"Yes," said Lutwich, thoughtfully, "I will send for one to-morrow;" and he followed the head jailer, with a turnkey at his heels, to the apartments destined for him.

"These two, colonel, with the room at the lodge for your man, will be ten guineas a week, you know," said the head Cerberus, after Lutwich had stood in the midst, gazing round for a minute or two.

"Very well," replied the prisoner, paying the money in advance, as usual in such cases; and then again he fell into thought.

"Can I do any thing further to serve you, colonel?" inquired the head jailer.

"Yes," answered Lutwich, abruptly: "pen, ink, and paper; some supper, and your best wine."

"Can I send for your dressing things?" was the next question; but the prisoner waved his hand impatiently, saying, "No, no; it is too far: I have sold off my house and goods in London, my good friend, realizing thereby, what with horses and plate, near seven thousand pounds."

He paused, for an idea passed through his mind of tempting the man's fidelity in order to effect his escape; but the jailer answered him with a smile, "What, sir, I suppose you intended to quit the road, and take another line? Ay, that's the reason they nabbed you. They never let a gentleman do that. They give him his swing as long as he keeps to business. It's the only trade from which a man can never retire."

"Too true!" said Lutwich, with a sigh; "and yet, methinks, every vice is the same. 'Tis like climbing a precipice, my good friend. The road up may be accomplished with that fiery pleasure which ever accompanies danger surmounted, if we look not down below us in the ascent; but the moment we try to turn back, we break our necks. Is this God's ordinance, or man's?"

"The devil's, sir, I should think," replied his companion, "for he gains by it."

"And the jailer," added Lutwich, with a bitter laugh. "Well, well, let me have the things I asked for, and good-night."

"Good-night, sir," said the jailer, and withdrew, securing the door behind him.

Lutwich was left alone; and oh! what language can describe the emotions which then took possession of him—the anguish of heart and spirit! None but his own. After gazing full ten minutes on the floor, as he stood like marble in the midst of the small room, he repeated one word several times with a groan, "Blighted, blighted, blighted!" he said, "all blighted!"

They were hopes, expectations, purposes, he spoke of; the dreams of love and tenderness, and reformation, and honor, and self-respect, and even domestic peace—all blighted, blighted! There seemed nothing else but blight over the whole world for him; and that which rendered the common agony of disappointed hope, and love frustrated, and despair confirmed, doubly agonizing, was the thought that he had worked the ruin of his own futurity; that in the wild, insane fury of many mingled passions, he had cut down the fruit-bearing tree of life; uprooted, harrowed over, and sown with salt the field of earth's expectations, and left nothing for the heart to long for but the peace of death—the slumber of the grave.

Such were the first dark, fearful thoughts which crowded upon him as he stood there alone. They lasted even while the jailer brought in his supper and the wine, the materials for writing, wax-lights, and all that could render a prison luxurious—even while the man spoke to him, and he answered; for there is a mechanical part of man, which goes through its functions while the will is far away.

Then, when the heavy door was finally locked and bolted for the night, he sat himself down and pondered. At first all was blank darkness—a night without a star; but gradually a pale, faint gleam, the dawn of Hope's renewed day, began to rise into a doubtful twilight.

"Will she love me still?" he asked himself. "I have heard of woman's deep devotion unto death, despising shame, insult, scorn; enduring even while it condemns, and clinging to the criminal even while it abhors the crime. If ever there was a being who could so love, methinks she is the one. I will write to her. I will try her. If her love still conquers, there is yet something to live for, something to struggle for. It is very strange, when I had no such feelings in my breast—when the light pleasures of the world, the follies, the vanities, the vices of this earth engrossed, though with empty levity, every thought, I never judged life unworthy of an effort, I was prepared to strive and combat to the last; and now, when higher objects have been placed before my view, and nobler purposes animated me, I feel cast down at the first check, dispirited and despairing while there is many a chance yet left. I will write to her; I will seek some object in living—ay, or perhaps some consolation in death."

He seated himself at the table; he took the paper and the pen; but innumerable difficulties presented themselves at the outset. He tried to think over what he would say, but he got impatient with thought; and murmuring, "Let the heart speak," he wrote:

"In the midst of anguish (I had almost said despair), I turn to my only remaining hope for one gleam of comfort. By letter I can explain nothing, account for nothing; and yet, how dare I venture to ask you to visit me in a prison? What excuse can I frame for such a request, except the impossibility of going forth to see you? There are heavy walls around me, bars upon my windows, locks and bolts upon the door. Yet I have much to say to you, Kate—my own Kate. Well may I call you so; for your spirit had infused into mine a new life, your love had become the star to guide me to right and honor, the hope of your approbation had become the beacon which was leading me onward to all that was good and high. A cloud has come over it for a time, a mist has obscured it; you only can make the light blaze up again. Come to me, then, for a few short minutes, if you still can love me. Give me counsel, give me hope, give me strength. I have some tidings also to give you; but that is nothing to the purpose: I can write them hereafter, if affection, if charity, if the memory of all you have bestowed upon him does not induce you to accede to this request—perhaps the last—of

"Yours till death,

"HENRY LUTWICH."

CHAPTER XXXII.

THE reader has perceived that somewhat more than a fortnight had passed since the day on which Major Brandrum and Reginald Lisle had met Sir Theodore Broughton and his friend Frederic Fitzgerald, Esquire—better known by the name of "Fighting Freddy Fitzgerald"—and had been interrupted in their hostile purposes by the opportune arrival of Doctor Gamble and Captain Donovan. The history of one of the antagonist parties is sufficiently known, but that of the other has ceased since we left him with Doctor Gamble at his inn, after an interesting conversation with that admirable person, Ben Plowshare. It is therefore absolutely necessary to take up again the thread of Sir Theodore's personal story, although I shall sketch it but lightly, from various considerations.

In the first place, let me say that he found the friendship of Mr. Fitzgerald somewhat more difficult to get rid of than to acquire. In a case of emergency, such as the affair between himself and Major Brandrum, Sir Theodore naturally clung to the person who first offered him assistance; but, at the same time, he was clear-sighted enough to see that his new-found friend was rather more ready with pistol or small-sword than even the evil customs of a society such as ours—mingling, in strange compound, barbarism and civilization—required. All that Fitzgerald seemed to desire or aim at in the whole business, was that Sir Theodore should shoot Major Brandrum, or Major Brandrum should shoot Sir Theodore; and, apparently, he did not much care which consummation was arrived at. Do not let the reader suppose, however, that he had any personal feeling in the matter, for such was not the case. He was actuated by a pure, disinterested love of bloodshed, and acted quite philanthropically upon a thorough conviction that it is best, in the abstract, for mankind, that when two human beings quarrel, one of them should be shot or run through the body. We have not quite got rid of this sort of philosophy yet; but it certainly is not as popular as it was.

However, as he could not have his fill of fighting or seeing fought, he thought he might quite as well have his fill of those good things which usually graced the table of the young baronet, and the very same day he presented himself, a few minutes before the usual dinner hour, to talk over the occurrences of the morning. As the table-cloth was already laid, Sir Theodore, notwithstanding a grimace on the part of Doctor Gamble, thought he could not do less than ask his volunteer second to dinner; and Mr. Fitzgerald was soon seated at the well-served board. Doctor Gamble he treated with undisguised contempt, as one of the uncombative portion of the community; but to Sir Theodore he showed great respect, both from the pugnacious qualities he had exhibited, and from a sense of the excellence of soup, fish, poultry, and other bounties of nature. After having taken a sufficient portion of wine, too, and when Doctor Gamble had quitted the room for a few minutes, his regard for Sir Theodore rose to such a pitch of enthusiasm, that he offered his best services once more to find out Major Brandrum, and give him cogent reasons for gratifying Sir Theodore by another meeting, undertaking to manage the whole matter in such a delicate and skillful way as to avoid all chance of a second interruption. He seemed, indeed, to believe that Sir Theodore must necessarily look upon this as the greatest possible favor, and the young gentleman was somewhat embarrassed as to how he should make him comprehend that his taste for such morning exercises was less than his own. Perhaps the very attempt which he made to do so might have forfeited Mr. Fitzgerald's friendship, had not the table and the wine rendered it very adhesive.

The young baronet, however, felt somewhat anxious to get rid of him, and not a little annoyed at the protracted absence of Gamble, which left him to the tender mercies of this gentleman. At length the doctor reappeared, and a minute or two after a waiter entered and informed Mr. Fitzgerald that somebody wished to speak with him. With a look of some alarm, he went out, taking hat and cane with him; but he did not appear again, and only sent his compliments to Sir Theodore, with an intimation he would call upon him another day.

"Rather droll!" said Sir Theodore; "what can be the meaning of this, doctor?"

"Only a friendly hint from a Bow-street officer," replied Gamble, dryly; "the man is a pest, and must be got rid of, my young friend. Life is a pleasant thing, depend upon it; and it was made for other occupations than fighting. Come, let us away to Vauxhall; you will find better amusement there than my Master Fitzgerald would provide for you."

Sir Theodore Broughton, to say the truth, was not at all sorry to be disembarrassed of the presence of his dearly beloved second, although he did not much like the manner in which it had been effected. Nevertheless, the memory of being very heartily horsewhipped rankled much more in his mind than in that of worthy Doctor Gamble. Perhaps it might be that he was less accustomed to the operation; but, as not unfrequently happens, a great portion of his resentment was transferred from his immediate castigator to the person whom he supposed to have suggested the castigation, or, at all events, to him who had been, to all appearance, the proximate cause thereof. Major Brandrum he hated much, but Colonel Lutwich more; and although the somewhat sullen and reserved character of his mind made his spontaneous communications, even with Doctor Gamble, somewhat niggardly, yet more than once the feelings fermenting within found voice in a few brief sentences soon interrupted, which served the good tutor as a foundation for longer replies, and as a means of drawing forth more of the secret feelings of his pupil's heart.

As they were on their way to Vauxhall—after an interval of silence, during which Sir Theodore seemed to be busy in looking at the buildings and lights that they passed—he broke forth abruptly, showing what was really the matter of his thoughts.

"I can not help thinking, doctor," he said, "that fellow Lutwich must have overheard what we were talking about that morning in my room. There was somebody sleeping just next door, and the partition must have been thin, for I heard whoever it was moving about after I was in bed."

"It is very likely," replied Gamble; "I can not conceive how he could find out any other way, for we let Hargrave know so little that he could not betray you. But what do you intend to do when you have talked to this post-boy? If he peaches of Lutwich, it will be no good to you. Unless—"

"I'll hang him if I can," replied the other, gloomily. "What business had he to meddle with my affairs? If I can not hang him for that, I'll hang him for something else, if I can."

"Perhaps he is in love with the girl himself," said Doctor Gamble, looking at Sir Theodore by the light of a globe lamp, which was shining into the carriage.

The young baronet gave a sudden start as if something pained him; but he remained silent for several minutes, till at length Doctor Gamble continued, "I am almost inclined to think, Sir Theodore, that it would be better for you to give the whole thing up. You may find more difficulties in the way than you or I see. This girl is well protected, and—"

An impatient exclamation from the young baronet stopped him, and Sir Theodore replied, "I tell you, difficulties shall not prevent me. I believe what you say is true—he is in love with her. I remember how he took her part at Dunstable—I never thought of it before; and she is in love with him, perhaps."

He paused for a moment or two in gloomy silence, and then asked, "What did you mean by saying 'unless' just now, and then stopping short?"

"Why, I only meant that I did not see, after all, what good your having any thing to do with this post-boy—this Hangingwood Billy, can do, unless you could, some way or another, make it serviceable to your soft suit and pursuit of pretty Kate Malcolm."

"Perhaps I may," replied Sir Theodore, "perhaps I may; but, at all events, doctor, I can make it turn to the punishment of the scoundrel Lutwich himself."

"He will never know that it was you who punished him," said Gamble; and he was going on to add something more, when the young baronet interrupted him by exclaiming. "Yes, he shall, by ——!"

"What I was going to say," continued the

tutor, "is only this, my dear young friend. If you can turn any information you can gain to advantage in winning the lady, why well; but if not, I would not meddle with the poor devil. It will do you no good to hang him."

"You are mighty forgiving," said the young man, with a sneer; "but perhaps I may turn it to advantage."

"I do not think it," said Doctor Gamble; "she may have a liking for the man; but it is not very probable that she would become your mistress to save his life. If it were marriage you offered her, the case might be different. Few women care much whom they marry, so they marry some one able to keep them well."

"Then I *will* marry her," replied Sir Theodore, sharply.

That was a consummation which Doctor Gamble had not expected, and did not at all desire. To be a tutor to a married man was not altogether the office that would suit him, even if it had been by any means usual; and during the remainder of the drive to Vauxhall, he revolved in his mind the various points of his own situation, and that of Sir Theodore, which bore upon the question at issue. He judged his pupil's character very accurately, and knew that to oppose him was but to strengthen his resolution, and to lose his own influence. On the other hand, to aid and abet a scheme which might bring about a marriage with Kate Malcolm would instantly produce his dismissal by Captain Donovan. To pursue the baser purposes with which he and his pupil had set out toward her, he was now convinced would be fruitless, protected as she was by many persons of power, character, and knowledge of the world; for it must be recollected that, at this time, Kate was still under the care of Lady Chevenix, and that both Major Brandrum and Captain Lisle were still in Great Britain.

Doctor Gamble was much embarrassed; and the only plan he could devise was, to lead Sir Theodore away from this passion by plunging him as deeply as possible, not only into the gayeties, but also into the debaucheries of the metropolis. "He is young," thought Gamble, "inexperienced, full of passions, and there are plenty of nymphs to be found who, with a little teaching, will tie him to their apron-strings for a month or two."

I must not trace his meditations further, nor even attempt to paint what followed during the next week. Suffice it to say, that Sir Theodore Broughton was initiated very rapidly into the various mysteries of dissipation with which London then, as now, abounded; and that, by excesses and late hours, the florid hue of health disappeared from his countenance, while weariness and feebleness took possession of his limbs. Doctor Gamble himself became somewhat alarmed at the proficiency which his pupil had attained in vice; but he consoled himself with the fallacious belief that his "boy's passion," as the tutor called it, for Kate Malcolm had altogether died away.

For a moment I must pause to look into the mind of the young man himself, for what was passing there is not without its interest. What, then, were the feelings of Sir Theodore Broughton, when, at the end of about eight days, he lay for more than half an hour after waking, heated, feverish, irritable, but too tired and enfeebled to rise with the elasticity of youth, and the eagerness for fresh enjoyment which he had experienced so short a time before? He was sick of himself, disgusted with his own acts, seeming degraded and contemptible in his own eyes. So much, at least, of the knowledge of right and wrong remained; and had there been any one near him whom he could have respected, to give counsel and warning, perhaps a change to better things might have been effected.

I say perhaps, for I will own that it was very doubtful.

There were no resolutions, founded upon any right principle, for the wise or the good to strengthen. He determined, indeed, to change his course to a certain degree; but the motive was all selfish. He resolved to be more moderate, but simply because he felt that excesses weakened and injured him. He never thought of abstaining, he never accused himself of vice, or dreamed of penitence or proposed reformation; and far, very far from his mind was that forgetfulness of his purposes which Doctor Gamble attributed to him. In the midst of all the wild scenes of profligacy into which he had plunged, he had often wondered why the St. Alban's post-boy had never appeared, and had revolved in his meditations many a scheme for seeking his objects without confiding in his worthless tutor. But in all his plans the assistance of Gamble seemed needful. He did not even know where to find the man Ben Plowshare without his aid. In this difficulty, he applied to one not less base than the other; but Hargrave had turned somewhat sullen and restive, and it was with considerable trouble that Sir Theodore got him to speak at all.

"Why, sir, I do not like to be blamed when I do my best to please you," said the man, "and as Doctor Gamble has taken all your affairs into his hands, I would rather you asked him any thing you want to know. Heaven forbid that I should be accused of trying to mislead you! We are all weak, sinful creatures, and apt to fall when we work by our own light. Perhaps I was very wrong in what I did, wishing to please an earthly rather than a heavenly master; but if I was wrong, Doctor Gamble was worse; and I don't think he served you a bit better either."

His hypocrisy was now even more disgusting to Sir Theodore than Gamble's barefaced licentiousness, and he was about to dismiss him from his presence sharply, when Hargrave threw in a word or two which changed the aspect of affairs. "Of course you know where the young lady is, sir?" he said, after a moment's pause. Sir Theodore instantly caught at his words, saying, "No; where is she?"

The man made new difficulties, and affected to be half afraid to tell his secret; but at length Sir Theodore extracted from him an account of his having met with old Joseph, Colonel Lutwich's servant, and learned from him that Miss Malcolm was now at the house of Captain's Lisle's mother. He saw his master's eyes kindle as he spoke, and with a degree of malicious satisfaction, he added, "She is to remain there, I hear, sir, till she is married to Colonel Lutwich."

It cost the young baronet a great effort to hide the emotion he felt; but he did so, even from the keen eyes of the hypocrite before him; and in further conversation he elicited that Captain Lisle and Major Brandrum were both absent from London, and that Lutwich himself had gone down into Yorkshire some days before.

The tumult of wild wishes and vague plans, which succeeded in the mind of Sir Theodore when the man had left the room, is indescribable; but, after more than half an hour spent in troubled thought, he came to the unpalatable conclusion that he could do nothing without the assistance of his tutor.

"I must speak with him," he thought; "but I must teach him that I will have my own way, and that, if he tries now to rule me by cunning, as he once ruled me by force, he will find himself mistaken, and have cause to rue it."

To his surprise, however, he found Gamble all compliance and frankness. "I have wished you, my dear Sir Theodore," said the tutor, "to get over this passion; but, if that is not to be done, we can not help it. There is only one stipulation I must make, namely, I will have nothing to do with a *real* marriage. At your age, such a thing is most inexpedient; it would subject me to the high indignation of your guardian, you would repent it yourself before twelve months were passed, and would reproach me for aiding you. In any thing else, you have nothing to do but to command me."

He had taken care to lay great stress upon the word "real," and his pupil did not fail to remark it, and ask an explanation. That explanation was soon given; and when Doctor Gamble saw a smile, a little cynical, indeed, but still expressive of satisfaction, come upon the hearer's face, he rose gayly from his chair, adding, "And now, Sir Theodore, let us order the horses and take a ride to St. Alban's. Country air and new pursuits will do you good, for, to say truth, I think you have, as the sailors say, carried a little too much sail for one so young. I have not opposed you, because I think there is a great deal of true philosophy in the practice of the confectioners, who, when they have a new apprentice, suffer him to eat as much of their confectionery as ever he pleases, quite certain that a surfeit is the best lesson of moderation."

Sir Theodore was not well pleased at all with the illustration; but he made no reply, and the horses were ordered.

CHAPTER XXXIII.

Few scenes upon the stage, and only one group in marble—I mean the famous one of the Niobe—could give, or have given, so beautiful a picture of deep grief as that presented by the two lovely girls whom Mrs. Lisle had left so suddenly, when the surgeon pronounced the words, "She is at peace!" Louisa drew back suddenly, and gazed in his face, confounded with terror, while Kate drew closer to her bereaved friend, and clasped her arm with her beautiful fingers, as if she feared that the orphan would fall. The one, always pale, was now white as alabaster; and though with the other some color remained in her cheek, it had faided till it was but like the faint blush in the inside of one of those small Indian shells. Both were silent; and the fine line of the features took that slight but all-changing alteration which, by the least possible variation of the forms, can convert at once the expression of joy into that of sorrow or despair.

"Oh no, no!" cried Louisa, at length; "do not, do not say it; she is not, she can not be gone; she is but fainting."

The surgeon shook his head sorrowfully, and then gently tried to lead the poor girl from the room; but with eager vehemence she rushed back, cast her arms round her mother's body, and wept profusely. The cheek against which her own rested was already as cold as marble; no breath waved her light hair; and Louisa Lisle felt that the surgeon's words were but too true, and that she was motherless.

"You had better lead her away," said the surgeon, speaking in a low tone to Kate; "it seems to have taken her completely by surprise. I wonder Mrs. Lisle did not in some degree prepare her for such an event."

"Was it to be expected, then?" asked Kate, wiping the tears from her own eyes.

"Assuredly," replied the surgeon; "she has had disease of the heart for some years, and was well aware that she should die suddenly, if much excited or distressed at any time."

"And to-night she was both," said Kate, with a sigh. "My sad fate strikes all who are kind to me."

"Induce her to come away," said the surgeon. But Kate could not make the effort; she remembered what she herself had felt; she knew that such tears are the heart's best relief. An old servant of the family, however, advanced to her young lady's side, and taking her arm, whispered, "Come, Miss Louisa, come! You will have to send after your brother, and there is no time to be lost."

It was a happy thought. Louisa Lisle started up from the bed, pushed back the hair from her face, and said, somewhat wildly, "So I must—so I must. Oh, Kate!" and she cast herself upon her young friend's bosom.

Gently leading, and partly supporting her, Kate Malcolm drew her from the chamber of death, and into a room on the other side of the landing-place, the surgeon and the old servant following.

The man of healing would fain have had her take some restorative, but she answered, "No, no, I shall be better soon, Mr. Slater. Oh, Kate! I can not write to him; write a few lines for me to Reginald, and send it off to Bristol. They may still be caught. Oh, dear Kate, I can feel for you more truly now. Will you write?"

"Certainly," replied Miss Malcolm. But the surgeon interposed, saying, "Perhaps I had better do it; and to your uncle too. He is in Warwickshire, I think?"

"Yes," replied Louisa, bending her head; "but first to Reginald. He is just about to sail for America."

"I will not lose a moment," said the surgeon. And, having procured pen, ink, and paper, he wrote a few lines rapidly, and dispatched them at once by Mrs. Lisle's man-servant, giving him money to pay his expenses. His labor was lost, however; for, half an hour before the servant reached the port, the ship carrying away Reginald Lisle and Major Brandrum had got under weigh.

Perhaps it was better for Kate Malcolm that her young companion's grief continued long unsubdued, for the anguish of her own mind, if not relieved, was in a degree suspended for the time by the task of consoling and supporting; and there were many painful hours coming rapidly forward out of the dim treasury of the future. All that night she sat by Louisa's bedside, and sleep visited the eyelids of neither. In the morning, however, Reginald's sister became somewhat more calm; and her little strength being exhausted, she slept.

Kate stole away to her own room, and, sitting down, gave way to the thoughts which had been banished. They were multitudinous as the waves of the sea, and dark and stormy too. Oh! what questions were there not ready for her fancy at every turn! Oh! what doubts, and fears, and vague, misty horrors rose up before her! It were endless to detail them; but ever and anon her lips murmured, and the low words they uttered were as an echo to some which Lutwich had once addressed to her.

"He had no faults toward me," she said; "he had no faults toward me!" and, with the true love of woman, she seemed to cling to him the more ardently when she thought of him, lonely, desolate, despairing, criminal—ay, even criminal, for still she thought, "he had no faults toward me;" and it seemed to her that the want of conscious innocence must be to him the summit of all misfortune—the crowning misery of all—that which required more than all else consolation and support. She never dreamed of erecting herself into his judge, of condemning him, of punishing him beyond all the punishments of the law, by snatching from him her love, in addition to all of which the law would deprive him.

Yet she was as pure and as innocent herself as human being can be, as high-principled, as virtuous; but there was nothing harsh in her virtue. Had she felt, had she wished, had she done any thing that was wrong, none would have judged more severely; but it was in her own case only that she felt a right to judge and to condemn. The character may be rare, but it does exist; it may be foolish, but there is much Christianity in it. She would have acted thus, felt thus, to any one, how much more to one whom she loved!

It may be thought that she would naturally have felt inclined to repel the very idea of his criminality with scorn and indignation if she loved him so well, and sometimes she was inclined to do so; but yet he had let fall words when they were together at his cottage which might well apply to his present situation; and she had seen how deadly pale he had turned when the officers appeared. I must not say that this created suspicion; for that is not the right name for the feeling which took possession of her: it created a dread—a terrible dread, indeed, that he might be guilty, that he might be proved so, that he might be made to suffer the punishment of guilt; and oh! how her heart sank at the thought of all that was to follow—of the dark, terrible future, hurrying on like a thunder-cloud, big with tempest and destruction. She felt that it was enough to turn her brain, if she remained thinking over it; and yet there was a strange, awful fascination in the serpent eyes of Fate, which made it impossible to withdraw from the contemplation, which glued her thoughts to that one subject; and for full two hours she remained there, with her head resting on her hand, and her eyes, sightless to present objects, fixed upon one spot, while the mind saw nothing but the dark shadow of the future.

At length a servant entered the room, and started at seeing her; for the girl had thought that she was still in the chamber of Louisa Lisle.

"La, miss!" she said, "I did not know you were here. Had you not better have some breakfast?"

"If you please, Bessy," replied Kate. "Your young lady is still asleep, I hope. She was so when I left her a few minutes ago."

A few minutes! It was two hours.

She descended to the drawing-room shortly after, and there every thing put her in mind of Mrs. Lisle, for whom, in the short space of their acquaintance, she had conceived a great reverence and affection; but these thoughts brought no relief, not even that of change. It was sorrow added to sorrow, and Kate sat down and wept. The housemaid placed the breakfast things before her, and, seeing her in tears, tried to comfort her; but how worse than idle were the words of consolation. They sounded even harsh to her; for could she have been comforted, she would have hated herself. Louisa's bell rang, and it was a good excuse for Kate to run up and leave the breakfast nearly untasted; and when, after sitting for an hour with her young friend, she came down again, a letter was put into her hand.

She paused and gazed at the address for two or three minutes before she opened it. Oh! how different is the fresh confidence of youth from the cold and chilly apprehension of experience. Sorrow after sorrow plants dread in the mind, till the world is a garden of fears. Kate was very young to know such things, but she had had many lessons in the bitter tasks of life, and even the sight of a strange handwriting made her heart sink. What fresh sorrows might lie beneath? At length she broke the seal, and read the sad words which Lutwich had written from his prison. She did not ask herself what she should do, for she resolved at once to go. But at the same time, she judged that it would be only right to tell Louisa all. She had no one to consult with, no one to communicate with, but her; and although she had been accustomed much to act for herself, and even for her father too, yet this was a new case, and she shrank from all the first steps. To Louisa she must speak, she thought; but still the task was not easy for her. She did not like to obtrude other thoughts upon one so completely overwhelmed with her own grief; and then she had to tell her love and her promises to an ear which she fancied quite unprepared to hear them.

Poor Kate hesitated, and delayed for some time, read and re-read the letter often, felt eager to set out, and yet dreaded the undertaking; and thus the day wore away toward evening before she could make up her mind to say what she intended to her friend. At length, accusing herself of weakness, she went up to Louisa's room, and, much to her relief, found her greatly calmed. She had a letter before her, and she had been weeping; but her eyes were now dry, and she looked up almost brightly as Kate entered.

"This is from my dear mother," she said. "It seems, Kate, like a message from her in heaven. Mrs. Jones found it in the drawer, and brought it to me. Oh! dear Kate, mamma was quite prepared for what has happened, and wrote this three or four months ago, to comfort me when she should be gone. Read that part."

Kate took it, and read the few concluding lines to which Louisa pointed.

"Give not way, then, to sorrow, my dear child," were the words, "for the only pang of death to me is parting from you and your dear brother; but when I consider how short a time we shall be separated, and how happy will be our reunion, even that grief is greatly mitigated. I am weak enough to feel much satisfaction in knowing that when death comes, it will be without any corporeal suffering, for I will own that I have always dreaded too much the bodily anguish of long sickness; and I know, my dear child, that it will be a comfort to you to feel that I have passed from life without pain. The shock for you will, I fear, be great, and I have considered much whether it were not better to prepare your mind for it, by telling you of the probable end of my earthly being. I trust I act wisely in abstaining; and I do so, because the period being altogether uncertain, I might only be inflicting upon you months and even years of hourly dread and intense anxiety, when you can do nothing to stay the time of separation. Farewell, then, my beloved child; grieve not for me more than nature compels you to grieve. Your mother has shown her love for you in the precepts she has given you; and you, I am quite sure, will show your love for her by keeping them in mind. Fortitude, benevolence, truth, are all needful in this world, and all tend to that whither I am going. Farewell, then, till we meet again in heaven."

The tears rose again in Kate Malcolm's eyes; but she felt that such a letter must be a comfort indeed, and when she compared it with the one she had herself received, she felt that Louisa's affliction might well be lighter than her own.

That gave her courage to speak; and after a few words on the subject of the dead, she said, "It grieves me much, dear Louisa, to be obliged to leave you this evening for a few hours; but I have a sad duty to perform—I know not how to explain it, or, rather, how to begin the explanation. But read that letter; it will save me, perhaps, some words painful to speak;" and, with a flushed cheek, she placed the note she had received before her friend.

Ere she looked at it, Louisa raised her eyes earnestly to Kate's face, and said, in a low, sweet voice, "Perhaps I can spare you more, my dear sister. I saw last night that your fate was a very sad one. I was sure, from the first, that I could not be mistaken, and when that terrible scene occurred, I had no longer a doubt."

Kate bent her blushing face on her friend's shoulder, and remained silent and anxious while Louisa read the letter. The first words Louisa spoke were a great relief to her. "You will go, of course," she said: "such an appeal as that you must not reject."

"I will go, certainly, dear Louisa," replied Kate. "I must not deny that affection leads me; but, even if it did not, I think duty would. I told you once how he had come to my rescue at a moment when I was reasonably alarmed by the shameful conduct of some bad men, whose motives I do not even now clearly comprehend; but I did not, and hardly can, tell all the delicate and kind attention he showed me, how his whole thoughts seemed directed to relieve me from that embarrassment which being forced to remain for a whole night in his house, without a friend near me, might well produce. Whatever may be his faults to others, Louisa, he has had none to me; and I should think myself selfish, and base, and cruel, if I refused him comfort in his distress."

"Oh! yes, go—go by all means," said Louisa Lisle; "but take the housekeeper with you, Kate. She can wait in the coach while you go in. It will be better to have some one with you."

"I do not know how to explain my errand to her," replied Kate, thoughtfully; "it is a strange situation, mine, Louisa. I am not afraid to go alone; but how should I be able to tell a stranger all that leads me thither?"

"I will explain," said Louisa Lisle; "ring the bell, my dear sister, and then go and get ready. I will tell the good old lady all that is needful for her to know."

About half an hour passed, and then Kate Malcolm set out for the prison in the only conveyance which could be procured in the neighborhood, a common post-chaise. She was accompanied, as Louisa had proposed, by Mrs. Jones, the housekeeper, a good, sensible, matter-of-fact kind of woman, who was benevolently inclined to comfort her young companion, as far as her qualities would allow her to do so; but there are times when trite motives of consolation jar sadly with the spirit; and Kate's mind was so full of anxieties, that even the words of hope sounded importunate.

"Don't be so sad, Miss Kate," said Mrs. Jones; "I dare say the gentleman will soon get out. Many a man is accused of things he never did; and then he is sure to get right when he proves his innocence."

What would not Kate have given to be sure that Lutwich could prove his innocence! "I trust it is so, Mrs. Jones," she answered; "but I have heard of many an innocent person being condemned."

"Oh! pooh, pooh!" said the housekeeper; "not when they have good friends, and plenty of money to pay the lawyers. Many a poor fellow, I dare say, without a friend or a guinea, is hanged for what he never did, and the more innocent and simple he is, the more likely to be condemned, for he is not shrewd enough to find out all the roguery. But when a man has wit, and money, and high relations, like this gentleman, he is sure to do very well."

Kate fell into thought again without reply, and after a weary drive of more than an hour, the chaise stopped before the gates of the prison. Kate looked up at the windowless brick walls, and how her heart sank beneath their frowning aspect! There were two or three people passing, a drunken-looking man among the rest, with an apron before him, and a two-foot rule in his hand, and they all stopped to see if a prisoner was about to be brought out of the chaise; but when the post-boy put down the step, and Kate alighted, the half-tipsy workman curled up his nose, saying aloud, "Only some pad's dolly come to see her pal," and walked away.

The poor girl's cheek turned as red as a rose; but Mrs. Jones, who had heard what passed, followed her, whispering, "Never mind him, ma'am; he's a low fellow, and drunk, moreover. I'll go up the steps and inquire."

The porter looked hard at both the old lady and Kate Malcolm, and something in the air and manner of the latter, as she stood on the steps in deep mourning, made him civil enough. "The colonel will be sorry, ma'am, you had the trouble," he said; "but, you see, you'll not be able to see him to-day, for he's been sent for to the justice's for examination, and no one can tell how long he may be, for I hear it's a queer case."

"I will come again to-morrow, then," said Kate, with a disappointed heart. "Will you tell him that Miss Malcolm, to whom he wrote, came as he wished?"

"Just put down the name on that there bit of paper," replied the porter; and, walking into his dingy den, Kate did as he asked.

He then gave her a hint to make her next visit somewhat earlier; and with a spirit more depressed than she had ever felt it, even in the midst of all the sorrows with which she had struggled, Kate re-entered the chaise, and ordered the driver to return whence he came. The distance back did not seem long; for deep and intense thought had taken such complete possession of Kate Malcolm, that she started when the driver stopped, unable to believe that the tedious way, as it had seemed an hour or two before, had dwindled into so small a space.

CHAPTER XXXIV.

In the days I write of, a London police-office was a very different utensil from that which it is now. It, itself, and every thing in it, were different. The justice was quite a different animal, the officers or constables were quite different, the clerk was different, the manner of conducting the business, the manner of bringing it there, the very inkstand, were all different. Law had very little to do with the business, and justice sometimes still less. One of the best magistrates who ever sat there was by nature and trade a saddler. Officers, as well as justices, were chosen for their wit and shrewdness more than for their learning or honesty. There was no preventive force, but an excellent detective one; and as the commission of crimes was the remote, while the capture of criminals was the proximate cause of emolument to all concerned, it very naturally happened that in the eyes of the police, robbery, house-breaking, picking pockets, and the higher branches of swindling, were professions which deserved encouragement and countenance. Petty larceny and such sorts of error were looked upon as apprenticeship.

As to the office itself, it had just emerged from the humble state of "the justice's parlor;" but it was now furnished with a bar, as one of the gentlemen on the bench had, not long before, had his head broken by a refractory felon, with whom he had often smoked his pipe, and who took a different view of their relative situations from the magistrate himself. A hint, too, had been given from a high power, that it would be better for those in authority not to be, like the princes of Israel, partakers with thieves; but still a great deal of the old leaven was left, and every day's sitting presented a scene which would have very much shocked our present notions of the administration of justice.

It was to the bar of one of these police-offices, then, that Colonel Lutwich was brought, at about three o'clock of the day on which Kate went to visit him in prison. The magistrate before whom he appeared did not like him, for Lutwich had never descended from his original station to seek the connivance of justice or officer, either by bribery or familiarity; but the justice had great reverence for him, for, though strongly suspected, he had set all the arts of Bow-street at defiance. He was glad, then, to have so distinguished a personage under his thumb; but, at the same time, inclined to treat him with all sort of ceremonious respect, and even with apparent indulgence, while he relaxed his grasp of him in no degree, and enjoyed in anticipation the satisfaction of frustrating all his wiles, and sending him for trial with a case which would insure condemnation.

The court was crowded, not alone with the usual attendants upon such scenes, but with several persons of a better class; and when Colonel Lutwich was brought forward between two officers, a number of heads were thrust out to look at him. The prisoner ran his eye over the crowd of spectators with a firm, haughty air; but suddenly his glance was arrested, and fixed upon one spot, and a strange change came over his expressive face. So marked was the alteration, that the persons standing near the place where his eyes rested turned round and looked at the group near them. There was nothing remarkable in it: a young gentleman, fashionably dressed, looking forward into the court; a stout, jolly-looking, middle-aged man in black, speaking in a low tone to a squinting man, habited like a post-boy, behind him, and the said post-boy, were all of which that group consisted. And yet the prisoner's eyes had lightened as if some sudden intelligence had been conveyed to him from that part of the court; or as if, with rapid combination, he had discovered, from something he saw there, facts which had before been dark and mysterious.

The blood mounted up into the cheek of Sir Theodore Broughton as the firm, steady gaze of Lutwich rested upon him, and the next moment a sarcastic smile curled the prisoner's lip, and he turned toward the magistrate. That smile stung the young baronet more than the lash of a horsewhip would have done.

"I am sorry to see you here, Colonel Lutwich," said the magistrate, resolved to make him feel all that was painful in his situation to the utmost, "and, of course, I feel that any charge brought against a gentleman of your station and respectability must be received with caution; but, at the same time, where there is information upon oath of a felony being committed by any man, whatever be his rank, a warrant must issue against him."

"Undoubtedly, sir," replied the prisoner, "you could do no less than you have done, if such information has been tendered to you. At the same time, I am glad to find that you allow the improbability of the story, as I shall soon, I doubt not, be able to show you that it is more than improbable."

The magistrate did not like the reply; but, after humming for a moment, he called upon Edward Warwick, one of the officers of the sheriff of Middlesex, to come forward and make his deposition.

The man, then, in a somewhat rambling and unconnected manner, stated the facts connected with the robbery, which must be fresh in the recollection of the reader, and ended by swearing that, to the best of his knowledge and belief, it had been committed by the prisoner at the bar.

When he had done, Colonel Lutwich fixed his eyes sternly upon him for a moment, and was about to speak, when a lawyer who was in the court stopped him, whispering, "Had you not better reserve your defense, colonel?"

"No," said Lutwich, sternly, "I have nothing to fear. Now answer me, Edward Warwick. Do you speak from my personal appearance?"

"Why, I mean to say, I think it was you," answered the man, doggedly.

"Sir, that will not do," replied Lutwich. "You shall give me a straightforward answer before you go, depend upon it. I ask you—and remember, you are upon your oath—I ask you if I bear any resemblance whatever to the man who robbed you?"

"Why, as to resemblance," said the bailiff, "people look so different at different times, that I can't say."

"Then you mean to say that it is not by any personal resemblance you identify me," rejoined Lutwich.

"Yes, there may be a likeness," replied the man.

"Do you mean to say you recognize me, as I stand here?" demanded Lutwich, sternly.

"Yes, I do," answered the officer.

"Then, sir, you are perjured," replied Lutwich, with a look of contempt.

"Nay, nay, colonel!" exclaimed the magistrate, in a bland tone, "that is going a little beyond the bounds allowable even to gentlemen in your unpleasant situation."

"Not, sir, when they can prove what they say," replied the prisoner: "this man—you will hardly believe it, for it is almost incredible—this man, in my presence, gave information of this very robbery to my excellent friend Sir Harry Jarvis, and then solemnly declared that he had never seen the highwayman before, describing him as a person as unlike myself as possible. It luckily happens that Sir Harry took down what he said; but I repeat that the statement was made in my presence, I sitting face to face with him."

"How happens this, sir?" asked the magistrate, sharply frowning at the bailiff; for he evidently thought a good case was about to break down.

The man paused in dull silence for a minute or two, and then answered, "I remember quite well going to Sir Harry Jarvis, and seeing him there, but I didn't recollect him at the minute."

"More marvelous still!" exclaimed Lutwich, with a scoff; "that you then did not recollect me a few minutes after, and now recollect me several weeks after. That you did not recognize me when I had had no time to change my dress, and recognize me now when my dress is quite different from what it was that night."

"Very extraordinary indeed!" said the magistrate; "what have you got to answer to this, witness?"

The man was silent; and, after having waited a minute, Lutwich addressed the bench: "Sir, I think you must see," he said, "that I am justified in saying this man is perjured; and the evidence of Sir Harry Jarvis will prove it. But there is something more: I am inclined to believe that there is something like a conspiracy here, and before I quit this place I trust you will give me an opportunity of sifting that matter to the bottom."

"You are at liberty to ask the witness any questions you think fit," replied the justice.

"Well, then, Mr. Warwick," said the prisoner, "will you have the goodness to say whether you do or do not recognize me by my face, figure, or appearance, as the man who robbed you?"

"No, not by that there," replied the bailiff, getting confused; "but I have reason to think it was you."

"What reason?" demanded Lutwich, vehemently.

"Why, a gentleman came and told me he had got a man who would swear to you," replied the bailiff.

"Oh ho!" said Lutwich; "now we are coming to the truth. What gentleman?"

"I don't know," said the man, looking round the court; "he was here just now."

"I know he was," answered the prisoner; "and he slipped away at my last two questions. Do you know his name?"

"No, I don't," said the bailiff.

"Another question, if you please," rejoined Lutwich; "did he show you the man *he had got?*" and he laid strong emphasis upon the words. "Did he show you this man he had got who would swear to me?"

"Yes," replied the bailiff; "and he said he would."

"So you got up your evidence together," said Lutwich. "Now, your worship, I think I have shown sufficiently what sort of a case this is. I will only further state that I once had the good fortune of frustrating a most infamous scheme concocted by a gentleman who was but now in court, and who takes his revenge by suborning evidence against me. I must contend that you have nothing to proceed upon."

"But there is the man who can swear to you?" exclaimed the bailiff.

"Where?" demanded Lutwich, gazing round.

"William Havant!" exclaimed an officer; but no William Havant appeared.

"We have certainly something in the form of a deposition," said the judge, "from a post-boy of St. Alban's. It shall be read over to you, if you like."

"If I have the opportunity of cross-examining him," replied Lutwich, "it may be of some avail; otherwise, I think, of none. Let him be produced; and I shall be able to show, I doubt not, that the same nefarious means have been used with him as with this perjurer. If he is not produced, I must contend that there is no pretense whatever for detaining me, and the warrant must be discharged."

"Too fast, colonel, too fast," said the magistrate, with a quiet smile. "Seek for William Havant, constable."

"He was here a minute ago, your worship," replied a man, "but somebody called him out on business."

"Then all I can do is to remand you for further examination, colonel," observed the justice.

"This is very hard!" said Lutwich, bitterly.

"I have a notion it might be harder," replied the magistrate. "Prisoner remanded to this day week."

The prisoner was accordingly removed from the bar, and, accompanied by two constables, was placed in a hackney coach, to be conveyed back to prison. As he was mounting the step, he perceived the post-boy, Hangingwood Bill, pushing his way back into the court through the little crowd that surrounded the door, and he was inclined to pause and demand that the investigation should proceed, feeling that he had gained an advantage which might be lost by delay. The officers hurried him in, however, and the coachman was ordered to drive on.

"Beg your pardon, colonel," said the chief constable, as soon as the lumbering vehicle was on its way, "but it's better for you to let it stop where it is. You've got a week to come and go upon."

"In which they may make up their story better than they have it now," replied Lutwich, gloomily.

"No, no, sir," replied the other, who was a stout, jolly-looking man; "that won't do. It's all for your advantage, I can tell you, if you work it well. I don't mean to say that your defense wasn't a good one. It was capital; and, if it comes to a trial, I dare say you'll be able to get out a few more facts to prove that Bill has been bribed. Indeed, there is no manner of doubt he has, for you are not a man to refuse him his fair snack, and so make him turn viperous. But you might say what you liked now, the old gentleman in the wig is determined to commit you; and so a week gained is somewhat. As for Master Hangingwood Bill, he shall swing himself within six months for this here very job. He has no business to come meddling with our affairs. He thought to patch it up by telling me all about it; but that won't do. If we suffered interlopers, we should never do no business."

"Ay, and what did he tell you?" asked Lutwich.

"Why, all about it," said the officer. "I don't mind letting you know, colonel, because it may help you, and I should like to spoil this job for him. He's going to blow the whole thing, how you put off your two coats and the padding in Ridge Hill copse, and how you used to rub your chin over with indigo, and put on a black wig, and where you stowed away the lantern and all. It will all come out this time, depend upon it."

Lutwich's heart sank; but still he continued the conversation, hoping to gain more information. "Did he tell you nothing about the bribery?" he inquired.

"No, no, he kept that snug enough," replied the officer; "but it was that young fellow, I am sure, that Sir Theodore, who, they say, has a grudge against you. But I'll find it out, close as he is."

"If you do," answered Lutwich, "and will enable me to prove it on my trial, you and your friend here shall have fifty pounds a piece the very day you bring me the full information; and, in the event of my being acquitted, you shall each have a hundred pounds a piece to make up for losses."

"Well, that's devilish handsome," said the man; "you seem to be flush of cash, colonel?"

"I have at this moment plenty," replied the prisoner, anxious to get every insight into his situation that he could. "The truth is, I have lately sold all my property, intending to lead a quieter life, and upon that score I did you good fellows some injustice; for I thought you were resolved I should not be quiet, and had taken me on that account, although I had resolved beforehand to make you each a handsome present, which would have put things square, as you call it. Indeed, I should have done so before now, only I was out of town till the night before last."

"No, we had nothing to do with it," replied the officer; "it was all that fellow's doing. You shall have the information, sure enough; and all we can do to help you we will; but I am afraid, now you've been had up, you'll not get off, do what we may. The old beak is against you. He has been looking after you a long while, 'cause you've been high with him, and he won't stand that. He's got a deal of information about you in his little book, and it will all come out this time. I don't see well what you can do, unless—"

"Unless what?" asked Lutwich, eagerly.

"Unless you would just compromise the affair with Billy, and get him out of the way before next Wednesday," replied the officer; "he has taken one bribe to 'peach; depend upon it, he'll take t'other to hold his tongue. But mind, don't pay all till after the trial, for he's not to be trusted. He shall swing in six months, for all that."

"Do you think you can manage it for me?" asked the prisoner, after thinking heavily for some minutes.

"No, that won't do," said the officer; "I might be caught; and he'd be very shy with me too. You must get some one he doesn't know, colonel; the lawyer, or some one, who will offer him a good round sum, half down, half after the trial. Send to him at night, for he's the greater part of the day kept quite close under the eyes of that barrownight, and t'other chap, the tutor. A pretty tutor! why, I once had him in custody for violence to a woman; but he compromised it, or he would never have been tutor to nobody."

"But where is this scoundrelly informer to be found?" asked Lutwich; "he must have left St. Alban's."

"Oh, ay, he's lodged quite genteel," said the officer; "he has a second floor in Swallow-street, No. 103, with a woman who sells hosiery. Her husband was once one of our people; but he's grown corpulent, and left off business; but he looks after Bill sharp enough; so you had better send about eight o'clock, when he comes to our club; for if you don't get Hangingwood Bill out of the way, you're done, take my word for it, colonel."

With this pleasant announcement the conversation closed, and soon after Lutwich was once more consigned to the gloomy walls, whence he had emerged only for examination.

CHAPTER XXXV.

The prisoner sat alone. Darkness and gloom were upon him. Conscience had been busily at work—conscience, which had been silent for years. The whirl and the confusion of the busy world, the sound of gay tongues, and music, and laughter, and revelry, the light joke, the gay scoff, the claims of business, pleasure, necessity, even of the light virtues, easily attended to by a kind and liberal heart, the loud call of passion, enterprise, excitement, make such a hubbub round the ears of the mind in the whirlpool of society, that *the small still voice within us* is unheard, though it speak never so plainly.

Who can attend to its counsels or its reproaches in the midst of life's turmoil? or who will?

Does your keen manufacturer, greedy of wealth, grinding the bones and sinews of his fellow-men in the hot mill—does he attend to it, while the steam-engine roars and hisses, and sounds at every heavy stroke "wealth! wealth! wealth! wealth!"

Does the care-worn lawyer in the crowded court or the dull chambers, amid the babble of technical terms, the rigmarole of forms, or even when poring over the rustling parchment? Do not the crabbed letters, traced with such care by the engrossing clerk, find tongues to drown that small still voice?

Does yonder landlord, with the poor of his domain consigned to the squalid dens and famishing pittance of the Union House, lest they should eat up his rents, while he rolls in his carriage from the sumptuous dinner to the noisy Commons—does he hear the voice? or do the rattle of infinite wheels and gay jokes, or the buzz of dull speeches, drown it? Does the merchant upon 'Change? Does the man of pleasure? Does the courtier? Does the statesman? Or do they not all find the thunder of their several callings outroar the quiet monitor within?

Oh, were the guilt of men but weighed by their opportunities, were the heaviness or lightness of those things which silence the voice of conscience within them but judged as well as their acts, who would not stand in the dock? And may it not be so hereafter? May not the thief be asked, What was it made you neglect the safeguard planted in your breast by Heaven? and may he not answer, Want, ignorance, evil associates, injustice, oppression? And may not the rich neglecter of all duties be so questioned likewise, and find nothing to reply but Pleasure, ambition, avarice? Then, with Omniscience for a judge, how will the more guilty tremble?

No, no, conscience is drowned in pleasant sounds even more easily than in the cries of want. It needs silence, solitude, the lull of passions, and the death of hopes, to let that still small voice reach the heart's ear, and awaken repentance and reformation.

Lutwich had sat in silence and in solitude, and the lamp of hope burned very dim—so dim that it had no glare to dazzle the eye. He thought with cold heart and clear mind of his situation and his prospects. He looked forward, he looked backward. All was dark except a small, bright spot just left behind; but he felt no power, he entertained no expectation of being able to turn back and stand on that bright oasis again. Oh, how he regretted the past! Oh, what would he not have given to have recalled that sad, that fatal hour, when, in a spirit of mad frolic more than deliberate crime, he had first tasted a cup from which he had never afterward been able to abstain, so strong had been its charm for his wild and adventurous spirit. But the hour was beyond recall; its deeds were done, its seed sown; and the harvest was to be reaped—its bitter harvest!

The future, what did it present? Despair. He pondered the words of the man who had accompanied him from the office to the prison. He knew him to be a keen judge of such cases, and he read his opinion of his own well and clearly. Moreover, he was conscious that he was open to the sword of justice upon so many points, that once it was raised to strike it could not fail to slay. And what was the faint, faint hope which had been held out to him? Was it real or illusory? To bribe a felon without honor, faith, or honesty, to conceal crimes which he had already denounced, to fly from his country, or to hide himself for months, and that, too, when there was an eager enemy urging him on. Was he likely to consent? Was he likely to keep his word if he promised? Was it not much more probable that he would use the very proposal only to wring a further reward from those who had already taught him to betray?

Yet it was the only hope. He thought of Kate Malcolm, and he clung to it. "If she shrinks from me," he thought, "I will abandon all, and bear my fate; but if she still clings to me, I will make that one effort."

Then came the terrible question, "Will she shrink from me?" But a voice in his heart instantly answered "No!" He had divined her nature, and he said No boldly. "She has come once," he thought, "and she will come again. But how shall I deal with her when she does come? Can I—dare I tell her truth? Can I—dare I tell her falsehood? No, no! That last I will not do, at all events!"

The heavy key turned in the lock, the bolts

above and below were withdrawn, and the turnkey said, "A lady, sir, wants to see you."

Lutwich started forward, and took Kate's hand in his. Hers was as cold as marble; for the very passages of a prison were enough to chill her to the heart. She gazed anxiously in his face, and saw how two short days had changed it. Her eye ran over his limbs, and a sensation of relief spread through her bosom. There were no fetters. He had been remanded, not committed; and the jailer had not thought it necessary to put that indignity upon him.

"Oh, Kate, this is kind—this is very kind," he said; "it is almost more than I dared hope for;" and he drew her gently to a chair, and seated himself beside her.

"Why, Henry," she said, "why should you doubt I would come? After the words you have spoken and I have spoken, there is nothing that I ought not to do for you. But let me pause a moment to recover, for the sights and sounds without there have made my heart beat sadly. How long will they let me stay?"

"As long as you please, dear girl," replied the prisoner; "but I will not let you stay long. This is no place for you, my Kate; and, though you bring sunshine with you to the poor captive's cell, yet he must not be selfish in your case, love."

"I am sure you will not," she answered; and then she added, with a sweet, sorrowful smile, "you have had no faults to me, Henry."

Lutwich pressed her for one moment to his heart, and the unwonted tears rose in his eyes. "And you remember those words," he said; "yes, Kate, yes, you have remembered them, and repeated them to yourself, and asked if he whom you love can have had grievous faults to others?"

"Perhaps I have," she answered, simply; "and yet it was foolish to do so, for it could make no difference to me. Besides, you told me long ago that you had many faults; but as they were not to me, I have naught to do with them: and now tell me, Henry, what can be done for you? The sight of this cheerful room gives me better hopes. It is hardly like a prison."

Lutwich silently raised his hand, and pointed to the barred windows, and Kate dropped her eyes toward the ground, and fell into bitter thought.

"But tell me," she said at length, "what can be done for you?"

"But little, I fear, dear girl," he replied, sadly; "very, very little." He paused with a sigh, and then added, "I know, my Kate, you will not ask me any questions which might be painful for me to answer; but I must give you, of my own free will, some explanation. Yet I hardly know how to do it without implying a falsehood, or relating all."

"Then do not do it at all," replied Kate, laying her small, fair hand on his; "only tell me what I can do for you."

"Nay, my Kate—my dear confiding girl," answered Lutwich, "do not be so kind to me. Your love is, indeed, a blessing undeserved; but oh, Kate! it makes my present situation almost more terrible. But I must tell you a part, at least, lest you should be taken too sadly unprepared. This charge is brought against me by a base conspiracy, and out of pure revenge—"

"Then surely you can frustrate it," exclaimed his beautiful companion, with a look of joy. "I have heard high praises of the English law; I have heard it called the perfection of human wisdom; surely, if it even approach to justice, it will not suffer an innocent man to fall before such means."

"Alas, Kate! I said not I was innocent," replied the prisoner, turning away his head. "All I said—all I do say is, that this charge would never have been brought had I not rescued you from the hands of that young scoundrel Broughton. He has me in a trap. He has, I fear, my life in his power."

Kate put her hands before her eyes, and trembled very much; and Lutwich continued, somewhat more collectedly, for the worst was now told: "He has got a man ready to swear a crime against me. I may struggle; I may turn; I may even prove that the basest means have been employed to bring that man's evidence against me; but the evidence itself I cannot rebut. The more I think of it, the more I see it will be impossible. Scoundrel as he is, his oath will be taken; and I know of no means of shaking his testimony."

"Oh, what is to be done?" cried Kate, raising her tearful eyes toward heaven; "oh, what is to be done?"

"The only thing I can do," said Lutwich, "is to endeavor by any means, were it by the sacrifice of all I have on earth, to bribe that man to absent himself both from the next examination and from the trial. Could that be done, I should be secure."

"Where is he to be found?" cried Kate, eagerly: "I will go to him—I will send to him. Tell me—tell me, Henry, where he lives, and what is his name?"

Lutwich told her, on the first impulse; but immediately after he said, "But, Kate, you must not go yourself. It is not a place to which you must venture. Six days must pass before the next examination, and there will be plenty of time to deal with him. I must find some lawyer or some friend who will undertake to negotiate with him—though it is not every one who will mix in such a business. You must not, nor, indeed, could you, properly."

Kate sat thoughtfully for a moment or two without reply; but at length she asked, "Have you the means, Henry? I have but little, yet all I have is yours."

"It is not needful, dearest girl," replied the prisoner. "I have more than seven thousand pounds in my banker's hands. Surely a thousand now and a thousand after the trial will be enough to make that low and drunken villain do any thing on earth. Oh, that seven thousand pounds! how I looked to it, my dear Kate, as the means of happy independence with her I love; and now it must go to purchase immunity for my offenses—even if it can do that."

"And if it can not," said Kate, catching fresh apprehension from his words and tone, "what is to be done then?"

Lutwich shook his head sadly. "There must be a parting," he said: "a parting more painful than that of soul and body. I may and will make a great effort, for you have rendered life dear and valuable to me, Kate; but I fear the effort will be in vain. I can prove the prosecutor to be perjured; I can prove the charge to be brought forward for revenge; I can throw doubt upon the facts by many a point of time and circumstance; but there is no use of hiding it from my own eyes or from yours—that man has me in his power! I can show that within half an hour of the time the offense was committed, I was in the house of Sir Harry Jarvis; that I was there talking with him—talking with you; but a stout horse would carry a bold rider thither in the time; and he knows too much not to be able to meet me at every turn. But, speaking of Sir Harry Jarvis, Kate—you must go to him, my love; you must take him a letter from me. I wrote it last night. See him yourself, dear girl; give it into his own hands, and hear what he says. Tell him, too, that I fear I must require his evidence on Wednesday next, to prove what took place at his house on the night I saw you there, and brought you the letter you had left at Dunstable. He will come, I am sure. Sir Charles Chevenix's evidence, too, might be needful, but whether it will be given or not, I doubt."

"Oh, he will give it," cried Kate, "I am quite sure. He is as generous and kind as man can be; and I will write about it myself. I have a right to do so, as this has fallen upon you, Henry, in consequence of the protection you afforded me. Sir Charles, knowing the facts, will see the motive of that base young man, and will, I am sure, do all that he can to frustrate him."

"Perhaps so," said Lutwich, thoughtfully; "yet I have my doubts. Still you can write, my Kate: to that there can be no objection; and I am very sure it will be a pleasure to you to feel that you are laboring for your poor prisoner."

"It will, indeed," said Kate; "and you must let me, Henry, labor in all I can, for it is the only relief I now can have. There is much to make me sad, even besides that which is here. I have not told you yet what has happened since you were taken away that fatal night."

"No!" exclaimed Lutwich. "What? No more misfortunes, I hope?"

"A very sad one," answered Kate. "From my childhood, an evil fate has seemed to pursue all who took interest in me. Poor Mrs. Lisle! who was so kind and good to me, was taken hence that very night. She fell back suddenly, and died in a moment, as we were all going up stairs gloomily to our beds."

"Good Heaven!" cried Lutwich; "that is sad indeed; and now you are left alone, without protection or a home."

"Oh no," answered Kate; "Louisa and I will live together for the present; and as for the rest, I have been so much accustomed—so much more than other girls of my age, I should say—to act for myself, and even for others, that I do not feel it strange, as some might do. And now tell me, Henry, when shall I see you again? Louisa's uncle is expected to-night, and I would fain be with her when he comes; for, though he is very kind and good, she says, yet he is quick and blunt, so that she is somewhat afraid of him; and there are many sad things for her to go through."

"Then come to-morrow, dear girl," said Lutwich.

"I had better go with this letter to Jarworth Park to-morrow," replied Kate, "and it may be late ere I return. If, then, there should be any thing of importance to tell you, I will come to-morrow; but if not, the next day about this hour."

"Yet stay a little longer, Kate," said the prisoner. "Oh, dear girl, you can not tell how long and dreary are the hours within these walls, with nothing to fill them but torturing thoughts of danger and disgrace, and wild, whirling schemes to meet the one and to avert the other. Your coming is like the morning beam, which steals through the window, wanders over the floor for a short hour, and then is lost. But I can not say to it as to you, Oh! stay a little longer."

Kate sat down again, for she had risen; but, ere she had been seated more than a minute, the turnkey opened the door, saying, "Mr. Keating, the solicitor, colonel, is in the lodge, asking to see you."

"Let him come in," said the prisoner. With one embrace Kate and he parted, and she betook herself to the chaise, turning from one scene of gloomy sadness to another.

CHAPTER XXXVI.

Since last we placed Mr. Mullins before the reader, time, business, some anxiety, and much grief had greatly altered him. Mr. Mullins had been a very prosperous man; but prosperity is not happiness, nor the principal ingredient in it. Mr. Mullins, between seven and eight years before, had known the enjoyment of a calm domestic home: he had seen a son and a daughter growing up by his fireside; and a wife, of whom he was very fond—though her insipidity somewhat worried him—always ready to receive him with a smile when he came home weary with thought. The son had been drowned in bathing; the daughter had died of small-pox; the mother had left the world with a broken heart; and Mr. Mullins, then one of the wealthiest solicitors in London, had retired into the country to live alone with his memories.

His nephew, Reginald Lisle, had been very kind to his dead boy, though a good deal older and Louisa had been a sister to his daughter. Mr. Mullins had been very fond of them both, even when his children lived, but after they had departed he grew fonder of them still; for the remembrance of his own loved ones clung round them, and they became to him as children: not that he would ever suffer himself to love them as much as he had loved others, for it is wonderful how the gentle tenderness of youth twines itself round the sturdy and firm heart of strong-minded men in the moments of sweet relaxation and idleness. He had felt too much when the ties snapped ever to seek willingly such ties again.

He had loved his sister, too, very much; had thought her a fool at one time, indeed, for marrying the son of a noble house, and had augured evil from the connection; but the result had justified her choice; and her conduct in every circumstance of life had won even her brother's reverence, though he was not much given to reverence any thing.

But to return: he was very much changed since the night of Sir Walter Broughton's death. At that period he had been as upright as an unstrung bow, and his eyebrows had been very black, his face displaying a good deal of healthy color. Now, he stooped not a little; his eyebrows, long and shaggy as they had always been, were as white as snow, his cheeks almost as colorless; but the same quick, almost stern air of decision was apparent in all he did, and the same activity in his movements.

When Kate Malcolm returned from the prison, she found the old solicitor seated by the side of Louisa Lisle, with the poor girl's hand in his; and Mr. Mullins raised his large, dark, brilliant eyes, and fixed them upon Kate's face as she entered, with a calm, steadfast, contemplative glance, which abashed her.

The next moment, however, as if satisfied with what he saw, he rose with a bland, grave smile, and took her hand. "So this is Kate Malcolm," he said; "my dear, I am very glad to see you. That old rascal Brandrum wrote to me about you; and Reginald wrote to me; and Louisa has been telling me about you; and my poor sister who lies in there—having left her cares behind, and taken her affections with her, I do believe—wrote to me also. Louisa, show that you have mind and Christianity, my dear girl, and weep not thus to hear your mother named. You must hear it frequently; begin betimes, and remember that her life has sanctified her death for us all; so that while we are sad for the parting, we may rejoice that she has found peace, and gone before us, whither we must all soon follow. A few short years—perhaps a few short months—and you will have to place me within the funeral wood, and lay me in the dusty grave. Then you yourself must follow; and the brightest and most glorious now upon the earth will tread quickly on your steps unto the grave. Believe me, Loo, when each one stands beside that small portal of the world to come, and looks back to the day when he placed the loved within it, the intervening time is shortened to a span, and he wonders how he could grieve at so brief a separation. It is six years on Midsummer-day since I buried my poor boy. I thought that life would be a long weary waste till I rejoined him; and now 'tis but as yesterday. Six years more will be the same, and we shall be together. I would not pain you, my dear child; but you must learn to endure what reason should lighten, and what time will certainly remove. And now to matters of worldly business."

With those I need not trouble the reader: they were not very complicated, nor very interesting. To Louisa, her uncle was kind, though somewhat, perhaps, too bluff and plain-spoken for the tenderness of grief. To Kate he was more gentle, and hardly less kind; but, had he been otherwise, she would not have felt his roughness as Louisa did, for she had been more accustomed to the hard hand of the world. The matters of business were all soon settled; and the solicitor went out to give directions which might be painful, and no way beneficial for Louisa to hear.

While he was absent, a letter came for him marked "immediate," and on his return at the end of about half an hour, it was given to him at once. He tore it open hastily, and read the contents with an eye of some anxiety apparently, for the shaggy eyebrow fell heavily over it, and the lid was high raised. In the end he bit his lip, crushed the letter in his hand, and rang the bell sharply.

"Get me a carriage of some kind," he said; "a post-chaise—a post-chaise is best. Louisa, my dear, I must run away from you for a while. I will call on Mr. Slater as I go, and ask him to do all for you that I can not stay to do. Miss Malcolm, you will be with her, and be kind to her, I am sure. Business—business calls me to a distance—very sudden and unexpected business."

"I am afraid, painful business too, sir," replied Kate.

"Ay, not pleasant," said Mr. Mullins; "it may be better, though, than it seems. I must go and lock my portmanteau;" and he hurried from the room.

A cold presentiment of further sorrow fell upon Kate's heart, she knew not well why; for we often gather indications from small signs which we take in the mass, without discriminating; and it might be that while Mr. Mullins was speaking, evidently more agitated than he wished to appear, she had seen his eye once or twice take a furtive glance to Louisa, and then to herself.

In a few minutes he came down again. The chaise was announced, his baggage put in, and he hurried to the door. The two girls heard him say to the driver, "To Craig's Court, Charing Cross."

"Why, that is where Reginald's agent lives," said Louisa, without any appearance of apprehension.

"Perhaps he is going there first, to give some directions," replied Kate; but she felt a dread of she knew not what.

In the mean time, Mr. Mullins was carried rapidly to Charing Cross, thrown back in the corner of the chaise, with his head bent forward, his hand up to his mouth, and his feet crossed. He stirred not in the slightest degree till the chaise stopped, so deeply was he buried in thought. As soon as the door was open, he ran quickly down the court, stopped at an office, the door of which was closed—for by this time it was growing late—and rang the bell.

A clerk opened it. "Is Mr. G—— at home?" demanded the solicitor.

"Yes, sir; he thought you might come, and stayed an hour longer than usual," replied the clerk; "pray walk in."

Mullins hurried forward without a pause, and, in the inner office, found a stout man looking over some papers. "This is terrible news, Mr. G——," said the old man at once; "is it quite sure?"

"I am afraid so," answered the agent: "but too true. We have no details, but the fact would seem indubitable. There is the letter we received."

Mr. Mullins read it twice. "Misfortune—

upon misfortune!" he said. "Why, when I saw you this morning you had not received this news, and yet the post had arrived."

"It came by express from Swansea," said Mr. G——. "I have sent into the city, but nothing further is known there. The letters *received are all* to the same effect — mere transcripts. We shall not hear any thing further till Saturday, I suppose, when the *Russell* is expected at Plymouth."

"I must hear more before that," said Mr. Mullins, who was much agitated. "I will go down myself at once. In the mean time, do not let any rumor of this reach poor Louisa's ears. While there is a hope, it would be cruel to agitate her, shaken as she is, with fears which may prove groundless. I will call here as I return; and, till then, send no news to the cottage unless it be good news. Good-by, for the present; and Heaven grant these tidings may be exaggerated."

Thus saying, he hurried out of the office, re-entered the chaise, gave the man directions where to drive, and proceeded on his way toward the west coast without pause. He neither stopped to eat nor to sleep, and when at length he reached Barnstaple, he was completely exhausted. There he swallowed a goblet full of wine, and eating a biscuit as he went, set out in a small gig down the Taw and along the sea-coast. He stopped at many a hut in Barnstaple Bay, and earnest was his conversation with the sea-faring people whom he met; but sadder and more sad became the expression of the old man's face as he went; and at length, when he ordered the driver to turn back, he sat with his eyes bent down in the vehicle, never uttering a word till he reached the door of the White Lion.

When he had entered the room prepared for him, he said, "Bring me pen, ink, and paper;" and while the waiter retired to get what he had demanded, the old solicitor walked slowly up and down the room, with deep grief written in every strong line of his face.

"That he should die just as such an unexpected piece of good fortune befell him!" he said. "God's will be done! God's will be done!"

When the paper was brought, he sat down, but paused ere he began to write.

"Do you take dinner, sir?" said the waiter.

"Yes."

"Will you please to order?"

"Any thing, any thing," said Mr. Mullins, and he wrote—

"My dear young lady, — I sit down to write what will shock your kind heart to read; but you have a firmer mind and more experience than our poor Louisa; and, therefore, I must ask you to break to her news that will dreadfully affect her. The ship *London*, of Bristol, in which my poor nephew, Reginald, embarked for America—a finer, more noble, more honorable young man never lived—was run down during the night of Tuesday last by the *Russell*, 80 gun ship.* She sank instantly, and every soul, I am assured, perished. I have labored all this day with no result but to blot out all remaining hope. There is none left, and I have only time, before the mail departs, to write these few lines. I must have one night's rest; but *to-morrow early I* cross the country to Plymouth, and thence go straight to London. In the mean time, for Heaven's sake, prepare poor Louisa gently for the terrible tidings, and believe me,

"My dear Miss Malcolm,

"Yours affectionately," &c.

* This event happened on the 28th of December, 1778. The reader will perceive that a little liberty has been taken with the date.

CHAPTER XXXVIII.

How the events of a single day affect not only the whole life of one individual, but the fate of many! and upon what a small circumstance will the whole turn! In the day which succeeded the departure of Mr. Mullins for the west of England lay the key-stone of Kate Malcolm's fate, and of that of almost every body who had become so strangely connected with her since the evening when, not knowing any of them, she had entered the yard of the Black Bull at Dunstable. I must, therefore, with somewhat more care than usual, relate her proceeding during those twelve hours.

Her first task was to write to Mary Chevenix, and she found it a more difficult one than she had anticipated. She had not remembered, when she undertook to do so, that she must necessarily display the love which existed between Lutwich and herself. Not that she would have shrunk from the task, even if she had remembered that fact; but when she sat down to fulfill her promise, it embarrassed her. She thought over the words she was to use more than she was accustomed to think of any act which she had determined to perform, and believed right. She weighed the expressions hesitatingly; but soon she started at her own feelings, and asked, "Am I going to be insincere—untrue? No, no! I will write what naturally comes from the heart, let Mary think what she will."

She did so; and when she read the letter over as a whole, found it far better than if she had used any art. It was sincere, straightforward, to the point. Her own feelings were not much touched upon, and though, perhaps, in a certain degree displayed, were far less so than if she had made an effort to conceal them. There was but one expression which spoke them plainly. After referring to the situation of Lutwich, she added, "You may imagine, Mary, that I am most wretched."

The letter was folded and sent; and after their sad breakfast, for it had grown a gloomy and sorrowful meal to those poor mournful girls, she explained to Louisa Lisle that she must go to Jarworth Park to see Sir Harry Jarvis upon business. "Then take the carriage, dear Kate," said Louisa Lisle, "instead of going in a post-chaise, which you will have to change. There is a carriage in the coach-house, though we have not had horses for some years; but it will be more convenient, and look more respectable than a hired vehicle. The servant, too, can go with you."

The latter offer Kate would not accept; but the carriage she took, with horses from a neighboring inn, and thus set out for the house of Sir Harry Jarvis. She felt pleasure at the thought of seeing him again—not exactly hope, for she knew not what he could do—but still she felt glad to go, for the good old man had been so kind and courteous, and even affectionate, toward her, that she was sure she should have sympathy, and thought that she might obtain advice, if not assistance.

The carriage rolled on; the road seemed long; and, given up to her own thoughts, Kate's heart fell lower and lower. The country looked bleak and bare. There was nothing to lead away the mind; heavy meditation settled *down upon* her, and every dark or painful word that Lutwich had spoken came back to memory. He had seen no hope but that one of removing the testimony of William Havant, and he had seemed puzzled how to accomplish that. Hours were flying fast, Kate thought; it might take long to negotiate such an affair. Should she remain idle, without making some effort for his service? It could do no harm to see the man; and she might, at all events, discover how he stood affected. Lutwich had only feared for her: for herself she had no fear. Oh, if she could save him! Oh, if she could aid to save him! Would not life itself be a light sacrifice for that? But there was no danger. The place in which the man lived was not one of those nests of vice and crime of which London was so full. If not the most fashionable part of the town, it was close to it; and there could not be the slightest risk, while there might be a great advantage.

She dwelt upon these thoughts all the way; she pondered, she meditated, and every moment she became more and more confirmed in her resolution of seeking out this William Havant. At length the carriage passed through the gates of Jarworth Park, and rolled up to the house. The postillion rang the bell, and a somewhat long pause ensued; but, in the end, the old butler, whom she knew well, opened the doors, and approached the side of the chaise.

"Oh! Miss Malcolm, I am glad to see you, ma'am," said the old man, in a kindly tone; and, ere she could ask if his master was at home, he went on, saying, "Poor Sir Harry is very bad, miss: he's no better to-day."

"Is he ill?" exclaimed Kate, with a look of surprise and grief which touched the attached dependant.

"Very ill, miss, indeed," said the man. "Dear me! have you not heard of it? He has been ill for the last week with a bad fever, which he caught, they think, from some vagrants who were brought before him."

"Oh! I should so much like to see him," said Kate, looking pained and bewildered.

"His cousin, ma'am, is with him," said the butler, with a look over his shoulder: "he is a very strict, hard gentleman. But I can go up, and ask if you can see Sir Harry."

"Do—do," said Kate; "but not if it will be injurious to him. I do not wish it, if it can hurt him."

The old man went away, leaving the door open behind him; and Kate could hear some talking at the top of the first flight of stairs. Then the butler came down, and stood at the further end of the vestibule, as if waiting for a reply to the message he had delivered; so that Kate hoped it had been sent in to Sir Harry himself. In a minute or two after, however, a man, looking like a gentleman's valet, came down part of the way, and said, somewhat rudely, "No: it is impossible that any body can be admitted to Sir Harry in his present state. You're to tell the lady that."

The old butler approached the side of the carriage again, as if to repeat the reply; but Kate stopped him, saying, "I heard—I heard the message."

"It is not my master's, Miss Malcolm," he said. "He would never have sent you such a message as that."

"Is he sensible?" asked Kate, in a low voice.

"Oh dear, yes—quite," answered the servant. "He did wander a good deal some days ago, but he's quite sensible now. I am sure he will be sorry that he has not seen you."

"I will come again," said Kate. "I have a letter to deliver to him, which I was told to give into his own hand."

"They will not let you see him, miss, if they can help it," said the butler, almost in a whisper. "If you will give me the letter, I will give it into my master's own hand, upon my word. You can trust me, indeed, ma'am."

"I am sure of that," replied Kate; "but they can have no greater objection to my seeing him than any one else, as soon as he is able."

"I do not know that, ma'm," said the other, shaking his head. "Master was speaking of you the other night; and I do not think it was very pleasant to those who heard it."

"I do not know what to do," said Kate, thoughtfully; "but perhaps it would be best to give you the letter, for I know it is of great importance. But you must promise me you will give it only to Sir Harry himself, when he is well enough to read it."

"That I will, upon my word!" replied the butler; "and when nobody else is by, too. But I did not mean to say you had better not come, Miss Malcolm. I am afraid they will not let you see him; but it would be as well to try. Only let me have the letter, in case of the worst."

"Well, there it is," replied Kate, with some hesitation still remaining; and the man, taking it quietly, slipped it into his pocket, looking round to see if he were observed. She then reiterated her injunctions, and he his promise; and the carriage drove away toward London again.

More and more depressed was poor Kate Malcolm's heart. Here was another evil chance for him she loved. The evidence of a man of such high character she had calculated much upon, for she had taken it for granted that his evidence must be favorable; and now it was clearly impossible that he could give it. Lutwich would be without the whole advantage of his testimony, at a time when, by his own acknowledgment, all that could be obtained would be hardly enough to save him. It seemed to poor Kate as if Fate decreed that every thing should be thrown into the scale against him; and as she thought of this new misfortune, the bitter tears ran down her cheeks. The carriage was at this moment upon the edge of Finchley Common, and there was a very sharp and abrupt descent at that time in the road, with a small water-course across it, not kept in the best possible order, for the sun of Mac-Adam had not yet dawned. The post-boy was driving quick, for Kate had told him to make haste, in order to report to the prisoner before she went home the result of her visit to Jarworth Park; and in descending the little dip in the ground—it was not more that fifty yards—he took the gutter or water-course at a right angle, and as hard as he could go. Kate felt a sharp concussion, and then saw the horses thrown upon their haunches, and the man almost pitched out of the saddle. The next instant he pulled up and dismounted, looked under the vehicle, and, approaching the window, said, "Please, ma'am, the axle's broken."

"Good Heaven! what am I to do?" cried Kate. "Where can we get it mended?" and she looked in the man's face, utterly bewildered.

"Why, it will be a long job," said the post-boy; "and there's never a blacksmith nearer than a mile and a half; but you see, ma'am, we can't go on as it is, for it's a-dragging with both ends."

"Where can I find the blacksmith?" asked Kate, anxiously. "Tell me the way, and I will bring him."

"Why, the way's not very straight, nohow," said the driver. "I'd go myself, but, you see, I shouldn't like to leave you with the horses, ma'am. But I'll tell you what: if you like to walk on about three quarters of a mile upon this here high road, you'll come to Mother Havant's—a little bit of a house, with lollipops and things in the window—and she'll send her girl down, for a sixpence, and tell Tom the blacksmith to come down here directly. We must contrive to get it spliced up somehow, for there's no use trying to weld it here. Then we can go on gently into town."

"What did you say was the woman's name?" asked Kate.

"Mrs. Havant, ma'am," replied the post-boy. "It's a little red brick house, just on the right-hand of the road, all by itself. You can't miss it. There's lollipops, and hard-bake, and all that there, in the window."

Kate got out, and walked on, musing and repeating to herself the name "Mrs. Havant—Mrs. Havant: it may be a common name about here. It is curious, too: I may as well make some inquiries."

The common looked lonely enough, and bleak, even under the full sunshine. There was not a tree to be seen; not a living creature but a stone-chat flitting from furze-bush to furze-bush, and from sandy bank to bank, with incessant motion, like a troubled spirit. Kate felt very sad and very solitary in that wide, arid heath. She was not alarmed, indeed, but there was something in the wild, desolate aspect of the place, between which and her own fate fancy drew sad parallels. She walked on quickly, however; and at length, by the side of the road, saw a small, narrow red house standing perfectly alone, but the long, flat, unfinished sides of which seemed to show that the builder had intended to give it companions. In the window she perceived the various little articles of sale with which many a poor woman ekes out her scanty means of livelihood, and over the door was written the name of Rebecca Havant. Satisfied that she was right, she entered the open door; but it can not be said that she was much prepossessed in favor of the respectability of the place, or its mistress, by the appearance of either. The little shop was dirty, and redolent of disagreeable odors; and the woman, who appeared behind the counter, was a thin, slatternly person, with a sharp, aquiline nose, very red at the point, and flanked by two keen black eyes, somewhat bleared. A boy was sitting near her, upon a high stool, moping sulkily over a greasy slate; and a girl, somewhat younger, who could not have been often washed since her birth, was pulling her mother's apron, and seemed petitioning for something.

"Well, ma'am, what's for you?" said the woman, in an impatient tone, not taking any notice of the child.

"An accident has happened to the carriage in which I am traveling," replied Kate, "and the post-boy, who did not like to leave the horses, told me that one of your children, Mrs. Havant, would run down and order the blacksmith to go and set it to rights."

"Lord! my children has plenty to do without running after blacksmiths," replied the woman, rudely.

"I did not intend that they should go without payment," answerd Kate. "I'll give that little man a shilling if he will send the blacksmith down to the carriage he will find nearly a mile on the way to Barnet."

"Ah, that alters the case," said the woman. "Bill, jump down this minute and run for Tom Smith—the lady says she will give you a shilling."

"I sha'n't go," answered the boy, sullenly: "you'd only take the shilling from me if she did give it."

The woman instantly boxed his ears, but that seemed not likely to have any more effect than words, till she promised him that he should have sixpence out of the shilling for himself. Nor would he go even then till he had made her give him a peg-top as earnest, with which he walked away, his mother wisely refusing him a string till he came back again, lest he should stop to spin his top by the way.

When he was gone, after some hesitation, Kate ventured to say, putting down the promised shilling on the counter, "Is your son's name William?"

"Yes, ma'am," answered the woman, in a much civiller tone; "and a troublesome, obstinate little devil he is."

"It is curious," said Kate; "I am looking for a person of the name of William Havant—I believe he's in London, though."

"It's my brother-in-law, I dare say," replied the woman; "he was post-boy at the Woolpack, at St. Alban's."

"The same," replied Kate.

"Lord 'a mercy! what can a young lady like you want with he?" exclaimed Mrs. Rebecca Havant.

"Perhaps something that may turn to his advantage," answered Kate; "do you think you could convey a message to him privately, without the people who have got him in London knowing it?"

"Why, Uncle Bill's up stairs," cried the little girl, "a drinking his gin and water."

It was now her turn to have her ears boxed; but that could not remedy the indiscretion which her mother seemed to think she had committed, and, therefore, the good lady turned again to Kate, saying, with a certain degree of menace in her tone, "I hope you wants to do him no harm, ma'am; for you see—"

Kate smiled: "What harm could I do him?" she said. "I am not very strong, my good lady; and all I want is to speak a few words with him, and tell him something that may be very serviceable to him, if he manages rightly."

The woman still looked doubtful; but at length, as if she had made up her mind, she said, with a laugh, "Well, I suppose we could manage you, if you did;" and, turning round, she passed through a swing door, and Kate could hear her step ascending the stairs. There was something unpleasant and threatening in the woman's words and manner, which in a degree alarmed her; for a moment she thought of quitting the shop and hastening back to the chaise. But the next instant she nerved her heart with the thought that she was serving Lutwich, and with a particle of that superstition which is kneaded more or less into the clay of every one, she dwelt with fanciful hopes upon the extraordinary fact of her having so unexpectedly fallen upon the very man she had made up her mind to seek. A long consultation seemed to be going on up stairs, for she heard a murmur of voices, protracted through nearly a quarter of an hour; but at length the woman came down again and said, "You just step in here, ma'am; he'll come down directly. I can't ask you up stairs, for the place ain't quite tidy;" and she led the way into a little dirty back parlor, separated from the shop by a glass door.

Here Kate remained alone for two or three minutes, the woman having betaken herself to the shop again; and at the end of that time a heavy clamping boot was heard descending. The next instant the short, spare figure, the low forehead, wide mouth, inturned eye, and twisted, hook-nose of Hangingwood Billy was before her.

The man, though not drunk, had evidently been drinking a good deal, and his first words were, "Well, ma'am, what do you want with me?"

"Is your name William Havant?" asked Kate, with a heart not quite devoid of fear, for the aspect of the scoundrel frightened her.

"Ay, ay; William Havant, or Hangingwood Bill—it's all the same," replied the post-boy.

"I think, then," said Kate, with a voice trembling with varied emotions, "you were one of the witnesses against Colonel Lutwich on Wednesday last."

"Oh ho! that's the go, is it?" replied the scoundrel; "and what if I was? I'm not a going to be frightened out of telling the truth by no one. I'm sure I wish people would let me alone. I had a man last night a threatening on me, and that's the reason they sent me down here, to keep me out of the way;" and he bestowed a very hearty and blasphemous imprecation upon the heads of those whom he designated by the comprehensive pronoun "they."

"Are you sure he did not come to offer you some better inducement than threats?" asked Kate, growing a little bolder as she went on.

"I don't know what you call inducements," said the other; "he talked a bit of something in hand, if I bolted for a month or two; but he wouldn't say how much, so I couldn't use it one way or t'other; and he said, plain enough, that he'd hang me if I didn't bolt—though it's not in his skin to do that; but that's threatening, I think, notwithstanding."

"Well, I do not seek to threaten at all," replied Kate, hesitating how much she should offer; "but, on the contrary, I think I can promise you a very large sum if you will go out of England for four or five months."

"What's the figure?" said the man, abruptly.

Kate gazed in his face for a moment, and then answered, "Why, a thousand pounds: half the money when you set out, and half as soon as the trial is over."

She saw, with joy indescribable, that the man was as if thunderstruck at the magnitude of the sum; but the demon of cupidity is never sated. He recovered himself immediately, and scratching his gray head, replied, "That won't quite do: I must have the whole of that there when I start, or curse me if I don't hang him. I'll tell you what, miss—you go and talk to the colonel about it, and I'll come and see you. When you have found out what he really can give, and have got the money all ready, I'll come and see you quietly. We'll settle it all at once, and I'll be off before any one can say Jack Robinson—you may see me start, if you like—but mind, I'll have a cool thousand down, or I don't stir a step."

"Well, so be it, then," answered Kate, repressing the joy that rose up in her breast. "Come to me to-morrow night just after dark. I shall see Colonel Lutwich previously."

"Ay, but where am I to come?" asked Hangingwood Bill. "I always like to do business with the ladies. One gets on at a gallop."

"If you will give me some paper and a pen, I will put down the address," replied the poor girl, trembling with agitation. The man grinned as he marked the emotions she suffered, and, going into the shop, returned with the stump of a pen full of ink, and a scrap of ruled paper. Kate wrote the address as clearly as possible, and put it into the post-boy's hands, saying, "You will not fail to come to-morrow, immediately after sunset."

How hard a lesson it is for a young heart to learn that it must never show its eagerness, whatever be the prize it aims at, however high and ennobling, just, wise, or generous be the motives. We live in a sea of selfishness, where every one is ready to devour the other, and the poor bleak, when it rises to a gilded fly upon the surface of the stream, is not so sure to be snapped up by the ravenous pike, as the inexperienced to be made a prey to the greedy the moment he displays the weakness of eagerness.

"I'll try," said the man, in an indifferent tone; "it makes no difference to me. I shall be well paid for what I am doing any way, and so I am in no hurry to drive a bargain. Besides, one has always somewhat in hand when one makes a deal. I think, ma'am, you ought to give me something to drink your health, if I promise to come."

Kate gave him a guinea, and then hurried out of the shop, and down the road, to the side of the carriage, glad to escape from people who excited both disgust and fear.

"I say, Becky," said the post-boy, as soon as she was gone, "I'm like to make a good thing of this job. I've had a fifty-pound note, and a promise of fifty more, for 'peaching of the colonel, and I shall now get a cool thousand for getting out of the way."

"I heard it all," answered the woman; "but I tell you what, Bill, you're a fool if you don't make it well-nigh double. You may see sure enough there's something under all this, and you've got the cards in your own hands."

"Why, what would you have me do?" asked Hangingwood Bill; "you're a keen hand, I know, Becky, though you haven't played your own cards very well neither."

"The luck's been against me," said the woman; "I saved your brother from swinging—you know that, Bill—and he drank himself to death in a year. However, if you promise me just a fifty out of all you get, I'll tell you how you may make as much again, or perhaps more."

The bargain was struck, and, retreating with her amiable brother-in-law into the back parlor, Mrs. Havant placed her hands on her knees, and looked at him impressively: "Now, Bill," she said, "if you will take my advice, you'll do just this; but mind, you must do it exactly, or there is no use of doing any thing. As soon as it's dark, you'll trot back to those two young fellows you told me of in London."

"They're not both young," said the post-boy, interrupting her; "one's an old un, and up to any thing."

"That makes no difference," replied the woman; "folks wouldn't give a fifty-pound note for nothing—nor for the amusement of hanging a man—and they're not surgeons, so they don't want to dissect him. There's more in it, I tell you, than you think. So just you trot back to them, and tell them that you can't just do what they want, because a young lady has offered you a thousand pounds down if you don't. You can be very civil, you know, and all that; but stick fast, and show them that even if they keep you by might and main, you'll spoil the evidence by the way of giving it. They'll pretend not to believe a word about it, and talk high, I dare say; but you can say, it don't matter to you which you get the money of—that, as for the young lady, you never clapped eyes on her before—that's true, you know—and then you can tell them her name. Take my word for it, they'll know all about her, and will see it's all true in a minute. Then they'll promise you what you want, be you sure."

"Then I shall lose t'other," said Bill, with a certain degree of contempt upon his face; "sha'n't get both that way, Becky."

"You're a fool," answered the lady; "stick out for one half down, and if they're afeard on you, offer to let them shut you up anyhow as soon as you have got it; but say you must just send to me for the things you've left here—"

"They'll send some of their own people," said Bill, shaking his head.

"What does that matter, you idiot?" asked the virago. "I shall know just as well that you've got the money from them if they send as if you do; and in five hours after you shall be out, if they stick you fast in the stone pitcher. Then down to the young lady's place as fast as you can go, get the money there, and be off. If they won't give the money, the pitiful scamps, take hers at all events. She's a nice young woman; and it'll be some pleasure to save the colonel. He's quite a gentleman, and as fine a man as ever I saw. How he used to go galloping past here sometimes, on his black horse, so tight and straight, as if they were all of a piece! He'd make a handsome corpus; but I should like him to be shot, or break his neck, or something of that kind, and not hanged by the neck like a dog."

"Well, I'll try your trick, Becky," said Hangingwood Billy; "it won't stop my getting t'other, so it can do me no harm."

"Not a snuff," answered Mrs. Havant; and so the conversation terminated for the time. During the course of the afternoon, sundry fresh hints were given by the lady to her companion as new lights broke upon her; but as they did not at all affect the course of this history, we may as well draw the curtain upon two persons whose sickening characters would never have been introduced here but that they were necessary to this tale.

CHAPTER XXXIX.

"The spirit of the power of the air!" What an idea that name gives of the all-prevailing influence of the mighty Principle of Evil! If we look, too, at the effects of that influence which are visible to our own eyes, which are felt in our own hearts, how strange and marvelous they are! Did you ever sit, reader, calmly thinking of things pure, perhaps, and elevating, and find suddenly something foreign and deteriorating stealing among your thoughts, something ludicrous mingling with the most high, something earthly with the most holy? Few of those who have the power and the habit of scanning the secrets of their own bosoms, have not had to detect and war against such impulses.

But look at that young man, seated at the table, still covered with the remains of a late dinner—a very late dinner for that period—with his cheek resting on his hand, and the eyes turned toward the vacant fire-place; look at the fine, high brow, the delicate features, the clear eye, the thoughtful, almost melancholy expression. What is he meditating now? It can not surely be evil.

Perhaps not; he may be even now tasting the drops of bitterness that spring up from the fountain of passions indulged. There may have come upon him that consciousness of there being better, brighter, happier things than he has ever sought and found, which is sent at longer and longer intervals, like an angel visit, to every one who goes on in a career of wrong. The aspirations may be now for higher objects, for more ennobling pursuits, for things of the spirit and the mind, rather than the animal and the flesh.

But see, there is a slight sneering smile comes upon the lip, naturally somewhat scornful! What is the secret movement of the heart which brings that expression to the face?

Does he congratulate himself upon success and triumph over an adversary? Does he ask himself if he shall be stopped and turned back at the very gates of fruition, by the dull scruples which dotards have instilled and fools are led by?

And see, another change of countenance! He sets his teeth hard together, the compressed lips are protruded, the broad brow gathers into a frown. The idea of failing, of being frustrated, of submitting to be baffled, laughed at, scorned, despised, must have presented itself; and he turns a glance toward the face of the other man who sits on the opposite side of the table, with two decanters at his elbow, and his head nodding to his chest. Oh, what a look of loathing contempt comes upon the young man's face as he gazes at that man—at once the tempter and the tool.

"Doctor! doctor!" exclaimed Sir Theodore Broughton.

"My dear sir," said Doctor Gamble, starting, "I was oblivious. What is it?"

"We were to settle our final plans," said the young man; "it is late, and there you sit sleeping after your food like a pig in a sty."

"What is to settle?" said Doctor Gamble. "I thought it was arranged that we were to suspend all proceedings till after the next examination and committal. Then we may do something."

"I should like to see her," said Sir Theodore, musing. "But you think we can not fail now, doctor?"

"I think not," replied the doctor, stretching himself. "Lutwich out of the way would be one step to success. These other two men gone is another great one already gained; and if the hint I got of old Mrs. Lisle being dead is true, I think we have pretty well the game in our own hands. Patience, perseverance, and smooth dealing on your part, my dear Sir Theodore; ambition, vanity, and even a small portion of womanly weakness on hers, and you have the honors and the odd trick. A fair and candid offer of your heart and hand will do wonders; a private marriage, on account of your not being of age, will but be reasonable; and neither you nor I can help it if the priest have not yet taken deacon's orders, and the license be signed by the wrong man, through mistake."

Sir Theodore smiled, and fell into a reverie again; but a moment or two after, Master Hargrave entered, saying, "Please, Sir Theodore, there's the man Bill Havant come back. He wishes to speak with you."

"What does he want now?" exclaimed the young baronet, starting up fiercely. "He promised, upon his honor, to stay there till Wednesday."

"His honor!" said Doctor Gamble, laughing. "Show him in, Zachary. Now, Master Havant, what do you want? Take a glass of wine, man, to clear your throat."

"No, thank you, sir," replied Hangingwood Bill, "I never drink wine;" and he looked over his shoulder to see if the door was shut.

"What has brought you back again?" asked Sir Theodore, sternly. "I gave you five guineas to go down to your sister's at Finchley Heath, and you promised neither to return, nor to let any one know where you were, till after Wednesday. I hope you are not trying to make a fool of me?"

Hangingwood Bill looked very shrewd, but he replied with all outward respect and deference, "No, sir, no. It's just because I do not want to make a fool of you that I have come up. I kept my promise, too, about not telling any one where I was; but, bless you, sir, some one found out."

"By an accident done on purpose, I suppose," said Doctor Gamble. "Was it the same man, Master Bill? What did he offer?"

"It wasn't no man at all," replied the postboy; "and as for the accident, if you had left me at my old trade I might have had some hand in it; but as I wasn't a driving, I hadn't The accident was the breaking of the carriage axle-tree right through the middle."

"But who was it?" exclaimed Sir Theodore, impatiently.

"Rat me, if I've a mind to tell!" said Mr. Havant, knitting his brows; "I sha'n't, either, unless I'm treated more civiller. I needn't go a begging if I give you back all I had o' ye."

"Let me talk to him, Sir Theodore," said Gamble; "you don't understand him. He's a very honest fellow, and has come to give us information that may be useful. Who was it came to see you, Bill?"

"A young lady, sir," answered the man, in a more placable tone; "and, my eye! what a pretty young lady too. She was dressed all in black, she was; but that did not stop her being wonderful handsome. Such teeth! just like so many little pearls. So, when the smash happened, she came into my sister-in-law's place to rest, and send for a blacksmith; and she soon found out the name, and that I was there; and she said she should like to speak to me, for she had just been going to find me out in Swallow-street. Well, when I came down, she took me into the back parlor, and talked to me about it, but quite different from the t'other one!"

"What did she say?" asked Gamble.

"Why, that's the very thing," replied Bill. "She was uncommon sad and low, poor thing, about the colonel, to be sure; and then she told me I should have a thousand pounds down in golden guineas, to-morrow night, and somewhat more after the trial, if I would but take myself off."

Sir Theodore looked at Gamble, and Gamble at Sir Theodore, and neither of them bore the best satisfied air in the world. But the tutor replied, after a moment's thought, "A thousand pounds! Pooh, pooh! that's a joke."

"Very well, sir. It's like to be a good joke for me," replied the man, coolly.

"Why, I tell you, she has not got a thousand pounds to give," cried Gamble.

"Some one has," said Hangingwood Bill. "I don't much care who gives it, so as I get it. But you seem to know the young lady, sir."

"No I don't," answered the tutor; "but I know that none of Lutwich's people have got any thing like that."

"Oh, I'm not sure of that, sir," answered the man; "the colonel himself is not badly off. Howsoever, what I want to know is, am I to take the money and bolt?"

Gamble put on a severe and determined air, and replied, "I think you had better, if you can. I tell you what, Master Bill, I believe the whole story is a make up. I don't believe there is such a young lady. It's all improbable together."

"Well, I can prove there is such a young lady," replied Hangingwood Bill, remembering the instructions of his sister-in-law, "for she wrote down her name and address for me to go and see her, and have the money just after dark to-morrow. There it is;" and he produced the paper, and showed it to Doctor Gamble.

"Well, good evening, gentlemen," he said, after the tutor had looked at it, and Sir Theodore too had read it over Gamble's shoulder. "I'm a going. I certainly would like better to stay in this here country than to go over the water, and live upon frogs and all that for a while; but no man can say I'm wrong to make my fortune where I can."

"To be sure not," replied Gamble, with a cold and scornful air. "Go and do it."

But Sir Theodore, less shrewd than his tutor, interposed very *mal à propos*. "Stay, stay," he cried; and the man, whose countenance had fallen a good deal under some vague apprehension, which the coolness of Doctor Gamble had suggested, turned round again with a more confident air.

"My dear Sir Theodore, do not suffer yourself to be imposed upon," said Gamble, aloud, that his words might reach Mr. Havant's ears; "you know that this girl has no such means at her disposal, and I know that Lutwich has none either. The man is either trying to cheat you himself, or she is cheating him."

"Well, let me speak to you in the next room for a moment," said Sir Theodore; and, turning his head as he walked toward the door, he added, "Stay here till I come back."

"You have spoiled all," said Doctor Gamble, with a gesture of impatience: "I would have called him back when it was needful, but you must not think of acceding to such terms. It is all nonsense about a thousand pounds. Depend upon it, he is offered nothing like it, and you must beat him down."

"But if he won't be beat down," said the young man. "I believe the man's story is true. You heard yourself that Lutwich had got a very large sum for his plate and horses, and of course he would pay any thing to save his life. What is to be done, I say, if it turns out really true?"

"Why, you must give it up, I suppose," said Gamble; "it would be paying rather too much for a toy; and, besides, where are you to get the money? Donovan gave you enough to last you for half a year. It is nearly all gone already."

"I can easily get it from the Jews," said Sir Theodore, "and I will not be balked now, doctor. I will not, by ——!" and he swore a vehement oath.

Gamble thought gravely. He did not like the affair in which he had plunged. The passions of his young companion had proved more vehement and headstrong than he had imagined them to be, and he felt that they were beyond his control.

"I will go and tell him he shall have the money," said the young baronet, seeing that his tutor did not answer.

"Stop, stop, stop!" cried Gamble; "let me think for one moment. Now tell me, Sir Theodore, which do you seek—the girl, or Lutwich's life? You can not have both."

"Can you ask the question?" replied the young man. "I have made that scoundrel smart already—perhaps not enough; but let him go. But I swear by Heaven, nothing shall ever make me give up the pursuit of that scornful girl till she is mine."

"Well, then," rejoined Gamble, "let me deal with this man, and you shall both have your way, and save your money. Do you promise not to interfere?"

"Yes, if you promise me not to fail me," replied Sir Theodore.

"If I do, kick me out of that door the next minute," replied Gamble; "now let us go back. Don't take any notice of what I say, however odd;" and, opening the door, he went in again, with a contemptuous shrug of the shoulders, saying, as if in continuation, "Well, if you will be such a fool, you must!"

Throwing himself into an arm-chair, with a dissatisfied look, while Sir Theodore resumed his seat, the tutor gazed for a moment or two at the post-boy with the corners of his mouth turned down, and at length said, "So you would have us believe she has promised you a thousand pounds?"

"Yes!" replied the man, boldly, "she did, too."

"I don't think you'd ever get one third of it," answered Gamble; "but, now, not to beat about the bush, Master Havant, tell me, at one word, what you will engage to stay for, and give your evidence properly and truly. We don't ask you to tell any lies, or do any thing that's wrong, remember. *We* are all on the side of the law. They want you to compound a felony. For what sum will you bind yourself to do what I say?"

"For a thousand pounds," replied the man; "your money is as good to me as theirs, and then I should be obliged to bolt."

"That's all nonsense," said Doctor Gamble; and he affected to labor hard to beat the man down. But Hangingwood Bill would give way but little, for he clearly saw that he had got Sir Theodore's weakness on his side, and the sum was at length fixed at eight hundred pounds.

"Now," said Gamble, "there is one thing more to be settled, Master Havant. We must have no more of these tricks, or you may be coming to make us bid up every day. We will have it down in black and white, if you please. You can write, I suppose?"

"I can write my name," replied the man.

"Well, that will do," said Gamble; "I will draw up the agreement, and you shall sign it."

"I won't sign nothing till I've got the money," said Bill.

"Then you'll get no money at all," said Gamble, resolutely.

"What is it you want me to sign?" asked the other, after a moment's thought.

"Nothing but a promise to stay and give your evidence truly and sincerely, if Sir Theodore here pays you eight hundred pounds," replied Gamble; "and, from the moment you have received the money, to remain constantly under the eye of one of his servants till your evidence is given."

The man hesitated a little, and then said, "I'm not a going to put myself in custody like that till I've got the money."

"I do not want you to," replied Gamble; "but the case is this: we have not, of course, got the money in the house; all the banks are shut, and we must get it to-morrow. You were not to see Miss Malcolm till after dusk to-morrow. Now, if you come here at three o'clock, the money will be all ready, and a servant too, to look after you; but you must sign the promise to-night, or we might have you coming and telling us some one had offered you fifteen hundred."

The consummation was so very likely that Hangingwood Bill could not help smiling; but still he hesitated a moment, for he was half afraid that the strict watch to which he was to be subjected might prevent the execution of the double game which his fair sister-in-law had suggested. It seemed very like a trap, in short, into which he could not avoid plunging without displaying the whole of his purposes. Under these circumstances, he resolved, like a bold man, to take his chance, recovering courage as he remembered that there were many ways of blinding a spy, and escaping from any human supervision, when not fortified by tall walls with spikes at the top.

"Well," he said, after some consideration, "I'll agree; let us have the paper."

But Doctor Gamble seemed inclined to dally more than himself, and he consequently only became eager to conclude a bargain which rendered the possession of eight hundred pounds certain—at least he thought so.

"Well, what like was this young lady, my good friend?" asked the tutor, when the man's assent had been signified, and the four or five first words of the agreement proposed had been written.

The scoundrel, who was by no means insensible to beauty, went over his former description, and added a few more commendations of form and feature.

"Did she seem very anxious to save the gallant colonel?" asked Doctor Gamble, with a sneering laugh.

"Ay, that she was," replied the man; "she'd give all she had in the world to get me out of the way, I'll answer for it."

"Indeed!" said the tutor, rather enjoying the torture to which he saw he was putting Sir Theodore Broughton; "then I suppose she is very much in love with him?"

"I don't know," replied Hangingwood Bill. "But I do know that she shook like a willow in the wind when she was talking to me, and turned red and white, and white and red, by turns. I thought she'd have gone down in a faint one time."

"Ha!" said Doctor Gamble, writing on; "poor thing! It is a pity she should set her heart upon a highwayman. We must cure her of that. The colonel, as you call him, is quite up to the mark, and if you did not bring him to Tyburn, some one else would."

"That's true enough, I should think," replied Mr. Havant, thoughtfully; "there is no use waiting and letting some one else get the reward."

"As for that, there is no reward offered, except what we intend to give," replied Doctor Gamble; "and if there was, you should be too old a bird not to know that no one ever gets it but the officers. However, you'll make your money of the thing. It is not every one has such a sweep as this. You can read writing, I suppose: I don't want to take you in at all, so you had better look over what I've put down. There it is."

The man took the paper and held it near the candle to see, but he was a long time in making out the true meaning of the worthy tutor's scrawl; for, though the hand was a large one, and not very indistinct, he had no great experience in the deciphering of manuscripts, and every now and then he stopped to ask, "What's that word?" or, "What's this?"

At length, however, the task was complete, and he said, "Very well; I'll sign it: give us a pen."

"Stop! stop!" said Gamble: "we must have a witness!" and Zachary Hargrave was called into the room. In his presence the man affixed his name in a wild, hilly kind of hand, and the groom added his as a witness.

"And now—where am I to go now?" asked Havant, with a stupid look.

"Wherever you like," replied Gamble. "To the devil, if you please; only come back to-morrow at three to get the money, and put yourself under watch and ward. There, take him away, Hargrave, and give him a dram."

"A fine way of saving the money," said Sir Theodore, gloomily; "but never mind. I have sworn, and I will not regret one step that is needful, be it what it may."

"The money will be saved, nevertheless," replied Gamble. "Were I not sure of that, I would not go one step further, for Heaven only knows what would be Donovan's rage if he found you had been intermeddling with Jews and usurers."

"But you have promised it to him in that paper," exclaimed Sir Theodore.

"Not a whit," exclaimed the tutor. "All the promises are on his side. He undertakes to stay and give evidence, and to put himself into our custody entirely—if you pay him the money. Now, I do not intend you should; but we must be careful about the refusal, or he will go and give evidence against Lutwich out of pure spite, if he dreams for one moment we want him to abstain. I shall quietly tell him I have seen the lady, and that his story is all nonsense. Then I'll offer him five pounds to stay, and make some one else give him ten or twenty to go."

"I do not understand your plan at all," replied the young baronet.

"All the better," answered Gamble. "It is the more likely to succeed. This depends upon myself alone; and I will carry it through, or my name is not Gamble. But now I'll to bed, for I must be up and doing early."

CHAPTER XL.

Kate Malcolm passed the evening after her return from Barnet partly by the side of Louisa, partly in her own room, schooling her heart. She looked back upon days not very long gone, and upon sorrows, anxieties, and even anguish of mind suffered therein, and she remembered that she had borne afflictions very differently then. She asked herself where was the spirit of calm endurance which had then animated and supported her; where that firm, quiet, unmurmuring devotion, with which she had borne poverty and adversity, and soothed and upheld her dying father? She had felt, she had grieved as much as human creature can feel and grieve, but still her courage and her tranquillity had never forsaken her; she had believed that it was her appointed lot, and she had bowed resigned to the will of God. Now, however, she had given way to agitation, terror, restless anxiety; her whole thoughts and mind had been in continual movement; her heart and her brain had labored, aching with intensity of exertion. A new element had mingled with her feelings. She loved, and with love came all love's strange and quick emotions. But hers was not an ordinary character. With all her gentle tenderness, there were strong powers of intellect; and when she resolutely said to her own spirit, "This must be conquered," it was conquered. Not the love, but the emotion. She prepared herself to act calmly, whatever she might be called upon to do; to suffer calmly, whatever she might be fated to suffer. She reproached herself for the agitation which she had allowed to master her while dealing with the base man whom she had met at Finchley, and she resolved to be upon her guard against herself more even than against others.

With these determinations she slept, and on the following morning woke early to put them in execution. Poor girl! she had much need of resolution.

Hardly was Kate down when a note was put into her hands. It was addressed in a stiff, lawyer-like hand, which she did not know, and, on opening it, she found the following words:

"Mr. Thomas Brown, attorney-at-law, presents his respectful compliments to Miss Catharine Malcolm, and begs to solicit an interview of a few minutes in the course of the morning, having some matters of much importance to communicate regarding the situation of Lieutenant-colonel Lutwich. Mr. Brown will not give Miss Malcolm the trouble of calling at his office, but will wait upon her toward ten o'clock."

The letter was dated from one of the inns of court, and Kate immediately gave orders that if a gentleman of the name of Brown called upon her, he was to be admitted. She felt her heart beat a little as fancy tried to discover what new turn in the strange path of Fate was before her; but she instantly—with strong resolution—repressed the thoughts that would agitate her, and prepared to go through whatever might be to be suffered calmly.

Punctually as the clock struck ten, it was announced to her, then sitting with Louisa, that Mr. Brown was in the dining-room, whither she had directed him to be shown, and, proceeding thither hurriedly, she found a stout man dressed in rusty black, with a pair of gray worsted stockings meeting the breeches at the knee. He wore a large pair of spectacles, too, and a bushy, well-powdered wig. He was a coarse-looking man, Kate thought, and not pleasant of aspect, but such as might well be employed about the police courts and at the Old Bailey.

"Mr. Brown, I believe," she said, as he stood and gazed at her through his spectacles.

"Yes," he replied, "my name is Brown, ma'am. Have I the honor of speaking to Miss Malcolm? I expected to see an elder person."

"My name is Malcolm," answered Kate; "pray be seated."

The visitor took a chair, hummed once or twice, drew a bundle of papers from his pocket tied with red tape, and then said, "I have come to you, ma'am, upon a very unpleasant, nay, painful piece of business—and quite in an unprofessional manner, to see if I can not make some arrangement which may save the life of poor Colonel Lutwich, in whom I know you take a deep interest, and for whom I imagine you would willingly do all that lies in your power."

Kate felt a sad tremor creeping over her; but she resisted her emotions, and quietly clasping her hands together without knowing that she did so, replied, "I would, indeed, sir—any thing—any thing."

"That is right," said Mr. Brown, with an approving nod; "will you allow me to ask you a question or two? You yesterday saw a man of the name of William Havant, I think?"

"I did," answered Kate, becoming more and more agitated; "but I was not aware that he would mention the fact."

"He related all the facts immediately," replied the other; "you offered him a thousand pounds, I think, my dear young lady, if he would abscond and withhold the fatal evidence against poor Colonel Lutwich."

Kate bowed her head, saying, in a voice hardly articulate, "Yes, sir."

"Do you know you acted a very imprudent part," said Brown, gravely; "by what you did, you neither more nor less than rendered yourself guilty of a breach of the law, made yourself an accessory to the crime after the fact, and placed yourself within the statutes regarding the compounding of felonies."

Kate trembled violently, not, indeed, so much from personal fear—although she felt acutely how terrible the situation in which, according to his statement, she had placed herself might become—as from apprehension that the very steps which she had taken might be disadvantageous to Lutwich himself.

The man before her did not altogether rightly understand the sensations which his words had produced; but he saw that she was greatly agitated, and after a moment's pause, he said, "Do not be alarmed. The man to whom you spoke is an infamous scoundrel, and of course he came and betrayed you at once. Luckily, however, it was to one who has the most friendly feelings toward you, and measures were immediately taken to shield you from the consequences of this indiscretion, which, doubtless, arose from a kind motive."

"It was committed, sir," replied Kate, with

a very pale cheek, "only with the view to save a gentleman who once laid me under a very great obligation."

"You are, indeed, the only person who could save him," replied the other; "but you did not take the right means."

"I could save him!" exclaimed Kate, eagerly; "I could save him! How? Oh, tell me how!"

"You would not do it, if I did," replied her companion, coldly.

"You are wrong, sir," replied Kate, almost indignantly; "there is hardly any thing on earth that I would not do to save him from the dreadful fate that seems before him."

"Ay! hardly," said the man, with a short laugh; "but this is one of the hardlies, my dear young lady."

"Well, then, sir, I will say nothing," replied Kate; "nothing but tell a falsehood or commit a crime. I beseech you, inform me what it is."

"There is no use of it, my dear young lady," replied the visitor; "I should only distress you and pain myself. I am not new to the views of womankind upon such subjects, and although, as I have said, you could save Colonel Lutwich from all risk and danger if you would, yet the sacrifice is too great for any woman to make."

"It can not be too great for me," said Kate, eagerly, with her eyes fixed imploringly upon his face: "once more I beseech you to tell me what it is."

"Well, I will do so, if you wish it," said the other, "but it is first necessary that you should know Colonel Lutwich's situation exactly. A highway robbery was committed on a night which you must well remember, for the colonel visited you the same evening, I find, at the house of Sir Harry Jarvis. Now, the only evidence before the magistrates at present is that of the person robbed, who swore last Wednesday that Colonel Lutwich was the man. His evidence unconfirmed, however, is not worth a rush, for he had before given a totally different description of the highwayman, and that in Lutwich's own presence, which can be proved. But then this man William Havant, *alias* Hangingwood Billy, who drove the chaise that was stopped, is ready not only to swear that the man who stopped it was Colonel Lutwich, but to give such explanations as to his change of dress and appearance in order to disguise himself, as will at once account for the other man's first mistake, and prove the crime beyond all doubt against the prisoner. His fate, as you ought to know, is irrevocably sealed if that man appears against him."

He paused, and Kate exclaimed, sorrowfully, "How can I prevent him from appearing? You blamed me a moment ago for having endeavored to do so."

"True," replied Mr. Brown, "because you did it imprudently, and by means that could not succeed. But hear me out. There are secrets in all things, my dear young lady. A gentleman of rank, station, and fortune has resolved to bring Lutwich to justice. This man, Havant, has placed himself entirely and totally at his disposal. He can put him in the witness-box to-morrow, or keep him away from it till the trial is over, and Lutwich acquitted, just as he pleases. Mind, I will prove all this to you before I have done. I assert nothing I can not prove. Now, I am sorry to say, this young gentleman is not moved by any abstract love of justice in his determined pursuit of your friend; nor must you suppose, either, that it is by revenge, even when I tell you that Lutwich has been an obstacle in the way of his love. You know—all women know—what an overpowering passion love is; what sacrifices it will induce people to make, what acts it will hurry them on to commit. The gentleman I speak of is mad with that passion, and resolved, let it cost what it will, to sweep every obstacle away that impedes its gratification. He has no hatred to Lutwich, no enmity toward him, except as one, and that the principal, obstacle to his success. Let his success be assured, and from that moment Lutwich is saved; this man, Havant, is sent out of England, and, once acquitted, the prisoner never can be tried again for the offense."

Kate had sat for some time with her hands covering her eyes, but now she started up with her cheek burning and her eyes bright. "Cease! cease, sir!" she cried, "and do not insult me further. I told you I would do any thing but commit a crime to serve him, ay, were it to lay down my own life for his. But if you suppose that I would become the mistress of Sir Theodore Broughton to save my own life, or that of any one else, you are mistaken. I beg you to leave me! What have I done to make this man think thus of me?"

"I knew it," said her companion, "I knew it. I did not wish to say any thing on this point, but you forced me. Let us drop the subject; but yet, before I do so, I must correct one error into which you have fallen. I neither supposed, nor proposed, that you should become the mistress of Sir Theodore. Indeed, he would not have ventured to charge me with any such commission. What he proposed was —what he has always sought—to make you his wife. His heart has been yours long. He offers you his hand, his name, and his fortune. He seeks nothing else, he never has sought any thing else, but your hand. Do not mistake him or me. He wished me to put his proposal plainly before you, and to leave not only his own happiness, but Colonel Lutwich's life or death, at your disposal. His fate is in *your* hands: *you* give him life and liberty, or condemn him to death. But I told Sir Theodore how it would be. I know that ladies may have a great regard for a man, and think they love him very much, but not be able to sacrifice their passion even to save him from death and disgrace. Let us speak no more upon the subject. I see how it is—I had better go," and he rose, put the papers in his pocket, and moved toward the door.

"Stay, stay, stay!" cried Kate, wildly; and, falling back into her seat, she burst into a passion of tears. "Oh, this is terrible! oh, this is cruel!" she murmured, under the first impulse of contending emotions. "Can this man expect to win a woman's love by such means?" and she sobbed so loudly that her companion seemed to fear the sound would call some one to her aid, and tried to calm and console her.

"My dear young lady, be tranquil, be composed," he said, in a tender tone, but gazing at her beautiful face and form, as she writhed under the mental agony she suffered, with a look that would have made her blood run cold, had her suffering given her power to observe it. "No one forces you to any line of conduct. You are the mistress of your own actions. Think calmly, think reasonably of your situation, and do not agitate yourself thus without cause. It is true," he continued, seeing her tears flow with less emotion, "it is true, your situation is a very painful one. You have to decide upon the life or death, to condemn or to acquit a man whom, perhaps, you love—to whom, perhaps, you have promised your hand; and if you would save him from a death of horror and disgrace, you must give that hand to another. It is a dreadful choice, indeed, for a young creature of ardent affections; but yet you have to consider that it may be looked upon in some sort as a boon, that, by this sacrifice of yourself, you have an opportunity of giving him life. If you refuse to make the sacrifice, he is lost to you by death; you can never be his, he can never be yours. You may rescue him from destruction by what we must consider the gift of a widowed hand."

"To his murderer!" replied Kate, bitterly. "Let me think, sir. Let me think in silence for a moment. My decision will soon be made, and when made it will be irrevocable;" and, once more pressing her hands upon her burning brow and eyes, she remained for several minutes without uttering a word. It is impossible to describe the anguish of that moment. To say that the thoughts which crossed her brain—the feelings that passed through her heart—seemed like brands of fire, scorching and withering as they went, were but a poor expression of her sufferings. There was a terrible struggle, too—a struggle for calmness, for a mastery over herself and her own emotions—a struggle for the full use of her own intellect, that she might see the whole, and act upon the united dictates of reason and affection, and yet the tumult of agitating passions almost drowned the voice of the mind.

At length she conquered; and, taking away her hands from her face, she said, abruptly, and in that tone of command which despair will sometimes assume, "You said you had proofs that this man is entirely at the command of Sir Theodore Broughton—that Colonel Lutwich's life or death, in short, are at his disposal. Show me the proofs."

"Read that paper, madam," said Mr. Brown, choosing one from the bundle in his hand: "it must satisfy you on that score, I think."

Kate took it—gazed at it—wiped away the tears that obscured her sight—gazed at it again, and read the promise given by the man Havant, and signed with his name, to place himself completely in the power of Sir Theodore Broughton. It seemed all too clear—too certain. There was no hope, no chance of removing the man's evidence without the consent of her persecutor. She shuddered as she read. Then, relapsing into thought again, she pressed one hand upon her heart, still holding the paper in the other, till her meditation was broken by her companion gently taking the document from her.

Kate started, gazed at him wildly for an instant, and then, resuming a cold, calm air, she said, "I see there is no other hope. I will not say, sir, what I think of the conduct which has been pursued toward me, for my resolution is taken. I will save him at any cost. Yet I must not and will not deceive Sir Theodore Broughton. I *have* loved—I do *love* Colonel Lutwich. Were I to say otherwise, I should tell a falsehood. You may tell Sir Theodore that if this cold, unwilling form is all he asks, I am ready to give it, as the price of the life he has aimed at but too well. Nay, more, I will strive to do my duty to him as his wife, and to forget the past. More I can not say. But I must have security, sir, that Colonel Lutwich is safe; for the man who would act thus, would commit any other act to gratify his passions. I neither can nor will marry him till the prisoner is acquitted."

"That will be easily arranged, my dear young lady," replied the other; "you do indeed make a noble and a generous sacrifice. This is real love. However, you must pardon me if I act as a lawyer, and take securities also. It might happen—though I am sure it would not happen with you—that by persuasions and representations of friends, a young lady so situated, when she saw her end accomplished and her lover acquitted, might refuse to ratify the contract."

"Be under no fear, sir," replied Kate, with a slightly scornful look; "I am not accustomed to violate my word; and I promise by all I hold sacred, so help me God, if, by Sir Theodore's means, and the removal of this base wretch from England, Colonel Lutwich is acquitted, I will become the wife of him who sent you, whenever he chooses to demand my hand."

"Then, of course, you will not object to give that pledge in writing," said Mr. Brown; "I must satisfy Sir Theodore by something more than my bare assurance; and, indeed, it were better, otherwise he may be tempted to keep the man in England till the trial, and then some fatal accident might happen, by which William Havant would be compelled to come forward and give evidence."

"What I have said that I will write," replied Kate; "but no more, sir."

"I must also require that you do not see Colonel Lutwich during his imprisonment," said the other; "people in his situation always entertain hopes that are only dispelled by a court of justice and the black cap."

Kate hesitated, but her spirit was weary and worn out, and she thought it was little worth while to struggle now. The man who was with her saw his advantage; and, as those who are much accustomed to deal with people of less cunning know well how, he gained step by step, she promised to consent that the marriage should be private, if Sir Theodore required it, in consideration of his being under age; and, indeed, there was nothing short of falsehood or evil which she would not have promised at that moment to save Lutwich from the fate that menaced him. The terrible engagement which she had entered into seemed to leave every other point in her fate quite in insignificance, and her whole heart was filled with the indifference of despair. She demanded, however, and steadily adhered to that demand, before she fixed her name to the paper which her visitor drew out, that he should sign a solemn pledge that William Havant should be sent at once out of England. Mr. Brown hesitated strangely, however, and thereby suggested doubts which confirmed her resolution.

He then affected anger, putting up the papers as if to go, and Kate, terrified, but yet determined, called him back, saying, "Stay, sir; I will myself write the promise you require, inserting in it the conditions I think fit. If it then suit you, well; if not, I can not help it, for I will not at once put my own fate and the life of Colonel Lutwich in the hands of a man who has shown how basely he can use an accidental advantage."

Sitting down at the table, on which were pen and ink, she wrote for a few minutes with a firm hand, then paused an instant, dated it, and affixed her name. "There," she said, "read it. If it will do, well; if not, tear it and leave me."

"It will do quite well, madam," replied her companion. "The man shall be sent out of the country before to-morrow night. I only hesitated because I could not affix Sir Theodore's name to the paper, or any other, indeed, except my own, for that would be forgery, and poor Thomas Brown, attorney-at-law, has no power. I may rely then, I think, completely upon your keeping this promise, if, in consequence of this witness's absence, Colonel Lutwich is liberated or acquitted."

"I have pledged myself as solemnly as words can do it," replied Kate, "and have called God to witness. I can say no more;" and she rose from her seat, as if to show that their interview was at an end.

Her visitor then withdrew, passed through the little vestibule, and entered a hackney-coach which was waiting for him. "Back again," he said, as the coachman closed the door; and, as soon as the vehicle drove on, he laughed gayly, and threw the wig and the spectacles into the opposite seat, displaying the merry, dissolute face of Doctor Gamble.

In the mean time, Louisa Lisle sat anxiously waiting for Kate Malcolm's return. She heard the door of the house shut, and the coach drive away, but Kate did not appear; and, after waiting five or ten minutes more, she timidly approached the dining-room and went in. Kate Malcolm was lying insensible on the floor, and some time elapsed before she could be restored to consciousness.

CHAPTER XLI.

For a time we must leave Kate Malcolm and the sad events which surrounded her, and turn to another scene not quite so gloomy as those in which she was placed, yet far from gay. It is true, the aspect of every thing around was cheerful. The morning light was shining upon the green leaves and through the old trees of Dunsmore Park; and it found its way, tempered, into the breakfast-room, where, with all the pleasant accessories of wealth, the family of Sir Charles Chevenix were assembled to partake of the bright first meal of the day. The whole air was tuneful with the songs of birds, and perfumed with the breath of flowers; and the herds of deer moving across the picture before the windows, the busy rooks cawing and fluttering in the distant rookery, a tall peacock sweeping the dewy grass with his gemmed train, and the squirrels running across the green, and then swarming up the pines, gave a gay and pleasant aspect to the whole. But Sir Charles himself was anxious for his daughter, and Lady Chevenix was very uneasy at Mary's changed looks, and grave, nay, melancholy mood. The objects that had pleased her, pleased her no more; the studies she had delighted in, wearied instead of amusing; the book and the pencil were thrown by; and the very wing of Fancy seemed heavy and oppressed, unless, indeed, it soared when she stood silently gazing forth from the window; but if it did, it must have been with a melancholy flight.

She was now seated opposite her father, tasting but little of that which was before her, and striving to talk cheerfully, but often losing herself in thought. Sir Charles saw the effort, and was pained, so that it was a relief to him when a servant brought in the letters.

"There, that is for you, Mary," he said. "What hands women are now learning to write, as tall, and stiff, and straight as a regiment of grenadiers. When I was young, the *o's* and the *a's* were as fat as aldermen, and the *l's* and *b's* as crooked as a dog's tail."

Thus saying, he threw the letter across the table to his daughter, gave another to Lady Chevenix, and proceeded to open one which was addressed to himself. It was merely some formal notification, and soon read; and when he had done, he raised his eyes again to Mary's face. They remained fixed upon her for some time, while she continued to read with a straining eye and changing color; and Sir Charles saw that there was something moved her greatly in the contents of the letter, but he took no notice.

"Sir Harry is somewhat better, Charles," said Lady Chevenix; and, as she spoke, she remarked how steadily her husband was gazing at Mary, and her eyes followed his. "What is the matter, my dear child?" cried Lady Chevenix at once; "something pains or agitates you?"

"Both, my dear mother, both," replied Mary; "but let me read it out. It is a sad letter, indeed."

Mary read on, and when she had done, she gave the letter to her father, and wiped some tears from her eyes.

"Who is it from?" asked Lady Chevenix, while Sir Charles read the letter almost as eagerly as his daughter.

"From poor Kate Malcolm," replied Mary, with her hand trembling as it lay lightly on the table. "Mrs. Lisle is dead! She died suddenly—in a moment; and, I am sorry to say, Colonel Lutwich is in prison upon some terrible charge affecting his life."

Great was Lady Chevenix's astonishment, for Colonel Lutwich had been an especial favorite of hers; and when Sir Charles had done, she also asked to see the letter.

"I must go to London directly," said Sir Charles, as he gave it to her. "If the facts be as Kate states them, my evidence will be most important to poor Lutwich. He could not have committed this crime at the time stated, for he was at Jarvis's within half an hour after, and it would take an hour to ride the distance by any road I know;" and he rose and rang the bell sharply.

"Pray let me go with you, papa," said Mary, raising her beautiful eyes to his face; "I may be of some use, at least as far as consolation goes, to poor Kate, for Mrs. Lisle's death must have made a terrible change. Pray let me go."

"With all my heart, my love," replied Sir Charles; "will you come too, mamma?"

But Lady Chevenix was not fond of sudden movements. She had so many things to do at home; it would take such a time to pack up her clothes; her maid was not prepared: in short, there were a hundred objections; and it was decided that Sir Charles and Mary should go together, while she remained at the Park. A servant was dispatched instantly to Stratton for post-horses, and after some common-place comments upon Kate's letter, Lady Chevenix left the room. Mary was about to follow; but her father called her back, and walked into the bay window. When, with a still varying cheek, she came near him, Sir Charles threw his arm round her, saying, "Did you observe nothing in that letter, my dear Mary, besides what we have spoken of?"

Mary was silent, and her father went on, saying, "Come, my dear child, let us have perfect confidence in each other. Your little friend, here, Kate, is evidently in love with Lutwich—I should think, engaged to him: I judge by the tone of her letter rather than the words she makes use of. If so, Mary, I have done injustice to Reginald Lisle. Have you not done so too, my love?"

Mary wept, and leaned her forehead against her father's bosom. He pressed her kindly to his heart; and that tender movement gave her strength to say, "I am bewildered; but I judged principally by what you told me, my dear father. Now, I do not know what to think."

"We have both been mistaken, dear Mary," said Sir Charles; "but this may be amended. Be assured, my love, your happiness shall ever be your father's first object; but I thought I was best consulting it when I told you what I believed to be the truth. I did not, indeed, know that this had gone so deeply as I have lately seen, with pain, it has gone; but of that, more as we drive along, my dear; now run away and get ready."

With all possible dispatch, Sir Charles Chevenix and his daughter set out, Mary with a heart much lightened, but still sorely agitated between hope and fear, and her father thoughtful, and, for him, very grave.

The first two miles passed nearly in silence; but at length Sir Charles laid his hand upon his daughter's, and said, "Now tell me all, my dear Mary. Shut not up your feelings in your own heart like a dormouse in a cage, but let me have a peep at them too, my child. You know, I think, that my love for you is not of that selfish kind which seeks the gratification either of passion or prejudice rather than the happiness of its object. What has passed between you and Lisle, Mary?"

"I can not recall his words, my dear father, or my own," replied Mary; "I have often tried to do so since, in vain; but I will own, I was convinced, from all he said, that he loved me, and would seek my hand."

"And you loved him, and told him so?" said Sir Charles.

Mary's cheek burned a good deal; but she replied frankly, "I did love him—I do love him; and I let him see that it was so, though, perhaps, I might not exactly say the words."

"You should have told me all this, Mary," said her father, gravely.

"I thought he would do so," answered Mary, simply.

"Ay, and we prevented him," said Sir Charles; "well, well, we are always making mistakes in life, and then mending what we have broken."

"Perhaps, too, mamma's conduct alarmed him," rejoined Mary, in a low tone; "she was certainly very cold to him when she discovered who he was. Indeed, her feelings frightened me, and make me fearful still. I do not think she would ever consent, even if he were to wish it now."

"Pooh, pooh!" said Sir Charles, "your dear mother will not oppose my wishes and yours too. As to Lisle himself, I must find some means of coming to an explanation with him."

"But he is out of England," said Mary, sadly; "did you not see, Kate mentions that he has gone abroad—sad, I dare say, and thinking me very capricious?"

Sir Charles had not seen or remarked the part of Kate's letter she spoke of, and it was re-read. "Well, I must write to him," he said, when he had done; but Mary exclaimed, "Oh, no! Do not, dear papa. He will think it very strange, and suppose, perhaps, that I—"

"Mary, Mary!" said Sir Charles, "take my word for it, my dear girl, perfect frankness in matters of love is ever the best, the noblest, and the surest way. I will say nothing that can compromise your delicacy, depend upon it; but I will tell him that you have now informed me of all that had passed between you, and that I—filled with a prepossession of his being engaged to Kate Malcolm—had given you the same mistaken impression I had received. That explained, he will see the motives on which we acted; and the rest must come from himself, my child. But I will not hold the worth of my Mary so cheap as to suppose that any man on earth with a free heart could possess her, and not strive to do so."

Thus ended their conversation for the time; and four horses and well-paid post-boys brought the father and daughter rapidly to London. It was near midnight, however, when the carriage stopped at the house of Sir Charles Chevenix, and, as his arrival was unexpected, the clock had struck two before Mary's head rested on her pillow. She was very much tired, but she was still agitated. She thought of how unkind her conduct must have appeared to Reginald Lisle; she thought of how sad his heart must have been, if she might judge from her own, when he left the shores of England; and tears and bitter meditations occupied many of the hours of darkness. She was up before her father, however, and waited for his appearance with anxiety, for Mary was not quite satisfied yet. There was a shade of doubt still upon her mind; she feared that she might be deluding herself with false hopes of Reginald's unchanged affections; and the smallest particle of uncertainty is a heavy load to the heart of love. When Sir Charles did come down, he was somewhat tardy at breakfast, and, Mary thought, very grave; but when he had done, it was arranged that he should proceed to see Lutwich, and take whatever steps might be necessary in order to be present at the next examination before the magistrates, while Mary, with a fresh pair of post-horses, set out to visit Kate Malcolm.

Mary's heart beat a good deal, poor girl, as the carriage rolled on, and her thoughts were very busy with the interview that was about to take place; but when she stopped before Mrs. Lisle's cottage, and, looking out, beheld the closed windows, she reproached herself with selfishness for having forgotten that she was approaching the house of mourning. When the bell was rung and the servant appeared, he said, in answer to her inquiries, that Miss Malcolm was ill in bed. "She has been very unwell, ma'am," he said, "since yesterday morning."

"I think if she is well enough to receive any one, she will admit me," said Mary, "and I much wish to see her. Pray send up word that Miss Chevenix is below."

"Will you step into the drawing-room for a moment, ma'am, and I will see?" said the man; and Mary followed him instinctively.

When the man opened the door of the room for her to enter, he paused suddenly, as if he saw something there he had not expected; but Mary was already on the threshold, and she beheld seated at a table, with her head resting on her hand, a young girl, pale, slight, and shadowy, but bearing in her features a sufficient resemblance to Reginald Lisle to show at once that she was his sister.

Mary gave way to the feelings of her heart; and, while the servant was beginning an excuse for showing her to that room, on the plea that he did not know Miss Lisle was down, she advanced at once toward her, and, taking her hand kindly, kissed her pale cheek.

"You do not know me," said Mary, "but I think your brother must have mentioned me. I am Mary Chevenix."

The least thing agitated Loor Louisa's shaken nerves, and she trembled without answering. "I did not intend to intrude upon you, dear Miss Lisle," continued Mary, "but, having come up to town to see our poor friend, Kate Malcolm, I am unwilling to go away without doing so, though the servant says she is ill. Shall I leave you?"

"Oh no, no, stay!" said Louisa; "I know all about you now; but the sight of a stranger frightened me. Send up, and let Miss Malcolm know that Miss Chevenix is here," she continued, speaking to the servant; and then turning to Mary again, she added, "Kate is indeed very ill. I never saw such a change as has taken place in her since yesterday."

"But what is the matter?" asked Mary, seating herself by Louisa's side. "Has any fresh misfortune happened?"

"I think I might tell you," replied Louisa, "for I know she loves you very much; but yet I am so ignorant of these things, I might do harm. I may at least say this, that poor Kate was yesterday called upon to make a most terrible sacrifice of all her dearest feelings, to save from destruction the man she loves. She will herself tell you more, however, I dare say. She spoke of rising, so I am sure she will see you; but I persuaded her to rest till dinner-time, for she is certainly very ill."

"If you will step up, madam," said old Mrs. Jones, appearing at the door, "Miss Malcolm will see you;" and, in another minute, Mary was by Kate's bedside. The poor girl was as pale as death; all her warm color gone, except when for a moment a slight flush crossed her cheek, and passed away again.

Mary kissed her tenderly, and her heart, as she did so, reproached her for the feelings with which she had parted from her. "Dear Kate!" she said, "I am really much grieved to find you so ill. But do not give way, Kate. Papa and I set out as soon as your letter arrived—we were not more than an hour in the house after it came—and he speaks with good hope; for he says that it is impossible this charge against Colonel Lutwich can be true, as there was not time for him to reach Jarworth Park, if he had been guilty. You know that there is some one very like him."

Kate smiled faintly, saying, "You are very kind, dear Mary, and so is Sir Charles also; but, alas! you do not know all. Colonel Lutwich is safe, I trust, but my peace is at an end forever."

She did not weep, but closed her eyes, and remained for some moments in bitter thought.

Mary gazed upon her sorrowfully, and asked herself, "How can I soothe and console her? No way without knowing the whole; and how can I learn that? Perhaps by making my own confession first, and trying to atone for my unkind feelings toward her when we parted."

"Kate," she continued aloud, "look at me, dear Kate. I have come to tell you a tale of my own weakness and folly, and to ask your pardon for coldness and unkindness which you did not merit. I am sure you will give it me; and I think, as a proof that you do forgive me, you will open your heart to me in return."

"I forgive you, Mary!" exclaimed Kate, turning round and gazing at her. "I have nothing to forgive, unless kindness and generosity be an offense."

"Listen to me, then, dear Kate," replied Mary Chevenix, "and you will soon see what you have to forgive. I have been jealous of you, Kate—foolishly, blindly jealous, and have made myself wretched by my own fault. I have wished I had never seen you—oh, I can not tell you what I have felt toward you. But listen, and I will try to explain all;" and, with a burning cheek, Mary poured forth her little history, concealing nothing, but, as if in expiation of the feelings with which she reproached herself, aggravating rather than diminishing any faults attributable to herself.

"I have but one excuse to offer," said Mary, in the end, "and that is, dear Kate, that some of your own words helped to deceive me, and your own looks still more. Do you remember a conversation we had on the evening of that day when you returned with my father to Jarworth Park, and when I spoke to you about Reginald's coming to your assistance at Dunstable?"

"No," said Kate, "it was Lady Chevenix spoke to me about that."

"Yes, but I spoke to you afterward, when mamma had left the room," replied Mary, "and asked you if he had not fallen a little in love with you?"

"Not Captain Lisle!" exclaimed Kate, eagerly; "you never mentioned his name."

Mary put her hand to her brow and thought.

"I remember I did not," she said; "but it was of him I spoke."

"I thought you meant Colonel Lutwich," said Kate, gazing at her.

"Fool that I have been!" cried Mary; "oh, far more foolish than I thought; and, if I am miserable, it is my own fault."

"Oh, do not think so," replied Kate; "I trust you will be very, very happy, dear Mary; and you must try to be so, for you have every thing to brighten hope. I have no hope; and yet I will endeavor to be contented as far as possible, for that is a duty, and to brood over disappointments is a sin."

"But why no hope?" asked Mary; and, with kind and gentle persuasions, she won from poor Kate Malcolm some detail of the facts with which the reader has already been made acquainted. Kate did not, indeed, tell all distinctly; first, because it was too painful to pause long upon; and, secondly, because she thought it better to conceal the actual motives which had been held out to induce her to promise her hand to a man she abhorred. What she did tell she told truly; and she did not even hide from Mary that she was concealing something; but when she spoke of the transaction with Doctor Gamble, whom she represented, as she believed him to be, as a lawyer of the name of Brown, she merely said that he had proved to her most distinctly that the only means of saving Lutwich from an ignominious death was to give in writing the pledge he dictated. She wept a little, but not much, and then added, "I was thus obliged, dear Mary, to choose between leaving him to his terrible fate, and being separated from him by his death, or to sacrifice the remaining years of my life to a fate, compared with which my own death would be a blessing. And yet I felt that there was no choice either; that I was bound by every principle to one course—that, if I really loved him, there was no alternative."

"Oh, noble, dear, generous girl!" exclaimed Mary. "All I hope, Kate, is, that they have not deceived you, and led you to make such a sacrifice of yourself without an absolute necessity."

"Oh no!" replied Kate Malcolm; "of that I am certain. Some words which Lutwich himself let drop accidentally, showed me that this man had him entirely in his power; but it is only an aggravation of my misery to think that I am doomed to be the wife of one who could act so basely as he has done. Come in!" she added, hearing a knock at her room door; and a maid-servant entered with two letters. One bore a distant post-mark, the other none; and the first Kate opened immediately. The effect produced upon her may be imagined by the reader when he knows that it was the letter of Mr. Mullins which then met her eye, with Mary Chevenix sitting beside her. For an instant she felt stunned; but, the next moment, the habitual devotion of years lent her strength. She had so often been called upon at once to endure and to support, that it was nothing new. She folded the letter carefully and placed it beneath her pillow, gazing sadly at Mary with tearful eyes, and then thought, "No! her father must break it to her. My task is with Louisa—the bereaved indeed."

She had not voice to speak; and the other letter lay upon the bed unopened, with the address uppermost, till Mary pointed to it, saying, "That is surely my father's hand." Kate took it up and opened it mechanically. She read it twice, the first time unable to fix her attention so far as even to gather the meaning; but at length, with a feeling of relief, she saw that it afforded an excuse for terminating an interview which, burdened as she was with the terrible tidings of Reginald Lisle's fate, she feared to protract. The note was very brief, and in the following terms:

"Dear Miss Malcolm,—Will you do me the favor, as soon as you receive this, to put yourself into a post-chaise, and meet me at the house of Sir Harry Jarvis? Your presence there is absolutely needful; and I shall wait your coming, for I have news of importance for you, and not a moment is to be lost. If Mary is with you when this arrives, tell her to go home, and not wait dinner or sit up for me, as I do not know when I shall be able to quit Jarworth. Lose no time, my dear Kate, for you may be assured that, without necessity, you would not be thus hurried by,

"Your affectionate friend,

"Charles Chevenix."

"I must rise directly, Mary," said Kate, giving her Sir Charles's note to read; but Mary proposed a plan which Kate had not thought of, yet could not well decline. "Our carriage is at the door with post-horses," she said; "dress yourself at once, Kate, and come with me. You can set me down in Grosvenor Square, and then go on."

"I must speak with poor Louisa first," said Kate; "I may detain you some time; I have a bitter task to perform toward her."

"No new misfortune?" said Mary.

"Yes, indeed," replied Kate; but Mary had no clew to guide her fears to the truth; and Kate rose and dressed herself almost in silence, for her thoughts were very busy and her frame was weak.

When her toilet was complete, she left Mary for a few minutes, and sent for the old housekeeper, Mrs. Jones, into another room. Their conversation was very earnest; but the good woman dissuaded her strongly from even hinting the facts to Louisa till after Mrs. Lisle's funeral. "Pray do not, miss," she said, with tears in her eyes; "it would kill my poor young lady. If Mr. Mullins is angry, I will take all the blame, for I know her better than he does."

It was difficult for Kate to decide. She saw that, notwithstanding Mr. Mullins's assurance that there was no hope left, he still entertained some, however faint and doubtful; and she knew what a terrible thing long-protracted apprehension is. How was she, then, she asked herself, to prepare Louisa's mind for what might be the fatal truth, without inflicting upon her anguish more severe than even the truth itself would produce? She paused, therefore, some time, in doubt; and at length, calculating that the poor girl's uncle could not travel to Plymouth, and thence to London, and arrive before the following night, she resolved to defer all reference to the subject till after her return from Jarworth Park, which plan would, at least, afford time for deliberation. Announcing this determination to the housekeeper, she proceeded to inform Louisa of her sudden call to the house of Sir Harry Jarvis; and, promising to return as early as possible, she set out with Mary Chevenix.

Mary's mind was lightened by all that had passed between her and Kate; hope dawned again in her heart; and though she sympathized sincerely with her fair companion, yet the brighter coloring which had come over her own prospects communicated itself to the view she took of Kate's situation. Hoping for herself, she hoped for Kate too—that Lutwich would be saved; that something might be done to annul the fatal promise which had been given; that she might yet see Kate as happy as she deserved to be. She had no grounds for such hopes, it is true; but yet, when her own fate seemed to be suddenly cleared of its darkest clouds, she could not but dream that it might be so also with that of Kate Malcolm. Her cheerfulness, quiet as it was, was painful to Kate; and more than once she said to herself, "Oh, if Mary did but know the terrible secret of that letter! But it will be told her only too soon."

The journey to Jarworth Park seemed longer than ever; but at length it was accomplished, and as the carriage drove up to the house, Kate saw a post-chaise just pulling up at the door. A gentleman sprang out and rang the bell; and then, turning round, Sir Charles Chevenix approached the side of his own carriage in which she was, and said, "I have seen Lutwich, my dear. He told me to say he had received your note, but did not quite understand it."

"I am not surprised, Sir Charles," said Kate; "I fear it was hardly intelligible."

"Of that, more hereafter," said Sir Charles, in his usual rapid way; "now alight, my dear, and come with me. The servant is at the door, I see."

CHAPTER XLII.

Drawing Kate's arm through his own, Sir Charles Chevenix walked up to the door of Sir Harry Jarvis's house, at which by this time was standing his old butler, with another of his servants, while in the vestibule beyond appeared the same valet-looking man whom Kate had seen when last she was at Jarworth Park.

"Oh, Sir Charles, I am exceedingly glad to see you," said the butler; "my poor master is very ill still."

"Is he awake?" demanded Sir Charles Chevenix.

"I believe so, sir," replied the servant; "but I have not been permitted to see or attend upon him for several days."

"He is awake, sir," said the footman; "for, as I passed the door this minute, I heard him speaking."

"Then I will see him," said Sir Charles; and, turning toward Kate, he added, in a low voice, "there is something wrong here."

At that moment the valet advanced, saying, without any mark of want of respect, "I am sorry, sir, you can not see Sir Harry Jarvis, as I was directed to say that no one could be admitted to him in his present state except the medical men."

"Indeed!" replied Sir Charles, looking at him from head to foot; "and, pray, who may you be? Your face is new to me."

"I am Mr. Eaton's servant, sir," replied the man: "Mr. Eaton is Sir Harry's cousin."

"Oh, I know him!" replied Sir Charles Chevenix; "but now, my good fellow, have the kindness to get out of my way, for it is my intention to see Sir Harry Jarvis, my oldest and dearest friend, whether you, or Mr. Eaton, or any one else in the world says 'Nay.'"

"I can not permit it, sir," said the man, still standing before him; "my orders are distinct."

"Are they?" said Sir Charles, slipping Kate's arm out of his own, and advancing upon the valet. "Now, sir, my orders to you are distinct. Out of the way this instant!"

The man remained firm, however; there was a step and a voice heard upon the landing-place above; and with one blow Sir Charles knocked the valet backward upon the large mat at the foot of the stairs.

At the same moment a thin, gentleman-like man, with an exceedingly keen, sharp-looking face, came down with a quick step, exclaiming, "What is all this? Sir Charles Chevenix! I am astonished, sir!"

"And so am I, Mr. Eaton," replied the baronet, "most exceedingly astonished that any one with your authority should attempt to prevent my entrance into the house of my oldest and dearest friend. I have, however, removed the impediment, and shall now go and see him: come, Kate, my dear."

"I must beg to say you can not, Sir Charles," replied Mr. Eaton, who had cast one glance to the face of Kate Malcolm, which was quite sufficient, however, to make him turn first very pale and then very red; "Sir Harry is sleeping, and must not be woke on any account. Perfect tranquillity, the physicians assure me, is absolutely necessary to his recovery. You can not, and you shall not disturb him."

"Shall not, sir!" exclaimed Sir Charles, with his eyes flashing: "think yourself lucky I do not throw you out of that door upon the drive."

"Sir, you shall be brought to account for this conduct!" cried Mr. Eaton, bristling up and looking very fierce.

"Whenever you please, Mr. Eaton," replied Sir Charles; "in an hour or two hence, if you like. In the mean while, you will have the goodness to move out of my way. Sir Harry Jarvis is awake—of that I already have information."

"But, sir, you are not aware—" said the

other, still keeping his place upon the last step of the stairs.

"I am aware of more than you imagine, Mr. Eaton," replied the baronet. "Now, sir, I should be very sorry to use your nose as a handle for leading you out of the house, but I shall be compelled to do so if you detain me one instant longer."

"Well, sir, well," cried the other; "you are responsible for the consequences to Sir Harry Jarvis, and shall be answerable to me for your language and ungentlemanly conduct. I am not disposed to increase the uproar you have already made in this house by opposing your mad and cruel proceedings further;" and he moved out of the way with a sullen air.

"Come, Kate," said Sir Charles, turning round; but as Kate, with a trembling and agitated frame, was following, the old butler stepped forward, and taking the letter she had given him out of his pocket, he said, "I have been prevented, ma'am, by that gentleman, from delivering this to Sir Harry, and received warning from him—which I do not choose to take—even for taking it from you, having been watched when you gave it."

"You are an impudent scoundrel!" exclaimed Mr. Eaton, vehemently; but, without taking any further notice of that gentleman, Sir Charles said, "Bring the letter with you, my dear. It may be needful. You follow us to the door of your master's room, my good fellow, and see that we are not interrupted."

"Oh, I have no intention of interrupting you, sir," said Mr. Eaton; "at least not at present. That young woman, however, may find her proceedings checked when she least expects it."

Kate's spirit rose. She remembered her father and that man's conduct toward him; and, looking him full in the face, she said, "For shame, sir! for shame!"

A reply seemed struggling to his lips, but he turned upon his heel suddenly, and, beckoning to his valet, walked into the library.

"A sharp engagement, my dear Kate," said Sir Charles, in a low tone, as he led her up the stairs; "but a complete victory, I trust. The field is clear of the enemy, at all events."

"I really do not understand it at all," said Kate.

"You will understand more presently," replied her gallant friend; "at present we must lose no time, for we can not depend upon the account of Sir Harry's health;" and he quietly approached a mahogany door at the end of the wide corridor in which they now were. "Keep a little behind me, Kate, but come in," he said; and then, turning the handle of the lock very gently, he opened the door.

The curtains of the room were partly drawn, and the windows were open to admit the air. There was sufficient light to display every thing in the room, which presented the ordinary aspect of a sick-chamber, with a large, massive, four-post bed at the further side, from which a nurse was just withdrawing with a teacup in her hand.

"Some one came in—who is that?" said a feeble voice from the bed; and, while the woman stared, Sir Charles advanced with a quick step, saying, "It is I, Jarvis—your old friend Chevenix. I thought you would be glad to see me, and that the face of an old companion could do you no harm: so I forced my way up, in spite of all sorts of remonstrances."

"I am delighted, Chevenix," said Sir Harry Jarvis, in a glad tone; "this is very kind of you, indeed. It will do me more good than all the medicines in the world. The foolish doctor wrote to Eaton when I was first attacked, and he has come up, and bores me to death."

Kate, as she stood near the door, could see Sir Charles Chevenix smile gayly as he sat down by the bedside. "Well, Jarvis, you do not seem so ill, after all," he said, leaning over the bed; "let us have a little more light, my good woman. I want to see my old friend's face somewhat better. You can bear a little more light, I dare say."

"Oh yes! the light does not hurt me," said the old baronet; "but do not lean over me or touch me, Chevenix. They say the fever is very infectious. I have been seriously ill; but I am somewhat better now, my dear boy, though weak as an infant—weaker than you were as an infant, for I recollect, when I had you in my arms at your christening, you kicked so that I could hardly hold you;" and the old man laughed.

"Well, you look better than I expected," said his friend, as some more light was admitted; "you'll do very well now, and we'll soon get your strength up."

"Seventy-three! seventy-three! my dear boy," said Sir Harry; "no getting over that disease, Charles," replied Sir Harry, but not at all sadly.

"Won't you take a seat, miss?" said the nurse, putting a chair for Kate.

"Who is that?" exclaimed the sick man; "have you got any one with you? Is it Mary?"

"No, not Mary," replied Sir Charles, "but one who is nearer and should be dearer to you, my dear friend, than Mary. It is Kate;" and he beckoned her forward.

"Keep away! keep away!" cried Sir Harry, as soon as she approached within his sight; "the fever is very infectious. Chevenix, you are mad."

"I am not at all afraid of it," said Kate, advancing quietly and gracefully.

"But I am for you, my dear young lady," said Sir Harry; "but what is it you mean, Charles? Nearer and dearer to me! A hint of the same kind was given to me before; but I made inquiries, and—"

"They were frustrated by a prearranged plan," replied Sir Charles Chevenix. "I neither wish to hurt any one, nor to prejudge any questions which I trust you will soon have an opportunity of investigating for yourself. But, in the mean time, I assure you—and you will take my word, I know—that this is Kate Malcolm, the only child of your favorite niece, who married, while you were in India, Ensign Marsham, of the Twenty-third. He afterward took the name of Malcolm, by permission of the crown, the warrant for which I have seen this day at the Herald's College."

"But the register of her burial as Lucy Marsham was shown to me," said Sir Harry; "she never took the name of Malcolm."

"No," replied Sir Charles, "but her husband and her daughter did. The warrant authorizes Frederic Marsham and his daughter Catharine, by his marriage with Lucy Carr, deceased, to take and assume the name and arms of Malcolm, and it is dated fourteen years ago, when this dear child was barely five years old."

"If that be any proof," said Kate, in a low, quiet tone—though she was much agitated, as the reader may suppose—"I have here Mr. Eaton's letter, in which he calls me 'cousin.'"

"The proof is there," said Sir Harry, raising his thin, pale hand, and pointing to her face; "I saw it from the first hour I beheld her: but what a villain this man must be! He always led me to believe that my poor Lucy had died without a child, a few years after her marriage, and that Marsham was dead too. But now, my dear Kate, go away into another room; you have been here too long already. Mrs. Ward, give her some of that stuff William Eaton uses to prevent infection."

"I have no fear, indeed," said Kate; "and do forgive me, my dear uncle, if I prove disobedient to your first commands. I am resolved to stay and help this good lady to nurse you till you are quite well. I am accustomed to nursing—indeed I am; and Mr. Eaton, I am sure, will not have the heart to prevent me."

"He will not have the power," said Sir Harry, with a bitter smile, which sat strangely upon his mild and gentle features: "he has imposed upon me, and tried to wrong you; but that is past, and he shall now quit my house. Well, stay, my child, stay, since you desire it. I trust God will not take you from me now."

"Shall I go and turn him out?" asked Sir Charles Chevenix.

"No, no, Charles," said the old man; "the physician and apothecary will soon be here, and they shall carry my message. They will be glad of it; for the good doctor was very angry at his preventing me from having the quantity of wine ordered when the complaint was at the worst. He pretended he thought it would heat me—and it saved my life. There is the doctor's carriage, I believe."

He was silent, and the whole party listened; but the carriage wheels seemed to roll away from, rather than to the house, and a moment after the sick man said, "I wish you would see for my old butler Dixon, Charles. I am afraid he must be ill; he has not been near me for three or four days."

"Mr. Eaton would not let him in, your worship," said the nurse. "He declared his shoes made such a creaking, it disturbed you."

"I rather think he was more afraid of the creaking of a certain letter in his pocket," said Sir Charles, rising; "for Kate was here three or four days ago, it seems, and gave Dixon a letter for you, from poor Lutwich, who hunted out all the facts. However, Dixon is now keeping guard at the door."

The old servant was called in, and approached the side of his master's bed with tears in his eyes. "I am very glad indeed, Sir Harry, to see your honor so much better," said the man, after gazing a moment in his face. "You look quite a different man."

"I am much better, my good old friend," replied the baronet; "but, as one can never tell what may happen from moment to moment, be so good, Dixon, as to tell John, the groom, to ride over to Barnet as fast as he can go, and bring me, in a post-chaise, Mr. Groves, the attorney. Tell him that I wish to make a new will, for I find I have been imposed upon, Dixon. Let him bring his clerk with him for a witness. I thought I heard the doctor's carriage—who was it?"

"It was Mr. Eaton, your worship," said the butler, with a broad grin. "Mr. Eaton and his valet, that Sir Charles knocked down because he would not let him see you. They knew the game was up as soon as he did see you, and so they took themselves off—Mr. Hicks with a precious black eye."

"Chevenix, Chevenix!" said Sir Harry, "you are always too hasty. Did not Mr. Eaton leave a letter or message for me, Dixon?"

"He only said, sir, that he would not remain in a house where he had been so insulted," replied the butler, "and that he would write to your honor."

"Well, well, send the groom, Dixon, as I have said," answered his master. "I shall, of course, be willing to hear reason; but I do not see, I confess, how his conduct and his words can be explained otherwise than as a gross imposition. And now, my dear niece, you go with Dixon and get some refreshment. You look very pale, my love—much paler than when you were here before. This is my grand-niece, Dixon; look upon her as your future mistress."

"She's wonderful like poor Miss Lucy, Sir Harry," said the old butler; "I thought so from the first, and told Mrs. Williams so. Lord! how well I remember Miss Lucy, when I was under-footman at your father's, and what a pretty girl she was, and what a nice young lady too—every one loved her."

"This is her child," said Sir Harry, wiping away a tear from his eyes. "Now go, my love, go with him. I want to speak with Chevenix, and get him to make a memorandum or two for me. I have not been able to do any thing since that man has been in the house."

"I may come back again soon?" asked Kate.

The invalid made a movement of assent with a bland smile, and she left him.

When she and the butler were in the corridor, the old man seemed quite overpowered by his feelings. He took her hand, and kissed it; but words failed him, and only muttering, "God bless you, God bless you!" he hurried down the stairs and disappeared. Kate found her way alone to the drawing-room, where more than one little incident of the past flashed back upon memory with one of those strange pangs which dart across the breast, as if an arrow were shot into it, when things gone present themselves in painful contrast with the present. It may be asked if she had been happier when there before, a mere dependent upon the bounty of strangers, without one being upon earth on whom she seemed to have any real claim, than now, the near relation of a kind and excellent man of great wealth, who acknowledged her with pride and pleasure? All her fate seemed totally changed, indeed, except in this one essential point of happiness, that strange chameleon gift varying under every circumstance of human life, different in different men, different in the same man at different periods, fixed and firm often in the midst of earthquake mutabilities, and yet changing, fading, vanishing, lost, under external alterations, which would seem to superficial eyes as mere dust and emptiness —the harmony of the heart, which one note out of tune will turn to discord.

Kate sat down, and wept with a long, painful, despairing flood of tears.

There were, however, certain principles in her heart which, however much she might be moved at times, always soon reasserted their sway. There were things which she considered duties; and yet she was not one of those cold slaves of formal precepts who act by rule, neglecting all the tenderer emotions, and the bright, real charities of life, in order to guide their conduct by a rigid measure. In truth, she extended far her notion of duties, taking in many things that the duty-mongers would judge superfluous. Kindness, gentleness, meekness, patience, forgiveness, forgetfulness of injuries, candor, frankness, love for her fellow-creatures, efforts to make them happy, abstinence from all that could pain unnecessarily, or wound by a light word, she looked upon as duties, full as much as truth and honor, justice and probity. We are very apt to select our duties in this world, and that, too, with a partial eye. Kate looked to her Savior's words for those she was to practice, and tried at least to perform all which his words inculcated or implied.

After she had given way to her tears for a few minutes, she suddenly wiped them away. "I must write to Louisa. I can not, I ought not to quit my uncle till he is somewhat better; but perhaps I can see her to-morrow for a few hours. I must tell Sir Charles Chevenix, too, of poor Captain Lisle's unhappy fate, and beg him to break it to Mary—perhaps to Louisa also. Lutwich, too, I must write to; he did not understand that incoherent note I sent. But I had better not tell him all till the trial is over, lest he should do some rash thing in despair. God give me strength to go through all this!" and, seeking for writing materials, she commenced her task at once, and was still so employed when the old butler and another servant brought her in some refreshment.

Kate felt a loathing of the food set before her, however; and though she forced down a mouthful, and took some wine when the men were gone, she could do no more, and recommenced the writing of her letters. As she went on, she heard more than one carriage drive up to the house; but no one disturbed her; and when she had concluded, she rang to inquire if she could return to the room of her uncle.

"He has got the two doctors and the lawyer with him, ma'am," said the butler; and Kate was obliged to rest satisfied. At length, however, just when the change had taken place in the landscape which announces that day is merging into evening, she heard steps approaching, and Sir Charles Chevenix, with three other gentlemen, entered the room. Her kind friend took her paternally in his arms, and kissed her.

"I wish you joy, my dear Kate," he said; "you are now, beyond all doubt and cavil, the heiress of my good friend Sir Harry; to the principal part of his landed estates in virtue of the entail, which, failing his issue, conveys them to you as the representative of his eldest sister; and to all his large personal property, in virtue of his will just signed. It is so simple that there can be no dispute; for ten lines, and a codicil referring to a few legacies, have done it all."

"But he is better?" asked Kate, eagerly looking to a grave man, whom she supposed to be the physician. "He will recover—oh! he will recover, will he not?"

"I trust so, madam," replied the physician. "With very careful nursing, I see every probability of his doing so."

"Leave her to nurse him," said Sir Charles Chevenix, "and he will soon be well enough."

After a few words more with the physician and the lawyer, Sir Charles Chevenix was left alone with Kate, who charged him with her letter to Louisa, and then proceeded to tell him the intelligence conveyed to her by Mr. Mullins. Much to her relief, she found that Sir Charles was not altogether unprepared for such tidings.

"I saw a rumor of the kind," he said, "in the morning paper, before I left the house to-day; but I would not tell Mary, my dear Kate, nor will I, unless at your particular desire, say any thing on the subject to Miss Lisle. Misfortunes never come too late, my dear girl; and when one must slay hope, it is better to do it at one blow than by slow torture. I was myself killed twice while I was in active service, and Lady Chevenix has since assured me that nothing could exceed the suffering she underwent during long alternations of hope and fear. Poor Lisle may yet be living, although it is certain that the *London* was run down a few nights ago by the *Russell*, and that a great number of persons perished. Let us have accurate information before we say any thing, and let us also trust that others will not carry the news to poor Miss Lisle till it is fully confirmed."

Kate could not but own that her opinion coincided with his, and Sir Charles went on in a kindly tone to speak of her own appearance, and to urge her to take care of herself. She had no heart to enter into any explanations, nor, indeed, to make any promises, for she felt that health of body could hardly be expected when peace of mind was gone. She would fain have asked questions regarding Lutwich too; but her voice failed her, and she was glad to fly from subjects which produced so many emotions, by proposing to return to the chamber of Sir Harry Jarvis.

I must now confine myself to a brief summary of the events affecting poor Kate Malcolm, which took place during the next fortnight or three weeks; for, as the reader may perceive, the work is waning to its close, and this inexorable volume is nearly at an end. For the two next days, Kate tended her sick relation with the utmost care and tenderness, passing the greater part of every day, and a part of every night, by his bedside. The wearied nurse thus had more opportunities of repose, and, when the period of her watch came, of course performed her duties better.

In these circumstances, Sir Harry Jarvis rallied rapidly, and on the third day of Kate's attendance the physician declared that all danger of a relapse had passed away. He even sat up for some hours in bed, and declared that his rapid progress was entirely attributable to his dear Kate; and, in truth, the joy of finding her might have something to do with it. The morning of that third day, however, was a very anxious one for poor Kate Malcolm; for the second examination of Colonel Lutwich had taken place on the preceding evening, and she had not heard the result. About twelve, a brief note arrived from Sir Charles Chevenix, telling her that he would be at Jarworth in the afternoon, and informing her that, although the principal witness was still absent, and the bulk of evidence was given in favor of the prisoner, the magistrate had determined to commit him for trial.

"This, perhaps, is quite as well for Lutwich," said Sir Charles, in conclusion, "for no jury can convict upon such evidence, and, once acquitted, he can never be troubled on the subject again."

The last words were certainly some consolation to poor Kate; but, nevertheless, the depression of her spirits seemed rather increasing than diminishing throughout the whole of that morning. Her head ached violently, too; a terrible, overpowering languor spread over all her frame. Slowly and with difficulty she dragged herself from place to place; and as she was sitting by the bedside of Sir Harry, while the physician was speaking to him, a fit of shuddering seized her which she could not restrain. The eye of the medical man was upon her at the moment; and, after having said all he had to say to his patient, he came round and felt her pulse.

His face was very grave while he did so; but in the end, he said, in a quiet tone, "If you will take my advice, my dear young lady, you will go to bed. You have fatigued yourself too much, and got a little cold. Sir Harry can quite well spare you, for to-morrow I shall let him rise for a few hours, and by timely care you may save yourself from a very bad cold."

"Perhaps it would be as well," replied Kate, who felt the impossibility of sitting up any longer, "if my dear uncle can really spare me."

Sir Harry took alarm immediately, and sent her to her room at once, asking the physician earnestly if he thought she was seriously ill. But the man of healing was also a very prudent man, and he replied according to the usual form, "No, I trust not—only a little cold." But when he quitted his patient's room, he called the nurse out, and with a very serious air inquired whether she felt herself able to go through the attendance upon another case. Significant looks passed between the doctor and the nurse; but the latter replied, "I dare say I can, sir. Do you think she has caught it?"

"Beyond a doubt," answered the physician; "she was apparently depressed and agitated when first she saw him, poor thing! and though she seems to have had no fear, yet she has now the fever upon her. Remember, however, Mrs. Ward, not a word to Sir Harry! If he inquires, say that it is a severe cold; tell him she is better—any thing rather than let him know for some days how ill she is."

"Is it a bad kind, do you think, sir?" inquired the nurse.

"I should think it may prove a much more severe case than his," answered the physician, "from the sharp and sudden rigors I observed. Upon second thoughts, I had better send another attendant, while you remain with Sir Harry; for I should not wonder if violent delirium were to come on to-night, and he must not know that you are wanted. Go and see if she is in bed, and I will come and speak with her."

As he prognosticated, before eleven o'clock that night Kate Malcolm's consciousness of all around her was at an end, and she was raving in that frightful delirium which attends the worst class of typhus fever. Wild and horrible fancies presented themselves to her mind, and all that was painful in her situation was constantly present, aggravated by the imaginings of a disturbed intellect. She strove to rise; she raved of Lutwich and Sir Theodore Broughton; she thought she beheld the one at the place of execution, and the other standing by her bedside. Gradually, however, with decreasing powers, the violence of her demeanor abated; low, incoherent mutterings succeeded; her long, delicate fingers picked at unseen objects on the bed-clothes; and, at the end of nine days, she fell into a state in which the flame of life hovered so faintly over the expiring lamp, that it was hardly possible to say whether she lived or not.

The physician himself had sat up with her during the whole of that night. It was the ninth; and the two nurses, as well as Sir Harry Jarvis—now well, though weak, and aware of her situation—stood round her bed. The doctor's hand was on the pulse, expecting, in truth, to find the faint, fluttering, hardly-perceptible thread cease to vibrate altogether. Suddenly, however, he felt a more distinct stroke, and then another. "Go and get me some brandy, Mrs. Ward," he said; "here is a slight reaction, which must be encouraged: make haste!"

The woman ran away with all speed, and brought what was required. A teaspoonful was poured between the dry and parched lips, and an involuntary movement of the throat to swallow was seen; another spoonful, and another, were given; and then the physician put his hand upon the pulse again. Now, for the first time, he looked at Sir Harry Jarvis with a smile. "There is an improvement," he said; "slight, but decided."

The old man made no reply, but, seating himself, continued to gaze upon her unconscious face for more than half an hour. "Does she not breathe more regularly?" he asked, at length, in a low voice.

"I think so," replied the physician, "and with a fuller inspiration."

"I think she is asleep," said the nurse; "you need not be afraid of waking her, for she got so deaf yesterday evening I could hardly make her hear."

"Indeed!" said the physician, with a well-satisfied look. "Now mix some of the brandy with equal parts of water."

Another quarter of an hour went by; the physician felt the pulse frequently, and once or twice put his ear down to listen to the respiration. At length he went round to the other side of the bed, and laid his hand upon Sir Harry's arm, saying, "Now, my dear sir, you had better retire to rest. A favorable change has certainly taken place; and I will remain to watch her, and administer the remedies myself, till noon, when I have an engagement."

"Is she safe?" asked the old man, fixing his eyes upon him.

"I hope and trust she is," said the doctor; "safety, however, is only God's giving. We will do our best under his will. Every symptom, however, shows a tendency to improvement; and with care, I am very confident of the result."

"Then see me before you go," said Sir Harry; and he retired to give thanks and to take some repose.

"How is she now?" asked the old man, entering Kate's room at a little after eleven.

"Sleeping as calmly as an infant," replied the physician; "the breathing, regular and calm; the pulse, slow and fuller: come and see. If we lose her now, it must be our own fault; but it has been the narrowest race between life and death I almost ever saw."

Life won it, however.

CHAPTER XLIII.

THERE was a ship sailing over the dark sea. Slowly it passed on through the waves, for the wind from the northwest, though not absolutely contrary, favored its progress but little. There were no stormy billows around it, though the large, heavy swell of the Atlantic where it meets the waters of St. George's Channel heaved it up and down as if it had been a feather on the bosom of the waters. Yet it was a goodly bark of many hundred tons burden, nearly new from the ship-builder's hands, and laden with a precious freight of human life. She was not a royal vessel, but nevertheless armed and manned as a ship of war; and with every sail set to catch the light breeze, she plowed her way onward toward the Far West.

The moon was still far below the horizon, for she rose very late, and there was a heavy mass of low cloud overhead; the feathery fringe of that dark veil, sometimes descending in mist till it swept the sea beneath, made the lamp over the compass glare like a hazy meteor. Yet, if the heaven denied its stars, the ocean seemed to have its lights; for ever and anon, as the waves broke upon the vessel's sides, flashes of fire, as they seemed, would spangle the foamy tide, and suddenly disappear. But still all was black, and solemn, and silent around; and there was something strange, and dream-like, and unreal in finding one's self borne thus stilly onward in the midst of that inscrutable darkness, over that wide and gloomy swell of waters. The rush, and the ripple, and the faint whisper of the wind amid the rigging were the only sounds; and the sights were but the phosphorescent sparkle of the waves, the glare of the lamp, and a phantom-like form walking here and there upon the deck.

Many were the emotions of which that ship had been the scene within the last few hours. There were some voyagers setting out with joy to meet friends, and relatives, and love long parted from; and some instinct with hope of brighter fortunes in a distant land; and some moved with yearnings for change; and some with high ambitions and aspirations for wealth, distinction, or renown. But, except the watch upon the deck, almost all had retired to the hammock or the close small berth, to dream that they were in the midst of happy meetings over the wide sea, or that they were still in their own homes, or that they were reaping glory, or winning wealth, or tasting some one or other of the sweet and bitter fruits of life.

A few, however, of the passengers still paced the deck, mostly keeping silence, as if in reverence of the solemn stillness round, and among the rest were two who had joined the vessel just on the eve of her sailing, who walked up and down with a steady step, as if not unaccustomed to the plank upon the sea. But if there was deep darkness in the air, there was a more oppressive night in the heart of Reginald Lisle; for the star of hope had gone out for him, and when he set his foot upon the ship's deck, he felt as if he had bidden adieu to happiness forever—as if he went with all the ties of human affection broken, a lonely struggler with Fate, to fight the fight with utter indifference to all things but his country's honor, perhaps to win, perhaps to lose, perhaps to live, perhaps to die, but without one personal feeling mingling in the motives.

Sometimes a few words passed between him and his companion, but they both soon fell into thought again; sometimes Reginald would pause, and, leaning over the bulwark, gaze down upon the turbulent waters rushing by, while his friend prolonged his steady course toward the stern, wrapped, like himself, in thought, but lighter far in the tone of his meditations; sometimes Brandrum would stop and speak to him, and then, receiving a short reply, would walk on again.

"I wonder if the great Moose is living yet?" said the old officer, pausing for a moment in one of his walks.

"Dead, most likely," was the reply; and on he went.

"Scalped, in all probability," Brandrum rejoined, at his next turn.

"I dare say he is," said Reginald; and the colonel pursued his way.

"I wish I had been born an Indian," said the colonel, a minute or two after.

"You do quite as well without," replied Reginald Lisle; "it were better to wish one had never been born at all."

"Pooh, pooh! my dear boy," said his friend, stopping; "all comes right in the end."

"By death," said the young man.

"Halloo! steersman! you fellow at the wheel!" shouted Brandrum, the next moment, in a voice that would have drowned a tempest, "what the devil is that upon our weather-bow!"

A mate who was upon watch caught a rope, and jumped upon one of the bulwarks; but at the same instant a bell was heard ringing, loud and sharp, at a little distance, and through the darkness of the misty night, sweeping down right upon them, appeared, dim and gigantic, like some enormous specter, the bows and bowsprit of a large ship, towering high above the deck of the ill-fated *London*.

Loud cries, commands, shouts, oaths, were heard, and various things were done, or attempted, which would be tedious and useless to describe. In vain—it was all in vain, or only served to render the disaster more fatal.

Driving on, the monster of the deep, becoming each second more distinct, came forward against the weather side of the barque, which was now brought right athwart her. The bowsprit passed over the bulwarks—tore through shrouds and rigging—grazed the main-mast. Then came a violent concussion, which threw the stoutest men off their feet, accompanied by a loud, crashing sound of breaking timbers, and then, heeling to one side, the deck was covered with water.

The noise, the tumult, in both vessels was beyond description. Ropes, buoys, hen-coops, were thrown from the man-of-war, as on she drove in her merciless course, crushing the merchant vessel down into the waves.

"Lisle! Lisle! are you safe?" cried the voice of Colonel Brandrum, as he was pulled up by a rope thrown from the larger vessel.

Lisle did not answer: he looked round—a feeling of despair was upon him. There were hundreds perishing to whom life was precious: why should he struggle, to whom existence was a burden? He saw a half-clothed figure running up from the cabin: it was the last thing he beheld distinctly; the water dashed over him, he was swept from his feet, and the next moment felt himself sucked down as if in the vortex of a whirlpool. The ill-fated *London* had gone to the bottom, with all its freight of hopes and fears, desires and aspirations.

The instinct of self-preservation, however, is most strong. For a few seconds the heavy waves rolled over Reginald Lisle's head; but then he rose, and instantly, without knowing or willing it, struck out with strength and skill. He was an expert and practiced swimmer, and the impulse was not to be resisted. Ere he had swam half a dozen yards, and before he had fully recovered thought, his hand struck against something hard. It was a hen-coop, and he clutched it tight. It rolled round with his weight; but he held fast, and soon found means to make it serviceable. Untying his cravat, he contrived to bind himself to it in such a manner as to keep his head and shoulders above water, without spending his strength in any further exertion than was necessary to prevent the coop from being rolled over by the waves. But the sea, as I have said, was not rough, and such small objects as the man and the frail wood-work that supported him were raised upon the bosom of the long swell, hardly feeling it.

Reginald had now time for thought, and better feelings had regained their influence. The remembrance of duties came back, the voice of Faith and Hope was heard in the midst of the waters. "If I perish, it shall be by God's will, not my own fault," he said. "Thank Heaven, Brandrum is safe! I saw him hauled up the ship's side."

His next thoughts turned to the chances of deliverance; and, first, he looked out for the vessel which had caused the disaster, thinking that she might probably bring-to (as indeed she did), in order to pick up any of the crew of the *London* who might be floating about. But the mist was still upon the sea, and the speed with which the *Russell* was going before a fair wind could not be stopped for some minutes. Reginald could see nothing of her. He knew, however, by the small way the *London* had made through the water, and by the objects he had seen just before sunset, that he could not be far from the mouth of the Bristol Channel, and he trusted that some of the many vessels continually leaving or returning to the port might come within hail after daylight. Luckily, the year was now so far advanced that night was not of long duration, and his sufferings were less than they might have been, had the accident occurred in the cold season of winter. In about an hour, or a little more, the mist cleared away, and the stars shone out clear and bright over head. In another hour they grew paler, and a faint gray light spread over the sky, showing Reginald where the east lay. That was something gained; but he now found that he was drifting to the southwest. At length the sun rose—oh, how calmly and beautifully!—and he could perceive to the eastward a low grayish line against the burning sky. It might be cloud, it might be land. He looked around to see if he had any companions in misfortune near. There was a barrel floating not far off, another hen-coop, and several pieces of timber, heaving up and down upon the bosom of the swell, but no living thing. An oar, which had been swept out of one of the ship's boats, then drifted by, and he contrived to catch it, and fasten his handkerchief to the end of it as a sort of flag of distress. He raised it up; but he was exhausted and dispirited; the oar was heavy, and he was forced to let the end fall again, and support itself upon the water. About three quarters of an hour passed by without his seeing any thing more, except some sea-birds rapidly skimming along, close to the waves, and then the swell heaved him up as on the ridge of a rounded hill.

"A ship! a ship!" and now, with better hope, he raised his signal as high as he could.

The ship sailed straight upon her course, coming nearer, it is true, for her path over the waters led her across that along which he was slowly borne, but at the distance of full half a mile. He could see no change whatever, and he did feel disappointment; but yet I must not ascribe to him feelings which he did not experience, in order to give deeper interest to my narrative. Reginald had not yet learned to value life so fully as to make the alternation of hope and fear very powerful. He watched the vessel, indeed, as he rose and fell upon the swell, with some degree of eagerness, but there are few men in his situation would have felt less.

Still there was a sensation of joy when he saw a sudden change of her course, and became convinced, from various indications, familiar to his eyes from having frequently voyaged far, that he was seen and she was bringing-to.

In five or ten minutes more he was on the deck of a brig of-war; but the language spoken all around him was French. He was well accustomed to the tongue, however, and spoke it almost as well as a native; for, during a long residence in Canada, it had been the tongue which he had principally been called upon to use. Every thing that kindness and courtesy could do to comfort and restore him was done, for the French were at that period the most polished people upon earth. A fierce revolution had not yet swept away, with a dark mass of evils, the courtesies and amenities of life. Many were the questions asked him, indeed, and much was the talking round him; but, though his dress bespoke him a British officer, and actual, though not yet declared, hostilities were taking place between France and England, yet he was treated with the utmost suavity and politeness. Dry clothes were found for him, food and wine were freely given, and the commander of the brig promised to put him on shore at the first French port, whence he could procure a passage for his own country. He was as good as his word, too; and, after a sojourn of three very pleasant days on board the brig, Lisle was landed at Calais, and the next day, without any of those lets and hinderances which would occur in the present time to a person so circumstanced, he obtained a passage in a packet-boat to Dover.

A voyage across the Channel in those days was not what it is now; neither had steamboats bridged the waves, nor had they egged on sailing vessels to go at tolerable speed out of pure emulation. Very often twelve mortal hours were consumed in going from the French to the English port, and sometimes nineteen, as the writer has known to his cost. On the present occasion the wind was fair but light, the day fine, the sea smooth; and Reginald Lisle—tell it not to the lovers of pure romance, or those who are fond of what is called, in the present day, "powerful writing"—Reginald Lisle did feel, and did acknowledge to himself, that it was much more comfortable to stand upon a dry, secure deck in the free sunshine, than to cling to a frail collection of planks and laths immersed in the wild waters, even though his heart was still heavy, and his thoughts sad with a bitter disappointment of the brightest of all early hopes.

He was pacing the small space of deck, on which were but few of the few passengers, and perhaps he might be thinking of Mary Chevenix—perhaps he might ask himself if she had heard the rumor, which he doubted not had spread, of his death—perhaps he might long to know if she had shed a tear or two over his supposed fate, and had regretted what he could not but call the caprice she had displayed—when suddenly a man of gentlemanly appearance was seen coming up the companion ladder, and the next moment Captain Donovan stood before him, gazing round with a look of indifference. His eye passed over Reginald; but, for a moment, either from absence of mind or some other cause, he did not seem to recognize him. The next instant, however, he gazed fixedly at him, and exclaimed, with a start, "Good Heaven! Major Lisle! Do my eyes deceive me? Not two days have passed since I received this letter, telling me that you had been lost in the unfortunate *London;*" and he produced from his pocket a soiled and ill-folded epistle, addressed in a very cramp and vulgar hand.

"Such a report might well get abroad, Captain Donovan," replied Lisle, somewhat coldly, "for I was several hours in the water, supported by a hen-coop, and was at last picked up by a French vessel, in which I was obliged to remain for several days. May I ask who thought it worth while to give you intelligence of the assumed fate of so insignificant a person as myself?"

Donovan colored a little, but replied, "It was Hargrave, a servant in attendance upon Sir Theodore Broughton;" and seeing Reginald turn, as if to pursue his walk up and down the deck, Donovan, for some reason or another, walked on at his side.

It is difficult to escape from a fellow-passenger on board a packet-boat without palpable rudeness, and, although Lisle did not like the man, and would have been well content to be rid of his company, he was forced to endure it.

Donovan, for his part, mused for several minutes; and then, seeming to have settled the plan of his speech—for speeches, even in common conversation, have often plans, as the reader learned in the heart may know—he said, somewhat abruptly, "Do you know, Major Lisle, there is more that may in some degree be interesting to you in that letter than the mere news of your own death?"

"That is a subject in which I take very little interest," replied Lisle, with a faint smile. "What more, Captain Donovan?"

"I am here informed," replied the other, raising the letter, which he still held in his hand, "that it is one of the goodly schemes of my young and troublesome ward, Sir Theodore Broughton, to marry a young lady named Miss Catharine Malcolm, in whom, I believe, you do feel a great interest."

"Decidedly," replied Reginald; "but I should strongly suspect, Captain Donovan, that it is not, by any means, one of her schemes to marry him. Make your mind easy upon that score. No such ill-assorted match is at all likely to mar your views for your ward. I do not believe, if he had the wealth of the Indies, Miss Malcolm would condescend to marry Sir Theodore Broughton, after having been insulted by him as she has been."

"I am happy to hear you say so," replied Donovan, in an altered tone; "it may save me from some embarrassment, as I have business which calls me to another part of the country; and yet I should have thought it a duty to go immediately to London, to stop such rash proceedings. I may, I suppose, depend upon your view of the case."

"You may depend upon what I say being my view of the case," answered Lisle; "and more, my dear sir, you may depend upon it that Colonel Brandrum—who must be now in London, as he was taken into the vessel which ran us down—will oppose such a union as you have mentioned to the utmost of his power, for, however light and careless he may have seemed to you, he is one who values honor and integrity above all wealth or station. He has a right, also, to oppose, as he promised the young lady's father, on his death-bed, to be a parent to his orphan child."

"You are somewhat severe upon my young ward," said Captain Donovan; "but, having these assurances, I shall not make myself uneasy;" and, indeed, during the rest of the journey he seemed greatly relieved. But Captain Donovan was not a man to trust to any guarantees but his own observation.

Before the boat reached the port of Dover, he had disappeared below the deck again, and Lisle certainly did not look for him to bid him adieu. As the young officer was passing up to the hotel, however, something caused him to turn back his head, and he beheld his late traveling companion, with a pretty-looking French woman on his arm. He turned his head away instantly, and pursued his course.

Dover was one of those places which, at the time I speak of, possessed a stage-coach traveling to and from London, and, as the money which was in Reginald's purse when the ship went down was not great in amount, he preferred the cheaper conveyance to the more comfortable and solitary one. The coach set out, on its return to the capital, about five o'clock, and, accomplishing the journey in eighteen hours, reached London at eleven on the following day. Nothing occurred on the road worthy of commemoration, unless it were that, while changing horses at Dartford, a post-chaise passed the vehicle on its way to town, and Reginald, who had got out to relieve himself from his cramped position in the coach, saw clearly that, notwithstanding all he had said, Captain Donovan was on his way to the great city.

In London, Lisle's first visit was to the Horse Guards, where he was detained some time. His next was to his agent's; not to transact business, for to relieve the anxieties of the dear who doubted, and to wipe away the tears of those who grieved, was his first care after duty. But he knew that it must be done cautiously, and therefore he wished to engage Mr. ——, in the first place, to go down and state to his mother and sister that some of the passengers in the *London* had been picked up at sea. The tidings that now met his ears were a cold, cold welcome back to his native land; and, by the feelings which he experienced himself, he learned, in part at least, what would have been the grief of his poor mother had she lived to hear the report of his death.

Sad and heavily he took his way to the inn at which he had informed the secretary of the commander-in-chief he should take up his abode, and was somewhat surprised when the waiter, to whom he was known, said, "Very glad to see you safe, sir. There is a letter for you in the bar."

"Some note, sent after I had set out," thought Reginald; and, taking it indifferently, he told the man to show him to a room. For a minute or two he did not open it: it looked like an invitation to a dinner or a ball; but at length he broke the seal, and saw a few words, which seemed written to change the whole current of his feelings. They were as follows:

"I am bold, perhaps, to write to you at all, but it is with my father's permission. I have asked him what I ought to say, and he tells me to say what I feel. I feel, then, that I have been wrong, but more deceived by circumstances than wrong; and I am ready to explain all, if you desire to hear, and to ask forgiveness, too, for having given pain where I could least have wished it. Though your trust in me, Reginald, may be shaken from what has passed, I have now learned that I ought not to have withdrawn my trust from you.

"But I am writing stiffly, coldly. Such are not my feelings, indeed; and I will only further say, if it will give you pleasure, come to us to-night—not till after eight o'clock, for I am setting out immediately to break to dear Louisa the tidings which we have somewhat abruptly, but yet kindly, received from Lord Granby, and to tell her that the tears we have shed together were causeless. I have still confidence enough in your generosity and your love to say, Yours,

"Mary Chevenix."

CHAPTER XLIV.

A state sometimes succeeds to typhus fever, during which, for a few days, the convalescent is plunged in utter forgetfulness of all that went before, with the exception of some scattered facts, generally referable to the period of infancy. I knew a young man who, having been seized with the malady at one of the universities not long before the time appointed for his examination for academical honors, found, when sense and consciousness returned, that he had totally forgotten every word of Latin and Greek; and, in a still more extraordinary instance, a lady, born in India, and brought up till she was six years old by a Hindoo nurse, during an attack of fever when she was twenty-seven, forgot entirely the English language, and for several days could speak nothing but Hindostanee, of which she had previously forgotten the very sound. Truly, we are fearfully and wonderfully made!

Such was, happily, the case with poor Kate Malcolm. She remembered nothing during the first ten days after the disease had passed its crisis of the events which had immediately preceded. She knew the persons around her, and spoke perfectly rationally of every subject brought before her; but not one particular fact regarding her own situation presented itself to her mind during that period. In the mean time, she recovered rapidly her bodily health and strength. The dim and painfully-distressed eye recovered its light and luster; the dry, parched lip once more became red, and full, and soft; and a faint, rosy hue began to spread itself over the pale cheek. The warm summer air breathing in at the ever-open windows seemed to bring healing upon its wings: she was permitted to rise, to walk about the room, and to go into that adjoining. Sir Harry Jarvis was with her all day long; and the joy and affection in the old man's face, as well as his cheerful conversation, aided not a little the efforts of youth and a good constitution to cast off all the remains of illness. Sir Charles Chevenix came to see her, too, several times; but he had wisely taken the instructions of the physician, and he followed them, by refraining from every thing which could produce agitation, even of a joyful kind.

At length the poor girl was permitted to drive out with her uncle, and then to walk for an hour in the park; but, to the surprise of Sir Harry, her spirits fell as her health rose: for memory, with all its pangs, returned; and dark, and hard, and clear to the eye of imagination appeared her sad future fate, like the burning mountain of the Eastern tales, at which were performed the human sacrifices to the God of Fire, rising before the eyes of the intended victims as the annual ship bore them toward it. With clearer remembrance came also the longing to know the fate of Lutwich. She did not, indeed, imagine that the day of his trial could yet be come; but she wished to inquire—to learn what others judged of the probable result. She dared not ask, however; she feared even to pronounce his name; and though she often resolved to make some effort to obtain information, yet the powerful determination which, hand in hand with affectionate gentleness, had dwelt in her heart while in health, had been enfeebled by illness, and was not yet restored.

At length, one day, Mary, who had been to see her twice without ever mentioning any subject that could recall the past, led the way herself toward the topic uppermost in Kate's thoughts.

"I have a whole budget of news to give you, dear Kate," she said, "but I am ordered only to dole it out to you by degrees, and we have matter for several days' conversation. Louisa would have come to see you with me, but she has been very ill, poor girl. The false report of Reginald's death, added to the grief she suffered before, quite overpowered her."

"The false report," said Kate, speaking to herself; "thank God for that! and Major Brandrum too, Mary, is he safe? They were in the same ship."

"He was one of the nine who were saved," replied Mary: "all but those who were on the deck perished; but poor Colonel Brandrum's thigh was broken by the falling of a spar, as the sailors call it, just as they were getting him into the *Russell*. He is doing well, however, but can not move, or he would have been to see you long ago."

"I must go to see him," replied Kate, thoughtfully; "but now tell me, dear Mary—between you and Captain Lisle, is all explained?"

"Yes, yes," replied her friend, with a blush and a smile, "all is explained, and he has quite forgiven me; but I will not talk of my own selfish happiness, Kate. I have other tidings for you, which I know will be joyful to you also, if you are strong enough to bear them."

"Oh yes," replied Kate, "any thing joyful will do me good, Mary, and give me strength for that which will be more difficult to bear."

"Well, then, Colonel Lutwich is acquitted," replied Mary, fixing her eyes eagerly on her young companion, in some doubt as to the effect of these tidings; but Kate only clasped her hands together, and with tearful eyes murmured, "Thank God! thank God! Then the sacrifice has not been unfruitful."

The next moment she looked up timidly, and asked, "Can you tell me, Mary, whether that man—that William Havant—appeared against him?"

"No, he did not," replied Mary Chevenix; and Kate's eyes fell again, and she sank into a profound reverie.

She seemed so calm, however, that Mary thought she might venture to go on. "Colonel Lutwich," she said, "gave my father this letter for you, Mary, but the doctors would not allow it to be delivered till to-day. Read it, dear Kate, if you like; I will sit here in the window till you have done."

Kate broke the seal and read. The letter was a long one, and it made the tears fall fast upon the paper; but still she was otherwise calm, and Mary did not interrupt her by a word.

When she had done, she sat for some moments with the letter on her knee, and then turning to her friend, she inquired, "Where is Lutwich now, Mary? I must write to him, for still it is clear he has either not received or not understood my last letter. Yet, I gave it to your father for him, Mary. I did not, indeed, venture to write the facts exactly, for fear the people of the prison should take it, and then find means to force the attendance of that man at the trial; but yet I thought he would comprehend."

"What makes you think he did not, dear Kate?" asked Mary, approaching her, and sitting down by her side; "the letter was certainly delivered."

"He says here," rejoined Kate, "that, through the generous kindness of the commander-in-chief, he is permitted to serve in America; that he will be absent for two years, and that during that time he will endeavor to prove that he is not unworthy of my love—"

Kate paused, for tears drowned her voice; but, after a moment or two, she added, "Alas! dear Mary, he must have understood that, ere those two years are over, I must never even think of him with love—must think of him at all as little as possible."

"He heard from my father your situation in every respect, Kate," replied Mary, laying her hand upon that of her fair companion; "but, at the same time, I know he was told that your friends would never consent to your keeping a promise so obtained, and which every one must consider perfectly invalid."

"It is registered there, Mary," said Kate, pointing to the sky. "I dare not break it."

"But it was obtained by the most infamous means," urged Mary; "it was drawn from you by compulsion and by a base conspiracy."

"It was a compact, dear Mary," replied Kate, in a low, quiet voice; "they have fulfilled their part—Lutwich is saved in consequence of it; I must not refuse to fulfill mine, when I called God to witness my pledge. I believe it was almost wrong to tell you any thing about it; but still, Mary, I must be true, whatever I be: I dare not falsify my word."

Mary Chevenix was deeply grieved; but she was a poor causist, and, though she still urged several arguments against her poor friend's vow, they failed to convince. Kate was nearly silent, indeed, but it was evident that she was unshaken to the end of their conference.

During the whole of that after afternoon Sir Harry Jarvis was peculiarly grave and thoughtful, and on the following morning he announced to Kate that he must go to London for some hours upon business. Kate saw him depart with a feeling almost of dread; she knew not why, indeed, but still she felt unwilling to be left alone. She passed part of the morning in reading, and part in writing, and then wandered out into the park, walking on slowly under the shade of the old trees. It was an extensive piece of ground, and she had gone nearly half a mile, when she turned suddenly, seeing two strangers apparently watching her. Taking her way back toward the house, she hurried her pace, hearing footsteps behind her; but she went so rapidly that she was within sight of the windows and the drive when those who were following overtook her. She was a good deal alarmed; but feeling that, if necessary, she could make her voice be heard, she paused to let the others pass, which they did, and then instantly turned. Kate, as they did so, saw before her a face which she could not easily forget, and with a shudder recognized Sir Theodore Broughton.

"Miss Malcolm," he said, biting his lip at the sight of feelings but too evident, "I have long been seeking an opportunity of speaking with you."

Kate hesitated for an instant, and then replied, "It would not have been denied you, sir, if you had applied at the house of my granduncle, Sir Harry Jarvis."

"I am aware of your newly-discovered relationship," replied the young man, sternly; "but that can make no difference in your promises to me, Miss Malcolm."

Kate was silent, and he went on: "Do you deny your promise? Here it is in your own hand-writing. I have fulfilled my part, and I claim the fulfillment of yours "

"I do not deny it," said Kate, with a faltering tongue; and then giving a glance to Doctor Gamble, she added, "I think I have been somewhat deceived, however. Did not that person come to me in disguise, representing himself as a lawyer?"

"That has nothing to do with the question," said Sir Theodore, sharply; "your promise was given upon certain conditions: you called God to witness you would fulfill it, if those conditions were accomplished. They are accomplished to the letter, and I require you to redeem your word."

"I beg you to let me pass, sir," said Kate, faintly, alarmed by his vehemence. "I am ill —I have been very ill: let me pass to the house; you can speak with me there. You shall not be denied, I promise you."

"I will have an answer first," replied Sir Theodore, vehemently; "you can say 'Yes' or 'No' here to a plain question. Will you fulfill your word?"

"I will," said Kate, in a tone of despair; "but let me pass, I beg. There is some one coming, and I am not in a fit state—"

Sir Theodore and Doctor Gamble instantly turned their eyes in the direction in which Kate was looking, and both turned somewhat pale.

"Donovan, by ——!" exclaimed the worthy tutor. "I'll be off; d—n it, she's fainted, upon my life!"

"Stay, sir!" exclaimed Sir Theodore, in a voice of thunder. "I don't care if it be Donovan or the devil. Help me to carry her into the house."

Doctor Gamble chose his part at once, and obeyed, although he would have given all he possessed to escape the eye of the guardian rather than assist the ward: but by this time the dominance of the more vehement character was fully established over the more cunning. Raising Kate in their arms, they bore her toward the house, which they had nearly reached before Captain Donovan came up.

That gentleman uttered not a word, but followed them in silence, with a frown upon his brow, and a sort of sarcastic smile upon his lip. Neither did Sir Theodore show that he saw him except by the firm shutting of the teeth together, with a look of determination which was not without its meaning. Determination with a strong and permanent motive, however, is a much more powerful thing than that founded upon a caprice or any transitory passion. And here let me remark, that all passions should be classified exactly like verbs—transitive, passive, and neuter, and the passive are the most dangerous and the most permanent.

They bore Kate Malcolm to the door of the house, then, and Captain Donovan rang the bell; but still, though they were necessarily detained a moment there, no one spoke. Doctor Gamble, indeed, did not at all like the dead silence of his two companions; but it overawed him, and he did not venture to open his lips, notwithstanding a constitutional tendency to loquacity. At length the butler and another servant appeared, and all was bustle, anxiety, and consternation at the sight of Miss Malcolm fainting. She was carried at once into the library, however, and the footman was sent in haste for the housekeeper, as Sir Harry's return was expected every moment, and Dixon declared that he would not, for the world, have his master come back, and find his young lady so unwell.

His precautions were vain, however; the old lady had just entered the room, and was giving her directions, and applying her approved restoratives, when wheels were heard rolling up without.

The same dull silence had been maintained by the three gentlemen who had carried or accompanied Miss Malcolm into the house, and to the housekeeper's inquiry of where they had found her, and how it had happened, Sir Theodore had replied nothing. The next moment, however, Captain Donovan looked at him sternly, saying, "Now, Sir Theodore, I think you and I, and this gentleman, had better retire."

But neither his stern look nor his words had any effect upon the young baronet. Sir Theodore had got a step further in his progress. He was resolved to resist, and he merely replied, "Not yet, sir."

The next moment Sir Harry Jarvis and Sir Charles Chevenix entered the room, and, of course, were not a little alarmed and astonished at what they beheld. Their first care was, of course, directed to Kate, who was beginning to revive, and who, in a few minutes, was able to sit up. None of the party present when he came in, except Kate and his own servants, was known to Sir Harry Jarvis, and when satisfied that his grand-niece was not seriously indisposed, he looked round with an inquiring glance.

Sir Charles Chevenix, however, who was slightly acquainted with one of the gentlemen, and thought he recollected the face of another, began the explanation, saying, "Captain Donovan, Sir Harry Jarvis. This, if I mistake not, is Sir Theodore Broughton?"

"The same, sir," said Sir Theodore, boldly.

"And this, sir," said Captain Donovan, with a sarcastic smile, "is Doctor Gamble—as serviceable a knave as any in Europe."

"For which excellent reason," replied Gamble, now goaded to retaliate, "you selected him as the tutor of your ward."

"Gentlemen," said Sir Harry Jarvis, "these are harsh words. Kate, my dear, remain here—lie upon the sofa—do not rise yet. These gentlemen and I will go into another room;" and, telling the housekeeper to remain with her, he opened the door with ceremonious courtesy, and requested the rest of the party to follow him.

As they were entering the dining-room, Sir Charles Chevenix whispered a word or two in the old baron's ear, who replied, "That is clear; I understand it all."

"And now, gentlemen," said Sir Harry, "pray be seated, for I have a few inquiries to make. I understand from my butler that Miss Malcolm, my niece, was brought in, fainting, by yourselves. Permit me to ask how this happened?"

"I know nothing of the circumstances, sir," answered Captain Donovan; "but, having heard of some rumors of proceedings I did not approve of, I followed Sir Theodore and Doctor Gamble hither. When first I caught sight of them, they were talking to the young lady in the park; but before I came up she had fainted, and they were carrying her toward your mansion."

"I trust, young gentleman," said the master of the house, fixing his eyes sternly upon Sir Theodore, "that you gave no occasion for emotions calculated to produce such a result. I have heard, sir, of some proceedings on former occasions, which lead me to suspect that you have yet to learn what is due from a gentleman and a man of honor to a lady."

Sir Theodore was evidently a good deal embarrassed; but, after a moment's pause, he replied, in a bold and decided tone, "Sir Harry Jarvis, I shall not go back to the past, whatever you may think fit to do. On the present occasion, I have only done what I have a right to do, and that, I trust, not in a discourteous manner. I came hither to see Miss Malcolm, and, meeting her in your park, I reminded her of a promise made by her some time ago to give me her hand. I have that promise in writing, and have a right to require its fulfillment. I think my station and my fortune entitle me to aspire to her, and that my demanding the accomplishment of a solemn pledge to which she called God to witness can not be considered either an insult or an injury."

"You do her and me much honor, sir," replied Sir Harry, calmly; "first, I will remark in passing, that Miss Malcolm is not of age to contract such engagements without my consent, being her nearest relative and natural guardian; and next, sir, I will request you to inform me what she replied to this application."

"Oh, she said several things I do not well recollect," answered Sir Theodore, with a confused manner; "yes, I do now remember," he continued; "she did not deny the promise, and then said that she would fulfill it."

"The devil she did!" exclaimed Sir Charles Chevenix; "and then I suppose she fainted, to show how pleasant she thought you."

Sir Theodore Broughton turned as red as fire, and replied, "Pleasant or unpleasant, sir, she expressed her willingness to fulfill her plighted word, and nobody has a right to prevent her."

"I beg your pardon, Theodore," said Captain Donovan, "I have that right, and shall exercise it. You are my ward, sir, and although, on the representation of several persons that I was keeping you too strictly, I have suffered you to go for a month or two with the bridle on your neck, to see if you were able to guide yourself, depend upon it my arm is strong enough to use that bridle, now that I find you are unfit for such liberty; and I tell you plainly that I will not consent to such a marriage."

"Such a marriage!" said Harry Jarvis, turning toward him; "may I inquire, sir, what you could object to in a marriage with my niece's child, if I condescended to agree to her giving her hand to this young man? Methinks one of my family, and the heiress of my property, might find a somewhat higher match, if she chose, than Sir Theodore Broughton."

"I beg your pardon, Sir Harry Jarvis," replied Donovan, who had turned singularly pale; "I did not at all mean to utter a word that could be offensive to you, or the young lady either. I merely wish to convey to my ward the information that, as long as my guardianship continues, he can contract such engagements with no one, and that I certainly shall not consent to his marriage till he is of age. Then he must do as he pleases."

"And then I will as certainly marry her as I stand here!" exclaimed Sir Theodore Broughton, calling down awful curses on his head if he did not fulfill his word. "If she have not a mind to be considered forever perjured and faithless, she will keep her engagement," he continued. "I shall preserve that written promise carefully, you may all depend upon it, and the very day I am of age I will demand its fulfillment. That day is not so far off, Captain Donovan."

"I know it is not," replied Donovan, looking at him with a very strange expression; "till then, you will obey me, if you please."

"A word or two more, Sir Theodore," said the old baronet; "I shall also object to my niece marrying till she is of age. You will mark me, I neither give my approval, nor, indeed, express any opinion in regard to this promise which you say she has made you; but between this time and the period I have mentioned, I will talk with her fully on the subject, and determine my own conduct by her replies."

"If you doubt that she gave me the promise, and called God to witness that she would fulfill it, ask herself," exclaimed Sir Theodore; "and I must request you, Sir Harry Jarvis, in fairness to her and to me, to tell her at once that, as soon as I am of age, whatever impediments be now thrown in my way, I will demand its fulfillment."

"I will," said the old baronet.

"And pray add, on my part," said Captain Donovan, "that I shall oppose its fulfillment as long as I have any authority, and that I protest against any idle words of this young gentleman being considered as an engagement."

"I will," replied Sir Harry, again, in a dry tone; and, rising from his chair, he stood with his hands behind his back, as if to intimate that the conference was finished.

The three gentlemen who, uninvited, had found their way into the old baronet's house, seemed to hesitate for an instant in regard to taking the hint; and, in fact, two at least of the party were unwilling to walk out, either individually or collectively, with the third. Captain Donovan, however, was the most cool, and, after a momentary pause, he said, "Now, Sir Theodore, I think we may as well depart." The young baronet turned from him, bowed to Sir Harry Jarvis, and walked to the door; Sir Harry rang the bell, and all three were ushered forth.

"You surely do not mean, Jarvis," said Sir Charles Chevenix, "to let that dear, excellent girl fulfill so rash a promise, and one so scandalously obtained, to a man whose whole conduct and demeanor proves that he is unworthy of her."

"My dear Charles," replied his old friend, "I shall certainly oppose her so doing by every argument I can use, when the time comes for him to demand the fulfillment of her word, but, at the same time, I will not control her. There are some people who would be rendered more unhappy by being forced to commit what they consider a wrong action, than by any personal suffering they could endure, and I believe my dear Kate is one of them. Then, on the other hand, as I told you the day before yesterday, this unfortunate attachment which has arisen between her and Lutwich is one of the most painful things to me that ever could have occurred."

"I would a thousand-fold rather see her marry Lutwich than that young scoundrel," exclaimed Sir Charles, warmly; "independent of his unprincipled conduct, his sullen, dogged character would make an angel miserable, while Lutwich, with all his faults, is a gallant, bold, open-hearted man, who never did a mean thing, though he may have done criminal things. I would rather give her to him a great deal than the other."

"So would I," said his friend; "but I would rather give her to neither; and I think that, by leaving her to suppose, for a time at least, that she is really bound to this Sir Theodore Broughton, I may wean her heart of its attachment to the other."

Sir Charles shook his head, and the old baronet proceeded: "Not that I dislike, or ever did dislike, Lutwich; far from it, I conceived a very great regard for him, Chevenix; but still, from the inquiries we have both made, there is very little doubt that he has not been suspected or accused wrongfully."

"Granted! granted!" replied Sir Charles Chevenix; "his is a Cumberland family, and he has got a touch of the old blood about him. Carry him two or three centuries back, and put a spear in his hand, and you have a border knight. He is not a bit worse than his ancestors, I am sure."

"The two or three centuries make all the difference," replied Sir Harry Jarvis.

"There is one thing to be said, however, which you have not considered, my good friend," rejoined his friend, "and that is, that if it had not been for Lutwich, you would never have had your pretty Kate to give or to refuse to any one, for he ferreted out all the facts; and had it not been for his generous protection of her from the infamous pursuit of this very young man who now seeks to marry her, the charge would never have been brought against him which has near cost him his life, and made him so distasteful to you. In considering his claims, you should never forget these two."

"Nor will I," replied Sir Harry; "but I much doubt, Chevenix, that Kate will ever be brought to violate her word, however rashly engaged, however shamefully wrung from her."

"So thinks Mary," said Sir Charles; "but time and proper representations, together with the soft pleadings of love for another, would, I am sure, make her view the case differently."

"I do not think it," replied Sir Harry; "but now let us go and see her."

CHAPTER XLV.

Sir Theodore Broughton, Captain Donovan, and Doctor Gamble walked along the road which led through Jarworth Park from the house to the lodge. The scenery was very beautiful, as some of the park scenery in green Hertfordshire is. The trees were old and fine, and so disposed along the road as to give every moment a new prospect, breaking in through some dell, or over some savanna narrowing toward its close; and the light of the afternoon sun, now somewhat more than half way in its descent from the meridian, cast long, blue shadows over the turf, and purpled the lines of distant country seen above the tree tops in the lower parts of the park.

Not one of the three men saw that they were surrounded by beautiful landscapes. It is one of the sad qualities of evil passions in the heart to shut out from man's faculties the impression of all those bright things in which a God of mercy created him to delight. Captain Donovan, calm, cold, and stern, was busy with thoughts dark and terrible enough. Sir Theodore, with many an angry feeling in his breast, was trying to nerve his mind to resistance, but, with that combination of willfulness and weakness which I have tried to depict, felt his courage unequal to his will, and his firmness giving way before the gloomy quietness of his guardian's demeanor. Doctor Gamble was preparing replies, and, with that sort of impudent indifference which formed part of his high philosophy, was making up his mind to what could not be avoided, and resolving to have his revenge in repartee for any blame that might fall upon him. He saw, too, that Sir Theodore was dispirited, and perhaps to relieve him a little, or perhaps merely to vent an overflow of impertinence, he said, when they had gone some five or six hundred yards in silence, "A very pretty place this, captain, and a capital house. A good cook, too, I dare say. There was a mighty savory smell. I think the old gentleman might have asked us to dinner."

"Be silent, sir!" replied Captain Donovan, without turning his head; "he does wisely to ask neither fools nor blackguards to his table."

Doctor Gamble was silenced for the time; and they walked on to the lodge without another word.

There was a carriage standing near the gates, and, when the driver saw Captain Donovan, he touched his hat and opened the door. "Be so good as to get in, Sir Theodore," said Captain Donovan.

"My own chaise is—"

"Gone back to Barnet," added his guardian, suddenly; "I discharged it."

Sir Theodore got in, Donovan followed, and Doctor Gamble paused for a moment, as if not quite sure whether to enter or not.

"Come in, sir," said the stern voice of the officer; "we shall want you;" and the tutor mounted the steps also. The driver shut the door, and, at a nod from Donovan, drove on without further directions.

The determination shown in all these preparations, the coolness with which all his purposes and plans had been prearranged, and the still, dull silence which he maintained, overpowered for the time the last efforts of the spirit of resistance in his ward's heart. The carriage rolled on during that long twelve miles without a single word being spoken, and stopped at length at the hotel where Sir Theodore and his tutor had resided in London. At the top of the stairs, near the door of the young baronet's sitting-room, they found Zachary Hargrave and the other servant, both equipped for a journey.

"Are all the things packed up, Hargrave?" asked Captain Donovan.

"All but Doctor Gamble's, sir," answered the man, with a grin; "I did not like to meddle with them."

"Quite right," said Captain Donovan; "order the horses, and let me have the bill;" and, walking into the sitting-room, he said, "Sir Theodore, I intend that you shall go with me into Warwickshire. If you have any preparations to make, you had better, perhaps, do so, as we set out in a quarter of an hour."

The young man glared at him, but after a momentary struggle with himself, made no reply, and left the room.

"And now, Doctor Gamble," continued Donovan, "a few words, and only a few words, with you."

"Quite at your service, captain," replied the tutor, in the easiest possible tone.

"Well, then, sir, you must be quite aware that, after what has happened," said Donovan, "you can be permitted to remain no longer with Sir Theodore Broughton."

"For obeying your directions, I suppose, sir," answered Gamble, with a sarcastic smile; "you told me to let him see a little of life, and I *have* let him see a little."

"A little too much, sir," replied Captain Donovan; "but, whatever I said on that score, I did not tell you that I wished a boy not twenty to marry. Now, sir, can you deny that you proposed and devised this marriage?"

"A sham marriage—a sham marriage, captain," replied Gamble, with the most perfect assurance; "nothing more did I ever propose or devise either; and that would have suited you, and him, and me quite well, I think. When he found that she was under such care and guardianship that a sham marriage was not to be done, it was he himself determined upon a real one, against all my arguments and persuasions. I went down to Barnet with him three or four days ago, quite as if I were going to put my neck into a halter instead of himself. But what is your objection to the young lady? She will be immensely rich—is of very good family; and, I will answer for it, all the world will say it was a very suitable match, and if they lay the arrangement of it at my door, will give me credit for more *savoir faire* than is my due."

There were two or three little touches in the tutor's speech which Captain Donovan did not like. He felt a sort of indefinite dread of his tool; but, at the same time, he was fully resolved that he should be separated from his young ward, and he replied in an indifferent tone, "All that may be very true, Doctor Gamble; and the world may praise you, and blame me, if it pleases. You should be aware by this time, I think, that I am very indifferent as to other people's opinions of my conduct. One thing, however, nobody can deny, that it was your duty not to have countenanced such a transaction without communicating with me, and receiving my sanction; therefore your superintendence of Sir Theodore is at an end. There is a somewhat long account to settle between us, as I furnished you with a large sum of money. You will be good enough to render a statement of its disbursement to my lawyers, where you have had business before now."

"I will trouble you, on my part, for my half-year's salary, captain," said the tutor, unblushingly; "and I will put down the items of account with my usual punctuality. As to the large sum of money you mention, it is all gone, with the exception of seven pounds three and sixpence. I have vouchers for all my disbursements. It has not gone in *fumus;* but, as the base and perpendicular of a triangle are always more in sum than the hypotheneuse, so do two persons expend more than one person, especially in *seeing a little of life*, as you aptly and expressively termed it."

Captain Donovan gazed at him with a strong inclination to knock him down; but, feeling that to do so might be dangerous, he merely replied, "You have let him see too much of money as well as life, I am afraid, sir. However, give me pen and ink, and you shall have a draft for the sum you claim. The account of your expenses must be given in, as I have said, for I shall have to account hereafter; but pray remember that the investigation of the account may be strict or otherwise, according to circumstances."

The pen and ink were given, the draft drawn, and a significant look interchanged between Captain Donovan and the tutor before Sir Theodore Broughton returned. There were then some bills to be paid, and a few other affairs to be settled; and at length, with a ceremonious air, Donovan begged his ward to proceed to the carriage.

Sir Theodore felt bitterly what it is to act under compulsion, and perhaps resolved to take his revenge some day; but, in the mean time, his detestation of his guardian revived a feeling, if not of regard, at least of companionship toward his tutor; and, going up to him, he shook hands with him, saying, in a low voice, "Write to me, doctor. I suppose I am not a state prisoner, and may read my own letters. Look after Kate, and let me hear all about her, especially if there be any talk of her marriage. At present, perhaps I had better submit; but it wants but a slight motive more to make me break my bonds. Where shall I write to you?"

"Good faith! my dear Theodore, that is a difficult question," replied Gamble; "I am like Milton's Adam, 'The world is all before me where to choose.' Well, address Post-office, Charing Cross. That is as good as any other. I trust, Captain Donovan, that in seeking for a new appointment, I shall not want your recommendation?"

"On any application, I will not fail to do justice to your merits," replied Donovan, with one of his faint sarcastic smiles. "Good morning, Doctor Gamble;" and he descended with his pupil to the carriage.

No delay was made upon the road. Donovan traveled all night, and the next day Sir Theodore Broughton found himself at his old ancestral hall. How dull and gloomy every thing looked! How different from that which it appeared before! Very few words had passed between him and his guardian on the journey, and the young gentleman fancied that the same cold, sullen demeanor was to last; that Donovan, displeased with all that had occurred in London, was resolved to resume the somewhat tyrannical sort of sway which had been exercised over him before. But he was mistaken. The dinner was served at the usual hour; the wine circulated in moderation; conversation, broken, but not altogether grave, succeeded; and at length, after filling his own glass and pushing over the decanter to his ward, Captain Donovan said, "Now, Sir Theodore, to prevent all misunderstanding, I think it better to state at once the manner in which I expect that we are to live during the time that you continue under my guardianship. As you may see, I am not satisfied with what has taken place in London, and I am consequently resolved that you shall stay here under my own eye till you are of age. You have injured your health, done no good to your reputation, and may, in some degree, have corrupted your mind; but, I trust, not much. These results I in some degree anticipated; but foolish and impertinent people thought fit to comment upon my conduct in keeping you in the country, and not being willing to adhere obstinately to my own opinions, I permitted you to make a trial, which has ended as I expected. I do not pretend, however, to treat you as a boy, after you have been acting as a man; and I shall neither watch your actions in small things, nor attempt to restrain them therein. I shall only interfere in matters of real importance, but then I expect my authority to be respected. You are fond of shooting, hunting, fishing. The seasons for those amusements rapidly succeed each other, and I have no wish to prevent your enlivening to the utmost the dullness of a country life. Roam where you will within twenty or thirty miles of the house; bring what guests home you may think fit, and endeavor to enjoy yourself and recover your health by prudence and moderation. I neither wish to act the part of a tyrant, nor even to let the necessary authority which I must exercise be visible to the eyes of others in a manner painful to yourself. The task, however, of preventing it from ever becoming so, rests principally with you. I will take care to interfere as little as possible; but when I do—even by a very slight hint—be assured that it is upon full consideration, and with a determination not to be changed. Then yield with a good grace, and no one will ever see that I interfere at all. Even that restraint will soon be over, and it is as well that the intervening time should pass pleasantly to us both."

This was much better than Sir Theodore Broughton had expected, and he soon began to try the extent of his liberty. To the sports of the country, in which he had always indulged with excess, he added many of the vices and evil habits which he had acquired in London, and that in a manner which could not fail to reach his guardian's ears. Captain Donovan took no notice. Sir Theodore would be absent from home all night—it called for neither inquiry nor remark. He brought home loose and riotous companions—Captain Donovan expressed no dissatisfaction, but retired from table at his own hour, and left the rest of the party to follow their course.

Indeed, the habits of that gentleman seemed a good deal changed. He was often, it is true, absent from the house for several days; but when he was there, he showed himself studious, thoughtful, frequently locked up in his own room for many hours, reading curious old books, and making various chemical experiments. Thus passed nearly a year, and summer had returned again, when the events took place which shall be recorded in the following chapter, premising merely that Donovan had been absent during a whole week, and that during three days of that time Sir Theodore had also been unseen in his own house, though he had neither servants nor baggage with him. When he returned, he looked ill and harassed, and sent for the apothecary from the neighboring town. Some medicine was brought for him the same evening, but he did not take it; and, after inquiring if any thing had been seen or heard of Captain Donovan, he drank somewhat more wine than was perhaps wise, and retired to bed.

CHAPTER XLVI.

In a small room, hot to suffocation, although the windows were all open, was seated Captain Donovan, with an elderly man, curiously dressed, considering that it was the middle of the day, for he had on an old, worn, and very dirty dressing-gown, with his unpowdered gray hair tied with a greasy black ribbon behind, slippers on his feet, and the gray stockings which covered his legs slipping down in large wrinkles from under the unbuttoned knees of his drab breeches. His eyes were keen and sharp, but there was a somewhat wild look of abstraction in their glance which was hardly sane. The room contained little furniture beyond bookshelves, furnaces, stills, retorts and crucibles; and while Donovan poured over the pages of an old book, the other, who seemed the master of the house, busied himself with what was going on in three of the small furnaces.

"You'll kill yourself, Amos, if you go on this way," said Donovan, looking up. "I can not think what a man of your competent fortune can want, stewing yourself to death in this way, unless it be to arrive at the happy consummation of putting yourself out of the world."

"No, no," answered the other with a laugh; "if I desired to do that, I would use the laurel water we were talking of some time ago. It is the speediest, quietest, most comfortable sort of death in the world; and then people would not have an opportunity of thrusting a stake through me either, for it leaves no mark. Have you found what you want? If you do not find it under the essences, look for the word rosemary in the index. Perhaps people may call it rosemary water; then you will come upon it just after the laurel water. I'll get it for you."

"I've got it—I've got it," said Donovan, turning over some pages hastily. "I wish you would lend me this book, Amos."

"To be sure," replied the other, "though you're but a dabbler in science, Donovan. Put it in your pocket; but send it back, mind;" and he applied himself to his furnaces again.

"Well, I must go," said Captain Donovan: "I can not stay in this infernal hot place any longer."

The other laughed, and they parted.

Donovan proceeded to the inn of the little town where this scene took place, mounted his horse, and rode away. He went very quick; but he did not use any great caution in riding, for his mind seemed very busy with some strong preoccupying thoughts, and his horse twice stumbled, and nearly fell. Two or three times, too, as he rode along, he murmured, "In two months—ay, in two months."

He thus journeyed on for more than five-and-twenty miles, and at length reached the house of Sir Theodore Broughton about three o'clock in the afternoon. After giving his horse to a servant, he inquired if the young baronet was at home.

"He is out just now, sir," replied the man; "but he came home yesterday, looking very ill, we all thought."

"Indeed!" said Donovan; "not seriously ill, I hope?"

"Oh no, sir; he is looking better to-day," replied the man; "but desperate cross."

"Let me have a fire lighted in my little room," said Donovan; and thither he retired. There were two letters lying on the table, and Captain Donovan took one up, read it with an indifferent air, and threw it down. The other, though much shorter, seemed of more importance, for it made his eye gaze eagerly, and his lips quiver. The few words it contained were to the following effect:

"Sir Harry Jarvis presents his compliments to Captain Donovan, and begs to inform him that Sir Theodore Broughton has been again at Jarworth Park to renew his application for the hand of Miss Malcolm. Sir Harry Jarvis is very desirous of having an interview with Captain Donovan upon this subject, as Sir Theodore now states that he is within two months of being of age; and Miss Malcolm, notwithstanding every argument of her friends, and her own strong disinclination to the alliance, seems to feel herself bound by the promise she so rashly made. Sir Harry Jarvis would propose to wait upon Captain Donovan, but the state of his health does not permit him to travel."

Donovan held the paper in his hand motionless for a moment or two, and then walked once or twice up and down the room.

"He will have it," he said, at length; "he will have it;" and, tearing the letter to pieces, he threw it under the grate.

A woman-servant entered to light the fire, saying, "I have not kept it in, sir, while you were gone, for it has been so hot."

"The room feels chilly to me," replied Donovan; "you had better light it. I will go and walk up and down in the sunshine till it is done. I have somewhat overheated myself with hard riding;" and he went out.

Instead of going into the sunshine, however, he betook himself to the shadiest part of the gardens, and walked slowly up and down a walk bordered with shrubs of the cherry-laurel. From time to time he picked a leaf and put it in his pocket, looked carefully around, and resumed his walk. At length he turned back to the house again, and, re-entering the little room which he had appropriated to the purposes of a study, locked the door behind him. He then took down from a shelf by the side of the fire a little portable still, put the laurel leaves into it, added some water, and placed it securely over the flame. When this was completed, a fit of indescribable agitation seized him. He trembled violently, sat down in a chair, placed his hands before his eyes, and opened his waistcoat, as if for air. After a time he became somewhat calmer. "No need of using it when it is made," he said: "there can be no harm in making it;" and, rising, he went out, locking the door behind him, and leaving the still over the fire.

As he was crossing the great hall toward the drawing-room, Sir Theodore came in; and, going up to him at once, Donovan shook hands with him, saying, "The servants tell me you have not been well; and you do not look it at all. Really, my dear Theodore, you must take care, or you will seriously injure a constitution naturally strong."

"Pooh, pooh!" said the young baronet, "I shall soon be better."

"Have you taken the medicine the doctor sent?" asked Captain Donovan.

"No; I could not get it down, it was so nauseous," replied the young man; "but he has sent me something better to-day, and I will take it to-morrow."

"Upon your word?" asked Donovan, with a smile.

"Upon my word, I will," answered Sir Theodore, laughing. "My stomach is out of order, that is all; but I will take it. Indeed, I have put it on my dressing-room mantel-piece on purpose."

But little more passed at that time. Sir Theodore went his own way, and Captain Donovan returned to his room; but there the agitation he had before suffered seemed to seize him again. Once he took the still off the fire, and then he put it back again, and then walked up and down for nearly half an hour. At length he examined the receiver, into which somewhat more than a wine-glassful of liquid had come over.

"Where shall I put it?" he asked himself. "I wish I had a vial."

Then, after pouring the liquid into a tumbler, he quietly walked out of the room, looked into the library, where Sir Theodore was lying on a sofa apparently asleep, and mounted the stairs. When Captain Donovan returned to his study with the same noiseless step, he found the door ajar, and Zachary Hargrave standing by the table with the tumbler in his hand.

Donovan snatched it from him instantly, exclaiming, vehemently, "You have not been drinking that? It might—good Heaven! it might—"

"No, no, sir," replied the man, "I have not drank any. I thought it was dirty water, and was going to carry it away."

"Never touch any thing in my room," said Donovan, gravely; "you do not know what might be the consequences. What do you want?"

"Why, I wanted to speak with you about Sir Theodore, sir," replied Hargrave.

Donovan pointed to the door. The man shut it, and proceeded to say, "He was dreadful angry with me this morning, sir, though, Heaven be praised! he had no cause. I have only humbly endeavored to open his mind to grace in regard to little—"

"Well, well, never mind what you have done," cried Donovan, impatiently; "tell me what he said to you."

"Why, sir, he said all manner of things," replied the man: "he abused me for a full hour, accused me of betraying him to you, and told me that, as soon as he was of age, he would not only kick me out of the house, but punish me for all those little fallings off into which the weakness of the flesh betrays every man."

"Upon my life, he is likely to do it, too," answered Donovan. "Had I the means, Hargrave, I would protect you as long as I lived; and I will do what I can for you, whatever happens; for what Sir Theodore imputes to you as a fault to him, was no more than a duty. When did he say all this?"

"Why, a few hours ago, sir, when I took the medicine up to his dressing-room," replied the man.

"Well, leave me now, Hargrave," answered Donovan: "it is near dinner-time. I will think what I can do for you. If I were master here, you should have a different prospect."

The man withdrew; but, for some reason or another, he remained close to the door, with his head bent down, and his eye very near the key-hole.

Shortly after, Captain Donovan joined Sir Theodore Broughton, and at dinner appeared calm and sedate, as usual. Again the young man drank a great deal of wine, and his spirits rose with the stimulus. His guardian remonstrated, in no very domineering tone, saying that he had better abstain, for a few days at least, till he was in better health; but the servants were in the room, and Sir Theodore, already bold on his approaching emancipation, answered sharply, "I shall drink as much as I think proper, sir."

"Very well—kill yourself, if you like," said Donovan, and shortly after dinner left him, and went to walk in the garden. He was no longer agitated, but a dull and somber gloom seemed to hang over him. His eyes were bent upon the ground, his hands clasped together behind his back, and from time to time his lips moved, as if he were internally discussing some dark question. "Either he or I," he said, and then walked on again; then paused and murmured, "If I could get rid of that bond—Ay, but how can that be done?" and again he resumed his perambulations.

It was nearly dark when he returned to the house, and his first question was in regard to Sir Theodore.

"He is out with the coachman and Brompton, sir, fishing," replied the footman, who was in the hall.

"What, at this time of the evening!" exclaimed Donovan; and then added, after a pause, "He will kill himself, that is clear. He is greatly changed. His death would not surprise me any day."

He then went into the drawing-room and ordered coffee, and there he sat till the young baronet's return, which did not take place till past nine. The servants heard some high words passing between guardian and ward; and shortly after Sir Theodore went to his bedroom, and ringing, ordered a tumbler of mulled wine to be brought him. He was evidently not in the most placable humor; and when Hargrave took him up what he had demanded, he asked him why the devil he ever came into his sight.

"Did I not tell you this morning," exclaimed the young gentlemen, "that you are a spy and an informer, a liar, and I dare say a thief into the bargain? Get out of the room this instant!"

The man looked at him doggedly, and walked away muttering.

"No insolence, sir, or I will kick you down the stairs!" exclaimed Sir Theodore, vehemently; and then, as Hargrave left the room, he added to himself, "By Heaven! when I am of age, I will teach these scoundrels a different story."

Captain Donovan remained in the drawing-room for more than an hour after his ward had left it, walking up and down incessantly. He then went to the door of his study; but he seemed to fear that room, and, turning back upon his steps, seated himself before a window not yet closed, and gazed out toward the starry sky. They have voices, those bright stars, and speak to the human heart, if we will but seek counsel of them—voices more sweet, more powerful, more true, than those which astrologers of old ascribed to them. The power and presence of divinity is spoken by them, if not to crush, to overawe man's passions; and deaf must be the ear that will not hear.

Donovan gazed, and, whatever was in his

thoughts, the fit of agitation seized him again. "What am I to do?" he murmured, as he stood in the midst of that large old room; "what am I to do?" and then he walked up and down, with his hand playing nervously with the seals of his watch. At length he stopped suddenly and said, "No, no, no!" and, turning sharply away, he lighted a candle, and walked straight to the little room where he had passed so much of the afternoon.

When there, he took down a vial from the shelf, which had not been there when Hargrave left him alone in the room. The tumbler on the table was empty, and the liquid it had contained was now in the vial. He held it up to the light, uncorked and smelled it, and then replaced it on the shelf. Then emptying the still of the laurel leaves, he cast them upon the fire, and watched them till they were consumed. He next, from a basket in the corner of the room, half filled the still with quicklime. That done, he turned to the door—paused—looked at the vial; and then murmuring once more, "No, no!" hurried away and went to bed.

The house became silent and still in about half an hour; but at the end of a quarter more, the door of the little study opened, and a figure entered, bearing a candle. It was not that of Donovan. With a still, quiet step, moving on his stocking stoles, it was Hargrave who entered.

"Ay," he said, "the bottle is there! He hasn't done it. He'd like, I'm sure, but he's afraid. I wonder if the stuff he poured in is poison, after all? I'll soon see;" and, taking the bottle down, he carried it to the kitchen. There was a large fire in the grate, before which, stretched at her ease, lay a large cat, which rose as the man came near, and rubbed herself against his legs. After looking about in various places, he found a jug with some milk in it, and, pouring a portion into a saucer, added about a teaspoonful of the liquid from the bottle, and set the mixture down before the cat. She began to lap it eagerly, but stopped.

"Ay, it's poison, sure enough," said Hargrave to himself; "they say cats won't take poison, though dogs will, sure enough."

The next moment, however, the animal returned to her drink, and had lapped up nearly the whole, when suddenly she drew back, staggered once or twice, as if she were drunk, and then the hind quarters dropped apparently paralyzed. An instant after she fell over upon her side, and after two or three convulsive movements expired.

"Ay, pussy, you've had enough, I think," said the man, with a grin; "and hang me if he sha'n't have the rest. Stay! I must wash out the saucer first; and he applied himself to put every thing in the same order as that in which he had found it.

He then walked quietly up stairs. At the top of the second flight, the first door was that of Sir Theodore Broughton's dressing-room, and it stood ajar. "That is a piece of luck!" said the scoundrel to himself.

Nevertheless, as he pushed it open, it creaked upon its hinges; and he started, prepared to run down stairs. All was silent, however; and, after waiting a moment or two to listen, he entered the room. Treading on tiptoe, he moved across to the fire-place, where stood the bottle of medicine which had been sent that day for Sir Theodore Broughton. The man was cautious, however, and he examined the bottle well. It was labeled in the same manner as that which he held in his hand, "The draught for Sir Theodore Broughton. To be taken before breakfast." But the color was very different; and, drawing out the cork, he poured some of the medicine into the other bottle, till he had filled it up. Then substituting the one for the other, he was going away; but, remembering that there had been two bottles there in the morning, he rubbed his head, and approaching a drawer in the dressing-table, he drew it out, saying to himself, "He used to have a number here."

What he sought was easily found; and, placing another vial by the side of the first, he crept quietly out of the room again. His next voyage was to the kitchen once more, where he emptied and washed the bottle he had taken away, filled it with clear water, and placed it in Captain Donovon's study.

"Now," said Zachary Hargrave, as he threaded the manifold windings in the old house back to his garret, "nobody can say I've poisoned him. If he takes it, it is his doing, not mine; and we're quit of him—the nasty young vermin!"

With such comfortable reflections, he lay down and slept quite quietly. Nor let the reader marvel; for none of us ever commit a wrong act without seeking, if not finding, some such evasion of the charge of conscience.

On the following morning, Captain Donovan was down early, and ordered his horse, saying he should ride out for an hour before breakfast. A minute or two after, he heard Sir Theodore's bell ring; and he asked one of the servants if he had seen the young baronet.

"Not yet, sir," replied the man. "I hope he will be better this morning."

"I do not think he is well at all," replied Captain Donovan. "Do you remark how his color is changed? It would not surprise me at all if he did not recover."

In the mean while, the under-footman had gone up the stairs to the young baronet's room, and Captain Donovan walked leisurely toward the stable-yard to mount there. He had got one foot in the stirrup when the man, who had gone out, came running up, exclaiming, "For Heaven's sake, stop, sir! Sir Theodore is very ill!"

"What is the matter?" demanded Donovan, pausing instantly. "What ails him?"

"I don't know, sir," replied the man: "he's all gasping, and heaving, and foaming at the mouth."

"An epileptic fit, I suppose," said Captain Donovan, turning toward the house. "You, Thomas, mount the horse, and gallop off for the doctor;" and, without further pause, he returned and ran up stairs.

There were two women-servants in the young baronet's room, called by the footman in his first alarm, and they exclaimed as Donovan entered, "Oh, sir! the stuff Thomas gave him out of the bottle has killed him."

Donovan ran hastily to the side of the bed, but there was now nothing but a corpse before him. The eyelids moved a little, and there was a convulsive movement of the chest, but the spirit had departed.

"Let me see the bottle," cried Donovan; and, taking it from the maid's hand, he instantly recognized the smell of laurel water. A cold, chilly, death-like feeling seized him. All his calmness and firmness forsook him in a moment. How could it have been given to him? Who could have given it? Could he himself have done it in his sleep? A thousand such mad questions suggested themselves to his mind in a moment. Conscious of what he had meditated, terror took possession of him entirely. All presence of mind was lost; he snatched both bottles from the maid, who had taken them up again, hurried with them to the basin, tasted the contents of one, and washed them both out with his own hands. Then running down to his study, without giving any directions to the women, he locked the door, and took down the vial from the spot where it stood. At first his face looked joyful as he gazed at it; but the next instant he opened it, and tasted the contents. It was pure water; and, setting it down, he clasped his hands with a look of bewildered despair.

CHAPTER XLVII.

There was sunshine of many kinds at Jarworth Park; for the bright beams of summer which poured in at the windows of the cheerful drawing-room were not more warm or gay than the hearts of most of those assembled there. It is true, there were some clouds in the heaven, and also some cares in the bosoms of two or three, much darker than the soft vapors which passed upon the breeze; but those who had cause for sadness tried to throw it off for the time, in order to grace the welcome of dear friends, who came on a joyful journey with nothing but smiles.

Mary Chevenix and Reginald Lisle—whose paternal uncle had died on the day after his mother's death, leaving him both wealth and rank—had passed a short time in London after their marriage, and now came down to the house of the kind-hearted Sir Harry Jarvis, in order to meet Mary's father and mother. The good old baronet, ever thoughtful of what would give pleasure to others, had sent his carriage to London for Colonel Brandrum. Louisa Lisle came with her brother and her sister-in-law; and thus a large party, each worthy and amiable in their several ways, was assembled under one roof.

Sir Harry Jarvis himself, though now somewhat feeble, was all smiles and gladness, and as active as his infirmities would permit in caring for the comfort of his guests. Kate was, for the time, not merely externally cheerful, for she was one who knew not seeming. The effort went deeper than the lips or the brow, and she forced her heart to throw away its dark memories and darker anticipations, and share in the joy of her friends.

The dinner passed very merrily; Sir Charles Chevenix was full of jest and gay good-humor. Colonel Brandrum told many an anecdote of Indian warfare, and vowed that, if it were not for his broken leg, which incapacitated him for active service, he would dress himself as the Ravenous Crow, and dance the war-dance in honor of Reginald's marriage. Lady Chevenix, now quite charmed with her son-in-law, was all urbanity and kindness; and though she did not comprehend Colonel Brandrum's character in the least, declared he was highly entertaining. Louisa, even pale, fragile Louisa, felt her gentle heart expand with joy at her brother's happiness; and Kate and Mary looked into each other's eyes, and whenever a sad thought returned, strove hard to banish it.

No excess was committed at the old baronet's table; and the gentlemen joined the ladies in the drawing-room as soon as Brandrum and Sir Charles had finished their allotted portion of claret. The fragrant coffee had been served, and Mary had been just besought to sing, when Dixon, the old butler, entered with two papers in his hand, which he presented to Sir Harry, saying, "Jenkins, the Barnet coachman, sir, brought these down from London for your honor. There's great news in town, he says, and he thought you would like to see the *Gazette*."

Sir Harry took the papers and called for his spectacles, and when he had got them, he applied himself to the "Extraordinary Gazette," handing the newspaper which accompanied it to Colonel Brandrum, with the remark, "It is very droll, my dear colonel, that the appetite for this world's news increases when we are going out of it."

"True, Sir Harry, true," replied the colonel; "you and I have little else to amuse us: those boys and girls find plenty;" and he applied himself to his paper.

Sir Harry, sitting under a luster, read on for some minutes gravely, but with a look of satisfaction; but then he suddenly stopped, and raised his eyes toward Kate, when, almost at the same moment, Colonel Brandrum did the same. The latter, however, was much more accustomed to vent his thoughts aloud than the old baronet, and sometimes added an unnecessary expletive. On this occasion he did both, saying, "By ——, that's curious. I could have sworn it of him."

"Hush!" said Sir Harry. "I suppose, my dear sir, our news is the same."

He spoke in a low voice, and Brandrum asked, "What is it?"

"The taking of Charleston by Sir Harry Clinton," said the old man, aloud, seeing that all eyes were turned upon him; but, at the same time, he pointed with his finger to a passage in the *Gazette*.

Brandrum limped up to his chair and looked over him, when he saw, at the spot where the baronet's finger rested, the following words in the dispatch: "I can not forbear expressing my high sense of the distinguished conduct of Lieutenant-colonel Lutwich in all the operations which preceded and accompanied this event, both in leading and encouraging the men, and maintaining order and discipline under very trying circumstances. Though wounded in the arm and in the knee, he refused to retire from his command, and rendered me the most efficient and gallant assistance at every period of the operations."

"That's worth a general's commission," said Brandrum; "but that is not my news, Sir Harry. It is well-nigh as good, though very horrible. There, you take that—it is more in your way, and give me this, which is more in mine; only the news of the fighting will make me long to be in the midst of it."

Mary's song had been stopped by all this; and now there was a general exclamation of "Pray, let us hear. Do not keep all the good news to yourselves."

"Charleston is taken by Sir Harry Clinton," repeated Sir Harry, looking at the newspaper which Brandrum had put into his hands at the same time; "Charleston is—Good Heaven! I had not heard of his death!"

"Nor I either," said the colonel.

"Whose death?" asked Lady Chevenix.

"Sir Theodore Broughton's," replied Colonel Brandrum; and Kate fell at once on the floor, as if he had shot her.

Of course, much confusion followed; and during the intervals of the attempts to recall poor Kate to herself, both ladies and gentlemen cried out upon the old officer for his indiscretion.

He bore it with great meekness and fortitude, however.

"Well, my dears," he said to Mary and Louisa, "I might have told her worse news for herself, though one can not help regretting that a young fool like that should be cut off in the midst of a career of folly and wickedness, without time to review his life, and make atonement as far as possible. After all, I believe my way of telling her was best: it was once for all. But she is coming to herself again. You English girls are dear creatures, but you are very weak and movable. If I had told one of the charming squaws such a piece of news, she would have got up and given the war-hoop."

Kate recovered speedily, and Mary and Louisa led her away to her own room. Sir Harry could not be content without following; and, with all his own kindness of heart and gentleness of manner, he soothed her tenderly and affectionately.

The emotions in the poor girl's bosom were very mixed, but they found relief in tears; and after Mary and Louisa were gone, she replied to her old relation's expressions of anxiety, "I shall be better soon, my dear uncle. I can not but feel that this is a relief, and yet I am half angry at myself for feeling it so. It is, indeed, terrible to think of this young man's death, and to know that he was but little prepared for it; but I do hope and trust that his rash pursuit—I might well call it persecution—of myself, has had no share in bringing about this fatal result."

"No, my dear child, no," replied Sir Harry, in a very sad tone; "I fear that there is a horrible history to be yet fully developed. All we know at present is, that a suspicion of poison exists, and that his guardian, Captain Donovan, has been apprehended."

He saw that Kate was very painfully affected, and he paused; but then added, "Without at all rejoicing at this unhappy man's death, my dear girl, we may reasonably thank God for relieving you from so dark and sad an engagement, without one step on your part, which even your too scrupulous heart might feel unworthy of you. You are now free, my Kate."

"To dedicate the rest of my life to you, my dear uncle," replied Kate, gazing at him with deep affection in her face.

"No, no—not quite so," said Sir Harry, with a smile; "you were formed for a happier fate, my love."

Kate shook her head somewhat sadly, and the old man went on to say, "Some one who may be worthy of your love may win it, and claim you of me."

She gazed upon the ground with tears in her eyes, and her lips murmured slowly, "No—no."

"Well, let us talk of brighter things," continued Sir Harry, anxious to give her every or any source of happiness. "I have some news of a far more pleasant and unmixed character for you, my love. In Sir Henry Clinton's last dispatch regarding the campaign in America, the name of our friend Colonel Lutwich is mentioned with the very highest encomiums, not only of his gallantry and military skill, but of his whole conduct. I have lived many years, my child, and never yet, that I remember, have seen higher praise given to any soldier by his commanding officer."

It was the first time he had ever mentioned the name of Lutwich in her hearing since she had dwelt under his roof, and she gazed in his face with an inquiring look. Sir Harry played for a moment with his seals, and lifting his eyes, he said, "Now, tell me, Kate, are you really resolved never to marry?"

Kate laid her hand upon his, and answered, "Never, if it is to take me from you; and never, never, without your consent."

The old man threw his arms round her, and kissed her tenderly. "My own Kate!" he said: "now tell me, in your own dear, frank way, do you love Lutwich?"

Kate kept her face upon his shoulder, and replied, in a low voice, "I have loved him well enough to sacrifice for him more than life—a whole life's happiness: I love him still well enough to do the same, were it needful; but not to disobey you, or do aught, I trust, that is wrong."

"My consent shall never be refused to your happiness, my love," replied Sir Harry, pressing her to his heart. "We will think, my dear, that Lutwich, during his earlier years, was mad; that the delirium of youth's high blood was in many of his acts: we will trust that he is now himself again; and if he still proves himself so, he shall not want his reward, if I can give it."

"He never had any faults toward me!" replied Kate; "and when others persecuted, he nobly protected me. Oh! my dear uncle, I can never forget that night I passed in his cottage: the kindness, the gentlemanly courtesy, the respectful tenderness, the consideration for every feeling which he displayed. Let others call him what they will, to me he was ever generous—noble—kind."

"Enough, enough, my Kate," said the old baronet; "you have said enough to decide my conduct. Now, Kate, wipe away those tears, and rejoin us soon."

I know not whether the reader will or will not wish to hear more of the personages of this tale. But lest he should, and be disappointed if he do not, I will add a few words.

Sir Harry Jarvis was busy writing all the following morning; and his letter, which was a long one, went to America. About nine months after, Kate stood in that bright drawing-room with Lutwich's arms around her; nor did any consequence of his past life ever appear to trouble their repose. She had changed, not his nature, but his conduct: her love had led him in the only road to true happiness; and he tried to make the present as happy to her, as she had rendered futurity to him.

Surely no one will ask if Reginald Lisle and Mary Chevenix were happy too.

Louisa made one of the most charming old maids that ever was seen; and if she had not spoiled a whole host of nephews and nieces, she would have been without a fault.

Doctor Gamble died in the Fleet Prison.

Colonel Brandrum lived to tell his stories of Indian warfare long, and Sir Harry Jarvis saw extreme old age; for, in both their cases, high hearts and pure had an embalming influence, which long preserved even the frail mortal body from the power of Time.

There is one other to be spoken of, and, alas! that the tale should close so sadly!

Captain Donovan, conscious of intended guilt, was betrayed into such doubtful conduct after the death of his ward, that suspicion was soon directed toward himself. He was tried by a judge who summed up harshly against him, convicted upon evidence that would not in our days be held conclusive, and executed for a crime he had meditated, but did not commit, protesting his innocence to the last.

I am not fond of dwelling upon painful scenes. Of his fate I have said enough, and the tale is done.

THE END.

THE

LAST OF THE FAIRIES;

A Christmas Tale.

BY G. P. R. JAMES, ESQ.,

AUTHOR OF

"THE CONVICT," "MARGARET GRAHAM," "RUSSELL," "THE CASTLE OF EHRENSTEIN," "BEAUCHAMP," "HEIDELBERG," ETC., ETC.

HARPER & BROTHERS, PUBLISHERS,

82 CLIFF STREET, NEW YORK.

1848.

THE LAST OF THE FAIRIES.

CHAPTER I.

There was an old house near Worcester on the very highest part of the hill, which is not very high after all. It was not a gentleman's house, nor a farm-house, nor a cottage. Heaven knows what it had been in former years. It was nothing at all in A. D. 1651, but a moderate sized brick building, lined with old wainscot, with broken windows and latchless doors, and one portion of it a great deal taller than the other.

There were eyes in the upper room of the tallest part of the old house; and to them was exposed an exceedingly beautiful scene, such as is rarely beheld, except in the vale of the Severn. Worcester, with its walls, and gates, and churches, and sunny fields, and pleasant places round; and the wide valley studded with little knolls, and monticules covered with turf still green, and plumed with feathery trees. It was a pleasant and a cheerful sight,—a sort of fairy scene; and indeed the rings left by the feet of the Good People, in their merry moonlight dances, attested their frequent revels in the meadows and under the trees.

But there were other objects besides those which nature's hand had formed that gave additional cheerfulness to the scene. On both banks of the Severn, the eyes gazing from that high window could discern colours flaunting in the light wind, banners tossed about, and plumes, and gay dresses, and glittering arms; so that in that part of the landscape, as a cloud or two passed over the sun, the effect was like that of rapid light and shade sweeping across a garden of flowers. And merry notes were there too: the fife, and the drum, and the clarion, rising up from below, softened and entendered by the air and the distance. The bells of the cathedral chimed cheerfully, and altogether it was a pleasant scene to look upon, and these were merry sounds to hear.

About ten of the clock, a horseman, followed by two or three others, spurred up from the bank of the Severn, towards that house upon the hill. He came gaily along at a good quick canter, and his horse was a fine one, and well caparisoned. His bearing, too, was firm and soldier-like: but when one saw his face nearer, although he could not have counted more than five or six and thirty years, there seemed to be traces of many cares and anxieties upon his countenance, as well, perhaps, as a certain degree of constitutional melancholy, not to say gloom. It was a very grave face —very grave, indeed, yet high and noble in expression, with a tall straight forehead, somewhat broader, perhaps, at the top of the temples than over the brow.

Some servants came round from the back of the house as he approached, and ran to hold his horse and his stirrup. He sprang lightly to the ground, and walked into the house, saying, "Take the basket from Matthews there behind me, and bring it up. Take care that you don't break the wine bottles, for there is but little to be had at Worcester. The Puritans have drank it all up in a very godly manner;" and mounting the old stairs as he spoke, he ran rather than walked up to the higher chamber. There was an embrace for each of the two persons it contained—a lady of seven or eight and twenty years of age, still in her full loveliness, and a little girl of nine or ten, exceedingly beautiful, and very like her mother. Their faces were full of affection towards him who came; but yet there could not be a greater contrast than between the expression of his countenance and theirs. Cheerful hope and glad expectation was upon the face of the girl and her mother, and melancholy thought upon his.

"Here is some breakfast for you, Lilla, dear," he said, "and for my little Kate too. I was resolved to come up for half an hour, and take it with you, for Heaven knows where our next meal may be."

"Will there be a battle to-day, father?" said the little girl; "and will the King win? Oh! yes, I am sure the King will win."

"I trust he will," replied the soldier, "if there is a battle, my Kate; but of that I begin to doubt, for the Roundheads have a long march before them, and cannot get here very early."

"Then we had better come back into the town," said the lady, looking to her husband inquiringly, while two of the servants laid a napkin in one of the broad, open window-seats, for table there was none. "I should not like Cromwell's people to cut us off."

"No, my Lilla," answered her husband, you must not come into the town again. There is much confusion there; and as soon as the enemy appear, you had better retire with the servants to Pershore, where you will have speedy tidings of what follows. If we have to stand a siege, or repel an assault, it would be a pain and a burden to me to have all I lóve pent up within those old and crumbling walls."

There was a look of remonstrance came upon the lady's face, but her husband interrupted her with a smile, saying, "Come—to breakfast! to breakfast! for I must soon get back. What, not a chair to sit down upon! Well, we must make the best of our campaigning;" and standing by the side of the window-seat, he proceeded to distribute the homely breakfast he had brought up from Worcester; ate a small portion, but not much, himself; and gazed with a look of thoughtful delight upon his innocent child, as she seemed to partake of the meal with double zest, from the rude and hasty way in which it was served.

Perhaps five minutes had elapsed while they were thus employed, when a quick light foot was heard coming up the stairs, and a lad some seventeen or eighteen years of age, richly dressed and accoutred, with his long dark hair flowing down over his laced collar to his shoulders, entered the room in haste, exclaiming, "Lord Eustace!—My lord! Cromwell is in sight—Hark! you can hear his trumpets!"

The gentleman he addressed instantly started to the window and looked out, while his young visitor, with a slight affectation of manhood, patted the little girl upon the head, saying, "Ah! my darling Kate, drinking wine at ten in the morning. That's to make you a fit wife for a dashing cavalier. I hope your ladyship is well this morning. You will soon see some warm work down below; but I trust before night we shall have one-half of the Roundheads in the Severn, and the rest in the gaol."

A slight cloud came over the lady's face, and she was answering, with a sigh, "I trust so," when her husband turned round from the window, saying, "I must to horse, dear ones. Remember, you must ride to Pershore, as soon as you have seen them upon the ground. Come, Denzil, we must away."

"Do you see them, Charles,—do you see them?" asked the lady, clinging to his arm.

"Not their whole force," replied her husband, "those trees there hide them; but I caught a glance of steel caps through the brake; and if you listen for a moment you will hear. There! there!"

The distant sounds of a trumpet rose upon the air; and with one brief embrace he tore himself away, ran down the stairs, followed by his young friend, mounted his horse, and galloped back to Worcester.

The lady's eyes were full of tears when she gazed forth from the window, first marking the course of her husband towards the town, and then turning an anxious look over the distant wooded landscape, where the forces of the Parliament were advancing towards the fatal field of Worcester. In a few minutes she beheld a dark moving mass—with catches of light here and there upon breast-plate or steel cap—come forth from behind one clump of trees and disappear again behind a little wood. Another, and another body passed, foot and horse in very equal numbers; but regiment after regiment, troop after troop, till the lady's heart sunk at the conviction of the great superiority of their numbers; and her eyes turned to the royal army below.

A good deal of bustle was then observable; and, by the aid of fancy, she thought she could discover her husband, and the King, and Leslie, and Middleton, and Hamilton, and Derby.

Long and anxious was her watch, till passing in and out, now seen, now lost as before, the army of the Commonwealth, growing more and more distinct in all its parts as it advanced, swept on —halted for a moment—marched forward again, and assumed its position as if for battle, taking possession of the slope of the very hill on which she stood, and interposing between herself and the town.

Her heart sank a little, and she gazed down upon her child; but then a look of high resolution came into her face, and putting her arm round the fair delicate form of the little girl, she said, "We will see it out, Kate; we will see it out."

"Oh! yes, mother, let us see it out," answered the child; "do not let us run away while my father is fighting."

"Never," answered the lady; and there they stood, while the servants gathered themselves together at another window, and gazed forth likewise.

All seemed tranquil for about half-an-hour. An occasional horseman galloped along the line, trumpets sounded from time to time, a slight movement took place amongst the infantry, some stragglers were seen moving about upon the rear of the Parliamentary army, and a stout heavy man, with ten or twelve other horsemen following him, moved slowly for a little distance up the hill. Then halting, he gazed over the plain, and over the town, for a moment or two, spoke a few words to one of those near him, and instantly a horseman dashed away, taking his course towards the left. A large body of cavalry detached itself at once, and rode along the bank of the river; a fire of musketry began from the centre of the line, and a cloud of smoke spread over the scene. It interrupted the sight sadly, but the lady saw several large squadrons of horse put into a charge, and they whirled down like a bolt from a cross-bow against the Royalist troops on the nearest side of the river.

From that moment all was confusion, to eyes unaccustomed to seek out and judge the events of a field of battle. Large bodies of men riding fast, were seen through the clouds of sulphurous vapour, the flashes of the musketry, the gleam of waving swords, and the slow movements of some bands of pikemen were caught indistinctly from time to time; but all that the lady and her child could gather as to the result of these movements was, that the Parliamentary army was pressing down steadily and strongly upon Worcester, and that the waves of battle rolled nearer and nearer to the town.

It was a sight that made her heart sink, and her eye ran along the course of the river, towards a spot where she knew that a large body of the Royalist cavalry had been posted. She saw them there all firm and in array upon the opposite bank, but a little further on she saw—what they could not see, on account of a thick copse and a wooded hill, which screened the operations of the enemy—two regiments of Parliamentary horse galloping rapidly towards a ford, where the stream took a sharp turn. She clasped her hands together, and pressed them tight. What would she have given at that moment for wings to fly and bear her friends intelligence of the manœuvre she had detected and understood right well. But it was all in vain. The enemy reached the ford, dashed in, gained the meadows on the other side, re-formed, and taking ground a little to the left, became suddenly apparent to the King's cavalry.

An instant movement was observable amongst the latter; two gentlemen drew out a little way from the rest, gazed at the squadrons which had so suddenly appeared, and rode to the opposite extremes of their own line. A slight change of disposition immediately followed. The right of the Royalists was somewhat extended, the left was brought a little forward at a slow pace, and then there came a temporary pause. The sound of trumpets was heard the moment after; and both parties dashed forward against each other with furious speed. They met in full career, while a fierce and wild hurrah rose up into the air and reached the lady's ears as she gazed upon the struggling mass, now all mingled and confused. Her hands pressed tighter and tighter together as she saw masterless horses break away from the line and gallop across the plain, and knew that some one, as loved and dear to others as he whom she loved best was to herself, had fallen beneath the chargers' feet in the midst of that fierce conflict.

"They give way, mother, they give way," cried the little girl, touching the lady's arm, "the Roundheads are routed —See, they fly, they fly!"

It was true. The temporary success of Middleton and the Duke of Hamilton for an instant promised to change the fate of the day. Cromwell's cavalry did give way, the Royalists pursued fiercely and drove them back fighting, almost to the very ford. But at that moment a small group was seen to separate itself from the rear of the King's soldiers, and the lady could distinguish two or three troopers supporting a gentleman upon his horse. "That looks like the Duke," she murmured; "No, it must be Middleton."

Another group detached itself, but these were on foot—dismounted soldiers bearing a dead or wounded man in their arms. Then the uncertain tide of battle turned. The Parliamentary forces rallied, charged again, the Royalists were beaten back over the ground they had just traversed, broken, scattered, and flying hither and thither in parties of ten and twelve.

The lady clasped the child's hand in her own—tight, very tight; and the little girl wept. They turned their eyes to the part of the field immediately below them. A terrible change had come over the scene. The Royalist forces were not to be discovered—unless, indeed, the fragments might be distinguished in those small bodies of horse that were seen galloping away over the distant fields. The troops of the Parliament were at the gates of Worcester.

"Pardon, my lady, but it is time for you to go," said an old servant, approaching from the other window; "the day is lost. You had better betake yourself to Pershore, as my lord directed. The horses are all ready."

The lady raised her eyes to heaven for an instant, and seemed to ask strength from above. "No," she said, at length, "we will hide in the wood, Isaac. I will not quit this ground till I know his fate. Come, Kate, we may help your dear father yet. God give us courage and success!"

CHAPTER II.

It was night—dark night. There were stars out but no moon, and across many parts of the sky long lines of dull grey clouds were drawn, hiding the twinklers of the heavens. The clocks of Worcester had struck nine, and the dull vibration of the great bell was sounding, as if with pulses, through the heavy feverish air. The scene around the city lay wrapt up in shadows, while the fugitives sped far away from the field of their defeat, and the pursuers with hot spur hurried after. The dead in their last rest lay in the meadows round—three thousand as gallant gentlemen as ever drew a sword. The wounded untended shared the couch of the dead, and lost part of their own sufferings in the sense of their royal master's disaster. Here and there was a light upon the field, sometimes seen wandering about, sometimes stationary; and the low creaking of rude cart-wheels could be heard seeking for the less dangerously wounded, or for those prisoners who had not yet been taken into the town of Worcester.

Near a low wood, broken and irregular in its external form, stood two or three Parliamentary musketeers, with a group of some seven or eight prisoners, disarmed and tied. A torch was stuck into a hole in the ground, casting its red unwholesome glare around, over the rough stern features of Cromwell's soldiers, and the sad countenances of the captives, and the green branches of the trees, and the turf dabbled with blood, and the corpses of five or six gallant companions fallen; for the spot was one where a fierce and last effort at resistance had been made.

The armed soldiers were standing, resting on their guns; the captives were generally seated, though some who had received wounds were stretched out upon the grass. Few of them spoke, but one man, a Scotchman, in the garb of a Royalist foot-soldier, who was upon his feet, nearest to the musketeers, seemed anxious to ascertain the fate reserved for them. He had put several questions without receiving an answer; but, at length, one of the men, seemingly irritated by his pertinacity, replied in a loud harsh tone, "If you want to know what is to become of you, Scot, I will tell you, though methinks you would learn soon enough: you are to be sold for slaves into the plantations."

The poor Scotchman hung his head, and sat down dejected by his fellows. At the same moment a heavy cart came grating along towards them, and one of the soldiers said, "Come, get up, get up; here is your conveyance."

The cart had not yet indeed become visible, but the next instant the faint outline thereof was descried wending slowly forward, and there seemed two or three people with it. The soldiers, as they looked forward, thought they perceived a woman's garments, and in about a minute after, they saw a child also.

That sight was seen by another likewise, and it told to a heart oppressed with grief and despair, the sweet consoling tale of love and devotion true to the last. He raised himself a little from the grass, and the light of the torch fell more strongly than before upon his fine form and noble countenance. The expression was still the same, and any close observer could not have doubted that there was a man of noble lineage, and of gentle breeding, although his gay and plumed hat was cast away, and the coat that he now wore was that of a common foot-soldier.

Slowly the cart rolled on, but when it came nigh, though the child still appeared, young, and fair, and graceful, the woman's form was no longer seen. It seemed to have dissolved into thin air, or as if the darkness had swallowed it up, even as she came forward. So suddenly and completely did it disappear, that one of the soldiers took two or three steps forward to meet the cart, bending his eyes fixedly upon the obscurity before him; and when he reached the little group walking together at the horse's head, he demanded, sharply, "Was there not a woman with you?"

"No," replied the carter, "there has been no woman here, unless you call this babe a woman."

"And what does she want here?" demanded the stern voice of the soldier; "this is no place for children, or women either."

"I am seeking my father, sir," said the sweet low voice of the little girl. "I am sure you will help me to find my father."

The soldier gazed at her for an instant, as the light of the torch, somewhat softened by the distance, fell upon her fair countenance and her rich dress; and he shook his head with a look not altogether unfeeling, replying, "Ah, poor child! your father is not here; we have none of your gay gallants amongst us; your ruffling cavaliers and dashing lords have all been taken into the town; we have got none but the poor foot-soldiers, who have been led like sheep to the slaughter by those who should know better."

"But I am sure he is here, living or dead," said the little girl in reply; one of our servants saw him here just after the battle, and he told me where to find him; pray let me look for him by the light of the torch;" and she clasped her fair small hands together with the gesture of earnest entreaty.

"I am here, my child, I am here, my Kate," cried a voice; for, although it was ruin to all his plans, the captive could resist no longer; and the child darted forward unopposed, for the soldiers had not the heart to restrain her under the impulse of filial affection.

The poor captive tried to rise from the ground to press her to his heart as she sprang towards him; but his hands were tied, and before he could effect that purpose, the child had cast herself upon his bosom with one arm round his neck, covering his face with kisses.

The stern soldiers looked on much moved; but the captive was surprised to find that while with her left arm she clung closely to him, the right sought out the bonds upon his hands, and something cold, like steel, glided down his wrist. The next instant the cord was severed, and his hands were free; and the child's mouth pressed close to his ear, whispered, low but clear, "There's a horse at the corner of the wood. Mount, father, and away!"

His brain seemed to turn giddy for a moment, and the pulsations of his heart to stop. But the child unclasped her arm from his neck, and whispered once more, "Away!"

It was the only chance for safety. The concealment he had hoped for was no longer possible. The bloody axe which had struck so many of his noble friends was the only fate before him;

and, springing suddenly on his feet, he darted away into the gloom.

As his tall figure disappeared, however, the stern soldiers, with a fierce cry of indignation, raised their muskets to their shoulders, and fired in the direction he had taken. A shrill scream burst from the darkness, at the very same instant that the sound of a horse's hoofs at the full gallop reached the spot where they stood.

"He is down, he is down!" cried some of the men, rushing forward, while two of their comrades remained with the prisoners. But they found no one, though they searched diligently around; and still the quick beating of the horse's hoofs was heard, growing fainter and fainter in the distance. When they returned to the spot where the captives were, they found the child lying prone upon the ground, pale as monumental marble; nor did she recover from the swoon into which she had fallen, till the prisoners had been all placed in the cart, and the party were about to proceed upon their way. The soldiers threatened and reproached; but they had not the heart to hurt her; and one of them, who was a father himself, took her by the hand, and led her into Worcester. He said he must take her before the Lord General, but she besought and prayed him to let her seek shelter in the house of an old servant, and when he left her at the door, he said to himself, "If I should be ever in such a case, may my child do as she has done."

"How the hours fleet away! Be they dull and heavy-footed, overburdened with sorrow—be they winged with joy and mirth—be they even-paced and tranquil in the path of life, still they go, they go; and when they are gone they diminish into a mere speck. Nine years have passed away and it seems but a span; and yet if I come to think, my hair, which is now white, was then just turning grey, and my eyes, that are dim now, were as clear as an eagle's. But come out of the way, lad, come out of the way. There's a stranger riding down the hill, and I have not liked the sight of a stranger for many a long year."

Such were the words of an old man, dressed in a black coat, with a broad-ended handkerchief round his neck, and bearing a respectable and even reverend appearance, to a good-looking country youth of two or three and twenty years of age, as they stood together upon the green sward beneath an old castle wall.

Many a strong fortified house had been besieged and ruined by the cannon of one or the other of the contending parties in the great civil war, but the dilapidation of this building dated from a period long anterior, and the ivy had grown thickly over even the fragments which had fallen from the walls, marking that centuries had passed. Yet these walls were very thick and strong, and one could not suppose, to look upon them, that the hand of time alone had broken them as they now appeared. It was evident, in short, that some of man's desolating devices had overthrown the place of strength before its time—when, I know not—perhaps during the contentions of York and Lancaster; but however, there it stood, a ruin. The most perfect part of the building was the old gateway, with its two tall machicolated towers, and guard-room over the arch; but yet, guard-room and towers were both unroofed, and the wind whistled through the empty window-frames—the voice of desolation calling to the dead.

From either side of this gateway stretched forth walls, with other towers, surrounding perhaps an acre and a half of ground; and the court within showed many a fragment of feudal times in the crumbling masonry of the late keep, and the broken tracery of the chapel windows. A seedling ash tree had planted itself here and there amongst the ruins, and three tall elms in a group stretched their wide branches over the well in the castle court. That well had once been covered by an arch of richly wrought stone-work; but some forty years before the period of which I speak, the mortar having fallen out and some of the stones dropped into the water, which was the finest, the clearest, and the best in the whole neighbourhood, the inhabitants of the adjacent village, who loved the well with a degree of almost superstitious affection, cleared away the ruined fragments from around it, and left it nearly as nature had formed it, with no covering but the branches of the three elms of which I have spoken.

The castle well was in fact a spring

of very beautiful water which issued bountifully from the turf in the castle-court. Old hands long gone had dug a little reservoir for the waters of this spring about three feet deep, and of the same width, with a length of about four feet—it might be five, but I never measured it. The sides of this reservoir were lined with flat stones, to prevent the earth from falling in; and a semi-circular piece cut out of the slab at the west side, suffered the superfluous water to flow away into a little conduit underneath the castle wall, and so over the side of the hill down to the stream in the valley. From the distance of more than a mile, people would come to fill the pitcher at this well; and, indeed, so limpid was the water, that although at most times the smooth surface reflected the leaves and branches of the trees above, yet through these transparent coloured images one could see the little pebbles at the bottom as distinctly as if no medium but thin air had been interposed: indeed, it only seemed to render them brighter, as if encasing them in polished crystal. All around, the turf was short and thick; and the elms and the well they shaded were so placed as to be clearly seen through the archway of the great gates, by any one who was standing on the castle-green in front.

I have been obliged to dwell upon these facts particularly; for the reader must remark and remember them as necessary to the due understanding of this tale. It may be also as well to point out that the castle stood alone, on what may be called the step of a hill, occupying a position about half way up the ascent, which was long but not steep. This step was a flat piece of some twenty or thirty acres; and upon it, at the distance of three or four hundred yards from the old castle, were built several neat cottages. Below them again, on both sides of the road, which, after crossing the castle-green in its descent, wound gently down to the bottom of the valley, appeared the village, following all the sinuosities of the path, and so closely embowered in trees, that from the old gates nothing could be perceived but a roof or a chimney here and there, and the tower of the church rising up from below.

It was as pretty a rural scene, indeed, as ever the eye fell upon; and, whether in sunshine or in shade, under the blue sky or the cloud, there was something of homely peace and tranquillity about it which had a tendency to soothe the mind of the beholder, and call up images of a calmer and happier kind than the heart was ordinarily conversant with in those days of strife and faction.

The village had fared well, too, in many respects. At some distance from any of the channels through which the tide of war had flowed, few of those pertinacious heart-burnings had been engendered in it which had sprung up in most parts of England, from the struggle of parties in the civil war. The old clergyman of the place, it is true, had been dispossessed; and a Presbyterian minister occupied his place; but good Doctor Aldover was a very meek, peaceful, timid man, and he had made no struggle to retain what the powers that were thought fit to take away from him, having been scared almost out of his senses by being apprehended as a malignant, while on a visit to a neighboring town, and examined by a party of Parliamentary Commissioners. He promised them on that occasion, with all the sincerity of terror, to conform as much as in him lay to their good will and pleasure, and, consequently, resigned his benefice, without a word, at the very first summons. He had studied medicine early, as a means of benefitting his parishioners; and now, as was frequently the case with dispossessed clergymen in their days, he studied the healing art more deeply, for the purpose of maintaining himself. He acquired skill and reputation, too, and, at the time I speak of, was the only physician or surgeon in the place. It can not be said that, though he bore his fate so meekly, he looked at his Presbyterian rival at first with any great affection: but it so happened that the minister, though somewhat starch and caustic in his manner, was a good man and a kind, at heart; and when he discovered all the high qualities of his predecessor, he felt half inclined to be sorry that he had been the means of depriving him of his cure. He made sundry attempts to win the friendship of good old Dr. Aldover, which, though shyly viewed at first, were rendered successful in the end by various accidental circumstances which tended to bring them together; and now they would not unfrequently sit in the parlour of the one or the other, drinking a moderate glass of good ale, and conversing learnedly of this or of that, sometimes with much simple shrewdness, when the topic was one with which their studies had rendered them familiar, and sometimes very nonsensically when they ventured upon ground of which they had no experience.

Such was the state of the village on the day I speak of.

I know not whether the poet intended it as the most perfect picture of human felicity when he described a man as "the world forgetting, by the world forgot," but certainly, dear reader, such is to many men, and to all men under certain circumstances, a very blissful mode or condition of life. We all know that in this great world that we inhabit, there are a great number of jealousies, fears, animosities, hatreds, strifes, confusions, riots, massacres, crimes—that men in the world pick each other's pockets of their purses, their snuff-boxes, their handkerchiefs, their reputation, their honour, their peace; and we all know, moreover, that there are certain times—stormy times in the world, party times—when the winds of faction blow high, and the clouds of rancour gather over the state, and men see in the fanciful vapours, strange images of patriotism and freedom, and devotion and renown, which after all turn out shapes formed of mist, that change with every puff of prevailing gale; we all know, I say, that there are such times, and that then the devil is exceedingly busy in stirring up the confused caldron of human passions and bringing hatred, malice, and all uncharitableness to the surface.

Surely, at such epochs as these, a man may well wish to live, "the world forgetting, by the world forgot." But it is not very often that he can find such a state in its completeness as might have been done at the time I speak of, in the village that I have mentioned. The Presbyterian minister was at the height of his ambition. There was nothing more for him to have or to desire. He had dispossessed an Episcopalian of his church and benefice, he had sat himself down amongst a knot of his co-religionists, to whom he could hold forth continually upon predestination, and election, and free grace. He met with no opposition and very little dissent from his doctrines, and he did not at all want to be disturbed in the exercise of functions which worked so easily by Baptists, Anabaptists, Independents, or Fifth Monarchy men.

Doctor Aldover had still greater objections to any interruptions of the quietude of the place; and he it was, to say the truth, who, standing before the castle gate, with a youth, the son of one of his patients, was struck with so much terror at the sight of a stranger, and hurried away so precipitately towards his own house in the village.

In the mean time, the horseman whom he had perceived coming down the hill, descended slowly; and it would appear that his quiet pace was the effect, more of curiosity in regard to the country, than of apprehension for his horse's knees, for he stopped altogether more than once, and seemed to gaze over the surrounding scene. He took no notice whatsoever of the two who turned away at his approach; and, at length, he reached the step in the hill which I have described, and drew in his rein before the castle gates. Whether it was the beauty of the scene that attracted him, or some personal interest in the spot, I cannot tell; but, after looking round him for a moment, he dismounted, threw the heavy stirrups across the saddle, and leading his horse under the shadow of the old walls at the northern angle, where the grass was luxuriant but somewhat rank, he left him to feed, as if there was a perfect understanding between man and beast, as to their pilgrimage together through this world. Then, coming round to the western side himself, on which the declining sun was beginning to shine, he seated himself in the shadow of the arch-way, crossed his arms upon his chest, and fell into a fit of meditation.

Now, whether meditation always ends in a conviction of its own inutility, and men, before it has gone on long, come to the conclusion of one of the best of our mocking-bird poets, that

"Thinking is nothing but a waste of thought,
And nought is everything, and everything is nought:"

or whether there be something of a retro-active mesmerism in the very operation of thinking, which sends the thinker asleep, as potently as the communication of his thoughts sometimes sends others; certain it is that reveries, especially after a long ride, are very apt—at least it is so with myself—to end in a nap. The traveller, if one might judge by his dress, which was very dusty, had come that day somewhat more than a good morning's march; and his meditations, after having continued profoundly for about five minutes, concluded in the abandonment of all meditations. His eyes closed, his head leaned back against the angle of the masonry, and his hat pressed off, formed an indifferent pillow, while his dark brown hair escaping from beneath, refuted without words the famous tract upon "The unloveliness of Lovelocks."

In short, he was a very handsome young man, of some seven or eight and twenty; and the bright glossy curls of his long abundant hair, suited his face much better than the short crop of the parliamentary soldier, or the sleek straight cut hair of the puritanical preacher.

He slept there undisturbed for nearly half an hour; and whether he dreamed at all, or did not dream, whether his slumbers were sweet and balmy, or troubled and restless, none knew so well as his horse; for the animal, after having cropped the grass for about a quarter of an hour, came quietly up to his master, and looked at him with a pensive seriousness, very edifying to behold, as if he were reasoning upon the quality of sleep, or wondering what the mischief his master could be about. At the end of the time I have mentioned, however, the horse gave a sudden start, and a stamp with his foot; and the traveller springing on his feet, found the sun upon the very verge of the horizon, pouring a rich stream of purple light straight through the great gates and over the green turf of the castle-yard.

As was very natural with a horse, after having been ridden throughout a dusty day, the beast's nose was extended straight towards the well in the castle-yard; and the young gentleman, turning his eyes in that direction likewise, beheld, with a strange peculiar feeling which he could not account for, a female form of exquisite beauty and grace standing on the opposite side of the little well, and gazing apparently towards the setting sun. She was clothed altogether in white, and though the shadow of the trees fell over her, yet there was at that moment a sort of airy lustre upon her face and person, which spread, as it seemed, through the atmosphere round her, catching even upon the rugged trunks of the elms and the leaves immediately over her head, very much after the fashion of the glory round the figures of saints in pictures of the second or third epoch of art. She was slight and small of stature; but it seemed to the dazzled and surprised eyes of the traveller, that never in mortal form had he beheld so much symmetry and grace. He could hardly believe that he was awake; and yet everything was clear and palpable around him: the old castle and its grey walls, and the green ivy, the yard, the chapel, the castle-green, the horse which had borne him so far. But still he almost fancied that he was sleeping, for the being before him, dressed in a fashion different from that of the day, looked so much like the creature of some brilliant dream, that he could hardly imagine it reality. He took a step or two towards her; and was convinced that he was waking, by seeing the reflection of the same figure in the limpid waters of the well near which she stood. The next instant, another sense was called upon to bear testimony to the truth of what his eyes avouched, for a sweet and musical voice, though somewhat melancholy in tone withal, pronounced three times the word "Back!" But as he still advanced, the figure retreated step by step before him, seeming to become thinner, less substantial, more shadowy; first losing its peculiar radiance, then becoming dimmer in outline, and then being but faintly seen, as it entered the dark shadows cast by the old chapel, still keeping, however, its face towards him.

He was one not easily daunted, and he exclaimed aloud, "Lady! lady! grant me one word of direction, for I am not sure of my way." At the same moment he sprang across the old well, bending down his eyes for a single instant to make sure of his leap. When he raised them again, the figure was gone, and he stood gazing upon the chapel like one bewildered.

In passing from the castle to the

higher part of the village, there was a little lane between two trimmed hedgerows, with gardens on either side, filled not only with fruit-bearing trees, but with several broad oaks and long-armed beeches, and here a poplar towering up and looking, in the shadowy evening, by no means unlike a cypress. The edge on the left ended in a neat paling, defending from the encroachment of dogs and urchins a small strip of flower-garden lying between the lane and a moderate-sized house. As soon as you had passed the house, you found yourself upon a good wide piece of broken turf, flanking the sandy main road, and ornamented with a row of elms; and the eye could range down the highway between houses and gardens and groups of trees and broad patches of waste green, dotted with sundry geese gobbling the short grass, into the more populous part of the village, till, taking a gentle turn, its further course was lost, just when the church came in sight, with the wall of the church-yard extending to the edge of the road.

The house on the left of the lane—I mean the house with the little strip of flower-garden—was both neat and picturesque—a combination not frequently found. The lower story—whether upon the consideration that land was dear and sky was cheap—had been so constructed as to occupy considerably less space than the upper story, which projected on every side nearly a foot and a half beyond the sub-structure, resting on massive beams, which were supported by the walls beneath. The roof was thatched, but in the most perfect order and repair, and the walls were nicely whitewashed, although an immense quantity of superfluous timber, forming a sort of curious pattern upon the front and sides, was still distinctly visible, giving the whole building the appearance of being covered with a damask table-cloth.

Here lived good Doctor Aldover; and towards the hour of sunset on the day I have mentioned, he was sitting, as was not at all uncommon in those times, before his own door, with a table by his side, and a jug of ale upon it.

Close to him, hat in hand, and ready to depart, was the youth with whom we have seen him speaking upon the green before the old castle; but upon the other side of the table, seated on a settle, was the Presbyterian minister—a thin, worn, ascetic-looking personage, of fifty-six or fifty-seven years of age, whose somewhat hard features and fallen cheeks gave an expression of sourness and implacability to his countenance, except at those moments when an accidental smile played upon his lips, serving as a better interpreter to his heart.

The good clerical doctor dismissed the youth with an assurance that his father would do very well if he would take the medicines ordered him. "You see to it yourself, John Brownlow," he said, "for I have a great notion, my man, that more of the potions go under the bed than into the mouth, and I'll call upon him again to-morrow. I shall find out—depend upon it."

"Then you don't think he's bewitched, sir?" said the young man, with a sly smile.

"Bewitched? befiddled!" exclaimed Doctor Aldover; "no such thing—it's all nonsense—get away with you."

The young man retired at his bidding; but the Rev. Gideon Samson shook his head with a grave and doubtful expression of countenance, observing, "I hope, my good and learned friend, your observation just now does not extend to imply a disbelief in the actual existence of witches or in the apparition of the spirits of the dead?"

"Nay, heaven forbid, reverend sir," replied Doctor Aldover. "That witches have existed we know from the Book of books; and that spirits have appeared and do appear is rendered positively certain by direct testimony which cannot be gainsayed; but whether these be mere astral spirits, or really and truly the disembodied soul of a departed person, sometimes puzzles me sorely to determine."

"Astral spirits!" exclaimed Mr. Gideon Samson. "That is a mere fantastic absurdity, Doctor Aldover, a mode of explaining away facts which both Scripture, common sense, and evidence require us to believe. I suppose your sceptical coxcombs would have it that this fairy of the castle is an astral spirit forsooth; but I will ever maintain that it is purely and simply the reappearance on this earth of a person long dead permitted, for some inscrutable purpose, to revisit scenes once familiar. I suppose, doctor, you do not think fit to disbelieve in this apparition, at least, when it has been seen by so many."

"Heaven forbid that I should disbelieve in the fairy," answered Doctor Aldover meekly. "Have I not seen her myself, which is better than all argument, my reverend friend?"

"I don't know that," answered Mr. Samson, who was in a disputatious mood; "there are some modes of argument, Doctor Aldover, which are more convincing than even the evidence of our own senses."

A sly smile came upon the worthy doctor's face, but the conversation was cut short by the appearance of a third personage on the scene; no other, in fact, than the young stranger, who had passed a portion of the evening in sleeping under the castle walls. He walked forward slowly and gravely in the twilight, leading his horse by the bridle, as if, either weary with a long ride, or busy with deep meditations; and, as he approached the spot where Doctor Aldover and his companion were sitting, he raised his eyes and looked at them steadily, and then, with a graceful salutation, addressed the worthy physician, inquiring if he could direct him to an inn, or any place where he could obtain accommodation for his beast and himself during the night.

"There are few inns or taverns in this neighbourhood, I thank God," said Mr. Gideon Samson, taking the words out of Dr. Aldover's mouth. "We have not here much to do with lewd travellers, and no habitual revellers of our own; those are evils we are free from at least."

The answer was certainly not civil, but yet the young stranger only heard it with a smile. "There may be other travellers, my good sir," he said, "besides those whom you designate by so harsh a name, and I trust I am one of them. There are travellers for business as well as for pleasure; and they needs must find some place of public entertainment if they have no friends in the part of the country where they may be. Such is my case at present, and I shall think it somewhat hard, if with a weary beast and tired limbs of my own, I am forced to journey many miles onward, because some people might make evil uses of an inn, were such a thing tolerated in the village."

This reply seemed somewhat to soothe the worthy Presbyterian, who, as has been before explained, was not by nature a harsh or unkind man, though, as is always the case with sects claiming the utmost extent of free judgment, he was somewhat intolerant of the opinions of others. His second reply, however, though couched in rather more courteous terms than the first, was but little more satisfactory to the stranger; for it only went to show him that there was but small chance of his obtaining any accommodation in a place where, for some reason or another, he was determined to remain.

His face displayed the mortification which he felt very clearly, and just as he was turning away with an expression of thanks for what little information he had obtained, good Doctor Aldover, who had been gazing at him with some interest, but without speaking, came to his relief, saying, "My dwelling is a very humble one, sir, but if you can content yourself with that, such accommodation as it can afford is very much at your service for the night."

The young man's countenance brightened instantly; and after some faint apologies for the trouble, et cetera, he agreed to take up his abode with the doctor, saying, "all that I require, kind sir, is a hard bed, a crust of bread, and a glass of water."

"Oh! we can do better for you than that," replied the worthy old man; "we can give you—"

The doctor did not conclude the sentence as he had intended, for he stood in some awe of his Presbyterian friend, and the catalogue of good things which he was about to enumerate being suspended on his lips, "We can give you," he said, "a cup of as good ale as any in the country, and a frugal supper—it may be of bread and cheese, or perhaps a rasher; and though my beds are not of down, yet they are soft enough to sleep upon, especially for a weary man."

The invitation thus given and received seemed the signal for worthy Mr. Gideon Samson's departure; and to say the truth, his going did not appear at all unpleasant to Doctor Aldover, whose face brightened at his departure. He let him be out of earshot, however, before he made any comment, talked to the stranger about stabling his horse, talked to himself as to what room he should lodge him in, and then, calling loudly for a personage named Joshua, declared repeatedly that he was very happy indeed to have the opportunity of showing his young guest some attention.

The stranger received his civilities calmly and gravely, waited with his bridle in his hand till Joshua appeared in a gardener's habit, and then, resigning the charge of his steed to him, walked with his host into the house, and entered a little parlour, to which one descended by a single step. When the door was closed, however, he too began to smile; and, taking the doctor's hand as he welcomed him courteously, he said, "I rather imagine, my kind friend, that your hospitality is shown to one not altogether unknown to you, although you have forgotten him. Time has changed you much too, but I can not be mistaken in thinking that I am right in calling you Mr. Aldover."

"To be sure, to be sure," answered that clerical physician. "I will never deny my name; but in good sooth, young gentleman, yours I cannot tell; and yet your face comes back upon my memory like a dream. I wish you would say where I have seen it."

"It matters not, my dear sir," replied the young gentleman. "You saw it last in terrible times, which it were safest both for you and me not to speak of."

Doctor Aldover looked all round the room with a timid glance, as if he expected to see protruding from the wainscot the secret ears which walls are reputed to have; and he murmured in a low voice, "Very true, very true; it is better not to talk of such things. They are a severe and suspicious people here, with very rank and hasty people amongst them. Lord love you! my dear sir, a tavern is an abomination in their eyes; and because the boys and girls used to dance at the inn-door, they called it a tabernacle for the devil, dispossessed the landlord, and shut up the house. I am very glad to see you, nevertheless, and we will have—we will have a bowl of punch. There can be no harm in that surely. I never could discover that there was any sin in a lemon, or the bitterness of malignancy in sugar, or that rum was an evil spirit; except when he got too strong for a man. We will have a bowl of punch, I declare, but with all moderation, for it is many a year since I took a ladle-full with a—a friend."

By what free-masonry it was that he discovered the stranger to be of the same party to which he himself had formerly belonged — whether by the long locks of curling hair, or by the cavalierish cut of his vest, or by the tie of his cravat—I cannot say, but certain it is, that good Doctor Aldover felt a moral conviction that his guest had a great deal more of the Cavalier than the Roundhead in him; and yet it was a sort of timid, half-frightened assurance, which required some sort of confirmation from his own lips. Such, however, the stranger did not vouchsafe to give, but merely replied in a somewhat thoughtful tone, "Punch is no bad mixture, my reverend friend, when both compounded and drank with due discretion;" and taking this admission as confirmation of the judgment he had formed, the worthy doctor hurried out to procure the ingredients for the fragrant bowl, while the stranger looked after him for a moment with a slight smile, and then leaned his brow upon his hands, and closed his eyes with the air of a man exhausted by fatigue either of mind or body. The short sleep which he had obtained under the castle walls was all that his eyes had known for two whole days and nights, and he certainly still felt drowsy. He struggled against it, however, for he was by no means a sleepy-headed hero, and when he felt himself inclined to nod he looked up and gazed round the chamber, trying to find some object sufficiently interesting to the eyes to keep them from closing. The aspect of the whole place, however, was not very enlivening. It was a tolerable sized low-roofed room, panelled with dark oak, and having on one side of it a range of ponderous book-cases of the same material, filled principally with large folios. There is a certain degree of sleepiness even in the very aspect of a great number of big books. They weigh upon the imagination, and make the very mind feel drowsy by anticipation; so that side of the room would not do. He then looked to the other, but he was almost worse off there. Each panel was surrounded by a wreath of carved flowers, each having been, to all appearance, cut out of the very piece of wood that formed the panel to which they were attached. They were by no means badly executed, but yet there was a certain degree of stiffness about them, a drowsy immobility, which fell oppressively upon the spirits; one would have given the world for a breath of air to stir them. It was worse still with the different carved heads with which the room was thickly ornamented. They all looked not alone as if they were going to sleep, but as if they were sound asleep already. A grim lion seemed to nod at him here; a sleepy-looking cherub hung over another corner, as if its eyes, according to the boys' phrase, were drawing straws; and the devil himself, who was perched up in the centre of the cornice with a fiddle in his hand, was the very picture of Morpheus.

As the stranger gazed the objects became indistinct; and leaning his head upon his hand, he gave himself up to the influence, rousing himself only twice, and at length bowed his head to his fate, and adding his other hand to support his brow likewise, enjoyed a few moments of perfect oblivion.

Oh! where do its waters flow? In what happy land, where the past is forgotten, and the future all unknown? Thirst for what he may in life, man will often desire no other beverage so much as for a few drops from that dark stream,

"The goddess dipped her mortal son in Styx,
A mortal mother would on Lethe fix."

Sleep, however, is not always oblivion; and although, as I have said, the young wanderer enjoyed for a few moments that blissful immunity from racking thought, it lasted no longer. The vision came to renew the past, to paint the future. He was in the saddle again, but not as he had lately ridden. There were plumes in his hat, and steel upon his breast, and weapons upon his side. He heard the clang of the trumpet, and the word of command, and the clash of swords, and the rattle of the musketry, and the roar of the cannon. His horse seemed to bound beneath him, his hand to grasp the reins, his arm to wave the bright and trenchant blade. The enemy went down before him, he trampled upon them as he went on in the furious charge—nothing could resist him, nothing stood against him; onward, onward he was hurried, as if some supernatural power gave him strength and command to smite down every thing before him. The pike, and the sword, and the musketoon, and the flaming mouth of the artillery, had no fears for him; victory was upon his arm and triumph upon his brow, and he thought but of success and conquest. But yet he saw his fellows fall around him; the fiery shot told amongst their ranks, the keen sabre hewed them down, they became thinner and more thin, till at length he was left alone in the midst of the fight, still conquering wherever he came, still seeing nothing stand before him. Onward, onward, through the hostile ranks he dashed, leaving a wide space cleft like a pathway through the heart of battalions bristling with arms. Onward, onward, from the front to the very rear, past their artillery, through their tents, till not even a straggler appeared before him. Then he strove to draw in his rein that he might turn again to the fight, but it was in vain he did so. The horse's jaws seemed of iron; and, impelled by a power no human strength could overcome or guide, forward he went at the same headlong pace, through the standing corn, over the fallow field, across the brown moor, and the high hill down into the valley, through the marsh and the deep stream. The forest impeded him not, the very rocks seemed to give way before him; his breath was as free in rushing up the mountain as in galloping across the plain; and miles, and miles, and miles, were left behind, as if the beast had the wings of thought or hoofs of the lightning.

The day seemed to go down, thunder-clouds gathered upon the evening sky; the night came on; but still, in the impervious darkness, forward rushed the steed as fresh as the morning, as unweary as the ever-wandering sun. The rider felt exhausted, fatigued; his limbs ached and lost their strength; he felt he could not sit his beast much longer, when, in the faint grey light of the morning, he saw a wood and an old abbey with its ruined arches and broken tracery, and there seemed thin and airy figures on the walls and at the windows beckoning him with shadowy hands, as if inviting him to enter. The reins dropped from his hand, his head turned giddy, and he fell upon the green sward, at the foot of the trees, saying to himself, "Here shall I die;" but suddenly a sweet voice, the voice of a young girl, cried, "Denzil, Denzil, rise up and listen!"

And, starting from his slumber, the wanderer found himself still sitting in Doctor Aldover's library. The twilight had faded away into night; but yet it was not dark, for the moon had risen and was looking in at the window. He could see every object around him as plainly as if it were day, but yet he could not perceive whence that voice came. "It was in a dream," he thought; but the moment after he heard it again repeating, "Denzil, Denzil, wake up and listen."

"Am I still dreaming?" he thought; and, to assure himself that such was not the case, he rose from his seat, exclaiming, "Who is it that speaks? Where are you?"

"Near to you, yet far from you," replied the voice; "where you can not come to me yet, though in time you must come."

"What would you, then?" cried the young man; "what would you with me now?"

"Come to the church at midnight," said the voice, "and you shall hear."

"Why not now?" demanded the young man; "why not here?"

"Come alone to the church at midnight," repeated the voice, "and wait in the nave till you are called."

"Who bids me do so?" demanded the traveller.

But before any answer could be given, the door of the library opened, and good Doctor Aldover himself appeared with a light in his hand.

"Why you are talking to yourself, my young friend," he said. "Yet, after so quiet a sleep as you have had for the last half hour, I should have thought you might have chosen some other collocutor."

The young gentleman put his hand to his brow and remained silent for a moment or two, while a neat maid-servant brought into the room a large bowl of punch, together with several plates and dishes loaded, if one might judge by the odour, with contents by no means unpalatable. He permitted her to set them down upon the table, and make all those little arrangements upon which maid-servants are so fond of spending more time than enough, without uttering a word in reply to the worthy doctor's observation; but when that was done, and the room once more clear, he laid his hand upon his host's arm, saying, "My dear sir, I was not talking to myself, and there is something that must be explained here. I was called by my name not two minutes ago; I answered, and received a reply in return. All this in a place where I know no one—am known to no one that I know of! Had it been a man's voice, I might have understood it in part at least; but it was a woman's tongue, and the whole is incomprehensible."

"Pooh! pooh!" said Doctor Aldover, "you have been dreaming, my good sir."

"Dreaming I have been, certainly," replied the stranger; "but this took place when I had awakened from my dream."

"A change in the vision, that is all," answered the worthy clerical physician, who did not seem to like the subject altogether; "it could be nothing else. When I looked at you half an hour ago, your hands were moving upon your face as if your thoughts were very busy, though sound asleep.—Come, let us to supper, my good friend. Here we have got, I think, a young fowl boiled with barley, and a leaf or two of taragon to give it good digestion, and there are some slices of bacon boiled to give a relish to our punch; sit you down, my good sir—nay, take an arm-chair."

The stranger did according to the bidding of his entertainer, and Doctor Aldover helped him liberally to the dish before him; but the young man's appetite seemed to fail, for ere he had eaten more than two or three mouthfuls, he laid down his knife and fell into a deep fit of thought.

"Mr. Aldover," he said, after this had continued for a minute or two, "I cannot rest satisfied with this mystery. I assure you I was awake, broad awake, and I received an injunction from the voice that spoke to me, to go down to the church at midnight."

"Indeed!" exclaimed Doctor Aldover with a look of some surprise; "do you intend to go?"

"I must have some further insight into the case before I determine, replied the guest; "and as this occurrence has taken place in your house, I cannot help thinking you can give me an explanation if you will."

"Have you seen any one since your arrival whom you know?" asked Doctor Aldover; "I mean before you reached my garden gate; for it seems you do know me."

"No one," replied his visitor; "I met no one of any kind, except indeed one personage who puzzled me much, a lady in the castle-yard standing just on the opposite side of the well. When I sought to speak with her, she retreated before me, and in the end seemed to vanish away—at least, I could discover no farther trace of her."

"The fairy of the castle well," said Doctor Aldover, in a low voice and in a very peculiar tone. "What was the hour?"

"Just as the sun was setting," replied the young man.

"Ay, ay! just the exact hour! It is very strange how rashly some people judge. Now I hold this to be merely an astral spirit, but good Mr. Gideon Samson and many of the inhabitants of this village maintain stoutly that it is the spirit of some one dead permitted to return for the purpose, doubtless, of frightening their friends and relations."

The guest leaned his head upon his hand and thought, while Doctor Aldover proceeded to discuss very learnedly the difference between astral spirits and what he termed Hammethim, or the spirits of the dead, and when his worthy entertainer paused for a moment he enquired, "Pray, when did this spirit or fairy first appear?"

"It is some years ago now," answered Doctor Aldover, "in the worst times of a bad age. When first the thing was talked of, we thought it but the melancholic superstitions of the old women of the place, for it was good Dame Deborah Higgins who first saw the apparition as she went to draw water at the well, just as the sun was setting, and left her pitcher there and came away in a great fright. But several have seen the fairy, as they call her, since, and all their doubts have vanished in the place."

"Has any effort been made to speak with or to follow her?" asked the stranger.

"Oh yes!" answered Doctor Aldover; "one young fellow half drunk vowed he would have a dance with the fairy, and went up to the castle for that purpose. The fairy seemed not inclined to disappoint him, for according to his story, he saw her by the well within three minutes after he was there, and followed her across the great court, and suddenly he received a buffet from an unseen hand which laid him at full length upon the grass."

The stranger smiled. "Somewhat more substantial than fairy favours usually are," he answered.

"Ay! I see you are an unbeliever," replied Doctor Aldover. "I, however, believe what I have seen, though you apparently doubt your own eyes, for you admit that they were witnesses of this sight."

"Nay, I doubt not," answered the young gentleman; "I only think it very strange. I see no sufficient reason to suppose either that there are not many intermediate grades of beings between God and man, or that some of these beings may not become visible to us even on the earth. At the same time, my dear sir, I entertain no dread of them; for although every man has many sins to atone for, yet the atonement which has been made is all-sufficient if we have but faith therein."

"Wisely and reasonably spoken," replied Doctor Aldover. "I feel the same. I acknowledge and entertain no apprehensions whatever; but the people of the place have very different feelings, so much so, that you find it very difficult to persuade any of them to visit the church or the castle either after night-fall."

"I am determined to do the former," replied the doctor's guest, "and must use your interest with the sexton to get the keys, which I suppose as rector you can command at any time."

"Alas! my young friend, I am rector no more," replied the doctor; "I was dispossessed just after the battle of Worcester. Nevertheless, I can get you the keys easily, for they are in the hands of one who is under some obligations to me, and I will walk down with you to his house, though it be somewhat far off, and I am not fond of the evening air. Let us finish our bowl first, however, for you will need all the courage that a stout heart and a good strong cup can supply, to walk amidst those old aisles and ghostly-looking monuments at midnight. There are strange stories about that church, and true ones I believe."

"Pray, let me hear some of them," said his guest; but Doctor Aldover said, "No, no, I never repeat them, though my good successor in the ministry is not a little fond of spreading them abroad, till there is scarcely a child in the village that does not go to bed with his knees shaking, or a girl that will open her eyes for a moment after her candle is out. Here, let me fill your glass."

The young man took his full share of the stout beverage very readily, and the doctor remarked, not without some satisfaction, that he looked grave and thoughtful during the rest of the time they remained in the house. Whether he really entertained any apprehensions or not, however, he steadily maintained his resolution, and in half an hour set out with his worthy host in search of the keys of the church.

There was a nice little cottage in the green lane that turned off from the high-road, about a hundred yards before you came to the castle green. The lane ploughed the side of the hill as with a deep furrow and descended rapidly, passed the cottage itself and a farm-house on the other hand, and then took a considerable circuit to reach the bank of the stream and the lower end of the village, which it accomplished by four or five little paths stretching out like the fingers of an open hand. This lane avoided all the turnings and windings which were taken by the high-road, for instead of circling round any obstruction which might come in its way in the shape of a rise or fall in the ground, it went straight over them all. The little cottage I have spoken of was about half-way between the castle and the stream, a neat, tidy, though lowly building, containing within itself more accommodation than the externals promised; and though it was somewhat lonely, yet in the clear summer days it had a pleasant view both of the church and the castle, and a part of the village, and in the winter a better view still, because the leaves were then off the trees. In the front towards the lane was a very neat parlour—for the personage to whom it belonged aped some of the usages of gentility—and separated by a thick partition that which to him was drawing-room, dining-room, and library, from the offices, although round the latter there ran a sort of trellised portico, which we, in the present day, should call verandah.

In this parlour, on the same night during which, for the first time in eight or nine years, Doctor Aldover consumed a bowl of punch with a guest, were seated two persons of very different age and appearance. We will take the one in the arm-chair first. He was a man of some sixty-eight years of age, but looking a good deal more—heavy, stout, and venerable, but with a dull sort of look, as if intellect, though not altogether gone, were a little drowsy. His face was reddish about the nose and on the cheeks, but rather pale in the intervening spaces; and his black eye, though not so sparking as it once had been, had a good deal of sharp cunning in it, perhaps natural, perhaps acquired by long dealing with the world, that great whetstone of the faculties.

On the broad capacious hearth, although it was summer time—that is to say, the later summer when evenings get somewhat cold—were two or three lighted logs of wood, and over them the old man bent in his arm-chair with his hands outspread, as if the warm flame cheered the icy blood of age.

Before I go farther, however, as I have talked of a parlour and an arm-chair, and a verandah, let me first explain what sort of room, what sort of chair, what sort of verandah it is that I mean. Well then, dearly beloved reader, the parlour was floored with brick; it was low in the ceiling; and a great number of beams, protruding far beyond the rest of the plasterer's work overhead, afforded convenient positions for driving in a nail or a screw to support a number of small articles and some large ones, such as hams, sides of bacon, a powder-flask, a pouch or two of shot, besides several of these things for which we acquire an affectionate regard in passing from youth to age—things which are as if they were friends to us, from our long familiarity with them. The arm-chair, indeed, derived its name from having two wooden arms, one on either side; but if examined closely, it was found to be nothing more than a settle with appendages. The verandah was a sort of little rustic portico with a trellis-work of rough branches, which in the summer evenings afforded shade to the old man when he thought fit to sit out and drink his glass of ale in the free air.

The other tenant of the room, standing behind the first, with a yard or two between them, and phial and a cup in his hand, was no other than the young man we have twice seen with Doctor Aldover, a good-looking, stout, well-formed peasant youth of about six or seven and twenty years of age, with nut-brown curly hair, a good deal of hardy color, a bright clear eye, and a look of shrewd and merry intelligence. He was in the present instance in the act of persuading his father to take the medicine ordered for him by Doctor Aldover; but the old man resisted stoutly.

"No, John, no," he said; "I'll take no more of it. What's the use, John? I'm bewitched, boy; there's not a doubt of it; and I am sure old Martha Unwin did it, because I took her chamber clock for rent."

"Pooh, pooh, father," answered the son, "you are not bewitched at all: Doctor Aldover says so, and he is both a divine and a physician, so he must know. As to Martha, she is a very good old woman, and would not hurt any one for the whole world. She thought you bewitched for being so hard upon her, but she never bewitched you."

"Then how came I to bring two tin tacks off my stomach?" asked the old man, as if that argument were conclusive; "you saw it yourself."

"Because you put half a dozen of them between your teeth, when you were mending the old coffer," answered his son; "I saw that, too, myself; and if six went in, only four came out of your mouth. Come, father, take the medicine; it will make you quite well the good doctor says."

It required much persuasion, however, before the medicine was taken, and it had certainly not been down three minutes when old Roger Brownlow, as he was called in the village, remarked, in a discontented tone, "I'm no better, John."

"If you go to bed, father, you soon will be," replied his son; and at the end of an argument of five or ten minutes more, the old gentleman was persuaded to follow this piece of good advice and retire to rest. The domestic labors of John Brownlow being thus concluded, he took down his tall, plain, steeple-crowned hat from a peg on which it hung; and, approaching a door which opened from the side of the room within a few feet of the fire-place, said, in a low voice, "Alice, Alice, I am going out for a while."

No answer was returned, and, after waiting for a moment, the young man quietly mounted the stairs and tapped at a door above. Still all was silent, and murmuring, "How provoking! she has gone out!" he returned, and seated himself in the parlour, and leaned his head upon his hand.

"Heaven knows when she will be back now," he said, in a murmur to himself; "and Jane will be gone to bed before I can get out. Then, all to-morrow I shall have no time. Where can she be gone to now, I wonder; she knew I was anxious to go."

He continued in this sort of vein to converse with himself, evidently not very well satisfied with the absence of the person he called Alice, till, at the end of about half an hour, some one knocked hard at the door, and John Brownlow exclaimed, sharply, "Come in."

Before the words were spoken, however, Doctor Aldover and his young companion were in the room; and the former at once began upon the business which brought him, saying, "I want the keys of the church, John. Has your father gone to bed?"

"Yes, sir," answered the young man, with a respectful air, "he has been in bed this half hour or more; but if he were up, I don't think he has got the keys himself, for Alice always keeps them now, and she's out, I don't know where."

"Wherever she is, she is in the right place," said Doctor Aldover, "and she won't be long, I dare say; so we will wait till she comes back, John."

"I was waiting for her, too, sir," said the young man; "for Betty, the girl, has gone to see her father at Crofton, and I did n't like to go out and leave my old father in the house alone for fear anything should happen, though I wanted to go out for a while very much too; but if you are going to stop, doctor, till Alice comes back, there will be no need of my remaining."

"Ah! Jane Unwin, Jane Unwin!" said Doctor Aldover. "I know where you are going, just as well as if you told me, John; and you are two silly young people, for your father will never consent. I am quite sure of that. Well, go along with you; it 's no use trying to make youth wise. Nature makes us fools, experience whips us into scholars, and then death takes us just as we are getting the last lesson by heart. Go along with you, go along with you. I will stay till Alice comes."

The young man was not slow in taking advantage of the permission he thus received, and without further ceremony or excuses, he put on his hat again and walked out of the door which had given admission to his two visitors.

"He 's a good lad," said Doctor Aldover, as soon as he was gone; "he 's a good lad as any in the parish, but his father is a nasty old curmudgeon, whose whole soul has been devoted to scraping money together all his life. The young man is in love too, like a fool, with a pretty little penniless thing whom his father will never consent to his marrying; so the poor boy is in a perilous way, as old Shakspere calls it. I know not what will come of it, I am sure, and sometimes think it almost a sin to prolong the old man's life, for it is a plague to himself and no good to any one. It is not my business, indeed, and God will take him when he thinks fit."

There was a slight rustle as the old gentleman spoke, and turning sharply round, as did also his young companion, they saw, coming down the stairs, the foot of which was visible through the door which John Brownlow had left open, the form of a young girl of seventeen or eighteen years of age, which well deserved their attention, and that of the reader also. It had all the lightness of youth, and those graces which, given by nature to a very early period of life, are but too frequently obliterated in the poorer classes of society by the labours and the toils to which poverty is exposed. In Alice Brownlow, however, not one of those graces had been effaced, and the perfect symmetry of every limb was only the more displayed by every movement that she made. Not even the prim and unbecoming dress of the day could in the least conceal it, nor the plain mob-cap, showing the smallest possible portion of the black, dark hair, hide or diminish the beauty of the face beneath. The young stranger, at least, thought it the fairest face he had ever seen, and while Doctor Aldover advanced and took her hand, saying, "Ah, Alice! my dear child, your cousin told us you were out, and we have been waiting your return. I thought you could not be playing truant at this hour of night."

"I have but this moment come back, sir," answered Alice Brownlow, "and, thinking I heard some one speaking, I came down to see who it was, or if my uncle wanted anything."

"He is gone to bed," said Doctor Aldover, "so John tells me; but what we want, my dear child, are the keys of the church, which are in your fair possession, I find. This gentleman is going to see if he can find a ghost or a fairy."

"He must go up to the castle for the fairy," said the beautiful girl, turning her eyes upon the young stranger, who then, for the first time, perceived that those eyes were deep blue; and, to say the truth, he gazed into them so earnestly, that the colour came a good deal into her cheek as she proceeded; "but I do not think he would find any fairy there either. I have never seen one, at least."

"Ah! you are a little sceptic," said Doctor Aldover. "Do not let your friend, Gideon Samson, hear you, or he will put you to penance for your incredulity."

The girl laughed, as if she did not much fear such a result, but merely replying, "I will go and fetch the keys directly," she ran away up the stairs again, leaving one at least of the party in wonder and admiration.

"She is marvellously beautiful," he said, as soon as he thought she was out of earshot.

"And not less beautiful than good," said Doctor Aldover; "but there is a very cold heart under that bright face—at least so say the youths of the village, I know not with what truth. She may be cold to love, but she is not cold to charity, that I can vouch for; for she goes about healing the wounds her uncle makes, and they are a good many. That old man was once the sexton here, and he has somehow contrived to amass sufficient wealth to make himself master of half the cottages in the village; but here she comes again with her foot of light. So here are the keys, my dear; but you must tell us which is which, for there seems a score of them."

Alice Brownlow smiled; "I will go with you and show you, sir," she said, "if you like."

"He is not going now," answered the good doctor, "but at an hour when even you, Alice, would be afraid to go."

"Oh, no!" replied the girl, "I have no fears at any time."

"What, at midnight?" asked the stranger.

"Oh yes! or at any time," she answered. "I do not know why people should be more afraid at midnight than any other hour, if they have good consciences."

"Then if you will, you shall be my guide," said the young gentleman somewhat eagerly; but Doctor Aldover looked a little grave, saying, "It is hardly fit, I think. What will your uncle say, Alice?"

"Nothing," replied the girl, looking up with a frank smile in Doctor Aldover's face. "He leaves me to do as I please in all things, and he knows I do not use my liberty amiss. Do you think I do, kind Doctor Aldover?"

"Heaven forbid!" exclaimed the old man; "but this gentleman is nearly a stranger to me, Alice. I beg your pardon, sir," he continued, turning to the stranger, "but I look upon this dear girl almost as my own child."

"She is perfectly safe with me," replied the stranger, warmly; "I trust the day will never come when the very thought of injuring or insulting one like her could even enter into my mind."

"I am quite certain of it," said Alice Brownlow; "I never met with insult from any one yet, and I do not think this gentleman would be the first.

"Not for aught on earth," he answered; "but as your kind friend here is still afraid, I see, though it may be a trespass on his time, why should he not come with us?"

"That must not be, I am afraid," replied Doctor Aldover. "My good friend Gideon is somewhat jealous, and were he to hear that I, his dispossessed predecessor, were visiting the church at midnight, there is no knowing what suspicions he might conceive. I must even trust you, I suppose."

"Trust is always best," said the fair girl beside him; "I have found it so, and it will be so to the end. My cousin John will not be home for an hour or more, but if the gentleman will then come down, I will show him the way to the church and open the doors for him. The way back he must find himself, I fear, for I cannot stay, and he can put the keys in the shed by the door."

"Farewell, then, for the present," said Doctor Aldover; and thus the conversation ended, with the exception of a few words of very little interest to the reader, though of more to the young stranger.

"Has your uncle let the two rooms above?" asked the good physician.

"Not yet," replied Alice.

"Nor ever will," said Doctor Aldover; "he asks too much for them, my dear."

The young stranger thought that he should very much like to make the worthy doctor's words prove false. It was a rash, bold fancy that he took to hire those two rooms, and he revolved the subject in his mind all the way back, not forgetting, however, to remark every turning of the road, that he might find his way to the cottage again at the appointed time.

The moon's short-lived reign was over, and the night was dark. There were many stars indeed in the zenith twinkling bright and clear, but round the horizon on every side there were heavy mists, not exactly amounting to clouds, but which shut out all the lesser lights of heaven. There were many trees over the road too, so that it was only now and then that Orion or the Bear could be seen; and the stranger and Alice Brownlow walked on almost in darkness. The whole world was silent around, except when from a great distance the baying of a dog was heard through the clear stillness of the night. There was a strong odour in the air too, as if the flowers were giving out their perfume more liberally to the cool night air than to the warm and eager day; but yet there was a kind of faint sensation crept over the frame under the overpowering sweetness which seemed to breathe from the flowers and shrubs,—a languor tending to fanciful imaginings, to which the absence of all sight and sound contributed also.

The stranger felt it gain upon him; the stories he had heard told and well authenticated came back to his mind; and many a curious question suggested itself as he walked on. To say that he was superstitious would not be correct, for in regard to beings beyond or above the earth, he believed rather less than more than the great majority of people in his day; but yet he could not help feeling that, in reasoning analogically, there was every cause for believing, first, that the interval between the All-creating Spirit and the first of corporeal creatures was not an unfilled gap—that the upper world, if I may so term it, was tenanted, like the inferior world in which we dwell, by innumerable classes, infinite gradations of spiritual beings; and he then asked himself, "Is it to be supposed that an impassable bar is placed against all communion between the purely spiritual and the next link in the great chain of creation?"

Reason instantly answered, "No;" and, whether he looked to the evidence of Scripture, or history, or the testimony of living men, he found an infinity of recorded facts to bear out the conclusion that communications of various kinds could and did take place, between the free spirit, detached from all earthly bonds, and the immortal essence prisoned in the clay. He thought of all the bold and daring carelessness with which he regarded such subjects at ordinary times, and again he asked himself, if it was not the daily round of business, the turmoil, and hurry of the strife of life, the worldliness of our whole existence, that withdrew us from a sense, a consciousness, a conviction that we were ever in the presence of multitudes of fellow-spirits unseen, unknown, but who might, if we were less absorbed in the dull things of earth, manifest themselves to us in some mode, to warn, to encourage, or to uphold?

Busied with these thoughts, he almost forgot his fair companion for some time, as she walked on beside him, in her grey dress, and with a black silk scarf shrouding her head, shadowy almost as his imaginations. At length, however, his thoughts seemed to oppress him. He asked himself if he were going to turn coward and be afraid; and, certainly, a degree of awe, such as he had never felt before, crept over him, and he felt cold and chilled. He thought conversation might dissipate such sensations, and breaking the long silence, he said, "You are sceptical about ghosts and spirits, I find. Do you not believe in the existence of such beings at all?"

"Certainly I do," replied the girl, with her sweet plaintive voice; "it is a belief I cherish and am fond of. I not only know that they exist, but I know that they appear; but that is very different from fearing them."

"Then have you ever seen one?" asked the stranger.

"Nay," she said, "I did not come to tell you ghost stories. You will see enough, perhaps, to-night to convince you, if you doubt or misbelieve; for many of the hard and incredulous have learned, in the very church-yard to which we are going, to know that there are other things worthy of men's thoughts besides the mere seeking after gain, the strife of ambition, or the empty toys with which grown children amuse the busy infancy of this life."

"You are a strange being," said the stranger, "and seem to have busied yourself with things very different from those which usually occupy girls of your age and station."

"I have," she answered. "Left an orphan at a very early age, my own thoughts have been my companions, and some old books, which, if they were more read, might render men and women wiser than they are. But yonder is the church-yard. Pray, remember, sir, that those who are good have nought to fear from either worse or better spirits. A free conscience and a bold heart need dread nothing on this earth or beyond it."

She spoke in a low and solemn tone, and certainly her words did serve to cheer, though they seemed intended to encourage. The stranger looked forward on the path which they were following; but the darkness was too profound for him to see any thing but the rounded forms of some large old trees, with the dark tower of the church rising above them. In another minute he stood beneath the wooden shedded portico of the church-yard, where, in the service of the Church of England, the clergyman first meets the corpse; and he could see the low crumbling wall that surrounded the cemetery stretching away far on either side.

"It seems very extensive," he said, in a low voice.

"It had need," replied his guide, "for there are many dead lie here: the great and the humble side by side, the good and the bad, the oppressor and the oppressed, the young and the old; the dust mingling with the dust through far-back centuries; the spirits to their several tasks as God shall appoint them."

As she spoke she unlocked the outer gate, and led the way on as if so familiar with the place that she could not miss her way; but her companion as he followed stumbled more than once over the little mounds of earth cast up upon the breasts of the dead. They passed through the tall old trees which nearly encircled the church-yard, and then the young stranger could see dark masses of the building itself through the dim faint air. It was a large and heavy pile, with many a projecting buttress, and many a tall narrow window, while high up in air rose the large square tower, solemn and mysterious in its look.

"What is that?" asked the traveller as they came near; "there seems a light there—a faint small light."

"Nothing but a glow-worm on a grave," replied the girl; "the image of fame after death;" and she walked quietly on till she stood beneath the low projecting porch. It was evident that the place and the hour had their impression with her—if not of fear, still of awe; and with hasty hand she sought the key of the church in the large bunch she carried, and applied it to the keyhole in the heavy door.

Before she turned it she asked almost in a whisper, "Is your heart still strong."

"Yes," replied her companion; and she opened the door.

"Take care how you go," said the girl, "for the chancel is full of tombs; and remember to shut the doors after you and lock them. I must now leave you."

For a moment he heard her light step retreating in the deep silence of the night, and then all was still again; and he stood before the open door of the church alone. He felt a hesitation—he asked himself if it were not folly to go on at a summons so strangely given; but something impelled him forward, and he stretched out his hand to push the door farther back. At that very instant there was a loud clang that made him start, as with a slow, swinging, wave-like sound the great clock began to strike the hour of midnight. He felt ashamed of his sensations, ashamed of having started; and with a determined step he entered.

All was dark within, and he had to feel his way. The first thing his hand touched was one of the small narrow pillars of a cluster-column, feeling cold and death-like; and then came an iron railing round a grave. That guided him on some way; but then putting forth his right arm, he suddenly laid his hand upon the icy fingers of a statue, and the first impulse was to draw back as if he had touched a corpse. The stillness was overpowering, too; it seemed more profound, more death-like than without. In the free air, there had been a light rustle amongst the trees; the very sigh of the night-wind had taken away from the solemnity of the silence. Here, everything was hushed and mournfully quiet, not a breath of air moved through the gloomy aisles, and there was a chilly sensation in the place, a close clinging coldness, that depressed the heart and filled the imagination with gloomy images. The grave and the worm, and the icy chill of death, and the everlasting silence, and the slow corruption, presented themselves involuntarily to the mind, and he wondered if the disembodied spirit could be permitted to see, and trace day by day the awful changes of that corporeal frame in the powers and beauty of which it perhaps once glorified itself. His thoughts were very dark, and his heart heavy, as he reached the spot as the transept by which he entered joined the nave. He turned to the right and to the left, endeavouring to see the objects around, but at first nothing was perceptible but the tall windows on either side, looking at him like dim strange-shaped eyes, as the less intense darkness without them gave some relief from the black obscurity of all the rest. The next moment, however, something white, of the size and in the form of a human figure, seemed to gleam upon him at the farther end of the nave; as he gazed towards it he could see it more distinctly. It moved not, but remained without any apparent change in one spot; and clasping the fingers of his left hand round the sheath of his sword, he took a step or two towards it. The figure was now more defined, apparently that of a woman, habited in a long white robe; but still it was perfectly motionless; and the young stranger said in a low voice, "I am here! what do you want with me?"

There was no answer, and with a hasty determination, advancing straight towards the object he beheld, he found that it was a figure of white marble upon a low sepulchral monument.

"Can I have been the sport of my own fancy?" the young man asked himself; "can I have been still dreaming as the good old man said when I thought I heard this voice calling me? no, no; that is impossible!" and turning towards the other end of the church, he repeated aloud, "I am here! who is it sent for me?"

There was a momentary silence, and then came a low, sweet, beautiful strain of music, solemn and sad, but exquisitely touching; and the young traveller stood listening in silent delight. But yet there was something unearthly about it too. Now it seemed far off, now it swelled nearer to the ear, now rose into the high treble, now sunk muttering down in the bass. Suddenly it ceased, and the same sweet tongue which had spoken to him before said, "Denzil, Denzil, follow, follow!"

"Where?" asked the stranger.

"To the grave," said the voice.

"To mine?" demanded the young man.

"To the grave of one who loved you in boyhood," replied the voice again. "Denzil, Denzil, follow, follow!"

"I will," he replied; "show me the way."

The moment he spoke a faint light gleamed through the church, and he could see dimly around him the gloomy aisles, and the tall columns, and the numerous tombs, with the sculptured memorials of the dead. His heart beat a good deal, but he had no time to question with himself, for the voice repeated from the other end of the church, "Denzil, Denzil, follow, follow!" and with a strong resolution, and a quick step, he hurried on, guided by the voice. The church had been stripped of many of its monuments, the rich screen had been torn down between the choir and the nave, the seats of sculptured oak had lighted the fires of the Puritans, and all was free and open from one end to the other. But just beyond the northern wing of the transept, Denzil could see the spot from which the light seemed to issue, still faint but stronger there than anywhere else; and as he approached, it appeared to him to rise from the ground. A step or two farther showed him a large flat stone, like the covering of a vault raised high, and the gleam coming up from beneath; and when he reached the edge of the aperture, he could perceive the first steps of a stone stair-case, descending apparently into the vaults or the crypt of the church. He hesitated for an instant as to whether he should descend, but the voice again called him by name, and repeated "Follow, follow!"

"I will," murmured the stranger to himself, "whatever be the consequence;" and with a feeling of awe, for I will not venture to call it fear, he leaped down to the top, or landing-place, of the small stair-case, and began the descent. "I shall soon see whence this light comes," he said; but he was mistaken, for he found the faint rays still gleaming up, casting a long shadow behind him as he went down. Near the top the steps seemed new and fresh, at least compared with those below; for although they were somewhat stained and green as if no foot had trod them for many years, yet they were sharp-cut and firmly set in the mortar. After the first ten or twelve, however, they became rough, broken and irregular, slippery with cold damp, and with many a foul insect crawling over them. A large toad, bloated and swollen, crept slowly across almost under the wanderer's feet, eyeing him in the unaccustomed light, with his large brilliant eyes, as if wondering what he did there; and numerous bats hanging together in clusters from the mildewed walls, took flight at his approach, and skimmed away upon their filmy wings.

The descent was long, at least fifty steps, turning upon a common centre, led him down, as if towards the very heart of the earth, and still the light receded before him, seeming as far off at the bottom as the beginning of the descent, till at length a small round arched door appeared at the foot of the staircase, and he saw the faint rays, gleaming as before amidst innumerable low pillars and intersecting lines of masonry. At the same moment the voice said again, "Follow, Denzil, follow!" but to obey was somewhat difficult, for the ground was obstructed, not only by loose scattered stones and fragments of falling masonry, but by the rolled up bones of the dead. Skulls with their grinning white teeth, and wide staring, eyeless sockets, lay upon the path, and more than once he felt the bones of beings like himself cranch and crumble under his tread as he marched along. It made his blood run cold to think that his steps were upon the ruined relics of mortal men, and he strove to see where he set his foot, but the light receding fast, left him in a sort of semi-darkness, while a hooting owl flapped past him on its downy wings, and stirred the damp-smelling air around.

Smothering his repugnance, he strode on hastily, perplexed and bewildered by the numerous arches and the low columns that supported them, and unable to perceive in what precise direction the light was carried, while a low murmuring sound, as if of a multitude of voices talking at a distance, met his ear, and a cool fresh air came and waved about the curls around his brow.

"This is indeed strange," he thought, "I know not whether I am dreaming or awake. What can be the object of bringing me hither! Yet it is vain to think of retreating now," and on he went till suddenly he came to what seemed the cold face of a rock, roughly hewn and fashioned, into what the old architects called rustic-work, with a small narrow archway through which the light still streamed, though it was partly obstructed by a heavy stone door, left half open. The young stranger pushed it back, using all his strength, but it rolled easily on the pivot which supported it, and striking against the masonry which lined the passage beyond, produced a hollow sound and a sharp clang like a groan and a scream. The light was before him still, and he could now see a small pale bluish white flame moving onward at a distance, but could distinguish no hand that bore it.

"Follow, Denzil, follow!" said a voice which came sweetly, almost in a whisper, along the passage, and the next instant there was a sound like the baying of a large dog, while another voice exclaimed, "Down, fiend, down!"

Silently the young man drew his sword out of the sheath, and paused for an instant, but immediately the voice he had first heard said, "Fear not, Denzil, follow! nothing living has ever cowed you; fear not the dead."

"I fear not," answered the young man, aloud; but yet, if the truth must be told, he felt cold and chill, and his heart beat quicker than was its wont. Onward, onward, he went for nearly a quarter of a mile, the light still preceding him, casting a bright glare upon the yellow brown damp that hung about the walls, and the drops of moisture that every here and there percolated through the stones of the vault overhead. At length the passage seemed to open out, and he caught a faint sight of what seemed a large octagonal chamber with something that looked at first view like an altar in the midst, and the moment after the light was suddenly extinguished, and he stood in total darkness.

"Twenty steps farther," said the voice, "then ask what questions you will, and they shall be answered."

With his sword still in his hand, the young man strode on till nineteen steps were measured, and as he took the twentieth the blade of his weapon struck against some hard substance, and produced a ringing sound around him.

"Why have I been brought hither?" he said aloud.

"To receive advice which may lead you to fortune," answered a deep stern voice.

"I must know the giver of the advice before I take it," said the young man; "yet let me hear it."

"It is written down," replied the same tongue which had before spoken. "Those who give it, know what you know not, see what you see not, understand what you do not understand. They are with you, but not of you; they have guided you, and will guide you, they have watched over you from youth to manhood; they would fain see that manhood great and good, but your fate must be of your own shaping, they can but help."

"Where shall I find this writing?" asked the young man.

"Will you obey the words that you shall find written?" demanded the voice.

"That will depend upon what they are," was the answer. "I will do nought against my country, or the cause which I have always served."

"If you would free your country from a yoke more burdensome than that of the bloodiest tyrant that ever ruled, if you would render triumphant the great cause in which you have fought and bled—if you would raise yourself high in honour, and merit gratitude and renown, you will follow the advice given, unquestioning and unhesitating."

"If I understand you right," answered the young man, "I will do so; but tell me who and what you are; I would fain see you face to face."

"Him you cannot see," said the sweeter voice which he had first heard. "Denzil Norman, ask not what is not permitted."

"But you, you," said the young man eagerly; "you, I think, I have already seen; show yourself now."

"So be it," replied the voice, and instantly a light shone through the old place, again displaying the octagon stone chamber, with its vaulted roof, and niches as if for statues, all around. Exactly in the centre was a plain stone tomb with an inscription on the slab of free-stone on the top, and over it were scattered a profusion of fresh flowers, in the midst of which lay a small roll of paper. One object, however, attracted the whole of the young man's attention. One of the large niches, some five or six feet from the ground, seemed open like a Gothic arch, and filled with light, in the midst of which stood the same beautiful figure he had beheld by the castle well, clothed as before entirely in white from head to foot, with long rich curls of glossy, light brown hair, falling over her neck, and breast, and shoulders. He paused in deep silence and amazement, and then, stretching out his hands towards the figure, he was about to speak, when the sweet voice said, "Pray for an instant by the side of the tomb of her who guarded your youth, and was a mother to you when your mother was laid in the grave. Then take up the paper, begone, and obey."

The young man knelt by the tomb, catching sight of one name inscribed upon it as he did so, and bending his head, with the tears streaming from his eyes, upon the cold gray stone, he prayed for an instant as fervently as he had ever prayed in life. Then, rising, he stretched out his hand and took the paper, and the moment he had done so all was darkness.

Denzil Norman stood bewildered for a moment or two beside the tomb, with his thoughts all troubled and his heart beating fast.

"Stretch forth your hand," said the deeper voice of the two which he had heard, and without reply he obeyed. The moment he did so, his fingers were clasped tight in the grasp of another hand; but it was not a hand of flesh and blood. The hardest-working artisan in all the world never had a hand like that—cold as that of the dead, and hard and stiff as adamant. He would have withdrawn his fingers from those that clutched them, but he could not; and the voice said, "Follow, follow!"

On he went, as the cold hand guided, slowly and silently; for though the young gentleman spoke twice, he received no answer. The way seemed interminable in the darkness and the silence, and there was an oppressive feeling in the air which showed him that he was still in the vault. At length, however, a gust of fresh night wind came upon the young man's cheek, and the moment after he perceived a low door open before him, with the faint external light just marking it out in the darkness. He turned quickly in the hope of seeing who was his guide, but at the same moment the hand relaxed its grasp, and the voice said, "Forward!"

Three steps more brought him upon the green grass of the church-yard, and the instant he had passed through the archway the door banged to with a loud clang, which made the whole of the old building echo with the sound.

At day-break Denzil Norman sat in his room at Doctor Aldover's alone with the dove-coloured light of dawn streaming in through the window, and falli upon a table before him, on which was stretched a scroll covered with characters written in very black ink. The paper was yellow as if with age, and part of the writing, at least, was in a tongue or a cypher which the eyes that looked upon it were unacquainted with. A few lines at the top and at the bottom of the page were in the ordinary English hand and language, though there was something cramped and stiff in the formation of the letters, which gave them a strange and antique look. The young gentleman gazed on the paper with a thoughtful air, and repeated in a low voice, "Stay here a week, and then journey as a messenger to the north! Well, it matters not where I stay or or whither I go. In all places there are dangers; in all places there is a Providence. I will obey these strange commands; but where can I find lodging in this place without an inn? I cannot trespass longer on the hospitality of this good old man."

He then remembered the conversation between Doctor Aldover and Alice Brownlow, just before they parted, regarding the rooms her uncle had to let, and his resolution was soon taken. Ere mid-day he was installed the tenant of Roger Brownlow's lodgings; and the old man acknowledged, with the simplicity which not unfrequently accompanies a single passion, especially that of avarice, that he did not know which had done him most good—the having let his rooms, or Doctor Aldover's last dose.

Alice, who was present, smiled gaily, and the good doctor laughed, saying, "The money, Roger; the money! that is your disease and medicine too. But come, Roger, the young gentleman has given you two gold twenty-shilling pieces, out of which you owe him ten; go and get him a couple of fresh Olivers out of your coffer, or you may forget that he has not had his change."

"I'll go, I'll go," answered the old man; "but just let me have a word with you, doctor, before you go;" and away he walked, taking Doctor Aldover with him. Left alone with his fair guide of the night before, Denzil Norman took the opportunity of thanking her; for he had remarked that not only no word of his visit to the church in old Roger Brownlow's presence, but that Doctor Aldover himself, no longer under the exhilarating influence of a good glass of punch, had been exceedingly shy of the subject. Not so Alice Brownlow, however, for she not only spoke freely of his expedition, but questioned him as to what he had seen, in a tone so light and gay as to form a strange contrast with her demeanour on the preceding night.

Denzil Norman found it somewhat difficult to parry her quick inquiries, and only succeeded in doing so by assuming the same tone himself. A little gallantry certainly mingled in his manner too, whether he would or not; for he thought her even more beautiful by daylight than he had done on the preceding evening, and the sparkling grace of her whole manner, in this more cheerful mood, seemed to render her only the more engaging. "I think," he said, "that I shall call you the fairy of the cottage, as we have got a fairy of the castle on the hill above."

"I wish I were a fairy," said the girl with a sigh; "I could do many things then, that I cannot do now."

As may be supposed, Denzil Norman did not let slip the occasion of inquiring how she would exercise her fairy powers if she possessed them; and she answered, "In healing wounds, in making the good and the wise happy, when an adverse fortune dooms them too frequently in this life to sorrow and disappointment."

"Nay," replied the young man, "that, according to the old legends, is more the function of one of the nine orders of angels than of an inferior being like a fairy. But have you no one in particular you would benefit?"

"Oh, to be sure!" replied Alice Brownlow, with a gay smile; "every one has somebody whom they would wish to serve."

"And who would be this favoured one with you?" asked Denzil Norman, not quite well satisfied with the reply. "It is perhaps a bold question to ask a fair lady like yourself."

The girl laughed. "How curious men are!" she said. "The lions are the painters, and they have represented women as all curiosity, while in truth it is man's peculiar vice; but you shall not be disappointed, noble sir. Some day I will show you the person I would wish to benefit, but it must be after longer acquaintance."

The young gentleman, as may be supposed, pressed hard for speedier knowledge, although, to say the truth, he had many doubts whether that knowledge would be pleasing to him; for since the day when Adam ate of the fruit of the forbidden tree, down to this present time, an insatiable thirst has been upon the mortal lip for knowledge, knowledge, knowledge—not only of good but of evil; it is knowledge that we want, whether it be a curse or a blessing, and the devil has ever, as then, an excuse ready for our seeking it.

"I would fain know," said the young man to himself, "whether her heart is given to any one, and to whom. I feel she might be a dangerous companion in this secluded place, and if I find her love has been won, I shall be sufficiently armed against the peril. It is strange that I, who have moved amid the brightest and the fairest, in courts and cities throughout one half of Europe, should never see one who seemed to me so fair and bright as the cottage girl; but it is nonsense thinking of such things—Denzil Norman in love with the niece of Roger Brownlow! That is out of the question. I would give a great deal to see her lover, and I will, please Heaven—some mere boor, I dare say;" and he continued to press her on the subject, till she answered, in the same gay tone in which she had hitherto spoken, "Well, well, sir, you shall be satisfied if you will take a walk forth with me this evening—quietly and secretly, remember, inasmuch as my good uncle must not know anything of the matter; for 'thereby hangs a tale.'"

The answer was not pleasant to him. He almost wished that he had refrained. He fancied he caught a fluttering blush upon her cheek—that he detected a slight embarrassment in her manner, gay and cheerful as it was; and yet he was determined to carry the inquiry to the end, for, let sceptics say what they will, uncertainty is the most painful state of life.

"Give me some sign, then," he said; but before he could finish, or Alice could reply, Doctor Aldover returned with old Roger Brownlow, and soon after took his leave, promising his late guest that his horse should be well cared for at his stable, and that his saddle-bags should be sent down immediately.

The rest of the day passed very pleasantly to Denzil Norman; for although he wandered forth for a short time, yet, as had been previously arranged, he returned to take a homely meal with the family of his host, and sat long, to say sooth, in the parlour of the cottage, conversing with the fair Alice; while the old man nodded in his chair hard by, and left his lodger and his niece to amuse themselves as best they might. Denzil found that that conversation was not without its peril; but there are some men fond of standing on the brink of a precipice, and though he felt a little giddy, yet he would not withdraw. It might be asked, what they talked of? but to be answered by another question, what did they not talk of? for, although he was evidently a high-bred cavalier, and she a country girl, she led him to a thousand themes, and through a thousand courses of thought, which her mind seemed to tread with ease when his had almost lost its way. Sometimes it seemed to him like the course of a butterfly, sporting from flower to flower, and resting but a moment on each; sometimes like some brilliant dance, through which the feet of imagination played sparklingly, seeming all wild and uncontrolled, and yet with a form and plan in every movement.

At length, however, she started up, saying, "I must away, I have an errand to perform;" and passing through the door which has been mentioned, on the left of the fire-place, she ascended the stairs, as it seemed, to her own apartment. A moment or two after, however, while Denzil was looking at the old man, who was just rousing himself from his slumber, he saw a wimple and hood pass the window of the cottage; and taking his hat, he issued forth and looked for the fair wearer. She was nowhere to be seen, however; but that was not at all wonderful, for the manifold lanes and alleys, and their thick hedge-rows, rendered it very easy to lose sight of any object of pursuit. For some time he wandered about in the hope of discovering which way she had taken; and then giving up the chase, bent his steps towards the castle, the grey towers of which he could perceive rising high over the trees.

"I will think no more of this fair young creature," he said to himself; "I have thought of her too much already;" and with a habit which he had acquired in perilous times, and many painful circumstances, he strove to force his mind away from the thoughts that would engross it, and fix them upon those calm external objects of nature's handy-work, from which it is difficult even for the perverse heart of man to extract anything that is evil or dangerous. "How beautiful the scene is!" he continued, in thought; "if I can find my way to the top of yon little hill, I shall get the best view of the castle, I fancy;" and following a path which seemed to lead thither, he was brought round under the old towers, at the distance of about a quarter of a mile. The way was steep, and walking quickly, as all men do who strive to fly from thought, he paused after a while to take breath, and looked up to the ivy-covered walls. As he did so, he suddenly beheld a form appear upon the battlements of the highest tower. It was the same he had seen the evening before at the well; the same that he had seen in the vaults. The white garments, the flowing hair, the light and airy form, which to the eye of fancy seemed almost transparent, were there, with the full light of the sun, not yet declined four hours, shining full upon them; and with a rapid, fearless step, she passed along upon the very edge of the crumbling walls, and amidst the tottering pinnacles, till she reached the top of a small watch-turret, overhanging the path which he was ascending, and there pausing, as if suspended in the air, with a grave and warning gesture she waved him back.

The young man paused and hesitated; and three times she repeated the sign, then suddenly disappeared from his sight, as if she had sunk at once through the tower. Denzil Norman gazed down upon the ground for a moment or two, then turned upon his steps, and found his way back to the cottage.

He found the old man with his son beside him; and John Brownlow, who seemed to have been informed of all that had taken place during his absence in the morning, eyed the stranger not uncivilly; and while finishing the meal to which he had come in late, inquired what way the stranger had directed his steps in his walk.

"By a small road to the eastward, which leads under the castle-walls," replied Denzil Norman.

"Then you must have met the soldiers, I suppose," replied John Brownlow. "I passed them on that road about an hour ago."

Denzil gazed at him steadily for an instant, and then replied in a calm tone, "No, I met no soldiers. What troops are they, pray?"

"They are Lambert's men," answered the other; "marching towards the north, they told me."

"Then they do not remain here," said Denzil Norman, with the same unconcerned manner.

"No," replied John Brownlow, "they must go five miles farther before night; but we are to have a company quartered upon us in a few days, I am told." As he spoke, he fixed his eyes upon his father's lodger; and when he had drank off his horn of beer, he rose, saying, "Have you seen our garden, sir? It is very pretty;" and he took a step or two towards the door of the kitchen, through which was the only exit to the back of the house. Denzil Norman followed, saying he should like to walk through the garden with him; but as soon as they had issued forth, and walked some little way amidst the quaint flower-beds which surrounded the apple trees, John Brownlow stopped, and said, in a low voice, "I think, sir, you had better keep yourself to the house till these men are gone on."

"What makes you think I have any cause to fear them?" asked Denzil Norman.

"Your hair, your French boots, and your gilt hilted sword," answered John Brownlow. "I know not what may be done in London, but here we do not see such things often; and, depend upon it, some of the officers would inquire who you are, and what brought you here. You, of course, know best your own business, but I have given you my advice honestly."

"And I will take it," answered Denzil Norman. "But how shall I know when they are gone?"

"I will let you know," replied the other. "You had better say nothing to my father, but just sit in your own room, and pretend to be busy writing."

The evening sun was just setting upon Landleigh Castle and village, when Denzil Norman once more walked up the hill with Alice Brownlow by his side. Their way lay through the shady lanes, athwart which the level sunbeams glanced, tinged with a rosy hue; as the sun sunk down to rest, and as they caught upon her beautiful figure and sweet face, they seemed to the eyes of her companion to draw forth strange graces and new charms, and his contemplation ended with a sigh. It might be fancy, but he could not help thinking that there was something strange about her altogether—a power, a captivating influence, which no one seemed able to resist. He had seen her that evening with her uncle and her cousin, and they seemed to feel the spell as much as he did. The old man was tame in her presence, strove to conceal before her even the ill qualities he was vain of, and yielded to her lightest word like a child. The young man, though frank and straightforward, still sprang to do her slightest bidding as if her commands were his law; but yet, there was a something in his whole manner to her, and in hers to him, which swept away at once the suspicion which had crossed the mind of Denzil Norman that her cousin might be her lover.

She had been very gay and cheerful throughout the day, but now, when they were alone together in those green lanes, the graver spirit had fallen over her again; and he found deep and strong thoughts, powerful often from their very simplicity, mingling in every answer which she made him, though from time to time a touch of sparkling lightness would cross the whole, like the sunbeams darting through the shade as they passed along. He strove to keep pace with the variations of her mood, and as she had heard of the arrival and halt for an hour of the soldiers in the village, Denzil told her, in gay and jesting strain, of his pursuit of her fair self some hours before, and the cause which had induced him to turn back. "I must be strangely favoured by this fairy," he said; "and as we seem passing near the castle, I should like to turn in at the gate for a moment, and see whether she will favour me again with her presence when I have got a companion with me fairer than herself."

Alice turned and gazed at him for a moment with a grave look. "Do not speak lightly," she replied, "of fairy favours, nor ever pretend to doubt wherever you do not; I will go with you to the castle, if you please, with all my heart, but it will be of little use, for we here know right well that the fairy never appears but once in the day to any one."

"Indeed!" replied Denzil, "she is very regular in her habits, then; I thought fairies were more capricious. Nevertheless, I should like to look through the castle with you, for fair scenes are ever fairer when we see them with one who can appreciate their beauty."

Alice looked in his face with a faint smile. "It is the return of thought for thought," she said, "which brings forth the treasures of the mind and the heart. What would the light be without the shade? and even an inferior mind may often, by the contrasts it affords, give greater brightness to the rays of a higher one. We have little of such interchange of thought here," she added with a sigh; "but here we are at the castle walls, and we can go in by this small gate as well as by the greater one."

They went in, and passing through what seemed to have been a narrow outer court, soon found themselves in the larger open space with the old castle well before them. The sun was shining straight through the arch upon the crystal water and the green trees above it, but no fairy form was there, and Alice stood by the side of the well, and gazed up thoughtfully at the old towers. "Here reigned the bright and noble in the days long gone," she said; "and all have passed away. Their very memories are like a faint echo amongst the hills of words spoken once aloud, and repeated farther and farther distant till they became indistinct. Thus perishes man and his memories! I wonder how many kings and warriors, now forgotten, once thought that they should live for ever in the minds of men."

"All things pass away, and all things are renewed, fair Alice," answered Denzil Norman. "We have—at least I have—seen all our institutions swept to the wind, kings proscribed and slain, princes banished, lords done away, parliaments reduced to a mere name, laws used to destroy laws, and injustice of every kind perpetrated in the name of justice. Yet from all this, as when the earth is ploughed with the deep share, and harrowed with the rough harrow, will, I doubt not, spring up the same institutions as those which went before."

"No, not the same," she answered; "things very much resembling past things, but not the same. I'll tell you how the course of the world seems to me to go," she continued, laying her hand familiarly on his arm. "A simple figure is always the best and the clearest. Did you ever tend a garden? If you did, you will know that each flower and each tree, if you take the seed thereof and sow it, will produce things of the same kind, but not exactly the same. Gather the seed of a tulip or a poppy, and put it in the ground; you will have tulips and poppies spring up the next year, but varied from those which went before. Thus, methinks, with worldly institutions; even when they perish they leave seed, but that seed never reproduces the same. Come, let us not stand speculating here. We are amongst dead things—I have living ones to show you;" and turning to the great gate she passed out; then took her way to the outskirts of the village, and followed by Denzil Norman entered a cottage, the door of which stood open. Within they found a woman in extreme old age, yet hale and healthy for her time of life, and by her side, busily spinning, as fast as her fingers could go, as beautiful a country girl as ever mortal eyes fell upon.

"Ah, Dame Unwin!" said Alice, "I am glad to see you back; I hope poor Bridget is better."

"She is better than any of us, my dear," replied the old woman, "for she is in heaven. The good doctor did all that man could to save her, for her poor husband's sake, and I did what little I could do, but it was of no avail, poor thing. God had called her to himself, and she went. The minister has taken two of the babes home to his house, and the doctor put the other one out to nurse, so the poor man's cares are lightened."

"I fear he could not repay you, granny," said Alice.

"She would not have taken a penny for the world, Alice," replied the girl, looking up from her work, and plying her fingers still. "Should the poor be hard upon the poor?"

"Heaven forbid," said Alice Brownlow; "but you seem very busy here, Jane. Who is it for?"

"Partly for us, partly for them," answered the girl; "but you see, Alice, we have got the clock again. We found the money in the window on Tuesday morning last. Granny would scarcely use it, for she said it was fairy gold, and it might turn to leaves or straws when old Roger Brownlow had got it."

"He would not take anything that was not full weight and tale," answered Alice; "be you sure of that, Jane. It is a good fairy, not a bad one; and if she ever brings me anything, I shall have no fears about it."

Some further conversation passed, and then Alice and her companion took their way homeward. "You have seen," she said, looking up in Denzil's face with a smile of some meaning, "those for whose sake I wish I was a fairy."

"They seem kind, good people," said Denzil Norman, a little confused with the memory of his own doubts.

"The old woman tends the sick poor," said Alice, in a slow and feeling tone, "when they have no one to tend them; and the girl works cheerfully from dawn till night to support her grandmother and herself. She will one day become John Brownlow's wife; but that day is afar, and I could wish to be a fairy, to abridge the long hours of expectation for them. Now, do you understand me?"

"I do, at length, entirely," answered Denzil Norman, warmly; "but such a heart as yours may not be easy to understand at once."

It was still dark, although there was a faint grey streak upon the edge of the eastern sky, and Denzil Norman's head was on the pillow, dreaming of Alice Brownlow. He had been at Landleigh six days, and more than once he had dreamed of her, both sleeping and waking, and each time the vision had become brighter. Suddenly, however, the dream was dispelled, and the sleep broken. There was some one knocking at the door, and starting up, he exclaimed, "Come in!"

The next moment John Brownlow entered, with a light in his hand. "Up and away, sir, as fast as possible," he said. "A company of Lambert's troops are in the place, and they were reading last night, where the officers are quartered, a proclamation, ordering the apprehension of several persons, amongst whom was named one stated to be passing under the name of Denzil Norman."

"Passing under my own name, then," said the young gentleman, with a smile.

"But not all your names, sir," replied the young man, "or else they are mistaken; for some one mentioned your being in the village, and they are to be here at day-break to take you out of your bed."

"Well, leave me then, good John," replied Denzil, "and I will rise and go. I have been in worse perils than this before now, and shall be in worse still before they make me lose heart. It is hard to be hunted thus like a hare before the hounds: but still we must abide our fate. Run up to Doctor Aldover's, if you would serve me, and have my horse ready."

"That is cared for," answered John Brownlow; "the horse is at the end of our garden. I will go out in the front and watch till you are ready. Alice is below."

Denzil Norman rose in haste and dressed himself; placed all his small portion of worldly goods in his saddle-bags, and was about to descend, when, by the growing light, he saw a paper lying on the window seat. He could not remember having left any there; and, on taking it up and looking at it closely, he perceived that it was in the same hand-writing as that which had been given him in the vaults. He had no time to examine it further, but hastily concealing it in a pocket between his vest and his shirt, he threw the saddle-bags over his arm, and went down to the room below.

The cottage windows were still closed; but Alice Brownlow was standing beside a table, on which was a light, with a grave and thoughtful face. She did not move when he entered; but Denzil advanced towards her at once, and took her hand, saying, "Alice, I must away, and that with all speed; but I shall never forget the hours I have passed here."

"Stay not to speak of such things," answered Alice; "every moment is precious for flight."

"I must stay to give you three commissions," replied the young gentleman: "first, give that gold Carolus to your uncle. I promised him something for attendance. Is it enough?"

"Too much," answered Alice.

"Next, there are five for good Dame Unwin," he continued, rapidly; "I am poor, or I would send her more. Will you give them to her for me?"

"I will," answered the beautiful girl, with an anxious look; "what is the third? speak quickly."

Denzil Norman still held her hand in his, and his fingers clasped more warmly round it, while he gazed in her beautiful face with a look of strong affection. "The last is," he said, "love me, as I will you, till we meet again."

Alice made no reply, but a warm glow, like that of the rising sun, sprung over her cheek and brow.

"Will you do that, too?" asked Denzil, in a low and agitated voice.

"It were soon promised," replied Alice; "for in a week you will forget the cottage girl."

"Never," he replied eagerly; "never while I have life. Perhaps there has been a struggle, Alice, between prejudice and love; but the struggle is over for ever, and if I escape—if I live, I will return to ask this dear hand. Oh! give me hope to cheer me by the way."

"Go, go," said Alice, turning away her face; "every moment brings you into danger."

Before he could answer, John Brownlow hurried into the cottage and locked the door behind him. "This way! this way!" he cried; "they are coming down the hill. Quick, quick!" and he caught Denzil's arm and drew him towards the door, which led through the kitchen to the garden behind. Alice, as if by an impulse she could not resist, started forward and laid her hand on that of the young fugitive. Denzil cast his arms round her, and pressed his lips upon her cheek. "Be true!" she whispered; "and you shall find me true."

The next instant he was in the garden, and he could distinctly hear the measured tramp of marching men. The ground sloped down on that side of the house towards the river and the valley, and the thick apple-trees afforded a complete screen from the road to almost all the little paths which had been formed in the garden. Through these John Brownlow led his companion with a quick step, till they reached a hedge with a little gate in it, within fifty yards of the stream.

To the gate was fastened Denzil Norman's horse; the saddle-bags were soon fastened to the saddle: and putting his foot in the stirrup, the young gentleman held out his hand to his companion, saying, "Farewell, John, with many, many thanks. We shall meet again, I trust, in happier days, when I can thank you better."

"God bless you, my lord," replied John Brownlow. "Hark! there is some one running down the hill—Away, away! Over the turf, that they may not hear you."

Denzil was in the saddle in a moment; his horse was fresh and full of fire; and bounding forward over the turf by the river side, he soon bore his rider beyond pursuit.

For two hours Denzil Norman rode on without drawing a rein; but often directing his course to the top of any high hill he came near, in order to examine the country he had passed, and ascertain if any one followed. He could see no signs of pursuit, however, and at length he halted in a meadow by a little stream, to let his horse drink and crop a mouthful of the green grass. His first thoughts were of Alice; but there were others that came soon and pressed for attention. "I will to the north," he said to himself, "but now for this other paper;" and drawing it forth he examined it more minutely than he had been able to do before. It was all legible enough, and he read the following directions, evidently intended for himself, although the paper bore neither address nor superscription.

"Go with all speed towards Newcastle," so ran the writing; "but avoid Lambert's posts. In the village of Corbridge, stable your horse at the inn called the Hart. You will meet there a short, stout, dark man, whom you shall ask if his name be Gideon. If he reply, 'Yea,' then tell him that Portsmouth holds out against the army, that the soldiers sent against it have declared for the Parliament, that the troops in London have done the same, that Lawson and the fleet will abandon the fanatics, and that Desborough's force is safe; but above all, let him know that Fairfax holds York, and that he may trust in him. Stir not from Corbridge till you see him."

"These are strange directions," thought Denzil Norman; "but yet I will follow them, although I doubt the accuracy of the tidings. Who can this short dark man be?"

His reverie was interrupted by the distant blast of a trumpet, and springing on his horse again, he was soon once more upon his way northward, nor stopped till he had put the distance of forty miles between himself and Landleigh. Still the journey before him was long; difficulties and obstacles interposed: now he found himself in the neighbourhood of some of Lambert's forces, and was obliged to take a circuit of several miles; now his horse cast a shoe, and no blacksmith was found to replace it; now he was impeded by finding no boat at a ferry; and thus eight days elapsed before he reached the fair banks of the Tyne.

It was late in the evening when, after descending the river for some fifteen or sixteen miles, he inquired for the village of Corbridge, and was told that it lay about a mile before him. Slackening his pace, then, that he might enter the place with the appearance of a mere traveller journeying leisurely on his way, he reached the inn door just as the sun was setting, and carefully attended to his horse before he entered the room of general reception. He found it entirely vacant, and a host without much custom anxious to show all attention to an unexpected guest. The best of everything was soon placed before him, and his meal was just finished, when he heard the sound of horses before the door. Some time elapsed without any one appearing, and expectation began to fade away, when he heard a voice without giving some orders, apparently to a servant. The next instant the door opened, and a stranger entered, who eyed him for a moment and then sat down at a distance. Denzil Norman examined him well. He was somewhat above the middle age, a stout man, and a dark one, but he could hardly be called short, although he was not so tall as the young cavalier himself. The expression of his countenance was somewhat grave and stern; but after the first look, he took no notice of his companion in the room until the landlord had served him a frugal supper, and a black jug full of some drink. As the latter was put upon the table, the stranger asked a question in a low voice; and when the room was again cleared, he turned his head towards Denzil Norman, and said, with a less surly expression of face, "The landlord tells me, sir, you come from the side of Carlisle. Is there anything stirring in those parts?"

"He is mistaken, sir," answered Denzil Norman, "I have not been near Carlisle; my journey has been from the southward."

"Ay, indeed," said the stranger, and he proceeded with his supper.

"Perhaps, if you belong to this part of the country," said Denzil, after a short pause, "you can inform me, sir, where I can find a person who calls himself Gideon."

"There might be more difficult things than that," said the stranger.

"Is your own name Gideon?" demanded the young gentleman.

"Yea," replied the other. "You have news for me it seems."

"I have," replied Denzil; and he proceeded to repeat to him precisely the information which had been contained in the paper. As he did so, he watched his companion's countenance; and, although he could see that the intelligence he conveyed was not without effect, yet the indications were too slight for him to judge whether that effect was pleasurable or otherwise.

"When did you set out?" demanded the stranger, after the detail was concluded; and, on being informed, he replied, "Methinks the fairies must have given you this information even before the events happened."

"They did," replied Denzil Norman. "At least I know no other source whence the intelligence came."

"Indeed!" said the other. "You are a good messenger to bring tidings without knowing whence they come. But methinks you should have some paper for me, young gentleman; have you it about you?"

"I have," replied Denzil Norman, somewhat drily, for he was not altogether pleased at the tone of authority which the other assumed. "Here it is;" and he laid it down upon the table before him without taking the trouble of rising to deliver it. The other man smiled, rose from his seat, crossed the room, and took the paper, examined the cypher by the light, and seemed to read it over attentively; his brow grew instantly dark, however, and he demanded sternly, "Do you know the contents of this paper, young man?"

"The part which is written in English I do know," answered Denzil Norman. "Of the rest I comprehend not one word."

"Happy for you, you do not," said the other; "happy for you that your want of reverence makes me believe that it is so, for, were it otherwise, I would have hanged you on the tree before the door. Nevertheless, you shall be taken care of; and as you would value your life, take care how you use your tongue with those people in whose hands I place you. Ho! without there! bring up a guard."

"Yes, my Lord General," answered a voice; and the next moment several soldiers appeared at the door.

As may easily be conceived, the feelings of Denzil Norman were of no very pleasant kind; but there was about the cavaliers of that period an assumption of indifference to the evils of life which was not of the best school of philosophy, but which affected even those of higher toned mind and character. "I should remonstrate, sir," he said, "upon being subjected to inconvenience for having very civilly borne you a message, the import of which I did not understand, if remonstrance were likely to be of any avail; but having lived long in a country where neither law nor reason are very available, I think it best to hold my tongue."

"You do wisely," replied the other, drily; and then added, addressing the officer of the guard, "Remove him."

"Shall we search his person or examine his papers, my Lord General?" demanded the officer.

"You will do at your peril any thing more than the strict letter of my commands," answered the other, "which are, to remove him, and keep him under arrest, with all due civility, till I make further inquiries. Send Mr. Clarges hither."

"One question before I go, sir," said Denzil Norman. "May I ask at whose command I am to be subjected to imprisonment, for amongst all the Lord Generals whom we have lately heard of, I am unacquainted with the name of General Gideon?"

"He was a famous man, too, in his day," replied the other, with a faint smile, "and a great general; but my name is Monk."

"Oh! very well," replied Denzil, with a mind a good deal relieved, and without farther comment or resistance he followed the officer of the guard out of the room.

The life of Denzil Norman for some time was a very unpleasant one, for it was a life of uncertainty and of confinement. The general prevalent belief that Monk was favourable to the royal cause of course had its effect in relieving his mind from any serious apprehensions for his personal safety; but yet to be in the midst of scenes where the great game of policy was playing without knowing any of the moves, and without the power to take any part, uncertain of his own fate, or the fate of his country and friends, was at once painful and exciting. Rumours he could not but hear, movements he could not but see; but the truth of the one, and the causes of the other, he could not in any degree divine. He was treated with general civility, and gradually had more liberty allowed him than at first; but still he was obliged to consider himself as a prisoner, and seemed more the sport of caprice than the object of just precaution. At one time he was permitted to go out for an hour or two on parole; at another was strictly confined in whatever place the army might be. Sometimes he fared well in his prison, sometimes had little more allowed him than mere bread and water.

From the small town where he had been captured, he was removed to Berwick, then to Edinburgh, then to Coldstream, and then advanced with the army into England in the midst of a severe winter. But that which struck him as most unaccountable was, that not the slightest inquiry was made with regard to his name, station, or quality; no examination took place of his small baggage, which was always carefully placed in the same room with himself: and had it not been for the guard at his door, and the occasional changes which occurred in his treatment, he should have thought that Monk had entirely forgotten him. At length, on a wintry and inclement evening, the army approached York, and the well-remembered cathedral appearing in the grey light, showed Denzil Norman that he was coming near a city where he was known to many, and threw him into meditation in regard to the chances of effecting his escape by their aid and assistance.

A little reflection, however, induced him to refrain from attempting it. There was something he could not help thinking very peculiar in Monk's conduct towards him. Perhaps, indeed, he was influenced in this view of the case by the treatment he had lately received; for, since the army reached Durham, his fare and his quarters had been very superior to those which he had met with before. However that might be, he was inclined to imagine that the general was not so harshly disposed towards him as his demeanour at first might have induced him to believe; and in the end he asked himself, "I wonder what effect perfect frankness will have upon this man?"

The opportunity of trying was soon afforded to him, for as he was riding with a trooper by his side, Monk himself passed by on horseback, gave him what seemed to be a casual glance, and rode on to the head of the army. In about ten minutes, however, a young officer appeared, and informed the prisoner that he would be permitted to choose his own lodging in the town, upon the condition that he presented himself every morning at the general's quarters.

"Give my humble duty to the Lord General," replied Denzil, "and tell him that, for particular reasons, I cannot avail myself of his permission till I have spoken with him for a moment."

"Ride on with me, then," said the young officer; "but you must be quick, for he is going forward into the town."

Monk was soon overtaken, however, for he had stopped to converse with some of his principal officers, and the message of his prisoner was delivered to him as soon as a pause took place. He looked at Denzil for a moment, from under his bent and somewhat shaggy eyebrows, and then beckoning him up, as he rode on, he asked him abruptly, "What is the meaning of this? Is your money expended?"

"Not so, sir," answered Denzil; "but you cautioned me to be careful of what I said and did, making me imagine that you would rather I should have no communication, public or private, with any of my friends. I have now to tell you that I have more than one acquaintance in York and its neighbourhood, with whom I shall most likely be brought into communication if I am at liberty in the city."

Monk mused, "It were well to avoid it," he said at last. "Who do you know at York?"

"I know the Lord Fairfax," replied Denzil, "and several others in the town."

"I will consider," answered Monk. "Retire for the present:" and without another word he rode on, leaving his prisoner in custody of the trooper. That night he was lodged at the quarters of the general, and remained two days a close prisoner. He was sitting at an early hour on the third morning, feeling some mortification at the result of his frankness—for though, according to the old copy-line, "virtue is its own reward," yet we are seldom inclined to be satisfied with that sort of recompense—when the door opened, and, with his slow step and sedate carriage, Monk himself entered the room and sat down.

"You are discreet, young gentleman," he said, "and honest—rare qualities in the world. I can trust you, which is what I can say to few men."

He paused for a moment or two, and Denzil asked himself what this preamble was to lead to. The stop was so long, however, that he had almost come to the conclusion that Monk had delivered himself of all he had to say, when that officer resumed, "Under these circumstances, and upon the assurance of Lord Fairfax, I have resolved to give you all personal freedom, notwithstanding your boldness in bringing me letters containing matter little short of high treason."

"I was perfectly ignorant of the contents," replied Denzil, "not being learned in Arabic, or whatever tongue they were written in."

"You knew who sent them at all events," replied General Monk; "and that was sufficient."

"Not so," answered Denzil Norman; "I was as ignorant of one as the other."

"Strange enough!" replied Monk. "But to the point: I will give you, as I have said, all reasonable freedom upon conditions, which are, first, that you accompany me soberly and quietly to London, presenting yourself at my quarters every morning; secondly, that you mention to no one who or what you are; and thirdly, that you make no attempt whatsoever in favour of persons who may be your friends without communicating with me."

Denzil marked with very strong emotions the last phrase in Monk's address. In difficult times, and circumstances most perilous to himself, he had learned from very small indications to guess at, if not divine, men's feelings and intentions, and with a heart greatly relieved, he replied, "I accept all the terms, my Lord General, and you shall find that I adhere to them punctually. Perhaps, when you find that I do so, you may grant me permission to absent myself for a short time, as I am anxious, on many personal accounts, to visit once more the place from which I brought those letters you have mentioned."

"All in good time, all in good time," answered Monk; "but now, remember, should you have occasion to speak with me, or any information to give, affecting the good of the state, say it not rashly, even should I seem alone; for there be men full of doubts and jealousies, who have not even scrupled, in this very town of York, to bore a hole through my chamber-door in order to gain a hearing of my private conversation. I warn one who will take a warning, I think; and I will beg you to remember, young man, that there is a certain name, which it is an offence to mention in the ears of many people in this land with whom I am at present compelled to deal, and therefore it must never be uttered between you and me."

"May I know, Lord General," said Denzil, "how I am to contrive to obtain private audience of you, should it be needful?"

"Merely say, when you come to me," replied Monk, "that it is your wish to speak with me in private, and I will find the means. Be ready at my call, however, whenever I may want you;" and thus saying, he left the room.

The thoughts of Denzil Norman, when Monk was gone, were of Alice Brownlow, and they were sweet.

It was a bright morning in the month of May, 1660, and the light and shade were skipping over the fair village of Landleigh, bringing out a thousand different beauties in their passage, when the sound of drum and trumpet was heard upon the castle green, and a small body of horse rode in and formed in line nearly opposite to the great gates. The smallest event has its rumour, and it is therefore no wonder that a full hour at least before the entrance of the soldiers, the tidings of their approach had reached Landleigh. Thus, although those were times of doubt and suspicion, and the sober citizens and peasantry, even when fanatically inclined themselves, looked upon the military hypocrites of the day with much awe and trepidation, a number of the inhabitants of Landleigh, amongst whom was many a stout young peasant and buxom country girl, were assembled on the castle green to see the arrival of the soldiers. The man at their head was no very favourable specimen of the class to which he belonged, either internally or externally. Though not absolutely ugly, his countenance was anything but prepossessing; and, though tall, and in reality strong, there was a shambling, ungainly look about his limbs which gave one no great idea of his corporeal vigour. His character was one not unfrequently met with in every age, but which was peculiarly developed by the times of which I speak. Excitable, sensual, and worldly, he had cunning enough to discover that his passions could be best served, and his interests advanced by an assumption of zeal for the predominant tenets of the day. He had pursued this course cunningly for many years, and there are few minds so incapable of enthusiasm, as not to obtain by long habit a tincture of the views they affect. As a man is sometimes deceived by his own lies, so are men frequently cheated by their own rogueries, and Colonel Okey doubtless believed himself a fanatic in religion, and a republican in policy.

But a truce to description. We have to do with a few of the man's actions, the springs of which will be easily understood by those who have at all studied the times. After marshalling his men and glancing his eyes round the villagers with a look which, when it rested upon the female part of the assembly, betokened no very unearthly feelings, he harangued his men with the common-place cant of the wilder and more enthusiastic sectaries, who then struggled to retain that power and predominance which they had for many years enjoyed and misused in the land, wresting texts of Scripture from their original meaning, and applying them in the most forced and extraordinary manner to the events of the times. With all the rest he mingled a confusion of commands and directions, which none but those accustomed to such strange oratory could at all comprehend, and from which the villagers, habituated to the homely, but intelligible preaching of Mr. Gideon Samson, could only make out that General Lambert was in arms for the repose and domination of the saints, and that the soldiers were exhorted to denounce every one wherever they met with him, who could even be suspected of favouring the malignant proceedings of Papists, Prelatists, and Presbyterians. He ended by a call upon the inhabitants of the place, under the most fearful denunciations of wrath, to give up without delay all persons who might harbour or conceal themselves in the village from the wrath of God and man; and then, dismissing his troopers to their quarters, rode slowly into the village himself, followed by one or two of his officers, after having commanded a muster of the troop at the same place, at the hour of five in the evening. He took his way straight down the high road, going at a slow pace, and examining the different houses as he went with the eye of one seeking a comfortable lodging, but it would seem that he had previously received some information concerning the characters and opinions of the inhabitants, for he at length fixed upon by no means the best house in the place, but one inhabited by a man after his own heart—the grocer, or, as we should call him, the chandler of the village, whose notions of predestination, saintly freedom, sufficiency of grace, and other dogmas were held in high detestation by Mr. Gideon Samson, whose own doctrines were uniformly pronounced cold, comfortless, and carnal by the more enthusiastic Mr. Culpeper. After feeding liberally, and drinking somewhat deep, considering the early hour in the morning, Colonel Okey held a long private conference with his worthy host, at the end of which he walked out into the village, and visited several of the houses and cottages, amongst which was that of Roger Brownlow, where he remained for some time in private conference with the *ci-devant* sexton. It might seem, indeed, that the subject matter of their conversation was of no great moment, for when they issued forth from the room formerly tenanted by Denzil Norman, John Brownlow, who was below, heard with consternation his worthy father assuring Colonel Okey that he had been bewitched by the old hag, under which denomination the young man naturally concluded was meant poor old Martha Unwin.

"Well, Master Brownlow," said the Colonel, "I will visit and interrogate her this very day, and on my return will proceed in her case and all others to put down the kingdom of Satan, and establish the reign of the Saints upon earth."

Thus saying, the worthy Colonel quitted the cottage, and a somewhat sharp dispute took place between father and son, in regard to the reputation of Dame Unwin. But the Colonel's last words implied a hint not lost to the ears of John Brownlow, who, as soon as the angry discussion was over with his father, hurried away into the cottage of the poor old woman, to warn her of the officer's friendly intentions towards her. As he approached the house, he thought he heard the voice of his fair Jane raised in higher and less gentle tones than usual; and, lifting the latch, he pushed the door sharply open. It struck with a violent clatter upon the steel back-piece of Colonel Okey, who was holding both Jane's hands tight in his own, and addressing words to her pure ear, which made the blood boil in the veins of her lover. The hypocrite let go his hold and started back, and, placing himself by Jane Unwin's side, John Brownlow stood gazing in the officer's face, strongly tempted to knock him down on the spot, yet dreading the consequences to all whom he loved.

With a swaggering and supercilious air, often assumed to cover confusion, Colonel Okey turned to the door and quitted the cottage without saying a word; and in an hour or so after, he was once more pouring forth the rapid strain of hypocrisy and cant, with which he was wont to delight the ears of his fanatical soldiers.

The following morning the troops marched out of the village, and the inhabitants rejoiced in the thoughts of having got rid of their unwelcome guests; but John Brownlow remembered the hint that Colonel Okey had given of his intentions to return, and with a degree of vigour, determination, and good sense which his fellow villagers had not expected of him, he took the first steps towards preparing the people of Landleigh for resisting, in case of need, the aggressions of the insolent soldiery. Presbyterians and Churchmen for once united together to make common cause against those who were enemies of both, and, with the exception of Mr. Culpeper and a few of his particular associates, all the inhabitants of the place prepared themselves, determined to resist to the last. But, alas! profession of resistance in peaceable men are not much to be depended on, and when, two nights after, a corporal's guard entered the village bringing intelligence that the Colonel and his men would be there early on the following morning, the scene of consternation that ensued amongst those who had been so bold but a few hours before was both ludicrous and lamentable. Rumours crept among them, whether spread by the soldiery or not I cannot tell, that the Lord General Lambert was in the immediate neighbourhood with a large force; that he had defeated the troops of the new Parliament, and proclaimed a pure and perfect Republic, the whole affairs of which were to be carried on by a committee of twelve saints. The people of Landleigh, it would appear, were in a very ungodly state, for they seemed to dread nothing so much as this saintly domination. Some were actually preparing to run away, but a mere hint from a single soldier was quite sufficient to make the most forward of them skulk back to their houses; and early the next morning, the report was spread through the village that both good Doctor Aldover and Mr. Gideon Samson had been apprehended in their beds without warrant.

By the grey daylight, John Brownlow was at the door of good Dame Unwin's cottage, and he was not kept long waiting, as it was opened for him. A hurried consultation ensued as to what was best to be done, and at length it was determined that Jane and the good dame should take refuge in a part of the ruins of the castle, where John Brownlow assured them that they might lie concealed till the soldiers departed. "I will come to you at sun-set, dear Jane," he said, "and bring you provisions, and all that I can think of to make you comfortable."

Jane seemed to entertain no apprehensions; but the old lady, all witch as she was, entertained a great dread of the fairy, and it was not without much persuasion that she was induced to go forth with her grand-daughter to make abode near the spirit's well. Their little journey was not without trepidation, for Jane fancied she saw a soldier in every bush they passed in the lane leading to the castle green; and by the time they reached the end of it all three became convinced that they heard steps following. Quickening their pace to a run, however, they passed the open space in safety, darted through the old portal, and were led by John Brownlow up a narrow and tottering stair to a small chamber in one of the gate towers.

"No one would ever think of seeking for you here," he said; "and as I go down, I will take away one of the stone steps that are loose, so as to make it seem more difficult than it is to get up. Don't be frightened, good Dame Martha, for the fairy is a kind fairy, and one soldier is worse than any that ever danced upon the green."

The good lady, however, made him repeat over and over again his promise to rejoin them at sun-set, and to sit up with them till the cock crowed in the dawn.

There had been a parade of the troops on the castle-green, and an examination of Mr. Gideon Samson and Doctor Aldover before Colonel Okey; and there had been a search for old Dame Unwin and Jane, and a proclamation with sound of trumpet against sundry malignant enemies of the state and commonwealth of England, amongst whom the principal person was Charles Brook, Lord Eustace, reported to be harbouring in or near the village of Landleigh. But the parade of the troops passed over, and the soldiers returned to their quarters. Nothing was extracted from Mr. Gideon Samson but fiery abuse of Anabaptists, and fanatics, and Fifth-monarchy men, or from Doctor Aldover but meekness and submission. Dame Unwin and her grand-daughter were not found; and at the name of Lord Eustace, the villagers shook their heads, and murmured that it would be long ere his enemies found that good, kind lord, for he had died at Worcester fight. The day, in short, went by with less results of any kind than had been expected; and all seemed quiet in the village when the sun touched the edge of the horizon.

At that moment John Brownlow was standing under the arch of the castle gateway, loaded with many things to make the two poor fugitives as comfortable as might be; and after taking a cautious look round, he entered the tower on the left, and began ascending the dilapidated stairs.

Hardly had he disappeared, when silently and quietly four men came forth from a part of the ruin on the right of the gate, showing the faces of Colonel Okey himself and three of his soldiers; and the commander whispered, "After him, quick and noiselessly. You will find them all together if you go quietly."

The soldiers hurried on, and were lost to sight under the low arched door of the stairs, while Colonel Okey himself remained under the gateway. In less than a minute he caught the sound of loud voices speaking above, and an unpleasant smile came upon his face. Then descending steps were heard through the loop-holes, and in a few moments more poor John Brownlow, with old Dame Unwin and Jane, appeared under the guard of the soldiers.

"Here, bring them here!" exclaimed the officer, taking a few steps into the great court. "Let me look at their faces. Here's a pretty one at least;" and he put his hand under Jane Unwin's chin.

It was more than John Brownlow could bear, and he was starting forward *with his fist clenched, when a voice ex*claimed, "Forbear!" in a tone sweet and musical, but loud and penetrating; and all eyes turned towards the spot whence the sound seemed to proceed. There, standing as before, on the other side of the well, appeared the same beautiful figure, clothed in white, with the sort of lustrous light upon her face and garments which Denzil Norman had seen when first he visited Landleigh.

"Forbear!" repeated the figure; "bad man, forbear!"

Every one was silent for an instant; but then, with an exclamation strangely mingling blasphemy with fanaticism, Colonel Okey darted forward towards the well.

"It is the fairy! it is the fairy!" cried Jane Unwin.

"Were it Beelzebub, I would bring him into captivity," said Colonel Okey; but the fairy receded before him, and, ere he could run round the well, had reached the same gloomy archway through which she had disappeared when followed by Denzil Norman.

"Keep them fast till I return," shouted the officer, turning his head to speak to the soldiers, and the next instant disappearing in the gloom.

"Verily, he is rash to trust himself with spiritual enemies," said one of the soldiers, gazing at the walls and towers opposite. "Mayhap she will lure him to some perilous place, and there seek to destroy him."

His words seemed to be verified the moment they were spoken; for hardly were they uttered when, in the clear evening twilight, the beautiful figure, in its floating white garments, was seen walking with a step of light along the very edge of the crumbling battlements, when the loose stones seemed hardly fitted to support the very softest tread; and the next instant the head of Colonel Okey protruded from a small door-way in a tower, looking upon that part of the curtain along which her course lay. The figure paused a moment, as if poised in air; and a clear short laugh was heard, followed by the words, "Come on, come on;" and instantly Colonel Okey sprang forward, several of the stones giving way under his feet, and rolling into the court below. At the same time the figure he was pursuing resumed its rapid course towards a round tower, in the western wall of which were still to be seen the fragments of a stone stair-case, which formerly led up to the higher apartments of the keep. She reached the foot of the tower, and then began to ascend by the broken steps, only supported on one side by the old wall into which they were built.

"Forbear, Colonel, forbear!" shouted one of the soldiers. "Do not sacrifice the life of one of the saints in pursuit of a shadow."

But the officer hurried recklessly on, and began to mount with a slower step, when suddenly a black arm was thrust through one of the loop-holes, and at a single blow hurled the fanatic down into the court below; while at the same moment the female figure disappeared, vanishing apparently into the body of the tower.

"I knew it, I knew it," cried one of the soldiers. "It was written in the Book that he should be so slain, even by the powers of darkness;" and at the same moment he sprang forward toward the spot where the unhappy man had fallen. The two others were following, when they were reminded of their charge of the prisoners by a somewhat untimely movement of Dame Unwin towards the gate; and, unceremoniously drawing their swords, they commanded the unwilling captives to march on before them to the spot where their unsanctified commander lay. To the surprise of all, however, on approaching, they found Colonel Okey endeavouring to raise himself upon his arm. His escape might indeed have been considered miraculous in a fall from such a height, had it not been that some thick and tangled bramble-bushes had gathered round the foot of the tower, and had received him on his descent from above as on a soft, though somewhat thorny, bed. Sorely bruised, indeed, he was, and stunned, and confused with the fall; but the evil spirit was by no means driven out of him, and his first exclamation was an order to look well to the prisoners. He remained some time upon the ground unable to rise; but when, with the assistance of one of his troopers, he succeeded in getting on his feet, he poured forth long and bitter complaints in regard to the misfortune which had befallen him, savouring very little of saintly resignation. Indeed, the expressions that he used were neither more nor less than imprecations in another form, and probably comforted him as much as a volley of oaths would have solaced a habitual swearer. With these complaints over his bruised body, he mingled orders for removing the three prisoners to the house where he had taken up his abode, and guarding them strictly till he should be well enough to deal with them as he thought fit. This done, he limped away, grumbling every step he took; and was fain to call for the assistance of Doctor Aldover to soothe his hurts as best he might.

Surely there is no faith to be found on earth. We trust not, we hope not, as we should trust and hope were we really and thoroughly convinced that there is an over-ruling Providence, a just Judge, a future state. We look to this world alone. If we trust, it is in our own strength; if we calculate, it is upon worldly chances; if we despair, it is because this life is our all.

The heart of John Brownlow burned within him as he sat during the livelong night in a small garret-room, with a soldier at the door, separated from his companions, and every moment fancying her he loved exposed to insult, and perhaps to injury, from a brutal and licentious hypocrite. It was in vain that he tried to console himself; it was in vain that he looked around for help or hope. He trusted not, he thought not of trusting where trust only is sure; and he passed the whole hours of darkness in the fever fits of cold despair and fiery indignation. He saw the day break at length without having closed an eye; and the soft light of the early morning was perhaps more painful to him than the shadows of the night. He heard people moving about, he heard voices speaking, he thought he could distinguish the tones of his dear Jane; and he would have given all that he possessed on earth for some intelligence of her fate. For many hours, however, he was kept in the bitterness of suspense. No one came near him, no one spoke to him, except when once he tried to open the door, and the voice of the sentinal without bade him keep quiet under the threat of the strapado. At length, however, the door was thrown back, and he was hurried with a good deal of rude brutality into a large room—a sort of hall, indeed, it might be called, which had been built by worthy Mr. Culpeper as a place of meeting for himself and his fellows. A table was stretched across the upper end of the room, beyond which was placed an arm-chair. A soldier, with an ink-horn and some paper, sat at one end of the table; and Colonel Okey himself, with his head bound up and his arm in a sling, was seated in the chair of state. At a little distance from the table stood old Martha Unwin and her daughter, both as pale as death. Several of the villagers, more especially of the Culpeper faction, were between them and the door; and behind all were a number of troopers, mostly with grave faces and arms crossed on the breast.

The room, indeed, had somewhat the aspect of a court of justice; and old Roger Brownlow, who stood before the table speaking, seemed acting the part of a witness. The sight of his father in such a capacity was no great consolation to the young prisoner; nor were the first words he heard at all calculated to relieve his anxiety.

"That is quite sufficient," said Colonel Okey, as he entered, apparently addressing his father. "She shall have a full trial by water. Take her away, Hezekiah Strong-i'-the arm, and worthy Good-fight-the-faith Perkins. Conduct her quietly to the river side at the deepest part, and cast her in, taking care that she reach not the land on the same side, but that if the fiend help her, she pass clearly over. If she succeed in doing so, we will give her over to the fire; for no witch must be suffered to dwell in our Israel."

The old woman uttered not a word; for, to say the truth, her senses were quite benumbed by terror at the prospect of a fate—to the disgrace of the land be it spoken—not at all uncommon in England at that period. Jane, however, cast herself upon her knees before the brutal tyrant who threatened her aged relation with the dreadful alternative of perishing by water or by fire, and poured forth wild entreaties for mercy, mingled with appeals to the villagers present to give some testimony of the acts of kindness and Christian charity which had so often been performed by her now brutally condemned.

Okey gazed at her with a fiend-like smile, and then beckoned to her to come round to the same side on which he was sitting; but at that moment John Brownlow's indignation mastered all prudence, and starting forward through the crowd, he caught Jane's arm, exclaiming, "Go not near him, Jane. He is a base, lewd hypocrite, and you know it. Go not near him, my love. He dare not do what he has threatened."

"Ha, ha! young viper's spawn!" exclaimed Okey. "Dare not! Do you think that we have girded up our loins and ridden forth with our swords upon our thigh for nothing? You shall soon learn what the saints of the Lord dare when the spirit moves them. Have you not aided to harbour and conceal that malignant traitor Charles Brooke, called of men Lord Eustace? Have you not comforted him and abetted him after proclamation made, and contrary to the laws of this land of England? Have you not received rents for him, and offerings from dark-minded and perverse men, who were once his tenants, but who now owe nothing to any one but the Commonwealth of England, and those to whom it shall give a portion in the marrow and fatness of the land? Dare not to deny it, for thine own father is a witness against thee, and against himself also, if we choose to be extreme with him; but, considering that he has given us a knowledge of these things, and how we may bring the most guilty to justice, we will spare the old adder, seeing that the poison is squeezed out of its fangs; but we will tread upon the head of the young adder, lest it bite the heel of the saints. In less than one hour shall the malignant Charles Brooke become the captive of our bow and spear; for we have surrounded his hiding-place with godly men, who will take care not to let him forth. In the mean time, however, we will smite his comforters and adherents hip and thigh; and thou and the prelatic malignant Aldover, who consorted with thee in thy evil deeds, shall die within ten minutes from this time, even upon the green before the castle gates. Here, Obadiah Jason, take the young man away, and bring the old man out of the prison where thou hast imprisoned him; and see that they be both shot upon the green within ten minutes, for which thou shalt have our warrant, according to the powers granted us by our commission under the seal of the Committee of Safety. What is it, Joshua Scroggs, thou man of valour? What causes that tumult at the door, and who is it thou halest along so sturdily?"

"Verily he is a captain whom we have taken, worthy colonel," replied the corporal, to whom he addressed himself, speaking in a harsh, rude voice. "I was hastening up with my men to relieve the guard at the gates of the castle, and I hurried my steps when I was upon the green, for methought I heard the voices of many men speaking loud and tumultuously; but, lo! the sentinel was walking calmly at his post, and he heard not the sounds that were revealed to my ears, when suddenly I beheld this youth walking slowly towards the castle, and I saw in him all the signs of the man of Belial. Behold his love-locks and his boots of French calf-skin, and his sword-knot of blue and white, and his G—d-d—mme hat, with a band of ostrich feather; and, meditating with myself, I said, 'Woe be to the land when such things walk abroad in open day,' and therewith I apprehended him, and brought him hither. Stand forth, thou man of Belial, and give an account of thyself." And he pulled roughly the arm of a man, the principal part of whose face and figure was concealed by the crowd which filled the lower part of the room.

"I will stand forth, if you will make way," replied a voice; "for, to tell you the truth, my good friend, you have only brought me where I was coming." And at the same time, putting the soldier somewhat roughly aside, Denzil Norman advanced into the little open space before the table, and took his place by the side of young John Brownlow.

"Who art thou, bold boy?" demanded Colonel Okey, gazing upon the young gentleman with some surprise, and not altogether without apprehension, as he marked the calm and almost contemptuous smile with which the young cavalier looked at him. "Take off thy hat. Knowest thou in whose presence thou standest?"

"Oh sir! I am sorry to see you here," said John Brownlow, with his fingers clasping tighter upon those of Jane, whose hand he held, and, unlike the generality of men, really feeling distressed to see a new companion destined to share in his misfortunes; but Denzil Norman, without noticing, replied to

Colonel Okey, "I know well in whose presence I stand, but, nevertheless, I shall keep my hat upon my head, as I have no reverence for any one I see before me. You asked my name, sir. It is Denzil Norman."

"Ha! ha! hast thou found me, mine enemy?" said Okey; "but now shalt thou know what it is to be in the hands of those who will not spare. Art thou, I ask thee, that Denzil Norman, Lord [illegible]unt, who slew my nephew, my sister's son, when thou wert but a boy at Worcester?"

"I am," replied the young cavalier, without the slightest sign of emotion; "but what of that, Master Okey? It was hand to hand in fair fight, a man of thirty against a lad of eighteen. He died fighting against his king; I lived to fight for my king another day."

"That thou shalt never do," answered Okey; "for thou hast seen the last sun thou ever shalt see. Take him away, Obadiah Jason, and do him to death with the rest."

"Nay, nay," answered Denzil Norman; "not quite so fast, Master Okey. A word or two more before we part."

"Take him away!" shouted Okey, by no means well pleased at the young nobleman's bold bearing and tranquil smile. "I know what he counts upon —the nest of traitors and scorpions in London, and the false and deceitful Monk; but he shall find himself deceived, for were it the last day I had to live, this hour shall he die. Take him away, I say!"

"Nay, then," answered Denzil Norman, putting his hand into his breast, "if you be so imperative, Master Okey, I must take another course," and drawing forth a pistol, he levelled it across the table at Okey's head, adding rapidly, "the man that lays a hand upon me signs your death-warrant. Bid them hold back!"

"Hold back, hold back!" cried Okey, his face turning pale; "hear what the young man has to say."

"It will be soon said, Master Okey," answered Denzil. "Listen, all men. In virtue of a commission under the hand and seal of General Monk, commander-in-chief of all the land forces of England, I hereby apprehend you, John Okey, for high treason, and I command you instantly to surrender. You, troopers of the seventh troop of Lilburn's regiment, by the same power and authority I command you to lay down your arms, and every man to betake himself peacefully to the house where he is quartered, to await the decision of the commissioners in your case, giving you, at the same time, to know that the commissions of Generals Fleetwood and Lambert have been revoked by the council of state, and that, six days ago, the latter, who resisted the authority of Parliament and the Council, was encountered near Daventry by Colonels Streater, Ingoldsby, and myself, his men routed, and himself taken prisoner, to be dealt with according to law. See that you obey! To you, villagers—if you move a hand or utter a word, Colonel Okey, I blow your brains out on the spot—I have more joyful tidings to announce. Your King is restored, bringing with him pardon and oblivion for all offences, toleration for all religions, and peace and happiness to his subjects. Neither have any fear of these misguided men who have quartered themselves amongst you; for know that the castle and the church are by this time in the hands of my regiment, and that the report of this pistol will fill this room in one minute with faithful subjects of his majesty. Long live King Charles!"

"Hark!" cried a voice from behind, "there is a drum."

As is usual in such cases, a momentary hesitation had come over those persons who an instant before had felt the greatest confidence in their own power and strength, when they perceived that the chances were turning against them. It was not, indeed, that they were utterly dismayed, but their minds hung in the balance, as it were, as to what course they should pursue, and the least weight thrown into either of the scales was certain to decide between the most opposite courses. The sound of that drum had wellnigh given the preponderance to the more timid policy, but there was more than one stout heart amongst Okey's troopers, and the stoutest of them all, because the most fanatical, was that of the corporal, Joshua Scroggs. "What!" he exclaimed, starting forward, while the rest stood round with looks of moody hesitation, "do our hearts wax faint because the battle rages strong against us? Shall we be deprived of the captives of our bow and spear because the Amorites triumph in the hill country? Did not Barak, the son of Abinoam, coming out of Kadesh-Naphthali, go up against the hosts of Jabin, King of Canaan, with few people, and did he not prevail against him even by the side of the river Kishon; and shall we be afraid because the castle and the steeple-house are in the hands of the Philistines? No, verily, this young man shalt die as thou hast said, and the other young man, and the old man with him, because they have brought the abominable things into our Israel, even a king and a king's crown, which the land had spued forth."

"Beware, Colonel Okey, beware!" cried Denzil Norman.

"Hark! they are in the streets before the house," cried a young man from the window, looking out.

"Call them up," shouted the young cavalier; and, instantly letting go Jane Unwin's hand, John Brownlow started towards the window.

One of the troopers, however, threw himself in the way, and knocked him down with the hilt of his sword, when at once the confusion became general. Some voices shouted, "Long live King Charles," some "Down with the men of Belial;" the crowd in the room swayed hither and thither as several strove to push forward, and not a few to escape; and, in the midst of the confusion, Joshua Scroggs threw himself upon the young Lord Blount, and endeavoured to pinion his arms; but Denzil was as strong and more active, and turning the pistol from Okey towards the head of his assailant, he fired, and the man fell back, knocking down with his ponderous weight one of the soldiers who was hurrying up to his assistance. A loud rushing tramp was heard from the door as of a multitude of feet hurrying up the stairs, and the next moment a number of steel caps and grim faces appeared pouring in, and the voice of Denzil Norman shouted aloud, "Arrest every man found in arms, and let the rest go. Quietly, quietly; we have had too much strife already."

"Take that, at least, for thy part," cried one of Okey's troopers, levelling a carbine towards him. A villager, however, who stood near, struck the man a blow on the arm at the very moment he was pulling the trigger, and the shot, passing by Denzil Norman's head, with one of those retributive accidents which we so often see occur, hit old Roger Brownlow on the temple, and laid him convulsed and prostrate on the ground.

No further resistance was offered; the troops, who might now be called Royalists, poured into the room, and although the scene of confusion, of which I will not attempt to give the details, continued for about a quarter of an hour longer, all was at length quieted, and Colonel Okey and his companions removed from the room, leaving Denzil Norman with some of his officers and one or two of the villagers. Amongst the latter was John Brownlow, who, notwithstanding his own deliverance from peril and immediate death, felt too keenly for all joy, not alone the sad fate which had befallen his father, but the treacherous course which that father had pursued.

"Be comforted, my good friend," said the young nobleman, after he had given orders to remove the body to the old man's cottage. "This was an accident which but shortened his days by a very brief space, and, perhaps, it is better to terminate life with one brief pang suddenly over, than to endure prolonged suffering, or the wearisome exhaustion of gradual decay."

John Brownlow was a simple and not very well educated peasant. He affected to be nothing more; but there is something in plain good sense superior to all education and to all talent, and he replied, "I think, my lord, that everything must depend upon preparation; and it is with grief I ask myself, 'Was he prepared?'"

Lord Blount felt rebuked, but it was done without the slightest assumption, and he replied at once, "That is too true. Nevertheless, my good friend, let us not, even in our thoughts, limit God's mercy; but go home now, and tell your fair cousin that I shall be at your house soon. I have many things to deal with, but I will not be long ere I visit you."

John Brownlow smiled faintly. "You will not find Alice there," he said; "but I will tell you more, my lord, when I see you. She, too, has had duties to perform, and has performed them well; but, if I might advise you, your lordship would look to the safety of Lord Eustace, he was your old friend, I understand, and if these men have dared such things here, what may they not have attempted there?"

"My old friend!" replied the young cavalier. "He was more than a father to me; but I fear not for him. They had no power to injure him. Now leave me, John. We will soon meet again."

An hour had passed, and while minute after minute of that time crept by, not less than a third part of the time had been spent by Denzil Norman Lord Blount in deep meditation, with his hands covering his eyes, as he sat in the chair so lately occupied by Colonel Okey. His orders had been given, his arrangements made, soldier after soldier had quitted the room, and no one remained on that floor of the house but the guard at the door. He was left all alone in the hall, where one of those little tragedies had taken place which, though enacted in a smaller space than the greater dramas performed on the wide stage of the world, often afford a deeper and more concentrated interest. The hall was large, as I have said, and looked larger in its vacancy. Benches and settles had been removed, and naught remained upon the floor but the dark-red stains of blood where the soldier and Roger Brownlow had fallen.

Twenty minutes may seem a long period for meditation, but who can tell how many were the different images which presented themselves to his mind during that time, how wide was the range of thought, how discursive and how erratic was the course that it pursued. In those twenty minutes the present and the past were revolved, and the future came in for its share of consideration; but memory, perhaps, was the most busy, and the eight or nine years last past presented a thousand objects to arrest the mind. It was only wonderful that so much was crowded into so small a space. Where did his thoughts wander? To Worcester field, the flight, the pursuit, the first battle he had ever seen, with its fiery strife, and its thrilling interest, the disastrous defeat, the breathless gallop for life and liberty, the long concealment, the passage to another land, the life of privation, adventure, and care, and all that had succeeded, seemed like a dream: painful, confused, irregular, yet full of dark and powerful emotions, and things which could never be blotted from memory. But if from the fountain rose up drops of bitterness, yet there was one sweet and balmy stream mingled with the less refreshing waters, and seemed to enrich and beautify the garden of the future. It sprang from the memories of the place in which he then was. In a humble cottage, with nothing to decorate, to enrich, or to beautify, there appeared to remembrance a form and a face never to be forgotten. His ear still seemed to hear the musical tones heard many months before, his heart to thrill, his imagination to take fire, with the high thoughts presented to him by a simple peasant girl. There was no hesitation, there was no doubt, as to his own conduct. He had learned a deep, a stern, a wholesome lesson in adversity, and he had not learned it in vain. *Worth is better than wealth, goodness greater than nobility, excellence brighter than distinction.* And, after that long pause of thought, he rose, and putting on his hat again, for he had removed it, as if to cool his heated brow while the furnace of thought worked within, he went to the door, and demanded, "Has the King been proclaimed in the village?"

"No, my lord," replied the man; "you gave no orders."

"Quick, order up my horse," replied the young nobleman, "and order the trumpeters to mount. Shame on me that I neglected it for a minute!"

Then descending to the door, where a number of the soldiers were waiting for his pleasure, he gave various orders for marching off the prisoners who had been taken in the town, and for communicating intelligence of all that had occurred both to Colonel Ingoldsby and to the Commander-in-Chief. He then mounted his horse, and with a small party of troops following, and three trumpeters preceding him, he rode through the village, proclaiming the King at every open space. His last halt was before the castle, where the whole of the regiment which had accompanied him, drawn up in battle array, occupied the right-hand side of the green, while the villagers, in a considerable number, stood with every sign of rejoicing beneath the castle walls. A loud shout greeted his approach, and, in answer to the proclamation, a hundred voices shouted, "God save the King!"—a sound which had not been heard in

Landleigh for many a year before. The young lord looked around over the faces of the country people, but he saw few that he recognised; for neither Alice Brownlow, nor her cousin, nor Jane, nor good Dame Unwin were present. In the front, indeed, was the thin, spare person of Mr. Gideon Samson, and spurring his fiery horse up to him, the young nobleman shook him kindly by the hand, expressing regret that he had suffered imprisonment by the fanatics; adding, however, "As it was for conscience sake, my dear sir, you will not, I am sure, regret it."

Mr. Samson was about to reply, in perhaps a sourer strain than usual, when good Doctor Aldover stood forward, and with tears in his eyes greeted his former guest. "Ah! my dear young lord," he said, "I remember you now right well. How could I be so stupid as to forget you; though, lack a day, you are much changed—but so, indeed, am I. I trust, however, that you will be my guest again, and take up your quarters with me while you stay."

Denzil Norman was answering kindly, and bending from his horse, with Doctor Aldover's hand in his, to speak a few words more privately to his old friend, when an officer rode up, saying, "We have examined every nook and cranny, my lord, but we can find nothing."

"That is strange," answered the young nobleman. "My information is positive, but I shall probably receive further intelligence soon. Let the matter pass for the present, and be with me at eight to-night. In the meanwhile, dismiss the troops to their quarters, but see that good order be strictly preserved, and that the prisoners be well treated."

As he spoke, Denzil Norman dismounted from his horse, and passing along the line, addressed a few words to the soldiers, brief but kind and energetic, and when he had done, and seeing them begin to file off, he turned again towards the villagers, looking apparently for Doctor Aldover. The worthy physician, however, had disappeared, and telling the peasantry that if they would meet him there on the following day at twelve, he would treat them to as much beef and ale as they could lay into their skins in honour of the King's restoration, Denzil walked slowly into the castle court, and gazed around him for a moment or two with an air in some degree melancholy.

Some of the villagers, before they departed, peeped in through the archway, to see what the young commander was about; but one by one they dropped away, some of them saying to each other as they went, "He is waiting to see the fairy, I will warrant."

In the meantime, Denzil Norman took out his watch, and communed with himself in a low murmur. "I should like to see," he said, with a slight smile, perhaps at his own credulity, "I should like to see whether this sight will appear again. It wants but half an hour to sunset. I will wait and watch, and go down to the cottage after night-fall. It is growing very sultry, methinks," and passing through the arch again, he looked forth over the sky. To the southward and eastward heavy clouds were rising up, and advancing with great rapidity, although, as he stood there beneath the ruined walls, not a breath of air fanned his cheek; and walking round to the further side of the building, he gazed out over the scene below, seeing the dark shadow of the clouds sweeping up over the sunshiny lands, while a long black fringe, stretching from the edge of the cloud to the very ground, told that the rain was descending in torrents not far off. A dull flash passed before his eyes as he gazed, and turning back towards the gates of the castle, he placed himself under the heavy arch, and gazed towards the well. The sunshine which, streaming through the portal, stretched out across the green grass of the court, growing longer and longer as the sun declined, had just reached the margin of the well, and the deep clouds, stretching far over the sky, seemed to gather the whole light under their gloomy canopy; the rays, from the warm yellow, first assumed a violet colour, and then a rosied red, so that some fragments of glass in the old window frames seemed actually to send forth flames. More than one flash had succeeded the first which Denzil Norman had seen, and one loud roll of the thunder had been heard, when suddenly a broad blue glow spread over the sky, and a thin line of zigzag light darted rapidly down before his eyes, and struck a pinnacle of the old keep which towered up on the right-hand side. In an instant a large mass of the stone-work was cast down, joining the crashing noise of its fall with the deafening roar of the thunder. Denzil Norman pressed his hands over his eyes, for the brightness of the flash seemed almost to have deprived him of sight. When he opened them again, and looked towards the well, the same figure he had seen before was standing there, but now a portion of the white garments was cast over the head, and the face was entirely veiled. The young gentleman sprang forward, but while he was yet some fifteen or twenty paces from the well, the figure, which had been perfectly motionless before, raised one arm with a warning motion, and a voice said, "Hold! no farther!"

"Tell me, then, extraordinary being, what you are!" exclaimed Denzil Norman, pausing in his advance.

"That matters not to you," she said. "Inquire not of things that concern you not, but listen to words that may benefit you. You have followed counsel, and you have prospered. Follow it now, and you shall have better than prosperity—peace! All things shall undergo a change in this land. The old have passed away; the new are coming. You stand upon the limits of two great epochs, with an impassable gulf between them. Men shall try to bring back that which has gone by, and they shall fail. Strife and bloodshed will follow, and corruption and wickedness shall reign; but do you mix in none of these things. Flee the court and the cities, and live amongst your own people on your own lands. Be a brother to some, a father to others, a friend to all, and suffer not yourself to be tempted into places where kings resort; for in this day of all days it is dangerous, if not wicked. Hold yourself aloof from every faction and every party, and let the gay and the light scoff if they will, the sober and the steadfast will love and approve. This I am commanded to tell you: will you obey as you before obeyed? If you do, you shall be rewarded."

"Most assuredly I will," replied Denzil Norman; "for, in truth, such was my determination ere you spoke. Now one word more—"

"Enough!" said the figure, waving its hand; "enough! You shall find him you seek before this night be over."

She took a step back as she spoke, and, as she did so, another vivid flash of lightning blazed through the castle court. He could see the livid fire play around the form before him, and, at the same moment, a loud crash was heard mingling with the thunder, and one of the large elms, shivered by the lightning, fell in a slanting direction across the well, brushing the garments of the young cavalier even as he started away.

"It must have fallen upon her," he exclaimed, and, advancing rapidly, he looked round in every direction, but the figure was no longer to be seen, and the next instant the sun went down, the dark clouds stretched over the sky, and all was darkness.

Through the thick shower of rain, with drenched garments and a somewhat disappointed heart, Denzil Norman took his way back from the cottage of John Brownlow toward the house of good Doctor Aldover. He had found no one at the cottage but the servant girl, and an old woman appointed to watch the body of the dead man. Neither could he obtain any information regarding Alice at all satisfactory to himself. The girl said she had not been at home for three days, and that she did not know where she was, but that was all the young nobleman could extract from her; and let those who are younger than I am imagine the disappointment which such tidings gave to one who, for months, had been dwelling in the thought of seeing her whom he loved, and calling her his own. The warm reception of good Doctor Aldover cheered him, it is true, and he was still more cheered by the worthy man's assurance that Alice Brownlow would soon be back again, and that she had only left the place in fear of the Roundhead soldiery—a term which the Doctor did not scruple to apply in the present instance, although he would rather have eaten his hand than have used it to the soldiers of the Commonwealth a month before. As soon as he had given this intelligence, however, Doctor Aldover thought fit to put on a grave look, and add, "I am not sure, my good lord, that I ought not to send word to Alice that she had better remain away, for I do not half like a noble lord taking such particular interest in a cottage girl."

"If you do, I shall not easily forgive you," answered Denzil Norman; "but be under no fear, my good doctor. I can act as a man of honour to a woman as well as to a man. I will now send for my luggage, and change my dress, for I am somewhat travel-stained and very wet."

"You will find all your luggage in your room, my lord," replied Doctor Aldover. "I took the liberty of telling your people that you should quarter nowhere else while you were here. I will light you up, and when you have done we will have another bowl of punch together, and drink the King's health with a worthy friend of mine who is anxious to be well acquainted with you."

"What! Mr. Gideon Samson?" said the young nobleman.

"No, no," replied the doctor; "one of a very different kidney; but this is the way;" and he led him up the low open stair-case to the room he had tenanted before. Some time elapsed before Denzil came down again, for, to say the truth, he passed several minutes in meditation. At length, however, he descended, and found his way easily enough to the door of the good doctor's library, guided partly by memory, partly by the sound of voices speaking. On opening the door, he beheld two persons seated by the small, square table in the window. Doctor Aldover was one, the other was a noble-looking man in black, with a pointed beard, which, as well as his hair, was nearly white; and yet, to judge both from form and face, he was by no means far advanced in life. He had a long rapier by his side, and his black cloak had not been cast off. The moment the young nobleman entered, he rose and gazed upon him steadfastly, while Denzil's eyes were busy with his features also. The next instant, however, Lord Blount started forward with extended hand, exclaiming, "Oh, my dear lord! this is indeed a joyful meeting. Where have you concealed yourself so long?"

"Welcome, welcome, Denzil," said Lord Eustace; "welcome, my dear boy. Well have you done your *devoir* as a loyal subject, a good soldier, and an honest man. What more need I for all the care that I bestowed upon your youth?" and at the same moment he took Denzil's hand with his own left.

The young man looked somewhat surprised. "Nay, my good lord," he said; "give me your right hand surely, if you love me as of old."

"You will know the touch of it right well," said Lord Eustace, stretching his right arm from beneath the cloak, and grasping Denzil's hand.

The young nobleman started back, exclaiming, "Good heaven! What is this? It is cold as iron!"

"Because it is iron," answered Lord Eustace. "On the bitterest day of all my life, Denzil, wounded in this right arm, and a prisoner on the field of battle, my escape was purchased at the dearest price that ever was paid for human safety—at a price which I call honour to witness I would not willingly have paid for a thousand years of the brightest existence that ever was given to mortal man. Untended for many days, the gangrene seized upon my wounded hand, and I lost it under the surgeon's knife. Thanks to this good old man, whom you must remember well as my chaplain when you were a boy, this contrivance was procured for me, on a model brought from far, serving me well-nigh as well as the hand I had lost; for by the movement of my arm, I can clasp and extend the fingers as you see, aye, wield a sword or strike a stout blow, should it be needful. I have struck one, too, and not long since."

"Yes, I have heard of it," replied Denzil. "Had it not been for that, I might have come somewhat too late."

"And for a dose of Thebiac tincture," added Doctor Aldover. "I had better intelligence than Master Okey thought for; and when he sent for me, after I had been kept many hours in prison in sore trepidation of mind and discomfort of body, I made bold to give him that which I knew would render the snake innocuous for eight or ten hours at least; but now, by the leave of both your lordships, I will retire and prepare a better potion than that which I gave the routed colonel—good punch, I mean. Perhaps, too, you may have matters well to be talked over in private."

Thus saying, he withdrew; and a long, a sad, and interesting conversation took place between the elder and younger nobleman, in which Denzil for the first time learned the events which had taken place on Worcester field an hour or two after night-fall; how a wife and a daughter had devoted themselves to save a husband and father; and how the shot which had been intended for the escaped captive, had struck her whose life was far dearer to him than his own, as has been shadowed out in the first chapter of this history.

"For nine years," continued Lord Eustace, "I have mourned as few men ever mourned. In secrecy and by night I caused the body of my departed saint to be brought hither to my old castle of Landleigh, where the reverend friend who has just left us performed the last office for the dead in the vaults beneath the castle. Every morning have I prayed beside her tomb, every evening have I wept over her, and strewed the cold stone with flowers. I have lived the life of a hermit within those old walls, concealed and aided by a few kind friends and faithful dependents, who befriended me in my adversity as I had befriended them in my prosperity. The most skilful and the most kind, because by nature the most timid, was good Doctor Aldover; and an idle story which the villagers got up of the castle being haunted by a fairy, contributed much to my long concealment."

"Nay, my good lord," replied Denzil; "it was no idle story got up by villagers. The fairy I have seen with my own eyes, and a right beautiful fairy she is. On the very same night when I saw your lordship in the vaults beneath the castle, I beheld that fairy, and you must have beheld her too."

He spoke with a smile, but Lord Eustace answered gravely, "I saw no fairy, Denzil. You must have been dreaming."

"Not so, upon my life," replied Denzil Norman. "I was called thither to that interview by the fairy's voice; I saw her with my own eyes that night; I have seen her twice since, ay, this very night, not much more than an hour ago. But, perhaps, my dear lord, the fairy was of flesh and blood. Had I not known that your dear daughter was in London, kept under the tutelage of Cromwell, I should have thought it was her whom I beheld."

Lord Eustace smiled with an incredulous shake of the head. "Well, Denzil," he said, "young men and young women are hard to disabuse of their errors; but as you have mentioned my daughter's name, let me speak at once before Aldover's return, on a subject near to my heart. You are well aware, I doubt not, that it was the dearest wish of my beloved Lilla that our Kate should be united to you, whom we had educated with so much care. The dear girl will soon be in my arms again. I find that her education has been in no degree neglected; and as Cromwell, with a generosity but little to be expected, saved my lands from confiscation for her sake, saying that he would not spoil the orphan, inasmuch as he believed me to be dead, the wealth, which was abundant in other days, has only increased. Beautiful she is. Denzil, beautiful she must be; and with a right good will, a father's blessing, and a dowry which might suit a princess, I will give her to you as soon as we reach London. But you look grave, good youth. What is the matter? Does not the match suit you?"

Denzil Norman paused for a moment ere he replied, and he felt his situation painful. For the man before him he felt, as well he might, a son's affection. Lord Eustace had been to him a father when his own father was no more. Lady Eustace had been more than a mother to him. For the sweet child, who, with such fortitude and presence of mind, had saved her father from imprisonment and death, he had felt in early years a brother's affection. But yet there was something stronger still than all this: there was love, the pure, high, first love of a warm and enthusiastic heart. That would have been enough; but there was something more. There was honour—that feeling, that principle, that prejudice, call it what you will, which had been early implanted in his heart by the man who now spoke to him, which had been cherished through life, and worshipped almost with idolatry. He had spoken words to Alice Brownlow that could never be unsaid, that he could not, that he would not, wish unsaid. What was to him the prejudices of the world, what the considerations of wealth, of rank, of station, in comparison with honour and love! He knew that the light and gay might laugh; he knew that the proud and the selfish might scorn and blame: but he was not the creature of other men's opinions, and he hesitated not a moment. He paused, indeed, but it was with no hesitation. It was merely to consider how he might tell his tale so as not to pain or offend the hearer.

"What is the matter, Denzil?" demanded Lord Eustace, after waiting some moments for an answer; and his brow was grave and almost stern as he put the question.

"I will tell you in few words, my dear lord," replied the young nobleman; "and you shall judge, and will judge, as you always do, nobly and rightly. It was my fate some time ago to meet in this very village, in a humble station of life, without fortune, without family, without anything to recommend her but the loveliness of her person, and the high qualities of her mind, the only woman for whom I ever felt love. In a moment of danger and difficulty, when I little thought to see the bright days that we now see, when I little thought to meet you or any of my old friends again, I told her of my love and won a promise from her. Yet I will own, had I known all that I now know—had I been a prophet to foresee the events which have taken place, I would have done the same."

"Have you considered well, young man," said Lord Eustace, with a very grave brow, "that which you are about? Have you bethought you of all that must follow? Remember that the beauty must fade, and all those charms and graces which captivate the eye will pass away; that passion itself may die in its own flame, and the more solid realities of the world may acquire weight even with a romantic spirit, as the hurry of the young blood is calmed by years, and thought takes place of passion. Have you thought what it will be to see the cold civility shown by your peers to the young Lord Blount's peasant wife? to hear it told how you had been caught by a pretty face? to bear all those petty slights and half-concealed contempts which follow surely in society upon an ill-assorted union?"

"My lord, I have thought of all this and more," replied Denzil. "I have put more questions to my own heart than you can or will put; and I have answered, that beautiful as she is, were it mere beauty, I should never have spoken to her the words I have spoken; but even had I done so for beauty alone, yet I would keep my word. I owe that to her and to myself. In doing so, however, I have no fears, no hesitation either for myself or her; for the mind is as lovely as the person, and the heart as beautiful as either. You smile, my dear lord."

"Because you speak as a lover, and will act as a lover," answered Lord Eustace. "May your love long continue; for in it only can you find happiness under such circumstances. But, good faith, I should like to see your paragon of perfection. You say that she lives in this village; I must surely know her. What is her name?"

The colour somewhat mounted in the young lord's cheek as he replied, "Alice Brownlow;" but Lord Eustace shook his head. "I know no such person," he said; "I never heard the name. There was old Roger Brownlow, a tenant of mine, who has since proved traitor to his lord, I find; and John Brownlow, his son, as good a youth as ever lived, who has served me well; but the old man had no daughter."

"He had a niece, though," answered Denzil.

"I never heard of her," replied Lord Eustace. "I must ask good Doctor Aldover about her; for I must see her, in good faith, Denzil; and if she proves as you have reported her, you shall have my blessing on your marriage as a father's. Ah! here comes the good doctor himself. Tell me, my old and valued friend, who is this Alice Brownlow that my young friend Denzil raves about?"

"She is all that is beautiful, bright, and excellent," replied Doctor Aldover; "and is in my house at this very moment."

"What, you too enthusiastic!" cried Lord Eustace. "Pray, let me have the fair lady's company, my dear friend. Nay, I will go and fetch her myself. Where shall I find her?"

"Nay, nay, I will bring her," answered Doctor Aldover; and going forth again, he returned a moment after, leading Alice by the hand. She was dressed as she had been when she went with Denzil to the church, with wimple and hood, almost like a nun; and, with a heart beating warmly, he sprang up to meet her so soon as that beautiful form appeared; but, without even looking towards him, Alice drew her hand from that of Doctor Aldover, and advanced with a quick and eager step towards Lord Eustace.

The old nobleman threw wide his arms, and, casting hers around his neck, she leaned her head upon his bosom, and sobbed aloud.

"Nay, Kate, nay," cried Lord Eustace; "nay, my sweet Kate, be not so moved. What though this ungrateful boy here refuses your hand, all for the love of one Alice Brownlow, we shall find you a better husband than him, no fear. Come, look up, my Kate. Well I know joy will have tears as well as sorrow, and we have shed many of the former together, so the latter must have way. Keep back, Lord Blount; you have refused her, you know. Lo! you repent, do you? Well, take her, then, and forget Alice Brownlow in the arms of Catharine Brooke."

"Never," answered Denzil, throwing his arms around her; "never, my good lord. My first love, and my last. Call her what name you will—add titles, rank, distinction, fortune, every thing that men hold dear—you cannot make me love her better than I loved my cottage girl."

"Thanks, Denzil, thanks for that," cried Alice, for so we must still call her, as he ever did. "But will you love me as well, Denzil, as Catharine Brooke, for look, I am very much changed," and she threw back the hood from her head. Somewhat to his surprise, he then beheld that the dark, black braided hair was gone, and in its place the bright glossy tresses of a warm, light brown, which he remembered hanging over the fair brow of the child. He only drew her closer to his breast. "Ay," he said, "as Alice Brownlow, as Catharine Brooke, and moreover, as—"

But she put her fair hand upon his lips, saying, "Hush, hush! not a word of that;" and she turned a timid glance to good Doctor Aldover, whose eyes were too full of joyful tears to notice one half of what passed.

L'ENVOYE.

Dearly-beloved reader, you have heard an old story as it was told by an old man upon an old Christmas night. For some reason of his own—you know old men are very whimsical—he did not choose to go any farther, and it was quite in vain questioning him. Perhaps the truth was he knew nothing more, for he was a man of scrupulous veracity, as I am. I would have been glad to hear the details, but nevertheless I contented myself with what I had got—an exceedingly good plan in all circumstances, dear reader, but for which on this occasion I had my particular reasons. In the first place, I could not at all doubt that, under the circumstances in which they married, Denzil Norman and the Lady Catharine Brooke, otherwise Alice Brownlow, were as happy as any two people can be in this place of pilgrimage. I was satisfied, therefore, in regard to them, and wished them joy as heartily as good Doctor Aldover did, I do not doubt, after giving them the nuptial benediction when he was restored to his old cure at Landleigh, which I find by the parish register was in July of the year 1660. As to John Brownlow, who, by the way, was Alice's foster-brother, I have not the slightest doubt in the world that he married Jane Unwin, and made her a very excellent husband. It is not a thing to be doubted at all; and I find in the records of the house of Fauconberg the following curious passage:

"Alice Brownlow, long educated by my Lady Mary as the Lady Catharine Brooke, she having been found in a house at Worcester after the battle at that place, and passed by her mother Janet for the daughter of Lord Eustace, was this day dismissed from her home with many presents, she having grown greatly in my lady's favour by reason of her gentleness and docility. Item, a silver saltcellar was given to her by my lord as a gift."

In regard to Mr. Gideon Samson, I might have made my mind uneasy, having no precise information concerning him, but that I find many of the Presbyterian clergy fled from England into Scotland, to avoid the plague and Episcopacy; and as Sir Walter Scott, in one of his true histories, records the life and actions of a worthy gentleman of the same name as our respected friend, I have no doubt that he left posterity to carry on his virtues to other generations. The only persons of importance to be provided for, therefore, were the old castle and the fairy. As to the old castle, its ruins were shown with pride within my remembrance, by the antiquaries of Landleigh, who pointed out to the curious a subterranean communication between the building and the church, together with some stone doors in the remaining towers of the old fortalice, fitting so nicely into the masonry as not to be distinguishable to any but a prepared eye. The building has lately been very much dilapidated by a greediness for stones which has come upon the population since numerous factories have been established by the banks of the stream; and some of the wags of the place have remarked that the castle is the best quarry in the neighbourhood.

Either from this desecration of her dwelling-place, or some other cause of disgust, the fairy has not appeared for many, many years by the side of Landleigh well, though its waters remain clear and limpid, and the setting sun shines upon it every evening as before. Her memory is still cherished, however, by the older and the younger inhabitants of the place. The boys and girls look through the old archway with timid expectation as they pass on the summer evenings; and I once gave great offence to an old lady by hinting a suspicion that the famous fairy of Landleigh well was no other than the beautiful daughter of Brooke, Lord Eustace.

On this important point I must leave all readers to judge for themselves; but, at all events, this was the last of the fairies, and the only one that ever appeared after William Churne of Staffordshire was dead, and "Wittie Bishop Corbet" took his "Farewell" of the Good People.

THE END

SAFIA;

OR,

THE MAGIC OF COUNT CAGLIOSTRO.

A Venetian Tale.

TRANSLATED FROM THE FRENCH OF

ROGER DE BEAUVOIR,

BY

P. F. CHRISTIN AND EUGENE LIES.

NEW-YORK:
PUBLISHED BY HARPER & BROTHERS,
No. 82 CLIFF-STREET.

1845.

SAFIA.

INTRODUCTION.

While residing at Venice, during the summer of 1832, with the worthy Counsellor Honorius Claas, he would often speak to me of the strange ideas that arose in his mind upon meeting a certain man called Mariano Calvi, then living at the hotel designated by the euphonical title of "The British Queen," situate near the bridge of Fuseri, directly opposite his house.

The counsellor had frequently observed this man enjoying himself, *al fresco*, at his window, clad in a long, loose flannel gown, apparently watching the eddies of the canal, or gazing on vacancy, and thought Calvi's the most singular countenance he had ever beheld.

At first sight, it was difficult to comprehend who this Mariano Calvi could be: a compound of baboon, abbé, and spy; his disposition naturally lively, eccentric, and multiform. At times he would leave his hotel, his costume in perfect keeping, his boots well polished, coat well made and brushed; a fashionable English frill, black dress-coat, and the gray hat latterly adopted by men of ton. On other occasions he would stalk forth, enveloped in the ample folds of an Italian cloak, a cigarillo in his mouth, a coral hand, with small gold chain, by way of breastpin, in his scarf, humming a cavatina of Bellini. What most tormented the counsellor was, that this Calvi was constantly standing, statue-like, at his window; so that he could neither undergo the process of having his hair dressed in that antiquated style to which the worthy Dutchman had religiously adhered, nor smoke his rosewood pipe, nor even spit into the canal, without encountering the scrutinizing glance of Mariano Calvi.

At night, especially, the Italian's eyes, his head half hidden beneath an enormous fur cap, such as we see in the portrait of Ruggieri or Laensberg, would flash fire. The figure of Mariano Calvi, leaning over the brink of the canal, was calculated to imbue the spectator with the idea that he was labouring under some singular hallucination of the brain; he would seem as if absorbed in thought, and holding mysterious converse with the green and sleepy waters beneath. For hours and hours he would thus commune with them, listening eagerly to the songs of the barcaroli, as they sought their nightly dormitories, to the murmur of the wind rushing through the space between those pillars whereon once waved the Venitian standard, now replaced by the Austrian flag, else watching the track of some swiftly-gliding gondola, or listening to the faint notes of a distant piano, whose touch served to while away the tedious hours of some lonely but lovely signora. If he raised his eyes aloft, it was only to gaze at the stars, with an indescribable air of abstraction and dreaminess in his attitude, or to notice to which side inclined the blossoms of the flowers covering the flat roofs of the surrounding dwellings. Daily he might be seen at the Florian coffee-house, a painted paper fan in his hand, swallowing inordinate quantities of ice-cream, and in the evening enjoying himself at the Benedetto theatre in his private stall, of which he kept the key.

One evening that La Pisaroni had sung the part of Arsace, which Calvi had applauded most extravagantly, upon leaving the theatre he was seized with an apoplectic fit. The counsellor happened to be at his side, and received his last dying words, which were, "Take this key, signor, and should I die, as you hope for salvation, deliver it to no one save my nephew; mark me—to him alone." These were the last expressions of the unfortunate man, who was carried home, and expired that night.

Vainly did the counsellor make inquiries in every quarter of the city in search of that nephew. Neither from friends nor from the police could he gain the slightest information relative to the Italian's habits of life, save that he had paid his hotel expenses regularly, had several chests in his apartment carefully padlocked, and frequently mailed letters for Florence, which, with its accustomed paternal solicitude, the Austrian government considered itself bound to open; but that despotic inquisition gained nothing for its pains, for the letters were invariably found to be *blank*.

Whether or not Mariano Calvi used sympathetic ink had not been ascertained. He was rather regarded as a madman, desirous of taxing some worthy Florentine with useless postage.

All these letters were addressed to some doge of the republic—some superscribed, "Al serenissimo principe Moncenigo;" some to "Alvise;" others to "Renier," from whence the madness of Mariano was generally, and not unreasonably inferred, inasmuch as these illustrious personages, renowned in the history of the Venitian Republic, had long slept that sleep from which no mortal can awake unless by the fiat of God, or by the resuscitating spell of the poet's imagination.

Honorius Claas, like a true counsellor and Dutch diplomatist, as in truth he was, kept this key as religiously as though it had been that of a chamberlain; it was, indeed, a charming little key, elaborately chased in the style of the age of Louis XIII. Eight months had elapsed, and no person had appeared to lay claim to it; the official seal remained affixed to the doors of his apartments, and, thanks to the superstitious terror of the hotel-keeper, might have remained there forever; but one evening, as Claas sat leaning over the canal, reflecting at ease upon the matter contained in a despatch he had just received, upon suddenly raising his eyes, he perceived a vivid light issuing from between the blinds of the apartment of Calvi.

Simultaneously a shadow was perceptible, moving up and down, as if intently searching for some object on the floor; then, all at once, the blinds of one window were thrown open, and the counsellor clearly distinguished a young man, apparently about thirty years old, trying the locks of several chests in the room with a bunch of keys. At length, glancing at and seizing a small casket from amid the confused mass of furniture and effects, he tried in vain the same manœuvre; none of the keys would fit.

"Demonio!" exclaimed the young man.

Honorius then perceived him pull the bell-rope violently. The landlord answered the summons; but, from the gestures of the parties, it was apparent that he could give no satisfactory information.

The counsellor, who was enjoying the freshness of the evening breeze, in summer undress, at his window, beckoned to him, holding up the key left in his care by Calvi. Instantly the young man rushed from the room, and, quickly descending the staircase, entered his gondola. They had no sooner met than the young stranger exclaimed, "My name is Juliani, nephew of Mariano Calvi; since chance has so befriended me, Signor Counsellor, allow me to share with you."

Then, placing the casket upon the counsellor's table, he opened it with the key which Honorius had given to him, and displayed to my friend two separate compartments. The first enclosed some bank notes tied round with pink tape; these Juliani appropriated to himself, as his share of the spoil; the contents of the other division were an infinite number of small cards covered with notes, and each adorned with an elegant and delicately-sketched pen and ink likeness of a doge of Venice. On the outside of the case containing these annotations were inscribed these words, written with a pen: "For the Prince of Albania."

"Who that prince was," continued Honorius, "I confess I was then unable to guess; but, as Signor Juliani had tendered to me such a windfall, I thought I might accept his offer without pangs of conscience. Juliani was a good-looking young man; he had gained possession of his uncle's fortune, which, from what he related to me, he richly deserved. As for myself, I inherited the notes of a singular being, who had employed himself in writing the secret history of Venice. Was my share destined to prove equal to that of Juliani? But that little concerned him, as he was making his arrangements to marry the Signora O****a, a rather handsome Florentine; so, after smoking a pipe, he bade me good-night, and left me.

"I must confess that I was anxious to peruse these papers. The handwriting was close, harshly defined, and portraying marks of insanity in the writer; but each one of these notes bore a character of mysterious authenticity, seemingly penned under momentary inspiration, and bearing semblance of the daily memoranda of a spy; there were passages sufficient to make one's hair stand on end—executions, murders, imprisonments, drownings beyond all conception; in few words, it was the history of Venice graven with the burin of its executioner—a list of crime so horrible, frightful, and yet fantastical, that each comma, stop, or mark assumed, in my eyes, the colour of blood: an inexplicable vertigo seized me; and when, next morning, my Hungarian valet brought my breakfast, he found me paler than the old papers before me, near which my lamp was still burning. Juliani followed close behind him.

"'I fear,' said he, waving in his hand the handsomest flower he had been able to find at the Sclavonian quay, 'that the follies of my uncle have caused you to pass a bad night; not but what he had opportunities of becoming acquainted with sundry mysteries of the archives of Venice, but, then, he had the mania of writing the History of the Venitian Republic in two volumes quarto.'

"'But who was that Prince of Albania?' I then inquired of Mariano's nephew.

"'Stefano Zannowick, who assumed the title of Prince of Albania,' he answered, 'was my uncle's protector, and died towards the end of the summer of 1786. He was born the 17th of February, 1752, at the town of Pastrovichio, on the borders of Turkish Albania, near Montenegro. In 1760 his father opened a small retail store in one of the obscure streets of Venice for the sale of various trifling articles, and especially of confectionery, suitable to the taste of the children of the neighbourhood. His talent for play soon procured him a more brilliant position; but the paternal government of Venice thought fit to put an end to his successful career by banishing him from the republic. He left the state, but invested his profits in landed property in his native country, and became even owner of the town of Pastrovichio; he caused his sons, Primislas and Stefano, to be educated at the University of Padua, and to that choice, undoubtedly, Stefano was indebted for his knowledge of literature.

"'My uncle then resided at Padua, and had the honour of being selected as Stefano's tutor. In spite of my uncle's advice, he soon gave proof that he inherited his father's talent, and by its exercise drew down upon himself a similar correction from the government. In 1773, at a time when Stefano Zannowick, after adventurously roving through France, England, and Holland, was preparing to play the part of Peter III. in the Montenegro, and to take advantage of his popularity in the country, my uncle, by his request, prepared for him several important papers relative to the history of Venice; he was then on terms of friendship with the keeper of the archives, Orio Contini, a man of shrewd abilities, who wrote of passing events with the utmost reserve. From him my uncle learned the secret of that mysterious ink that he used afterward in his correspondence with several persons of distinction, and latterly with me; for Mariano Calvi had acquired so strong a habit of using it, that he considered it indispensable even in communications of the most simple and ordinary nature. The various letters which he mailed at Venice, bearing the superscription of doges, were not the less a sign of madness in my worthy uncle, for they were all intended for one identical individual, myself. The mystery he observed, Signor Counsellor, was occasioned by a dark adventure, the secret of which he alone possessed, and related to me with terror.'

"'What was that adventure?'

"'It must be comprised in the notes in your

possession, and you will find it either under the title of Alessandro or Safia, I forget which.'

"'True enough,' I remarked, 'that mysterious story concerns a doge, and one whose name is new to me. It is extraordinary.'

"'Remember,' continued the young man, 'that Mariano Calvi has written only of the last three doges of the republic; the pseudoname of Alessandro, therefore, designates one of them. As to the history of Venice, as we see it printed in books, he had certain fixed and determined ideas, which, although not lacking weight, were clearly considered preposterous by those who did not consider isolated facts as sufficient authority.

"'When visiting together the hall of the Ducal Palace, where hang the portraits of the doges, he would often say to me, "Juliani, all those personages you behold here with the *corna* on their heads, the brocade robe covering their shoulders, and the wedding ring of the Adriatic Sea upon their fingers, died not the death ascribed to them in history. The true history of Venice is all that has not been written about it—the sealed book, not the open one;" and thereupon he one day related to me the story of a certain doge whom he called Alessandro. That curious portion of the memoirs he was to leave was written for the instruction of the Prince of Albania, who had left him at Venice when going to spend the winter at Groningen. When the French invasion swept away, at one breath, our shadow of the shadow of a government, and the abdication adopted on the 12th of May, 1797, surrendering Venice as a conquered territory, the Prince of Albania had already, twelve years previously, opened his veins in the prisons of Amsterdam, under rather curious circumstances. Being arrested for debt, he held out threats to his creditors that he would kill himself if too harshly prosecuted. The regency of Amsterdam, in consequence, caused him to be stripped, and had him clad in entirely new garments, in order to be assured that he could secrete upon his person neither poison nor murderous weapon. In spite of all these precautions, he was found dead in his bed, bathed in blood, with an incision in his right arm, his head thrust under his pillow.

"'Convicted of having practised fraud at Amsterdam upon their high mightinesses, and upon other individuals, the unfortunate Zannowick was wholly without information from abroad. His body was drawn upon the hurdle at Amsterdam. Upon hearing this intelligence, my uncle became almost crazy. He had always reckoned upon the protection of his pupil, whom he persisted in loving with all his vices. The notes collected by my uncle might compromise many families. Give me your word, Signor Counsellor, that, should you make use of these materials, the names of the principal actors in this singular drama, however transparent the veil thrown over their identity, shall not be divulged. Although there no longer exist doges, and we live under the merciful dispensation of the Austrian government, there still remain some descendants of that family, whose chief my uncle has designated under the name of Alessandro. This history will probably be more highly appreciated in Germany, where all that appertains to magic, or the wonderful, is prized and cherished; therefore I leave it with you. As for myself, my worthy uncle has bequeathed me gold: to me far preferable to all fairy tales, or wondrous stories, even those penned by Tieck or Hoffman.'"

It was the Counsellor Honorius Claas, therefore, who arranged the story that follows; and it is to vindicate its authenticity that we have thought it best to lay these explanations before the public. We are gratified that, instead of presenting it under the somewhat equivocal patronage of the Prince of Albania, we are enabled to give it under that of our readers.

CHAPTER I.

THE ALMS GATHERER.

This day, the 29th of June, was at Venice, as throughout Christendom, the holyday consecrated in honour of the Keeper of Heaven—in honour of Saint Peter, who possessed, in the City of the Doges, the principal church in the quarter Del Castillo—not to mention the Cathedral of Saint Peter at Rome, where the saint enjoys more extensive lodgings.

The tower clock situate at one of the angles of the Piazza fronting the sea—built after the design of Carlo Rinaldi from Reggio—had just struck 7 A.M.; the populace of Venice were on the alert, and the bells of the various churches were gladdening the air with their merry chimes.

In the grand square already were the numerous showmen anxiously assembling their customers to the sound of their ivory whistles, their attendants at intervals beating the drum; pedlers, displaying their wares of every description, citron, ribands, and whatever was likely to attract the attention of the crowd around, with their baskets, were passing and repassing the bridges; the Turks and Armenians vended their perfumes; the gondoliers, in their holyday attire, sat indolently smoking upon the wide marble steps of the palaces leading to the waterside, waiting the call of any stranger.

All was bustle and excitement: shopkeepers opened wide their doors, the coffee-houses displayed all their attractions, each house seemed ready for the reception of guests; while the variegated awnings of the palaces were stretched forth to shade their inmates from the penetrating rays of the sun, and lovely young girls of the district of Piacetta came to draw water from the well in the ducal palace-yard.

As the clock struck seven, a lady issued from the water-gate of the palace, richly habited, and wearing a white mask attached to her three-cornered hat—for the Venitian ladies then wore a small hat with the bahuta, a sort of black mantle, trimmed with lace, and descending to the hips, leaving the arm exposed from the elbow downward. They also wore a sort of petticoat of yellow or white, spreading out after the fashion of an ecclesiastical robe, and scarcely discovering the extremity of their small feet, encased in a tiny slipper. They carried in their hands either a white or black mask, in order to preserve their complexion from the heat of the sun, and wore powder, as in the days of Madame Du Bany.

It was in the costume so often reproduced by Il Tiepolo and Canaletti, and of which the engravings of Peter Longhus have preserved the general idea, that the signora of whom we have spoken issued that very morning from the water-gate of her palace, to the steps descending from which her gondola was attached.

A negro boy bore her train, a duenna carried her missal and ample purse upon a cushion: the gondola was steered towards the patriarchal church of Saint Peter.

The Signora Grimani was wedded to one of the most noble patricians of Venice. Her age was forty — but she was still handsome; yet, had it been necessary to establish her reputation for virtue by test of the ballot-box, in senatorial parlance, she might have found herself blackballed. However, she was selected upon this day to repair to the church of Saint Peter, in order to take up the collection.

She was what is now called a *well-preserved* woman of a certain age. Her severe and prudish looks, her rouge carefully and artistically laid on, her haughty lip, and her large and piercing jet-black eyes, rendered her, no less than her age, an object of respect and terror to the younger portion of the nobility of Venice, while those of riper years, and more experienced, gave credit to the Marchioness Apollonia as possessing incontestable traces of former beauty. Her prudishness and dread of her husband's ire alone kept them aloof.

The fact was, that the marchioness had become religious; this might serve as an excuse for no longer loving her husband, a man past fifty, brutal, dissolute, and ambitious withal, who continued to indulge to excess in all those vices with which, at this period, Venice so luxuriantly abounded. He seldom inhabited his palace, preferring that he owned at Padua on terra firma; left the marchioness to her devotions, and gave himself up entirely to his pleasures; and yet it was asserted in Venice that the Marquis Grimani was jealous.

The gondola stopped at the square of San Pietro del Castello. This ancient edifice, which, from the first centuries of the Republic, had been regarded as the Cathedral of Venice, might metaphorically be said to exhibit upon that day with pride, to the assembled spectators, its fine portico, in the style of Palladio. Beggars were sitting upon the steps, and the leathern curtains, at the very threshold of the door of entrance, discovered to the eye of the beholder the perfumed vapour of the incense from the censers, gracefully curling upward, and spreading among the Corinthian columns and above the pulpit of the Holy Apostle, brought from the city of Antioch.

When the Marchioness Apollonia Grimani entered the church, the patriarch, with his canons, issued from the sacristy. The church was crowded with priests, choristers, and novices. Three mace-bearers opened a passage through the throng, and conducted the lady alms-gatherer to her seat near the great chapel.

The marchioness folded her fan, opened her missal, and first casting her eyes downward, then raised them, and took a survey of the assembled multitude.

A murmur of approbation was audible around, which possibly recalled to mind her youthful days; but, insensibly, her thoughts reverted to spiritual ideas, doubtlessly influenced by the solemnity of the scene. She soon prayed fervently—apparently wholly abstracted from worldly ideas—until the proper moment arrived for taking up the collection. A credulous and bigoted Italian, she had long placed her sole devotion in Saint Peter, from innate conviction of his power; indeed, the protection of that holy saint had never failed her.

The marchioness farther imagined that, as Saint Peter held the keys of Paradise, it was to him she should apply for hope of admission; she whose pious life seemed to shame the reckless and profligate career of her husband, and who was cited in Venice as a woman who had renounced the errors of vanity and the world. "Is not Saint Peter," she would say to herself, "the celestial guardian of Paradise? the sun of the popes? the king of the Apostles? Is he not greater than Saint Mark?" The signora's father bore the name of the sainted Peter; this was an additional incentive to veneration, rendering her's doubly enthusiastic. Finally, there hung in the private apartment of the marchioness a magnificent copy of the painting representing Saint John the Evangelist, with Saint Peter and Saint Paul, the original of which, by Paul Veronese, might be seen in the church.

When the marchioness left her seat, the clanging halberds of the Swiss ringing upon the pavement, the loud swell of the organ, caused all the ladies assembled, whether Venitians or foreigners, to rise, in order to catch a glimpse of the lady alms-gatherer: all habited in holyday attire — their heads adorned with flowers on either side—standing upon tiptoe, and wearing the high-heeled shoe then in fashion: a fashion which the subtle policy of husbands had alone contrived to introduce within the precincts of the Adriatic city. The female attendant of the marchioness handed to her her purse, and, followed by her little negro boy, she made her way to the bench of the magnates and senators, to whom she first applied.

The shower of sequins dropped into the signora's purse was truly marvellous. She bowed to each patrician, and even to each mere citizen, with an air so charming, and so blended with grace, that it excited envy among the female spectators. The collection being over, she returned to her seat; and, to conceal the pride her triumph had created in her breast, had recourse to her missal. In opening it, she probably reflected that the procurator Grimani, her worthless husband, was not present, and was about offering up prayers to Saint Peter for his conversion, when, among the leaves, a small but charming note on vellum, with an embossed border of miniature flowers, similar to those used to frame the pious orisons of saints, and two doves—resembling those fed by Saint Mark in the court-yard of the Ducal Palace, and for which Venice displayed so particular and exclusive a regard—cooing over a cross, and two hearts consuming with the celestial fire of charity. The note was traced in golden characters, and read as follows:

"Signora—Your prayers, equally as your collection, have deservedly earned for you the favour of Heaven, where it is registered that for three years you have abjured your former errors, and that you differ from most women of Venice by the prudence and reserve of your conduct. As a mark of the divine and ineffable goodness (the knowledge of which must be held sacred by you, and imparted to no profane ear), permission has been granted to the first and best beloved apostle, upon his own request, to descend upon earth and sup with you to-night. He desires that there may be no witness of this sacred interview, and from his lips you shall hear what never before was uttered to mortal.

"(Signed), PETER, *Apostle, and patron of the Church of San Pietro del Castello.*

"Paradise, June 29."

The signora's surprise was so great that it nearly betrayed her; she cast a hesitating glance around, but saw no persons, save a few devout old women, wholly absorbed in the passing solemnities. The patriarch was officiating, and the ceremony merely lacked the presence of the doge.

In the fulness of pride and joy, the marchioness read over two or three times the holy epistle, which seemed to her fragrant with seraphic odour. Her first thought was to confide all to some worthy canon, but the celestial missive so expressly recommended implicit secrecy, that, upon leaving the church, she imposed upon herself the obligation of mentioning the circumstance to no one; she even appeared to converse upon indifferent subjects with her female attendant and her black page.

When the prow of her gondola touched the marble steps leading to Grimani's palace, "Morenita," said she to her waiting woman, "it has been very warm to-day; follow me to my apartment and unlace me."

Morenita obeyed the summons. Upon entering the chamber, the most conspicuous object was a large and elaborately-carved bedstead, with wrought pillars, surmounted by plumes of variegated feathers: the portrait of the noble Marquis Grimani faced the sacred painting before mentioned.

"What is the matter, madam?" asked Morenita, seeing her mistress affected to tears. "Does the prayer you are reading recall to mind any excusable error of your youth, to one so adored as you have been?"

"Silence, Morenita; remind me not of aught terrestrial. Let the Countess d'Azola enjoy the infantile glitter of conquests and worldly pleasures. My regards are fixed upon Heaven, and you shall see one of the most illustrious of its representatives come down this night."

Morenita looked mechanically towards the ceiling; it represented Venus and Adonis surrounded by a group of Cupids, in the style of Albano. The painting sufficiently portrayed the ancient Olympus, at the shrine of whose frailest goddess, according to the scandalous chronicles of Venice, the signora had too often worshipped.

"You can read," resumed the Marchioness Grimani; "well, my dear, peruse this letter."

"This letter, madam," answered Morenita; "probably the petition of some handsome lover, or a snare of Signor Grimani! he is so suspicious."

"Read, I say."

Morenita took the paper; her knees sunk upon the floor; her tongue became parched, and she crossed herself.

"So holy a guest, madam," she exclaimed, upon recovering herself; "where can we find a restaurateur sufficiently skilful to prepare supper for your apostle? Guaspolo, our cook, is the most talkative man in Venice; besides, he is a spy of the marquis, and will be determined to ascertain."

"You are right; we should either have some discreet man, or else one wholly ignorant."

"I conceive your idea: that young Armenian who has just left the service of the reverend Father Pasquali, and who used to make such exquisite ice-creams. He has been a week out of employ, and is unacquainted with your husband. We can tell him to make all the arrangements in the lower rooms, and can afterward have him reconducted, in a gondola, through the water-gate of the palace. As for our cook, Guaspol, there are to-day entertainments enough in the Place of Saint Mark to keep him amused; let him have his own way, and you may remain tranquil. He will surely meet some barcaroli of his acquaintance, and spend the night with them drinking."

"But the plate! You know, Morenita, that the marquis, through spite, has only left us three covers and a few dishes, enough, as he said, to suit the necessities of pious women wrapped up in their devotions, maliciously adding, that the Lord's Supper, by Paul Veronese, with its gold and silver ornaments, savoured strongly of the pharisee. How can I receive Saint Peter with a table so meanly appointed?"

"Is there not in Venice a district called the Ghetto, inhabited by the Jews? Leave all to me, madam: I know a certain goldsmith there—"

"What! Place Israelitish plate before an apostle? Never!"

"Be composed, madam, the plate is ducal—senatorial and most Christian. Venice, in these degenerate days, glitters with the show of wealth; but that show is a cloak to poverty, and many a time has the marquis himself—"

"The thought is excellent: we might then, at least, present a decent appearance. There is one of my caskets of jewels. Take it, and pledge it with the Jew."

"Still, madam, you forget the bill of fare."

"You are right; but first, is there not capital wine in the cellar? Summon Honorio, the butler."

"Him, madam! Why, Honorio received orders from your beloved husband to meet him this morning at Padua. He is, by this time, on his way thither."

"I have often heard Grimani say that there is excellent Cyprus wine to be had at the Aquila coffee-house. He often—perhaps too often — enjoys himself there in the accursed company of Trevisani, Monsenigo, and other dissolute lords of his acquaintance. We will send for six bottles of Cyprus, three of Montefiascone, some Rosolio, and a few flasks of Maraschino."

"Well, but for the supper?"

"As regards the supper, we may desire the Armenian to serve before the King of Apostles an excellent soup, a *poulet au riz*, a dozen of ortolans, and a larded capon. with Constantia sauce. Think you that will suffice, Morenita?"

"For the appetite of a saint I scarcely know, they fare so well in Paradise; besides, consider the distance from our gate to that of which Saint Peter keeps the key is a thousand times longer than from here to Morano."

"True, Morenita. You will, then, see the goldsmith and the Armenian. Beseech the latter to make his sauces palatable to the most fastidious taste."

"I have told you that he comes from a canon's house. For a few ducats he will surpass himself."

"Begone, then, and lose no time. Ah! what think you? were it not well, in order to keep the matter more secret, that from this moment we barricade each door and shut the blinds of each window? Light betrays, by its reflection upon the canal. Tell the street porter that I feel fatigued, and have retired for the night. Leave the land-gate ajar; I have a surmise that the holy apostle may come that way. It is said, however, that saints sometimes tumble down the chimney, or fall through the ceiling."

"Are you sure, madam, that no one will harm him? peregrinating the streets of Venice at night is so unsafe and dangerous."

"I have no fear of that. Did not Saint Peter cut off the ears of Malthus?"

"You remind me, there is a great painting so representing him near the Fondaco of the Turks. What shall I ask from the blessed saint?" continued Morenita, putting on her veil and her out-door finery.

At this moment a soft voice, essaying one of the songs of the gondoliers so common among the Venitians, was heard nearing the palace. Morenita peeped from the window, and recognised the young Armenian.

"There goes our *cuisinier*, madam, sent to us by Providence. I'll away and give him his lesson, then hie to the goldsmith Isaac, at the Ghetto, to borrow his handsomest plate."

Morenita went off, leaving to the marchioness herself the care of laying the table of the apostle, which, with charming gallantry, she prepared in the state bedchamber, the handsomest apartment in the palace.

CHAPTER II

THE SUPPER.

At the appointed hour, and as the marchioness, by a refinement of politeness towards her apostolic guest, was reading his fifteenth epistle to the Corinthians, a slight noise was heard at the land-gate of the palace, and Morenita entered, with awe depicted upon her pallid countenance, preceding a grave personage, whose features the obscurity had prevented her discerning.

Following the instructions of her mistress, Morenita had introduced this venerable guest in the dark, and caused him to grope his way through the antechamber, offering in excuse the secrecy his note had exacted from her mistress. But when she threw open the door of the bedchamber, wherein the marchioness stood, she had but time to fall prostrate at the feet of the sainted apostle, so radiant did he appear under the bright rays of the chandelier lighted for this occasion.

He was attired in the long and flowing Judaical robe with which painters represent the Prince of Apostles; a thick beard hung down, partly over his breast; and from his girdle were suspended the keys of the celestial kingdom. His deportment was solemn, but tempered with a certain air of mild benignity; his hands were fair, and upon his forefinger he wore a ring similar to that of his apostolical and Roman holiness the pope. He laid aside his staff, and smiled affectionately upon his hostess.

The marchioness, imitating the example of her attendant, threw herself at the feet of Saint Peter, and fervently kissed the hem of his garment.

"Are you sure that you are quite alone, daughter?" asked the apostle, surveying the apartment with a scrutinizing look.

Morenita locked all the doors, advanced a fauteuil, covered with satin fringed with gold, for Saint Peter, and, upon a sign from the marchioness, retired as the saint took his seat at the sumptuously furnished table.

Thereon was displayed the richest gold and silver plate of the richest goldsmith in the Ghetto, and the most savory repast ever offered to the epicurean palate of the most fastidious father confessor.

Saint Peter acknowledged that he had never witnessed the like since the miraculous draught which whilom destroyed his fishing nets.

"You are indulgent, holy saint," said the marchioness; "this modest supper was prepared by a young Armenian, who thrice devoutly crossed himself previously to commencing his operations. He is a discreet young man, and perfectly to be relied upon, for which reason Morenita selected him in preference to a certain Guaspolo, who would surely have betrayed our interview to my husband."

"A husband unworthy of so virtuous a woman! I know it," answered the apostle, carving a fowl. "Your charity is in such good repute above, that it has become proverbial there. My daughter, you are not the woman ever to leave the altar without flame, or the temple without attendance. Even this morning the collection you took up, and are to send to the parish—"

"Alas! holy apostle," answered the Marchioness Apollonia Grimani, with a sigh, "the collection produced little in comparison with the wants of the patriarchal church. I intend to add a few sequins myself to complete the sum required; for to-morrow morning the purse is to be claimed. It is the duty of the Primiciero Daniel to do this."

"The Primiciero Daniel?" resumed the apostle. "Are you sure that he will fulfil his office as becomes a pious ecclesiastic?"

"Nothing can induce me to suspect the primiciero," said the marchioness. "However, more is known in heaven than on earth, and possibly the Signor Daniel—"

Saint Peter drew from his pocket a set of tablets, and appeared to peruse attentively certain memoranda. "The Primiciero Daniel," resumed the apostle, sipping from a tolerably large goblet filled with Cyprus wine, "has as bad a name above as the Canon Zobeni."

"Zobeni?" exclaimed the marchioness, "Zobeni, my confessor?"

"I am sorry he is, my dear lamb; but Zobeni does not suit you. He sends me daily to Paradise fair penitents whom, conscientiously, I am compelled to leave to shiver and freeze outside the gate. Sad chaff the list of good deeds upon which they ground their claims to admission. Not one of them would part with a necklace, or other ornament, towards repairing the broken thumb or heel of my mutilated statue. Charity, my daughter, charity is the balm that unlocks the gates of heaven: open your door, and the door shall be opened to you. You have done so, of which I make minute."

Saint Peter took up his tablet, and inscribed thereon some notes.

"What are you doing?"

"Nothing! You shall know hereafter."

"But yet—"

"Daughter, beware of the curiosity of Eve. Suffice it to you to know that the day you dismiss Zobeni and the Primiciero Daniel, I will myself bear you to the steps of the throne of the angels. There are men who destroy the souls of others while blasting their own: *descendunt in infernum viventes*."

The apostle was discussing his fourth ortolan, and had broached a flask of Maraschino.

"Alas!" he resumed, "must I confess, my dear daughter, that this morning I found my chapel meanly endowed, while that of Saint Justinian, where his ashes repose, was much more munificently supplied. Why this? I cannot divine, for he is far from equalling Saint John, or even Saint Andrew, my brother, and yet a few ducats—"

"You are right," exclaimed the marchioness, suddenly enlightened; "but, great saint, since I have the inestimable honour of entertaining you, there is no farther need of any intermediate hand to convey this alms. Yourself can take charge of the purse containing the collection. I will add a few of my bracelets, and you can give the whole into the hands of the patriarch himself towards the expenses of worship."

"On condition, my daughter, that I give you a receipt; business must be transacted with regularity."

The marchioness opened a magnificent casket inlaid with mother-of-pearl and marqueterie, and took from it a parchment, which she handed to the apostle.

"Here is a receipt in due form," said Saint Peter. "I would not use a leaf from my own tablets in order to leave strong proof that I have descended upon earth. Previous to my return to heaven, I shall also call on the patriarch, with whom I shall have an explanation. For the present, I have a slight favour to request from you, madam."

"Name it, great saint," answered she, courtesying.

"One of my followers, a man of deeply religious feeling, but relentlessly persecuted by the Secret Council of Venice, has just returned to this city to collect an inheritance. You are the wife of the Procurator Grimani, and he is likely to become inquisitor. Could you not obtain from him for my protégé a permit to reside in this city? It is said that he is in the habit of signing such documents for small sums; a practice I infinitely disapprove; but at Venice justice is so corrupt."

"Since it is impossible to conceal anything from you, great saint," answered the marchioness, with her hand upon a drawer, "it is true, my husband carries on a scandalous traffic in these permits; I have mastered his secrets, and know the receptacles wherein he keeps his private papers. From one day to another the senate may gain information by spies, and he be led into difficulty."

"The very contingency you must avoid, daughter, trust me; purge your house of all fraud; the Marquis Grimani might some day have to pay dearly for such artifices. Besides, he is careless in dispensing those permits; and if the arragador Cesare Morini, his mortal enemy, or Casanova de Seigngalt, a rake banished from Venice, should chance to gain information—"

At the name of Casanova, the marchioness turned pale; however, she merely answered, with trembling lips,

"Then Casanova did not die at Corfu?"

"Nothing is less proved," replied the apostle, observing the agitation of the marchioness; "he is a cunning rogue, who daily sends to Satan the prettiest sinners about the Adriatic. Besides, he still has friends at Venice—friends who will never forgive the council for banishing him, well as he deserved it. The faithful worshipper at my altar, in whose behalf I now apply to you, is, on the contrary, unjustly accused; a permit would save him during his brief sojourn in Venice; without it, madam, his life is in danger."

"His life!" exclaimed the marchioness, with much excitement; "his life! Ah! great saint, take these permits; you may carry them all away; may they redeem all my errors!"

"Well said, my daughter, well said!" continued the apostle, as he gathered the blank signatures which the marchioness handed him; "but this," continued he, as he pocketed the purse, "will prove no less agreeable an offering. Now, in my turn, I wish to reward your zeal by a gift that is worth all terrestrial gifts; you have opened your door to me; mine shall not be closed against you."

The apostle then tearing from his tablet the leaf whereon he had written a few lines, presented it to the Signora Grimani.

"Here is a permit," added he, "that secures to you all the joys of heaven. With this paper—"

Saint Peter did not conclude; for at that moment Morenita rushed into the room; and she had hardly entered and bolted the door, when three violent knocks were struck upon it.

"Who can come at such an hour?" cried the marchioness, pale with terror.

"I know not, madam," answered Morenita; "he is a tall, bald man, with a robe like that of this gentleman. He says—he pretends that he wishes to speak with you."

"His name?" asked Saint Peter.

"Faith! Mr. Saint, he did not see fit to tell me; but hear him knock, louder still! Why, he will break down the door!"

Saint Peter arranged his dress, and, going in person to the door, asked firmly,

"Who knocks?"

"Saint Paul!" answered a voice; "open the door!"

"Saint Paul!" said the marchioness, with an indescribable expression of joy. "What! Saint Paul too? Am I, then, to be honoured to-night with the visit of the whole college of apostles?"

"Do not open, marchioness, do not open!" cried Saint Peter, trying to keep her from the door.

But at this moment the door received such a vigorous push, that Morenita, dreading the consequences of the noise, sprang towards it, opened, and Saint Paul was in sight.

Saint Paul wore the Israelitish costume; he held under his arm a book with silver clasps —wore large sandals on his feet—his eyes flashed fire.

"Apostle, unworthy of the name," cried he, "who permitted you to come here, and mingle terrestrial interests with the sublime truths which we defend? Sent by our common Prince and Master, I notify to you the decree from above. Follow me!"

"You!" grumbled Saint Peter. "You! my inferior! Bah!"

"I expected that, after thrice denying Christ, you would deny me also, guilty apostle! but I have taken my measures, and these gentlemen, my supporters, will show you the effect of the victorious grace that compels you to submit."

Upon a gesture of Saint Paul, three men, masked, appeared upon the threshold. Saint Paul bade them do their duty with due respect for the holy character of the saint they had to arrest. They gagged him, and bound his hands.

The marchioness fell, fainting, into an arm-chair, and Morenita hastened to follow her example; mean while the holy posse entered a large gondola with their prisoner, and the barcaroli rowed speedily away.

CHAPTER III.

THE TWO APOSTLES.

The gondola had just passed the angle of Grimani's palace, lighted on her course by the bright moon of an Italian sky, when it stopped before a dwelling of rather modest appearance, buried among a labyrinth of small streets, in the vicinity of the Reggio canal, near the Church of Saint Job. The three cavaliers politely handed Saint Peter from the gondola, and introduced him through the grated door of a dimly-lighted vestibule, upon which several doors opened. Saint Paul ordered his brother apostle to follow him into his room, and motioned the cavaliers to leave them alone. When they both found themselves in a large apartment, whose only furniture consisted of a variety of instruments of alchemy, furnaces, and crucibles, Saint Paul jerked off the beard of his prisoner, and flinging away his own,

"A thousand pardons," said he, "Signor Casanova!"

"Cagliostro!" cried the false Saint Peter, retreating.

They gazed at each other in mute astonishment, until Casanova first broke silence.

"What miserable jest is this?" said he to Saint Paul; "and how did you learn? Be that as it may, you will have to give me satisfaction for such a proceeding; I am not a man to bear it!"

Cagliostro looked at him maliciously, and, taking his hand as he would that of a pupil,

"Signor Casanova," said he, "you were getting into a scrape; for the procurator returns from Padua this night; he received information from his cook Guaspolo; but for his return I should not have interrupted your tête-à-tête."

"In that case, my dear master, I owe you an apology; but who told you I was to sup with the signora?"

"The Armenian who prepared the supper, and who sometimes comes in to prepare for me furnaces of another description. Yes, those I use for chemistry, my dear fellow! Have you not employed him on sundry errands since his dismissal from the prebendary Pasquale's house? You had stationed him, had you not, opposite Grimani's palace, with instructions to keep good watch?"

"True! and I swear I'll break his bones if I chance to meet him."

"Why so? because he gave me information of a fortunate adventure? Is it not one for me to have the honour of renewing acquaintance with a person of such merit as yourself? Were we not friends in Germany? and have you forgotten that, at Berlin, I had the honour of winning from you sundry small sums?"

"Three thousand florins, I think. I owe them to you still; I do not hesitate to acknowledge the debt. But, then, you play with such luck!"

"I do not deny that. Now I have made up my mind to lose to-night, and to you. Your pockets are well furnished; I heard the ring of gold as you were carried into the gondola. You shall play against my bank, here in my house. I reside at Venice, under the name of Count Lippone; and the only way to win confidence is to appear to lose; then you excite compassion even to admiration; therefore, you must punish my purse severely. The three cavaliers you have seen, and who arrested you so politely at the signora's celestial supper, will decoy some dupes for us this night, and I will take care afterward to make up for my losses."

"So you reside in Venice, Count Cagliostro—I beg pardon, Count Lippone?"

"I have been here a week; and you?"

"I arrived the day before yesterday, and I confess that I came here with fear. I lodge in a small room near the *Ponte del Paradiso*. The last doge, through the importunity of others, banished me. I have been abroad three years, and were it not for the fortune I hope to inherit from my old aunt, the Countess d'Agnati—I need it sadly, my dear fellow, for nowadays there is not even the smallest German count to pluck."

"Shameful! that we should meet so ill-favoured by fortune. You say you are banished from Venice? Give me your hand; I have just been banished from France."

"Indeed!"

"Yes, for mere trifling matters too tedious to narrate. I always had a bad opinion of that country. It swarms with philosophers, who will soon know as much as ourselves; and nobles, whose ingratitude and avarice are discouraging to true genius. And may I confide to you, whom I regard as a pupil, from the period when a certain female slave, some fifteen years since, caused me the loss of a fortune, I hardly think myself longer fit for anything?"

"You jest; remember your late trick upon me."

"That was the only means of renewing our acquaintance. Diamond cut diamond. If we only understood each other—"

"I intend we shall. You once gave me some lessons. If I could now return the compliment—"

"You are ingenious, Signor Casanova."

"What is better still, I have that which will save us from the hands of the Venitian police."

"What do you mean?"

"We are both in search of fortune here in Venice, against wind and tide. You ever curious to try experiments in magic, and all methods of imposing upon the strong or weak mind; I eternally seeking money and women. We are like two summer clouds, swiftly passing: I represent Pleasure, you Intrigue."

"It is, then, our interest to enter into partnership, dear Casanova. What do I seek at Venice? I hardly know; mean while, I try to force fortune in my favour; and in that I only follow the example of the first personages of the republic. I must, this night, bring you in contact with an excellent dupe I have discovered—a French marquis who used to visit me formerly in Paris, and who, not having the same reasons as I for changing his name, has retained his own; from this circumstance I recognised him the other evening at the Casino. The madcap has come to Venice, as most Parisians would go to Saint Cloud or the Porcherons: without being able to boast of much learning, he knows what all the world is doing, is fond of women, enterprising, and perfectly unsuspicious. I plucked his feathers in Paris, and shall spit the bird in Venice. He eulogizes without reserve the house of the Count Lippone, and every night rolls under the tables of the Aquila coffee-house. But be not alarmed about him; he is one of your little French lordlings, who can bear any quantity of wine, and play as people play only in Paris."

"I should be delighted to know him. His name—"

"The Marquis Eusebe de Saluces, a man of noble birth, and moving in the best society. You would never guess who is the uncle of this noble gambler."

"Some lord of the court of Versailles, whose inheritance he squanders."

"Not at all. His uncle is Monsieur de Sartines."

"Who is so powerful, and so feared?"

"Alas! yes, my dear friend, that same M. de Sartines who found fault with my magic, my secrets at faro, and, above all, the mysterious hotel which I kept open day and night in the *Marais.* While Louis XV., a king who did some good, whatever the world may say to the contrary, gave the Count of Saint Germains an apartment at Chambord, with one hundred thousand francs, that he might have ample means to prepare the dyes that were to secure superiority for French cloths, the present minister orders me to quit France, dreading my washes, my cosmetics, my magic! Why I might either have killed him with a glass of *aqua tofana*, or have restored his youth, as I listed."

"Truly, I had nearly forgotten, count, your boundless reputation as a restorer of youth! You ought to impart the benefit of your knowledge to the Marchioness Grimani, who seems to have grown terribly old. By-the-by, I have with me certain permits of residence, which, in case of misfortune, may prove of service to you. We will share equally as brothers; and now let us part. Since yesterday I have made a discovery in the district of the Ghetto."

"What?" asked Cagliostro, hastily, as he threw off his long apostle's gown, under which he wore an elegant dress-coat, trimmed with the finest embroidery. "Is it an old Jewish usurer, able to support us here for some time respectably, or a treasure buried in the cellars of those sons of Israel, who keep their houses as closely shut up as their purses?"

"You have hit the mark, count; it is a treasure; one a thousand times more precious to me than Saint Mark's own treasury—a young and beautiful girl, who dwells near the Church of Saint Jeremiah."

"Her name?"

"That, indeed, I know not as yet. It was nightfall as I caught a glimpse of her through the gratings of her window; I fancied I saw that angel whom Raphael represents illumining with radiance the dark dungeon of the saint whose beard I wore just now. If you like, we will take a stroll, to-morrow morning, in that direction, and, as you are no longer as inflammable as I am, I reckon on your assistance towards the accomplishment of that *great work.* But have you not yourself some fair Venitian that you think of?"

"Perhaps," stammered Cagliostro, emptying a bottle of essence on his hands, and ringing for one of his servants.

A footman appeared, and informed the Count Lippone that his company had arrived.

"You will soon behold that august assembly," said the count to Casanova. "Under what name shall I present you to my players?"

"Why, marquis, under my own, to be sure, if you had rather. Have I not, as well as yourself, a talisman of safety?"

"Yes, but trust me; use it only in case of absolute necessity. The doge Alessandro is not like other doges; and, although he is only about thirty-five years old—"

"The doge Alessandro thirty-five! Parbleu! I am sure he will be anxious to become acquainted with the most undoubted rake in all Venice! Devil take prudence! If I chance to meet him to-morrow in Venice, I would tell him boldly my name."

"Yes, and get shut up under the Leads, or exiled to Bohemia; and your Jewess—your idol—who must equal, I should think, in your eyes, that Theresa Irmer, a comedian's daughter, who once turned your senses—would you thus freely give her up?"

"Call me Doctor Celsus or Paracelsus, as you like; only lend me some clothes, for I have nothing about me save Saint Peter's tunic."

Cagliostro touched a spring behind the tapestry; the door closed on his friend, who presently reappeared, dressed quite splendidly. Casanova had with him the product of the collection; he lined therewith the pockets of his vest, intending to make it yield well at the bank founded by himself and Cagliostro.

The Count de Lippone's play-room was near at hand; Casanova and Cagliostro repaired thither soon after, and found there a numerous assemblage. Parties soon gathered and formed faro tables; several ladies prepared to stake a ducat at a time. Rather high sums were lost in this place; but the Count Lippone, among others, appeared so ill-treated by fortune, that, on going out, every one offered him his purse.

When Cagliostro and his friend were alone,

"All goes well," said Casanova; "you suit me; and now I shall tell you a secret; you hardly deserve it, however, after so cruelly interrupting my apostolic supper. I was on the scent of an important discovery at Signora Grimani's—"

"Speak—speak quickly," answered Cagliostro, trying the power of his fascinating glance upon the Venitian.

"This is it. I came here in search of a treasure—"

"You have told me that; the daughter of a Jew, is it not, who lives near the Church of Saint Jeremiah?"

"That is an affair of the heart—a whim—a true-love fancy. But, first of all, I must take care of the substantial."

"Well spoken."

"Be it known to you, then, that there exists at Venice—though, unfortunately, I don't know the spot—a treasure that might enrich us both, and put us on a par with the first players of the Rialto."

"I know it."

"Who told you?"

"The old procurator, Morosini—six years ago—under the most solemn pledge of secrecy. But I know, at the same time, the nature and origin of that treasure."

"I know also. It cost the doge dearly. You know the name of that doge?"

"Yes," answered Cagliostro; and he whispered in Casanova's ear a name which the latter knew well. "But how can we tell where the republic of Venice caused that gold to be buried? Yes, by what means?" continued Cagliostro, apparently musing.

"That is precisely the point," answered Casanova, "I hoped to discover; the private library of Signor Grimani is famous in Venice; it is said to contain an infinite number of sacred documents, stolen by him from the records under the reign of the last doge. One of us must—"

"Rest assured, I will take care of that. Only, after this night's adventure at Signora Grimani's, it were prudent to wait a few days, were it not?"

"The manuscript must be in Arabic, and I do not understand that language. The procurator Morosini, exiled from Venice, must have told you in France—"

"He told me that the Venitian Inquisition at that time had in its employ, as secretary, a man acquainted with that language; so that, supposing the book should fall into the hands of a profane person, or be subtracted from the records, it would be a useless treasure. Did Signor Grimani know that language?"

"No more than I do," answered Casanova, laughing; "then, by both abstaining a few days from going to see the signora—"

They were still conversing when the gray light of dawn peeped through the windows of the apartment. Cagliostro and Casanova parted, after mutual vows of friendship, existing less in their hearts than upon their lips.

CHAPTER IV.

AN INQUISITOR.

The same morning, and as the grated doors of the Ghetto creaked slowly on their hinges, three young patricians, followed by a servant bearing several bags of money, issued from a house, forming the angle of the small square where stands the Church of Saint Jeremiah.

In front of this church, which separates the district of the Jews from the Christian part of the city, some lean-faced Israelites passed and repassed, wearing the red hat which had taken place of the patch of yellow linen worn by their ancestors, as a distinctive sign, upon their breasts: children were repairing to the synagogue, and water-carriers forced, with their unmelodious rattles, the notice of their customers. The house whence the young lords issued belonged to the Jew Ottale, one of the richest money-lenders of the republic. It looked upon a narrow canal, whose green waters no bark then disturbed; the neighbourhood of the spot wore a stern, mistrustful aspect. A bridge of few steps ended near the house, every window of which was closed with enormous padlocks.

"Battista," said one of the young men to his servant, "carry this to the Trevisani Palace. We need a good breakfast to raise our spirits after the night's fatigue. Tell the keeper of the Aquila coffee-house to get it ready: we shall follow quickly after you."

"Two thousand ducats lost to that French marquis introduced to me last night at Count Lippone's. Do you know that that is something?" muttered the most elegant of the young patricians, whose name was Moncenigo, as he sat down on the stone bench beneath the house they had just left.

"True enough," answered Trevisani, glancing sideways at his servant, who had just started towards his palace; "but I lost three thousand ducats to that German called Doctor Paracelsus. Devil take me if I have not seen that face before somewhere: a rogue who can say nothing but *mein herr*, and does not seem to know one word of Italian. But you, Ranuzzi, who were not at play last night, how is it that you come to borrow from our Jews of Venice?"

"I will tell you at breakfast; I must prepare for a journey; yes, this night I leave Venice."

"Is it to go back to Padua, my terra firma noble? Padua, where you like so much to reside? It is said you keep, in a seraglio there, several handsome slaves from India; of course there is some favourite sultana among the number; confess it, you rogue!"

"Come," said Ranuzzi, affecting to appear gay, "your jests are ill-timed. I go; that is enough; believe me, I do not leave Venice without a tear."

"Hold on! we will not let you go. What the devil! Ranuzzi, you love pleasure; do you forget that you are engaged, and must come to-night to the ball of the fair Countess d'Azola? To-morrow, at break of day, you may leave for Constantinople or the Indies; but this night you belong to us."

"I bet that Ranuzzi does not relish the air of Venice at this moment," said Trevisani, regarding him fixedly; "for, with those old statutes, just revised by the Inquisition of State, do you know, Ranuzzi, that, by merely importing your yellow women from India, you expose the Venitian patriciate to the shame of having, some day, the blood of slaves mingled in their veins? The Inquisition does not trifle on that point."

"Bah!" resumed Moncenigo, seeing that Ranuzzi turned pale; "the power of the Inquisition is every day declining; its hands are not yet upon you; mean while let us go and open a few bottles of Cyprus; that Battista is a fellow to breakfast before us, and I feel my stomach as empty as my purse was this morning."

The three patricians took the road towards the Aquila, without minding the various sounds that were already rife in that district. The house of the Jew Ottale was still closed, when a gondola stopped near the bridge, whence a veiled lady issued, with a cavalier who held her prayer-book, and who gallantly handed it to her as she stepped from the gondola.

"Countess," said he, "your bark, faith! is as light as the wind, soft as a swan's neck. Here is Saint Jeremiah's Church; you will have time to pray for our sins; for, look! it is scarcely eight o'clock, and more than an hour will elapse before the bishop comes to give his blessing to the young couple so earnestly protected by the doge and yourself. Scarcely had I arrived from Padua, and before even entering my house, I found at home an order from the doge, bidding me offer you my hand to church during his absence; state affairs, I suppose, countess—"

"That is an admirable excuse, with which you patricians habitually cover your tender avocations! Confess, Grimani, that state affairs answer your purpose marvellously well! You are never engaged in business except when you wish to deceive us. For instance, might we not often translate an extra session of the senate by an amorous cruise on the Canalazzo? and a full council by a masquerade at Fusina? I know some high-born ladies who are disrespectful enough to laugh when their noble husbands affect to use pompously, in their presence, the words election, college, quarantia; each lady knows, then, that the next day her husband's senatorial gown will smell of Cyprus wine—that his wig will be awry, and his ruffled wristbands soiled; too lucky even if the severe magistrate does not return from the Ducal Palace disguised as a Turk or a Scaramouch."

"You entertain, madam, a rather bad opinion of the patrician order."

"Between us, Grimani, you entertain no better. To plant the standard of Saint Mark on the walls of Constantinople, like old Dandolo; to beat the infidels at sea and on land, like Morosini; to humble Genoa; to construct basilics; to cast cannons at the arsenal; launch vessels filled with armed seamen—oh! that was suitable for the heroic times; but now what is required to perpetuate those high names? To frequent masquerades and coffee-houses; to draw the sword under a street lamp in behalf of some low courtesan; to gamble all they possess, and often what they do not. Such is the exemplary life of the Venitian gentlemen."

The personage to whom the countess's bitter criticism was addressed cast a look upon his wig, as though he had found himself attacked in his inmost trenches, and, looking at the countess with his scrutinizing glance, said,

"Thus, madam, your criticism spares no one, not even the doge?"

"Is not Alessandro present at all your parties—all your feasts?"

"True, madam; but he appears also first at the council and at business: he is found under the double livery of pleasure and work, at the same time the model of the young and idle of the Broglio, and of the old counsellors of the Seignory. When I gave my vote for him at the ballot of the Great Council, I deemed, as my colleagues did, that I was electing a doge who loved nothing but luxury and indolence, desirous, at the most, of having carried before him the silver trumpets, the gold chair, the cushions, and the spurs—those symbols of his dignity—a doge, in short, such as we required in Venice!"

"You found yourselves quite disappointed," resumed the countess, maliciously; "did you not?"

"Thanks to him, madam, our offices are becoming sinecures. Alessandro knows everything in the state, men and things; walls and consciences are made of crystal for his penetrating eye; he outspies the spies whom we set upon his track; and it is often in the midst of some gay supper that he laughingly corrects our errors of the preceding day, or, in anticipation, our blunders of the next."

"Such he is, indeed!"

"Besides, he possesses the love of the people: he has made himself one of them by the interest he takes in their welfare: one day the first man in Venice, under the golden brocade canopy; the next a simple workman, handling the file and the plane in the arsenal's workshops. Oh! he is a strange doge, impenetrable to all, even an inquisitor of state."

"It is so said."

"You alone, madam, however, hold the key of that heart, locked to all others. The doge loves you! The only subject of conversation in Venice is the love with which the beautiful Countess d'Azola has inspired the sovereign of the republic; and, therefore, the homages of your adorer glide past you like the waves of the sea by the sides of your gondola—"

"Grimani," resumed the countess, fixing on the procurator the glance with which an Italian woman might eye a soothsayer she was consulting, "do you think that the doge loves me?"

"Who doubts it, madam?" rejoined Grimani, warmly. "What charm do you lack for pleasing him? he, what power for fulfilling all your wishes? You are as submissive to him as the Adriatic Sea to her spouse; and therefore I must tell you my mind. It is believed in Venice that you will be dogaressa. The doge Alessandro will give to you the ring with which he weds the sea!"

"Silence, Grimani!" exclaimed the countess, with a strange expression of melancholy and terror. "Think not that I am ambitious of a title whose lustre makes its danger—a title which, while it ensured me the possession of Alessandro's heart, might subject him to a yoke. I am happy, Grimani, very happy; Alessandro is young, handsome; he is a doge. I am the only woman in Venice he has been pleased to distinguish; I ask nothing of him save his love. It is true, my love is not like the love of those degenerate Venitian ladies who surround me," continued the countess, raising her head proudly. "The feeling I bear Alessandro is jealous, anxious, mistrustful. That feeling, I know it, is the penalty of my error and of my weakness; therefore I go, sometimes, and pray to God to protect me against its transports, and to give me back, alas! that peace which I have lost!"

Thus speaking, the countess had already lifted the tapestry leading to the church. Standing on the marble steps of the temple, she seemed one of those fair goddesses under whose features Veronese so often personified Venice, his city. Her figure, closely fitted by a long black satin bodice, gave indication of that soft, undulating motion common to Asiatic women who are ever reclining; her skin, slightly tinged with amber hue, the lustre of her large blue eyes, almond-shaped, her hair, black as jet, and the classic cast of her profile, caused the beholder to dream softly of the daughters of Greece; her hands were fair and delicate as Leda's, her nails just touched with *henna*, that carmine dye sold at Venice by the Armenians of the port; her foot was finely shaped, and quite at ease in a tiny slipper; for the fashion of wearing high-heeled shoes, she thought, should be abolished.

"I shall await patiently the coming of his highness to his tribune," said she to Grimani as she left him; "you, my dear procurator, do not forget that you have accepted an invitation for my supper to-night."

"Nor that I am permitted to kiss the fair hand that penned it!"

Grimani imprinted a respectful kiss upon the fair hand of the countess, and his eyes followed her to the tribune of the doge, which she entered. The countess quickly closed its gratings, unwillingly, doubtless, to expose herself to the curiosity of the inhabitants of the neighbourhood before the doge's arrival.

It was not the intention of the procurator Grimani to enter Saint Jeremiah's previous to the hour of the betrothal; he stood, therefore, in the square looking towards the Gindeua; he saw coming towards him a man dressed in livery, who hurried his steps as soon as he perceived him.

"What news, Guaspolo?"

"Alas! excellency, bad news. I had left this very night to meet you in Padua and tell you what was taking place."

"What took place?"

"Your house, or, rather, your palace, excellency, was last night the scene of singular occurrences. But this is not the place to relate them to you. Come with me, and you shall see with your own eyes."

The procurator hastened to follow Guaspolo; but, as he turned the corner of this piazzetta, he was met by two ushers in red gowns from the Ducal Palace, who handed him a sealed package; Grimani's hand trembled as he opened it, but a ray of gratification soon illumined his sallow brow, furrowed with previous wrinkles; he even drew from his pocket a few ducats, which he saw fit to give the two ushers.

"Let us hurry on, Guaspolo," said he to his cook; "for the affiancing will soon take place at the church, and I must, you know, again meet the Countess d'Azola at Saint Jeremiah's."

A quarter of an hour had elapsed since the procurator had taken one of the streets that led to his palace, when three patricians, issuing from the Aquila coffee-house, came back to the square. Their very countenances attested sufficiently the copious meal they had just indulged in; their purple faces, the mirth of their remarks, their laughter and sallies gave sufficient evidence that they had just left the Aquila, where they might, at this moment, have answered as a sign instead of the Bacchus that adorned it.

"Ha! ha!" said Trevisani, "what a capital adventure!"

"Excellent trick!" joined Moncenigo.

"Our friend Grimani himself will surely laugh about it. What an honour, gentlemen—Saint Peter and Saint Paul for his guests!"

"Silence, gentlemen; their goes the marchioness with her beloved husband. They are coming by yonder canal. Grimani has probably felt desirous of showing himself: he must be in high spirits!"

The procurator then crossed the square: he was escorting his wife to the Church of Saint Jeremiah.

"Faith, Ranuzzi, you ought to hire that little Armenian; he has cooked for a saint: what better can you ask?"

"Speak lower, Moncenigo; here comes the procurator back!"

"Faith, let us congratulate him; I can't hold in."

"That's it; let us ask him about Saint Peter."

"And Saint Paul too; they are the talk of the whole neighbourhood. The duenna could not keep the secret."

"All hail to the noble Marquis Grimani," continued they, affecting so serious a composure that it discomposed the procurator. "How fares his excellency to-day?"

"Rather poorly: I spent the night travelling. Yes, letters from the doge recalled me to Venice."

"And on your return from Padua you hardly anticipated that supper."

"What supper?" asked Grimani, affecting surprise.

"Why, to speak the truth, the supper—which—the supper that—you must be sanctified from top to toe this morning. How is the signora? indeed, she has good reason to be returning thanks at church."

"A letter for Signor Grimani," here interrupted a *sbirro*, dressed in black, who brought a large portfolio to the procurator.

"Well," said the procurator, smiling.

"How now, Grimani, do you know such people?" asked Moncenigo, after the *sbirro* had withdrawn; "Saint Peter will not forgive you."

"Nor Saint Paul either; they are police officers."

"You think so?" rejoined Grimani, in a freezing tone; "the notes they bring me may be useful. This, for instance: read the address."

Moncenigo took the letter.

"'*To Signor Grimani, inquisitor.*' What! are you an inquisitor?"

"It would seem so," answered Grimani, coldly; "that gives me the opportunity of knowing that you played *biribi* the other night with two Sweedish barons, Signor Moncenigo."

"True enough, and I happened to win."

"Well, but you used marked cards in your play."

"Sir!"

"You were wrong, however, in forgetting them at the house of the courtesan Lucrezia: that's all!"

"Who dares to accuse me?"

"Here is the complaint; read it yourself."

"I render thanks to the senate, who have appointed you inquisitor," rejoined Moncenigo, with a hypocritical effusion; "we shall have some one now to protect us! You know," added he, in a whisper, "that I promised you a good share in the will of Count Orio, my uncle?"

"I have sundry pipes of Malmsey and Spanish wine buried in a safe place; I wish you to taste them," said Trevisani, embracing the new inquisitor.

"Trevisani, the keeper of the Aquila coffee-house insists on levying on your palace. He claims that you owe him."

"Ungrateful wretch! he himself owes me—his reputation! But say, dear Grimani, who are these *sbirri*, with their cloaks, that I see yet lurking around the church?"

"I have some one to arrest this very day. As for you, Ranuzzi, if I may venture to give you a piece of advice," said Grimani, stepping up to one of the young men who surrounded him, "do not stay to-night for the ball of the Countess d'Azola. You must foresee yourself what danger threatens you."

"Come, now, Grimani, you wouldn't be hard on the poor fellow," said Moncenigo, showing him how pale his words had made Ranuzzi's brow; "don't you know he has a love affair here upon his mind—a certain lady, who lives, I think, at the angle of the Rialto? And, then, is it his fault if that celestial supper of Saint Peter and Saint Paul—"

Grimani's lips quivered with rage; but Moncenigo went on:

"Since it is urgent that you should this day arrest somebody, why don't you rather arrest a certain French marquis, who won three thousand ducats last night from me at faro? He played against me at Count Lippone's; and last night I had not taken, I must confess, my measures, as I have this day."

And Moncenigo drew from his vest a pack of marked cards.

"Will you hide that pack?" said Grimani, "or I'll have you arrested."

"No! you won't; haven't you and I used them frequently at play at Lucrezia's? I have a letter of yours even, in which you recommend her to keep the matter secret! She gave it to me. But rest easy; although you are an inquisitor, I shall remain your friend."

"Give me proof, then," answered Grimani, "by helping me to discover the authors of the scandal that took place last night at my house."

"How can you call it a scandal, so honourable a visit?"

"Yes, indeed! they broke my door, borrowed plate and eatables in my name; in short, Moncenigo—shall I say it to you—they purloined my wife's gold. This morning she was unable to give either her collection or the purse that contained it."

"They might have been out of change, like myself. Why, you see, there are no Jews in Paradise—"

Just then, a hubbub in the Israelitish district, occasioned by the arrival of a somewhat ludicrous personage, interrupted the inquisitor's conversation, and his eyes, like those of the patrician's, were soon turned towards a stranger who was coming across the bridge with a book in his hand.

The new comer's appearance was surely one to claim notice, for his dress was entirely different from that of the young Venitian lords. He wore the dress-coat of a marquis, cut after the last fashion of the *œil-de-bœuf*. He was a French gentleman in all the Italian meaning of the word; that is, he affected those wild, reckless airs which were then fashionable only at Versailles, and which contrasted with the rather *German* levity of the signory of Venice. His blue dress-coat was embroidered with humming birds and parrots, who were nibbling cherries even into his pockets. His fingers were covered with marcasite rings; and the tie of his irreproachably white cravat shamed the linen bands of the procurator Grimani. He might be about thirty-eight.

"That's the man," whispered Moncenigo to the inquisitor; "think of the three thousand ducats I lost at Count Lippone's. It is not at all unlikely that cursed marquis might have used marked cards!"

"We shall see," answered Grimani to the young patrician; "let me only converse a few minutes with him while I wait for the Countess d'Azola's coming from church. I must have a victim; and by Saint Mark! this one shall pay for Saint Peter and Saint Paul."

Moncenigo took the arm of Ranuzzi, who appeared to be musing; and, giving the French marquis a last look, exclaimed,

"What a funny figure! what a queer mask, though carnival is past!"

Trevisani, still tottering on his legs, followed them; and all three promised the inquisitor to seek him as soon as the church service should be concluded.

CHAPTER V.

THE CICERONE.

Upon reaching the foot of the bridge, the French marquis looked around with an air of abstraction; his eyes then reverted to the book he was perusing. It was a traveller's guide;

the very one, perhaps, which John Baptist Albrizzi fancied to write in his day, to enable foreigners the more easily to find whatever rare and curious objects Venice contained; the marquis was still perusing it with particular attention, when he perceived Grimani seated upon a stone bench close by the dwelling of the Jew Ottale.

"'There are in Venice honest ciceroni, whose officious ministry it is to pilot strangers to the threefold object of their search: inspecting monuments, gambling, and flirtation. What denotes their calling is, that they are usually to be found sitting alone on benches in the public squares, awaiting the arrival of some foreigner sufficiently well furnished with cash.' Good! there is my man," continued the marquis, after reading this passage; "a man seated on that bench, alone, and apparently waiting—he must be one of them." Then replacing the book in his pocket, the marquis, with much courtesy, approached Grimani.

"What would he with me?" said the inquisitor to himself, eyeing the new comer.

"Hem! hem!" began the marquis, coughing; "cool morning, sir. Nonsense! what am I talking about? The thermometer is at thirty; I am always imagining myself at the Tuileries, or at Cours-la-Reine!"

"I presume you are looking after one of your servants, sir?"

"I left both my servants near the bridge opposite when I alighted from my cab—I mean gondola—wonderful conveyances those gondolas, my dear sir; the government should make a pond of the Place Vendome, if merely to afford the nobility the chance of displaying themselves as navigators."

"Do you really think so?"

"I will not gainsay it. I was bound to see Venice. Faith! it is as brilliant as the Rue Saint Honoré, especially the Place of Saint Mark. I have not spared myself—my gondola is nearly foundered. As to this suburb, there is a stern, frowning, Bastille-like look about it. Has it a name?"

"It is called the Ghetto."

"Here she lives, then, no doubt," said the marquis, making a note upon tablets. "Tell me, my dear fellow," continued he, offering a purse to Grimani, who indignantly retreated; "did a lady land here but half an hour since, accompanied by a cavalier?"

"The ladies of Venice are always attended by a cavalier," answered Grimani, with indifference.

"Yes, I know, some even have two! The cavalier was dressed nearly as yourself; he carried the lady's missal, and she wore a black veil."

"Can he mean my wife?" thought Grimani, eyeing the marquis with terror; "I must draw him out. Give me, at least, some particulars," said Grimani, "and I shall be happy—"

"A most accommodating gentleman!" muttered the marquis. "The affair is very simple. Enjoying an excursion the other day upon the grand canal, I ventured to peep from out my gondola, which was run against by another, and nearly upset. Some of our gondoliers are very awkward indeed. This accident which happened to my carriage—gondola I would say—caused me to take a glance at the persons who had just passed me. The lady, who sat on the front cushions, was just then giving some order to the barcarole. I thought I recognised her voice, for, according to the custom of your country, a veil concealed her face. As I have come to Venice merely as a handsome man, whose aim is gallantry, I should like to have some conversation with the lady. Come, give me your advice: and be not afraid of getting me into a scrape, for I am just arrived from France, a mirror of bravery from head to foot."

"Suppose the lady has a husband?"

"A fig for husbands! I look upon them as a set of importunate creditors. The lady has won my heart, my dear fellow, and I am on the lookout for a chance to shine before her."

The ridiculous excitement with which the marquis spoke, his questions, and his ignorance of the manners of Venice, would have been enough to ease the mind of a less suspicious man than the inquisitor; but he was bent on sifting the matter; and, besides, as we have said, he was seeking an opportunity for revenge.

"You are rather hasty," said Grimani to the marquis; "but I like your spirit. Since you insist upon it, I can tell you where you can meet the lady."

"Speak! speak! I entreat," answered the marquis, again offering his purse; "I won last night at Count Lippone's—the first time for a week—and half of this gold is yours. Where can I see the object of my passion?"

"In this square."

"What! in front of this church? What am I to do when she appears?"

"Can you ask me that?"

"To be sure."

"That is your affair. You assert yourself to be a brave man; act as such, marquis; approach the lady, and raise her veil."

"Her veil! I declare," said the marquis, casting a wondering look at the man he still persisted in considering as his guide and cicerone, "that were bold—excessively bold."

The marquis turned a pirouette, then turning to Grimani, with a dubious look, said,

"Do you think she will be offended?"

"Boldness never offends a woman. At Paris it might compromise you, but at Venice it aids your desire."

"Take my purse."

"Like our great physicians, or celebrated lawyers, I receive no pay until after the event, and then only if successful," said Grimani. "I have him," continued he to himself, withdrawing; "now I'll give the *sbirri* their cue. A formal arrest on the first day of my term of office will prevent my enemies here from talking of my last night's adventure. I am at your orders, excellenza," he added, aloud. "I shall be back immediately. Permit me to go and meet a young bridegroom whom I am to accompany this day to church—a mere sculptor—who is to marry the daughter of Ottale the Jew."

Grimani withdrew, and the marquis remained, delighted at meeting so honest a man.

"Books of travels," said the latter, as the inquisitor retired, "are all false; they pretend that these men are venal. There goes a cicerone who puts their falsehoods to the blush. How delightful is the life of Venice. That I am now in a fair way is very clear."

The marquis was still pondering with delight upon the happy adventure he now felt certain of achieving, when he heard one of the windows fronting upon the canal open; he looked up: a fair young girl stood leaning over her balcony, and gazing at the water.

"A lovely girl," thought the marquis; "what a sweet, innocent countenance for a Jewess. If all at the Ghetto resemble her!"

The young girl seemed to be listening anxiously to the clock of Saint Jeremiah, which was striking eight.

"This beauty is evidently waiting for some one," soliloquized the marquis. "How sadly she shook her head. There! she has gone back into her room. Bah! she is a reserved, timid creature; she will not suit me."

A slight cough from the balcony presently attracted his attention. The young girl, partly dressed in white satin, was again gazing along the canal.

"Odds my life! I think she calls me. No! I am wrong," continued the marquis, carefully advancing on tiptoe upon the bridge; "it was some one else. A pretty affair: a masked cavalier, with his gondola, stop at the water-gate of the house! What is he about? Faith! he takes from his pocket a key, yet seems to hesitate before entering. No! he is only pulling off his ring; a large ring, and of a most unusual shape. The door is closed, he has entered; the young girl also has just closed that window. I must remember this series of manœuvres, as characteristic of the manners of the people!"

The scene upon which the marquis thus commented had passed rapidly before his eyes, when, turning round, he found himself in presence of Grimani. Grimani was followed by a rather good-looking young man, who wore a bridal bouquet in his workman's vest. The latter cast a hurried look around, and, going towards the door,

"If, as your lordship thinks," said he, addressing Grimani, "my betrothed Ziana has not yet come down, I shall knock at her door; the clock has struck eight."

"Well," thought the marquis, "here is the bridegroom following close upon the other. In all decency, that masked cavalier, a lover, no doubt, must have time to escape. The husband has come earlier than expected. What is your name, my dear fellow?" asked the marquis of the young man, who was resolutely knocking at the Jew's door.

"Taddeo, sir, the sculptor. To-morrow I shall be quite at your service; but to-day I am to be affianced at church. Farewell! I must seek my bride, to take her thither."

"One single word, young man. I have an affair of honour on my hands. Are you willing to act as my second? Now, even now."

"You may inquire of any one about the arsenal whether Taddeo ever refused to give assistance."

"Give me proof!" ejaculated the marquis, pretending to be violently excited; "this is the spot where I expect to meet my adversary. I swear, I'll go no farther to fight than yonder alley. Come, follow me; it will take but a moment."

"You are mad!" answered the young workman, still knocking at the Jew's door.

"Ha! do you insult me? would you provoke me? still insist upon entering this house!" exclaimed the marquis, raising his voice, so as to be heard by the masked cavalier inside. "You leave me to fight a duel without a second because I am a foreigner. Well, let me tell you, unfortunate young man," continued he, at the highest pitch of his voice, "it was in behalf of your mistress that I engaged in this quarrel; you are indebted to me for silencing the impertinent man who pretended that she received a lover into her house."

"Thank you, my fine gentleman," answered Taddeo; "but we of the people attend to our own matters."

"Good!" said the marquis to himself, looking towards the canal; "I have given my masked friend time to escape; his bark is already at a distance; if he is a man, he will do the same for me some day."

Just at the close of this farce, which the marquis had extemporized for his own gratification, partly inspired by the fumes of the Cyprus wine he had drunk in the morning, Ziana appeared at the threshold of Ottale's house, led by her father, a venerable old man, famed in Venice for his honesty and his exemplary life, who was still at this time the keeper of the mint at the Zecca. "Taddeo," she said, as she came near the young man, "what means this noise?"

"It was not my fault," answered the bridegroom; "this stranger would not let me enter."

"That person?" replied Ziana, looking towards the marquis; "I cannot conceive why."

Grimani led the way, and she followed, towards the church. As she crossed the threshold with Taddeo, her betrothed, she dropped her veil, and blushed; for, amid the crowd whom curiosity gathered around the door, she had encountered the bold, steady glance of a person unknown to her: this stranger was Casanova, who kept his eyes riveted on her like a snake trying to fascinate his prey.

"She is truly the pearl of the Ghetto," said he to a man who seemed to be waiting like himself in the square. "Look at her, count; was I wrong?"

"And there goes the Queen of Venice," replied Cagliostro, pointing to the Countess d'Azola, who was hurrying out of the church, supported by Grimani's arm.

The countess was pale, agitated; she longed, doubtless, to be fairly out of the crowd; for, addressing the inquisitor, "Grimani," she said, "the ceremony is nearly over, and he has not yet come."

"Who do you mean, madam?"

"The doge; could you not guess, from my excitement?"

"How could I know?"

"Grimani, what can he be doing at this hour? where can he be? Speak! This is a month in which masks are allowed to be worn in Venice. Did he go out with a mask? Your police ought to know."

The features of the countess wore the expression of anxiety, fear, and jealousy; her bosom heaved; she seemed ready to weep or faint; she was overcome.

"Have I not informed you that this was council day at the palace, madam? His serene highness has a thousand things to attend to, what with the preparations necessary for the sailing of the fleet, and our difficulties with Barbary."

"I must see him, Grimani; I must speak with him. I shall go to the palace. Where are my servants—my gondola?"

While Grimani was acting in conformity with the imperious commands of the countess, and giving the necessary orders, the marquis stood rubbing his hands. "Well," said he to himself, "here is a good beginning; that honest man yonder has kept his word with me;" and, seizing the moment when the countess, in order to conceal her features from the gaze of the importunate throng, had lowered her veil, "Madam," said he, with much emphasis, "deign to raise your veil."

"Admirably well," whispered Grimani, encouraging him with a hypocritical smile; "capital! go on!"

"You mistake, sir," disdainfully objected the countess, drawing back.

"No, indeed, divine creature! I do not mistake. Once more, lift your veil!" And before the countess had time to enter her gondola he boldly took the liberty of raising it.

"What insolence! Signor Inquisitor, have this man arrested."

This injunction so well suited Grimani's wishes, that he hastened to obey it; addressing then one of his *sbirri*, "Seize him," said he; "he is a criminal; but before taking him to prison, let his correspondence be searched; obey the inquisitor."

"The inquisitor!" echoed the unfortunate marquis; "into whose hands have I fallen?"

While the *sbirri* were executing Grimani's orders, the crowd had left the church; and the bold attempt of the marquis was the theme of general remark.

"He is a foreigner!" shouted the seafaring men; "he has dared offer insult to the countess! Away with him to the canal!"

The excitement increased; the marquis had drawn his sword, but was soon disarmed by the *sbirri*.

"To the canal with him!" yelled the multitude. Meanwhile the poor marquis had been searched. The first object produced was a purse full of ducats; this purse in nowise resembled such as commonly carried; it was one of that kind used to gather alms: Grimani immediately identified it as the one his wife had lost.

"I was not deceived," thought Grimani; "I have at last caught the man; but his examination must not take place so publicly."

"My purse! that is my purse!" exclaimed the Marchioness Grimani, who at that moment came from the church. "Signor Inquisitor, I recommend you to punish severely so bold a thief."

"Who the deuse could have thrust that in my pocket?" muttered the marquis; "perhaps last night, at Count Lippone's."

"Poor marquis," whispered Casanova to Cagliostro; "he will suffer for us, that is clear. He is in for it."

A look of intelligence passed between the worthy confederates.

"Search the gentleman farther," said the inquisitor to his people. "Let us see—what is this? letters bound with rose-coloured riband. What says this?"

Grimani opened one of them, and read:

"'My dear little Marquis—Lend me a hundred crowns I need, and forget forever,

"'Yours, Olympia,

"'Of the Italian Theatre.'"

"What a strong smell of jonquils here!" remarked Moncenigo, as, with his friends, he drew near the scene of the arrest. "Why, it is that odd personage we met this morning—our last night's friend, the marquis: poor fellow! he has got into a serious scrape."

"Countess!" said Grimani, with a solemn tone, "decide yourself upon this man's fate. This letter," he continued, addressing the prisoner, "is addressed to the Marquis Eusebe de Saluces."

"That is myself," answered he, throwing himself into a theatrical attitude.

"The Marquis de Saluces," murmured the countess, with surprise, "at Venice! Heaven!" And approaching the marquis, who was at least as much astonished as herself, "To-night," said she, "at nine o'clock, come to the palace of the Countess d'Azola, who wishes to see you in private. Silence!"

The countess added a few words in a whisper to Grimani, who escorted her back to the church, where the young couple had remained. It was evident that, while the inquisitor obeyed the Countess d'Azola, he had made up his mind to recapture the marquis at the earliest opportunity. Without waiting to see the end of the ceremony, the marquis, who considered himself lucky in escaping so easily, fled as fast as his gondola could carry him.

CHAPTER VI.

THE INTERVIEW.

The palace which the fair Countess d'Azola inhabited formed the angle of the Procuratie; it was one of the largest, handsomest, and most splendid palaces of Venice.

From one of the numerous windows the countess could, at a glance, discover the piazzetta, the ducal church, and the magnificent prospect of the sea; she could enjoy the sight of the Fresco* on the Murano Canal, and the many entertainments in the Place of Saint Mark, which the first ladies in Venice witnessed from boxes erected along the sides of the square.

Whether the king of the butchers, arrayed in fantastic magnificence, went through the ceremony of decapitating the bull with an ancient *spadone;* whether some agile nicolotto was to perform the perilous feat of descending a rope stretched from the top of the Campanello to the ducal galley placed between its two columns; or whether fireworks were to be displayed at midday at the risk of burning the lion's wings, or even singing the beard of Saint Theodorus, the main balcony of the palace of the countess was sure to be as crowded as any of the platforms around the place. Thither would the

* A promenade in Venice.

fairest ladies of Venice repair, masked and attired in white, in their gondolas decked with wreaths of roses, to clap their little hands in token of applause at the wonted performances, so that, on such occasions, the palace of the mistress of the doge presented the appearance of a vast garland of flowers.

Beneath the vestibule, severe and somewhat heavy in style, might be seen antique statues of the palmiest days of sculpture, basso relievos of animals, paintings of Salviati and Baptista Franco, surrounded by grotesque ornaments and foliage. The most sumptuous carpets covered the marble steps of the staircase; its balusters glittering with gilded fret-work, and enormous chandeliers hung from the various compartments of the ceiling.

The interior of the palace displayed the utmost magnificence; there was a profusion of velvet hangings embroidered in silver, with many-coloured fringes, and tables, mirrors, and other furniture, in the most expensive style. The bedroom of the countess alone was deemed a prodigy; it was decked with the rarest stuffs of the East; a bead of pearls wound around its cornice. There hung from the ceiling a chandelier of painted crystal, which, at the celebrated works of Murano, had been made to represent Venice surrounded by a group of cupids, nymphs, and tritons, some with their conches, others with baskets and scarfs. Daily, in this fairy abode of voluptuousness, the choicest perfumes exhaled their fragrant odours; everything displayed that exquisite delicacy which the magic spell of wealth alone can produce when wielded by woman in the pride of happiness and prosperity. In the midst of this Eldorado, where every country of the globe was represented by its rarest productions, the countess led a life of tranquil felicity; and, as if to exclude all ideas save those of peace and happiness, the Ducal Palace spread forth its large wings to intercept the view of the Bridge of Sighs, and its graceful range of slight columns, to mask the Giant's Staircase, where Faliero fell.

The marquis took especial care to be punctual to his appointment. Saint Mark's clock was striking nine as he entered the palace. With the habits and train of thought of a true French nobleman of the day, whose only experience of women had been acquired in the easy routine of gallantry at Versailles, he naturally considered himself a happy man; for the handsomest woman in Venice had given him a *rendezvous;* consequently, he had spared neither time nor pains about his dress; not a jewel or ornament was omitted.

Being admitted through a private door, where a Greek girl, a slave of the countess, awaited him, he followed her through a suite of richly-illuminated apartments; at the end of a gallery his guide stopped, lifted a tapestry, and introduced the marquis into that rich apartment we have described as the bedchamber of the countess.

This room communicated, through wide folding doors, with a drawing-room of considerable size; the only sound audible proceeded from a richly ornamented clock on the mantle. Here the marquis threw off his cloak.

"Faith," said he, looking around, "a most magnificent palace. Two seats, I perceive, have been placed. . Well, I shall wait."

The marquis had not time even to sit, for the countess came in dressed magnificently, as for a ball.

In spite of the paleness of her countenance, her beauty was dazzling; a very slight quantity of powder served only to soften the jetty hue of her hair and eyebrows. Her skin resembled that peculiar whiteness of the cameo.

"Why are you thus in full dress?" asked the marquis, with astonishment. "For a *tête-à-tête*, was there any need—"

On any other occasion the countess would have punished such conceit with a cold and disdainful silence; but she seemed determined to indulge the marquis; for, glancing at him, she merely replied,

"I perceive, with pleasure, that you also have taken unusual pains with your dress; and, indeed, after this morning's adventure, it was urgent that you should no more rove about Venice in undress costume."

"Do not mention it; it was a lucky escape."

"Could you not have named yourself sooner? But, then, what madness it was to raise my veil!"

"I was in error. But there remains another veil I desire to raise; and I suppose that this night's interview—Doubtless you had some motive for making this appointment?"

"My motive," she said, regarding him with a look of peculiar anxiety, "was to secure the safe keeping of a secret."

"Of what secret," answered the marquis, in a trifling tone, "am I depositary? A state secret? I neither am nor wish to be a diplomatist."

"But you are generous, marquis; yes, fully as generous as brave. Have you not already given me proof? The Countess d'Azola must not be the subject of this interview. I wish to —I must speak of a certain Safia—"

"Safia, madam? Well, if you desire it, let us speak of her," interrupted the marquis, with an air of assurance that wounded the countess deeply.

"You still remember her?" she asked, in a voice of anguish.

"Most assuredly! I have excellent reasons. It is true that Safia, whom that pretty Greek name so well became, was not then mistress of a sumptuous palace opposite to the residence of the doge; and when she had the imprudence to write those fatal letters, those models of passion, which I had to dare the devil himself to recover. Certainly at that time I should have travelled from one end of the world to the other to please the young, the beautiful Safia. She subjected me, you know, to a somewhat more dangerous task. For her it was that I, the Marquis de Saluces, was compelled to draw my sword against that sorcerer, that Cagliostro!"

"You fought in my behalf, I know," answered the countess, with much emotion. "The Count Cagliostro was forced by you to give up those fatal letters."

"Yes, but I came near giving up the ghost! You do not know that Cagliostro was a practised swordsman; he wounded me, and I was for two months confined to my bed; and all in order to have the honour of returning love-letters written by you to other people!"

"I will not gainsay it."

"If, at least, I had met you in Germany, as your letter intimated would be my reward—but no! I have vainly travelled the world over in search of you. I have been in England, in Sweden; wherever, in short, I hoped to hear from, or of you. You never addressed me even a word of thanks! Is that your way of treating people who are wounded for your sake?"

The marquis drew himself back, and fixed upon the countess a look of profound self-satisfaction. He had preferred a charge against her, and awaited her answer. The countess understood that the moment had come requiring all her strength, and she spoke thus in a low tone, as if making a painful avowal:

"You are right, marquis; but I pray you listen to me: my error consists in thanking you at Venice only for a kindness rendered by you at Paris. Do but hear me: you know but a portion of my story; the remainder might justify me in your eyes."

"Madame, I am all attention," answered the marquis, listening as if much flattered by such a confidence.

The countess proceeded:

"In close connexion with the name of Cagliostro, just pronounced by you, stands that of Safia, my own. You can hardly help remembering the count's wonderful dwelling in France: the abode of magic, sudden darkness, soft lights, elixirs of life, apparitions, and wonders of all kinds; thither, at stated hours, repaired, ostensibly to cultivate the hidden sciences, a number of lords, foreigners, a world of idle people drawn by the attraction of artificial darkness, costly experiments of chemistry, and sleights of hand that passed for miracles. I soon made one of the captivating troop of those he called his *doves*. In a short time I became one of the queens of those mysterious suppers, where it was believed spirits attended. It is fifteen years since; I was but a mere child, but already handsome; at least I was told so. I had just arrived from Adrianopolis, where Count Tekeli had purchased me. When we landed at Venice, a woman came to demand me; she showed a letter to the count, who instantly delivered me up to her. I was ignorant of her name, but she seemed as generous as she was handsome. I heard it rumoured around me that she was a Genoese marchioness."

"'We leave to-morrow for France, Safia,' said she, embracing me; 'would you decline following me to that land of freedom?'

"'Do I not belong to you, madam?' I answered; 'and have I not just been told by Count Tekeli that he had yielded to you all his right in his slave?'

"'Trust yourself with me,' she replied; 'I am going to France with my husband. To-morrow, by daybreak, we shall reach Fusina.'

"I kissed her hands; I felt overpowered with joy and happiness at the sudden prospect of liberty set before me. The Countess Tekeli, however, did not share my exultation: she had always proved herself a kind and indulgent mistress, and shed tears when, on the following day, I was about to leave her.

"'Poor Safia!' she said, as soon as we were alone together, 'I do not know this woman; I only know that my husband has often been duped by worthless and intriguing persons. His passion for gambling often endangers his fortune. I am acquainted neither with the man nor the woman with whom you are to go; but Heaven protect you, Safia! and may you never repent having obtained your freedom.'

"I attributed these words to the regret she naturally felt at losing me: I was under the influence of feelings till then unknown to me. It seemed to me that I breathed then for the first time, that purer breezes fanned my cheeks; I longed for the hour of our departure. I remember well that I spent that whole night on deck: I deemed it an age. Hardly had our vessel reached Venice, ere already Heaven seemed to have taken pity on me. I was free! The Count Tekeli had assigned no reason for the sudden transfer, or, rather, emancipation, which I realized, as yet, but as a dream. From our anchorage I could see the maritime city, Venice, whose outline, uprising before me, wooed by the sea-breeze, reminded me of the wide expanse of ocean, with whose waves my tears had so often mingled. Venice! at the sound my heart thrilled as if it had been my home; for of my own native city I could think only as of a harsh parent who had sold me to slavery! I wished to tread her pavements, visit her quays, manufactories, and contemplate the august and venerable old man, the then doge! But such happiness was denied me. I saw the marble city only in the dim shadows of night. I was compelled to wait on board the return of the marchioness. He alone who has been chained, bartered, and sold at noonday, as I had been in a bazar at Adrianopolis, could realize the sense of joy that swelled my bosom at the sight of yonder lion, spreading forth his wings as a symbol of redemption and freedom. I knelt on the frigate's deck that night, and poured forth thanksgivings to Heaven; I communed with God, as a happy daughter with a cherished father; I thanked and worshipped him for the secret dispensation of his bountiful Providence. I had just sat down—I remember it well—and was listening to the stories which our pilots were relating among themselves concerning that familiar spirit of the lagunes, the Oreo, when I saw a six-oared barge stemming the moon-lit waves. At the prow stood a man, wrapped in a large cloak embroidered with gold: he, like myself, was gazing at the splendid scene around; but I remember, also, that he laughed several times, and there was something in the sound so harsh and fiend-like, that I thought for a moment I had heard the Oreo's laugh. When he boarded our vessel, I saw him turn around and offer his arm to a woman whom I recognised as the marchioness. The man went forward, and spoke a few words to the servants of Count Tekeli, who had himself given them his orders previous to landing. The individual with the cloak came towards me, and spoke a few words in Italian, using the Sicilian dialect—that of Palermo. A few moments sufficed me to gather what few effects the generosity of the countess had bestowed upon me; and free, at last, I bade farewell to the vessel I had entered as a slave. When we arrived at Fusina, I was informed that the name of the marchioness was Serafina—"

"Serafina Feliciani!" interrupted the marquis, whose countenance reflected the livid pallor which the mention of that name had called on the lips of the countess.

"Serafina Feliciani," she resumed, still shuddering, "was the name of that woman whom Cagliostro had taken from some obscure *ridotto* in Venice; a fit person to seduce and develop vice while speaking of virtue. Paris was the scene on which they had determined to act. They were both well qualified to meet success there, and such was my destiny that I was fated to accompany them thither with a heart overflowing with happiness and hope.

"During the whole journey, Serafina Feliciani showed herself so well disposed towards me that I could scarcely suspect that her friendship was the result of a deliberate plan of villany; she and her husband loaded me with caresses and attentions. Remember, I was a young girl just escaped from a long and tedious bondage, accustomed to be treated as an object of traffic by any one who might choose to address me; in my younger days, bending beneath the lash of a pirate; afterward having to bear the haughty and arrogant temper of that dreaded Count Tekeli, whom the grand signor had just invested with the principalities of Vidino, Carausibes, and Lugos, to indemnify him for the loss of his Hungarian estates. The Countess Tekeli, it is true, had ordered me to be treated with more delicacy than my companions in misfortune; but she herself, who has since given such proofs of courage by her defence of Mongatz, trembled before the count, and might be considered as his slave. Therefore she who called herself the Marchioness Feliciani appeared to me an angel of clemency and kindness; she described Paris as the city of wonders; once in France, I was to see the land of romance and pleasure; there beauty alone had sway; and she often repeated to me that I was beautiful. During the whole journey I remained under the influence of delirious dreams and supernatural fancies; sometimes I fell asleep upon her shoulder dreaming of courts, noblemen, and princes. At such times a glow of conscious pride would alight on my brow, and I awoke with a fevered pulse from visions of palaces whose splendor had no parallel even in the Arabian tales.

"At other times my mind would wander with ingenuous delight in the contemplation of another and different prospect of happiness; then, under the eyes of the count, I was admitted to mysteries that I was not allowed, as yet, to understand; I stood in a temple resplendent with lights, where incense and varied perfumes burned in golden censers; where, upon a throne of rubies and sapphires, sat he whose words had conjured up these wonders to my imagination. The Count Cagliostro had an expressive physiognomy; there was something electrifying in his voice, his glance, his breath. He spoke of dwellings I had never beheld; of palaces, the residence of heavenly spirits; their attendants, young girls, who possessed that purity, that virginity of heart which were mine, since I had never known love, and no passions had ever enchained my heart, so early and rudely schooled by adversity, save an eager curiosity that made me listen with avidity to his words. There was, then, a land of liberal minds and generous hearts! I felt raised in my own estimation by learning that there was. In these interviews I opened my soul before him; I concealed none of my sensations; he was my teacher, and yet I, his pupil, would often shudder and tremble in his presence. Was I to expect happiness or misery from him? what price was he to exact in return for his kindness? had I a right to call in question his powers as a guardian over me? When we reached Paris my bosom could scarcely contain the crowd of varied feelings with which it throbbed tumultuously.

"On entering the hotel of the count, I found myself treated as the Marchioness Feliciani's own daughter. It was a solitary mansion, hid in the silent solitude of a distant suburb; at first it looked to me as gloomy as a dungeon. I thought of my little room on board the ship: there, at least, I could look through the small cabin windows, and smile as the waves dashed against the sides of the vessel, scattering around the sparkling spray. Such thoughts made me so sad that I shed tears, which the marchioness perceiving, would say,

"'Cheer up, my child: but a few days, and this gloomy habitation will be enlivened by the richest entertainments; a thousand lights will give brightness to the gilded ceilings. Weep no more, but preserve your beauty; to-morrow we are to receive a few friends of the count noblemen, courtiers. You may, at first, wonde at their manners; but I will watch over you Safia, as a mother. To-morrow, then, you mus dress in that Ionian costume given to you by the Countess Tekeli!'

"At the first words of the marchioness I felt an unaccountable shudder of vague fear: there was something unusually authoritative in he tone; but the thought of wearing a dress I ha received from my dear benefactress thrilled me with childish joy.

"Such, then, was my costume when, upon the following day, I made my appearance in the drawing-room of the marchioness, led by Count Cagliostro himself, who constantly riveted upon me his embarrassing glance. I was surrounded, flattered by every one; their language was unknown to me, a poor stranger: could not, therefore, understand their arden proffers of worship; but I guessed that they thought me handsome. I listened—and I wa lost!

"In short, marquis, ignorant as I was o everything, and even of the dangers, I followe but too well the lessons of Serafina Felician and became unwittingly her accomplice—"

"Her accomplice?"

"Yes, indeed. Cagliostro was scarcely eve a week without dictating to us himself som of those letters which he compelled us to sigr He would fold them and leave the addres blank, reserving to himself to direct them a terward, either to some marquis, some rich ir tendant, or some foreign prince, whom he thu allured in the evening to his splendid cavern Those letters enabled him to set a price upo our dishonour. He would either trust to th somniferous properties of his wines to surrer der his helpless and slumbering victims, or con fine us to a narrow cell, where he would con and bid us choose between the most seve poverty or a fortune too easy to acquire. However, my eyes were soon opened. In the little room, or, rather, prison I occupied, my eyes would sometimes meet a sword-knot, a ring, a cloak, or some other article forgotten, that told me my shame. One night the whole truth flashed upon me! I fell upon my knees and implored Heaven to save me. The same evening, at Cagliostro's table, when I sat down, as usual, to be gazed at by all the guests, a Venitian nobleman seated himself opposite to me. His first glance threw me into strange confusion. I trembled without knowing the cause. When he approached me, I could scarcely stand up: his words were the reverse of the language of those other lords, whose shameless remarks had so often caused me to blush; they were respectful, and uttered in those sweet sounds whose music seems the organ of the melodious inspiration of Italian climes. His kindness, his generosity, restored to me my self-respect. In short, he taught me to hate myself—to love and to fly with him, far from the odious domination of my tyrant, Cagliostro. He was about departing for Italy; thither I accompanied him. Our journey was a period of enchanting happiness; it ended at Rome where we resided a year."

"But Cagliostro?"

"He, irritated at the loss of one by whose dishonour he had hoped to secure his fortune, followed us to Rome to claim me. He begged—threatened—but without success. One day, as I was coming out of the Church of Santa Maria Maggiore, leaning on the arm of my deliverer, Cagliostro took advantage of a sudden rush of the crowd to approach him, and, with a sarcastic glance, whispered a word in his ear. What that word was, I did not know; but, to my astonishment, my liberator turned deadly pale; nor did he draw his sword to chastise such insolence. Since that day, we have never seen Cagliostro."

"What followed?"

"We soon returned to Venice. He to whom I had devoted my whole being, had been promoted to an unexpected dignity. He was elected doge!"

"The doge!" murmured the marquis, with profound astonishment.

"In order to blot out all reminiscences of my past life, together with that name of Safia, under which no one save yourself knows me at Venice, the doge Alessandro had caused me to be named Countess d'Azola by the pope. I found here all the enjoyments of wealth, a palace, a crowd of servants, a whole nation at my feet. But yet, a sadness came over me. Alessandro's temper was changed. At times I surprised him deeply musing; at other times he was irritable. Cagliostro's name was often on his lips. He knew that, while in Paris, I had written those fatal letters which the count had gathered and kept so carefully. Vainly did I urge that the change in my name had made them harmless. 'Your handwriting!' would he object, with terrible impressiveness. He shuddered at the name of Safia as at that of Cagliostro. His reproaches overpowered me. Had I lost his love? I often asked myself. A prey to doubt and anguish, I wished for wings to fly to Paris and take possession of those letters. Could I but destroy those traces of my past life, my future prospects were happy indeed. An honourable marriage would have secured Alessandro's love. But I could not dream of going without him—of leaving him here to his suspicions! Then it was that I remembered you—shall I acknowledge it, marquis, before I met Alessandro, I had often thought of you as of a deliverer—one who could understand what pride I still preserved in my debased condition. I knew that you had access to Cagliostro's house. I did not hesitate to appeal to your courage; marquis, you know the rest!"

"Yes, countess," answered he, slowly, and casting upon Safia a look of bitter irony, "I know the rest, and I thank you for the candour of your confession. You love a prince. I do not object to that, although I myself still hold to mere nobility. He has delivered you from Cagliostro's claws, fair dove; he has made you queen—the fairy queen of Venice; that was nobly and generously done on his part! But, then, inasmuch as the trade of *bravo* exists here, it is not right that a cavalier of my figure should exercise it for nothing."

"What mean you?" asked the countess, with visible alarm.

"That I may have in my possession," answered the marquis, with assumed indifference, "the second part of a book of love, the first of which alone you have received. These letters," he added, producing his pocket-book.

"What of them?"

"Are such as I had reserved to secure my share of the bargain, and to protect myself in case you failed to meet your engagements. Business is business, you know."

"Do you mean to abuse that advantage?"

"Confess that many others would, in my place."

"But you will not," answered the countess, rising.

"You owe me for two items: a wound and my discretion. Come, beautiful Safia, a little gratitude!"

"Those letters, marquis; those letters!"

"To-morrow, madam, they will be returned to you, but on one condition only: that you accompany me, in a masked party, to Fusina."

"So long a journey!" exclaimed the countess, slyly approaching the marquis; "how can you think of it? Dear marquis, your pocket-book is out of fashion; this one will suit you better."

With a rapid gesture the countess exchanged her tablets against those of the marquis, and snatching the package of letters, she held them with one hand over the flame of a chandelier, while with the other she rang the bell.

CHAPTER VII.

A DOGE.

A YOUNG girl answered the summons. "Do you want me, signora?" she asked, with a charming look of ingenuousness. "I was tired of waiting, and came here with my father. Taddeo is to meet us here."

She was dressed in the full costume of a novizza; a bouquet of silver flowers was coquettishly placed in a girdle of the same material. The ladies of the Celestia employ their leisure hours in working these bouquets with wonderful freshness and delicacy for nuptial occasions; long pearl ear-rings, crescent-shaped, hung down to her shoulders, and she wore around her arm a coral bracelet clasped by a green stone, on which was engraven, in triangular letters, a sentence from the Koran.

"Deuse take the girl!" grumbled the marquis, still astounded by the abrupt victory of the countess. "But," added he to himself, "this is the young bride I saw this morning at the Ghetto."

"Look, sir, what a beautiful bracelet the countess has just presented to me; I intended to preserve it for my bridal day, but I could scarcely have patience enough to wait so long. On coming to the palace, I looked at it more than twenty times."

While thus speaking, Ziana showed to the marquis the bracelet she had received from the countess, laughing at the same time, and capering like a young fawn.

"Where is Taddeo?" asked the countess.

"Do not mention him; he has been all day strangely out of temper; he, who is usually so good and kind to me, takes every occasion to quarrel with me; and a little while ago, even—"

"Well, what occurred then?" asked the marquis, probably recollecting the singular sight he had witnessed in the morning.

"Why, he left me a little while ago, saying that there were certain events passing at Venice which required his presence; that he was one of the people, and that their interests were in danger; and thereupon he left me to join a set of Nicolotti and Castellani hurrying towards the arsenal. However, I think it was only a pretext for witnessing their game of the *morerea*."

"What means this noise?" interrupted the marquis, looking out from the balcony. "Behold! a man with a turban upon his head, escorted by Algerines, and apparently striving to escape; the multitude seem to rise against him; they gain upon him; there is no discerning his features; he comes this way; knocks at the palace-gate."

The countess and Ziana had watched the scene thus described by the marquis. Indeed, the riot without increased each moment in intensity; one of the illuminated scaffoldings near the palace-gate had just been torn down.

At this moment, also, several patricians, in the utmost disorder, entered the apartments prepared for the fête of the countess.

"What signifies this?" asked she of Grimani, who was one of the first who entered. "Does any danger threaten his serene highness?"

"None whatever for the present, countess; for I have taken upon myself to order the doors of your palace to be bolted; the doge has this moment come in; he follows me; I hear his footsteps."

"Lead me instantly to him, Grimani!" cried the countess. "I have no fear; my place is at the side of the doge; and if any one should dare—"

With a rapid gesture she seized, from beneath a rich Venitian mirror, a jasper-handled poniard, and concealed it in her bosom.

"I repeat to you, madam," answered Grimani, "his serene highness is in no danger. I merely give you notice that, for a few hours, this palace, prepared for a fête, must be used as a hall of council. The district of the arsenal is in motion; the man pursued by the multitude, who took refuge here, is an emissary from the Barbary powers; he who just saved him from impending death was the doge—"

The noise of many voices now overpowered Grimani's: it proceeded from a crowd of signors and noblemen, who had come to the palace upon the first intelligence of the tumult. Some came in carriages, others in gondolas, others on foot; some with, and some without masks.

The countess sprang forward towards the vast and extensive gallery, whose doors she had ordered to be thrown open; it was already crowded. In the midst of that eager throng of noblemen an old man, bent by age, approached Ziana; this was the Jew Ottale, her father, who had long exercised the office of keeper of the mint of the republic. He embraced his daughter, and pointed to her Taddeo, who was endeavouring to force a passage through the crowd gathered in the vestibule.

At this moment one of the doors leading to the gallery opened, and gave entrance to several Venitian noblemen, in the midst of whom was the doge Alessandro, followed by a personage who wore the costume of Tunis. A Persian poniard glittered in his girdle; his turban lacked the usual regularity of its folds; his silver-wrought slippers were soiled; he was deadly pale, and trembled with fear as the increasing yells from the mob outside reached his ears; he looked more like a detected spy than the delegate of the deys who ruled the three regencies.

The tumult was still raging without; but, like the storm, it had intervals of violence and calm.

"Ambassador, you are under my protection," said the doge, "but you are also in presence of the nobility of Venice. They listen—speak!"

These words were pronounced with that firmness which indicated a man who needed not the adventitious aid of the ducal dignity to exact respect and obedience. The person thus addressed seized the prince's robe with both hands, and begged him to excuse him.

"You have saved my life," said he, "and now might as well bid me die as to give me such an order. If I concealed myself at Venice until discovered by some of the multitude; if I have landed here at night, and clandestinely, it was because I was the bearer of such proposals to your highness and the senate, from the three regencies, that my mission must needs be enveloped in mystery. I am not aware who has betrayed my incognito, since the costume I wear is common to many inhabitants of Venice; but, surely, this is not a fit place or time—"

"This is a time of popular commotion, sir; speak! speak!" resumed the doge; "I am waiting, and yonder multitude also."

The assembly was now as silent as it had been tumultuous shortly before. The delegate from Tunis seemed to collect himself, and take courage; then, presenting a letter to the doge.

"Read, your highness! I fear that my voice—"

The doge seized the paper; it bore the triple seal of Tripoli, Tunis, and Algiers; it was a letter signed by the deys of the three regencies, and contained for the senate proposals of conciliation and treaty. They asked a suspension of all hostilities against the powers of Barbary; but in such terms as more implied superiority than submission on their part. They required that the vessels the doge was preparing to chastise these piratical sovereignties should be disarmed; and, without denying that they had captured by surprise, and against every law, several islands and castles belonging to the republic, they assumed that, in the present penury of the Venitian finances, peace ought to be deemed preferable, by the latter power, to an expensive war. When the doge had imparted aloud, to the assembled nobility, the contents of this missive,

"You were right, sir," he resumed, with a disdainful look at the delegate, "to wear arms while bearing such despatches. You might well need the poniard you carry, to defend yourself against the populace of Venice, if you should read such propositions to them. The reception they have already greeted you with may have given you to understand how they relish the thought of coming to terms with rebels and pirates. You need take no farther trouble in the matter. You propose peace; we answer, war!"

"War! war!" exclaimed some of the patricians.

"Is it to be thought of?" murmured others; "the treasury is empty! the Jews themselves have no money left!"

"War! war!" yelled the multitude outside, who had invaded the piazzetta.

"You hear!" said the doge, fixing his penetrating glance upon the undecided assembly. "The sight of our ancient standard, so long idle, now waving over our fleet, has recalled to the memory of the children of Venice her former power—her former victories. Money, you say, is wanting; but are you not yourselves indebted to the state? Thank Heaven, the Adriatic has pearls enough left on her robe to scatter over every ocean in the universe! Venice shall buckle on her armour? Venice shall be avenged! I swear!"

And, leaning over the balcony, the doge, followed by all the procuratori, the sages of the council, and the noblemen of the republic, was the first to utter, within the hearing of the people of Venice, that war-cry they seemed so eagerly to require. In three days the fleet was to sail for the coast of Africa.

Presently, by order from one of the Council of Ten, the crowd dispersed; a few distant cries alone were heard in the direction of the arsenal.

Separated from the doge by a crowd of patricians, Ottale had beheld the scene with visible anxiety. Vainly he sought to speak with the doge. Taddeo, with no less impatience, riveted his glance upon Alessandro.

He alone who has beheld at Rome the magnificent portrait of Cæsar Borgia can appreciate the resemblance between his features and those of Alessandro, the Doge of Venice. Every lineament of his beautiful countenance bespoke a brave and noble heart. He was a rare instance of devoted patriotism, ardent love for the glory of his country, and deep and keen resentment of her injuries. He was not the patrician who would stop in the street to gaze at shows or listen to an itinerant musician; pure blood flowed in his veins; he had still faith in his country; he entertained for Venice the attachment of a pilot for his vessel. With lamentable infatuation, he had placed his love upon that rotten, worn-out, decrepit city! Undermined by the vice and debauchery of her patricians, ruined by their indolence and weakness, the city of the doges was already stricken to the heart. The Angel of Destruction had wrenched from Saint Theodore his lance, to strike a death-blow at the lion sleeping at his feet. Within those walls that once re-echoed the victorious cannon of Macalo and Lepanto lived a people enslaved by recklessness and disgrace, and a corrupt, irreligious nobility. All was matter of bargain and sale, from the senatorial offices to the innocence of the virgin. Corruption had hurled glory from her throne; sons mocked the white hair of their fathers; nobles speculated upon their rank by marrying the daughters of Jews. Day and night, bending over the gaming tables at the Casino, young patricians dissipated the gold yet left them, exhibiting symptoms of premature old age, and turning with disgust from the frescoes of the Ducal Palace representing the victories of their ancestors. But one wave was wanting to ingulf fair Venice; the vessel of state had lost her rudder, and her hull was shattered.

Meanwhile, the delegate of Tunis had been conducted to the college by an imposing escort; the doge had secured his retreat, and the fête of the countess, somewhat disturbed, as it well might be by such an event, had insensibly and partially resumed its splendour. Lively conversations had divided the assembled parties into several distinct groups. In one, composed of young lords in full dress, and wearing swords, the marquis soon recognised Moncenigo, a libertine, gambler, and profligate, who bore one of the most illustrious names of the Venitian republic; farther off, Trevisani's brow exhibited marks of idleness, effrontery, and disorder. Here was a Dandolo speaking of war, and ranting like a Cæsar, fear and egotism betrayed upon his countenance.

"Is the doge mad," said one, "to war against the three regencies? War, indeed, when we, the first in the republic, have not enough left to settle our differences at play at the Ridotto, and our creditors refuse to trust us longer."

"Has the Republic of Venice inherited the estate and fortune of the Grand Mogul?" added another.

"Possibly his serene highness possesses the secret of making gold!"

"Or else his private fortune may suffice for the expense of the expedition!"

"After all, faith," said Moncenigo, admiring himself in one of the large mirrors, "we are not to start with the expedition: that may do for the seafaring men and the rabble of Venice. However, it would not be amiss to show ourselves arrayed in purple robes, and in gondolas without gilded hoops, for that day. Upon my honour, I mean to order a dress expressly for the occasion; but such a dress!"

"And we," answered Trevisani and Ranuzzi, "intend to turn out our entire households in new suits. I mean that my livery shall do me credit, and on that day my cook shall wear a turban."

In the midst of these degenerate sons of Venice, Alessandro's countenance glowed with a proud sense of superiority. He knew well that he could not rely upon them. They inwardly blamed him for that exercise of power which had thus abruptly awakened them from their lethargy and indolence; they avoided his glance. Was the play at the Ridotto, which was to have taken place a few days hence, to be adjourned? Would Venice have no more fêtes to satisfy her patricians' love of pleasure? Such were the questions that preoccupied the minds of the Sybarite noblemen, who would have felt wounded by the fold of a rose-leaf upon their couch. Venice, for them, consisted of the Place of Saint Mark and the Ridotto, open at night for such senators as could yet borrow.

The astonishment of some men of a serious turn, who claimed to have a thorough knowledge of the resources of Venice, at least equalled the wonder of these thoughtless young men.

The ambassadors of the several powers, who had heard the speech of the doge, remained thunderstruck. They were aware of the naval preparations; they had seen the arsenal crowded with workmen, provisions, and implements of war; but they all presumed that this display would end in vain show; they knew that gold was wanting, and that the Lion of Saint Mark was sculptured in brass.

Yet the doge had pledged his royal word; he appeared calm, confident.

A young man approached Alessandro, and begged the favour of a few moments' interview.

He was a simple child of Venice, one of the people, a mechanic—Taddeo, the sculptor at the arsenal—Taddeo, the betrothed of Ziana.

CHAPTER VIII.

THE BRACELET

Taddeo was pale, agitated: the throng had just separated him from Ziana and her father. He knelt before the doge.

"What do you wish from me, Taddeo?" said Alessandro, raising him. "Do you seek any favour from my hands? Speak, it is granted."

"Yes, prince," answered the young man, in a low tone; "I ask to sail with the fleet."

"Have you well considered your request, Taddeo? At such a time? betrothed but this morning?"

"My betrothed can wait—"

The sculptor spoke these words with trembling lips; he seemed a prey to the most violent emotions; some internal struggle was wringing his very soul.

"You are mad," continued Alessandro. "Are you not my protégé? the artist whose works I most admire? But yesterday I stopped to gaze at your sculpture on the Bucentaur.* Trust me, war is not a profession to suit you."

"Again, I beseech your highness, do not oppose the determination of one who, however obscure he may be, still reveres and loves you! The atmosphere of this city oppresses me; its pavements scorch my feet! Close not against me alone the path you have just opened."

"Leave your betrothed, your wife?"

"Your highness," resumed Taddeo, "may Heaven, whose blessing this morning consecrated our union, bear witness to the purity of my love. Yes, I cherish Ziana, and for that very reason I wish to become worthy of her. She may perhaps bestow more tenderness, more happiness on the soldier who has fought for his prince than the mere workman of the arsenal, whose chisel has not the attraction of a sword. Besides, the Bohemian gipsy whom I have just consulted at the Largo del Castello has told me that my vocation was for higher attainments than ornamenting galleys: a foe to combat, an African standard to bear back with me in triumph! Oh! let me, let me go from Venice, since I ever had more faith in glory than in love!"

The inexpressible sadness of Taddeo, the feverish emotion with which he spoke, had for a moment clouded the brow of the doge. The sight of the Jew and his daughter soon cleared it, however; and, pointing to Ziana, whom the countess at this moment was embracing, with a smile,

"Look, Taddeo," said he, "how beautiful she is!"

"Beautiful, indeed," answered the young man, with a sigh; "beautiful as the Esther of Paul Veronese."

"Do not tremble thus, Ziana," said the doge, approaching her. "The events that have just taken place have not made me lose sight of the ancient customs of our republic. It is usual, you know, for the doge to make a present to the novizza. You have been surnamed the Rose of the Ghetto. May this remind you of your title."

And the doge, with winning affability, presented the beautiful girl with a diamond rose. Ziana blushed, and could not help thinking how superior the doge's present was to the bracelet she had received from the countess.

Alessandro stood contemplating her for a few seconds in silence, as if the sight of this young girl had put every other feeling of his bosom at rest. He seemed to take singular pleasure in gazing at this angel, whose beauty, radiant with innocence, contrasted so strongly with the hideous vice around him.

Thus the star that glitters alone, pearl-like amid the dreary clouds, attracts the sailor's eye. The hunter will stop to gaze at the snow-like wings of the dove. Ziana was beautiful, and

* *Note of the translators.*—The Bucentaur was a large vessel richly carved and gilt, and used on occasions of ceremony. The etymology of the word is not known; some derive it from the augmentative particle *Bu* and *Centaur*, the latter word being the name of a celebrated vessel in ancient times. Others recognise it as the name of the vessel of Æneas, which was called *Bis Taurus;* while many insist that it is only a corruption of *ducentorum*, that is to say, a vessel with 200 oarsmen.—*Daru, Histoire de Venice.*

D

the personal advantages of the doge had raised him many envious and bitter rivals among the nobility of Venice.

"Do you not think, Grimani, that our doge looks somewhat amorously at his handsome protégé yonder?" said Moncenigo, touching the arm of the inquisitor.

"Yes; and that French marquis we came so near drowning this morning makes good use of his time with the countess."

"True, Grimani; but who is yonder importunate valet who seems to be seeking to draw your attention."

"That man," resumed the inquisitor, looking in the direction indicated by Moncenigo, "is—Pray, Moncenigo, leave me for a moment. I will explain all presently."

The valet, who was carrying a tray of sorbets and other refreshments, whispered to Grimani. Within a few steps from the latter, the doge himself placed his hand upon the shoulder of a young nobleman, and said,

"One word of advice, Signor Ranuzzi. You have enemies. It would be prudent in you to escape through the crowd—believe me."

"Many thanks, your highness; but I have promised to dance a *Françoise* with the Signora Sabina, and with your permission—"

While Ranuzzi offered his hand to the lady, Grimani stood perusing a letter the valet had slipped into his hand.

"Well, you are one of ours," said he to the man. "Beppo, let one of the faithful be in attendance—enough! This is a serious affair: an arrest in the midst of a ball!"

"It is absolutely necessary, signor," answered Beppo, mysteriously. "He intends to leave Venice at daybreak."

Grimani and the man carrying the salver exchanged a few words. Dancing had begun in the gallery of the countess; iced wines were in request. The Marquis de Saluces noticed with surprise Grimani writing upon his knee, then folding a paper, which he handed to the valet.

"Some billet-doux, I suppose?" lisped the marquis, with irony, as he bowed to the inquisitor. "We became acquainted, my dear sir, in a rather eccentric manner this morning."

Grimani coldly returned the salute of the marquis.

"I understand you," added the marquis. "You suspect me on account of that purse found in one of my pockets; but some one must have exchanged it last night for mine at Count Lippone's.'

"Silence, marquis," said a mask, wearing a three-cornered hat and a pink domino of rather handsome appearance. "Do not mention the names of any whom you met at Count Lippone's, else."

The individual with the pink domino was lost in the crowd after showing the marquis the blade of a stiletto. "

"You are acquainted with Count Lippone?" resumed the inquisitor.

"Yes; or, rather, no," stammered the marquis; "he is—that is, they pretend that he is—I have heard—"

"Who is he? what do they pretend? what have you heard? I insist upon knowing. Where did you become acquainted with that count?"

"I will tell you all: since my misfortunes at play in Paris, and while I was risking some rather heavy sums at the bank of a certain Cagliostro—"

"Cagliostro? we have received some notes relative to that individual."

"Very likely; in that case, you would oblige me much by communicating them to me. I have lost in the house of that Cagliostro more than 37,000 francs in one night. They played infernally high there. I was excusable, therefore, for trying to redeem my losses at Count Lippone's."

"I advise you to calculate no longer upon that resource, for this night we shall close his gambling-house."

"I am glad to know that," murmured a mask, who stood fanning himself behind them.

This individual soon afterward went to a table covered with viands and fruit, surrounded by several guests of the countess; and, leaning upon his elbow with affected indifference, listened to their conversation.

"You may believe me or not, as you like, gentlemen," said a cavalier; "but that poor Casanova will never get possession of his aunt's estate."

"Why?" asked another.

"Because he is in Holland this very hour.

"You know him?" asked the mask.

"I flatter myself I do."

"Are you not the Chevalier de Talvis?"

"I am."

"He who was in Hungary last year, and swindled the prime bishop of Presburgh?"

"Sir!"

"I have a piece of advice to give you: it is not at all unlikely that Casanova may return from Holland purposely to break your neck; so do not meddle quite so much with his affairs! You were wounded once by Casanova: beware of the next thrust."

And as a group of promenaders passed by, the mask glided among them, and soon joined the pink domino, who stood silently, and in pensive mood, waiting for him under one of the paintings in the gallery.

"Dear count," said he, "you are still the same. While I flutter like a butterfly among the guests, you make your observations. I rush headlong into all the pleasures of Venitian life, while you stand meditating upon the age and decline of a republic, which not all your elixers and secret preparations combined can restore to youth. Your nodding Chinese figures—your speaking automata—have more skill than those senators, whose titles of nobility are passports for stupidity. You seem absent; you do not answer."

Indeed, Cagliostro was at the moment scrutinizing the Countess d'Azola.

As the alligator watches every motion of the victim for whose blood he thirsts, the count had that night followed with his eyes every movement, every gesture of the beautiful Safia. Not that he recognised the former slave of his infernal harem; not that the Marquis de Saluces had been indiscreet, nor that, after fifteen years of fruitless search, Cagliostro could have suspected that at a ball in Venice, in his sight, within his reach, stood the precious jewel—the loadstar of his vile ambition!

He beheld in the Countess d'Azola merely a

beautiful Venitian lady; a woman in all the pride of splendour and gracefulness; the delicate whiteness of her skin, the lustre of her eyes, the choice perfumes her dress exhaled—all had acted upon his mind, and caused his lascivious imagination to revel in exciting reminiscences of that voluptuous flock of lovely young damsels—his *doves*, as he called them, among whom Safia was the youngest and the fairest.

What might have become of his fugitive fair one? Where was his Safia now?

While Casanova tried, by the variety of intrigues which his mask facilitated, to console himself for the temporary absence of Ziana—who had repaired to an adjoining room with her father—Cagliostro still gazed upon the countess. Suddenly a rumour spread among the dancers that an arrest had just taken place by order of the Council of Ten.

"Poor Ranuzzi," said Moncenigo to a senator; "he has disappeared. What did I tell you? At the very moment he was leading his partner to the floor—"

"How so?"

"A person in a domino beckoned him to the door. He was hurried into a gondola, which steered towards the prisons: that is all."

"May I ask," inquired the French marquis, advancing on tiptoe, "why this gentleman has been thus unceremoniously disposed of?"

"Signor Marquis," answered Moncenigo, "look around; you see nothing but joy, luxury, noise: this is one view of Venitian life. Reverse the medal, and you find the best-regulated police in the universe. Your Monsieur de Sartines could do no better."

"Truly, my worthy uncle might well envy the celerity and neatness of that proceeding," thought the marquis. "Now, if he knew what I do concerning one of the principal ladies in Venice, the countess—but my happiness depends on my discretion; and, besides, Safia, from what I have just witnessed, might find a way of silencing me forever. On due consideration, I will say nothing; for Safia is almost a doge's wife."

"Signor Marquis," said Moncenigo, pressing the hand of Saluces most cordially, "we are at war with Barbary, but not with France; the Ridotto is to open in three days; you will see whether we are wealthy; you will play, I hope; and if fortune favour you as she did at Count Lippone's—"

"Against whom it is proposed to proceed, as I was informed just now by the inquisitor Grimani."

"I shall not be sorry for that," resumed Moncenigo; "for, after all, no one knows where that *soi disant* count comes from. Venice is deluged with marquises and counts of the Holy Empire! At all events, there is no lack of prisons here, equally for the count as for that poor Ranuzzi who has just been taken away In that line we are truly prodigal."

"Indeed!"

"Yes. First, we have the Leads," said Moncenigo, counting on his fingers; "you know, Trevisani, those Leads wherein Casanova was locked up, and from which he found means of escaping. Under the Leads the prisoner is half suffocated alive; under the Wells he is frozen to death; true antipodes of punishment."

"What a waste of blessings! In France, we have only the Bastille!"

"The Orfano Canal is quite different, and deserves attention," resumed Moncenigo, sipping a sorbet: "a gentleman, like you or myself, for instance—a gentleman of good family—is sent to take an airing in a gondola for his health. The gondola is a charming affair; but it opens beneath, and—"

"You take a bath! I understand. Very ingenious, 'pon my word!"

"Then there is a variety of other ways: poisoned oranges, sweetmeats, or sorbets. Frequently a gentleman disappears from Venice: he is seized in his bed, at table, in the senate, or at a ball; a quarter of an hour afterward his family goes into mourning. No more."

"Well, then," thought the marquis, "I will beware of mentioning what I know to any one; women, after all, may find means of revenge as well as doges."

The countess, who had been absent a moment to give orders, re-entered the ball-room, more handsome and dazzling than ever; she leaned on the arm of Ziana, who, followed by Taddeo and her father, proceeded to the banqueting-hall. The doors had just been thrown open by order of the doge.

In the centre of a table glittering with plate and crystal was a vase, magnificently chased by the chisel of Taddeo. The doge was pointing it out to the admiration of the senators around him, when the mask with the pink domino approached Ziana, and asked, in Hebrew, permission to examine the bracelet she wore. After a brief inspection, the stranger seemed startled, and begged the young girl to tell him by whom it had been given to her.

"By the countess, sir, my protectress," answered Ziana, joining her father, with a vague presentiment of fear; for the mask was wholly a stranger to her.

This scene had passed unnoticed, and the stranger, approaching the countess at a moment when the banqueting-hall was thronged, said,

"One question, countess: are you certain you never lived in France?"

"France, sir!" answered the countess, with singular confusion. "Who are you, sir?"

"No matter; I am what I wish to be."

At the sound of that voice she shuddered; but, distrusting her half-awakened recollections, she answered, with doubtful confidence,

"No, sir, I never resided in France."

"Safia," resumed the stranger, withdrawing, "you ought to take more care of the presents of the Count Cagliostro. That bracelet was one."

He had disappeared; the countess remained in a state of stupor unequal to the attempt of preventing his escape: her trembling lips refused utterance.

"What ails you, countess?" asked the marquis, coming rapidly towards her, as he noticed her pale cheek.

"Nothing, Marquis de Saluces—the heat, probably. Lead me to that window: the air will restore me."

The marquis led her to the balcony.

CHAPTER IX.

ZIANA.

"Where can the doge be?" asked the countess, looking anxiously around.

"I think that I saw his highness, in company with the Jew Ottale, take the direction of the Zecca."

"The mint of Venice?" resumed the countess, casting a dispirited look on the canal.

Safia remained under the influence of the terrible words of the unknown: she could not assume strength enough to relate this meeting to the marquis. The ball still continued, although many of the dancers had already departed; but the more eager and reckless devotees of pleasure deemed themselves in honour bound to prolong the festivity. Lost to all sense of their country's fame, they cared but little for the announcement of war, the arming of troops, the equipment of fleets.

An orchestra, concealed behind long silken curtains, had just concluded a symphony, when the countess, leaning on the arm of the marquis, advanced towards the table spread for the midnight repast.

At this table, although at some distance from the titled guests, sat Taddeo beside Ziana; his hand timidly held that of his betrothed, and he eyed suspiciously those Venitian noblemen, whom he had hated from childhood. His hatred for them was that of the slave for his master, mingled with unforgiving contempt. By birth one of the people, Taddeo cherished so exclusive and jealous a love for his class, that, excepting the doge, he would never bow to a partrician in the street. He had heard so many and such tragical stories of the signoria of Venice, of their secret executions, their snares, their perfidiousness, that, yielding to a vague instinct of superstitious fear, he kept studiously aloof from the great; his profession favoured that disposition, inasmuch as it confined his residence to the arsenal, one of the remotest localities of Venice; his studio for sculpture was situated within that naval fortress, which, as is well known, extends three miles in circumference. Among the special and separate population of this district, its foundrymen, sail-makers, wheelwrights, and seafaring men, he passed his life, toiling daily on iron and brass. It was his pride to know that no stranger could be admitted within its precincts wearing a sword, unless a prince, or one on whom the doge himself had conferred nobility. Taddeo looked upon the arsenal as the haughty bulwark of Venice. Often, as he crossed the marble bridge that leads to the celebrated land-gate, erected in 1475, by Geronimo Campagna, under the doge Pascal Malipiero, he felt his heart beat more freely, as if relieved from the noxious atmosphere of the city: at such times, he preferred the songs of the workmen in the rope-walks of the Tana to the miraculous entertainments of the Place of Saint Mark. The front arch of the land-gate of the arsenal presented to his eye the winged lion, that symbol of Venitian daring; the galleries were decked with Turkish trophies in memory of Venitian victories; and the docks presented a warlike array of vessels and galleys that, to awake from their repose, awaited only the spell of the Venitian war-cry. In short, everything in this remote quarter of Venice, from the sight of yonder Bucentaur, whose high decks lay rotting in stately gloom, and whose sculptures he had been employed by the doge in restoring, to the sound of the bell that recalled or dismissed the workmen, teemed with memories of former greatness and victory.

He would often sit on one of the batteries that look towards the sea, motionless as a fisherman of the lagunes, indulging in thoughts which he dared to confide only to the waves and the clouds—thoughts whose depth Ziana herself had never fathomed, far as she might read into her lover's dreams of future greatness. Taddeo well understood that Venice was wasting, in debauchery and voluptuousness, the last hectic energies of her political agony, whose close was marked for no distant period, and might be witnessed by the young generation to which he belonged.

"And yet," he would say, communing with himself, "there are still those, among the sons of Venice, who cherish her fame. The patricians have outlived their time; now shall our reign begin! Are we not the trusty sentinels of our city? and shall we permit her to lose her rank among nations? Let our noblemen throng around those tables piled with gold, and hide their shame beneath the mask which the law commands gamblers to wear — let foreigners enjoy the sad privilege of ruining themselves at faro-tables kept by senators! well may they convert night into day, for they could not bear the sunlight! let them destroy their constitutions in debauchery and criminal pleasures! We must lift up our heads, since our noblemen plunge theirs into the excesses of shame and degradation. We must upraise the standard of Foscarini, which they trample in the dust. Yes, their soft hands could never handle the cannon upon the ship's deck to scatter death among the pirates; they are fit only to hold the banker's cards at the Ridotto; let their idle sloth sink into the slumber preceding death! Noblemen of Venice, be it your privilege to sink in inglorious repose—ours to live indeed; to breathe the inspiriting element of strife; to wade in blood over the turbaned dead spurned by the conqueror's foot! ours the national emblem — the angry lion at our galley's prow! The day will come, lordly masters, when nothing shall remain of the people of Venice save *the* people! The hour is fast approaching when, the batteries of Venice being silenced, the republic lost to all sense of honour, the nation without chiefs, we shall arise in our might — we, the obscure sons of this ancient and mournful city—at the head of the Sclavonian and Albanian regiments, in the service of Saint Mark, and, in our turn, dictate to the senate! Then rest, descendants of Pietro Gionani and Alvise Moncenigo! rest still! consume, in daily excesses, the worthless remnants of your existence! We are at the helm, noble signors! we will try desperate measures in your behalf. Your Council of Ten—so powerful, so mournful, so dreadful—may give way, some day, to democratic rule. Yonder Lion of Saint Mark, your Corinthian trophies, yonder Golden Book itself, which a conqueror would cast into the flames while he declared you unfit for liberty—

all these we will preserve and save, even in behalf of our oppressors! Such noble and generous revenge may confound your understandings, and be deemed an error by posterity; but so magnanimous a feeling is the love of country, that it casts the veil of oblivion over private wrongs. Fear not, senators and patricians, nor shake with causeless dread! we will only—forget you!"

While his mind thus wandered in such flighty visions, Taddeo felt his heart expand within him; his large blue eye, as he surveyed the moving assemblage, glowed with such pure, though melancholy light, that the star nightly casting its network of silver beams over the lagunes, the crystal polished by the artist's skilful hand, or even the choicest diamonds of Saint Mark's treasury, could scarcely emulate its steady, bright, and placid lustre. Absorbed in the contemplation of that anxious, ardent dream, which, in imagination, carried him into another world, the creation of his fancy, he had wellnigh forgotten Ziana, who filled his imagination, by night and day, with soft dreams of happiness, and now sat beside him.

The refusal of his request by the doge had much grieved him; yet he could but regard it as a mark of peculiar friendship; indeed, on more than one occasion, Alessandro had bestowed upon him proofs of paternal benevolence. Often, while employed in renovating the carved ornaments of that immense vessel, the Bucentaur, he had heard praise uttered, and, looking around, recognised the doge. The friendship of the prince of the republic for Ottale was also notorious. The Jew was the keeper of the mint of Venice; every one held him in high esteem for his integrity and skill. The more inconsiderate among the young noblemen of Venice reproached him for keeping his daughter, the young and beautiful Ziana, in close confinement at home, like a choice pearl within a casket, and could not forgive his causing her to embrace the Catholic religion. They conceived his policy in this to have in view the means of raising his posterity to the rank of nobility; for, in those days, as we have stated, everything in Venice might be effected by bargain and sale.

"Jews in the council! what think you of that?" said Moncenigo to Trevisani.

"That it will make them more liberal in loans; but who is that green domino regarding the Jew's daughter so fixedly?"

"I know not. There is nothing unusual in his disguise, but its mysterious wearer has really a very fair hand, and upon his finger a magnificent diamond ring."

The silent personage alluded to seemed gazing upon Ziana with rapture; seated near the Marchioness Grimani, whose jewels resembled Saint Peter's own reliquary, he appeared ironically engaged in instituting disrespectful comparisons between her faded beauty and the blooming countenance of Ziana, towards whom his lorgnette was so continually directed, that Taddeo, in a fit of jealousy, was about inducing the fair Jewess to withdraw. But, noticing the motion, the domino, rising, glass in hand, said,

"Not so fast, my handsome child. We have not yet spoken to you. There is luck, 'tis said, in a betrothal day; now, Ziana, three days hence the fleet sails; drink to the safety of the republic!"

"After which we shall imprint a kiss upon your lips all around," added Trevisani, under the influence of the wine he had drunk.

The unknown held his glass; he had risen from his seat, and several of the guests also.

"This goblet," he continued, "will hereafter be so precious to me, that I will have it set in jewels."

"Are you serious, your excellency?" said Ziana, fearfully drawing back; "what! from your glass?"

"Ziana," negligently answered the unknown, "a patrician's glass is an honour to the lips of a Jewess; we wish an augury, be you our priestess; we desire omens of victory; drink, then, to the defeat of our foes!"

"Wretch!" cried Taddeo, grinding his teeth with rage. But ere he had time to snatch the glass from Ziana, a stronger arm had thrown it in fragments to the floor, and a deep voice thus spoke,

"Wo to the abandoned wretch who would pollute the lips of innocence! Are there not mistresses enough for you in Venice without desecrating this hall with your profligate advances? must intoxication and insolence revel where but a few hours past an ambassador goaded our national pride with humiliating proposals?"

"The doge!" exclaimed Taddeo and Ziana in the same breath, regarding the speaker.

"Who is the man," continued the doge, "dare treat Ziana as a courtesan, and Ottale's daughter as a submissive mistress—slave to his caprice. Signor Inquisitor, I would know the names of the noblemen who have lost all self-respect. Tear off his mask."

Grimani obeyed, and the unknown, after a slight resistance, was compelled to exhibit his face to the assembled crowd. He appeared about forty; his features had that characteristic beauty so peculiar to the Italian; and his glance, cold as that of the basilisk, boldly surveyed the by-standers.

"Casanova!" exclaimed several young roués, who recognised in him a friend and companion of their pleasures.

It was, indeed, Casanova, the hero of frivolous amours, miraculous escapes, the day-dream of many a romantic signora, the terror of uncles and guardians; Casanova the duellist, or the languid minstrel, as circumstance required; as ready with his sword as with a jest, and, sooth to say, as reckless of infamy as skilful to escape from prison. He was the man, and so long had he been absent that any other would have been forgotten; but Venice could not forget Casanova.

Was not Casanova the favourite son of that corrupt city? He was no longer young; his cheeks were rouged, his language grossly lascivious; an image, in short, of cynical licentiousness, he stood there the faithful representative of his parent city.

Thus returning to his beloved Adriatic, he had hoped to reign there sovereign, a master and model; he had expected to act as the monitor of those he called his pupils, and who were the most vicious among the nobility. To ride with a mistress at the Lido, or stem at night the waters of the Brenta, give concerts to courtesans, hold fraudulent banks in suspicious palaces, scatter gold in return for infamous pleasures, and immortalize himself by notorious love affairs, and conspicuous deeds of eventful treachery; such was the brilliant part he had intended to play, and he longed to signalize his return to his beloved country by some dazzling adventure that might at once restore him to rank as the leader of Venitian fashion.

He had selected the Jew's daughter as his intended victim; her angelic beauty had acted upon him as the sight of some sweet fresh-blown flower upon the senses of a fastidious botanist.

He had left the city under the reign of Alessandro's immediate predecessor; he found in the new doge a severity to his mind unaccountable. Of what, after all, had he been guilty? his boldness had been in keeping with the gayeties of the occasion; his proposal to a Jewess was rather a condescension on the part of a patrician; in fact, the doge's anger had overturned all his ideas.

He had taken off his mask before Grimani had had time to tear it from his face, and as we have said, all had thronged eagerly around him, curiosity mastering their fears at the eventful moment. Trevisani and Moncenigo greeted him with looks of intelligence, and Signora Grimani had hid her face behind her fan at the removal of Casanova's fatal mask.

"We were not aware of your being in Venice, sir," said the doge, severely; "the inquisitor will probably ascertain by whose permission."

"With this, your highness," replied Casanova, negligently. And he exhibited to Grimani the passport signed by himself, which the officious lady of the inquisitor had, the night before, bestowed upon Saint Peter.

"I suppose," whispered he to the astounded and enraged inquisitor, "that you will not arrest one so sumptuously entertained last night by the signora, your wife. I have wit enough, you may well suppose, to publish a most particular and interesting account of that transaction. Be wise enough to be silent upon the subject, or—"

Grimani could scarcely realize to himself that he was not dreaming. He had found, indeed, one of his nocturnal guests, but he wanted the other. He resumed:

"Bravo! Signor Casanova; you have lost nothing by travelling, I perceive. You have returned younger and more alert than ever. You shall enjoy your liberty, but under securities. Tell me only the name of your accomplice!"

The abruptness of the question caused hesitation on the part of the guilty apostle. He cast a rapid glance around him, and, having ascertained that the mask in the pink domino was no longer in the room,

"Faith," said he, "Signor Inquisitor, your question is difficult to answer; however, disguise would be of no avail. It was that rogue Ranuzzi; I do not see him here, or else he himself—"

Grimani frowned like a man who finds himself grossly imposed upon. Indeed, no one knew better than he for what crime Ranuzzi, one of the noblest patricians in Venice, had been transferred from the ball-room to a prison.

The doge had retired, accompanied by several senators, after ordering that one of the gondolas of the palace should be in waiting to convey the young couple home. A smile of inexpressible sadness passed over his features as he bade farewell to the Rose of the Ghetto, as if he had parted with the object of his fondest and purest joys, of his most anxious dreams, his most earnest cares.

The countess had not yet recovered from the varied sensations of the evening. In a state of stupor, she awaited, with increasing anxiety, the return of a trusty slave, to whom she had given a private order at the departure of the individual with the pink domino.

After Ziana and Taddeo had left, the doge approached the countess, and conversed with her in a low voice. The lights of the ball-room had been gradually extinguished; Safia's guests had dispersed; the clock of the Ducal Palace struck twelve. The marquis, leaning over the quay, could count, like so many floating stars, the retreating gondolas, whose lanterns alone illumined the dark waves of the canal. Large masses of clouds had gathered over the sky, furrowed at intervals by lurid streaks of lightning; the atmosphere was heavy, the darkness intense, and a few waves broke with ominous sound against the marble steps of the palace.

"I must leave you, Safia," whispered the doge; "this night is not mine: I am expected at the council. On my return, let me learn that you are at rest; that is all I ask. Your hand is feverish: the fatigue of the ball, I presume; and then, so many incidents have happened within a few hours!"

"You seemed much moved, Alessandro, when you broke that glass?"

Without answering, the doge imprinted so soft and pure a kiss on her brow, that Safia blushed for her doubts. Besides, her mind was too uneasy to heed anything save the sinister sound of that voice, whose words, cold and sharp as steel, had been breathed in her ear that evening.

Leaning on Alessandro's shoulder, she accompanied him to the door of the gallery. Her eyes followed him under the dark arches of the procuratie, where several nobles stood waiting for him; then, rapidly retracing her steps, she approached the marquis, who, already wrapped in his dark cloak, was preparing to take his leave of her.

"Marquis," said she, "I need your assistance: remain!"

CHAPTER X.

LA CA' MALDETTA.*

WHILE listening to these words, the marquis could scarcely trust the report of his senses.

"Remain!" repeated Safia, authoritatively; "you must! Would you refuse to accompany me?"

She seized hold of a japanned case, and drew from it a poniard, which she placed in her girdle.

* Venitian dialect, signifying "house accursed."

"Accompany you, madam! Where, and wherefore?" asked the marquis, scanning her pallid countenance.

"Where, I cannot say; but I expect a messenger who will probably inform me. The cause I will tell you now. A mask addressed me at the ball. I do not know him; but he knows me. He called me, as yourself, by a name which no one save the doge, Alessandro, knows in Venice. That mask was the fiend!"

"Did you cause him to be followed?"

"Yes, by Azael, my Moorish slave; but the mask had gained some distance in advance. Yet, whether my messenger has succeeded in tracing him or not, I must see—ay, speak to him this night!"

"But consider, countess, leaving the palace at such an hour, what will the doge surmise?"

"One of my attendants will leave the note I am now writing upon Alessandro's table. He will not return to the palace before two o'clock; this note will inform him that I retired in better health. Alessandro has too much to think of; he will suspect nothing."

The countess folded the note she had just written, and rung for one of her women, to whom she intrusted it.

"Has Azael returned?"

"He is here, madam; I see him approaching."

Azael entered, jaded and wet. He had been unable to gather any positive information concerning the man with the pink domino. He had come up with him near the Rialto, seen him disappear through a narrow street, where there was a fight among the rabble, so that, impeded by the conflict, he had lost all trace of the unknown.

"So," said the countess, "there is no hope! no one in Venice who could tell us—"

"Wait a moment," interrupted the marquis, as if struck with a sudden idea; "on the contrary, there may be one in Venice who may be able to point out to us the retreat of the unknown. Said you not, Azael, that the mask passed over the bridge of the Rialto?"

"Yes, excellency," answered Azael; "he walked so fast that I could scarcely follow him."

"Azael, does not the Rialto lead to the Cá Maldetta?"

"It does, excellency; that is for those who fancy going there by land. A storm was brewing, and the individual, perhaps, preferred trusting to his feet than risk the danger of a gondola."

"Do you know the Cá Maldetta, Azael?"

"Excellency, who in Venice does not? There are stories told of that house sufficiently horrible to make your blood curdle."

"Have you ever seen the Count Lippone, its new tenant?"

"No, excellency."

"I know him well, madam," resumed the marquis, addressing the countess, who hung breathlessly on every word he uttered. Then, turning to the slave,

"Azael," said he, "you shall follow me."

"Thanks, excellency, craving your pardon, I had rather stand all night between the columns of Saint Theodore and the Lion, exposed to the rain about to fall—"

"Coward! In that case, find me a gondola. The Count Lippone is my friend; I have been several times his guest; I played at his house the other night, and from him, countess, I expect to receive information concerning our unknown."

"The Count Lippone?" answered the countess; "the name is not familiar to me; some stranger, I presume."

"In truth, countess, I am as ignorant as yourself who he may be; he is an ugly, stooping old man, who stammers the most horrible Dutch, and keeps a faro-bank: that is all I have seen of him. What I know besides is, that there is neither an Italian nor a stranger of note residing in Venice of whom I have not heard him speak in full detail. Between ourselves, I think he belongs to the police. Odds my life! if I had my uncle's *estafiers* here, how quickly I could get the information you desire! Yet, this being the hour of the count's faro, I am going to ask him for it."

"But is there no danger? I know, marquis, that you are brave; yet, at Venice, bravery avails little against a stiletto."

"I have taken my measures," answered the marquis—"yes, since my arrest this morning, and," he added, in a whisper, "the flattering appointment you gave me for this night."

While speaking, the marquis produced from either pocket of his vest a beautiful pistol, wrought in damask.

Meanwhile the storm raged, rain fell in torrents, and mournful gusts of wind awoke the echoes of each vestibule. The marquis, scarcely suspecting the countess would persevere in her insane resolution of following him, was preparing to leave with Azael alone, when Safia seized her veil, and motioned him to be silent with a determined gesture.

In a short time Azael had unfastened a gondola, that danced on the bounding waves of the canal.

"Truly," muttered the marquis, "people are right in saying that, when once women entertain an idea—what beautiful weather to be navigating the canals! What a delightful excursion we shall have!"

A dazzling flash of lightning illumined the cushions of the gondola whereupon Safia had just seated herself, and was succeeded by impenetrable darkness. The barcarole turned into the first *cœllc* that offered itself, frightened, probably, by the increasing agitation of the waves in the Grand Canal. He avoided the bridge of the Rialto, and the quarter of Saint Paul; and, with infinite precautions, reached at last—adjacent to the Church of Saint Job—a palace more dark and mournful in aspect than any other on the Reggio Canal. A faint light glimmered from one solitary window of this edifice, whose dark marble front was made visible at intervals by lurid streaks of lightning. The marquis pointed to the window, and said,

"That light shows that my dear friend, the count, is at home; but I wonder there are no gondolas about the palace. His usual company of gamesters have, I presume, come by land."

"La cá Maldetta!" murmured the countess; "I have heard the senator Andrea Galvagna say several times that it was intended to raze that palace. Many people persist in believing that sorcery is practised there in this enlightened age. Do you think, marquis, that upon so vague an indication as a pink domino—"

"Leave that to me; I may meet your man among the crowd of players. Permit me only to give you this advice: now that you have accompanied me to Count Lippone's, return to your palace, dear countess; for, from what I have seen of the temper of your doge, I promise to call on you in the morning early, or will send you a message. Leave all to me."

"Marquis," resumed the countess, with energy, "you can see whether my spirit equals that of their Italian ladies. That man who is in Venice; that man whom I do not even know, but who might speak to the Doge of Venice; that man, marquis, must not be alive tomorrow; do you understand? else I, Safia, shall be the laughter of the nobility."

"Who is he, countess? an agent of Cagliostro? but Cagliostro is at Venice! A French nobleman? no, for he would have come to me first and embraced me, even in the open Place of Saint Mark. At all events, my arm is at your service; of this I think I have given you proof. I have still on my mind the thrust that devilish Cagliostro gave me, and should not be sorry to reciprocate upon one of the count's friends."

"Look, marquis, how like an ignis fatuus that light wavers through the apartments; one would think it was the perturbed spirit of some lord of that palace."

"Since you are so mindful, madam, await me here. Azael, I hope, is armed?"

Azael pointed to the ataghan he wore in his belt.

"Well!" said the marquis. "Now, barcarole, fasten your gondola to this ring, for the waves rush tempestuously."

Indeed, the storm now raged with the utmost violence; the rain streamed down the window-panes of the gondola; the barcarole crossed himself. Two valets, wearing the livery of Count Lippone, appeared upon the vestibule, sheltering, as well as they could with boards, the burnished gold upon the palace-gate.

"The Count Lippone?" inquired the marquis.

"His excellency has just returned! who are you?"

"There is my name, scoundrels!" answered the marquis, tossing his purse to them.

One of the valets picked it up, and, after duly poising its weight, motioned the marquis to enter, saying,

"Our master is about to retire; we will let him know."

"You need not; the count already knows."

"Yet, your excellency—"

"I know very well that he desires this interview as much as I do; enough!"

Conquering their doubts by the mere force of his assurance, he ascended rapidly the double-balustered staircase, traversed the play-gallery, and, throwing open the door of an apartment wherein a lamp was still burning, found himself in the presence of a man who, clad in a flowing robe-de-chambre, was then passing before a large Venitian mirror. This personage turned round precipitately at the interruption. The footsteps of the marquis had fallen noiseless upon the carpets of the intermediate apartments, and the party intruded upon seemed suddenly surprised and unprepared, for he hastened to resume a mask that lay upon a chair near a pink domino. Prompt and skilful as his motion was, nevertheless the marquis had time to recognise his features.

"Cagliostro!" exclaimed he, retreating.

"Cagliostro! much at your service, Marquis de Saluces," answered the mask, affecting great coolness. "What do you wish? speak!"

"Revenge for the dastardly sword-thrust I received from you, and punishment for your villany! That is all I have to say, Count Cagliostro!"

The marquis drew from his vest his pistols, took aim at the count's breast, and fired. The balls fell harmless upon the ground; a half-suppressed, scornful laugh escaped the count. He then stamped his foot upon the boards whereon the marquis was standing, who suddenly disappeared through the sliding floor.

CHAPTER XI.

THE DOVE.

A QUARTER of an hour had elapsed, which the anguish of expectation had made appear an age to the countess, when she heard her name uttered by one of the servants from the dark and tomb-like palace. At first she hesitated, but, soon taking courage, she followed her unknown guide: grasping with one hand the poniard she wore, and with the other adjusting the folds of her veil over her mask, drenched with rain, she was led by the count's valet through several cold, unfurnished, and deserted apartments, which seemed as if long untenanted.

"Whither do you lead me?" asked she of the negro, who, clad in a blue tunic, carried a horn lantern before her.

"To the apartment of Count Lippone," answered the negro.

Encouraged by the answer, she overcame her fears, and, almost without dread, beheld a door leading from the gallery open, and give egress to a man, who advanced towards her. Suddenly her limbs refused her support; for she recognised in this man he who was the terror of her dreams—her inmost thoughts—the Count Cagliostro.

At a sign from the count, the negro opened a silver dressing-case, and, handing to Cagliostro a small vial, withdrew, carefully closing behind him the damask hangings screening the entrance. The countess had swooned; the negro had carried her to a spacious couch; no sound was audible in this immense apartment, save the splashing of the rain against the windows. Cagliostro was himself pale; frightened, perhaps, spite of his usual precautions, by the sudden assault of the marquis, or, rather, trembling in presence of Safia, half dead with terror, like a sacrilegious robber before the altar.

Truly, Safia, extended upon that couch, was admirably beautiful. Her hair, damped by the storm, fell in disordered ringlets over her brow; her bosom heaved; her bare arms hung lifeless. She resembled a statue of Niobe in the calm of grief and despair. Her eyes sought heaven, but a resistless power seemed to bow her down to the earth.

Cagliostro gazed upon her as the high-priest of a sensual worship would gaze upon his victim, the master on his slave, the evil angel on one he would woo to his fiendish embrace. There are temperaments thus gifted with a fatal power. All the offspring of Satan are not confined to their eternal prison. Some range the earth with fire in their eyes, and astounding power in their glance. The eye of Cagliostro then glowed with lurid, magnetic flashes; a silent but strong influence was binding the insensible slumberer. As the daring tempter appeared to the first woman, so stood Cagliostro, the lover of the Greek slave, the mistress of the doge.

However, so suddenly had the occurrence which brought her within his power taken place, perhaps again to baffle his ambitious dreams, that he was not wholly free from that incredulous wonder with which a French nobleman of the period might have looked upon Rugguri's magic mirror. He was astounded, almost frightened. But a few moments ago his Safia was the admired hostess of the Venitian patricians, the fairy queen of the glittering ball-room, dazzling in beauty, worshipped by a numerous train of followers; while, from the Ducal Palace to the lowly huts of the gondoliers at Murano, all invoked blessings upon her. This was the woman whom Cagliostro now held in his power, whom he was at liberty to claim as his slave. The count hesitated a moment; mysterious shadows passed confusedly before his sight, reviving reminiscences of those noble and fascinating beauties of the French court who had fallen a prey to his jealous avarice, to his unquenchable thirst for gold.

"I have read," said he to himself, "that formerly, at Nuremberg, the executioner caused his victim to be masked before striking the fatal blow! I grant that this was almost a cowardly compromise with his courage, but at least he had no shadowy, threatening visitations to dread for the future. He performed the duty of his office, whether upon veil or mask, that was all; and I, the accursed paria of all countries—I, who ever considered this woman as my talisman, my loadstar—I must now claim her as a fugitive slave, and revenge upon her the wreck of all my hope of the fortune I once nearly grasped and lost—lost through her! The die is cast; I am doomed to be her judge!"

Before proceeding to her trial, or awaking her from that lethargic, deathlike sleep, he once more halted before Safia; and, while the insidious influence of his mind hovered shadow-like over the cold and silent slumberer, he shuddered at the sight of her bloodless lips and pale cheeks as she lay before him, livid and mute as marble.

"You sleep, Safia?" asked he, in a winning tone.

The countess opened her eyes, and, through their tearful lashes, cast on him a pleading look of heavenly softness. Thus looks the bird at the hunter who holds its bloodstained feathers; thus the deer, with her dying tears, almost moves to compassion the savage conqueror who makes sport of her agony. Safia acknowledged that this man possessed a terrible, infernal power; her Eden was destroyed, and she had once more fallen into the power of the fiend.

"You here!" exclaimed she, with a sigh; "from what accursed ocean do you rise in Venice?"

"Is it thus you greet me, Safia? I might, however, have expected your bitter, unjust upbraidings. It was not me you sought here, but the Marquis de Saluces."

"It was the marquis, my protector, I sought," replied she, rising from the couch; "what have you done with him?"

"The marquis is safe," answered Cagliostro, ironically; "he will not intrude upon our interview. Let me speak of you, Safia; yourself, my dove. Thanks to chance, I may yet deem myself your master; thanks to the stormy night, I may still be Cagliostro!"

"Cagliostro!" resumed she, with a bitter smile, that betrayed her secret fear. "Yes, you are Cagliostro! Who else could compel with one word a lady to seek this mansion, there to wring her mind with anguish, and destroy her every hope of happiness?"

"Heaven forbid, madam!" answered the count, with a penetrating glance, "that I should change the course of your new destiny. Are you not mistress of the doge? Have not our relative positions been inverted, Safia? Fifteen years since you were my subject—my favourite—before your noble Italian lover had invaded the sacred precincts of my abode, as the thief who would rob me of my treasure."

"Speak not thus of him who opposed to your infamous claims the claims of high and noble birth!"

"Birth!—nobility! mere words, Safia. You were mine, and he dared to rob me of my most highly valued prize!"

"Rob you! you, Cagliostro, the robber! What right, noble count, did you possess over my person or liberty?" answered Safia, with haughty and energetic gesture. "When my foot touched the soil of France, did I not at once acquire freedom? We are no longer at Adrianopolis, but in Venice!"

Cagliostro's laugh was so peculiar in expression, that the blood of the countess froze in her veins.

"Venice!" exclaimed he, "Venice! how simple you must be to trust to the protection of Venice!"

"Yet I reign here! I am a sovereign! I may this very day have you thrown into a dungeon."

"You can do nothing, Safia, against him who can compass everything," resumed the count, with a look of pity. "It is your turn to submit and implore, Safia; mine to command. I repeat, you belong to me!"

"Rather belong to Satan! with whom thou must dwell ere long!" answered she, raising her stiletto. "Insult me again, and see whether I am or not a Venitian!"

"Greek or Venitian," said he, parrying her poniard, "matters but little. Within this palace strange things have occurred—unknown and frightful crimes. One mere look at these walls alone makes thee afraid—"

"Of disgrace alone. If thou wouldst fill to the brim the measure of thy crimes, murder me! I am prepared!"

So beautiful and imposing looked Safia as she spoke, that Cagliostro, in turn, became pale.

"I would save thee," said he.

"Save me?"

"Yes, Safia; but thou must first obey my commands."

"What would my former master bid me do?" resumed she, ironically, and glancing at him as if she would penetrate the very soul of the Jew, Balsamo, under his assumed character of count.

"The easiest thing in the world; follow me, Safia."

"Follow you, noble count? I, the mistress of the doge—wife if I list! Yes, I shall follow thee," continued she, folding her arms across her breast; "but it will be upon the day when the executioner shall lay his hands upon thee; the day when I shall be able to say to all Venice, 'Look at yonder villain, yonder cowardly suborner passing: he is Balsamo of Palermo, Count Lippone of Venice, Cagliostro of France.'"

The count trembled with rage, but constrained his emotion; and casting upon her that glance, of whose power he was well aware,

"Fifteen years!" muttered he; "fifteen years!"

"Yes, fifteen years of peace! happiness far removed from thy polluted home! Fifteen years! during which I have striven to redeem the errors of my former life," continued she, "while thou wast pursuing thy criminal career. Begone! I am beyond thy power now, although thou wouldst still intimidate me! Hast thou neither pity nor remorse? Thou, an Italian, dost thou not fear death? What wrong have I done thee? Answer me. What fault of mine wouldst thou pretend to punish?"

"Your fault and his," answered he. "He first engaged in a struggle against me, which can end but with my life."

"He is powerful, Cagliostro; noble. I love him!"

"The very acknowledgment I awaited," resumed the count, his clear, penetrating eye fixed upon Safia. "Thou hast now pronounced a double sentence—aye, double!—for I will be revenged on both."

"Begin with me, then, Cagliostro; I listen; fear not to unfold thy plans of revenge."

"Again, I say, if thou wilt leave that man and follow me, I will carry away with me the weapon I have in my possession, and which would cause a surer death than the poniard. As for him, no harm shall be done him."

Safia shuddered, so much assurance and conviction did every word of the count evince. Should she now try what effect her prayers might have upon a man she had just loaded with contumely? Was her last hope to rest upon his pity? The coolness of Cagliostro amazed and frightened her.

On the other hand, her aspect had caused all the chords of hatred and passion to vibrate in Cagliostro's breast. He considered her flight from him a horrible treason. Finding her so beautiful, he could not console himself for his loss.

"Safia," said he, "you are a rebellious angel. You dare to brave me, when I have braved Heaven! Yet, remember, I have brought low higher fortunes, ruined more powerful enemies. My revenge is my secret."

"I repeat that I am willing to shed my blood, and give up my life for my deliverer," exclaimed Safia, with a burst of passionate anguish; "but you, who would propose me to follow you, fly, Cagliostro! oh, fly!"

"Fly! and why?" asked he. "Is not Venice your residence, Safia? I cannot leave it without you. In your turn, countess, examine your own heart; ask yourself what you would be to-morrow if the only object of your love, your dreams, that Alessandro, whose life you protect with so much zeal, were taken away from you, without possibility of discovering his traces: when neither breeze nor sea would ever waft you the sound of his voice? The day your mother, clasping you to her bosom, vainly resisted the avaricious cupidity of a slave-driver; the hour when your beautiful locks first fell under the shears of a Moorish owner—when the garb of slavery was first upon you—that day, that hour, had less bitterness than the dreadful moment when I became aware of your flight, Safia! You were my life, my idol, my treasure; another possesses you; another, who now curses me, and has taught you to curse me. And when chance, or the fiend, has brought me once again in presence of that man, when I may still, after a lapse of fifteen years, contend with my rival for your person, you would bid me quit Venice, and yield you up to him! No, Safia! I can hate as well as love. Safia, I hate him! but, alas! I love you!"

While speaking he had thrown himself at her feet. There was in his whole demeanour a cruel and fatal influence. There was something almost supernatural in his glance, an unaccountable spell in the very terror he inspired. Alarmed by the despotic control which that absolute and mysterious tyrant seemed to be regaining over her, Safia was alarmed; she rushed towards the window.

The storm had ceased, but the night was still dark. She drew aside the curtains. She could not see beyond the gloomy marble of the large palaces along the Reggio Canal; but she deemed she heard the sound of footsteps coming towards the little Place of Saint Job.

The clock of the neighbouring church now struck two. The countess turned round; she saw Cagliostro kneeling before her, still praying and imploring. She repulsed him with disgust.

"So," resumed he, rising, "the magician has lost his spell; the master his power? Then, Safia, the executioner remains!"

The countess shuddered. She knew his malice and his skill, and she anticipated being the victim of some of his well-laid snares. She mechanically grasped the handle of her stiletto.

"Safia," resumed the count, in a sinister tone, "do you refuse to follow me?"

"I do!" said she. "Now I must away. Was it not two that struck?"

"It was," murmured Cagliostro; "and this, Safia, is the hour of taking counsel of what is about to happen. Come, put on thy mask; come hither and look!"

Cagliostro opened the window of the apartment; the countess approached it with trembling footsteps.

CHAPTER XII.

THE BLANK PAPER.

The square in front of the circular steps of the Church of Saint Job was suddenly illumined; the light of torches streamed over the pavement.

A man, wrapped in a black cloak, surrounded by eight soldiers, advanced leaning upon a monk, whose face was veiled with crape, and who bore a long crucifix. He was followed by a woman and a young girl, perhaps fifteen or sixteen. Both were bound. A few familiars of the Council of Ten, and several spies in pay of the State Inquisition, closed the procession.

Night and its silence spread a horrible calm over this scene. No sound was heard save the shuffling of sandals over the pavement. The culprit, his wife, and daughter entered the church.

This man, who appeared scarcely over thirty, preserved in his features those noble lines denoting the patrician class, and which habits of dissipation and indolence had not yet effaced. His complexion was of that peculiar paleness indicative of a life of dissolute leisure passed within a palace, and abroad only at night. He wore no mask; his brow was uncovered; despair had settled upon it. He was doomed to die, but cast several glances behind upon his wife and child.

She was truly a beautiful woman; her complexion had that dark hue, the pride of the Hindu females. Her jet-black hair waved in glossy curls over her shoulders; her lips were purple, like coral when altered by exposure. The breeze played with the long sleeves of striped silk which fell over the bracelets and gold circlets covering her arms. Safia shuddered as she recognised the indelible mark of a slave. Her lustreless eyes constantly rested on her daughter, whose tears were enough to pierce a mother's heart. The daughter wore an amulet attached to her dress.

The door of the church was suddenly thrown wide open; and the light from the interior, strongly relieved by the darkness of the portico, streamed in yellow, uncertain rays over the whole group, producing one of those effects of *chiarò oscuro* which Rembrandt introduces with such happy skill in his paintings. At this moment, also, the culprit, by a sudden impulse, turned round at the threshold, and embraced his wife and child.

It was an eloquent, a sublime sight to witness that frantic, heart-rending farewell! He wept as one who felt he must die in youth, in happiness, in the midst of all the enjoyments of life. But, as if suddenly ashamed of his tears, he mastered his courage, and raised his brow. As he did so, the countess recognised him; she grasped the balcony, and exclaimed,

"Ranuzzi!"

The cry she uttered sounded like the voice of agony; Safia seemed as if she felt herself dying.

It was, indeed, the patrician Ranuzzi, whose graceful figure every one in the rooms of the countess had admired a few hours before—Ranuzzi, with his hair still perfumed as for the ball from whose dazzling splendour he had so suddenly passed to the mournful darkness of night—Ranuzzi, who was now to suffer within that church a death so horrible, that it could only have been invented by the genius of a Venitian tormentor or a Spanish inquisitor.

The only vestiges of that mode of death now in existence are a few stones that once formed the covering of a well. There are still indications of it at the old Palace of the Inquisition at Seville. It consisted in the agony we will now describe, and whose details Safia had often heard with a shudder of horror.

The sufferer was led to the *pozzo* (well), lined inside with long iron hooks; he was then stripped, and hurled to the bottom of the horrible abyss. The victim, by his own weight, was thus borne from one hook to the other to the very bottom of the well. The covering was then replaced, and sealed with three seals of the Inquisition, and none save the familiars of the council had a right to raise it.

The doors of the church were closed; the three victims had entered.

"Ranuzzi! Ranuzzi!" exclaimed the countess, with convulsive despair. "What crime has he, then, committed?" continued she, interrogating Cagliostro, who, silent and impassible, had witnessed this scene.

"A crime which the law of Venice punishes with death."

"But the female foreigner and the young girl who followed him?"

"They will both perish likewise. Both belonged to Ranuzzi; the one was his wife, the other his daughter! Do you now understand, Safia, why I urged you to fly? It was because the same fate may be yours to-morrow; yours, Countess d'Azola, and also that of the doge, your lover. Yes! Pride, the sovereign master here, has dictated this law, inscribed among the statutes of the State Inquisition:

"'A noble of Venice who has commerce with a slave alters the blood of Venice. He and his accomplice, and his children, shall die the death of the slave in the *pozzo* of the Church of Saint Job.'"

"How!" exclaimed the countess, shaking off her stupor, "this is but an infamous murder! Let me go forth! I will inform the doge!"

"Inform the doge, and obtain from his clemency the pardon of these three victims! Safia, you forget that your Alessandro is powerless. The Doge of Venice! *he* is the ghost of Venice—the puppet of the multitude—the scorn of the nobility—a slave in a brocade robe; and although he may not, by a decree, save yonder victims, he may, in his turn, be dragged, some day, to this very square; may turn around, as Ranuzzi did a short time ago, and find behind him a woman bathed with tears—his slave Safia, his fair Greek girl, condemned to the same death!"

"But I am not a slave! I!" exclaimed Safia, trembling with rage.

"Thou liest! Safia, thou art a slave! Thou wast sold to me by the magnificent Count Tekeli, fifteen years ago, after a game at cards at Venice! I had noticed thee, my fair Greek girl, inhaling the sea breeze on the deck of thy vessel; I had admired, in secret, that beauty which no one save the count was aware of in Venice; soon as I saw thee, I guessed how useful thou mightst become, and I doomed thee, sweet dove, to my eagle's nest!"

"To thy vulture's nest! thy hell! Again I repeat, I am free now, miserable villain!"

"Look at this paper!" said Cagliostro, producing a paper, carefully folded, from his pocket-book. "It is now white and pure as thy own brow, fair Safia; but, beware! I am the very fiend, when forced to become so."

"I brave thy sorcery and thy falsehood!" resumed the countess, glancing at the paper Cagliostro held. "No more shalt thou intimidate me with thy tricks, nor govern me by fear. I am free, I say! Room for thy mistress, slave! Let me go forth!"

Safia advanced to the door, but was unable to find its lock; and, as she turned around in despair, Cagliostro again burst into that harsh laughter, whose tones resembled the guttural screech of the night-owl.

"For the last time, Safia, wilt thou follow me?" said he, still holding the mysterious paper. "Wilt thou save thy Alessandro, or die with him?"

"I say to thy face that I despise thee, sovereign conjurer of the dead! imperfect sorcerer, who boasted thyself the rival and the contemporary of God!"

"Safia!" he said, stamping his foot.

"Yes, threaten me, because I am at thy mercy alone, now that thou hast disposed of the marquis, my protector! Dost thou forget that I need but utter a cry, and the executioners of Ranuzzi will come in and cast thee into yonder canal? But, rather, thou hast guessed that I had come here without the knowledge of Alessandro, and that I am compelled to be silent! Miserable outcast from every land! now a refugee at Venice! But, Cagliostro, since, as thou hast just seen with thy own eyes," continued she, pointing to the square where Ranuzzi had just passed, "if Venice is so barbarously severe to her own nobility—if she invents for the slave a death complicated by a thousand tortures—what will she do with thee, a vile spy! a ghostly impostor, over whose back many a noble of Vienna and Paris has broken his cane? Why, she will send him back to the police of France, muzzled like one of the bears of the Place of Saint Mark, an iron collar around his neck, and led, with a rope, by my servants! Thou turnest pale, noble count! such is the fate that awaits thee! that sight will console me for the one thou hast made me witness here; the doge and I will witness thy departure from the Ducal balcony!"

"Safia!"

"Thou tremblest, I see! thou beginnest to believe in a woman's revenge. Mine will not fail me through lack of courage; thou wilt leave this city only branded on the forehead by her who hates and despises thee! of her who would follow thee, as thou wouldst have her, only to denounce and betray thee to thy judges!"

"Safia, thou bravest me, but know, in thy turn, that thou art lost! Look at this paper!"

"What paper? Thou mayest begin to write thy confessions on it; it seems to wait for them; it is yet unsoiled."

"Safia, say only thou wilt obey me, and I will tear this fatal paper! Dost thou still refuse?"

"What then?"

"I have only to hold it near this light, and thou wilt see letters flash like fire upon it."

While thus speaking, Cagliostro had seized a taper from the table. Safia uttered a half-smothered sigh.

"What paper is that, and what the contents?" asked she, shuddering with fear, and gasping with anguish.

"Thy sentence! Look!"

He held the paper near the light, and the countess could see, one by one, letters appear, forming lines. When the heat had rendered the whole visible, Cagliostro pointed to the signature at the foot of the infernal instrument; it bore the name of Tekeli, the former master of Safia.

"What means this?" inquired she, her voice trembling with fear.

"It means, Safia, that, since thou wouldst have it so, thy sentence is now written, in letters that nothing can efface. Yes, this instrument is the deed of sale of the Greek slave Safia, signed, fifteen years ago, by Count Tekeli, at Venice. I might consign you to the fate of the wife of Ranuzzi, but I prefer taking you again into my service. Say but one word, and I will abandon my just revenge!"

"Villain!" exclaimed she, endeavouring to snatch the paper from him; but failing in the attempt, and irritated almost to madness, she spat in his face.

"Safia, you have fulfilled your destiny! you are mine!" cried the count, in the short, abrupt tones of rage. "Upon your knees, countess, obey me!"

His iron arms had nearly grasped her, when suddenly the sound of footsteps was heard at the door of the remote apartment; the count's negro came in, and hurriedly uttered these brief words:

"The palace is surrounded, dear master; he is there—he comes."

"Who comes?"

"The inquisitor."

"Grimani?"

"Yes, master, and we have but one way left; the subterranean passage that leads beyond the Church of Saint Job. Your valets are all captured. I will not leave you."

"You see that woman," resumed the count, opening one of the panels of the apartment; "carry her this way; follow me!"

But at this instant one of the window panes was dashed in pieces, a hand protruded and pressed the iron latch on the inside; a man leaped into the room; it was Azael, followed by two barcarolie; they seized the half-fainting countess in their strong arms, while Cagliostro and his negro vanished, unobserved, through the leather panel which, falling back in its place, marked their flight.

CHAPTER XIII.

THE RETURN.

Once more in her gondola, gliding with fearful rapidity over the waters, the countess soon revived under the care of Azael and the cooling night breeze, and inwardly congratulated herself upon her escape from the spies of the council, who had followed Grimani to the Cá Maldetta.

This nightly attack upon the palace of Count Lippone had raised the whole neighbourhood; the valets had to offer resistance; the report of pistols had awakened all the inhabitants of the vicinity of Saint Job. In the midst of the tumult, Azael had had presence of mind enough to replace the velvet mask of the countess which he had picked up from the floor; Safia, therefore, hoped to enter her palace without her absence being suspected.

In the agitation produced by this scene, the fair Greek thought less of the Marquis de Saluces than of Cagliostro; she soon reached the Palace d'Azola, which had been bestowed upon her by the munificence of the doge. Upon entering the mansion where Alessandro sometimes sought rest from his fatigue upon the breaking up of the nocturnal council, at the angle of the Place of Saint Mark, she trembled like a guilty creature; yet she was apprized by a confidential servant that the doge was asleep; it was an hour even since he had returned.

With light step she glided through those halls and galleries, still fragrant with the perfumes of a fête, pressed the spring of a secret door, and found herself in an apartment lighted by the flickering flame of a lamp near a bed.

Many a time within this room had the lover forgotten the cares of the prince; the countess, therefore, had caused it to be decorated in similar style to that which the Count Tekeli, her former master, once occupied. The walls were hung with Persian tapestry; Turkish arms disposed as trophies, vases filled with perfumes, Oriental agate, and flower baskets containing the most choice and rare exotics completed the furniture of this apartment, whose general character seemed but little in keeping with the appearance of him who lay stretched upon a bed of carved ivory.

For in this boudoir, decorated with woman's delicate taste, Alessandro, by the manly beauty of his features, nearly resembled a severe patrician, under the effect of an elixir, in the apartment of some titled courtesan. He had thrown himself dressed upon the bed, and Safia's noiseless footsteps could not awake him to consciousness. He appeared to be struggling against a heavy, painful sleep; at times he uttered inarticulate sounds.

"Ottale, Ottale!" was the first name Safia could distinguish. She had long known the Jew Ottale as a man of unblemished character, and as one who, in the long exercise of his office of keeper of the Mint, with which he had been invested by Alessandro, had borne himself beyond the reach of suspicion. Yet he was not free from the contempt and prejudice which still existed in Venice against his nation, although offices had then become merchandise, and the nobles of Venice the traders who dispensed them. It was therefore but seldom he left the house where he dwelt, amid the dark, ruinous, winding streets of the Ghetto; he went abroad only upon great national festivals, the banquets of the doge, public entertainments, and promenades, and then only with repugnance, and to please Ziana his daughter, whom he loved as a father loves the only joy of his home; he trembled at the thought of ever parting from her, his treasure. Often had the countess wandered with delight through the windings of the Jewish quarter to visit the old man's dwelling. Ziana was her favourite; and never had a jealous thought visited the heart of Safia when the doge spoke of the Rose of the Ghetto.

There was, even in the humble condition of the Jewess, something that caused Safia's pride to exult as she instituted the obvious comparison: she, also, had known grief in spite of youth and beauty, and she, also, had experienced from Alessandro the same protection and the same goodness.

"He dreams of Ottale," murmured she; "Ottale is his friend, his adviser; he has doubtless been with him, and fancies himself still conversing with him."

The doge stirred slightly.

"I have often been reminded," said the countess to herself, still gazing on the slumberer, "of what was related to me by the old senator Gandone, one of the most dreaded of the Venitian inquisitors. He said that he most trusted to the sleep of the accused to reveal their guilt. That of my beloved Alessandro could reveal nothing but love! for, if he has caused my misfortunes, he has also been the source of the sweetest and most thrilling joys of my life. How often, in this room, his head pillowed upon my heart, I have heard him speak of that other mistress of his soul, whom I hate, because she deprives me of much of his love—my only rival in his heart—Venice! But rest; dream of her even at my side, Alessandro! I will not so far forget thine honour as a prince, as to attempt to quench that fire which burns and consumes thee! I still hope that there may be days of joy and happiness yet in store for us, although Satan has brought back to Venice that foe who threatens my ruin! My trust is still more in Heaven than my lover."

Safia had knelt before a painting of the Byzantine school that hung in one corner of the room, representing Christ. She took it down with tremulous hand, fearing to be surprised by Alessandro. Then drawing aside the sliding board on which the divine features were portrayed, she uncovered a piece of sandal-wood, to which a lock of black hair was fastened. Safia gazed several moments on that lock, and kissed it several times with tears in her eyes. She sobbed, and stood contemplating that lock of hair as if it had been some pious relic.

"*Poveretta!*" murmured she, "it was well that thou didst not live. Thy mother has now to contend with grief and anguish. If thou art an angel, as I doubt not thou art, oh! thou so often cradled on my bosom, pray for me, whom so many perils environ! Each hair appears to me like a ray from the holy crown of the blessed Virgin! Farewell! farewell, angel—*Poveretta!*"

The countess replaced the painting, and suspended it in its former place. She looked a silent image of discouragement and inexpressible grief. She bent again, motionless and cold, over the bed of the doge, and was enabled to hear these words, uttered in a slow, panting breath:

"Gold! yes, gold! where are we to find it? Gold, Ottale! gold!"

The doge raised his hands with convulsive

terror, as in appeal to some unknown power, whose aid he invoked. Then his arms fell as if in discouragement, cold drops glistened on his brow, his lips were closed, he appeared inanimate.

"She!" exclaimed he suddenly; "ever, ever she!"

Safia examined Alessandro's face; it was radiant now. All the joys of hope illumined his beautiful features. A soft, superhuman thought seemed to have reanimated that brow, so pale and sad a short time since. His lips parted with a smile, and in their slight motion Safia deemed she read her own name.

"He dreams of me," thought she.

Suddenly she drew back with a convulsive instinct, as if she had felt the cold touch of steel.

"Ziana! Ziana!" whispered Alessandro.

"Ziana the Jewess!" repeated the countess, with lustreless eyes and parched lips.

"Ziana! Ziana—oh! Heaven—why must we still—" continued the doge.

Safia listened breathlessly to these half-uttered exclamations, and trembled with fear at the expected revelation of a horrible secret.

At this moment of solemn uncertainty, the clock upon the mantle struck with so loud and sharp a sound that Alessandro was startled. At the same time a slight noise was heard at the door, a gleam of light flashed through the keyhole, and before the countess could utter a sound, the door was thrown open, and a man appeared, wrapped in a cloak, a large hat covering his face, and a lantern in his hand. He withdrew a step at the sight of Safia, standing, statue-like, by the bed where Alessandro lay.

The doge had raised himself, and cast wondering glances from the man with the lantern to the countess.

"Taddeo!" cried he, as the man discovered his features.

"Myself, your highness. Pray excuse so late an intrusion. I come from Ottale, who, owing to his age and the importance of the occasion, would not trust himself at night to the dangerous streets of Venice. Although you left him a short time ago at the Zecca, he wishes to speak with you. You may trust, I think, to the guide he sends you."

The young man then threw open his cloak to show that he was armed.

"I follow you presently," answered Alessandro. "One word only, Safia; how is it that you are still up at so late an hour?"

"I had not retired," answered she. "I stood watching you while you slept."

Safia was dreadfully pale.

"Alessandro," resumed she, on seeing that the doge kept silence, "can you grant me a few moment's conversation?"

"I must follow that young man instantly, Safia."

"Could you not postpone that interview till to-morrow?"

"Impossible; for to-morrow depends on that interview."

"Will you leave me, then?"

"I leave you, soon to return."

Hurriedly withdrawing, the doge followed his guide from the room and down the staircase. By the faint light of breaking day, Safia, leaning over her balcony, could see the gondola vigorously propelled along the Grand Canal.

She heaved a deep sigh, cast a look in a mirror, and, alarmed at her paleness, rung for one of her attendants. No rest visited the unfortunate woman's couch that night; the incidents that had succeeded each other during the former part of the night were reproduced in gloomy colours to her imagination. Now, a terrible voice whispered threats in her ear: it was the voice of Cagliostro. At other times she heard deep moanings, that seemed to arise from the grave; then the thought of Ranuzzi, his wife, and child. Finally, a shadow, dim and pale as a ghost, seemed bending over her couch; and as she scanned the features of that waving shade, a smile passed over them that went to her heart like a poniard; and she recognised a confused likeness of Ziana, the Jewess who had usurped her share of Alessandro's agitated dreams! At last, worn out by these horrible visions, she fell into a heavy, death-like sleep.

CHAPTER XIV.

THE POLICE.

In a small room of an inn situated on the Rialto, two individuals were conversing together the afternoon of the ensuing day.

One was rather reclining upon than seated in a large arm-chair wheeled close to the window, overlooking the Rialto. His feet rested upon an ottoman; and, from the deep potations he occasionally indulged from a decanter placed on a little table within his reach, containing steeped lemonade, he seemed determined to adhere strictly to a wholesome, though unpleasant diet. His companion wore a black *bahuta* and a three-cornered hat.

The latter had gravely rested his chin upon his gold-headed cane, and appeared somewhat bored with his sick friend's company, when, suddenly, the patient, striking a blow on the table with his fist that made the teaspoon fly upon the floor, cried out in a terrible passion,

"It shall not be said that I will not write all this to my uncle, M. de Sartines."

"Write whatever you please, Signor Marquis; but it is not my fault if you have taken upon yourself the care of the police of this city. Venice is not Paris; and you are not yet an inquisitor, I believe!"

"Go to the devil! you can discover nothing—not even the cunning rogues who personated the apostles at a supper at your house. How, then, can you hope to ensnare an impostor of Cagliostro's ability. You have allowed him to escape! Bravo! You will have trouble for your pains."

"But first," answered Grimani, assuming an air of dignity, and evidently vexed at the allusion of the marquis to the famous supper at which his wife had been honoured by the presence of Saint Peter and Saint Paul, "we have been only two days searching for the count! I have given my man eight days; and if, within that time, he is not captured, dead or alive, I will give them to the care of Master Grande, who will quickly despatch this business."

"All that will not hasten my recovery! I

must have fallen thirty feet at least. I compliment you, I confess, upon your traps; although, in conscience, I cannot upon your police."

"You need not, sir; you have not yet had the opportunity of testing its activity."

"Indeed, but I have; I was arrested the very day I arrived."

"I called to apologize for that."

"Apologies! will they heal my broken back? Come, give me your word as an honest man, that, before leaving this room, I shall see Cagliostro hanged."

"My men have hunted throughout Venice, and from his description—"

"What description? He has twenty. Now you may imagine that he is disguised as an Armenian monk, when, in the garb of a noble, he stands in a box at the opera. Another day you station your men all around the Garden of Saint Birsias—the favourite walking-lounge of Venitian gentlemen and their lady-loves—while he will be promenading, masked, the Prato delle Valle, or sipping his coffee in company with one of your spies. His description, forsooth! Cagliostro may transform himself into a devil or a woman, to escape from you. He may be at present at the Convent of Murano in the shape of a nun. Trust me, Signor Inquisitor, you are no better off than I am, save that you have not turned such a somerset as I did at the house of that accursed Piedmontese, Sicilian, or Jew. Heaven confound him!"

With a visible expression of pain, the marquis felt of his bruises; then with the tip of his finger applied to the part a certain liniment, which one Doctor Fiaramosca—whom he had sent for in the morning—had prescribed, promising, at the same time, that he should be well in a week.

"A week!" repeated he, impatiently, resting on Grimani his twinkling gray eyes, flashing anger; "a week! when I was upon the eve of winning one of the handsomest women in Venice!"

"Who might that be?" inquired Grimani, insinuatingly.

"Faith! not your wife," replied the marquis, peevishly, "rest assured; not that the Signora Grimani might not have many a senator at her feet; those who know her affirm that she is accomplished; but, then, since that mysterious supper given to apostles, unknown to all Venice—"

Grimani bit his lips; the marquis had twice vexed him; his turn had now come.

"The marquis," said he, "imagines that the police of Venice is inefficient. I might, perhaps, satisfy him that he is wrong. While, last night, he was parading about the city with a masked lady, and I, at the head of my men, was entering the Cá Maldetta to seize the fictitious Count Lippone, there took place here, in this room, a rather funny occurrence."

"What was it?"

"I scarcely know whether I ought to inform you; the police here is so inefficient!"

"I admit that it deserves all praise."

"No, indeed; it never knows anything."

"But still, I beseech you—"

"You insist upon it? then let the blame rest on yourself! But, first, would you be so kind, marquis, as to ring the bell?"

"Why?"

"No matter; pull that bell-rope!"

"Willingly; but I begin to think—"

"That I am jesting? Come, I hear Master Olivario, your host, coming up; interrogate him yourself; ask whether, last night, you did not return here, after the ball at the Countess d'Azola's. A charming ball, faith; pity that stupid ambassador from Tunis—"

"I here last night?"

"Certainly; you returned, masked, to your hotel, and went up the stairs to your room."

"This is cool; I never returned to my room till I was carried into it this morning."

"Only ask Olivario there, your host. Olivario, my friend," continued the impassible Italian, "what did the marquis say to thee last night on returning home?"

"Faith! nothing, sir," answered Olivario, who at this moment entered politely, cap in hand; "the signor took his key; then, supporting himself by the balusters of the staircase, sought his own room, where he remained till morning. In passing me, the signor had drawn his hat over his eyes with the air of a despairing gamester; I dared not speak to him."

"You confounded rascal! dare you speak thus to my face?" interrupted the marquis, throwing himself into a pugilistic attitude before poor Olivario.

"He speaks truth!" coolly observed Grimani.

"I am robbed!" suddenly exclaimed the marquis, rushing to his bureau. "Luckily," added he, so as not to be heard by Grimani, "I secured my pocket-book when going to the countess's."

A short investigation convinced the Marquis Eusebe de Saluces of the hiatus of Louis and ducats in his escritoir, which, with true Parisian thoughtlessness and unlimited faith in the probity of Venitian inn-keepers, he had left unlocked. His rings and diamond buttons were gone; his trunk alone had been respected, in all probability owing to the two enormous padlocks which secured its contents.

"Robbed!" exclaimed the marquis, passionately. "Robbed! by the holy rod! Signor Grimani, tell me who is the offender?"

"Softly, my dear marquis," answered the inquisitor, with vexatious coolness; "do not get enraged; inquire of Olivario. Was it not the signor himself who called last night for his gold and rings?"

"I'll take my oath it was either he or his counterfeit in flesh and blood," answered the host; "I even remember that he waved his hand—à la Française—thus! to my wife, as the signor always does when he feels himself en verve."

"May Satan confound thee!" exclaimed the marquis, seizing hold of mine host's cravat, as though he would have strangled him; "you have allowed a mean, disreputable thief to invade the sacred precincts of my apartment!"

"In—capa—ble!" gasped Olivario, who, but for Grimani's intercession, had been choked; "my house is safe as a church."

"Nevertheless, I must find out and secure the thief," muttered the marquis, with clinched teeth.

"You shall, marquis, you shall," said Olivario; "the inquisitor will surely take extra trouble in your behalf; but abate your anger; it will only make you worse; I have about me a cordial, better, I think, than all your physician's prescriptions; I mean this pretty little billet, which, to judge from the perfumed paper, must be from a lady of rank. An old female slave handed it to me, about noon, at the market, to deliver to you. Thinking you were reposing, I did not come up."

"Say rather, rascal, you dreaded the sound threshing you knew your impudence deserved. No doubt you are in connivance with the thief?"

"Ah! Signor Marquis, stealing is, in the abstract, decidedly wrong; but to be content with once in the crime, I call *mean!*"

"Give me your letter; a dozen of the same description I receive daily; I will read this with the rest."

"Signor, your dinner is on the table; does the Signor Grimani dine with you?"

"I have more important business to attend to; art thou mad, Olivario? must I not hunt up the thief who has robbed the marquis? Let me consider!" continued Grimani to himself. "Arrest Cagliostro! secure the thief who has robbed the marquis. Decidedly, I must confine myself to the capture of Cagliostro."

"Confine yourself? What mean you, Signor Grimani? Is that doing justice? Give orders to your *sbirri*, and take my deposition."

"Such trifling accidents will happen in the best-governed countries."

"True; but you have a fashion here of wearing masks—a mode of civilization altogether in advance of the age; disguised beneath that piece of taffeta covering your faces, you rob and murder with impunity."

"You, at least, have no reason to complain; I obtained the earliest information of your loss; and, since you absolutely insist upon it, here is a letter that will convince you that he who has borrowed your property is a gentleman as conversant with the French language as yourself, and who, besides, has some pretensions to delicacy and refinement of manners."

"Explain!" said the marquis.

From a number of papers, Grimani produced one neatly folded, directed to himself; he read it aloud to the marquis; it was as follows:

"'While the doge launches his fleet to wage war against the Moorish pirates, we fancy, Signor Grimani, that the seignory of Venice should not remain inactive; consequently, we shall, as heretofore, indulge ourselves in the pleasures of our beloved city: we shall war against husbands, inquisitors, Jewish bankers, instead of the distant foes of the republic. Give notice, then, Signor Grimani, to all foreigners now in Venice, that, unless they make their appearance, in grand style and fashion, at the Casino, to give us a fair opportunity of visiting their purses, we shall find ourselves compelled to levy private contributions upon them.'"

"A most perspicuous document," resumed the marquis, "and in no wise ambiguous."

"No one denies it," said Grimani; "but here is one still more explicit. It came to hand this morning, and the notice yesterday; there is no time lost, you see, in this country:

"'Signor Grimani—I must inform you that, pursuant to previous notice, one of our brotherhood has made a trifling levy upon the purse of a certain Marquis de Saluces, a vain, silly individual, who imagined that, upon his arrival here, every woman would throw herself into his arms, and who, mean while, provides the female portion of the community with gloves, oranges, and ear-rings from all the shops in the city. Be it known to that finical and self-sufficient gentleman that, in order to succeed here, he must be the Caneletti of painting, the Casanova of gallantry. While giving this piece of advice, I would also beg him to keep his escritoir, at the house of Master Olivario, locked. If ever I have luck at *biribi*, I will return him his money at any Ridotto, whenever I may chance to meet him. Meanwhile, please inform him that there will be deep play, a few days hence, at the Casino of Venice, and that we dare him to stake against our bank. Farewell.'

"So you perceive, marquis," continued Grimani, "that your suspicions were unfounded. You have only favoured with a loan a gentleman who happened to be hard-up, and who will repay you at any time. As to the sarcastic expressions contained in the foregoing missive, they only show that you are already making a conspicuous figure in Venice, that people here are jealous of you, and would be glad to hear of your death."

"Death! faith, Signor Grimani, I was near dying in earnest in your palace of the Cá Maldetta! I never was so astonished in my life as when, after firing both my pistols at Signor Cagliostro, I found myself in a cave, on a level with the canal. Finally, I shouted so long and so loudly through the skylight, like the judge, in Racine's comedy, from his cellar, that, at last, your *sbirri* heard me; and, to crown all, upon my return I find that I have been plundered."

"Look in that glass," said the inquisitor, whose mock gravity completely deceived the marquis; "look, and tell me whether you ought to confine yourself to your room with such a countenance? Your complexion is charming. By-the-by, that *billet-doux* which Olivario handed to you—I would not be indiscreet, yet I would wager that your fair one—Come, now, I read in your eyes that you have some appointment this evening."

"I! who can scarcely move?"

"So much the better; you will seem a hero of gallantry. But tell me, had you not two servants?"

"Two scoundrels, you mean, called *facchini*, here or at Naples, I forget which. It was frightful to see them drink, and they wore a most absurd omelet-coloured livery. I dismissed them on my return. Do you intend me a servant?"

"No; but I would not have any accidents befall you on your excursion to-night to visit your lady-love. I will select two men—"

"That were a good method of discovering the residence of my dulcinea; but I will spare you that trouble. I go alone," resumed he, after perusing the note of Olivario; "for in that palace, I presume, I shall be safer than in the Cá Maldetta."

Fearful of being intrusive, Grimani left the marquis, dressing and perfuming himself while waiting for the hair-dresser. The latter soon arrived, and flourishing his implements,

"Great news, marquis," said he. "War de-declared, and the fleet about to sail."

"I knew that yesterday, fool."

"In that case, signor, I have other news for you: Casanova de Seingalt has returned to Venice."

"I am aware of that; what next?"

"Nothing; only it is lucky for you, Signor Marquis, that you are unmarried, else that wily serpent, Casanova, would be likely to get up a family revival of the Temptation of Eve for your special benefit."

"Know you aught of one Cagliostro?"

"Nothing, signor."

"Seek me a conveyance."

"Your orders, signor, shall be obeyed."

Soon afterward the marquis, forgetting, or, rather, mastering his sufferings, was on his way to the Palace d'Azola, where the countess expected him.

CHAPTER XV

THE BLACK BOOK.

That same evening, returning, as usual, from service, a venerable lady, not yet, we trust, forgotten by our readers, the Signora Grimani, ordered her duenna Morenita to attract, as much as possible, the attention of her servants, and all other spies of her husband, to another quarter, while she improved the absence of the inquisitor, whose presence was necessary at an extra session of the great council, by preparing, as well as she could, for the reception of a mysterious personage who had requested her to grant him an interview.

The Signora Grimani was, as may be seen, destined for adventures since the apostolical supper. She had, however, grown suspicious, and nothing short of the marvellous and universal fame of her expected guest would have induced her to receive him at her house. He was known as Doctor Phœnix.

Eight struck as this remarkable person was ushered, with the utmost precaution, into that same apartment which had witnessed the untoward catastrophe of the apostolical supper before related.

He was a fine old man, with trembling head, stooping gait, and hands of aristocratic whiteness. His frill and lace ruffles were unexceptionable, his wig two thousand years old at least, his coat cut in the most antique fashion, and its trimmings most venerably obsolete. A band of taffeta covered his left eye; his thick-soled shoes were unadorned with buckles; but he wore a large diamond on his forefinger, and the insignia of the order of Malta and Saint John of Jerusalem upon his breast.

"*I am what I am!*" said he, seating himself in a large fauteuil; "my dear child, what do you desire from me?"

The Signora Grimani started at the sound of his voice, as though it were familiar to her; but, mastering the impression, answered,

"I desire that we have agreed upon."

"You have no repugnance, then, to the water?"

"Certainly not; is it not from the Fountain of Youth? the treasure of beauty in her spring? to use the most amiable doctor's own words."

"True," murmured Cagliostro, "it is the most potent of elixirs; one drop would make you ten years younger."

"Ten years younger!" exclaimed Signora Grimani; "that were admirable indeed; it is just ten years, dear Doctor Phœnix, since I became acquainted with Casanova in Venice."

"Casanova?" answered the doctor; "who is he? some frequenter of gambling-houses, some young nobleman seeking unenviable notoriety at the Casino, and whose education you have undertaken, I dare say, dear countess," continued Cagliostro, with a hypocritical smile.

"Alas! dear doctor, that Casanova, who, it seems, is not known to you—and Heaven grant he never may be—is no novice. It is ten years since he touched my fond heart, ten years since he abandoned me; he scarcely recognised me last night at the house of that impertinent Countess d'Azola, where all the nobility of Venice had assembled to conciliate the favour of the doge; so lost to good manners, so eager after novelty are the patricians of Venice, young and old. I do not deny," added the signora, "that the Countess d'Azola is very handsome; she lives luxuriously in the vortex of pleasure and flattery; but what woman would not appear handsome residing in a rich palace on the Grand Canal, basking in the sunshine of Venice, enjoying the smiles of its doge? On the contrary, one leading, as I do, the life of a hermit, with a suspicious, jealous, cruel husband like Signor Grimani—"

The inquisitor's wife checked herself, and cast a glance at her looking-glass; she had formerly been handsome, and, though warned by increasing years and the neglect of her former lovers, still persisted in believing herself so; the doctor quickly perceived how much her regrets might suit his views.

"The Countess d'Azola," said he, "is certainly one of the most fashionable beauties in Venice; but you have it in your power to be as beautiful."

"How?"

"By swallowing a few drops from this vial. I must, however, ask one question: have you either daughter or niece?"

"I have a daughter, beautiful as Allori painted his Judith; but, doctor, a daughter is an invidious date, suggesting ill-natured surmises as to her mother's age, and making her appear older. Mine is confined in a convent at Padua."

"This water, madam, would in a few moments render you as young, to all appearance, as your daughter."

"You jest?"

"Not so. I have travelled in France, England, and Holland. In all those countries my specific produced marvellous effects. There was a certain margravine of Anspach, who, after swallowing a few drops, found herself so young, that a family council was held the same evening to take into consideration the propriety of dressing her in baby linen, and putting her out to nurse."

"Dear doctor, can it be possible?"

"True, every word. That Casanova still holds sway over your mind; he is not yet so much sought after in Venice as to prevent your resuming your rights over him."

"Ah, no! I met him at the Garden of the Zuecca, and he pretended not to know me. The wretch! when I have exhausted a fortune to support his extravagance, and he still wears my rings upon his fingers."

"Insufferably insolent, certainly," answered Doctor Phœnix. "But, madam, you have ink and paper before you; let us conspire to confound the perjured Casanova."

"Willingly," answered the signora; "but what shall I write?"

"Anything you think of—that you love him—have met him at the promenade; deem it strange he did not recognise and address you."

"That is no more than truth," said she; "what else?"

"Say that you have an account to settle with him—wish to see him—that he must come. As to the address, I cannot inform you, as I am wholly unacquainted with that Casanova. But such is the power of my art, that he will receive your epistle before leaving the gaming-table: he will come."

"Come, say you? and I shall see him, and be able to say—" inquired Signora Grimani, with an anxious glance at her looking-glass.

"He shall come," replied the doctor, with an air of conviction that put at rest the doubts the signora could entertain; "but to obtain that result, I repeat, you must write."

The Signora Grimani sat down before an inlaid rose-wood writing-desk; meanwhile, Doctor Phœnix employed his time in taking an accurate survey of the furniture of the apartment. During the pious entertainment he received from the Signora Grimani in his apostolical character, Casanova had noticed a door leading to the inquisitor's library. Beyond, mysteriously concealed from profane gaze by a large tapestry, probably slumbered, in the mist of obscurity, the secrets of many families. Doctor Phœnix, with the concurrence of his friend, had resolved to improve the discovery, inasmuch as he hoped to find in that library means to guide him to the treasure both were seeking.

"Have you written?" inquired he.

"I have," answered she, presenting him a letter whose seal bore her motto, "*Amor è zelo.*"

"Very well," replied the doctor. "Now allow me to put it into the despatch post."

He then cast the letter into a sort of brazier burning in the apartment; and, seeing that she was about to ask an explanation,

"That is my way," said he. "Astaroth, the spirit of fire, is at my orders; and within a quarter of an hour your perfidious lover—"

The Signora Grimani looked at him with the awe with which all Italian women behold a supposed sorcerer. The doctor drew from his pocket a small vial, ornamented with pink ribands, and handed it to his patient, after swallowing a portion of its contents.

"What I do," he resumed, "is from particular regard for you; for if I tasted my elixir for all who apply to me, I should soon be a child again."

The signora, at one draught, swallowed the contents, encouraged in this marvellous experiment by the fascinating glance of the doctor, as well as by her desire of again captivating her beloved Casanova. After drinking the precious beverage, she exclaimed,

"What sum, doctor, can cancel my obligation to you?"

"You do not speak seriously, I hope, madam," said the doctor, with an air of offended dignity. "Do you take me for a common physician? Thank Heaven, I do not traffic in such matters. Have that liquid analyzed, if it so please you; it defies chemistry. A few words only pronounced over it. But, hark! my orders have been executed already. I hear your lover's footsteps; allow me to take refuge for a moment in your library."

"But, dear doctor, really I scarcely know how to explain," stammered the signora, with embarrassment.

"Rest assured, madam, I am not a man to pry into your husband's secret archives; the only book I read is that of nature; and observe," added he, leading her to a large Venitian glass, "is it not the sweetest one can see? Surely you represent, this evening, nature's loveliest work."

It might be confidence in the doctor's magic preparation, or her own innate vanity; but Signora Grimani fancied herself so charming, the roses of her complexion so blooming, and the youthful elasticity of her gait so alluring, that, without farther hesitation, she locked Doctor Phœnix in her husband's library, and hastened to open the other door to give entrance to a cavalier.

He was a fine Venitian noble, in every sense of the word; his dress, his rings were in a style far superior to those of Doctor Phœnix; he was still young, and formed to please. There was a resistless attraction in his looks and gesture. Had the poor Marquis de Saluces been there, he might have recognised those rings. Signora Grimani could scarcely conceive how he could possibly have received her letter so soon; but her amazement was boundless when the newcomer, after surveying her a few seconds, exclaimed,

"Signorita!"

"Whom, think you, you address, Signor Casanova," inquired she; "do you not recognise me?"

"Signorita, a thousand pardons; you should be daughter of Signora Grimani, whom I had once the honour of knowing. Your mother—"

"My daughter," murmured the countess, half distracted with wonder; "he takes me for my daughter! well, I declare, Signor Casanova, no more jesting. I am the Marchioness Grimani; she in whose behalf you once fought a duel that became so celebrated. I love you still, ungrateful man; do you ever think of me?"

"Think! Apollonia; I have never ceased thinking of you, believe me; but finding you so young—so beautiful—"

"Really!" said she, with a gesture of wondering ecstasy unhoped for; "am I so young, so handsome? Are you not deceiving me? do you still think me worthy of a lover like yourself?"

"You might have judged, signora, merely by my mistake, that you have lost no charm. Time, the destroyer of all, even of the ocean foundations of Venice—Time, that saps palaces, and has already slightly furrowed my brow, has respected you. I understand now why your daughter persists in residing at Padua; her complexion would look pale compared with yours. I swear, that of all the beauty of Venice, yours is the noblest, softest, most delicate. Although the other day the Countess d'Azola was pointed out to me—"

"The countess!" interrupted Signora Grimani, dryly; "the countess! you think her handsome; have you fallen in love with her?"

"Had I not seen you, signora, that might have been possible; but this evening—"

"This evening! tell me who informed you? Do you know Doctor Phœnix?"

"No; some physician."

"A wonderful man, indeed," exclaimed the old lady, with enthusiasm; "I will introduce you to him."

"Excuse me; I am not ill, but might become so at the bare sight of him. However, I received information that you desired to see me; I was then at the play at the Countess d'Agnati's; but I came—"

"Who told you that I sought you?"

"An ill-shapen dwarf—a mandragora. He escorted me to your door, then vanished through the wall. Heaven forgive me! he left behind a smell of sulphur that little suited the gallantry of his message. If I were at all superstitious, this were enough to make me believe in supernatural agencies."

The Signora Grimani stood wonderstruck. There was in the sincere tone of Casanova, the seriousness of his gesture, and even the admiration he seemed to entertain of her youth and beauty, enough to assail her reason more strongly than the fumes of Cyprus wine. She looked proudly at her former lover; she deemed it unnecessary to sermonize him, since she was yet young enough to sin; she listened imprudently to Casanova, and was still listening when ten o'clock struck. The inquisitor was to return from the council before twelve; Morenita entered to say to her mistress that she thought she had recognised her master's lantern at the next turning.

"Farewell," said the signora, "till to-morrow! I will send you notice of time and place. Follow Morenita; she will conduct you out by the land-gate."

In her exultation, the signora had wellnigh forgotten Doctor Phœnix; she opened the door of the library, and, presenting Casanova to him, who, of course, did not recognise him, said,

"Dear doctor, I leave you, or, rather, I trust you to this gentleman, who will lead and protect you to your hotel: Signor Casanova de Seingalt!"

The doctor bowed, and the signora's gallant returned the civility. Morenita was at her post. She effected their escape through the land-gate, while the inquisitor's gondola bore him homeward by the canal.

The two actors in this farce soon found themselves on the Place of Saint John. Casanova then hastened to ask Cagliostro whether he had found the object of his search.

"Certainly!" stammered Doctor Phœnix, with some embarrassment; "here is the book!"

The book was bound in black morocco, closed by two silver clasps. Cagliostro handed it to his friend; then showing him that there was a page torn out in the middle of the manuscript,

"Unfortunately though," resumed he, "the page is gone. The one next before indicated the chapter where mention was made of the buried treasure which was to have enriched us, and which, even yesterday, we still hoped to discover! Grimani himself has probably torn out the page. Here is the book, my dear fellow; do as you will with it!"

And, with a dismayed look, he left the book with Casanova. Had Grimani or Cagliostro torn out that leaf?

CHAPTER XVI.

THE MAN WITH THE RING.

During this same evening, in the apartment of the fair Safia, the Marquis Eusebe de Saluces urged his suit to the beautiful countess, by presenting the list of his services with the eagerness of an anxious office-seeker bent upon obtaining what has long been denied.

"Let us recapitulate!" he said, while the countess seemed scarcely to endure the importunate loquacity of her Parisian gallant: "*Primo*, a wound received, in your behalf, from Cagliostro, sixteen years ago; in damp weather it pains me still. Next, firing a brace of pistols at the aforesaid Cagliostro. Last night, add to this, my fall into a trap—worthy of the opera of *Proserpina*."

"Poor marquis! you say truly," answered the countess, smiling; "you have bad luck in whatever you undertake in my behalf; therefore, trust me, we had better let the matter rest."

"How can you speak so, when, for your sake, I would dare everything, undertake everything? Would I leave you exposed to the infernal malice of Cagliostro, who still lurks in Venice, after frustrating Grimani's search? He may, any day, under the mask, speak to the doge. He may tell him—"

"You are in error, marquis; Count Cagliostro is now lost forever. Read this letter from M. de Sartines, your uncle."

"My uncle!" exclaimed the marquis, amazed.

"Himself; the letter was directed to the care of the avogador Andrea Gradenigo, who left it with me this morning for you."

"But how is it?" inquired the marquis, after perusing it.

"Nothing more simple," interrupted the countess. "You have been three months travelling all over Italy, without ever writing to your family. M. de Sartines, your uncle, being anxious concerning you, has taken the opportunity of an express bearer of important despatches. One of these was a formal demand to the police of Venice for the arrest of Cagliostro. He will be banished or imprisoned, if no worse fate befall him. I was mad, I perceive, to feel alarmed; the Inquisition is now aware of his character. His description has been given at Fusine and Padua; those two gates of Venice are closed against him. I may breathe!"

The countess fell back on the sofa, affecting a tranquillity that was far from her heart. The marquis was too well accustomed to fathom at one glance the conscience of a woman not to perceive that she was ill at ease.

"Countess," resumed he, "I really hope that the accursed magician will no more interfere with either of us; but are you certain the doge knows nothing of last night's expedition? For my part, I tremble lest Grimani's spies—"

"Alessandro has this moment left me," answered she. "No report, no suspicion, no cloud is there to disturb our happiness. Thank Heaven, Cagliostro has not spoken; and as for yourself, marquis, the elevation of your feeling and your friendship for me warrant your silence."

"My friendship, Safia? How much more lively, more profound the sentiment I feel towards you! have not my eyes revealed?"

"They reveal a very gallant disposition, marquis, I will not deny; but, after withstanding their fire so long in Paris, I would advise you to let them rest here on worthier objects."

"What worthier, fairer, more divine object could they find than yourself, Safia, though you so haughtily disdain their worship? Since I arrived at Venice, in vain have I striven to anticipate your least desires; so severe you continue, that I feel inclined to go and turn monk at the Armenians' convent! Really, now I am in earnest. If things go on at this rate, the only thing I have to ask of you is to be present on the day of my taking orders."

"You forget, marquis, that I am determined to preserve you for the world! The Marquis Eusebe de Saluces a monk! What would your uncle say of the nobility of Venice for depriving fashion of one of her most distinguished and brilliant votaries?"

"That may be in Paris, perhaps; but here—"

"Surely you have had no lack of adventures."

"You call them adventures? Think how near I came being food for the fishes of the Adriatic Sea! 'Pon my honour, your police is a strange affair, as I said this morning to the noble Signor Grimani. Your palaces are all admirably contrived, all provided with two entrances: one on the water, the other on land. Good that! while one person comes in another goes out; every one is suited, and there are no disagreeable rencounters. The women are masked, their husbands and their lovers also; not only on particular occasions, but at all times, by special order of the most serene republic; your arrangement is much superior, in point of convenience at least, to ours."

"Do you really think so?"

"Certainly; and, therefore, since M. de Sartines, my uncle, has had the goodness to concern himself about me, I intend to give a downright proof of gratitude to that affectionate relative—that unswerving magistrate—who, out of mere principle, has constantly declined paying my debts. I purchased, under the Procuratie Nuove, a delightful little memorandum-book, wherein I record, day by day, my adventures. When it is sufficiently scribbled over, I will send it to him: he will be able to understand the life of Venice, and his nephew's into the bargain. That's an idea—"

"A most moral idea, and one that I highly approve," answered the countess; "your uncle will be delighted, I have no doubt. You begin your journal by a trait of courage that will make him exult in you. May I not peruse—"

"Not until I have recorded there a conquest over yourself, fair Safia. Will you still refuse me, cruel fair one?"

"Cease your jesting, sir. I say again to you that I am not one to add my name to your amateur's collection."

"As to your name, countess, you may depend upon me, I will only use initials. I know full well that you are not free, that your rank, your exalted station—"

"Again, marquis," interrupted Safia, offended, "I love the doge; I thought I had already told you so."

"So you have, most clearly; I am aware of it. The Prince of Venice is in the prime of youth, he has rank, beauty—in short, numberless advantages over me; but do you imagine, perchance, that he is as tender, as devoted to you, as impervious to seduction, as he was when first he looked upon you at Cagliostro's table?"

This commonplace remark, which roués never fail to employ, either as an experimental trial to measure their distance, or as a reserve master-stroke in case of absolute necessity, startled the countess. She looked back to the time when she had first known Alessandro, and shuddered at measuring the years that had elapsed since; for the first time, perhaps, doubt found place in her mind. This impression was strengthened by the remembrance of the half-articulated expressions she had surprised during the doge's sleep; her voice at first failed her, but she soon resumed, with an effort:

"To suspect Alessandro, marquis, were like suspecting the pure gold inlaid in Saint Mark's cross: he is all mine, as I am all his. But let us drop that subject," said she, checking herself, and struggling against the anxious feeling that was gnawing at her heart. "Let us speak of yourself, dear marquis; come, read me the detail of your first day's experience at Venice: just imagine that I am M. de Sartines, your uncle. I listen."

"The first page," replied the marquis, opening his tablets with an indifferent air, "presents nothing very interesting, as far as I remember. Before the moment I so imprudently accosted one of the handsomest women of Venice—yourself, countess—I stood observing, opposite Saint Jeremiah, a series of gallant manœuvres, that may be all the fashion here, but which I thought best to note down, if only to satisfy my friends at Paris (who imagine they have done all because they own a *petite maison*) of the immense advantages of your system of land-gate and water-gate, which I eulogized a short time since."

"Let us hear it, marquis. What does it consist of?"

"It consists," continued the marquis, barely glancing at his notes, "or, rather, it consisted—for I saw it all with my own eyes—of a cavalier of good appearance, who, with a mask over his face, visited a little girl of the quarter of the Jews."

"A little girl of the quarter of the Jews?"

"Precisely; and, now I think of it," continued the marquis, still assuming his air of unconcern, "that little girl—she might be fourteen or fifteen—was young and blooming as your *protégée*, the little Ziana."

"Proceed."

"The said masked cavalier then entered at the water-gate of the house, which was situated—so is Ziana's, I believe—opposite a wing of the Church of Saint Jeremiah."

"Saint Jeremiah?"

"Exactly. You call that place, I think, the Ghetto."

"True."

"Said cavalier wore upon the second finger of his right hand a large gold ring, like that worn by the doge—"

"The doge, you say? Come now," interrupted the countess, with a forced laugh, "you wish to make me jealous with your story."

"You give me credit for more wit than I possess; but since you seem to doubt the accuracy of my narrative, why not leave it to your young protégée herself? I have just seen her under your vestibule with her betrothed, Taddeo. I noticed at the same time some Turk or other, with a black beard, who sold Venice lace and beads, while a female slave sang *Canzonette* by his side. Would you please send for the fair Jewess? To-morrow, you know, is to decide her fate and Taddeo's. To-morrow, according to the Venitian custom, the husband will have a right either to take his wife with him from the city, or take up his residence here with her."

"Why would you suppose, marquis, that the young sculptor of the arsenal should leave Venice? Why suppose that he would take Ziana from it?"

"You are perfectly right," replied the marquis, with an assumed air of indolent carelessness in his manner; "it is his own business. After all, that cavalier—the man with the ring, as I told you before—may have become tired of going there. Whether at Venice or Paris, change is necessary in love, or else it settles into the monotony of passion! Faith! I must keep watch to-morrow at the Ghetto to see if that cavalier—the girl deserves it, though. Fourteen—soft, lustrous eyes. When I saw the doge give her that kiss the other night, I really regretted not being a prince!"

The martyrdom of the countess might have endured much longer, for every word of the marquis went to her heart. As she was about to request him to escort her down the steps, where the wild notes of fantastic music were still audible, Ziana herself appeared at the door. Her liquid eyes beamed with ingenuous delight. She held a chaplet of alabaster beads, separated at intervals by gilt beads, which, upon entering, she exhibited to the countess.

"That Turkish merchant yonder gave it to me," she exclaimed, addressing Safia, "because I was handsome, he said. Taddeo was angry; but I told him it was for the countess, whence the cause of my intrusion."

She presented the chaplet to the countess. She was dressed in white, as the day before. Her face, however, was somewhat pale, and she looked fatigued; a sleepless night seemed to have left traces of unusual exertion upon cheeks that were wont to wear the bloom of the peach blossom.

"How pale you are to-day," remarked the countess.

"True, madam," answered Ziana; and as she spoke a healthy glow again suffused her cheeks. "I sat up waiting for my father the greater part of last night. He was, he said, at the Zecca with the doge."

"Listen to me, Ziana! At the eve of parting from me, perhaps forever," said the countess, with marked interest, "have you nothing to confide to me?"

"Nothing that I know of, madam," answered the maiden, with signs of embarrassment.

"Well, Ziana, I have something to ask from you. You may speak before this gentleman; he feels great interest in you. Does not a masked cavalier occasionally visit your father's dwelling?"

"A cavalier, madam?" exclaimed Ziana, with evident confusion.

"Yes, a cavalier? Answer me. Do you hesitate?"

"Why, madam, I have never yet spoken of this to any one. Oh! but to you," added Ziana, feelingly, "my benefactress, I may tell all. Yes, madam, a masked cavalier does sometimes come to my father's house."

"At night?"

"At night. At first his visits were at distant intervals, but for the last month he has come every evening. He has a key that opens the water-gate; he enters softly, and never fails, upon entering, to present me with a bouquet. He then speaks a few words to me, and afterward, with tremulous emotion, takes me by the hand, and leads me, without raising his mask, to my room. There—"

"Well!"

"He locks me in alone."

"No great harm as yet?" said the countess, with a smile, to the marquis.

"Wait the result, countess. Fair child, proceed."

"After retiring, I hear him in conversation with my father, but can never distinguish their words. My father's laboratory, you may perhaps know, madam, is situated in a remote part of the house. I know nothing of that room, which for years has been closed to all except my father and that cavalier. I have no idea what transactions take place between them there; but sometimes, on awaking, a strange smell of smoke and furnaces has pervaded the house. I know nothing farther."

"A most singular story!" resumed the countess.

"The more singular, madam, that it agrees pretty well with what I was telling you," insisted the marquis, still bent upon his object. "Recollect and call to mind whether the doge does not leave you thus every night."

"True!" murmured Safia; "he leaves me each evening at the same hour."

"Ah! I am an observer! But, then, the doge may have a taste for alchemy. Does not the Jew's laboratory contain crucibles and alembics?"

"I have often caught a glimpse of such instruments through the fissures of the door," said Ziana.

"The doge an alchemist!" thought the countess. "What folly! No; some other motive—"

"You appear to be musing," resumed the marquis. "Why, countess, I see no grounds for anxiety on your part. The doge may be in search of the philosopher's stone. Did not even that accursed Cagliostro employ me under him in pursuit of that great object? But," resumed he, closely scrutinizing the features of the countess, "we forget this beautiful child. She must be sent back to her intended, who is probably waiting for her. She appears to be much agitated by her narrative. With your permission, I will escort her."

"Do not give yourself the trouble," answered Safia, ringing the bell; "one of my servants will accompany her. I want Taddeo," whispered she to Ziana, as she kissed her; "I will send word to him."

"Taddeo, madam?"

"Fear nothing, he will soon be with you."

The countess then gave an order to Azael, who came in, pressed again the hands of the fair Jewess, and pointing from the balcony to a gondola waiting for her, intrusted her to the care of a female servant. The shadows of night were fast closing in, like silent waves under the numerous bridges of the Adriatic city.

"This, then," said the countess to herself, "is his reason for leaving me, such the motive of his continual absence, of the cruel solitude to which he condemns me, and which so deeply wounds me. I am determined to unravel the secret. Marquis," continued she, aloud, "my eyes feel heavy; farewell. To-morrow, if you are so disposed, we may together watch the Jew's house from the canal. I will send Azael for you."

"I am ever at your orders, countess; even now. I wish to convince you that, for your sake, I would brave any danger. Dispose of me, I beseech you."

"The doge!" exclaimed the countess, looking out of the window, "the doge! fly! Azael will lead you to your hotel; you will find him below."

The marquis kissed the fair hand of the countess and withdrew; a footstep was heard in the gallery; the doge entered, and found himself alone with Safia.

CHAPTER XVII.

"Not yet retired, Safia?" said Alessandro, softly, taking her hand; "strange," continued he; "you tremble."

"Waiting for you, Alessandro; I felt anxious."

"Anxious? why? Did not your reception last night gratify your utmost wishes? did not all your guests admire the splendour of your table, the richness of your apartments, glittering with superb dresses? Do you fear that Venice has already forgotten the magnificence of that entertainment?"

"It was suddenly interrupted, Alessandro; you left it first to go to the palace; and again, during the evening, a messenger summoned you to the Zecca."

"Yes; the arrival of that ambassador—I scarcely had time, Safia, to admire your dress! I regret, for it was truly splendid. But you must be exhausted; are you not going to rest?"

"Not to-night; I scarcely know what I feel; my head swims.

"You are suffering; you do not take proper care of yourself. Remember that the day after to-morrow I wish you to look well and handsome, Safia. On that day our fleet is to sail under the blessing of the Patriarch of Venice. As, on the day when the Bucentaur sets sail, I shall be standing upon deck, you shall appear by my side, your hair adorned with sapphires, clad in the richest silks of the East, an object of worship and of jealous admiration. On that day you must be dazzling—nay, eclipse yourself, Safia, that all may exclaim, There is the queen. You are almost consort of a doge, Safia!"

"Almost! If you loved me I should soon be so indeed; but vain have been my supplications; you refuse to make our union legitimate—that would be too great a sacrifice for you; you will some day break the bond that unites us because it exposes me to malice and envy."

"Speak not thus, Safia; are we not secretly married? Did we not, in church at Rome, exchange the sacred vow which no church here would have allowed? It is not in my power to solemnize our marriage openly. Nay, the statutes of the Venitian Inquisition make my duty imperious, never to give you the title of wife. The arrest of Ranuzzi at your ball—"

"Ranuzzi!" exclaimed the countess, affecting surprise; "the patrician Ranuzzi?"

"Two innocent beings, his wife and his child, shared his doom; think you, Safia, such an example of severity—"

"You are right, Alessandro: I must to the world seem only your mistress; the only angel who might have pleaded for me is no more; my daughter is in heaven. It pleased Heaven to take her from us, Alessandro!"

Safia covered her face with both hands.

"You weep!" said the doge, whose livid pallor revealed his secret anguish, "you weep, Safia; am I, then, no longer anything to you?"

"No," answered she, with a look of desponding grief; "no longer, since you enjoy a cruel pleasure in leaving me alone, since you forsake me without even giving me a reason."

"What could I give, Safia, that would not prove repulsive? That public business which absorbs all my attention would cause wrinkles upon your fair brow, make you prematurely old, Safia, as myself! What do you require? Does not your palace abound with costly furniture? are not your jewels and lace the richest and rarest in the world? your servants clad in the most splendid liveries? Have I not, in short, made you the wealthiest woman in Venice? Be content with so much happiness."

"Can I be happy, Alessandro, when you are absent from my side? I was happy once, when, in the earliest period of our union, our hearts ever beat against each other, when you even neglected business for my sake, and that I had but to look into your eyes to read that love which was the pride of my life. You were then only the young senator, Alessandro; you are a doge now!"

"What would you have me do?"

"Remain with me, my Alessandro," said she, half smiling through her tears. "Dear prince, seat yourself here, by my side. Yes, the day after to-morrow, I promise you I shall look well; but let me look on you, my Alessandro! It seems an age since I have seen you."

"I found you last night by my bed, Safia; how happened it you were not yet at rest?"

"I have already told you. When you leave me, I cannot sleep. You will stay now, will you not?" continued she, throwing her arms around his neck.

"Impossible," answered he, with an effort that Safia could not understand.

"Why impossible?"

"To-morrow—yes, to-morrow," murmured Alessandro.

"To-morrow; ever to-morrow! Why am I not like that ring now, for ever inseparable from you?"

Had Alessandro seen the fiery glance she then cast upon his ring, he would have shuddered.

"You never part from that ring?" inquired she, closely examining it.

"The ducal ring may never leave the doge's finger."

"The work is beautiful, especially that setting made to open; let me examine it."

"Wherefore?"

"Because it might contain a woman's hair, for instance."

"Are you mad?" said the doge. "I see, you only wish to detain me; let me go," continued he, glancing at the clock.

"What if I do, Alessandro? whither?"

"To the council that sits to-night, for the purpose of preparing instructions for the admiral of the fleet."

"There is no session to-night, I know; the avogador, Gradenigo, told me so himself."

"He was in error."

"Whither can you go at such an hour?" inquired Safia, in a freezing tone; "to some gaming-house?"

"Countess!" exclaimed the doge, with dignity.

"If you do not gamble, it must be love that calls you out so dark a night; secret, deep love. Do you not sometimes visit the Ghetto, Alessandro?"

The doge turned as pale as the countess herself: cold drops stood upon his brow; still he answered,

"I sometimes go there to visit the keeper of the Mint of Venice: the Hebrew exchange broker, Ottale."

"Very well," said she, resolutely locking the door of the apartment; "you shall not go out to-night, Alessandro."

"Let me go, Safia; I must go out."

"You shall not, I say. It is no more a helpless, injured woman who pleads; it is a mistress who commands. You shall remain. You must!"

"Madam!"

"If you attempt to go, I kill myself! from this balcony, overlooking the great canal. Take but one step towards that door—"

"Safia!"

"I shall not have loved in vain a man whose cold, gloomy nature resembles those suits of armour in the Ducal Hall, silent and chilling as the tomb! I will fathom that soul which none can penetrate; that enigma of Venice, which fifteen years I have vainly striven to solve, the doge—the doge Alessandro!"

"Countess!"

"Look you! it were better to acknowledge to me your love; I might, perhaps, make up my mind to it; but if you render me the laughing-stock of Venice, wo to you—wo to you, Alessandro!"

The doge kept his eye fixed on the clock. The convict, watching in his cell the progress of the hand that will soon point to his last hour; the lover, impatiently waiting the appointed time for a tender meeting; the young soldier, longing for the signal of attack: all these never felt their souls leap with such varied and tumultuous feelings as now assailed the doge. He approached the countess, and, dashing off a furtive tear,

"Safia," said he, "let me go where I am expected to-night. I must go."

These words were pronounced in a tone of inexpressible softness and resignation. Alessandro's features then beamed with so pure and noble an expression; his voice was so calm, that any one would have placed trust in him. But Safia, accustomed to overcome all resistance, could not account for his perseverance: she suspected his motives, and therefore refused to yield.

"The night is mine," answered she, "as well as yours, Alessandro. I will follow you."

"Follow me, Safia, to the council!"

"Yes, I will; I must follow you. Let me be denied admittance where you are going; let me be repulsed, trampled upon—what is it to you? Alessandro, your life belongs to me. I must, I will know it."

"What madness! No, you must never know that life which is my secret, as it must, as it shall ever be," answered the doge, bitterly. "You are right, mine is a double nature."

"A double nature, and a double love," answered she, ironically.

"A double nature, with a heart and lips that have nothing of duplicity. Attempt no longer to fathom the fathomless. You deem me a gambler? Pity me; I *am* a gambler. Yes, as you say, I repair to those ridotti of Venice, where all must go masked—to hide their shame, doubtless—I go thither at night. I deceive you. I love, say you? Go, then, take your mask, and visit every house in Venice; discover my mistress, if you can! Ah! women, women!" continued he, with a scornful, mocking laugh; "unless you stand ever at their sides, they think you a deceiver. Unless you kneel forever before them to worship, they deem you infamous! You might suspect me, Safia, if, like the other patricians of Venice, I spent my life in raising or lowering, according to the sun or shade, the gilded hoops of a gondola over the brow of a mistress! *They* traverse the lagunes to the sound of soft music; my element is the high sea, the raging storm, the sombre night! *They* are the careless passengers; I am at the helm! Arise, Safia. Again I say it, I must go; the hour is striking."

"Twelve! oh yes, twelve!" cried the countess, highly excited.

She was kneeling before Alessandro, but she arose on hearing the sound of the clock.

"She is waiting for you, Alessandro! mind you do not keep her waiting."

"Safia! let me go."

The countess had placed herself, pale and motionless, against the door.

"Again, Alessandro, I repeat, you shall not go," she murmured, in a voice trembling with anger.

"I say to you, Safia, that there is a person waiting for me. I must go."

The doge, by a rapid movement, disengaged himself from her arms.

Safia, whose limbs hardly supported her, slowly proceeded to her balcony; so dark was the night, so chill the breeze, that she closed the window, shuddering.

"Gone!" she exclaimed — "gone! Oh Heaven! am I becoming insane?" Then pressing her hand to her forehead, "Ah! I remember now, there was some one I asked to wait for me."

She proceeded towards the gallery, and cried, "Taddeo, Taddeo!"

"Here, madam," answered Taddeo, who seemed delighted to be called out at last.

"Taddeo, go into that room; you will find there a cloak and a sword."

"I obey, madam."

He soon re-entered the room, wrapped in a large cloak, under which a sword glittered.

The countess had precipitately thrown her *bahuta* over her shoulders, her veil over her hair; she took her mask, and descended the steps.

"Whither are we going, madam?" asked the young man.

"Follow me; you will soon know."

Then motioning him forward, the countess was soon lost, in the darkness of the murky night, amid the labyrinth of narrow streets which environ the Ducal Palace.

CHAPTER XVIII.

AT THE GHETTO.

The quarter of the Ghetto, whither we now lead our readers, was, as we have stated, that containing the Hebrew synagogues and schools. These establishments were, at that time, only seven in number; and their varied chimes had just struck one o'clock, as Ziana, anxious at the protracted absence of Ottale, ventured, in spite of the wind and rain, to open the window that overlooked the canal. The silence of night had succeeded to the busy hum of the city during the day; the clouds were spreading the shroud of darkness over the waters; the Church of Saint Jeremiah only looked a darker mass of shadows. The maiden, leaning forward, listened intently for the arrival of her father; but no sound of oars upon the canal broke the stillness; no lights from the prows of gondolas were in sight.

The air was bleak and chill; the wind blew in fitful gusts from the direction of the Malamocco. The rain fell in torrents, and the buzzing of insects, attracted to her light as towards a shelter, compelled the fair Jewess to close the casement.

Ziana seated herself, with a look of disappointment, at her little table, and resumed her work. It was a veil—her bridal veil—she was embroidering. She had piously deposited her bouquet of silver flowers at the feet of a little sculptured Madonna, before which a lamp was burning; she had drawn the curtain over this niche, which was habitually kept veiled, from delicacy for the Jew.

The room where sat the fair girl was very spacious; adjoining it, on the left, was Ottale's laboratory. The apartments were separated by a leaden casement framing of small pieces of dark glass, through which rich vases, and several articles of plate, could be perceived.

This laboratory had a low door, over which hung a large drapery; there was, at this moment, no light in that apartment. A little to the right was another door, somewhat similar to the latter; it opened upon a large corridor which led to Ziana's chamber.

The apartment where Ziana now watched was dark and smoky, the exact background Rembrandt would have chosen for the portrait of an alchemist. A large pillar stood in the middle of the floor. In a nook of this pillar was placed Ziana's Madonna; for, as we have said, the Jew's daughter was a Catholic. An old clock fixed to the wall, a few leather chairs, and a large oaken arm-chair placed before Ottale's desk, completed the furniture. The floor was covered with warm mattings, the walls bare and dark. An enormous bunch of keys hung by the window, and, in a wire cage, a pigeon—whom Ziana held sacred, as if he had been one of Saint Mark's own doves—slept, sheltered from the light by an old brocade covering.

"The business of the seignory probabla detains my father at the Zecca," thought the betrothed of Taddeo: "he returns not—he may not return till dawn! Poor father! what a life of labour and grief! Those Venitian nobles regard a Jew as they would a slave. How often have I seen him return worn, faint, exhausted! They treat him like a servant; yet what a noble, elevated nature is his! His least desire is to me a sacred order, and when he presented Taddeo to me—"

The maiden paused from her work for a moment, and appeared musing.

"Will our mysterious friend," continued she to herself, in a low voice, trembling with secret emotion; "will he come to-night? he scarcely ever comes save at night. Shall I see him enter, as usual, the beloved unknown? not so, since my father knows him. Yes, he will come; in darker nights than this he has found our humble dwelling, despite the lightning and the wave. When aught delays him, I know not why, but I always shudder. At night the streets and canals are infested with drunken sailors and Sclavonian banditti. Should he run any danger to-night—Holy Madonna! for him, at least, I can pray to you without veiling your dear image! he is a Christian, like myself."

Then trimming the dim lamp, the beautiful creature knelt before the Virgin's image; lovely as an angel form she looked, amid the dim shadows of the half-lighted room. She prayed long and fervently. At last she arose.

"Yes," said she, "let us wait; he will come! The day on which the patriarch blessed me as the betrothed of Taddeo, at Saint Jeremiah's, he made it a point to call and embrace me before the pious ceremony. He loves Ottale; he loves me also; and yet, such a love—"

Ziana fell into another fit of soft revery,

when suddenly she heard the sound of footsteps.

"Can it be he?" thought she.

The door opened, and the maiden recognised her father.

The Jew was pale and care-worn; his limbs could scarce support him. He threw aside his drenched cloak.

Ziana had had time to draw the curtain over the Madonna's image, unseen by her father.

"How tired you seem," said she, taking from him his scarlet hat; "why did you not come in your gondola?"

"My dear child," answered Ottale, seating himself before her, and fondly kissing her hand, on which he nearly dropped a tear; "the reason is, that the seignory of Venice have no respect for the age and sufferings of their servants. I was obliged, to-night, to call at every house in the Ghetto to ascertain the means of my brethren, to solicit or threaten, according to the orders I had received. To-morrow, you know, Venice sends forth an expedition. To-morrow the fleet, whose equipment had been interrupted, will sail from the port with streaming colours and Saint Mark's lion, blessed by the patriarch. To-morrow, ay, to-morrow!" murmured the Jew. "But, Ziana, the hour of God's vengeance has come; no fleet will sail to-morrow."

"What mean you?"

"That it is time Venice should bear the penalty due to her errors. Venice, my child, has filled the measure of crime and profligacy; and now, as a punishment, she is poor and forsaken. There was a day when the inhabitants of the superb city alone had monopolized the commerce of the Levant and the East Indies; their vessels brought from Aleppo and Alexandria those rare articles conveyed by the Red Sea into Syria and Egypt; and, exclusive masters of all European ports, commanded their own prices. Soon, however, they lost all, save the trade of Constantinople and Germany. Hence those Turks and Dalmatians, whom you see listlessly lying on the quays; hence that old palace on the great canal was built for those idle Levantine merchants who are still in daily relations with Asia. The Germans, also, have, you know, their royal residence near the bridge of the Rialto. They have special statutes and privileges. Giorgione and Titian have painted frescoes on the outside of their palace; and the gilt leather hangings of their stores have been decorated by the brush of Paul Veronese. These are the chosen—the favourites of the republic! The revenues of their counters furnish the prince and officers of Venice with their annual salaries; her senators with the silks and velvets they wear; and the bank of the Giro, with the means of preserving its credit inviolate. And yet, what are they, Ziana, compared with the Jews of Venice? These, without any acknowledged counting-houses of their own, deal with every counting-house in Europe; without having any special privileges, they receive mysteriously at their houses, the lords and masters of this great republic. At first, they lurked in poverty and obscurity upon the island formerly called Longa Spina, which from them took its name of Gindeua. The former decrees did not allow them to reside more than a fortnight at a time at Venice; each week they were compelled to appear before a procurator. Insensibly Venice called them forward, flattered them. Although some outward signs distinguish them from the Armenians on the quays, yet by them are treaties made and broken; to them the younger nobles apply for assistance; for them new leaves have been added to the Golden Book. We need no longer complain of national degradation. We reign, we command. The hour of retribution has come. The coffers of the Germans, the Turks, the Dalmatians, and the Greeks being exhausted, we have been applied to since yesterday. We have been implored to save the honour of Venice!"

"You will not hesitate, father; I trust you will not hesitate," exclaimed Ziana. "You will forget your injuries—your resentment. I know as well as yourself what bitter cup has been often forced to your lips; but, as yourself, I love instead of hating Venice. I cannot but remember that I am betrothed to one of her sons."

"Taddeo has not been here to-night?" inquired the old man, striving to forget the serious subject that occupied his thoughts. "Yet he was, the other night, at the Zecca with his serene highness."

"Taddeo had not mentioned it to me, probably owing to your orders; the Countess d'Azola gave him some commands to-night, and he remained at her house."

"The countess!" murmured the Jew; "what need could she have of him?"

The storm had now increased in violence. Ziana thought she heard the sound of oars beneath the window; she looked out, but the darkness was impenetrable.

"Ziana," resumed Ottale, "to-morrow the bells will toll their joyful peals; the duties of my office command my attendance at the ceremony, which is still more magnificent than that of the Bucentaur. You have often heard that the pilot who steers that floating palace to sea shudders at a cloud; judge, then, Ziana, what must be my feelings when I think of the doge, who to-morrow will be the pilot of Venice! when I see him taking his solemn and public oath as admiral, that the fleet may sail from the port! This stormy night has chilled my blood. Did no one call? Has no letter been left for me?"

"None, father, to my knowledge; yet I did see some person lurking about the house."

"A spy of the seignory—a *sbirro*, undoubtedly! Come, speak without reserve. They imagine I have buried treasures here—that I am wealthy. Alas! my child, you are my only wealth," resumed the Jew, pressing Ziana to his bosom; "but who was it you saw?"

"A Jew, father, like yourself. He wore the robe and the scarlet hat prescribed to the inhabitants of the Ghetto; I stood at the window near the land-gate; he approached it to-night about dusk, and spoke to me in Hebrew."

"What said he?"

"That he had known you during a voyage to Palermo; that he had partaken of your hospitality. His name—let me see—Gruss!"

"David Gruss!" murmured the old man. "He in Venice! True, he is of my religion—a strange man!" continued he, musing.

"He added, 'Tell your father that I will soon call again; to-night, perhaps.'"

"To-night?"

"He then left me, and disappeared in a neighbouring alley. He appeared about your age; his gait was slow; his beard long as a monk's."

"David Gruss!" exclaimed the old man, approaching his table, strewed with books. He took up one, and read eagerly. No sound could be heard save the pattering of the rain against the windows and the howling of the wind.

"Are your books in order, father?" inquired the maiden; "you know I am sometimes your clerk when your sight fails you."

"Dear child, I am not consulting my loan-books; they are, truly, records of shame! the first names of the republic reduced to borrow! the descendants of noble ancestors giving their signatures for gold! Among those idle nobles who mortgage the future for present vicious indulgence, or to gratify the whim of a mistress, and who crave my assistance, there is one, Ziana—but one—who looks, as I do, with sorrow upon the misfortunes of this land. He, Ziana, is a last heroic remnant of patrician virtue. The day when Venice shall fall, never to rise again, he will ascend to heaven like the soul separated from the body. The soul of Venice, Ziana, is the doge."

"I have not forgotten, father, that the doge once saved your life."

"You were very young then," answered the old man, with a sigh. "Famine had raised the populace of Venice against the Jews. Your father was forced from his bed in this very house, beaten, dragged to the place of execution, and hanged like a malefactor. There seemed no opportunity of escape. Through the darkness around me I saw nothing but weapons, torches, and men who yelled for vengeance. One man forced a passage through the furious multitude, drew his poniard, and deliberately cut the rope asunder. A thousand arms were raised against him; a thousand voices yelled; but he exclaimed, 'Justice for all! I am the Doge of Venice, elected this night by the council.' I fell breathless at his feet, Ziana, embraced his knees with sobs of joy! Oh! why may I not shed my blood for him who saved me?"

"You know, father, that in all the prayers I address to Heaven the name of the doge is ever remembered."

"Kiss me, daughter! the will of Heaven is impenetrable; but let us change the subject," continued the old man, striving to disguise his emotion; "let us speak of you, my daughter—of your future happiness."

"Can I, dear father, be happy separated from you?"

"So speak all maidens at your age, Ziana; but one day suffices to change all their resolutions."

"Alas! I am not like the maidens of Venice—I who, in the solitude of this dwelling, have never had the opportunity of pouring into a mother or a sister's bosom the effusions of my soul. All my feelings have centred in yourself; for never have your lips told who was my mother!"

"Let us speak of the future, Ziana; the past is no longer ours."

"My mother!" continued the maiden, musing mournfully—"my mother—is she in heaven or on earth? No answer. Alas! you are ever silent to that question."

"Ziana," resumed Ottale, with a painful effort, "the husband I give you is an honest, loyal man; you know it. Brilliant vices could never characterize one to whom I intrust the care of your happiness."

"I am ready to follow Taddeo wherever he may lead me," answered the maiden, with a sigh, fixing on Ottale a glance of heavenly sweetness; "but the thought of never seeing you save at rare intervals—of bidding farewell to Venice forever—that, father, saddens my heart!"

"Dear child!"

"Father," said Ziana, "this is the hour at which that friend, unknown to me, usually comes; since he appears to feel interested in me, since he knows that I am soon to leave you, why does he delay coming to-night?"

"That cavalier, Ziana, indeed merits the feeling of gratitude he has inspired in you. He will come to-night. Some one knocks, I think."

A slight knock was heard at the hall door on the right. The sound of the waves splashing under the weight of a gondola was heard; the old man opened the door; he appeared surprised at the sight of the person who entered. Ziana, with no less astonishment, first gazed upon the new comer, then placed a chair for him.

The unexpected visiter wore a black robe and peruke; an inkstand in his girdle. The dress indicated a notary.

"Be seated, sir, if you please," said the Jew; "I will presently be with you."

Then, taking his daughter by the hand, Ottale whispered,

"An affair of importance, Ziana, obliges me to speak a few words in private with that man."

"I never before saw him in our house, father!"

"Leave us, I pray, for a short time."

Ziana obeyed, and taking her embroidery, seated herself at the extremity of the room, suspiciously glancing at intervals towards the notary.

"Pardon me, sir," whispered Ottale, as soon as Ziana was out of hearing. "I regret that my involuntary absence—I know that you have called already once to-day."

"Pursuant to your orders. I deemed the business important; and therefore—"

"I will not trespass on your time. Your reputation warrants your fidelity."

"What do you wish of me?"

"To take charge of some papers," answered the Jew, opening a casket, which he presented to the notary. "Those papers are important, and I desire to deposite them with you. I am old; I may die very soon. These papers are not mine. They were deposited with me. Let it suffice you to know that the prospects of several persons—their lives, perhaps—depend on the secret which those papers contain. The late proclamation of war, and the sailing of the fleet, oblige me to give them to you without delay. They will be safer in the hands of a notary than here. Take them. I need not recommend the utmost secrecy."

"Depend upon me," answered the notary, taking the papers.

"At Venice, you know," continued the old man, "we live in continual dread of spies and informers. At Venice treachery abides everywhere, as well under the magisterial gown as the garb of livery."

"To whom, when the time comes, must these documents be rendered?"

"To the person whose name is written upon the envelope."

"Very well. Have you no farther instructions to give?"

"None."

"Then depend upon me," resumed the notary, retiring.

CHAPTER XIX.

"I SHALL now rest more tranquilly," murmured Ottale, as the notary withdrew. "Such a trust, and under such circumstances—But it is late. Will he not be able to come to-night?"

Turning suddenly round, he saw Ziana, her eyes fixed on the inner door, half opened, and through which was visible the corridor leading to the maiden's apartment.

"What were your thoughts?" he asked, with a kind, though scrutinous glance.

"Father, since you question me, I must say that my eyes are irresistibly attracted to that door, and to the secret passage that opens upon the canal, and through which our friend is admitted—that entrance, unknown even to Taddeo."

"Yes, through that entrance once the nobles of Venice brought to my predecessors and to myself," added the old man, with a sigh, "their plate, that it might be melted for the wants of the republic. Now play and dissipation have so impoverished them that they have forgotten the route. What a singular house this is, Ziana! It would seem that under each reign, under every doge, these cracking walls were destined to witness mysterious scenes, the secret of which has never been violated. Before me Daniel Vimfen was keeper of the mint, and here held his obscure counting-room. His predecessor was Sebastian Gonzales, a Portuguese Jew. I found numerous names inscribed on yonder pillar. These bolts and gratings make the house resemble a state-prison; and yet we have no more gold to watch over. We must ourselves borrow, in order to loan to the nobles! A few gold vases, some plate chased by Benvenuto Cellini, the Florentine—naught else. The treasury of Saint Mark still has the two crowns of the kingdoms of Candia and Cyprus, several agate, emerald, and rock crystal vases, sapphires, gold armour enriched with pearls, grenate seals, and the autograph Gospel of St. Mark. One Candi Stemati once found passage through the wall of the adjoining church into the treasury, and robbed it; but who, Ziana, would venture here, into the Jew's cavern? What step save that of our friend is ever heard to tread these floors? For no one save my liberator, would I consent to watch when sleep weighs heavily upon my eyelids, to sit, old and infirm as I am, listening to the slightest sound from the canal, joyful or terrified, according as his visit is early or late. I feel it, alas! Ziana, my life rests with him!"

"Mine also, father. At night, when locked in my chamber, before the door of which he passes in departing from the house, I still listen to the echo of his footsteps."

"Will you, then, think of him sometimes when you no more can see him?"

"See him no more? Is he about leaving? Perhaps he has already left? Oh! father, conceal not the truth from me."

A tear glistened in the maiden's eye; she was earnest in her inquiries; but Ottale doubtless preferred not to explain himself.

"Yes, father," resumed Ziana; "I will ever think of that friend, who has shown himself so devoted to you, so kind, so tender, so generous to me! His thoughts, though melancholy, are so elevated! The impenetrable mystery under which he shrouds himself, the care with which he withholds from me his name, the mask which ever disguises his features, and yet has sometimes betrayed a tear—oh! I love him with love mingled with respect, like the love I bear to you."

"Well you may, daughter. He is our providence. You know that when he is present, blessings from above enter with him into our dwelling."

"Yet to-morrow I depart, perhaps forever, with my husband, without even being acquainted with the name or features of that man! I tremble for him, unconscious what danger threatens him, or whether the soil he treads is that of friendly asylum or proscription. Venice! Venice! how terrible are thy mysteries!"

Ziana had scarcely finished this sentence, to which the Jew listened with a sad look of assent, when a slight noise was heard at the half-opened door; the door which admitted the mask every night.

Really, at the sight of that man, wrapped in a large black domino, silent and mournful as the grave, any woman, save Ziana, would have shuddered. There flashed such fire from his eyes through his mask, there was something in his whole appearance that betrayed such deep, settled melancholy, that he might have claimed attention from the most thoughtless. Was he an angel or a fiend? Did he repair to this house to tempt its beauteous Eve, or did he descend to Ottale's dark retreat, a messenger of goodness and superior intelligence? All Ziana knew was that, in his presence, she trembled and was thoughtful; the empire he exercised over her was unaccountable.

As he entered, he slowly approached Ziana; he held a bouquet of flowers and presented it to the maiden, on whose forehead he imprinted a kiss.

"These flowers," said he, in a slow and painful tone, "are the last you will receive from your friend, Ziana; for you are about to quit Venice, and I remain."

He sighed as he spoke, and rested his hands on Ottale's chair, as if he felt faint.

"You remain?" said she, mournfully. "Do you remain here forever?"

"Forever!"

"Has Venice, then, such charms for our friend, that he may not leave it even for a short time?"

"Venice, child, so dear to patrician idleness, weighs as heavily upon my head as a prison's roof; and yet I love that prison as others love their freedom. My life and death belong to Venice; to her I must account for the air I breathe; I live at her feet like a slave under the eyes of her spies. Having nothing of my own, not even the deep secrecy of my thoughts, I ever dread, Ziana, lest informers might penetrate the double mask which I wear over my face and my soul, and lest Venice should some day punish me for the ardent wishes I form for her happiness."

"You are much to be pitied."

"Such is my fate."

"Perhaps it may change?"

"Never."

"Ah, sir! permit me, before I leave this city, to throw myself at the feet of the doge. If you are proscribed, he alone may absolve you; he is powerful and kind; my father has some influence with him."

"Fond child! you know not that the doge is nothing in Venice. Faliero and Foscari, alas! are sad examples of the fact."

"Well, then, the Countess d'Azola, my protectress."

"Hush! as well might you cast a denunciation against me into the marble lion's mouth as invoke the aid of the countess."

"You make me shudder," said the maiden, with impassioned anguish.

"Ottale," said the mask, sorrowfully approaching the Jew, "Ziana and her bridegroom must go to Ferrara without delay."

"What, do you insist upon my very exile?" said Ziana to the unknown.

"She is no longer safe, even in your house," whispered the mask in Ottale's ear.

"They shall leave to-morrow," answered the Jew.

"How dejected you look, my child," said the mask, taking the hand of Ziana.

"I am ready to go," answered she, with emotion, "since you wish it."

"I wish it, Ziana. Ah! if you could but know what suffering the parting causes me—how hard it will be for me, after your departure, to struggle alone through the night of my existence, no more cheered by the soft star towards which I nightly proceeded."

"Your words comfort me! at least, I shall bear with me the hope that our friend will not forget me."

"Forget you! never, never!"

"Grant me one prayer."

"What is it?"

"Will you consent?"

"Were it my life, child, I would grant it freely."

"For my sake alone, then, allow me to see you once unmasked."

"Hold, Ziana; should this mask be removed a head must follow."

"Keep, then, your mask."

"Retire, Ziana; I have to converse to-night with your father concerning an affair of importance."

"Till to-morrow, then. I could not go, and I should lose all my courage if I had not seen you."

"Yes, yes; farewell until to-morrow!" said the mask, smothering his convulsive sobs.

He hastily led Ziana to the door of her apartment, and softly withdrew the key from the door of the passage. The storm had ceased, the silence of night was undisturbed; no sound was audible save the ticking of the pendulum of the old clock.

"Ottale," said the doge, taking off his mask, "what news?"

"Bad, your highness. The Jews, who number, as you know, some three thousand here, speak of raising the populace."

"Do they forget, Ottale, that if to-day I supplicate, to-morrow I may punish?"

"They know it, your highness; but you also know that their loans to the state have never been refunded. The Jews are bold and insidious; they trust in the antipathy which the nobles feel for war. I have visited them at their synagogues, in their offices; they know full well that the Zecca has no more wealth, that the Bank of the Giro, the Venetian Exchange, will vainly claim from the republic the moneys deposited with the prince."

"Those moneys have paid for the first preparations of the fleet; I intended to return it from my private funds."

"Not only do the Jews claim payment of the sums they have loaned, but they claim it before any moneys are disbursed for an expedition which they suppose may last long. You know that several, taking advantage of the distress of Venice, have found means of being ennobled, and of having their names inscribed in the Golden Book."

"A most infamous traffic; I know it."

"To-morrow, the wealthiest among them have agreed to wait, in a body, upon the senate, and to reveal the state of the treasury."

"What will they say?"

"They will say, your highness, that the treasury of Saint Mark has already been pawned or coined by you, without the knowledge even of its keeper, the procurator of Saint Mark's Church; they will say, what is known but to you and myself," said Ottale, lowering his tone, "that false jewels have been substituted for the true ones; they will show this in the face of the sun, before the ambassadors of all powers, gratified on that day to witness the humiliations of Venice."

"Then wo to them, Ottale! for I will arm my patricians against them, and bind, hands and feet, those who dare to glory in our shame."

"The patricians will turn in their favour, for they are all against you. They need the Jews; and those insolvent noblemen are oftener at the Ghetto than at church."

"But the people—the army?"

"The sailors have declared that they will not sail upon this expedition unless their wages are paid. The nobles will lock themselves up within their palaces; the workmen of the navy-yard will rise in arms by daybreak; and the ambassador from Tunis, in spite of the haughty words you made use of to him the other night, has raised his head, and now receives the visits of senators. A deputation from the sages of the council has been addressed to him this very day, begging him to come to terms."

"Terms with pirates! Such humiliation in the presence of ambassadors from all parts of the world! Have, then, those degraded compounds of vice and meanness forgotten the rupture of treaties, the seizure of our merchandise, the insults offered to our flag, the shameful tributes imposed upon Venice?"

"Highness, the day has come: Venice will, must die."

"Venice shall not die while I live! Venice, Ottale, needs a war; to rouse her from her lethargy, we must have another Lepante."

"Are you a god, to save Venice? Have not cities, like men, their fate recorded above? You are doubtless great, sincere, generous; but can you save those who desire perdition, give glory to those who seek shame?"

"So, then, there is no more hope; no gold in the treasury, no resource left. To-morrow the cannon of the forts shall thunder—to-morrow the whole city shall hasten to the ports! Day of wo and shame! It were enough to make me envy the fate of Foscari, who died while listening to the sound of the bells that tolled for his deposition; it were enough to make me ask that a stone, cast by the hand of a woman, might crush me to earth, like Tiepolo!"

"You are no alchemist, signor. You may wed the sea by casting your ring into it; you may wield that shadow of a sceptre still allowed you in Venice; but you cannot make plenty replace misery, nor cause the coffers of the state to be replenished when, alas! they are exhausted."

"Ottale," resumed the doge, "have you, then, knocked at the door of every Jew in Venice?"

"I know them all; I know their ability, and I know also what they dare."

"But you do not know that I might to-night set fire to the Ghetto; the gates are closed already. Fire would rid me of that vile herd whom former doges had banished far from Venice, and with whom they never even condescended to speak, in dread of contamination."

"Highness," rejoined Ottale, with composed grief, "you forget that I am a Jew, and that I have left the Ghetto of Rome for the Ghetto of Venice."

"Yes," answered the doge; "you remind me of a tie so dear that I could never wish to offend you. I honour and esteem you. You received from me a trust, and you have guarded it faithfully. Ottale, dear Ottale, I wear a double character: one, scrupulously jealous of the honour of his country, severe to himself, and walking as if in the sight of the Eternal Judge—that is the doge; the other, miserable and anxious, ever suffering from wounds which your eye alone discovers—that latter is the lover of Safia."

"Oh! you remind me of it. To-night I dreamed of Ranuzzi."

On hearing that fatal name the doge shuddered. It seemed as if the spirit of death, in its terrible implacability, had already laid its hand upon him.

He stood erect, motionless, scarcely breathing, when three knocks were heard at the landgate of the dwelling. Ottale, with a shudder, arose and hastened to unfasten the door.

CHAPTER XX.

THE MAGICIAN.

"David Gruss!" exclaimed the Jew, looking at the new-comer.

The doge then beheld a man apparently sixty years of age; his dress sufficiently denoted the class to which he belonged: he wore the distinctive patch of yellow linen over his Israelitish robe, the red hat, and long beard. A pair of piercing gray eyes, sunk deep in their orbits, imparted to his physiognomy a strange expression of cunning and subtlety; his person was bent, like that of a usurer who stoops all day over his counter; his leather sandals were soiled and worn.

"David Gruss!" repeated Ottale, fixing upon him a glance of mingled fear, interest, and astonishment.

"Yes, David Gruss, your former friend," answered the new visiter. "I come to see you first, and then this gentleman," said he, pointing to the doge, who had had time to resume his mask prior to his entrance.

"What is there in common between us?" inquired Alessandro, in a tone of mingled contempt and suspicion.

"Many things, Signor Mask."

"Speak, then, I listen: time is precious."

"It is; and I mean to use it so as to escape the reproach of wasting it. You have visited my co-religionist here for the purpose of finding money, have you not?" he continued, fixing the doge with his piercing, deceitful eye.

"True; what next?"

"Next, signor, you are about to return as you came, without your errand. Distressing, is it not?"

"Abominably so for a gamester, as I am," said the doge, endeavouring to lead the inquirer upon a false track.

"The game *you* play is a dangerous one."

"I think it is."

"Doubtless; you play that of a prince."

"Do you know me?"

"You visit the Casino and the ridotti of Venice, I am certain."

"Well?"

"What would you give an honest man who could enable you to find gold?"

"My word; and that were worth the gold."

"No doubt; but would you swear never to reveal his secret?"

"I swear. Proceed."

"Well, signor, I can give you gold.'

"You are an alchemist?" said Alessandro, doubtfully.

"Wrong, your excellency; alchemists are madmen. I know you are hard to persuade, but I will give you convincing proof. Ottale, do you remember Palermo?"

"I remember David Gruss, a man who had more skill than all the physicians in the world; a man who, finding me dangerously ill, came to my aid when not only the most esteemed physicians, but the very quacks had given me over. He sat by my pillow, locked up the house, and, without ever leaving me, acted as my physician. In each crisis of pain he fixed on me a wondrous glance; his brow paled; he would slowly extend his hand over me, and I soon fell into a heavy, unaccountable sleep: his mere approach dispelled all pain; and when his eyes fixed upon mine—as yours do at this moment, David Gruss—I felt, even in my sleep, that my lips moved unbidden, as if I were about to speak."

"These are facts to confound and perplex the imagination of men," murmured Alessandro. "Did that physician cure you?"

"He saved me from certain death," resumed Ottale: "that wondrous sleep alone has survived my illness. It terrifies me sometimes when it absorbs my senses. Ziana is alone aware of this."

"What mysterious influence belongs, then, to that man?" asked the doge, immersed in thought, and as if attempting to fathom the depth of a new order of things suddenly revealed to his mind.

"Inquire of himself," answered Ottale; "that man is now in your presence; he is David Gruss."

David Gruss nodded assent.

"What, sir, do you mean to accomplish here by the aid of that power whose secret is your own?"

The Jew drew near the doge, and whispered. As he spoke, he kept his eyes fixed on Ottale, who, evidently under some resistless power, had sunk upon his chair; David Gruss soon approached the old man, and passed his hand over him; from his eyes, constantly bent upon Ottale, were emitted bright magnetic sparks that glowed like the flashes of the diamond; their liquid, absorbing flame startled even the doge, who leaned against the pillar with half-suppressed breath, as a man who expects to witness some scene that he cannot completely realize.

"Are you ready?" inquired Gruss.

"Yes, master, I am," answered the old man, in a feeble voice.

"To obey me, Ottale?"

"To obey you," reiterated he, letting fall his arms.

"Ottale," resumed David Gruss, "you are the state broker of the public Mint, and keeper also?"

"I am."

"Ottale, is there no deposite of money at the Zecca?"

"None."

"But here?"

"Here?" uttered Ottale, in a trembling voice. An icy shudder seemed to thrill through his aged limbs, big drops of perspiration burst upon his brow.

"Here?" reiterated David Gruss.

"Master, master!" stammered the old man. "I may not—I pray you, do not—cause me not to—"

He appeared struggling convulsively against the will of David Gruss.

"Ottale, I pray, and if necessary, I command you, tell me whether this house contains a deposite of money, a treasure; do you understand?"

"A deposite? yes."

"In silver? in gold?"

"Gold; but," resumed the old man, rising, "that deposite, that gold is—"

"*I* know what you know. Silence! where is the gold—the deposite?" said David Gruss, forcing him back to his seat.

"Master, I beseech you—"

"Obey! Where is the gold? Answer!"

"There, master, beneath that wall," resumed Ottale, pointing to the pillar against which the doge was leaning. "It is the fourth square beyond the pillar; but—"

"Silence! Sleep! I will it! Sleep, Ottale, sleep!"

David Gruss then, placing both hands on the bald forehead of the Jew, soon absorbed him in the dim heaviness of that slumber so resembling death. After a few spasmodic palpitations, the old man soon sunk into deep repose.

"To think," murmured David Gruss, contemplating the slumberer, "that this soul is now beyond the control of its conscience—its Creator! that my will is now the soul of that mass of clay! All around is silent! no gondola disturbs the calm of the sleepy waves! the heavens are veiled in dark clouds! Come, noble signor," said he to the doge, "assist me, and wo befall any intruder!"

David Gruss drew a poniard, till then concealed beneath his robe. Alessandro did the like from beneath his *cahuta.*

"The fourth square beyond the pillar said Ottale? Well, here is the spot! let us make haste!"

The doge listened like a man bewildered.

"You do not doff your mask, excellency? Why?"

No answer was returned.

"Have no false shame. I know you!"

"You?"

"Certainly! I saw you pass, this morning, the quay of Maria Rosa. You purchased some pomegranate flowers at a flower-stand."

"Perchance you are a spy in the employ of the Ten?"

"You wrong me; I am but a poor Jew. You love gold, so do I. There is deposited here a treasure; we will share it. I have your word—enough! the Doge Alessandro would not deal falsely."

"Well," said Alessandro, resolutely tearing off his mask, "note my features, David Gruss, and imprint them well upon your memory. Upon the first word—the first sign or indication of treachery that escapes you, I will deal with you as with a prevaricating Jew. You shall be led through the city by the executioner, and expire beneath his lash between the pillars of Saint Mark and Saint Theodore."

"Thanks, your highness! you will have no occasion to treat Venice to so pleasurable a scene. I will be silent as yourself; our common interest compels us. By Heaven! I stand as much in need of sequins as yourself; for I play under mask; and, at the casinoes of Padua and Venice, I am accounted a patrician, thanks to that mask allowed to players. The other day I won five hundred sequins in four deals; but subsequently I lost ten thousand in partnership with a friend. Therefore I want gold as much as you; although it is not true, as you would wish me to suppose, that you play at the Ridotti."

"For what purpose, then, think you, I need this gold?"

"For a noble, elevated purpose, altogether worthy of your high spirit," rejoined the Jew, with a smile, the irony of which escaped Alessandro unnoticed. "You wish the fleet to sail to-morrow, with its streaming pennons, and the patriarch at the head. Upon the decks of that fleet the power and pride of Venice will throng, and you, prince, from the Bucentaur, will bid the Adriatic, your spouse, spread her submissive waters for the passage of your high-spirited battalions; you, with the admiral, will accompany them, all the vessels steering towards Tunis; and you will leave them but at the Lido point. When you ascended the throne, everything revealed to you the decay of the republic; the public mind is in a state of fermentation, and rife for sedition; Bergama, Brescia, Salo, and Cremona, are in intelligence with Milano. Your game, your highness, is to punish, crush, conquer. Mine is that of a wretch panting with the thirst of gold—pressed by avaricious employers; for, at the Casino, I am the representative of a large number of patricians! To our task, then, my master, and let us pursue our object! The Jew is asleep—he will never speak! Unfasten your lamp, and let us examine the spot indicated by Ottale!"

Alessandro obeyed mechanically. He felt as if addressed by some fiend; he knelt beside David Gruss, and proceeded to lift the flag.

This part of the room was covered by a large mat, which they drew aside. Alessandro chanced to break his poniard. David Gruss then sneered, and shrugged his shoulders, saying, in a half-contemptuous tone,

"After all, your highness, this is not your habitual trade. Come, take that crowbar near the laboratory, and lift this flag; it is as heavy as a tomb-stone."

The flag-stone soon yielded to their joint efforts. They perceived two large iron coffers, sealed with the threefold seals of the Inquisition, the patriarch, and the doge. Rust had covered the locks, and there was no key.

David Gruss then produced a glass vial of middling size, containing a reddish fluid. He rubbed it over the locks, and, with a screw, forced out the nails. Then seizing the crowbar, he applied it, with Herculean strength, to one of the coffers, whose lid he succeeded in forcing open. A heap of ducats, as bright as if just coined at the Zecca, struck their view. David Gruss plunged his arms among them like a diver.

The doge, despite all his efforts, had not yet succeeded in opening his coffer. David Gruss soon overcame its resistance, and both uttered a cry of admiration at the sight of a quantity of gold far superior in value to the contents of the other coffer.

"Give unto Cæsar that which is Cæsar's. I give you the best share, your excellency; I shall have enough with this to hold the bank the day after to-morrow, and to satisfy my partners' demands. Now listen: I caused four Armenians to row beneath this window one of those flat boats on which wares are transported to Fusina. With the aid of a rope, we may let these coffers slide down; I will take you to the point of Fusina, opposite which the fleet is to pass to-morrow; there dwells the Jew Sperone, a man, I think, entirely devoted to you; you may leave the coffer with him. I will then carry you in the boat to the first marble steps whereon you choose to alight, and then we part."

"Venice! it is for thee!" murmured the doge, bending from the window illumined by the first dawn of day. "Come, let us go, I will follow." David Gruss had replaced the stone, and recovered it with its mat, after lifting from it the two coffers. Then, from the window that looked on the canal, he hailed the gondoliers. They threw up a rope; the Jew skilfully let the two coffers slide down to the bark. Meanwhile the doge kept his eyes riveted on the aged slumberer, with an air of religious dread.

"Yes! now rest in peace, poor old man; and awake to-morrow unconscious of what has been done to-night. Oh! for thy blissful ignorance. Hasten," said he, "day will soon dawn upon Venice. Venice, my fair, my well-beloved city, awake now without fear; thou art saved! One more day of splendour for thee!"

Alessandro and his companion then directed their steps to the gate leading to the canal, when suddenly a young man, wrapped in a black cloak, entered abruptly through the door of the passage upon which Ziana's apartment opened. A female followed him, covered with one of those veils called, in Venice, zindaletta. The doge and David Gruss had barely time to extinguish the light and hide themselves behind the pillar.

"Taddeo, what room is this?" inquired the countess.

"The counting-room of Ottale," said Taddeo, groping his way in the dark.

"Where is Ziana's apartment?"

"It opens upon the passage, madam; the Jew and his daughter doubtlessly have both retired."

"But there is a gondola moored beneath the Jew's window, at that little door that seems to communicate with his dwelling; a flat, uncovered gondola, like those of the Albanians. He is here."

"Madam, the key has been taken from Ziana's door."

"Taddeo, you must either open or burst that door."

"Let us fly, signor; let us fly!" whispered David Gruss to Alessandro.

"I cannot mistake, it is the voice of the countess; what can cause her visit hither?"

"Taddeo," said Safia, "burst open that door; there is a man concealed there, the lover of thy betrothed!"

"The lover of Ziana! can you think so, madam? Infamy!" The young man seized a stool and struck vigorously against the door.

"Who knocks?" cried Ziana, in a trembling voice.

At this instant the sound of oars was heard upon the water. David Gruss and the doge had fled through the open window.

"Escaped!" exclaimed the countess, with frantic rage, "escaped! see yonder bark that glides away."

"Escaped!" reiterated Taddeo.

"I will be revenged!" exclaimed Safia, with a suppressed sigh as she picked from the floor something against which she had stumbled in the dark. It was a poniard with an agate handle. "Yes, I will be revenged; follow me; day is breaking, we can easily find a gondola." And forcing Taddeo before her, she rapidly descended the steps that led to the gate opening upon the canal.

CHAPTER XXI.

THE FLEET.

The following day was one of great excitement in Venice. The throng of spectators was incredible.

A vast procession of barks, shallops, and gondolas covered the waters of the port, situated opposite the lesser Place of Saint Mark.

Those who have admired the paintings of Canaletti, of Tiepolo, or the engravings of Petrus Longhi, representing the ceremonies of the day of the Accession, or of the Bucentaur, can alone conceive an idea of the spectacle we shall endeavour to describe.

First, the ushers, called *commandadori*, opened the march upon the quay of the Sclavonians. Eight of them bore a like number of banners, two white, two red, two blue, and two purple. They were followed by the rest of the *commandadori*, the last six bearing each a large silver trumpet similar to those formerly used upon the vessels of the republic.

Next followed six fifers in red uniform, and the squires of the doge, the latter being attended by his seneschal on the right, and the capitan grande on the left.

The clerk of the private chapel of his highness came next, alone, preceding the master of ceremonies of the Church of Saint Mark, attended by six canons in golden vestments. These were followed by two officers, called *Gastaldi ducali*, and four secretaries of the senate, behind whom followed the doge's own secretary, bearing a silver candelabra, with extinguished tapers.

After these, most conspicuous were the two chancellors of his serene highness, the grand chancellor, and then the doge, escorted by all the foreign ambassadors. Near the doge were two squires, bearing the chair and the cushion of gold cloth. A third followed, holding over the prince the golden fringed umbrella.

One noble and one patrician closed the private escort of Alessandro, who wore the state sword in its velvet scabbard.

One of the magistrates of the *Proprio*, accompanied by the senior counsellor, headed the second division of the procession.

This consisted of counsellors in full dress, the president of the Criminal Quarantia, those of the other quarantias, the avogadores, the president of the Council of Ten, the censors of the Broglio, the patrons of the arsenal, the consulta, the *pregadio*, or senate, and the procurators of Saint Mark, two by two.

This noble procession, in gala robes, descended in most admirable order the Giant's Staircase, and embarked upon their respective gondolas and galiots, decked with flags and banners; a few armed barks were their escort. The oarsmen wore livery, consisting of the Albanian cap, with gold tassels, heavily-embroidered vest and jacket. A small number of persons, who composed the more immediate escort of the doge, hastened to the bridge, forty feet in length, which had been erected for the occasion, leading from the quay to the galley of the proveditor or naval admiral, who stood on deck, surrounded by his officers, in full uniform. Each gondola, with its golden ornaments, and freight of magnificent costumes, glittered in the sun; the skiffs of the povejotes and fishermen of Saint Nicholas stemmed in every direction the waves of the great canal. The spectator could at one glance behold the magnificent, gilded barks of the ambassadors, the painted cloths of the Muranese, and the virgins adorning their prows, decked with flowers and ribands.

These various barks passed in majestic array along the grand canal, escorted by a number of vessels of war, with streaming banners and pennons, awaiting but the admiral's signal to fire the salute.

The *Furta* of Saint Mark gave the first salute, which was responded to by the galiots and all the other vessels.

The Patriarch of Venice stood on the deck of the main galley, accompanied by the canons of Castello and those of his own court; he was decked with the patriarchal robes and mitre, as for the ceremony of the Bucentaur. He blessed the sea, kissed the cross, and withdrew.

The fleet was ordered to await the return of the doge near Saint Nicholas of the Lido.

Upon a bench, over which was spread a cloth of velvet, gemmed with pearls, a man, dressed in the French style, seated beside a masked lady, looked on the *funcion* with eager curiosity. The sides of the gondola were richly carved and gilded; its panels were filled with resplendent mirrors; the upholstery, silk and silver.

"Really, countess, there is nothing so elegant, and so charming and soft as your conveyance. Compare with this our hack-carriages and sedans of the Place Royale; they are vulgar in the lowest degree. The duchesses of our court would envy you so delightful a mode of reclining."

Safia made no answer to the Marquis de Saluces; her attention was absorbed upon the galley of the Proveditor-general of the Sea, whereon the doge exhibited himself to the gaze of the astounded multitude. Never, perhaps, had Alessandro looked more noble, or more worthy of admiration, than on that day; never had the radiant sovereignty of his mien beamed with loftier beauty.

In spite of the unconquerable disorder of her mind, the pangs of jealousy, the countess could not but acknowledge the infinite fascination which the doge exercised over every pulsation of her heart; she remembered him, seated under the gilded awnings of the Bucentaur, the day when he threw his ducal ring into the sea, a young and handsome senator, still astonished at his sudden elevation, and at the clamorous greetings of a whole nation. And now, as she gazed at his severe features, whose harsh, imperial beauty contrasted with the effeminate looks of other Venetian noblemen, it seemed as if the galley that bore Alessandro was the pedestal of some heroic statue.

"And yet," said the countess to herself, "but a night since he deceived me—falsely deceived me—and for that Jewess! That poniard I found, whose sheath I discovered in his room, was his. It was rumoured yesterday that the populace would rebel, as the sea-foam that lashes the rocks of Fusina. Alas! my heart alone rebels! To have loved so fondly, and be deceived! Yes, I loved him; I love him still. With one word I might have revenge, and recall him, repentant, at my feet. No! I must know from his mistress herself what all-powerful charm she possesses, that she dare rival her sovereign! I have ordered Azael to bid her come; she will come."

Safia, with Asiatic indolence, had reclined beneath the shade of the parasol held over her by her negro; the rich carpets of the gondola dipped into the waves; the oarsmen already began to feel fatigued; the distant city appeared but a confused mass of roofs and steeples, when the Marquis de Saluces abruptly interrupted the course of her meditations by requesting her to tell him what had been the motive of her being, at three o'clock in the morning, upon the canal of Saint Jeremiah.

"You appeared, madam, so strangely agitated, and the cavalier in the black cloak escorting you evinced so little of the expansive in his disposition, that I was compelled to adjourn all inquiries until this morning. Countess, such adventures happen but to myself. I had left you with a promise of watching for your interest; for, on due reflection, I am little else than your spy. A barcarole on the Piazzetta was ridiculous enough to ask me eight sequins for a night gondola. 'Go to the devil,' said I to him; 'for such a price I might sup with a nymph of the opera at Paris.' Thereupon I was walking backward and forward, sad and thoughtful, under the arcades of the Procuratias, when a mask, rather elegantly attired in a pink cahuta, threw his arms around my neck, with a vigorous hug, exclaiming,

"'Parbleu! I am delighted to see you, dear marquis.'

"'Whom have I the honour of addressing?' inquired I, with most justifiable suspiciousness.

"'One of the best friends of your uncle, M. de Sartines, my dear Saluces; but fear not, I come not to this city of pleasures to teaze you with advice and moral lectures. No, dear marquis, I know your disposition too well; you are the hero of fêtes, play, and suppers! You have no idea how lonely your absence has left us! The opera, without your presence, is a bore; the theatre has become positively insufferable since you are no more to be seen seated at the side of the stage, upon the *banc des marquis*, both hands in your vest pockets, or leaning like a Cyrus by the orchestra.'

"'You are very polite,' said I; 'but may I request your name?'

"'Certainly, my dear fellow: I am the Chevalier de la Plumardiere. No scholar, true, but well versed in almost everything. I have one of those faces which women love, and husbands abhor; besides, so very lucky at play! But come, let us sup. They have not the worst Sillery in the world at the Aquila! here is the bill of fare; order yourself, and I shall approve.'

"I was astonished at the singular manner of this person. I noticed he had a beautiful, most aristocratic hand. You had dismissed me so cruelly, fair countess, that the bacchanalian consolations offered me by my new friend could not have come more opportunely. I yielded to the allurements of his proposal; his conversation I found most agreeable, the supper unexceptionable, and, sooth to say, I forgot the Ghetto and my promises in the company of the Chevalier de la Plumardiere."

"'I beg your pardon,' he remarked, as he poured out for me a fifteenth glass of Malmsey; 'I do not treat you to anything very exquisite; but I fancy we shall be able to offer you something quite superior to-morrow at the play at the Casino.'

"'There is to be play, then?' I inquired.

"'Play and masks yet for a fortnight. After that time, Venice again sinks into darkness and obscurity; then, if you like, we will start for Vienna.'

"'Shall you play to-morrow?'

"'Certainly; and if you like, you shall be one of our bankers. We have secured high names already: Moncenigo, Croce, several Poles, and a few Swedes, who roll in gold.'

"'Bravo!' replied I; 'I will trust you with my funds.'

"'Nobody can deal like me, as you will see!'

"I was delighted with my new friend, and regretted parting with him. It was near daybreak, and on the Piazzetta I met the same gondolier whose prices were so extravagant. After vainly waiting to procure a passenger, his bad luck had made him quite tractable. He approached me, cap in hand, and asked if I still wished to use his gondola.

"The sight of this man at once cleared my head from the fumes of our revel; I remembered my promise, and, throwing myself headlong into his gondóla, I bade him cruise along the Jews' quarter, the Ghetto.

"'Your honour is aware,' he exclaimed, 'that the Ghetto is an accursed spot, where the fiend of the lagunes, whom we call Orco, delights in laying his snares. Sometimes he assumes the appearance of a beautiful dark-eyed girl, and, seating himself in that shape upon the marble steps of some landing, he inveigles you into the accursed cave of some son of Israel, who then compels you to sign a usurious bond to him. Again, assuming the form of a cavalier drowning, that devilish Orco drowns his rescuer. One day, an uncle of mine—a brave Nicolotte he was—passing, at three in the morning, through the Ghetto, saw a beggar who, with his staff, attempted to stop up the street. My uncle at first thought him a thief or a drunken man, but was soon undeceived by a strong smell of brimstone, that almost knocked him down. "Wretch!" cried the man, "were you not one of those who witnessed the execution of the Jew, Roboam Ber, who rode hind foremost through the city upon an ass? Roboam Ber was my friend, and he left a legacy for you: here it is." My uncle then felt blows rain thick and heavy on his shoulders; and all at once the beggar took the shape of the wandering Jew, and followed him to the limits of the Ghetto, where he left him half dead.'

"These stories of my gondolier were little calculated to cheer me. Yielding to that heavy, peaceful sleep which Cyprus wine habitually induces, I sunk upon the cushions of the bark, when suddenly I heard cries, and soon after I perceived a white shadow—a woman.

"'The Orco!' cried my gondolier.

"I examined the object of his superstitious

fear for some time: it was a woman veiled, escorted by a cavalier in a black cloak. You know the rest. I recognised you by your voice, and ordered my barcarole to row near to you. Your companion remained silent while you pressed my gondolier to take the direction of Fusina, towards which an open bark was making then all speed. Who it was you could be following thus I know not; but my fool of a gondolier, fully satisfied that you were the Orco, refused to row in that direction. Will you now explain to me the mystery of that adventure?"

"How can I explain shadows that escape even myself? What your gondolier related of the Ghetto is not altogether unlikely: unaccountable things happen there, and henceforward I shall no longer require your services to discover them."

"Meaning to say, I presume, that you are on the track of some infidelity? After all, princes are no better than other men; the gallantries of Louis XV. may have spread their contagion as far as Venice. Nevertheless, I maintain that it is here difficult to discern the truth! so many masks, intrigues, canals! a man loses his way, 'pon honour. The doge has a handsome person: observe only how the ladies of the seignory regard him."

Several shallops with gilded panels, and filled with patrician ladies, were cruising lightly around the ducal galley. The procession was nearing Fusina, where the squadron was in sight, skimming the blue waves of the Adriatic. It was an imposing sight to see those decks thronged with soldiers, waving the standards conquered from the Turks. The workmen of the docks, called *squeri*, all wore the red and yellow jacket; the cannon of the forts thundered over the sea, and the bells of the city tolled responsive. The doge, wearing upon his head the *como*, spoke and waved his hand encouragingly to each officer and workman of the Tana. Venice rose in the distance, with her cloud-capped towers, her magic palaces, and balconies thronged with spectators.

By express order of the doge, it had been published throughout the city, during the morning, that wages would be paid in advance. Yet, although the prince seemed perfectly composed, strange rumours were already circulating.

"It seems the doge intends to pay all from his private funds," said Moncenigo to Trevisani, with a skeptic tone.

"Remark how his eyes are riveted upon the house of the Jew Sperone. Can it be possible such a wretch has deceived the doge? Notice how haughty an air the ambassadors assume; they doubt us, and would be as astonished as ourselves at such a result."

"Silence, Trevisani! See those Greek slaves bearing a large iron coffer upon deck! The patriarch opens the lid. Heaven forgive me! His hand now distributes a harvest of sequins among the soldiers and sailors."

"You speak truth. How they rush upon the gold!"

"In all this the Jews will be robbed, you will see. For my part, I should not complain: it would be one way to put me even with them."

A herald wearing the ducal livery ascended the deck of the vessel; he motioned the two bearers of silver trumpets to sound a blast.

"Good! Moncenigo, a decree. The herald unfolds a parchment received from the doge."

The herald read the decree, as follows:

"The Jews of Venice have dared attempt sedition. The most guilty of them are known to us. Justice will be dealt upon them this day. The Republic of Venice has resolved to punish their insolence as she has that of the powers of Barbary. The Criminal Quarantia met this morning, and sentenced two thousand Jews to banishment; and now, victory and fame to the winged lion of Saint Mark. The fleet is weighing anchor, but has received orders to admit all voluntee s."

A large number of sailors and workmen responded to this appeal, while a shallop manned by forty oarsmen approached to carry back the doge. The cries of joy and applause of the assembled multitude recalled a ray of pride and happiness to the brow of Alessandro. As he passed the vessel of the volunteers, he started suddenly. A young man was clinging to the rigging, whom the captain seemed disposed to drive away, probably because he wore neither the sailor's vest nor uniform.

"For pity's sake, admit me," cried he, "or I will let myself fall into the sea."

He was lifted in, and dashed away a tear as he reached the deck. The doge made a motion, but the vessel was already far behind, and carried with her Taddeo.

CHAPTER XXII.

PLAY AT VENICE.

On the night of that day, and after a sumptuous repast given by the doge to the ambassadors, the seignory, and nobles who had attended the ceremony, an immense multitude thronged the avenues of the Casino, which was to open at twelve.

The exterior was brilliantly illuminated. The Sclavonian detachment were on guard at the door, and kept back the Nicolottes and the Castellans who were striving to sell refreshments around.

In a hall hung exclusively with leather of Cordova, and every entrance of which was closed with brocade curtains, was the orchestra, in a sort of gallery, suspended at one end, to which two circular staircases of fine Carrara marble led, the balusters terminating in four magnificently carved lions, bearing between their paws the Book and the sword.

Two hundred stands for torches, and as many chandeliers of stained glass of Murano, shed an immense stream of light over this apartment, showing, with finer effect, several paintings of Tiepolo that hung over the doors.

Before reaching this hall, denominated the play-room, there were three galleries less splendidly decorated, but in which several negroes were arranging salvers with fruit, refreshments, and viands, while other servants, and several handsome female store-keepers of the Rialto, attracted the attention of customers to their stands filled with glass ware, enamel chains, flowers, ribands, and embroidered lace.

Numerous tables were disposed around the hall, at one of which each noble who intended to keep a private bank was to sit close to the wall, surrounded with lights and packs of cards, a bag of gold pieces, and one of silver ducats, ready to stand against all comers, whether masked or Venetian gentlemen. Besides these, directly beneath the orchestra was an immense table covered with cloth, around which chairs were placed, and whereon lay several packs of cards, tied with riband, as customary at faro.

Faro and bassette were then the only games in vogue. The French had lately introduced faro en revanche for the introduction of bassette into France, under Louis XIV., by the Marquis Justiniani, ambassador from Venice.

As we have said before, the players were masked; but before entering they were compelled to deliver checks to door-keepers wearing perukes.

Behind a grating similar to that in a broker's office, the keeper of the Mint was to sit, who alone had the key.

The dial of the clock pointed to half past eleven when Ottale, accompanied by his daughter, made his way through the crowd pressing around the doors of the Casino, in order to repair to his habitual post.

The old man had been unable to witness the departure of the fleet, owing, first, to the painful torpor that he had felt during a part of the day, and subsequently to a note received from the doge, in which Alessandro, while intimating the resolution passed by the council in the morning relative to those of his creed, assured him, at the same time, that he was safe both in person and office. The evident protection he had always granted to the old man was, as well as his friendship, a guarantee for his security.

However surprised at receiving such a missive, he was still more so when Ziana related to him what strange sounds she had heard during the night: hurried steps and confused voices in the lower room. Taddeo had been there, threatening to break open the door; and when, with justifiable terror, she called aloud to her father, she had received no answer. At last, half dead with fear, but finding, in her anguish, a supernatural courage, she had succeeded in forcing open her door. She had then reached her father only to find him in a profound sleep, and yet the window on the canal was open.

She pressed Ottale with anxious inquiries; but he knew nothing, had heard nothing. All was in order in the laboratory, the plate deposited there, the tools, the scales of exchange; nothing was missing. There was nothing to induce a belief that David Gruss had introduced himself into the house with felonious intent. Besides, the note from the doge set all fears at rest on that score.

After vainly interrogating the neighbours, unable to obtain any clew to satisfy her painful uncertainty, she had determined, as a last extremity, to apply to Taddeo himself, were he even to upbraid and reproach.

The poor girl proceeded towards the arsenal; but, besides the inevitable confusion of that day, the admiral had given orders that no one should be admitted; she was then compelled to wait outside clinging to its grated enclosure, in the midst of a crowd of women and superannuated sailors, who were waiting, like herself, the hour at which the workmen came out.

But Taddeo, the sculptor of the arsenal, did not come; he was nowhere to be seen. Ziana was weeping, when she met a Bohemian woman.

The grief of the Jew's daughter contrasted with the hideous joy of the frightful old beggar, who, leaning over the parapet of a neighbouring bridge, thus spoke to one of her cronies, at the same time showing two bright gold sequins that glittered in the sunlight.

"Poor fellow! he gave me this for telling him the truth; I do not know his name, but he sometimes visited me at Santa Maria Maggiòre. He was a singular young man, who never smiled, even when luck favoured him at cards. 'I have no faith in my star,' he would say. Well, this morning he came to me, with a cloak and sword. 'Take these,' said he, 'sell them, and here are two gold sequins besides; I want no more money: I am betrayed, deceived by a Jewess of the Ghetto! All I want is to know whether I shall ever return to Venice; for, you see, I enlist: I am to sail to-day in the fleet bound for Tunis.'

"I looked at him sadly," continued the Bohemian, "for we sorcerers guess at all; I had imagined what he most wished, so I answered, 'I know not your fair one's name; but I see her meeting you a month hence at the Sclavonians' quay! You will then forgive, and no more upbraid; for you will then return as powerful and proud as is now the doge himself!'

"Thereupon, my darling, the young man went off like an arrow; he is now, no doubt, on board the fleet."

Upon hearing those words, Ziana uttered a fearful cry, and rushing towards the port, had barely time to see the far horizon dotted with the vessels of the fleet which carried off her betrothed.

"Why did you bring me hither, father?" she asked, as Ottale led her through the splendid rooms of the Casino, where as yet only domestics were to be seen arranging the tables. "How beautiful everything looks here! but how sad I am! I feel as one in a dream. On my return from the seashore I had not strength enough left to call upon the Countess d'Azola, who had sent for me. What can she have to say to me? Here comes the Signor Inquisitor, he may inform us."

Grimani, his mask in hand, was indeed then entering the play-room, and giving some orders to the overseers. He wore the *bahuta* and peruke.

The inquisitor seemed astonished at the paleness of the Jew's daughter. He had just left the banquet of the doge, and as soon as he perceived Ziana, said,

"The countess wishes to speak with you, signorita: follow me. You, Ottale, are aware the doge intends to honour the play with his presence; his serene highness has bidden me assure you of his continued favour. I take this opportunity to ask you to lend me two hundred pistoles."

"Signor Inquisitor," answered Ottale, hesitating.

"Well, well, I will pay you. I am partner

in the bank of Signor Arnolfo, who has just arrived from Florence. He is said to be immensely wealthy. I will lead Ziana to the countess, and be back with her immediately."

Ottale followed with his eyes the maiden, who had but to cross the square to reach the palace, so short was its distance from the Casino.

"I had perhaps better have left her at home," thought he; "but this show will raise her spirits. Really, the dear child occupies my mind more than my own danger; and yet, with their edicts against the Jews, how did the doge manage to obtain such subsidies?" continued he to himself, as he returned to his stand. "I will see him during this fête; and although his rank forbids him to wear the mask, he will, I hope, find means to speak with me!"

As Ottale disappeared, two masks came in, both wearing dominoes and three-cornered hats.

"*Parbleu!* my dear Chevalier de la Plumardière, I am very much obliged to you for procuring me admittance in advance to the scene of our future exploits. We are partners: fortune must smile upon us."

"Fortune is fickle," answered the chevalier; "but if she treats you as well as the Countess d'Azola, my dear marquis—"

"Hush, chevalier! Do you forget that we are no more at Paris, and that here walls have ears? True, the countess bestows upon me most indulgent glances. What would you? Good looks and smartness such as mine have their effect."

"You are a charming man," said the mask, in a jeering tone, which the marquis did not perceive. "By-the-by, we have to play against a gamester of eminent fame, one Arnolfo, of whom nobody had ever heard until, all at once, he secured enormous bets by correspondence with our strongest bankers."

"I hold him a dead man if he wins our funds. I have most extraordinary luck whenever I play abroad; yet, were I to play again at Paris, against that rascal, Cagliostro—how easily that fellow plucked me—"

"Have you heard nothing of him? It has been stated he was at Venice, with one Casanova."

"Yes, a libertine! a roué! I do not know him, but I am sure you think with me. The police here have caged them, but will not acknowledge it."

"Ah! you think that the police—"

"Certainly; I filed my complaint with Messer Grimani. By-the-by, chevalier, shall we not take off our masks? I am half smothered with this piece of pasteboard, and that domino, which you adorn with the name of *bahuta!*"

"You may do as you like, marquis. As to myself, I intend to preserve this incognito: an affair of some celebrity, a duel in which I was unfortunately involved in Padua—"

"Indeed! With whom?"

"A Milanese officer, *morbleu!* who spoke ill of France. Some day I will tell you all particulars; but just now we had better retain our places; the rush will soon begin."

Twelve had, indeed, just struck, and the marquis had to take refuge prudently against the wall to avoid the tumultuous entrance of a throng of masks, who only stopped at the door to deliver their cross-marked checks. Amid that crowd, all dressed alike, there were some *gentil donne*, with their muffs, their black velvet masks, arms and shoulders bare. Some of these held their ear-rings for fear of being robbed; others played with their fans on account of the excessive heat. Meanwhile the heralds of the Casino announced, with loud voices, that the play had begun.

When the crowd had disposed themselves around the table, the marquis was enabled to see several valets hurriedly carrying coffers bearing the name of Signor Arnolfo. They were followed by more bearers, who protected the coffers until the arrival of that player, whose place was retained for him at the faro-table.

At this moment, also, the Chevalier de la Plumardière was surrounded by several gentlemen, some masked, others not. Among these were Moncenigo, Trevisani, and other nobles. All seemed to be acquainted with the Chevalier de la Plumardière, and to treat him with great familiarity.

"So we are in time, all of us, gentlemen, even with the clock! The circumstance of war in the morning; evening, play. The Marquis de Saluces holds our bank, does he not, dear chevalier?"

"I have that honour, gentlemen, and will hold it against all comers. But pray, what are we waiting for now?"

"The arrival of one Signor Arnolfo. Some think that name disguises Teodoro Cornaro, banished by the former doge for his excessive debts. You know, Trevisani, that Teodoro Cornaro, to whom you are still indebted."

Moncenigo had scarcely concluded when a domino, habited like the rest, and masked with a wide piece of pasteboard that concealed even the lower part of the face, arrived, somewhat intoxicated, and fanning himself with a handkerchief, at the spot where the valets guarded the coffers. He whispered to them, and quietly sat down. His wig was so redolent of Cyprus-perfumed powder, his wristbands were so long, his sword-knots so eccentric and unfashionable, that he looked as if just emerged from some obscure Venetian province, whither he had retired to economize.

"Permit us, signor," said Trevisani, approaching the unknown, "to salute in your person one of the most celebrated of all players."

"The most magnificent," added Moncenigo.

"The most rare," chimed in the Chevalier de la Plumardière.

"The most dangerous," interposed the marquis, glancing at the enormous quantities of sequins that were piled in pyramids before the mask.

The new comer, without answering, waited until his opponents had seated themselves, and then said,

"The game is made!"

At this solemn moment the hangings covering the two doors facing each other at either extremity of the hall were drawn aside; one gave passage to the doge, escorted by the seignory; the other to the Countess d'Azola, leaning on the arm of Grimani.

CHAPTER XXIII.

THE MONEY OF THE GHETTO.

The countess was pale; she glanced at the splendour of the Casino; then, with several noble ladies in her suite, took her seat upon a velvet settee near the principal table.

It seemed as though some violent, passionate scene had exhausted Safia's strength. She had, indeed, had an interview with the Jew's daughter; but, too irritated to listen to her, too jealous to believe her, she had vainly used prayers and threats without obtaining from Ziana any other confession than that of a mystery which she herself could not unravel.

Then, from a protectress she became a rival. She disgracefully expelled Ziana from her presence; and the poor girl was at this moment hiding her tears in her father's bosom, who himself, trembling with rage and indignation, strove to console her.

"What do you say—expelled you!" continued he, pressing the maiden's hands within his own. "She, the Countess d'Azola! Oh Heaven! if I were at liberty to speak, to say to her—But what is your crime? of what does she accuse you?"

"She charges me, father, with having myself excited Taddeo's jealousy, in order that he might leave; when I desired nothing so much as to render him happy!"

"What next?"

"She pretends that the mysterious cavalier who visited us, and who is known to you, at least, was—oh, father! I blush to repeat it. She said he was my lover!"

Ziana covered her face with her hands, and wept so abundantly, that the poor Jew, himself moved to tears, promised to speak with the doge.

"Venice!" resumed he, "Venice! accursed, ungrateful city! How, my Ziana, can one believe in innocence here, when vice triumphs impudently in sight of all—when it has become a crime to give hospitality to a friend? Be comforted, however, I will see the doge—speak with him. He will restore to you the protection of the Countess d'Azola. Meanwhile forget her harsh words. She thought well of Taddeo, and on his leaving so abruptly—"

"Good father, you are my only refuge! Yes, Heaven is my witness that I am not guilty; that the feeling my heart entertained for our friendly visiter was that of compassion. If he still abides in Venice, let him bear witness for me. Taddeo, Taddeo!" continued the maiden, "will he ever return?"

Thus speaking, Ziana leaned her sweet face upon the old man's shoulder. The Jew had closed the door of his counting-room in order to be more at liberty, when several voices were heard at the grating.

"Jew, exchange these orders for me."

"Jew, here is a bill for a hundred ducats."

"Jew, I am the Marquis Malatesta."

"And I, the Procurator Steno."

Ottale, without opening, passed his withered hand under the gratings, and exchanged the bills that were presented to him.

"Ziana," resumed he, "time presses; I fear I may not be able to speak to-night to his highness the doge. Go to him, and excuse me with him. You know his kindness. I hope he does not intimidate you when he addresses you!"

"I will, father, I will; but instead of being, to-night, among the multitude of the Casino, I had rather—I confess it—be with the venerable ladies at the convent of the Celestia, praying for Taddeo."

Ziana came out, her mind agitated by tumultuous thoughts: the play was then at its height, but yet, as customary even in the ridotti of Venice, silence reigned profound.

Standing near the faro-table, Alessandro observed the players with visible indifference, when, all at once, the mask with the coffers excited his curiosity.

So rapidly did gold and silver accumulate under his hands, that it seemed as if he had a familiar devil in his service, and that he was in partnership with some invisible power. Owing to the strict rule of silence, not a word had passed between him and the Marquis de Saluces, who dealt, or the different nobles who played.

"D—n the domino!" muttered the marquis between his teeth. "Do you know, Chevalier de la Plumardière, that I begin to think I have a sorcerer to deal with?"

"Marquis de Saluces," answered the chevalier, "I am a seafaring man, accustomed to all sorts of weather; let Fortune be propitious or adverse, I contemplate with equal indifference the calm or the tempest: do likewise."

"Parbleu! chevalier, it is easy for you to say so; but when one has, like myself, six thousand sequins at stake—"

"Indeed, marquis, the coffers of that singular gamester seem always open, and always full. It seems as if some fairy power were engaged in emptying its contents upon our table only to fill it again with our spoils. I have seen many players in Venice, but this one surpasses them all; who can he be?"

The unknown mask, indeed, was playing like a man on whom the ambassadors of all the powers had had their eyes fixed: he said, "*Vado, knave loses, ten wins*," as coolly as an agent playing for a principal. True it was, that by his side several coffers were open, and while the croupiers raked the gold across the table, he carefully placed the remnant of his casket on the cloth.

"What sum does this stand for on the queen?" inquired the marquis, laying his hand on the player's casket.

"Twenty thousand ducats."

"Twenty thousand ducats!" exclaimed the players, agitated and astounded.

"Twenty thousand, gentlemen," rejoined the player, pursuing his victorious course of doubling on his losses.

"Signor Mask," said the doge to him, drawing him aside—before the croupier called the game—"one who plays as you do must be either Teodoro Cornaro, banished some time ago on account of his debts, or a certain man, named, I believe, David Gruss."

The doge awaited with visible emotion and growing anxiety the answer of the mysterious domino.

"Neither, your highness," he answered, taking his leave, and coolly resuming his seat.

Whether the unknown gamester's voice was smothered by his mask, or whether he purposely disguised it, the doge did not recognise him as his acquaintance of the preceding night.

"Some young fool from Padua," said he to himself, "hurrying to his ruin, or some insolvent noble, I suppose. Why the state Mint would scarcely satisfy his cupidity: he is playing for his house or his mistress; he plays without sign, without word, without accomplice; that is his secret! Have I not also a secret that weighs on me with tyrannical influence? Did not I last night accomplish the deed of a thief, of a ruffian? I robbed the Jew during his sleep, to bestow on Venice his deep-buried treasure: that treasure has been blessed by the patriarch, and distributed among my soldiers. Who was its owner I do not know; but Venice had an insult to avenge, Venice had to arm herself; gold was denied her, and I took it. But, once more, who is yonder strange being?" continued Alessandro, self-communing, and fixing his eye upon the mysterious gamester. "Come, then, my idle senators, play, play against that man. I, the doge, the prince, played for the honour of Venice, and won! Yesternight still Saint Mark's lion might not unfold his wings; and this morning he soared afar to avenge the misfortunes, the contumely of his city. He soared in the strength of his victorious youth, angry as of yore in the days of Carmagnola! Play on, play still, my patricians, play! for it was but a day since the treasury of Venice was empty; play, for had it not been for that unknown mask, who plays aloof from all, I could not have buckled her armour upon Venice."

"*Vado!*" cried the marquis; "knave loses, ten wins!"

"Ever playing," continued the doge; "what shame! They play, and their stakes are idleness, pleasure, luxury, creditors, all that is ignominious! How much more, more exalted was my stake last night; but Heaven! how much more fearful! I staked Venice and her fame—against a Jew called David Gruss! David Gruss! who is David Gruss?" resumed the doge, still fixing his eyes upon the faro-table. "Some vain, contemptible usurer, some one of those Ghetto leeches; a man delighted to loan to a doge!"

"We have lost!" cried Moncenigo, in a tone of despair.

"We are cleaned out!" added the Chevalier de la Plumardière.

"Dead to all eternity!" joined Trevisani.

"Bravo! bravo! keep on, my dear Cornaro," said several patricians to the mask, whom they believed to be Cornaro. The new Crœsus of the Casino remained immoveable; he had but a sign to make, and directly a docile valet brought him a coffer filled with sequins.

The play had now really reached that solemn crisis which puts the most unyielding temper to the severest test, when the mask, approaching the doge, said,

"Your highness does not play?"

"Never."

The mask returned to his seat. There had now settled around the table one of those moments of deep, convulsive silence which play alone can produce; for the marquis and his associates were staking large sums against the unknown gamester.

"The game is made!" again cried the voice of the croupier.

At this moment Alessandro was approached at the same time by *two different* persons: the countess, but masked, and Ziana, who was timidly drawing over her shoulders the folds of a thick zendaletto, or veil.

The maiden withdrew at the sight of the haughty lady before her.

Safia took the arm of Alessandro; she was pale as marble.

"Two words only."

"The countess!" murmured the doge to himself.

He had forgotten her, as a prince may well forget when state affairs have more claims on his time than love—when, before becoming slave to a woman, he governs a state threatened with danger. Her authoritative air, however—that air which a mistress never loses—sufficiently appealed to his memory. With somewhat of awe in his manner, he replied,

"Two words, then, so be it; but I give you warning your confidence must be short."

"Would you make me your own confidences?"

"Not at present, for I am in haste."

The doge observed Ziana, who stood timidly aloof, like a slave fearing to intrude upon her master.

"Your highness," resumed the masked lady, wrapping herself more closely in her large *bahuta*, "it is hardly past midnight; there is yet time for you to traverse the canals, as you did last night about the same hour."

"What mean you?"

"Darkness is deep and discreet; the gondolier safe; the spurred prow of the bark leaves no track over the waters, even when speeding to Fusina."

"Madam—"

"The houses of the Jews at the Ghetto are like tombs, whence no secrets arise."

"Really, madam, I do not know what you mean," said the doge, soon conquering an involuntary shudder.

"Won!" cried together the marquis, Trevisani, and Moncenigo, in a tone of exulting hope.

"Why, surely," resumed the countess, "it was you I met the other night at the house of the Jew Ottale."

"It is herself; I was not deceived!" murmured the doge.

"True, the mask preserved the secret of your highness; but then you dropped this poniard there?"

The countess drew forth, before her astonished listener, a poniard adorned with turquoises and Oriental pearls, which she had herself given to the doge, and whose blade had been broken in the efforts he had made to reach the buried treasure.

"You suppose, then, it was I?" resumed he, striving to speak with an assurance which his conscience belied.

"No, it was not you," continued the relentless Safia, "whom the Jew's daughter, your paramour, aided in escaping furtively by the canal!"

"Saw you naught else?"

"An open window! a tented gondola rowed rapidly towards Fusina!"

"Speak lower!"

"I saw also a locked door, that of Ziana's apartment—"

"Silence!"

"And I was escorted in my nocturnal expedition by a young man, the betrothed of your paramour. He, maddened with despair, enlisted this morning."

"Enough, madam! What is your pleasure with me?"

"That this very moment that girl, who dares to brave me even here, be expelled the Casino of Venice."

"You are mad!"

"There she is. I see her waiting for you, and covered with her zendoletto. Obey! Alessandro," added she, "farther disguise between us is useless; let this end. I am your slave, or your mistress, my lord; I am Safia! Look at me: we may here, at this Casino, speak to each other face to face. Well, listen: drive that woman from the Casino, from Venice—exile her wherever you choose: to Padua, Vicenza, anywhere! but let her go, I beseech you! have pity on yourself, or on me!"

"Safia," resumed Alessandro, bitterly, "you know me not, since you accuse me!"

"I do accuse you; I charge you with deception. Last night, at the Jew's house, you fled at my approach! Your life is wrapped in mystery; your life would defy the glance of inquisitor or spy, as I have told you; but, Alessandro, I will be revenged. Go, Alessandro, go and speak with your mistress; here will I await your decision. If she goes, I remain; if she remain, our intercourse is ended."

Safia at this moment looked so jealous and commanding; her muscles, rigid with revengeful resolve, had imparted to her countenance so imperious an air of authority, that the doge made no answer. The consciousness of his innocence, and the uncertain nature of the information obtained by the countess, made him heedless of her threats. Besides, he wished to fulfil another appointment, that with Ziana, then surrounded by Moncenigo, Casanova, and Grimani. Casanova, disguised as La Plumardière, despite the golden chain that bound him to the inquisitor's aged dame, felt himself irresistibly attracted towards the Jew's daughter, and scarcely heeded the play, although himself a constant loser.

"You look sad, my beauteous child," said he to the betrothed of Taddeo.

Ziana made no answer. She watched an opportunity of addressing the doge as soon as he should be disengaged from the importunity of the domino. The poor girl shuddered with terror when she recognised the countess.

"Expelled! expelled by her from her house!" said she to herself, bitterly. "Of what have I been guilty?"

Mechanically she turned towards the play. The varied incidents that had lately changed the tenor of her life filled her mind. She thought of her intended husband's abrupt departure; of the mysterious friend who visited her father at night.

Suddenly a soft, familiar voice startled her by whispering in her ear words of sad and melting tenderness. She turned around, and recognised the doge.

Meanwhile, and as the players at the faro-table were consulting together, and meditating a last and decisive attempt to rally fortune, the mask with the three-cornered hat, he of the daring and hazardous game, abruptly rose from the table and approached Safia:

"Countess," said he, "you love the doge, and he loves you no more."

"Who are you, sir?"

"A gamester, well aware of the privileges of the mask. I come to give you safe advice. You are in danger of death, unless this night you abandon his highness."

"Explain."

"I will be brief, but perspicuous. You were last night where he was, at the house of Ottale, at the Ghetto."

"Who am I now addressing?"

"One who knows everybody, and whom no one here knows; one who takes compassion upon the doge, and is aware that the mad love which now leads him astray must prove fatal."

"Explain."

"Explain first to yourself the flight of his gondola; his obstinate silence when last night you entered the Jew's house with Taddeo. Ziana's door was closed; he had taken the key. Every night he repaired thither. Every night he betrayed you with another."

"True!"

"But what is also true, madam, is, that, with heedless restlessness, he incurred the greatest perils. He went," continued the mask, lowering his voice, "he went to a house—he visited people—"

In an almost inaudible whisper, he made Safia the confidant of a horrible, frightful secret, which called a livid pallor on the features of the countess. Scarcely breathing, she listened. Each word uttered by the mask sounded as dreadfully, as lugubriously as an information drawn from the marble mouth of the lion of the Ducal Palace.

"Thanks!" said she, "thanks! You give arms to my revenge. Whoever you may be, friend or spy, return to your seat. I know enough."

The mask regained his seat at the faro-table. As we have said before, a decisive coup was preparing. It might be the last. The attention of the players was intense; bets were enormous; stakes were tripled."

"Will you not bring us luck?" said Casanova to the Jew's daughter. "Yet I think the hand of a fair young maiden may wring from Fortune many favours. Come, now that the doge has spoken to you, your pretty face is radiant with happiness and hope! Ziana, you are like a rainbow among these clouds. This unknown gentleman will surely lend you a purse of sequins. He is liberal and generous, of course, since he wins. Accept, then, the offer of that wealthy wrestler of the Casino, and play."

"Signor Mask, you are in error," answered the Jew's daughter. "I am not happy enough myself to-night to bring you luck."

"Then play for your secret thought," resumed the dauntless roué. "Play, fair one, for the fortunes of him you love! Take these ducats."

Ziana now found herself an object of general notice to the crowd. She felt a proud and pure inspiration. While the nobles around were risking their gold for unworthy objects, the artless girl threw on the table a few gold pieces of the unknown; but it was for *him* who was far away —to ascertain his fate—to know if he should ever return. She played for Taddeo.

Had angels been hovering over that hell of Venice, watching whether in the guilty throng there was not one sweet and fair vision, they would have smiled on the Rose of the Ghetto, decked in the freshness of graceful youth, and standing, with a gamester's purse in her hand, in the midst of all those masked libertines. With her beauty, her ingenuous air, and timidity she resembled a fair girl suddenly enslaved, a Grecian captive amid a group of corsairs.

The Marquis de Saluces cut the cards with chill silence; no sound was to be heard save the rustling of silk dresses and dominoes. The doge had disappeared. He wished to speak with Ottale, and had proceeded to his counting-room. The countess observed the game, cold and motionless.

"*Vado!*" cried the marquis, cutting for the last time.

Heaps of gold streamed like water over the tables; each player's breath was suspended; the masks pressed closely together in the utmost anxiety. Suddenly a moment of solemn expectation ensued; hands covered with rings trembled convulsively; awful suspense was as clearly legible through the masks as on uncovered countenances; then the Marquis de Saluces arose, and exclaimed,

"Gentlemen, the bank is broken!"

Then followed a unanimous concert of exclamations, outcries, and murmurs. Those who had lost vented their rage in imprecations, while the winners hastened to gather their gold in anticipation of the croupier's rakes; when the countess, seeing the doge returning, exclaimed,

"Gentlemen, hold! The republic has been basely deceived to-night. The gold which has been staked here to-night, that gold now heaped on these tables, is counterfeit!"

"Counterfeit!" reiterated the crowd.

"Let every one resume his seat," uttered Grimani. "Masks off! obey the Inquisition! Guard the doors. Let no one enter nor go out. Call the broker Ottale to test this coin. If such a deed has been committed, its author shall be discovered, and incur the penalty of the law. Here is the broker; his highness the doge will interrogate him."

Deep silence prevailed. Ottale, led by one of the officers of the seignory, then appeared. He took several of the coins, and bent them on the card-table.

"Well?" exclaimed the players.

"Well, noble masters, all these coins are counterfeit."

"Counterfeit!" echoed the crowd.

"Who gave these?" inquired Grimani. "Do *you* know, madam?" continued he, addressing the countess.

"That woman," said she, pointing to Ziana.

"I!" exclaimed the Jew's daughter.

"Yourself. Who gave you that gold?"

Ziana vainly searched the crowd of dominoes. All, alas! were alike. The player with the coffers had escaped; he was nowhere to be found.

"In the name of the Inquisition of State," resumed Grimani, "arrest that woman. Seize the gold on these tables."

These words were addressed to a file of soldiers, who entered with fixed bayonets. They struggled a while with the players, who tried to recover possession of their gold. Several masks drew their swords. The tumult was at its height. The tables were upset, gold rolled on the floor. Shortly after, the throng rushed down the stairs with loud cries, after having repulsed the guard.

"'Pon my honour," said the marquis, coolly surveying the various groups, "this will make a charming chapter in my book of travels."

"Justice! justice! your highness," cried several nobles, who had gathered around the doge.

"Signors, justice will be done," answered Alessandro.

CHAPTER XXIV.

A FIRST MASTER.

On returning to her palace, leaning upon the arm of the marquis, Safia felt alarmed at herself.

"I have revenged myself," she said; "but upon information from an unknown. Who was he? I know not; yet the means which he offered were so easy that I cheerfully employed them. Alessandro deceived me; yet until this hour he had given me no cause for suspicion: I trusted as I loved him. Was the Jewess guilty? I was told so; and Ottale's evidence is overwhelming. No doubt remains; the doge, in his nightly visits at the house of the keeper of the Mint, was in secret intelligence with his daughter. What pallor spread over his features when Grimani seized Ziana. She and her father are now cast into a dungeon."

"You will confess, countess, that you denounced their guilt at the proper moment. But for you, Safia, I had been ruined. Really, the unknown mask who so cleverly fleeced us all, was one of Satan's own progeny. Amid the confusion he made his escape, and doubtless by this time—Do you know, countess, that your Casino is really a cut-throat place? We play against masked faces."

"Ziana! Ziana!" resumed the countess, lost in deep revery; "you saw her, marquis. Yesterday she was a sweet, ingenuous creature, whom I delighted to protect; an angel, with chaste brow, and pure and innocent look, a child whom every mother would have been proud to claim as a daughter: to-day, an evil influence from the realms of darkness, a personification of guile, deceit, robbery, with pencilled eyebrows! After that, trust to seraphic smiles, the mask of ingenuousness, the veil which beauty wears till purchased by gold! The betrothed upon the eve of her wedding, daughter of a Jew brought up as a nun! Fathom her heart—how soon you reach the mire! Approach the lily, and you will find it black with contamination. A gaming-house was a fitting spot for the wreck of such virtue. The doge, too, was in that den! the grave, the superb Alessandro, whom I had ever loved, and would have loved forever. Alessandro has become the slave of a vile receiver of stolen goods! Can that be? yes; men are so formed. Let woman be loving as I was ever, blindly trusting as I am still, young and fair as but yesterday he called me, and yet she will find some day, in spite of her virtue, in spite of her blind confidence, in spite of her devotion to an ingrate, that hatred and jealousy will bring treachery to her door. You may laugh at my complaints, marquis, but I am justifiable: laugh at my revenge; it is holy."

"No, madam, I think not of laughing," answered the marquis; "provoked as it may have been, your vengeance is severe. Because the doge takes Ottale under his protection, his house becomes the abode of crime, his daughter guilty, and himself her accomplice! Who revealed this to you? who sullied your hands with all this shame and contumely? Ottale yields his gray hairs to the executioner equally as Ziana. I laugh no more, countess, though a Frenchman—a French noble—I laugh no more; I tremble for the accused and for the doge."

"The doge?"

"Listen, countess: the republic has this day caused the banishment of many Jews; Ottale, the severe and honest Ottale, was excepted. By whom? the doge. You are not ignorant that the Venetian patricians bear with difficulty the sway of Alessandro: they cry out for vengeance to-night; to-morrow they will inculpate him. He was the friend of the man whose daughter staked her coin at the Casino; whence came it? I know not; but the keeper of the Mint of Venice must know and reveal. By Grimani's triumphant air, I fancied I discovered that the inquisitor held the clew to the mystery. As he verified the coffers and coin, he started. Now, then, why should not the doge be tried as well as Ottale? Why should not the hatred of the nobles reach unto the friend of the Jew? Trust me, countess, you are no longer in safety here; Venice is not like Paris: justice is here too often done in the dark. You were the protectress of Ziana, the mistress of the doge; you will be called upon to reveal the secrets of your protégée. Fly, then, fly! I see around you but informers and snares. Fly! for to-morrow you may cross the Bridge of Sighs; to-morrow you may share the gloom of Ziana's dungeon."

"You frighten me, marquis. Fly! with whom? The doge? You might as well tear out a leaf from the tree as expatriate Alessandro. Yes, I feel it but too well; he loves me next only to Venice; he could not live in banishment. Strange is his life: by day, at the council, he is the stern senator of former times, devoted to his country as to a jealous deity; while night finds him wandering through the dark streets, a reckless adventurer, who seeks pleasure as others seek rest. Fatal, unaccountable genius! never have I been able to grasp his hidden thought. Heretofore, marquis, I had thought, indeed, that glory was his only passion. I compared him to a stern religionist, prematurely old, but still beautiful, standing in some dark cathedral's aisle, and listening to the voice of God through the impressive peal of the solemn organ. Alessandro has those occasional bursts of generous passion which women love so well; sudden flashes lighten his pale cheek and brow; his heart swells with noble ambition and aspiring energy. His tears are to me invaluable; for when alone with me he sometimes weeps: on such rare occasions I shed tears also. Why does he weep? I know not. He speaks of his country, of Venice, of things in which I scarcely feel an interest. Whatever the cause, I saw that he was slowly decaying; wherefore I had determined to know; and now, by Heaven, I do know! Nobles must have their plebeian, their secret loves. Never had I heard him address even the lady of a sage of the council, and yet this Jewess—"

"Countess," interrupted the marquis, "I have known at Paris a courtesan from Rome, called Anna Flora, who boasted that she had boundless influence over the minds of the great, merely from the fact of her being the daughter of an obscure inn-keeper of Parma. There is an attraction towards inferiority that drags down elevated natures with irresistible force: superior men entertain really but one ambition—that of living in quiet."

"A Jewess!" murmured the countess; "a girl upon whom I had showered favours and benefits. I remember how he gazed on her the day of her betrothal. It is all over, marquis; I have lost all courage. He should be here; he is not. Where can he be? doubtless with her."

"Countess, I have pointed out to you the only remaining path of safety; you will not charge me with striving to deprive you of the love of the doge. There was a man who had scarcely landed in Venice ere you trembled at finding yourself in his power. Cagliostro might have ruined you. Who knows but the doge, warned by his advice, intimidated by his threats—"

"Marquis," resumed the countess, "Cagliostro is no longer in Venice; he has found means of escaping. It has not been in the power of the doge to see or question him. Thank Heaven, that man no longer sways my destiny, or his!"

"A letter for the signora," said Azael, entering the apartment, and presenting upon a silver tray a note given him by a Sclavonian.

With contracted eyebrows the countess opened the missive, which she supposed contained tidings from Alessandro. Suddenly a cold moisture suffused her hand and brow: she looked as if the last star had fallen from the heaven of her hopes. Handing the note to the marquis, she folded her arms with the determination of anguish. Its hastily-traced characters ran thus:

"The doge is lost, fair Safia; come to me. I heard of the scandalous incident at the play-table, the perfidiousness of your lover, and your shame. Alessandro betrayed you. I can put you in possession of correct and positive particulars. My gondola awaits you at the landing of the Bridge of Sighs; I did not wish to stop near your palace. A carriage is in readiness at Fusina to convey us to Milan. It is no longer your master, but your slave who awaits you."

The letter was unsigned, but the countess knew the writing; the marquis could also guess from whom it came.

On reading that note, Safia understood that a last snare had been spread for her by Cagliostro, whose boldness and unprincipled skill she dreaded. She knew better than any one else the astute mind of her former master, and feared she was lost beyond hope.

"He will speak, he will say that, while at Paris, I was still less than the daughter of that Jew; he will crush me, make me the laughing-stock of Venice. Contemptible wretch! At one word, marquis, I could have him seized, thrown into a dungeon!"

"Yes, indeed," answered Saluces, "with a police so delightfully organized as yours! I have lost all faith in it since my mishap. On the contrary, you must answer Cagliostro that you will go; send him word to wait, and leave the rest to me."

"What do you intend?"

"That is my secret."

"But still—"

"Trust to me; merely write a word desiring him to wait. *Aspetta!*"

"I am willing," said the countess; "but afterward—"

"Afterward," continued the marquis, "you will send this (he then folded the note) to Count Cagliostro by your usual trusty messenger, Azael. His eyes are sharp as those of a Greek, and a few minutes will suffice him to take accurate observation of the count's gondola. Do you see these weapons?" resumed the marquis, producing a stiletto and a brace of loaded pistols; "with these a woman in a gondola is safe."

Azael soon returned; he had critically scanned the count's gondola. The two *barcaroli* were known to him; the passenger was in a superb dress, concealed by a black bahuta, an enormous wig, and a three-cornered hat. The night was serene, and the crystal bosom of the lagunes shone like a mirror.

A quarter of an hour later, a woman, wrapped in a long brown mantle, issued from the Palace d'Azola, masked; she was escorted by Azael, who gave her his hand to aid her in entering the gondola.

CHAPTER XXV.

FROM VENICE TO FUSINA.

Never had a more lovely night spread its star-spangled canopy over the flight of a loving couple. Venice, now far behind, looked like a vessel framed in stone, at anchor in the distance.

The gondola ploughed its silver furrow through the phosphorescent waves of the Adriatic, the barcaroli chanted, the breeze sighed faintly around the Lido, the illumined stores of the Place of Saint Mark sent forth across the waves long streaks of lurid flame. Venice, with her thousand lights, seemed to the enraptured beholder a fairy city, bound to earth by wreaths of glittering diamonds and emeralds. Cagliostro himself, as he looked back, sighed like one leaving his home. He was conquered by the matchless magic of that unparalleled sight, that fête given in honour of the sea, for which the waves had decked themselves with glittering lights.

Echoes of music still came from the ancient City of the Doges, the taverns remained open, the arrest at the Casino had as yet caused only vague and uncertain rumours.

"What a night, Safia! what a night for our departure! See, everything invites us, the propitious waves and the sombre palace, yonder palace, where the doge is now meditating the means of saving his beloved; for he loved her, Safia, he loved her. I met him myself under the roof of the Jew, my banker."

Much elated as he uttered this ironical sentence, Cagliostro placed his hand upon a coffer of considerable size, in which the lucky player was transporting his wealth. For, in return for the counterfeit coin, he had received pure virgin gold, with which he had filled his pockets, and which, after his flight, he transferred to a box purchased by him at the Sclavonian quay.

"You are agitated—trembling. You do not answer, countess? Do you fancy I do not appreciate the treasure I am carrying away? Compose yourself, fair Safia. Count Cagliostro is a different adorer from your doge and your marquis. Are you ill? Here is an excellent bottle of smelling salt. I had it from Madame d'Ursé, one of my initiated at Paris.

"Paris!" continued Cagliostro; "we shall both, then, behold it once more. This time, however, without my wife. She did not understand apparitions, so I dropped her. You, on the contrary, will produce a sensation at the court of France. With your beauty, grace, and accomplishments you will be the pearl of the city, the magnet of attraction."

The countess bowed her head. She made frequent applications of the smelling-bottle Cagliostro had given her, yet cast many and watchful glances at the two gondoliers as they rowed towards Fusina.

"You regret your beloved city! You, perhaps, shed tears of farewell. But, Safia, what is the mournful palace of the Countess d'Azola, compared with the fairy abode that awaits you? Your life at Venice was one of continual fear and anxiety. You feared me; you feared the doge. At Paris a crowd of brilliant noblemen will stand trembling before you—the king himself. A king, countess: a King of France is surely more than the Doge of Venice! Once at Paris, you shall occupy by yourself alone a part of the large mansion I inhabit. There you will live, under whatever name you please to adopt, a life of happiness, of joy, and rapturous pleasure! Paris now lives under the sway and will of Madame Dubarry. You shall eclipse her. Paris is infested with philosophers. You shall muzzle the tigers! Painting and poetry will lay tribute at your feet; and when Venice is mentioned before you, you will exclaim,

"'Venice! What is Venice? Yes,' you will add, 'I remember a province laved by the waters, a city, a miracle of nature, with her seventy-two islands, bound together by eight hundred bridges. It is rather a singular than a handsome city, a mass of marble and porphyry, where splenetic nobles dwell. I remember leaving that city one lovely, star-lit night. That night, I also remember, my lover had deceived me, and a young girl had been arrested at the play-table for passing counterfeit money.'"

While thus speaking, Cagliostro listened whether, through the silk of her mantle he could not detect by the loud beatings of her heart, the thousand wounds his words were inflicting. Her sudden and unexpected decision;

her obstinate silence, interrupted only by passionate sighs, threw his mind into a maze of tumultuous thoughts. Before Safia his reason was confounded, as if supernatural agency had been necessary to explain her presence.

"It was well I took advantage of her first impulse," thought he; "to-morrow might have been too late."

Still finding her obstinately silent, he resumed, with counterfeit humility,

"You think me, perhaps, madam, a jailer, a wretch who would make traffic of your person? Dispel such thoughts. Thank Heaven, I am rich; and that wealth," added he, pointing to the coffer, "I lay at your feet. Again I say, I am but the most humble of your adorers. Perish the thought of my ever again becoming your master! I have found you again, beautiful and noble. Now I am your squire, your servant; command me, and I obey."

He then glanced upon the countess with his flaming eyes, resorting to his habitual power of snake-like fascination, and not without effect, it would seem; for although the countess still persevered in her silence, when he took her hand, she did not withdraw it.

Unhoped-for as was this happiness, Cagliostro secretly solved the enigma. He had heard at play the sound of her jealous, haughty voice; he had seen her approach, with quivering lips, the faro-table. Had he not himself dictated what she should say? Was not he the cause of Ziana's arrest? When Grimani had extended his staff over Ziana, to signify that she was a prisoner, Alessandro had uttered a half-suppressed cry, which had found an echo in Safia's heart. She could no longer doubt Alessandro's inconstancy, and the thought was death. Cagliostro took infernal delight in spreading before her the whole in detail, and he used all the arts of a vile informer to persuade his silent listener.

"Two o'clock!" exclaimed he, taking out his watch. "The night is dark; it will be difficult for the custom-house officers at Fusina to know me under this disguise!"

Then, casting off his bahuta and his wig, and concealing them under the cushions, he exhibited himself to his companion apparelled in the latest style of Versailles, a costume which the Marquis de Saluces alone in Venice could have produced. He no longer wore the enormous wig he had worn at the Casino; his hair artificially powdered, his coat impregnated with perfume, his breast glittering with ribands, he looked a true *seigneur* from the court of France.

"I thought I could not do better, madam, to please you, than to assume the dress and appearance of the Marquis de Saluces, your *cavalier serviente*. If it amuse you, I will imitate his lisp, and dance French *courantes!* Poor marquis!" continued Cagliostro, laughing heartily, "how desolate will he be to-morrow when he learns your departure! The fellow has an Amadis turn, and it would not be astonishing if he drowned himself, 'pon honour!"

"Hem! hem!" uttered the countess, coughing, and taking from Cagliostro's box a jujube.

"You cough violently—the night air—allow me to close this window."

"I was saying," resumed the count, shutting the window of the gondola, "that it will surely be the death of the marquis. For my part, I should advise him to make an end of it—a man of doubtful courage, a fool, a fop, a—"

The count would have continued, but at this moment they reached Fusina: the custom-house officer hailed with his speaking trumpet for a night gondola.

The overseer came out, and asked the count his destination.

"Milan."

"Who accompanies you?"

"My wife."

"Without passports?"

"Here is mine."

Cagliostro then produced from his pocket-book a passport carefully folded, and scrupulously correct in all particulars. It was no other than that which Casanova had so skilfully stolen from the unfortunate marquis, and sold to Cagliostro the same evening.

At sight of this passport the officer frowned, and read it twice through.

"Arrest that man and the female with him," said he to one of his attendant *sbirri*.

Cagliostro attempted to resist; he drew his sword, but was quickly disarmed, and deprived of all means of doing harm. The lady made no difficulty, but laughed long and loud.

"The Marquis de Saluces! the marquis!" exclaimed Cagliostro, as his mystifier doffed the mantle and the mask that concealed his person.

"Myself, my dear friend; I am delighted to have eloped once in my life as a female. I was never run away with before! Have the kindness to return me my passport."

"Who, then, denounced me?" said the count to the custom-house officer.

"One of your friends, Signor Count. You aee, we are never betrayed save by friends."

"A friend?"

"You are acquainted, I presume, with Signor Casanova de Seingalt?"

"Certainly."

"Did he not give you the passport of the Marquis de Saluces?"

"For six hundred sequins," murmured Cagliostro, aside, "if he calls that giving."

"Well, Signor Count, the Signor Casanova de Seingalt, your intimate friend, had given us notice at the same time, that from day to day you might be expected to attempt leaving Venice with a false passport. Therefore, signor, as we cannot bear the thought of losing you, we have provided you with a delightful retreat, neither the Casino nor the Place of Saint Mark, but the Leads—you understand."

"The Leads! for me! what means this ill-timed jest?"

"We never jest, signor, when Messer Grimani gives us orders to execute. Reserve your thanks for him when he visits you in the morning: it is he, this time, who provides you with lodging."

Cagliostro stamped with rage, while Saluces laughed immoderately.

"My dear friend," said the marquis, "you forget your money—that money, you know, with which I was to make such a figure at Paris!"

"What! then the count has been lucky at play to-night," said the officer: "let us see."

Upon an order from him, three *sbirri*, guided by the marquis himself, entered the gondola. They found there a coffer full of shining gold pieces, half sequins and half ducats; the whole was placed aside to be sent to Messer Grande the inquisitor, by the same bark that was to convey Cagliostro back to the Leads of Venice.

While passing beneath that dreadful portal by torch-light, Cagliostro more than once tried to escape from his watchful keepers. But the most severe one was the marquis himself, in his female headdress, who appeared overjoyed, at last, at securing the count. As he crossed the threshold of the room which was destined to be his prison, a sarcastic peal of laughter re-echoed from the vaulted roof of the Ducal Palace, under which this room was situated; at the same time a man, wrapped in a bahuta, as if recently risen from the faro-table, appeared before him, and, with ironical politeness, did the honours of the place to the new guest.

"Casanova!" exclaimed Cagliostro; "well played!"

"We are locked in together," answered Casanova; "the night will be long; let us talk, dear count."

CHAPTER XXVI.

UNDER THE LEADS.

"Yes, talk," answered Cagliostro, striving to disguise his rage; "talk."

The count seated himself upon a worn straw chair. They eyed each other suspiciously.

Casanova and the count were both in full ball dress under their dominoes; a lamp, suspended from the iron ring in the centre of the vault above, made their tinselled dresses glitter.

They looked like two itinerant country quacks settling the bill for their first night's performance.

The room offered to the eye nothing but a tiresome monotony of roofs. The ceiling, inclined like that of an attic, was composed of sheets of lead. The heat was intense and suffocating; no sea-breeze reached it. Four signors of the night had just visited the prison, and as they went out drew the bolts upon them.

"This more resembles an oven than a dungeon," said Cagliostro, wiping his brow with a fine linen handkerchief. "What procures me the pleasure, my dear friend, of meeting you here?"

"Faith, my dear friend, I was about to ask you the same question. A husband's, an inquisitor's revenge, perhaps, together with that devilish coin which I handed, most unsuspectingly, I assure you, to that little girl. That Signor Arnolfo, who gave it me, was a great rascal."

"Of course, I did not play that night, because I had no money to play with; but at the mere name of Arnolfo I started, as I remembered a certain Florentine by birth, though Greek by profession, who bore that name at Rome."

"You might perhaps give information concerning him?"

"For what purpose, since he found means to escape before the *finale*? Nevertheless, the police of Venice must be very inefficient."

"Not so much so since we are in its clutches. But who denounced you?"

"I know not; but what I do know is, that I do not intend to remain here long. Did you not once escape from this place?"

"Yes; ten years ago, under the former doge. But the arrangements have since been altered, and I doubt—"

"Will Signor Casanova de Seingalt allow me a simple question?"

"Certainly. Why, we are here merely for the purpose of asking and answering questions. Nothing else to do, save drinking or cards."

"Very well. What would he think of a man who should denounce his bosom friend?"

"His bosom friend?"

"Ay."

"I should think the bosom friend must have deserved it."

"In what way?"

"By not assisting those who assisted him."

"Did I not assist you under the wig and the costume of Doctor Phœnix? and Signora Grimani—"

"True; but did I not cause you to find a most valuable book, one that was surely worth more than your powders and your philosopher's stone?"

"I showed you that there was a cruel gap in that book; the most interesting leaf for us had been torn out."

"By whom?"

"By Signor Grimani, doubtless."

"Nothing can rid me of the idea—since here we speak openly—that you sold it to some one; to that Signor Arnolfo, for instance."

"Suppose it were true?"

"You would have played a handsome trick: he will be arrested, and confess the whole truth. If that affair had been in my hands, we should not be where we are."

"Why, Casanova, I have not been seen at the Signora Grimani's palace. I entered it in a disguise when in search of that book; but the inquisitor's wife knows *you*."

"Well?"

"Well! she will denounce you. You have it in your power to make amends for your conduct towards me; write to Signora Grimani, and ask her to release us from this place. It is true—I will confess it—I ought to have shared with you the price of the book; but I was at Padua, and durst not come back. That Arnolfo cannot recognise me; I am not afraid of being confronted with him; but I have worse affairs on my hands: I am persecuted by the hatred of the countess; the Marquis de Saluces is the mortal enemy of both of us. Obtain, I say, from Signora Grimani—"

"Charming speech! Do you imagine that women have power to release captives from the Leads of Venice?"

"Why not? The signora is enough of a heroine to visit you here with her duenna; we will take their dresses, and let them remain in our stead. Grimani will hush up the affair; he will not assemble the Council of the Ten against his wife."

"Grimani watches her, and us too. We commenced our life at Venice with an apostolical supper; we shall end it with a foretaste of hell. I don't know whether you are aware of it, but this leaden vault is anything but cool."

Casanova now industriously plied a fan which he produced from under his bahuta.

"Nothing to be done, to be attempted!" resumed he. "Bars like the Lion's Column!

walls as thick as the dike of Murano! It has been my misfortune to become acquainted with you, Signor Count; you play too deep a game for me!"

He paused then, as to listen to the silence of his cage. Through a grated loop the eye could gaze at the starry dome above, that shone in all the splendour of a most lovely night. Casanova carelessly began pacing the floor back and forth. As for Cagliostro, he was dispirited, and sat with his brow between his hands.

"Hush!" said he, interrupping Casanova in his walk; "there are some persons beneath. List! two voices in conversation."

Casanova kneeled on the floor, and, bringing his ear close to it, heard a sweet, clear maiden's voice singing, in a melancholy tone, the following stanza:

"Our Lady with the comb of gold,
Holy Madonna, sainted queen!
Whose arms, all deck'd with flowrets, hold
The boy-god smiling and serene;
Bright Star! whose soft beams lead
The vessel o'er the main,
Safe from the wars our sailors speed
Home, home again!"

The voice was now silent, and a deep sigh was heard. Another voice soon interrupted the silence, and in aged, hoarse tones, repeated a Hebrew prayer.

"Ottale!" murmured Cagliostro.

"Ziana!" joined Casanova.

The Jew and his daughter were indeed locked in the Ducal Palace, whose mournful privilege it was to have a certain class of prisoners confined beneath its roof of lead. The president of the criminal Quarantia had just introduced them into a narrow apartment situated directly beneath that occupied by our worthy pair.

Ziana, on her entrance, found there another prisoner, one of Saint Mark's pigeons, which the jailer doubtless had brought up for a pastime. She asked the privilege of keeping it. The bird alighted familiarly upon her shoulder.

Ottale's stupor at his sudden arrest was indescribable; he thought himself in a dream; he looked at Ziana; then, as if overpowered by the certainty of his misfortune, he burst into bitter and indignant tears.

"To be arrested like a thief! After sixty years of virtue and probity, to be doomed to infamy at Venice! To be accused of a crime that I do not even understand."

The old man sank despairingly on the wretched bed of his cell, which, however, he shortly after yielded to Ziana, who soon fell into a deep and calm sleep. She had found hung on the wall of the prison an image of *our Lady with the Golden Comb*, which had suggested her humble prayer.

Ottale contemplated the slumbering girl; she resembled a fair statue. Her transparent complexion discovered the blue tracery of the veins of her temples and neck; her lips were pale as those of a closing lily. She wore the ordinary dress of Venetian maidens, a white veil, and high shoes laced with gold. Her hands were locked over her breast, which heaved at intervals with a sigh, and where the jailer's dove had nestled. She looked one of those maidens idealized by Greuse. The old man was tempted to kneel by her side, and pray to the God to whom she had prayed.

"On whose protection may we now depend? Who will vindicate innocence? The Doge of Venice? But he is only a mask of power and authority. Taddeo? But he has gone to seek death afar. What infernal genius has wrought the ruin of both of us, my Ziana?"

After a pause he resumed, with cold composure,

"As for myself, the sacrifice of my life is accomplished. That life belonged to this dear child; her joys were my joys, and her smile my smile. The education I gave her was severe, but necessarily so. I was bound to watch over so young a heart, so charming a beauty! My love was jealous, anxious as a father's love. No, she shall not die. I shall, I must acquit my debt towards her! Rest in peace, then, my noble, sweet girl; Ottale watches over thee!"

The old man sat down on a stool, and while Ziana slept, he recalled slowly from memory every circumstance of his life. That self-examination brought back a tranquil sereneness to his brow. He had fathomed his soul, and had found there neither treachery nor hatred. The life of Ottale had been a peaceful field over which no storms had yet passed. He could remember no one bad action for which he would have to blush. Thus the souls of the just, like the earth, exhale towards the evening rare and heavenly perfumes; thus the urn of the heart gushes towards God, and makes the angels weep for joy. Ottale was the representative of virtues long erased from the book of Venice, exact and scrupulous probity.

"Star of the lowly, immutable, and sacred rule," resumed he, "thou hast guided me to this day! The corruption of the patricians has made *me* a better man. I have been ennobled by contact with their daily degradation. God alone has seen me; He alone may judge. I trust to his providence. After all, this poor, artless child has the protection of the doge. This is the hour at which he proceeded, masked, towards my dwelling, to visit me—he! the prince, the true Signor of the Night. Strange city! unfortunate prince! I feel my heart bleed with all the wounds inflicted upon his."

After a dark and painful contemplation of his prospects, the Jew, soon yielding to the oppressive heat of the room, reclined his head on the foot of Ziana's bed, and fell into that calm sleep which was never given to a guilty being. Raphael, in his painting at the Vatican of Saint Peter in his prison, would have taken delight in observing the flickering lights and shades which the dim lamp threw over that worn, open brow. Ottale slept, while Casanova was still awake.

Casanova, the unprincipled libertine—Casanova, the rake, thought at that moment of anything but sleep: he thought of Ziana's captivating beauty.

His fired blood rushed violently to his brain; he pictured to himself the lovely girl, separated by a few boards only from his own cell, tearful, forsaken; lost by his fault, since it was he who had induced her to play! Casanova could not repress his feelings at the sight of that image. He saw her, mournful and pensive, at the small window of her cell, faintly inhaling some dying breeze from the Lido, and shrinking with dread if some one of the keepers chanced to lay his hand on her shoulder. He accused himself with the most odious perfidy for being the author of that lovely being's ruin, for causing the Rose of the Ghetto to wither under that roof of misery.

Then, suddenly, his imagination made him fancy he was in her presence. In his delicious dreams, he spoke to Ziana the soft language of love, which no one could ever speak to woman like Casanova. The door of his prison had vanished before him; hushed were the voices of death and lugubrious broodings. He was afar with the Jew's daughter, in some vine-canopied arbour of a Venetian garden; the inspiriting nectar foamed in her goblet; her hair hung in loose waves, and wooed the breeze. She was no longer the timid Ziana, but the captivating queen of pleasure, with alluring smiles and glances.

Dreams, frantic dreams! dreams that brought madness to his brain and agony to his heart. Casanova, in that prison, was suffering all the tortures of love: he, the resistless Casanova, who had ever trifled with love. It is by a heavenly retribution that those hearts, long sated with easy pleasure, sometimes kindle at last into a blaze of passion. The wretch did not even struggle against the agony of his feelings, but suffered in silence.

"True," murmured he, "this is the same window through which, ten years ago, I accomplished my escape with amazing boldness; but then I only sighed for liberty; to-day I should be miserable if I conquered it again. That Jewess is beautiful. I love her! With her I must escape hence."

Then overcoming all obstacles, he saw the walls of his prison open a passage for him; he was with Ziana at Malta, at Smyrna, at Constantinople! Such were the powers of seduction of that matchless suborner, that to deceive and conquer had ever been for him but the work of an hour; so easily had the cooped vulture always succeeded in bursting the iron fetters of his cage, that one day, one night perhaps, would suffice now, and his mind already grasped the fearful distance that separated him from his object.

Cagliostro contrasted strangely with him. He seemed to consider the walls of his prison as a profane violation of his inborn rights and power; he could not forgive Venice for avenging France by confining him under the Leads. His countenance alone sufficiently indicated that he no more considered Casanova as a friend: his lips had opened only to ask the latter to hand him the Treatise on Consolation, by Boëce, at which request the incorrigible Venetian laughed till he cried.

"For what purpose, my dear fellow?" he answered. "Since you boast of conjuring up the dead, why do you not call forth Seneca, Charron, and a multitude of philosophers besides? They would make a handsome appearance to-morrow about noon, the thermometer at thirty-seven in these apartments which the bounty of the Grand Council has provided for us! Believe me, you had better think of inventing some pleasant and cooling acid beverage—some sorbet that were worthy of the Aquila, for instance."

Safia's master, the count, Doctor Phœnix, was about to reply, when the door opened and gave passage to the inquisitor Grimani.

The inquisitor was in full costume, as if just coming out from a ball; such, indeed, was the case, for he still held in his hand a bouquet presented by Casanova to the Signora Grimani, his wife.

"Faith, gentlemen, I am very sorry to interrupt so sweet an intimacy; you were probably engaged in administering mutual consolations to each other. Men of such cultivated understandings could not fail to do so. But the council requires your immediate separation. M. Casanova de Seingalt, your marvellous agility is well known: you already escaped once from the Leads; we must now give you lodgings under the wells!"

As Casanova was about to remonstrate,

"Excuse me, sir," pursued the inquisitor, "it is only for one night. By to-morrow your case shall be attended to. As for you," resumed Grimani, turning round to Cagliostro, "yours is a capital case, my good friend. The gold pieces found in your bark at Fusina are exactly like those gathered on the play-table at the Casino: you will have to answer this before the Three."

The two friends being once separated, the jailer introduced a man of middle size, bearing the usual dress of the notaries of Venice, and who appeared to be as much amazed as frightened.

"Do you know this person?" inquired Grimani of Cagliostro.

"Not at all; but, judging from the inky smell of his robe, his crooked fingers, and his face more dry than an antiquary's parchment, he must be a notary. Really, Messer Grimani, I am astonished that you should mix gentlemen with such people."

The new prisoner did not see fit to answer the count's disdainful remark. He sat down quietly at one extremity of the room, like a man long accustomed to respect the decrees of law. Grimani withdrew, taking his leave with an ironical smile; he closed the door, and placed three sentries before it, an unusual extravagance of precaution in this place.

The two captives for a moment kept an icy silence, as two persons unknown to and suspicious of each other.

The notary soon drew a package from his pocket; it was a parcel of papers carefully folded and sealed.

Then, by the light of a little taper, which he lighted from the lamp of the prison, he read the following superscription: "To be given, after my death, to the Countess d'Azola."

"What means this?" thought the notary, as he examined the seal. "No crest on that wax: it is not from a noble. It is a deposite—no more. What induced me to go to that nocturnal man-trap in the Ghetto? Thanks to that visit of mine, I am arrested to give evidence as to what took place in his house at night! I am not curious, and yet I should like to know. After all, those Jews have always meddled with all conspiracies; they have poisoned, several times, the wells of Venice, and were in correspondence last year with Milan, and this paper may perhaps—"

"You seem to be musing, Sir Notary," observed Cagliostro, in an insidious tone; "have you, like myself, been made a victim to that Signor Arnolfo, who has dared to circulate such peculiar coin in Venice? I will not conceal from you the fact that I have something of a dislike for men of your profession; but I feel prepossessed by your physiognomy. You are not guilty, I am certain."

The notary attentively examined the count, and the survey inspired him with confidence in Cagliostro, who, as we have said, could assume any mask.

"Sir," replied he, "I acknowledge that I find myself in a strange perplexity. The night before that of the play, I called at the house of the Jew on his own request. He then intrusted me with a deposite, of which this is the address. I am not acquainted with the countess, but her name is well known in Venice."

"What woman do you refer to?"

"Read yourself. The Countess d'Azola."

"Safia!" murmured the count, starting with astonishment, "Safia! What can there be in common between her and the Jew?"

"I am well aware what danger there is," continued the notary, "in a breach of trust. Heaven forbid that I should ever think of prying into the secrecy of this one; but the Jew is under arrest; this package might compromise me. What do you think of it?"

"I think it is absolutely necessary to become acquainted with its contents; not for yourself, sir, who appear to be beyond reach of charge or suspicion, but for the countess. It may compromise her—establish, perhaps, her complicity in his guilt! Beware, sir; there are a thousand ways at Venice of ruining those whose ruin has been resolved upon!"

"But can I break a seal?"

"The seal, it would seem, is without any crest: it is mere red wax; and if you will permit me to examine—"

"Who are you, sir?"

"A friend of the Countess d'Azola, one of the players denounced by her; but her charge was against masked persons, and she would not have accused me had she seen my features. How much did the Jew Ottale give you, sir, for keeping these papers?"

"A bag of ducats, which I have not even counted," answered the notary, assuming the ingenuous blush of conscious virtue.

"Rare instance of disinterestedness! But I repeat it, you place yourself in danger. The Inquisition will insist on knowing what package was placed in your charge, and there can be no harm in ascertaining what it contains. A count of Harberg was poisoned by opening a paper; a noble lady, Maria Cattaneo, suffered the same fate, to say nothing of the Duchess of Chateauroux, who is supposed, in France, to have met a similar death. Only recapitulate the circumstances of this case. On the eve of the banishment of the Jews, on the night before the promulgation of the edict of the doge, one of that nation gives you papers addressed to the countess. Believe me, under the circumstances, there is no breach of trust; it is a mere measure of safety. If you dread to open the package yourself, let me have it, and were it even to poison me, I tear it open!"

Before the notary had time to oppose his rapid gesture, Cagliostro tore away the seal of the envelope.

"It is in Hebrew characters," said he, scarcely able to conceal his emotion.

"I do not know that language; but does the countess?"

"Perhaps," proceeded Cagliostro, perusing again, with increased surprise, the writing which he held. "However that may be," he added, with a demoniacal smile, "we are saved now; we are both free; this paper has saved us: one head shall fall, but it will be neither yours nor mine."

"What do you mean?"

"I will tell you to-morrow."

CHAPTER XXVII.

THE APARTMENT OF THE DOGE.

Meanwhile Alessandro, rather pursued than surrounded by all the patricians and nobles who were present at the play, had repaired from the Casino to the Ducal Palace, after engaging, as has been said, his royal word that the author of that crime would soon be punished.

But where was he to meet that accursed Jew named David Gruss? What cavern, what subterranean retreat was his refuge? Alessandro even doubted his presence at the play; the man he had addressed there spoke without the least Hebrew accent, and none of the gamesters at the Casino knew David Gruss.

On the other hand, the imprisonment of the keeper of the Mint and his daughter overwhelmed Alessandro with grief. Safia's jealousy had done all—that jealousy had caused an awful discovery. It was owing to her that over the Jew's head and Ziana was now suspended the executioner's axe.

A prey to such thoughts, the doge had returned to his apartment in a state of alarm and anxiety which allowed him no rest.

Five now struck from the clock of his apartment, a bare, unfurnished room, on which two doors opened, one at its farther end, the other opposite its only window. Both these doors were covered with hangings of worn and tattered brocade; for Alessandro, under the ducal corno and purple, led the life of an austere senator of former days; nothing betrayed the splendour and the ostentation of the patrician order. A bed, covered with a purple canopy, a few leather chairs, and a crucifix suspended to the wall, composed the only ornaments of this room.

As he entered, the doge threw his mask and bahuta over a chair, and pushed open the window; day was already breaking.

"Five! how calm and cold everything looks around! Who are those early pedestrians in the street? A few masks going home. They converse doubtless of the events of this night, that fatal night, which opened so well, but now looks like a dark stain on my life! By this time, the sails of my fleet woo the winds of the open sea, my sailors can look over the vessels' sides at waves which are not the Adriatic waves. A glorious night to them, but bitter and sinister to me. All my hopes wrecked by a woman! Will that woman dare again to appear before the doge? She has ruined the only man I venerated, the only child whose smile still bound me to life. Did she know that David Gruss? did she induce him to work my ruin? What am I to think, what to fear? My soul refuses to think or fear save for Ziana's pale and soft features! I see my guard enter prison: Ziana and Ottale will soon be here. I must see, I must interrogate the Jew, and reveal to him the mysteries of that night. All-powerful, all-merciful God," added the doge, kneeling before the image of Christ, "help me, inspire me: you alone know Alessandro!"

"But do I hear aright? Yes, they are cries of a tumultuous crowd. What signifies this?" continued he, going to the balcony; "a stone strikes the angle of this wall; the multitude throngs around the Ducal Palace. Ah! whatever happens, they will see what man I am."

Alessandro took down an old Castilian sword from the wall, where it hung close by a bunch of withered flowers, suspended with a riband. Near the pommel of that blade was engraved the famous Castilian motto:

"No me saques sin razon,
No me embaines sin honor!"

"No, I shall not unsheath thee without reason, thou sacred sword, the gift of a duke of Alba. Ottale, Ziana, I will protect you, or die in the attempt."

Quivering with rage and impatience, like a wounded lion, he proceeded to the door, where repeated knocks were heard.

"Ziana!" exclaimed he, seeing the Jew's daughter pale and almost beside herself.

Her limbs trembled with emotion, and the doge was obliged to support her.

The maiden was accompanied by an officer of the household of the prince, followed himself by an old man with torn garments, uplifted hands, and blood-stained brow.

"Ottale! merciful Heaven! Ottale wounded! What has happened?"

"Highness," answered the Jew, calmly, "at the moment when, by your orders, this officer came to seek us in our prison, the Jews still remaining at Venice, those of the Ghetto and of the surrounding islands attempted, most imprudently, to rescue me. Instead of being introduced by the secret passage, I was led, by the express order of *Messer Grande* Grimani, through the courtyard."

"What happened then?"

"A collision then took place between the Jews and the populace; a stone wounded me on the head. But," proceeded Ottale, "think no longer of myself, think of this dear child. Our moments are numbered: you wished to interrogate me; I am ready."

"To interrogate you, Ottale!" answered the doge, bitterly. "I wish to save you first. Dispel your fears; I swear that no harm will befall you while you are near me with this dear girl."

"Highness," resumed the Jew, "I have no need, I presume, of any defence in your eyes; but it is not enough of life, you must also save my honour."

"That is uppermost in my thoughts, Ottale: you are right. Truth must plunge to the bottom of that gulf of mystery, and unmask guilt."

"Except yourself, signor, no one at Venice," said Ottale, with some hesitation, "ever entered, at night, my laboratory."

"No one, save the man whom you admitted, in my presence, that very night."

"What man do you mean?" asked the Jew, tremulously.

"David Gruss."

"You say true; that man has been within my house."

"Do you remember seeing him go out?"

"I remember the habitual fixedness of his glance, then a heavy, all-absorbing slumber; after that, nothing."

"Interrogate carefully your memory."

"My memory, highness, presents a sad scene after I awoke; Ziana was in tears; Ziana said that Taddeo had knocked repeatedly at the door of her room about daybreak. If that man, in concert with Taddeo, had penetrated my laboratory to coin false pieces at the effigy of Saint Mark — But, highness, besides that Taddeo is almost my son, and that his honesty and upright life have won my esteem, what interest could he have had in aiding David Gruss in such an infernal work? He is now on the high seas, to combat, and die, perhaps, for Venice. And, then, these pieces are old; they were struck under the pedestal Mano Rinio of Padua, by the Venetian Dominico Camelo. Witness this sequin."

Ottale then produced one of the sequins he had taken from the play-table at the Casino; it bore the appearance of the most masterly imitation. So skilful was the counterfeit, that Ottale alone, owing to his special knowledge as keeper of the Mint, could have discerned the fraud.

"I am the more astonished," he resumed, "that immediately after the execution of the pedestal of Padua, Mano Rinio, denounced by a Greek of Torcello to the Inquisition of Venice, this coin was buried within the city, in some safe spot, which I never knew, and of which the procurator Grimani, now messer grande, alone may perhaps be aware."

"How! did you not know that in your own house, under that pillar—"

"What would you say?"

"That it is time to inform you, Ottale, of the crime of David Gruss. Know, then, that the other night, taking advantage of your sleep, to make you the unwilling instrument of his own will, that man dared to make me his accomplice by sharing with me moneys buried in the same room where he had forced you to sleep. I have every reason to think that David Gruss is a hidden foe, yours or mine, I scarcely know which. But his aim was to ruin us, and he has succeeded but too well."

"Your words, highness, confound my reason. Who can that man be, and what interest—"

"I know not; but again, leave to me the care of justifying you. One thing is certain: David Gruss became possessed of that secret; during your sleep he forced your thoughts towards that place of concealment: you are lost, and I must save you."

"Highness, I will remain. You speak of saving; will your patricians allow it? The patricians of Venice, they our masters as to probity and justice! because the gold on their play-tables chances to be counterfeit, the Jews of Venice must bear the penalty! Have the

Jews exacting mistresses, palaces, and tables that drain the revenues of whole provinces? Are they seen to sell at auction their paternal roofs? to play and spend their nights in dissipation? No, gold in their hands is a river whose source the nobles alone exhaust: the Jews are the slaves of Venice; their masters, as to crimes, are the patricians!"

"Ottale, we have but a moment to save Ziana and yourself from the perils that threaten you. This devoted servant," said the doge, pointing to the officer, who kept himself aloof, "will soon tell you what you are to do: you are here under my protection, but the minutes are numbered. I have caused the palace guard to be doubled; the vestibule and the gratings of the marble staircase are closed. There resides at Venice, in the Island of Saint Angelo, a mute from Abyssinia, whose pardon I procured a year ago. He resides with the monks of the Cross of Judea; he is in relation with Smyrniot vessels; he is devoted to me; he will lead you, with Ziana, on board of a Greek vessel. This paper will be handed to him by this officer. The rest is for myself to attend to. Be cheerful, then, Ottale; you are in the presence of your prince, and in that of your God."

"Highness," exclaimed Ziana, in a tearful voice, "if you may not save us both, save, at least, my old father; save my protector, save Ottale! Besides, I alone have, as yet, been accused."

"I will save you both," exclaimed the doge, with unutterable anguish, and striving to speak with that confidence which he lacked; "I will discover the true culprit, wherever he may lurk."

"Highness, you whose goodness is so exalted," continued the maiden, fixing on the prince a glance which embarrassed him, "you know all the mysteries of Venice. Before I leave you, you may discover to me a mystery that has been the torment of my life."

"Who told you, Ziana, that I knew your secret?"

"You do know it!"

"I?"

"Certainly! That masked cavalier who, in the darkest nights, visited my father; that man whose words were ever of protection and defence, whom I loved as the guardian angel of our house—"

"Well?"

"Signor, that mask, that cavalier was yourself."

"You are beside yourself, child," resumed the doge, calmly.

"Seek no longer to deceive me, prince. To make that mystery impenetrable to my eyes, it was not enough of a mask; you should have deprived my mind of that intelligent anxiety which interrogated the gestures and features of all. I should not have felt, when, in that horrid night, the inquisitor Grimani laid his hand upon me, and when I dared, with the courage of fear, to seize the hem of your ducal robe—I should not have felt your heart beat with much more than compassion as you so kindly bade me rise. In short, you should have kept your voice, your eyes, your soul, under perfect control, to conceal that secret from me."

"What if it were so?" inquired the doge, with evident alarm.

"Oh! then I should have the right to call you my protector, to account for that strange guardianship. What can there be in common between us, that the Jew's daughter should receive so exalted a guest? What in common between the doge and Ottale, that Ottale, the scrupulous money dealer, should nightly open his doors to him? Oh! who will tell me why it was that when you had been a single day without coming, I wished to die, and that now I love you, and wish to live?"

"Listen, Ziana," answered the doge, resuming his composure with a painful effort. "If ever human lips, heretofore inviolably closed, were ready to break the silence, mine are at this moment. But if you in your soul feel any compassion for me, beware of making any farther inquiries. There lies between us a secret of death. Beware of guessing it, Ziana; and if ever a suspicion of the truth should flash upon your mind, dispel it, and pray God, child, to make doubly obscure that night which envelops our chaste and mysterious friendship."

"Proceed, oh! proceed! Your voice sounds so sweet to poor Ziana."

"You know not how much I love you. Under that mask, which was my only safety, I have run many a danger, escaped many a snare. Often, mid snow or rain, I arose; I took my cloak to go to you, to see you, if but for a moment, and bring back with me the flowers you had worn in your hair! Look. They are here, pining like yourself."

Alessandro, opening a casket, showed Ziana a few withered, blighted flowers.

The maiden looked sadly at the doge without yet understanding the nature of the connexion that existed between them. There were in his beautiful physiognomy marks of strong emotion that invincibly attracted her towards him. Alessandro had, in a few moments, gained over Ziana an influence which neither Ottale, nor even Taddeo, had ever possessed. She looked upon him with a sort of religious terror akin to that feeling with which she had seen oftentimes those lugubrious processions passing through the city. Never had Love or Glory circled a fairer brow than his with their wreaths; and yet that princely brow was contracted by grief, and tears now fell from his eyes.

"It is evident," murmured the maiden, "that there are two men in him, one that encourages, and one that awes me. Life may cease to-morrow for me, but even in that dread moment will the remembrance of that friend be alive in my heart. Ottale stands looking upon us in mute sympathy. Poor father! venerable parent! how often I have discouraged his kind heart! When that cavalier was to come, I often remained for whole hours without speaking to him, without seeing him, sadly watching from our little window that part of the canal where the bark was to appear. Heaven! what means all this?"

Overcome by that desperate self-examination, and startled by the sudden gush of compassion, sympathy, and tender sadness that she felt within her heart, Ziana burst into a flood of tears, while the Jew remained speechless, motionless, and as if thunder-struck, in the presence of the prince.

"Weep not thus, Ziana," resumed the doge,

himself dashing away a tear, "weep no more. You will yet live happy."

"Happy! How may I be? Oh, my protector! my friend! I feel that I shall always lack a sheltering bosom, a voice to tell me, 'Ziana, you shall know all.'"

The doge cast an imploring look of mingled misery and resignation towards the sacred sign of Redemption to man, and murmured,

"Oh, Saviour! you also have suffered! Ziana," continued he, struggling not to betray his emotions, "you must leave me: leave me until to-morrow, and then you shall be free. You shall go from Venice—go with Ottale!"

"Then, signor," said the maiden, clasping her hands with grief, "you will not allow me even to carry with me a secret whose knowledge is of more importance to me than even liberty? I am not, then, to know by what link of his mysterious chain God has bound you to the existence of a wretched being like myself, nor by what inscrutable decree of His providence my life is in the hands of the Countess d'Azola? Oh! how shall I express what I now feel? Look at that old man, who weeps now like you and myself; he is one I have ever loved, and who has ever taught me to love you! Well, when I count the beatings of my heart between you and him, it is towards you that it leaps, towards you that it aspires. Everything tells me, oh Heaven! that, while I belong to you both, one of you is but the depositary, while the other is the master. I was startled on the day of my betrothal by that thought: how is it that I am a Christian? At night, before Ottale, I hide myself to pray; before you I can pray, and still look upon you! Oh God!" cried then the maiden, falling prostrate before the crucifix, "since he I love is silent still, and will not speak, reveal yourself the truth!"

Ziana, in that passionate invocation, seemed to have concentrated all the powers of her soul; breathless, broken-hearted, she seemed to expect that by some miraculous dispensation the sacred image would open its lips, and let its words fall like dew upon her brow. The doge looked upon her with anguish and consternation; but, like the wrestler, Alessandro had long nerved himself for that heart-rending contest: he merely took the Jew's hand, sadly pointing to Ziana on her knees; then turning towards her,

"Yes," said he; "yes, child, ask from Heaven what is Fortitude, that virtue which has long winged its flight back to the skies; it may be that a secret voice will then whisper to you that there are sufferings above the strength of man, that there are victims who suffer in silence, and do not smite their breasts; souls doomed to live apart from their dearest joy—their treasure, their all!"

While he spoke thus, in a voice oppressed with sobs, the doge gazed lovingly upon Ziana: that flame, which heavenly love kindled in the eyes of Joseph as he extended his paternal hands over the fair head of Jesus, now glowed with electric warmth in the eyes of Alessandro. The doge, with mingled delight and anguish, pressed the maiden to his heart; a silent pause then took place, which their sighs alone interrupted.

"Oh! my glance now probes the whole depth of your sacrifice," murmured Ziana, while her hands were pressed between those of the prince. "Yes, I will go; I will leave. I will do whatever you command, but let me call you my—"

"Never! not even here," said he, laying his hand upon her lips; "the walls of this palace have ears and tongues. Go, poor child! I guess your meaning from the beams of joy in your eye: to-morrow you shall be free, and then, perhaps, will you remember me in your prayers."

"Oh! now, now!" answered she, kissing his hands. "Now I can wait!"

"Ottale," said the doge, "their excellencies the state inquisitors have requested me to wait for them here; they must not meet you in this room with Ziana. Fly! both of you."

"The inquisitors!" murmured the Jew; "would they dare to interrogate their prince?"

"Ottale, whatever may be my fate, I promise soon to meet you here. Watch over her," he added, in a whisper; "if any important revelation reaches me as to David Gruss, I will inform you of it."

The doge, fixing a last sad glance upon Ziana, drew aside the hangings of one of the doors, and bade the officers take back the prisoners.

A moment after, the three inquisitors entered his room.

CHAPTER XXVIII.

A BARGAIN.

The three inquisitors entered in silence; they bowed to the doge, and seated themselves on stools, which were presented by a *sbirro* in a red jacket, who attended them.

"Speak, signors, speak; the Doge of Venice is ready to hear you. Have you any petition to present?"

"Is it necessary to remind his highness, then," said Grimani, "that the Inquisition of Venice never petition, but command?"

"And that its judgments are without appeal," added a second personage, in whom the doge recognised Moncenigo.

"We are here to proceed, by all means, to the discovery of the truth," joined the third, who presented to Alessandro the no less familiar features of Trevisani.

"I know better than any one the power of the State Inquisition," calmly answered the doge, as he bent on his judges a look of dignified courage. "The tribunal of the Three may even, at will, decree that the head of their prince shall fall. Now, what is your wish?"

"To call upon your highness for a strict and severe account of the protection with which you favoured the Jew Ottale and his daughter Ziana. Your benevolence towards them wore the appearance of injustice and guilt. The house of the Jew contained a deposite of counterfeit coin; a book was stolen from Signor Grimani's library which indicated the quarter, and even the house where the republic had seen fit, two hundred years ago, to cause those proscribed coins to be buried. You often repaired at night to the house of Ottale; did you never meet any one there? Do you know the author of the crime? If such be the case, denounce him."

"A man by the name of David Gruss is the only person I ever met at that house."

"As yet the Inquisition has been unable to discover his trace. The Countess d'Azola is ignorant even of the name of that man, although she was the first to enlighten our justice—"

"Enlighten your justice!" interrupted the doge, with bitter irony; "say, rather, that she denounced the purest and holiest virtue."

"It does not belong to us to investigate the motives that may have induced the countess to bring so precise a charge. We ask you whether the Jew ever spoke to you of a treasure buried in his house?"

"Never. I am certain even that he was ignorant of its existence."

"It becomes our duty to inform you of an incident of which you are ignorant. One Count Cagliostro has been seized at Fusina, bearing with him a considerable number of gold pieces resembling those found at the Casino. That adventurer asks to see you; he pretends that he has important revelations to make. As we respect in you the supreme majesty of the chief of the republic, we consent that you shall yourself interrogate him, trusting to your highness for the care of our honour and our privileges; remember only that this is to be a decisive interview. That man sent for us to his prison, and uttered these most positive words: 'I know the culprit, but to the doge alone will I reveal his name.'"

"Cagliostro!" murmured the doge, stupified. "Oh! I am accursed. Is Satan, then, at Venice? What can he have to say to me?" added he, in an inaudible voice.

"Highness," resumed Grimani, "should Ottale or his daughter be named by that man—if he designates to you either these or any other persons as the authors of that crime, you swear on this cross to inform us of it."

"I swear!" said the doge.

"Introduce the prisoner of room No. 2, under the Leads," said Grimani to the *sbirro* who waited outside the door. "We give you one hour; only one hour, highness, mark!"

The inquisitors withdrew then one by one, and the doge was alone. A personage in a cloak was introduced by a *sbirro* of the Inquisition. Alessandro bolted the door, and raised the cover of his lamp as if to lose nothing of the features of the singular man who had requested this interview.

"Cagliostro!" cried the doge, surveying the count. "You are at Venice, then, and, scarcely at Venice, you are imprisoned, sir."

A cold, fearful smile glided over the lips of the count. Alessandro shuddered; it was long since he had seen that dreaded tyrant of Safia, and now he stood before him, calm, collected, almost threatening.

"You wish to speak with me," resumed Alessandro; "be brief."

"I am at your orders, highness," answered Cagliostro, in a voice that caused Alessandro to turn pale; he had recognised David Gruss.

"Then," said he, "you have no mercy: ever implacable and treacherous, you have attempted to betray me, and now you come to implore—"

"A criminal never implores his accomplice."

"Dare you establish any comparison between us?"

"Why not? There are two men whom the law of Venice claims: the one staked the gold of Venice at play, the other staked Venice herself!"

"Wretch!"

"Yes, doge, I confess it: I am David Gruss; but are you not yourself the senator Alessandro, who married a slave?"

"What next?"

"Next, signor? Here is the deed of sale of the Countess d'Azola! Two heads fall with mine! If I suffer the fate of the counterfeiter, Dominico Camela, you shall suffer the fate of the noble Ranuzzi!"

"Do you hope to intimidate me? What to me is the countess? what Safia, the dastardly informer? Safia, your worthy pupil, has filled the measure—she has called the sword of justice down upon an innocent head. Do you likewise! Denounce me with her, and let one torture unite in death those whom hell alone could have united!"

"Very well, highness; but there is another person whom the fate of Ranuzzi must reach. Together with these papers, which prove the sale of Safia, I have also this instrument, written in Hebrew by Ottale, and delivered by him, in safe keeping, to the notary Bernardi. Read there the name of her whom the instrument concerns, and whom it will deliver to the executioner."

"Oh! wo, wo upon me!" said the doge, after reading. "Are you, then, the fiend?"

"I am Cagliostro, the same Cagliostro whom you spurned at Paris, and who now makes you tremble at Venice! Highness, you took from me a woman who was completely under my power; you have annihilated that power. I have now demonstrated to you that one charge uttered by you before the tribunal against me would ruin you, and cause two heads to fall besides your own. Now make your own choice. Whichever way you turn, you are lost! The same fate awaits the doge or the husband of Safia; therefore set me free, and I will annihilate these papers, which compromise, besides yourself, two persons dear to you. I will then spurn Venice and leave it; or, if you prefer that the robber of the Ghetto should suffer, mark, signor, I will inform against the doge."

"Are you not frightened at your own impudence, wretched impostor? Do you forget that you are in my power?"

"It is yourself, signor, who are in my power. To end at Paris, or end at Venice, is all the same to me; at least, here I shall have the satisfaction of knowing that three deaths will follow mine. After suffering what I have, that vengeance is no more than due!"

The satanic expression of the count's features, his tranquil coolness, but most of all, those fatal proofs which he held, united to strike terror into the soul of Alessandro. He fixed Cagliostro with a look like that which Don Juan bends on the commander's statue; then pressing his heart with his hand, as if to repress its loud beatings,

"Rest assured," said he, "I will name another."

"Whom?"

"That is my secret."

"Will you swear?"

"Upon those papers you hold, upon that Christ who some day will judge us both!"

"I have your word, signor; here is the deed of sale of Count Tekeli, and here the writing of Ottale."

"At last!" murmured the doge, seizing the papers, which he burned in the flame of his lamp.

Then, seeing Cagliostro still in his presence, he said,

"In a few minutes I will call in the inquisitors. Concealed in this closet, you may hear every word I shall utter. Farewell; leave me. A door communicates from them with the gallery."

He pushed the count into the cabinet, and then remained for a few minutes on the threshold, erect, motionless, and pale, as if just awaking from some horrid dream.

"I owed to myself, to my God, that dark but pure sacrifice! She need now fear no longer, she, the sole object of my thoughts, of my life, till this day! I will now write to the Three, promise them entire satisfaction, and ask for a last, a short interview. Ziana, Ziana, I shall have saved you; yes, the man from Saint Angelo must be in readiness; let us see."

The doge rang, and one of his officers appeared, the same who had led Ziana and her father to the prison. A few minutes sufficed Alessandro to write to the inquisitors, who waited in the great council hall: an usher was intrusted with the letter, and while he went on his errand the doge asked of the officer,

"Well, Andrea, what news?"

"Prince, the mute of the Island of Saint Angelo, to whom I bore your letter, is here. According to your orders, he has arranged all for the passage of the Jew and his daughter on a Smyrniot vessel. He undertakes to see them on board."

"Well; but time presses. Andrea, lead hither the prisoners again, and tell the mute to come to me instantly."

"He is there, signor; with his caftan, his poniard, and his black countenance, he looks like a true corsair. I was told that he prayed all the way with his beads. His gondola is at the corner of the Bridge of Sighs."

"I know his worth in time of need. Introduce him, then speed to the Leads; here is the key of my apartment; return quickly with Ottale and Ziana."

The officer sped on his errand, after motioning the mute to the doge's apartment.

The Abyssinian came in, bowing to the floor.

He was still a young man; his complexion was dark, his stature tall; he wore a striped vest with hanging sleeves, the turban and a sailor's caftan, then lowered over his face. In his belt was a sharp Venetian blade, with the Lion of Saint Mark engraved on it, and in his right hand he held the copper medal which all Abyssinians were obliged to produce in order to obtain admittance to the palace.

"It is you, Orsato?" said the doge. "You received my note?"

The mute handed to the prince his letter.

"You know the dangerous mission on which I would employ you?"

The mute smiled, and pointed to his poniard.

"Mark, I intrust you with what I hold dearest in the world. Orsato, you were sentenced to the ordinary and extraordinary question, when I saved you. You still wear the bracelet I gave you for attending me in that riot at Ferrara?"

The mute showed a bracelet which he wore around his wrist.

"Be ready, then; I hear Andrea," said the doge, listening.

The officer was indeed returning with the Jew and his daughter. Ziana wept no more; her beautiful eyes then beamed with the smile of hope.

"All is lost," whispered the doge, in Ottale's ear; "a man, a foe, has gained possession of the instrument you had imprudently intrusted with the notary Bernardi. Bernardi was a secret spy of the Inquisition; of this you were not aware. Now listen: Orsato will lead you both to a place of safety; I will remain to speak with the inquisitors. Ottale, you have followed me long enough in my sad and heavy existence to know whether I loved you. Ziana's happiness I intrust with you. You are free!"

"Free!" exclaimed the Jew. "But who, then, was guilty? I must know."

"The Inquisition of Venice has its secrets; but it has its powers also, and those, you know, are absolute, tyrannical. Ottale, you are free, but you are no longer safe in Venice. Follow, then, this man, and be sure that before the Three I will clear you of all suspicion."

The doge now shuddered as, glancing at the clock, he marked how few were the moments he might still call his own. His features presented a singular expression of mingled sadness, elevation, and regret. While pressing Ziana's hand, he dropped upon it a scalding tear. His strength deserted him.

"Free! but free without you!" repeated the maiden, bending an anguished look of despair upon the doge.

"Free without me, Ziana," said he, printing a last kiss on her angelic brow. His lips felt cold, as if death had been there already.

Ottale, quivering with emotion, fell at the feet of the doge.

"Let the girl go first," said he. "I will overtake her, signor; but I have the right of being present at the secret tribunal. I will—I must."

"Ottale," said the doge, "you must obey me. Look, the hour has struck." The rustling of their robes announced the passage of the inquisitors through the gallery.

Alessandro quickly motioned away the Abyssinian, who bore the fainting maiden to his gondola.

"One part of the sacrifice has been consummated," said the doge, looking at the door through which Ziana had disappeared; "the other part now remains!"

Turning around, the doge perceived Ottale.

"For the first time," said the Jew, "I disobey your highness. I will remain. The vessel will not sail yet under an hour."

CHAPTER XXIX.

THE TRIBUNAL OF THE THREE.

When the inquisitors entered, they found the doge calm and dignified. He had hurriedly placed his brocade robe upon his shoulders, his ducal *corno* upon his head.

"The better to show my deference to the choice of the Ten, it is meet, signors, that I should forget none of the exigencies which ceremony imposes upon my rank as prince. It is in ducal robes that I must answer you. I am ready."

"Before all, we must bid that Jew withdraw. His presence is contrary to the statutes of the State Inquisition."

"This man is innocent, signors, I attest," resumed the doge, warmly.

"Meanwhile he remains our prisoner."

"But you will respect his aged head when you learn who is really guilty."

"The Jew's life will be spared, we swear it," answered the Three, after a short conference in whispers. "He will be led to the hall of deliberations, and, according to what we shall now hear, dismissed with his liberty."

"Highness," said the Jew, extending his arms towards the doge.

Alessandro encouraged the old man with a benevolent smile, while two familiars of the Inquisition led him out; then, turning to his judges,

"It is a patrician," said he, "who has committed this deed, signors."

"A patrician! You know him?" inquired Grimani.

"I know him."

"On your head, then, doge, I adjure you to name him."

"Yes, I will name him; I will unmask him. Yes, the mere mention of his name will make you all turn pale on your seats."

"Speak."

"Listen, then, you who claim to be his judges. Venice was ruined, lost beyond hope, cankered by vice, a prey to usury, which tore away, piecemeal, the last spoils of that dying city, once the pride and the love of Italy. We were all humbled. Our old palaces and our old names presented nothing but crumbling ruins. Our mercenary defenders mutinied for want of pay. The people cried famine in the public squares. No resource, no energy, no shame was left in the discouraged, sinking, humbled nation. Hope itself had fled from among us. An ambassador —what do I say?—a pirate had come purposely from Tunis to ascertain the state of our means. A son of Venice, heir of an illustrious house, one who felt the insults inflicted upon his native city as if they had been outrages offered to his own mother, meditated, meanwhile, the means of sustaining yet for a time, in the sight of Europe, the rotten frame of a sovereign state now at the eve of crumbling into dust. He wished to save his country from misery, from contumely. Gold was wanted in order to wing for its victorious flight our fleet, distined to drive before it a herd of slaves, to destroy the possessions of the powers of Barbary, and return home with one more victory to be inscribed on the republican banners. For lack of gold that fleet itself was captive in our port. That man first called upon the nobles of Venice. His messengers were sent back with disdainful answers. He implored Heaven, and Heaven was deaf to his prayers. The counters of the Jews were exhausted, and those avaricious money dealers, tired with loaning forever to patricians sums which they were compelled themselves to refund, had seen the gold of Venice melt away through their hands. Thereupon, that man called at night on the Jew Ottale, and there, unseen, unheard by the Jew, he exhumed that gold, that buried, concealed treasure."

"Counterfeit coin," interrupted Grimani, with contemptuous irony.

"The Jews of Venice were satisfied with it on the day of the sailing of the fleet; and the Lion of Saint Mark, free from the fetters of usury, opened his wings upon the Adriatic."

"His name! his name!" inquired altogether Trevisani, Moncenigo, and Grimani.

"Hold! I have not said all yet. Surely there is no one among you who would have consumed his nights and days indefatigably at work. You would not have condescended to become the first labourers of Venice, nor dared that awful attempt to save a degraded country shorn of her wreath of glory; you, the living representatives of the vices that undermine Italy; you, the three incarnate symbols of our fallen Venice! You, Moncenigo, who are Play! you, Trevisani, who are Drunkenness! and you, Grimani, Lust!"

"This is too much," said the three inquisitors, rising; "you insult the senate!"

"Doge," resumed Grimani, "who is the culprit?"

"The culprit? I!"

"You!" exclaimed they, terrified.

"I—I, your doge! Now punish me! now erase my name from the Golden Book; cause the executioner to deface my coat of arms. You are right," continued he, with increased irony, "I should die, since I failed to save you!"

The voice of the doge now sounded like a funeral toll; his brow was erect and proud, and the three inquisitors themselves trembled in the presence of this strange culprit.

"You know all," resumed he: "I have accused myself: it was my duty; but spare the Jew: he is innocent! Grimani," resumed the doge, softly, "you must set the old man free; he awaits."

Grimani arose, and, after exchanging a sign of intelligence with his colleagues, proceeded towards the window of the apartment that looked upon the courtyard of the palace.

"We have sworn it," said he. "Highness, the blood of the Jew shall not be shed."

Then calling in a *sbirro*, he spoke to him in a low tone.

"In a few minutes," resumed he, "you will see the Jew crossing that portico; he will be brought forth from his prison."

Grimani had scarcely done speaking when the doge saw the Jew coming out, preceded by a man who was covered with a black veil.

Ottale wore a similar veil; he raised it a moment, to cast a farewell glance towards the window of the doge.

"Hold, signors!" cried Alessandro. "No, that must not be!"

"Excuse, highness; the Jew must bear the penalty of the prince. Venice must have a victim: Ottale will be led through the city, then taken to the Lazaretto, where he will be employed during his whole life in subterranean labour. His age and his reputation for honesty will shelter him from the fury of the populace."

"Sacrilegious blasphemers! lying, impious judges! exhaust upon me your tortures; but doom not that old man to the endless night of such a dungeon, I charge you!" exclaimed the doge, rushing from the window towards the door.

But Moncenigo and Trevisani held him back, while Grimani, his arms folded over his breast, looked upon the contest with impassible eye.

"Doge," said he, slowly advancing towards Alessandro, "your life is forfeited to the Three. What are your last requests?"

"I have but one," answered the doge, with awful calmness."

"What is it?"

"That the people—my people—may be allowed to approach my scaffold, that my dying look may rest on Venice: that is all."

Grimani opened the door; he called in two familiars of the Three, who stood in waiting in the gallery. The inquisitors, after a short conversation aside, transmitted their orders. After the *sbirri* had gone out,

"Listen, highness, to the decision of the tribunal," resumed Grimani, advancing towards the doge. "The punishment of the doge shall be kept secret, like his crime. While the people feast their eyes upon the Jew Ottale, designated as the only culprit, the heralds of the palace shall proclaim, throughout the city, the sudden death of the doge. Venice shall be clad in mourning; prayers shall be offered for the rest of your soul in all the churches of the republic; the patriarch shall pronounce your funeral oration; your obsequies shall be attended with the usual pomp to the basilic of Saint Mark; your bier shall be borne from the Ducal Palace to the Church of Saint John and Paul; the Great Council shall meet to appoint your successor."

"I have heard," said the doge, with dignified composure. "And now, what mode of death do you assign to me? Is it water, steel, or poison?"

"Prince, you shall leave this room no more. Every issue shall be walled up."

"I understand you. Famine is a silent executioner!"

"If there is any one in Venice who loves you enough to call on you here, he may come; but he goes out no more!"

"Doge," whispered Moncenigo, approaching Alessandro with hypocritical marks of respect, "we preserve the honour of your name."

"Doge," added Grimani, in the same tone, "we have not forgotten that the culprit was once our friend."

"Trevisani, Moncenigo," resumed the doge, with bitter, but dignified irony, "if you have no loftier virtues, you have yet gratitude. How deeply thankful I am to you! Yet, if you consult your memory—if you search the past, you will remember that often a mysterious protector paid your debts, redeemed your hypothecated estates, supplied, like an indulgent father, the wants of your extravagance. I was that unknown friend!"

"You!" exclaimed the three patricians, with amazement.

"Do you still doubt it?" resumed the doge, snatching a few papers that lay scattered on a table. "Look, Grimani! here is your estate of Boveredo redeemed from the Jew Samuel! Here, Trevisani—here, Moncenigo, behold the secret of the indulgence of your creditors!"

"It is even so!" exclaimed the judges, looking at each other with stupor.

"I have, then, rent one corner of the veil which concealed my life from every eye; now, do you comprehend me? I, the doge, dwelt in this wretched room; I slept on that bed, which is harder than a soldier's couch. While you dissipated your nights in pleasures, I spent mine in labour; and oftentimes has the sun, when he rose over Venice, found us face to face, you worn out by play and voluptuousness, me by unrelenting application. Like your divine Redeemer," continued he, pointing to the image on the wall, "I have often felt as if nailed to a cross, with bleeding hands and feet, and sorrow-stricken heart; I prayed then the Father of all to take from me the chalice of suffering! He has heard me at last: I shall soon be free!"

The doge was now silent; a tear moistened his eyes, upturned towards the heavenly sign of suffering and affliction; but he was resigned to his sacrifice. Meanwhile, the masons were at work, walling up the outside of the window; vague and indefinite rumours were heard in the Hall dello Scudo, near the doge's apartment, where the government usually give notice of the death of the prince by raising a sable banner; the bells tolled throughout the city.

"I tremble, Moncenigo," said Trevisani to his colleague.

"I am panic-struck, Trevisani; I thought I saw blood issue from the wounds of yonder Christ."

"Come, signors, let us away," said Grimani, yielding, in spite of himself, to his emotions; "we have accomplished a duty!"

The three inquisitors then withdrew, much agitated. The voice of a herald was heard from without; the sounds of hammers were already audible at the exterior; daylight had insensibly passed away.

An usher appeared, bowed to the prince, and placed a lamp on his table.

CHAPTER XXX.

THE DUCAL RING.

"Night!" murmured the doge, looking at the lamp, whose wick smoked in the gloomy solitude of his room; "night! dreadful, eternal night! such is their decree! To die in this tomb, while the sun shines yonder under so pure a sky! To die here, while there, beneath my feet, Venice weeps over the empty bier of her doge.

"I was quite young still," resumed he, seating himself near the table where stood the lamp, "when passed before me the statue of the man whose successor I was destined to be. This body, according to the usual rites, had been borne without pomp to his ancestral sepulture; the bells of the city tolled responsive to that of Saint Mark's, to inform the people of the death of their prince. He was a noble old man, an aged remnant of the now degenerate blood of the Dandolos. The statue, whose waxen face bore his likeness, was laid, I remember it well, on a high scaffolding arrayed in the ducal robes; he wore, as I do, the gold brocade gown, the ermin mantle, and over his head the *corno*. His spurs were inverted; I saw him thus in the hall of the Auditor Nuovo, guarded by twenty nobles in scarlet robes. The commanders of the vessels of the fleet then came to seek him, followed by all the confraternities, and forty electors in deep mourning. The waxen statue was then borne under a canopy—I remember it well—preceded by the scutcheon of the republic, covered with a sable gauze. The relations of the doge followed the statue; his funeral took place at Saint John and Paul. On the eve of that fatal day I arrived at Venice with Safia—Safia, who has caused my ruin! I was elected soon after; but for a month that waxen statue was before my eyes! Bitter derision! But the Doge of Venice was really dead, and I still live in all my strength! Is it a dream of hell? Has my heart ceased to beat within my breast? Am I no longer the doge, no longer Alessandro?"

Instinctively he drew near to the window. The herald's voice was then heard in the courtyard of the palace, crying,

"The doge is dead! pray for his soul! the doge is dead!"

Alessandro listened again through the gloomy darkness. The drums and the silver trumpets, that are used at the ceremony of the Bucentaur, now mingled with the deep-toned bells.

"It is a lie! no, the doge is not dead!" exclaimed he, opening his window, and, with a half-suppressed cry of rage, he smote his hands against the masonry that left now only a small blue patch of sky to be seen. "It is a lie! no, the doge is not dead! give him way, and through this window he will fall mutilated in the midst of your hypocritical pageantry of mourning."

"Vain efforts!" resumed he, tearing his bleeding hands from the window; "my voice and my arms are alike powerless against those stones! Oh! to think that I did not smite those infamous judges in the face! But what? what man am I to be angry now? Has not my whole life been one struggle with sorrow? Can I no longer bear the decrees of Heaven? Shall my iron will now bend at the sight of death? Do I shed tears?" resumed he, drawing his hand across his eyes; "*I* weep—weep like a woman! Come, this is unworthy of me."

He took a few strides, and stopped before the window. A single spot of blue still hung over the prison; upon that the glance of the doge now rested with watchful eagerness. The silence was deep, deep as the grave; the steps of the captive alone were to be heard, Alessandro still fixing his eyes on that corner through which he could still behold the last flickering rays from above.

"Farewell!" cried he, "farewell, Venice, for whom I lay down my life! farewell, my dearly loved city, my pride, the cherished object of my thoughts, of that dream from which I now awake to die! You who now weep over my bier to forget even my name to-morrow! Ungrateful Venice, I love you! let me still behold a little of your blue sky—or, rather, let it vanish from my sight; for if, through the darkness in which I am about to leap, I could see one of your soft stars gleaming, Venice, I should have no longer any strength to die!

"To you my last thought, my own city," added the doge, retreating from the window, "and to you, young maiden, whom I have saved from death, for whom I bear the whole of this burden of sorrow, rather than let you share it with me! Ziana, be happy, and compensate me for the forgetfulness of Venice, your twin sister in my love!

"But I am not deceived; a slight sound, the sound of steps is heard in the gallery. The door of it is not yet walled up, and affords a slight passage. A woman's voice! what woman can be coming here, to her grave?"

The doge leaned forward; he dimly saw through the darkness a white veil, a woman's dress.

"What a thought! heaven! Ziana; yes, Ziana alone. Have I not succeeded in saving her? You, madam!" exclaimed the doge, suddenly recognising her who entered the room; "you here!"

"Myself!" answered the countess, drawing her veil aside.

"Safia! Ah! God is just! you know not where you come!"

"I care not to know; I have a secret to tell you, therefore I have come!"

"Look at this window, it is walled in," answered the doge, drawing aside the curtain; "that door will be so before long; you go hence no more."

"Doge, the guilty alone need fear the touch of the executioner's axe. I am not guilty; I may go forth."

"Insane woman! you have not seen the snare! I have also a secret to impart; a soft and consoling thought, which I have kept for you, as the last sacrament is reserved for the dying."

"What would you impart?" inquired she, fixing a look of terror on the face of Alessandro, that looked still more pale by the light of the lamp which he now held himself.

"Safia! you were once a mother!" continued he, with a glance that seemed to explore her inmost heart.

"Ah! strike not the most painful string of my soul," answered she.

"Fifteen years ago, at Rome, I entered one night your room, and informed you that our only child had died in its cradle."

"Hush! I pray you, hush! Do you forget the tears I shed? *You* did not weep; and I myself was then too young fully to realize my loss."

"Well, Safia, I deceived you then!"

"Deceived me?"

"Your daughter lives!"

"She lives!" cried the countess, highly excited, then retreating suddenly with terror; "she lives!" said she. "Oh! do not deceive me again."

"So near God, one would not speak false."

"My daughter alive!" said Safia, drawing nearer to the doge. "Where have you kept her concealed, Alessandro? say," continued she, wringing her hands with anguish. "Make me not pay for that secret with an age of torture!

No; although you have despised my love, betrayed me, and given me every cause for hating you, I ever recognised in you, Alessandro, a noble and great nature; surely you would not trifle with a mother's love; you will tell me where you have concealed my daughter; for again I say, *I* may leave this living tomb! Must I go from Venice, traverse the whole world, I am ready."

"You have time enough to hear me."

"Speak, I beseech you; I will curse you no longer. If you knew how much I shall love that child—your child! I shall be so proud of her, so loving to her! Surely you had your reasons for inflicting upon me so great a sorrow. You feared to see that pure, cherished being exposed daily to the corruption of Venice. You took my treasure away to hide it in some solitary spot, far distant from the palaces and the scandals of this city—far from the example of her mother—under some calm, humble roof, such a roof as you would have delighted yourself to dwell under, had not your country required the sacrifice of your rest. That is what you have done, is it not? But had you, instead of deceiving me thus, informed me of your plans, Alessandro, I should have approved them; I should have felt as you did—that a mother's stainless name is a daughter's fairest ornament."

"Speak you true?" inquired the doge, with emotion.

"Yes; I should have kissed and wept over the cradle of my daughter, and covered my eyes with my hands, that I might not know whither you had carried her."

"Do you not deceive me, Safia?"

"Look at me!"

"You weep!"

"Yes, I weep because you never knew me; because, relying on the past, which was beyond my control, you have never taken into account my repentance, my faithfulness, my love for you—you, who have so cruelly betrayed me!"

"Safia!"

"Yes, I weep for your harshness, your pitiless silence, your cowardly courage in trampling me under your feet, in causing my poor heart to bleed, through all the wounds you had yourself inflicted. You did not understand that a mother's love is a flame that purifies whatever it touches: you have looked upon me only as a slave, purchased, or, rather, stolen by you, carried away like a precious toy to please the eyes of your people. Alessandro! you loved me not; you judged me at Paris to be the fairest, and you dragged me away through France and Italy. You gave me palaces, titles; you made of me a gaudy show, like your Bucentaur; but at this supreme instant, when, for what crime I know not, you await the last blow of human justice, doubtless you will tell me where you have concealed my daughter. If you refuse, I will start to-night, and search every spot of the earth, and ask for my Safia—my Safia, whom they have stolen from me."

"Your daughter no longer bears that name."

"That name you had already taken from me; you exchanged it for a title the day when we left Rome, after that horrid scene."

"The day when Cagliostro whispered into mine ear, at Santa Maria Maggiore, that word which made me tremble and turn pale, you remember. That word made me wish to purify you from the name of Safia; that word caused me to take from you your child; that word is to-day the signal of the death of us both!"

"What a look!" murmured the countess, seeing the burning fire that glowed then from the eye of the doge.

"Do you know what your magician said to me, Safia? with what proof, the night after that interview, he accompanied that dreadful word? He showed me the deed of sale of a slave, purchased when very young by him, and he whispered the name of Safia, the name which you bore."

"True, true!" said she, hiding her face with both hands.

"Remember now the arrest of Ranuzzi in your own palace; he was executed at Saint Job that same night, together with a foreign woman and her daughter. Your own fate, and the fate of your daughter, were written down by that example. Do you understand now how that rival, that Cagliostro, who threatened me at Rome, has revenged himself at Venice? But a moment ago he was here, holding in one hand the deed of sale from Tekeli, your former master, and another instrument, still more important, that proved the birth of our daughter, her true name, her titles, that she might claim them thereafter, should better days dawn upon her and ourselves."

"He was here?" inquired the countess, with wandering eyes and livid brow.

"Here, before me, Safia; he arose before me like a snake. Know that Cagliostro was David Gruss, who had sworn your ruin and mine; Cagliostro, whom the justice of man has never yet been able to reach, dared, in this spot, to tempt the justice of God. He swore that, unless I consented to take his own crime upon myself, he would produce before the state inquisitors those overwhelming proofs by which three heads were to fall. Could I hesitate? I thought of my daughter, whose innocence would not save her. I accused myself alone; alone I took upon myself the burden of the crime, and its disgrace. But, at least, my daughter is saved; yes, owing to my forethought—"

"Thanks! thanks!" murmured the countess, wildly sobbing with joy; "thanks!"

"She is now far from Venice. A safe guide—"

"From Venice, did you say?" inquired Safia, suddenly turning pale and agitated.

"Yes; I made her escape from the palace in a gondola. She is to sail in a Greek vessel for Adrianopolis."

"Her name, I implore you! Her name?" repeated the countess, wringing her arms with impatience.

"You understand now, Safia, that under sentence of the law, which menaced your child and yourself, I could not, I might not tell you—"

"Proceed!"

"That supposed rival, that Ziana—"

"Ziana!"

"Is your daughter and mine."

"Ah!" exclaimed the countess, with a deep-drawn sigh, and leaning for support on the table where stood the lamp. Sobs came from her breast—her heart was broken.

"You know now my secret," resumed Alessandro; "may the one you have to impart—"

"Ah! let me go forth!" exclaimed the countess, as if just awaking from a horrid dream; "let me go, Alessandro!"

Rushing to the door, she rapidly drew aside the curtain; and then, horror-struck, fell back with a terrible shriek, at the sight of the wall which had now closed the opening.

"Walled—walled in!" she cried, as she fell fainting on her knees.

"I had told you," said the doge, calmly.

"But," she cried, raising herself with the energy of despair, "you know not yet what I had to impart, Alessandro!"

"I listen."

"My fatal jealousy has ruined us all!" continued she, raving.

"I tell you that I have saved your daughter."

"And I tell you that *I* have killed her!"

"Wretch!" cried the doge, casting her from him. "No, no! it is only madness. Say it again."

"Yes, killed her! Since that horrid night at the Casino, I had been a prey to jealousy. I watched: I saw the mute Orsato come in, then go out, with a veiled female. I spoke to Grimani, and the bark, instead of going towards the open sea, took the direction of the Orfano Canal!"

"Ah! my deep curse upon thee!" said the doge, retreating from her.

She had fallen at his feet, exhausted by the horrid confession; her eye seemed to follow her victim, still struggling with the waves of the canal as they rushed into the opening gondola.

"It is she—I see her!" murmured she, in frantic delirium; "she struggles, she calls you! she curses me as you have cursed me! Oh! God, God! I am mad. I hear a dim sound of groans and plaintive sobs amid the deadly waters, and just above them I see an angel's head, the head of Ziana!"

Her voice, which scarcely articulated these words, broken by terror, soon became audible only as the rattle that precedes death.

Alessandro gazed on her motionless, as one who has done with the joys and sorrows of the earth. His brow was moist with a chilly perspiration, his heavy brocade robe weighed upon him like the leaden cloak which Dante assigns to the damned.

"Strike!" resumed the countess; "let me suffer no longer! Strike, I say, Alessandro. Ziana, my daughter, I go to meet thee."

"Blaspheme not, madam," answered he, with a voice of stern command; "blaspheme not, Safia, my daughter has gone to heaven! Dead! dead! Heaven! the bitter cup is full!"

Now the fibres of his soul were rent as those of an instrument when strung too tightly. That man, who forgot the gloom of his own fate, who had so generously accused himself under the threatening echoes of this room, that man, who died to save his daughter, now wept because he had failed to save her whom he had so dearly loved. He looked towards death, that horrid death, which drew near to him, with longing, tender eagerness. Vainly did Safia kiss his hands and feet; he saw her not, he saw only Ziana. A boundless, ethereal, indescribable sense of voluptuousness stole upon the senses of Alessandro with absorbing, urging influence. He was overpowered; he saw, amid a choir of angels such as Murillo alone ever painted, a virgin, stainless soul, with tiny wings, that, fluttering, brushed his lips and brow, a radiant soul, animated with breath divine—Ziana, his Ziana, shedding fragrant dews upon him! No longer a captive within the gloomy prison walls, he soared amid clouds gilded by a sweet April sun. No longer he wore the ducal *corno*, but the white wreath of the sons of heaven. No longer he saw judges coming towards him, but Doria, Faliero, Zeno, Carmagnola welcoming him with a triumphant apotheosis. For a time the joyous vision dwelt within his mind; he listened to those friendly voices conjured up by that sovereign fairy; but insensibly the vision faded away, and the doge found himself alone with that woman who lay at his feet in frantic disorder, with her hair streaming loose adown his feet. Safia had thrown back her brow, as pale as the veil she wore; she implored him as a convict would implore the executioner.

"Away!" cried he, abruptly turning towards her.

"Yet, my Alessandro," answered she, with melting grief, "I came here determined not to leave you again! This tomb is mine as well as yours, for those men have obeyed me, they have walled it in!"

Seizing the lamp, she pointed again to the insuperable barrier.

"Mercy!" cried she, "mercy!"

"Have you had mercy on Ziana, say?"

"Ah! my heart bursts! my daughter! my daughter!"

The miserable woman, seized with a sudden sensation of cold, approached the bed, and wrapped her shoulders within its curtains with a spasmodic, convulsive laugh.

"Dead! Ziana, my daughter! Venice, my city! farewell," murmured the doge, leaning upon the bed. Then drawing his ducal ring from his finger, he raised it to his lips.

"Alessandro," said the countess, creeping on her knees towards him, "speak to me, speak! one word, if but to curse me!"

"You asked me the other day what was contained within the setting of my ring? Look, Safia!"

He threw her his ring. The bells of the palace were now heard dimly tolling.

"It is empty," said she, after opening the ring. "What have you done?"

Alessandro uttered a faint cry; he raised himself, ghastly, dreadful to behold. Safia retreated, shuddering.

"Cagliostro," murmured the doge, faintly, "I thank thee; that poison is thy most precious secret."

"Poison! and none, none left for me! to die slowly here with hunger!" repeated the countess, still holding the ring.

The voice of the herald was now heard in the courtyard of the palace, proclaiming,

"The doge is dead! pray for his soul! the doge is dead!"

"You say true," murmured Alessandro, dropping his head upon the bed; "the doge is dead!"

CONCLUSION.

THREE months later, by a beautiful night, while waves and skies rivalled each other in freshness, beauty, and splendour, a young man of bronzed complexion and black, flowing hair leaned with his elbow on the stern of a bark impelled by three oarsmen. He looked behind towards a number of fine vessels in the distance, decked with a thousand banners, and leaving their silvery tracks on the blue carpet of the deep, while the sailors sang the national hymn composed in honour of Marc Antonio Colonna, on the occasion of the battle of Lepante.

The architecture of Venice, with its Oriental roofs and domes bathed in the hazy light of the moon, uprose then to the eyes of the young man like a fairy city long seen in his dreams. He seemed, however, familiar with it; for, as he landed at the Lazaretto, his first care was to give some orders to several slaves who stood at the point of that island formerly called Santa Maria of Nazareth.

Since the deadly plague that afflicted Venice in 1576, a rigid station near this island was exacted for all vessels coming from Tunis, even those bearing the flag of the republic. The young man, who wore the sailor's caftan, leaped ashore opposite the pavilion, beyond which it was not permitted to cross, and which faced the celebrated gallows erected by the prior within this fortress to punish any infractions of the public orders.

"Let this flag be hoisted instead of that!" cried he, with a firm voice, and pointing to a banner embroidered with gold, upon which appeared the name of Alessandro and his family arms.

"Who are you, to give orders here?" inquired a voice that seemed to come from a tomb rather than from a human breast.

"A Venetian like yourself! Taddeo, the former sculptor at the Arsenal; now appointed an officer by the naval commander-in-chief."

"Taddeo!" repeated the voice, with a low and mournful accent.

The officer then saw a man of some sixty years, with shackles around his hands and feet, whom a Moor of equal age was leading over the open space in front of the Lazaretto.

"Taddeo!" murmured the old man, drawing his hand across his forehead; "yes, in my better days—formerly—I knew some one by that name."

The moon now fell upon the prisoner's features. Taddeo started back. He had recognised Ottale.

"My father! my good father! Heavens! you here? You bound in fetters? What means this? And Ziana—Ziana, my beloved?"

The old man glanced at the Moor who usually led him, and murmured between his teeth, "That man is insane!"

"I am not insane," resumed Taddeo. "Recognise me, my father! I precede in Venice a victorious fleet. But you, you here? Oh, I I will set you free! I have that right. It is one of the privileges of the first sailor who lands after a victory."

Now the guns of the fleet spoke in thunder, and were answered from the forts of Venice.

"Do you hear, *padre?*" cried Taddeo, pressing the old man to his heart. "It is we, the sons of Venice, who have returned, loaded with spoils and banners, from Barbary. Look at those flags, those trophies; see the name of the doge embroidered in the midst of these warlike pennons."

"The doge is dead!" murmured the old man; "the doge is dead! Pray for his soul! The doge is dead!"

He smiled the smile of madness, and drew the Moor's attention to the flag which Taddeo bore.

"Wo to us!" cried the young man, drawing his hand across his brow. "And Ziana! Ziana! where is she? Speak! We may not enter the city until to-morrow; but, even if I have to swim from here to the Ghetto, I will be the first to carry her the news of a victory."

The old man held in his hand a soiled, ragged riband made of silver threads He sang a verse of the ballad of the Paludes, beating the time with this riband.

"Dark or fair,
To his lair
The Orco takes them all, to dwell
In his cave,
'Neath the wave,
Where the last laguna breasts the swell!"

"Damnation!" resumed the young man; "there is nothing to hope from him; but you, his guide!"

The Moor whispered for some time in Taddeo's ear. While he spoke, the countenance of the young man expressed at once stupor and anxiety. Suddenly, he dropped his head upon his breast, and wept abundantly.

"Sentenced by the Three! Impossible to free him," resumed he; "that is impossible! But Ziana?"

"Excellency, it is not known what became of the poor girl. The Leads and the Wells are tombs that keep well their dead."

The young man was silent; but a week later the following incidents took place within the Ducal Palace.

* * * * * * *

That part of the *Cortile* which the young officer, wrapped in a cloak, was now crossing, was robed in shadowy darkness, when, under those porticoes, closed at that hour, and guarded on the outside by the sentries of the palace, he met a human form stretched at the foot of the staircase that leads to the ducal gallery. This phantom uttered a faint scream at the sight of the uniform and countenance of Taddeo.

"There! this way! go up!" murmured he, taking hold of the officer's belt.

The latter then distinguished in his strange interlocutor an old man, whose scanty hair, wet with perspiration, clung to his brow; his nails were bleeding; his face was bruised as if he had been engaged in some long and toilsome labour. He held in his hand one of those iron bars which the water-carriers of Venice use to carry their pails to the copper wells of Saint Mark.

"There!" resumed he; "there, I say. I have seen—hush!"

He held his finger on his lips, with a dreadful, mysterious, and sinister look.

"They are there—both there!" resumed he "I have seen them—her and him. She has her white veil on, and he his mantle. I replaced the stone. Never fear; they will not find it out."

In spite of the active searches of Taddeo, he had been unable to discover any trace of the unfortunate Ziana. He had searched the quays, the canals, all in vain. A resistless sadness consumed him ; an imperious desire of discovering.

"Ottale !" cried he, recognising the Jew.

It was he indeed.

"Gracious Heaven !" thought Taddeo, "have I met, then, with what I sought? All powerful God, lead me towards Ziana !"

This thought shot so rapidly athwart his mind, that he blindly followed Ottale. Dark was the vaulted passage, and both glided like shadows over the pavement. When they reached the spot where formerly was the apartment of Alessandro, the Jew stopped, with a shudder, before a wall of newly-laid masonry. He then drew the iron bar from beneath his cloak, and introducing it within one of the fissures, he loosened first one stone, then two. He now interrupted his toil to breathe.

Taddeo's soul now hung with devouring anxiety on every one of his motions. With a lover's inconsistency, he expected to see Ziana herself issue from amid those crumbling stones.

"Is it a crime that I am about to witness?" murmured he. "I know not; but I tremble here like a sacrilegious thief before his holy booty. Come, Ottale, proceed."

The two stones having yielded, there was room for one person only to pass. Ottale went in first, and then drew the young man in after him.

The Venetian navy officer then saw a sight as singular as fearful. Two corpses, disfigured by the mephitic atmosphere of that room, clung yet to each other as in a last embrace. The man was livid and purple ; his countenance had that muscular contraction indicative of a violent death. The female held between her fingers a ring of uncommon size, on which were engraven the arms of the doge.

In mute despair, Taddeo contemplated that sepulchre and its two inmates, when he heard a half-suppressed scream ; it was uttered by the Jew, as he threw himself upon the already-decaying hand of Alessandro.

"To the Lazaretto !" said he, after replacing both the stones, and casting his iron bar into the courtyard. "To the Lazaretto! At last I have escaped from it, but I must die there."

He had recovered a lucid interval of reason, but lost it again as soon as his hands and feet were manacled, in spite of Taddeo's supplications. Two of the keepers had discovered his escape, and recaptured him in the ducal courtyard. Ottale expired the same day on which Cagliostro died in his prison at Fort Saint Angelo.

There is yet to be seen at Venice, near the main gate of the Ghetto, a dark house, with doors always closed, where a glass-ware merchant has opened a shop. On the first story there is a little window, that still preserves the leaden sash and trellis-work of the olden times. The spider weaves his web in its corners, for the window opens no more: it has been nailed down This was Ziana's window. The house worthy of Joyant's pencil is sad as a *lamento.* At evening, where Ziana once leaned out, eagerly listening to the slightest noise upon the canal, the police of Venice now allow a shameless courtesan to appear with flowers in her hair and a paper fan in her hand. This woman allures thither sailors and foreigners.

Fitting conclusion for that singular government. A record of vice and corruption.

THE END.

AMERICAN NOTES

FOR

GENERAL CIRCULATION.

BY CHARLES DICKENS.

NEW-YORK:
PUBLISHED BY HARPER & BROTHERS, 82 CLIFF-ST.
1842.

I DEDICATE

THIS BOOK

THOSE FRIENDS OF MINE

IN AMERICA

WHO,

[illegible] ME A WELCOME I MUST EVER GRATEFULLY AND

PROUDLY REMEMBER,

LEFT MY JUDGMENT

FREE;

AND WHO,

LOVING THEIR COUNTRY, CAN BEAR THE TRUTH,

WHEN IT IS TOLD GOOD-HUMOUREDLY,

AND IN A KIND SPIRIT.

CONTENTS.

NOTES ON AMERICA.

CHAPTER I.

GOING AWAY.

I SHALL never forget the one fourth serious and three fourths comical astonishment with which, on the morning of the third of January, eighteen hundred and forty-two, I opened the door of, and put my head into, a "stateroom" on board the Britannia steam-packet, twelve hundred tons per register, bound for Halifax and Boston, and carrying her majesty's mails.

That this stateroom had been specially engaged for "Charles Dickens, Esquire, and Lady," was rendered sufficiently clear, even to my scared intellect, by a very small manuscript announcing the fact, which was pinned on a very flat quilt, covering a very thin mattress, spread like a surgical plaster on a most inaccessible shelf. But that this was the stateroom concerning which, Charles Dickens, Esquire, and Lady, had held daily and nightly conferences for at least four months preceding: that this could by any possibility be that small snug chamber of the imagination, which Charles Dickens, Esquire, with the spirit of prophecy strong upon him, had always foretold would contain, at least, one little sofa, and which his lady, with a modest yet most magnificent sense of its limited dimensions, had, from the first, opined would not hold more than two enormous portmanteaus in some odd corner out of sight (portmanteaus which could now no more be got in at the door, not to say stowed away, than a giraffe could be persuaded or forced into a flower-pot): that this utterly impracticable, thoroughly hopeless, and profoundly preposterous box, had the remotest reference to, or connexion with, those chaste and pretty, not to say gorgeous little bowers, sketched by a masterly hand, in the highly varnished lithographic plan hanging up in the agent's counting-house in the city of London: that this room of state, in short, could be anything but a pleasant fiction and cheerful jest of the captain's, invented and put in practice for the better relish and enjoyment of the real stateroom presently to be disclosed: these were truths which I really could not, for the moment, bring my mind at all to bear upon or comprehend. And I sat down upon a kind of horsehair slab, or perch, of which there were two within; and looked, without any expression of countenance whatever, at some friends who had come on board with us, and who were crushing their faces into all manner of shapes by endeavouring to squeeze them through the small doorway.

We had experienced a pretty smart shock before coming below, which, but that we were the most sanguine people living, might have prepared us for the worst. The imaginative artist to whom I have already made allusion, has depicted, in the same great work, a chamber of almost interminable perspective, furnished, as Mr. Robins would say, in a style of more than Eastern splendour, and filled (but not conveniently so) with groups of ladies and gentlemen, in the very highest state of enjoyment and vivacity. Before descending into the bowels of the ship, we had passed from the deck into a long, narrow apartment, not unlike a gigantic hearse with windows in the sides; having at the upper end a melancholy stove, at which three or four chilly stewards were warming their hands, while on either side, extending down its whole dreary length, was a long, long table, over each of which a rack, fixed to the low roof, and stuck full of drinking-glasses and cruet-stands, hinted dismally at rolling seas and heavy weather. I had not, at that time, seen the ideal presentment of this chamber, which has since gratified me so much, but I observed that one of our friends who had made the arrangements for our voyage, turned pale on entering, retreated on the friend behind him, smote his forehead involuntarily, and said, below his breath, "Impossible! it cannot be!" or words to that effect. He recovered himself, however, by a great effort, and after a preparatory cough or two, cried, with a ghastly smile, which is still before me, looking at the same time round the walls, "Ha! the breakfast-room, steward—eh?" We all foresaw what the answer must be; we knew the agony he suffered. He had often spoken of *the saloon;* had taken in and lived upon the pictorial idea; had usually given us to understand, at home, that to form a just conception of it, it would be necessary to multiply the size and furniture of an ordinary drawing-room by seven, and then fall short of the reality. When the man in reply avowed the truth; the blunt, remorseless, naked truth; "This is the saloon, sir," he actually reeled beneath the blow.

In persons who were so soon to part, and interpose between their else daily communication the formidable barrier of many thousand miles of stormy space, and who were, for that reason, anxious to cast no other cloud, not even the passing shadow of a moment's disappointment or discomfiture, upon the short interval of happy companionship that yet remained to them—in persons so situated, the natural transition from these first surprises was obviously into peals of hearty laughter; and I can report that I, for one, being still seated upon the slab or perch before mentioned, roared outright until the vessel rang again. Thus, in less than two minutes after coming upon it for the first time, we all by common consent agreed, that this stateroom was the pleasantest and most facetious and capital contrivance possible; and that, to have had it one inch larger, would have been quite a disagreeable and deplorable state of things. And with this, and with showing how, by very nearly closing the door, and twining in and out like serpents, and by counting the little washing slab as standing-room, we could manage to insinuate four people into it, all at one time; and entreating each other to observe how very airy it was (in dock), and how there was a beautiful port-hole which could be kept open all day (weather permitting), and how there was quite a large bull's-eye just over the looking-glass which would render shaving a perfectly easy and delightful process (when the ship didn't roll too much); we arrived, at last, at the unanimous conclusion that it was rather spacious than otherwise; though I do verily believe that, deducting the two berths, one above the other, than which nothing smaller for sleeping in was ever made except coffins, it was no bigger than one of those hackney cabriolets which have the door behind, and shoot their fares out, like sacks of coals, upon the pavement.

Having settled this point to the perfect satisfaction of all parties, concerned and unconcerned, we sat down round the fire in the ladies' cabin, just to try the effect. It was rather dark, certainly, but somebody said, "of course it would be light at sea," a proposition to which we all assented; echoing "of course, of course;" though it would be exceedingly difficult to say why we thought so. I remember, too, when we had discovered and exhausted another topic of consolation in the circumstance of this ladies' cabin adjoining our stateroom, and the consequently immense feasibility of sitting there at all times and seasons, and had fallen into a momentary silence, leaning our faces on our hands and looking at the fire, one of our party said, with the solemn air of a man who had made a discovery, "What a relish mulled claret will have down here!" which appeared to strike us all so forcibly, as though there were something spicy and high-flavoured in cabins, which essentially improved that composition, and rendered it quite incapable of perfection anywhere else.

There was a stewardess, too, actively engaged in producing clean sheets and tablecloths from the very entrails of the sofas, and from unexpected lockers, of such artful mechanism, that it made one's head ache to see them opened one after another, and rendered it quite a distracting circumstance to follow her proceedings, and to find that every nook and corner and individual piece of furniture was something else besides what it pretended to be, and was a mere trap and deception, and place of secret stowage, whose ostensible purpose was its least useful one.

God bless that stewardess for her piously fraudulent account of January voyages! God bless her for her clear recollection of the companion passage of last year, when nobody was ill, and everybody danced from morning to night, and it was a "run" of twelve days, and a piece of the purest frolic, delight, and jollity! All happiness be with her for her bright face and pleasant Scotch tongue, which had sounds of old Home in it for my fellow-traveller; and for her predictions of fair winds and fine weather (all wrong, or I shouldn't be half so fond of her); and for the ten thousand small fragments of genuine womanly tact, by which, without piecing them elaborately together, and patching them up into shape, and form, and case, and pointed application, she nevertheless did plainly show that all young mothers on one side of the Atlantic were near and close at hand to their little children left upon the other; and that what seemed to the uninitiated a serious journey, was, to those who were in the secret, a mere frolic, to be sung about and whistled at! Light be her heart, and gay her merry eyes, for years!

The state-room had grown pretty fast; but by this time it had expanded into something quite bulky, and almost boasted a bay-window to view the sea from. So we went upon the deck again in high spirits; and there, everything was in such a state of bustle and active preparation, that the blood quickened its pace, and whirled through one's veins on that clear, frosty morning with involuntary mirthfulness. For every gallant ship was riding slowly up and down, and every little boat was plashing noisily in the water; and knots of people stood upon the wharf, gazing with a kind of "dread delight" on the far-famed fast American steamer; and one party of men were "taking in the milk," or, in other words, getting the cow on board; and another were filling the icehouses to the very throat with fresh provisions; with butchers' meat and garden-stuff, pale sucking-pigs, calves' heads in scores, beef, veal, and pork, and poultry out of all proportion; and others were coiling ropes, and busy with oakum yarns; and others were lowering heavy packages into the hold; and the purser's head was barely visible as it loomed in a state of exquisite perplexity from the midst of a vast pile of passengers' luggage; and there seemed to be nothing going on anywhere, or uppermost in the mind of anybody, but preparation for this mighty voyage. This, with the bright, cold sun, the bracing air, the crisply-curled water, the thin, white crust of morning ice upon the decks, which crackled with a sharp and cheerful sound beneath the lightest tread, was irresistible. And when, again upon the shore, we turned and saw from the vessel's mast her name signalled in flags of joyous colours, and, fluttering by their side, the beautiful American banner with its stars and stripes, the long three thousand miles and more, and, longer still, the six whole months of absence, so dwindled and faded, that the ship had gone out and come home again, and it was broad spring already in the Coburg Dock at Liverpool.

I had not inquired among my medical acquaintance whether turtle, and cold punch, with hock, Champagne, and claret, and all the slight et cetera usually included in an unlimited order for a good dinner—especially when it is left to the liberal construction of my faultless friend, Mr. Radley, of the Adelphi Hotel—are peculiarly calculated to suffer a sea-change; or whether a plain mutton-chop, and a glass or two of sherry, would be less likely of conversion into foreign and disconcerting material. My own opinion is, that whether one is discreet or indiscreet in these particulars, on the eve of a sea-voyage, is a matter of little consequence; and that, to use a common phrase, "it comes to very much the same thing in the end." Be this as it may, I know that the dinner of that day was undeniably perfect; that it comprehended all these items, and a great many more; and that we all did ample justice to it. And I know too, that, bating a certain tacit avoidance of any allusion to-morrow, such as may be supposed to prevail between delicate-minded turnkeys, and a sensitive prisoner who is to be hanged next morning, we got on very well, and, all things considered, were merry enough.

When the morning—*the* morning—came, and we met at breakfast, it was curious to see how eager all were to prevent a moment's pause in the conversation, and how astoundingly gay everybody was: the forced spirits of each member of the little party having as much likeness to his natural mirth, as hothouse pease at five guineas the quart resemble in flavour the growth of the dews, and air, and rain of Heaven. But as one o'clock, the hour for going aboard, drew near, this volubility dwindled away by little and little, despite the most persevering efforts to the contrary, until at last, the matter being now quite desperate, we threw off all disguise; openly speculated upon where we should be this time to-morrow, this time next day, and so forth; and intrusted a vast number of messages to those who intended returning to town that night, which were to be delivered at home and elsewhere without fail, within the very shortest possible space of time after the arrival of the railway train at Euston Square. And commissions and remembrances do so crowd upon one at such a time, that we were still busied with this employment when we found ourselves fused, as it were, into a dense conglomeration of passengers, and passengers' friends, and passengers' luggage, all jumbled together on the deck of a small steamboat, and panting and snorting off to the packet, which had worked out of dock yesterday afternoon, and was now lying at her moorings in the river.

And there she is! all eyes are turned to where she lies, dimly discernible through the gathering fog of the early winter afternoon; every finger is pointed in the same direction; and murmurs of interest and admiration, as, "How beautiful she looks!" "How trim she is!" are heard on every side. Even the lazy gentleman, with his hat on one side and his hands in his pockets, who has dispensed so much consolation by inquiring with a yawn of another gentleman whether he is "going across," as if it were a ferry—even he condescends to look that way and nod his head, as who should say, "No mistake about *that;*" and not even the sage Lord Burleigh, in his nod, included half so much as this lazy gentleman of might, who has made the passage (as everybody on board has found out already, it's impossible to say how) thirteen times without a single accident! There is another passenger very much wrapped up, who has been frowned down by the rest, and morally trampled upon and crushed, for presuming to inquire, with a timid interest, how long it is since the poor President went down. He is standing close to the lazy gentleman, and says, with a faint smile, that he believes she is a very strong ship; to which the lazy gentleman, looking first in his questioner's eye and then very hard in the wind's, answers unexpectedly and ominously that she need be. Upon this, the lazy gentleman instantly falls very low in the popular estimation, and the passengers, with looks of defiance, whisper to each other that he is an ass and an impostor, and clearly don't know anything at all about it.

But we are made fast alongside the packet, whose huge red funnel is smoking bravely, giving rich promise of serious intentions. Packing-cases, portmanteaus, carpet-bags, and boxes, are already passed from hand to hand, and hauled on board with breathless rapidity. The officers, smartly dressed, are at the gangway, handing the passengers up the side, and hurrying the men. In five minutes' time the little steamer is utterly deserted, and the packet is beset and overrun by its late freight, who instantly pervade the whole ship, and are to be met with by the dozen in every nook and corner; swarming down below with their own baggage, and stumbling over other people's; disposing themselves comfortably in wrong cabins, and creating a most horrible confusion by having to turn out again; madly bent upon opening locked doors, and on forcing a passage into all kinds of out-of-the-way places, where there is no thoroughfare; sending wild stewards, with elfin hair, to and fro upon the breezy decks on unintelligible errands, impossible of execution; and, in short, creating the most extraordinary and bewildering tumult. In the midst of all this, the lazy gentleman, who seems to have no luggage of any kind—not so much as a friend, even—lounges up and down the hurricane-deck, coolly puffing a cigar; and, as this unconcerned demeanour again exalts him in the opinion of those who have leisure to observe his proceedings, every time he looks up at the masts, or down at the decks, or over the side, they look there too, as wondering whether he sees anything wrong anywhere, and hoping that, in case he should, he will have the goodness to mention it.

What have we here? The captain's boat! and yonder the captain himself. Now, by all our hopes and wishes, the very man he ought to be! A well-made, tight-built, dapper little fellow, with a ruddy face, which is a letter of invitation to shake him by both hands at once; and with a clear blue honest eye, that it does one good to see one's sparkling image in. "Ring the bell!" "Ding, ding, ding!" the very bell is in a hurry. "Now for the shore; who's for the shore?" These gentlemen, I am sorry to say." They are away, and never said good-by. Ah! now they wave it from the little boat. "Good-by! Good-by!" Three cheers from them; three more from us; three more from them; and they are gone.

To and fro, to and fro, to and fro again a hundred times! This waiting for the latest mailbags is worse than all. If we could have gone off in the midst of that last burst, we should have started triumphantly; but to lie here, two hours and more, in the damp fog, neither staying at home nor going abroad, is letting one gradually down into the very depth of dulness and low spirits. A speck in the mist at last! That's something. It is the boat we wait for! That's more to the purpose. The captain appears on the paddle-box with his speaking-trumpet; the officers take their stations; all hands are on the alert; the flagging hopes of the passengers revive; the cooks pause in their savoury work, and look out with faces full of interest. The boat comes alongside; the bags are dragged in anyhow, and flung down for the moment anywhere. Three cheers more; and as the first one rings upon our ears, the vessel throbs like a strong giant that has just received the breath of life; the two great wheels turn fiercely round for the first time; and the noble ship, with wind and tide astern, breaks proudly through the lashed and foaming water.

CHAPTER II.

THE PASSAGE OUT.

We all dined together that day; and a rather formidable party we were: no fewer than eighty-six strong. The vessel being pretty deep in the water, with all her coals on board and so many passengers, and the weather being calm and quiet, there was but little motion; so that before the dinner was half over, even those passengers who were most distrustful of themselves plucked up amazingly; and those who in the morning had returned to the universal question, "Are you a good sailor?" a very decided negative, now either parried the inquiry with the evasive reply, "Oh! I suppose I'm no worse than anybody else;" or, reckless of all moral obligations, answered boldly, "Yes:" and with some irritation too, as though they would add, "I should like to know what you see in *me*, sir, particularly, to justify suspicion!"

Notwithstanding this high tone of courage and confidence, I could not but observe that very few remained long over their wine; and that everybody had an unusual love of the open air; and that the favourite and most coveted seats were invariably those nearest to the door. The tea-table, too, was by no means as well attended as the dinner-table; and there was less whist-playing than might have been expected. Still, with the exception of one lady, who had retired with some precipitation at dinner-time, immediately after being assisted to the finest cut of a very yellow boiled leg of mutton with very green capers, there were no invalids as yet; and walking, and smoking, and drinking of brandy-and-water (but always in the open air) went on with unabated spirit, until eleven o'clock or thereabouts, when "turning in"—no sailor of seven hours' experience talks of going to bed—became the order of the night. The perpetual tramp of boot-heels on the decks gave place to a heavy silence, and the whole human freight was stowed away below, excepting a very few stragglers, like myself, who were probably, like me, afraid to go there.

To one unaccustomed to such scenes, this is a very striking time on shipboard. Afterward, and when its novelty had long worn off, it never ceased to have a peculiar interest and charm for me. The gloom through which the great black mass holds its direct and certain course; the rushing water, plainly heard, but dimly seen; the broad, white, glistening track, that follows in the vessel's wake; the men on the look-out forward, who would be scarcely visible against the dark sky but for their blotting out some score of glistening stars; the helmsman at the wheel, with the illuminated card before him, shining, a speck of light amid the darkness, like something sentient and of Divine intelligence; the melancholy sighing of the wind through block, and rope, and chain; the gleaming forth of light from every crevice, nook, and tiny piece of glass about the decks, as though the ship were filled with fire in hiding, ready to burst through any outlet, wild with its resistless power of death and ruin. At first, too, and even when the hour, and all the objects it exalts, have come to be familiar, it is difficult, alone and thoughtful, to hold them to their proper shapes and forms. They change with the wandering fancy; assume the semblance of things left far away; put on the well-remembered aspect of favourite places dearly loved; and even people them with shadows. Streets, houses, rooms—figures so like their usual occupants, that they have startled me by their reality, which far exceeded, as it seemed to me, all power of mine to conjure up the absent—have, many and many a time, at such an hour, grown suddenly out of objects with whose real look, and use, and purpose I was as well acquainted as with my own two hands.

My own two hands, and feet likewise, being very cold, however, on this particular occasion, I crept below at midnight. It was not exactly comfortable below. It was decidedly close; and it was impossible to be unconscious of the presence of that extraordinary compound of strange smells, which is to be found nowhere but on board ship, and which is such a subtle perfume that it seems to enter at every pore of the skin, and whisper of the hold. Two passengers' wives (one of them my own) lay already in silent agonies on the sofa; and one lady's maid (*my* lady's) was a mere bundle on the floor, execrating her destiny, and pounding her curl-papers among the stray boxes. Everything sloped the wrong way—which in itself was an aggravation scarcely to be borne. I had left the door open, a moment before, in the bosom of a gentle declivity, and, when I turned to shut it, it was on the summit of a lofty eminence. Now every plank and timber creaked, as if the ship were made of wicker-work; and now crackled, like an enormous fire of the driest possible twigs. There was nothing for it but bed; so I went to bed.

It was pretty much the same for the next two days, with a tolerably fair wind and dry weather. I read in bed (but to this hour I don't know what) a good deal; and reeled on deck a little; drank cold brandy-and-water with an unspeakable disgust, and ate hard biscuit perseveringly: not ill, but going to be.

It is the third morning. I am awakened out of my sleep by a dismal shriek from my wife, who demands to know whether there's any danger. I rouse myself, and look out of bed. The water-jug is plunging and leaping like a lively dolphin; all the smaller articles are afloat, except my shoes, which are stranded on a carpet-bag, high and dry, like a couple of coal-barges. Suddenly I see them spring into the air, and behold the looking-glass, which is nailed to the wall, sticking fast upon the ceiling. At the same time the door entirely disappears, and a new one is opened in the floor. Then I begin to comprehend that the state-room is standing on its head.

Before it is possible to make any arrangement at all compatible with this novel state of things, the ship rights. Before one can say "Thank Heaven!" she wrongs again. Before one can cry she *is* wrong, she seems to have started forward, and to be a creature actively running of its own accord, with broken knees and failing legs, through every variety of hole and pitfall, and stumbling constantly. Before one can so much as wonder, she takes a high leap into the air. Before she has well done that, she takes a deep dive into the water. Before she has gained the surface, she throws a summerset. The instant she is on her legs, she rushes backward. And so she goes on staggering, heaving, wrestling, leaping, diving, jumping, pitching, throbbing, rolling, and rocking: and going through all these movements, sometimes by turns, and sometimes all together: until one feels disposed to roar for mercy.

A steward passes. "Steward!" "Sir?" "What *is* the matter? what *do* you call this?" "Rather a heavy sea on, sir, and a head wind."

A head wind! Imagine a human face upon the vessel's prow, with fifteen thousand Sampsons in one bent upon driving her back, and hitting her exactly between the eyes whenever she attempts to advance an inch. Imagine the ship herself, with every pulse and artery of her huge body swollen and bursting under this maltreatment, sworn to go on or die. Imagine the wind howling, the sea roaring, the rain beating: all in furious array against her. Picture the sky both dark and wild, and the clouds, in fearful sympathy with the waves, making another ocean in the air. Add to all this the clattering on deck and down below; the tread of hurried feet; the loud, hoarse shouts of seamen; the gurgling in and out of water through the scuppers; with, every now and then, the striking of a heavy sea upon the planks above, with the deep, dead, heavy sound of thunder heard within a vault — and there is the head-wind of that January morning.

I say nothing of what may be called the domestic noises of the ship: such as the breaking of glass and crockery, the tumbling down of stewards, the gambols, overhead, of loose casks and truant dozens of bottled porter, and the very remarkable and far from exhilarating sounds raised in their various state-rooms by the seventy passengers who were too ill to get up to breakfast. I say nothing of them; for, although I lay listening to this concert for three or four days, I don't think I heard it for more than a quarter of a minute, at the expiration of which term I lay down again excessively sea-sick.

Not sea-sick, be it understood, in the ordinary acceptation of the term—I wish I had been—but in a form which I have never seen or heard described, though I have no doubt it is very common. I lay there, all the day long, quite coolly and contentedly; with no sense of weariness, with no desire to get up, or get better, or take the air; with no curiosity, or care, or regret, of any sort or degree, saving that I think I can remember, in this universal indifference, having a kind of lazy joy—of fiendish delight, if anything so lethargic can be dignified with the title—in the fact of my wife being too ill to talk to me. If I may be allowed to illustrate my state of mind by such an example, I should say that I was exactly in the condition of the elder Mr. Willet after the incursion of the rioters into his bar at Chigwell. Nothing would have surprised me. If, in the momentary illumination of any ray of intelligence that may have come upon me in the way of thoughts of home, a goblin postman, with a scarlet coat and bell, had come into that little kennel before me, broad awake in broad day, and, apologizing for being damp through walking in the sea, had handed me a letter, directed to myself in familiar characters, I am certain I should not have felt one atom of astonishment: I should have been perfectly satisfied. If Neptune himself had walked in, with a toasted shark on his trident, I should have looked upon the event as one of the very commonest every-day occurrences.

Once—once—I found myself on deck. I don't know how I got there, or what possessed me to go there, but there I was; and completely dressed too, with a huge peacoat on, and a pair of boots such as no weak man in his senses could ever have got into. I found myself standing, when a gleam of consciousness came upon me, holding on to something; I don't know what. I think it was the boatswain; or it may have been the pump; or possibly the cow. I can't say how long I had been there; whether a day or a minute. I recollect trying to think about something (about anything in the whole wide world, I was not particular) without the smallest effect. I could not even make out which was the sea, and which the sky; for the horizon seemed drunk, and was flying wildly about in all directions. Even in that incapable state, however, I recognised the lazy gentleman standing before me, nautically clad in a suit of shaggy blue, with an oilskin hat; but I was too imbecile, although I knew it to be he, to separate him from his dress, and tried to call him, I remember, *Pilot*. After another interval of total unconsciousness, I found he had gone, and recognised another figure in its place. It seemed to wave and fluctuate before me as though I saw it reflected in an unsteady looking-glass; but I knew it for the captain; and such was the cheerful influence of his face, that I tried to smile; yes, even then I tried to smile. I saw by his gestures that he addressed me; but it was a long time before I could make out that he remonstrated against my standing up to my knees in water—as I was; of course I don't know why. I tried to thank him, but couldn't. I could only point to my boots—or wherever I supposed my boots to be—and say, in a plaintive voice, "Cork soles;" at the same time endeavouring, I am told, to sit down in the pool. Finding that I was quite insensible, and for the time a maniac, he humanely conducted me below.

There I remained until I got better; suffering, whenever I was recommended to eat anything, an amount of anguish only second to that which is said to be endured by the apparently drowned in the process of restoration to life. One gentleman on board had a letter of introduction to me from a mutual friend in London. He sent it below with his card on the morning of the head-wind; and I was long troubled with the idea that he might be up and well, and a hundred times a day expecting me to call upon him in the saloon. I imagined him one of those cast-iron images—I will not call them men—who ask, with red faces and lusty voices, what sea-sickness means, and whether it really is as bad as it is represented to be. This was very torturing indeed; and I don't think I ever felt such perfect gratification and gratitude of heart as I did when I heard from the ship's doctor that he had been obliged to put a large mustard poultice on this very gentleman's stomach. I date my recovery from the receipt of that intelligence.

It was materially assisted though, I have no doubt, by a heavy gale of wind, which came slowly up at sunset, when we were about ten days out, and raged with gradually increasing fury until morning, saving that it lulled for an hour a little before midnight. There was something in the unnatural repose of that hour, and in the after-gathering of the storm, so inconceivably awful and tremendous, that its bursting into full violence was almost a relief.

The labouring of the ship in the troubled sea on this night I shall never forget. "Will it ever be worse than this?" was a question I had often heard asked, when everything was sliding and bumping about, and when it certainly did seem difficult to comprehend the possibility of anything afloat being more disturbed without toppling over and going down. But what the agitation of a steam-vessel is, on a bad winter's night in the wild Atlantic, it is impossible for the most vivid imagination to conceive. To say that she is flung down on her side in the waves, with her masts dipping into them, and that, springing up again, she rolls over on the other side, until a heavy sea strikes her with the noise of a hundred great guns and hurls her back—that she stops, and staggers, and shivers, as though stunned, and then, with a violent throbbing at her heart, darts onward like a monster goaded into madness, to be beaten down, and battered, and crushed, and leaped on by the angry sea—that thunder, lightning, hail, and rain, and wind, are all in fierce contention for the mastery—that every plank has its groan, every nail its shriek, and every drop of water in the great ocean its howling voice—is nothing. To say that all is grand, and all appalling and horrible in the last degree, is nothing. Words cannot express it; thoughts cannot convey it. Only a dream can call it up again in all its fury, rage, and passion.

And yet, in the very midst of these terrors, I was placed in a situation so exquisitely ridiculous, that even then I had as strong a sense of its absurdity as I have now, and could no more help laughing than I can at any other comical incident happening under circumstances the most favourable to its enjoyment. About midnight we shipped a sea, which forced its way through the skylights, burst open the doors above, and came raging and roaring down into the ladies' cabin, to the unspeakable consternation of my wife and a little Scotch lady—who, by the way, had previously sent a message to the captain by the stewardess, requesting him, with her compliments, to have a steel conductor immediately attached to the top of every mast, and to the chimney, in order that the ship might not be struck by lightning. They, and the handmaid before mentioned, being in such ecstacies of fear that I scarcely knew what to do with them, I naturally bethought myself of some restorative or comfortable cordial; and nothing better occurring to me at the moment than hot brandy-and-water, I procured a tumbler-full without delay. It being impossible to stand or sit without holding on, they were all heaped together in one corner of a long sofa—a fixture extending entirely across the cabin—where they clung to each other in momentary expectation of being drowned. When I approached this place with my specific, and was about to administer it, with many consolatory expressions, to the nearest sufferer, what was my dismay to see them all roll slowly down to the other end! And when I staggered to that end, and held out the glass once more, how immensely baffled were my good intentions by the ship giving another lurch, and their all rolling back again! I suppose I dodged them up and down this sofa for at least a quarter of an hour without reaching them once; and by the time I did catch them, the brandy-and-water was diminished, by constant spilling, to a tea-spoonful. To complete the group, it is necessary to recognise in this disconcerted dodger a very pale individual, who had shaved his beard and brushed his hair last at Liverpool, and whose only articles of dress (linen not included) were a pair of dreadnaught trousers, a blue jacket, formerly admired upon the Thames at Richmond, no stockings, and one slipper.

Of the outrageous antics performed by that ship next morning; which made bed a practical joke, and getting up, by any process short of falling out, an impossibility, I say nothing. But anything like the utter dreariness and desolation that met my eyes when I, literally, "tumbled up" on deck at noon, I never saw. Ocean and sky were all of one dull, heavy, uniform, lead colour. There was no extent of prospect even over the dreary waste that lay around us, for the sea ran high, and the horizon encompassed us like a large black hoop. Viewed from the air, or some tall bluff on shore, it would have been imposing and stupendous no doubt; but seen from the wet and rolling decks, it only impressed one giddily and painfully. In the gale of last night the lifeboat had been crushed by one blow of the sea like a walnut-shell; and there it hung dangling in the air: a mere fagot of crazy boards. The planking of the paddle-boxes had been torn sheer away. The wheels were exposed and bare; and they whirled and dashed their spray about the decks at random. Chimney, white with crusted salt; topmasts struck; storm-sails set; rigging all knotted, tangled, wet, and drooping: a gloomier picture it would be hard to look upon.

I was now comfortably established by courtesy in the ladies' cabin, where, besides ourselves, there were only four other passengers. First, the little Scotch lady before-mentioned, on her way to join her husband at New-York, who had settled there three years before. Secondly and thirdly, an honest young Yorkshireman, connected with some American house; domiciled in that same city, and carrying thither his beautiful young wife, to whom he had been married but a fortnight, and who was the fairest specimen of a comely English country girl I have ever seen. Fourthly, fifthly, and lastly, another couple: newly married too, if one might judge from the endearments they frequently interchanged: of whom I know no more than that they were rather a mysterious, run-away kind of couple; that the lady had great personal attractions also; and that the gentleman carried more guns with him than Robinson Crusoe, wore a shooting-coat, and had two great dogs on board. On farther consideration, I remember that he tried hot roast pig and bottled ale as a cure for sea-sickness; and that he took these remedies (usually in bed) day after day, with astonishing perseverance. I may add, for the information of the curious, that they decidedly failed.

The weather continuing obstinately and almost unprecedently bad, we usually straggled into this cabin, more or less faint and miserable, about an hour before noon, and lay down on the sofas to recover; during which interval, the captain would look in to communicate the state of the wind, the moral certainty of its changing to-morrow (the weather is always going to improve to-morrow, at sea), the vessel's rate of sailing, and so forth. Observations there were none to tell us of, for there was no sun to take them by. But a description of one day will serve for all the rest. Here it is.

The captain being gone, we compose ourselves to read, if the place be light enough; and if not, we doze and talk alternately. At one, a bell rings, and the stewardess comes down with a steaming dish of baked potatoes, and another of roasted apples; and plates of pig's face, cold ham, salt beef; or perhaps a smoking mess of rare hot collops. We fall to upon these dainties; eat as much as we can (we have great appetites now); and are as long as possible about it. If the fire will burn (it *will* sometimes) we are pretty cheerful. If it won't, we all remark to each other that it's very cold, rub our hands, cover ourselves with coats and cloaks, and lie down again to doze, talk, and read (provided as aforesaid) until dinner-time. At five, another bell rings, and the stewardess reappears with another dish of potatoes—boiled, this time—and store of hot meat of various kinds: not forgetting the roast pig, to be taken medicinally. We sit down at table again (rather more cheerfully than before); prolong the meal with a rather mouldy dessert of apples, grapes, and oranges; and drink our wine and brandy-and-water. The bottles and glasses are still upon the table, and the oranges, and so forth, are rolling about according to their fancy and the ship's way, when the doctor comes down, by special nightly invitation, to join our evening rubber: immediately on whose arrival we make a party at whist, and as it is a rough night and the cards will not lie on the cloth, we put the tricks in our pockets as we take them. At whist we remain with exemplary gravity (deducting a short time for tea and toast) until eleven o'clock, or thereabout; when the captain comes down again, in a sou'-wester hat tied under his chin, and a pilot-coat: making the ground wet where he stands. By this time the card-playing is over, and the bottles and glasses are again upon the table; and after an hour's pleasant conversation about the ship, the passengers, and things in general, the captain (who never goes to bed, and is never out of humour) turns up his coat collar for the deck again; shakes hands all around; and goes laughing out into the weather as merrily as to a birth-day party.

As to daily news, there is no dearth of that commodity. This passenger is reported to have lost fourteen pounds at Vingt-et-un in the saloon yesterday, and that passenger drinks his bottle of Champagne every day, and how he does it (being only a clerk), nobody knows. The head engineer has distinctly said that there never was such times—meaning weather—and four good hands are ill, and have given in, dead beat. Several berths are full of water, and all the cabins are leaky. The ship's cook, secretly swigging damaged whiskey, has been found drunk; and has been played upon by the fire-engine until quite sober. All the stewards have fallen down stairs at various dinner-times, and go about with plasters in various places. The baker is ill, and so is the pastry-cook. A new man, horribly indisposed, has been required to fill the place of the latter officer; and has been propped and jammed up with empty casks in a little house upon deck, and commanded to roll out pie-crust, which he protests (being highly bilious) it is death to him to look at. News! A dozen murders on shore would lack the interest of these slight incidents at sea.

Divided between our rubber and such topics as these, we were running (as we thought) into Halifax Harbour, on the fifteenth night, with little wind and a bright moon—indeed, we had made the Light at its outer entrance, and put the pilot in charge—when suddenly the ship struck upon a bank of mud. An immediate rush on deck took place of course; the sides were crowded in an instant; and for a few minutes we were in as lively a state of confusion as the greatest lover of disorder would desire to see. The passengers, and guns, and water-casks, and other heavy matters, being all huddled together aft, however, to lighten her in the head, she was soon got off; and after some driving on towards an uncomfortable line of objects (whose vicinity had been announced very early in the disaster by a loud cry of "Breakers a-head!") and much backing of paddles, and heaving of the lead into a constantly decreasing depth of water, we dropped anchor in a strange, outlandish-looking nook which nobody on board could recognise, although there was land all about us, and so close that we could plainly see the waving branches of the trees.

It was strange enough, in the silence of midnight, and the dead stillness that seemed to be created by the sudden and unexpected stoppage of the engine, which had been clanking and blasting in our ears incessantly for so many days, to watch the look of blank astonishment expressed in every face: beginning with the officers, tracing it through all the passengers, and descending to the very stokers and furnace-men, who emerged from below, one by one, and clustered together in a smoky group about the hatchway of the engine-room, comparing notes in whispers. After throwing up a few rockets and firing signal-guns in the hopes of being hailed from the land, or at least of seeing a light—but without any other sight or sound presenting itself—it was determined to send a boat on shore. It was amusing to observe how very kind some of the passengers were, in volunteering to go ashore in this same boat: for the general good, of course: not by any means because they thought the ship in an unsafe position, or contemplated the possibility of her heeling over in case the tide were running out Nor was it less amusing to remark how desperately unpopular the poor pilot became in one short minute. He had had his passage out from Liverpool, and during the whole voyage had been quite a notorious character, as a teller of anecdotes and cracker of jokes. Yet here were the very men who had laughed the loudest at his jests, now flourishing their fists in his face, loading him with imprecations, and defying him to his teeth as a villain!

The boat soon shoved off, with a lantern and sundry blue lights on board; and in less than an hour returned; the officer in command bringing with him a tolerably tall young tree, which he had plucked up by the roots, to satisfy certain distrustful passengers whose minds misgave them that they were to be imposed upon and shipwrecked, and who would on no other terms believe that he had been ashore, or had done anything but fraudulently row a little way into the mist, especially to deceive them, and compass their deaths. Our captain had foreseen from the first that we must be in a place called the Eastern Passage; and so we were. It was about the last place in the world in which we had any business or reason to be, but a sudden fog, and some error on the pilot's part, were the cause. We were surrounded by banks and rocks, and shoals of all kinds, but had happily drifted, it seemed, upon the only safe speck that was to be found thereabout. Eased by this report, and by the assurance that the tide was past the ebb, we turned in at three o'clock in the morning.

I was dressing about half past nine next day, when the noise above hurried me on deck. When I had left it over night, it was dark, foggy, and damp, and there were bleak hills all round us. Now, we were gliding down a smooth, broad stream, at the rate of eleven miles an hour: our colours flying gayly; our crew rigged out in their smartest clothes; our officers in uniform again; the sun shining as on a brilliant April day in England; the land stretched out on either side, streaked with light patches of snow; white wooden houses; people at their doors; telegraphs working; flags hoisted; wharfs appearing; ships; quays crowded with people; distant noises; shouts; men and boys running down steep places towards the pier: all more bright and gay and fresh to our unused eyes than words can paint them. We came to a wharf, paved with uplifted faces; got alongside, and were made fast, after some shouting and straining of cables; darted, a score of us, along the gangway, almost as soon as it was thrust out to meet us, and before it had reached the ship, and leaped upon the firm glad earth again!

I suppose this Halifax would have appeared an Elysium, though it had been a curiosity of ugly dullness. But I carried away with me a most pleasant impression of the town and its inhabitants, and have preserved it to this hour. Nor was it without regret that I came home, without having found an opportunity of returning thither, and once more shaking hands with the friends I made that day.

It happened to be the opening of the Legislative Council and General Assembly, at which ceremonial the forms observed on the commencement of a new session of Parliament in England were so closely copied, and so gravely presented on a small scale, that it was like looking at Westminster through the wrong end of a telescope. The governor, as her majesty's representative, delivered what may be called the speech from the throne. He said what he had to say manfully and well. The military band outside the building struck up "God save the Queen" with great vigour before his excellency had quite finished; the people shouted; the in's rubbed their hands; the out's shook their heads; the government party said there never was such a good speech; the opposition declared there never was such a bad one; the speaker and members of the House of Assembly withdrew from the bar to say a great deal among themselves and do a little; and, in short, everything went on, and promised to go on, just as it does at home upon the like occasions.

The town is built on the side of a hill, the highest point being commanded by a strong fortress, not yet quite finished. Several streets of good breadth and appearance extend from its summit to the water-side, and are intersected by cross streets running parallel with the river. The houses are chiefly of wood. The market is abundantly supplied; and provisions are exceedingly cheap. The weather being unusually mild at that time for the season of the year, there was no sleighing; but there were plenty of those vehicles in yards and by-places, and some of them, from the gorgeous quality of their decorations, might have "gone on" without alteration as triumphal cars in a melo-drama at Astley's. The day was uncommonly fine; the air bracing and healthful; the whole aspect of the town cheerful, thriving, and industrious.

We lay there seven hours to deliver and exchange the mails. At length, having collected all our bags and all our passengers (including two or three choice spirits, who, having indulged too freely in oysters and Champagne, were found lying insensible on their backs in unfrequented streets), the engines were again put in motion, and we stood off for Boston.

Encountering squally weather again in the Bay of Fundy, we tumbled and rolled about as usual all that night and all next day. On the next afternoon, that is to say, on Saturday, the twenty-second of January, an American pilot-boat came alongside, and soon afterward, the Britannia steam-packet, from Liverpool, eighteen days out, was telegraphed at Boston.

The indescribable interest with which I strained my eyes, as the first patches of American soil peeped like molehills from the green sea, and followed them, as they swelled, by slow and almost imperceptible degrees, into a continuous line of coast, can hardly be exaggerated. A sharp, keen wind, blew dead against us; a hard frost prevailed on shore; and the cold was most severe; yet the air was so intensely clear, and dry, and bright, that the temperature was not only endurable, but delicious.

How I remained on deck staring about me until we came alongside the dock, and how, though I had had as many eyes as Argus, I should have had them all wide open, and all employed on new objects, are topics which I will not prolong this chapter to discuss. Neither will I more than hint at my foreigner-like mistake in supposing that a party of most active persons, who scrambled on board at the peril of their lives as we approached the wharf, were newsmen, answering to that industrious class at home; whereas, despite the leathern wallets of news slung about the necks of some, and the broad sheets in the hands of all, they were editors, who boarded ships in person (as one gentleman in a worsted comforter informed me), "because they liked the excitement of it." Suffice it in this place to say, that one of these invaders, with a ready courtesy for which I thank him here most gratefully, went on before to order rooms at the hotel; and that when I followed, as I soon did, I found myself rolling through the long passages with an involuntary imitation of the gait of Mr. T. P. Cooke, in a new nautical melodrama.

"Dinner, if you please," said I to the waiter.

"When?" said the waiter.

"As quick as possible," said I.

"Right away?" said the waiter.

After a moment's hesitation, I answered, "No," at hazard.

"*Not* right away?" cried the waiter, with an amount of surprise that made me start.

I looked at him doubtfully, and returned, "No, I would rather have it in this private room. I like it very much."

At this, I really thought the waiter must have gone out of his mind; as I believe he would have done, but for the interposition of another man, who whispered in his ear, "Directly."

"Well! and that's a fact!" said the waiter, looking helplessly at me: "Right away."

I saw now that "Right away" and "Directly" were one and the same thing. So I reversed my previous answer, and sat down to dinner in ten minutes afterward; and a capital dinner it was.

The hotel (a very excellent one), is called the Tremont House. It has more galleries, colonnades, piazzas, and passages, than I can remember, or the reader would believe; and is some trifle smaller than Bedford Square.

CHAPTER THE THIRD.

BOSTON.

In all the public establishments of America

the utmost courtesy prevails. Most of our departments are susceptible of considerable improvement in this respect, but the Custom-house, above all others, would do well to take example from the United States, and render itself somewhat less odious and offensive to foreigners. The servile rapacity of the French officials is sufficiently contemptible, but there is a surly, boorish incivility about our men, alike disgusting to all persons who fall into their hands, and discreditable to the nation that keeps such ill-conditioned curs snarling about its gates.

When I landed in America, I could not help being strongly impressed with the contrast their Custom-house presented, and the attention, politeness, and good humour with which its officers discharged their duty.

As we did not land at Boston, in consequence of some detention at the wharf, until after dark, I received my first impressions of the city in walking down to the Custom-house on the morning after our arrival, which was Sunday. I am afraid to say, by-the-way, how many offers of pews and seats in church for that morning were made to us, by formal note of invitation, before we had half finished our first dinner in America, but, if I may be allowed to make a moderate guess, without going into nicer calculation, I should say that, at least, as many sittings were proffered us as would have accommodated a score or two of grown-up families. The number of creeds and forms of religion to which the pleasure of our company was requested was in very fair proportion

Not being able, in the absence of any change of clothes, to go to church that day, we were compelled to decline these kindnesses one and all; and I was reluctantly obliged to forego the delight of hearing Dr. Channing, who happened to preach that morning for the first time in a very long interval. I mention the name of this distinguished and accomplished man (with whom I soon afterward had the pleasure of becoming personally acquainted), that I may have the gratification of recording my humble tribute of admiration and respect for his high abilities and character, and for the bold philanthropy with which he has ever opposed himself to that most hideous blot and foul disgrace—Slavery.

To return to Boston. When I got into the streets upon this Sunday morning, the air was so clear, the houses were so bright and gay, the signboards were painted in such gaudy colours, the gilded letters were so very golden, the bricks were so very red, the stone was so very white, the blinds and area railings were so very green, the knobs and plates upon the street-doors so marvellously bright and twinkling, and all so slight and unsubstantial in appearance, that every thoroughfare in the city looked exactly like a scene in a pantomime. It rarely happens in the business streets that a tradesman, if I may venture to call anybody a tradesman, where everybody is a merchant, resides above his store, so that many occupations are carried on in one house, and the whole front is covered with boards and inscriptions. As I walked along, I kept glancing up at these boards, confidently expecting to see a few of them change into something; and I never turned a corner suddenly without looking out for the clown and pantaloon, who, I had no doubt, were hiding in a doorway or behind some pillar close at hand. As to Harlequin and Columbine, I discovered immediately that they lodged (they are always looking after lodgings in a pantomime) at a very small clock-maker's, one story high, near the hotel; which, in addition to various symbols and devices, almost covering the whole front, had a great dial hanging out—to be jumped through, of course.

The suburbs are, if possible, even more unsubstantial-looking than the city. The white wooden houses (so white that it makes one wink to look at them), with their green jalousie blinds, are so sprinkled and dropped about in all directions, without seeming to have any root at all in the ground, and the small churches and chapels are so prim, and bright, and highly varnished, that I almost believed the whole affair could be taken up piecemeal like a child's toy, and crammed into a little box.

The city is a beautiful one, and cannot fail, I should imagine, to impress all strangers very favourably. The private dwelling-houses are, for the most part, large and elegant, the shops extremely good, and the public buildings handsome. The State House is built upon the summit of a hill, which rises gradually at first, and afterward by a steep ascent, almost from the water's edge. In front is a green enclosure, called the Common. The site is beautiful, and from the top there is a charming panoramic view of the whole town and neighbourhood. In addition to a variety of commodious offices, it contains two handsome chambers: in one the House of Representatives of the State hold their meetings, in the other, the Senate. Such proceedings as I saw here were conducted with perfect gravity and decorum, and were certainly calculated to inspire attention and respect.

There is no doubt that much of the intellectual refinement and superiority of Boston is referable to the quiet influence of the University of Cambridge, which is within three or four miles of the city. The resident professors at that university are gentlemen of learning and varied attainments, and are, without one exception that I can call to mind, men who would shed a grace upon, and do honour to, any society in the civilized world. Many of the resident gentry in Boston and its neighbourhood, and I think I am not mistaken in adding a large majority of those who are attached to the liberal professions there, have been educated at this same school. Whatever the defects of American universities may be, they disseminate no prejudices; rear no bigots; dig up the buried ashes of no old superstitions; never interpose between the people and their improvement; exclude no man because of his religious opinions; above all, in their whole course of study and instruction, recognise a world, and a broad one too, lying beyond the college walls.

It was a source of inexpressible pleasure to me to observe the almost imperceptible, but not less certain effect wrought by this institution among the small community of Boston, and to note at every turn the humanizing tastes and desires it has engendered; the affectionate friendships to which it has given rise; the amount of vanity and prejudice it has dispelled. The golden calf they worship at Boston is a pigmy compared with the giant effigies set up in other parts of that vast counting-house which lies beyond the Atlantic; and the almighty dollar sinks into something comparatively insignificant amid a whole Pantheon of better gods.

Above all, I sincerely believe that the public institutions and charities of this capital of Massachusetts are as nearly perfect as the most considerate wisdom, benevolence, and humanity can make them. I never in my life was more affected by the contemplation of happiness, under circumstances of privation and bereavement, than in my visits to these establishments.

It is a great and pleasant feature of all such institutions in America, that they are either supported by the state or assisted by the state, or (in the event of their not needing its helping hand) that they act in concert with it, and are emphatically the people's. I cannot but think, with a view to the principle and its tendency to elevate or depress the character of the industrious classes, that a public charity is immeasurably better than a private foundation, no matter how munificently the latter may be endowed. In our own country, where it has not, until within these later days, been a very popular fashion with governments to display any extraordinary regard for the great mass of the people, or to recognise their existence as improvable creatures, private charities, unexampled in the history of the earth, have arisen, to do an incalculable amount of good among the destitute and afflicted. But the government of the country, having neither act nor part in them, is not in the receipt of any portion of the gratitude they inspire; and, offering very little shelter or relief beyond that which is to be found in the workhouse and the jail, has come, not unnaturally, to be looked upon by the poor rather as a stern master, quick to correct and punish, than a kind protector, merciful and vigilant in their hour of need.

The maxim that out of evil cometh good, is strongly illustrated by these establishments at home, as the records of the Prerogative Office in Doctors' Commons can abundantly prove. Some immensely rich old gentleman or lady, surrounded by needy relatives, makes, upon a low average, a will a week. The old gentleman or lady, never very remarkable, in the best of times, for good temper, is full of aches and pains from head to foot; full of fancies and caprices; full of spleen, distrust, suspicion, and dislike. To cancel old wills and invent new ones, is, at last, the sole business of such a testator's existence; and relations and friends (some of whom have been bred up distinctly to inherit a large share of the property, and have been, from their cradles, specially disqualified from devoting themselves to any useful pursuit on that account), are so often and so unexpectedly and summarily cut off, and reinstated, and cut off again, that the whole family, down to the remotest cousin, is kept in a perpetual fever. At length it becomes plain that the old lady or gentleman has not long to live; and the plainer this becomes, the more clearly the old lady or gentleman perceives that everybody is in a conspiracy against their poor old dying relative; wherefore the old lady or gentleman makes another last will—positively the last this time—conceals the same in a china teapot, and expires next day. Then it turns out that the whole of the real and personal estate is divided between half a dozen charities; and that the dead and gone testator has, in pure spite, helped to do a great deal of good, at the cost of an immense amount of evil passion and misery.

The Perkins Institution and Massachusetts Asylum for the Blind, at Boston, is superintended by a body of trustees, who make an annual report to the corporation. The indigent blind of that state are admitted gratuitously. Those from the adjoining state of Connecticut, or from the states of Maine, Vermont, or New-Hampshire, are admitted by a warrant from the state to which they respectively belong; or, failing that, must find security among their friends for the payment of about twenty pounds English, for their first year's board and instruction, and ten for the second. "After the first year," say the trustees, "an account current will be opened with each pupil: he will be charged with the actual cost of his board, which will not exceed two dollars per week," a trifle more than eight shillings English; "and he will be credited with the amount paid for him by the state, or by his friends; also with his earnings over and above the cost of the stock which he uses; so that all his earnings over one dollar per week, will be his own. By the third year it will be known whether his earnings will more than pay the actual cost of his board; if they should, he will have it at his option to remain and receive his earnings, or not. Those who prove unable to earn their own livelihood will not be retained, as it is not desirable to convert the establishment into an almshouse, or to retain any but working-bees in the hive. Those who, by physical or mental imbecility, are disqualified for work, are thereby disqualified from being members of an industrious community; and they can be better provided for in establishments fitted for the infirm."

I went to see this place one very fine winter morning; an Italian sky above, and the air so clear and bright on every side, that even my eyes, which are none of the best, could follow the minute lines and scraps of tracery in distant buildings. Like most other public institutions in America of the same class, it stands a mile or two without the town, in a cheerful, healthy spot, and is an airy, spacious, handsome edifice. It is built upon a height commanding the harbour. When I paused for a moment at the door, and marked how fresh and free the whole scene was, what sparkling bubbles glanced upon the waves, and welled up every moment to the surface, as though the world below, like that above, were radiant with the bright day, and gushing over in its fulness of light; when I gazed from sail to sail away upon a ship at sea, a tiny speck of shining white, the only cloud upon the still, deep, distant blue—and, turning, saw a blind boy with his sightless face addressed that way, as though he too had some sense within him of the glorious distance. I felt a kind of sorrow that the place should be so very light, and a strange wish that, for his sake, it were darker. It was but momentary of course, and a mere fancy, but I felt it keenly for all that.

The children were at their daily tasks in different rooms, except a few who were already dismissed, and were at play. Here, as in many institutions, no uniform is worn; and I was very glad of it, for two reasons. First, because I am sure that nothing but senseless custom and want of thought would reconcile us to the liveries and badges we are so fond of at home. Secondly, because the absence of these things presents each child to the visiter in his or her own proper character, with its individuality unimpaired; not lost in a dull, ugly mono onous repetition of the same unmeaning garb, which is really an important consideration. The wisdom of encouraging a little harmless pride in personal appearance even among the blind, or the whimsical absurdity of considering charity and leather breeches inseparable companions, as we do, requires no comment.

Good order, cleanliness, and comfort, pervaded every corner of the building. The various classes, who were gathered round their teachers, answered the questions put to them with readiness and intelligence, and in a spirit of cheerful contest for precedence which pleased me very much. Those who were at play were gleesome and noisy as other children. More spiritual and affectionate friendships appeared to exist among them than would be found among other young persons suffering under no deprivation; but this I expected, and was prepared to find. It is a part of the great scheme of Heaven's merciful consideration for the afflicted.

In a portion of the building set apart for that purpose, are workshops for blind persons whose education is finished, and who have acquired a trade, but who cannot pursue it in an ordinary manufactory because of their deprivation. Several people were work at here, making brushes, mattresses, and so forth; and the cheerfulness, industry, and good order discernible in every other part of the building, extended to this department also.

On the ringing of a bell, the pupils all repaired, without any guide or leader, to a spacious music-hall, where they took their seats in an orchestra erected for that purpose, and listened, with manifest delight, to a voluntary on the organ played by one of themselves. At its conclusion, the performer, a boy of nineteen or twenty, gave place to a girl, and to her accompaniment they all sang a hymn, and afterward a sort of chorus. It was very sad to look upon and hear them, happy though their condition unquestionably was; and I saw that one blind girl who (being for the time deprived of the use of her limbs, by illness), sat close beside me with her face towards them, wept silently while she listened.

It is strange to watch the faces of the blind, and see how free they are from all concealment of what is passing in their thoughts; observing which, a man with eyes may blush to contemplate the mask he wears. Allowing for one shade of anxious expression which is never absent from their countenances, and the like of which we may readily detect in our own faces if we try to feel our way in the dark, every idea, as it rises within them, is expressed with the lightning's speed and nature's truth. If the company at a rout or drawing-room at court could only for one time be as unconscious of the eyes upon them as blind men and women are, what secrets would come out, and what a worker of hypocrisy this sight, the loss of which we so much pity, would appear to be!

The thought occurred to me as I sat down in another room before a girl, blind, deaf, and dumb; destitute of smell, and nearly so of taste; before a fair young creature with every human faculty, and hope, and power of goodness and affection, enclosed within her delicate frame, and but one outward sense, the sense of touch. There she was before me, built up, as it were, in a marble cell, impervious to any ray of light or particle of sound, with her poor white hand peeping through a chink in the wall, beckoning to some good man for help, that an immortal soul might be awakened.

Long before I looked upon her the help had come. Her face was radiant with intelligence and pleasure. Her hair, braided by her own hands, was bound about a head whose intellectual capacity and development were beautifully expressed in its graceful outline and its broad, open brow; her dress, arranged by herself, was a pattern of neatness and simplicity; the work she had knitted lay beside her; her writing-book was on the desk she leaned upon. From the mournful ruin of such bereavement there had slowly risen up this gentle, tender, guileless, grateful-hearted being.

Like other inmates of that house, she had a green riband bound round her eyelids. A doll she had dressed lay near her upon the ground. I took it up, and saw that she had made a green fillet such as she wore herself, and fastened it about its mimic eyes.

She was seated in a little inclosure, made by school-desks and forms, writing her dayly journal. But soon finishing this pursuit, she engaged in an animated communication with a teacher who sat beside her. This was a favourite mistress with the poor pupil. If she could see the face of her fair instructress, she would not love her less, I am sure.

I have extracted a few disjointed fragments of her history, from an account, written by that one man who has made her what she is. It is a very beautiful and touching narrative; and I wish I could present it entire.

Her name is Laura Bridgman. "She was born in Hanover, New-Hampshire, on the twenty-first of December, 1829. She is described as having been a very sprightly and pretty infant, with bright blue eyes. She was, however, so puny and feeble until she was a year and a half old, that her parents hardly hoped to rear her. She was subject to severe fits, which seemed to rack her frame almost beyond her power of endurance; and life was held by the feeblest tenure: but when a year and a half old, she seemed to rally; the dangerous symptoms subsided; and at twenty months old, she was perfectly well."

"Then her mental powers, hither stinted in their growth, rapidly developed themselves; and during the four months of health which she enjoyed, she appears (making due allowance for a fond mother's account) to have displayed a considerable degree of intelligence."

"But suddenly she sickened again; her disease raged with great violence during five weeks, when her eyes and ears were inflamed, suppurated, and their contents were discharged. But though sight and hearing were gone for ever, the poor child's sufferings were not ended. The fever raged during seven weeks; for five months she was kept in bed in a darkened room; it was a year before she could walk unsupported, and two years before she could sit up all day. It was now observed that her sense of smell was almost entirely destroyed; and, consequently, that her taste was much blunted."

"It was not until four years of age that the poor child's bodily health seemed restored, and she was able to enter upon her apprenticeship of life and the world."

"But what a situation was hers! The darkness and the silence of the tomb were around her: no mother's smile called forth her answering smile, no father's voice taught her to imitate his sounds: they, brothers and sisters, were but forms of matter which resisted her touch, but which differed not from the furniture of the house, save in warmth, and in the power of locomation; and not even in these respects from the dog and the cat.

"But the immortal spirit which had been implanted within her could not die, nor be maimed nor mutilated; and, though most of its avenues of communication with the world were cut off, it began to manifest itself through the others. As soon as she could walk, she began to explore the room, and then the house; she became familiar with the form, density, and weight, and heat, of every article she could lay her hands upon. She followed her mother, and felt her hands and arms, as she was occupied about the house; and her disposition to imitate, led her to repeat everything herself. She even learned to sew a little, and to knit."

The reader will scarcely need to be told, however, that the opportunities of communicating with her, were very, very limited; and that the moral effects of her wretched state soon began to appear. Those who cannot be enlightened by reason, can only be controlled by force; and this, coupled with her great privations, must soon have reduced her to a worse condition than that of the beasts that perish, but for timely and unhoped-for aid.

"At this time, I was so fortunate as to hear of the child, and immediately hastened to Hanover to see her. I found her with a well-formed figure; a strongly-marked, nervous-sanguine temperament; a large and beautiful shaped head, and the whole system in healthy action. The parents were easily induced to consent to her coming to Boston, and on the 4th of October, 1837, they brought her to the Institution.

"For a while, she was much bewildered; and after waiting about two weeks, until she became acquainted with her new locality, and somewhat familiar with the inmates, the attempt was made to give her knowledge of arbitrary signs, by which she could interchange thoughts with others.

"There was one of two ways to be adopted: either to go on to build up a language of signs on the basis of the natural language which she had already commenced herself, or to teach her the purely arbitrary language in common use: that is, to give her a sign for every individual thing, or to give her a knowledge of letters by combination of which, she might express her idea of the existence, and the mode and condition of existence of any thing. The former would have been easy, but very ineffectual; the latter seemed very difficult, but, if accomplished, very effectual. I determined therefore to try the latter.

"The first experiments were made by taking articles in common use, such as knives, forks, spoons, keys, &c., and pasting upon them labels with their names printed in raised letters. These she felt very carefully, and soon, of course, distinguished that the crooked lines *spoon*, differed as much from the crooked lines *key*, as the spoon differed from the key in form.

"Then small detached labels, with the same words printed upon them, were put into her hands; and she soon observed that they were similar to the ones pasted on the articles. She showed her perception of this similarity by laying the label *key* upon the key, and the label *spoon* upon the spoon. She was encouraged here by the natural sign of approbation, patting on the head.

"The same process was then repeated with all the articles which she could handle; and she very easily learned to place the proper labels upon them. It was evident, however, that the only intellectual exercise, was that of imitation and memory. She recollected that the label *book* was placed upon a book, and she repeated the process first from imitation, next from memory, with only the motive of love of approbation, but apparently without the intellectual perception of any relation between the things.

"After a while, instead of labels, the individual letters were given to her on detached bits of paper: they were arranged side by side so as to spell *book*, *key*, &c.; then they were mixed up in a heap, and a sign was made for her to ar range them herself, so as to express the words *book*, *key*, &c.; and she did so.

"Hitherto, the process had been mechanical, and the success about as great as teaching a very knowing dog a variety of tricks. The poor child had sat in mute amazement, and patiently imitated everything her teacher did; but now the truth began to flash upon her: her intellect began to work: she perceived that here was a way by which she could herself make up a sign of anything that was in her own mind, and show it to another mind; and at once her countenance lighted up with a human expression: it was no longer a dog, or parrot: it was an immortal spirit, eagerly seizing upon a new link of union with other spirits! I could almost fix upon the moment when this truth dawned upon her mind, and spread its light to her countenance; I saw that the great obstacle was overcome; and that henceforward nothing but patient and persevering, but plain and straightforward efforts were to be used.

"The result thus far, is quickly related, and easily conceived; but not so was the process; for many weeks of apparently unprofitable labour were passed before it was effected.

"When it was said above, that a sign was made, it was intended to say, that the action was performed by her teacher, she feeling his his hands, and then imitating the motion.

"The next step was to procure a set of metal types, with the different letters of the alphabet cast upon their ends; also a board, in which were square holes, into which holes she could set the types; so that the letters on their ends could alone be felt above the surface.

"Then, on any article being handed to her, for instance, a pencil, or a watch, she would select the component letters, and arrange them on her board, and read them with apparent pleasure.

"She was exercised for several weeks in this way, until her vocabulary became extensive; and then the important step was taken of teaching her how to represent the different letters by the position of her fingers, instead of the cumbrous apparatus of the board and types. She accomplished this speedily and easily, for her intellect had begun to work in aid of her teacher, and her progress was rapid.

"This was the period, about three months after she had commenced, that the first report of her case was made, in which it is stated that 'she has just learned the manual alphabet, as used by the deaf mutes, and it is a subject of delight and wonder to see how rapidly, correctly, and eagerly, she goes on with her labours. Her teacher gives her a new object, for instance, a pencil, first lets her examine it, and get an idea of its use, then teaches her how to spell it by making the signs for the letters with her own fingers: the child grasps her hand, and feels her fingers, as the different letters are formed; she turns her head a little on one side, like a person listening closely; her lips are apart; she seems scarcely to breathe; and her countenance, at first anxious, gradually changes to a smile, as she comprehends a lesson. She then holds up her tiny fingers, and spells the word in the manual alphabet; next, she takes her types and arranges her letters; and last, to make sure that she is right, she takes the whole of the types composing the word, and places them upon or in contact with the pencil, or whatever the object may be.'

"The whole of the succeeding year was passed in gratifying her eager inquiries for the names of every object which she could possibly handle; in exercising her in the use of the manual alphabet; in extending in every possible way her knowledge of the physical relations of things; and in proper care of her health.

"At the end of the year a report of her case was made, from which the following is an extract.

"'It has been ascertained beyond the possibility of doubt, that she cannot see a ray of light, cannot hear the least sound, and never exercises her sense of smell, if she have any. Thus her mind dwells in darkness and stillness, as profound as that of a closed tomb at midnight. Of beautiful sights, and sweet sounds, and pleasant odours, she has no conception: nevertheless, she seems as happy and playful as a bird or a lamb; and the employment of her intellectual faculties, or the acquirement of a new idea, gives her a vivid pleasure, which is plainly marked in her expressive features. She never seems to repine, but has all the buoyancy and gayety of childhood. She is fond of fun and frolic, and when playing with the rest of the children, her shrill laugh sounds loudest of the group.

"'When left alone, she seems very happy if she have her knitting or sewing, and will busy herself for hours: if she have no occupation, she evidently amuses herself by imaginary dialogues, or by recalling past impressions; she counts with her fingers, or spells out names of things which she has recently learned, in the manual alphabet of the deaf mutes. In this lonely self-communion she seems to reason, reflect, and argue: if she spell a word wrong with the fingers of her right hand, she instantly strikes it with her left, as her teacher does, in sign of disapprobation; if right, then she pats herself upon the head, and looks pleased. She sometimes purposely spells a word wrong with the left hand, looks roguish and laughs, and then with the right hand strikes the left, as if to correct it.

"'During the year she has attained great dexterity in the use of the manual alphabet of the deaf mutes; and she spells out the words and sentences which she knows, so fast and so deftly, that only those accustomed to this language can follow with the eye the rapid motions of her fingers.

"'But wonderful as is the rapidity with which she writes her thoughts upon the air, still more so is the ease and accuracy with which she reads the words thus written by another; grasping their hands in hers, and following every movement of their fingers, as letter after letter conveys their meaning to her mind. It is in this way that she converses with her blind playmates, and nothing can more forcibly show the power of mind in forcing matter to its purpose, than a meeting between them. For if great talent and skill are necessary for two pantomimes to paint their thoughts and feelings by the movements of the body, and the expression of the countenance, how much greater the difficulty when darkness shrouds them both, and the one can hear no sound!

"'When Laura is walking through a passageway, with her hands spread before her, she knows instantly every one she meets, and passes them with a sign of recognition: but if it be a girl of her own age, and especially if it be one of her favourites, there is instantly a bright smile of recognition, and a twining of arms, a grasping of hands, and a swift telegraphing upon the tiny fingers; whose rapid evolution convey the thoughts and feelings from the outposts of one mind to those of the other. There are questions and answers, exchanges of joy or sorrow, there are kissings and partings, just as between little children with all their senses.'

"During this year, and six months after she had left home, her mother came to visit her, and the scene of their meeting was an interesting one.

"The mother stood some time, gazing with overflowing eyes upon her unfortunate child, who, all unconscious of her presence, was playing about the room. Presently Laura ran against her, and at once began feeling her hands, examining her dress, and trying to find out if she knew her; but not succeeding in this, she turned away as from a stranger, and the poor woman could not conceal the pang she felt at finding that her beloved child did not know her.

"She then gave Laura a string of beads which she used to wear at home, which were recognised by the child at once, who, with much joy, put them around her neck, and sought me eagerly to say she understood the string was from her home.

"The mother now tried to caress her, but poor Laura repelled her, preferring to be with her acquaintances.

"Another article from home was now given her, and she began to look much interested; she examined the stranger much closer, and gave me to understand that she knew she came from Hanover: she even endured her caresses, but would leave her with indifference at the slightest signal. The distress of the mother was now painful to behold; for, although she had feared that she should not be recognised, the painful reality of being treated with cold indifference by a darling child, was too much for woman's nature to bear.

"After a while, on the mother taking hold of her again, a vague idea seemed to flit across Laura's mind, that this could not be a stranger; she therefore felt her hands very eagerly, while her countenance assumed an expression of intense interest; she became very pale, and then suddenly red; hope seemed struggling with doubt and anxiety, and never were contending emotions more strongly painted upon the human face; at this moment of painful uncertainty, the mother drew her close to her side, and kissed her fondly, when at once the truth flashed upon the child, and all mistrust and anxiety disappeared from her face, as with an expression of exceeding joy she eagerly nestled to the bosom of her parent, and yielded herself to her fond embraces.

"After this, the beads were all unheeded; the playthings which were offered to her were utterly disregarded: her playmates, for whom but a moment before she gladly left the stranger, now vainly strove to pull her from her mother; and though she yielded her usual instantaneous obedience to my signal to follow me, it was evidently with painful reluctance. She clung close to me, as if bewildered and fearful; and when, after a moment, I took her to her mother, she sprang to her arms, and clung to her with eager joy.

"The subsequent parting between them, showed alike the affection, the intelligence, and the resolution of the child.

"Laura accompanied her mother to the door, clinging close to her all the way, until they arrived at the threshold, where she paused, and felt around, to ascertain who was near her. Perceiving the matron, of whom she is very fond, she grasped her with one hand, holding on convulsively to her mother with the other; and thus she stood for a moment: then she dropped her mother's hand; put her handkerchief to her eyes; and turning round, clung sobbing to the matron; while her mother departed, with emotions as deep as those of her child.

* * * * * * *

"It has been remarked in former reports, that she can distinguish different degrees of intellect in others, and that she soon regarded almost with contempt, a newcomer, when, after a few days, she discovered her weakness of mind. This unamiable part of her character has been more strongly developed during the past year.

"She chooses for her friends and companions those children who are intelligent, and can talk best with her; and she evidently dislikes to be with those who are deficient in intellect, unless, indeed, she can make them serve her purposes, which she is evidently inclined to do. She takes advantage of them, and makes them wait upon her, in a manner that she knows she could not exact of others; and in various ways she shows her Saxon blood.

"She is fond of having other children noticed and caressed by the teachers, and those whom she respects; but this must not be carried too far, or she becomes jealous. She wants to have her share, which, if not the lion's, is the greater part; and if she does not get it, she says, '*My Mother will love me.*'

"Her tendency to imitation is so strong, that it leads her to actions which must be entirely incomprehensible to her, and which can give her no other pleasure than the gratification of an internal faculty. She has been known to sit for half an hour, holding a book before her sightless eyes, and moving her lips, as she has observed seeing people do when reading.

She one day pretended that her doll was sick, and went through all the motions of tending it and giving it medicine; she then put it carefully to bed, and placed a bottle of hot water to its feet, laughing all the time most heartily. When I came home she insisted upon my going to see it and feel its pulse; and when I told her to put a blister on its back, she seemed to enjoy it amazingly, and almost screamed with delight.

"Her social feelings and her affections are very strong; and when she is sitting at work, or at her studies, by the side of one of her little friends, she will break off from her task every few moments to hug and kiss them with an earnestness and warmth that is touching to behold.

"When left alone, she occupies and apparently amuses herself, and seems quite contented; and so strong seems to be the natural tendency of thought to put on the garb of language, that she often soliloquizes in the *finger language*, slow and tedious as it is. But it is only when alone that she is quiet: for if she become sensible of the presence of any one near her, she is restless until she can sit close beside them, hold their hand, and converse with them by signs.

"In her intellectual character it is pleasing to observe an insatiable thirst for knowledge, and a quick perception of the relations of things. In her moral character it is beautiful to behold her continual gladness, her keen enjoyment of existence, her expansive love, her unhesitating confidence, her sympathy with suffering, her conscientiousness, truthfulness, and hopefulness."

Such are a few fragments from the simple but most interesting and instructive history of Laura Bridgman. The name of her great benefactor and friend, who writes it, is Dr. Howe. There are not many persons, I hope and believe, who, after reading these passages, can ever hear that name with indifference.

A farther account has been published by Dr. Howe, since the report from which I have just quoted. It describes her rapid mental growth and improvement during twelve months more, and brings her little history down to the end of last year. It is very remarkable, that, as we dream in words, and carry on imaginary conversations, in which we speak both for ourselves and for the shadows who appear to us in those visions of the night, so she, having no words, uses her finger alphabet in her sleep. And it has been ascertained that when her slumber is broken, and is much disturbed by dreams, she expresses her thoughts in an irregular and confused manner on her fingers, just as we should murmur and mutter them indistinctly in the like circumstances.

I turned over the leaves of her diary, and found

it written in a fair legible square hand, and expressed in terms which were quite intelligible without any explanation. On my saying that I should like to see her write again, the teacher, who sat beside her, bade her, in their language, sign her name upon a slip of paper twice or thrice. In doing so, I observed that she kept the left hand always touching and following up the right, in which, of course, she held the pen. No line was indicated by any contrivance; but she wrote straight and freely.

She had, until now, been quite unconscious of the presence of visiters; but, having her hand placed in that of the gentleman who accompanied me, she immediately expressed his name upon her teacher's palm. Indeed her sense of touch is now so exquisite, that, having been acquainted with a person once, she can recognise him or her after almost any interval. This gentleman had been in her company, I believe, but very seldom, and certainly had not seen her for many months. My hand she rejected at once, as she does that of any man who is a stranger to her; but she retained my wife's with evident pleasure, kissed her, and examined her dress with a girl's curiosity and interest.

She was merry and cheerful, and showed much innocent playfulness in her intercourse with her teacher. Her delight on recognising a favourite playfellow and companion—herself a blind girl—who silently, and with an equal enjoyment of the coming surprise, took a seat beside her, was beautiful to witness. It elicited from her at first, as other slight circumstances did twice or thrice during my visit, an uncouth noise, which was rather painful to hear; but, on her teacher touching her lips, she immediately desisted, and embraced her laughingly and affectionately.

I had previously been into another chamber, where a number of blind boys were swinging and climbing, and engaged in various sports. They all clamoured, as we entered, to the assistant master, who accompanied us, "Look at me, Mr. Hart! Please, Mr. Hart, look at me!" evincing, I thought, even in this, an anxiety peculiar to their condition, that their little feats of agility should be *seen*. Among them was a small laughing fellow, who stood aloof, entertaining himself with a gymnastic exercise for bringing the arms and chest into play, which he enjoyed mightily, especially when, in thrusting out his right arm, he brought it into contact with another boy. Like Laura Bridgman, this young child was deaf, and dumb, and blind.

Dr. Howe's account of this pupil's first instruction is so very striking, and so intimately connected with Laura herself, that I cannot refrain from a short extract I may premise that the poor boy's name is Oliver Caswell; that he is thirteen years of age; and that he was in full possession of all his faculties until three years and four months old. He was then attacked by scarlet fever—in four weeks became deaf; in a few weeks more, blind; in six months, dumb. He showed his anxious sense of this last deprivation by often feeling the lips of other persons when they were talking, and then putting his hand upon his own, as if to assure himself that he had them in the right position.

"His thirst for knowledge," says Dr Howe, "proclaimed itself as soon as he entered the house, by his eager examination of everything he could feel or smell in his new location. For instance, treading upon the register of a furnace, he instantly stooped down and began to feel it, and soon discovered the way in which the upper plate moved upon the lower one; but this was not enough for him: so, lying down upon his face, he applied his tongue first to one, then to the other, and seemed to discover that they were of different kinds of metal.

"His signs were expressive; and the strictly natural language, laughing, crying, sighing, kissing, embracing, &c., was perfect.

"Some of the analogical signs which (guided by his faculty of imitation) he had contrived were comprehensible—such as the waving motion of his hand for the motion of a boat, the circular one for a wheel, &c.

"The first object was to break up the use of these signs, and to substitute for them the use of purely arbitrary ones.

"Profiting by the experience I had gained in the other cases, I omitted several steps of the process before employed, and commenced at once with the finger language. Taking, therefore, several articles having short names, such as key, cup, mug, &c., and with Laura for an auxiliary, I sat down, and, taking his hand, placed it upon one of them, and then, with his own, made the letters *k e y*. He felt my hands eagerly with both of his; and, on my repeating the process, he evidently tried to imitate the motions of my fingers. In a few minutes he contrived to feel the motions of my fingers with one hand and, holding out the other, he tried to imitate them, laughing most heartily when he succeeded. Laura was by, interested even to agitation; and the two presented a singular sight: her face was flushed and anxious, and her fingers twined in among ours so closely as to follow every motion, but so lightly as not to embarrass them; while Oliver stood attentive, his head a little aside, his face turned up, his left hand grasping mine, and his right held out. At every motion of my fingers his countenance betokened keen attention; there was an expression of anxiety as he tried to imitate the motions; then a smile came stealing out as he thought he could do so, and spread into a joyous laugh the moment he succeeded, and felt me pat his head and Laura clap him heartily upon the back, and jump up and down in her joy.

"He learned more than half a dozen letters in half an hour, and seemed delighted with his success, at least in gaining approbation. His attention then began to flag, and I commenced playing with him. It was evident that in all this he had merely been imitating the motions of my fingers, and placing his hand upon the key, cup, &c., as part of the process, without any perception of the relation between the sign and the object.

"When he was tired with play I took him back to the table, and he was quite ready to begin again his process of imitation. He soon learned to make the letters for *key*, *pen*, *pin*; and, by having the object repeatedly placed in his hand, he at last perceived the relation I wished to establish between them. This was evident, because, when I would make the letters *p i n*, or *p e n*, or *c u p*, he would select the article.

"The perception of this relation was not accompanied by that radiant flash of intelligence, and that glow of joy, which marked the delightful moment when Laura first perceived it. I then placed all the articles on the table, and, going away a little distance with the children, placed Oliver's fingers in the position to spell *key*, on which Laura went and brought the article. The little fellow seemed to be much amused by this, and looked very attentive and smiling. I then caused him to make the letters *b r e a d*, and in an instant Laura went and brought him a piece. He smelled it, put it to his lips, cocked up his head with a most knowing look, seemed to reflect a moment, and then laughed outright, as much as to say, 'Aha! I understand now how something may be made out of this.'

"It was now clear that he had the capacity and inclination to learn, that he was a proper subject for instruction, and needed only persevering attention. I therefore put him in the hands of an intelligent teacher, nothing doubting of his rapid progress."

Well may this gentleman call that a delightful moment in which some distant promise of her present state first gleamed upon the darkened mind of Laura Bridgman. Throughout his life the recollection of that moment will be to him a source of pure, unfading happiness; nor will it shine least brightly on the evening of his days of Noble Usefulness.

The affection that exists between these two—the master and the pupil—is as far removed from all ordinary care and regard, as the circumstances in which it has its growth, are apart from the common occurrences of life. He is occupied now, in devising means of imparting to her, higher knowledge; and of conveying to her some adequate idea of the Great Creator of that universe in which, dark and silent and scentless though it be to her, she has such deep delight and glad enjoyment.

Ye who have eyes and see not, and have ears and hear not; ye who are as the hypocrites of sad countenances, and disfigure your faces that ye may seem unto men to fast; learn healthy cheerfulness, and mild contentment, from the deaf, and dumb, and blind! Self-elected saints with gloomy brows, this sightless, earless, voiceless child may teach you lessons you will do well to follow. Let that poor hand of hers lie gently on your hearts; for there may be something in its healing touch akin to that of the Great Master whose precepts you misconstrue, whose lessons you pervert, of whose charity and sympathy with all the world, not one among you in his daily practice knows as much as many of the worst among those fallen sinners, to whom you are liberal in nothing but the preachment of perdition!

As I rose to quit the room, a pretty little child of one of the attendants came running in to greet its father. For the moment, a child with eyes, among the sightless crowd, impressed me almost as painfully as the blind boy in the porch had done, two hours ago. Ah! how much brighter and more deeply blue, glowing and rich though it had been before, was the scene without, contrasting with the darkness of so many youthful lives within!

At South Boston, as it is called, in a situation excellently adapted for the purpose, several charitable institutions are clustered together. One of these, is the State Hospital for the insame; admirably conducted on those enlightened principles of conciliation and kindness, which twenty years ago would have been worse than heretical, and which have been acted upon with so much success in our own pauper asylum at Hanwell. "Evince a desire to show some confidence, and repose some trust, even in mad people," said the resident physician, as we walked along the galleries, his patients flocking round us unrestrained. Of those who deny or doubt the wisdom of this maxim after witnessing its effects, if there be such people still alive, I can only say that I hope I may never be summoned as a juryman on a Commission of Lunacy whereof they are the subjects; for I should certainly find them out of their senses, on such evidence alone.

Each ward in this institution is shaped like a long gallery or hall, with the dormitories of the patients opening from it on either hand. Here they work, read, play at skittles, and other games; and when the weather does not admit of their taking exercise out of doors, pass the day together. In one of these rooms, seated, calmly, and quite as a matter of course, among a throng of madwomen, black and white, were the physician's wife and another lady, with a couple of children. These ladies were graceful and handsome; and it was not difficult to perceive at a glance that even their presence there, had a highly beneficial influence on the patients who were grouped about them.

Leaning her head against the chimney-piece, with a great assumption of dignity and refinement of manner, sat an elderly female, in as many scraps of finery as Madge Wildfire herself. Her head in particular was so strewn with scraps of gauze, and cotton, and bits of paper, and had so many queer odds and ends stuck all about it, that it looked like a bird's-nest. She was radiant with imaginary jewels; wore a rich pair of undoubted gold spectacles; and gracefully dropped upon her lap, as we approached, a very old greasy newspaper, in which I dare say she had been reading an account of her own presentation at some foreign court.

I have been thus particular in describing her, because she will serve to exemplify the physician's manner of acquiring and retaining the confidence of his patients.

"This," he said aloud, taking me by the hand, and advancing to the fantastic figure with great politeness—not raising her suspicions by the slightest look or whisper, or any kind of aside, to me: "This is the lady hostess of this mansion, sir. It belongs to her. Nobody else has anything whatever to do with it. It is a large establishment, as you see, and requires a great number of attendants. She lives, you observe, in the very first style. She is kind enough to receive my visits, and to permit my wife and family to reside here; for which, it is hardly necessary to say, we are much indebted to her. She is exceedingly courteous, you perceive," on this hint she bowed, condescendingly, "and will permit me to have the pleasure of introducing you: a gentleman from England, ma'am: newly arrived from England, after a very tempestuous passage: Mr. Dickens—the lady of the house!"

We exchanged the most dignified salutations with profound gravity and respect, and so went on. The rest of the madwomen seemed to understand the joke perfectly (not only in this case, but in all the others, except their own), and to be highly amused by it. The nature of their several kinds of insanity was made known to me in the same way, and we left each of them in high good humour. Not only is a thorough confidence established, by these means, between physician and patient, in respect of the nature and extent of their hallucinations, but it is easy to understand that opportunities are afforded for seizing any moment of reason, to startle them by placing their own delusion before them in its most incongruous and ridiculous light.

Every patient in this asylum sits down to dinner every day with a knife and fork; and in the midst of them sits the gentleman, whose manner of dealing with his charges, I have just described. At every meal, moral influence alone restrains the more violent among them from cutting the throats of the rest; but the effect of that influence is reduced to an absolute certainty, and is found, even as a means of restraint, to say nothing of it as a means of cure, a hundred times more efficacious than all the strait-waistcoats, fetters, and handcuffs, that ignorance, prejudice, and cruelty have manufactured since the creation of the world.

In the labour department, every patient is as freely trusted with the tools of his trade as if he were a sane man. In the garden, and on the farm, they work with spades rakes, and hoes. For amusement, they walk, run, fish, paint, read, and ride out to take the air in carriages provided for the purpose. They have among themselves a sewing society to make clothes for the poor, which holds meetings, passes resolutions, never comes to fisty cuffs or bowie-knives as sane assemblies have been known to do elsewhere; and conducts all its proceedings with the greatest decorum. The irritability, which would otherwise be expended on their own flesh, clothes, and furniture, is dissipated in these pursuits. They are cheerful, tranquil, and healthy.

Once a week, they have a ball, in which the doctor and his family, with all the nurses and attendants, take an active part. Dances and marches are performed alternately, to the enlivening strains of a piano; and now and then some gentleman or lady (whose proficiency has been previously ascertained) obliges the company with a song: nor does it ever degenerate, at a tender crisis, into a screech or howl; wherein, I must confess, I should have thought the danger lay. At an early hour they all meet together for these festive purposes; at eight o'clock refreshments are served; and at nine they separate.

Immense politeness and good-breeding are observed throughout. They all take their tone from the doctor; and he moves a very Chesterfield among the company. Like other assemblies, these entertainments afford a fruitful topic of conversation among the ladies for some days; and the gentlemen are so anxious to shine on these occasions, that they have been sometimes found "practising their steps" in private, to cut a more distinguished figure in the dance.

It is obvious that one great feature in this system, is the inculcation and encouragement, even among such unhappy persons, of a decent self-respect. Something of the same spirit pervades all the institutions at South Boston.

There is the House of Industry. In that branch of it which is devoted to the reception of old or otherwise helpless paupers, these words are painted on the walls: "Worthy of Notice. Self-Government, Quietude, and Peace, are Blessings." It is not assumed and taken for granted that being there they must be evil-disposed and wicked people, before whose vicious eyes it is necessary to flourish threats and harsh restraints. They are met at the very threshold with this mild appeal. All within-doors is very plain and simple, as it ought to be, but arranged with a view to peace and comfort. It costs no more than any other plan of arrangement, but it bespeaks an amount of consideration for those who are reduced to seek a shelter there, which puts them at once upon their gratitude and good behaviour. Instead of being parcelled out in great long, rambling wards, where a certain amount of weazen life may mope, and pine, and shiver, all day long, the building is divided into separate rooms, each with its share of light and air. In these the better kind of paupers live. They have a motive for exertion and becoming pride, in the desire to make these little chambers comfortable and decent. I do not remember one but it was clean and neat, and had its plant or two upon the window-sill, or row of crockery upon the shelf, or small display of coloured prints upon the white-washed wall, or, perhaps, its wooden clock behind the door.

The orphans and young children are in an adjoining building; separate from this, but a part of the same institution. Some are such little creatures that the stairs are of lilliputian measurement, fitted to their tiny strides. The same consideration for their years and weakness is expressed in their very seats, which are perfect curiosities, and look like articles of furniture for a pauper doll's-house. I can imagine the glee of our Poor Law Commissioners at the notion of these seats having arms and backs; but small spines being of older date than their occupation of the Board-room at Somerset House, I thought even this provision very merciful and kind.

Here again I was greatly pleased with the inscriptions on the wall, which were scraps of plain morality, easily remembered and understood: such as "Love one another." "God remembers the smallest creature in his creation:" and straightforward advice of that nature. The books and tasks of these smallest of scholars were adapted, in the same judicious manner, to their childish powers. When we had examined these lessons, four morsels of girls (of whom one was blind) sang a little song about the merry month of May, which I thought (being extremely dismal) would have suited an English November better. That done, we went to see their sleeping-rooms on the floor above, in which the arrangements were no less excellent and gentle than those we had seen below. And after observing that the teachers were of a class and character well suited to the spirit of the place, I took leave of the infants with a lighter heart than ever I have taken leave of pauper infants yet.

Connected with the House of Industry there is also a Hospital, which was in the best order, and had, I am glad to say, many beds unoccupied. It had one fault, however, which is common to all American interiors: the presence of the eternal, accursed, suffocating, red-hot demon of a stove, whose breath would blight the purest air under Heaven.

There are two establishments for boys in this same neighbourhood. One is called the Boylston school, and is an asylum for neglected and indigent boys who have committed no crime, but who, in the ordinary course of things, would very soon be purged of that distinction if they were not taken from the hungry streets and sent here. The other is a House of Reformation for Juvenile Offenders. They are both under the same roof, but the two classes of boys never come in contact.

The Boylston boys, as may be readily supposed, have very much the advantage of the others in point of personal appearance. They were in their school-room when I came upon them, and answered correctly, without book, such questions as where was England; how far was it; what was its population; its capital city; its form of government, and so forth. They sang a song, too, about a farmer sowing his seed: with corresponding action at such parts as "'tis thus he sows," "he turns him round," "he claps his hands:" which gave it greater interest for them, and accustomed them to act together in an orderly manner. They appeared exceedingly well taught, and not better taught than fed; for a more chubby-looking, full-waistcoated set of boys I never saw.

The juvenile offenders had not such pleasant faces by a great deal, and in this establishment there were many boys of colour. I saw them first at their work (basket-making, and the manufacture of palm-leaf hats), afterward in their school, where they sang a chorus in praise of Liberty: an odd, and, one would think, rather aggravating theme for prisoners. The boys are divided into four classes, each denoted by a numeral, worn on a badge upon the arm. On the arrival of a new comer, he is put into the fourth or lowest class, and left, by good behaviour, to work his way up into the first. The design and object of this institution are to reclaim the youthful criminal by firm but kind and judicious treatment; to make his prison a place of purification and improvement, not of demoralization and corruption; to impress upon him that there is but one path, and that one sober industry, which can ever lead him to happiness; to teach him how it may be trodden, if his footsteps have never yet been led that way; and to lure him back to it if they have strayed: in a word, to snatch him from destruction, and restore him to society a penitent and useful member. The importance of such an establishment, in every point of view, and with reference to every consideration of humanity and social policy, requires no comment.

One other establishment closes the catalogue. It is the House of Correction for the State, in which silence is strictly maintained, but where the prisoners have the comfort and mental relief of seeing each other, and of working together. This is the improved system of prison discipline which we have imported into England, and which has been in successful operation among us for some years past.

America, as a new, and not over-populated country, has, in all her prisons, the one great advantage, of being enabled to find useful and profitable work for the inmates; whereas, with us, the prejudice against prison labour is naturally very strong, and almost insurmountable, when honest men, who have not offended against the laws, are frequently doomed to seek employment in vain. Even in the United States, the principle of bringing convict labour and free labour into a competition which must obviously be to the disadvantage of the latter, has already found many opponents, whose number is not likely to diminish with access of years.

For this very reason though, our best prisons would seem at the first glance to be better conducted than those of America. The treadmill is accompanied with liitle or no noise; five hundred men may pick oakum in the same room without a sonnd; and both kinds of labour admit of such keen and vigilant superintendence as will render even a word of personal communication among the prisoners almost impossible. On the other hand, the noise of the loom, the forge, the carpenter's hammer, or the stone-mason's saw, greatly favour those opportunities of intercourse—hurried and brief no doubt, but opportunities still—which these several kinds of work, by rendering it necessary for men to be employed very near to each other, and often side by side, without any barrier or partition between them, in their very nature present. A visiter, too, requires to reason and reflect a little, before the sight of a number of men engaged in ordinary labour, such as he is accustomed to out of doors, will impress him half as strongly as the contemplation of the same persons in the same place and garb would, if they were occupied in some task, marked and degraded everywhere as belonging only to felons in jails. In an American state prison or house of correction I found it difficult at first to persuade myself that I was really in a jail: a place of ignominious punishment and endurance. And to this hour I very much question whether the humane boast that it is not like one, has its root in the true wisdom or philosophy of the matter.

I hope I may not be misunderstood on this subject, for it is one in which I take a strong and deep interest. I incline as little to the sickly feeling which makes every canting lie or maudlin speech of a notorious criminal a subject of newspaper report and general sympathy, as I do to those good old customs of the good old times which made England, even so recently as in the reign of the third King George, in respect of her criminal code and her prison regulations, one of the most bloody-minded and barbarous countries on the earth. If I thought it would do any good to the rising generation, I would cheerfully give my consent to the disinterment of the bones of any genteel highwayman (the more genteel, the more cheerfully), and to their exposure, piecemeal, on any sign-post, gate, or gibbet, that might be deemed a good elevation for the purpose. My reason is as well convinced that these gentry were utterly worthless and debauched villains, as it is that the laws and jails hardened them in their evil courses, or that their wonderful escapes were effected by the prison-turnkeys, who, in those admirable days, had always been felons themselves, and were, to the last, their bosom-friends and pot-companions. At the same time I know, as all men do or should, that the subject of Prison Discipline is one of the highest importance to any community, and that in her sweeping reform and bright example to other countries on this head, America has shown great wisdom, great benevolence, and exalted policy. In contrasting her system with that which we have modelled upon it, I merely seek to show that, with all its drawbacks, ours has some advantages of its own.*

The House of Correction, which has led to these remarks, is not walled, like other prisons, but is palisaded round about with tall, rough stakes, something after the manner of an enclosure for keeping elephants in, as we see it represented in Eastern prints and pictures. The prisoners wear a particoloured dress; and those who are sentenced to hard labour, work at nail-making or stone-cutting. When I was there, the latter class of labourers were employed upon the stone for a new custom-house in course of erection at Boston. They appeared to shape it skilfully and with expedition, though there were very few among them (if any) who had not acquired the art within the prison gates.

The women, all in one large room, were employed in making light clothing, for New-Orleans and the Southern States. They did their work in silence, like the men, and, like them, were overlooked by the person contracting for their labour, or by some agent of his appointment. In addition to this, they are every moment liable to be visited by the prison officers appointed for that purpose.

The arrangements for cooking, washing of clothes, and so forth, are much upon the plan of those I have seen at home. Their mode of bestowing the prisoners at night (which is of general adoption) differs from ours, and is both simple and effective. In the centre of a lofty area, lighted by windows in the four walls, are five tiers of cells, one above the other; each tier having before it a light iron gallery, attainable by stairs of the same construction and material: excepting the lower one, which is on the ground. Behind these, back to back with them and facing the opposite wall, are five corresponding rows of cells, accessible by similar means: so that supposing the prisoners locked up in their cells, an officer stationed on the ground, with his back to the wall, has half their number under his eye at once; the remaining half being equally under the observation of another officer on the opposite side; and all in one great apartment. Unless this watch be corrupted or sleeping on his post, it is impossible for a man to escape: for even in the event of his forcing the iron door of his cell without noise (which is exceedingly improbable), the moment he appears outside, and steps into that one of the five galleries on which it is situated, he must be plainly and fully visible to the officer below. Each of these cells holds a small truckle-bed, in which one prisoner sleeps; never more. It is small, of course; and the door being not solid, but grated, and without blind or curtain, the prisoner within is at all times exposed to the observation and inspection of any guard who may pass along that tier at any hour or minute of the night. Every day the prisoners receive their dinner, singly, through a trap in the kitchen wall; and each man carries his to his sleeping cell to eat it, where he is locked up, alone, for that purpose, one hour. The whole of this arrangement struck me as being admirable; and I hope that the next new prison we erect in England may be built on this plan.

I was given to understand that in this prison no swords or firearms, or even cudgels, are kept; nor is it probable that, so long as its present excellent management continues, any weapon, offensive or defensive, will ever be required within its bounds.

Such are the Institutions at South Boston! In all of them, the unfortunate or degenerate citizens of the State are carefully instructed in their duties both to God and man; are surrounded by all reasonable means of comfort and happiness that their condition will admit of; are appealed to, as members of the great human family, however afflicted, indigent, or fallen; are ruled by the strong Heart, and not by the strong (though immeasurably weaker) Hand. I have described them at some length: first, because their worth demanded it; and secondly, because I mean to take them for a model, and to content myself with saying of others we may come to, whose design and purpose are the same, that in this or that respect they practically fail, or differ.

I wish by this account of them, imperfect in its execution, but in its just intention honest, I could hope to convey to my readers one hundredth part of the gratification, the sights I have described, afforded me.

To an Englishman, accustomed to the paraphernalia of Westminster Hall, an American Court of Law is as odd a sight as, I suppose, an English Court of Law would be to an American. Except in the Supreme Court at Washington (where the judges wear a plain black robe), there is no such thing as a wig or gown connected with the administration of justice. The gentlemen of the bar being barristers and attorneys too (for there is no division of those functions as in England), are no more removed from their clients than attorneys in our Court for the Relief of Insolvent Debtors are, from theirs. The jury are quite at home, and make themselves as comfortable as circumstances will permit. The witness is so little elevated above, or put aloof from, the crowd in the court, that a stranger entering during a pause in the proceedings would find it difficult to pick him out from the rest.

* Apart from profit made by the useful labour of prisoners, which we can never hope to realize to any great extent, and which it is perhaps not expedient for us to try to gain, there are two prisons in London, in all respects equal, and in some decidedly superior, to any I saw or have ever heard or read of in America. One is the Tothill Fields Bridewell, conducted by Lieutenant A. F. Tracey, R.N.; the other the Middlesex House of Correction, superintended by Mr. Chesterton. This gentleman also holds an appointment in the Public Service. Both are enlightened and superior men: and it would be as difficult to find persons better qualified for the functions they discharge with firmness, zeal, intelligence, and humanity, as it would be to exceed the perfect order and arrangement of the institutions they govern.

And if it chanced to be a criminal trial, his eyes, in nine cases out of ten, would wander to the dock in search of the prisoner, in vain; for that gentleman would most likely be lounging among the most distinguished ornaments of the legal profession, whispering suggestions in his counsel's ear, or making a toothpick out of an old quill with his penknife.

I could not but notice these differences, when I visited the courts at Boston. I was much surprised at first, too, to observe that the counsel who interrogated the witness under examination at the time, did so *sitting*. But seeing that he was also occupied in writing down the answers, and remembering that he was alone and had no "junior," I quickly consoled myself with the reflection that law was not quite so expensive an article here, as at home; and that the absence of sundry formalities which we regard as indispensable, had doubtless a very favourable influence upon the bill of costs.

In every court, ample and commodious provision is made for the accommodation of the citizens. This is the case all through America. In every public institution, the right of the people to attend, and to have an interest in the proceedings, is most fully and distinctly recognised. There are no grim door-keepers to dole out their tardy civility by the sixpenny-worth; nor is there, I sincerely believe, any insolence of office of any kind. Nothing national is exhibited for money; and no public officer is a showman. We have begun of late years to imitate this good example. I hope we shall continue to do so; and that in the fulness of time, even deans and chapters may be converted.

In the civil court, an action was trying, for damages sustained in some accident upon a railway. The witness had been examined, and counsel was addressing the jury. The learned gentleman (like a few of his English brethren) was desperately long-winded, and had a remarkable capacity of saying the same thing over and over again. His great theme was "Warren the ĕn*gine* driver," whom he pressed into the service of every sentence he uttered. I listened to him for about a quarter of an hour; and, coming out of court at the expiration of that time, without the faintest ray of enlightenment as to the merits of the case, felt as if I were at home again.

In the prisoners' cell, waiting to be examined by the magistrate on a charge of theft, was a boy. This lad, instead of being committed to a common jail, would be sent to the Asylum at South Boston, and there taught a trade; and in the course of time, he would be bound apprentice to some respectable master. Thus, his detection in this offence, instead of being the prelude to a life of infamy and a miserable death, would lead, there was a reasonable hope, to his being reclaimed from vice, and becoming a worthy member of society.

I am by no means a wholesale admirer of our legal solemnities, many of which impress me as being exceedingly ludicrous. Strange as it may seem, too, there is undoubtedly a degree of protection in the wig and gown—a dismissal of individual responsibility in dressing for the part—which encourages that insolent bearing and language, and that gross perversion of the office of a pleader for The Truth, so frequent in our courts of law. Still, I cannot help doubting whether America, in her desire to shake off the absurdities and abuses of the old system, may not have gone too far into the opposite extreme; and, whether it is not desirable, especially in the small community of a city like this, where each man knows the other, to surround the administration of justice with some artificial barriers against the "Hail fellow, well met" deportment of everyday life. All the aid it can have in the very high character and ability of the Bench, not only here but elsewhere, it has, and well deserves to have; but it may need something more: not to impress the thoughtful and the well-informed, but the ignorant and heedless; a class which includes some prisoners and many witnesses. These institutions were established, no doubt, upon the principle, that those who had so large a share in making the laws would certainly respect them. But experience has proved this hope to be fallacious; for no men know better than the Judges of America, that on the occasion of any great popular excitement, the law is powerless, and cannot, for the time, assert its own supremacy.

The tone of society, in Boston, is one of perfect politeness, courtesy, and good breeding. The ladies are unquestionably very beautiful—in face: but there I am compelled to stop. Their education is much as with us; neither better nor worse. I had heard some very marvellous stories in this respect; but not believing them, was not disappointed. Blue ladies there are, in Boston; but like philosophers of that colour and sex in most other latitudes, they rather desire to be thought superior than to be so. Evangelical ladies there are, likewise, whose attachment to the forms of religion, and horror of theatrical entertainments, are most exemplary. Ladies who have a passion for attending lectures are to be found among all classes and all conditions. In the kind of provincial life which prevails in cities such as this, the Pulpit has great influence. The peculiar province of the Pulpit in New England (always excepting the Unitarian ministry) would appear to be the denouncement of all innocent and rational amusements. The church, the chapel, and the lecture-room, are the only means of excitement excepted; and to the church, the chapel, and the lecture-room, the ladies resort in crowds.

Wherever religion is resorted to, as a strong drink, and as an escape from the dull, monotonous round of home, those of its ministers who pepper the highest will be the surest to please. They who strew the Eternal Path with the greatest amount of brimstone, and who most ruthlessly tread down the flowers and leaves that grow by the way-side, will be voted the most righteous; and they who enlarge with the greatest pertinacity on the difficulty of getting into heaven, will be considered, by all true believers, certain of going there: though it would be hard to say by what process of reasoning this conclusion is arrived at. It is so at home, and it is so abroad. With regard to the other means of excitement, the Lecture, it has at least the merit of being always new. One lecture treads so quickly on the heels of another, that none are remembered; and the course of this month may be safely repeated next, with its charm of novelty unbroken, and its interest unabated.

The fruits of the earth have their growth in corruption. Out of the rottenness of these things, there has sprung up, in Boston, a sect of philosophers known as Transcendentalists. On inquiring what this appellation might be supposed to signify, I was given to understand that whatever was unintelligible would be certainly transcendental. Not deriving much comfort from this elucidation, I pursued the inquiry still farther, and found that the Transcendentalists are followers of my friend, Mr. Carlyle, or, I should rather say, of a follower of his, Mr. Ralph Waldo Emerson. This gentleman has written a volume of Essays, in which, among much that is dreamy and fanciful (if he will pardon me for saying so), there is much more that is true and manly, honest and bold. Transcendentalism has its occasional vagaries (what school has not?) but it has good healthful qualities in spite of them; not least among the number a hearty disgust of cant, and an aptitude to detect her in all the million varieties of her everlasting wardrobe. And therefore if I were a Bostonian, I think I would be a Transcendentalist.

The only preacher I heard in Boston was Mr. Taylor, who addresses himself peculiarly to seamen, and who was once a mariner himself. I found his chapel down among the shipping, in one of the narrow, old, water-side streets, with a gay blue flag waving freely from its roof. In the gallery opposite to the pulpit were a little choir of male and female singers, a violoncello, and a violin. The preacher already sat in the pulpit, which was raised on pillars, and ornamented behind him with painted drapery of a lively and somewhat theatrical appearance. He looked a weather-beaten, hard-featured man, of about six or eight and fifty; with deep lines graven as it were into his face, dark hair, and a stern, keen eye. Yet the general character of his countenance was pleasant and agreeable.

The service commenced with a hymn, to which succeeded an extemporary prayer. It had the fault of frequent repetition, incidental to all such prayers; but it was plain and comprehensive in its doctrines, and breathed a tone of general sympathy and charity, which is not so commonly a characteristic of this form of address to the Deity as it might be. That done, he opened his discourse, taking for his text a passage from the Songs of Solomon, laid upon the desk before the commencement of the service by some unknown member of the congregation: "Who is this coming up from the wilderness, leaning on the arm of her beloved!"

He handled this text in all kinds of ways, and twisted it into all manner of shapes; but always ingeniously, and with a rude eloquence, well-adapted to the comprehension of his hearers. Indeed, if I be not mistaken, he studied their sympathies and understandings much more than the display of his own powers. His imagery was all drawn from the sea, and from the incidents of a seamen's life; and was often remarkably good. He spoke to them of "that glorious man, Lord Nelson," and of Collingwood; and drew nothing in, as the saying is, by the head and shoulders, but brought it to bear upon his purpose naturally, and with a sharp mind to its effect. Sometimes, when much excited with his subject, he had an odd way—compounded of John Bunyan and Balfour of Burley—of taking his great quarto Bible under his arm and pacing up down the pulpit with it; looking steadily down, meantime, into the midst of the congregation. Thus, when he applied his text to the first assemblage of his hearers, and pictured the wonder of the church at their presumption in forming a congregation among themselves, he stopped short with his Bible under his arm in the manner I have described, and pursued his discourse after this manner:

"Who are these—who are they—who are these fellows? where do they come from? where are they going to? Come from! What's the answer?" leaning out of the pulpit, and pointing downward with his right hand: "From below!" starting back again, and looking at the sailors before him: "From below, my brethren. From under the hatches of sin, battened down above you by the evil one. That's where you came from!" a walk up and down the pulpit: "and where are you going"—stopping abruptly, "where are you going? Aloft!"—very softly, and pointing upward: "Aloft!"—louder: "aloft!"—louder still: "That's where you are going—with a fair wind—all taut and trim, steering direct for Heaven in its glory, where there are no storms or foul weather, and where the wicked cease from troubling, and the weary are at rest."—Another walk: "That's where you're going to, my friends. That's it. That's the place. That's the port. That's the haven. It's a blessed harbour—still water there, in all changes of the winds and tides; no driving ashore upon the rocks, or slipping your cables and running out to sea, there: Peace—peace—peace—all peace!"—Another walk, and patting the Bible under his left arm: "What! These fellows are coming from the wilderness, are they? Yes. From the dreary, blighted wilderness of Iniquity, whose only crop is Death. But do they lean upon anything—do they lean upon nothing, these poor seamen?"—Three raps upon the Bible: "Oh yes. Yes. They lean upon the arm of their Beloved"—three more raps: "upon the arm of their Beloved"—three more, and a walk: "Pilot, guiding-star, and compass, all in one, to all hands—here it is"—three more: "Here it is. They can do their seamen's duty manfully, and be easy in their minds in the utmost peril and danger, with this"—two more: "They can come, even these poor fellows can come, from the wilderness leaning on the arm of their Beloved, and go up—up—up!"—raising his hand higher and higher at every repetition of the word, so that he stood with it at last stretched above his head, regarding them in a strange, rapt manner, and pressing the book triumphantly to his breast, until he gradually subsided into some other portion of his discourse.

I have cited this rather as an instance of the preacher's eccentricities than his merits, though, taken in connexion with his look and manner, and the character of his audience, even this was striking. It is possible, however, that my favourable impression of him may have been greatly influenced and strengthened, firstly, by his impressing upon his hearers that the true observance of religion was not inconsistent with a cheerful deportment and an exact discharge of the duties of their station, which, indeed, it scrupulously required of them; and secondly, by his cautioning them not to set up any monopoly in Paradise and its mercies. I never heard these two points so wisely touched (if, indeed, I have ever heard them touched at all), by any preacher of that kind before.

Having passed the time I spent in Boston in making myself acquainted with these things, in settling the course I should take in my future travels, and mixing constantly with its society, I am not aware that I have any occasion to prolong this chapter. Such of its social customs as I have not mentioned, however, may be told in a very few words.

The usual dinner-hour is two o'clock. A dinner party takes place at five; and at an evening party, they seldom sup later than eleven; so that it goes hard but one get home, even from a rout, by midnight. I never could find out any difference between a party at Boston and a party in London, saving that at the former place all assemblies are held at more rational hours; that the conversation may possibly be a little louder and more cheerful; that a guest is usually expected to ascend to the very top of the house to take his cloak off; that he is certain to see at every dinner an unusual amount of poultry on the table; and at every supper, at least two mighty bowls of hot stewed oysters, in any one of which a half grown Duke of Clarence might be smothered easily.

There are two theatres in Boston, of good size and construction, but sadly in want of patronage. The few ladies who resort to them sit, as of right, in the front rows of the boxes.

There is no smoking-room in any hotel, and there was none consequently in ours; but the bar is a large room with a stone floor, and there people stand and smoke, and lounge about, all the evening: dropping in and out as the humour takes them. There, too, the stranger is initiated inot the mysteries of Gin-sling, Cocktail, Sangaree, Mint Julep, Sherry-cobbler, Timber Doodle, and other rare drinks. The house is full of boarders, both married and single, many of whom sleep upon the premises, and contract by the week for their board and lodging: the charge for which diminishes as they go nearer the sky to roost. A public table is laid in a very handsome hall for breakfast, and for dinner, and for supper. The party sitting down together to these meals will vary in number from one to two hundred: sometimes more. The advent of each of these epochs in the day is proclaimed by an awful gong, which shakes the very window frames as it reverberates through the house, and horribly disturbs nervous foreigners. There is an ordinary for ladies, and an ordinary for gentlemen.

In our private room the cloth could not, for any earthly consideration, have been laid for dinner without a huge glass dish of cranberries in the middle of the table; and breakfast would have been no breakfast unless the principal dish were a deformed beefsteak with a great flat bone in the centre, swimming in hot butter, and sprinkled with the very blackest of all possible pepper. Our bedroom was spacious and airy, but (like every bedroom on this side of the Atlantic) very bare of furniture, having no curtains to the French bedstead or to the window. It had one unusual luxury, however, in the shape of a wardrobe of painted wood, something smaller than an English watchbox: or, if this comparison be insufficient to convey a just idea of its dimensions, they may be estimated from the fact of my having lived for fourteen days and nights in the firm belief that it was a shower-bath.

CHAPTER IV.

AN AMERICAN RAILROAD. LOWELL AND ITS FACTORY SYSTEM.

Before leaving Boston, I devoted one day to an excursion to Lowell. I assign a separate chapter to this visit; not because I am about to describe it at any great length, but because I remember it as a thing by itself, and am desirous that my readers should do the same.

I made acquaintance with an American railroad, on this occasion, for the first time. As these works are pretty much alike all through the States, their general characteristics are easily described.

There are no first and second class carriages as with us; but there is a gentlemen's car and a ladies' car; the main distinction between which is that in the first, everybody smokes; and in the second, nobody does. As a black man never travels with a white one, there is also a negro car; which is a great blundering clumsy chest, such as Gulliver put to sea in, from the kingdom of Brobdignag. There is a great deal of jolting, a great deal of noise, a great deal of wall, not much window, a locomotive engine, a shriek, and a bell.

The cars are like shabby omnibusses, but larger; holding thirty, forty, fifty, people. The seats, instead of stretching from end to end, are placed crosswise. Each seat holds two persons. There is a long row of them on each side of the caravan, a narrow passage up the middle, and a door at both ends. In the centre of the carriage there is usually a stove, fed with charcoal or anthracite coal; which is for the most part red-hot. It is insufferably close; and you see the hot air fluttering between yourself and any other object you may happen to look at, like the ghost of smoke.

In the ladies' car, there are a great many gentlemen who have ladies with them. There are also a great many ladies who have nobody with them; for any lady may travel alone, from one end of the United States to the other, and be certain of the most courteous and considerate treatment everywhere. The conductor or check-taker, or guard, or whatever he may be, wears no uniform. He walks up and down the car, and in and out of it, as his fancy dictates; leans against the door with his hands in his pockets and stares at you, if you chance to be a stranger; or enters into conversation with the passengers about him. A great many newspapers are pulled out, and a few of them are read. Everybody talks to you, or to anybody else who hits his fancy. If you are an Englishman, he expects that that railroad is pretty much like an English railroad. If you say "No," he says "Yes?" (interrogatively,) and asks in what respect they differ. You enumerate the heads of difference, one by one, and he says "Yes?" (still interrogatively) to each. Then he guesses that you don't travel faster in England; and on your replying that you do, says "Yes?" again (still interrogatively), and, it is quite evident, don't believe it. After a long pause he remarks, partly to you, and partly to the knob on the top of his stick, that "Yankees are reckoned to be considerable of a go-ahead people too;" upon which you say "Yes," and then he says "Yes" again (affirmatively this time); and upon your looking out of window, tells you that behind that hill, and some three miles from the next station, there is a clever town in a smart lo-cation, where he expects you have con-cluded to stop. Your answer in the negative naturally leads to more questions in reference to your intended route (always pronounced rout); and wherever you are going, you invariably learn that you can't get there without immense difficulty and danger, and that all the great sights are somewhere else.

If a lady take a fancy to any male passenger's seat, the gentleman who accompanies her gives him notice of the fact, and he immediately vacates it with great politeness. Politics are much discussed, so are banks, so is cotton. Quiet people avoid the question of the Presidency, for there will be a new election in three years and a half, and party feeling runs very high: the great constitutional feature of this institution being, that directly the acrimony of the last election is over, the acrimony of the next one begins; which is an unspeakable comfort to all strong politicians and true lovers of their country: that is to say, to ninety-nine men and boys out of every ninety-nine and a quarter.

Except when a branch road joins the main one, there is seldom more than one track of rails; so that the road is very narrow, and the view, where there is a deep cutting, by no means extensive. When there is not, the character of the scenery is always the same. Mile after mile of stunted trees: some hewn down by the axe, some blown down by the wind, some half fallen and resting on their neighbours, many mere logs half hidden in the swamp, others mouldered away to spongy chips. The very soil of the earth is made up of minute fragments such as these; each pool of stagnant water has its crust of vegetable rottenness; on every side there are the boughs, and trunks, and stumps of trees, in every possible stage of decay, decomposition, and neglect. Now you emerge for a few brief minutes on an open country, glittering with some bright lake or pool, broad as many an English river, but so small here that it scarcely has a name; now catch hasty glimpses of a distant town, with its clean white houses and their cool piazzas, its prim New-England church and schoolhouse; when whir-r-r-r! almost before you have seen them, comes the same dark screen: the stunted trees, the stumps, the logs, the stagnant water—all so like the last that you seem to have been transported back again by magic.

The train calls at stations in the woods, where the wild impossibility of anybody having the smallest reason to get out, is only to be equalled by the apparently desperate hopelessness of there being anybody to get in. It rushes across the turnpike road, where there is no gate, no policeman, no signal: nothing but a rough wooden arch, on which is painted "WHEN THE BELL RINGS, LOOK OUT FOR THE LOCOMOTIVE." On it whirls headlong, dives through the woods again, emerges in the light, clatters over frail arches, rumbles upon the heavy ground, shoots beneath a wooden bridge which intercepts the light for a second like a wink, suddenly awakens all the slumbering echoes in the main street of a large town, and dashes on hap-hazard, pell-mell, neck or nothing, down the middle of the road. There—with mechanics working at their trades, and people leaning from their doors and windows, and boys flying kites and playing marbles, and men smoking, and women talking, and children crawling, and pigs burrowing, and unaccustomed horses plunging and rearing, close to the very rails—there—on, on, on—tears the mad dragon of an engine with its train of cars; scattering in all directions a shower of burning sparks from its wood fire; screeching, hissing, yelling, panting: until at last the thirsty monster stops beneath a covered way to drink, the people cluster round, and you have time to breathe again.

I was met at the station at Lowell by a gentleman intimately connected with the management of the factories there; and gladly putting myself under his guidance, drove off at once to that quarter of the town in which the works, the object of my visit, were situated. Although only just of age—for if my recollection serve me, it has been a manufacturing town barely one-and-twenty years—Lowell is a large, populous, thriving place. Those indications of its youth which first attract the eye, give it a quaintness and oddity of character which, to a visiter from the old country, is amusing enough. It was a very dirty winter's day, and nothing in the whole town looked old to me, except the mud, which in some parts was almost knee-deep, and might have been deposited there on the subsiding of the waters after the Deluge. In one place, there was a new wooden church, which, having no steeple, and being yet unpainted, looked like an enormous packing-case without any direction upon it. In another there was a large hotel, whose walls and colonnades were so crisp, and thin, and slight, that it had exactly the appearance of being built with cards. I was careful not to draw my breath as we passed, and trembled when I saw a workman come out upon the roof, lest with one thoughtless stamp of his foot he should crush the structure beneath him, and bring it rattling down. The very river that moves the machinery in the mills (for they are all worked by water power), seems to acquire a new character from the fresh buildings of bright red brick and painted wood among which it takes its course; and to be as light-headed, thoughtless, and brisk a young river, in its murmurings and tumblings, as one would desire to see. One would swear that every "Bakery," "Grocery," and "Bookbindery," and other kind of store, took its shutters down for the first time, and started in business yesterday. The golden pestles and mortars fixed as signs upon the sun-blind frames outside the druggist's, appear to have been just turned out of the United States' Mint; and when I saw a baby of some week or ten days old in a woman's arms at a street corner, I found myself unconsciously wondering where it came from: never supposing for an instant that it could have been born in such a young town as that.

There are several factories in Lowell, each of which belongs to what we should term a Company of Proprietors, but what they call in America a corporation. I went over several of these; such as a woollen factory, a carpet factory, and a cotton factory: examined them in every part; and saw them in their ordinary working aspect, with no preparation of any kind, or departure from their ordinary every-day proceedings. I may add that I am well acquainted with our manufacturing towns in England, and have visited many mills in Manchester and elsewhere in the same manner.

I happened to arrive at the first factory just as the dinner-hour was over, and the girls were returning to their work; indeed, the stairs of the mill were thronged with them as I ascended. They were all well-dressed, but not to my thinking above their condition: for I like to see the humbler classes of society careful of their dress and appearance, and even, if they please, decorated with such little trinkets as come within the compass of their means. Supposing it confined within reasonable limits, I would always encourage this kind of pride, as a worthy element of self-respect, in any person I employed; and should no more be deterred from doing so, because some wretched female referred her fall to a love of dress, than I would allow my construction of the real intent and meaning of the Sabbath to be influenced by any warning to the well-disposed, founded on his backslidings on that particular day, which might emanate from the rather doubtful authority of a murderer in Newgate.

These girls, as I have said, were all well dressed: and that phrase necessarily includes extreme cleanliness. They had serviceable bonnets, good warm cloaks, and shawls; and were not above clogs and pattens. Moreover, there were places in the mill in which they could deposite these things without injury; and there were conveniences for washing. They were healthy in appearance, many of them remarkably so, and had the manners and deportment of young women: not of degraded brutes of burden. If I had seen in one of those mills (but I did not, though I looked for something of this kind with a sharp eye), the most lisping, mincing, affected, and ridiculous young creature that my imagination could suggest, I should have thought of the careless, moping, slatternly, degraded, dull reverse (I *have* seen that), and should have been still well pleased to look upon her.

The rooms in which they worked were as well ordered as themselves. In the windows of some there were green plants, which were trained to shade the glass; in all, there was as much fresh air, cleanliness, and comfort as the nature of the occupation would possibly admit of. Out of so large a number of females, many of whom were only then just verging upon womanhood, it may be reasonably supposed that some were delicate and fragile in appearance: no doubt there were. But I solemnly declare, that from all the crowd I saw in the different factories that day, I cannot recall or separate one young face that gave me a painful impression; not one young girl whom, assuming it to be matter of necessity that she should gain her daily bread by the labour of her hands, I would have removed from those works if I had had the power.

They reside at various boarding-houses near at hand. The owners of the mills are particularly careful to allow no persons to enter upon the possession of these houses, whose characters have not undergone the most searching and thorough inquiry. Any complaint that is made against them by the boarders or by anybody else, is fully investigated; and if good ground of complaint be shown to exist against them, they are removed, and their occupation is handed over to some more deserving person. There are a few children employed in these factories, but not many. The laws of the state forbid their working more than nine months in the year, and require that they be educated during the other three. For this purpose there are schools in Lowell; and there are churches and chapels of various persuasions, in which the young women may observe that form of worship in which they have been educated.

At some distance from the factories, and on the highest and pleasantest ground in the neighbourhood, stands their hospital, or boarding-house for the sick: it is the best house in those parts, and was built by an eminent merchant for his own residence. Like that institution at Boston which I have before described, it is not parcelled out into wards, but is divided into convenient chambers, each of which has all the comforts of a very comfortable home. The principal medical attendant resides under the same roof; and were the patients members of his own family, they could not be better cared for, or attended with greater gentleness and consideration. The weekly charge in this establishment for each patient is three dollars, or twelve shillings English; but no girl employed by any of the corporations is ever excluded for want of the means of payment. That they do not very often want the means, may be gathered from the fact, that in July, 1841, no fewer than nine hundred and seventy-eight of these girls were depositors in the Lowell Savings Bank: the amount of whose joint savings was estimated at one hundred thousand dollars, or twenty thousand English pounds.

I am now going to state three facts, which will startle a large class of readers on this side of the Atlantic, very much.

Firstly, there is a joint-stock piano in a great many of the boarding-houses. Secondly, nearly all these young ladies subscribe to circulating libraries. Thirdly, they have got up among themselves a periodical called THE LOWELL OFFERING, "A repository of original articles, written exclusively by females actively employed in the mills," which is duly printed, published, and sold; and whereof I brought away from Lowell four hundred good solid pages, which I have read from beginning to end.

The large class of readers, startled by these facts, will exclaim, with one voice, "How very preposterous!" On my deferentially inquiring why, they will answer, "These things are above their station." In reply to that objection, I would beg to ask what their station is.

It is their station to work. And they *do* work. They labour in these mills, upon an average, twelve hours a day, which is unquestionably work, and pretty tight work too. Perhaps it is above their station to indulge in such amusements, on any terms. Are we quite sure that we in England have not formed our ideas of the "station" of working people, from accustoming ourselves to the contemplation of that class as they are, and not as they might be? I think that if we examine our own feelings, we shall find that the pianos, and the circulating-libraries, and even the Lowell Offering, startle us by their novelty, and not by their bearing upon any abstract question of right or wrong.

For myself, I know no station in which, the occupation of to-day cheerfully done and the occupation of to-morrow cheerfully looked to, any one of these pursuits is not most humanizing and laudable. I know no station which is rendered more endurable to the person in it, or more safe to the person out of it, by having ignorance for its associate. I know no station which has a right to monopolize the means of mutual instruction, improvement, and rational entertainment; or which has ever continued to be a station very long, after seeking to do so.

Of the merits of the Lowell Offering as a literary production, I will only observe, putting entirely out of sight the fact of the articles having been written by these girls after the arduous labours of the day, that it will compare advantageously with a great many English Annuals. It is pleasant to find that many of its Tales are of the Mills and of those who work in them; that they inculcate habits of self-denial and contentment, and teach good doctrines of enlarged benevolence. A strong feeling for the beauties of nature, as displayed in the solitudes the writers have left at home, breathes through its pages like wholesome village air; and though a circulating library is a favourable school for the study of such topics, it has very scanty allusion to fine clothes, fine marriages, fine houses, or fine life. Some persons might object to the papers being signed occasionally with rather fine names, but this is an American fashion. One of the provinces of the state legislature of Massachusetts is to alter ugly names into pretty ones, as the children improve upon the tastes of their parents. These changes costing little or nothing, scores of Mary Annes are solemnly converted into Bevelinas every session.

It is said that on the occasion of a visit from General Jackson or General Harrison to this town (I forget which, but it is not to the purpose), he walked through three miles and a half of these young ladies, all dressed out with parasols and silk stockings. But as I am not aware that any worse consequence ensued, than a sudden looking-up of all the parasols and silk stockings in the market; and perhaps the bankruptcy of some speculative New-Englander who bought them all up at one price, in expectation of a demand that never came; I set no great store by the circumstance.

In this brief account of Lowell, and inadequate expression of the gratification it yielded me, and cannot fail to afford to any foreigner to whom the condition of such people at home is a subject of interest and anxious speculation, I have carefully abstained from drawing a comparison between these factories and those of our own land. Many of the circumstances whose strong influence has been at work for years in our manufacturing towns have not arisen here; and there is no manufacturing population in Lowell, so to speak: for these girls (often the daughters of small farmers) come from other states, remain a few years in the mills, and then go home for good.

The contrast would be a strong one, for it would be between the Good and Evil, the living light and deepest shadow. I abstain from it, because I deem it just to do so. But I only the more earnestly adjure all those whose eyes may rest on these pages, to pause and reflect upon the difference between this town aud those great haunts of desperate misery: to call to mind, if they can in the midst of party strife and squabble, the efforts that must be made to purge them of their suffering and danger: and last, and foremost, to remember how the precious Time is rushing by.

I returned at night by the same railroad and in the same kind of car. One of the passengers being exceedingly anxious to expound at great length to my companion (not to me, of course) the true principles on which books of travel in America should be written by Englishmen, I feigned to fall asleep. But glancing all the way out at window from the corners of my eyes, I found abundance of entertainment for the rest of the ride in watching the effects of the wood fire, which had been invisible in the morning, but were now brought out in full relief by the darkness: for we were travelling in a whirlwind of bright sparks, which showered about us like a storm of fiery snow.

CHAPTER V.

WORCESTER.—THE CONNECTICUT RIVER.—HARTFORD—HEW-HAVEN.—TO NEW-YORK.

Leaving Boston on the afternoon of Saturday, the fifth of February, we proceeded by another railroad to Worcester: a pretty New-England town, where we had arranged to remain under the hospitable roof of the governor of the state until Monday morning.

These towns and cities of New-England (many of which would be villages in Old England), are as favourable specimens of rural America, as their people are of rural Americans. The well-trimmed lawns and green meadows of home are not there; and the grass, compared with our ornamental plots and pastures, is rank, and rough, and wild: but delicate slopes of land, gently-swelling hills, wooded valleys, and slender streams abound. Every little colony of houses has its church and school-house peeping from among the white roofs and shady trees; every house is the whitest of the white; every Venetian blind the greenest of the green; every fine day's sky the bluest of the blue. A sharp, dry wind and a slight frost had so hardened the roads when we alighted at Worcester, that their furrowed tracks were like ridges of granite. There was the usual aspect of newness on every object, of course. All the buildings looked as if they had been built and painted that morning, and could be taken down on Monday with very little trouble. In the keen evening air, every sharp outline looked a hundred times sharper than ever. The clean, cardboard colonnades had no more perspective than a Chinese bridge on a teacup, and appeared equally well calculated for use. The razor-like edges of the detached cottages seemed to cut the very wind as it whistled against them, and to send it smarting on its way with a shriller cry than before. Those slightly-built wooden dwellings, behind which the sun was setting with a brilliant lustre, could be so looked through and through, that the idea of any inhabitant being able to hide himself from the public gaze, or to have any secrets from the public eye, was not entertainable for a moment. Even where a blazing fire shone through the uncurtained windows of some distant house, it had the air of being newly-lighted, and of lacking warmth; and instead of awakening thoughts of a snug chamber bright with faces that first saw the light round that same hearth, and ruddy with warm hangings, it came upon one suggestive with the smell of new mortar and damp walls.

So I thought, at least, that evening. Next morning, when the sun was shining brightly, and the clear church bells were ringing, and sedate people in their best clothes enlivened the pathway near at hand, and dotted the distant thread of road, there was a pleasant Sabbath peacefulness on everything, which it was good to feel. It would have been better for an old church; better still for some old graves; but as it was, a wholesome repose and tranquillity pervaded the scene, which, after the restless ocean and the hurried city, had a doubly grateful influence on the spirits.

We went on next morning, still by railroad, to Springfield. From that place to Hartford, whither we were bound, is a distance of only five-and-twenty miles, but at that time of the year the roads were so bad that the journey would probably have occupied ten or twelve hours. Fortunately, however, the winter having been unusually mild, the Connecticut River was "open," or, in other words, not frozen. The captain of a small steamboat was going to make his first trip for the season that day (the second February trip, I believe, within the memory of man), and only waited for us to go on board. Accordingly, we went on board, with as little delay as might be. He was as good as his word, and started directly.

It certainly was not called a small steamboat without reason. I omitted to ask the question, but I should think it must have been of about half a pony power. Mr. Paap, the celebrated dwarf, might have lived and died happily in the cabin, which was fitted with common sash-windows like an ordinary dwelling-house. These windows had bright red curtains, too, hung on slack strings across the lower panes; so that it looked like the parlour of a lilliputian public-house, which had got afloat in a flood, or some other water accident, and was drifting nobody knew where. But even in this chamber there was a rocking-chair. It would be impossible to get on anywhere in America without a rockingchair.

I am afraid to tell how many feet short this vessel was, or how many feet narrow: to apply the words length and width to such measurement would be a contradiction in terms. But I may state that we all kept the middle of the deck, lest the boat should unexpectedly tip over; and that the machinery, by some surprising process of condensation, worked between it and the keel: the whole forming a warm sandwich, about three feet thick.

It rained all day as I once thought it never did rain anywhere but in the Highlands of Scotland. The river was full of floating blocks of ice, which were constantly crunching and cracking under us; and the depth of water, in the course we took to avoid the larger masses, carried down the middle of the river by the current, did not exceed a few inches. Nevertheless, we moved onward dexterously; and, being well wrapped up, bade defiance to the weather, and enjoyed the journey. The Connecticut River is a fine stream; and the banks in summer-time, are, I have no doubt, beautiful: at all events, I was told so by a young lady in the cabin; and she should be a judge of beauty, if the possession of a quality include the appreciation of it, for a more beautiful creature I never looked upon.

After two hours and a half of this odd travelling (including a stoppage at a small town, where we were saluted by a gun considerably bigger than our own chimney), we reached Hartford, and straightway repaired to an extremely comfortable hotel: except, as usual, in the article of bedrooms, which, in almost every place we visited, were very conducive to early rising.

We tarried here four days. The town is beautifully situated in a basin of green hills; the soil is rich, well-wooded, and carefully improved. It is the seat of the local legislature of Connecticut, which sage body enacted in bygone times, the renowned code of "Blue Laws," in virtue whereof, among other enlightened provisions, any citizen who could be proved to have kissed his wife on Sunday, was punishable, I believe, with the stocks. Too much of the old Puritan spirit exists in these parts to the present hour; but its influence has not tended, that I know, to make the people less hard in their bargains, or more equal in their dealings. As I never heard of its working that effect anywhere else, I infer that it never will here. Indeed, I am accustomed, with reference to great professions and severe faces, to judge of the goods of the other world pretty much as I judge of the goods of this; and whenever I see a dealer in such commodities with too great a display of them in his window, I doubt the quality of the article within.

In Hartford stands the famous oak in which the charter of King Charles was hidden. It is now enclosed in a gentleman's garden. In the State House is the charter itself. I found the courts of law here just the same as at Boston; the public institutions almost as good. The Insane Asylum is admirably conducted, and so is the Institution for the Deaf and Dumb.

I very much questioned within myself, as I walked through the Insane Asylum, whether I should have known the attendants from the patients, but for the few words which passed between the former and the doctor, in reference to the persons under their charge. Of course I limit this remark merely to their looks; for the conversation of the mad people was mad enough.

There was one little prim old lady, of very smiling and good-humoured appearance, who came sidling up to me from the end of a long passage, and with a courtesy of inexpressible condescension, propounded this unaccountable inquiry:

"Does Pontefract still flourish, Sir, upon the soil of England?"

"He does, Ma'am," I rejoined,

"When you last saw him, Sir, he was—"

"Well, Ma'am," said I, "extremely well. He begged me to present his compliments. I never saw him looking better."

At this the old lady was very much delighted. After glancing at me for a moment, as if to be quite sure that I was serious in my respectful air, she sidled back some paces; sidled forward again; made a sudden skip (at which I precipitately retreated a step or two), and said:

"*I* am an antediluvian, Sir."

I thought the best thing to say was, that I had suspected as much from the first. Therefore I said so.

"It is an extremely proud and pleasant thing, Sir, to be an antediluvian," said the old lady.

"I should think it was, Ma'am," I rejoined.

The old lady kissed her hand, gave another skip, smirked and sidled down the gallery in a most extraordinary manner, and ambled gracefully into her own bed-chamber.

In another part of the building there was a male patient in bed; very much flushed and heated.

"Well!" said he, starting up, and pulling off his night-cap: "It's all settled at last. I have arranged it with Queen Victoria."

"Arranged what?" asked the Doctor.

"Why, that business," passing his hand wearily across his forehead, "about the siege of New-York."

"Oh!" said I, like a man suddenly enlightened. For he looked at me for an answer.

"Yes. Every house without a signal will be fired upon by the British troops. No harm will be done to the others. No harm at all. Those that want to be safe must hoist flags. That's all they'll have to do. They must hoist flags."

Even while he was speaking, he seemed, I thought, to have some faint idea that his talk was incoherent. Directly he had said these words, he lay down again; gave a kind of groan, and covered his hot head with the blankets.

These was another: a young man, whose madness was love and music. After playing on the accordion a march he had composed, he was very anxious that I should walk into his chamber, which I immediately did.

By way of being very knowing, and humouring him to the top of his bent, I went to the window, which commanded a beautiful prospect, and remarked, with an address upon which I greatly plumed myself:

"What a delicious country you have about these lodgings of yours."

"Poh!" said he, moving his fingers carelessly over the notes of his instrument: "*Well enough for such an Institution as this!*"

I don't think I was ever so taken aback in all my life.

"I come here just for a whim," he said, coolly. "That's all."

"Oh! that's all!" said I. all

"Yes. That's all. The Doctor's a smart man. He quite enters into it. It's a joke of mine. I like it for a time. You needn't mention it, but I think I shall go out next Tuesday!"

I assured him that I would consider our interview perfectly confidential; and rejoined the Doctor. As we were passing through a gallery on our way out, a well-dressed lady, of quiet and composed manners, came up, and proffering a slip of paper and a pen, begged that I would oblige her with an autograph. I complied, and we parted.

"I think I remember having had a few interviews like that with ladies out of doors. I hope *she* is not mad?"

"Yes."

"On what subject? Autographs?"

"No. She hears voices in the air."

"Well!" thought I, "it would be well if we could shut up a few false prophets of these later times, who have professed to do the same; and I should like to try the experiment on a Mormonist or two to begin with."

In this place there is the best jail for untried offenders in the world. There is also a very well-ordered state prison, arranged upon the same plan as that at Boston, except that here, there is always a sentry on the wall with a loaded gun. It contained at that time about two hundred prisoners. A spot was shown me in the sleeping ward, where a watchman was murdered some years since in the dead of night, in a desperate attempt to escape, made by a prisoner who had broken from his cell. A woman, too, was pointed out to me, who, for the murder of her husband, had been a close prisoner for sixteen years.

"Do you think," I asked of my conductor, "that after so very long an imprisonment, she has any thought or hope of ever regaining her liberty?"

"Oh dear, yes," he answered. "To be sure she has."

"She has no chance of obtaining it, I suppose?"

"Well, I don't know:" which, by-the-by, is a national answer. "Her friends mistrust her."

"What have *they* to do with it?" I naturally inquired.

"Well, they won't petition."

"But if they did they couldn't get her out, I suppose?"

"Well, not the first time, perhaps, nor yet the second, but tiring and wearying for a few years might do it."

"Does that ever do it?"

"Why yes, that'll do it sometimes. Political friends 'll do it sometimes. It's pretty often done, one way or another."

I shall always entertain a very pleasant and grateful recollection of Hartford. It is a lovely place, and I had many friends there, whom I can never remember with indifference. We left it with no little regret on the evening of Friday the 11th, and travelled that night by railroad to New Haven. Upon the way, the guard and I were formally introduced to each other (as we usually were on such occasions), and exchanged a variety of small-talk. We reached New Haven at about eight o'clock, after a journey of three hours, and put up for the night at the best inn.

New Haven, known also as the City of Elms, is a fine town. Many of its streets (as its *alias* sufficiently imports) are planted with rows of grand old elm-trees; and the same natural ornaments surround Yale College, an establishment of considerable eminence and reputation. The various departments of this Institution are erected in a kind of park or common in the middle of the town, where they are dimly visible among the shadowing trees. The effect is very like that of an old cathedral yard in England; and when their branches are in full leaf, must be extremely picturesque. Even in the winter time, these groups of well-grown trees, clustering among the busy streets and houses of a thriving city, have a very quaint appearance: seeming to bring about a kind of compromise between town and country; as if each had met the other half way, and shaken hands upon it; which is at once novel and pleasant.

After a night's rest, we rose early, and in good time went down to the wharf, and on board the packet New-York, *for* New-York. This was the first American steamboat of any size that I had seen; and certainly to an English eye it was infinitely less like a steamboat than a huge floating bath. I could hardly persuade myself, indeed, but that the bathing establishment off Westminster Bridge, which I had left a baby, had suddenly grown to an enormous size; run away from home; and set up in foreign parts as a steamer. Being in America too, which our vagabonds do so particularly favour, it seemed the more probable.

The great difference in appearance between these packets and ours, is, that there is so much of them out of the water: the main-deck being enclosed on all sides, and filled with casks and goods, like any second or third floor in a stack of warehouses; and the promenade or hurricane-deck being a-top of that again. A part of the machinery is always above this deck: where the connecting-rod, in a strong and lofty frame, is seen working away like an iron top-sawyer. There is seldom any mast or tackle: nothing aloft but two tall black chimneys. The man at the helm is shut up in a little house in the fore part of the boat (the wheel being connected with the rudder by iron chains, working the whole length of the deck); and the passengers, unless the weather be very fine indeed, usually congregate below. Directly you have left the wharf, all the life, and stir, and bustle of a packet cease. You wonder for a long time how she goes on, for there seems to be nobody in charge of her; and when another of these dull machines comes splashing by, you feel quite indignant with it, as a sudden cumbrous, ungraceful, unshiplike leviathan: quite forgetting that the vessel you are on board of, is its very counterpart.

There is always a clerk's office on the lower deck, where you pay your fare; a ladies' cabin; baggage and stowage rooms; engineer's room; and in short a great variety of perplexities which render the discovery of the gentleman's cabin, a matter of some difficulty. It often occupies the whole length of the boat (as it did in this case), and has three or four tiers of berths on each side. When I first descended into the cabin of the New-York, it looked, in my unaccustomed eyes, about as long as the Burlington Arcade.

The Sound which has to be crossed on this passage, is not always a very safe or pleasant navigation, and has been the scene of some unfortunate accidents. It was a wet morning, and very misty, and we soon lost sight of land. The day was calm, however, and brightened towards noon. After exhausting (with good help from a friend) the larder, and the stock of bottled beer, I lay down to sleep: being very much tired with the fatigues of yesterday. But I awoke from my nap in time to hurry up, and see Hell Gate, the Hog's Back, the Frying Pan, and other notorious localities, attractive to all readers of famous Diedrich Knickerbocker's History. We were now in a narrow channel, with sloping banks on either side, besprinkled with pleasant villas, and made refreshing to the sight by turf and trees. Soon we shot in quick succession, past a lighthouse; a madhouse (how the lunatics flung up their caps, and roared in sympathy with the headlong engine and the driving tide)! a jail; and other buildings; and so emerged into a noble bay, whose waters sparkled in the now cloudless sunshine like Nature's eyes turned up to Heaven.

Then there lay stretched out before us, to the right, confused heaps of buildings, with here and there a spire or steeple, looking down upon the herd below; and here and there, again, a cloud of lazy smoke; and in the foreground a forest of ships' masts, cheery with flapping sails and waving flags. Crossing from among them to the opposite shore, were steam ferry-boats laden with people, coaches, horses, wagons, baskets, boxes: crossing and recrossing by other ferry-boats: all travelling to and fro: and never idle. Stately among these restless Insects, were two or three large ships, moving with slow majestic pace, as creatures of a prouder kind, disdainful of their puny journeys, and making for the broad sea. Beyond, were shining heights, and islands in the glancing river, and a distance scarcely less blue and bright than the sky it seemed to meet. The city's hum and buzz, the clinking of capstains, the ringing of bells, the barking of dogs, the clattering of wheels, tingled in the listening ear. All of which life and stir, coming across the stirring water, caught new life and animation from its free companionship; and, sympathizing with its buoyant spirits, glistening as it seemed in sport upon its surface, and hemmed the vessel round, and plashed the water high about her sides, and, floating her gallantly into the dock, flew off again to welcome other comers, and speed before them to the busy Port.

CHAPTER VI.

NEW-YORK.

The beautiful metropolis of America is by no means so clean a city as Boston, but many of its streets have the same charactesistics; except that the houses are not quite so fresh-coloured, the sign-boards are not quite so gaudy, the gilded letters not quite so golden, the bricks not quite so red, the stone not quite so white, the blinds and area railings not quite so green, the knobs and plates upon the street doors, not quite so bright and twinkling. There are many by-streets, almost as neutral in clean colours, and positive in dirty ones, as by-streets in London; and there is one quarter, commonly called the Five Points, which, in respect of filth and wretchedness, may be safely backed against Seven Dials, or any other part of famed St. Giles's.

The great promenade and thoroughfare, as most people know, is Broadway; a wide and bustling street, which, from the Battery Gardens to its opposite termination in a country road, may be four miles long. Shall we sit down in an upper floor of the Carlton House Hotel (situated in the best part of this main artery of New-York), and when we are tired of looking down upon the life below, sally forth arm-in-arm, and mingle with the stream?

Warm weather! The sun strikes upon our heads at this open window, as though its rays were concentrated through a burning-glass; but the day is in its zenith, and the season an unusual one. Was there ever such a sunny street as this Broadway? The pavement stones are polished with the tread of feet until they shine again; the red bricks of the houses might be yet in the dry, hot kilns; and the roofs of those omnibuses look as though, if water were poured on them, they would hiss and smoke, and smell like half-quenched fires. No stint of omnibuses here! Half a dozen have gone by within as many minutes. Plenty of hackney cabs and coaches too; gigs, phaetons, large-wheeled tilburies, and private carriages—rather of a clumsy make, and not very different from the public vehicles, but built for the heavy roads beyond the city pavement. Negro coachmen and white; in straw hats, black hats, white hats, glazed caps, fur caps; in coats of drab, black, brown, green, blue, nankeen, striped jean and linen; and there, in that one instance (look while it passes, or it will be too late), in suits of livery. Some southern republican that, who puts his blacks in uniform, and swells with Sultan pomp and power. Yonder, where that phaeton with the well-clipped pair of grays has stopped—standing at their heads now —is a Yorkshire groom, who has not been very long in these parts, and looks sorrowfully round for a companion pair of top-boots, which he may traverse the city half a year without meeting. Heaven save the ladies, how they dress! We have seen more colours in these ten minutes, than we should have seen elsewhere, in as many days. What various parasols! what rainbow silks and satins! what pinking of thin stockings, and pinching of thin shoes, and fluttering of ribands and silk tassels, and display of rich cloaks with gaudy hoods and linings! The young gentlemen are fond, you see, of turning down their shirt-collars and cultivating their whiskers, especially under the chin; but they cannot approach the ladies in their dress or bearing, being, to say the truth, humanity of quite another sort. Byrons of the desk and counter, pass on, and let us see what kind of men those are behind ye: those two labourers in holyday clothes, of whom one carries in his hand a crumpled scrap of paper from which he tries to spell out a hard name, while the other looks about for it, on all the doors and windows.

Irishmen both! You might know them, if they were masked, by their long-tailed blue coats and bright buttons, and their drab trousers, which they wear like men well used to working dresses, who are easy in no others. It would be hard to keep your model republics going, without the countrymen and countrywomen of those two labourers. For who else would dig, and delve, and drudge, and do domestic work, and make canals and roads, and execute great lines of Internal Improvement! Irishmen both, and sorely puzzled too, to find out what they seek. Let us go down, and help them, for the love of home, and that spirit of liberty which admits of honest service to honest men, and honest work for honest bread, no matter what it be.

That's well! We have got at the right address at last, though it is written in strange characters truly, and might have been scrawled with the blunt handle of the spade the writer betters knows the use of, than a pen. Their way lies yonder, but what business takes them there? They carry savings: to hoard up? No. They are brothers, those men. One crossed the sea alone, and working very hard for one half year, and living harder, saved funds enough to bring the other out. That done, they worked together, side by side, contentedly sharing hard labour and hard living for another term, and then their sisters came, and then another brother, and, lastly, their old mother. And what now? Why, the poor old crone is restless in a strange land, and yearns to lay her bones, she says, among her people in the old graveyard at home: and so they go to pay her passage back: and God help her and them, and every simple heart, and all who turn to the Jerusalem of their younger days, and have an altar-fire upon the cold hearth of their fathers.

This narrow thoroughfare, baking and blistering in the sun, is Wall-street: the Stock Exchange and Lombard-street of New-York. Many a rapid fortune has been made in this street, and many a no less rapid ruin. Some of these very merchants whom you see hanging about here now, have locked up Money in their strong-boxes, like the man in the Arabian Nights, and opening them again, have found but whithered leaves. Below, here by the water side, where the bowsprits of ships stretch across the footway, and almost thrust themselves into the windows, lie the noble American vessels which have made their Packet Service the finest in the world. They have brought hither the foreigners who abound in all the streets: not perhaps, that there are more here than in other commercial cities; but elsewhere, they have particular haunts, and you must find them out; here, they pervade the town.

We must cross Broadway again; gaining some refreshment from the heat, in the sight of the great blocks of clean ice which are being carried into shops and bar-rooms; and the pineapples and water-melons profusely displayed for sale. Fine streets of spacious houses here, you see!—Wall Street has furnished and dismantled many of them very often—and here a deep green leafy square. Be sure that is a hospitable house with inmates to be affectionately remembered always, where they have the open door and pretty show of plants within, and where the child with laughing eyes is peeping out of window at the little dog below. You wonder what may be the use of this tall flagstaff in the by street, with something like Liberty's head-dress on its top: so do I. But there is a passion for tall flagstaffs hereabout, and you may see its twin brother in five minutes, if you have a mind.

Again cross Broadway, and so—passing from the many-coloured crowd and glittering shops—into another long main street, the Bowery. A railroad yonder, see, where two stout horses trot along, drawing a score or two of people and a great wooden ark, with ease. The stores are poorer here; the passengers less gay. Clothes ready-made, and meat ready-cooked, are to be bought in these parts; and the lively whirl of carriages is exchanged for the deep rumble of carts and wagons. These signs which are so plentiful, in shape like river buoys, or small balloons, hoisted by cords to poles, and dangling there, announce, as you may see by looking up, "OYSTERS IN EVERY STYLE." They tempt the hungry most at night, for then dull candles glimmering inside, illuminate these dainty words, and make the mouths of idlers water, as they read and linger.

What is this dismal-fronted pile of bastard Egyptian, like an enchanter's palace in a melo drama!—a famous prison, called The Tombs. Shall we go in?

So. A long narrow lofty building, stove-heated as usual, with four galleries, one above the other, going round it, and communicating by stairs. Between the two sides of each gallery, and in its centre, a bridge, for the greater convenience of crossing. On each of these bridges sits a man: dozing or reading, or talking to an idle companion. On each tier, are two opposite rows of small iron doors. They look like furnace doors, but are cold and black, as though the fires within had all gone out. Some two or three are open, and women, with drooping heads bent down, are talking to the inmates. The whole is lighted by a skylight, but it is fast closed: and from the roof there dangle, limp and drooping, two useless windsails.

A man with keys appears, to show us round. A good-looking fellow, and, in his way, civil and obliging.

"Are those black doors the cells?"

"Yes."

"Are they all full?"

"Well, they're pretty nigh full, and that's a fact, and no two ways about it."

"Those at the bottom are unwholesome, surely?"

"Why, we *do* only put coloured people in 'em. That's the truth."

"When do the prisoners take exercise?"

"Well, they do without it pretty much."

"Do they never walk in the yard?"

"Considerable seldom."

"Sometimes, I suppose?"

"Well, it's rare they do. They keep pretty bright without it."

"But suppose a man were here for a twelvemonth. I know this is only a prison for criminals who are charged with grave offences, while they are awaiting their trial, or are under remand, but the law here, affords criminals many means of delay. What with motions for new trial, and in arrest of judgment, and what not, a prisoner might be here for twelve months, I take it, might he not?"

"Well, I guess he might."

"Do you mean to say that in all that time he would never come out at that little iron door, for exercise?"

"He might walk some, perhaps—not much."

"Will you open one of the doors?"

"All, if you like."

The fastenings jar and rattle, and one of the doors turns slowly on its hinges. Let us look in. A small bare cell, into which the light enters through a high chink in the wall. There is a rude means of washing, a table, and a bedstead. Upon the latter, sits a man of sixty; reading. He looks up for a moment; gives an impatient dogged shake; and fixes his eyes upon his book again. As we withdraw our heads, the door closes on him, and is fastened as before. This man has murdered his wife, and will probably be hanged.

"How long has he been here?"

"A month."

"When will he be tried?"

"Next term."

"When is that?"

"Next month."

"In England, if a man be under sentence of death, even, he has air and exercise at certain periods of the day."

"Possible?"

With what stupendous and untranslatable coolness he says this, and how loungingly he leads on to the women's side: making, as he goes, a kind of iron castanet of the key and the stair-rail!

Each cell door on this side has a square aperture in it. Some of the women peep anxiously through it at the sound of footsteps; others shrink away in shame.—For what offence can that lonely child, of ten or twelve years old, be shut up here? Oh! that boy? He is the son of the prisoner we saw just now; is a witness against his father; and is detained here for safe-keeping, until the trail: that's all.

But it is a dreadful place for the child to pass the long days and nights in. This is rather hard treatment for a young witness, is it not?—What says our conductor?

"Well, it ain't a very rowdy life, and *that's* a fact!"

Again he clinks his metal castanet, and leads us leisurely away. I have a question to ask him as we go.

"Pray, why do they call this place The Tombs?"

"Well, it's the cant name."

"I know it is. Why?"

"Some suicides happened here, when it was first built. I expect it come about from that."

"I saw just now, that that man's clothes were scattered about the floor of his cell. Don't you oblige the prisoners to be orderly, and put such things away?"

"Where should they put 'em?"

"Not on the ground surely. What do you say to hanging them up?"

He stops, and looks round to emphasize his answer:

"Why, I say that's just it. When they had hooks they *would* hang themselves, so they're taken out of every cell, and there's only the marks left where they used to be!"

The prison-yard in which he pauses now, has been the scene of terrible performances. Into this narrow, grave-like place, men are brought out to die. The wretched creature stands beneath the gibbet on the ground; the rope about his neck; and when the sign is given, a weight at its other end comes running down, and swings him up into the air—a corpse.

The law requires that there be present at this dismal spectacle, the judge, the jury, and citizens to the amount of twenty-five. From the community it is hidden. To the dissolute and bad, the thing remains a frightful mystery. Between the criminal and them, the prison-wall is interposed as a thick gloomy veil. It is the curtain to his bed of death, his winding-sheet, and grave. From him it shuts out life, and all the motives to unrepenting hardihood in that last hour, which its mere sight and presence is often all-sufficient to sustain. There are no bold eyes to make him bold; no ruffians to uphold a ruffian's name before. All beyond the pitiless stone wall, is unknown space.

Let us go forth again into the cheerful streets.

Once more in Broadway! Here are the same ladies in bright colours, walking to and fro, in pairs and singly; yonder the very same light blue parasol which passed and repassed the hotel window twenty times while we were sitting there. We are going to cross here. Take care of the pigs. Two portly sows are trotting up behind this carriage, and a select party of half a-dozen gentlemen-hogs have just now turned the corner.

Here is a solitary swine, lounging homeward by himself. He has only one ear; having parted with the other to vagrant-dogs in the course of his city rambles. But he gets on very well without it; and leads a roving, gentlemanly, vagabond kind of life, somewhat answering to that of our club-men at home. He leaves his lodgings every morning at a certain hour, throws himself upon the town, gets through his day in some manner quite satisfactory to himself, and regularly appears at the door of his own house again at night, like the mysterious master of Gil Blas. He is a free-and-easy, careless, indifferent kind of pig, having a very large acquaintance among other pigs of the same character, whom he rather knows by sight than conversation, as he seldom troubles himself to stop and exchange civilities, but goes grunting down the kennel, turning up the news and small-talk of the city, in the shape of cabbage-stalks and offal, and bearing no tails but his own: which is a very short one, for his old enemies, the dogs, have been at that too, and have left him hardly enough to swear by. He is in every respect a republican pig, going wherever he pleases, and mingling with the best society, on an equal, if not superior footing, for every one makes way when he appears, and the haughtiest give him the wall if he prefer it. He is a great philosopher, and seldom moved, unless by the dogs before mentioned. Sometimes, indeed, you may see his small eye twinkling on a slaughtered friend, whose carcase garnishes a butcher's door-post, but he grunts out, "Such is life: all flesh is pork!" buries his nose in the mire again, and waddles down the gutter: comforting himself with the reflection that there is one snout the less to anticipate stray cabbage-stalks, at any rate.

They are the city scavengers, these pigs. Ugly brutes they are; having, for the most part, scanty, brown backs, like the lids of old horse-hair trunks: spotted with unwholesome black blotches. They have long, gaunt legs, too, and such peaked snouts, that if one of them could be persuaded to sit for his profile, nobody would recognise it for a pig's likeness. They are never attended upon, or fed, or driven, or caught, but are thrown upon their own resources in early life, and become preternaturally knowing in consequence. Every pig knows where he lives, much better than anybody could tell him. At this hour, just as evening is closing in, you will see them roaming towards bed by scores, eating their way to the last. Occasionally, some youth among them who has over-eaten himself, or has been much worried by dogs, trots shrinkingly homeward, like a prodigal son: but this is a rare case: perfect self-possession and self-reliance, and immovable composure, being their foremost attributes.

The streets and shops are lighted now; and as the eye travels down the long thoroughfare, dotted with bright jets of gas, it is reminded of Oxford Street or Piccadilly. Here and there, a flight of broad stone cellar-steps appears, and a painted lamp directs you to the Bowling Saloon, or Ten-Pin alley: Ten-Pins being a game of mingled chance and skill, invented when the legislature passed an act forbidding Nine-Pins. At other downward flights of steps, are other lamps, marking the whereabout of oyster-cellars—pleasant retreats, say I: not only by reason of their wonderful cookery of oysters, pretty nigh as large as cheese-plates (or for thy dear sake, heartiest of Greek Professors!) but because of all kinds of eaters of fish, or flesh, or fowl, in these latitudes, the swallower of oysters alone are not gregarious; but subduing themselves, as it were, to the nature of what they work in, and copying the coyness of the thing they eat, do sit apart in curtained boxes, and consort by twos, not by two hundreds.

But how quiet the streets are! Are there no itinerant bands; no wind or stringed instruments? No, not one. By day, are there no Punches, Fantoccinis, Dancing-dogs, Jugglers, Conjurors, Orchestrinas, or even Barrel-organs? No, not one. Yes, I remember one. One barrel-organ and a dancing monkey—sportive by nature, but fast fading into a dull, lumpish monkey, of the Utilitarian school. Beyond that, nothing lively; no, not so much as a white mouse in a twirling cage.

Are there no amusements? Yes. There is a lecture-room across the way, from which that glare of light proceeds, and there may be evening service for the ladies thrice a week, or oftener. For the young gentlemen, there is the counting-house, the store, the bar-room: the latter, as you may see through these windows, pretty full. Hark! to the clicking sound of hammers breaking lumps of ice, and to the cool gurgling of the pounded bits, as, in the process of mixing, they are poured from glass to glass! No amusements? What are these suckers of cigars and swallowers of strong drinks, whose hats and legs we see in every possible variety of twist, doing, but amusing themselves? What are the fifty newspapers, which those precocious urchins are bawling down the street, and which are kept filed within, what are they but amusements? Not vapid waterish amusements, but good strong stuff; dealing in round abuse and blackguard names; pulling off the roofs of private houses, as the Halting Devil did in Spain; pimping and pandering for all degrees of vicious taste, and gorging with coined lies the most voracious maw; imputing to every man in public life the coarsest and the vilest motives; scaring away from the stabbed and prostrate body-politic, every Samaritan of clear conscience and good deeds; and setting on, with yell and whistle and the clapping of foul hands, the vilest vermin and worst birds of prey.—No amusements!

Let us go on again; and passing this wilderness of a hotel with stores about its base, like some continental theatre, or the London Opera House shorn of its colonnade, plunge into the Five Points. But it is needful, first, that we take as our escort these two heads of the police, whom you would know for sharp and well-trained officers if you met them in the Great Desert. So true it is, that certain pursuits, wherever carried on, will stamp men with the same character. These two might have been begotten, born, and bred, in Bow Street.

We have seen no beggars in the streets by night or day; but of other kind of strollers, plenty. Poverty, wretchedness, and vice, are rife enough where we are going now.

This is the place: these narrow ways, diverging to the right and left, and reeking everywhere with dirt and filth. Such lives as are led here, bear the same fruits here as elsewhere. The coarse and bloated faces at the doors, have counterparts at home, and all the wide world over. Debauchery has made the very houses prematurely old. See how the rotten beams are tumbling down, and how the patched and broken windows seem to scowl dimly, like eyes that have been hurt in drunken frays. Many of those pigs live here. Do they ever wonder why their masters walk upright in lieu of going on all fours? and why they talk instead of grunting?

So far, nearly every house is a low tavern; and on the bar-room walls, are coloured prints of Washington, and Queen Victoria of England, and the American Eagle. Among the pigeon-holes that hold the bottles, are pieces of plate-glass and coloured paper, for there is, in some *sort, a taste for decoration*, even here. And as seamen frequent these haunts, there are maritime pictures by the dozen: of partings between sailors and their lady-loves, por raits of William, of the ballad, and his Black-Eyed Susan; of Will Watch, the Bold Smuggler; of Paul Jones the Pirate, and the like: on which the painted eyes of Queen Victoria, and of Washington to boot, rest in as strange companionship, as on most of the scenes that are enacted in their wondering presence.

What place is this, to which the squalid street conducts us? A kind of square of leprous houses, some of which are attainable only by crazy wooden stairs without. What lies beyond this tottering flight of steps, that creak beneath our tread? a miserable room, lighted by one dim candle, and destitute of all comfort, save that which may be hidden in a wretched bed. Beside it, sits a man: his elbows on his knees: his forehead hidden in his hands. "What ails that man!" asks the foremost officer. "Fever," he sullenly replies, without looking up. Conceive the fancies of a fevered brain, in such a place as this!

Ascend these pitch-dark stairs, heedful of a false footing on the trembling boards, and grope your way with me into this wolfish den, where neither ray of light nor breath of air, appears to come. A negro lad, startled from his sleep by the officer's voice—he knows it well—but comforted by his assurance that he has not come on business, officiously bestirs himself to light a candle. The match flickers for a moment, and shows great mounds of dusky rags upon the ground; then dies away and leaves a denser darkness than before, if there can be degrees in such extremes. He stumbles down the stairs and presently comes back, shading a flaring taper with his hand. Then the mounds of rags are seen to be astir, and rise slowly up, and the floor is covered with heaps of negro women, waking from their sleep: their white teeth chattering, and their bright eyes glistening and winking on all sides with surprise and fear, like the countless repetition of one astonished African face in some strange mirror.

Mount up these other stairs with no less caution (there are traps and pitfalls here, for those who are not so well escorted as ourselves) into the housetop: where the bare beams and rafters meet over-head, and calm night looks down through the crevices in the roof. Open the door of one of these cramped hutches full of sleeping negroes. Pah! They have a charcoal fire within; there is a smell of singeing clothes, or flesh, so close they gather round the brazier; and vapours issue forth that blind and suffocate. From every corner, as you glance about you in these dark retreats, some figure crawls half awakened, as if the judgment-hour were near at hand, and every obscene grave were giving up its dead. Where dogs would howl to lie, women, and men, and boys slink off to sleep, forcing the dislodged rats to move away in quest of better lodgings.

Here too are lanes and alleys, paved with mud knee-deep: underground chambers, where they dance and game; the walls bedecked with rough designs of ships, and forts, and flags, and American Eagles out of number: ruined houses, open to the streets, whence through wide gaps in the walls, other ruins loom upon the eye, as though the world of vice and misery had nothing else to show: hideous tenements which take their name from robbery and murder: all that is loathsome, drooping, and decayed is here.

Our leader has his hand upon the latch of "Almack's," and calls to us from the bottom of the steps; for the assembly-room of the Five-Point fashionables is approached by a descent. Shall we go in? It is but a moment.

Heyday! the landlady of Almack's thrives! A buxom fat mulatto woman, with sparkling eyes, whose head is daintily ornamented with a handkerchief of many colours. Nor is the landlord much behind her in his finery, being attired in a smart blue jacket, like a ship's steward, with a thick gold ring upon his little finger, and round his neck a gleaming golden watch-guard. How glad he is to see us! What will we please to call for? A dance? It shall be done directly, sir: "a regular break-down."

The corpulent black fiddler, and his friend who plays the tambourine, stamp upon the boarding of the small raised orchestra in which they sit, and play a lively measure. Five or six couple come upon the floor, marshalled by a lively young negro, who is the wit of the assembly, and the greatest dancer known. He never leaves off making queer faces, and is the delight of all the rest, who grin from ear to ear incessantly. Among the dancers are two young mulatto girls, with large, black, drooping eyes, and head-gear after the fashion of the hostess, who are as shy or feign to be, as though they never danced before, and so look down before the visiters, that their partners can see nothing but the long fringed lashes.

But the dance commences. Every gentleman sets as long as he likes to the opposite lady, and the opposite lady to him, and all are so long about it that the sport begins to languish, when suddenly the lively hero dashes in to the rescue. Instantly the fiddler grins, and goes at it tooth and nail; there is new energy in the tambourine; new laughter in the dancers; new smiles in the landlady; new confidence in the landlord; new brightness in the very candles. Single shuffle, double shuffle, cut and cross-cut: snapping his fingers, rolling his eyes, turning in his knees, presenting the backs of his legs in front, spinning about on his toes and heels like nothing but the man's fingers on the tambourine; dancing with two left legs, two right legs, two wooden legs, two wire legs, two spring legs—all sorts of legs and no legs—what is this to him? And in what walk of life, or dance of life, does man ever get such stimulating applause as thunders about him, when, having danced his partner off her feet, and himself too, he finishes by leaping gloriously on the bar-counter, and calling for something to drink, with the chuckle of a million of counterfeit Jim Crows, in one inimitable sound!

The air, even in these distempered parts, is fresh after the stifling atmosphere of the houses; and now, as we emerge into a broader street, it blows upon us with a purer breath, and the stars look bright again. Here are The Tombs once more. The city watch-house is a part of the building. It follows naturally on the sights we have just left. Let us see that, and then to bed.

What! do you thrust your common offenders against the police discipline of the town, into such holes as these? Do men and women, against whom no crime is proved, lie here all night in perfect darkness, surrounded by the noisome vapours which encircle that flagging lamp you light us with, and breathing this filthy and offensive stench! Why, such indecent and disgusting dungeons as these cells, would bring disgrace upon the most despotic empire in the world! Look at them, man—you, who see them every night, and keep the keys. Do you see what they are? Do you know how drains are made below the streets, and wherein these human sewers differ, except in being always stagnant?

Well, he don't know. He has had five-and-twenty young women locked up in this very cell at one time, and you'd hardly realize what handsome faces there were among 'em.

In God's name! shut the door upon the wretched creature who is in it now, and put its screen before a place, quite unsurpassed in all the vice, neglect, and devilry, of the worst old town in Europe.

Are people really left all night, untried, in those black sties?—Every night. The watch is set at seven in the evening. The magistrate opens his court at five in the morning. That is the earliest hour at which the first prisoner can be released; and if an officer appear against him, he is not taken out till nine o'clock or ten.—But if any one among them die in the interval, as one man did, not long ago? Then he is half eaten by the rats in an hour's time; as that man was; and there an end.

What is this intolerable tolling of great bells, and crashing of wheels, and shouting in the distance? A fire. And what that deep red light in the opposite direction? Another fire. And what these charred and blackened walls we stand before? A dwelling where a fire has been. It was more than hinted, in an official report, not long ago, that some of these conflagrations were not wholly accidental, and that speculation and enterprise found a field of exertion, even in flames: but be this as it may, there was a fire last night, there are two to-night, and you may lay an even wager there will be at least one, tomorrow. So, carrying that with us for our comfort, let us say, Good night, and climb up stairs to bed.

One day, during my stay in New-York, I paid a visit to the different public institutions on Long Island. One of them is a Lunatic Asylum. The building is handsome; and is remarkable for a spacious and elegant staircase. The whole structure is not yet finished, but it is already one of considerable size and extent, and is capable of accommodating a very large number of patients.

I cannot say that I derived much comfort from the inspection of this charity. The different wards might have been cleaner and better ordered; I saw nothing of that salutary system which had impressed me so favourably elsewhere; and everything had a lounging, listless, madhouse air, which was very painful. The moping idiot, cowering down with long dishevelled hair; the gibbering maniac, with his hideou laugh and pointed finger; the vacant eye, the fierce wild face, the gloomy picking of the hands and lips, and munching of the nails: there they were all, without disguise, in naked ugliness and horror. In the dining-room, a bare, dull, dreary place, with nothing for the eye to rest on but the empty walls, a woman was locked up alone. She was bent, they told me, on committing suicide. If anything could have strengthened her in her resolution, it would certainly have been the insupportable monotony of such an existence.

The terrible crowd with which these halls and galleries were filled, so shocked me, that I abridged my stay within the shortest limits, and declined to see that portion of the building in which the refractory and violent were under closer restraint. I have no doubt that the gentleman who presided over this establishment at the time I write of, was competent to manage it, and had done all in his power to promote its usefulness: but will it be believed that the miserable strife of Party feeling is carried even into this sad refuge of afflicted and degraded humanity? Will it be believed that the eyes which are to watch over and control the wanderings of minds on which the most dreadful visitation to which our nature is exposed has fallen, must wear the glasses of some wretched side in Politics? Will it be believed that the governor of such a house as this, is appointed, and deposed, and changed perpetually, as Parties fluctuate and vary, and as their despicable weathercocks are blown this way or that? A hundred times in every week, some new most paltry exhibition of that narrow-minded and injurious Party Spirit, which is the Simoom of America, sickening and blighting everything of wholesome life within its reach, was forced upon my notice; but I never turned my back upon it with feelings of such deep disgust and measureless contempt, as when I crossed the threshold of this mad-house on Long Island.

At a short distance from this building is another called the Alms House, that is to say, the workhouse of New-York. This is a large Institution also: lodging, I believe, when I was there, nearly a thousand poor. It was badly ventilated, and badly lighted; was not too clean; and impressed me, on the whole, very uncomfortably. But it must be remembered that New-York, as a great emporium of commerce, and as a place of general resort, not only from all parts of the States, but from most parts of the world, has always a large pauper population to provide for; and labours, therefore, under peculiar difficulties in this respect. Nor must it be forgotten that New-York is a large town, and that in all large towns a vast amount of good and evil is intermixed and jumbled up together.

In the same neighbourhood is the Long Island Farm, where young orphans are nursed and bred. I did not see it, but I believe it is well conducted; and I can the more easily credit it, from knowing how mindful they usually are, in America, of that beautiful passage in the Litany which remembers all sick persons and young children.

I was taken to these Institutions by water, in a boat belonging to the Long Island Jail, and rowed by a crew of prisoners, who were dressed in a striped uniform of black and buff, in which they looked like faded tigers. They took me by the same conveyance, to the jail itself.

It is an old prison, and quite a pioneer establishment, on the plan I have already described. I was glad to hear this, for it is unquestionably a very indifferent one. The most is made, however, of the means it possesses, and it is as well regulated as such a place can be.

The women work in covered sheds, erected for that purpose. If I remember right, there are no shops for the men, but be that as it may, the greater part of them labour in certain stone-quarries near at hand. The day being very wet indeed, this labour was suspended, and the prisoners were in their cells. Imagine these cells, some two or three hundred in number, and in every one a man, locked up: this one at the door for air, with his hands thrust through the grate; this one in bed (in the middle of the day, remember); and this one flung down in a heap upon the ground, with his head against the bars like a wild beast. Make the rain pour down, outside, in torrents. Put the everlasting stove in the midst: hot, and suffocating, and vaporous, as a witch's caldron. Add a collection of gentle odours, such as would arise from a thousand mildewed umbrellas wet through, and a thousand buck-baskets full of half-washed linen; and there is the prison as it was that day.

The prison for the state at Sing Sing, is, on the other hand, a model jail. That, and Mount Auburn, are the largest and best examples of the silent system.

In another part of the city, is the Refuge for the Destitute: an institution whose object is to reclaim youthful offenders, male and female, black and white, without distinction; to teach them useful trades, apprentice them to respectable masters, and make them worthy members of society. Its design, it will be seen, is similar to that at Boston; and it is a no less meritorious and admirable establishment. A suspicion crossed my mind during my inspection of this noble charity, whether the superintendent had quite sufficient knowledge of the world and wordly characters; and whether he did not commit a great mistake in treating ome young girls, who were to all intent and purposes, by their years and their past lives, women, as though they were little children; which certainly had a ludicrous effect in my eyes, and, or I am much mistaken, in theirs also. As the institution, however, is always under the vigilant examination of a body of gentlemen of great intelligence and experience, it cannot fail to be well-conducted; and whether I am right or wrong in this slight particular, is unimportant to its deserts and character, which it would be too difficult to estimate too highly.

In addition to these establishment, there are, in New-York, excellent hospitals and schools, literary institutions and libraries; an admirable fire department (as indeed it should be, having constant practice), and charities of every sort and kind. In the suburbs there is a spacious cemetery; unfinished yet, but every day improving. The saddest tomb I saw there was "The Strangers' Grave. Dedicated to the different hotels, in this city."

There are three theatres. Two of them, the Park and the Bowery, are large, elegant, and handsome buildings, and are, I grieve to write it, generally deserted. The third, the Olympic, is a tiny show-box for vaudevilles and burlesques. It is singularly well-conducted by Mr. Mitchell, a comic actor of great quiet humour and originality, who is well remembered and esteemed by London playgoers. I am happy to report of this deserving gentleman, that his benches are usually well filled, and that his theatre rings with merriment every night. I had almost forgotten a small summer theatre, called Niblo's, with gardens and open air amusements attached; but I believe it is not exempt from the general depression under which Theatrical Property, or what is humorously called by that name, unfortunately labours.

The country round New-York, is surpassingly and exquisitely picturesque. The climate, as I have already intimated, is somewhat of the warmest. What it would be, without the sea breezes which come from its beautiful bay in the evening time, I will not throw myself or my readers into a fever by inquiring.

The tone of the best society in this city, is like that of Boston; here and there it maybe, with a greater infusion of the mercantile spirit, but generally polished and refined, and always most hospitable. The houses and tables are elegant; the hours later and more rakish; and there is perhaps, a greater spirit of contention in reference to appearances, and the display of wealth and costly living. The ladies are singularly beautiful.

Before I left New-York I made arrangements for securing a passage home in the George Washington packet-ship, which was advertised to sail in June: that being the month in which I had determined, if prevented by no accident in the course of my ramblings, to leave America.

I never thought that going back to England returning to all who are dear to me, and to pursuits that have insensibly grown to be a part of my nature, I could have felt so much sorrow as I endured, when I parted at last, on board this ship, with the friends who had accompanied me from this city. I never thought the name of any place, so far away and so lately known, could ever associate itself in my mind with the crowd of affectionate remembrances that now cluster about it. There are those in this city who would brighten to me, the darkest winter-day that ever glimmered and went out in Lapland; and before whose presence even Home grew dim, when they and I exchanged that painful word which mingles with our every thought and deed; which haunts our cradle-heads in infancy, and closes up the vista of our lives in age.

CHAPTER VII.

PHILADELPHIA, AND ITS SOLITARY PRISON.

The journey from New-York to Philadelphia is made by railroad and two ferries; and usually occupies between five and six hours. It was a fine evening when we were passengers in the train: and, watching the bright sunset from a little window near the door by which we sat, my attention was attracted to a remarkable appearance issuing from the windows of the gentlemen's car immediately in front of us, which I supposed for some time was occasioned by a number of industrious persons inside ripping open feather-beds, and giving the feathers to the wind. At length it occurred to me that they were only spitting, which was indeed the case, though how any number of passengers which it was possible for that car to contain could have maintained such a playful and incessant shower of expectoration, I am still at a loss to understand, notwithstanding the experience in all salivatory phenomena which I afterward acquired.

I made acquaintance on this journey with a mild and modest young Quaker, who opened the discourse by informing me, in a grave whisper, that his grandfather was the inventor of cold-drawn castor oil. I mention this circumstance here, thinking it probable that this is the first occasion on which the valuable medicine in question was ever used as a conversational aperient.

We reached the city late that night. Looking

out of my chamber window, before going to bed, I saw, on the opposite side of the way, a handsome building of white marble, which had a mournful, ghostlike aspect, dreary to behold. I attributed this to the sombre influence of the night, and on rising in the morning, looked out again, expecting to see its steps and portico thronged with groups of people passing in and out. The door was still tight shut, however; the same cold, cheerless air prevailed; and the buildidg looked as if the marble statue of Don Guzman could alone have any business to transact within its gloomy walls. I hastened to inquire its name and purpose, and then my surprise vanished. It was the tomb of many fortunes, the great catacomb of investment, the United States Bank.

The stoppage of this bank, with all its ruinous consequences, had cast (as I was told on every side) a gloom on Philadelphia, under the depressing effect of which it yet laboured. It certainly did seem rather dull and out of spirits.

It is a handsome city, but distractingly regular. After walking about it for an hour or two, I felt that I would have given the world for a crooked street. The collar of my coat appeared to stiffen, and the brim of my hat to expand, beneath its Quakerly influence. My hair shrunk into a sleek, short crop, my hands folded themselves upon my breast of their own calm accord, and thoughts of taking lodgings in Mark Lane, over against the Market-place, and of making a large fortune by speculations in corn, came over me involuntarily.

Philadelphia is most bountifully provided with fresh water, which is showered and jerked about, and turned on, and poured off, everywhere. The Waterworks, which are on a height near the city, are no less ornamental than useful, being tastefully laid out as a public garden, and kept in the best and neatest order. The river is dammed at this point, and forced by its own power into certain high tanks or reservoirs, whence the whole city, to top stories of the houses, is supplied at a very trifling expense.

There are various public institutions. Among them a most excellent hospital—a Quaker establishment, but not sectarian in the great benefits it confers; a quiet, quaint old library, named after Franklin; a handsome exchange and post-office, and so forth. In connexion with the Quaker hospital, there is a picture by West, which is exhibited for the benefit of the funds of the institution. The subject is our Saviour healing the sick, and it is, perhaps, as favourable a specimen of the master as can be seen anywhere. Whether this be high or low praise depends upon the reader's taste.

In the same room there is a very characteristic and lifelike portrait by Mr. Sully, a distinguished American artist.

My stay in Philadelphia was very short, but what I saw of its society I greatly liked. Treating of its general characteristics, I should be disposed to say that it is more provincial than Boston or New-York, and that there is afloat in the fair city an assumption of taste and criticism, savouring rather of those genteel discussions upon the same themes, in connexion with Shakspeare and the musical glasses, of which we read in the Vicar of Wakefield. Near the city is a most splendid unfinished marble structure for the Girard College, founded by a deceased gentleman of that name and of enormous wealth, which, if completed according to the original design, will be perhaps the richest edifice of modern times. But the bequest is involved in legal disputes, and pending them the work has stopped; so that, like many other great undertakings in America, even this is rather going to be done one of these days than doing now.

In the outskirts stands a great prison, called the Eastern Penitentiary: conducted on a plan peculiar to the state of Pennsylvania. The system here is rigid, strict, and hopeless solitary confinement. I believe it, in its effects, to be cruel and wrong.

In its intention, I am well convinced that it is kind, humane, and meant for reformation; but I am persuaded that those who devised this system of prison discipline, and those benevolent gentlemen who carry it into execution, do not know what it is that they are doing. I believe that very few men are capable of estimating the immense amount of torture and agony which this dreadful punishment, prolonged for years, inflicts upon the sufferers; and, in guessing at it myself, and in reasoning from what I have seen written upon their faces, and what to my certain knowledge they feel within, I am only the more convinced that there is a depth of terrible endurance in it which none but the sufferers themselves can fathom, and which no man has a right to inflict upon his fellow-creature. I hold this slow and daily tampering with the mysteries of the brain, to be immeasurably worse than any torture of the body: and because its ghastly signs and tokens are not so palpable to the eye and sense of touch as scars upon the flesh; because its wounds are not upon the surface, and it extorts few cries that human ears can hear; therefore I the more denounce it, as a secret punishment which slumbering humanity is not roused up to stay. I hesitated once, debating with myself, whether, if I had the power of saying "Yes" or "No," I would allow it to be tried in certain cases, where the terms of imprisonment were short; but now I solemnly declare, that with no rewards or honours could I walk a happy man beneath the open sky by day, or lie me down upon my bed at night, with the consciousness that one human creature, for any length of time, no matter what, lay suffering this unknown punishment in his silent cell, and I the cause, or I consenting to it in the least degree.

I was accompanied to this prison by two gentlemen officially connected with its management, and passed the day in going from cell to cell, and talking with the inmates. Every facility was afforded me that the utmost courtesy could suggest. Nothing was concealed or hidden from my view, and every piece of information that I sought was openly and frankly given. The perfect order of the building cannot be praised too highly, and of the excellent motives of all who are immediately concerned in the administration of the system, there can be no kind of question.

Between the body of the prison and the outer wall there is a spacious garden. Entering it by a wicket in the massive gate, we pursued the path before us to its other termination, and passed into a large chamber, from which seven long passages radiate. On either side of each is a long, long row of low cell-doors, with a certain number over every one. Above, a gallery of cells like those below, except that they have no narrow yard attached (as those on the ground tier have), and are somewhat smaller. The possession of two of these is supposed to compensate for the absence of so much air and exercise as can be had in the dull strip attached to each of the others in an hour's time every day; and therefore every prisoner in this upper story has two cells adjoining and communicating with each other.

Standing at the central point, and looking down these dreary passages, the dull repose and quiet that prevails, is awful. Occasionally, there is a drowsy sound from some lone weaver's shuttle, or shoemaker's last, but it is stifled by the thick walls and heavy dungeon-door, and only serves to make the general stillness more profound. Over the head and face of every prisoner who comes into this melancholy house, a black hood is drawn; and in this dark shroud, an emblem of the curtain dropped between him and the living world, he is led to the cell from which he never again comes forth, until his whole term of imprisonment has expired. He never hears of wife or children; home or friends; the life or death of any single creature. He sees the prison-officers, but with that exception he never looks upon a human countenance, or hears a human voice. He is a man buried alive; to be dug out in the slow round of years; and in the mean time dead to everything but torturing anxieties and horrible despair.

His name, and crime, and term of suffering, are unknown, even to the officer who delivers him his daily food. There is a number over his cell-door, and in a book of which the governor of the prison has one copy, and the moral instructor another: this is the index to his history. Beyond these pages the prison has no record of his existence: and though he live to be in the same cell ten weary years, he has no means of knowing, down to the very last hour, in what part of the building it is situated; what kind of men there are about him; whether in the long winter nights there are living people near, or he is in some lonely corner of the great jail, with walls, and passages, and iron doors between him and the nearest sharer in its solitary horrors.

Every cell has double doors: the outer one of sturdy oak, the other of grated iron, wherein there is a trap through which his food is handed. He has a Bible, and a slate and pencil, and, under certain restrictions, has sometimes other books, provided for the purpose, and pen and ink and paper. His razor, plate, and can, and basin, hang upon the wall, or shine upon the little shelf. Fresh water is laid on in every cell, and he can draw it at his pleasure. During the day, his bedstead turns up against the wall, and leaves more space for him to work in. His loom or bench, or wheel is there, and there he labours, sleeps and wakes, and counts the seasons as they change, and grows old.

The first man I saw, was seated at his loom, at work. He had been there six years, and was to remain, I think, three more. He had been convicted as a receiver of stolen goods, but even after this long imprisonment, denied his guilt, and said he had been hardly dealt by. It was his second offence.

He stopped his work when we went in, took off his spectacles, and answered freely to everything that was said to him, but always with a strange kind of pause first, and in a low, thoughtful voice. He wore a paper hat of his own making, and was pleased to have it noticed and commended. He had very ingeniously manufactured a sort of Dutch clock from some disregarded odds and ends; and his vinegar-bottle served for the pendulum. Seeing me interested in this contrivance, he looked up at it with a good deal of pride, and said that he had been thinking of improving it, and that he hoped the hammer and a little piece of broken glass beside it "would play music before long." He had extracted some colours from the yarn with which he worked, and painted a few poor figures on the wall. One, of a female, over the door, he called "The Lady of the Lake."

He smiled as I looked at these contrivances to while away the time; but when I looked from them to him, I saw that his lip trembled, and could have counted the beating of his heart. I forget how it came about, but some allusion was made to his having a wife. He shook his head at the word, turned aside, and covered his face with his hands.

"But you are resigned now!" said one of the gentlemen after a short pause, during which he had resumed his formed manner. He answered with a sigh that seemed quite reckless in its hopelessness, "Oh yes, oh yes! I am resigned to it." "And are a better man, you think?" "Well, I hope so: I'm sure I hope I may be." "And time goes pretty quickly?" "Time is very long, gentlemen, within these four walls!"

He gazed about him—Heaven only knows how wearily!—as he said these words; and in the act of doing so, fell into a strange stare as if he had forgotten something. A moment afterward he sighed heavily, put on his spectacles, and went about his work again.

In another cell, there was a German, sentenced to five years' imprisonment for larceny, two of which had just expired. With colours procured in the same manner, he had painted every inch of the walls and ceiling quite beautifully. He had laid out the few feet of ground, behind, with exquisite neatness, and had made a little bed in the centre, that looked, by-the-by, like a grave. The taste and ingenuity he had displayed in everything were most extraordinary; and yet a more rejected, heart-broken, wretched creature, it would be difficult to imagine. I never saw such a picture of forlorn affliction and distress of mind. My heart bled for him; and when the tears ran down his cheeks, and he took one of the visiters aside, to ask, with his trembling hands nervously clutching at his coat to detain him, whether there was no hope of his dismal sentence being commuted, the spectacle was really too painful to witness. I never saw or heard of any kind of misery that impressed me more than the wretchedness of this man.

In a third cell, was a tall, strong black, a burglar, working at his proper trade of making screws and the like. His time was nearly out. He was not only a very dexterous thief, but was notorious for his boldness and hardihood, and for the number of his previous convictions. He entertained us with a long account of his achievements, which he narrated with such infinite relish, that he actually seemed to lick his lips as he told us racy anecdotes of stolen plate, and of old ladies whom he had watched as they sat at windows in silver spectacles (he had plainly had an eye to their metal even from the other side of the street), and had afterward robbed. This fellow, upon the slightest encouragement, would have mingled with his professional recollections the most detestable cant; but I am very much mistaken if he could have surpassed the unmitigated hypocrisy with which he declared that he blessed the day on which he came into that prison, and that he never would commit another robbery as long as he lived.

There was one man who was allowed, as an indulgence, to keep rabbits. His room having rather a close smell in consequence, they called to him at the door to come out into the passage. He complied, of course, and stood shading his haggard face in the unwonted sunlight of the great window, looking as wan and unearthly as if he had been summoned from the grave. He had a white rabbit in his breast; and when the little creature, getting down upon the ground, stole back into the cell, and he, being dismissed, crept timidly after it, I thought it would have been very hard to say in what respect the man was the nobler animal of the two.

There was an English thief, who had been there but a few days out of seven years; a villanous, low-browed, thin-lipped fellow, with a white face, who had, as yet, no relish for visiters, and who, but for the additional penalty, would have gladly stabbed me with his shoemaker's knife. There was another German who had entered the jail but yesterday, and who started from his bed when we looked in, and pleaded, in his broken English, very hard for work. There was a poet, who, after doing two days' work in every four-and-twenty hours, one for himself and one for the prison, wrote verses about ships (he was by trade a mariner), and "the maddening wine-cup," and his friends at home. There were very many of them. Some reddened at the sight of visiters, and some turned very pale. Some two or three had prisoner nurses with them, for they were very sick; and one, a fat old negro, whose leg had been taken off within the jail, had for his attendant a classical scholar and an accomplished surgeon, himself a prisoner likewise. Sitting upon the stairs, engaged in some slight work, was a pretty coloured boy. "Is there no refuge for young criminals in Philadelphia, then?" said I. "Yes, but only for white children." Noble aristocracy in crime!

There was a sailor who had been there upward of eleven years, and who in a few months' time would be free. Eleven years of solitary confinement!

"I am very glad to hear your time is nearly out." What does he say? Nothing. Why does he stare at his hands, and pick the flesh upon his fingers, and raise his eyes for an instant, every now and then, to those bare walls which have seen his head turn gray? It is a way he has sometimes.

Does he never look men in the face, and does he always pluck at those hands of his, as though he were bent on parting skin and bone? It is his humour: nothing more.

It is his humour too, to say that he does not look forward to going out; that he is not glad the time is drawlng near; that he did look forward to it once, but that was very long ago; that he has lost all care for everything. It is his humour to be a helpless, crushed, and broken man. And Heaven be his witness that he has his humour thoroughly gratified!

There were three young women in adjoining cells, all convicted at the same time of a conspiracy to rob their prosecutor. In the silence and solitude of their lives they had grown to be quite beautiful. Their looks were very sad, and might have moved the sternest visiter to tears, but not to that kind of sorrow which the contemplation of the men awakens. One was a young girl, not twenty, as I recollect, whose snow-white room was hung with the work of some former prisoner, and upon whose downcast face the sun in all its splendour shone down through the high chink in the wall, where one narrow strip of bright blue sky was visible. She was very penitent and quiet; had come to be resigned, she said (and I believe her), and had a mind at peace. "In a word, you are happy here?" said one of my companions. She struggled—she did struggle very hard—to answer, Yes; but raising her eyes, and meeting that glimpse of freedom overhead, she burst into tears, and said, "She tried to be; she uttered no complaint; but it was natural that she should sometimes long to go out of that one cell; she could not help *that:*" she sobbed, poor thing!

I went from cell to cell that day; and every face I saw, or word I heard, or incident I noted, is present to my mind in all its painfulness. But let me pass them by, for one, more pleasant, glance of a prison on the same plan which I afterward saw at Pittsburgh.

When I had gone over that, in the same manner, I asked the governor if he had any person in his charge who was shortly going out. He had one, he said, whose time was up next day; but he had only been a prisoner two years.

Two years! I looked back through two years in my own life—out of jail, prosperous, happy, surrounded by blessings, comforts, and good fortune—and thought how wide a gap it was, and how long those two years passed in solitary captivity would have been. I have the face of this man, who was going to be released next day, before me now. It is almost more memorable in its happiness than the other faces in their misery. How easy and how natural it was for him to say that the system was a good one; and that the time went "pretty quick—considering;" and that when a man once felt he had offended the law, and must satisfy it, "he got along, somehow:" and so forth!

"What did he call you back to say to you, in that strange flutter?" I asked of my conductor, when he had locked the door and joined me in the passage.

"Oh! That he was afraid the soles of his boots were not fit for walking, as they were a good deal worn when he came in; and that he would thank me very much to have them mended, ready."

Those boots had been taken off his feet, and put away with the rest of his clothes, two years before!

I took that opportunity of inquiring how they conducted themselves immediately before going out; adding, that I presumed they trembled very much.

"Well, it's not so much a trembling," was the answer—"though they do quiver—as a complete derangement of the nervous system. They can't sign their names to the book; sometimes can't even hold the pen; look about 'em without appearing to know why, or where they are; and sometimes get up and sit down again twenty times in a minute. This is when they're in the office, where they are taken with the hood on, as they were brought in. When they get outside the gate, they stop, and look first one way and then the other, not knowing which to take. Sometimes they stagger as if they were drunk, and sometimes are forced to lean against the fence, they're so bad; but they clear off in course of time."

As I walked among these solitary cells, and looked at the faces of the men within them, I tried to picture to myself the thoughts and feelings natural to their condition. I imagined the hood just taken off, and the scene of their captivity disclosed to them in all its dismal monotony.

At first, the man is stunned. His confinement is a hideous vision, and his old life a reality. He throws himself upon his bed, and lies there abandoned to despair. By degrees the insupportable solitude and barrenness of the place rouses him from this stupor, and when the trap in his grated door is opened, he humbly begs and prays for work. "Give me some work to do, or I shall go raving mad!"

He has it; and by fits and starts applies himself to labour; but every now and then there comes upon him a burning sense of the years that must be wasted in that stone coffin, and an agony so piercing in the recollection of those who are hidden from his view and knowledge, that he starts from his seat, and striding up and down the narrow room with both hands clasped on his uplifted head, hears spirits tempting him to beat his brains out on the wall.

Again he falls upon his bed, and lies there, moaning. Suddenly he starts up, wondering whether any other man is near; whether there is another cell like that on either side of him; and listens keenly.

There is no sound, but other prisoners may be near for all that. He remembers to have heard once, when he little thought of coming here himself, that the cells were so constructed that the prisoners could not hear each other, though the officers could hear them. Where is the nearest man—upon the right or on the left? or is there one in both directions? Where is he sitting now—with his face to the light? or is he walking to and fro? How is he dressed? Has he been here long? Is he much worn away? Is he very white and spectre-like? Does *he* think of his neighbour too?

Scarcely venturing to breathe, and listening while he thinks, he conjures up a figure with its back towards him, and imagines it moving about in this next cell. He has no idea of the face, but he is certain of the dark form of a stooping man. In the cell upon the other side he puts another figure, whose face is hidden from him also. Day after day, and often when he wakes up in the middle of the night, he thinks of these two men until he is almost distracted. He never changes them. There they are always as he first imagined them—an old man on the right, a younger man upon the left—whose hidden features torture him to death, and have a mystery that makes him tremble.

The weary days pass on with solemn pace, like mourners at a funeral; and slowly he begins to feel that the white walls of the cell have something dreadful in them: that their colour is horrible; that their smooth surface chills his blood: that there is one hateful corner which torments him. Every morning when he wakes, he hides his head beneath the coverlet, and shudders to see the ghastly ceiling looking down upon him. The blessed light of day itself peeps in, an ugly phantom face, through the unchangeable crevice which is his prison window.

By slow but sure degrees, the terrors of that hateful corner swell until they beset him at all times; invade his rest, make his dreams hideous, and his nights dreadful. At first, he took a strange dislike to it: feeling as though it gave birth in his brain to something of corresponding shape, which ought not to be there, and racked his head with pains. Then he began to fear it, then to dream of it, and of men whispering its name and pointing to it. Then he could not bear to look at it, nor yet to turn his back upon it. Now, it is every night the lurking-place of a ghost; a shadow; a silent something, horrible to see, but whether bird, or beast, or muffled human shape, he cannot tell.

When he is in his cell by day, he fears the little yard without. When he is in the yard, he dreads to re-enter the cell. When night comes, there stands the phantom in the corner. If he have the courage to stand in its place, and drive it out (he had once, being desperate), it broods upon his bed. In the twilight, and always at the same hour, a voice calls to him by name; as the darkness thickens his Loom begins to live; and even that, his comfort, is a hideous figure, watching him till daybreak.

Again, by slow degrees, these horrible fancies depart from him one by one; returning sometimes, unexpectedly, but at longer intervals, and in less alarming shapes. He has talked upon religious matters with the gentleman who visits him, and has read his Bible, and has written a prayer upon his slate, and hung it up, as a kind of protection, and an assurance of Heavenly companionship. He dreams now, sometimes, of his children or his wife, but is sure that they are dead or have deserted him. He is easily moved to tears; is gentle, submissive, and broken-spirited. Occasionally, the old agony comes back: a very little thing will revive it; even a familiar sound, or the scent of summer flowers in the air; but it does not last long, now; for the world without, has come to be the vision, and this solitary life, the sad reality.

If his term of imprisonment be short—I mean comparatively, for short it cannot be—the last half year is almost worse than all; for then he thinks the prison will take fire and he be burned in the ruins, or that he is doomed to die within the walls, or that he will be detained on some false charge and sentenced for another term: or that something, no matter what, must happen to prevent his going at large. And this is natural and impossible to be reasoned against, because, after his long separation from human life, and his great suffering, any event will appear to him more probable in the contemplation, than the being restored to liberty and his fellow-creatures.

If his period of confinement have been very long, the prospect of release bewilders and confuses him. His broken heart may flutter for a moment, when he thinks of the world outside, and what it might have been to him in all those lonely years, but that is all. The cell-door has been closed too long on all its hopes and cares. Better to have hanged him in the beginning than bring him to this pass, and send him forth to mingle with his kind, who are his kind no more.

On the haggard face of every man among these prisoners, the same expression sat. I know not what to liken it to. It had something of that strained attention which we see upon the faces of the blind and deaf, mingled with a kind of horror, as though they had all been secretly terrified. In every little chamber that I entered, and at every grate through which I looked, I seemed to see the same appalling countenance. It lives in my memory with the fascination of a remarkable picture. Parade before my eyes a hundred men, with one among them newly released from this solitary suffering, and I would point him out.

The faces of the women, as I have said, it humanizes and refines. Whether this be, because of their better nature, which is elicited in solitude, or because of their being gentler creatures, of greater patience and longer suffering, I do not know; but so it is. That the punishment is nevertheless, to my thinking, fully as cruel and as wrong in their case as in that of the men, I need scarcely add.

My firm conviction is that, independent of the mental anguish it occasions—an anguish so acute and so tremendous, that all imagination of it must fall far short of the reality—it wears the mind into a morbid state, which renders it unfit for the rough contact and busy action of the world. It is my fixed opinion that those who have undergone this punishment, MUST pass into society again morally unhealthy and diseased. There are many instances on record, of men who have chosen, or have been condemned, to lives of perfect solitude, but I scarcely remember one, even among sages of strong and vigorous intellect, where its effect has not become apparent, in some disordered train of thought, or some gloomy hallucination. What monstrous phantoms, bred of despondency and doubt, and born and reared in solitude, have stalked upon the earth, making creation ugly, and darkening the face of Heaven!

Suicides are rare among these prisoners; are almost, indeed, unknown. But no argument in favour of the system can reasonably be deduced from this circumstance, although it is very often urged. All men who have made diseases of the mind their study, know perfectly well that such extreme depression and despair as will change the whole character, and beat down all its powers of elasticity and self-resistance, may be at work within a man, and yet stop short of self-destruction. This is a common case.

That it makes the senses dull, and by degrees impairs the bodily faculties, I am quite sure. I remarked to those who were with me in this very establishment at Philadelphia, that the criminals who had been there long were deaf. They who were in the habit of seeing these men constantly were perfectly amazed at the idea, which they regarded as groundless and fanciful. And yet, the very first prisoner to whom they appealed—one of their own selection—confirmed my impression (which was unknown to him) instantly, and said, with a genuine air it was impossible to doubt, that he couldn't think how it happened, but he *was* growing very dull of hearing.

That it is a singularly unequal punishment, and affects the worst man least, there is no doubt. In its superior efficacy as a means of reformation, compared with that other code of regulations which allows the prisoners to work in company without communicating together, I have not the smallest faith. All the instances of reformation that were mentioned to me were of a kind that might have been—and I have no doubt whatever, in my own mind, would have been—equally well brought about by the Silent System. With regard to such men as the negro burglar and the English thief, even the most enthusiastic have scarcely any hope of their conversion.

It seems to me that the objection that nothing wholesome or good has ever had its growth in such unnatural solitude, and that even a dog or any of the more intelligent among beasts would pine, and mope, and rust away beneath its influence, would be in itself a sufficient argument against this system. But when we recollect, in addition, how very cruel and severe it is, and that a solitary life is always liable to peculiar and distinct objections of a most deplorable nature, which have arisen here; and call to mind, moreover, that the choice is not between this system and a bad or ill-considered one, but between it and another which has worked well, and is, in its whole design and practice, excellent; there is surely more than sufficient reason for abandoning a mode of punishment attended by so little hope or promise, and fraught beyond dispute with such a host of evils.

As a relief to its contemplation, I will close this chapter with a curious story, arising out of the same theme, which was related to me, on the occasion of this visit, by some of the gentlemen concerned.

At one of the periodical meetings of the inspectors of this prison, a working man of Philadelphia presented himself before the Board, and earnestly requested to be placed in solitary confinement. On being asked what motive could possibly prompt him to make this strange demand, he answered that he had an irresistible propensity to get drunk; that he was constantly indulging it, to his great misery and ruin; that he had no power of resistance; that he wished to be put beyond the reach of temptation; and that he could think of no better way than this. It was pointed out to him, in reply, that the prison was for criminals who had been tried and sentenced by the law, and could not be made available for any such fanciful purposes; he was exhorted to abstain from intoxicating drinks, as he surely might if he would; and received other very good advice, with which he retired, exceedingly dissatisfied with the result of his application.

He came again, and again, and again, and was so very earnest and importunate, that at last they took counsel together, and said, "He will certainly qualify himself for admission, if we reject him any more. Let us shut him up. He will soon be glad to go away, and then we shall get rid of him." So they made him sign a statement which would prevent his ever sustaining an action for false imprisonment, to the effect that his incarceration was voluntary, and of his own seeking; they requested him to take notice that the officer in attendance had orders to release him at any hour of the day or night when he might knock upon his door for that purpose; but desired him to understand that, once going out, he would not be admitted any more. These conditions agreed upon, and he still remaining in the same mind, he was conducted to the prison, and shut up in one of the cells.

In this cell, the man who had not the firmness to leave a glass of liquor standing untasted on a table before him—in this cell, in solitary confinement, and working every day at his trade of shoemaking, this man remained nearly two years. His health beginning to fail at the expiration of that time, the surgeon recommended that he should work occasionally in the garden; and as he liked the notion very much, he went about this new occupation with great cheerfulness.

He was digging here, one summer day, very industriously, when the wicket in the outer gate chanced to be left open; showing, beyond, the well-remembered dusty road and sunburnt fields. The way was as free to him as to any man living, but he no sooner raised his head and caught sight of it, all shining in the light, than, with the involuntary instinct of a prisoner, he cast away his spade, scampered off as fast as his legs would carry him, and never once looked back.

CHAPTER VIII.

WASHINGTON. — THE LEGISLATURE. — AND THE PRESIDENT'S HOUSE.

We left Philadelphia by steamboat at six o'clock one very cold morning, and turned our faces towards Washington.

In the course of this day's journey, as on subsequent occasions, we encountered some Englishmen (small farmers, perhaps, or country publicans at home) who were settled in America, and were travelling on their own affairs. Of all grades and kinds of men that jostle one in the public conveyances of the States, these are often the most intolerable and the most insufferable companions. United to every disagreeable characteristic that the worst kind of American travellers possess, these countrymen of ours display an amount of insolent conceit and cool assumption of superiority quite monstrous to behold. In the coarse familiarity of their approach, and the effrontery of their inquisitiveness (which they are in great haste to assert, as if they panted to revenge themselves upon the decent old restraints of home), they surpass any native specimens that came within my range of observation; and I often grew so patriotic when I saw and heard them, that I would cheerfully have submitted to a reasonable fine, if I could have given any other country in the whole world the honour of claiming them for its children.

As Washington may be called the headquarters of tobacco-tinctured saliva, the time is come when I must confess, without any disguise, that the prevalence of those two odious practices of chewing and expectorating began about this time to be anything but agreeable, and soon became most offensive and sickening. In all the public places of America this filthy custom is recognised. In the courts of law, the judge has his spittoon, the crier his, the witness his, and the prisoner his: while the jurymen and spectators are provided for, as so many men who, in the course of nature, must desire to spit incessantly. In the hospitals, the students of medicine are requested, by notices upon the wall, to eject their tobacco juice into the boxes provided for that purpose, and not to discolour the stairs. In public buildings visiters are implored, through the same agency, to squirt the essence of their quids, or "plugs," as I have heard them called by gentlemen learned in this kind of sweetmeat, into the national spittoons, and not about the bases of the marble colums. But in some parts this custom is inseparably mixed up with every meal and morning call, and with all the transactions of social life. The stranger, who follows in the track I took myself, will find it in its full bloom and glory, luxuriant in all its alarming recklessness, at Washington. And let him not persuade himself (as I once did, to my shame) that previous tourists have exaggerated its extent. The thing itself is an exaggeration of nastiness, which cannot be outdone.

On board this steamboat, there were two young gentlemen, with shirt-collars reversed as usual, and armed with very big walking sticks; who planted two seats in the middle of the deck, at a distance of some four paces apart; took out their tobacco-boxes, and sat down opposite each other, to chew. In less than a quarter of an hour's time, these hopeful youths had shed about them on the clean boards, a copious shower of yellow rain: clearing, by that means, a kind of magic circle, within whose limits no intruders dared to come, and which they never failed to refresh and refresh before a spot was dry. This being before breakfast, rather disposed me, I confess, to nausea; but looking attentively at one of the expectoraters, I plainly saw that he was young in chewing, and felt inwardly uneasy, himself. A glow of delight came over me at this discovery; and as I marked his face turn paler and paler, and saw the ball of tobacco in his left cheek, quiver with his suppressed agony, while yet he spat, and chewed, and spat again, in emulation of his older friend, I could have fallen on his neck and implored him to go on for hours.

We all sat down to a comfortable breakfast in the cabin below, where there was no more hurry or confusion than at such a meal in England, and where there was certainly greater politeness exhibited than at most of our stage-coach banquets. At about nine o'clock we arrived at the railroad station, and went on by the cars. At noon we turned out again, to cross a wide river in another steamboat; landed at a continuation of the railroad on the opposite shore, and went on by other cars; in which, in the course of the next hour or so, we crossed, by wooden bridges, each a mile in length, two creeks, called respecttvely Great and little Gunpowder. The water in both was blackened with flights of canvass-backed ducks, which are most delicious eating, and abound hereabout at that season of the year.

These bridges are of wood, have no parapet, and are only just wide enough for the passage of the trains; which, in the event of the smallest accident, would inevitably be plunged into the river. They are startling contrivances, and are most agreeable when passed.

We stopped to dine at Baltimore, and being now in Maryland, were waited on, for the first time, by slaves. The sensation of exacting any service from human creatures who are bought and sold, and being, for the time, a party as it were to their condition, is not an enviable one. The institution exists, perhaps, in its least repulsive and most mitigated form in such a town as this; but it *is* slavery; and though I was, with respect to it, an innocent man, its presence filled me with a sense of shame and self-reproach.

After dinner, we went down to the railroad again, and took our seats in the cars for Washington. Being rather early, those men and boys who happened to have nothing particular to do, and were curious in foreigners, came (according to custom) round the carriage in which I sat; let down all the windows; thrust in their heads and shoulders; hooked themselves on conveniently, by their elbows; and fell to comparing notes on the subject of my personal appearance, with as much indifference as if I were a stuffed figure. I never gained so much uncompromising information with reference to my own nose and eyes, the various impressions wrought by my mouth and chin on different minds, and how my head looks when it is viewed from behind, as on these occasions. Some gentlemen were only satisfied by exercising their sense of touch; and the boys (who are surprisingly precocious in America) were seldom satisfied, even by that, but would return to the charge over and over again. Many a budding president has walked into my room with his cap on his head and his hands in his pockets, and stared at me for two whole hours: occasionally refreshing himself with a tweak at his nose, or a draught from the water-jug; or by walking to the windows and inviting other boys in the street below, to come up and do likewise: crying, "here he is!" "come on!" "bring all your brothers!" with other hospitable entreaties of that nature.

We reached Washington at about half past six that evening, and had upon the way a beautiful view of the Capitol, which is a fine building of the Corinthian order, and placed upon a noble and commanding eminence. Arrived at the hotel, I saw no more of the place that night; being very tired, and glad to get to bed.

Breakfast over next morning, I walk about the streets for an hour or two, and, coming home, throw up the window in the front and back, and look out. Here is Washington, fresh in my mind and under my eye.

Take the worst parts of the city road and Pentonville, preserving all their oddities, but especially the small shops and dwellings, occupied there (but not in Washington) by furniture brokers, keepers of poor eating-houses, and fanciers of birds. Burn the whole down; build it up again in wood and plaster; widen it a little: throw in part of St. John's wood; put green blinds outside all the private houses, with a red curtain and a white one in every window; plough up all the roads; plant a great deal of coarse turf in every place where it ought not to be; erect three handsome buildings in stone and marble, anywhere, but the more entirely out of everybody's way the better; call one the Post Office, one the Patent Office, and one the Treasury; make it scorching hot in the morning, and freezing cold in the afternoon, with an occasional tornado of wind and dust; leave a brick-field without the bricks, in all central places where a street may naturally be expected: and that is Washington.

The hotel in which we live, is a long row of small houses fronting on the street, and opening at the back upon a common yard, in which hangs a great triangle. Whenever a servant is wanted, somebody beats on this triangle from one stroke up to seven, according to the number of the house in which his presence is required: and as all the servants are always being wanted, and none of them ever come, this enlivening engine is in full performance the whole day through. Clothes are drying in the same yard; female slaves, with cotton handkerchiefs twisted round their heads, are running to and fro on the hotel business; black waiters cross and recross with dishes in their hands; two great dogs are playing upon a mound of loose bricks in the centre of the little square; a pig is turning up his stomach to the sun, and grunting "that's comfortable!" and neither the men, nor the women, nor the dogs, nor the pig, nor any created creature, takes the smallest notice of the triangle, which is tingling madly all the time.

I walk to the front window, and look across the road upon a long, straggling row of houses, one story high, terminating, nearly opposite, but a little to the left, in a melancholy piece of waste ground with frowzy grass, which looks like a small piece of country that has taken to drinking, and has quite lost itself. Standing anyhow and all wrong, upon this open space, like something meteoric that has fallen down from the moon, is an odd, lop-sided, one-eyed kind of wooden building, that looks like a church, with a flag-staff as long as itself sticking out of a steeple something larger than a tea-chest. Under the window, is a small stand of coaches, whose slave-drivers are sunning themselves on the steps of our door, and talking idly together. The three most obtrusive houses near at hand, are the three meanest. On one—a shop, which never has anything in the window, and never has the door open—is painted in large characters, "THE CITY LUNCH." At another, which looks like the backway to somewhere else, but is an independent building in itself, oysters are procurable in every style. At the third, which is a very, very little tailor's shop, pants are fixed to order: or, in other words, pantaloons are made to measure. And that is our street in Washington.

It is sometimes called the City of Magnificent Distances, but it might with greater propriety be termed the City of Magnificent Intentions; for it is only on taking a bird's-eye view of it from the top of the Capitol, that one can at all comprehend the vast designs of its projector, an aspiring Frenchman. Spacious avenues, that begin in nothing, and lead nowhere; streets, mile-long, that only want houses, roads, and inhabitants; public buildings that need but a public to be complete; and ornaments of great thoroughfares, which only lack great thoroughfares to ornament, are its leading features. One might fancy the season over, and most of the houses gone out of town forever with their masters. To the admirers of cities it is a Barmecide Feast; a pleasant field for the imagination to rove in; a monument raised to a deceased object, with not even a legible inscription to record its departed greatness.

Such as it is, it is likely to remain. It was originally chosen for the seat of Government, as a means of averting the conflicting jealousies and interests of the different States; and very probably, too, as being remote from mobs: a consideration not to be slighted, even in America. It has no trade or commerce of its own: having little or no population beyond the President and his establishment; the members of the legislature who reside there during the session; the Government clerks and officers employed in the various departments; the keepers of the hotels and boarding-houses; and the tradesmen who supply their tables. It is very unhealthy. Few people would live in Washington, I take it, who were not obliged to reside there; and the tides of emigration and speculation, those rapid and regardless currents, are little likely to flow at any time towards such dull and sluggish water.

The principal features of the Capitol are, of course, the two Houses of Assembly. But there is, besides, in the centre of the building, a fine rotunda, ninety-six feet in diameter, and ninety-six high, whose circular wall is divided into compartments, ornamented by historical pictures. Four of these have for their subjects prominent events in the revolutionary struggle. They were painted by Colonel Trumbull, himself a member of Washington's staff at the time of their occurrence; from which circumstance they derive a peculiar interest of their own. In this same hall Mr. Greenough's large statue of Washington has been lately placed. It has great merits of course, but it struck me as being rather strained and violent for its subject. I could wish, however, to have seen it in a better light than it ever can be viewed in, where it stands.

There is a very pleasant and commodious library in the Capitol; and, from a balcony in front, the bird's-eye view, of which I have just spoken, may be had, together with a beautiful prospect of the adjacent country. In one of the ornamented portions of the building, there is a figure of Justice; whereunto the Guide Book says, "the artist first contemplated giving more of nudity, but he was warned that the public sentiment in this country would not admit of it, and in his caution he has gone, perhaps, into the opposite extreme." Poor Justice! she has been made to wear much stranger garments in America than those she pines in, in the Capitol. Let us hope that she has changed her dress-maker since they were fashioned, and that the public sentiment of the country did not cut out the clothes she hides her lovely figure in, just now.

The House of Representatives is a beautiful and spacious hall, of semi-circular shape, supported by handsome pillars. One part of the gallery is appropriated to the ladies, and there they sit in front rows, and come in, and go out, as at a play or concert. The chair is canopied, and raised considerably above the floor of the House; and every member has an easy chair and a writing-desk to himself; which is denounced by some people out of doors as a most unfortunate and injudicious arrangement, tending to long sitting and prosaic speeches. It is an elegant chamber to look at, but a singularly bad one for all purposes of hearing. The Senate, which is smaller, is free from this objection, and is exceedingly well adapted to the uses for which it is designed. The sittings, I need hardly add, take place in the day; and the parliamentary forms are modelled on those of the old country.

I was sometimes asked, in my progress through other places, whether I had not been very much impressed by the *heads* of the lawmakers at Washington; meaning not their chiefs and leaders, but literally their individual and personal heads, whereon their hair grew, and whereby the phrenological character of each legislator was expressed: and I almost as often struck my questioner dumb with indignant consternation by answering "No, that I didn't remember being at all overcome." As I must, at whatever hazard, repeat the avowal here, I will follow it up by relating my impressions on this subject in as few words as possible.

In the first place—it may be from some imperfect development of my organ of veneration—I do not remember having ever fainted away, or having even been moved to tears of joyful pride, at sight of any legislative body. I have borne the House of Commons like a man, and have yielded to no weakness, but slumber, in the House of Lords. I have seen elections for borough and county, and have never been impelled (no matter which party won) to damage my hat by throwing it up into the air in triumph, or to crack my voice by shouting forth any reference to our Glorious Constitution, to the noble purity of our independent voters, or the unimpeachable integrity of our independent members. Having withstood such strong attacks upon my fortitude, it is possible that I may be of a cold and insensible temperament, amounting to iciness, in such matters; and therefore my impressions of the live pillars of the Capitol at Washington must be received with such grains of allowance as this free confession may seem to demand.

Did I see in this public body, an assemblage of men, bound together in the sacred names of Liberty and Freedom, and so asserting the chaste dignity of those twin goddesses, in all their discussions, as to exalt at once the Eternal Principles to which their names are given, and their own character, and the character of their countrymen, in the admiring eyes of the whole world?

It was but a week, since an aged, gray-haired man, a lasting honour to the land that gave him birth, who has done good service to his country, as his forefathers did, and who will be remembered scores upon scores of years after the worms bred in its corruption, are but so many grains of dust—it was but a week, since this old man had stood for days upon his trial before this very body, charged with having dared to assert the infamy of that traffic, which has, for its accursed merchandize, men and women, and their unborn children. Yes. And publicly exhibited in the same city all the while; gilded, framed and glazed; hung up for general admiration; shown to strangers, not with shame, but pride; its face not turned towards the wall, itself not taken down and burned; is the Unanimous Declaration of the The Thirteen United States of America, which solemnly declares that All Men are created Equal; and are endowed by their Creator with the Inalienable Rights of Life, Liberty, and the Pursuit of Happiness!

It was not a month, since this same body had sat calmly by, and heard a man, one of themselves, with oaths, which beggars in their drink reject, threaten to cut another's throat from ear to ear. There he sat, among them; not crushed by the general feeling of the assembly, but as good a man as any.

There was but a week to come, and another of that body, for doing his duty to those who sent him there; for claiming in a Republic the Liberty and Freedom of expressing their sentiments, and making known their prayer; would be tried, found guilty, and have strong censure passed upon him by the rest. His was a grave offence indeed; for years before, he had risen up and said, "A gang of male and female slaves for sale, warranted to breed like cattle, linked to each other by iron fetters, are passing now along the open street beneath the windows of your Temple of Equality! Look!" But there are many kinds of hunters engaged in the Pursuit of Happiness, and they go variously armed. It is the Inalienable Right of some among them, to take the field after *their* Happiness, equipped with cat and cartwhip, stocks, and iron collar, and to shout their view halloa! (always in praise of Liberty), to the music of clanking chains and bloody stripes.

Where sat the many legislators of coarse threats; of words and blows such as coal-heavers deal upon each other, when they forgot their breeding? On every side. Every session had its anecdotes of that kind, and the actors were all there.

Did I recognise in this assembly, a body of men, who applying themselves in a new world to correct some of the falsehoods and vices of the old, purified the avenues to Public Life, paved the dirty ways to Place and Power, debated and made laws for the Common Good, and had no party but their Country?

I saw in them, the wheels that move the meanest perversion of virtuous Political Machinery that the worst tools ever wrought. Despicable trickery at elections; under-handed tamperings with public officers; cowardly attacks upon opponents, with scurrilous newspapers for shields, and hired pens for daggers; shameful truckling to mercenary knaves whose claim to be considered, is, that every day and week they sow new crops of ruin with their venal types, which are the dragon's teeth of yore, in everything but sharpness; aidings and abettings of every bad inclination in the popular mind, and artful suppressions of all its good influences: such things as these, and in a word, Dishonest Faction in its most depraved and most unblushing form, stared out from every corner of the crowded hall.

Did I see among them, the intelligence and refinement: the true, honest, patriotic heart of America? Here and there, were drops of its blood and life, but they scarcely coloured the stream of desperate adventurers which sets that way for profit and for pay. It is the game of these men, and of their profligate organs, to make the strife of politics so fierce and brutal, and so destructive of all self-respect in worthy men, that sensitive and delicate-minded persons shall be kept aloof, and they, and such as they, be left to battle out their selfish views, unchecked. And thus this lowest of all scrambling fights goes on, and they who in other countries would, from their intelligence and station, most aspire to make laws, do here recoil the farthest from that degradation.

That there are, among the representatives of the people in both houses, and among all parties, some men of high character and great abilities, I need not say. The foremost among these politicians who are known in Europe, have been already described, and I see no reason to depart from the rule I have laid down for my guidance, of abstaining from all mention of individuals. It will be sufficient to add, that to the most favourable accounts that have been written of them, I more than fully and most heartily subscribe; and that personal intercourse and free communication have bred within me, not the result predicted in the very doubtful proverb, but increased admiration and respect. They are striking men to look at, hard to deceive, prompt to act, lions in energy, Crichtons in varied accomplishments, Indians in fire of eye and gesture, Americans in strong and generous impulse; and they as well represent the honour and wisdom of their country at home, as the distinguished gentleman who is now its minister at the British Court sustains its highest character abroad.

I visited both houses nearly every day, during my stay in Washington. On my initiatory visit to the House of Representatives, they divided against a decision of the chair; but the chair won. The second time I went, the member who was speaking, being interrupted by a laugh, mimicked it, as one child would in quarrelling with another, and added, "that he would make honourable gentlemen opposite, sing out a little more on the other side of their mouths presently." But interruptions are rare; the speaker being usually heard in silence. There are more quarrels than with us, and more threatenings than gentlemen are accustomed to exchange in any civilized society of which we have record; but farmyard imitations have not as yet been imported from the Parliament of the United Kingdom. The feature in oratory which appears to be the most practised, and most relished, is the constant repetition of the same idea or shadow of an idea in fresh words; and the inquiry out of doors is not, "What did he say?" but, "How long did he speak?" These, however, are but enlargements of a principle which prevails elsewhere.

The Senate is a dignified and decorous body, and its proceedings are conducted with much gravity and order. Both houses are handsomely carpeted; but the state to which these carpets are reduced by the universal disregard of the spittoon with which every honourable member is accommodated, and the extraordinary improvements on the pattern which are squirted and dabbled upon it in every direction, do not admit of being described. I will merely observe, that I strongly recommend all strangers not to look at the floor; and if they happen to drop anything, though it be their purse, not to pick it up with an ungloved hand on any account.

It is somewhat remarkable, too, at first, to say the least, to see so many honourable members with swelled faces; and it is scarcely less remarkable to discover that this appearance is caused by the quantity of tobacco they contrive to stow within the hollow of the cheek. It is strange enough too, to see an honourable gentleman leaning back in his tilted chair with his legs on the desk before him, shaping a convenient "plug" with his penknife, and when it is quite ready for use, shooting the old one from his mouth, as from a pop-gun, and clapping the new one in its place.

I was surprised to observe that even steady old chewers of great experience, are not always good marksmen, which has rather inclined me to doubt that general proficiency with the rifle, of which we have heard so much in England. Several gentlemen called upon me who, in the course of conversation, frequently missed the spittoon at five paces; and one (but he was certainly short-sighted) mistook the closed sash for the open window, at three. On another occasion, when I dined out, and was sitting with two ladies and some gentlemen round a fire before dinner, one of the company fell short of the fireplace six distinct times. I am disposed to think, however, that this was occasioned by his not aiming at that object; as there was a white marble hearth before the fender, which was more convenient, and may have suited his purpose better.

The Patent Office at Washington, furnishes an extraordinary example of American enterprise and ingenuity; for the immense number of models it contains, are the accumulated inventions of only five years: the whole of the previous collection having been destroyed by fire. The elegant structure in which they are arranged, is one of design rather than execution, for there is but one side erected out of four, though the works are stopped. The Post Office is a very compact, and very beautiful building. In one of the departments, among a collection of rare and curious articles, are deposited the presents which have been made from time to time to the American ambassadors at foreign courts by the various potentates to whom they were the accredited agents of the Republic: gifts which by the law they are not permitted to retain. I confess that I looked upon this as a very painful exhibition, and one by no means flattering to the national standard of honesty and honour. That can scarcely be a high state of moral feeling which imagines a gentleman of repute and station, likely to be corrupted, in the discharge of his duty, by the present of a snuff-box, or a richly-mounted sword, or an Eastern shawl: and surely the Nation who reposes confidence in her appointed servants, is likely to be better served, than she who makes them the subject of such very mean and paltry suspicions.

At George Town, in the suburbs, there is a Jesuit College; delightfully situated, and, so far as I had an opportunity of seeing, well managed. Many persons who are not members of the Romish Church, avail themselves, I believe, of these institutions, and of the advantageous opportunities they afford for the education of their children. The heights in this neighbourhood, above the Potomac River, are very picturesque; and are free, I should conceive, from some of the insalubrities of Washington. The air, at that elevation, was quite cool and refreshing, when in the city it was burning hot.

The President's mansion is more like an English club-house, both within and without, than any other kind of establishment with which I can compare it. The ornamental ground about it has been laid out in garden walks; they are pretty, and agreeable to the eye; though they have that uncomfortable air of having been made yesterday, which is far from favourable to the display of such beauties.

My first visit to this house was on the morning after my arrival, when I was carried thither by an official gentleman, who was so kind as to charge himself with my presentation to the President.

We entered a large hall, and having twice or thrice rung a bell which nobody answered, walked without farther ceremony through the rooms on the ground floor, as divers other gentlemen (mostly with their hats on, and their hands in their pockets) were doing very leisurely. Some of these had ladies with them, to whom they were showing the premises; others were lounging on the chairs and sofas; others, in a perfect state of exhaustion from listlessness, were yawning drearily. The greater portion of this assemblage were rather asserting their supremacy than doing anything else, as they had no particular business there, that anybody knew of. A few were closely eying the movables, as if to make sure that the President (who was far from popular) had not made away with any of the furniture, or sold the fixtures for his private benefit.

After glancing at these loungers; who were scattered over a pretty drawing-room, opening upon a terrace which commanded a beautiful prospect of the river and the adjacent country; and who were sauntering, too, about a larger state room called the Eastern Drawing-room; we went up stairs into another chamber, where were certain visitors, waiting for audiences. At sight of my conductor, a black in plain clothes and yellow slippers who was gliding noiselessly about, and whispering messages in the ears of the more impatient, made a sign of recognition, and glided off to announce him.

We had previously looked into another chamber fitted all round with a great bare wooden desk or counter, whereon lay files of newspapers, to which sundry gentlemen were referring. But there were no such means of beguiling the time in this apartment, which was as unpromising and tiresome as any waiting room in one of our public establishments, or any physician's dining-room during his hours of consultation at home.

There were some fifteen or twenty persons in the room. One, a tall, wiry, muscular old man, from the west; sunburnt and swarthy; with a brown-white hat on his knees, and a giant umbrella resting between his legs; who sat bolt upright in his chair, frowning steadily at the carpet, and twitching the hard lines about his mouth, as if he had made up his mind to "fix" the President on what he had to say, and wouldn't bate him a grain. Another, a Kentucky farmer, six feet six in height, with his hat on, and his hands under his coat-tails, who leaned against the wall and kicked the floor with his heel, as though he had Time's head under his shoe, and were literally "killing" him. A third, an oval-faced, bilious-looking man, with sleek black hair cropped close, and whiskers and beard shaved down to blue dots, who sucked the head of a thick stick, and from tima to time took it out of his mouth, to see how it was getting on. A fourth did nothing but whistle. A fifth did nothing but spit. And indeed all these gentlemen were so very persevering and energetic in this latter particular, and bestowed their favours so abundantly upon the carpet, that I take it for granted the Presidential housemaids have high wages, or, to speak more genteelly, an ample amount of "compensation:" which is the American word for salary, in the case of all public servants.

We had not waited in this room many minutes, before the black messenger returned, and conducted us into another of smaller dimensions, where, at a business-like table covered with papers, sat the President himself. He looked somewhat worn and anxious, and well he might: being at war with everybody—but the expression of his face was mild and pleasant, and his manner was remarkably unaffected, gentlemanly, and agreeable. I thought that in his whole carriage and demeanour, he became his station singularly well.

Being advised that the sensible etiquette of the republican court, admitted of a traveller, like myself, declining, without any impropriety, an invitation to dinner, which did not reach me until I had concluded my arrangements for leaving Washington some days before that to which it referred, I only returned to this house once. It was on the occasion of one of those general assemblies which are held on certain nights between the hours of nine and twelve o'clock, and are called, rather oddly, Levees.

I went, with my wife, at about ten. There was a pretty dense crowd of carriages and people in the court-yard, and so far as I could make out, there were no very clear regulations for the taking up or setting down of company. There were certainly no policemen to soothe startled horses, either by sawing at their bridles or flourishing truncheons in their eyes; and I am ready to make oath that no inoffensive persons were knocked violently on the head, or poked acutely in their backs or stomachs; or brought to a stand-still by any such gentle means, and then taken into custody for not moving on. But there was no confusion or disorder. Our carriage reached the porch in its turn, without any blustering, swearing, shouting, backing, or other disturbance; and we dismounted with as much ease and comfort as though we had been escorted by the whole Metropolitan Force from A to Z inclusive.

The suite of rooms on the ground-floor were lighted up; and a military band was playing in the hall. In the smaller drawing-room, the centre of a circle of company, were the President and his daughter-in-law, who acted as the lady of the mansion: and a very interesting, graceful, and accomplished lady too. One gentleman who stood among this group, appeared to take upon himself the functions of a master of the ceremonies. I saw no other officers or attendants, and none were needed.

The great drawing-room, which I have already mentioned, and the other chambers on the ground-floor, were crowded to excess. The company was not, in our sense of the term, select, for it comprehended persons of very many grades and classes; nor was there any great display of costly attire: indeed some of the costumes may have been, for aught I know, grotesque enough. But the decorum and propriety of behaviour which prevailed, were unbroken by any rude or disagreeable incident; and every man, even among the miscellaneous crowd in the hall who were admitted without any orders or tickets to look on, appeared to feel that he was a part of the Institution, and was responsible for its preserving a becoming character, and appeared to the best advantage.

That these visiters, too, whatever their station, were not without some refinement of taste and appreciation of intellectual gifts, and gratitude to those men who, by the peaceful exercise of great abilities, shed new charms and associations upon the homes of their countrymen, and elevate their character in other lands, was most earnestly testified by their reception of Washington Irving, my dear frieud, who had recently been appointed Minister at the court of Spain, and who was among them that night, in his new character, for the first and last time before going abroad. I sincerely believe that in all the madness of American politics, few public men would have been so earnestly, devotedly, and affectionately caressed, as this most charming writer; and I have seldom respected a public assembly more, than I did this eager throng, when I saw them turning with one mind from noisy orators and officers of state, and flocking with a generous and honest impulse round the man of quiet pursuits; proud in his promotion as reflecting back upon their country; and grateful to him with their whole hearts for the store of graceful fancies he had poured out among them. Long may he dispense such treasures with unsparing hand; and long may they remember him as worthily!

The term we had assigned for the duration of our stay in Washington, was now at an end, and we were to begin to travel; for the railroad distances we had traversed yet, in journeying among these older towns, are on that great continent looked upon as nothing.

I had at first intended going South—to Charleston. But when I came to consider the length of time which this journey would occupy, and the premature heat of the season, which even at Washington had beeu often very trying; and weighed moreover, in my own mind, the pain of living in the constant contemplation of slavery, against the more than doubtful chances of my ever seeing it, in the time I had to spare, stripped of the disguises in which it would certainly be dressed, and so adding any item to the host of facts already heaped together on the subject; I began to listen to old whisperings which had often been present to me at home in England, when I little thought of ever being here; and to dream again of cities growing up, like palaces in fairy tales, among the wilds and forests of the west.

The advice I received in most quarters when I began to yield to my desire of travelling towards that point of the compass was, according to custom, sufficiently cheerless; my companion being threatened with more perils, dangers, and discomforts, than I can remember or would catalogue if I could; but of which it will be sufficient to remark that blowings-up in steamboats and breakings down in coaches were among the least. But, having a western route sketched out for me by the best and kindest authority to which I could have resorted, and putting no great faith in these discouragements, I soon determined on my plan of action.

This was to travel south, only to Richmond in Virginia; and then to turn, and shape our course for the Far West; whither I beseech the reader's company.

CHAPTER IX.

A NIGHT-STEAMER ON THE POTOMAC RIVER.—A VIRGINIA ROAD, AND A BLACK DRIVER.—RICHMOND.—BALTIMORE.—THE HARRISBURGH MAIL, AND A GLIMPSE OF THE CITY.—A CANAL-BOAT.

We were to proceed in the first instance by steamboat: and as it is usual to sleep on board, in consequence of the starting hour being four o'clock in the morning, we went down to where she lay, at that very uncomfortable time for such expeditions when slippers are most valuable, and a familiar bed, in the perspective of an hour or two, looks uncommonly pleasant.

It is ten o'clock at night: say half past ten; moonlight, warm, and dull enough. The steamer (not unlike a child's Noah's ark in form, with the machinery on the top of the roof) is riding lazily up and down, and bumping clumsily against the wooden pier, as the ripple of the river trifles with its unwieldy carcase. The wharf is some distance from the city. There is nobody down here; and one or two dull lamps upon the steamer's decks are the only signs of life remaining, when our coach has driven away. As soon as our footsteps are heard upon the planks, a fat negress, particularly favoured by Nature in respect of bustle, emerges from some dark stairs, and marshals my wife towards the ladies' cabin, to which retreat she goes, followed by a mighty bale of cloaks and great coats. I valiantly resolve not to go to bed at all, but to walk up and down the pier till morning.

I begin my promenade—thinking of all kinds of distant things and persons, and of nothing near—and pace up and down for half an hour. Then I go on board again; and getting into the light of one of the lamps, look at my watch, and think it must have stopped; and wonder what has become of the faithful secretary whom I brought along with me from Boston. He is supping with our late landlord (a field-marshal, at least, no doubt) in honour of our departure, and may be two hours longer. I walk again, but it gets duller and duller: the moon goes down: next June seems farther off in the dark, and the echoes of my footsteps make me nervous. It has turned cold too; and walking up and down without any companion in such lonely circumstances, is but poor amusement. So I break my stanch resolution, and think it may be, perhaps, as well to go to bed.

I go on board again; open the door of the gentleman's cabin, and walk in. Somehow or other—from its being so quiet I suppose—I have taken it into my head that there is nobody there. To my horror and amazement it is full of sleepers in every stage, shape, attitude, and variety of slumber: in the berths, on the chairs, on the floors, on the tables, and particularly round the stove, my detested enemy. I take another step forward, and slip upon the shining face of a black steward, who lies rolled in a blanket on the floor. He jumps up, grins, half in pain and half in hospitality; whispers my own name in my ear; and groping among the sleepers, leads me to my berth. Standing beside it, I count these slumbering passengers, and get past forty. There is no use in going farther, so I begin to undress. As the chairs are all occupied, and there is nothing else to put my clothes on, I deposite them upon the ground: not without soiling my hands, for it is in the same condition as the carpets in the Capitol, and from the same cause. Having but partially undressed, I clamber on my shelf, and hold the curtain open for a few minutes while I look round on all my fellow-travellers again. That done, I let it fall on them, and on the world: turn round, and go to sleep.

I wake, of course, when we get under weigh, for there is a good deal of noise. The day is then just breaking. Everybody wakes at the same time. Some are self-possessed directly, and some are much perplexed to make out where they are until they have rubbed their eyes, and, leaning on one elbow, look about them. Some yawn, some groan, nearly all spit, and a few get up. I am among the risers: for it is easy to feel, without going into the fresh air, that the atmosphere in the cabin is vile in the last degree. I huddle on my clothes, go down into the fore-cabin, get shaved by the barber, and wash myself. The washing and dressing apparatus for the passengers generally, consists of two jack towels, three small wooden basins, a keg of water and a ladle to serve it out with, six square inches of looking-glass, two ditto ditto of yellow soap, a comb and brush for the head, and nothing for the teeth. Everybody uses the comb and brush except myself. Everybody stares to see me using my own; and two or three gentlemen are strongly disposed to banter me on my prejudices, but don't. When I have made my toilet, I go upon the hurricane-deck, and set in for two hours of hard walking up and down. The sun is rising brilliantly; we are passing Mount Vernon, where Washington lies buried; the river is wide and rapid; and its banks are beautiful. All the glory and splendour of the day are coming on, and growing brighter every minute.

At eight o'clock, we breakfast in the cabin where I passed the night, but the windows and doors are all thrown open, and now it is fresh enough. There is no hurry or greediness apparent in the despatch of the meal. It is longer than a travelling breakfast with us; more orderly, and more polite,

Soon after nine o'clock we come to Potomac Creek, where we are to land: and then comes the oddest part of the journey. Seven stage-coaches are preparing to carry us on. Some of them are ready, some of them are not ready. Some of the drivers are blacks, some whites. There are four horses to eace coach, and all the horses, harnessed or unharnessed, are there. The passengers are getting out of the steam-boat, and into the coaches; the luggage is being transferred in noisy wheelbarrows, the horses are frightened, and impatient to start; the black drivers are chattering to them like so many monkeys; and the white ones whooping like so many drovers; for the main thing to be done in all kinds of hostering here, is to make as much noise as possible. The coaches are something like the French coaches, but not nearly so good. In lieu of springs, they are hung on bands of the strongest leather. There is very little choice or difference between them; and they may be likened to the car portion of the swings at an English fair, roofed, put upon axle-trees and wheels, and curtained with painted canvass. They are covered with mud from the roof to the wheel-tire, and have never been cleaned since they were first built.

The tickets we have received on board the steamboat are marked No. 1, so we belong to coach No. 1. I throw my coat on the box, and hoist my wife and her maid into the inside. It has only one step, and that being about a yard from the ground, is usually approached by a chair: when there is no chair, ladies trust in Providence. The coach holds nine inside, having a seat across from door to door, where we in England put our legs: so that there is only one feat more difficult in the performance than getting in, and that is, getting out again. There is only one outside passenger, and he sits upon the box. As I am that one, I climb up; and while they are strapping the luggage on the roof, and heaping it into a kind of tray behind, have a good opportunity of looking at the driver.

He is a negro—very black indeed. He is dressed in a coarse pepper-and-salt suit excessively patched and darned (particularly at the knees); gray stockings, enormous unblacked high-low shoes, and very short trousers. He has two odd gloves: one of parti-coloured worsted, and one of leather. He has a very short whip, broken in the middle and bandaged up with string. And yet he wears a low-crowned, broad-brimmed, black hat: faintly shadowing forth a kind of insane imitation of an English coachman! But somebody in authority cries "Go ahead!" as I am making these observations. The mail takes the lead in a four-horse wagon, and all the coaches follow in procession, headed by No. 1.

By-the-way, whenever an Englishman would cry "All right!" an American cries "Go ahead!" which is somewhat expressive of the national character of the two countries.

The first half mile of the road is over bridges made of loose planks laid across two parallel poles, which tilt up as the wheels roll over them, and IN the river. The river has a clayey bottom, and is full of holes, so that half a horse is constantly disappearing unexpectedly, and can't be found again for some time.

But we get past even this, and come to the road itself, which is a series of alternate swamps and gravel-pits. A tremendous place is close before us, the black driver rolls his eyes, screws his mouth up very round, and looks straight between the two leaders, as if he were saying to himself, "We have done this often before, but *now* I think we shall have a crash." He takes a rein in each hand, jerks and pulls at both, and dances on the splashboard with both feet (keeping his seat, of course) like the lamented Ducrow on two of his fiery coursers. We come to the spot, sink down in the mire nearly to the coach windows, tilt on one side at an angle of forty-five degrees, and stick there. The insides scream dismally; the coach stops; the horses flounder; all the other six coaches stop; and their four-and-twenty horses flounder likewise, but merely for company, and in sympathy with ours. Then the following circumstances occur:

Black Driver (to the horses). "Hi!"

Nothing happens. Insides scream again.

Black Driver (to the horses). "Ho!"

Horses plunge, and splash the black driver.

Gentleman inside (looking out). "Why, what on airth—"

Gentleman receives a variety of splashes, and draws his head in again, without finishing his question or waiting for an answer.

Black Driver (still to the horses). "Jiddy! Jiddy!"

Horses pull violently, drag the coach out of the hole, and draw it up a bank, so steep that the black driver's legs fly up into the air, and he goes back among the luggage on the roof. But he immediately recovers himself, and cries (still to the horses),

"Pill!"

No effect. On the contrary, the coach begins to roll back upon No. 2, which rolls back upon No 3, which rolls back upon No. 4, and so on, until No. 7 is heard to curse and swear, nearly a quarter of a mile behind.

Black Driver (louder than before). "Pill!"

Horses make another struggle to get up the bank, and again the coach rolls backward.

Black Driver (louder than before). "Pe-e-e-ill!"

Horses make a desperate struggle.

Black Driver (recovering spirits). "Hi, Jiddy, Jiddy, Pill!"

Horses make another effort.

Black Driver (with great vigour). "Ally Loo! Hi. Jiddy, Jiddy. Pill. Ally Loo!"

Horses almost do it.

Black Driver (with his eyes starting out of his head). "Lee, den. Lee, dere. Hi. Jiddy, Jiddy Pill. Ally Loo. Lee-e-e-e-e!"

They run up the bank, and go down again on the other side at a fearful pace. It is impossible to stop them, and at the bottom there is a deep hollow full of water. The coach rolls frightfully. The insides scream. The mud and water fly about us. The black driver dances like a madman. Suddenly we are all right by some extraordinary means, and stop to breathe.

A black friend of the black driver is sitting on a fence. The black driver recognises him by twirling his head round and round like a harlequin, rolling his eyes, shrugging his shoulders, and grinning from ear to ear. He stops short, turns to me, and says,

"We shall get you through, sa, like a fiddle, and hope a please you when we get you through, sa. Old 'ooman at home, sir;" chuckling very much. "Outside gentleman, sa, he often remember old 'ooman at home, sa," grinning again.

"Ay, ay, we'll take care of the old woman. Don't be afraid."

The black driver grins again, but there is another hole, and, beyond that, another bank close before us. So he stops short; cries (to the horses again) "Easy. Easy, den. Ease. Steady. Hi. Jiddy. Pill. Ally. Loo," but never "Lee!" until we are reduced to the very last extremity, and are in the midst of difficulties, extrication from which appears to be all but impossible.

And so we do the ten miles or thereabout in two hours and a half; breaking no bones, though bruising a great many; and, in short, getting through the distance "like a fiddle."

This singular kind of coaching terminates at Fredericksburgh, whence there is a railway to Richmond. The tract of country through which it takes its course was once productive; but the soil has been exhausted by the system of employing a great amount of slave labour in forcing crops without strengthening the land, and it is now little better than a sandy desert overgrown with trees. Dreary and uninteresting as its aspect is, I was glad to the heart to find anything on which one of the curses of this horrible institution has fallen, and had greater pleasure in contemplating the withered ground than the richest and most thriving cultivation in the same place could possibly have afforded me.

In this district, as in all others where slavery sits brooding (I have frequently heard this admitted, even by those who are its warmest advocates), there is an air of ruin and decay abroad which is inseparable from the system. The barns and outhouses are mouldering away; the sheds are patched, and half roofless; the log cabins (built in Virginia with external chimneys made of clay or wood) are squalid in the last degree. There is no look of decent comfort anywhere. The miserable stations by the railway side; the great wild woodyards, whence the engine is supplied with fuel; the negro children rolling on the ground before the cabin doors, with dogs and pigs; the biped beasts of burden slinking past; gloom and dejection are upon them all.

In the negro-car belonging to the train in which we made this journey were a mother and her children, who had just been purchased, the husband and father being left behind with their old owner. The children cried the whole way, and the mother was misery's picture. The champion of Life, Liberty, and the Pursuit of Happiness, who had bought them, rode in the same train, and every time we stopped got down to see that they were safe. The black in Sinbad's Travels, with one eye in the middle of his forehead, which shone like a burning coal, was nature's aristocrat compared with this white gentleman.

It was between six and seven o'clock in the evening when we drove to the hotel, in front of which, and on the top of the broad flight of steps leading to the door, two or three citizens were balancing themselves on rocking-chairs, and smoking cigars. We found it a very large and elegant establishment, and were as well entertained as travellers need desire to be. The climate being a thirsty one, there was never, at any hour of the day, a scarcity of loungers in the spacious bar, or a cessation of the mixing of cool liquors; but they were a merrier people here, and had musical instruments playing to them o' nights, which it was a treat to hear again.

The next day, and the next, we rode and walked about the town, which is delightfully situated on eight hills overhanging James River, a sparkling stream, studded here and there with bright islands, or brawling over broken rocks.

Although it was yet but the middle of March, the weather in this southern temperature was extremely warm; the peach-trees and magnolias were in full bloom, and the trees were green. In a low ground among the hills is a valley known as "Bloody Run," from a terrible conflict with the Indians which once occurred there. It is a good place for such a struggle, and, like every other spot I saw associated with any legend of that wild people now so rapidly fading from the earth, interested me very much.

The city is the seat of the local parliament of Virginia; and in its shady legislative halls some orators were drowsily holding forth to the hot noonday. By dint of constant repetition, however, these constitutional sights had very little more interest for me than so many parochial vestries; and I was glad to exchange this one for a lounge in a well-arranged public library of some ten thousand volumes, and a visit to a tobacco manufactory, where the workmen were all slaves.

I saw in this place the whole process of picking, rolling, pressing, drying, packing in casks, and branding. All the tobacco thus dealt with was in course of manufacture for chewing; and one would have supposed there was enough in that one storehouse to have filled even the comprehensive jaws of America. In this form, the weed looks like the oilcake on which we fatten cattle, and, even without reference to its consequences, is sufficiently uninviting.

Many of the workmen appeared to be strong men, and it is hardly necessary to add that they were all labouring quietly then. After two o'clock in the day, they are allowed to sing, a certain number at a time. The hour striking while I was there, some twenty sang a hymn in parts, and sang it by no means ill; pursuing their work meanwhile. A bell rang as I was about to leave, and they all poured forth into a building on the opposite side of the street to dinner. I said several times that I should like to see them at their meal; but as the gentleman to whom I mentioned this desire appeared to be suddenly taken rather deaf, I did not pursue the request. Of their appearance I shall have something to say presently.

On the following day, I visited a plantation or farm, of about twelve hundred acres, on the opposite bank of the river. Here again, although I went down with the owner of the estate to "the quarter," as that part of it in which the slaves live is called, I was not invited to enter into any of their huts. All I saw of them was that they were crazy, wretched cabins, near to which groups of half-naked children basked in the sun, or wallowed on the dusty ground. But I believe that this gentleman is a considerate and excellent master, who inherited his fifty slaves, and is neither a buyer nor a seller of human stock; and I am sure, from my own observation and conviction, that he is a kind-hearted, worthy man.

The planter's house was an airy rustic dwelling, that brought Defoe's description of such places strongly to my recollection. The day was very warm, but the blinds being all closed, and the windows and doors set wide open, a shady coolness rustled through the rooms, which was exquisitely refreshing after the glare and heat without. Before the windows was an open piazza, where, in what they call the hot weather—whatever that may be—they sling hammocks, and drink and doze luxuriously. I do not know how their cool refections may taste within the hammocks, but, having experience, I can report that, out of them, the mounds of ices and the bowls of mint-julep and sherry-cobbler they make in these latitudes, are refreshments never to be thought of afterward in summer, by those who would preserve contented minds.

There are two bridges across the river: one belongs to the railroad, and the other, which is a very crazy affair, is the private property of some old lady in the neighbourhood, who levies tolls upon the town's people. Crossing this bridge, on my way back, I saw a notice painted on the gate, cautioning all persons to drive slowly, under a penalty, if the offender were a white man, of five dollars; if a negro, fifteen stripes.

The same decay and gloom that overhang the way by which it is approached, hover above the town of Richmond. There are pretty villas and cheerful houses in its streets, and Nature smiles upon the country round; but jostling its handsome residences, like slavery itself going hand in hand with many lofty virtues, are deplorable tenements, fences unrepaired, walls crumbling into ruinous heaps. Hinting gloomily at things below the surface, these and many other tokens of the same description force themselves upon the notice, and are remembered with depressing influence, when livelier features are forgotten.

To those who are happily unaccustomed to them, the countenances in the streets and labouring-places, too, are shocking. All men who know that there are laws against instructing slaves, of which the pains and penalties greatly exceed in amount the fines imposed on those who maim and torture them, must be prepared to find their faces very low in the scale of intellectual expression. But the darkness—not of skin, but mind—which meets the stranger's eye at every turn; the brutalizing and blotting out of all the fairer characters traced by Nature's hand; immeasurably outdo his worst belief. That travelled creation of the great satirist's brain, who, fresh from living among horses, peered from a high casement down upon his own kind with trembling horror, was scarcely more repelled and daunted by the sight, than those who look upon some of these faces for the first time must surely be.

I left the last of them behind me in the person of a wretched drudge, who, after running to and fro all day till midnight, and moping in his stealthy winks of sleep upon the stairs between whiles, was washing the dark passages at four o'clock in the morning; and went upon my way with a grateful heart that I was not doomed to live where slavery was, and had never had my senses blunted to its wrongs and horrors in a slave-rocked cradle.

It had been my intention to proceed by James River and Chesapeake Bay to Baltimore; but one of the steamboats being absent from her station through some accident, and the means of conveyance consequently rendered uncertain, we returned to Washington by the way we had come (there were two constables on board the steamboat, in pursuit of runaway slaves), and, halting there again for one night, went on to Baltimore next afternoon.

The most comfortable of all the hotels of which I had any experience in the United States, and they were not a few, is Barnum's in that city: where the English traveller will find curtains to his bed, for the first and probably the last time, in America; and where he will be likely to have enough water for washing himself, which is not at all a common case."

This capital of the state of Maryland is a bustling, busy town, with a great deal of traffic of various kinds, and in particular of water commerce. That portion of the town which it most favours is none of the cleanest, it is true; but the upper part is of a very different character, and has many agreeable streets and public buildings. The Washington Monument, which is a handsome pillar with a statue on its summit; the Medical College; and the Battle Monument in memory of an engagement with the British at North Point; are the most conspicuous among them.

There is a very good prison in this city, and the state Penitentiary is also among its institutions. In this latter establishment there were two curious cases.

One, was that of a young man who had been tried for the murder of his father. The evidence was entirely circumstantial, and was very conflicting and doubtful; nor was it possible to assign any motive which could have tempted him to the commission of so tremendous a crime. He had been tried twice; and on the second occasion the jury felt so much hesitation in convicting him, that they found a verdict of manslaughter, or murder in the second degree; which it could not possibly be, as there had, beyond all doubt, been no quarrel or provocation, and if he were guilty at all, he was unquestionably guilty of murder in its broadest and worst signification.

The remarkable feature in the case was, that if the unfortunate deceased were not really murdered by this own son of his, he must have been murdered by his own brother. The evidence lay, in a most remarkable manner, between those two. On all the suspicious points, the dead man's brother was the witness; all the explanations for the prisoner (some of them extremely plausible) went, by construction and inference, to implicate him as plotting to fix the guilt upon his nephew. It must have been one of them: and the jury had to decide between two sets of suspicions, almost equally unnatural, unaccountable, and strange.

The other case, was that of a man who once went to a certain distiller's and stole a copper measure containing a quantity of liquor. He was pursued and taken with the property in his possession, and was sentenced to two years' imprisonment. On coming out of the jail, at the expiration of that term, he went back to the same distiller's, and stole the same copper measure containing the same quantity of liquor. There was not the slightest reason to suppose that the man wished to return to prison: indeed, everything, but the commission of the offence, made directly against that assumption. There are only two ways of accounting for this extraordinary proceeding. One is, that, after undergoing so much for this copper measure, he conceived he had established a sort of claim and right to it. The other that, by dint of long thinking about it, it had become a monomania with him, and had acquired a fascination which he found it impossible to resist: swelling from an Earthly Copper Gallon into an Ethereal Golden Vat.

After remaining here a couple of days I bound myself to a rigid adherence to the plan I had laid down so recently, and resolved to set forward on our western journey without any more delay. Accordingly, having reduced the luggage within the smallest possible compass (by sending back to New-York, to be afterward forwarded to us in Canada, so much of it as was not absolutely wanted); and having procured the necessary credentials to banking-houses on the way; and having, moreover, looked for two evenings at the setting sun, with as well-defined an idea of the country before us as if we had been going to travel to the very centre of that planet; we left Baltimore by another railway at half past eight in the morning, and reached the town of York, some sixty miles off, by the early dinner-time of the hotel, which was the starting-place of the four-horse coach wherein we were to proceed to Harrisburgh.

This conveyance, the box of which I was fortunate enough to secure, had come down to meet us at the railroad station, and was as muddy and cumbersome as usual. As more passengers were waiting for us at the inn door, the coachman observed under his breath, in the usual self-communicative voice, looking the while at his mouldy harness as if it were to that he was addressing himself,

"I expect we shall want *the big* coach."

I could not help wondering within myself what the size of this big coach might be, and how many persons it might be designed to hold, for the vehicle which was too small for our purpose was something larger than two English heavy night coaches. My speculations were speedily set at rest, however, for as soon as we had dined there came rumbling up the street, shaking its sides like a corpulent giant, a kind of barge on wheels. After much blundering and backing, it stopped at the door, rolling heavily from side to side when its other motion had ceased, as if it had taken cold in its damp stable, and between that and the having been required in its dropsical old age to move at any faster pace than a walk, were distressed by shortness of wind.

"If here ain't the Harrisburgh mail at last, and dreadful bright and smart to look at too," cried an elderly gentleman, in some excitement, "darn my mother!"

I don't know what the sensation of being darned may be, or whether a man's mother has a keener relish or disrelish of the process than anybody else; but if the endurance of this mysterious ceremony by the old lady in question had depended on the accuracy of her son's vision in respect to the abstract brightness and smartness of the Harrisburgh mail, she would certainly have undergone its infliction. However, they packed twelve people inside, and the luggage (including such trifles as a large rocking-horse and a good sized dining-table) being at last made fast upon the roof, we started off in great state.

At the door of another hotel there was another passenger to be taken up.

"Any room, sir?" cries the new passenger *to the coachman.*

"Well, there's room enough," replies the coachman, without getting down, or even looking at him.

"There an't no room at all, sir," bawls a gentleman inside. Which another gentleman (also inside) confirms, by predicting that the attempt to introduce any more passengers "won't fit nohow."

The new passenger, without any expression of anxiety, looks into the coach, and then looks up at the coachman: "Now, how do you mean to fix it?" says he, after a pause, "for I *must* go."

The coachman employs himself in twisting the lash of the whip into a knot, and takes no more notice of the question, clearly signifying that it is anybody's business but his, and that the passengers would do well to fix it among themselves. In this state of things, matters seem to be approximating to a fix of another kind, when another inside passenger in a corner, who is nearly suffocated, cries faintly, "I'll get out."

This is no matter of relief or self-congratulation to the driver, for his immovable philosophy is perfectly undisturbed by anything that happens in the coach. Of all things in the world, the coach would seem to be the very last upon his mind. The exchange is made, however, and then the passenger who has given up his seat makes a third upon the box, seating himself in what he calls the middle; that is, with half his person on my legs and the other half on the driver's.

"Go ahead, cap'en," cries the colonel, who directs.

"Gŏ lāng!" cries the cap'en to his company, the horses, and away we go.

We took up at a rural bar-room, after we had gone a few miles, an intoxicated gentleman, who climbed upon the roof among the luggage, and, subsequently slipping off without hurting himself, was seen in the distant perspective reeling back to the grogshop where we had found him. We also parted with more of our freight at different times, so that, when we came to change horses, I was again alone outside.

The coachmen always change with the horses, and are usually as dirty as the coach. The first was dressed like a very shabby English baker; the second like a Russian peasant, for he wore a loose purple camlet robe with a fur collar, tied round his waist with a party-coloured worsted sash; gray trousers, light blue gloves, and a cap of bearskin. It had by this time come on to rain very heavily, and there was a cold damp mist besides, which penetrated to the skin. I was very glad to take advantage of a stoppage and get down to stretch my legs, shake the water off my greatcoat, and swallow the usual anti-temperance recipe for keeping out the cold.

When I mounted to my seat again, I observed a new parcel lying on the coach roof, which I took to be a rather large fiddle in a brown bag. In the course of a few miles, however, I discovered that it had a glazed cap at one end and a pair of muddy shoes at the other; and farther observation demonstrated it to be a small boy in a snuff-coloured coat, with his arms quite pinioned to his sides by deep forcing into his pockets. He was, I presume, a relative or friend of the coachman's, as he lay a-top of the luggage with his face towards the rain; and, except when a changs of position brought his shoes in contact with my hat, he appeared to be asleep. At last, on some occasion of our stopping, this thing slowly upreared itself to the height of three feet six, and, fixing its eyes on me, observed, in piping accents, with a complacent yawn half quenched in an obliging air of friendly patronage, "Well now, stranger, I guess you find this a'most like an English arternoon, hey?"

The scenery, which had been tame enough at first, was, for the last ten or twelve miles, beautiful. Our road wound through the pleasant valley of the Susquehanna; the river, dotted with innumerable green islands, lay upon our right; and on the left, a steep ascent, craggy with broken rock, and dark with pine trees. The mist, wreathing itself into a hundred fantastic shapes, moved solemnly upon the water; and the gloom of evening gave to all an air of mystery and silence which greatly enhanced its natural interest.

We crossed this river by a wooden bridge, roofed and covered in on all sides, and nearly a mile in length. It was profoundly dark; perplexed, with great beams, crossing and recrossing it at every possible angle; and through the broad chinks and crevices in the floor, the rapid river gleamed, far down below, like a legion of eyes. We had no lamps; and as the horses stumbled and floundered through this place, towards the distant speck of dying light, it seemed interminable. I really could not at first persuade myself, as we rumbled heavily on, filling the bridge with the hollow noises, and I held down my head to save it from the rafters above but that I was in a painful dream; for I have often dreamed of toiling through such places, and as often argued, even at the time, "this cannot be reality."

At length, however, we emerged upon the streets of Harrisburgh, whose feeble lights, reflected dismally from the wet ground, did not shine out upon a very cheerful city. We were soon established in a snug hotel, which, though smaller and far less splendid than many we put up at, is raised above them all in my remembrance, by having for its landlord the most obliging, considerate, and gentlemanly person I ever had to deal with.

As we were not to proceed upon our journey until the afternoon, I walked out, after breakfast the next morning, to look about me; and was duly shown a model prison on the solitary system, just erected, and as yet without an inmate; the trunk of an ald tree to which Harris, the first settler here (afterward buried under it) was tied by hostile Indians, with his funeral pile about him, when he was saved by the timely appearance of a friendly party on the opposite shore of the river; the local legislature (for there was another of those bodies here, again, in full debate); and the other curiosities of the town.

I was very much interested in looking over a number of treaties made from time to time with the poor Indians, signed by the different chiefs at the period of their ratification, and preserved in the office of the Secretary to the Commonwealth. These signatures, traced of course by their own hands, are rough drawings of the creatures or weapons they were called after. Thus, the Great Turtle makes a crooked pen-and-ink outline of a great turtle; the Buffalo sketches a buffalo; the War Hatchet sets a rough image of that weapon for his mark. So with the Arrow, the Fish, the Scalp, the Big Canoe, and all of them.

I could not but think—as I looked at these feeble and tremulous productions of hands which could draw the longest arrow to the head in a stout elkhorn bow, or split a head or feather with a rifle-ball—of Crabbe's musings over the Parish Register, and the irregular scratches made with a pen, by men who would plough a lengthy furrow straight from end to end. Nor could I help bestowing many sorrowful thoughts upon the simple warriors whose hands and hearts were set there, in all truth and honesty; and who only learnt in the course of time from white men how to break their faith, and quibble out of forms and bonds. I wondered, too, how many times the credulous Big Turtle, or trusting Little Hatchet, had put his mark to treaties which were falsely read to him; and had signed away, he knew not what, until it went and cast him loose upon the new possessors of the land, a savage indeed.

Our host announced, before our early dinner, that some members of the legislative body proposed to do us the honour of calling. He had kindly yielded up to us his wife's own little parlour, and when I begged that he would show them in, I saw him look with painful apprehension at its pretty carpet; though, being otherwise occupied at the time, the cause of his uneasiness did not occur to me.

It certainly would have been more pleasant to all parties concerned, and would not, I think, have compromised their independence in any material degree, if some of these gentlemen had not only yielded to the prejudice in favour of spittoons, but had abandoned themselves, for the moment, even to the conventional absurdity of pocket-handkerchiefs.

It still continued to rain heavily, and when we went down to the Canal Boat (for that was the mode of conveyance by which we were to proceed) after dinner, the weather was as unpromising and obstinately wet as one would desire to see. Nor was the sight of this canal boat, in which we were to spend three or four days, by any means a cheerful one; as it involved some uneasy speculations concerning the disposal of the passengers at night, and opened a wide field of inquiry touching the other domestic arrangements of the establishment, which was sufficiently disconcerting.

However, there it was—a barge with a little house in it, viewed from the outside; and a caravan at a fair, viewed from within: the gentlemen being accommodated, as the spectators usually are, in one of those locomotive museums of penny wonders; and the ladies being partitioned off by a red curtain, after the manner of the dwarfs and giants in the same establishments, whose private lives are passed in rather close exclusiveness.

We sat here, looking silently at the row of little tables, which extended down both sides of the cabin, and listened to the rain as it dripped and pattered on the boat, and plashed with a dismal merriment in the water, until the arrival of the railway train, for whose final contribution to our stock of passengers, our departure was alone deferred. It brought a great many boxes, which were bumped and tossed upon the roof, almost as painfully as if they had been deposited on one's own head, without the intervention of a porter's knot; and several damp gentlemen, whose clothes, on their drawing round the stove, began to steam again. No doubt it would have been a thought more comfortable if the driving rain, which now poured down more soakingly than ever, had admitted of a window being opened, or if our number had been something less than thirty; but there was scarcely time to think as much, when a train of three horses was attached to the tow-rope, the boy upon the leader smacked his whip, the rudder creaked and groaned complainingly, and we had begun our journey.

CHAPTER X.

SOME FARTHER ACCOUNT OF THE CANAL-BOAT, ITS DOMESTIC ECONOMY, AND ITS PASSENGERS.—JOURNEY TO PITTSBURG ACROSS THE ALLEGHANY MOUNTAINS.—PITTSBURG.

As it continued to rain most perseveringly, we all remained below: the damp gentlemen round the stove, gradually becoming mildewed by the action of the fire; and the dry gentlemen lying at full length upon the seats, or slumbering uneasily with their faces on the tables, or walking up and down the cabin, which it was barely possible for a man of the middle height to do, without making bald places on his head by scraping it against the roof. At about six o'clock, all the small tables were put together to form one long table, and everybody sat down to tea, coffee, bread, butter, salmon, shad, liver, steak, potatoes, pickles, ham, chops, black puddings, and sausages.

"Will you try," said my opposite neighbour, handing me a dish of potatoes, broken up in milk and butter, "will you try some of these fixings?"

There are few words which perform such various duties as this word "fix." It is the Caleb Quotem of the American vocabulary. You call upon a gentleman in a country town, and his help informs you that he is "fixing himself" just now, but will be down directly: by which you are to understand that he is dressing. You inquire, on board a steamboat, of a fellow-passenger, whether breakfast will be ready soon, and he tells you he should think so, for when he was last below, they were "fixing the tables:" in other words, laying the cloth. You beg a porter to collect your luggage, and he entreats you not to be uneasy, for he'll "fix it presently:" and if you complain of indisposition, you are advised to have recourse to Doctor so and so, who will "fix you" in no time.

One night, I ordered a bottle of mulled wine at a hotel where I was staying, and waited a long time for it; at length it was put upon the table with an apology from the landlord that he feared it wasn't "fixed properly." And I recollect once, at a stage-coach dinner, overhearing a very stern gentleman demand of a waiter who presented him with a plate of underdone roast beef, "whether he called *that*, fixing God A'mighty's vittles?"

There is no doubt that the meal, at which the invitation was tendered to me which has occasioned this digression, was disposed of somewhat ravenously; and that the gentlemen thrust the broad-bladed knives and the two-pronged forks farther down their throats than I ever saw the same weapons go before, except in the hands of a skilful juggler: but no man sat down until the ladies were seated; or omitted any little act of politeness which could contribute to their comfort. Nor did I ever once, on any occasion, anywhere, during my rambles in America, see a woman exposed to the slightest act of rudeness, incivility, or even inattention.

By the time the meal was over, the rain, which seemed to have worn itself out by coming down so fast, was nearly over too; and it became feasible to go on deck: which was a great relief, notwithstanding its being a very small deck, and being rendered still smaller by the luggage which was heaped together in the middle under a tarpaulin covering; leaving, on either side, a path so narrow, that it became a science to walk to and fro without tumbling overboard into the canal. It was somewhat embarrassing at first, too, to have to duck nimbly, every five minutes, whenever the man at the helm cried "Bridge!" and sometimes, when the cry was "Low Bridge," to lie down nearly flat. But custom familiarizes one to anything, and there were so many bridges that it took a very short time to get used to this.

As night came on, and we drew in sight of the first range of hills, which are the outposts of the Alleghany Mountains, the scenery, which had been uninteresting hitherto, became more bold and striking. The wet ground reeked and smoked, after the heavy fall of rain; and the croaking of the frogs (whose noise in these parts is almost incredible) sounded as though a million of fairy teams with bells were travelling through the air, and keeping pace with us. The night was cloudy yet, but moonlight too: and when we crossed the Susquehanna river—over which there is an extraordinary wooden bridge with two galleries, one above the other, so that even there, two boat teams meeting, may pass without confusion—it was wild and grand.

I have mentioned my having been in some uncertainty and doubt, at first, relative to the sleeping arrangements on board this boat. I remained in the same vague state of mind until ten o'clock or thereabout, when, going below, I found suspended on either side of the cabin, three long tiers of hanging book-shelves, designed apparently for volumes of the small octavo size. Looking with greater attention at these contrivances (wondering to find such literary preparations in such a place), I descried on each shelf a sort of microscopic sheet and blanket; then I began dimly to comprehend that the passengers were the library, and that they were to be arranged, edgewise, on these shelves, till morning.

I was assisted to this conclusion by seeing some of them gathered round the master of the boat, at one of the tables, drawing lots with all the anxieties and passions of gamesters depicted in their countenances; while others, with small pieces of cardboard in their hands, were groping among the shelves in search of numbers corresponding with those they had drawn. As soon as any gentleman found his number, he took possession of it by immediately undressing himself and crawling into bed. The rapidity with which an agitated gambler subsided into a snoring slumberer, was one of the most singular effects I have ever witnessed. As to the ladies, they were already abed, behind the red curtain, which was carefully drawn and pinned up the centre; though as every cough, or sneeze, or whisper, behind this curtain, was perfectly audible before it, we had still a lively consciousness of their society.

The politeness of the person in authority had secured to me a shelf in a nook near this red curtain, in some degree removed from the great body of sleepers: to which place I retired, with many acknowledgments to him for his attention. I found it, on after measurement, just the width of an ordinary sheet of Bath post-letter paper; and I was at first in some uncertainty as to the best means of getting into it. But the shelf being a bottom one, I finally determined on lying upon the floor, rolling gently in, stopping immediately I touched the mattress, and remaining for the night with that side uppermost, whatever it might be. Luckily, I came upon my back at exactly the right moment. I was much alarmed on looking upward, to see, by the shape of his half yard of sacking (which his weight had bent into an exceedingly tight bag), that there was a very heavy gentleman above me, whom the slender cords seemed quite incapable of holding; and I could not help reflecting upon the grief of my wife and family in the event of his coming down in the night. But as I could not have got up again without a severe bodily struggle, which might have alarmed the ladies, and as I had nowhere to go to, even if I had, I shut my eyes upon the danger and remained there.

One of two remarkable circumstances is indisputably a fact, with reference to that class of society who travel in these boats. Either they carry their restlessness to such a pitch that they never sleep at all, or they expectorate in dreams, which would be a remarkable mingling of the real and ideal. All night long, and every night, on this canal, there was a perfect storm and tempest of spitting; and once my coat, being in the very centre of a hurricane sustained by five gentlemen (which moved vertically, strictly carrying out Reid's Theory of the Law of Storms), I was fain the next morning to lap it on the deck, and rub it down with fair water before it was in a condition to be worn again.

Between five and six o'clock in the morning, we got up, and some of us went on deck, to give them an opportunity of taking the shelves down; while others, the morning being very cold, crowded round the rusty stove, cherishing the newly-kindled fire, and filling the grate with those voluntary contributions of which they had been so liberal all night. The washing accommodations were primitive. There was a tin ladle chained to the deck, with which every gentleman who thought it necessary to cleanse himself (some were superior to this weakness), fished the dirty water out of the canal, and poured it into a tin basin, secured in like manner. There was also a jack-towel. And, hanging up before a little looking-glass in the bar, in the immediate vicinity of the bread and cheese and biscuits, were a public comb and hair-brush.

At eight o'clock, the shelves being taken down and put away, and the tables joined together, everybody sat down to the tea, coffee, bread, butter, salmon, shad, liver, steak, potatoes, pickles, ham, chops, black-puddings, sausages, all over again. Some were fond of compounding this variety, and having it all on their plates at once. As each gentleman got through his own personal amount of tea, coffee, bread, butter, salmon, shad, liver, steak, potatoes, pickles, ham, chops, black-puddings, and sausages, he rose up and walked off. When everybody had done with everything, the fragments were cleared away; and one of the waiters appearing anew in the character of a barber, shaved such of the company as desired to be shaved; while the remainder looked on, or yawned over their newspapers. Dinner was breakfast again, without the tea and coffee; and supper and breakfast were identical.

There was a man on board this boat, with a light fresh-coloured face, and a pepper-and-salt suit of clothes, who was the most inquisitive fellow that can possibly be imagined. He never spoke otherwise than interrogatively. He was an imbodied inquiry. Sitting down or standing up, still or moving, walking the deck or taking his meals, there he was, with a great note of interrogation in each eye, two in his cocked ears, two more in his turned-up nose and chin, at least half a dozen more about the corners of his mouth, and the largest one of all in his hair, which was brushed pertly off his forehead in a flaxen clump. Every button in his clothes said "Eh? What's that? Did you speak? Say that again, will you?" He was always wide awake, like the enchanted bride who drove her husband frantic; always restless; always thirsting for answers; perpetually seeking and never finding. There never was such a curious man.

I wore a fur great-coat at that time, and before we were well clear of the wharf, he questioned me concerning it, and its price, and where I bought it, and when, and what fur it was, and what it weighed, and what it cost. Then he took notice of my watch, and asked what that cost, and whether it was a French watch, and where I got it, and how I got it, and whether I bought it or had it given me, and how it went, and where the keyhole was, and when I wound it, every night or every morning, and whether I ever forgot to wind it at all, and if I did, what then? Where had I been to last, and where was I going next, and where was I going after that, and had I seen the President, and what did he say, and what did I say, and what did he say when I had said that? Eh? Lor now! do tell!

Finding that nothing would satisfy him, I evaded his questions after the first score or two, and in particular pleaded ignorance respecting the name of the fur whereof the coat was made. I am unable to say whether this was the reason, but that coat fascinated him ever afterward; he usually kept close behind me as I walked, and moved as I moved, that he might look at it the better: and he frequently dived into narrow places after me at the risk of his life, that he might have the satisfaction of passing his hand up the back, and rubbing it the wrong way.

We had another odd specimen on board, of a different kind. This was a thin-faced, spare figured man of middle age and stature, dressed in a dusty drabbish-coloured suit, such as I never saw before. He was perfectly quiet during the first part of the journey: indeed I don't remember having so much as seen him until he was brought out by circumstances, as great men often are. The conjunction of events which made him famous, happened, briefly, thus.

The canal extends to the foot of the mountain, and there, of course, it stops: the passengers being conveyed across it by land carriage, and taken on afterward by another canal-boat, the counterpart of the first, which awaits them on the other side. There are two canal lines of passage-boat; one is called The Express, and one (a cheaper one) The Pioneer. The Pioneer gets first to the mountain, and waits for The Express people to come up: both sets of passengers being conveyed across it at the same time. We were the Express company: but when we had crossed the mountain, and had come to the second boat, the proprietors took it into their heads to draught all the Pioneers into it likewise, so that we were five-and-forty at least, and the accession of passengers was not at all of that kind which improved the prospect of sleeping at night. Our people grumbled at this, as people do in such cases: but suffered the boat to be towed off with the whole freight aboard nevertheless: and away we went down the canal At home, I should have protested lustily, but being a foreigner here, I held my peace. Not so this passenger. He cleft a path among the people on deck (we were nearly all on deck), and without addressing anybody whomsoever, soliloquized as follows:

"This may suit you, this may, but it don't suit me. This may be all very well with Down Easters and men of Boston raising, but it won't suit my figure no how; and no two ways about that: and so I tell you. Now! I'm from the brown forests of the Mississippi, I am, and when the sun shines on me, it does shine—a little. It don't glimmer where I live, the sun don't. No. I'm a brown forester, I am. I ain't a Johnny Cake. There are no smooth skins where I live. We're rough men there. Rather. If Down Easters and men of Boston raising like this, I'm glad of it, but I'm none of that raising nor of that breed. No. This company wants a little fixing, it does. I'm the wrong sort of man for 'em, *I* am. They won't like me, *they* won't. This is piling of it up, a little too mountainous, this is." At the end of every one of these short sentences he turned upon his heel, and walked the other way: checking himself abruptly when he had finished another short sentence, and turning back again.

It is impossible for me to say what terrific meaning was hidden in the words of this brown forester, but I know that the other passengers looked on in a sort of admiring horror, and that presently the boat was put back to the wharf, and as many of the Pioneers as could be coaxed or bullied into going away, were got rid of.

When we started again, some of the boldest spirits on board, made bold to say to the obvious occasion of this improvement in our prospects, "Much obliged to you, sir:" whereunto the brown forester (waving his hand, and still walking up and down as before), replied, "No you an't. You're none o' my raising. You may act for yourselves, *you* may. I have pinted out the way. Down Easters and Johnny Cakes can follow if they please. I an't a Johnny Cake, *I* an't. I am from the brown forests of the Mississippi, *I* am"—and so on, as before. He was unanimously voted one of the tables for his bed at night—there is a great contest for the tables—in consideration of his public services: and he had the warmest corner by the stove throughout the rest of the journey. But I never could find out that he did anything except sit there: nor did I hear him speak again until, in the midst of the bustle and turmoil of getting the luggage ashore in the dark at Pittsburg, I stumbled over him as he sat smoking a cigar on the cabin steps, and heard him muttering to himself, with a short laugh of defiance, "I an't a Johnny Cake, *I* an't. I'm from the brown forests of the Mississippi, *I* am, damme!" I am inclined to argue from this, that he had never left off saying so; but I could not make affidavit of that part of the story, if required to do so by my Queen and Country.

As we have not reached Pittsburg yet, however, in the order of our narrative, I may go on to remark that breakfast was perhaps the least desirable meal of the day, as in addition to the many savoury odours arising from the eatables already mentioned, there were whiffs of gin, whiskey, brandy, and rum, from the little bar hard by, and a decided seasoning of stale tobacco. Many of the gentlemen passengers were far from particular in respect of their linen, which was in some cases as yellow as the little rivulets that had trickled from the corners of their mouths in chewing, and dried there. Nor was the atmosphere quite free from zephyr whisperings of the thirty beds which had just been cleared away, and of which we were farther and more pressingly reminded by the occasional appearance on the table-cloth of a kind of Game, not mentioned in the Bill of Fare.

And yet, despite these oddities—and even they had, for me at least, a humour of their own—there was much in this mode of travelling which I heartily enjoyed at the time, and look back upon with great pleasure. Even the running up, bare-necked, at five o'clock in the morning, from the tainted cabin to the dirty deck: scooping up the icy water, plunging one's head into it, and drawing it out, all fresh and glowing with the cold: was a good thing. The fast, brisk walk upon the towing-path, between that time and breakfast, when every vein and artery seemed to tingle with health: the exquisite beauty of the opening day, when light came gleaming off from everything; the lazy motion of the boat, when one lay idly on the deck, looking through, rather than at, the deep blue sky; the gliding on, at night, so noiselessly, past frowning hills, sullen with dark trees, and sometimes angry in one red burning spot high up, where unseen men lay crouching ronnd a fire: the shining out of the bright stars, undisturbed by noise of wheels or steam, or any other sound than the liquid rippling of the water as the boat went on: all these were pure delights.

Then, there were new settlements and detached log-cabins and frame-houses, full of interest for strangers from an old country; cabins with simple ovens outside, made of clay; and lodgings for the pigs, nearly as good as many of the human quarters; broken windows, patched with worn-out hats, old clothes, old boards, fragments of blankets, and paper; and home-made dressers standing in the open air without the door, whereon was ranged the household store, not hard to count, of earthen jars and pots. The eye was pained to see the stumps of great trees thickly strewn in every field of wheat, and seldom to lose the eternal swamp and dull morass, with hundreds of rotten trunks and twisted branches steeped in its unwholesome water. It was quite sad and oppressive, to come upon great tracts where settlers had been burning down the trees, and where their wounded bodies lay about, like those of murdered creatures, while here and there some charred and blackened giant reared aloft two withered arms, and seemed to call down curses on his foes. Sometimes, at night, the way wound through some lonely gorge, like a mountain pass in Scotland, shining and coldly glittering in the light of the moon, and so closed in by high steep hills all around, that there seemed to be no egress save through the narrow path by which we had come, until one ragged hillside seemed to open, and, shutting out the moonlight as we passed into its gloomy throat, wrapped our new couse in shade and darkness.

We had left Harrisburgh on Friday. On Sunday morning we arrived at the foot of the mountain, which is crossed by railroad. There are ten inclined planes; five *a*scending, and five *de*scending; the carriages are dragged up the former, and let slowly down the latter, by means of stationary engines; the comparatively level spaces between, being traversed, sometimes by horse, and sometimes by engine power, as the case demands. Occasionally the rails are laid upon the extreme verge of a giddy precipice; and looking from the carriage window, the traveller gazes sheer down, without a stone or scrap of fence between, into the mountain depths below. The journey is very cheerfully made, however; only two carriages travelling together; and while proper precautions are taken, is not to be dreaded for its dangers.

It was very pretty travelling thus, at a rapid pace along the heights of the mountain in a keen wind, to look down into a valley full of light and softness: catching glimpses, through the tree-tops, of scattered cabins; children running to the doors; dogs bursting out to bark, whom we could see without hearing; terrified pigs scampering homeward; families sitting out in their rude gardens; cows gazing upward with a stupid indifference; men in their shirt-sleeves looking on at their unfinished houses, planning out to-morrow's work; and we riding onward, high above them, like a whirlwind. It was amusing, too, when we had dined, and rattled down a steep pass, having no other moving power than the weight of the carriages themselves, to see the engine released, long after us, come buzzing down alone, like a great insect, its back of green and gold so shining in the sun, that if it had spread a pair of wings and soared away, no one would have had occasion, as I fancied, for the least surprise. But it stopped short of us in a very business-like manner when we reached the canal; and, before we left the wharf, went panting up this hill again, with the passengers who had waited our arrival for the means of traversing the road by which we had come.

On the Monday evening, furnace fires and clanking hammers on the banks of the canal, warned us that we approached the termination of this part of our journey. After going through another dreamy place—a long aqueduct across the Alleghany River, which was stranger than the bridge at Harrisburgh, being a vast low wooden chamber full of water—we emerged upon that ugly confusion of backs of buildings and crazy galleries and stairs, which always abuts on water, whether it be river, sea, canal, or ditch: and were at Pittsburg.

Pittsburg is like Birmingham in England; at least its townspeople say so. Setting aside the streets, the shops, the houses, wagons, factories, public buildings, and population, perhaps it may be. It certainly has a great quantity of smoke hanging about it, and is famous for its iron-works. Besides the prison to which I have already referred, this town contains a pretty arsenal and other institutions. It is very beautifully situated on the Alleghany River, over which there are two bridges; and the villas of the wealthier citizens sprinkled about the high grounds in the neighourhood, are pretty enough. We lodged at a most excellent hotel, and were admirably served. As usual, it was full of boarders, was very large, and had a broad colonnade to every story of the house.

We tarried here three days. Our next point was Cincinnati: and as this was a steamboat journey, and western steamboats usually blow up one or two a week in the season, it was advisable to collect opinions in reference to the comparative safety of the vessels bound that way, then lying in the river. One called The Messenger was the best recommended. She had been advertised to start positively, every day for a fortnight or so, and had not gone yet, nor did her captain seem to have any very fixed intention on the subject. But this is the custom: for if the law were to bind down a free and independent citizen to keep his word with the public, what would become of the liberty of the subject? Besides, it is in the way of trade. And if passengers be decoyed in the way of trade, and people be inconvenienced in the way of trade, what man, who is a sharp tradesman himself, shall say "We must put a stop to this?"

Impressed by the deep solemnity of the public announcement, I (being then ignorant of these usages) was for hurrying on board in a breathless state, immediately; but receiving private and confidential information that the boat would certainly not start until Friday, April the first, we made ourselves very comfortable in the mean while, and went on board at noon that day.

CHAPTER XI.

FROM PITTSBURG TO CINCINNATI IN A WESTERN STEAMBOAT. CINCINNATI.

The Messenger was one among a crowd of high-pressure steamboats, clustered together by the wharf-side, which, looked down upon from the rising ground that forms the landing-place, and backed by the lofty bank on the opposite side of the river, appeared no larger than so many floating models. She had some forty passengers on board, exclusive of the poorer pessons on the lower deck; and in half an hour, or less, proceeded on her way.

We had, for ourselves, a tiny state-room with two berths in it, opening out of the ladies' cabin. There was, undoubtedly, something satisfactory in this "location," inasmuch as it was in the stern, and we had been a great many times very gravely recommended to keep as far aft as possible, "because the steamboats generally blew up forward." Nor was this an unnecessary caution, as the occurrence and circumstances of more than one such fatality during our stay sufficiently testified. Apart from this source of self-congratulation, it was an unspeakable relief to have any place, no matter how confined, where one could be alone; and as the row of little chambers of which this was one, had each a second glass-door besides that in the ladies' cabin, which opened on a narrow gallery outside the vessel, where the other passengers seldom came, and where one could sit in peace and gaze upon the shifting prospect, we took possession of our new quarters with much pleasure.

If the native packets I have already described be unlike anything we are in the habit of seeing on water, these western vessels are still more foreign to all the ideas we are accustomed to entertain of boats. I hardly know what to liken them to, or how to describe them.

In the first place, they have no mast, cordage, tackle, rigging, or other such boat-like gear; nor have they anything in their shape at all calculated to remind one of a boat's head, stern, sides, or keel. Except that they are in the water, and display a couple of paddle-boxes, they might be intended, for anything that appears to the contrary, to perform some unknown service, high and dry, upon a mountain top. There is no visible deck, even: nothing but a long, black, ugly roof, covered with burnt-out feathery sparks; above which, tower two iron chimneys, and a hoarse escape-valve, and a glass steerage-house. Then, in order as the eye descends towards the water, are the sides, and doors, and windows of the state-rooms, jumbled as oddly together as though they formed a small street, built by the varying tastes of a dozen men: the whole is supported on beams and pillars resting on a dirty barge, but a few inches above the water's edge: and in the narrow space between this upper structure and this barge's deck, are the furnace fires and machinery, open at the sides to every wind that blows, and every storm of rain it drives along its path.

Passing one of these boats at night, and seeing the great body of fire, exposed as I have just described, that rages and roars beneath the frail pile of painted wood: the machinery, not warded off or guarded in any way, but doing its work in the midst of the crowd of idlers and emigrants and children, who throng the lower deck; under the management, too, of reckless men, whose acquaintance with its mysteries may have been of six months' standing: one feels directly that the wonder is, not that there should be so many fatal accidents, but that any journey should be safely made.

Within, there is one long narrow cabin, the whole length of the boat; from which the state-rooms open, on both sides. A small portion of it at the stern, is partitioned off for the ladies; and the bar is at the opposite extreme. There is a long table down the centre, and at either end a stove. The washing apparatus is forward, on the deck. It is a little better than on board the canal-boat, but not much. In all modes of travelling, the American customs, with reference to the means of personal cleanliness and wholesome ablution, are extremely negligent and filthy; and I strongly incline to the belief that a considerable amount of illness is referable to this cause.

We are to be on board the Messenger three days: arriving at Cincinnati (barring accidents) on Monday morning. There are three meals a day. Breakfast at seven, dinner at half-past twelve, supper about six. At each, there are a great many small dishes and plates upon the table, with very little in them; so that although there is every appearance of a mighty "spread," there is seldom really more than a joint: except for those who fancy slices of beet-root, shreds of dried beef, complicated entanglements of yellow pickle; maize, Indian corn, apple-sauce, and pumpkin.

Some people fancy all these little dainties together (and sweet preserves besides), by way of relish to their roast pig. They are generally those dyspectic ladies and gentlemen who eat unheard of quantities of hot corn bread (almost as good for the digestion as a kneaded pin-cushion,) for breakfast, and for supper. Those who do not observe this custom, and who help themselves several times instead, usually suck their knives and forks meditatively, until they have decided what to take next: then pull them out of their mouths; put them in the dish; help themselves; and fall to work again. At dinner, there is nothing to drink upon the table, but great jugs full of cold water. Nobody says anything, at any meal, to anybody. All the passengers are very dismal, and seem to have tremendous secrets weighing on their minds. There is no conversation, no laughter, no cheerfulness, no sociality, except in spitting; and that is done in silent fellowship round the stone, when the meal is over. Every man sits down, dull and languid; swallows his fare as if breakfasts, dinners, and suppers, were necessities of nature never to be coupled with recreation or enjoyment; and having bolted his food in a gloomy silence, bolts himself, in the same state. But for these animal observances, you might suppose the whole male portion of the company to be the melancholy ghosts of departed book-keepers, who had fallen dead at the desk; such is their weary air of business and calculation. Undertakers on duty would be sprightly beside them; and a collation of funeral-baked meats, in comparison with these meals, would be a sparkling festivity.

The people are all alike, too. There is no diversity of character. They travel about on the same errands, say and do the same things in exactly the same manner, and follow in the same dull cheerless round. All down the long table, there is scarcely a man who is in anything different from his neighbour. It is quite a relief to have, sitting opposite, that little girl of fifteen with the loquacious chin: who, to do her justice, acts up to it, and fully identifies nature's handwriting, for of all the small chatterboxes that ever invaded the repose of a drowsy ladies' cabin, she is the first and foremost. The beautiful girl, who sits a little beyond her—farther down the table there—married the young man with the dark whiskers, who sits beyond *her*, only last month. They are going to settle in the very Far West, where he has lived four years, but where she has never been. They were both overturned in a stage-coach the other day (a bad omen anywhere else, where overturns are not so common), and his head, which bears the marks of a recent wound, is bound up still. She was hurt too, at the same time, and lay insensible for some days; bright as her eyes are, now.

Farther down still, sits a man who is going some miles beyond their place of destination, to "improve" a newly discovered copper mine. He carries the village—that is to be—with him: a few frame cottages, and an apparatus for smelting the copper. He carries its people too. They are partly American and partly Irish, and herd together on the lower deck; where they amused themselves last evening till the night was pretty far advanced, by alternately firing off pistols and singing hymns.

They, and the very few who have been left at table twenty minutes, rise, and go away. We do so too; and passing through our little stateroom, resume our seats in the quiet gallery without.

A fine broad river always, but in some parts much wider than in others: and then there is usually a green island, covered with trees, dividing it into two streams. Occasionally, we stop for a few minutes, maybe to take in wood, maybe for passengers, at some small town or village (I ought to say city, every place is a city here); but the banks are for the most part deep solitudes, overgrown with trees, which, hereaabout, are already in leaf and very green. For miles, and miles, and miles, these solitudes are unbroken by any sign of human life or trace of human footstep; nor is anything seen to move about them but the blue jay, whose colour is so bright, and yet so delicate, that it looks like a flying flower. At lengthened intervals a log cabin, with its little space of cleared land about it, nestles under a rising ground, and sends its thread of blue smoke curling up into the sky. It stands in the corner of the poor field of wheat, which is full of great unsightly stumps, like earthy butchers'-blocks. Sometimes the ground is only just now cleared: the felled trees lying yet upon the soil: and the log-house only this morning begun. As we pass this clearing, the settler leans upon his axe or hammer, and looks wistfully at the people from the world. The children creep out of the temporary hut, which is like a gipsy tent upon the ground, and clap their hands and shout. The dog only glances round at us; and then looks up into his master's face again, as if he were rendered uneasy by any suspension of the common business, and had nothing more to do with pleasurers. And still there is the same, eternal foreground. The river has washed away its banks, and stately trees have fallen down into the stream. Some have been there so long, that they are mere dry grisly skeletons. Some have just toppled over, and having earth yet about their roots, are bathing their green heads in the river, and putting forth new shoots and branches. Some are almost sliding down, as you look at them. And some were drowned so long ago, that their bleached arms start out from the middle of the current, and seem to try to grasp the boat, and drag it under water.

Through such a scene as this, the unwieldy machine takes its hoarse sullen way: venting, at every revolution of the paddles, a loud high-pressure blast; enough, one would think, to waken up the host of Indians who lie buried in a great mound yonder: so old, that mighty oaks and other forest trees have struck their roots into its earth; and so high, that it is a hill, even among the hills that Nature planted round it. The very river, as though it shared one's feelings of compassion for the extinct tribes who lived so pleasantly here, in their blessed ignorance of white existence, hundreds of years ago, steals out of its way to ripple near this mound: and there are few places where the Ohio sparkles more brightly than in Big Grave Creek.

All this I see, as I sit in the little stern-gallery, mentioned just now. Evening slowly steals upon the landscape, and changes it before me, when we stop to set some emigrants ashore.

Five men, as many women, and a little girl. All their worldly goods are a bag, a large chest, and an old chair: one, old, high-backed, rush-bottomed chair: a solitary settler in itself. They are rowed ashore in the boat, while the vesssl stands a little off awaiting its return, the water being shallow. They are landed at the foot of a high bank, on the summit of which are a few log cabins, attainable only by a long winding path. It is growing dusk; but the sun is very red, and shines in the water and on some of the tree-tops, like fire.

The men get out of the boat first; help out the women; take out the bag, the chest, the chair; bid the rowers "good by;" and shove the boat off for them. At the first plash of the oars in the water, the oldest woman of the party sits down in the old chair, close to the water's edge, without speaking a word. None of the others sit down, though the chest is large enough for many seats. They all stand where they landed, as if stricken into stone; and look after the boat. So they remain, quite still and silent: the old woman and her old chair in the centre; the bag and chest upon the shore, without anybody heeding them: all eyes fixed upon the boat. It comes alongside, is made fast, the men jump on board, the engine is put in motion, and we go hoarsely on again. There they stand yet, without the motion of a hand. I can see them, through my glass, when, in the distance and increasing darkness, they are mere specks to the eye: lingering there still: the old woman in the old chair, and all the rest about her: not stirring in the least degree. And thus I slowly lose them.

The night is dark, and we proceed within the shadow of the wooded bank, which makes it darker. After gliding past the sombre maze of boughs for a long time, we come upon an open space where the tall trees are burning. The shape of every branch and twig is expressed in a deep red glow, and as the light wind stirs and ruffles it, they seem to vegetate in fire. It is such a sight as we read of in legends of enchanted forests: saving that it is sad to see these noble works wasting away so awfully, alone; and to think how many years must come and go before the magic that created them will rear their like upon this ground again. But the time will come: and when, in their changed ashes, the growth of centuries unborn has struck its roots, the restless men of distant ages will repair to these again unpeopled solitudes; and their fellows, in cities far away, that slumber now, perhaps, beneath the rolling sea, will read, in language strange to any ears in being now but very old to them, of primeval forests where the axe was never heard, and where the jungled ground was never trodden by a human foot.

Midnight and sleep blot out these scenes and thoughts: and when the morning shines again, it gilds the house-tops of a lively city, before whose broad paved wharf the boat is moored; with other boats, and flags, and moving wheels, and hum of men around it; as though there were not a solitary or silent rood of ground within the compass of a thousand miles.

Cincinnati is a beautiful city; cheerful, thriving, and animated. I have not often seen a place that commends itself so favourably and pleasantly to a stranger at the first glance as this does: with its clean houses of red and white, its well-paved roads, and footways of bright tile. Nor does it become less prepossessing on a closer acquaintance. The streets are broad and airy, the shops extremely good, the private residences remarkable for their elegance and neatness. There is something of invention and fancy in the varying styles of these latter erections, which, after the dull company of the steamboat, is perfectly delightful, as conveying an assurance that there are such qualities still in existence. The disposition to ornament these pretty villas and render them attractive, leads to the culture of trees and flowers, and the laying out of well-kept gardens, the sight of which, to those who walk along the streets, is inexpressibly refreshing and agreeable. I was quite charmed with the appearance of the town, and its adjoining suburb of Mount Auburn; from which the city, lying in an amphitheatre of hills, forms a picture of remarkable beauty, and is seen to great advantage.

There happened to be a great Temperance Convention held here on the day after our arrival; and as the order of march brought the procession under the windows of the hotel in which we lodged, when they started in the morning, I had a good opportunity of seeing it. It comprised several thousand men; the members of various "Washington Auxiliary Temperance Societies;" and was marshalled by officers on horseback, who cantered briskly up and down the line, with scarves and ribands of bright colours fluttering out behind them gayly. There were bands of music, too, and banners out of number; and it was a fresh, holyday-looking concourse altogether.

I was particularly pleased to see the Irishmen, who formed a distinct society among themselves, and mustered very strong with their green scarves; carrying their national Harp and their Portrait of Father Mathew, high above the people's heads. They looked as jolly and good-humoured as ever; and, working the hardest for their living and doing any kind of sturdy labour that came in their way, were the most independent fellows there, I thought.

The banners were very well painted and flaunted down the street famously. There was the smiting of the rock, and the gushing forth of the waters; and there was a temperate man with "considerable of a hatchet" (as the standard-bearer would probably have said), aiming a deadly blow at a serpent which was apparently about to spring upon him from the top of a barrrel of spirits. But the chief feature of this part of the show was a huge allegorical device, borne among the ship-carpenters, on one side whereof the steamboat Alcohol was represented bursting her boiler and exploding with a great crash, while upon the other, the good ship Temperance sailed away with a fair wind, to the heart's content of the captain, crew, and passengers.

After going round the town, the procession repaired to a certain appointed place, where, as the printed programme set forth, it would be received by the children of the different free-schools, "singing Temperance Songs." I was prevented from getting there, in time to hear these Little Warblers, or to report upon this novel kind of vocal entertainment: novel, at least, to me: but I found, in a large open space, each society gathered round its own banners, and listening in silent attention to its own orator. The speeches, judging from the little I could hear of them, were certainly adapted to the occasion, as having that degree of relationship to cold water which wet blankets may claim: but the main thing was the conduct and appearance of the audience throughout the day; and that was admirable and full of promise.

Cincinnati is honourably famous for its free-schools, of which it has so many that no person's child among its population can, by possibility, want the means of education, which are extended, upon an average, to four thousand pupils, annually. I was only present in one of these establishments during the hours of instruction. In the boys' department, which was full of little urchins (varying in their ages, I should say, from six years old to ten or twelve), the master offered to institute an extemporary examination of the pupils in algebra; a proposal, which, as I was by no means confident of my ability to detect mistakes in that science, I declined with some alarm. In the girls' school, reading was proposed, and as I felt tolerably equal to that art, I expressed my willingness to hear a class.—Books were distributed accordingly, and some half dozen girls relieved each other in reading paragraphs from English History. But it was a dry compilation, infinitely above their powers; and when they had blundered through three or four dreary passages concerning the Treaty of Amiens, and other thrilling topics of the same nature (obviously without comprehending ten words), I expressed myself quite satisfied. It is very possible that they only mounted to this exalted stave in the Ladder of Learning, for the astonishment of a visiter; and that at other times they keep upon its lower rounds; but I should have been much better pleased and satisfied if I had heard them exercised in simpler lessons, which they understood.

As in every other place I visited, the Judges here were gentlemen of high character and attainments. I was in one of the courts for a few minutes, and found it like those to which I have already referred. A nuisance cause was trying; there were not many spectators; and the witnesses, counsel, and jury, formed a sort of family circle, sufficiently jocose and snug.

The society with which I mingled, was intelligent, courteous and agreeable. The inhabitants of Cincinnati are proud of their city, as one of the most interesting in America: and with reason: for beautiful and thriving as it is now, and containing, as it does, a population of fifty thousand souls, but two-and-fifty years have passed away since the ground on which it stands (bought at that time for a few dollars) was a wild wood, and its citizens were but a handful of dwellers in scattered log huts upon the river's shore.

CHAPTER XII.

FROM CINCINNATI TO LOUISVILLE IN ANOTHER WESTERN STEAMBOAT; AND FROM LOUISVILLE TO ST. LOUIS IN ANOTHER. ST. LOUIS.

Leaving Cincinnati at eleven o'clock in the forenoon, we embarked for Louisville in the Pike steamboat, which, carrying the mails, was a packet of a much better class than that in which we had come from Pittsburg. As this passage does not occupy more than twelve or thirteen hours, we arranged to go ashore that night: not coveting the distinction of sleeping in a state-room, when it was possible to sleep anywhere else.

There chanced to be on board this boat, in addition to the usual dreary crowd of passengers, one Pitchlynn, a chief of the Choctaw tribe of Indians, who *sent in his card* to me, and with whom I had the pleasure of a long conversation.

He spoke English perfectly well, though he had not begun to learn the language, he told me, until he was a young man grown. He had read many books; and Scott's poetry appeared to have left a strong impression on his mind; especially the opening of The Lady of the Lake, and the great battle scene in Marmion, in which, no doubt from the congeniality of the subjects to his own pursuits and tastes, he had great interest and delight. He appeared to understand correctly, all he had read; and whatever fiction had enlisted his sympathy in its belief, had done so keenly and earnestly, I might almost say fiercely. He was dressed in our ordinary every-day costume, which hung about his fine figure loosely, and with indifferent grace. On my telling him that I regretted not to see him in his own attire, he threw up his right arm, for a moment, as though he were brandishing some heavy weapon, and answered, as he let it fall again, that his race were losing many things besides their dress, and would soon be seen upon the earth no more; but he wore it at home, he added proudly.

He told me that he had been away from his home, west of the Mississippi, seventeen months: and was now returning. He had been chiefly at Washington on some negotiations pending between his Tribe and the Government; which were not settled yet (he said in a melancholy way), and he feared never would be; for what could a few poor Indians do, against such well-skilled men of business as the whites? He had no love for Washington; tired of towns and cities very soon; and longed for the Forest and the Prairie.

I asked him what he thought of Congress? He answered, with a smile, that it wanted dignity, in an Indian's eyes.

He would very much like, he said, to see England before he died; and spoke with much interest about the great things to be seen there. When I told him of that chamber in the British Museum wherein are preserved household memorials of a race that ceased to be, thousands of years ago, he was very attentive, and it was not hard to see that he had a reference in his mind to the gradual fading away of his own people.

This led us to speak of Mr. Catlin's gallery, which he praised highly: observing that his own portrait was among the collection, and that all the likenesses were "elegant." Mr. Cooper, he said, had painted the Red Man well; and so would I, he knew, if I would go home with him and hunt buffaloes, which he was quite anxious I should do. When I told him that supposing I went, I should not be very likely to damage the buffaloes much, he took it as a great joke and laughed heartily.

He was a remarkably handsome man: some years past forty I should judge; with long black hair, an aquiline nose, broad cheek bones, a sunburnt complexion, and a very bright, keen, dark, and piercing eye. There were but twenty thousand of the Choctaws left, he said, and their number was decreasing every day. A few of his brother chiefs had been obliged to become civilized, and to make themselves acquainted with what the whites knew, for it was their only chance of existence. But they were not many; and the rest were as they always had been. He dwelt on this: and said several times that unless they tried to assimilate themselves to their conquerors, they must be swept away before the strides of civilized society.

When we shook hands at parting, I told him he must come to England, as he longed to see the land so much; that I should hope to see him there, one day; and that I could promise him he would be well received and kindly treated. He was evidently pleased by this assurance, though he rejoined with a good-humoured smile and an arch shake of his head, that the English used to be very fond of the Red Man when they wanted their help, but had not cared much for them since.

He took his leave; as stately and complete a gentleman of Nature's making, as ever I beheld; and moved among the people in the boat, another kind of being. He sent me a lithographed portrait of himself soon afterward; very like, though scarcely handsome enough; which I have carefully preserved in memory of our brief acquaintance.

There was nothing very interesting in the scenery of this day's journey, which brought us, at midnight, to Louisville. We slept at the Galt House; a splendid hotel; and were as handsomely lodged as though we had been in Paris, rather than hundreds of miles beyond the Alleghanies.

The city presenting no objects of sufficient interest to detain us on our way, we resolved to proceed next day by another steamboat, the Fulton, and to join it, about noon, at a suburb called Portland, where it would be delayed some time in passing through a canal.

The interval, after breakfast, we devoted to riding through the town, which is regular and cheerful: the streets being laid out at right angles, and planted with young trees. The buildings are smoky and blackened, from the use of bituminous coal, but an Englishman is well used to that appearance, and indisposed to quarrel with it. There did not appear to be much business stirring; and some unfinished buildings and improvements seemed to intimate that the city had been over-built in the ardour of "going ahead," and was suffering under the reaction consequent upon such feverish forcing of its powers.

On our way to Portland, we passed a "Magistrate's office," which amused me, as looking far more like a dame school than any police establishment; for this awful Institution was nothing but a little lazy, good-for-nothing front parlour, open to the street; wherein two or three figures (I presume the magistrate and his myrmidons) were basking in the sunshine, the very effigies of languor and repose. It was a perfect picture of Justice retired from business for want of customers; her sword and scales sold off; napping comfortably with her legs upon the table.

Here, as elsewhere in these parts, the road was perfectly alive with pigs of all ages, lying about in every direction, fast asleep; or grunting along in quest of hidden dainties. I had always a sneaking kindness for these odd animals, and found a constant source of amusement, when all others failed, in watching their proceedings. As we were riding along this morning, I observed a little incident between two youthful pigs, which was so very human as to be inexpressibly comical and grotesque at the time, though I dare say, in telling, it is same enough.

One young gentleman (a very delicate porker with several straws sticking about his nose, betokening recent investigations in a dunghill) was walking deliberately on, profoundly thinking, when suddenly his brother, who was lying in a miry hole, unseen by him, rose up immediately before his startled eyes, ghostly with damp mud. Never was pig's whole mass of blood so turned. He started back at least three feet, gazed for a moment, and then shot off as hard as he could go: his excessively little tail vibrating with speed and terror like a distraced pendulum. But before he had gone very far, he began to reason with himself as to the nature of this frightful appearance; and as he reasoned, he relaxed his speed by gradual degrees; until at last he stopped, and faced about. There was his brother, with the mud upon him, glazing in the sun, yet staring out of the very same hole, perfectly amazed at his proceedings! He was no sooner assured of this; and he assured himself so carefully that one may almost say he shaded his eyes with his hand to see the better; than he came back at a round trot, pounced upon him, and summarily took off a piece of his tail, as a caution to him to be careful what he was about for the future, and never to play tricks with his family any more.

We found the steamboat in the canal, waiting for the slow process of getting through the lock, and went on board, where we shortly afterward had a new kind of visiter in the person of a certain Kentucky giant, whose name is Porter, and who is of the moderate height of seven feet eight inches in his stockings.

There never was a race of people who so completely gave the lie to history as these giants, or whom all the chroniclers have so cruelly libelled. Instead of roaring and ravaging about the world, constantly catering for their cannibal larders, and perpetually going to market in an unlawful manner, they are the meekest people in any man's acquaintance: rather inclining to milk and vegetable diet, and bearing anything for a quiet life. So decidedly are amiability and mildness their characteristics, that I confess I look upon that youth who distinguished himself by the slaughter of these inoffensive persons, as a false-hearted brigand, who, pretending to philanthropic motives, was secretly influenced only by the wealth stored up within their castles, and the hope of plunder. And I lean the more to this opinion from finding that even the historian of those exploits, with all his partiality for his hero, is fain to admit that the slaughtered monsters in question were of a very innocent and simple turn; extremely guileless and ready of belief; lending a credulous ear to the most improbable tales; suffering themselves to be easily entrapped into pits; and even (as in the Welsh giant), with an excess of the hospitable politeness of a landlord, ripping themselves open, rather than hint at the possiblity of their guests being versed in the vagabond arts of sleight-of-hand and hocus-pocus.

The Kentucky giant was but another illustration of the truth of this position. He had a weakness in the region of the knees, and a trustfulness in his long face, which appealed even to five feet nine for encouragement and support. He was only twenty-five years old, he said, and had grown recently, for it had been found necessary to make an addition to the legs of his inexpressibles. At fifteen he was a short boy, and in those days his English father and his Irish mother had rather snubbed him, as being too small of stature to sustain the credit of the family. He added that his health had not been good, though it was better now; but short people are not wanting who whisper that he drinks too hard.

I understand he drives a hackney-coach, though how he does it, unless he stands on the footboard behind, and lies along the roof upon his chest, with his chin in the box, it would be difficult to comprehend. He brought his gun with him, as a curiosity. Christened "The Little Rifle," and displayed outside a shop-window, it would make the fortune of any retail business in Holborn. When he had shown himself, and talked a little while, he withdrew with this pocket instrument, and went bobbing down the cabin, among men of six feet high and upward, like a lighthouse walking among lampposts.

Within a few minutes afterward we were out of the canal and in the Ohio River again.

The arrangements of the boat were like those of the Messenger, and the passengers were of the same order of people. We fed at the same times, on the same kind of viands, in the same dull manner, and with the same observances. The company appeared to be oppressed by the same tremendous concealments, and had as little capacity of enjoyment or light-heartedness. I never in my life did see such listless, heavy dulness as brooded over these meals: the very recollection of it weighs me down, and makes me for the moment wretched. Reading and writing on my knee, in our little cabin, I really dreaded the coming of the hour that summoned us to table; and was as glad to escape from it again, as if it had been a penance or a punishment. Healthy cheerfulness and good spirits forming a part of the banquet, I could soak my crusts in the fountain with Le Sage's strolling player, and revel in their glad enjoyment: but sitting down with so many fellow-animals to ward off thirst and hunger as a business; to empty, each creature, his Yahoo's trough as quickly as he can, and then slink sullenly away; to have these social sacraments stripped of everything but the mere greedy satisfaction of the natural cravings, goes so against the grain with me, that I seriously believe the recollection of these funeral feasts will be a waking nightmare to me all my life.

There was some relief in this boat, too, which there had not been in the other, for the captain (a blunt, good-natured fellow) had his handsome wife with him, who was disposed to be lively and agreeable, as were a few other lady-passengers who had their seats about us at the same end of the table. But nothing could have made head against the depressing influence of the general bod . There was a magnetism of dulness in them which would have beaten down the most facetious companion that the earth ever knew. A jest would have been a crime, and a smile would have faded into a grinning horror. Such deadly, leaden people; such systematic, plodding, weary, insupportable heaviness; such a mass of indigestion in respect of all that was genial, jovial, frank, social, or hearty, never, sure, was brought together elsewhere since the world began.

Nor was the scenery, as we approached the junction of the Ohio and Mississippi Rivers, at all inspiriting in its influence. The trees were stunted in their growth; the banks were low and flat; the settlements and log cabins fewer in number; their inhabitants more wan and wretched than any we had encountered yet. No songs of birds were in the air, no pleasant scents, no moving lights and shadows from swift passing clouds. Hour after hour, the changeless glare of the hot, unwinking sky, shone upon the same monotonous objects. Hour after hour, the river rolled along, as wearily and slowly as the time itself.

At length, on the morning of the third day, we arrived at a spot so much more desolate than any we had yet beheld, that the forlornest places we had passed, were, in comparison with it, full of interest. At the junction of the two rivers, on ground so flat, and low, and marshy, that at certain seasons of the year it is inundated to the house-tops, lies a breeding-place of fever, ague, and death; vaunted in England as a mine of golden hope, and speculated in, on the faith of monstrous representations, to many people's ruin. A dismal swamp, on which the half-built houses rot away: cleared here and there for the space of a few yards, and teeming then with rank, unwholesome vegetation, in whose baleful shade the wretched wanderers who are tempted hither, droop, and die, and lay their bones; the hateful Mississippi circling and eddying before it, and turning off upon its southern course, a slimy monster hideous to behold; a hotbed of disease, an ugly sepulchre, a grave uncheered by any gleam of promise: a place without one single quality in earth, or air, or water, to commend it: such is this dismal Cairo.

But what words shall describe the Mississippi, great father of rivers, who (praise be to Heaven) has no young children like him! An enormous ditch, sometimes two or three miles wide, running liquid mud six miles an hour; its strong and frothy current choked and obstructed everywhere by huge logs and whole forest trees; now twining themselves together in great rafts, from the interstices of which a sedgy, lazy foam works up, to float upon the water's top; now rolling past like monstrous bodies, their tangled roots showing like matted hair; now glancing singly by like giant leeches, and now writhing round and round in the vortex of some small whirlpool like wounded snakes. The banks low, the trees dwarfish, the marshes swarming with frogs, the wretched cabins, few and far apart, their inmates hollow-cheeked and pale, the weather very hot, moschetoes penetrating into every crack and crevice of the boat, mud and slime on everything: nothing pleasant in its aspect but the harmless lightning which flickers every night upon the dark horizon.

For two days we toiled up this foul stream, striking constantly against the floating timber, or stopping to avoid those more dangerous obtacles, the snags, or sawyers, which are the hidden trunks of trees that have their roots below the tide. When the nights are very dark, the look-out, stationed in the head of the boat, knows by the ripple of the water if any great impediment be near at hand, and rings a bell beside him, which is the signal for the engine to be stopped; but always in the night this bell has work to do, and after every ring there comes a blow, which renders it no easy matter to remain in bed.

The decline of day here was very gorgeous; tinging the firmament deeply with red and gold, up to the very keystone of the arch above us. As the sun went down behind the bank, the slightest blades of grass upon it seemed to become as distinctly visible as the arteries in the skeleton of a leaf; and when, as it slowly sank, the red and golden bars upon the water grew dimmer and dimmer yet, as if they were sinking, too; and all the glowing colours of departing day paled inch by inch before the sombre night; the scene became a thousand times more lonesome and more dreary than before, and all its influences darkened with the sky.

We drank the muddy water of this river while we were upon it. It is considered wholesome by the natives, and is something more opaque than gruel. I have seen water like it at the filter-shops, but nowhere else.

On the fourth night after leaving Louisville, we reached St. Louis, and here I witnessed the conclusion of an incident, trifling enough in itself, but very pleasant to see, which had interested me during the whole journey.

There was a little woman on board, with a little baby, and both little woman and little child were cheerful, good-looking, bright-eyed, and fair to see. The little woman had been passing a long time with her sick mother in New-York, and had left her home in St. Louis, in that condition in which ladies who truly love their lords desire to be. The baby was born in her mother's house; and she had not seen her husband (to whom she was now returning) for twelve months, having left him a month or two after their marriage.

Well, to be sure there never was a little woman so full of hope, and tenderness, and love, and anxiety, as this little woman was: and all day long she wondered whether "He" would be at the wharf; and whether "He" had got her letter; and whether, if she sent the baby ashore by somebody else, "He" would know it, meeting it in the street: which, seeing that he had never set eyes upon it in his life, was not very likely in the abstract, but was probable enough to the young mother. She was such an artless little creature; and was in such a sunny, beaming, hopeful state; and let out all this matter clinging close about her heart, so freely; that all the other lady passengers entered into the spirit of it as much as she; and the captain (who heard all about it from his wife), was wondrous sly, I promise you: inquiring, every time we met at table, as in forgetfulness, whether she expected anybody to meet her at St. Louis, and whether she would want to go ashore the night we reached it (but he supposed she wouldn't), and cutting many other dry jokes of that nature. There was one little weazen, dried-apple-faced old woman, who took occasion to doubt the constancy of husbands in such circumstances of bereavement; and there was another lady (with a lap-dog) old enough to moralize on the lightness of human affections, and yet not so old that she could help nursing the baby now and then, or laughing with the rest, when the little woman called it by its father's name, and asked it all manner of fantastic questions concerning him in the joy of her heart.

It was something of a blow to the little woman, that when we were within twenty miles of our destination, it became clearly necessary to put this baby to bed. But she got over it with the same good-humour; tied a handkerchief round her head; and came out into the little gallery with the rest. Then, such an oracle as she became in reference to the localities! and such facetiousness as was displayed by the married ladies! and such sympathy as was shown by the single ones! and such peals of laughter as the little woman herself (who would just as soon have cried) greeted every jest with!

At last, there were the lights of St. Louis, and here was the wharf, and those were the steps: and the little woman, covering her face with her hands, and laughing (or seeming to laugh) more than ever, ran into her own cabin, and shut herself up. I have no doubt that in the charming inconsistency of such excitement, she stopped her ears, lest she should hear "Him" asking for her: but I did not see her do it.

Then, a great crowd of people rushed on board, though the boat was not yet made fast, but was wandering about among the other boats to find a landing-place: and everybody looked for the husband: and nobody saw him: when, in the midst of all—Heaven knows how she ever got there—there was the little woman clinging with both arms tight round the neck of a fine, good-looking, sturdy young fellow! and, in a moment afterward, there she was again, actually clapping her little hands for joy, as she dragged him through the small door of her small cabin, to look at the baby as he lay asleep!

We went to a large hotel, called the Planter's House: built like an English hospital, with long passages and bare walls, and sky-lights above the room-doors for the free circulation of air. There were a great many boarders in it; and as many lights sparkled and glistened from the windows down into the street below, when we drove up, as if it had been illuminated on some occasion of rejoicing. It is an excellent house, and the proprietors have most bountiful notions of providing the creature comforts. Dining alone with my wife in our own room one day, I counted fourteen dishes on the table at once.

In the old French portion of the town, the thoroughfares are narrow and crooked, and some of the houses are very quaint and picturesque: being built of wood, with tumble-down galleries before the windows, approachable by stairs, or rather ladders, from the street. There are queer little barbers' shops and drinking-houses too, in this quarter; and abundance of crazy old tenements with blinking casements, such as may be seen in Flanders. Some of these ancient habitations, with high garret gable-windows perking into the roofs, have a kind of French shrug about them; and being lop-sided with age, appear to hold their heads askew, besides, as if they were grimacing in astonishment at the American Improvements.

It is hardly necessary to say, that these consist of wharfs and warehouses, and new buildings in all directions; and of a great many vast plans which are still "progressing." Already, however, some very good houses, broad streets, and marble-fronted shops, have gone so far ahead as to be in a state of completion; and the town bids fair in a few years to improve considerably: though it is not likely ever to vie, in point of elegance or beauty, with Cincinnati.

The Roman Catholic religion, introduced here by the early French settlers, prevails extensively. Among the public institutions are a Jesuit college; a convent for "the Ladies of the Sacred Heart;" and a large chapel attached to the college, which was in course of erection at the time of my visit, and was intended to be consecrated on the second of December in the present year. The architect of this building is one of the reverend fathers of the school, and the works proceed under his sole direction. The organ will be sent from Belgium.

In addition to these establishments, there is a Roman Catholic cathedral, dedicated to Saint Francis Xavier; and an hospital, founded by the munificence of a deceased resident, who was a member of that church. It also sends missionaries from hence among the Indian tribes.

The Unitarian church is represented in this remote place, as in most other parts of America, by a gentleman of great worth and excellence. The poor have good reason to remember and bless it; for it befriends them, and aids the cause of rational education, without any sectarian or selfish views. It is liberal in all its actions; of kind construction; and of wide benevolence.

There are three free-schools already erected, and in full operation in this city. A fourth is building, and will soon be opened.

No man ever admits the unhealthiness of the place he dwells in (unless he is going away from it), and I shall therefore, I have no doubt, be at issue with the inhabitants of Saint Louis, in questioning the perfect salubrity of its climate, and in hinting that I think it must rather dispose to fever in the summer and autumnal seasons. Just adding, that it is very hot, lies among great rivers, and has vast tracts of undrained swampy land around it, I leave the reader to form his own opinion.

As I had a great desire to see a Prairie before turning back from the farthest point of my wanderings; and, as some gentlemen of the town had, in their hospitable consideration, an equal desire to gratify me; a day was fixed before my departure, for an expedition to the Looking-Glass Prairie, which is within thirty miles of the town. Deeming it possible that my readers may not object to know what kind of thing such a gipsy party may be at that distance from home, and among what sort of objects it moves, I will describe the jaunt in another chapter.

CHAPTER XIII.

A JAUNT TO THE LOOKING-GLASS PRAIRIE AND BACK.

I MAY premise that the word Prairie is variously pronounced *paraaer*, *parearer*, and *paroarer*. The latter mode of pronunciation is perhaps the most in favour.

We were fourteen in all, and all young men: indeed it is a singular though very natural feature in the society of these distant settlements, that it is mainly composed of adventurous persons in the prime of life, and has very few gray heads among it. There were no ladies: the trip being a fatiguing one; and we were to start at five o'clock in the morning, punctually.

I was called at four, that I might be certain of keeping nobody waiting; and having got some bread and milk for breakfast, threw up the window and looked down into the street, expecting to see the whole party busily astir, and great preparations going on below. But as everything was very quiet, and the street presented that hopeless aspect with which five o'clock in the morning is familiar elsewhere, I deemed it as well to go to bed again, and went accordingly.

I awoke again at seven o'clock, and by that time the party had assembled, and were gathered round, one light carriage, with a very stout axletree; one something on wheels like an amateur carrier's cart; one double phaeton of great antiquity and unearthly construction; one gig with a great hole in its back and a broken head; and one rider on horseback who was to go on before. I got into the first coach with three companions; the rest bestowed themselves in the other vehicles; two large baskets were made fast to the lightest; two large stone jars in wicker cases, technically known as demi-johns, were consigned to the "least rowdy" of the party for safe keeping; and the procession moved off to the ferry-boat, in which it was to cross the river bodily, men, horses, carriages, and all, as the manner in these parts is.

We got over the river in due course, and mustered again before a little wooden box on wheels, hove down, all-aslant, in a morass, with "MERCHANT TAILOR" painted in very large letters over the door. Having settled the order of proceeding, and the road to be taken, we started off once more, and began to make our way through an ill-favoured Black Hollow, called, less expressively, the American Bottom.

The previous day had been—not to say hot, for the term is weak and lukewarm in its power of conveying an idea of the temperature. The town had been on fire; in a blaze. But at night it had come on to rain in torrents, and all night long it had rained without cessation. We had a pair of very strong horses, but travelled at the rate of little more than a couple of miles an hour, through one unbroken slough of black mud and water. It had no variety but in depth. Now it was only half over the wheels, now it hid the axletree, and now the coach sank down in it almost to the windows. The air resounded in all directions with the loud chirping of the frogs, who, with the pigs (a coarse, ugly breed, as unwholesome looking as though they were the spontaneous growth of the country), had the whole scene to themselves. Here and there we passed a log-hut; but the wretched cabins were wide apart and thinly scattered, for, though the soil is very rich in this place, few people can exist in such a deadly atmosphere. On either side of the track, if it deserved the name, was the thick "bush;" and everywhere was stagnant, slimy, rotten, filthy water.

As it is the custom in these parts to give a horse a gallon or so of cold water whenever he is in a foam with heat, we halted for that purpose, at a log-inn in the wood, far removed from any other residence. It consisted of one room, bare-roofed and bare-walled, of course, with a loft above. The ministering priest was a swarthy young savage, in a shirt of cotton print like bed-furniture, and a pair of ragged trousers. There were a couple of young boys, too, nearly naked, lying idly by the well; and they, and he, and *the* traveller at the inn, turned out to look at us.

The traveller was an old man with a gray, grizzly beard two inches long, a shaggy mustache of the same hue, and enormous eyebrows, which almost obscured his lazy, semi-drunken glance, as he stood regarding us with folded arms, poising himself alternately upon his toes and heels. On being addressed by one of the party, he drew nearer, and said, rubbing his chin (which scraped under his horny hand like fresh gravel beneath a nailed shoe), that he was from Delaware, and had lately bought a farm "down there," pointing into one of the marshes where the stunted trees were thickest. He was "going," he added, to St. Louis, to fetch his family, whom he had left behind; but he seemed in no great hurry to bring on these encumbrances, for when we moved away, he loitered back into the cabin, and was plainly bent on stopping there so long as his money lasted. He was a great politician, of course, and explained his opinions at some length to one of our company; but I only remember that he concluded with two sentiments, one of which was, Somebody forever! and the other, Blast everybody else! which is by no means a bad abstract of the general creed in these matters.

When the horses were swollen out to about twice their natural dimensions (there seems to be an idea here that this kind of inflation improves their going), we went forward again, through mud and mire, and damp, and festering heat, and brake and bush, attended always by the music of the frogs and pigs, until nearly noon, when we halted at a place called Belleville.

Belleville was a small collection of wooden houses, huddled together in the very heart of the bush and swamp. Many of them had singularly bright doors of read and yellow; for the place had been lately visited by a travelling painter, "who got along," as I was told, "by eating his way." The criminal court was sitting, and was at that moment trying some criminals for horse-stealing, with whom it would most likely go hard; for live-stock of all kinds being necessarily very much exposed in the woods, is held by the community in rather higher value than human life; and for this reason juries generally make a point of finding all men indicted for cattle-stealing guilty, whether or no.

The horses belonging to the bar, the judge, and witnesses, were tied to temporary racks set up roughly in the road, by which is to be understood a forest path, nearly knee-deep in mud and slime.

There was a hotel in this place which, like all hotels in America, had its large dining-room for the public table. It was an odd, shambling, low-roofed outhouse, half cowshed and half kitchen, with a coarse brown canvass table-cloth, and tin sconces stuck against the walls, to hold candles at supper-time. The horseman had gone forward to have coffee and some eatables prepared, and they this were by time nearly ready. He had ordered "wheat-bread and chicken fixings," in preference to "corn-bread and common doings." The latter kind of refection includes only pork and bacon. The former comprehends broiled ham, sausages, veal-cutlets, steaks, and such other viands of that nature as may be supposed, by a tolerably wide poetical construction, to "fix" a chicken comfortably in the digestive organs of any lady or gentleman.

On one of the door-posts at this inn was a tin plate, whereon was inscribed in characters of gold "Doctor Crocus;" and on a sheet of paper, pasted up by the side of this plate, was a written announcement that Dr. Crocus would that evening deliver a lecture on Phrenology for the benefit of the Belleville public, at a charge, for admission, of so much a head.

Straying up stairs, during the preparation of the chicken fixings, I happened to pass the doctor's chamber; and as the door stood wide open, and the room was empty, I made bold to peep in.

It was a bare, unfurnished, comfortless room, with an unframed portrait hanging up at the head of the bed; a likeness, I take it, of the doctor, for the forehead was fully displayed, and great stress was laid by the artist upon its phrenological developments. The bed itself was covered with an old patchwork counterpane. The room was destitute of carpet or of curtain. There was a damp fireplace without any stove, full of wood-ashes; a chair, and a very small table; and on the last-named piece of furniture was displayed, in grand array, the doctor's library, consisting of some half a dozen greasy old books.

Now it certainly looked about the last apartment on the whole earth out of which any man would be likely to get anything to do him good. But the door, as I have said, stood coaxingly open, and plainly said, in conjunction with the chair, the portrait, the table, and the books, "Walk in, gentlemen, walk in! Don't be ill, gentlemen, when you may be well in no time. Doctor Crocus is here, gentlemen, the celebrated Doctor Crocus! Doctor Crocus has come all this way to cure you, gentlemen. If you haven't heard of Doctor Crocus, it's your fault, gentlemen, who live a little way out of the world here, not Doctor Crocus's. Walk in, gentlemen, walk in!"

In the passage below, when I went down stairs again, was Doctor Crocus himself. A crowd had flocked in from the Court-house, and a voice from among them called out to the landlord, "Colonel! introduce Doctor Crocus."

"Mr. Dickens," says the colonel, "Doctor Crocus."

Upon which Doctor Crocus, who is a tall, fine-looking Scotchman, but rather fierce and warlike in appearance for a professor of the peaceful art of healing, bursts out of the concourse with his right arm extended, and his chest thrown out as far as it will possibly come, and says,

"Your countryman, sir!"

Whereupon Doctor Crocus and I shake hands; and Doctor Crocus looks as if I didn't by any means realize his expectations, which, in a linen blouse, and a great straw hat with a green riband, and no gloves, and my face and nose profusely ornamented with the stings of moschetoes and the bites of bugs, it is very likely I did not.

"Long in these parts, sir?" says I.

"Three or four months, sir," says the doctor.

"Do you think of soon returning to the old country, sir?" says I.

Doctor Crocus makes no verbal answer, but gives me an imploring look, which says so plainly "Will you ask me that again, a little louder, if you please?" that I repeat the question.

"Think of soon returning to the old country, sir!" repeats the doctor.

"To the old country, sir," I rejoin.

Doctor Crocus looks round upon the crowd to observe the effect he produces, rubs his hands, and says in a very loud voice,

"Not yet a while, sir, not yet. You won't catch me at that just yet, sir. I am a little too fond of freedom for *that*, sir. Ha, ha! It's not so easy for a man to tear himself from a free country such as this is, sir. Ha, ha! No, no! Ha, ha! None of that till one's obliged to do it, sir. No, no!"

As Doctor Crocus says these latter words, he shakes his head knowingly, and laughs again. Many of the by-standers shake their heads in concert with the doctor, and laugh too, and look at each other as much as to say, "A pretty bright and first-rate sort of chap is Crocus!" and unless I am very much mistaken, a good many people went to the lecture that night who never thought about phrenology, or about Doctor Crocus either, in all their lives before.

From Belleville, we went on through the same desolate kind of waste, and constantly attended, without the interval of a moment, by the same music, until, at three o'clock in the afternoon, we halted once more at a village called Lebanon to inflate the horses again, and give them some corn besides, of which they stood much in need. Pending this ceremony, I walked into the village, where I met a full-sized dwelling-house coming down-hill at a round trot, drawn by a score or more of oxen.

The public-house was so very clean and good a one, that the managers of the jaunt resolved to return to it, and put up there for the night, if possible. This course decided on, and the horses being well refreshed, we again pushed forward, and came upon the prairie at sunset.

It would be difficult to say why or how though it was possibly from having heard and read so much about it—but the effect on me was disappointment. Looking towards the setting sun, there lay, stretched out before my view, a vast expanse of level ground, unbroken, save by one thin line of trees, which scarcely amounted to a scratch upon the great blank, until it met the glowing sky, wherein it seemed to dip, mingling with its rich colours, and mellowing in its distant blue. There it lay, a tranquil sea or lake without water, if such a simile be admissible, with the day going down upon it; a few birds wheeling here and there: and solitude and silence reigning paramount around. But the grass was not yet high; there were bare black patches on the ground; and the few wild flowers that the eye could see, were poor and scanty. Great as the picture was, its very flatness and extent, which left nothing to the imagination, tamed it down and cramped its interest. I felt little of that sense of freedom and exhilaration which a Scottish heath inspires, or even our English downs awaken. It was lonely and wild, but oppressive in its barren monotony. I felt that in traversing the prairies I could never abandon myself to the scene, forgetful of all else, as I should do instinctively, were the heather underneath my feet, or an iron-bound coast beyond; but should often glance towards the distant and frequently-receding line of the horizon, and wished it gained and passed. It is not a scene to be forgotten, but it is scarcely one, I think (at all events, as I saw it), to remember with much pleasure, or to covet the looking-on again, in after life.

We encamped near a solitary log-house, for the sake of its water, and dined upon the plain. The baskets contained roast fowls, buffalo's tongue (an exquisite dainty, by-the-way), ham, bread, cheese, and butter; biscuits, Champagne, sherry; lemons and sugar for punch; and abundance of rough ice. The meal was delicious, and the entertainers were the soul of kindness and good humour. I have often recalled that cheerful party to my pleasant recollection since, and shall not easily forget, in junketings nearer home with friends of older date, my boon companions on the prairie.

Returning to Lebanon that night, we lay at the little inn at which we had halted in the afternoon. In point of cleanliness and comfort it would have suffered by no comparison with any village ale-house, of a homely kind, in England.

Rising at five o'clock next morning, I took a walk about the village; none of the houses were strolling about to-day, but it was early for them yet, perhaps; and then amused myself by lounging in a kind of farm-yard behind the tavern, of which the leading features were, a strange jumble of rough sheds for stables; a rude colonnade, built as a cool place of summer resort; a deep well; a great earthen mound for keeping vegetables in, in winter time; and a pigeon-house, whose little apertures looked, as they do in all pigeon-houses, very much too small for the admission of the plump and swelling-breasted birds who were strutting about it, though they tried to get in ever so hard. That interest exhausted, I took a survey of the inn's two parlours, which were decorated with coloured prints of Washington and President Madison, and of a white-faced young lady (much speckled by the flies), who held up her gold neck-chain for the admiration of the spectator, and informed all admiring comers that she was "Just Seventeen;" although I should have thought her older. In the best room were two oil portraits of the kit-cat size, representing the landlord and his infant son; both looking as bold as lions, and staring out of the canvass with an intensity that would have been cheap at any price. They were painted, I think, by the artist who had touched up the Belleville doors with red and gold; for I seemed to recognise his style immediately.

After breakfast, we started to return by a different way from that which we had taken yesterday, and coming up at ten o'clock with an encampment of German emigrants carrying their goods in carts, who had made a rousing fire which they were just quitting, stopped there to refresh. And very pleasant the fire was; for, hot though it had been yesterday, it was quite cold to-day, and the wind blew keenly. Looming in the distance, as we rode along, was another of the ancient Indian burial-places, called The Monks' Mound; in memory of a body of fanatics of the order of La Trappe, who founded a desolate convent there, many years ago, when there were no settlers within a thousand miles, and were all swept off by the pernicious climate; in which lamentable fatality, few rational people will suppose, perhaps, that society experienced any very severe deprivation.

The track of to-day had the same features as the track of yesterday. There were the swamp, the bush, the perpetual chorus of frogs, the rank unseemly growth, the unwholesome steaming earth. Here and there, and frequently too, we encountered a solitary broken-down wagon, full of some new settler's goods. It was a pitiful sight to see one of these vehicles deep in the mire; the axle-tree broken; a wheel lying idly by its side; the man gone miles away, to look for assistance; the woman seated among their wandering household gods with a baby at her breast, a picture of forlorn, dejected patience; the team of oxen crouching down mournfully in the mud, and breathing forth such clouds of vapour from their mouths and nostrils, that all the damp mist and fog around seemed to have come direct from them.

In due time we mustered once again before the merchant tailor's, and having done so, crossed over to the city in the ferry-boat; passing, on the way, a spot called Bloody Island, the duelling ground of St. Louis, and so designated in honour of the last fatal combat fought there, which was with pistols, breast to breast. Both combatants fell dead upon the ground; and possibly some rational people may think of them, as of the gloomy madmen on the Monks' Mound, that they were no great loss to the community.

CHAPTER XIV.

RETURN TO CINCINNATI. A STAGE-COACH RIDE FROM THAT CITY TO COLUMBUS, AND THENCE TO SANDUSKY. SO, BY LAKE ERIE, TO THE FALLS OF NIAGARA.

As I had a desire to travel through the interior of the state of Ohio, and to "strike the lakes," as the phrase is, at a small town called Sandusky, to which that route would conduct us on our way to Niagara, we had to return from St. Louis by the way we had come, and to retrace our former track as far as Cincinnati.

The day on which we were to take leave of St. Louis being very fine; and the steamboat, which was to have started I don't know how early in the morning, postponing, for the third or fourth time, her departure until the afternoon; we rode forward to an old French village on the river, called properly Carondelet, and nicknamed Vide Poche, and arranged that the packet should call for us there.

The place consisted of a few poor cottages, and two or three public-houses; the state of whose larders certainly seemed to justify the second designation of the village, for there was nothing to eat in any of them. At length, however, by going back some half mile or so, we found a solitary house where ham and coffee were procurable; and there we tarried to await the advent of the boat, which would come in sight from the green before the door, a long way off.

It was a neat, unpretending village tavern, and we took our repast in a quaint little room with a bed in it, decorated with some old oil paintings, which in their time had probably done duty in a Catholic chapel or monastery. The fare was very good, and served with great cleanliness. The house was kept by a characteristic old couple, with whom we had a long talk, and who were perhaps a very good sample of that kind of people in the West.

The landlord was a dry, tough, hard-faced old fellow (not so very old either, for he was but just turned sixty, I should think), who had been out with the militia in the last war with England, and had seen all kinds of service—except a battle; and he had been very near seeing that, he added; very near. He had all his life been restless and locomotive, with an irresistible desire of change; and was still the son of his old self; for if he had nothing to keep him at home, he said (slightly jerking his hat and his thumb towards the window of the room in which the old lady sat, as we stood talking in front of the house) he would clean up his musket, and be off to Texas to-morrow morning. He was one of the very many descendants of Cain proper to this continent, who seemed destined from their birth to serve as pioneers in the great human army; who gladly go on from year to year extending its outposst, and leaving home after home behind them; and die at last, utterly regardless of their graves being left thousands of miles behind, by the wandering generation who succeed.

His wife was a domesticated, kind-hearted old soul, who had come with him "from the queen city of the world," which, it seemed, was Philadelphia; but had no love for this Western country, and indeed had little reason to bear it any; having seen her children, one by one, die here of fever in the full prime and beauty of their youth. Her heart was sore, she said, to think of them; and to talk on this theme, even to strangers, in that blighted place, so far from her old home, eased it somewhat, and became a melancholy pleasure.

The boat appearing towards evening, we bade adieu to the poor old lady and her vagrant spouse, and making for the nearest landing-place, were soon on board The Messenger again, in our old cabin, and steaming down the Mississippi.

If the coming up this river, slowly making head against the stream, be an irksome journey, the shooting down it with the turbid current is almost worse; for then the boat, proceeding at the rate of twelve or fifteen miles an hour, has to force its passage through a labyrinth of floating logs, which, in the dark, it is often impossible to see before-hand or avoid. All that night, the bell was never silent for five minutes at a time; and after every ring the vessel reeled again, sometimes beneath a single blow, sometimes beneath a dozen dealt in quick succession, the lightest of which seemed more than enough to beat in her frail keel, as though it had been pie-crust. Looking down upon the filthy river after dark, it seemed to be alive with monsters, as these black masses rolled upon the surface, or came starting up again, head first, when the boat, in ploughing her way among a shoal of such obstructions, drove a few among them for the moment under water. Sometimes, the engine stopped during a long interval, and then before her and behind, and gathering close about her on all sides, were so many of these ill-favoured obstacles that she was fairly hemmed in; the centre of a floating island; and was constrained to pause until they parted somewhere, as dark clouds will do before the wind, and opened by degrees a channel out.

In good time next morning, however, we came again in sight of the detestable morass called Cairo; and stopping there to take in wood, lay alongside a barge, whose starting timbers scarcely held together. It was moored to the bank, and on its side was painted, "Coffee House;" that being, I suppose, the floating paradise to which the people fly for shelter when they lose their houses for a month or two beneath the hideous waters of the Mississippi. But looking southward from this point, we had the satisfaction of seeing that intolerable river dragging its slimy length and ugly freight abruptly off towards New Orleans; and passing a yellow line which stretched across the current, were again upon the clear Ohio, never, I trust, to see the Mississippi more, saving in troubled dreams and nightmares. Leaving it for the company of its sparkling neighbour, was like the transition from pain to ease, or the awakening from a horrible vision to cheerful realities.

We arrived at Louisville on the fourth night, and gladly availed ourselves of its excellent hotel. Next day, we went on in the Ben Franklin, a beautiful mail steamboat, and reached Cincinnati shortly after midnight. Being by this time nearly tired of sleeping upon shelves, we had remained awake, to go ashore straightway;

and groping a passage across the dark decks of other boats, and among labyrinths of engine-machinery and leaking casks of molasses, we reached the streets, knocked up the porter at the hotel where we had stayed before, and were, to our great joy, safely housed soon afterward.

We rested but one day at Cincinnati, and then resumed our journey to Sandusky. As it comprised two varieties of stage-coach travelling, which, with those I have already glanced at, comprehend the main characteristics of this mode of transit in America, I will take the reader as our fellow-passenger, and pledge myself to perform the distance with all possible despatch.

Our place of destination in the first instance is Columbus. It is distant about a hundred and twenty miles from Cincinnati, but there is a macadamized road (rare blessing!) the whole way, and the rate of travelling upon it is six miles an hour.

We start at eight o'clock in the morning, in a great mail-coach, whose huge cheeks are so very ruddy and plethoric, that it appears to be troubled with a tendency of blood to the head. Dropsical it certainly is, for it will hold a dozen passengers inside. But, wonderful to add, it is very clean and bright, being nearly new, and rattles through the streets of Cincinnati gayly.

Our way lies through a beautiful country, richly cultivated, and luxuriant in its promise of an abundant harvest. Sometimes we pass a field where the strong bristling stalks of Indian corn look like a crop of walking-sticks, and sometimes an enclosure where the green wheat is springing up among a labyrinth of stumps; the primitive worm-fence is universal, and an ugly thing it is; but the farms are neatly kept, and, save for these differences, one might be travelling just now in Kent.

We often stop to water at a roadside inn, which is always dull and silent. The coachman dismounts and fills his bucket, and holds it to the horses' heads. There is scarcely ever any one to help him; there are seldom any loungers standing round, and never any stable-company with jokes to crack. Sometimes, when we have changed our team, there is a difficulty in starting again, arising out of the prevalent mode of breaking a young horse; which is to catch him, harness him against his will, and put him in a stage-coach without farther notice; but we get on somehow or other, after a great many kicks and a violent struggle, and jog on as before again.

Occasionally, when we stop to change, some two or three half-drunken loafers will come loitering out with their hands in their pockets, or will be seen kicking their heels in rocking-chairs, or lounging on the window-sill, or sitting on a rail within the colonnade; they have not often anything to say though, either to us or to each other, but sit there, idly staring at the coach and horses. The landlord of the inn is usually among them, and seems, of all the party, to be the least connected with the business of the house. Indeed he is with reference to the tavern, what the driver is in relation to the coach and passengers; whatever happens in his sphere of action, he is quite indifferent, and perfectly easy in his mind.

The frequent change of coachmen works no change or variety in the coachman's character. He is always dirty, sullen, and taciturn. If he be capable of smartness of any kind, moral or physical, he has a faculty of concealing it which is truly marvellous. He never speaks to you as you sit beside him on the box, and if you speak to him, he answers (if at all) in monosyllables. He points out nothing on the road, and seldom looks at anything; being, to all appearance, thoroughly weary of it, and of existence generally. As to doing the honours of his coach, his business, as I have said, is with the horses. The coach follows because it is attached to them and goes on wheels, not because you are in it. Sometimes, towards the end of a long stage, he suddenly breaks out into a discordant fragment of an election song, but his face never sings along with him; it is only his voice, and not often that.

He always chews and always spits, and never encumbers himself with a pocket-handkerchief. The consequences to the box passenger, especially when the wind blows towards him, are not agreeable.

Whenever the coach stops, and you can hear the voices of the inside passengers; or whenever any by-stander addresses them, or any one among them, or they address each other, you will hear one phrase repeated over and over, and over again, to the most extraordinary extent. It is an ordinary and unpromising phrase enough, being neither more nor less than "Yes, sir;" but it is adapted to every variety of circumstance, and fills up every pause in the conversation. Thus:

The time is one o'clock at noon. The scene, a place where we are to stay to dine, on this journey. The coach drives up to the door of an inn. The day is warm, and there are several idlers lingering about the tavern, and waiting for the public dinner. Among them, is a stout gentleman in a brown hat, swinging himself to and fro in a rocking-chair on the pavement.

As the coach stops, a gentleman in a straw hat looks out of the window.

STRAW HAT (To the stout gentleman in the rocking-chair). I reckon that's Judge Jefferson, a'nt it?

BROWN HAT (Still swinging, speaking very slowly, and without any emotion whatever). Yes, sir.

STRAW HAT. Warm weather, Judge.

BROWN HAT. Yes, sir.

STRAW HAT. There was a snap of cold last week.

BROWN HAT. Yes, sir.

STRAW HAT. Yes, sir.

A pause. They look at each other very seriously.

STRAW HAT. I calculate you'll have got through that case of the corporation judge, by this time, now?

BROWN HAT. Yes, sir.

STRAW HAT. How did the verdict go, sir?

BROWN HAT. For the defendant, sir.

STRAW HAT (Interrogatively). Yes, sir?

BROWN HAT (Affirmatively). Yes, sir.

BOTH (Musingly, as each gazes down the street). Yes, sir.

Another pause. They look at each other again, still more seriously than before.

BROWN HAT. This coach is rather behind its time to-day, I guess.

STRAW HAT (Doubtingly). Yes, sir.

BROWN HAT (Looking at his watch). Yes, sir; nigh upon two hours.

STRAW HAT (Raising his eyebrows in very great surprise). Yes, sir.

BROWN HAT (Decisively, as he puts up his watch). Yes, sir.

ALL THE OTHER INSIDE PASSENGERS (among themselves). Yes, sir.

COACHMAN (in a very surly tone). No it a'nt.

STRAW HAT (to the coachman). Well, I don't know, sir. We were a pretty tall time coming that last fifteen mile. That's a fact.

The coachman making no reply, and plainly declining to enter into any controversy on a subject so far removed from his sympathies and feelings, another passenger says "Yes, sir;" and the gentleman in the straw hat, in acknowledgment of his courtesy, says "Yes, sir" to him, in return. The straw hat then inquires of the brown hat, whether that coach in which he (the straw hat) then sits, is not a new one. To which the brown hat again makes answer, "Yes, sir."

STRAW HAT. I thought so. Pretty loud smell of varnish, sir?

BROWN HAT. Yes, sir.

ALL THE OTHER INSIDE PASSENGERS. Yes, sir.

BROWN HAT (to the company in general). Yes, sir.

The conversational powers of the company having been by this time pretty heavily taxed, straw hat opens the door and gets out, and all the rest alight also. We dine soon afterward with the boarders in the house, and have nothing to drink but tea and coffee. As they are both very bad, and the water is worse, I ask for brandy; but it is a Temperance Hotel, and spirits are not to be had for love or money. This preposterous forcing of unpleasant drinks down the reluctant throats of travellers is not at all uncommon in America, but I never discovered that the scruples of such wincing landlords induced them to preserve any unusually nice balance between the quality of their fare and their scale of charges: on the contrary, I rather suspected them of diminishing the one and exalting the other, by way of recompense for the loss of their profit on the sale of spirituous liquors. After all, perhaps, the plainest course for persons of such tender consciences would be, a total abstinence from tavern-keeping.

Dinner over, we get into another vehicle which is ready at the door (for the coach has been changed in the interval), and resume our journey, which continues through the same kind of country until evening, when we come to the town where we are to stop for tea and supper; and having delivered the mail-bags at the post-office, ride through the usual wide street, lined with the usual stores and houses (the drapers always having hung up at their door, by way of sign, a piece of bright red cloth), to the hotel where this meal is prepared. There being many boarders here, we sit down, a very large party, and a very melancholy one as usual. But there is a buxom hostess at the head of the table, and opposite, a simple Welsh schoolmaster with his wife and child, who came here, on a speculation of greater promise than performance, to teach the classics: and they are sufficient subjects of interest until the meal is over, and another coach is ready. In it we go on once more, lighted by a bright moon, until midnight; when we stop to change the coach again, and remain for half an hour or so in a miserable room, with a blurred lithograph of Washington over the smoky fire-place, and a mighty jug of cold water on the table; to which refreshment the moody passengers do so apply themselves, that they would seem to be, one and all, keen patients of Doctor Sangrado. Among them is a very little boy, who chews tobacco like a very big one; and a droning gentleman, who talks arithmetically and statistically on all subjects, from poetry downward; and who always speaks in the same key, with exactly the same emphasis, and with very grave deliberation. He came outside just now, and told me how that the uncle of a certain young lady who had been spirited away and married by a certain captain, lived in these parts; and how this uncle was so valiant and ferocious, that he shouldn't wonder if he were to follow the said captain to England, "and shoot him down in the street, wherever he found him;" in the feasibility of which strong measure I, being for the moment rather prone to contradiction, from feeling half asleep and very tired, declined to acquiesce: assuring him that if the uncle did resort to it, or gratified any other little whim of the like nature, he would find himself one morning prematurely throttled at the Old Bailey; and that he would do well to make his will before he went, as he would certainly want it before he had been in Britain very long.

On we go, all night, and by-and-by the day begins to break, and presently the first cheerful rays of the warm sun come slanting on us brightly. It sheds its light upon a miserable waste of sodden grass, and dull trees, and squalid huts, whose aspect is forlorn and grievous in the last degree. A very desert in the wood, whose growth of green is dank and noxious, like that upon the top of standing water; where poisonous fungus grows in the rare footprint on the oozy ground, and sprouts like witches' coral from the crevices in the cabin wall and floor; it is a hideous thing to lie upon the very threshold of a city. But it was purchased years ago, and as the owner cannot be discovered, the State has been unable to reclaim it. So there it remains, in the midst of cultivation and improvement, like ground accursed, and made obscene and rank by some great crime.

We reached Columbus shortly before seven o'clock, and stayed there, to refresh, that day and night: having excellent apartments in a very large unfinished hotel called the Neill House, which were richly fitted with the polished wood of the black walnut, and opened on a handsome portico and stone verandah, like rooms in some Italian mansion. The town is clean, and pretty, and, of course, is "going to be" much larger. It is the seat of the State Legisture of Ohio, and lays claim, in consequence, to some consideration and importance.

There being no stage-coach next day, upon the road we wished to take, I hired "an extra," at a reasonable charge, to carry us to Tiffin; a small town from whence there is a railroad to Sandusky. This extra was an ordinary four-horse stage-coach, such as I have described, changing horses and drivers, as the stage-coach would, but was exclusively our own for the journey. To ensure our having horses at the proper stations, and being incommoded by no strangers, the proprietors sent an agent on the box, who was to accompany us the whole way through; and thus attended, and bearing with us, besides, a hamper full of savoury cold meats, and fruit, and wine, we started off again, in high spirits, at half past six o'clock next morning, very much delighted to be by ourselves, and disposed to enjoy even the roughest journey.

It was well for us that we were in this humour, for the road we went over that day, was certainly enough to have shaken tempers that were not resolutely at Set Fair, down to some inches below Stormy. At one time we were all flung together in a heap at the bottom of the coach, and at another we were crushing our heads against the roof. Now, one side was down deep in the mire, and we were holding on to the other. Now, the coach was lying on the tails of the two wheelers; and now it was rearing up in the air, in a frantic state, with all four horses standing on the top of an insurmountable eminence, looking coolly back at it, as though they would say "Unharness us. It can't be done." The drivers on these roads, who certainly get over the ground in a manner which is quite miraculous, so twist and turn the team about in forcing a passage, corkscrew fashion, through the bogs and swamps, that it was quite a common circumstance on looking out of the window, to see the coachman with the ends of a pair of reins in his hands, apparently driving nothing, or playing at horses, and the leaders staring at one unexpectedly from the back of the coach, as if they had some idea of getting up behind. A great portion of the way was over what is called a corduroy road, which is made by throwing trunks of trees into a marsh, and leaving them to settle there. The very slightest of the jolts with which the ponderous carriage fell from log to log, was enough, it seemed, to have dislocated all the bones in the human body. It would be impossible to experience a similar set of sensations, in any other circumstances, unless perhaps in attempting to go up to the top of Saint Paul's in an omnibus. Never, never once, that day, was the coach in any position, attitude, or kind of motion to which we are accustomed in coaches. Never did it make the smallest approach to one's experience of the proceedings of any sort of vehicle that goes on wheels.

Still, it was a fine day, and the temperature was delicious, and though we had left Summer behind us in the west, and were fast leaving Spring, we were moving towards Niagara, and home. We alighted in a pleasant wood towards the middle of the day, dined on a fallen tree, and leaving our best fragments with a cottager, and our worst with the pigs (who swarm in this part of the country like grains of sand on the seashore, to the great comfort of our commissariat in Canada), we went forward again gayly.

As night came on, the track grew narrower and narrower, until at last it so lost itself among the trees, that the driver seemed to find his way by instinct. We had the comfort of knowing, at least, that there was no danger of his falling asleep, for every now and then a wheel would strike against an unseen stump with such a jerk, that he was fain to hold on pretty tight and pretty quick, to keep himself upon the box. Nor was there any reason to dread the least danger from furious driving, inasmuch as over that broken ground the horses had enough to do to walk; as to shying, there was no room for that; and a herd of wild elephants could not have run away in such a wood, with such a coach at their heels. So we stumbled along, quite satisfied.

These stumps of trees are a curious feature in American travelling. The varying illusions they present to the unaccustomed eye as it grows dark, are quite astonishing in their number and reality. Now, there is a Grecian urn erected in the centre of a lonely field; now there is a woman weeping at a tomb; now a very commonplace old gentleman in a white waistcoat, with a thumb thrust into each arm-hole of his coat; now a student poring on a book; now a crouching negro; now a horse, a dog, a cannon, an armed man; a hunch-back throwing off his cloak and stepping forth into the light. They were often as entertaining to me as so many glasses in a magic lantern, and never took their shapes at my bidding, but seemed to force themselves upon me, whether I would or no; and strange to say, I sometimes recognised in them, counterparts of figures once familiar to me in pictures attached to childish books, forgotten long ago.

It soon became too dark, however, even for this amusement, and the trees were so close together that the dry branches rattled against the coach on either side, and obliged us all to keep our heads within. It lightened, too, for three whole hours; each flash being very bright, and blue, and long; and as the vivid streaks came darting in among the crowded branches, and the thunder rolled gloomily above the tree tops, one could scarcely help thinking that there were better neighbourhoods at such a time than thick woods afforded.

At length, between ten and eleven o'clock at night, a few feeble lights appeared in the distance, and Upper Sandusky, an Indian village, where we were to stay till morning, lay before us.

They were gone to bed at the log inn, which was the only house of entertainment in the place, but soon answered to our knocking, and got some tea for us in a sort of kitchen or common room, tapestried with old newspapers, pasted against the wall. The bed-chamber to which my wife and I were shown, was a large, low, ghostly room; with a quantity of withered branches on the hearth, and two doors without any fastening, opposite to each other, both opening on the black night and wild country, and so contrived, tha one of them always blew the other open: a novelty in domestic architecture which I do not remember to have seen before, and which I was somewhat disconcerted to have forced on my attention after getting into bed, as I had a considerable sum in gold for our travelling expenses, in my dressing-case. Some of the luggage, however, piled against the panels, soon settled this difficulty, and my sleep would have been very much affected that night, I believe, though it had failed to do so.

My Boston friend climbed up to bed somewhere in the roof, where another guest was already snoring hugely. But being bitten beyond his power of endurance, he turned out again, and fled for shelter to the coach, which was airing itself in front of the house. This was not a very politic step, as it turned out; for the pigs scenting him, and looking upon the coach as a kind of pie with some manner of meat inside, grunted round it so hideously, that he was afraid to come out again, and lay there shivering till morning. Nor was it possible to warm him when he did come out, by means of a glass of brandy; for in Indian villages, the legislature, with a very good and wise intention, forbids the sale of spirits by tavern keepers. The precaution, however, is quite inefficacious, for the Indians never fail to procure liquor of a worse kind, at a dearer price, from travelling pedlers.

It is a settlement of the Wyoming Indians who inhabit this place. Among the company at breakfast was a mild old gentleman, who had been for many years employed by the United States Government in conducting negotiations with the Indians, and who had just concluded a treaty with these people, by which they bound themselves, in consideration of a certain annual sum, to remove next year to some land provided for them, west of the Mississippi, and a little way beyond St. Louis. He gave me a moving account of their strong attachment to the familiar scenes of their infancy, and in particular of their burial-places of their kindred; and of their great reluctance to leave them. He had witnessed many such removals, and always with pain, though he knew that they departed for their own good. The question whether this tribe should go or stay had been discussed among them a day or two before, in a hut erected for the purpose, the logs of which still lay upon the ground before the inn. When the speaking was done, the ayes and noes were ranged on opposite sides, and every male adult voted in his turn. The moment the result was known, the minority (a large one) cheerfully yielded to the rest, and withdrew all kind of opposition.

We met some of these poor Indians afterward, riding on shaggy ponies. They were so like gipsies, that if I could have seen any of them in England, I should have concluded, as a matter of course, that they belonged to that wandering and restless people.

Leaving this town directly after breakfast, we pushed forward again, over a rather worse road than yesterday, if possible, and arrived about noon at Tiffin, where we parted with the extra. At two o'clock we took the railroad; the travelling on which was very slow, its construction being indifferent, and the ground wet and marshy; and arrived at Sandusky in time to dine that evening. We put up at a comfortable little hotel on the brink of Lake Erie, lay there that night, and had no choice but to wait there next day, until a steamboat bound for Buffalo appeared. The town, which was sluggish and uninteresting enough, was something like the back of an English watering-place, out of the season.

Our host, who was very attentive and anxious to make us comfortable, was a handsome middle-aged man, who had come to this town from New England, in which part of the country he was "raised." When I say that he constantly walked in and out of the room with his hat on; and stopped to converse in the same free-and-easy state; and lay down on our sofa, and pulled his newspaper out of his pocket, and read it at his ease; I merely mention these traits as characteristic of the country: not at all as being matter of complaint, or as having been disagreeable to me. I should undoubtedly be offended by such proceedings at home, because there they are not the custom, and where they are not, they would be impertinences; but in America, the only desire of a good-natured fellow of this kind, is to treat his guests hospitably and well; and I have no more right, and I can truly say no more disposition, to measure his conduct by our English rule and standard, than I had to quarrel with him for not being of the exact stature which would qualify him for admission into the queen's grenadier guards. As little inclination had I to find fault with a funny old lady who was an upper domestic in this establishment, and who, when she came to wait upon us at any meal, sat herself down comfortably ln the most convenient chair, and producing a large pin to pick her teeth with, remained performing that ceremony, and steadfastly regarding us meanwhile with much gravity and composure (now and then pressing us to eat a little more), until it was time to clear away. It was enough for us, that whatever we wished done was done with great civility and readiness, and a desire to oblige, not only here, but everywhere else; and that all our wants were, in general, zealously anticipated.

We were taking an early dinner at this house, on the day after our arrival, which was Sunday, when a steamboat came in sight, and presently touched at the wharf. As she proved to be on her way to Buffalo, we hurried on board with all speed, and soon left Sandusky far behind us.

She was a large vessel of five hundred tons, and handsomely fitted up, though with high-pressure engines; which always conveyed that kind of feeling to me, which I should be likely to experience, I think, if I had lodgings on the first floor of a powder-mill. She was laden with flour, some casks of which commodity were stored upon the deck. The captain coming up to have a little conversation, and to introduce a friend, seated himself astride of one of these barrels, like a Bacchus of private life; and pulling a great clasp-knife out of his pocket, began to "whittle" it as he talked, by paring thin slices off the edges. And he whittled with such industry and hearty good will, that but for his being called away very soon, it must have disappeared bodily, and left nothing in its place but grist and shavings.

After calling at one or two flat places, with low dams stretching out into the lake, whereon were stumpy lighthouses, like windmills without sails, the whole looking like a Dutch vignette, we came at midnight to Cleveland, where we lay all night, and until nine o'clock next morning.

I entertained quite a curiosity in reference to this place, from having seen at Sandusky a specimen of its literature in the shape of a newspaper, which was very strong indeed upon the subject of Lord Ashburton's recent arrival at Washington, to adjust the points in dispute between the United States Government and Great Britain; informing its readers that as America had "whipped" England in her infancy, and whipped her again in her youth, so it was clearly necessary that she must whip her once again in her maturity; and pledging its credit to all true Americans, that if Mr. Webster did his duty in the approaching negotiations, and sent the English lord home again in double quick time, they should, within two years, "sing Yankee Doodle in Hyde Park, and Hail Columbia in the scarlet courts of Westminster!" I found it a pretty town, and had the satisfaction of beholding the outside of the office of the journal from which I have just quoted. I did not enjoy the delight of seeing the wit who indited the paragraphs in question, but I have no doubt he is a prodigious man in his way, and held in high repute by a select circle.

There was a gentleman on board, to whom, as I unintentionally learned through the thin partition which divided our state-room from the cabin in which he and his wife conversed together, I was unwittingly the occasion of very great uneasiness. I don't know why or wherefore, but I appeared to run in his mind perpetually, and to dissatisfy him very much. First of all I heard him say: and the most ludicrous part of the business was, that he said it in my very ear, and could not have communicated more directly with me, if he had leaned upon my shoulder, and whispered me: "Boz is on board still, my dear." After a considerable pause, he added, complainingly, "Boz keeps himself very close;" which was true enough, for I was not very well, and was lying down with a book. I thought he had done with me after this, but I was deceived; for a long interval having elapsed, during which I imagine him to have been turning restlessly from side to side, and trying to go to sleep; he broke out again with, "I suppose that Boz will be writing a book by-and-by, and putting all our names in it!" at which imaginary consequence of being on board a boat with Boz, he groaned, and became silent.

We called at the town of Erie, at eight o'clock that night, and lay there an hour. Between five and six next morning, we arrived at Buffalo, where we breakfasted; and being too near the Great Falls to wait patiently anywhere else, we set off by the train, the same morning at nine o'clock, to Niagara.

It was a miserable day; chilly and raw; a damp mist falling; and the trees in that northern region quite bare and wintry. Whenever the train halted, I listened for the roar; and was constantly straining my eyes in the direction where I knew the Falls must be, from seeing the river rolling on towards them; every moment expecting to behold the spray. Within a few minutes of our stopping, not before, I saw two great white clouds rising up slowly and majestically from the depths of the earth. That was all. At length we alighted: and then for the first time, I heard the mighty rush of water, and felt the ground tremble underneath my feet.

The bank is very steep, and was slippery with rain, and half-melted ice. I hardly know how I got down, but I was soon at the bottom, and climbing, with two English officers who were crossing and had joined me, over some broken rocks, deafened by the noise, half-blinded by the spray, and wet to the skin. We were at the foot of the American Fall. I could see an immense torrent of water tearing headlong down from some great height, but had no idea of shape, or situation, or anything but vague immensity.

When we were seated in the little ferry-boat, and were crossing the swollen river immediately before both cataracts, I began to feel what it was: but I was in a manner stunned, and unable to comprehend the vastness of the scene. It was not until I came on Table Rock, and looked—Great Heaven, on what a fall of bright-green water!—that it came upon me in its full might and majesty.

Then, when I felt how near to my Creator I was standing, the first effect, and the enduring one—instant and lasting—of the tremendous spectacle, was Peace. Peace of Mind: Tranquillty: calm recollections of the Dead: Great Thoughts of Eternal Rest and Happiness: nothing of Gloom or Terror. Niagara was at once stamped upon my heart, an Image of Beauty; to remain there, changeless and indelible, until its pulses cease to beat, forever.

Oh, how the strife and trouble of our daily life receded from my view, and lessened in the distance, during the ten memorable days we passed on that Enchanted Ground! What voices spoke from out the thundering water; what faces, faded from the earth, looked out upon me from its gleaming depths; what Heavenly promise glistened in those angels' tears, the drops of many hues, that showered around, and twined themselves about the gorgeous arches which the changing rainbows made!

I never stirred in all that time from the Canadian side, whither I had gone at first. I never crossed the river again; for I knew there were people on the other shore, and in such a place it is natural to shun strange company. To wander to and fro all day, and see the cataracts from all points of view; to stand upon the edge of the Great Horse Shoe Fall, marking the hurried water gathering strength as it approached the verge, yet seeming, too, to pause before it shot into the gulf below; to gaze from the river's level up to the torrent as it came streaming down; to climb the neighbouring heights and watch it through the trees, and see the wreathing water in the rapids hurrying on to take its fearful plunge; to linger in the shadow of the solemn rocks three miles below; watching the river as, stirred by no visible cause, it heaved and eddied and awoke the echoes, being troubled yet, far down beneath the surface, by its giant leap; to have Niagara before me, lighted by the sun and by the moon, red in the day's decline, and gray as evening slowly fell upon it; to look upon it every day, and wake up in the night and hear its ceaseless voice: this was enough.

I think in every quiet season now, still do those waters roll and leap, and roar and tumble, all day long; still are the rainbows spanning them, a hundred feet below. Still, when the sun is on them, do they shine and glow like molten gold. Still, when the day is gloomy, do they fall like snow, or seem to crumble away like the front of a great chalk cliff, or roll adown the rock like dense white smoke. But always does the mighty stream appear to die as it comes down, and always from the unfathomable grave arises that tremendous ghost of spray and mist which is never laid: which has haunted this place with the same dread solemnity since Darkness brooded on the deep, and that first flood before the Deluge—Light—came rushing on Creation at the word of God.

CHAPTER XV.

IN CANADA; TORONTO; KINGSTON; MONTREAL; QUEBEC; ST JOHN'S. IN THE UNITED STATES AGAIN; LEBANON; THE SHAKER VILLAGE; AND WEST POINT.

I WISH to abstain from insinuating any comparison, or drawing any parallel whatever, between the social features of the United States and those of the British Possessions in Canada. For this reason, I shall confine myself to a very brief account of our journeyings in the latter territory.

But before I leave Niagara, I must advert to one disgusting circumstance which can hardly have escaped the observation of any decent traveller who has visited the Falls.

On Table Rock, there is a cottage belonging to a Guide, where little relics of the place are sold, and where visiters register their names in a book kept for the purpose. On the wall of the room in which a great many of these volumes are preserved, the following request is posted: "Visitors will please not copy nor extract the remarks and poetical effusions from the registers and albums kept here."

But for this intimation, I should have let them lie upon the tables on which they were strewn with careful negligence, like books in a drawing-room: being quite satisfied with the stupendous silliness of certain stanzas with an anti-climax at the end of each, which were framed and hung up on the wall. Curious, however, after reading this announcement, to see what kind of morsels were so carefully preserved, I turned a few leaves, and found them scrawled all over with the vilest and the filthiest ribaldry that ever human hogs delighted in.

It is humiliating enough to know that there are among men, brutes so obscene and worthless, that they can delight in laying their miserable profanations upon the very steps of Nature's greatest altar. But that these should be hoarded up for the delight of their fellow swine, and kept in a public place where any eyes may see them, is a disgrace to the English language in which they are written (though I hope fow of these entries have been made by Englishmen), and a reproach to the English side, on which they are preserved.

The quarters of our soldiers at Niagara are finely and airily situated. Some of them are large detached houses on the plain above the Falls, which were originally designed for hotels, and in the evening time, when the women and children were leaning over the balconies watching the men as they played at ball and other games upon the grass before the door, they often presented a little picture of cheerfulness and animation which made it quite a pleasure to pass that way.

At any garrisoned point where the line of demarcation between one country and another is so very narrow as at Niagara, desertion from the ranks can scarcely fail to be of frequent occurrence; and it may be reasonably supposed that, when the soldiers entertain the wildest and maddest hopes of the fortune and independence that await them on the other side, the impulse to play traitor, which such a place suggests to dishonest minds, is not weakened. But it very rarely happens that the men who do desert are happy and contented afterward; and many instances have been known in which they have confessed their grievous disappointment, and their earnest desire to return to their old service, if they could but be assured of pardon, or of lenient treatment. Many of their comrades, notwithstanding, do the like from time to time; and instances of loss of life, in the effort to cross the river with this object, are far from being uncommon. Several men were drowned in the attempt to swim across not long ago; and one, who had the madness to trust himself upon a table as a raft, was swept down to the whirlpool, where his mangled body eddied round and round some days.

I am inclined to think that the noise of the Falls is very much exaggerated; and this will appear the more probable when the depth of the great basin, in which the water is received, is taken into account. At no time during our stay here was the wind at all high or boisterous, but we never heard them three miles off, even at the very quiet time of sunset, though we often tried.

Queenston, at which place the steamboats start for Toronto (or, I should rather say, at which place they call, for their wharf is at Lewiston, on the opposite shore), is situated in a delicious valley, through which the Niagara river, in colour a very deep green, pursues its course. It is approached by a road that takes its winding way among the heights by which the town is sheltered; and, seen from this point, is extremely beautiful and picturesque. On the most conspicuous of these heights stood a monument erected by the provincial legislature in memory of General Brock, who was slain in a battle with the Amercan forces, after having won the victory. Some vagabond, supposed to be a fellow of the name of Lett, who is now, or who lately was in prison as a felon, blew up this monument two years ago, and it is now a melancholy ruin, with a long fragment of iron railing hanging dejectedly from its top, and waving to and fro like a wild ivy branch or broken vine stem. It is of much higher importance than it may seem that this statue should be repaired at the public cost, as it ought to have been long ago. Firstly, because it is beneath the dignity of England to allow a memorial raised in honour of one of her defenders to remain in this condition on the very spot where he died. Secondly, because the sight of it in its present state, and the recollection of the unpunished outrage which brought it to this pass, is not very likely to soothe down border feelings among English subjects here, or compose their border quarrels and dislikes.

I was standing on the wharf at this place, watching the passengers embarking in a steamboat, which preceded that whose coming we awaited, and participating in the anxiety with which a sergeant's wife was collecting her few goods together—keeping one distracted eye hard upon the porters, who were hurrying them on board, and the other on a hoopless washing-tub, for which, as being the most utterly worthless of all her movables, she seemed to entertain particular affection—when three or four soldiers with a recruit came up, and went on board.

The recruit was a likely young fellow enough, strongly built and well made, but by no means sober; indeed he had all the air of a man who had been more or less drunk for some days. He carried a small bundle over his shoulder, slung at the end of a walking-stick, and had a short pipe in his mouth. He was as dusty and dirty as recruits usually are, and his shoes betokened that he had travelled on foot some distance; but he was in a very jocose state, and shook hands with this soldier, and clapped that one on the back, and talked and laughed continually, like a roaring idle dog as he was.

The soldiers rather laughed at this blade than with him; seeming to say, as they stood straightening their canes in their hands, and looking cooly at him over their glazed stocks, "Go on, my boy, while you may! you'll know better by-and-by;" when suddenly the novice, who had been backing towards the gangway in his noisy merriment, fell overboard before their eyes, and splashed heavily down into the river between the vessel and the dock.

I never saw such a good thing as the change that came over these soldiers in an instant. Almost before the man was down, their professional manner, their stiffness and constraint, were gone, and they were filled with the most violent energy. In less time than is required to tell it, they had him out again, feet first, with the tails of his coat flapping over his eyes, everything about him hanging the wrong way, and the water streaming off at every thread in his threadbare dress. But the moment they set him upright, and found that he was none the worse, they were soldiers again, looking over their glazed stocks more composedly than ever.

The half-sobered recruit glanced round for a moment, as if his first impulse were to express some gratitude for his preservation; but seeing them with this air of total unconcern, and having his wet pipe presented to him, with an oath, by the soldier who had been by far the most anxious of the party, he stuck it in his mouth, thrust his hands into his moist pockets, and without even shaking the water off his clothes, walked on board whistling; not to say as if nothing had happened, but as if he had meant to do it, and it had been a perfect success.

Our steamboat came up directly this had left the whrrf, and soon bore us to the mouth of the Niagara, where the stars and stripes of America fluttter on one side, and the Union Jack of England on the other; and so narrow is the space between them that the sentinels in either fort can often hear the watchword of the other country given. Thence we emerged on Lake Ontario, an inland sea, and by half past 6 o'clock were at Toronto.

The country round this town being very flat, is bare of scenic interest; but the town itself is full of life and motion, bustle, bussiness, and improvement. The streets are well paved, and lighted with gas; the houses are large and good; the shops excellent. Many of them have a display of goods in their windows, such as may be seen in thriving county towns in England; and there are some which would do no discredit to the metropolis itself. There is a good stone prison here; and there are, besides, a handsome church, a court-house, public offices, many commodious private residences, and a government observatory for noting and recording the magnetic variations. In the College of Upper Canuda, which is one of the public establishments of the city, a sound education in every department of polite learning can be had, at a very moderate expense, the annual charge for the instruction of each pupil not exceeding nine pounds sterling. It has pretty good endowments in the way of land, and is a valuable and useful institution.

The first stone of a new college had been laid but a few days before, by the Governor General. It will be a handsome, spacious edifice, approached by a long avenue, which is already planted and made available as a public walk. The town is well adapted for wholesome exercise at all seasons, for the footways in the thoroughfares which lie beyond the principal street, are planked like floors, and kept in very good and clean repair.

It is matter of deep regret that political differences should have run high in this place, and led to most discreditable and disgraceful results. It is not long since guns were discharged from a window in this town at the successful candidates in an election, and the coachman of one of them was actually shot in the body, though not dangerously wounded. But one man was killed on the same occasion; and from the very window whence he received his death, the very flag which shielded his murderer (not only in the commission o' his crime, but from its consequences), w lisplayed again on the occasion of the [illegible] remony performed by the governor general, to which I have just adverted. Of all the colours in the rainbow, there is but one which could be so employed; I need not say that flag was orange.

The time of leaving Toronto for Kingston, is noon. By 8 o'clock next morning the traveller is at the end of his journey, which is performed by steamboat upon Lake Ontario, calling at Port Hope and Coburg, the latter a cheerful thriving little town. Vast quantities of flour form the chief item in the freight of these vessels. We had no fewer than one thousand and eighty barrels on board between Coburg and Kingston.

The latter place, which is now the seat of government in Canada, is a very poor town, rendered still poorer in the appearance of its market-place by the ravages of a recent fire, Indeed, it may be said of Kingston, that one half of it appears to be burned down, and the other half not to be built up The Government House is neither elegant nor commodious, yet it is almost the only house of any importance in the neighbourhood.

There is an admirable jail here, well and wisely governed, and excellently regulated in every respect. The men were employed as shoemakers, ropemakers, blacksmiths, tailors, carpenters, and stonecutters, and in building a new prison, which was pretty far advanced towards completion. Tho female prisoners were occupied in needlework. Among them was a beautiful girl of twenty, who had been there nearly three years. She acted as bearer of secret despatches for the self-styled Patriots on Navy Island, during the Canadian insurrection, sometimes dressing as a girl, and carrying them in her stays—sometimes attiring herself as a boy, and secreting them in the lining of her hat. In the latter character she always rode as a boy would, which was nothing to her, for she could govern any horse that any man could ride, and could drive four-in-hand with the best whip in those parts. Setting forth on one of her patriotic missions, she appropriated to herself the first horse she could lay her hands on; and this offence had brought her where I saw her. She had quite a lovely face, though, as the reader may suppose from this sketch of her history, there was a lurking devil in her bright eye, which looked out pretty sharply from between her prison bars.

There is a bomb-proof fort here of great strength, which occupies a bold position, and is capable, doubtless, of doing good service; though the town is much too close upon the frontier to be long held, I should imagine, for its present purpose in troubled times. There is also a small navy-yard, where a couple of government steamboats were building, and getting on vigorously.

We left Kingston for Montreal on the tenth of May, at half past nine in the morning and proceeded in a steamboat down the St. Lawrence River. The beauty of this noble stream at almost any point, but especially in the commencement of this journey, when it winds its way among the thousand islands, can hardly be imagined. The number and constant succession of these islands, all green and richly wooded—their fluctuating sizes, some so large that for half an hour together one among them will appear as the opposite bank of the river, and some so small that they are mere dimples on its broad bosom; their infinite variety of shapes, and the numberless combinations of beautiful forms which the trees growing on them present, all form a picture fraught with uncommon interest and pleasure.

In the afternoon we shot down some rapids, where the river boiled and bubbled strangely, and where the force and headlong violence of the current were tremendous. At seven o'clock we reached Dickenson's Landing, whence travellers proceed for two or three hours by stage-coach, the navigation of the river being rendered so dangerous and difficult in the interval, by rapids, that steamboats do not make the passage. The number and length of those *portages*, over which the roads are bad and the travelling slow, render the way between the towns of Montreal and Kingston somewhat tedious.

Our course lay over a wide, unenclosed tract of country at a little distance from the river side, whence the bright warning lights on the dangerous parts of the St. Lawrence shone vividly. The night was dark and raw, and the way dreary enough. It was nearly ten o'clock when we reached the wharf where the next steamboat lay, and went on board and to bed.

She lay there all night, and started as soon as it was day. The morning was ushered in by a violent thunder-storm, and was very wet, but gradually improved and brightened up. Going on deck after breakfast, I was amazed to see, floating down with the stream, a most gigantic raft, with some thirty or forty wooden houses upon it, and at least as many flag masts, so that it looked like a nautical street. I saw many of these rafts afterward, but never one so large. All the timber, or "lumber," as it is called in America, which is brought down the St. Lawrence, is floated down in this manner. When the raft reaches its destination it is broken up, the materials are sold, and the boatmen return for more.

At eight we landed again, and travelled by a stage-coach for four hours, through a pleasant and well-cultivated country, perfectly French in every respect: in the appearance of the cottages, the air, language, and dress of the peasantry—the sign-boards on the shops and taverns, and the Virgin's shrines and crosses by the wayside. Nearly every common labourer and boy, though he had no shoes to his feet, wore round his waist a sash of some bright colour, generally red; and the women who were working in the fields and gardens, and doing all kinds of husbandry, wore, one and all, great flat straw hats with most capacious brims. There were Catholic priests and sisters of charity in the village streets, and images of the Saviour at the corners of cross roads and in other public places.

At noon we went on board another steamboat, and reached the village of Lachine, nine miles from Montreal, by three o'clock. There we left the river, and went on by land.

Montreal is pleasantly situated on the margin of the St. Lawrence, and is backed by some bold heights, about which there are charming rides and drives. The streets are generally narrow and irregular, as in most French towns of any age; but in the more modern parts of the city they are wide and airy. They display a great variety of very good shops, and both in the town and suburbs there are many excellent private dwellings. The granite quays are remarkable for their beauty, solidity, and extent.

There is a very large Catholic cathedral here, recently erected, with two tall spires, of which one is yet unfinished. In the open space in front of this edifice stands a solitary, grim-looking, square brick tower, which has a quaint and remarkable appearance, and which the wiseacres of the place have consequently determined to pull down immediately. The Government House is very superior to that at Kingston, and the town is full of life and bustle. In one of the suburbs is a plank road—not footpath—five or six miles long, and a famous road it is too. All the rides in the vicinity were made doubly interesting by the bursting out of spring, which is here so rapid, that it is but a day's leap from barren winter to the blooming youth of summer.

The steamboats to Quebec perform the journey in the night: that is to say, they leave Montreal at six in the evening, and arrive in Quebec at six next morning. We made this excursion during our stay in Montreal (which exceeded a fortnight), and were charmed by its interest and beauty.

The impression made upon the visiter by this Gibraltar of America—its giddy heights—its citadel suspended, as it were, in the air—its picturesque steep streets and frowning gateways, and the splendid views which burst upon the eye at every turn—is at once unique and lasting. It is a place not to be forgotten or mixed up in the mind with other places, or altered for a moment in the crowd of scenes a traveller can recall. Apart from the realities of this most picturesque city, there are associations clustering about it which would make a desert rich in interest. The dangerous precipice along whose rocky front Wolfe and his brave companions climbed to glory; the Plains of Abraham, where he received his mortal wound; the fortress, so chivalrously defended by Montcalm; and his soldier's grave, dug for him while yet alive, by the bursting of a shell, are not the least among them, or among the gallant incidents of history. That is a noble monument too, and worthy of two great nations, which perpetuates the memory of both brave generals, and on which their names are jointly written.

The city is rich in public institutions and in Catholic churches and charities; but it is mainly in the prospect from the site of the Old Government House, and from the Citadel, that its surprising beauty lies. The exquisite expanse of country, rich in field and forest, mountain-height and water, which lies stretched out before the view, with miles of Canadian villages, glancing in long whites treaks, like veins, along the landscape; the motley crowd of gables, roofs, and chimney tops in the old hilly:town immediately at hand; the beautiful St. Lawrence sparkling and flashing in the sunlight; and the tiny ships below the rock from which you gaze, whose distant riggiug looks like spiders' webs against the light, while casks and barrels on their decks dwindle into toys, and busy mariners become so many puppets: all this, framed by a sunken window in the fortress and looked at from the shadowed room within, forms one of the brightest and most enchanting pictures that the eye can rest upon.

In the spring of the year vast numbers of emi grants who have newly arrived from England or from Ireland, pass between Quebec and Montreal, on their way to the back woods and new settlements of Canada. If it be an entertaining lounge (as I very often found it) to take a morning stroll upon the quay at Montreal, and see them grouped in hundreds on the public wharfs, about their chests and boxes, it is matter of deep interest to be their fellow-passenger on one of these steamboats, and, mingling with the concourse, see and hear them unobserved.

The vessel in which we returned from Quebec to Montreal was crowded with them, and at night they spread their beds between decks (those who had beds, at least,) and slept so close and thick about our cabin door, that the passage to and fro was quite blocked up. They were nearly all English—from Gloucestershire the greater part, and had had a long winter passage out; but it was wonderful to see how clean the children had been kept, and how untiring in their love and self-denial all the poor parents were.

Cant as we may, and as we shall to the end of all things, it is very much harder for the poor to be virtuous than it is for the rich; and the good that is in them shines the brighter for it. In many a noble mansion lives a man, the best of husbands and of fathers, whose private worth in both capacities is justly lauded to the skies. But bring him here, upon this crowded deck. Strip from his fair young wife her silken dress and jewels, unbind her braided hair, stamp early wrinkles on her brow, pinch her pale cheek with care and much privation, array her faded form in coarsely patched attire, let there be nothing but his love to set her forth or deck her out, and you shall put it to the proof indeed. So change his station in the world that he shall see in those young things who climb about his knee not records of his wealth and name, but little wrestlers with him for his daily bread, so many poachers on his scanty meal, so many units to divide his every sum of comfort, and farther to reduce its small amount. In lieu of the endearments of childhood in its sweetest aspect, heap upon him all its pains and wants, its sicknesses and ills, its fretfulness, caprice, and querulous endurance; let its prattle be not of engaging infant fancies, but of cold, and thirst, and hunger; and if his fatherly affection outlive all this, and he be patient, watchful, tender, careful of his children's lives and mindful always of their joys and sorrows—then send him back to parliament, and pulpit, and to quarter sessions, and when he hears fine talk of the depravity of those who live from hand to mouth, and labour hard to do it, let him speak up, as one who knows, and tell those holders forth that they, by parallel with such a class, should be high angels in their daily lives, and lay but humble siege to Heaven at last.

Which of us shall say what he would be, if such realities, with small relief or change all through his days, were his! Looking round upon these people; far from home, houseless, indigent, wandering, weary with travel and hard living; and seeing how patiently they nursed and tended their young children; how they consulted ever their wants first, then half supplied their own; what gentle ministers of hope and faith the women were; how the men profited by their example; and how very, very seldom even a moment's petulance or harsh complaint broke out among them; I felt a stronger love and honour of my kind come glowing on my heart, and wished to God there had been many Atheists in the better part of human nature there, to read with me this simple lesson in the book of Life.

We left Montreal for New York again, on the thirtieth of May; crossing to La Prairie, on the opposite shore of the St. Lawrence, in a steamboat; we then took the railroad to St. John's, which is on the brink of Lake Champlain. Our last greeting in Canada was from the English officers in the pleasant barracks at that place (a class of gentlemen who had made every hour of our visit memorable by their hospitality and friendship); and with "Rule Britannia" sounding in our ears, soon left it far behind.

But Canada has held, and always will retain a foremost place in my remembrance. Few Englishmen are prepared to find it what it is. Advancing quietly; old differences settling down, and being fast forgotten; public feeling and private enterprise alike in a sound and wholesome state; nothing of flush or fever in its system, but health and vigour throbbing in its steady pulse: it is full of hope and promise. To me—who had been accustomed to think of it as something left behind in the strides of advancing society, as something neglected and forgotten, slumbering and wasting in its sleep—the demand for labour and the rates of wages; the busy quays of Montreal; the vessels taking in their cargoes, and discharging them; the amount of shipping in the different ports; the commerce, roads, and public works, all made to last; the respectability and character of the public journals; and the amount of rational comfort and happiness which honest industry may earn; were very great surprises. The steamboats on the lakes, in their conveniences, cleanliness, and safety; in the gentlemanly character and bearing of their captains: and in the politeness and perfect comfort of their social regulations; are unsurpassed even by the famous Scotch vessels, deservedly so much esteemed at home. The inns are usually bad; because the custom of boarding at hotels is not so general here as in the States, and the British officers, who form a large portion of the society of every town, live chiefly at the regimental messes; but in every other respect, the traveller in Canada will find as good provision for his comfort as in any place I know.

There is one American boat—the vessel which carried us on Lake Champlain, from St. John's to Whitehall—which I praise very highly, but no more than it deserves, when I say that it is superior even to that in which we went from Queenston to Toronto, or to that in which we travelled from the latter place to Kingston, or I have no doubt I may add, to any other in the world. This steamboat, which is called the Burlington, is a perfectly exquisite achievement of neatness, elegance, and order. The decks are drawing-rooms; the cabins are boudoirs, choicely furnished and adorned with prints, pictures, and musical instruments; every nook and corner in the vessel is a perfect curiosity of graceful comfort and beautiful contrivance. Captain Sherman, her commander, to whose ingenuity and excellent taste these results are solely attributable, has bravely and worthily distinguished himself on more than one trying occasion; not least among them, in having the moral courage to carry British troops, at a time (during the Canadian rebellion) when no other conveyance was open to them. He and his vessel are held in universal respect, both by his own countrymen and ours; and no man ever enjoyed the popular esteem, who, in his sphere of action, won and wore it better than this gentleman.

By means of this floating palace we were soon in the United States again, and called that evening at Burlington; a pretty town, where we lay an hour or so. We reached Whitehall, where we were to disembark, at six next morning; and might have done so earlier, but that these steamboats lie by for some hours in the night, in consequence of the lake becoming very narrow at that part of the journey, and difficult of navigation in the dark. Its width is so contracted at one point, indeed, that they are obliged to warp round by means of a rope.

After breakfasting at Whitehall, we took the stage-coach for Albany: a large and busy town, where we arrived between five and six o'clock that afternoon, after a very hot day's journey, for we were now in the height of summer again. At seven we started for New-York on board a great North River steamboat, which was so crowded with passengers that the upper deck was like the box lobby of a theatre between the pieces, and the lower one like Tottenham Court Road on a Saturday night. But we slept soundly, notwithstanding, and soon after five o'clock next morning, reached New-York.

Tarrying here only that day and night to recruit after our late fatigues, we started off once more upon our last journey in America. We had yet five days to spare before embarking for England, and I had a great desire to see "the Shaker Village," which is peopled by a religious sect from whom it takes its name.

To this end we went up the North River again, as far as the town of Hudson, and there hired an extra to carry us to Lebanon, thirty miles distant: and of course another and a different Lebanon from that village where I slept on the night of the prairie trip.

The country through which the road meandered was rich and beautiful; the weather very fine; and for many miles the Caatskill Mountains, where Rip Van Winkle and the ghastly Dutchmen played at ninepins one memorable gusty afternoon, towered in the blue distance like stately clouds. At one point, as we ascended a steep hill, athwart whose base a railroad, yet constructing, took its course, we came upon an Irish colony. With means at hand of building decent cabins, it was wonderful to see how clumsy, rough, and wretched, its hovels were. The best were poor protection from the weather; the worst let in the wind and rain through wide breaches in the roofs of sodden grass, and in the walls of mud; some had neither door nor window; some had nearly fallen down, and were imperfectly propped up by stakes and poles, all were ruinous and filthy. Hideously ugly old women and very buxom young ones, pigs, dogs, men, children, babies, pots, kettles, dunghills, vile refuse, rank straw, and standing water, all wallowing together in an inseparable heap, composed the furniture of every dark and dirty hut.

Between nine and ten o'clock at night we arrived at Lebanon: which is renowned for its warm baths, and for a great hotel, well adapted, I have no doubt, to the gregarious taste of those seekers after health or pleasure who repair here, but inexpressibly comfortless to me. We were shown into an immense apartment, lighted by two dim candles, called the drawing-room, from which there was a descent by a flight of steps to another vast desert called the dining-room: our bed-chambers were among certain long rows of little whitewashed cells, which opened from either side of a dreary passage; and were so like rooms in a prison that I half expected to be locked up when I went to bed, and listened involuntarily for the turning of the key on the outside. There need be baths somewhere in the neighbourhood, for the other washing arrangements were on as limited a scale as I ever saw, even in America: indeed, these bed-rooms were so very bare of even such common luxuries as chairs, that I should say they were not provided with enough of anything, but that I bethink myself of our having been most bountifully bitten all night.

The house is very pleasantly situated, however, and we had a good breakfast. That done, we went to visit our place of destination, which was some two miles off, and the way to which was soon indicated by a finger-post, whereon was painted "To the Shaker Village."

As we rode along we passed a party of Shakers, who were at work upon the road; who wore the broadest of all broad-brimmed hats; and were in all visible respects such very wooden men, that I felt about as much sympathy for them, and as much interest in them, as if they had been so many figure-heads of ships. Presently we came to the beginning of the village, and alighting at the door of the house where the Shaker manufactures are sold, and which is the head-quarters of the elders, requested permission to see the Shaker worship.

Pending the conveyance of this request to some person in authority, we walked into a grim room, where several grim hats were hanging on grim pegs, and the time was grimly told by a grim clock, which uttered evey tick with a kind of struggle, as if it broke the grim silence reluctantly, and under protest. Ranged against the wall were six or eight stiff, high-backed chairs, and they partook so strongly of the general grimness, that one would much rather have sat on the floor than incurred the smallest obligation to any of them.

Presently there stalked into this apartment a grim old Shaker, with eyes as hard, and dull, and cold, as the great round metal buttons on his coat and waistcoat: a sort of calm goblin. Being informed of our desire, he produced a newspaper wherin the body of elders, whereof he was a member, had advertised but a few days before, that in consequence of certain unseemly interruptions which their worship had received from strangers, their chapel was closed to the public for the space of one year.

As nothing was to be urged in opposition to this reasonable arrangement, we requested leave to make some trifling purchases of Shaker goods, which was grimly conceded. We accordingly repaired to a store in the same house and on the opposite side of the passage, where the stock was presided over by something alive in a russet case, which the elder said was a woman; and which I suppose *was* a woman, though I should not have suspected it.

On the opposite side of the road was their place of worship: a cool, clean edifice of wood, with large windows and green blinds: like a spacious summer-house. As there was no getting into this place, and nothing was to be done but walk up and down, and look at it and the other buildings in the village (which were chiefly of wood, painted a dark red like English barns, and composed of many stories like English factories), I have nothing to communicate to the reader, beyond the scanty results I gleaned the while our purchases were making. These people are called Shakers from their peculiar form of adoration, which consists of a dance, performed by the men and women of all ages, who arrange themselves for that purpose in opposite parties: the men first divesting themselves of their hats and coats, which they gravely hang against the wall before they begin; and tying a riband round their shirt sleeves, as though they were going to be bled. They accompany themselves with a droning, humming noise, and dance until they are quite exhausted, alternately advancing and retiring in a preposterous sort of trot. The effect is said to be unspeakably absurd: and if I may judge from a print of this ceremony which I have in my possession, and which I am informed by those who have visited the chapel, is perfectly accurate, it must be infinitely grotesque.

They are governed by a woman, and her rule is understood to be absolute, though she has the assistance of a council of elders. She lives, it is said, in strict seclusion, in certain rooms above the chapel, and is never shown to profane eyes. If she at all resembled the lady who presided over the store, it is a great charity to keep her as close as possible, and I cannot too strongly express my perfect concurrence in this benevolent proceeding.

All the possessions and revenues of the settlement are thrown into a common stock, which is managed by the elders. As they have made converts among people who were well to do in the world, and are frugal and thrifty, it is understood that this fund prospers: the more especially as they have made large purchases of land. Nor is this at Lebanon the only Shaker settlement: there are, I think, at least, three others.

They are good farmers, and all their produce is eagerly purchased and highly esteemed. "Shaker seeds," "Shaker herbs," and "Shaker distilled waters," are commonly announced for sale in the shops of towns and cities. They are good breeders of cattle, and are kind and merciful to the brute creation. Consequently, Shaker beasts seldom fail to find a ready market.

They eat and drink together, after the Spartan model, at a great public table. There is no union of the sexes; and every Shaker, male and female, is devoted to a life of celibacy. Rumour has been busy upon this theme, but here again I must refer to the lady of the store, and say, that if many of the sister Shakers resemble her, I treat all such slander as bearing on its face the strongest marks of wild improbability. But that they take as proselytes, persons so young that they cannot know their own minds, and cannot possess much strength of resolution in this or any other respect, I can assert from my own observation of the extreme juvenility of certain youthful Shakers whom I saw at work among the party on the road.

They are said to be good drivers of bargains, but to be honest and just in their transactions, and even in horse-dealing to resist those thievish tendencies which would seem, for some undiscovered reason, to be almost inseparable from that branch of traffic. In all matters they hold their own course quietly, live in their gloomy, silent commonwealth, and show little desire to interfere with other people.

This is well enough, but nevertheless I cannot, I confess, incline towards the Shakers; view them with much favour, or extend towards them any very lenient construction. I so abhor, and from my soul detest that bad spirit, no matter by what class or sect it may be entertained, which would strip life of its healthful graces, rob youth of its innocent pleasures, pluck from maturity and age their pleasant ornaments, and make existence but a narrow path towards the grave: that odious spirit which, if it could have had full scope and sway upon the earth, must have blasted and made barren the imaginations of the greatest men, and left them, in their power of raising up enduring images before their fellow creatures yet unborn, no better than the beasts: that, in these very broad-brimmed hats and very sombre coats—in stiff-necked, solemn-visaged piety, in short, no matter what its garb, whether it have cropped hair as in a Shaker village, or long nails as in a Hindoo temple—I recognise the worst among the enemies of Heaven and Earth, who turn the water at the marriage feasts of this poor world not into wine, but gall. And if there must be people vowed to crush the harmless fancies and the love of innocent delights and gayeties, which are a part of human nature: as much a part of it as any other love or hope that is our common portion: let them, for me, stand openly revealed among the ribald and licentious; the very idiots know that *they* are not on the Immortal road, and will despise them, and avoid them readily.

Leaving the Shaker village with a hearty dislike of the old Shakers, and a hearty pity for the young ones: tempered by the strong probability of their running away as they grow older and wiser, which they not uncommonly do: we returned to Lebanon, and so to Hudson, by the way we had come upon the previous day. There, we took steamboat down the North River towards New-York, but stopped, some four hours' journey short of it, at West Point, where we remained that night, and all next day, and next night too.

In this beautiful place: the fairest among the fair and lovely Highlands of the North River: shut in by deep green heights and ruined forts, and looking down upon the distant town of Newburgh, along a glittering path of sunlit water, with here and there a skiff, whose white sail often bends on some new tack as sudden flaws of wind come down upon her from the gullies in the hills: hemmed in, besides, all round with memories of Washington, and events of the revolutionary war: is the Military School of America.

It could not stand on more appropriate ground, and any ground more beautiful can hardly be. The course of education is severe, but well-devised, and manly. Through June, July, and August, the young men encamp upon the spacious plain whereon the college stands; and all the year their military exercises are performed there daily. The term of study at this institution, which the State requires from all cadets, is four years; but whether it be from the rigid nature of the discipline, or the national impatience of restraint, or both causes combined, not more than half the number who begin their studies here, ever remain to finish them.

The number of cadets being about equal to that of the members of Congress, one is sent here from every Congressional district: its member influencing the selection. Commissions in the service are distributed on the same principle. The dwellings of the various professors are beautifully situated; and there is a most excellent hotel for strangers, though it has the two drawbacks of being a total abstinence house (wines and spirits being forbidden to the students), and of serving the public meals at rather uncomfortable hours: to wit, breakfast at seven, dinner at one, and supper at sunset.

The beauty and freshness of this calm retreat, in the very dawn and greenness of summer—it was then the beginning of June—were exquisite indeed. Leaving it upon the sixth, and returning to New-York, to embark for England on the succeeding day, I was glad to think that among the last memorable beauties which had glided past us, and softened in the bright perspective, were those whose pictures, traced by no common hand, are fresh in most men's minds: not easily to grow old, or fade beneath the dust of Time: The Caatskill Mountains, Sleepy Hollow, and the Tappaan Zee.

CHAPTER XVI.

THE PASSAGE HOME.

I NEVER had so much interest before, and very likely I shall never have so much interest again, in the state of the wind, as on the long-looked-for morning of Tuesday, the seventh of June. Some nautical authority had told me a day or two previous, "anything with west in it, will do;" so when I darted out of bed at daylight, and throwing up the window, was saluted by a lively breeze from the northwest which had sprung up in the night, it came upon me so freshly, rustling with so many happy associations, that I conceived upon the spot a special regard for all airs blowing from that quarter of the compass, which I shall cherish, I dare say, until my own wind has breathed its last frail puff, and withdrawn itself forever from the mortal calendar.

The pilot had not been slow to take advantage of this favourable weather, and the ship which yesterday had lain in such a crowded dock that she might have retired from trade for good and all, for any chance she seemed to have of going to sea, was now full sixteen miles away. A gallant sight she was, when we, fast gaining on her in a steamboat, saw her in the distance riding at anchor: her tall masts pointing up in graceful lines against the sky, and every rope and spar expressed in delicate and thread-like outline: gallant, too, when we, being all aboard, the anchor came up to the sturdy chorus "Cheerily, men, oh cheerily!" and she followed proudly in the towing steamboat's wake: but bravest and most gallant of all, when the tow-rope being cast adrift, the canvass fluttered from her masts, and, spreading her white wings, she soared away upon her free and solitary course.

In the after-cabin we were only fifteen passengers in all, and the greater part were from Canada, where some of us had known each other. The night was rough and squally, so were the next two days, but they flew by quickly, and we were soon as cheerful and as snug a party, with an honest, manly-hearted captain at our head, as ever came to the resolution of being mutually agreeable, on land or water.

We breakfasted at eight, lunched at twelve, dined at three, and took our tea at half past seven. We had abundance of amusements, and dinner was not the least among them: firstly, for its own sake; secondly, because of its extraordinary length: its duration, inclusive of all the long pauses between the courses, being seldom less than two hours and a half; which was a subject of never-failing entertainment. By way of beguiling the tediousness of these banquets, a select association was formed at the lower end of the table, below the mast, to whose distinguished president modesty forbids me to make any farther allusion, which, being a very hilarious and jovial institution, was (prejudice apart) in high favour with the rest of the community, and particularly with a black steward, who lived for three weeks in a broad grin at the marvellous humour of these incorporated worthies.

Then we had chess for those who played it, whist, cribbage, books, backgammon, and shovel-board. In all weathers, fair or foul, calm or windy, we were every one on deck, walking up and down in pairs, lying in the boats, leaning over the side, or chatting in a lazy group together. We had no lack of music, for one played the accordion, another the violin, and another (who usually began at six o'clock A.M.) the key-bugle; the combined effect of which instruments, when they all played different tunes, in different parts of the ship, at the same time, and within hearing of each other, as they sometimes did (everybody being intensely satisfied with his own performance), was sublimely hideous.

When all these means of entertainment failed, a sail would heave in sight; looming, perhaps, the very spirit of a ship, in the misty distance, or passing us so close that through our glasses we could see the people on her decks, and easily make out her name, and whither she was bound. For hours together we could watch the dolphins and porpoises as they rolled, and leaped, and dived around the vessel; or those small creatures ever on the wing, the Mother Carey's chickens, which had borne us company from New-York Bay, and for a whole fortnight fluttered about the vessel's stern. For some days we had a dead calm, or very light winds, during which the crew amused themselves with fishing, and hooked an unlucky dolphin, who expired in all his rainbow colours, on the deck: an event of such importance in our barren calendar, that afterward we dated from the dolphin, and made the day on which he died an era.

Besides all this, when we were five or six days out, there began to be much talk of icebergs, of which wandering islands an unusual number had been seen by vessels that had come into New-York a day or two before we left that port, and of whose dangerous neighbourhood we were warned by the sudden coldness of the weather, and the sinking of the mercury in the barometer. While these tokens lasted, a double look-out was kept, and many dismal tales were whispered, after dark, of ships that had struck upon the ice and gone down in the night; but the wind obliging us to hold a southward course, we saw none of them, and the weather soon grew bright and warm again.

The observation every day at noon, and the subsequent working of the vessel's course, was, as may be supposed, a feature in our lives of paramount importance; nor were there wanting (as there never are) sagacious doubters of the captain's calculations, who, so soon as his back was turned, would, in the absence of compasses, measure the chart with bits of string, and ends of pocket-handkerchiefs, and points of snuffers, and clearly prove him to be wrong by an odd thousand miles or so. It was very edifying to see these unbelievers shake their heads and frown, and hear them hold forth strongly upon navigation: not that they knew anything about it, but that they always mistrusted the captain in calm weather, or when the wind was adverse. Indeed, the mercury itself is not so variable as this class of passengers, whom you will see, when the ship is going nobly through the water, quite pale with admiration, swearing that the captain beats all captains ever known, and even hinting at subscriptions for a piece of plate: and who, next morning, when the breeze has lulled, and all the sails hang useless in the idle air, shake their despondent heads again, and say, with screwed-up lips, they hope that captain is a sailor, but they shrewdly doubt him; that they do.

It even became an occupation in the calm to wonder when the wind *would* spring up in the favourable quarter, where, it was clearly shown by all the rules and precedents, it ought to have sprung up long ago. The first mate, who whistled for it zealously, was much respected for his perseverance, and was regarded even by the unbelievers as a first-rate sailor. Many gloomy looks would he cast upward through the cabin skylights at the flapping sails while dinner was in progress; and some, growing bold in ruefulness, predicted that we should land about the middle of July. There are always on board ship, a Sanguine One, and a Despondent One. The latter character carried it hollow at this period of the voyage, and triumphed over the Sanguine One at every meal, by inquiring where he supposed the Great Western (which left New-York a week after us) was *now;* and where he supposed the "Cunard" steam-packet was *now;* and what he thought of sailing vessels as compared with steamships *now;* and so beset his life with pestilent attacks of that kind, that he too was obliged to affect despondency for very peace and quietude.

These were additions to the list of entertaining incidents, but there was still another source of interest. We carried in the steerage nearly a hundred passengers; a little world of poverty; and as we came to know individuals among them by sight, from looking down upon the deck where they took the air in the daytime, and cooked their food, and very often ate it too, we became curious to know their histories, and with what expectations they had gone out to America, and on what errands they were going home, and what their circumstances were. The information we got on these heads from the carpenter, who had charge of these people, was often of the strangest kind. Some of them had been in America but three days, some but three months, and some had gone out in the last voyage of that very ship in which they were now returning home. Others had sold their clothes to raise the passage-money, and had hardly rags to cover them; others had no food, and lived upon the charity of the rest; and one man, it was discovered nearly at the end of the voyage, not before—for he kept his secret close, and did not court compassion—had had no sustenance whatever but the bones and scraps of fat he took from the plates used in the after-cabin dinner when they were put out to be washed.

The whole system of shipping and conveying these unfortunate persons is one that stands in need of thorough revision. If any class deserve to be protected and assisted by the government, it is that class who are banished from their native land in search of the bare means of subsistence. All that could be done for these poor people by the great compassion and humanity of the captain and officers was done, but they require much more. The law is bound, at least upon the English side, to see that too many of them are not put on board one ship; and that their accommodations are decent; not demoralizing and profligate. It is bound, too, in common humanity, to declare that no man shall be taken on board without his stock of provisions being previously inspected by some proper officer, and pronounced moderately sufficient for his support upon the voyage. It is bound to provide, or to require that there be provided a medical attendant; whereas in these ships there are none, though sickness of adults and deaths of children on the passage are matters of the very commonest occurrence. Above all, it is the duty of any government, be it monarchy or republic, to interpose and put an end to that system by which a firm of traders in emigrants purchase of the owners the whole 'tween-decks of a ship, and send on board as many wretched people as they can lay hold of, on any terms they can get, without the smallest reference to the conveniences of the steerage, the number of berths, the slightest separation of the sexes, or anything but their own immediate profit. Nor is even this the worst of the vicious system; for certain crimping agents of these houses, who have a per centage on all the passengers they inveigle, are constantly travelling about those districts where poverty and discontent are rife, and tempting the credulous into more misery by holding out monstrous inducements to emigration which never can be realized.

The history of every family we had on board was pretty much the same. After hoarding up, and borrowing, and begging, and selling everything to pay the passage, they had gone out to New-York, expecting to find its streets paved with gold, and had found them paved with very hard and very real stones. Enterprise was dull; labourers were not wanted; jobs of work were to be got, but the payment was not. They were coming back, even poorer than they went. One of them was carrying an open letter from a young English artisan, who had been in New-York a fortnight, to a friend near Manchester, whom he strongly urged to follow him. One of the officers brought it to me as a curiosity. "This is the country, Jem," said the writer. "I like America. There is no despotism here; that's the great thing. Employment of all sorts is going a-begging, and wages are capital. You have only to choose a trade, Jem, and be it. I haven't made a choice of one yet, but I shall soon. *At present I haven't quite made up my mind whether to be a carpenter—or a tailor.*"

There was yet another kind of passenger, and but one more, who, in the calm and the light winds, was a constant theme of conversation and observation among us. This was an English sailor, a smart, thorough-built English man-of-war's-man from his hat to his shoes, who was serving in the American navy, and, having got leave of absence, was on his way home to see his friends. When he presented himself to take and pay for his passage, it had been suggested to him that, being an able seaman, he might as well work it and save the money; but this piece of advice he very indignantly rejected, saying, "He'd be damned but for once he'd go aboard ship as a gentleman." Accordingly, they took his money, but he no sooner came aboard than he stowed his kit in the forecastle, arranged to mess with the crew, and the very first time the hands were turned up went aloft like a cat, before anybody. And all through the passage there he was, first at the braces, outermost on the yards, perpetually lending a hand everywhere, but always with a sober dignity in his manner, and a sober grin on his face, which plainly said, "I do it as a gentleman. For my own pleasure, mind you!"

At length, and at last, the promised wind came up in right good earnest, and away we went before it, with every stitch of canvass set, slashing through the water nobly. There was a grandeur in the motion of the splendid ship, as, overshadowed by her mass of sails, she rode at a furious pace upon the waves, which filled one with an indescribable sense of pride and exultation. As she plunged into a foaming valley, how I loved to see the green waves, bordered deep with white, come rushing on astern, to buoy her upward at their pleasure, and curl about her as she stooped again, but always own her for their haughty mistress still! On, on we flew, with changing lights upon the water, being now in the blessed region of fleecy skies; a bright sun lighting us by day, and a bright moon by night; the vane pointing directly homeward, alike the truthful index to the favouring wind and to our cheerful hearts; until at sunrise, one fair Monday morning—the twenty-seventh of June, I shall not easily forget the day—there lay before us old Cape Clear, God bless it, showing, in the mist of early morning, like a cloud; the brightest and most welcome cloud, to us, that ever hid the face of Heaven's fallen sister—Home.

Dim speck as it was in the wide prospect, it made the sunrise a more cheerful sight, and gave to it that sort of human interest which it seems to want at sea. There, as elsewhere, the return of day is inseparable from some sense of renewed hope and gladness; but the light shining on the weary waste of water, and showing it in all its vast extent of loneliness, presents a solemn spectacle, which even night, veiling it in darkness and uncertainty, does not surpass. The rising of the moon is more in keeping with the solitary ocean; and has an air of melancholy grandeur, which, in its soft and gentle influence, seems to comfort while it saddens. I recollect when I was a very young child having a fancy that the reflection of the moon in water was a path to Heaven, trodden by the spirits of good people on their way to God: and this old feeling often came over me again when I watched it on a tranquil night at sea.

The wind was very light on this same Monday morning, but it was still in the right quarter, and so, by slow degrees, we left Cape Clear behind, and sailed along, within sight of the coast of Ireland. And how merry we all were, and how loyal to the George Washington, and how full of mutual congratulations, and how venturesome in predicting the exact hour at which we should arrive at Liverpool, may be easily imagined and readily understood. Also, how heartily we drank the captain's health that day at dinner; and how restless we became about packing up; and how two or three of the most sanguine spirits rejected the idea of going to bed at all that night as something it was not worth while to do so near the shore, but went nevertheless, and slept soundly; and how to be so near our journey's end was like a pleasant dream, from which one feared to wake.

The friendly breeze freshened again next day, and on we went once more before it gallantly: descrying now and then an English ship going homeward under shortened sail, while we, with every inch of canvass crowded on, dashed gayly past, and left her far behind. Towards evening, the weather turned hazy, with a drizzling rain; and soon became so thick, that we sailed, as it were, in a cloud. Still we swept onward like a phantom ship, and many an eager eye glanced up to where the look-out on the mast kept watch for Holyhead.

At length his long-expected cry was heard, and at the same moment there shone out from the haze and mist ahead a gleaming light, which presently was gone, and soon returned, and soon was gone again. Whenever it came back, the eyes of all on board brightened, and sparkled like itself: and there we all stood, watching this revolving light upon the rock at Holyhead, and praising it for its brightness and its friendly warning, and lauding it, in short, above all other signal lights that ever were displayed, until it once more glimmered faintly in the distance far behind us.

Then it was time to fire a gun for a pilot; and almost before its smoke had cleared away, a little boat with a light at her masthead came bearing down upon us, through the darkness, swiftly. And presently, our sails being backed, she ran alongside; and the hoarse pilot, wrapped and muffled in peacoats and shawls to the very bridge of his weather-ploughed-up nose, stood bodily among us on the deck. And I think if that pilot had wanted to borrow fifty pounds for an indefinite period on no security, we should have engaged to lend it to him among us before his boat had dropped astern, or (which is the same thing) before every scrap of news in the paper he brrought with him had become the common property of all on board.

We turned in pretty late that night, and turned out pretty soon next morning. By six o'clock we clustered on the deck, prepared to go ashore; and looked upon the spires, and roofs, and smoke of Liverpool. By eight we all sat down in one of its hotels, to eat and drink together for the last time. And by nine we had shaken hands all round, and broken up our social company forever.

The country, by the railroad, seemed, as we rattled through it, like a luxuriant garden. The beauty of the fields (so small they looked!), the hedge-rows, and the trees; the pretty cottages, the beds of flowers, the old churchyards, the antique houses, and every well-known object: the exquisite delights of that one journey, crowding in the short compass of a summer's day the joy of many years, and winding up with Home and all that makes it dear: no tongue can tell, or pen of mine describe.

CHAPTER XVII.

SLAVERY.

The upholders of slavery in America—of the atrocities of which system, I shall not write one word for which I have not ample proof and warrant—may be divided into three great classes.

The first, are those more moderate and rational owners of human cattle, who have come into the possession of them as so many coins in their trading capital, but who admit the frightful nature of the Institution in the abstract, and perceive the dangers to society with which it is fraught, dangers which, however distant they may be, or howsoever tardy in their coming on, are as certain to fall upon its guilty head, as is the Day of Judgment.

The second, consists of all those owners, breeders, users, buyers, and sellers of slaves, who will, until the bloody chapter has a bloody end, own, breed, use, buy, and sell them at all hazards; who doggedly deny the horrors of the system, in the teeth of such a mass of evidence as never was brought to bear on any other subject, and to which the experience of every day contributes its immense amount; who would at this or any other moment, gladly involve America in a war, civil or foreign, provided that it had, for its sole end and object the assertion of their right to perpetuate slavery, and to whip, and work, and torture slaves, unquestioned by any human authority, and unassailed by any human power; who, when they speak of Freedom, mean the Freedom to oppress their kind, and to be savage, merciless, and cruel; and of whom every man on his own ground, in republican America, is a more exacting, and a sterner and less responsible despot, than the Caliph Haroun al Raschid in his angry robe of scarlet.

The third, and not the least numerous or influential, is composed of all that delicate gentility which cannot bear a superior, and cannot brook an equal: of that class whose Republicanism means, "I will not tolerate a man above me; and of those below, none must approach too near;" whose pride, in a land where voluntary servitude is shunned as a disgrace, must be ministered to by slaves; and whose inalienable rights can only have their growth in negro wrongs.

It has been sometimes urged that, in the unavailing efforts which have been made to advance the cause of Human Freedom in the republic of America (strange cause for history to treat of!), sufficient regard has not been had to the existence of the first class of persons; and it has been contended that they are hardly used, in being confounded with the second. This is, no doubt, the case; noble instances of pecuniary and personal sacrifice have already had their growth among them; and it is much to be regretted that the gulf between them and the advocates of emancipation should have been widened and deepened by any means: the rather, as there are, beyond dispute, among these slave-owners, many kind masters who are tender in the exercise of their unnatural power. Still it is to be feared that this injustice is inseparable from the state of things with which humanity and truth are called upon to deal. Slavery is not a whit the more endurable because some hearts are to be found which can partially resist its hardening influences; nor can the indignant tide of honest wrath stand still, because in its onward course it overwhelms a few who are comparatively innocent, among a host of guilty.

The ground most commonly taken by these better men among the advocates of slavery, is this: "It is a bad system; and for myself I would willingly get rid of it, if I could; most willingly. But it is not so bad, as you in England take it to be. You are deceived by the representations of the emancipationists. The greater part of my slaves are much attached to me. You will say that I do not allow them to be severely treated; but I will put it to you whether you believe that it can be a general practice to treat them inhumanly, when it would impair their value, and would be obviously against the interests of their masters."

Is it the interest of any man to steal, to game, to waste his health and mental faculties by drunkenness, to lie, forswear himself, indulge hatred, seek desperate revengé, or do murder? No. All these are roads to ruin. And why, then, do men tread them? Because such inclinations are among the vicious qualities of mankind. Blot out, ye friends of slavery, from the catalogue of human passions, brutal lust, cruelty, and the abuse of irresponsible power (of all earthly temptations the most difficult to be resisted), and when ye have done so, and not before, we will inquire whether it be the interest of a master to lash and maim the slaves, over whose lives and limbs he has an absolute control.

But again: this class, together with that last one I have named, the miserable aristocracy spawned of a false republic, lift up their voices and exclaim, "Public opinion is all sufficient to prevent such cruelty as you denounce." Public opinion! Why, public opinion in the slave States *is* slavery, is it not? Public opinion in the slave States has delivered the slaves over to the gentle mercies of their masters. Public opinion has made the laws, and denied them legislative protection. Public opinion has knotted the lash, heated the branding-iron, loaded the rifle, and shielded the murderer. Public opinion threatens the abolitionist with death, if he venture to the South; and drags him with a rope about his middle, in a broad unblushing noon, through the first city in the East. Public opinion has, within a few years, burned a slave alive at a slow fire in the city of St. Louis; and public opinion has to this day maintained upon the bench that estimable judge who charged the jury, impanelled there to try his murderers, that their most horrid deed was an act of public opinion, and being so, must not be punished by the laws the public sentiment had made. Public opinion hailed this doctrine with a howl of wild applause, and set the prisoners free, to walk the city, men of mark, and influence, and station, as they had been before.

Public opinion! what class of men have an immense preponderance over the rest of the community, in their power of representing public opinion in the legislature? The slave owners. They send from their twelve States, one hundred members, while the fourteen free States, with a free population nearly double, return but a hundred and forty-two. Before whom do the presidential candidates bow down the most humbly, on whom do they fawn the most fondly, and for whose tastes do they cater the most assiduously in their servile protestations? The slave owners always.

Public opinion! hear the public opinion of the free South, as expressed by its own members in the House of Representatives at Washington. "I have a great respect for the chair," quoth North Carolina, "I have a great respect for the chair as an officer of the house, and a great respect for him personally; nothing but that respect prevents me from rushing to the table and tearing that petition which has just been presented for the abolition of slavery in the District of Columbia, to pieces." "I warn the abolitionists," says South Carolina, "ignorant, infuriated barbarians as they are, that if chance shall throw any of them into our hands, he may expect a felon's death." "Let an abolitionist come within the borders of South Carolina," cries a third, mild Carolina's colleague, "and if we can catch him we will try him, and notwithstanding the interference of all the governments on earth, including the federal government, we will HANG him."

Public opinion has made this law: it has declared that in Washington, in that city which takes its name from the father of American liberty, any justice of the peace may bind with fetters any negro passing down the street and thrust him into jail; no offence on the black man's part is necessary. The justice says, "I choose to think this man a runaway;" and locks him up. Public opinion impowers the man of law when this is done to advertise the negro in the newspapers, warning his owner to come and claim him, or he will be sold to pay the jail fees. But supposing he is a free black, and has no owner, it may naturally be presumed that he is set at liberty. No; HE IS SOLD TO RECOMPENSE HIS JAILER. This has been done again, and again, and again. He has no means of proving his freedom; has no adviser, messenger, or assistance of any sort or kind; no investigation into his case is made, or inquiry instituted. He, a free man, who may have served for years, and bought his liberty, is thrown into jail on no process, for no crime, and on no pretence of crime, and is sold to pay the jail fees. This seems incredible, even of America, but it is the law.

Public opinion is deferred in such cases as the following, which is headed in the newspapers

"*Interesting Law Case.*

"An interesting case is now on trial in the Supreme Court, arising out of the following facts: a gentleman residing in Maryland had allowed an aged pair of his slaves substantial though not legal freedom for several years. While thus living a daughter was born to them, who grew up in the same liberty until she married a free negro, and went with him to reside in Pennsylvania. They had several children, and lived unmolested until the original owner died, when his heir attempted to regain them; but the magistrate before whom they were brought, decided that he had no jurisdiction in the case. *The owner seized the woman and children in the night, and carried them to Maryland.*"

"Cash for negroes," "cash for negroes," "cash for negroes," is the heading of advertisements in great capitals down the long columns of the crowded journals. Woodcuts of a runaway negro with manacled hands, crouching beneath a bluff pursuer in top boots, who, having caught him, grasps him by the throat, agreeably diversify the pleasant text. The leading article protests against "that abominable and hellish doctrine of abolition, which is repugnant alike to every law of God and Nature." The delicate mamma, who smiles her acquiescence in this sprightly writing as she reads the paper in her cool piazza, quiets her youngest child who clings about her skirts, by promising the boy "a whip to beat the little niggers with."—But the negroes, little and big, are protected by public opinion.

Let us try this public opinion by another test, which is important in three points of view: first, as showing how desperately timid of the public opinion slave owners are, in their delicate descriptions of fugitive slaves in widely-circulated newspapers; secondly, as showing how perfectly contented the slaves are, and how very seldom they run away; thirdly, as exhibiting their entire freedom from scar, or blemish, or any mark of cruel infliction, as their pictures are drawn, not by lying abolitionists, but by their own truthful masters.

The following are a few specimens of the advertisements in the public papers. It is only four years since the oldest among them appeared, and others of the same nature continue to be published every day in shoals.

"Ran away negress Caroline. Had on a collar with one prong turned down."

"Ran away, a black woman, Betsy. Had an iron bar on her right leg."

"Ran away, the negro Manuel, much marked with irons."

"Ran away, the negress Fanny. Had on an iron band about her neck."

"Ran away, a negro boy about twelve years old. Had round his neck a chain dog-collar with 'De Lampert' engraved on it."

"Ran away, the negro Hown. Has a ring of tron on his left foot. Also Grise, *his wife*, having a ring and chain on the left leg."

"Ran away, a negro boy, named James. Said boy was ironed when he left me."

"Committed to jail, a man who calls his name

John. He has a clog of iron on his right foot which will weigh four or five pounds."

"Detained at the police jail, the negro wench Myra. Has several marks of LASHING, and has irons on her feet."

"Ran away, a negro woman and two children; a few days before she went off I burned her with a hot iron on the left side of her face. I tried to make the letter M."

"Ran away, a negro man named Henry; his left eye out, some scars from a dirk on and under his left arm, and much scarred with the whip."

"One hundred dollars reward, for a negro fellow, Pompey, 40 years old. He is branded on the left jaw."

"Committed to jail, a negro man. Has no toes on the left foot."

"Ran away, a negro woman named Rachel. Has lost all her toes except the large one."

"Ran away, Sam. He was shot a short time since through the hand, and has several shots in his left arm and side."

"Ran away, my negro man Dennis. Said negro has been shot in the left arm between the shoulder and elbow, which has paralyzed the left hand."

"Ran away, my negro man named Simon. He has been shot badly in his back and right arm."

"Ran away, a negro named Arthur. Has a considerable scar across his breast and each arm, made by a knife; loves to talk much of the goodness of God."

"Twenty-five dollars reward for my man Isaac. He has a scar on his forehead, caused by a blow; and one on his back, made by a shot from a pistol."

"Ran away, negro girl called Mary. Has a small scar over her eye, a good many teeth missing, the letter A is branded on her cheek and forehead."

"Ran away, negro Ben. Has a scar on his right hand; his thumb and forefinger being injured by being shot last fall. A part of the bone came out. He has also one or two large scars on his back and hips."

"Detained at the jail, a mulatto, named Tom. Has a scar on the right cheek, and appears to have been burned with powder on the face."

"Ran away, a negro man named Ned. Three of his fingers are drawn into the palm of his hand by a cut. Has a scar on the back of his neck, nearly half round, done by a knife."

"Was committed to jail, a negro man. Says his name is Josiah. His back very much scarred by the whip; and branded on the thigh and hips in three or four places thus (J M). The rim of his right ear has been bit or cut off."

"Fifty dollars reward, for my fellow Edward. He has a scar on the corner of his mouth, two cuts on and under his arm, and the letter E on his arm."

"Ran away, negro boy Ellie. Has a scar on one of his arms from the bite of a dog."

"Ran away, from the plantation of James Surgette, the following negroes: Randal, has one ear cropped; Bob, has lost one eye; Kentucky Tom, has one jaw broken."

"Ran away, Anthony. One of his ears cut off, and his left hand cut with an axe."

"Fifty dollars reward for the negro Jim Blake. Has a piece cut out of each ear, and the middle finger of the left hand cut off to the second joint."

"Ran away, a negro woman named Maria. Has a scar on one side of her cheek, by a cut. Some scars on her back,"

"Ran away, the mulatto wench Mary. Has a cut on the left arm, a scar on the left shoulder, and two upper teeth missing."

I should say, perhaps, in explanation of this latter piece of description, that among the other blessings which public opinion secures to the negroes, is the common practice of violently punching out their teeth. To make them wear iron collars by day and night, and to worry them with dogs, are practices almost too ordinary to deserve mention.

"Ran away, my man Fountain. Has holes in his ears, a scar on the right side of his forehead, has been shot in the hind parts of his legs, and is marked on the back with the whip."

"Two hundred and fifty dollars reward for my negro man Jim. He is much marked with shot in his right thigh. The shot entered on the outside, half way between the hip and knee joints."

"Brought to jail, John. Left ear cropped."

"Taken up, a negro man. Is very much scarred about the face and body, and has the left ear bit off."

"Ran away, a black girl, named Mary. Has a scar on her cheek, and the end of one of her toes cut off."

"Ran away, my mulatto woman, Judy. She has had her right arm broken."

"Ran away, my negro man, Levi. His left hand has been burned, and I think the end of his forefinger is off."

"Ran away, a negro man, NAMED WASHINGTON. Has lost a part of his middle finger, and the end of his little finger."

"Twenty-five dollars reward for my man John. The tip of his nose is bit off."

"Twenty-five dollars reward for the negro slave, Sally. Walks *as though* crippled in the back."

"Ran away, Joe Dennis. Has a small notch in one of his ears."

"Ran away, negro boy, Jack. Has a small crop out of his left ear."

"Ran away, a negro man, named Ivory. Has a small piece cut out of the top of each ear."

While upon the subject of ears, I may observe that a distinguished abolitionist in New-York once received a negro's ear, which had been cut off close to the head, in a general post letter. It was forwarded by the free and independent gentleman who had caused it to be amputated, with a polite request that he would place the specimen in his "collection."

I could enlarge this catalogue with broken arms and broken legs, and gashed flesh, and missing teeth, and lacerated backs, and bites of dogs, and brands of red-hot irons innumerable; but as my readers will be sufficiently sickened and repelled already, I will turn to another branch of the subject.

These advertisements, of which a similar collection might be made for every year, and month, and week, and day; and which are coolly read in families as things of course, and as a part of the current news and small-talk; will serve to show how very much the slaves profit by public opinion, and how tender it is in their behalf. But it may be worth while to inquire how the slave owners, and the class of society, to which great numbers of them belong, defer to public opinion in their conduct, not to their slaves, but to each other; how they are accustomed to restrain their passions; what their bearing is among themselves; whether they are fierce or gentle; whether their social customs be brutal, sanguinary, and violent, or bear the impress of civilization and refinement.

That we may have no partial evidence from abolitionists in this inquiry, either, I will once more turn to their own newspapers, and I will confine myself, this time, to a selection from paragraphs which appeared from day to day, during my visit to America, and which refer to occurrences happening while I was there. The italics in these extracts, as in the foregoing, are my own.

These cases did not all occur, it will be seen, in territory actually belonging to legalized Slave States, though most, and those the very worst among them did, as their counterparts constantly do; but the position of the scenes of action in reference to places immediately at hand, where slavery is the law; and the strong resemblance between that class of outrages and the rest; lead to the just presumption that the character of the parties concerned was formed in slave districts, and brutalized by slave customs.

"*Horrible Tragedy.*

"By a slip from *The Southport Telegraph*, Wisconsin, we learn that the Hon. Charles C. P. Arndt, Member of the Council for Brown county, was shot dead *on the floor of the Council chamber*, by James R. Vinyard, Member from Grant county. *The affair* grew out of a nomination for Sheriff of Grant county. Mr. E. S. Baker was nominated and supported by Mr. Arndt. This nomination was opposed by Vinyard, who wanted the appointment to vest in his own brother. In the course of debate, the deceased made some statements which Vinyard pronounced false, and made use of violent and insulting language, dealing largely in personalities, to which Mr. A. made no reply. After the adjournment, Mr. A. stepped up to Vinyard, and requested him to retract, which he refused to do, repeating the offensive words. Mr. Arndt then made a blow at Vinyard, who stepped back a pace, drew a pistol, and shot him dead.

"The issue appears to have been provoked on the part of Vinyard, who was determined at all hazards to defeat the appointment of Baker, and who, himself defeated, turned his ire and revenge upon the unfortunate Arndt."

"*The Wisconsin Tragedy.*

"Public indignation runs high in the territory of Wisconsin, in relation to the murder of C. C. P. Arndt, in the Legislative Hall of the Territory. Meetings have been held in different counties of Wisconsin, denouncing *the practice of secretly bearing arms in the Legislative chambers of the country*. We have seen the account of the expulsion of James R. Vinyard, the perpetrator of the bloody deed, and are amazed to hear, that, after this expulsion by those who saw Vinyard kill Mr. Arndt in the presence of his aged father, who was on a visit to see his son, little dreaming that he was to witness his murder, *Judge Dunn has discharged Vinyard on bail.* The Miners' Free Press speaks *in terms of merited rebuke* at the outrage upon the feelings of the people of Wisconsin. Vinyard was within arm's length of Mr. Arndt, when he took such deadly aim at him, that he never spoke. Vinyard might at pleasure, being so near, have only wounded him, but he chose to kill him."

"*Murder.*

"By a letter in a St. Louis paper of the 14th, we notice a terrible outrage at Burlington, Iowa. A Mr. Bridgman having had a difficulty with a citizen of the place, Mr. Ross; a brother-in-law of the latter provided himself with one of Colt's revolving pistols, met Mr. B. in the street, *and discharged the contents of five of the barrels at him; each shot taking effect.* Mr. B., though horribly wounded, and dying, returned the fire, and killed Ross on the spot."

"*Terrible Death of Robert Potter.*

"From the 'Caddo Gazette' of the 12th inst., we learn the frightful death of Colonel Robert Potter. . . . He was beset in his house by an enemy, named Rose. He sprang from his couch, seized his gun, and, in his night clothes, rushed from the house. For about two hundred yards his speed seemed to defy his pursuers; but, getting entangled in a thicket, he was captured. Rose told him *that he intended to act a generous part*, and give him a chance for his life. He then told Potter he might run, and he should not be interrupted till he reached a certain distance. Potter started at the word of command, and before a gun was fired he had reached the lake. His first impulse was to jump in the water and dive for it, which he did. Rose was close behind him, and formed his men on the bank ready to shoot him as he rose. In a few seconds he came up to breathe; and scarce had his head reached the surface of the water when it was completely riddled with the shot of their guns, and he sunk, to rise no more!"

"*Murder in Arkansas.* '

"We understand *that a severe rencounter came off* a few days since in the Seneca Nation, between Mr. Loose, the sub-agent of the mixed band of the Senecas, Quapaw, and Shawnees, and Mr. James Gillespie, of the mercantile firm of Thomas G. Allison and Co., of Maysville, Benton, County Ark, in which the latter was slain with a bowie-knife. Some difficulty had for some time existed between the parties. It is said that Major Gillespie brought on the attack with a cane. A severe conflict ensued, during which two pistols were fired by Gillespie and one by Loose. Loose then stabbed Gillespie with one of those never, falling weapons a bowie-knife. The death of Major G. is much regretted, as he was a liberal-minded and energetic man. Since the above was in type, we have learned that Major Allison has stated to some of our citizens in town that Mr. Loose gave the first blow. We forbear to give any particulars, as *the matter will be the subject of judicial investigation.*"

"*Foul Deed.*

"The steamer Thames, just from Missouri River, brought us a handbill, offering a reward of 500 dollars for the person who assassinated Lilburn W. Baggs, late Governor of this State, at Independence, on the night of the 6th inst. Governor Baggs, it is stated in a written memorandum, was not dead, but mortally wounded.

"Since the above was written we received a note from the clerk of the Thames, giving the following particulars. Gov. Baggs was shot by some villain on Friday, 6th inst., in the evening, while sitting in a room in his own house in Independence. His son, a boy, hearing a report, ran into the room, and found the governor sitting in his chair, with his jaw fallen down, and his head leaning back; on discovering the injury done his father, he gave the alarm. Foot tracks were found in the garden below the window, and a pistol picked up supposed to have been overloaded, and thrown from the hand of the scoundrel who fired it. Three buck shots, of a heavy load, took effect; one going through his mouth, one into the brain, and another probably in or near the brain: all going into the back part of the neck and head. The governor was still alive on the morning of the 7th; but no hopes for his recovery by his friends, and but slight hopes from his physicians.

"A man was suspected, and the sheriff most probably has possession of him by this time.

"The pistol was one of a pair stolen some days previous from a baker in Independence, and the legal authorities have the description of the other."

"*Rencounter.*

"An unfortunate *affair* took place on Friday evening in Chatres Street, in which one of our most respectable citizens received a dangerous wound, from a poignard in the abdomen. From the Bee (New Orleans) of yesterday, we learn the following particulars. It appears that an article was published in the French side of the paper on Monday last, containing some strictures on the Artillery Battalion for firing their guns on Sunday morning, in answer to those from the Ontario and Woodbury, and thereby much alarm was caused to the families of those persons who were out all night preserving the peace of the city. Major C. Gally, Commander of the battalion resenting this, called at the office and demanded the author's name; that of M. P. Arpin was given to him, who was absent at the time. Some angry words then passed with one of the proprietors, and a challenge followed; the friends of both parties tried to arrange the affair, but failed to do so. On Friday evening, about seven o'clock, Major Gally met Mr. P. Arpin in Chatres Street, and accosted him. 'Are you Mr. Arpin?'

"'Yes, sir.'

"'Then I have to tell you that you are a —'" (applying an appropriate epithet.)

"'I shall remind you of your words, sir.'

"'But I have said I would break my cane on your shoulders.'

"'I know it, but I have not yet received the blow.'

"At these words, Major Gally, having a cane in his hands, struck Mr. Arpin across the face, and the latter drew a poignard from his pocket and stabbed Major Gally in the abdomen.

"Fears are entertained that the wound will be mortal. *We understand that Mr. Arpin has given security for his appearance at the Criminal Court to answer the charge.*"

"*Affray in Mississippi.*

"On the 27th ult., in an affray near Carthage, Leake county, Mississippi, between James Cottingham and John Wilburn, the latter was shot by the former, and so horribly wounded, that there was no hope of his recovery. On the 2d instant, there was an affray at Carthage between A. C. Sharkey and George Goff, in which the latter was shot, and thought mortally wounded. Sharkey delivered himself up to the authorities, *but changed his mind and escaped!*"

"*Personal Encounter.*

"An encounter took place in Sparta, a few days since, between the barkeeper of a hotel, and a man named Bury. It appears that Bury had become somewhat noisy, *and that the barkeeper, determined to preserve order, had threatened to shoot Bury*, whereupon Bury drew a pistol and shot the barkeeper down. He was not dead at the last accounts, but slight hopes were entertained of his recovery."

"*Duel.*

"The clerk of the steamboat *Tribune* informs us that another duel was fought on Tuesday last, by Mr. Robbins, a bank officer in Vicksburg, and Mr. Fall, the editor of the Vicksbug Sentinel. According to the arrangement, the parties had six pistols each, which, after the word 'Fire!' *they were to discharge as fast as they pleased.* Fall fired two pistols without effect. Mr. Robbins' first shot took effect in Fall's thigh, who fell, and was unable to continue the combat."

"*Affray in Clarke County.*

"An *unfortunate affray* occurred in Clarke County (Mo.) near Waterloo, on Tuesday the 19th ult., which originated in settling the partnership concerns of Messrs. M'Kane and M'Allister, who had been engaged in the business of distilling, and resulted in the death of the latter, who was shot down by Mr. M'Kane, because of his attempting to take possession of seven barrels of whiskey, the property of M'Kane, which had been knocked off to M'Allister at a sheriff's rale at one dollar per barrel. M'Kane immediately fled, *and at the latest dates had not been taken.*

"*This unfortunate affray* caused considerable excitement in the neighbourhood, as both the parties were men with large families depending upon them and stood well in the community."

I will quote but one more paragraph, which, by reason of its monstrous absurdity, may be a relief to these atrocious deeds.

"*Affair of Honour.*

"We have just heard the particulars of a meeting which took place on Six Mile Island, on Tuesday, between two young bloods of our city: Samuel Thurston, *aged fifteen*, and William Hine, *aged thirteen* years. They were attended by young gentleman of the same age. The weapons used on the occasion, were a couple of Dickson's best rifles; the distance, thirty yards. They took one fire, without any damage being sustained by either party, except the ball of Thurston's gun passing through the crown of Hine's hat. *Through the intercession of the Board of Honour*, the challenge was withdrawn, and the difference amicably adjusted."

If the reader will picture to himself the kind of Board of Honour which amicably adjusted the difference between these two little boys, who in any other part of the world would have been amicably adjusted on two porters' backs and soundly flogged with birchen rods, he will be possessed, no doubt, with as strong a sense of its ludicrous character, as that which sets me laughing whenever its image rises up before me.

Now, I appeal to every human mind, imbued with the commonest of common sense, and the commonest of common humanity; to all dispassionate, reasoning creatures, of any shade of opinion; and ask, with these revolting evidences of the state of society which exists in and about the slave districts of America before them, can they have a doubt of the real condition of the slave, or can they for a moment make a compromise between the institution or any of its flagrant fearful features, and their own just consciences? Will they say of any tale of cruelty and horror, however aggravated in degree, that it is improbable, when they can turn to the public prints, and, running, read such signs as these, laid before them by the men who rule the slaves: in their own acts and under their own hands?

Do we not know that the worst deformity and ugliness of slavery are at once the cause and the effect of the reckless license taken by these free-born outlaws? Do we not know that the man who has been born and bred among its wrongs; who has seen in his childhood husbands obliged at the word of command to flog their wives; women indecently compelled to hold up their own garments that men might lay the heavier stripes upon their legs, driven and harried by brutal overseers in their time of travail, and becoming mothers on the field of toil, under the very lash itself; who has read in youth, and seen his virgin sisters read, descriptions of runaway men and women, and their disfigured persons, which could not be published elsewhere, of so much stock upon a farm, or at a show of beasts—do we not know that that man, whenever his wrath is kindled up, will be a brutal savage? Do we not know that as he is a coward in his domestic life, stalking among his shrinking men and women slaves armed with his heavy whip, so he will be a coward out of doors, and carrying cowards' weapons hidden in his breast, will shoot men down and stab them when he quarrels? And if our reason did not teach us this and much beyond; if we were such idiots as to close our eyes to that fine mode of training which rears up such men; should we not know that they who among their equals stab and pistol in the legislative hall, and in the counting-house, and on the market-place, and in all the elsewhere peaceful pursuits of life, must be to their dependants, even though they were free servants, so many merciless and unrelenting tyrants?

What! shall we declaim against the ignorant peasantry of Ireland, and mince the matter when these American taskmasters are in question? Shall we cry shame on the brutality of those who ham-string cattle: and spare the lights of Freedom upon earth who notch the ears of men and women, cut pleasant posies in the shrinking flesh, learn to write with pens of red-hot iron on the human face, rack their poetic fancies for liveries of mutilation which their slaves shall wear for life and carry to the grave, break living limbs as did the soldiery who mocked and slew the Saviour of the world, and set defenceless creatures for targets! Shall we whimper over legends of the tortures practised on each other by the pagan Indians, and smile upon the cruelties of Christian men! Shall we, so long as these things last, exult above the scattered remnants of that stately race, and triumph in the white enjoyment of their broad possessions? Rather, for me, restore the forest and the Indian village; in lieu of stars and stripes, let some poor feather flutter in the breeze; replace the streets and squares by wigwams; and though the death-song of a hundred haughty warriors fill the air, it will be music to the shriek of one unhappy slave.

On one theme, which is commonly before our eyes, and in respect of which our national character is changing fast, let the plain Truth be spoken, and let us not, like dastards, beat about the bush by hinting at the Spaniard and the fierce Italian. When knives are drawn by Englishmen in conflict, let it be said and known: "We owe this change to Republican Slavery. These are the weapons of Freedom. With sharp points and edges such as these, Liberty in America doth hew and hack her slaves; or, failing that pursuit, her sons devote them to a better use, and turn them on each other."

CHAPTER XVIII.

CONCLUDING REMARKS.

There are many passages in this book, where I have been at some pains to resist the temptation of troubling my readers with my own deductions and conclusions; preferring that they should judge for themselves, from such premises as I have laid before them. My only object in the outset, was, to carry them with me faithfully wheresoever I went, and that task I have discharged.

But I may be pardoned, if on such a theme as the general character of the American people, and the general character of their social system, as presented to a stranger's eyes, I desire to express my own opinions in a few words, before I bring the volume to a close.

They are, by nature, frank, brave, cordial, hospitable, and affectionate. Cultivation and refinement seem but to enhance their warmth of heart and ardent enthusiasm; and it is the possession of these latter qualities in a most remarkable degree, which renders an educated American one of the most endearing and most generous of friends. I never was so won upon, as by this class; never yielded up my full confidence and esteem so readily and pleasuarbly, as to them; never can make again, in half a year, so many friends for whom I seem to entertain the regard of half a life.

These qualities are natural, I implicitly believe, to the whole people. That they are, however, sadly sapped and blighted in their growth among the mass; and that there are influences at work which endanger them still more, and give but little present promise of their healthy restoration; is a truth that ought to be told.

It is an essential part of every national character to pique itself mightily upon its faults, and to deduce tokens of its virtue or its wisdom from their very exaggeration. One great blemish in the popular mind of America, and the prolific parent of an innumerable brood of evils, is Universal Distrust. Yet, the American citizen plumes himself upon this spirit, even when he is sufficiently dispassionate to perceive the ruin it works; and will often adduce it, in spite of his own reason, as an instance of the great sagacity and acuteness of the people, and their superior shrewdness and independence.

"You carry," says the stranger, "this jealousy and distrust into every transaction of public life. By repelling worthy men from your legislative assemblies, it has bred up a class of candidates for the suffrage, who, in their every act, disgrace your Institutions and your people's choice. It has rendered you so fickle, and so given to change, that your inconstancy has passed into a proverb, for you no sooner set up an idol firmly, than you are sure to pull it down and dash it into fragments; and this, because directly you reward a benefactor, or a public servant, you distrust him, merely because he *is* rewarded; and immediately apply yourselves to find out, either that you have been too bountiful in your acknowledgements, or he remiss in his deserts. Any man who attains a high place among you, from the President downward, may date his downfall from that moment; for any printed lie that any notorious villain pens, although it militate directly against the character and conduct of a life, appeals at once to your distrust, and is believed. You will strain at a gnat in the way of trustfulness and confidence, however fairly won and well deserved; but you will swallow a whole caravan of camels, if they be laden with unworthy doubts and mean suspicions. Is this well, think you, or likely to elevate the character of the governors or the governed among you?"

The answer is invariably the same: "There's freedom of opinion here, you know Every man thinks for himself, and we are not to be easily overreached. That's how our people come to be suspicious."

Another prominent feature is the love of "smart" dealing, which gilds over many a swindle and gross breach of trust; many a defalcation, public and private; and enables many a knave to hold his head up with the best, who well deserves a halter—though it has not been without its retributive operation, for this smartness has done more in a few years to impair the public credit, and to cripple the public resources, than dull honesty, however rash, could have effected in a century. The merits of a broken speculation, or a bankruptcy, or of a successful scoundrel, are not guaged by its or his observance of the golden rule, "Do as you would be done by," but are considered with reference to their smartness. I recollect, on both occasions of our passing that ill-fated Cairo on the Mississippi, remarking on the bad effects such gross deceits must have when they exploded, in generating a want of confidence abroad, and discouraging foreign investment; but I was given to understand that this was a very smart scheme by which a deal of money had been made; and that its smartest feature was, that they forgot these things abroad in a very short time, and speculated again as freely as ever. The following dialogue I have held a hundred times: "Is it not a very disgraceful circumstance that such a man as So-and-so should be acquiring a large property by the most infamous and odious means, and, notwithstanding all the crimes of which he has been guilty, should be tolerated and abetted by your citizens? He is a public nuisance, is he not?" "Yes, sir," "A convicted liar?" "Yes, sir." "He has been kicked, and cuffed, and caned?" "Yes, sir." "And he is utterly dishonourable, debased, and profligate?" "Yes, sir." "In the name of wonder, then, what is his merit?" "Well, sir, he is a smart man."

In like manner, all kinds of deficient and impolitic usages are referred to the national love of trade; though, oddly enough, it would be a weighty charge against a foreigner, that he regarded the Americans as a trading people. The love of trade is assigned as a reason for that comfortless custom, so very prevalent in country towns, of married persons living in hotels, having no fireside of their own, and seldom meeting from early morning until late at night, but at the hasty public meals. The love of trade is a reason why the literature of America is to remain forever unprotected: "For we are a trading people, and don't care for poetry," though we *do*, by-the-way, profess to be very proud of our poets; while healthful amusements, cheerful means of recreation, and wholesome fancies, must fade before the stern utilitarian joys of trade.

These three characteristice are strongly presented at every turn full in the stranger's view. But the foul growth of America has a more tangled root than this, and it strikes its fibres deep in its licentious Press.

Schools may be erected east, west, north, and south; pupils be taught, and masters reared, by scores upon scores of thousands; colleges may thrive, churches may be crammed, temperance may be diffused, and advancing knowledge in all other forms walk through the land with giant strides; but, while the newspaper press of America is in, or near, its present abject state, high moral improvement in that country is hopeless. Year by year it must and will go back; year by year the tone of public feeling must sink lower down; year by year the Congress and the Senate must become of less account before all decent men; and, year by year, the memory of the Great Fathers of the Revolution must be outraged more and more in the bad life of their degenerate child.

Among the herd of journals which are published in the States, there are some, the reader scarcely need be told, of character and credit. From personal intercourse with accomplished gentlemen connected with publications of this class I have derived both pleasure and profit. But the name of these is Few, and of the others Legion; and the influence of the good is powerless to counteract the mortal poison of the bad.

Among the gentry of America; among the well-informed and moderate; in the learned professions; at the bar and on the bench, there is, as there can be, but one opinion in reference to the vicious character of these infamous journals. It is sometimes contended—I will not say strangely, for it is natural to seek excuses for such a disgrace—that their influence is not so great as a visiter would suppose. I must be pardoned for sayiug that there is no warrant for this plea, and that every fact and circumstance tends directly to the opposite conclusion.

When any man, of any grade of desert in intellect or character, can climb to any public distinction, no matter what, in America, without first grovelling down upon the earth, and bending the knee before this monster of depravity; when any private excellence is safe from its attacks, and when any social confidence is left unbroken by it, or any tie of social decency and honour is held in the least regard; when any man in that Free Country has freedom of opinion, and presumes to think for himself, and speak for himself, without humble reference to a censorship which, for its rampant ignorance and base dishonesty, he utterly loathes and despises in his heart; when those who most acutely feel its infamy and the reproach it casts upon the nation, and who most denounce it to each other, dare to set their heels upon and crush it openly, in the sight of all men; then, I will believe that its influence is lessening, and men are returning to their manly senses. But while that Press has its evil eye in every house, and its black hand in everp appointment in the state, from a president to a postman; while, with ribald slander for its only stock in trade, it is the standard literature of an enormous class, who must find their reading in a newspaper, or they will not read at all; so long must its odium be upon the country's head, and so long must the evil it works, be plainly visible in the Republic.

To those who are accustomed to the leading English Journals, or to the respectable journals of the Continent of Europe; to those who are accustomed to anything else in print and paper; it would be impossible, without an amount of extract for which I have neither space nor inclination, to convey an adequate idea of this frightful engine in America. But if any man desire confirmation of my statement on this head, let him repair to any place in this city of London where scattered numbers of these publications are to be found; and there let him form his own opinion.*

It would be well, there can be no doubt, for the American people as a whole, if they loved the Real less, and the Ideal somewhat more. It would be well, if there were greater encouragement to lightness of heart and gayety, and a wider cultivation of what is beautiful, without being eminently and directly useful. But then, I think the general remonstrance, "we are a new country," which is so often advanced as an excuse for defects which are quite unjustifiable, as being, of right, only the slow growth of an old one, may be very reasonably urged; and I yet hope to hear of there being some other national amusement in the United States, besides newspaper politics.

They certainly are not a humorous people, and their temperament always impressed me as being of a dull and gloomy character. In shrewdness of remark, and a certain cast-iron quaintness, the Yankees, or people of New-England, unquestionably take the lead; as they do in most other evidences of intelligence. But in travelling about, out of the large cities; as I have remarked in former parts of this volume; I was quite oppressed by the prevailing seriousness and melancholy air af business: which was so general and unvarying, that at every new town I came to, I seemed to meet the very same people whom I had left behind me, at the last. Such defects as are perceptibly in the national manners, seem, to me, to be referable, in a great degree, to this cause: which has generated a dull, sullen persistence in coarse usages, and rejected the graces of life as undeserving of attention. There is no doubt that Washington, who was always most scrupulous and exact on points of ceremony, perceived the tendency towards this mistake, even in his time; and did his utmost to correct it.

I cannot hold with other writers on these subjects that the prevalence of various forms of dissent in America, is in any way attributable to the non-existence there, of an established church: indeed, I think the temper of the people, if it admitted of such an Institution being founded among them, would lead them to desert it, as a matter of course, merely because it was established. But, supposing it to exist, I doubt its probable efficacy in summoning the wandering sheep to one great fold, simply because of the immense amount of dissent which prevails at home: and because I do not find in America any one form of religion with which we in Europe, or even in England, are unacquainted. Dissenters resort thither in great numbers, as other people do, simply because it is a land of resort: and great settlements of them are founded, because ground can be purchased, and towns and villages reared, where there were none of the human creation before. But even the Shakers emigrated from England: our country is not unknown to Mr. Joseph Smith, the opostle of Mormonism, or to his benighted disciples: I have heheld religious scenes myself in some of our populous towns which can hardly be surpassed by an American camp-meeting; and I am not aware that any instance of superstitious imposture on the one hand, and superstitious credulity on the other, has had its origin in the United States, which we cannot more than parallel by the precedents of Mrs. Southcote, Mary Tofts, the rabbit-breeder, or even Mr. Thom of Canterbury: which latter case arose, some time after the dark ages had passed away.

The Republican Institutions of America undoubtedly lead the people to assert their self-respect and their equality; but a traveller is bound to bear those Institutions in his mind, and not hastily to resent the near approach of a class of strangers, who, at home, would keep aloof. This characteristic, when it was tinctureed with no foolish pride, and stopped short of no honest service, never offended me: and I very seldom, if ever, experienced its rude or unbecoming display. Once or twice it was comically developed, as in the following case: but this was an amusing incident, and not the rule nor near it.

I wanted a pair of boots at a certain town, for I had none to travel in, but those with the memorable cork soles, which were much too hot for the fiery decks of a steamboat. I therefore sent a message to an artist in boots, importing, with my compliments, that I should be happy to see him, if he would do me the polite favour to call. He very kindly returned for answer that he would "look round" at six o'clock that evening.

I was lying on the sofa, with a book and a wineglass, at about that time, when the door opened, and a gentleman in a stiff cravat, within a year or two on either side of thirty, entered, in his hat and gloves; walked up to the looking-glass; arranged his hair; took off his gloves; slowly produced a measure from the uttermost depths of his coat-pocket; and requested me, in a languid tone, to "unfix" my

* Or, let him refer to an able, and perfectly truthful article, in *The Foreign Quarterly Review*, published in the present month of October; to which my attention has been attracted, since these sheets have been passing through the press. He will find some specimens there, by no means remarkable to any man who has been in America, but sufficiently striking to one who has not.

straps. I complied, but looked with some curiosity at his hat, which was still upon his head. It might have been that, or it might have been the heat—but he took it off. Then he sat himself down on a chair opposite to me; rested an arm on each knee; and, leaning forward very much, took from the ground, by a great effort, the specimen of metropolitan workmanship which I had just pulled off—whistling, pleasantly, as he did so. He turned it over and over; surveyed it with a contempt no language can express; and inquired if I wished him to fix me a boot like *that?* I courteously replied, that provided the boots were large enough, I would leave the rest to him; that if convenient and practicable, I should not object to their bearing some resemblance to the model then before him; but that I would be entirely guided by, and would beg to leave the whole subject to his judgment and discretion. "You an't partickler about this scoop in the heel, I suppose then?" says he: "we don't foller that, here." I repeated my last observation. He looked at himself in the glass again; went closer to it to dash a grain or two of dust out of the corner of his eye; and settled his cravat. All this time, my leg and foot were in the air. "Nearly ready, sir?" I inquired. "Well, pretty nigh," he said; "keep steady." I kept as steady as I could, both in foot and face; and having by this time got the dust out, and found his pencil-case, he measured me, and made the necessary notes. When he had finished, he fell into his old attitude, and taking up the boot again, mused for some time. "And this," he said, at last, "is an English boot, is it? This is a London boot, eh?" "That, sir," I replied, "is a London boot." He mused over it again, after the manner of Hamlet with Yorick's scull; nodded his head, as who should say "I pity the institutions that led to the production of this boot!" rose; put up his pencil, notes, and paper—glancing at himself in the glass, all the time—put on his hat, drew on his gloves very slowly, and finally walked out. When he had been gone about a minute, the door reopened, and his hat and his head reappeared. He looked round the room, and at the boot again, which was still lying on the floor; appeared thoughtful for a minute; and then said, "Well, good arternoon." "Good afternoon, sir," said I; and that was the end of the interview.

There is but one other head on which I wish to offer a remark: and that has reference to the public health. In so vast a country, where there are thousands of millions of acres of land yet unsettled and uncleared, and on every rood of which, vegetable decomposition is annually taking place; where there are so many great rivers, and such opposite varieties of climate; there cannot fail to be a great amount of sickness at certain seasons. But I may venture to say, after conversing with many members of the medical profession in America, that I am not singular in the opinion that much of the disease which does prevail, might be avoided, if a few common precautions were observed. Greater means of personal cleanliness are indispensable to this end; the custom of hastily swallowing large quantities of animal food, three times a day, and rushing back to sedentary pursuits after each meal, must be changed; the gentler sex must go more wisely clad, and take more healthy exercise; and in the latter clause, the males must be included also. Above all, in public institutions, and throughout the whole of every town and city, the system of ventilation, and drainage, and removal of impurities, requires to be thoroughly revised. There is no local legislature in America which may not study Mr. Chadwick's excellent Report upon the Sanitary condition of our Labouring Classes, with immense advantage.

I HAVE now arrived at the close of this book. I have little reason to believe, from certain warnings I have had since I returned to England, that it will be tenderly or favourably received by the American people; and as I have written the truth in relation to the mass of those who form their judgment and express their opinions, it will be seen that I have no desire to court, by any adventitious means, the popular applause.

It is enough for me to know, that what I have set down in these pages, cannot cost me a single friend on the other side of the Atlantic, who is, in anything, deserving of the name. For the rest, I put my trust implicitly in the spirit in which they have been conceived and penned, and I can bide my time.

I have made no reference to my reception, nor have I suffered it to influence me in what I have written; for, in either case, I should have offered but a sorry acknowledgment, compared with that I bear within my breast, towards those partial readers of my former books across the water, who met me with an open hand, and not with one that closed upon an iron muzzle.

MOTHER

AND

STEP-MOTHER.

IN TWELVE CHAPTERS.

FROM DICKENS' HOUSEHOLD WORDS.

Philadelphia:
T. B. PETERSON, NO. 102 CHESTNUT STREET.

MOTHER AND STEPMOTHER.

CHAPTER I.

"WELL, after all, I suppose it is not very much to be wondered at! Your disconsolate widowers are always the first to take comfort. Poor dear Ann! not dead two years till September, and Edward married again. The doctors ought to be ashamed of themselves, putting it into one's head that he was going into a decline. I am sure I couldn't rest day or night for thinking of him."

"I congratulate you on the relief this news must be to you, Fanny. Thomson says your brother is looking better than he ever did in his life; and he tells me his wife is a decided beauty."

"I cannot help thinking that he might have given us warning of his intentions earlier. It looks so awkward to know nothing of one's own brother's affairs. I talked so much about his grief that I shall get finely laughed at when he comes home with a young wife."

"You must endure with your usual patience, Fanny. I do not think he has used us particularly well; but it seems she was furious for him, and when a beauty of eighteen falls violently in love with a man of six-and-thirty, it must be allowed that it is sufficient to turn his head."

"O, you men always attach so much importance to youth. For my part, I should have thought Edward would have had too much sense to be caught by a miss in her teens; besides what can such a girl know about the management of children."

"I suppose she cannot know very much at present; but that comes by instinct. I do not think she is likely to make the worse stepmother because she is young; and Frank is such a pretty child that the danger will be of her spoiling him."

"O, it will be well enough till she has children of her own. Poor little Frank's good looks will not do him much service then; and you may take my word for it, Wilton, that it was a bad day for the poor child when his father first saw this Helen Macdonald."

Sir Edward Irwin, the subject of the foregoing tête-à-tête, was a baronet descended from a respectable family, and possessed of very considerable estates in the north of England. He had married, early in life, a lady of a sweet and amiable temper, and eschewing fashionable gaities, had found his happiness in domestic enjoyment, and in literary and scientific pursuits. The premature death of his wife startled him from the even tenor of his life. It was the first sorrow that had befallen him, and he was overwhelmed by it. His wife had been so constantly his companion; she had met all his requirements with a sympathy so ready and so intelligent; that he felt as though the dearer half of his soul was taken away, and as if it were impossible for the other half to linger behind. The caresses and necessities of his son, a child of some three years old, were powerless to rouse him. He was unhappy in having nothing to force him from his sorrow. His ample means, his obsequious retainers, his anxious friends—all ministered to it. Toil, the hard but sweet necessity of the sorrowing multitude, brought no aid to him: he nursed his woe, and fed it till his bodily strength gave way. Friends interfered; doctors were consulted; his affection for his child was appealed to; and he submitted passively to be sent to Italy, that change of scene and change of climate might be tried. He went without hope—without desire of recovery. Italy or England—what mattered it to him? The world was one graveyard, with one barren mound of earth, by which his heart sat and wept. So he said, and so he thought.

He took his child with him; for, though in his saddened mood the sight of the pretty boy only served to whet his sorrow, he clung to him as all that remained of her he had lost! and watched over him with a nervous solicitude grievous to behold. The contrast between the healthy child and the sorrow-stricken father could hardly fail to strike the most careless observer; it very quickly awakened the attention of Mrs. and Miss Macdonald, who happened to occupy an adjoining palazzo in Florence, whither Sir Edward had betaken himself by the direction of his physicians. The simple story of his bereavement roused the interest of both ladies—an interest which, in the younger, quickly assumed the character of passion.

Young, beautiful and undisciplined, Helen Macdonald revelled in wild notions of an all-consuming and imperious love. Her ardent temperament had been exaggerated by the loose morality of the unprincipled South, and she easily accepted the handsome stranger as the incarnation of an ideal, which already at eighteen she had despaired of meeting. Sir Edward's sunken eye and wan cheeks, his tall, worn person, and his rare and sorrowful smile, moved her, as the perfection of health and manly vigor might have failed to move her. What was not the love worth which could set such a mark on the bereaved one? She sympathised with, she admired his sorrow; and to soften it, to pour balm into the wound which he loved to keep open, became the ambition—the object of her life.

Occasion is rarely wanting to those who heartily seek it. In the present instance the child naturally opened the way to the father. The little boy's heart was easily won by the smiles and caresses of the beautiful stranger, who spoke to him in the language of his mother, and folded him in her arms almost as tenderly. The name of Helen Macdonald was constantly on his lips, until it became familiar and grateful to his father's ears. Courtesy required that Sir Edward should rouse himself to show some sense of the kindness lavished on his child. The first step taken, the rest followed naturally. Secure in his grief, Sir Edward submitted to the attentions of his neighbour. Her profound admiration, her sympathy unuttered, but spoken in every look, in every gesture, were a flattery which he accepted without suspicion. The meeting with her became the event of the day, until the sweet pale image of his lost love passed from his mind like breath from the face of a mirror, and the living, passionate Helen, reigned supreme. One bitter struggle he endured—one sickening attempt to return to his past state of feeling; but the flesh overcame the spirit, and with a sigh, half of sorrow at his instability, half of relief, he yielded himself to the intoxicating rapture of his new passion.

Helen was so very beautiful; so tender, yet withal so jealous, so imperious, that she kindled for a time his more placid temper into a semblance of her own. She was his tyrant and his slave; but in all her moods, so full of witchery, that she left him no time for backward thought, but filled him heart and soul with her own image.

No obstacles stood in the way of their union except such imaginary difficulties as the restless fancy of Helen created. Her mother, who in many respects resembled her daughter, was still in the meridian of her beauty, and was not ill-pleased to be relieved of a child whom she could not govern, and who had become a rival, and to have her creditably established as the wife of one of the oldest baronets in England. Sir Edward, on his side, had no near relations but his sister, and he had been so little in the habit of consulting her, that it was only on the eve of his marriage that he wrote to her. And the same letter which announced to her his complete recovery and approaching marriage, informed her of his intention of bringing his wife immediately to England.

CHAPTER II.

In spite of the dissatisfaction which Mrs. Wilton Brook had expressed at her brother's marriage, she was by no means deficient in anxiety to see her new sister-in-law, and she appreciated her brother's position too highly not to be anxious to ingratiate herself with a wife who she felt would exercise a strong influence over him. She accordingly dressed her pretty person in the most approved fashion, and prepared her lips for smiles and compliments, as she drove to visit the bride at Mivart's Hotel.

If her prejudice had been stronger than it was, it must have yielded to the grace and beauty of the stranger. Mrs. Brook, too, could not but be struck by the improvement in her brother's appearance, and she was grateful to her who had effected it; for, though a worldly woman, she was not deficient in natural affection. Sir Edward was her only brother, the head of her family, and she almost forgot poor Ann when she gazed on his renovated form, and saw the tender pride with which he watched the movements and listened to the words of his young wife.

The appearance of the child awoke the train of old recollections in the mind of his aunt, and when she had admired his growth, and caressed his fair long hair, she could not refrain from whispering to his father:

"How like poor Ann!"

Lady Irwin caught the whisper; her lip quivered, and the colour deepened on her cheek; she drew the child closer within the circle of her arm, and said softly—"I think him so like Edward."

"So he is," returned Mrs. Brook. "He is like Edward about the nose and mouth; but he has his mother's eyes."

It did not please Lady Irwin that the child's eyes were so large and tender.

"They are very beautiful," she said, with an anxious, half fearful look at her husband; but there was no sorrowful recollection in his countenance—nothing but present love and happiness.

"You can form no idea, Fanny, of what a mother Frank has in this dear little sister I have brought you. I cannot understand it, such a child as she is. Well might the poet say

φιλοτεκνον πως παν γοναικειον γενος."*

"What! you haven't cured him yet of his abominable habit of quoting what nobody can understand, Helen?"

"Oh no!" I don't wish to do it, either. You will laugh at us, I dare say, when I tell you that he is to give me regular lessons when we get home. I know a little Latin already, but not enough to be of any use. We have arranged our occupations for the winter. Edward's wife ought not to be a smatterer, you know."

"But I hope you are not going to let him bury you and himself down at Swallowfield. It was bad enough before, but to hide you in the country would be a crying scandal indeed."

"O, we have not the smallest intention of doing anything of the kind—have we, Edward? Do not alarm yourself, dear Mrs. Brook, I am quite as fond of society as you can desire."

"Well, that's some comfort. I only hope and trust that you do not intend to lay yourself out for a literary lady; that will do some twenty years hence; at present it would be a positive sacrifice. I am not sorry that you are only passing through town now; it would not have done to take off the gloss of your debut by appearing at the end of the season."

"O no! that would be an improvidence indeed," returned Helen, laughing. "I haven't tired Edward out yet, and we intend to live demurely and properly this winter, that I may come out span new with country cheeks next spring. We are going home to-morrow. It sounds so strange to talk of going home to a place one has never seen, but I almost seem to know it, I have made Edward tell me so much about it, from the lime avenue by the river's side, to the old oak cabinet in his study. I shall soon know the ways of the house, and then I hope you will come and see us."

"That's a very civil speech of yours, my dear," said Mrs. Brook, in high good humor; "and you may trust to my discretion not to break in upon you too soon. But what do you say to leaving me the boy for the present? I will take great care of him, and my girls will be nice playmates for him."

This invitation was declined with thanks, but with a haste which showed that neither Sir Edward nor his wife were inclined to forego the pleasure each derived from the presence of the child. Perhaps Mrs. Brook had given the invitation to test the real state of her sister-in-law's feelings towards her little nephew; certainly she did not seem displeased that it was not accepted, and took her leave, enraptured with the bride, and perfectly reconciled to her brother.

* The love of children is a woman's instinct.

CHAPTER III.

A FEW weeks saw Sir Edward Irwin and his lady established for the winter in their handsome country mansion. When the pleasant task of showing his estates to his wife was over, and the excitement of returning in joy to the home which he had left in sorrow and weakness, had subsided, Sir Edward resumed his old, but long interrupted pursuits; and his wife, true to her intention, entered on a course of study which should enable her to share them. Nor did her energies flag after a few weeks of strenuous exertion; her mind, vigorous and inquiring, demanded a pursuit which called its powers into action, and her proud spirit rose with the difficulties which presented themselves. Her husband smiled at her eagerness, and was delighted at her intelligence; so that the hours he spent in assisting her in the severe studies she undertook, were the pleasantest of his day.

And Lady Irwin was happy. Her husband had no thought beyond her, the boy throve and loved her; but yet her happiness was not perfect. Mere passion never brings happiness; it is of the earth, earthy, and bears the elements of corruption in itself. The love that does not come from Heaven, that does not look to Heaven for its perfection, cannot raise, cannot purify the heart—it is a restless wind that stirs the troubled soul, and will not let it be at peace—it is unquiet and ingenious as self-torture. So it was with Helen Irwin; between her and her happiness came a shadow, the phantom of one who had ceased to be.

The picture of the first Lady Irwin hung in the drawing-room, and she would sit and gaze at it until the canvass seemed to glow, and the sweet thoughtful face to live, smiling down upon her in secure triumph. She tortured herself by imagining the tenderness with which those large gray eyes had hung upon her husband, the loving words which those lips had uttered. If at any time his eyes dwelt on the picture, or if he involuntarily compared the features of his son with it, she could hardly control her impatience; and she would break from the boy in the midst of his caresses, if the resemblance he bore to his mother happened to strike her.

So time passed till a little girl was born to her, and the disquiet of her soul was hushed for awhile; the infant stole the trouble from its mother's heart, and wakened in her bosom strange yearnings for something better and purer than she had yet known. The great mystery of that new life, made so dear by suffering, and still so dependent upon her, stirred her to meditation on the great mystery of our being—the weakness incidental to her condition—while it humbled her pride, softened her heart to receive with meekness the only doctrine that can explain it. But in a few months the frail infant sickened and died. No tear wetted the mother's cheek, she endured in silence the affliction to which she would not submit, impiously arraigning the Hand that sent it, and the vague conception of religious truth which she had begun to entertain vanished, and darkness closed in upon her soul.

She had her child buried in a quiet corner of the churchyard, away from the vault where Lady Irwin lay, and thither she would wander at lonely hours, and sit on the little mound with dry eyes and an angry heart. The harebells that grew spontaneously about it she plucked and bore away, but she hung no garlands on the stone, and planted no flowers over the place of her infant's rest.

Her studies, which she had rather neglected during the little one's life, she now resumed with increased ardor, seeking distraction for her aching heart in mental exercise. Her husband, aware that all was not as it should be, though far from apprehending the true nature of the grief of which she never spoke, willingly lent her his aid, hoping that the pursuits which yielded him such satisfaction would act with medicinal virtue upon her. Her mind thus acquired strength, but her heart did not keep pace with its progress; the circle of her affections narrowed, no interchange of friendly sympathies with her equals drew her from herself, no tender acts of personal charity to the poor about her softened her sorrow. She became cold and stately, and proud of her secret grief, unprofaned by common pity, and unlike that of any other.

A young woman in the village, who had been married shortly after Lady Irwin's arrival at Swallowfield, lost her baby soon after the death of Helen's daughter. She was a simple creature, and the affliction lay sore upon her, for her husband was often rough, sometimes unkind to her, and being from a distant part of the country, she had few friends in the village. Many a summer evening did she spend in the churchyard, and many a tasteful garland of wild flowers did she weave to dress her baby's grave. More than once Lady Irwin passed her in the gloaming, but her heart never softened with a feeling of kindred sorrow; she rather despised the grief which could find relief in such childish demonstrations, and the poor woman—with the one thing that loved her laid in the dust, with clothes barely sufficient to cover her, and a cold hearth at home—was richer and happier than the beautiful lady whose costly robes brushed her as she passed, for, in the depth of her desolation, she could look to One, who had promised to bear her sorrow, in the light of whose presence she might hope to be re-united to her darling.

The world, as it is called, occupied a due share of Lady Irwin's time and attention: her tastes inclined her to magnificence, her beauty and her talents to display, while her husband's fortune justified her in assuming a leading position in society. No parties were more brilliant, no dinners better appointed than hers. Science, literature, and art were duly honored at her house, her husband was an accomplished conversationalist, and she herself possessed the rarer virtue of being an excellent listener. Thus her house was the resort of men of the highest intellectual attainments in town, and when at Swallowfield she was rarely without visitors whose names were known and honoured.

But though Lady Irwin had many admirers she had no friends; she asked no sympathy, and had none to give—none, at least, for the sorrows and joys of daily life—she was self-contained. In a man such a character is hard and sad—how much harder, how much sadder, in a woman, whose vocation it is to temper the stern realities of life, who, to be strong, must have some touch of weakness, who, if by too easy credulity, she opened the way to sin and death, should also point the road to life by faith perfected in the sense of her infirmity.

Aware of the violence of her passions, and falsely believing that unsubdued vigor of natural instinct was a proof of greatness of character, there was nothing of which Lady Irwin stood in such dread as the compassion of people of a tamer temperament. She, therefore, learnt, not indeed to govern her feelings, but to repress all outward manifestation of them, and to hide the tumult of her bosom under a cold and stately bearing.—She became silent and inclined to solitude, or to the dangerous intimacy of Agnese, a waiting-woman who had followed her from Italy, and to whom more than to any other creature she was in the habit of unveiling her emotions.

It seems to be an imperative law of our nature that the heart should unburthen itself to some one. When he whom we trust is indeed a friend, faithful in counsel and strong in comfort, obedience to his law is the sweetest solace of our earthly pilgrimage, but when we hide the ugly portions of our character from those who love us, and expose them only to those of whose judgment we stand in no awe, who, our inferiors in intellect and station, pander to our passions and foster our evil tendencies, there is no perverted blessing which may be turned to more deadly account.

Agnese Pistorella was the natural daughter of a Venetian nobleman, who had been assassinated by her mother in a fit of jealous des pair. Having accomplished her crime, the murderess was overwhelmed with remorse, and, far from attempting to make her escape, herself sent to summon the officers of justice, and lay with her loosened hair falling like a pall over her victim till they arrived. Her youth, her beauty, and the violence of her passions, drew much attention to her case, but she was executed—submitting to her fate with the constancy of one who knew it to be the natural consequence of her deed, the compensation due to the Manes of her lover. The child she left was completely abandoned by its father's friends, and became dependent on its maternal grandmother—a woman of infamous character. Taking advantage of the interest excited by her daughter, this woman made a loathsome traffic by exhibiting her child; but curiosity soon died away—the sooner, as the grandmother thought, that the girl inherited the swarthy countenance and beetling brows of her father. Nursed early and often with the terrible story of her parents, and tutored to assume a look of melancholy, Agnese gradually acquired that low cunning with which Nature arms the oppressed, passing from infancy to womanhood subject to the caprices of the abandoned old woman, who even in her dotage meditated crime.

A deep-lying love for her mother was the poetry of Agnese's life; whatever was sweet or soft in her memories gathered around the image of the beautiful, sumptuously-apparelled woman dwelling in luxurious chambers, who had fondled and caressed her; of those sunny, far-off times she had a vague recollection, but well did she remember the last time her mother's arms were folded about her—well did she remember the bare dungeon walls, the darkness, the bloodshot eyes, the pale, haggard cheeks, and the long, lingering kiss of the white tremulous lips.

On her grandmother's death she was forced to seek the means of living, and accident placed her in the family of Mrs. Macdonald, where she filled one of the lowest grades in the household. Here her haughty silence, while it made her unpopular among the servants, but excited the interest of Helen, who, in the loneliness of spirit engendered by the absence of confidence between herself and her mother, readily turned her thoughts to the outcast, and made it her earnest request that the girl might be given to her as her special attendant—a request which her mother, ever careless of her true interests, and blameably lax where her discipline should have been the strictest, never thought of denying her. The kindness thus unexpectedly shown to her, Agnese repaid with blind devotion. To Helen, in the dark twilight of a winter night, she told the story of her parents, lingering with fond minuteness over all the details with which her memory was stored. It was a story Helen well loved to hear; she never pointed out the heinous sin, and how the last evil was the fruit of the first—neither for herself nor for the poor orphan did she read this lesson.

Through Helen's courtship, Agnes had watched with jealous care, for the smallest sign of faithlessness in Sir Edward, resolved if need were, to prove her devotion to her mistress by sacrificing herself to avenge her; but the need did not arise. He had loved before—dearly loved, it was said; but she and Helen were both persuaded that true passion was now, for the first time, awakened in his bosom. When they were married, and Sir Edward gradually relapsed into his old habits, the ascendancy which his wife exercised over him left no room for jealousy, however much she might fret at the evenness and placidity of his temper.

How mutually injurious these two women were, may easily be conjectured. Neither acted as a corrective to the other; but each strengthened and confirmed the other's evil tendencies.

CHAPTER IV.

Little Frank Irwin would have been sadly starved for affection and sympathy, if he had been entirely dependent for both on his stepmother; for, though at times she oppressed him with her caresses, and indulged him even beyond what was wholesome for him, she grew so capricious in her treatment of him, after the death of her infant, that his naturally sweet and trustful temper must have been injured. But when they were in the country, which was generally for nine months in the year, Frank found a playfellow and friend in the little daughter of the clergyman, a blue-eyed child, something less than a year his junior.

The rectory was not a quarter of a mile from the gates of Sir Edward's park; and Mr. Birkby, the rector, was a distant relative of the Irwin's; so the intimacy of the children was quite natural; and whenever his mamma was busy—whenever Agnese was cross—whenever, in short, anything happened to disquiet him at home—away ran little Frank, to forget his trouble in the company of Kitty Birkby; and many a sunny afternoon did they sit together, under the large apple-tree in the orchard, or in the shadow of the old cedar, making daisy garlands, and mingling their hearts in innocent prattle.

Frank was a great hero to Kitty. Frank went to London and to all kinds of places with long names, which he knew quite well, and could repeat as easily as she could repeat the names of the field and hedge flowers. Frank went to the theatres, where he saw all sorts of wonderful things, which he described to her with indefatigable patience. There was not a marvellous feat of harlequin that she was not familiar with; and she even dreamt of the fairy—in pink, with silver wings—who always came down in a chariot, drawn by peacocks, just in time to save the prince and princess from the deep-laid plots of the cruel ogre with green hair, a bulbous nose, and a cavernous mouth, who had announced it to be his intention to dine off the prince, and promote the little trembling princess to the honour of Mrs. Ogress. O, with what eloquence did he describe, to the round-eyed, eager auditress, the final scene of the drama, when the fairy, having made the prince and princess happy, and consigned their wicked aunts and uncles to well-merited punishment, ascended out of mortal ken, seated on a many-coloured cloud, which seemed heavily charged with electricity—a mode of travelling highly unpleasant to any one but a fairy, but which, of course, afforded her unalloyed delight, as she took care to communicate to the prince and princess that they must expect nothing further from her; it being her intention to retire into private life among the stars, where she (very rationally, as the world goes,) did not wish to be disturbed.

By the time he had related the story six or seven times to Kitty, Frank became so enamoured of it, that he conceived the bold idea of acting it; he was to be the prince, Kitty the princess, and Sara, her nurse, a particularly solid young woman, the fairy; the other dramatis personæ might be imagined.

Kitty took very kindly to being the princess; she stuck a flower in her hair; sat herself down on a bank and pretended it was a throne; but when Frank tried to induce her to personate the agony of the princess when her lover was torn away from her by the savage ogre, here represented by a crabbed old tree, he was almost discomfited. Very much urged, Kitty rushed fiercely up to the tree, and beating its knotty stem with her chubby hands, cried, "Naughty ogre, take away my prince!" It was in vain that Frank explained the truculent nature of the ogre, and the timid character of the princess. This, however, was nothing in comparison to the trouble he had with Sara, who was always deeply engaged in reading a dilapidated copy of the Old English Baron, in devouring sour apples, or darning stockings, when she was required to make her graceful descent upon earth.

But there were other things which Frank delighted to impart to Kitty: the grand mystery of hic, hæc, hoc, in which he was at an early age indoctrinated; yet Kitty was no prodigy; at five years old she hardly knew her letters; and if any one had told her that the earth was like an orange, flattened at the poles, she would have opened her blue eyes in most profound astonishment. Like Frank, she had lost her mother in her infancy, and was in great measure dependent on a maiden sister of her father, who resided with him, and who loved her dearly. But Miss Selina Birkby was now in the winter of her days, and having spent the prime of her life in the dreary state called, in derision, single blessedness, she knew no more of the rearing and training of children than a day-labourer, accustomed to no sort of horticulture but the sowing of turnips, might be supposed to know of the rearing of delicate exotics.

Kitty, nevertheless, had a most charming little countenance, which changed from smiles to tears with the rapidity of an April day. She was a great favourite with Sir Edward Irwin, who liked to take her on his knee, and to play with her soft curls; but she never pleased Lady Irwin—perhaps because the sight of her wakened the memories of her own lost little girl—perhaps from the increasing jealousy of her disposition, which nothing seemed too small, nothing too innocent, to excite. She wondered what Sir Edward and Frank could see to interest them in a little creature neither remarkable for beauty, nor distinguished for intelligence; and Kitty, for her part, had an instinctive dread of Lady Irwin; she was almost completely silent in her presence, and approached her only with effort and unwillingness.

But if her instinct led her to avoid Lady Irwin, it operated yet more strongly in the case of Agnese. The child absolutely trembled if Agnese touched her; and once, when she insisted on kissing her, she was almost convulsed with terror. Agnese, as may be imagined, was not slow to repay dislike with dislike. She chose to believe, that, being the child of an ecclesiastic, Kitty was peculiarly under the ban of heaven; for, though destitute of anything like true religion, she clung with pertinacity to the superstitions which she had been taught in childhood, and especially delighted to believe that the marriage of a priest was a sacrilegious thing, and that, therefore, little Kitty was nothing but a foredoomed child of Satan.

CHAPTER V.

Frank was just nine years old, and in the middle of the veritable history of Pyramus and Thisbe, which he read with Mr. Birkby and duly performed with Kitty, when Lady Irwin again became a mother, the mother of a son of singular promise and beauty. Her heart swelled with joyful pride, but it seemed as if happiness for her was never to be without alloy. A conversation which she overheard between the nurse and Agnese completely damped her pleasure, and awakened discontented thoughts in her bosom.

They were speaking of the child, admiring his beauty, and commenting on the joy of his parents.

"Ah!" cried the old nurse, "Sir Edward's well pleased enough now; but, Lord love ye, if you'd seen the fuss there was when Master Frank was born—he worn't nothing to compare to this here lamb, but then he was the heir—Lord, the ringing of bells and the driving up of carriages! I made nigh twenty pound at the christening—and all the village was invited to dine; there was an ox roasted whole—and as to the ale, it was quite a sin to see it flowing about everywhere like water."

Nothing could exceed the tenderness of Sir Edward; he could not have shown more joy at the birth of his eldest son; the inquiries were numerous, the christening splendid; but the old nurse's words rankled in Lady Irwin's heart. She still loved Frank, but she could not at all times bear to see him caress his half-brother, though, if he showed the least indifference, she tortured herself by thinking how much the child's fate depended on his affection. As soon as the baby began to take notice, he showed a very decided affection for Frank; there was only one person whom he preferred, and that person was Kitty Birkby.

With all her passionate affection, Lady Irwin wanted the art to accommodate herself to the weaknesses of a little child; she could not talk the fond nonsense which the ordinary mother makes the vehicle of her tenderness, and by which she wakes the dimples in her infant's cheek. Kitty, on the other hand, was distinguished by an extraordinary power of sympathy; she seemed to know intuitively what was wanted of her, and with happy and unconscious grace to meet the requirement. She loved all children, so it was very natural that she could feel especial delight in the beautiful child who crowed and clapped his little hands at her appearance.

In spite of her dissatisfaction that her son was not his father's heir, Lady Irwin was made much happier by his birth: the boy was all her own—he had her fitful eyes, her square brow, the shape of his mouth was like hers, with a shadow of his father's smile; and before long it became evident that he inherited her temper. He was wilful and impatient, he never let his mother fret herself for want of excitement; it was never possible to tell in what mood the young autocrat might choose to show himself; he was like a mountain-girdled lake, now laughing to the summer sun, now lashing its crested billows into fury. Kitty Birkby was the only person whose influence with him never failed: his mother might waste her strength in the attempt to storm him down; she never gained her point; he would scream till she was terrified for his health, but he would not yield; yet Kitty, without violence, by some subtle charm in her touch or in her voice, brought back the smiles in five minutes, and won him obedience.

For two years longer Frank Irwin pursued his studies at home, under the direction of Mr. Birkby; he was then sent to Rugby, at the time under the wise government of Dr. Arnold. His departure caused Kitty great sorrow, but it made little interruption in her visits to the hall; for Edward, as the boy was named from his father, was growing fast, and became daily more imperious in his demands upon her time. It was not in the nature of things, that Lady Irwin should not feel some touch of tenderness to the sweet child to whom she owed so much; perhaps she regretted that she could not love her, and strove by the lavish profusion of her gifts to atone for the want of real affection. In one respect only did the little girl and the woman sympathise. Lady Irwin possessed a musical genius of a high order; her knowledge of the art was profound, and the harp or piano under her hand produced thrilling or stirring harmonies, the transcript of her state of feeling; she was a poet of sound, and the pulsations of her passionate temperament thus found immediate and ample expression.

Now, Kitty Birkby early evinced great taste for music; her voice was peculiarly clear and sweet; she owed much to the careful instruction of Lady Irwin, who was pleased to have a pupil so docile and so apt in her favorite science. In other respects, Kitty's education was not systematised; her aunt taught her needlework and what she knew of French; while her father instructed her in arithmetic, and formed her taste in literature. His eyes failing him he was often glad to use her younger sight, and thus she learned to read with expression and without fatigue, while she imbibed a fund of general knowledge, which lay in her mind like seed destined to bring forth a rich harvest in future years. And thus her childhood passed in ever-recurring works of tenderness and love. She was so gentle and so modest that it was only by her absence that her friends knew how much they needed her.

CHAPTER VI.

"Mother," cried Edward Irwin, now a fine boy of fourteen, "why does every one think so much more of Frank than of me?"

"He is the heir, and is just come of age, and when the heir comes of age there is always great rejoicing."

"It must be a fine thing to be the heir!" exclaimed Edward, after a pause, fixing his eyes thoughtfully on his mother's face.

"Why do you think so?" inquired she.

"Why? What a question! Why, the world is before you, to be sure; you can do exactly what you please, and everybody thinks you a fine fellow."

"It is better to make a fortune than barely to inherit one."

"O yes, of course; but that takes such a time. Just fancy, mother, how splendid it must be for Frank. Every one says how handsome he is, and every one admires his cleverness and his riding, and everything he does. Now I'm every bit as handsome and as clever for my age, and father says Frank couldn't have ridden Mad Tom before he went to Rugby; yet nobody takes the trouble to find out my perfections."

"Would you rather have been your father's heir than my son?" As Lady Irwin asked the boy the question, her cheek flushed, and her brow, to which a slight frown had become habitual, darkened.

"Why, no, mother, I don't mean that. I'd rather have my own stately mother, for all her fierce looks and angry words, than the pretty pale lady in the picture; but suppose there had been no Lady Irwin before you, I'm sure you're wife enough for one man any day."

"I should never have known your father if he hadn't come to Florence when he was in sorrow for the loss of Frank's mother."

"Which proves, I suppose, that it didn't please the Fates that I should be an eldest son. I always thought them a stupid set of spinsters. Don't you know any ricketty old Earl or Duke who might be coaxed into adopting me?"

"Do not talk so foolishly, Edward," returned his mother, with displeasure, "learn to have some respect for those to whom you owe your being; learn to have some regard for the talents with which you are endowed, and the legitimate exercise of which cannot fail to make you known and distinguished."

"In spite of all that," pursued the boy recklessly, "I believe, mother, you would like to see me in Frank's shoes. Only think, this grand old house, the woods, the lands, all mine. But there, don't bring down the thunder clouds! I'm sure, if the old Parcæ have ill-used me in condemning me to be a hewer of wood and a drawer of water, they are ten times more to blame for making you anything but an empress. If they had only done you justice now, I could have accommodated myself so nicely to the character of a royal duke."

"Doubtless, you foolish boy," said his mother, caressing his full dark curls.

"But only fancy, mother, you sweeping along in velvet and diamonds, issuing your commands to your generals and counsellors; ordering one man to lose his head, making a governor of a province of another; and me riding about on a cream-colored Arabian pony, at the head of an army, going to chastise some rebellious barbarians."

"Silly boy!" cried Lady Irwin, "what a shock you will feel when you descend from your Pegasus, and know yourself nothing but plain Edward Irwin, with not a sou to help you but what your father or brother may choose to give you."

"Considering the state of the case, mother, I think you might have let me give the reins to my fancy a little longer. I wish you hadn't pulled me up with such a jerk. I declare I felt the Arab under me, and the air fanning my cheek, and you and all your court ladies looking down from your balcony. It was too bad to bring me down such a thump into this seedy old room, with nothing out of doors but that wet blanket of a sky. I don't believe it ever intends to leave off raining till all the branches are washed off the trees.—Why, if there isn't Kitty! Only think, mother, of her coming all through this rain. See how daintily she holds up her dress, and what little pools of water her pretty pattering feet leave every step she takes. She's worth my cloud palace, Arab pony and all! There's a smile, now, would make sunshine anywhere. O mother, stir the fire and make it blaze, while I run down and help her off with her cloak."

Away he ran, leaving his mother sunk in gloomy meditation. The impatience he had expressed, and forgotten as soon as expressed, awakened the discontent in her own heart, and roused the old bitterness and jealousy that slumbered in her bosom. She was essentially an ambitious woman; her very love partook of the passion by which the angels fell; and the beauty and promise of her son, while it increased the idolatrous affection which she bore him, aggravated her discontent at the inferior position to which he was destined. But the fire smouldered in her own bosom, and even Agnese knew not into how fierce a blaze a little breath might kindle it.

When Edward returned, bringing in Catherine Birkby, despoiled of her wet garments, and glowing with exercise, the cloud had passed from Lady Irwin's countenance, if not from her spirit, and she welcomed her young visiter with courtesy, even with kindness.

"And now, mother," said Edward, when he had established the guest in a warm corner of a sofa, and supplied her with a footstool and all imaginable comforts; "and now, mother, would you like to know what has brought my princess out this fine November morning? It's a good story, and I'll tell Frank as sure as fate."

"Suppose you begin by telling me," said his mother, smiling.

"You tell her, Kitty. Doesn't she look a nice tutor, now? Just look at her; she wants nothing but a pair of spectacles and a stout cane."

"The boy's distracted," said Lady Irwin. "He is so delighted that you are come to break the dull tête-à-tête with his prosy old mother, Kate, that he can't speak an intelligible word."

"Well then, mother—neither prosy nor old, much younger than Kitty, I'll be bound—would you believe it? the abominable creature has come out through this weather to bring me my Arnold's Exercise book."

"She is a great deal too good to you, sir;

and we must get Mr. Birkby to be more strict with you, if you continue so careless."

"But only think of her malignity, mother, when I had forgotten the stupid book so cleverly, and persuaded myself that it would be cruel to send Brade and the ragged old pony for it, she must come through the cold and wet for no other purpose than to make me ashamed of myself. There's only one thing to be said for her; she never did Arnold herself, and so she doesn't know what a tremendous bore he is."

"Now I have brought the book, I hope you intend to do the exercise," said Kitty, smiling.

"Well, that depends. You must fold the paper and mend the pens, and look out the words in the index. But no, let's go and have a game at billiards. I'll hunt up Frank, and mother will come."

"No, no," said Kitty. "I'll play no billiards till you've done your exercise."

"Well, we can play without you, you know."

"You will have to play by yourself then," said his mother. "You'll find no one here to play with you, if you are rude to Kitty."

"Rude to Kitty!" repeated the boy, the color flushing to his cheek. "Rude to Kitty, whom I love better than anything in the whole world? I don't know what you mean, mother."

"He only wanted to show me that I was not quite so important as I thought myself," said Kate, apologetically. "Come, Edward, let us go into the school-room; the exercise won't take half an hour, and there will be plenty of time for billiards afterwards."

The boy obeyed, but his cheek still glowed. He got together what was necessary for his work in silence, and wrote quickly and attentively for some time; then suddenly flinging down his pen, he threw himself on the floor, and hiding his face on Catherine's knees, burst into tears.

"Hush, Edward, is this right—is this Christian?" remonstrated Kitty.

"Rude to you, my own dearest Kitty?" sobbed the boy. "If I was, I didn't mean it. Of course you know we can't play without you—at least, I can't; and I'm sure Frank wouldn't. O, you don't know how dull and stupid the house is when you are not here. Father sits in his study, making discoveries about meteoric phenomena or something or other; and Frank thinks he's doing a great deal with Plato, though I believe half the time he does nothing but smoke and dream; and mother and I talk ourselves into a horrible dislike of everything. O Kitty, I hate myself so sometimes, and you would hate me too, if you knew what wicked thoughts come into my head."

"Wicked thoughts come to all of us, Edward; and you know there is only one mode of driving them away."

"If I were only Frank, now," said the boy, "I should be quite happy."

"Oh no, you would not, if you are discontented now. And your brother loves you so dearly. I cannot think how you can find it in your heart to envy him."

"I do though, Kitty. I envy him his fortune and his rank; but that is not what I envy him most. I envy him because everybody loves him. Why, even you love him more than you love me."

"Don't you know what good reason I have to love him?" returned Kitty, firmly, but with some little embarrassment. "I have often told you what a friend he has been to me all my life long."

"Yes, I know that you don't love him because he is rich and will be called Sir Francis. O, I wish he had been cross and ugly, for then you could not have loved him."

"O, dear Edward, think how wrong it is to be vexed that your brother is loved."

"Well, it's not exactly that. I don't want people not to like Frank, for I know he's a splendid fellow; but I do wish somebody would love me better than him or anybody or anything else in the whole world."

"You know your mother does; and for her sake you should try to be contented and happy."

"Well, I am very happy, if the days were not so confoundedly long and everything so stupid. Do you know, I did something this morning. I am sure you will say it was very wrong—I felt it was wrong myself. I didn't mean to do it, but somehow I couldn't stop. I told mother I wished I was Frank. She did look so vexed—there came a strange fierceness into her face. Don't you think she is very handsome, Kitty?"

"Yes, especially when she smiles."

"No, when she frowns: it's my treasure of a Kate that looks lovely when she smiles. Mother looks magnificent when she's fierce. I feel a sort of creeping of the flesh and burning at the heart when she looks like that. Is it wrong to like to see her so?"

"It must be wrong," replied Kitty, gravely. "She cannot look so unless she feels unhappy; besides, I do not think it reverent in you to speculate on your mother's looks, and to put your own interpretation on a passing expression."

"Do not look so sorry, Kate—I can't bear to see you. I know I am very wicked, but you must not hate me. I try to pray, indeed I do, and I will yet more. Is it not strange," he added presently, in a lower tone—"is it not very strange that I never like to make you look sorry; but when I vex mother the blood leaps in my veins, and I feel as if I couldn't stop, it makes me feel so near to her. Look at my forehead: don't you see I am getting a frown like mother's? I frown so at night sometimes that it wakes me out of my sleep. I dream of nothing but battles and fighting. Dear Kitty, tell me, do you really think I could ever go to Heaven?"

"Remember who gave His precious life a ransom for sinners, Edward! Remember Him who loves you, and who is touched with a feeling for your infirmities."

"Sometimes," said the boy, looking out of the window, and speaking in a soft, dreamy tone—"sometimes all that is written in the Testament seems so true, that I feel strong for anything; but then, all in a moment, away it goes, and the old bad thoughts come back. I suppose, Kitty, it is the Devil taking away the Word out of my heart."

Thus, in the dark November day, they talked together.

CHAPTER VII.

"My dear Kitty, we must think of getting you some new clothes to go to London with. Of course, you will like to buy the principal things there; but you must have a new gown to go in. Morley has a lovely dove-colored silk, which I'm sure would just become you, and he only wants three-and ninepence a yard for it. It's rather a short length, but he said if I'd take it he'd allow me something."

"I am not going to London, my dear aunt," replied Catherine, in a low voice.

"Not going to London!" exclaimed Miss Birkby, looking over her spectacles in amazement. "Why, Lady Irwin has been here herself, and your papa and I accepted the invitation."

"I told Lady Irwin I was not going. I did not know she would ask me till just now. Edward talked of it, but she never mentioned it before."

"But why you won't go I can't understand," pursued Miss Birkby. "You may never have such another opportunity in your life. You would see everything and be in the first society without any trouble or fatigue. I'm sure Lady Irwin won't be pleased. I can't understand it. Why, when I was your age, I used to go wherever any one asked me. I hope you are not thinking about leaving your papa and me, because, you know, we could manage perfectly well by ourselves, and of course we can't expect to keep you always."

"I think you and papa would be lonely if I went," returned Catherine, slowly; "but that is not the only reason—that is not the principal reason. I don't think it would be well for me to go, and I hope you and papa will let me stay at home."

"Of course, dear, we are only too glad to have you. I'm sure I don't know what we should do without you for three months: I am only sorry about Lady Irwin."

"Well, now, this is too bad," cried Edward Irwin, brushing into the room, his face flushed and his eyes bright with tears of vexation. "Only think, Miss Birkby—only imagine—mother says Kitty won't go."

"She has just been telling me so, my dear, and I am quite as much surprised as you can be."

"But she doesn't know what she's refusing," returned Edward, impetuously—"how should she? She has never been out of this stupid little village in her life; and you can't think what trouble father and I had to get mother to ask her. She's horribly cross now, and says she knew she wouln't come, though how she could tell that I can't think. Why won't you come, Kitty dear?" he continued, changing at once from anger to entreaty. "You don't know what a splendid place London is. Mother goes everywhere, and every one comes to our house; and I'll work so hard—I'll do my lessons every morning before I go out. Do come, that's a dear!"

"I should like it very much," said Catherine, making an attempt to conceal the sadness with which she spoke. "I should like to see what we have so often talked of, and to hear the clever and famous men whom you know, but I do not think it would be right for me to go."

"But why, Kitty, why? We won't do anything wrong. You can go to church three times on a Sunday, if you like; and there's a church close to us where they have service every day. Then there are lots of beggars, ten times more miserable than any you can find at Swallowfield, who come and ask you for money without you're having the trouble of hunting them up. Isn't she tiresome, Miss Birkby? She thinks it such a clencher to say she does not think it would be right. There's no good to be got out of her after that; and the beauty of it is, she does not condescend to tell us why she does not think it would be right—O, Kitty! you can't think what a rage Frank is in. He turned as white as a sheet, and got up from the table where we were all sitting at lunch. He didn't say a word; but I wouldn't be in your shoes for something!"

"It does seem a pity, doesn't it, Kitty?" put in her aunt. "I'm sure your papa and I could manage very well. I could get Jane Thorpe to read to him; she reads particularly well for a person in her condition, and he would soon get accustomed to her."

"Oh, Miss Birkby, it's of no use," cried Edward, sorrowfully. He had been studying Catherine's half-averted face. "She don't wish to come, and, of course, we cannot wish to compel her, however sorry we may be."

Kitty sighed heavily, but said nothing.

"If you'd only give a reason," pursued Edward, after a pause, and in a softer tone. "If you would only say why you don't wish to come."

"That I cannot do, Edward; but will you not put faith in me? Will you not believe me when I say that it is not for want of love to you that I have refused,—that I should have enjoyed it more than I can tell? Will you not believe this on my simple word, and trust and love me still? You do not know how sad it will make me when you are away, to think that you are judging hardly of me."

The boy was silent—his face worked with various emotions. At length, it grew clear and firm. He took Kitty's hand, and, pressing it firmly between his own, exclaimed,

"It is hard, but I'll do it. I'll do it for you, Kitty. I'll believe what you say; I won't think hardly of you myself; and I won't let any one else think hardly of you. You never deceived me; you have always been dearer and kinder than any sister could have been, I am sure; so, if you say it's not for want of love, I will believe you, and love you all the same; but you won't mind writing to me?"

Catherine assured him that she looked forward to his letters as a great source of amusement during his absence; and the boy at last departed, much comforted, and firmly resolved to maintain the virtue of Kitty's incomprehensible determination against all assailants.

But another and a harder struggle yet awaited her—a struggle she gladly would have avoided, had it been possible. The intimate friendship which had subsisted from infancy between herself and Frank Irwin gave him a right to some further explanation of the motives of her conduct—a right which, whatever the difficulty in which she might be placed by the assertion of it, she felt no inclination to question.

To avoid, or at least postpone, her meeting with Frank, she took occasion to pay a visit to her old nurse, who, with her husband, occupied a small farm, at some distance from Swallowfield. She did not leave Mrs. Price's dwelling till past five, and the early spring day was waning fast, as she sadly bent her steps homeward. The soft and humid air was fragrant from banks of violets and primroses, and the distant moon hung in the ether. It was an evening for tender thoughts, and as Catherine pursued her way, her mind wandered back to the old days of her childhood, and to the countless pleasant hours which she and Frank had spent together.

When a turn in the road brought her face to face with him of whom she was thinking, she beheld him without surprise, though the tide of blood setting tumultuously to her heart deprived her for the moment of speech or motion.

"I came to meet you, Kitty," said Frank Irwin, "your aunt told me where you were gone—she asked me to come—I hope you are not displeased."

"Oh, no!" said Catherine, trembling yet more, and only daring to deprecate his anger by a look of supplication; for there was a restraint and haughtiness in his tone and manner which were quite new to her. He turned to walk with her, and they had proceeded some way before he again addressed her. At length he said,

"I want to say a few words to you Catherine." He spoke slowly and with manifest effort. "I need not tell you that your refusal to accompany my mother to London was a sad disappointment, yes, and an unexpected disappointment to me. I am not going to distress you by an inquiry into the motives of your refusal. You act upon them so decidedly that you must be satisfied with them. I only wish to say that I am aware from your conduct on this occasion, and from the manner of your behaviour to me since my return from Germany, that I have been so unhappy as to incur your displeasure. I have in vain examined myself to discover the reason, you have given me no clue, though I daily feel how strong that displeasure must be which has so completely changed our mutual relations and destroyed a friendship so close, so old. You must not imagine that I am so preposterously conceited as to suppose that your refusal to go to London was entirely occasioned by your unwillingness to be distressed by my presence. If that were the only obstacle, you need no longer hesitate, for I have to-day asked and obtained my father's permission to make an extensive tour in America; I hope even to extend my travels as far as the Rocky Mountains."

He had spoken in a hard, dull tone, never once looking at his companion, but nervously switching his riding-cane to and fro, and following its motion with his eyes. Each sentence struck harder and harder on poor Catherine's heart, and when the last abrupt announcement was made, she was compelled to stop, for her faltering limbs refused to support her, a deadly pallor overspread her countenance, and her lips quivered with the vain attempt to articulate a sound.

Terrified out of his anger, Frank hastened to support her, and gazed with stupefied amazement on an emotion such as he had never before witnessed, while his heart smote him for the selfishness of his reproaches.

"O, Kitty," cried Frank, passionately, "forget what I have said. Of course, I know, dear, you can't help it; I was a fool to hope it; but you know, Kitty, every one in this world is selfish but you."

"You shall know the whole truth," said Kitty, who, in her anxiety to master her emotion, hardly understood the import of his words. "I have never trusted you and repented of it, and, hard as it is, I will trust you now."

"No, Kitty; I will know nothing; you shall put no force upon yourself, dear. I know that I am in every respect unworthy your regard. I can well understand what a distasteful companion I must be to a gentle and accomplished woman like you."

"Frank, how can you talk so strangely? you know the inequality is all on my side. Listen to me a few moments, and I will try to tell you my reasons, that you may not think me altogether capricious and unworthy your friendship. You see my father has spent his life in such retirement that he thinks and cares little about what is said or done in the world. He is accustomed to see you, and he loves you dearly. My aunt knows, perhaps, something more about such things; but, I dare say, if either of them thought about it at all, they would consider that I was quite your equal."

"Well," said Frank, earnestly, though not impatiently.

"You see their affection for me would blind them to the truth." Kitty spoke with increasing effort, but still with a certain energy. "I tried to speak to Lady Irwin, and to ask her help; but I could not. I do not think it is right to speak to you, Frank; but you will help me, as you always have done, all your life, and for the sake of our old, old friendship. I cannot lose your friendship."

"Come what may, that will never be, Kitty," said Frank earnestly.

"Thank you for that comfort. And now you understand my motives."

"Forgive me, dear, I do not understand them in the least. You talk about the world, and about your father being blinded by his affection for you; but I honestly confess myself unable to make out the sequence of ideas, or to see what bearing your observations have on your refusal to go to London with my mother."

"Don't you see that, if I were to go, I should be, almost of necessity, a great deal in your company, and people might think—or, to speak the simple truth, it might not be well for me."

"O! why did you not tell me that before? Of course, it was hard for you to say it. I was a blockhead not to think of it myself. But I am going away now, you know, Kitty, so far, to another hemisphere; you will go now? No one can make observations, no one can misinterpret you now!"

"I will go if you wish it," she replied, in a very low, heart-broken voice.

"There is something still which you hide from me," said Frank, looking steadily at her; "and it is something which makes you unhappy. Even if I go to America, you do not wish to go to London."

"How can I wish to go if you are not there?" returned Catherine, almost angrily; "would not everything I saw remind me of you and of your kindness long ago?"

"And yet you deny me the pleasure of being there with you? I have heard that women are riddles; and I've been puzzled sometimes to understand my mother; but it's new to me to find *you* incomprehensible and inconsistent."

"Only let me stay at home," said Kitty, entreatingly; "don't ask me to go to London—don't show any interest about me; and, when you come back, you will find me once more your old friend and playfellow."

"No, Kate; do not let us deceive ourselves. That can never be again. The happy time when we were all in all to each other is gone; and the cold friendship you offer me is but a sorry substitute for the love you once bore me. As for me, I cannot cease to love you; but I cannot pretend to be satisfied with being less than all to you. Time may possibly modify my feelings, and I may grow accustomed to the thought that I am nothing to you; but we cannot become children again, and the memory of those joyous days only makes the sorrow of to-day the heavier."

"Do not say so!" said Kitty, in a tremulous tone, "we may be as brother and sister to each other."

"Brother and sister!" he replied, almost fiercely. "Do not deceive yourself, as you cannot deceive me, by that miserable delusion! Brother and sister! Brother and sister we never have been, and never can be. I love you, Kitty, cruel as you are. You know that I love you,—not with the temperate affection born of habit and of instinct, which knits together those of kindred blood; but I love you with that passion, which, if you do not know, you have at least read of. You were the dream of my boyhood, the hope of my youth. All that sisters are or may be to others, you are a thousand times to me. I do not importune you to do impossibilities. I love you too dearly to seek to influence you by appeals to your compassion. Yes, and I value myself too much for that; but do not mock me by comparing that which is life of my life to a feeling, however pure and sacred, which may, without difficulty, be divided among half-a-dozen. Some day, Kitty, you may know what it is. God grant that when you love you may never know the bitterness of having your passion unrequited!"

"There are many, many, worthier your affection than I."

"If there are, I don't care for them. I love you. I have loved you from the hour when I first steadied your infant steps in your father's orchard. I never called you sister. I never felt the love of a brother towards you. The love I then bore you was a faint foreshadowing of that which now possesses me. I, presumptuously, made sure of my happiness. Till this winter, I never questioned that you returned my love, absurd as it may appear to you. Never, till this winter—never, fully till to-day—did I contemplate the possibility of this agony."

"If I were but nearer to you in any one thing," faltered Kitty.

"What then?" said Frank, impatiently; "it would not bring your heart nearer to me. I should love you like a lover, and you would look upon me as a brother."

"How little you know!" exclaimed Kate. "Do you think I have had no struggles? Do you think I have shed no tears? Do you think it is easy to me to lose one turn of your countenance—one tone of your voice! O, you must not think that all, or even the heaviest of the pain is on your side. You will have much to comfort you—much to drive me from your thoughts. I shall have only the memory of the past, and prayer, to help me."

"You are more and more inexplicable, Kitty. If I could trust the seeming sense of your words, I should almost hope that you indeed love me, even as I would be loved. Yet you make the confession in a voice so sad, and with a look so hopeless, that I dare not rejoice at it. What barrier is there between us? What unknown hindrance which turns this, which should be the sweetest moment of our lives, into sorrow and bitterness?"

"You know! Oh, why compel me to repeat what you know so well? I am a simple country girl, without protection, without accomplishments. You have talents and rank which fit you to form an alliance with any of the noblest families of the land; and such an alliance Sir Edward and Lady Irwin naturally expect you to form."

"And is this the only hindrance, Kitty?"

"Yes. Even for your sake I would not creep into your family by stealth; or enter it only on suffrance. I will not deserve the reproaches of those to whom I owe gratitude and affection."

"By Heaven, Kitty, you wrong my father and mother if you think that they would value rank or fortune in comparison with such a true and pure heart—such a cultivated mind—as yours! Besides, if they were blind to your merit, do you think they set no value on my happiness—that they have no regard to my wishes? Put such unworthy thoughts away from you! My mother may sometimes seem capricious—she may be uncertain in trifles, but her own affections are too strong to allow her to endanger the happiness of both our lives for a prejudice. I am sure both she and my father will welcome with delight a prospect so full of reasonable happiness for both of us."

But Catherine could not think so. In the midst of her tremulous joy her heart remained heavy with foreboding. She felt that Lady Irwin would disapprove of their union, and a prescience of sorrow weighed upon her spirit.

Frank, though not entirely free from the same instinctive apprehension, could not restrain his delight at the acknowledgment he had drawn from her, he overwhelmed her with endearing words, demanded explanations of a thousand trifles which had pained him, as evidences of indifference, and learned, with rapture, that they were so many tokens of conscious love. Then he had arguments—unanswerable arguments—to prove the absurdity of her apprehension of Lady Irwin's disapproval, till Catherine, though unconvinced, was soothed into a sympathy in his delight; and when they parted at her father's gate, it would have been hard to tell which was the happier of the two.

CHAPTER VIII.

Sir Edward was reading when his son entered the dining-room. He was not a man who habitually wasted much of his conversation on his children; and he hardly looked up on Frank's entrance, merely showing his consciousness of his presence, and his satisfaction thereat by a commonplace question about the weather. Having replied to this, and taken a seat on the opposite side of the fire, Frank began to cast about in his mind how to introduce the great subject which engrossed his thoughts. He did not doubt that his father would hear him with indulgence and interest; but it was with considerable difficulty that he at length stammered out a request that he would give him his serious attention for a few minutes.

"What, again, Frank!" said Sir Edward, laying down his book, with a look of amazement. "You seem very impatient. Not that I blame you. I think travel does a young man good, provided he travels with a purpose, and not merely for the sake of wasting time and money. I was speaking to your mother about your plan just now. She thinks I ought to have taken time to consider it before I consented to your undertaking a journey so long and perilous; but, as I proved to her, it's nothing to the Argonautic expedition. Notwithstanding the danger of the adventure, I confess I am not sorry you have fixed on the Rocky Mountains as your Ultima Thule; for I shall be glad to have some geological specimens from them; and an authentic account of Mormanism—one of the most remarkable phenomena of the age. The accounts we have must be, to a certain extent, partial. Now, you will take a clear head and young eyes with you. All I would warn you against is too strong a leaning to the old-world prejudices, with which our good friend, Birkby, has taken such pains to fortify you."

"I have just parted from Kitty, sir," said Frank, breaking in at last, with desperate resolution.

"Why didn't you bring her up here? The little puss, I don't wonder she's ashamed to show her face. Your mother is by no means pleased, I can tell you. She never was very fond of poor Kitty. Very strange, though I don't know—perhaps it's natural, after all. I dare say Portia would have thought Imogen rather milk-and-waterish. I really begin to apprehend that my little friend is putting on her womanhood. Kitty, the sweetest piece of Nature's handiwork that ever gladdened human heart,—it is too bad for her to be having her whimsies and caprices."

Here was a good opening for Frank. These warm expressions of tenderness and affection loosened the powers of speech. He defended Catherine from the charge of caprice. He then, with more difficulty, explained the motive which had led her to refuse Lady Irwin's invitation, and concluded with an earnest avowal of his own passion, and an entreaty that his father would aid him with his countenance.

"So I am to remain in my present benighted

ignorance of the real estate of the Mormon colony," said Sir Edward, when his son at length ended; "and I shall not be able to enrich my collection with specimens from the Rocky Mountains! Do you think that Kitty could be persuaded to make it her bridal tour? But seriously, Master Frank, this is a grave matter. You and Kitty are over young to be running your heads into the yoke matrimonial. Kitty is a wife for an emperor; and you'll be a lucky fellow if you get her. Still, you know it is a matter to be carefully considered for both your sakes."

"Certainly, sir, if you will only give us your countenance, we shall be willing to wait."

"Oh, yes! I dare say! As willing as the hoar frost when the sun is shining. I wasn't many months older than you when I married your mother. I was very happy 'bonæ sub Cynaræ regno.' Kitty is not unlike her in many things. But I'll tell you what, Frank, we must talk to Lady Irwin; she does not like to have things done without her. I wish Kitty hadn't had her pretty fit of prudery just now. Helen does not like to have her invitations refused, especially when she fancies she is conferring a favor in giving them."

When the matter was broached to Lady Irwin, she listened with mingled astonishment and indignation. Her countenance sufficiently expressed her displeasure, though she controlled her utterance, and replied, only in a few cold words of disapprobation, to her husband's kindly representations of the wishes of the lovers. Strange as it may seem, she had never contemplated the probability of Frank's marriage, or only as a possible distant evil, to be prevented when it arose. That he would form an attachment to Catherine Birkby had never once occurred to her. Indeed, she held Kitty's beauty and accomplishments in very low esteem, and hardly thought of her except as a useful playfellow for Edward—an agreeable domestic animal, whom it was convenient to have about the house. To discover in this soft-voiced tender girl the enemy whom she should most sedulously have guarded against, was a bitter aggravation of her annoyance.

Turn the subject which way she would, she could discover no reasonable hope of averting the evil; Sir Edward had already given a quasi consent; she knew that, though generally complaisant, he was occasionally capable of firmness; that his affection for his eldest son was strong, his sense of justice strict, and that he had always regarded Kitty herself with peculiar tenderness. But none of these considerations shook her resolution to prevent the marriage, cost what it might; on the contrary, the difficulties that lay in her way rather strengthened her determination, and sharpened her ingenuity.

The sympathetic indignation of Agnese, to whom she disclosed the subject of her uneasiness during her evening toilette, confirmed her in the idea that Catherine had abused her hospitality, and under the guise of innocence had successfully carried out her wily designs upon the heir. She determined to meet craft with craft, and, by using her great influence with her husband, to retard the union of the lovers, and, while seeming to be only anxious for their welfare, to counteract, and finally to subvert their designs.

The youth of the lovers naturally formed the burden of her objections; she touched slightly on Catherine's want of fortune, and inferior rank; she urged the curtailment of Sir Edward's expenses which would become necessary if two families were to be supported on an income, handsome indeed, but every sixpence of which was annually spent; she dwelt on the injury it would be to Edward, if he were deprived of the advantages of such an education as his brother had enjoyed,—advantages more necessary to him, since his position must depend on his own exertions. She frankly acknowledged she could not comprehend Frank's attachment, and insinuated a doubt of its continuance, urging how often the pretty face and sweet temper, which were sufficient for the youth, palled upon the matured taste of the man. To this Sir Edward replied, that it was not probable that an attachment founded on such intimate knowledge, and so fortified by esteem, would be of a transitory character; he said that for his part he was quite satisfied with little Kitty for a daughter-in-law, but he acknowledged that he had not contemplated the necessity of a separate establishment, and ended by expressing his belief that the young people were in no hurry, and would make no difficulty of waiting a year or two.

When Frank found that Catherine's apprehensions were, in a measure at least, realised, and that Lady Irwin seemed determined to retard, if not openly to oppose their union, the antagonism of his nature was roused, and he could not altogether control his impatience in replying to her representations. He rejected with indignation the idea that his feelings might change; he thought the house was large enough for him and Kitty, but if his father and mother thought otherwise, his father had interest to get him some appointment which would enable him to take the burden of his own maintenance, and that of his wife, upon himself; he had no idea of an immediate marriage, but he could see no reason to justify him in submitting Catherine to the anxieties of an engagement of uncertain duration.

In Catherine herself Lady Irwin found the most pliant listener, she was so prepared for anger in the dreaded Lady of the Manor, in the event of her passion becoming known, that when she assailed her with arguments, persuasion and entreaties, coupled even with caresses, she yielded only too readily, and grateful for permission to love, assented to any terms, thinking delay scarcely an evil in the greatness of her unhoped-for happiness.

They were betrothed, and it was an acknowledged fact in the neighborhood, that Miss Birkby was engaged to Mr. Irwin. One or two sour spinsters and intriguing mammas were highly indignant, and by the community at large, it was regarded as a very natural and very desirable arrangement.

Mr. Birkby, when asked for his consent, gave it heartily, telling Frank, with tears of pleasure, that he was glad to show the love he bore him, by giving into his keeping his dearest earthly treasure; he was a little displeased at Lady Irwin's desire for the postponement of the marriage, for his affection took alarm at the idea that his child's excellence was not duly appreciated, but a few words from Catherine tranquillised his doubts, and he could not be long angry at what gave him longer possession of her who was so dear, so necessary to him.

As to Miss Birkby, the intelligence threw her into a flutter of delight. She had a happy knack of never seeing what was going on before her eyes, of course she knew that Kitty and Frank liked each other very much, but as to anything more than friendship, the idea had never suggested itself to her. She wished them happy with all her heart, and could see no reason why they should not be happy, since they had always been dear good children, both of them.

And so the matter rested. Lady Irwin, satisfied with having averted the evil for the present, revolved her plans at her leisure, and was content to bide her time. She was not, however, permitted to enjoy much repose, for she was harassed by the mute solicitations of Frank's anxious looks, and by the open remonstrances of her own son.

Edward heard the news at first with displeasure, and was inclined to feel himself aggrieved because Catherine loved any one better than himself; but when the first emotions of dissatisfaction were over, he entered with spirit into the interests of the lovers, and, having espoused their cause, he supported it with a warmth characteristic of his temperament, and which increased with opposition.—Proud of the victory he had gained over himself, and irritated by a suspicion that his mother was actuated by love to him, he was never weary of urging his brother's claims, till his galling solicitations goaded her to madness, and confirmed her in her resolution.

"Inconsiderate and thankless boy!" she exclaimed one day, thrown off her guard by his importunity; "blind to your own interest, as you are careless of the affections of your mother."

"My interest!" retorted Edward, "how can it affect my interest; except that it must be my interest to see Frank and Kitty happy."

"And yourself a beggar, and your mother a pensioner on the bounty of a country parson's daughter! Foolish child, how will it be with you when you are but an inmate on sufferance in the house beneath whose roof you were born?"

"Mother, that'll never be! You don't know of what true stuff Kitty's heart is made; if I ever want a home, and she has one, never fear that she'll grudge me a share of hers. Besides, have I not hands, arms and wits; can't I hire myself out for so much a day to be shot at, or get a handsome income for wearing a fine coat, and a sword at some foreign court, and writing lying letters about nothing? Frank and Mr. Birkby, both say I've capital abilities, and I'm sure if I take after you, I must be a long-headed fellow with a first-rate genius for politics. Only think now, mother, would it not be more gratifying to be pointed out as the mother of the eminent diplomatist, Mr. Edward Irwin, in time Sir Edward, and soon my lord viscount, or what not, than to look handsome in your black velvet and diamonds as the maternal relative of Sir Francis?"

"It is because I long to see you crowned with self-won honors, that I am impatient of this preposterous scheme of your brother's. Hampered with him, his wife, and perhaps a host of children—women who bring their husbands no fortune, always have large families—how is your father to give you the necessary start? How is he to put you properly forward in the world? On the next ten years the fortunes of your life must depend."

"Ten years! then Frank and Kitty are to wait ten years? Come, mother, that's too bad—why she'll be quite elderly by that time; just think, you are only five-and-thirty now, and you've been married these sixteen years. Depend upon it, I shall never get on the better for Kitty's fretting herself to fiddle-strings. No, no, mother, it won't do; there's no romance in a bride over twenty. If I were Frank, I'd carry her off in a chaise and four, and bring her home a married wife—I declare it would be splendid—I'd be postilion, and I don't think you'd have much chance of overtaking us, unless you swept after us in a whirlwind."

The idea of an elopement, and the exciting adventures by which it could not fail to be accompanied, was so agreeable to Edward, that, though it had occurred to him as a jest, he did not fail to suggest it seriously to his brother.

"You may look as grave as you please, Frank," he said, impatiently; "I tell you my father would be delighted to have it settled—the dear old fellow is as fond of Kitty as she deserves—you'd be gone just a couple of days, and I'd undertake to draw mother off while you begged pardon, he'd forgive you almost before you could ask him. Mother is splendid for holidays, but you know we sadly want a little household deity to nurse us when we are ill, and put us in good-humor when we are cross. Mother couldn't say anything when it was done, or if she did, it wouldn't so much matter."

"She would never forgive us, Edward," returned Frank, with a grave smile; "and we should feel that we had given her reason for her displeasure. Kitty's heart would break under the weight of such a resentment as my mother can feel, and all my love and yours would not support her under it. It is hard, but we must be patient."

"Then I'll tell you what it is, Frank, you'll have plenty of exercise for your patience; you may wait and wait till you are both old and cross. Mother will not give her consent; she'll mock you with vain hope, like that scoundrel Pygmalion and his poor sister Dido in Virgil. She has made up her mind—she says you are too young now, she'll find reasons just as good to keep you asunder till she can say you are too old, and ought to be thinking of the other world."

"Kitty would never consent," said Frank, not unimpressed by the boy's representations. The thought was not new to him, the shadow of such a fear had been darkening on his mind for some time.

"Don't ask her!" cried Edward, with animation; "of course, I know as well as you that she won't, if she can help it; but you know she loves you with all her heart—you know that though she tries to be gay, and deceives her poor old aunt and her father, who is always dreaming about some old Greek lovers instead of minding his own dear little girl; you know that when she thinks no one sees her the tears come welling up into her eyes, and she is grown so thin that I could almost span her waist, which used to be of a proper natural size. I do not doubt that she would protest and be very miserable, but you are her natural guardian now, and it is your business to take care of her health. Now, if you carry her off, and marry her against her will, she can't blame any one but you and me, and I don't think she can be long angry with either of us."

Frank smiled and loved his brother very dearly for his vehemence. And when he detailed to Catherine his proposal in all its extravagant wildness, there was a touch of sadness in the smile with which he related it, and in that with which she listened—a sadness perhaps inseparable from love so deep as theirs, yet showing that a foreboding of evil was in the heart of each.

CHAPTER IX.

Sir Edward, observing that his son's habits had become unsettled, and that his old pursuits now seemed to have lost their interest for him, became anxious that he should employ the time which was to intervene before his marriage in acquiring a more extensive acquaintance with foreign countries, and thus complete his education before sinking down into the even tenor of a country gentleman's life. Lady Irwin eagerly caught at and seconded the proposal; she was weary of the mute appeals of Frank's anxious looks, and of the importunity of her own son. Frank would be employed, interested and amused, his passion, the fruit of effervescent youth, might cool down, he would see other women of a very different stamp from the modest country girl to whom he was betrothed, women with glorious eyes, every glance of which must make a man's blood leap in his veins, and who would not disdain to flatter and court the handsome and accomplished heir to an English baronetcy, women skilled with specious talk to sap the groundwork of principle, and to beguile their victim into a slough of treacherous delight, after which the simple Kitty would have entirely lost her power to charm him. Failing this, there was ambition, there were a thousand allurements to bring out the evil of his nature and render him unfit or unwilling to fulfil his engagement. At all events, it was delay—at all events, it was separation; it would be strange, she thought, if in a year or eighteen months some occasion of mistrust did not arise, which she could foster into lasting estrangement.

The idea of travel was not without attractions to Frank. The irritation excited by his passion, and by the obstacles thrown in his way had given him a distaste for his old studies, the vapid life of the fashionable world in London was wearisome to him, bodily activity would, he thought, counteract his nervous restlessness of mind and allay the feverish excitement under which he labored. True, he must part from Kitty, but he hoped that his mother might soften to her when he was away, and that when he returned she would be his own for ever. Now, the dark shadow of his stepmother seemed to come between them, even when they were alone, so powerfully was each impressed by the consciousness of her unavowed purpose, though even to each other they hardly ventured to breathe the fear, lest, by uttering it, they should give it substance.

For one long happy week before he went abroad, Frank staid alone at Swallowfield—for one week of glorious sunshine his feet brushed the dew from the grass as he came across the field to the Parsonage—for one week of soft summer weather the leaves of the old elm outside the garden-gate whispered over his nightly farewell, and then he went, with smiles on his lips, though with tears in his eyes, to be away until another spring and summer were past, and until the leaves of that other summer were yellow with decay.

Catherine composed herself to wait, and devoted herself with increased earnestness to her various occupations. But though she conscientiously employed her time and indulged in no vain repinings, she could not restrain a feeling of joy when a day was past, at the thought that the term of their separation was by so much shortened. Her prayers seemed always to bring her near to him, and she had his letters, long, frequent, and inexpressibly delightful for the evidence they bore of a heart turning ever truly to her. Once in the winter there was an interval of sad anxiety—a long three weeks, and no letter; then, at last, a short note, written from a sick bed, but in good spirits, and in the near hope of approaching restoration to health.

Sir Edward and Lady Irwin remained in town until the end of the summer, and when they did return their attention was occupied by a succession of visitors. Edward was gone to Rugby, so Catherine was left with little interruption to the enjoyment of her own thoughts, and to her ordinary occupations.

"You don't mean to say, Helen, that that quiet little thing is Frank's fiancée?" said Mrs. Wilton Brook, Sir Edward's fashionable sister, now a well-preserved matron, who, with two full-blown daughters, was on a visit to her brother. "What a sacrifice! A man of his expectations, such a handsome fellow, too; why he might have married any one."

"He is going to marry according to his choice," replied Lady Irwin, drily.

"Oh! that's well enough for an old man with a broken constitution, a country curate, or something of that sort—but in Frank's position, with such opportunities, it is inexcusable. Really, a man owes something to his family. No one cares less for money than I do, but rank, fashion, beauty, or something, surely, he should require."

"Your brother and your nephews consider Catherine Birkby beautiful, I believe?"

"Beautiful! What? A girl who has no idea of setting herself off—no air—no manner! Her eyes are certainly not bad, if she had the least idea how to use them; and, I dare say, something might be made of her hair, it looks soft, and it certainly is a pretty color, just the brun-doré which was all the rage last year. Clementina has it almost—her's is a trifle too light, but, when properly brushed and oiled, it has very much the shade, I assure you. Really, Helen, you should give the poor child a hint or two—it is high time something should be done to civilise her."

"I confess I cannot avoid feeling some regret that Frank did not look about him a little before he tied himself down," said Lady Irwin. "Catherine Birkby is just the sort of barley-sugar sweetheart that a boy fancies himself in love with. I would have saved him if I could; but he must buy his experience, like the rest of us."

"His father ought not to have given his consent. I wonder you did not stop it before it came to a declaration, Helen."

"How could I apprehend the danger? She had been backwards and forwards at the house ever since I married. I never dreamt of anything more than brotherly regard. However, it is no affair of mine: when Edward grows up I shall do my best to avoid such a catastrophe."

"Edward will make a handsome fellow, Helen. He will make many a heart ache. He will beat Frank out-and out—he has so much more of the devil in him. I am heartily glad my girls have a dozen years the start of him."

"Edward's good looks will not avail him much. A younger son has little chance of distinguishing himself in this age of gain and calculation."

Mrs. Brook replied by extolling Edward's talents and acquirements. Lady Irwin, pleased to hear his praises even from one whose judgment she despised, incited her to further commendation by affecting to speak slightingly of him. Mrs. Brook was essentially a worldly-wise woman, though of a low order of mind, and debased by perpetual striving after petty ends. She was not without a certain acuteness, which enabled her to discover the assailable points of those characters, the dignity and strength of which she could not appreciate. She was an adroit and unscrupulous flatterer; and Lady Irwin, because she saw through and despised her, thought she could listen uninjured to her well-bred toadyism. She never perceived how lowering to the moral feelings, intercourse with persons of Mrs. Wilton Brook's class must always be—how it helped to maintain in her an extraordinary opinion of her own endowments, and kept her in suicidal ignorance of her true moral state.

Catherine, meanwhile, grew daily more and more conscious of the dislike with which Lady Irwin regarded her, and she consequently became more silent and depressed in that lady's presence. It was a great relief when Edward came home from school, full of his new experience, overflowing with anecdotes of masters and companions, lavish of caresses to his mother, and imperiously affectionate to Kitty. The jealousy which had at one time characterised his love to her had now quite passed away; she was no longer the principal object of his thoughts, and he began to have a perception, that charming as she was, she might be more desirable as a sister than as a wife. And now Frank was away Kitty could always listen to his stories; she was never too much engaged to walk or ride with him; she was a better listener than ever, and soon knew the distinctive characters of Brown, Sinclair, and Tomlins, Edward's particular friends, and could talk about them as if she were familiarly acquainted with them herself; while the arguments she employed to mollify his indignation against "that bully" Houseman, and to qualify his contempt for "Uncle" Bobbins, the pawnbroker's son, only gave additional gusto to the conversation by supplying the spice of a little contradiction.

Catherine's altered looks had struck Edward on his first arrival, and it was not long before he discovered that her spirits had lost much of their elasticity, and that in his mother's company she was always depressed and nervous. With unusual self-command, he kept his thoughts to himself, and carried on his observations in silence for several days, when he had ascertained that a coldness and distance in his mother's manner aggravated, if it did not cause this suffering, he resolved at once to appeal to her better nature, and to plead with her for worthier treatment of his brother's affianced wife. Accordingly, he entered her dressing-room one morning, and flinging himself on the rug at her feet, laid his head in her lap—an old childish habit of his, which she loved—and stroking her hand, caressingly, said,

"What a charming Christmas party we have, mother? I wish Frank were here."

"Frank is much better where he is," replied Lady Irwin.

"Of course, it's very nice to be at Rome; and if Kitty were with him, I don't suppose he would be in any hurry to get back. But as it is——"

"Don't distress yourself Edward; Frank's love will never break his slumbers, or spoil his appetite. Catherine did not give him much trouble, you know."

"No, I don't know what you mean by that, mother. If Kitty loved him with all her heart, as it was just and natural she should, would you have had her tell a lie, and say she didn't care for him?"

"I do not blame her. I say nothing.—Your brother's honor's engaged. I only say that he does not appear to suffer much from home-sickness."

"I don't think you can tell that, unless you were to see the letters he writes to Kitty. Of course he doesn't let out his feelings to you, or my father; but if he is so happy in Rome, which I don't believe, you can hardly say the same of her. O mother, I do so wish you would take pity on her, and comfort her with a few kind words. She will have quite lost her pretty looks before Frank comes back."

"You are very much mistaken, Edward, if you think that Catherine's happiness depends at all on me; and as to her fretting, I do not believe she has sufficient depth of feeling to fret for more than half a day about anything or any one. Agnese tells me, that on the very day of Frank's departure she went and took tea with that stupid paralytic old woman who lives at Hopwood."

"Is that the only bit of scandal Agnese has been able to pick up? She'd be much better employed in putting bows into your caps, instead of poking her ugly face into all the poor people's cottages, and prying into the affairs of her betters. What comfort Kitty could have found in going to see that cross old woman, I can't pretend to say.—Poor child, what a sorrowful heart she must have had coming all down Hopwood Lane in the gloaming, with no Frank to meet her! I tell you, mother, I can see the trouble in her eyes; and take my word for it, three nights out of the seven her pillow is not dry when she goes to sleep."

"What an extraordinary infatuation it is that you labour under about such a matter of fact person as Kitty. If she does look pale sometimes, it can be no wonder when Mr. Birkby keeps her so many hours reading to him. You should appeal to him, not to me. Catherine's feelings are never likely to injure her health."

"Oh, my dear mother, if you did but know her!"—cried Edward, rising on his knees in his eagerness, and looking with earnest entreaty into his mother's face—"if you would but open your heart to her! It would make you so much happier."

"My happiness is beyond her reach, either to diminish or increase," replied Lady Irwin, haughtily. It cut her to the heart to hear her boy pleading for the tender girl whom she hated.

"Only look at her, mother, pursued Edward, undaunted by her coldness. "Where did you ever see a sweeter smile? And as to her hands and feet, they are fifty times smaller and prettier than Clementina's, that Aunt Fanny is always making such a fuss about. Then, for a companion,—who is always sweet-tempered, always at leisure, like Kitty? I'm sure you have reason to thank her, mother; I don't know what I should have been, if she hadn't taken so much trouble with me. I never heard any one teach a fellow his duty to his neighbour, as Kitty does; and it's all the better because she does not seem to be teaching at all. Oh, mother! you do not know what you do when you shut her from your heart. She would be a dear daughter to you."

"I had a daughter once," returned Lady Irwin, bitterly, "who might have been what it seems my son will never be."

"Do not be angry, mother. I love you—you know I love you dearly; but, as Kitty says, love opens and does not narrow the heart."

"That is just the sort of speech I should have expected her to make—just the idea I should suppose her to entertain. Those who are incapable of profound passion generally seek to hide the shallowness of their feelings by high sounding theories of catholic affection.

"I wanted to persuade you, mother,—I wanted to entreat you; but it seems I only make you stronger in your own opinion. I am going down to have my lesson, now; perhaps I may not be home to dinner."

Lady Irwin said nothing. Edward lingered at the door, probably in expectation of a conciliatory word or look; then, with a heavy heart, he turned on his heel, and went his way.

CHAPTER X.

In spite of his resolution to keep hts uneasiness to himself, Edward was too much irritated by the ill success of his interference, to conceal from Catherine all his disquiet; and he told her enough to add weight to her former conviction, and to increase the burden of her sorrow. Loving her the better from the consciousness of the effort he had made to defend her, and dreading his mother's displeasure, he remained at the Parsonage until late in the evening; and having spent a few minutes in the drawing-room, where Lady Irwin's manner gave him little encouragement to remain, he went off to his own room.—There he wrote the following letter to his brother, which he carried to the post next morning himself:

Dear Brother—I came home last Tuesday week. I dare say you know that I didn't do so badly at the examination after all. I brought home a prize which pleased mother and delighted dear old Birkby. Father did not say much, but he looked as if he liked it, and made me bring it out to show Lord Allason when he called. I found all well at home: going on much as usual; father deep in some stratum or other at the bottom of the Dead Sea—I shouldn't much wonder if he were off to Palestine next week. I wish to Heaven he would, and take mother with him! A pilgrimage would do her a tremendous deal of good just now. I wish with all my heart you and Kitty were married!—What is the reason it would puzzle a much wiser head than mine to discover; but of this I'm sure; she—mother, I mean—has taken a positive dislike to Kitty. The worst of it is that Kitty knows it; and you may believe that she looks none the better for it. Of course, it's bad enough for her to have you so long away, and if any one sees her look sad, she puts it upon that; but mother has more to do with it. Aunt Fanny is here with Clem and Ada, all flounces and finery as usual. If it wasn't for father, no one would take any notice of dear Kitty, but he's as true as steel, and mother dares not say a word against her to him. I'm sure he has a notion that there's something wrong, for he pets Kitty like a child—much more than he pets me, which does not please mother. If you had only taken my advice, all the trouble would have been over by this time; you may take my word for it, that if you don't do something yourself, and before long, mother will find some means to break it off yet. You have no idea what a timid, nervous creature Kitty is become in her presence.

I dare say you find it extremely jolly at Rome; it must be nice to have lots of money and nothing to do. I suppose I'm not likely to have much experience of either of these pleasures. Father asked me, the other day, if I should like to be a parson. I suppose he was in joke; I took it so, for I only made a wry face. Fancy mother sitting demurely to hear her son deal out divinity! Don't forget dear Kitty, and when you write don't say a word of what I have told you. Mother always likes to read my letters, and it won't do to make her angry. Do you get any skating? The ice is four inches thick on the pond. Tomlins, a first-rate fellow, who works in my room, is coming down next week, if the frost only holds on, we shall have glorious fun. Good night, old fellow, I'm so sleepy I can hardly see. I wish you'd send me something about some of the temples—the ruins, I mean. Finch dotes on ruins.

Your affectionate brother,

Edward Irwin.

When this letter reached Frank he was recovering from an attack of fever, brought on by the climate, and perhaps by anxiety. He was consequently labouring under severe depression of spirits. His fears had already been excited by a coldness and constraint in the letters he received from his mother, and by the plaintiff tenderness which struggled through the assumed cheerfulness of Catherine's. He had promised his father to travel. He was to visit Greece and parts of Asia, perhaps to penetrate even to the land of joy and desolation—the glorious and wasted Palestine. He had been as yet only three quarters of a year absent, and this was his second illness.—It was evident that the climate of Italy did not agree with him. The image of her he loved pining for him, and crushed by the dislike of his stepmother, rose vividly before him. He saw her paler and thinner, watching with tearful eyes the embers as they fell, and thinking of him so far away, with a heart growing daily fainter, and wearying for the comfort of his cheering voice. He read those parts of his brother's letter, which related to her, again and again. To be so clear to the eyes of the boy, it must be bad indeed. He himself, too, was lonely and sorrowful. The sweet communion of thought and feeling to which he had become habituated, was checked, and the deepest emotions of his soul lay, unexpressed, a heavy burden on his spirit. One bold stroke, and she was his own for ever. He knew his father's indulgence, and that his mother's influence, though great, was not unlimited.

The yearning to England once indulged, became irresistible. Arguments readily presented themselves, not only excusing, but justifying, the apparent disobedience; and the next morning saw him already on his return. Once started, his impatience knew no bounds. No railway, no steamboat, was sufficiently expeditious for him; almost before an answer could have been received to his brother's letter, he arrived in person at his father's door.

Amazement was the first emotion produced by his unlooked-for appearance—amazement, quickly succeeded by pleasurable sensations in the breast of his father, by angry consternation in that of Lady Irwin, while Edward could hardly restrain his admiration and satisfaction at a promptitude so much in harmony with his wishes.

The tumult of feeling with which he beheld his son, travel-worn and haggard from recent illness, prevented Sir Edward from remarking the uncontrollable emotion of Lady Irwin. But Frank, whose perception was sharpened by anxiety, read her unspoken anger. His quivering lips hardly touched the cheek she mechanically presented to him; and she felt that if not before, now, at least, he knew the purpose lying in her heart. As by mutual consent, they shrunk from each other's gaze; for each felt the need of concealment. But Lady Irwin was stung almost to madness by the unrestrained joy with which his brother's return was welcomed by the child for whose aggrandisement she was prepared to jeopardise soul and body.

"Helen, you look pale, love," said Sir Edward, when the first excitement was over, and he had leisure to think of his wife. "This mad freak of Frank's has startled the blood from your cheeks. No wonder, either, —the silly fellow to come back without a single word of warning. Bringing such haggard looks, too. Your mother was growing anxious about you, Frank, and had just persuaded me that it would be pleasant to go and have a look at the old places again, when you must needs come blundering back. I am heartily glad to see you, nevertheless; and Kate, I've a shrewd guess, will not be sorry. She is not quite so rosy as she was, poor little girl, but your absence has told more on yourself than on her."

"She'll be all right, now," exclaimed Edward, unable to keep silence longer. "I'll be up betimes in the morning, and run over and give her a hint. She is not a colossus of strength; and there's no telling what might happen if she saw you all at once and unexpectedly. She might take you for a pallidaimago, instead of a true flesh and blood lover."

"I have not heard Catherine complain of illness," said Lady Irwin, "you should not frighten your brother without reason, Edward."

"Yes, yes; Kitty will be well enough now," said Sir Edward, "never fear, Frank. Love tortures, but he seldom kills, if the poor victims only continue of one mind."

"I acknowledge that I was drawn home, in great measure, by anxiety for Catherine," said Frank, cheered by his father's cordial kindness. "Not that I doubted your indulgence to one so very dear to me, or that I should have ventured to return without your permission if I had been in health to use my time either profitably or agreeably."

"Well, we should have liked a little notice, if it were only to have the opportunity of welcoming you with proper honor; but who has a greater right to be here than you? I thought a little travelling would be of use to you. Besides, I had a fancy to test the quality of your love, which your mother thought might possibly have no more stuff in it than first attachments often have. But since it was strong enough to render Italy, with all its charms of climate and association, distasteful, we are quite satisfied, are we not, Helen?"

"I assert no authority over Frank," said Lady Irwin, "however my interest in his welfare may have induced me to offer him unpalatable advice."

"So the young signor is returned," said Agnese, as she combed her lady's hair, "without warning, and unexpected!"

"He knows that he can insult me with impunity," returned Lady Irwin, "and that my influence over his father is gone."

"His love for the Curé's daughter has made him mad," said Agnese.

"Yes; and not him alone. She has won my husband from me. My very child she would not leave to me."

"He knows not what he does. She has won him with her false smiles, and he is entangled in her meshes; but fear not, Madonna; we are not yet overcome."

"The joy of life is gone," returned Lady Irwin, with fierce depression, "it were well for me to die."

"Be not troubled, Madonna, or let your purpose be shaken by the pride of this self-willed boy. Rouse your great heart. Let it never be said that you have been wronged with impunity."

"Do not tempt me, Agnese. Leave the dark thoughts in my soul, and do not make them more familiar by clothing them in words. I am sick and weary. I am alone—my very child arrays himself with my enemies."

"O! he knows not the interests at stake; he is still a child. No blood of mine flows in his veins; yet for your sake, Madonna, and for the memory of the long days and nights when he lay cradled in my arms, I would count life little to serve him!"

"Senseless as you are!" cried Lady Irwin, with an impatience not unlike that of an untamed horse excited beyond endurance by the application of the spur, "do you talk of what *you* would do, you who have never borne a child—who have only rocked to rest the child of others? Is he not mine—mine in mind and body? The hair that clusters on his brow he had from me; and in which of the tame Irwins would you see the flash of such an eye as his? He is the one thing on earth that is mine; and do you think there is anything I would not do for his sake? But were he nothing, I have still sufficient motives. They have treated me with scorn—almost with open defiance. They have turned from me the affections of my husband! But if I must be miserable, they at least shall not rejoice."

"There the signora spoke worthily of herself," cried Agnese, her dark eyes flashing; "but strong deeds are the language that she must learn to use to her enemies. The blood of the south is hot as its sun; that of the north cold as its winter streams."

"Agnese," replied Lady Irwin, rising and fixing a look upon her that made her quail, so stern—so cruel—it was, "there is blood flowing in my veins hot and impetuous as in those of the fiercest barbarian of the south. There are tales told of the clansmen of my house which would make even your Italian heart stand still. The snows of ten thousand winters will never cool the blood of the fiery Celt. The days of strong deeds are past, and this puny generation drags the chain its fathers burst. Nevertheless, fear not. I am no unworthy daughter of the Macdonalds."

CHAPTER XI.

It was a bright morning; the sky was cloudless, and the genial west wind sweeping over the grass, crisped with hoar frost, seemed to antedate the return of spring. In some sheltered nooks which Catherine well knew, the violets were already in blossom, and she was returning from an early ramble, with a small bunch of these precious flowers, when Edward came bounding along to meet her: now followed, now preceded by his favorite hound, who had caught the joyousness of his master's spirit, and emulated his activity.

"Good news, Kitty!" he cried, as soon as she came within earshot. "Good news, little sister; what will you give me for my news?"

"Have you got your pony?" asked Kate in reply.

"Pony!" retorted Edward, scornfully. "Don't I tell you it's great news—news for you, my darling!" and he flung his arms about her and kissed her.

There was a fluttering motion at Kitty's heart; the color left her cheeks, and she looked at him trembling.

"Well, why don't you guess? Why don't you laugh, or cry, or do something, Kitty? You couldn't look worse if I had said the news was bad. Come, haven't you a bit of Pandora's curiosity? Must I take my glorious news home again, because you won't give the least touch to the lid?"

"I know you are going to see Frank," said Kitty, tremulously. "Lady Irwin told me about it yesterday morning."

"No, that's not it. Guess again? But there, I won't torture you, dear. Strange, isn't it, Kate, that a man of taste like Frank, shouldn't like Italy?"

"If that's your news Edward, I had a shrewd guess of it before."

"Why, of course you had, when he began at the top of the sheet with, O! how am I to exist another day without you! and ended at the bottom of the fourth side with—I feel convinced I must expire if I don't see you tomorrow—all four sides written close and crossed, and all to the same tune."

"You are a saucy boy, Edward, and want to provoke me to show you Frank's letters. You know well enough he never crosses them, and that there is often room for a great deal more when he finishes."

"With 'Yours till death, eternally, and for ever.' Well, I'm sure I don't know what a love-letter is like, and I don't suppose I ever shall. I dare say Frank's letters are just what they should be, or that you think them so—which is quite as good; but I can tell you, you are not likely to have any more of them just at present, so you'd better make the most of what you have. I'll bet you Mad Tom to your father's old cob, that he won't write to you for a month to come."

"Have they heard from him at the Hall, then?" said Kate, bewildered.

"Yes, truly, have they. In a most substantial manner has he forced on their astounded minds the fact that he has a good stout will of his own, and that he has no idea of being sent out of the way that people may worry his little bride out of her pretty looks. I'll tell you what, Kitty, Frank has a great deal more spirit than I ever gave him credit for. You ought to be proud of him. He has done the very thing I should have done myself!"

"But what has he done?" cried Catherine, impatiently.

"O, you're coming up at last, are you, like a shy bottle of ale when it is held to the fire? Know, O sweet Kitty, that your future lord has shown himself a fine fellow, and won't be hoodwinked by my revered and incomprehensible mamma, and that I came off this morning to impart to you the intelligence, that he came home last night, to the confusion of his enemies, the delight of his affectionate father, of his devoted brother, and of his blushing bride. But I say, dear, what's the matter? Kitty, I say, dear Kitty, don't be a little fool, please, dear!"

The abrupt announcement of the return of her lover—a joy so sudden, so unlooked for, was indeed too much for Catherine's strength, enfeebled as she was by long separation, and by the wearing sickness of hope deferred; she would have fallen had not the boy caught her in his arms. He bore her with difficulty to the bank at the side of the road, and was running to seek assistance, when his brother, whose impatience had become uncontrollable, and who had wandered thus far in search of his betrothed, came up. A little water, brought, from a neighboring rivulet in Edward's cap, and dashed on Catherine's face, aided in reviving her: the sight of her lover bending over her with a look of earnest solicitude did more. He folded her in his arms, and all the troubled past seemed to vanish like a dream, or only to be remembered to intensify the happiness of re-union.

There was a long silence. Tears falling like genial rain, and a joy so solemn, that they held their breath as they stood locked hand in hand beneath the arch of the spring heavens.

When the first rapture of their meeting was over, Catherine's anxious eyes detected marks of uncontrollable suffering in her lover's countenance. His eyes, which looked larger and brighter than they were wont to look, were circled with black rings, his hands were parched, and the bronzed hue of his complexion told of fatigue and exposure rather than of health.

The imprudence with which he had acted was too evident. The marsh fever was still hanging about him when he set out on his hasty journey. The excitement produced by Edward's letter, which confirmed his worst fears, had rendered him for the time superior and insensible to his bodily infirmity. A troubled night, hardly visited by rare snatches of sleep, at last brought the morning, when he was once again to see her, made so much dearer by absence and by sorrow, borne for his sake. The cold water with which he bathed his burning temples stilled their throbbing for awhile; the fresh air, and the near hope of seeing his beloved, deadened the aching of his limbs and the fever in his throat; but now that the first joy of meeting was over, that he had held her in his arms, and felt her still all his own, he was obliged to succumb to the lassitude that oppressed him, and to acknowledge the too evident fact that he was not well.

He returned home in the hope that a few hours' rest might restore him; but Nature is a stern avenger, and exacts a heavy fine for over-taxed or abused powers. The excitement and disquietude in which he had lived for the last eighteen months had gradually undermined his vigorous constitution. The unexpressed displeasure of his stepmother weighed upon his heart with a foreboding which defied all his efforts to shake it off, and filled him with vague and paralyzing alarm. During the first few months of his residence abroad the variety of interests which crowded upon him had distracted his attention; Catherine's letters, full of hopeful tenderness, quieted his anxiety on her account; while Lady Irwin herself, relieved by his absence, wrote with cordiality, almost with affection. But when the novelty of foreign life began to wear off, when Lady Irwin had returned to Swallowfield, and, irritated by Catherine's frequent presence, and by the affection with which Sir Edward treated her, either ceased to write to the traveller, or wrote only letters so hard and dry, that the effort they had cost was too palpable to be mistaken; when Catherine's depression became evident in spite of her attempted cheerfulness; Frank's buoyancy of spirit gave way, and he began to succumb to the effects of the climate, which, trying as it is to many English constitutions, did not suit him, and neglected such precautions as might, perhaps, have preserved him in health and inured him to it.

So, now the fever, which had been checked, flew to the head; the overtaxed brain ceased to discharge its healthy office; his ravings were wild and incessant; his heart troubles mixing themselves up incongruously with scenes of foreign adventure; he called often and piteously on the name of his beloved, who seemed to his distempered fancy to be in fearful danger; with wild supplication or stormy menace he sought to protect her from a powerful but unnamed enemy. The whole household was filled with consternation. Sir Edward stood gazing on his fiery vacant eyes with an anguish too big for tears. Poor Edward ran vainly to and fro, overwhelming himself with reproaches for the heedless rashness with which he had communicated his suspicions to his brother. Catherine, pale and tremulous, crept from the Parsonage to the Hall, seeking for tidings she dare not ask for; her still woe-begone countenance and eager tearless eyes, were not the least grievous sight in all those grievous days. Sir Edward meeting her, lost the recollection of his own sorrow, and wept for the poor child who had no tears for herself.

Strange and strong was the conflict of Lady Irwin's feelings. The moment when the dear wish of her heart would be gratified seemed to have arrived; the life which stood between her son and the inheritance was fluttering on the verge of eternity. Agnese did not fail to offer congratulations, and with dark pupils distending to suggest that a slight mistake in the giving of a potion might make that certain which was already probable. Lady Irwin rejected the suggestion with indignation, and devoted herself with energy to the care of the sufferer; she shrunk from the presence of her confidante, and if by chance they met, she hurried by her as if she had been some venomous creature: above all, she sedulously guarded the approach to the sick man's chamber, gave him medicines herself, and administering nothing without previously subjecting it to a careful examination.

She seemed insensible to fatigue. Hour after hour, day after day, she went to and fro in the sick room, with pale, set features, like one acting under strong excitement, or afraid to break a spell. She hardly spoke, either in answer to the grateful thanks of her husband, or to the passionate caresses of her ton; but one day, when Catherine crept to her, and kissed her hand in token of the gratitude she could not speak, Lady Irwin stopped as she was traversing the corridor, and bending her head, pressed her lips on the brow of the trembling girl.

"Poor child," she said, "go and pray, and see if that will comfort thee."

It was at the time when the fever was at its height; the Doctors, of whom two had been fetched from London, had almost given up hope. The patient's strength seemed exhausted; he lay motionless, almost lifeless; his nervous hands were wan and passive, or convulsed by feeble twitterings; the wavy hair, which used to fall in such comely masses about his face, was all gone; his manly beauty withered like the leaves in autumn.

Who can tell what were Lady Irwin's thoughts as she sat through these long nights and days by the wreck of him whom she had taught herself by slow degrees to regard as the enemy of her son? Who can tell how much of her old tenderness to the fair motherless boy returned; how the helplessness of the suffering man recalled the weakness and dependence of the child; how the fever-parched lips awakened memories of the sweet firm lips that had so often pressed hers, and the joyous love of the child's close embrace.

Prostrate—helpless—there was nothing antagonistic there. Helen Irwin was of a temper too lofty to war with the powerless.

After a long time there came a dawn of hope. The youthful constitution, the careful tending, the earnest prayers, prevailed, and Death released his prey. Deep thankfulness and silent joy succeeded to despair in Catherine's heart. Sir Edward came out of his study and walked again among his trees; Edward scampered over hill and dale, to tame the spirit of his horse, wanton with too long idleness. The crisis was past; Frank would recover—slowly, tediously—but he would recover.

With the danger, Lady Irwin's care ceased. No sooner did he open his eyes upon her, animated by intelligence; no sooner did health-bringing sleep return to him than she withdrew from his chamber, leaving him to the attendance of the hired nurses, and only paying occasional visits to his room, which became shorter and rarer as he progressed in his recovery. His convalescence was tedious and wearisome, with many lets and hindrances, much lassitude and frequent suffering; but whatever aid, art or science could afford to alleviate the one or remove the other was used unsparingly, and the light of love gladdened him. Catherine seemed to have lost all recollection of her own worn health and spirits in the necessity for encouraging and strengthening him. Full of gratitude for the great mercy vouchsafed to her in his preservation, her joy manifested itself in a sweet and innocent gaiety—a cheerful lovingness of spirit, that shed sunshine over the life of her betrothed, and helped him more than anything else to the recovery of his strength. Her gratitude to Lady Irwin was so warm that it overcame the dread she had been accustomed to feel in her presence; and though Lady Irwin was still cold and stately in her manner towards her, Catherine had won something upon her regard. She could no longer look upon her as a being without passion; the feeling she had shown was unmistakable, and just of the kind which Lady Irwin could appreciate, Loud lamentations or stormy grief she would have despised; but she sympathised with the stony agony of her countenance and her voiceless despair. She could no longer think her impassive or commonplace. She might hate, but she could not now despise her.

Her mind at that period was in a struggling, combatting, fluctuating condition. Agnese revenged her late slight by almost unbroken silence, which Lady Irwin, too proud to make concessions, repaid with haughty contempt. Sir Edward, charmed out of all suspicion by the extraordinary devotion of her attendance on his son, had returned to something like a lover's tenderness. It seemed almost as if the evil thought which had long nestled in the depths of her heart might be crushed—perhaps, but for the Italian woman, it might have been. But Satan little loves to quit a tenement in which he has been welcomed and cherished; and evil acts are the legitimate offspring of evil thoughts.

CHAPTER XII.

It was some two months since the favorable turn had taken place, and Frank had begun to amend, when, coming home from his usual evening stroll to the Parsonage, he met his father, smoking his cigar, under the lime-trees, by the river-side.

"Well, my boy," said Sir Edward, "you don't look very brilliant yet. A month or so in Devonshire would set you up nicely."

"Indeed, sir, I am perfectly well,' returned his son in alarm. "The evening is unusually warm, and we walked a little too far. I hope you are not thinking of sending me away again so soon?"

"Why, to tell you the truth, I've been hatching a little plan that I don't think you'll object to. You know there is a small estate in Devonshire, which belonged to your mother. The house is not much more than a cottage, but it is very pretty and compact. Captain Martyn, who has rented it for these fifteen years, has been for some time in failing health; and I have this evening received intimation of his death. As I supposed probable, his widow does not wish to continue my tenant; and it has occurred to me that if the house were brightened up a little—it's very pretty, and the scenery about it splendid—it might not be so bad for you and Kitty, just for a year or two, till my shoes are ready for you. This would make everything smooth. Not that I want to send you away. my dear fellow. God knows, the house will be dull enough without you both!"

"We cannot expect you to make such a sacrifice for us, sir," said Frank, his cheek glowing with surprise and pleasure.

"O, as to that, the less we say of that the better. The property was your mother's; so it is a matter of mere justice. My idea is, that if I allow you three hundred-a-year, you may manage to live quietly down there. The estate itself is not unproductive, and might be improved if any one were resident upon it who would undertake to study agriculture as a science. So much is doing in that way now, that extraordinary obstinacy and stupidity may soon cease to be regarded as necessary qualifications for a farmer."

This scheme had been maturing for some time in Sir Edward's mind. The anxiety he had endured during his son's illness, and during his rather slow recovery, had determined him to expedite a marriage which he saw to be indispensable to his happiness. It had been his purpose to communicate his project to his wife, and to obtain her concurrence before mentioning it to his son; but coming unexpectedly on Frank just when he had received intelligence of the removal of the only obstacle that stood in his way, he had yielded to the impulse of the moment, and had spoken to him of a plan which he knew would give him extreme pleasure, and which, he hoped, would accelerate his recovery.

When they had discussed the subject for a little while, Sir Edward went in search of his wife, while Frank retired to his chamber. Lady Irwin sat by the fire, drawing. She drew finely, and she loved the art. Sir Edward stood over her for a while, and admired the design, pointing out at the same time some defects in the execution; then, turning to the fire, he stood some time in silence, and, taking up a book, seemed lost in the perusal of it, till at last he suddenly said, not without a slight tremor in his voice,

"By the way, Helen, did I tell you Martyn was dead?"

Lady Irwin answered in the negative; but she did not feel sufficient interest in the intelligence to interrupt her occupation.

"Yes, poor fellow! he is gone at last," continued Sir Edward. "It is surprising that he lasted so long, considering the rough usage the French gave him in the last war. He must have been nearly eighty. He was a bit of true British oak, tough to the last chip. Of course, Mrs. Martyn does not stay at Elington. Her nephew writes me word that she wishes to give it up at once, which is fortunate, for I could not well have turned her out."

"Do you think you are likely to get a higher rent for the place, then?"

"O, no! the rent Martyn paid was well enough. I have been thinking it would do for Frank and Kitty. To be sure, the house is small, and I dare say will want something done to it; but it is a snug little place, and Devonshire will probably suit Frank, now that terrible fever has made him delicate. You know it is, in a manner, his native air. His mother was born and brought up there."

Lady Irwin bent lower over her drawing. Sir Edward continued speaking, fast, but with a sense of growing uneasiness.

"I know that you are as anxious as I am to promote his happiness; and it is very fortunate that we are able to gratify him without trenching materially on our income. For my own part, I acknowledge that at first I did not feel the necessity of a second establishment. But I dare say you were right, and I am sure you will share my satisfaction in an arrangement which meets all the requirements of the case."

"They cannot live there without an income," said Lady Irwin, after a long pause.

"As to that, I should wish to consult you; for you know so much better than I do what would be necessary. I do not think they will require more than two hundred and fifty, or three hundred at first; for Frank must take care of himself; and Kitty has no extravagant notions, I suppose they can stay with us when they come to town."

Lady Irwin made no reply. Her husband, oppressed by the ominous silence, drew his chair closer to the hearth, and stirred the fire, with an attempt to seem unconcerned. There was something irresistibly overwhelming in Lady Irwin's silence, and in the continued but irregular movement of her pencil. After some minutes, she gathered her drawing materials together, and was leaving the room, when Sir Edward, taking her by the hand, looked up into her face with an attempt at a smile, saying,

"Come, sit down, Helen, and let us talk it over."

"There can be no need to talk over what you have already arranged," she returned, coldly disengaging her hand; and without another word, or a backward look, she left the room.

"Here's a pretty storm," muttered Sir Edward. "If Helen did but know how like Tisiphone she looks in that angry mood of her's, she would not be angry so often. Who could have anticipated such a reception of a plan which sets everything to rights? O, woman, woman, incomprehensible, irrational, contradictory!"

So saying, or rather so thinking, he turned for consolation to his book, and contrived to lose, for a while, the sense of domestic disquiet in the brilliant and witty pleading of one of his favorite essayists.

Not so, Lady Irwin. The burning indignation which she had violently repressed, burst out in fiery words as soon as she reached her chamber, and stood face to face with Agnese, busied there with duties of her office.

"Urge what you will now, Agnese, you shall not find me flagging. I was a fool to spurn your advice before; but his weakness made me childish. Now, all that is past, and you need not fear me; I am despised, and counted as nothing by my husband and by the boy I saved from the jaws of death. They hold their consultations; they determine what they will do; and, when it is done, they bid me receive with joy the intelligence that my child is counted as nothing in his father's sight, and that we are to be robbed of a third of our income. O! had I but harkened to the voice that bade me listen to you, when he lay senseless and powerless—when disease had done the work ready to my hand, and only to leave undone was needful. Now, he is strong again in mind and body, and the strength he has regained, through my help, he uses to insult and injure me! He must needs enter on the estate at once, He must sow enmity between me and my husband. When was it before, since the day when he first called me wife, that Sir Edward decided on even the smallest of his affairs without me? Now he consults, he decides, he portions out his income; and, when it is done, he tells me thus and thus it is to be. Devise what you will—fear no flinching in me now."

"Noble Madonna," cried Agnese, with a look of triumph, "now you are yourself again, all will be well; the daughter of the Curé shall never queen it here; and Edward shall inherit the lands of his father."

"We must be careful what we do, Agnese; we must be subtle and secret. Sir Edward has given to his son, to this Frank, who, but for me, might be lying in the vault beside his mother, the house in Devonshire, because it was his mother's, and he is quite sure that I must approve of so equitable an arrangement. The poor simpleton, Ann Irwin, left the house to her husband, thinking, I suppose, that no second love would banish her pale image from his heart, and that he could soar to no higher passion. This house is to be rendered back to her son, that he may live there with his wife; and that they may enjoy their Paradise, three hundred pounds a-year is to be taken from our income. Listen, Agnese, I will urge my husband to send his son to Elington; he shall alter and furnish to his taste. I will have liberal means placed at his disposal; the garden and the pleasure-grounds shall be re-arranged to his fancy; and he shall dream of the happiness he is never to know, as he wanders through the newly-adorned rooms, and lingers under the trees. He shall return to fetch his bride—she shall twine the orange-flowers in her hair—the wedding guests shall assemble—but the ringers who were to ring out the wedding peal shall toll for a death."

"Will you not destroy the girl with her lover?" inquired Agnese, eagerly.

"No, I hate her too much; she has won from me the hearts of all I love; but for her smiles and soft voice I might have lived happy and innocent. She loves him, Agnese; he is as dear to her as the light of heaven. She shall live to pine for him in hopeless sorrow."

"We must be wise and secret," said Agnese. "The crime shall be mine, the vengeance yours."

"Never fear, Agnese. The vengeance I will take shall be sudden and certain as the swoop of the eagle. But, enough, we have time to spare; to deceive them into security must be our present labor."

CHAPTER XIII.

"Kitty," cried Edward, bursting into the drawing-room, at the Parsonage, where Catherine sat with an open book before her, but thoughts wandering far away, "Kitty, my dear sister, what am I to do? Here I have been puzzling my brain for the last ten days to compose an Epithalamium for you and Frank! I tried Greek first, but you know I've only read the Prometheus, and Iambics don't come easy. I tried Latin next, but I couldn't determine whether it should be in Sapphics or Alcaics, and owing to the confusion of my mind, half the stanza was in one and half in the other; so down I fell to English, plain, wholesome English, as father calls it—which is, after all, the most Christian language of the three. I shall have a couple of hours' hard fighting with the Muse, by and by, and I'll bring her coy ladyship to terms, depend upon it. If you could but help me to a rhyme, now and then—but, of course, that is not to be expected. Mother is tremendously grand to-day. I can't get a word out of her, or I'd have pressed her into the service. She is glorious at finding rhymes. She has got a splendid gown for to-morrow, and a bonnet my aunt would give her ears for"

"I wish I could show her how grateful I am for all her goodness to us," said Catherine.

"I don't think you need feel oppressed by the weight of the obligation," replied Edward, gaily; "though I must say mother has behaved splendidly about Elington; and one must not mind her being a little cross sometimes. But come, Kitty! If I go and fetch the horses, you'll have one more ride with me, won't you, before you join the formidable corps of matrons. Just one last ride?"

Catherine not unwillingly consented, for she loved the boy dearly; and, in the near approach of an event so important, she felt herself unable to exercise her habitual control over her thoughts. It was a day in early autumn. The foliage had lost nothing of its summer fullness, though it was colored here and there with the beautiful shades that herald its decay. Roses clustered round the cottage doors, and the air was fragrant with clematis, while the stately autumn flowers nodded queenly greetings to each other, and the ripe fruits basked in the sunshine. The fresh wind, the blue sky, the rich landscape, combined to raise the spirits of the riders. Never had Edward looked so handsome; never had the play of his mind been so graceful. Catherine could not help gazing with admiration on his dark animated countenance, and on the supple grace of his movements.

"I will be with you before breakfast to-morrow, Kitty," he gaily cried as he rode away, leading the pony she had been riding, "as soon as ever Frank is off my hands! And never fear but I'll finish the Epithalamium, if I invoke all the Nine, at once, to my aid."

She lingered to look after him as he rode down the lane, on his glossy chestnut hunter, singing joyously, and with many a bright backward look and glad farewell.

CHAPTER XIV.

The autumn day had long since closed. Lurid clouds shut in the horizon; and the full harvest moon waded through majestic clouds—now walled in dense masses—now in fragments of grotesque shape. Lady Irwin stood on the balcony on which her dressing-room opened. The heavy shade of the trees; the stillness, broken fitfully by the moanings of the rising wind, and the jagged clouds; were in grand harmony with her spirit. The weight at her heart seemed a little lightened as she contemplated, in the deepening night, this tempest hatching in apparent calm, and ready to burst.

The door of the chamber opened, but so softly, that it was only by the current of air produced that Lady Irwin was aware of it. Agnese entered the room, her olive cheek pale, and her thin lips compressed.

Lady Irwin stepped slowly from the balcony, her eyes fixed in eager inquiry on her attendant.

"It is done," said the Italian, speaking with difficulty from her parched throat. Then, after a pause, she added, more quickly, "it was quite easy. The glass was on the table where Elton had placed it, with the Seltzer water. It was all as usual. The night is hot; he will certainly drink."

"If he should discover it," said Lady Irwin.

"I placed the powder in the glass as you bade me. It is impalpable,—if there is only enough."

"What I gave you would destroy half a dozen lives. But what, if he should not drink?"

"I do not fear that. He will be weary. And lest that cold drink should be insufficient to tempt him, I got some claret, and placed it hard by. The Curé has no great choice of wines. He will not fail to drink."

"Is he not yet come home? He lingers to-night. I wish it were over. This suspense is unendurable. Did you hear nothing then?"

"Only the sighing of the wind through the trees. There will be wild work among them to-night. Wild work within and wild work without: stout young branches rent and snapped, like a tulip by the hand of a child."

"Be silent, Agnese," cried Lady Irwin, fiercely; "the sound of your voice makes me mad! Be silent, and let me listen."

In obedience to her command Agnese was silent. The agony of expectation became every moment more intense. Yet there was no touch of remorse—no timely repentance. Every nerve was stimulated to the highest pitch of sensibility. Sounds, in general scarcely audible, seemed so loud and importunate, as to be almost unendurable. Every pulsation of the great clock on the staircase, the fluttering of a moth against the window, the whizzing of a bat's wing in its tortuous flight, were all so many sources of agony.

"The glass must be changed, and the wine taken away," said Lady Irwin, at last, unable longer to endure the silence. "Have you thought of that, Agnese? They will betray us."

"I shall not dare to go in," cried Agnese, shrinking with terrror.

"Not dare to go in!" repeated Lady Irwin, with surprise. "Why not? What should you fear?"

"When he is dead!" said Agnese, in a low voice.

"What harm can the poor clay do you, simpleton?" cried Lady Irwin, scornfully. "What! the daughter of Beatrice Pisterella!"

Agnese hung her head and was silent.

"He will only look like one in a deep sleep—like one in a deep leaden sleep. We have only lulled him to sleep—to the sweet dreamless sleep that knows no waking. His individual essence—that in him which groaned and suffered—will be resumed into the great all-pervading soul. He is but rocked to sleep a little before his time, to be reproduced in some other form of being. It is she who will suffer; the pain and the woe will be all hers. But hark! I hear Sir Edward's door open. He will be amazed to find me still dressed. Quick, Agnese. Give me my dressing-gown, and let down my hair."

As she hastened the operations of her waiting-woman, whose hands, cold and clammy with excitement, were little apt to render her service, the clock struck eleven.

"He cannot be long now," said Lady Irwin, assisting her maid to unfasten the long coils of her hair. "If you are afraid to go alone, wait for me, and, when Sir Edward is asleep, I will come to your room, and we will go together. How awkward you are to-night, Agnese. Comb my hair carefully instead of tearing it. Do you forget we are to have a wedding to-morrow?"

At this moment Sir Edward came through the dressing-room. He paused to say a few words to his wife, and to make some inquiries as to the arrangements for the morrow.—Lady Irwin's face reflected in the mirror, shaded though it was by the profuse masses of her hair, struck him by its extreme pallor, made the more remarkable by the feverish brilliancy of her eyes. He lingered to observe her, and, tenderly chiding her negligence of her health, closed the window.

It seemed to Lady Irwin and to Agense that he would never go. In vain she returned short answers. He was evidently disturded about her. He would not go, but began to talk of other things. Aware of the extreme danger of awakening his suspicions, she did her best to stimulate an interest she did not feel. But when she became aware that some one was moving in the room above, which was Frank's, her excitement became uncontrollable. At length, shaking her hair over her face, so as almost to conceal her features, she said, with a desperate attempt at playfulness,

"Come, Edward, I shall quarrel with you, if you do not go quickly. Here I have kept poor Agnese for half-an-hour over my hair. Remember, we must be up betimes in the morning."

As she spoke there was a slight tumult overhead, and a sound as of something falling.

"Frank is noisy," said Sir Edward, with a smile. "I suppose he doesn't feel particularly sleepy. I didn't know he was come home." And so saying, he took up his candle and went into the bedroom.

When he was gone, Lady Irwin closed the door, and turned her face towards Agnese. The two guilty creatures looked at each other in speechless but eager inquiry. They listened breathlessly, but there was nothing more to break the stillness above. The great clock ticked, the wind wailed among the trees, and the rain came in heavy drops, splashing on the terrace and ploughing up the earth. With these sounds, mingled the peaceful movements of Sir Edward as he prepared for repose. The lightning flashed across the windows in fierce succession, disclosing the ruffled landscape and the pale eager faces of the wicked women.

All at once there was a noise of opening and shutting doors; a quick step mounted the stairs; it passed Lady Irwin's door, and ascended to the room above. The women looked at each other in an agony of expectation; who can imagine the inexpressible terror of that moment!

Who was it that came so swiftly?—who had fallen a few minutes before? The steps in the chamber above went rapidly to and fro.—Then there was a momentary pause—a great cry of surprise or terror—hasty movements—the flinging open of a window—the violent ringing of a bell—the heavy step of one carrying a burden; then a hasty running down stairs, and a pause at Sir Edward's door.

"For God's sake, get up, sir!" cried Frank's voice, in a whisper, a whisper terribly audible to Lady Irwin. "Don't alarm my mother: Edward is ill."

"Where? What is the matter?" cried Sir Edward, starting up in alarm.

"I don't know—he seems to have fainted. He is in my room. I'll go ——"

But here he was interrupted by a shriek so loud, so terrible, that it seemed like the rending asunder of soul and body, and Lady Irwin rushed in with fierce desperate eyes, demanding the truth.

Wildly raving, and followed by Sir Edward and his son, who strove in vain to restrain her, and wondered at her strange and terrible words, she rushed to the chamber where the awful punishment of her crime awaited her. Little wonder that the sight which there blasted her vision overthrew her reason; for there he lay, the gallant boy just on the verge of manhood, not half an hour ago so full of joy and promise, dead on a couch beside the opened window, the stormy wind blowing his long hair wildly to and fro.

On the table stood the glass, and by it lay the copy of verses which had been the occasion of his visit to his brother's room. He had gone to rest early, as his mother thought, but he had set his heart on finishing his poem, and having succeeded beyond his expectation, had taken it to read to his brother: entering his room by a study common to the two. The wine which was to ensure the destruction of his brother had tempted the boy, weary with excitement, and he had drunk.

Consternation and dismay spread through the house and village. The facts of the case were too notorious to be concealed. Lady Irwin's reason was destroyed by the frightful catastrophe; and she now bemoaned her child—now demanded vengeance on his murderess. Agnese, overwhelmed by her reproaches, attempted neither escape nor defence. With a curious self-devotion, she found some solace in her misery by arrogating to herself the guilt which she shared with her mistress; and in her shameful death felt a glow of triumph in the thought that she suffered for the only being she loved.

Sir Edward, overwhelmed by the loss of his child, and by the crime of his wife, humbled himself at the foot of the cross, and in the depth of his misery learned to prize the light which, if he had not despised, he had disregarded. The marriage between Frank and Catherine was solemnized by his desire, when a year had passed; and they retired to Devonshire, where, in works of active benevolence, and in a fervent but humble spirit, they endeavored to live by the precepts of the great Master, whose kingdom is yet to come.

THE END.

FRANKENSTEIN;

OR,

THE MODERN PROMETHEUS.

BY MRS. MARY W. SHELLEY,

WIFE OF PERCY BYSSHE SHELLEY, THE POET.

> Did I request thee, Maker, from my clay,
> To mould me man? Did I solicit thee
> From darkness to promote me?
>
> PARADISE LOST.

NEW-YORK:
PUBLISHED BY H. G. DAGGERS,
No. 30 ANN-STREET.

1845.

TO

WILLIAM GODWIN,

AUTHOR OF "POLITICAL JUSTICE," "CALEB WILLIAMS," &c.

THESE VOLUMES

ARE RESPECTFULLY INSCRIBED BY

THE AUTHOR.

TO

WILLIAM GODWIN,

AUTHOR OF "POLITICAL JUSTICE," "CALEB WILLIAMS," &c.

THESE VOLUMES

ARE RESPECTFULLY INSCRIBED BY

THE AUTHOR.

humble novelist, who seeks to confer or receive amusement from his labors, may, without presumption, apply to prose fiction a license, or rather a rule, from the adoption of which so many exquisite combinations of human feeling have resulted in the highest specimens of poetry.

The circumstance on which my story rests was suggested in casual conversation. It was commenced, partly as a source of amusement, and partly as an expedient for exercising any untried resources of mind. Other motives were mingled with these, as the work proceeded. I am by no means indifferent to the manner in which whatever moral tendencies exist in the sentiments or characters it contains shall affect the reader; yet my chief concern in this respect has been limited to the avoiding the enervating effects of the novels of the present day, and to the exhibition of the amiableness of domestic affection, and the excellence of universal virtue. The opinions which naturally spring from the character and situation of the hero are by no means to be conceived as existing always in my own conviction; nor is any inference justly to be drawn from the following pages as prejudicing any philosophical doctrine of whatever kind.

It is a subject also of additional interest to the author, that this story was begun in the majestic region where the scene is principally laid, and in society which cannot cease to be regretted. I passed the summer of 1816 in the environs of Geneva. The season was cold and rainy, and in the evenings we crowded around a blazing wood fire, and occasionally amused ourselves with some German stories of ghosts, which happened to fall into our hands. These tales excited in us a playful desire of imitation. Two other friends (a tale from the pen of one of whom would be far more acceptable to the public than anything I can ever hope to produce) and myself agreed to write each a story, founded on some supernatural occurrence.

The weather, however, suddenly became serene; and my two friends left me on a journey among the Alps, and lost, in the magnificent scenes which they present, all memory of their ghostly visions. The following tale is the only one which has been completed."

The following is the preface to the last London edition, published in Ritchie's Library of Standard Novels. It is as intensely interesting as the work itself.

"The Publishers of the Standard Novels, in selecting "Frankenstein" for one of their series, expressed a wish that I should furnish them with some account of the origin of the story. I am the more willing to comply because I shall thus give a general answer to the question so very frequently asked me—"How I, then a young girl, came to think of, and to dilate upon so very hideous an idea?" It is true that I am very averse to bringing myself forward in print; but as my account will only appear as an appendage to a former production, and as it will be confined to such topics as have connection with my authorship alone, I can scarcely accuse myself of a personal intrusion.

It is not singular, that, as the daughter of two persons of distinguished literary celebrity, I should very early in life have thought of writing. As a child, I scribbled; and my favorite pastime, during the hours given me for recreation, was "to write stories." Still I had a dearer pleasure than this, which was the formation of castles in the air—the indulging in waking dreams—the following up trains of thought, which had for their subject the formation of a succession of imaginary incidents. My dreams were at once more fantastic and agreeable than my writings. In the latter I was a close imitator—rather doing as others had done than putting down the suggestions of my own mind. What I wrote was intended at least for one other eye—my childhood's companion and friend—but my dreams were all my own; I accounted for them to nobody; they were my refuge when annoyed—my dearest pleasure when free.

I lived principally in the country as a girl, and passed a considerable time in Scotland. I made occasional visits to the more picturesque parts; but my habitual residence was on the blank and dreary northern shores of the Tay, near Dundee. Blank and dreary, on retrospection, I call them; they were not so to me then. They were the eyry of freedom, and the pleasant region where unheeded I could commune with the creatures of my fancy. I wrote then—but in a most common-place style. It was beneath the trees of the grounds belonging to our house, or on the bleak sides of the woodless mountains near, that my true compositions, the airy flights of my imagination, were born and fostered. I did not make myself the heroine of my tales. Life appeared to me too common-place an affair as regarded myself. I could not figure to myself that romantic woes or wonderful events would ever be my lot; but I was not confined to my own identity; and I could people the hours with creations far more interesting to me at that age, than my own sensations.

After this, my life became busier, and reality stood in place of fiction. My husband, however, was from the first very anxious that I should prove myself worthy of my parentage, and enrol myself on the page of fame. He was for ever inciting me to obtain literary reputation, which, even on my own part, I cared for then, though since I have become infinitely indifferent to it. At this time he desired that I should write, not so much with the idea that I could produce any thing worthy of notice, but that he might himself judge how far I possessed the promise of better things hereafter. Still I did nothing. Travelling, and the cares of a family, occupied my time; and study, in the way of reading, or improving my ideas in communication with his far more cultivated mind, was all of literary employment that engaged my attention.

In the summer of 1816, we visited Switzerland, and became the neighbors of Lord Byron. At first we spent our pleasant hours on the lake, or wandering on its shores; and Lord Byron, who was writing his third canto of Childe Harold, was the only one among us who put his thoughts upon paper. These, as he brought them successively to us, clothed in all the light and harmony of poetry, seemed to stamp as divine the glories of heaven and earth, whose influences we partook with him.

But it proved a wet, ungenial summer, and incessant rain often confined us for days to the house. Some volumes of ghost stories, translated from the German and French, fell into our hands. There was the History of the Inconstant Lover, who, when he thought to clasp the bride to whom he had pledged his vows, found himself in the arms of the pale ghost of her whom he had deserted. There was the tale of the sinful founder of his race, whose miserable doom it was to bestow the kiss of death on all the younger sons of his ill-fated house, just when they reached the age of promise. His gigantic, shadowy form, clothed like the ghost in Hamlet, in complete armor, but with the beaver up, was seen at midnight by the moon's fitful beams, to advance slowly along the gloomy avenue. The shape was lost beneath the shadow of the castle walls: but soon a gate swung back, a step was heard, the door of the chamber opened, and he advanced to the couch of the blooming youths, cradled in healthy sleep. Eternal sorrow sat upon his face as he bent down and kissed the forehead of the boys, who from that hour withered like flowers snapped upon the stalk. I have not seen these stories since then; but their incidents are as fresh in my mind as if I had read them yesterday.

"We will each write a ghost-story," said Lord Byron; and his proposition was acceded to. There were four of us. The noble author began a tale, a fragment of which he printed at the end of his poem of Mazeppa. Shelley, more apt to embody ideas and sentiments in the radiance of brilliant imagery, and in the music of the most melodious verse that adorns our language, than to invent the machinery of a story, commenced one founded on the experiences of his early life. Poor Polidori had some terrible idea about a skull-headed lady, who was so punished for peeping through a key-hole—what to see I forget—something very shocking and wrong, of course: but when she was reduced to a worse condition than the renowned Tom of Coventry, he did not know what to do with her, and was obliged to despatch her to the tomb of the Capulets, the only place for which she was fitted. The illustrious poets, also annoyed by the platitude of prose, speedily relinquished their uncongenial task.

I busied myself *to think of a story*—a story to rival those which had excited us to this task. One which would speak to the mysterious fears of our nature, and awaking thrilling horror—one to make the reader dread to look round, to curdle the blood, and quicken the beatings of the heart. If I did not accomplish these things, my ghost story would be unworthy of its name. I thought and pondered—vainly. I felt that blank incapability of invention which is the greatest misery of authorship, when dull Nothing replies to our anxious invocations. *Have you thought of a story?* I was asked each morning, and each morning I was forced to reply with a mortifying negative.

Everything must have a beginning, to speak in Sanchean phrase; and that beginning must be linked to something that went before. The Hindoos give the elephant a world to support it, but they make an elephant to stand upon a tortoise. Invention, it must be humbly admitted, does not exist in creating out of void, but out of chaos; the materials must, in the first place, be afforded: it can give form to dark, shapeless substances, but cannot bring into being the substance itself. In all matters of discovery and invention, even of those that appertain to the imagination, we are continually reminded of the story of Columbus and his egg. Invention consists in the capacity of seizing on the capabilities of a subject, and in the power of moulding and fashioning ideas suggested to it.

Many and long were the conversations between Lord Byron and Shelley, to which I was a devout, but nearly silent listener. During one of these, various philosophical doctrines were discussed, and among others, the nature of the principle of life, and whether there was any probability of its ever being discovered and communicated. They talked of the experiments of Dr. Darwin. (I speak not of what the Doctor really did, or said he did, but, as more to my purpose, of what was then spoken of as having been done by him,) who preserved a piece of vermicelli in a glass cage, till by some extraordinary means it began to move with voluntary motion. Not thus, after all, would life be given. Perhaps a corpse would be re-animated; galvanism had given token of such things; perhaps the component parts of a creature might be manufactured, brought together, and endued with vital warmth.

Night waned upon this talk, and even the witching hour had gone by, before we retired to rest. When I had placed my head on my pillow, I did not sleep, nor could I be said to think. My imagination, unbidden, possessed and guided me, gifting the successive images that arose in my mind with a vividness far beyond the usual bound of reverie. I saw—with shut eyes, but acute mental vision—I saw the pale student of unhallowed arts kneeling beside the thing he had put together. I saw the hideous phantasm of a man stretched out, and then, on the working of some powerful engine, show signs of life, and stir with an uneasy, half vital motion. Frightful must it be; for supremely frightful would be the effect of any human endeavor to mock the stupendous mechanism of the Creator of the world. His success would terrify the artist; he would rush away from his odious handywork, horror-stricken. He would hope that, left to itself, the slight spark of life which he had communicated, would fade; that this thing which had received such imperfect animation, would subside into dead matter; and he might sleep in the belief that the silence of the grave would quench for ever the transient existence of the hideous corps which he had looked upon as the cradle of life. He sleeps: but he is awakened; he opens his eyes: behold the horrid thing stands at his bedside, opening his curtains, and looking on him with yellow, watery, but speculative eyes.

I opened mine in terror. The idea so possessed my mind, that a thrill of fear ran through me and I wished to exchange the ghastly image of my fancy for the realities around. I see them still; the very room, the dark *parquet*, the closed shutters, with the moonlight struggling through, and the sense I had that the glassy lake and white high Alps were beyond. I could not so easily get rid of my hideous phantom; still it haunted me. I must try to think of something else. I recurred to my ghost story—my tiresome, unlucky ghost story! O! if I could only contrive one which would frighten my reader as I myself had been frightened that night!

Swift as light, and as cheering, was the idea that broke in upon me. "I have found it! What terrified me will terrify others; and I need only describe the spectre which had haunted my midnight pillow." On the morrow I announced that I had *thought of a story*. I began that day with the words, *It was on a dreary night in November*, making only a transcript of the grim terrors of my waking dream.

At first I thought but of a few pages—of a short tale; but Shelley urged me to develope the idea at greater length. I certainly did not owe the suggestion of one incident, nor scarcely of one train of feeling, to my husband, and yet, but for his incitement, it would never have taken the form in which it was presented to the world. From this declaration I must except the preface. As far as I can recollect, it was entirely written by him.

And now, once again, I bid my hideous progeny go forth and prosper. I have an affection for it, for it was the offspring of happy days, when death and grief were but words, which found no true echo in my heart. Its several pages speak of many a walk, many a drive, and many a conversation, when I was not alone; and my companion was one who, in this world, I shall never see more. But this is for myself; my readers have nothing to do with these associations.

FRANKENSTEIN;

OR,

THE MODERN PROMETHEUS.

LETTER I.

TO MRS. SAVILLE, ENGLAND.

St. Petersburg, Dec. 11th, 17—.

You will rejoice to hear that no disaster has accompanied the commencement of an enterprise which you have regarded with such evil forebodings. I arrived here yesterday; and my first task is to assure my dear sister of my welfare, and increasing confidence in the success of my undertaking.

I am already far north of London; and as I walk in the streets of Petersburg, I feel a cold northern breeze play upon my cheeks, which braces my nerves, and fills me with delight. Do you understand this feeling? This breeze, which has travelled from the regions towards which I am advancing, gives me a foretaste of those icy climes. Inspirited by this wind of promise, my day dreams become more fervent and vivid. I try in vain to be persuaded that the pole is the seat of frost and desolation; it ever presents itself to my imagination as the region of beauty and delight. There, Margaret, the sun is forever visible; its broad disk just skirting the horizon, and diffusing a perpetual splendor. There—for with your leave, my sister, I will put some trust in preceding navigators—there snow and frost are banished; and, sailing over a calm sea, we may be wafted to a land surpassing in wonders and in beauty every region hitherto discovered on the habitable globe. Its productions and features may be without example, as the phenomena of the heavenly bodies undoubtedly are in those undiscovered solitudes. What may not be expected in a country of eternal light? I may there discover the wondrous power which attracts the needle; and may regulate a thousand celestial observations, that require only this voyage to render their seeming eccentricities consistent for ever. I shall satiate my ardent curiosity with the sight of a part of the world never before visited, and may tread a land never before imprinted by the foot of man. These are my enticements, and they are sufficient to conquer all fear of danger or death, and to induce me to commence this laborious voyage with the joy a child feels when he embarks in a little boat, with his holiday mates, on an expedition of discovery up his native river. But, supposing all these conjectures to be false, you cannot contest the inestimable benefit which I shall confer on all mankind to the last generation, by discovering a passage near the pole to those countries, to reach which at present so many months are requisite; or by ascertaining the secret of the magnet, which, if at all possible, can only be effected by an undertaking such as mine.

These reflections have dispelled the agitation with which I began my letter, and I feel my heart glow with an enthusiasm which elevates me to Heaven; for nothing contributes so much to tranquillize the mind as a steady purpose—a point on which the soul may fix its intellectual eye. This expedition has been the favorite dream of my early years. I have read with ardor the accounts of the various voyages which have been made in the prospect of arriving at the North Pacific Ocean through the seas which surround the pole. You may remember, that a history of all the voyages made for purposes of discovery composed the whole of our good uncle Thomas's library. My education was neglected, yet I was passionately fond of reading. These volumes were my study day and night, and my familiarity with them increased that regret which I had felt, as a child, on learning that my father's dying injunction had forbidden my uncle to allow me to embark in a seafaring life.

These visions faded when I perused, for the first time, those poets whose effusions entranced my soul, and lifted it to Heaven. I also became a poet, and for one year lived in a Paradise of my own creation; I imagined that I also might obtain a niche in the temple where the names of Homer and Shakspeare are consecrated. You are well acquainted with my failure, and how heavily I bore the disappointment. But just at that time I inherited the fortune of my cousin, and my thoughts were turned into the channel of their earlier bent.

Six years have passed since I resolved on my present undertaking. I can, even now, remember the hour from which I dedicated myself to this great enterprise. I commenced by inuring my body to hardship. I accompanied the whale-fishers on several expeditions to the North Sea; I voluntarily endured cold, famine, thirst, and want of sleep; I often worked harder than the common sailors during the day, and devoted my nights to the study of mathematics, the theory of medicine, and those branches of physical science from which a naval adventurer might derive the greatest practical advantage. Twice I actually hired myself as an undermate in a Greenland whaler, and acquitted myself to admiration. I must own I felt a little proud, when my captain offered me the second dignity in the vessel, and entreated me to remain with the greatest earnestness; so valuable did he consider my services.

And now, dear Margaret, do I not deserve to accomplish some great purpose? My life might have been passed in ease and luxury; but I preferred glory to every enticement that wealth placed in my path. Oh, that some encouraging voice would answer in the affirmative! My courage and my resolution is firm; but my hopes fluctuate, and my spirits are often depressed. I am about to proceed on a long and difficult voyage; the emergencies of which will demand all my fortitude: I am required not only to raise the spirits of others, but sometimes to sustain my own, when theirs are failing.

This is the most favorable period for travelling in Russia. They fly quickly over the snow in their sledges; the motion is pleasant, and, in my opinion, far more agreeable than that of an English stage-coach. The cold is not excessive, if you are wrapt in furs, a dress which I have already adopted; for there is a great difference between walking the deck and remaining seated motionless for hours, when no exercise prevents the blood from actually freezing in your veins. I have no ambition to lose my life on the post-road between St. Petersburg and Archangel.

I shall depart for the latter town in a fortnight or three weeks; and my intention is to hire a ship there, which can easily be done by paying the insurance for the owner, and to engage as many sailors as I think necessary among those who are accustomed to the whale-fishing. I do not intend to sail until the month of June: and when shall I return? Ah, dear sister, how can I answer this question? If I succeed, many, many months, perhaps years, will pass before you and I may meet. If I fail, you will see me again soon, or never.

Farewell, my dear, excellent Margaret. Heaven shower down blessings on you, and save me, that I may again and again testify my gratitude for all your love and kindness.

Your affectionate brother,

R. WALTON.

LETTER II.

TO MRS. SAVILLE, ENGLAND.

ARCHANGEL, 28th March, 17—.

How slowly the time passes here, encompassed as I am by frost and snow; yet a second step is taken towards my enterprise. I have hired a vessel, and am occupied in collecting my sailors; those whom I have already engaged appear to be men on whom I can depend, and are certainly possessed of dauntless courage.

But I have one want which I have never yet been able to satisfy; and the absence of the object of which I now feel as a most severe evil. I have no friend, Margaret: when I am glowing with the enthusiasm of success, there will be none to participate my joy; if I am assailed by disappointment, no one will endeavor to sustain me in dejection. I shall commit my thoughts to paper, it is true; but that is a poor medium for the communication of feeling. I desire the company of a man who could sympathize with me; whose eyes would reply to mine. You may deem me romantic, my dear sister, but I bitterly feel the want of a friend. I have no one near me, gentle yet courageous, possessed of a cultivated as well as of a capacious mind, whose tastes are like my own, to approve or amend my plans. How would such a friend repair the faults of your poor brother! I am too ardent in execution, and too impatient of difficulties. But it is a still greater evil to me that I am self-educated: for the first fourteen years of my life I ran wild on a common, and read nothing but our uncle Thomas's books of voyages. At that age I became acquainted with the celebrated poets of our own country; but it was only when it had ceased to be in my power to derive its most important benefits from such a conviction, that I perceived the necessity of becoming acquainted with more languages than that of my native country. Now I am twenty-eight, and am in reality more illiterate than many school-boys of fifteen. It is true that I have thought more, and that my day dreams are more extended and magnificent; but they want (as the painters call it) *keeping;* and I greatly need a friend who would have sense enough not to despise me as romantic, and affection enough for me to endeavor to regulate my mind.

Well, these are useless complaints; I shall certainly find no friend on the wide ocean, nor even here in Archangel, among merchants and seamen. Yet some feelings, unallied to the dross of human nature, beat even in these rugged bosoms. My lieutenant, for instance, is a man of wonderful courage and enterprise; he is madly desirous of glory. He is an Englishman, and in the midst of national and professional prejudices, unsoftened by cultivation, retains some of the noblest endowments of humanity. I first became acquainted with him on board a whale vessel: finding that he was unemployed in this city, I easily engaged him to assist in my enterprise.

The master is a person of an excellent disposition, and is remarkable in the ship for his gentleness, and the mildness of his discipline. He is, indeed, of so amiable a nature that he will not hunt (a favorite, and almost the only amusement here,) because he cannot endure to spill blood. He is, moreover, heroically generous. Some years ago he loved a young Russian lady, of moderate fortune; and having amassed a considerable sum in prize-money, the father of the girl consented to the match. He saw his mistress once more before the destined ceremony; but she was bathed in tears, and, throwing herself at his feet, entreated him to spare her, confessing at the same time that she loved another, but that he was poor, and that her father would never consent to the union. My generous friend re-assured the suppliant, and on being informed of the name of her lover, instantly abandoned his pursuit. He had already bought a farm with his money, on which he had designed to pass the remainder of his life; but he bestowed the whole on his rival, together with the remains of his prize-money, to purchase stock, and then himself solicited the young woman's father to consent to her marriage with her lover. But the old man decidedly refused, thinking himself bound in honor to my friend; who, when he found the father inexorable, quitted his country, nor returned until he heard that his former mistress was married according to her inclinations. "What a noble fellow!" you will exclaim. He is so; but then he has passed all his life on board a vessel, and has scarcely an idea beyond the rope and the shroud.

But do not suppose that, because I complain a little, or because I can conceive a consolation for my toils which I may never know, that I am wavering in my resolutions. Those are as fixed as fate; and my voyage is now only delayed until the weather shall permit my embarkation. The winter has been dreadfully severe; but the spring promises well, and it is considered as a remarkably early season; so that, perhaps, I may sail sooner than I expected. I shall do nothing rashly; you know me sufficiently to confide in my prudence and considerateness whenever the safety of others is committed to my care.

I cannot describe to you my sensations on the near prospect of my undertaking. It is impossible to communicate to you a conception of the trembling sensation, half fearful, with which I am preparing to depart. I am going to unexplored regions, to "the land of mist and snow;" but I shall kill no albatross, therefore do not be alarmed for my safety.

Shall I meet you again, after having traversed immense seas, and returned by the most southern cape of Africa or America? I dare not expect such success, yet I cannot bear to look on the reverse of the picture. Continue to write to me by every opportunity: I may receive your letters (though the chance is very doubtful) on some occasions when I need them most to support my spirits. I love you very tenderly. Remember me with affection, should you never hear from me again.

Your affectionate brother,

ROBERT WALTON.

LETTER III.

TO MRS. SAVILLE, ENGLAND.

JULY 7th, 17—.

MY DEAR SISTER: I write you a few lines in haste, to say that I am safe, and well advanced on my voyage. This letter will reach England by a merchant-man now on its homeward voyage from Archangel; more fortunate than I, who may not see my native land, perhaps, for many years. I am, however, in good spirits: my men are bold, and apparently firm of purpose; nor do the floating sheets of ice that continually pass us, indicating the dangers of the region toward which we are advancing, appear to dismay them. We have already reached a very high latitude; but it is the height of summer, and although not so warm as England, the southern gales, which blow us speedily toward those shores which I so ardently desire to attain, breathe a degree of renovating warmth which I had not expected.

No incidents have hitherto befallen us, that would make a figure in a letter. One or two stiff gales, and the breaking of a mast, are accidents which experienced navigators scarcely remember to record; and I shall be well content, if nothing worse happens to us during our voyage.

Adieu, my dear Margaret, Be assured that, for my own sake, as well as yours, I will rashly encounter danger. I will be cool, persevering, and prudent.

Remember me to all my English friends.

Most affectionately yours,

R. W.

LETTER IV.

TO MRS. SAVILLE, ENGLAND.

August 5th, 17—.

So strange an accident has happened to us, that I cannot forbear recording it, although it is very probable that you will see me before these papers can come into your possession.

Last Monday (July 31st,) we were nearly surrounded by ice, which closed in the ship on all sides, scarcely leaving her the sea-room in which she floated. Our situation was somewhat dangerous, especially as we were compassed round by a very thick fog. We accordingly lay to, hoping that some change would take place in the atmosphere and weather.

About two o'clock the mist cleared away, and we beheld, stretched out in every direction, vast and irregular plains of ice, which seemed to have no end. Some of my comrades groaned, and my own mind began to grow watchful with anxious thoughts, when a strange sight suddenly attracted our attention, and diverted our solicitude from our own situation. We perceived a low carriage, fixed on a sledge and drawn by dogs, pass on towards the north, at the distance of half a mile: a being which had the shape of a man, but apparently of gigantic stature, sat in the sledge, and guided the dogs. We watched the rapid progress of the traveller with our telescopes, until he was lost among among the distant inequalities of the ice.

This appearance excited our unqualified wonder. We were, as we believed, many hundred miles from any land; but this apparition seemed to denote that it was not, in reality, so distant as we had supposed. Shut in, however, by ice, it was impossible to follow his track, which we had observed with the greatest attention.

About two hours after this occurrence, we heard the ground sea; and before night the ice broke, and freed our ship. We, however, lay to until the morning, fearing to encounter in the dark those large loose masses which float about after the breaking up of the ice. I profited of this time to rest for a few hours.

In the morning, however, as soon as it was light, I went upon deck, and found all the sailors busy on one side of the vessel, apparently talking to some one in the sea. It was, in fact, a sledge, like that we had seen before, which had drifted towards us in the night, on a large fragment of ice. Only one dog remained alive; but there was a human being within it, whom the sailors were persuading to enter the vessel. He was not, as the other traveller seemed to be, a savage inhabitant of some undiscovered island, but an European. When I appeared on deck, the master said, "Here is our captain, and he will not allow you to perish on the open sea."

On perceiving me, the stranger addressed me in English, although with a foreign accent. "Before I come on board your vessel," said he, "will you have the kindness to inform me whither you are bound?"

You may conceive my astonishment on hearing such a question addressed to me from a man on the brink of destruction, and to whom I should have supposed that my vessel would have been a resource which he would not have exchanged for the most precious wealth the earth can afford. I replied, however, that we were on a voyage of discovery towards the northern pole.

Upon hearing this he appeared satisfied, and consented to come on board. Good God! Margaret, if you had seen the man who thus capitulated for his safety, your surprise would have been boundless. His limbs were nearly frozen, and his body dreadfully emaciated by fatigue and suffering. I never saw a man in so wretched a condition. We attempted to carry him into the cabin, but as soon as he had quitted the fresh air, he fainted. We accordingly brought him back to the deck, and restored him to animation by rubbing him with brandy, and forcing him to swallow a small quantity. As soon as he showed signs of life, we wrapped him up in blankets, and placed him near the chimney of the kitchen-stove. By slow degrees he recovered, and ate a little soup, which restored him wonderfully.

Two days passed in this manner before he was able to speak ; and I often feared that his sufferings had deprived him of his understanding. When he had in some measure recovered, I removed him to my own cabin, and attended on him as much as my duty would permit. I never saw a more interesting creature : his eyes have generally an expression of wildness, and even madness ; but there are moments when, if any one performs an act of kindness towards him, or does him any the most trifling service, his whole countenance is lighted up, as it were, with a beam of benevolence and sweetness that I never saw equalled. But he is generally melancholy and despairing ; and sometimes he gnashes his teeth, as if impatient of the weigh of woes that oppress him.

When my guest was a little recovered, I had great trouble to keep off the men, who wished to ask him a thousand questions ; but I would not allow him to be tormented by their idle curiosity, in a state of body and mind whose restoration evidently depended upon entire repose. Once, however, the lieutenant asked, Why he had come so far upon the ice in so strange a vehicle ?

His countenance instantly assumed an aspect of the deepest gloom ; and he replied, " To seek one who fled from me."

" And did the man whom you pursued travel in the same fashion ?"

" Yes."

" Then I fancy we have seen him ; for, the day before we picked you up, we saw some dogs drawing a sledge, with a man in it, across the ice."

This aroused the stranger's attention ; and he asked a multitude of questions concerning the route which the dæmon, as he called him, had pursued. Soon after, when he was alone with me, he said, " I have, doubtless, excited your curiosity, as well as that of these good people ; but you are too considerate to make inquiries."

" Certainly ; it would indeed be very impertinent and inhuman in me to trouble you with any inquisitiveness of mine."

" And yet you rescued me from a strange and perilous situation ; you have benevolently restored me to life."

Soon after this he inquired, if I thought that the breaking up of the ice had destroyed the other sledge ? I replied, that I could not answer with any degree of certainty ; for the ice had not broken until near midnight, and the traveller might have arrived at a place of safety before that time ; but of this I could not judge.

From this time the stranger seemed very eager to be upon deck, to watch for the sledge which had before appeared ; but I have persuaded him to remain in the cabin, for he is far too weak to sustain the rawness of the atmosphere. And I have promised that some one should watch for him, and give him instant notice if any new object should appear in sight.

Such is my journal of what relates to this strange occurrence up to the present day. The stranger has gradually improved in health, but is very silent, and appears uneasy when any one except myself enters his cabin. Yet his manners are so conciliating and gentle, that the sailors are all interested in him, although they have have very little communication with him. For my own part, I begin to love him as a brother ; and his constant and deep grief fills me with sympathy and compassion. He must have been a noble creature in his better days, being even now in wreck so attractive and amiable.

I said in one of my letters, my dear Margaret, that I should find no friend on the wide ocean; yet I have found a man who, before his spirit had been broken by misery, I should have been happy to have possessed as the brother of my heart.

I shall continue my journal concerning the stranger at intervals, should I have any fresh incidents to record.

August 13th, 17—.

My affection for my guest increases every day. He excites at once my admiration and my pity to an astonishing degree. How can I see so noble a creature destroyed by misery, without feeling the most poignant grief? He is so gentle, yet so wise; his mind is so cultivated; and when he speaks, although his words are culled with the choicest art, yet they flow with rapidity and unparalleled eloquence.

He is now much recovered from his illness, and is continually on deck, apparently watching for the sledge that preceded his own. Yet, although unhappy, he is not so utterly occupied by his own misery, but that he interests himself deeply in the employments of others. He has asked me many questions concerning my design; and I have related my little history frankly to him. He appeared pleased with the confidence, and suggested several alterations in my plan, which I shall find exceedingly useful. There is no pedantry in his manner; but all he does appears to spring solely from the interest he instinctively takes in the welfare of those who surround him. He is often overcome by gloom, and then he sits by himself, and tries to overcome all that is sullen or unsocial in his humor. These paroxysms pass from him like a cloud from before the sun, though his dejection never leaves him. I have endeavored to win his confidence; and I trust that I have succeeded. One day I mentioned to him the desire I had always felt of finding a friend who might sympathize with me, and direct me by his counsel. I said I did not belong to that class of men who are offended by advice. I am self-educated, and perhaps I hardly rely sufficiently upon my own powers. I wish therefore that my companion should be wiser and more experienced than myself, to confirm and support me; nor have I believed it impossible to find a true friend.

"I agree with you," replied the stranger, "in believing that friendship is not only a desirable, but a possible acquisition. I once had a friend, the most noble of human creatures, and am entitled, therefore, to judge respecting friendship. You have hope, and the world before you, and have no cause for despair. But I—I have lost everything, and cannot begin life anew."

As he said this, his countenance became expressive of a calm settled grief, which touched me to the heart. But he was silent, and presently retired to his cabin.

Even broken in spirit as he is, no one can feel more deeply than he does the beauties of nature. The starry sky, the sea, and every sight afforded by these wonderful regions, seem still to have the power of elevating his soul from earth. Such a man has a double existence: he may suffer misery, and be overwhelmed by disappointments; yet when he has retired into himself, he will be like a celestial spirit, that has a halo around him, within whose circle no grief or folly ventures.

Will you laugh at the enthusiasm I express concerning this divine wanderer? If you do, you must certainly have lost that simplicity which was once your characteristic charm. Yet, if you will, smile at the warmth of my expressions, while I find every day new causes for repeating them.

August 19th, 17—.

Yesterday the stranger said to me, "You may easily perceive, Captain Walton, that I have suffered great and unparalleled misfortunes. I had determined, once, that the memory of these evils should die with me; but you have won me to alter my determination. You seek for knowledge and wisdom, as I once did; and I ardently hope that the gratification of your wishes may not be a serpent to sting you, as mine has been to me. I do not know that the relation of my misfortunes will be useful to you, yet, if you are inclined, listen to my tale. I believe that the strange incidents connected with it will afford a view of nature, which may enlarge your faculties and understanding. You will hear of powers and occurrences, such as you have been accustomed to think impossible; but I do not doubt that my tale conveys in its series internal evidence of the truth of the events of which it is composed."

You may easily conceive that I was much gratified by the offered communication; yet I could not endure that he should renew his grief by a recital of his misfortunes. I felt the greatest eagerness to hear the promised narrative, partly from curiosity, and partly from a strong desire to ameliorate his fate, if it were in my power. I expressed these feelings in my answer.

"I thank you," he replied, "for your sympathy, but it is useless; my fate is nearly fulfilled. I wait for but one event, and then I shall repose in peace. I understand your feeling," continued he, perceiving that I wished to interrupt him; "but you are mistaken, my friend, if thus you will allow me to name you; nothing can alter my destiny. Listen to my history, and you will perceive how irrevocably it is determined."

He then told me, that he would commence his narrative the next day, when I should be at leisure. This promise drew from me the warmest thanks. I have resolved every night to record, as nearly as possible in his own words, what he has related during the day. If I should be engaged, I will at least make notes. This manuscript will doubtless afford you the greatest pleasure: but to me, who know him, and who hear it from his own lips, with what interest and sympathy shall I read it at some future day!

FRANKENSTEIN;

OR,

THE MODERN PROMETHEUS.

CHAPTER I.

I AM by birth a Genevese; and my family is one of the most distinguished of that republic. My ancestors had been for many years counsellors and syndics; and my father had filled several public situations with honor and reputation. He was respected by all who knew him, for his integrity and indefatigable attention to public business. He passed his younger days perpetually occupied by the affairs of his country; and it was not until the decline of life that he thought of marrying, and bestowing on the state sons who might carry his virtues and his name down to posterity.

As the circumstances of his marriage illustrate his character, I cannot refrain from relating them. One of his most intimate friends was a merchant who, from a flourishing state, fell, through numerous mischances, into poverty. This man, whose name was Beaufort, was of a proud and unbending disposition, and could not bear to live in poverty and oblivion in the same country where he had formerly been distinguished for his rank and magnificence. Having paid his debts, therefore, in the most honorable manner, he retreated with his daughter to the town of Lucerne, where he lived unknown and in wretchedness. My father loved Beaufort with the truest friendship, and was deeply grieved by his retreat in these unfortunate circumstances. He grieved also for the loss of his society, and resolved to seek him out and endeavor to persuade him to begin the world again through his credit and assistance.

Beaufort had taken effectual measures to conceal himself; and it was ten months before my father discovered his abode. Overjoyed at this discovery, he hastened to the house, which was situated in a mean street, near the Reuss. But when he entered, misery and despair alone welcomed him. Beaufort had saved but a very small sum of money from the wreck of his fortunes; but it was sufficient to provide him with sustenance for some months, and in the mean time he hoped to procure some respectable employment in a merchant's house. The interval was consequently spent in inaction. His grief only became more deep and rankling, when he had leisure for reflection; and at length it took so fast hold of his mind, that at the end of three months he lay on a bed of sickness, incapable of any exertion.

His daughter attended him with the greatest tenderness; but she saw with despair that their little fund was rapidly decreasing, and that there was no other prospect of support. But Caroline Beaufort possessed a mind of an uncommon mould; and her courage rose to support her in her adversity. She procured plain work; she plaited straw; and by various means contrived to earn a pittance scarcely sufficient to support life.

Several months passed in this manner. Her father grew worse; her time was more entirely occupied in attending him; her means of subsistence decreased; and in the tenth month her father died in her arms, leaving her an orphan and a beggar. This last blow overcame her; and she was kneeling by Beaufort's coffin, when my father entered the chamber. He came like a protecting spirit to the poor girl, who committed herself to his care, and after the interment of his friend he conducted her to Geneva, and placed her under the protection of a relation. Two years after this event, Caroline became his wife.

When my father became a husband and a parent, he found his time so occupied by the duties of his new situation, that he relinquished many of his public employments, and devoted himself to the education of his children. Of these I was the eldest, and the destined successor to all his labors and utility. No creature could have more tender parents than mine. My improvement and health were their constant care, especially as I remained for several years their only child. But before I continue my narrative, I must record an incident which took place when I was four years of age.

My father had a sister, whom he tenderly loved, and who had married early in life an Italian gentleman. Soon after her marriage, she had accompanied her husband into his native country, and for some years my father had very little communication with her. About the time I mentioned she died; and a few months afterwards he received a letter from her husband, acquainting him with his intention of marrying an Italian lady, and requesting my father to take charge of the infant Elizabeth, the only child of his deceased sister. "It is my wish," he said, "that you should consider her as your own daughter, and educate her thus. Her mother's fortune is secured to her, the documents of which I will commit to your keeping. Reflect upon this proposition; and decide whether you would prefer educating your niece yourself, to her being brought up by a stepmother."

My father did not hesitate, and immediately went to Italy, that he might accompany the little Elizabeth to her future home. I have often heard my mother say, that she was at that time the most beautiful child she had ever seen, and showed signs even then, of a gentle and affectionate disposition, These indications, and a desire to bind as closely as possible the ties of domestic love, determined my mother to consider Elizabeth as my future wife; a design which she never found reason to repent.

From this time Elizabeth Lavenza became my playfellow, and, as we grew older, my friend. She was docile and good tempered, yet gay and playful as a summer insect. Although she was lively and animated, her feelings were strong and deep, and her disposition uncommonly affectionate. No one could better enjoy liberty, yet no one could submit with more grace than she did to constraint and caprice. Her imagination was luxuriant, yet her capability of application was great. Her person was the image of her mind; her hazel eyes, although as lively as a bird's, possessed an attractive softness. Her figure was light and airy; and though capable of enduring great fatigue, she appeared the most fragile creature in the world. While I admired her understanding and fancy, I loved to tend on her, as I should on a favorite animal; and I never saw so much grace both of person and mind united to so little pretension.

Every one adored Elizabeth. If the servants had any request to make, it was always through her intercession. We were strangers to any species of disunion or dispute; for, although there was a great dissimilitude in our characters, there was a harmony in that very dissimilitude. I was more calm and philosophical than my companion; yet my temper was not so yielding. My application was of longer endurance; but it was not so severe while it endured. I delighted in investigating facts relative to the actual world; she busied herself in following the ærial creations of the poets. The world was to me a secret which I desired to discover; to her it was a vacancy which she sought to people with imaginations of her own.

My brothers were considerably younger than myself, but I had a friend in one of my school-fellows, who compensated for this deficiency. Henry Clerval was the son of a merchant of Geneva, an intimate friend of my father. He was a boy of singular talent and fancy. I remember, when he was nine years old, he wrote a fairy tale, which was the delight and amazement of all his companions. His favorite study consisted in books of chivalry and romance; and when very young, I can remember, that we used to act plays composed by him out of these favorite books, the principal characters of which were Orlando, Robin Hood, Amadis, and St. George.

No youth could have passed more happily than mine. My parents were indulgent, and my companions amiable. Our studies were never forced; and by some means we always had an end placed in view, which excited us to ardor in the prosecution of them. It was by this method, and not by emulation, that we were urged to application. Elizabeth was not incited to apply herself to drawing, that her companions might not outstrip her; but through the desire of pleasing her aunt by the representation of some favorite scene done by her own hand. We learned Latin and English, that we might read the writings of those languages; and so far from study being made odious to us by punishment, we loved application, and our amusements have been the labors of other children. Perhaps we did not read so many books, or learn languages so quickly, as those who are disciplined according to the ordinary methods; but what we learned was impressed the more deeply on our memories.

In this description of our domestic circle I include Henry Clerval, for he was almost constantly with us. He went to school with me, and generally passed the afternoon at our house; for being an only child, and destitute of companions at home, his father was well pleased that he should find associates at our house; and we were never completely happy when Clerval was absent.

I feel pleasure in dwelling on the recollections of childhood, before misfortune had tainted my mind, and changed its bright visions of extensive usefulness into gloomy and narrow reflections upon self. But, in drawing the picture of my early days, I must not omit to record those events which led, by insensible steps, to my after tale of misery: for when I would account to myself for the birth of that passion, which afterwards ruled my destiny, I find it arose, like a mountain river, from ignoble and almost forgotten sources; but, swelling as it proceeded, it became the torrent which, in its course, has swept away all my hopes and joys.

Natural Philosophy is the genius that has regulated my fate; I desire, therefore, in this narration, to state those facts which led to my predilection for that science. When I was thirteen years of age, we all went on a party of pleasure to the baths near Thonon: the inclemency of the weather obliged us to remain a day confin- to the inn. In this house I chanced to find a volume of the works of Cornelius Agrippa. I opened it with apathy; the theory which he attempts to demonstrate, and the wonderful facts which he relates, soon changed this feeling into enthusiasm. A new light seemed to dawn upon my mind; and, bounding with joy, I communicated my discovery to my father. I cannot help remarking here the many opportunities instructers possess of directing the attention of their pupils to useful knowledge, which they utterly neglect. My father looked carelessly at the title page of my book, and said, "Ah! Cornelius Agrippa! My dear Victor, do not waste your time upon this; it is sad trash!"

If, instead of this remark, my father had taken the pains to explain to me, that the principles of Agrippa had been entirely exploded, and that a modern system of science had been introduced, which possessed much greater powers than the ancient, because the powers of the latter were chimerical, while those of the former were real and practical; under such circumstances, I should certainly have thrown Agrippa aside, and, with my imagination warmed as it was, should probably have applied mself to the more rational theory of chemistry which has resulted from modern discoveries. It is even possible, that the train of my ideas would never have received the fatal impulse that led to my ruin. But the cursory glance my father had taken of my volume by no means assured me that he was acquainted with its contents; and I continued to read with the greatest avidity.

When I returned home, my first care was to procure the whole works of this author, and afterwards of Paracelsus and Albertus Magnus. I read and studied the wild fancies of these writers with delight; they appeared to me treasures known to few beside myself; and although I often wished to communicate these secret stores of knowledge to my father, yet his indefinite censure of my favorite Agrippa always withheld me. I disclosed my discoveries to Elizabeth, therefore, under a promise of strict secrecy; but she did not interest herself in the subject, and I was left by her to pursue my studies alone.

It may appear very strange that a disciple of Albertus Magnus, should arise in the eighteenth century; but our family was not scientifical, and I had not attended any of the lectures given at the public schools of Geneva. My dreams were therefore undisturbed by reality; and I entered with the greatest diligence into the search for the philosopher's stone and the elixir of life. But the latter obtained my most undivided attention: wealth was an inferior object; but what glory would attend the discovery, if I could banish disease from the human frame, and render man invulnerable to any but a violent death.

Nor were these my only visions. The raising of ghosts or devils was a promise liberally accorded by my favorite authors, the fulfilment of which I most eagerly sought; and if my incantations were always unsuccessful, I attributed the failure rather to my own inexperience and mistake, than to a want of skill or fidelity in my instructors.

The natural phenomena that take place every day before our eyes did not escape my examination. Distillation, and the wonderful effects of steam, processes of which my favorite authors were utterly ignorant, excited my astonishment; but my utmost wonder was engaged by some experiments on an air-pump, which I saw employed by a gentleman whom we were in the habit of visiting.

The ignorance of the early philosophers on these and several other points served to decrease their credit with me: but I could not entirely throw them aside, before some other system should occupy their place in my mind,

When I was about fifteen years old, we had retired to our house near Belrive, when we witnessed a most violent and terrible thunder-storm. It advanced from behind the mountains of Jura; and the thunder burst at once with frightful loud ness from various duarters of the heavens. I remained, while the storm lasted, watching its progress with curiosity and delight. As I stood at the door, on a sudd n I beheld a stream of fire issue from an old and beautiful oak, which stood about twenty yards from our house; and so soon as the dazzling light vanished the oak had disappeared, and nothing remained but a blasted stump. When we visited it the next morning, we found the tree shattered in a singular manner. It was not splintered by the shock, but entirely reduced to thin ribands of wood. I never beheld any thing so utterly destroyed.

The catastrophe of this tree excited my extreme astonishment; and I eagerly inquired of my father the nature and origin of thunder and lightning. He replied "Electricity;" describing at the same time the various effects of that power. He constructed a small electrical machine, and exhibited a few experiments; he made also a kite, with a wire and spring, which drew down that fluid from the clouds.

This last stroke completed the overthrow of Cornelius Agrippa, Albertus Magnus, and Paracelsus, who had so long reigned the lords of my imagination. But by some fatality I did not feel inclined to commence the study of any modern system; and this disinclination was influenced by the following circumstance.

My father expressed a wish that I should attend a course of lectures upon natural philosophy, to which I cheerfully consented. Some accident prevented my attending these lectures until the course was nearly finished. The lecture being therefore one of the last, was entirely incomprehensible to me. The professor discoursed with the greatest fluency of potassium and boron, of sulphates and oxyds, terms to which I could affix no idea; and I became disgusted with the science of natural philosophy, although I still read Pliny and Buffon with delight, authors, in my estimation, of nearly equal interest and utility.

My occupations at this age were principally the mathematics, and most of the branches of study appertaining to that science. I was busily employed in learning languages; Latin was already familiar to me, and I began to read some of the easiest Greek authors without the help of a lexicon. I also perfectly understood English and German. This is the list of my accomplishments at the age of seventeen; and you may conceive that my hours were fully employed in acquiring and maintaining a knowledge of this various literature.

Another task also devolved upon me, when I became the instructor of my brothers. Ernest was six years younger than myself, and was my principal pupil. He had been afflicted with ill health from his infancy, through which Elizabeth and I had been his constant nurses: his disposition was gentle, but he was incapable of any severe application. William, the youngest of our family was yet an infant, and the most beautiful little fellow in the world; his lively blue eyes, dimpled cheeks, and endearing manners, inspired the tenderest affection.

Such was our domestic circle, from which care and pain seemed forever banished. My father directed our studies, and my mother partook of our enjoyments. Neither of us possessed the slightest preeminence over the other; the voice of command was never heard among us; but mutual affection engaged us all to comply with and obey the slightest desire of each other.

CHAPTER II.

When I had attained the age of seventeen, my parents resolved that I should become a student at the university of Ingolstadt. I had hitherto attended the schools of Geneva; but my father thought it necessary, for the completion of my education, that I should be made acquainted with other customs than those of my native country. My departure was therefore fixed at an early date; but before the day resolved upon could arrive, the first misfyrtune of my life occurred—an omen, as it were, of my future misery.

Elizabeth had caught the scarlet fever;

but her illness was not severe, and she quickly recovered. During her confinement, many arguments had been urged to persuade my mother to refrain from attending upon her. She had, at first, yielded to our entreaties; but when she heard that her favorite was recovering, she could no longer debar herself from her society, and entered her chamber long before the danger of infection was past. The consequences of this imprudence were fatal. On the third day my mother sickened; her fever was very malignant, and the looks of her attendants prognosticated the worst event. On her death-bed the fortitude and benignity of this admirable woman did not desert her. She joined the hands of Elizabeth and myself: "My children," she said, "my firmest hopes of future happiness were placed on the prospect of your union. This expectation will now be the consolation of your father. Elizabeth, my love, you must supply my place to your younger cousins. Alas! I regret that I am taken from you; and, happy and beloved as I have been, is it not hard to quit you all? But these are not thoughts befitting me; I will endeavor to resign myself cheerfully to death, and will indulge a hope of meeting you in another world."

She died calmly; and her countenance expressed affection even in death. I need not describe the feelings of those whose dearest ties are rent by that most irreparable evil, the void that presents itself to the soul, and the despair that is exhibited on the countenance. It is so long before the mind can persuade itself that she, whom we saw every day, and whose very existence appeared a part of our own, can have departed for ever—that the brightness of a beloved eye can have been extinguished, and the sound of a voice so familiar, and dear to the ear, can be hushed never more to be heard. These are the reflections of the first days; but when the lapse of time proves the reality of the evil, then the actual bitterness of grief commences. Yet from whom has not that rude hand rent away some dear connection; and why should I describe a sorrow which all have felt, and must feel? The time at length arrives, when grief is rather an indulgence than a necessity; and the smile that plays upon the lips, although it may be deemed a sacrilege, is not banished. My mother was dead, but we had still duties which we ought to perform; we must continue our course with the rest, and learn to think ourselves fortunate, while one remains whom the spoiler has not seized.

My journey to Ingolstadt, which had been deferred by these events, was now again determined upon. I obtained from my father a respite of some weeks. This period was spent sadly; my mother's death, and my speedy departure, depressed our spirits; but Elizabeth endeavored to renew the spirit of cheerfulness in our little society. Since the death of her aunt, her mind had acquired new firmness and vigor. She determined to fulfil her duties with the greatest exactness; and she felt that the most imperious duty, of rendering her uncle and cousins happy, had devolved upon her. She consoled me, amused her uncle, instructed my brothers; and I never beheld her so enchanting as at this time, when she was continually endeavoring to contribute to the happiness of others, entirely forgetful of herself.

The day of my departure at length arrived. I had taken leave of all my friends excepting Clerval, who had spent the last evening with us. He bitterly lamented that he was unable to accompany me: but his father could not be persuaded to part with him, intending that he should become a partner with him in business, in compliance with his favorite theory, that learning was superfluous in the commerce of ordinary life. Henry had a refined mind; he had no desire to be idle, and was well pleased to become his father's partner, but he believed that a man might be a very good trader, and yet possess a cultivated understanding.

We sat late, listening to his complaints, and making many little arrangements for the future. The next morning early I departed. Tears gushed from the eyes of Elizabeth; they proceeded partly from sorrow at my departure, and partly because she reflected that the same journey was to have taken place three months before, when a mother's blessing would have accompanied me.

I threw myself into the chaise that was to convey me away, and indulged in the most melancholy reflections. I, who had ever been surrounded by amiable companions, continually engaged in endeavoring to bestow mutual pleasure, I was now alone. In the university, whither I was going, I must form my own friends, and be my own protector. My life had hitherto been remarkably secluded and domestic; and this had given me invincible repugnance to new countenances. I loved my brothers, Elizabeth, and Clerval; these were "old familiar faces;" but I believed myself totally unfitted for the company of strangers. Such were my reflections as I commenced my journey; but as I proceeded, my spirits and hopes rose. I ardently desired the acquisition of knowledge. I had often, when at home, thought it hard to remain during my youth cooped up in one place, and had longed to enter the world, and take my station among other human beings. Now my desires were complied with, and it would, indeed, have been folly to repent.

I had sufficient leisure for these and many other reflections during my journey to Ingolstadt, which was long and fatiguing. At length the high white steeple of the town met my eyes. I alighted, and was conducted to my solitary apartment to spend the evening as I pleased.

The next morning I delivered my letters of introduction, and paid a visit to some of the principal professors, and among others to M. Krempe, professor of natural philosophy. He received me with politeness, and asked me several questions concerning my progress in the different branches of science appertaining to natural philosophy. I mentioned, it is true, with fear and trembling, the only authors I had ever read upon those subjects. The professor stared: "Have you," he said, "really spent your time in studying such nonsense?"

I replied in the affirmative. "Every minute," continued M. Krempe with warmth, "every instant that you have wasted on those books is utterly and entirely lost. You have burdened your memory with exploded systems, and useless names. Good God! in what desert land have you lived, where no one was kind enough to inform you that these fancies, which you have so greedily imbibed, are a thousand years old, and as musty as they are ancient? I little expected in this enlightened and scientific age to find a disciple of Albertus Magnus and Paracelsus. My dear Sir, you must begin your studies entirely anew."

So saying, he stept aside, and wrote down a list of several books treating of natural philosophy, which he desired me to procure, and dismissed me, after mentioning that in the beginning of the following week he intended to commence a course of lectures upon natural philosophy in its general relations, and that M. Waldman, a fellow-professor, would lecture upon chemistry the alternate days that he missed.

I returned home, not disappointed, for I had long considered those authors useless whom the professor had so strongly reprobated; but I did not feel much inclined to study the books which I procured at his recommendation. M. Krempe was a little squat man, with a gruff voice and repulsive countenance; the teacher, therefore, did not prepossess me in favor of his doctrine. Besides, I had a contempt for the uses of modern natural philosophy. It was very different, when the masters of the science sought immortality and power; such views, although futile, were grand: but now the scene was changed. The ambition of the inquirer seemed to limit itself to the annihilation of those visions on which my interest in science was chiefly founded. I was required to exchange chimeras of boundless grandeur for realities of little worth.

Such were my reflections during the first two or three days spent almost in solitude. But as the ensuing week commenced, I thought of the information which M. Krempe had given me concerning the lectures. And although I could not consent to go and hear that little conceited fellow deliver sentences out of a pulpit, I recollected what he had said of M. Waldman, whom I had never seen, as he had hitherto been out of town.

Partly from curiosity, and partly from idleness, I went into the lecturing room, which M. Waldman entered shortly after. This professor was very unlike his colleague. He appeared about fifty years of age, but with an aspect expressive of the greatest benevolence; a few gray hairs covered his temples, but those at the back of his head were nearly black. His person was short, but remarkably erect; and his voice the sweetest I had ever heard. He began his lecture by a recapitulation of the history of chemistry and the various improvements made by different men of learning, pronouncing with fervor the names of the most distinguished discoverers. He then took a cursory view of the present state of the science, and explained many of its elementary terms. After having made a few preparatory experiments, he concluded with a panegyric upon modern chemistry, the terms of which I shall never forget:

"The ancient teachers of this science," said he, "promised impossibilities, and performed nothing. The modern masters promise very little; they know that metals cannot be transmuted, and that the elixir of life is a chimera. But these philosophers, whose hands seem only made to dabble in dirt, and their eyes to pore over the microscope or crucible, have indeed performed miracles. They penetrate into the recesses of nature, and show how she works in her hiding places. They ascend into the heavens; they have discovered how the blood circulates, and the nature of the air we breathe. They have acquired new and almost unlimited powers; they can command the thunders of the heaven, mimic the earthquake, and even mock the invisible world with its own shadows."

I departed highly pleased with the professor and his lecture, and paid him a visit the same evening. His manners in private were even more mild and attractive than in public; for there was a certain dignity in his mien during his lecture, which in his own house was replaced by the greatest affability and kindness. He heard with attention my little narration concerning my studies, and smiled at the names of Cornelius Aggrippa, and Paracelsus, but without the contempt that M. Krempe had exhibited. He said, that "these were men to whose indefatigable zeal modern philosophers were indebted for most of the foundations of their knowledge. They had left us an easier task, to give new names, and arrange in connected classifications, the facts which they in a great degree had been the instruments of bringing to light. The labors of men of genius, however erroneously directed, scarcely ever fail in ultimately turning to the solid advantage of mankind." I listened to his statement, which was delivered without any presumption or affectation; and then added, that his lecture had removed my prejudices against modern chemists; and I, at the same time, requested his advice concerning the books I ought to procure.

"I am happy," said M. Waldman, "to have gained a disciple; and if your application equals your ability, I have no doubt of your success. Chemistry is that branch of natural philosophy in which the greatest improvements have been made, and may be made; it is on that account that I have made it my peculiar study; but at the same time I have not neglected other branches of science. A man would make but a very sorry chemist, if he attended to that department of human knowledge alone. If your wish is to become really a man of science, and not a petty experamentalist, I should advise you to apply to every branch of natural philosophy, including mathematics."

He then took me into his laboratory, and explained to me the uses of his various machines; instructing me as to what I ought to procure, and promising me the use of his own, when I should have advanced far enough in the science not to derange their mechanism. He also gave me the list of books which I had requested; and I took my leave.

Thus ended a day memorable to me; it decided my future destiny.

CHAPTER III.

From this day natural philosophy, and particularly chemistry, in the most comprehensive sense of the term, became nearly my sole occupation. I read with ardor those works, so full of genius and discrimination, which modern inquirers have written on these subjects. I attended the lectures, and cultivated the acquaintance, of the men of science of the university; and I found even in M. Krempe a great deal of sound sense and real information, combined, it is true, with a repulsive physiognomy and manners, but not on that account the less valuable. In M. Waldman I found a true friend. His gentleness was never tinged by dogmatism; and his instructions were given with an air of frankness and good nature, that banished every idea of pedantry. It was perhaps, the amiable character of this man that inclined me more to that branch of natural philosophy which he professed, than an intrinsic love for the science itself. But this state of mind had place only in the first steps towards knowledge: the more fully I entered into the science, the more exclusively I pursued it for its own sake. That application, which at first had been a matter of duty and resolution, now became so ardent and eager that the stars often appeared in the light of morning while I was yet engaged in my laboratory.

As I applied so closely, it may be easily conceived that I improved rapidly. My ardor was indeed the astonishment of the students; and my proficiency, that of the masters. Professor Krempe often asked me, with a sly smile, how Cornelius Agrippa went on? while M. Waldman expressed the most heartfelt exultation in my progress. Two years passed in this manner, during which I paid no visit to Geneva, but was engaged, heart and soul, in the pursuit of some discoveries, which I hoped to make. None but those who have experienced them can conceive of the enticements of Science. In other studies you go as far as others have gone before you, and there is nothing more to know; but in a scientific pursuit there is continual food for discovery and wonder. A mind of moderate capacity, which closely pursues one study, must infallibly arrive at great proficiency in that study; and I who continually sought the attainment of one object of pursuit, and was solely wrapt up in this, improved so rapidly, that, at the end of two years, I made some discoveries in the improvement of some chemical instruments, which procured me great esteem and admiration at the university. When I arrived at this point, and had become as well acquainted with the theory and practice of natural philosophy as depended on the lessons of any of the professors at Ingolstadt, my residence there being no longer conducive to my improvement, I thought of returning to my friends and my native town, when an incident happened that protracted my stay.

One of the phenomena which had peculiarly attracted my attention was the structure of the human frame, and, indeed, any animal endued with life. Whence I often asked myself, did the principle of life proceed? It was a bold question, and one which has ever been considered as a mystery; yet with how many things are we upon the brink of becoming acquainted, if cowardice or carelessness did not restrain our inquiries. I revolved these circumstances in my mind, and determined thenceforth to apply myself more particularly to those branches of natural philosophy which relate to physiology. Unless I had been animated by an almost supernatural enthusiasm, my application to this study would have been irksome, and almost intolerable. To examine the causes of life, we must first have recourse to death. I became acquainted with the science of anatomy; but this was not sufficient; I must also observe the natural decay and corruption of the human body. In my education my father had taken the greatest precautions that my mind should be impressed with no supernatural horrors. I do not ever remember to have trembled at a tale of superstition, or to have feared the apparition of a spirit. Darkness had no effect upon my fancy: and a churchyard was to me merely the receptacle of bodies deprived of life, which, from being the seat of beauty and strength, had become food for the worm. Now I was led to examine the cause and progress of this decay, and forced to spend days and nights in vaults and charnel-houses. My attention was fixed upon every object the most insupportable to the delicacy of the human feelings. I saw how the fine form of man was degraded and wasted; I beheld the corruption of death succeed to the blooming cheek of life; I saw how the worm inherited the wonders of the eye and brain. I paused, examining and analysing all the minutiæ of causation, as exemplified in the change from life to death, and death to life, until from the midst of this darkness a sudden light broke in upon me—a light so brilliant and wondrous, yet so simple, that while I became dizzy with the immensity of prospect which it illustrated, I was surprized that among so many men of genius, who had directed their inquiries towards the same science, that I alone should be reserved to discover so astonishing a secret.

Remember, I am not recording the vision of a madman. The sun does not more certainly shine in the heavens, than that which I now affirm is true. Some miracle might have produced it, yet the stages of discovery were distinct and probable. After days and nights of incredible labor and fatigue, I succeeded in discovering the cause of generation and life; nay, more, I became myself capable of bestowing animation upon lifeless matter.

The astonishment which I had at first experienced on this discovery soon gave place to delight and rapture. After so much time spent in painful labor, to arrive at once at the summit of my desires was the most gratifying consummation of my toils. But this discovery was so great and overwhelming, that all the steps by which I had been progressively led to it were obliterated, and I beheld only the result. What had been the study and desire of the wisest men since the creation of the world, was now within my grasp. Not that, like a magic scene, it all opened upon me at once: the information I had obtained was of a nature rather to direct my endeavors so soon as I should point them towards the object of my search, than to exhibit that object already accomplished. I was like the Arabian who had been buried with the dead, and found a passage to life aided only by one glimmering, and seemingly ineffectual, light.

I see by your eagerness, and the wonder and hope which your eyes express, my friend, that you expect to be informed of the secret with which I am acquainted; that cannot be; listen patiently until the end of my story, and you will easily perceive why I am reserved upon that subject. I will not lead you on unguarded and ardent as I then was, to your destruction and infallible misery. Learn from me, if not by my precepts, at least by my example, how dangerous is the acquirement of knowledge, and how much happier that man is who believes his native town to be the world, than he who aspires to become greater than his nature will allow.

When I found so astonishing a power placed within my hands, I hesitated a long time concerning the manner in which I should employ it. Although I possessed the capacity of bestowing animation, yet to prepare a frame for the reception of it, with all its intricacies of fibres, muscles, and veins, still remained a work of inconceivable difficulty and labor. I doubted at first whether I should attempt the creation of a being like myself or one of simpler organization; but my imagination was too much exalted by my first success to permit me to doubt of my ability to give life to an animal as complex and wonderful as man. The materials at present within my command hardly appeared adequate to so arduous an undertaking; but I doubted not that I should ultimately succeed. I prepared myself for a multitude of reverses; my operations might be incessantly baffled, and at last my work be imperfect: yet, when I considered the improvement which every day takes place in science and mechanics, I was encouraged to hope my present attempts would at least lay the foundations of future success. Nor could I consider the magnitude and complexity of my plan as any argument of its impracticability. It was with these feelings that I began the creation of a human being. As the minuteness of the parts formed a great hindrance to my speed, I resolved, contrary to my first intention, to make the being of a gigantic stature; that is to say, about eight feet in height, and proportionably large. After having formed this determination, and having spent some months in successfully collecting and arranging my materials, I began.

No one can conceive the variety of feelings which bore me onwards, like a hurricane, in the first enthusiasm of success. Life and death appeared to me ideal bounds, which I should first break through, and pour a torrent of light into our dark world. A new species would bless me as its creator and source; many happy and excellent natures would owe their being to me. No father could claim the gratitude of his child so completely as I should deserve theirs. Pursuing these reflections, I thought, that if I could bestow animation upon lifeless matter, I might in process of time (although I now found it impossible) renew life where death had apparently devoted the body to corruption.

These thoughts supported my spirits, while I pursued my undertaking with unremitting ardor. My cheek had grown pale with study, and my person had become emaciated with confinement. Sometimes, on the very brink of certainty, I failed; yet still I clung to the hope which the next day or the next hour might realize. One secret which I alone possessed was the hope to which I had dedicated myself; and the moon gazed on my midnight labors, while, with unrelaxed and breathless eagerness, I pursued nature to her hiding-places. Who shall conceive the horrors of my secret toil, as I dabbled among the unhallowed damps of the grave, or tortured the living animal to animate the lifeless clay? My limbs now tremble, and my eyes swim with the remembrance; but then a resistless, and almost frantic impulse, urged me forward; I seemed to have lost all soul or sensation but for this one pursuit. It was indeed but a passing trance, that only made me feel with renewed acuteness so soon as, the unnatural stimulus ceasing to operate, I had returned to my old habits. I collected bones from charnel houses; and disturbed, with profane fingers, the tremendous secrets of the human frame. In a solitary chamber, or rather cell, at the top of the house, and separated from all the other apartments by a gallery and staircase, I kept my workshop of filthy creation; my eyeballs were starting from their sockets in attending to the details of my employment. The dissecting-room and the slaughter-house furnished many of my materials; and often did my human nature turn with loathing from my occupation, while, still urged on by an eagerness which perpetually increased, I brought my work near to a conclusion.

The summer months passed while I was thus engaged, heart and soul, in one pursuit. It was a most beautiful season; never did the fields bestow a more plentiful harvest, or the vines yield a more luxuriant vintage: but my eyes were insensible to the charms of nature. And the same feelings which made me neglect the scenes around me caused me also to forget those friends who were so many miles absent, and whom I had not seen for so long a time. I knew my silence disquieted them; and I well remembered the words of my father: "I know that while you are pleased with yourself, you will remember us with affection, and we shall hear regularly from you. You must pardon me, if I regard any interruption in your correspondence as a proof that your other duties are equally neglected."

I knew well therefore what would be my father's feelings; but I could not tear my thoughts from my employment, loathsome in itself, but which had taken an irresistible hold of my imagination. I wished, as it were, to procrastinate all that related to my feelings of affection until the great object, which swallowed up every habit of my nature, should be completed.

I then thought that my father would be unjust if he ascribed my neglect to vice, or faultiness on my part; but I am now convinced that he was justified in conceiving that I should not be altogether free from blame. A human being in perfection ought always to preserve a calm and peaceful mind, and never to allow passion or a transitory desire to disturb his tranquillity. I do not think that the pursuit of knowledge is an exception to this rule. If the study to which you apply yourself has a tendency to weaken your affections, and to destroy your taste for those simple pleasures in which no alloy can possibly mix, then that study is certainly unlawful, that is to say, not befitting the human mind. If this rule were always observed; if no man allowed any pursuit whatsoever to interfere with the tranquillity of his domestic affections, Greece had not been enslaved; Cæsar would have spared his country; America would have been discovered more gradually; and the empires of Mexico and Peru had not been destroyed.

But I forget that I am moralizing in the most interesting part of my tale; and your looks remind me to proceed.

My father made no reproach in his letters; and only took notice of my silence by inquiring into my occupations more particularly than before. Winter, Spring, and Summer, passed during my labors; but I did not watch the blossom or the expanding leaves—sights which before always yielded me supreme delight, so deeply was I engrossed in my occupation. The leaves of that year had withered before my work drew near to a close; and now every day showed me more plainly how well I had succeeded. But my enthusiasm was checked by my anxiety, and I appeared rather like one doomed by slavery to toil in the mines, or any other unwholesome trade, than an artist occupied by his favorite employment. Every night I was oppressed by a slow fever, and I became nervous to a most painful degree; a disease that I dreaded the more because I had hitherto enjoyed most excellent health, and had always boasted of the firmness of my nerves. But I believed that exercise and amusement would soon drive away such symptoms; and I promised myself both of these, when my creation should be complete.

CHAPTER IV.

It was on a dreary night of November, that I beheld the accomplishment of my toils. With an anxiety that almost amounted to agony, I collected the instruments of life around me, that I might infuse a spark of being into the lifeless thing that lay at my feet. It was already one in the morning; the rain pattered dismally against the panes, and my candle was nearly burnt out, when, by the glimmer of the half-extinguished light, I saw the dull yellow eye of the creature open; it breathed hard, and a convulsive motion agitated its limbs.

How can I describe my emotions at this catastrophe, or how delineate the wretch whom, with such infinite pains and care, I had endeavored to form? His limbs were in proportion, and I had selected his features as beautiful. Beautiful! Great God! His yellow skin scarcely covered the work of muscles and arteries beneath; his hair was of a lustrous black, and flowing; his teeth of a pearly whiteness; but these luxuriances only formed a more horrid contrast with his watery eyes, that seemed almost of the same color as the dun white sockets in which they were set, his shriveled complexion, and straight black lips.

The different accidents of life are not so changeable as the feelings of human nature. I had worked hard for nearly two years, for the sole purpose of infusing life into an inanimate body. For this I had deprived myself of rest and health. I had desired it with an ardor that far exceeded moderation; but now that I had finished, the beauty of the dream vanished, and breathless horror and disgust filled my heart. Unable to endure the aspect of the being I had created, I rushed out of the room, and continued a long time traversing my bed-chamber, unable to compose my mind to sleep. At length lassitude succeeded to the tumult I had before endured; and I threw myself on the bed in my clothes, endeavoring to seek a few moments of forgetfulness. But it was in vain: I slept indeed, but I was disturbed by the wildest dreams. I thought I saw Elizabeth, in the bloom of health, walking in the streets of Ingolstadt. Delighted and surprised, I embraced her; but as I imprinted the first kiss on her lips, they became livid with the hue of death; her features appeared to change, and I thought that I held the corpse of my dead mother in my arms; a shroud enveloped her form, and I saw the grave-worms crawling in the folds of the flannel. I started from my sleep with horror; a cold dew covered my forehead, my teeth chattered, and every limb became convulsed; when, by the dim and yellow light of the moon, as it forced its way through the window-shutters, I beheld the wretch—the miserable monster whom I had created. He held up the curtain of the bed; and his eyes, if eyes they may be called, were fixed on me. His jaws opened, and he muttered some inarticulate sounds, while a grin wrinkled his cheeks.

He might have spoken, but I did not hear; one hand was stretched out, seemingly to detain me, but I escaped, and rushed down stairs. I took refuge in the court-yard belonging to the house which I inhabited; where I remained during the rest of the night, walking up and down in the greatest agitation, listening attentively, catching and fearing each sound as if it were to announce the approach of the demoniacal corse to which I had so miserably given life.

Oh! no mortal could support the horror of that countenance. A mummy again endued with animation could not be so hideous as that wretch. I had gazed on him while unfinished; he was ugly then; but when those muscles and joints were rendered capable of motion, it became a thing such as even Dante could not have conceived.

I passed the night wretchedly. Sometimes my pulse beat so quickly and hardly, that I felt the palpitation of every artery; at others, I nearly sank to the ground through langor and extreme weakness. Mingled with this horror, I felt the bitterness of disappointment: dreams that had been my food and pleasant rest for so long a space, were now become a hell to me; and the change was so rapid, the overthrow so complete!

Morning, dismal and wet, at length dawned, and discovered to my sleepless and aching eyes the church of Ingolstadt, its white steeple and clock, which indicated the sixth hour. The porter opened the gates of the court, which had that night been my asylum, and I issued into the streets, pacing them with quick steps, as if I sought to avoid the wretch whom I feared every turning of the street would present to my view. I did not dare return to the apartment which I inhabited, but felt impelled to hurry on, although wetted by the rain, which poured from a black and comfortless sky.

I continued walking in this manner for some time, endeavoring, by bodily exercise, to ease the load that weighed upon my mind. I traversed the streets, without any clear conception of where I was, or what I was doing. My heart palpitated in the sickness of fear: and I hurried on with irregular steps, not daring to look about me:

Like one who, on a lonely road,
 Doth walk in fear and dread,
And, having once turn'd round, walks on,
 And turns no more his head;
Because he knows a frightful fiend
 Doth close behind him tread.*

* Coleridge's "Ancient Mariner."

Continuing thus, I came at length opposite to the inn at which the various diligences and carriages usually stopped. Here I paused, I knew not why; but I remained some minutes with my eyes fixed on a coach that was coming towards me from the other end of the street. As it drew nearer, I observed that it was the Swiss diligence: it stopped just where I was standing; and, on the door being opened, I perceived Henry Clerval, who, on seeing me, instantly sprung out. "My dear Frankenstein," exclaimed he, "how glad I am to see you! how fortunate that you should be here at the very moment of my alighting!"

Nothing could equal my delight on seeing Clerval; his presence brought back to my thoughts my father, Elizabeth, and all those scenes of home so dear to my recollection. I grasped his hand, and in a moment forgot my horror and misfortune; I felt suddenly, and for the first time during many months, calm and serene joy. I welcomed my friend, therefore, in the most cordial manner, and we walked towards my college. Clerval continued talking for some time about our mutual friends, and his own good fortune in being permitted to come to Ingolstadt. "You may easily believe," said he, "how great was the difficulty to persuade my father that it was not absolutely necessary for a merchant not to understand anything except book-keeping; and, indeed, I believe I left him incredulous to the last, for his constant answer to my unwearied entreaties was the same as that of the Dutch schoolmaster in the Vicar of Wakefield: 'I have ten thousand florins a year without Greek, I eat heartily without Greek.' But his affection for me at length overcame his dislike of learning, and he has permitted me to undertake a voyage of discovery to the land of knowledge."

"It gives me the greatest delight to see you; but tell me how you left my father, brothers, and Elizabeth."

"Very well, and very happy, only a little uneasy that they hear from you so seldom. By-the-bye, I mean to lecture you a little upon their account myself. But, my dear Frankenstein," continued he, stopping short, and gazing full in my face, "I did not before remark how very ill you appear; so thin and pale; you look as if you had been watching for several nights."

"You have guessed right; I have lately been so deeply engaged in one occupation, that I have not allowed myself sufficient rest, as you see: but I hope, I sincerely hope, that all these employments are now at an end, and that I am at length free."

I trembled excessively; I could not endure to think of, and far less to allude to the occurrences of the preceding night. I walked with a quick pace, and we soon arrived at my college. I then reflected, and the thought made me shiver, that the creature whom I had left in my apartment might still be there, alive, and walking about. I dreaded to behold this monster; but I feared still more that Henry should see him. Entreating him therefore to remain a few minutes at the bottom of the stairs, I darted up towards my own room. My hand was already on the lock of the door before I recollected myself. I then paused; and a cold shivering came over me. I threw the door forcibly open, as children are accustomed to do when they expect a spectre to stand in waiting for them on the other side; but nothing appeared. I stepped fearfully in: the apartment was empty; and my bed-room was also freed from its hideous guest. I could hardly believe that so great a good-fortune could have befallen me; but when I became assured that my enemy had indeed fled, I clapped my hands for joy, and ran down to Clerval.

We ascended into my room, and the servant presently brought breakfast; but I was unable to contain myself. It was not joy only that possessed me; I felt my flesh tingle with excess of sensitiveness, and my pulse beat rapidly. I was unable to remain for a single instant in the same place; I jumped over the chairs, clapped my hands and laughed aloud. Clerval at first attributed my unusual spirits to joy on his arrival; but when he observed me more attentively, he saw a wildness in my eyes for which he could not account; and my loud, unrestrained, heartless laughter, frightened and astonished him.

"My dear Victor," cried he, "what, for God's sake, is the matter? Do not laugh in that manner. How ill you are! What is the cause of all this?"

"Do not ask me," cried I, putting my hands before my eyes, for I thought I saw the dreaded spectre glide into the room; "*he* can tell. Oh, save me! save me!" I imagined that the monster seized me; I struggled furiously, and fell down in a fit.

Poor Clerval! what must have been his feelings? A meeting, which he anticipated with such joy, so strangely turned to bitterness. But I was not the witness of his grief; for I was lifeless, and did not recover my senses for a long, long time.

This was the commencement of a nervous fever, which confined me for several months. During all that time Henry was my only nurse. I afterwards learned that, knowing my father's advanced age, and unfitness for so long a journey, and how wretched my sickness would make Elizabeth, he spared them this grief by concealing the extent of my disorder. He knew that I could not have a more kind and attentive nurse than himself; and, firm in the hope he felt of my recovery, he did not doubt that, instead of doing harm, he performed the kindest action that he could towards them.

But I was in reality very ill; and surely nothing but the unbounded and unremitting attentions of my friend could have restored me to life. The form of the monster on whom I had bestowed existence was for ever before my eyes, and I raved incessantly concerning him. Doubtless my words surprised Henry; he at first believed them to be the wanderings of my disturbed imagination; but the pertinacity with which I continually recurred to the same subject persuaded him that my disorder indeed owed its origin to some uncommon and terrible event.

By very slow degrees, and with frequent relapses, that alarmed and grieved my friend, I recovered. I remember the first time I became capable of observing outward objects with any kind of pleasure, I perceived that the fallen leaves had disappeared, and that the young buds were shooting forth from the trees that shaded my window. It was a divine spring; and the season contributed greatly to my convalescence. I felt also sentiments of joy and affection revive in my bosom; my gloom disappeared, and in a short time I became as cheerful as before I was attacked by the fatal passion.

"Dearest Clerval," exclaimed I, "how kind, how very good you are to me. This whole winter, instead of being spent in study, as you promised yourself, has been consumed in my sick room. How shall I ever repay you? I feel the greatest remorse for the disappointment of which I have been the occasion; but you will forgive me."

"You will repay me entirely, if you do not discompose yourself, but get well as fast as you can; and since you appear in such good spirits, I may speak to you on one subject, may I not?"

I trembled. One subject! what could it be? Could he allude to an object on whom I dared not even think?

"Compose yourself," said Clerval, who observed my change of color, "I will not mention it, if it agitates you; but your father and cousin would be very happy if they received a letter from you in your own hand-writing. They hardly know how ill you have been, and are uneasy at your long silence."

"Is that all? my dear Henry. How could you suppose that my first thought would not fly towards those dear, dear friends, whom I love, and who are so deserving of my love."

"If this is your present temper, my friend, you will perhaps be glad to see a letter that has been lying here some days for you: it is from your cousin, I believe."

CHAPTER V.

CLERVAL then put the following letter into my hands.

"TO V. FRANKENSTEIN.

"MY DEAR COUSIN: I cannot describe to you the uneasiness we have all felt concerning your health. We cannot help imagining that your friend Clerval conceals the extent of your disorder: for it is now several months since we have seen your handwriting; and all this time you have been obliged to dictate your letters to Henry. Surely, Victor, you must have been exceedingly ill; and this makes us all very wretched, as much so nearly as after the death of your dear mother. My uncle was almost persuaded that you were indeed dangerously ill, and could hardly be restrained from undertaking a journey to Ingolstadt. Clerval always writes that you are getting better; I eagerly hope that you will confirm this intelligence soon in your own hand-writing; for indeed, indeed, Victor, we are all very miserable on this account. Relieve us from this fear, and we shall be the happiest creatures in the world. Your father's health is now so vigorous, that he appears ten years younger since last winter. Ernest also is so much improved, that you would hardly know him: he is now nearly sixteen, and has lost that sickly appearance which he had some years ago: he is grown quite robust and active.

"My uncle and I conversed a long time last night about what profession Ernest should follow. His constant illness when young has deprived him of the habits of application; and now that he enjoys good health, he is continually in the open air, climbing the hills, or rowing on the lake. I therefore proposed that he should be a farmer; which you know, cousin, is a favorite scheme of mine. A farmer's is a very healthy happy life; and the least hurtful, or rather the most beneficial profession of any. My uncle had an idea of his being educated as an advocate, that through his interest he might become a judge. But beside that he is not at all fitted for such an occupation, it is certainly more creditable to cultivate the earth for the sustenance of man, than to be the confidant, and sometimes the accomplice, of his vices; which is the profession of a lawyer. I said, that the employments of a prosperous farmer, if they were not a more honorable, they were at least a happier species of occupation than that of a judge, whose misfortune it was always to meddle with the dark side of human nature. My uncle smiled, and said, that I ought to be an advocate myself, which put an end to the conversation on that subject.

"And now I must tell you a little story that will please and perhaps amuse you. Do you not remember Justine Moritz? Probably you do not; I will relate her history, therefore, in a few words. Madame Moritz, her mother, was a widow with four children, of whom Justine was the third. This girl had always been the favorite of her father; but, through a strange perversity, her mother could not endure her, and, after the death of M. Moritz, treated her very ill. My aunt observed this; and, when Justine was twelve years of age, prevailed on her mother to allow her to live at her house. The republican institutions of our country have produced simpler and happier manners than those which prevail in the great monarchies that surround it. Hence there is less distinction between the several classes of its inhabitants; and the lower orders being neither so poor nor so despised, their manners are more refined and moral. A servant in Geneva does not mean the same thing as a servant in France or England. Justine, thus received in our family, learned the duties of servant; a condition which, in our fortunate country, does not include the idea of ignorance, and a sacrifice of the dignity of a human being.

"After what I have said, I dare say you well remember the heroine of my little tale: for Justine was a great favorite of yours; and I recollect you once remarked, that if you were in an ill humor, one glance from Justine could dissipate it, for the same reason that Ariosto gives concerning the beauty of Angelica—she looked so frank-hearted and happy. My aunt conceived a great attachment for her, by which she was induced to give her an education superior to that which she had at first intended. This benefit was fully repaid; Justine was the most grateful little creature in the world: I do not mean that she made any professions, I never heard one pass her lips; but you could see by her eyes that she almost adored her protectress. Although her disposition was gay, and in many respects inconsiderate, yet she paid the greatest attention to every gesture of my aunt. She thought her the model of all excellence, and endeavored to imitate her phraseology and manners, so that even now she often reminds me of her.

"When my dearest aunt died, every one was too much occupied in their own grief to notice poor Justine, who had attended her during her illness with the most anxious affection. Poor Justine was very ill; but other trials were reserved for her.

"One by one, her brothers and sister died; and her mother, with the exception of her neglected daughter, was left childless. The conscience of the woman was troubled; she began to think that the deaths of her favorites was a judgment from Heaven to chastise her partiality. She was a Roman Catholic; and I believe her confessor confirmed the idea which she had conceived. Accordingly, a few months after your departure for Ingolstadt, Justine was called home by her repentant mother. Poor girl! she wept when she quitted our house: she was much altered since the death of my aunt; grief had given softness and a winning mildness to her manners, which had before been remarkable for vivacity. Nor was her residence at her mother's house of a nature to restore her gayety. The poor woman was very vascillating in her repentance. She sometimes begged Justine to forgive her unkindness, but much oftener accused her of having caused the deaths of her brothers and sister. Perpetual fretting at length threw Madame Moritz into a decline, which at first increased her irritability, but she is now at peace for ever. She died on the first approach of cold weather, at the beginning of this last winter. Justine has returned to us; and I assure you I love her tenderly. She is very clever and gentle, and extremely pretty; as I mentioned before, her mien and her expressions continually remind me of my dear aunt.

"I must say also a few words to you, my dear cousin, of little darling William. I wish you could see him; he is very tall of his age, with sweet laughing blue eyes, dark eye-lashes, and curling hair. When he smiles, two little dimples appear on each cheek, which are rosy with health. He has already had one or two little *wives*, but Louisa Biron is his favorite, a pretty little girl of five years of age.

"Now, dear Victor, I dare say you wish to be indulged in a little gossip concerning the good people of Geneva. The pretty Miss Mansfield has already received the congratulatory visits on her approaching marriage with a young Englishman, John Melbourne, Esq. Her ugly sister, Manon, married M. Duvillard, the rich banker, last autumn. Your favorite schoolfellow, Louis Manoir, has suffered several misfortunes since the departure of Clerval from Geneva. But he has already recovered his spirits, and is reported to be on the point of marrying a very lively pretty French woman, Madame Tavernier. She is a widow, and much older than Manoir; but she is very much admired, and a favorite with everybody.

"I have written myself into good spirits, dear cousin; yet I cannot conclude without again anxiously inquiring concerning your health. Dear Victor, if you are not very ill, write yourself, and make your father and all of us happy; or—I cannot bear to think of the other side of the question; my tears already flow. Adieu, my dearest cousin. ELIZABETH LAVENZA.

"Geneva, March 18th, 17—."

"Dear, dear Elizabeth!" I exclaimed when I had read her letter; "I will write instantly, and relieve them from the anxiety they must feel." I wrote, and this exertion greatly fatigued me; but my convalescence had commenced, and proceeded regularly. In another fortnight I was able to leave my chamber.

One of my first duties on my recovery was to introduce Clerval to the several professors of the university. In doing this, I underwent a kind of rough usage, ill befitting the wounds that my mind had sustained. Ever since the fatal night, the end of my labors, and the beginning of my misfortunes, I had conceived a violent antipathy even to the name of natural philosophy. When I was otherwise quite restored to health, the sight of a chemical instrument would renew all the agony of my nervous symptoms. Henry saw this, and had removed all my apparatus from my view. He had also changed my apartment; for he perceived that I had acquired a dislike for the room which had previously been my laboratory. But these cares of Clerval were made of no avail when I visited the professors. M. Waldman inflicted torture when he praised, with kindness and warmth, the astonishing progress I had made in the sciences. He soon perceived that I disliked the subject; but not guessing the real cause, he attributed my feelings to modesty, and changed the subject from my improvement to the science itself, with a desire, as I evidently saw, of drawing me out. What could I do? He meant to please and he tormented me. I felt as if he had placed carefully, one by one, in my view those instruments which were to be afterwards used in putting me to a slow and cruel death. I writhed under his words, yet dared not exhibit the pain I felt. Clerval, whose eyes and feelings were always quick in discerning the sensations of others, declined the subject, alleging in excuse his total ignorance; and the conversation took a more general turn. I thanked my friend from my heart, but I did not speak. I saw plainly that he was surprised, but he never attempted to draw my secret from me; and although I loved him with a mixture of affection and reverence that knew no bounds, yet I could never persuade myself to confide to him that event which was so often present to my recollection, but which I feared the detail to another would only impress more deeply.

Mr. Krempe was not equally docile; and in my condition at that time, of almost insupportable sensitiveness, his harsh blunt encomiums gave me even more pain than the benevolent approbation of M. Waldman. "D—n the fellow!" cried he; "why, M. Clerval, I assure you he has outstript us all. Aye, aye, stare if you please; but it is nevertheless true. A youngster who, but a few years ago, believed Cornelius Agrippa as firmly as the gospel, has now set himself at the head of the university; and if he is not soon pulled down, we shall all be out of countenance. Aye, aye," continued he, observing my face expressive of suffering, "M. Frankenstein is modest; an excellent quality in a young man. Young men should be diffident of themselves, you know, M. Clerval; I was myself when young: but that wears out in a very short time."

M. Krempe had now commenced an eulogy on himself, which happily turned the conversation from a subject that was so annoying to me.

Clerval was no natural philosopher. His imagination was too vivid for the minutiæ of science. Languages were his principal study; and he sought, by acquiring their elements, to open a field for self-instruction on his return to Geneva. Persian, Arabic, and Hebrew gained his attention, after he had made himself perfectly master of Greek and Latin. For my own part, idleness had ever been irksome to me; and now that I wished to fly from reflection, and hated my former studies, I felt great relief in being the fellow-pupil with my friend, and found not only instruction but consolation in the works of the Orientalists. Their melancholy is soothing, and their joy elevating, to a degree I never experienced in studying the authors of any other country. When you read their writings, life appears to consist in a warm sun and a garden of roses—in the smiles and frowns of a fair enemy, and the fire that consumes your own heart. How different from the manly and heroical poetry of Greece and Rome.

Summer passed away in these occupations, and my return to Geneva was fixed for the latter end of autumn; but being delayed by several accidents, winter and snow arrived, the roads were deemed impassable, and my journey was retarded until the ensuing spring. I felt this delay very severely; for I longed to see my native town, and my beloved friends. My return had only been delayed so long from an unwillingness to leave Clerval in a strange place before he had become acquainted with any of its inhabitants. The winter, however, was spent cheerfully; and although the spring was uncommonly late, when it came, its beauty compensated for its dilatoriness.

The month of May had already commenced, and I expected the letter daily which was to fix the date of my departure, when Henry proposed a pedestrian tour through the environs of Ingoldstadt, that I might bid a personal farewell to the country I had so long inhabited. I acceded with pleasure to this proposition: I was fond of exercise, and Clerval had always been my favorite companion in the rambles of this nature that I had taken among the scenes in my native country.

We passed a fortnight in these perambulations: my health and spirits had long been restored, and they gained additional strength from the salubrious air I breathed, the natural incidents of our progress, and the conversation of my friend. Study had before secluded me from the intercourse of my fellow-creatures, and rendered me unsocial; but Clerval called forth the better feelings of my heart; he again taught me to love the aspect of nature, and the cheerful faces of children. Excellent friend! how sincerely did you love me, and endeavor to elevate my mind, until it was on a level with your own. A selfish pursuit had cramped and narrowed me, until your gentleness and affection warmed and opened my senses; I became the same happy creature who, a few years ago, loving and beloved by all, had no sorrow or care. When happy, inanimate nature had the power of bestowing on me the most delightful sensations. A serene sky and verdant fields filled me with ecstacy. The present season was indeed divine; the flowers of spring bloomed in the hedges, while those of summer were already in bud: I was undisturbed by thoughts which during the preceding year had pressed upon me, notwithstanding my endeavors to throw them off, with an invincible burden.

Henry rejoiced in my gayety, and sincerely sympathized in my feelings: he exerted himself to amuse me, while he expressed the sensations that filled his soul. The resources of his mind on this occasion were truly astonishing: his conversation was full of imagination, and very often, in imitation of the Persian and Arabic writers, he invented tales of wonderful fancy and passion. At other times he repeated my favorite poems, or drew me out into arguments, which he supported with great ingenuity.

We returned to our college on a Sunday afternoon: the peasants were dancing, and every one we met appeared gay and happy. My own spirits were high, and I bounded along with feelings of unbridled joy and hilarity.

CHAPTER VI.

On my return, I found the following letter from my father:

"To V. Frankenstein.

"My dear Victor: You have probably waited impatiently for a letter to fix the date of your return to us; and I was at first tempted to write only a few lines, merely mentioning the day on which I should expect you. But that would be a cruel kindness, and I dare not do it. But what would be your surprise, my son, when you expected a happy and gay welcome, to behold, on the contrary, tears and wretchedness! And how, Victor, can I relate your misfortune? Absence cannot have rendered you callous to our joys and griefs; and how shall I inflict pain on an absent child? I wish to prepare you for the woeful news, but I know it is impossible; even now your eye skims over the page, to seek the words which are to convey to you the horrible tidings.

"William is dead! that sweet child, whose smiles delighted and warmed my heart, who was so gentle yet so gay! Victor, he is murdered!

"I will not attempt to console you; but I will simply relate the circumstances of the transaction.

"Last Thursday, (May 7th,) I, my niece, and your two brothers, went to walk in Plainpalais. The evening was warm and serene, and we prolonged our walk farther than usual. It was already dusk before we thought of returning; and then we discovered that William and Ernest, who had gone on before, were not to be found. We accordingly rested on a seat until they should return. Presently Ernest came, and inquired if we had seen his brother: he said that they had been playing together, that William had ran away to hide himself, and that he vainly sought for him, and afterwards waited for him a long time, but that he did not return.

"This account rather alarmed us, and we continued to search for him until night fell, when Elizabeth conjectured that he might have returned to the house. He was not there. We returned again with torches; for I could not rest when I thought that my sweet boy had lost himself, and was exposed to all the damps and dews of night: Elizabeth also suffered extreme anguish. About five in the morning I discovered my lovely boy, whom the night before I had seen blooming and active in health, stretched on the grass livid and motionless: the print of the murderer's finger was on his neck.

"He was conveyed home, and the anguish that was visible on my countenance betrayed the secret to Elizabeth. She was very earnest to see the corpse. At first I attempted to prevent her; but she persisted, and entering the room where it lay, hastily examined the neck of the victim, and clasping her hands, exclaimed, 'O God! I have murdered my darling infant!'

"She fainted, and was restored with extreme difficulty. When she again lived, it was only to weep and sigh. She told me, that that same evening William had teased her to let him wear a very valuable miniature that she posssessed of your mother. The picture is gone, and was doubtless the temptation which urged the murderer to the deed. We have no trace of him at present, although our exertions to discover him are unremitted; but they will not restore my beloved William.

"Come, dearest Victor; you alone can console Elizabeth. She weeps continually, and accuses herself unjustly as the cause of his death; her words pierce my heart. We are all unhappy; but will not that be an additional motive for you, my son, to return and be our comforter? Your dear mother! Alas, Victor! I now say, thank God she did not live to witness the cruel, miserable death of her youngest darling!

"Come, Victor; not brooding thoughts of vengeance against the assassin, but with feelings of peace and gentleness, that will heal instead of festering the wounds of our minds. Enter the house of mourning, my friend, but with kindness and affection for those who love you, and not with hatred for your enemies.

"Your affectionate and afflicted father,

ALPHONSE FRANKENSTEIN.

"Geneva, May 12th, 17—."

Clerval, who had watched my countenance as I read this letter, was surprised to observe the despair that succeeded to the joy I at first expressed on receiving news from my friends. I threw the letter on the table, and covered my face with my hands.

"My dear Frankenstein," exclaimed Henry, when he perceived me weep with bitterness, "are you always to be unhappy? My dear friend, what has happened?"

I motioned to him to take up the letter, while I walked up and down the room in the extremest agitation. Tears also gushed from the eyes of Clerval, as he read the account of my misfortune.

"I can offer you no consolation, my friend," said he; "your disaster is irreparable. What do you intend to do?"

"To go instantly to Genexa: come with me, Henry, to order the horses."

During our walk, Clerval endeavored to raise my spirits. He did not do this by common topics of consolation. Those maxims of the Stoics, that death was no evil, and that the mind of man ought to be superior to despair on the eternal absence of a beloved object, ought not to be urged. Even Cato wept over the dead body of his brother."

Clerval spoke thus as we hurried through the streets; the words impressed themselves on my mind, and I remembered them afterwards in my solitude. But now, as soon as the horses arrived, I hurried into a cabriole, and bade farewell to my friend.

My journey was very melancholy. At first I wished to hurry on, for I longed to console and sympathize with my loved and sorrowing friends; But when I drew near my native town, I slackened my progress. I could hardly sustain the multitude of feelings that crowded into my mind. I passed through scenes familiar to my youth, but which I had not seen for nearly six years. How altered everything might be during that time? One sudden and desolating change had taken place; but a thousand little circumstances might have by degrees worked other alterations, which, although they were done more tranquilly, might not be the less decisive. Fear overcame me; I dared not advance, dreading a thousand nameless evils that made me tremble, although I was unable to define them.

I remained two days at Lausanne, in this painful state of mind. I contemplated the lake: the waters were placid; all around was calm, and the snowy mountains, "the palaces of nature," were not changed. By degrees the calm and heavenly scene restored me, and I continued my journey towards Geneva.

The road ran by the side of the lake, which became narrower as I approached my native town. I discovered more distinctly the black sides of Jura, and the bright summit of Mount Blanc; I wept like a child: "Dear mountains! my own beautiful lake! how do you welcome your wanderer? Your summits are clear; the sky and lake are blue and placid. Is this to prognosticate peace, or to mock at my unhappiness?"

I fear, my friend, that I shall render myself tedious by dwelling on these preliminary circumstances; but they were days of comparative happiness, and I think of them with pleasure. My country, my beloved country! who but a native can tell the delight I took in again beholding thy streams, thy mountains, and, more than all, thy lovely lake.

Yet, as I drew nearer home, grief and fear again overcame me. Night also closed around; and when I could hardly see the dark mountains, I felt still more gloomily. The picture appeared a vast and dim scene of evil, and I foresaw obscurely that I was destined to become the most wretched of human beings. Alas! I prophesied truly, and failed only in one single circumstance, that in all the misery I imagined and dreaded, I did not conceive the hundreth part of the anguish that I was destined to endure.

It was completely dark when I arrived in the environs of Geneva; the gates of the town were already shut; and I was obliged to pass the night at Secheron, a village half a league to the east of the city. The sky was serene; and, as I was unable to rest, I resolved to visit the spot where my poor William had been murdered. As I could not pass through the town I was obliged to cross the lake in a boat to arrive at Plainpalais. During this short voyage I saw the lightnings playing on the summit of Mount Blanc in the most beautiful figures. The storm appeared to approach rapidly; and, on landing, I ascended a low hill, that I might observe its progress. It advanced; the heavens were clouded, and I soon felt the rain coming slowly in large drops, but its violence quickly increased.

I quitted my seat and walked on, although the darkness and storm increased every minute, and the thunder burst with a terrific crash over my head. It was echoed from Salêve, the Juras, and the Alps of Savoy; vivid flashes of lightning dazzled my eyes, illuminating the lake, making it appear like a vast sheet of fire; then for an instant everything seemed of a pitchy darkness, until the eye recovered itself from the preceding flash. The storm, as is often the case in Switzerland, appeared at once in various parts of the heavens. The most violent storm hung exactly north of the town, over that part of the lake which lies between the promontory of Belrive and the village of Copet. Another storm enlightened Jura with faint flashes; and another darkened and sometimes disclosed the Mole, a peaked mountain to the east of the lake.

While I watched the storm, so beautiful yet terrific, I wandered on with a hasty step. This noble war in the sky elevated my spirits; I clasped my hands and exclaimed aloud, "William, dear angel! this is thy funeral, this thy dirge!" As I said these words, I perceived a figure which stole from behind a a clump of trees near me: I stood fixed, gazing intently: I could not be mistaken. A flash of lightning illuminated the object, and discovered its shape plainly to me; its gigantic stature, and the deformity of its aspect, more hideous than belongs to humanity, instantly informed me that it was the wretch, the filthy dæmon to whom I had given life. What did he there? Could he be (I shuddered at the conception) the murderer of my brother? No sooner did that idea cross my imagination than I became convinced of its truth; my teeth chattered, and I was forced to lean against a tree for support. The figure passed me quickly, and I lost it in the gloom. Nothing in human shape could have destroyed that fair child. He was the murderer! I could not doubt it. The mere presence of the idea was an irresistible proof of the fact. I thought of pursuing the devil; but it would have been in vain, for another flash discovered him to me hanging among the rocks of the nearly perpendicular ascent of Mount Saêlve, a hill that bounds Plainpalais on the south. He soon reached the summit and disappeared.

I remained motionless. The thunder ceased; but the rain still continued, and the scene was enveloped in impenetrable darkness. I revolved in my mind the events which I had until now sought to forget; the whole train of my progress towards the creation; the appearance of the work of my own hands alive at my bedside; its departure. Two years had now elapsed since the night on which he first received life; and was this his first crime? Alas, I had turned loose into the world a depraved wretch, whose delight was in carnage and misery; had he not murdered my brother?

No one can conceive the anguish I suffered during the remainder of the night, which I spent cold and wet in the open air. But I did not feel the inconvenience of the weather; my imagination was busy in scenes of evil and despair. I considered the being whom I had cast among mankind, and endowed with the will and power to effect purposes of horror, such as the deed which he had now done, nearly in the light of my own vampire, my own spirit let loose from the grave, and forced to destroy all that was dear to me.

Day dawned, and I directed my steps towards the town. The gates were open, and I hastened to my father's house. My first thought was to discover what I knew of the murderer, and cause instant pursuit to be made. But I paused when I reflected on the story that I had to tell. A being whom I myself had formed, and endued with life, had met me at midnight among the precipices of an inaccessible mountain. I remembered also the nervous fever with which I had had been seized just at the time that I dated my creation, and which would give an air of delirium to a tale otherwise so improbable. I well knew that if any other had communicated such a relation to me, I should have looked upon it as the ravings of insanity. Besides the strange nature of the animal would elude all pursuit, even if I were so far credited as to persuade my relatives to commence it. Besides, of what use would be pursuit? Who could arrest a creature capable of scaling the overhanging sides of Mont Salêve? These reflections determined me, and I resolved to remain silent.

It was about five in the morning when I entered my father's house. I told the servants not to disturb the family, and went into the library to attend their usual hour of rising.

Six years had elapsed, passed as a dream but for for one indellible trace, and I stood in the same place where I had last embraced my father, before my departure for Ingoldstadt. Beloved and respected parent! He still remained to me. I gazed on the picture of my mother, which stood over the mantlepiece. It was an historical subject, painted at my father's desire, and represented Caroline Beaufort in an agony of despair kneeling by the coffin of her dead father. Her garb was rustic, and her cheek pale; but there was an air of dignity and beauty, that hardly permitted the sentiment of pity. Below this picture was a miniature of William, and my tears flowed when I looked upon it. While I was thus engaged Ernest entered: he had heard me arrive, and hastened to welcome me. He expressed a sorrowful delight to see me. "Welcome, my dearest Victor," said he. "Ah! I wish you had come three months ago, and then you would have found us all joyous and delighted. But we are now unhappy, and I am afraid tears instead of smiles will be your welcome. Our father looks so sorrowful: this dreadful event seems to have revived in his mind his grief at the death of Mamma. Poor Elizabeth also is quite inconsolable." Ernest began to weep as he said these words.

"Do not," said I, "welcome me thus; try to be more calm, that I may not be absolutely miserable the moment I enter my father's house after so long an absence. But, tell me, how does my father support his misfortunes? and how is my poor Elizabeth?"

"She indeed requires consolation; she accused herself of having caused the death of my brother, and that made her very wretched. But since the murderer has been discovered——"

"The murderer discovered! Good God! how can that be? who could attempt to pursue him? It is impossible; one might as well attempt to overtake the winds, or confine a mountain stream with a straw."

"I do not know what you mean; but we were all very unhappy when she was discovered. No one would believe it at first, and even now Elizabeth will not be convinced, notwithstanding all the evidence. Indeed who would credit that Justine Moritz, who was so amiable, and fond of all the family, could all at once become so extremely wicked?"

"Justine Moritz! Poor, poor girl, is she the accused? But it is wrongfully; every one knows that; no one believes it, surely, Ernest?"

"No one did at first; but several circumstances came out, that have almost forced conviction upon us; and her own behavior has been so confused as to add to the evidence of facts a weight, that, I fear, leaves no hope for doubt. But she will be tried to-day, and you will then hear all."

He related that the morning upon which the murder of poor William had been discovered, Justine had been taken ill, and confined to her bed; and, after several days, one of the servants happening to examine the apparel she had worn on the night of the murder, had discovered in her pocket the picture of my mother, which had been judged to be the temptation of the murderer. The servant instantly showed it to one of the others, who, without saying a word to any of the family, went to a magistrate, and, upon their deposition, Justine was apprehended. On being charged with the fact, the poor girl confirmed the suspicion in a great measure by her extreme confusion of manner.

This was a strange tale, but it did not shake my faith; and I replied earnestly, "You are all mistaken; I know the murderer. Justine, poor good Justine, is innocent."

At that instant my father entered. I saw unhappiness deeply impressed on his countenance, but he endeavored to welcome me cheerfully; and after we had exchanged our mournful greeting, would have introduced some other topic than that of our disaster, had not Ernest exclaimed, "Good God, Papa! Victor says that he knows who was the murderer of poor William."

"We do also, unfortunately," relied my father; "for indeed I had rather have been forever ignorant than have discovered so much depravity and ingratitude in one I valued so highly."

"My dear father, you are mistaken; Justine is innocent."

"If she is, God forbid that she should suffer as guilty. She is to be tried to-day, and I hope, I sincerely hope that she will be acquitted."

This speech calmed me. I was firmly convinced in my own mind that Justine, and indeed every human being, was guiltless of this murder. I had no fear, therefore, that any circumstantial evidence could be brought forward strong enough to convict her; and, in this assurance, I calmed myself, expecting the trial with eagerness, but without prognosticating an evil result.

We were soon joined by Elizabeth. Time had made great alterations in her form since I last beheld her. Six years before she had been a pretty, good-humored girl, whom every one loved and caressed. She was now a woman in stature and expression of countenance, which was uncommonly lovely. An open and capacious forehead gave indications of a good understanding, joined to great frankness of disposition. Her eyes were hazle, and expressive of mildness, now through recent affliction allied to sadness. Her hair was of a rich dark auburn, her complexion fair, and her figure slight and graceful. She welcomed me with the greatest affection. "Your arrival, my dear cousin," said she, "fills me with hope. You perhaps will find some means to justify my poor guiltless Justine. Alas! who is safe, if she be convicted of crime? I rely on her innocence as certainly as I do upon my own. Our misfortune is doubly hard to us; we have not only lost that lovely darling boy, but this poor girl, whom I sincerely love, is to be torn away even by a worse fate. If she is condemned, I never shall know joy more. But she will not, I am sure she will not; and then I shall be happy again, even after the sad death of my little William."

"She is innocent, my Elizabeth," said I, "and that shall be proved; fear nothing, but let your spirits be cheered by the assurance of her acquittal."

"How kind you are! every one else believes in her guilt, and that made me wretched; for I knew that it was impossible: and to see every one else prejudiced in so deadly a manner, rendered me hopeless and despairing." She wept.

"Sweet niece," said my father, "dry your tears. If she is, as you believe, innocent, rely on the justice of our judges, and the activity with which I shall prevent the slightest shadow of partiality."

CHAPTER VII.

We passed a few sad hours, until eleven o'clock, when the trial was to commence. My father and the rest of the family being obliged to attend as witnesses, I accompanied them to the court. During the whole of this wretched mockery of justice, I suffered living torture. It was to be decided, whether the result of my curiosity and lawless devices would cause the death of two of my fellow-beings: one a smiling babe, full of joy and innocence: the other far more dreadfully murdered, with every aggravation of infamy that could make the murder memorable in horror. Justine also was a girl of merit, and possessed qualities which promised to render her life happy: now all was to be obliterated in an ignominious grave; and I the cause! A thousand times rather would I have confessed myself guilty of the crime ascribed to Justine; but I was absent when it was committed, and such a declaration would have been considered as the ravings of a madman, and would not have exculpated her who suffered through me.

The appearance of Justine was calm. She was dressed in mourning; and her countenance, always engaging, was rendered, by the solemnity of her feelings, exquisitely beautiful. Yet she appeared confident in innocence, and did not tremble, although gazed on and execrated by thousands; for all the kindness which her beauty might otherwise have excited, was obliterated in the minds of the spectators by the imagination of the enormity she was supposed to have committed. She was tranquil, yet her tranquillity was evidently constrained: and as her confusion had before been adduced as a proof of her guilt, she worked up her mind to an appearance of courage. When she entered the court, she threw her eyes round it, and quickly discovered where we were seated. A tear seemed to dim her eye when she saw us; but she quickly recovered herself, and a look of sorrowful affection seemed to attest her utter guiltlesness.

The trial began; and after the advocate against her had stated the charge, several witnesses were called. Several strange facts combined against her, which might have staggered any one who had not such proof of her innocence as I had. She had been out the whole of the night on which the murder had been committed, and towards morning had been perceived by a market-woman not far from the spot where the body of the murdered child had been found. The woman asked her what she did there; but she looked very strangly, and only returned a confused and unintelligible answer. She returned to the house about eight o'clock; and when one inquired where she had passed the night, she replied, that she had been looking for the child, and demanded earnestly, if anything had been heard concerning him. When shown the body, she fell into violent hysterics, and kept her bed for several days. The picture was then produced, which the servant had found in her pocket; and when Elizabeth, in a faltering voice, proved that it was the same which, an hour before the child had been missed, she had placed round his neck, a murmur of horror and indignation filled the court.

Justine was called on for her defence. As the trial had proceeded, her countenance had altered. Surprise, sorrow, and misery, were strongly expressed. Sometimes she struggled with her tears; but when she was desired to plead, she collected her powers, and spoke in an audible although variable voice:

"God knows," she said, "how entirely I am innocent. But I do not pretend that my protestations should acquit me: I rest my innocence on a plain and simple explanation of the facts which have been adduced against me; and I hope the character I have always borne will incline my judges to a favorable interpretation, where any circumstance appears doubtful or suspicious."

She then related that, by the permission of Elizabeth, she had passed the evening of the night on which the murder had been committed, at the house of an aunt at Chene, a village situated at about a league from Geneva. On her return, at about nine o'clock, she met a man, who asked her if she had seen anything of the child who was lost. She was alarmed by this account, and passed several hours in looking for him, when the gates of Geneva were shut, and she was forced to remain several hours of the night in a barn belonging to a cottage, being unwilling to call up the inhabitants, to whom she was well known. Unable to rest or sleep, she quitted her asylum early, that she might endeavor to find my brother. If she had gone near the spot where his body lay, it was without her knowledge. That she had been bewildered when questioned by the market-woman, was not surprising, since she had passed a sleepless night, and the fate of poor William was yet uncertain. Concerning the picture she could give no account.

"I know," continued the unhappy victim, "how heavily and fatally this one circumstance weighs against me, but I have no power of explaining it; and when I have expressed my utter ignorance, I am only left to conjecture concerning the probabilities by which it might have been placed in my pocket. But here also I am checked. I believe that I have no enemy on earth, and none surely would have been so wicked as to destroy me wantonly. Did the murderer place it there? I know of no opportunity afforded him for so doing; or if I had, why should he have stolen the jewel, to part with it so soon?

"I commit my cause to the justice of my judges, yet I see no room for hope. I beg permission to have a few witnesses examined concerning my character; and if their testimony shall not overweigh my supposed guilt, I must be condemned, although I would pledge my salvation on my innocence."

Several witnesses were called, who had known her for many years, and they spoke well of her; but fear, and hatred of the crime of which they supposed her guilty, rendered them timorous, and unwilling to come forward. Elizabeth saw even this last resource, her excellent dispositions and irreproachable conduct, about to fail the accused, when, although violently agitated, she desired permission to address the court.

"I am," said she, "the cousin of the unhappy child who was murdered, or rather his sister, for I was educated by and have lived with his parents ever since and even long before his death. It may therefore be judged indecent in me to come forward on this occasion; but when I see a fellow-creature about to perish through the cowardice of her pretended friends, I wish to be allowed to speak, that I may say what I know of her character. I am well acquainted with the accused. I have lived in the same house with her, at one time for five, and at another for nearly two years. During all that period she appeared to me the most amiable and benevolent of human creatures. She nursed Madame Frankenstein, my aunt, in her last illness with the greatest affection and care; and afterwards attended her own mother during a tedious illness, in a manner that excited the admiration of all who knew her. After which she again lived in my uncle's house, where she was beloved by all the family. She was warmly attached to the child who is now dead, and acted towards him like a most affectionate mother. For my own part, I do not hesitate to say, that, notwithstanding all the evidence produced against her, I believe and rely on her perfect innocence. She had no temptation for such an action: as to the bauble on which the chief proof rests, if she had earnestly desired it, I should have willingly given it to her; so much do I esteem and value her."

Excellent Elizabeth! A murmur of approbation was heard; but it was excited by her generous interference, and not in favor of poor Justine, on whom the public indignation was turned with renewed violence, charging her with the blackest ingratitude. She herself wept as Elizabeth spoke, but she did not answer. My own agitation and anguish was extreme during the whole trial. I believed in her innocence; I knew it. Could the dæmon, who had (I did not for a minute doubt,) murdered my brother, also in his hellish sport have betrayed the innocent to death and ignominy. I could not sustain the horror of my situation; and when I perceived that the popular voice, and the countenances of the judges, had already condemned my unhappy victim, I rushed out of the court in agony. The tortures of the accused did not equal mine; she was sustained by innocence, and the fangs of remorse tore my bosom, and would not forego their hold.

I passed a night of unmingled wretchedness. In the morning I went to the court; my lips and throat were parched. I dared not ask the fatal question; but I was known, and the officer guessed the cause of my visit. The ballots had been thrown; they were all black, and Justine was condemned.

I cannot pretend to describe what I then felt. I had before experienced sensations of horror; and I have endeavored to bestow upon them adequate expressions, but words cannot convey an idea of the heart-sickening despair that I then endured. The person to whom I addressed myself added, that Justine had already confessed her guilt. "That evidence," he observed, "was hardly required in so glaring a case, but I am glad of it; and, indeed, none of our judges like to condemn a criminal upon circumstantial evidence, be it ever so decisive."

When I returned home, Elizabeth eagerly demanded the result.

"My cousin," replied I, "it is decided as you may have expected; all judges had rather that ten innocent should suffer, than that one guilty should escape. But she has confessed."

This was a dire blow to poor Elizabeth, who had relied with firmness upon Justine's innocence. "Alas!" said she, "how shall I ever again believe in human benevolence? Justine, whom I loved and esteemed as my sister, how could she put on those smiles of innocence only to betray; her mild eyes seemed incapable of any severity or ill-humor, and yet she has committed a murder."

Soon after we heard that the poor victim had expressed a wish to see my cousin. My father wished her not to go; but said, that he left it to her own judgment and feelings to decide.

"Yes," said Elizabeth, "I will go, although she is guilty; and you, Victor, shall accompany me: I cannot go alone." The idea of this visit was torture to me, yet I could not refuse.

We entered the gloomy prison-chamber, and beheld Justine sitting on some straw at the further end; her hands were manacled, and her head rested on her knees. She rose on seeing us enter; and when we were left alone with her, she threw herself at the feet of Elizabeth, weeping bitterly. My cousin wept also.

"Oh, Justine!" said she, "why did you rob me of my last consolation. I relied on your innocence; and although I was then very wretched, I was not so miserable as I am now."

"And do you also believe that I am so very, very wicked? Do you also join with my enemies to crush me?" Her voice was suffocated with sobs.

"Rise, my poor girl," said Elizabeth, "why do you kneel, if you are innocent? I am not one of your enemies; I believed you guiltless, notwithstanding every evidence, until I heard that you had yourself declared your guilt. That report, you say, is false; and be assured, dear Justine, that nothing can shake my confidence in you for a moment, but your own confession."

"I did confess; but I confessed a lie. I confessed, that I might obtain absolution; but now that falsehood lies heavier at my heart than all my other sins. The God of Heaven forgive me! Ever since I was condemned, my confessor has besieged me; he threatened and menaced, until I almost began to think that I was the monster that he said I was. He threatened excommunication and hell-fire in my last moments, if I continued obdurate. Dear lady, I had none to support me; all looked on me as a wretch doomed to ignominy and perdition. What could I do? In an evil hour I subscribed to a lie; and now only am I truly miserable."

She paused, weeping, and then continued—"I thought with horror, my sweet lady, that you should believe your Justine, whom your blessed aunt had so highly honored, and whom you loved, was a creature capable of a crime which none but the devil himself could have perpetrated. Dear William! dearest blessed child! I soon shall see you again in heaven, where we shall all be happy; and that consoles me, going as I am to suffer ignominy and death."

"Oh Justine! forgive me for having for one moment distrusted you. Why did you confess? But do not mourn, my dear girl; I will everywhere proclaim your innocence, and force belief. Yet you must die; you, my playfellow, my companion, my more than sister. I never can survive so horrible a misfortune."

"Dear, sweet Elizabeth, do not weep. You ought to raise me with thoughts of a better life, and elevate me from the petty cares of this world of injustice and strife. Do you not, excellent friend, drive me to despair."

"I will try to comfort you; but this, I fear, is an evil too deep and poignant to admit of consolation, for there is no hope. Yet Heaven bless thee, my dearest Justine, with resignation, and a confidence elevated beyond this world. Oh! how I hate its shows and mockeries! when one creature is murdered, another is immediately deprived of life in a slow torturing manner; then the executioners, their hands yet reeking with the blood of innocence, believe that they have done a great deed. They call this *retribution*. Hateful name! When that word is pronounced, I know greater and more horrid punishments are going to be inflicted than the gloomiest tyrant has ever invented to satiate his utmost revenge. Yet this is not consolation for you, my Justine, unless indeed that you may glory in escaping from so miserable a den. Alas! I would I were in peace with my aunt and my lovely William, escaped from a world which is hateful to me, and the visages of men which I abhor."

Justine smiled languidly. "This, dear lady, is despair, and not resignation. I must not learn the lesson that you would teach me. Talk of something else, something that will bring peace, and not increase of misery."

During the conversation I had retired to a corner of the prison-room, where I could conceal the horrid anguish that possessed me! Despair! who dared talk of that? The poor victim, who on the morrow was to pass the dreary boundary between life and death, felt not as I did, such deep and bitter agony. I gnashed my teeth, and ground them together, uttering a groan that came from my inmost soul. Justine started. When she saw who it was, she approached me, and said, "Dear sir, you are very kind to visit me; you, I hope, do not believe that I am guilty."

I could not answer. "No, Justine," said Elizabeth; "he is more convinced of your innocence than I was; for even when he heard that you had confessed, he did not credit it."

"I truly thank him. In these last moments I feel the sincerest gratitude towards those who think of me with kindness. How sweet is the affection of others to such a wretch as I am! It removes more than half my misfortune; and I feel as if I could die in peace, now that my innocence is acknowledged by you, dear lady, and your cousin."

Thus the poor sufferer tried to comfort others and herself. She indeed gained the resignation she desired. But I, the true murderer, felt the never dying worm alive in my bosom, which allowed of no hope or consolation. Elizabeth also wept, and was unhappy; but her's also was the misery of innocence, which like a cloud that passes over the fair moon, for a while hides, but cannot tarnish its brightness. Anguish and despair had penetrated into the core of my heart; I bore a hell within me, which nothing could extinguish. We stayed several hours with Justine; and it was with great difficulty that Elizabeth could tear herself away. "I wish," cried she, "that I were to die with you; I cannot live in this world of misery."

Justine assumed an air of cheerfulness, while she with difficulty repressed her bitter tears. She embraced Elizabeth, and said, in a voice of half-suppressed emotion, "Farewell, sweet lady, dearest Elizabeth, my beloved and only friend; may Heaven in its bounty bless and preserve you; may this be the last misfortune that you will ever suffer. Live, and be happy, and make others so."

As we returned, Elizabeth said, "You know not, my dear Victor, how much I am relieved, now that I trust in the innocence of this unfortunate girl. I never could again have known peace, if I had been deceived in my reliance on her. For the moment that I did believe her guilty, I felt an anguish that I could not have long sustained. Now my heart is lightened. The innocent suffers; but she whom I thought amiable and good has not betrayed the trust I reposed in her, and I am consoled."

Amiable cousin! such were your thoughts, mild and gentle as your own dear eyes and voice. But I—I was a wretch, and none ever conceived of the misery that I then endured.

CHAPTER VIII.

Nothing is more painful to the human mind, than, after the feelings have been worked up by a quick succession of events, the dead calmness of inaction and certainty which follows, and deprives the soul both of hope and fear. Justine died; she rested; and I was alive. The blood flowed freely in my veins, but a weight of despair and remorse pressed on my heart, which nothing could remove. Sleep fled from my eyes; I wandered like an evil spirit, for I had committed deeds of mischief beyond description horrible, and more, much more, (I persuaded myself) was yet behind. Yet my heart overflowed with kindness, and the love of virtue. I had begun life with benevolent intentions, and thirsted for the moment when I should put them in practice, and make myself useful to my fellow-beings. Now all was blasted; instead of that serenity of conscience, which allowed me to look back upon the past with self-satisfaction, and from thence to gather promise of new hopes, I was seized by remorse and the sense of guilt, which hurried me away to a hell of intense tortures, such as no language can describe.

This state of mind preyed upon my health, which had entirely recovered from the first shock it had sustained. I shunned the face of man; all sound of joy and complacency was torture to me; solitude was my only consolation—deep, dark, death-like solitude.

My father observed with pain the alteration perceptible in my disposition and habits, and endeavored to reason with me on the folly of giving way to immoderate grief. "Do you think, Victor," said he, "that I do not suffer also? No one could love a child more than I loved your brother;" (tears came into his eyes as he spoke;) "but is it not a duty to the survivors, that we should refrain from augmenting their unhappiness by an appearance of immoderate grief? It is also a duty owed to yourself; for excessive sorrow prevents improvement or enjoyment, or even the discharge of daily usefulness, without which no man is fit for society."

This advice, although good, was totally inapplicable to my case; I should have been the first to hide my grief, and console my friends, if remorse had not mingled its bitterness with my other sensations. Now I could only answer my father with a look of despair, and endeavor to hide myself from his view.

About this time we retired to our house at Belrive. This change was particularly agreeable to me. The shutting of the gates regularly at ten o'clock, and the impossibility of remaining on the lake after that hour, had rendered our residence within the walls of Geneva very irksome to me. I was now free. Often, after the rest of the family had retired for the night, I took the boat, and passed many hours upon the water. Sometimes, with my sails set, I was carried by the wind, and sometimes, after rowing into the middle of the lake, I left the boat to pursue its own course, and gave way to my own miserable reflections. I was often tempted, when all was at peace around me, and I the only unquiet thing that wandered restless in a scene so beautiful and heavenly, if I except some bat, or the frogs, whose harsh and interrupted croaking was heard only when I approached the shore—often, I say, I was tempted to plunge into the silent lake, that the waters might close over me and my calamities for ever. But I was restrained, when I thought of the heroic and suffering Elizabeth, whom I tenderly loved, and whose existence was bound up in mine. I thought also of my father, and surviving brother : should I by my base desertion leave them exposed and unprotected to the malice of the fiend whom I let loose among them ?

At these moments I wept bitterly, and wished that peace would revisit my mind only that I might afford them consolation and happiness. But that could not be. Remorse extinguished every hope. I had been the author of unalterable evils ; and I lived in daily fear, lest the monster whom I had created should perpetuate some new wickedness. I had an obscure feeling that all was not over, and that he would still commit some signal crime, which by its enormity should almost efface the recollection of the past. There was always scope for fear, so long as anything I loved remained behind. My abhorrence of this fiend cannot be conceived. When I thought of him, I gnashed my teeth, my eyes became inflamed, and I ardently wished to extinguish that life which I had so thoughtlessly bestowed. When I reflected on his crimes and malice, my hatred and revenge burst all bounds of moderation. I would have made a pilgrimage to the highest peak of the Andes, could I, when there, have precipitated him to their base. I wished to see him again, that I might wreak the utmost extent of anger on his head, and avenge the deaths of William and Justine.

Our house was the house of mourning. My father's health was deeply shaken by the horror of recent events. Elizabeth was sad and desponding ; she no longer took delight in her ordinary occupations ; all pleasure seemed to her sacrilege towards the dead ; eternal woe and tears she then thought was the just tribute she should pay to innocence so blasted and destroyed. She was no longer that happy creature, who in earlier youth wandered with me on the banks of the lake, and talked with ecstacy of our future prospects. She had become grave, and often conversed on the inconstancy of fortune, and the instability of human life.

" When I reflect, my dear cousin," said she, " on the miserable death of Justine Moritz, I no longer see the world and its works as they before appeared to me. Before, I looked upon the accounts of vice and injustice, that I read in books or heard from others, as tales of ancient days, or imaginary evils ; at least they were remote, and more familiar to reason than to the imagination : but now misery has come home, and men appear to me as monsters thirsting for each other's blood. Yet I am certainly unjust. Every body believed that poor girl to be guilty ; and if she could have committed the crime for which she suffered, assuredly she would have been the most depraved of human creatures. For the sake of a few jewels to have murdered the son of her benefactor and friend, a child whom she had nursed from its birth, and appeared to love as if it had been her own ! I could not consent to the death of any human being ; but certainly I should have thought such a creature unfit to remain in the society of men. Yet she was innocent ; you are of the same opinion, and that confirms me. Alas ! Victor, when falsehood can look so like the truth, who can assure themselves of certain happiness ? I feel as if I were walking on the edge of a precipice, towards which thousands are crowding, and endeavoring to plunge me into the abyss. William and Justine were assassinated, and the murderer escapes ; he walks about the world free, and perhaps respected But even if I were condemned to suffer on the scaffold for the same crimes, I would not change places with such a wretch."

I listened to this discourse with the extremest agony. I, not in deed, but in effect, was the true murderer. Elizabeth read my anguish in my countenance, and kindly taking my hand said, " My dearest cousin, you must calm yourself. These events have affected me, God knows how deeply ; but I am not so wretched as you are. There is an expression of despair, and sometimes of revenge in your countenance, that makes me tremble. Be calm, my dear Victor; I would sacrifice my life to your peace. We surely shall be happy: quiet in our native country, and not mingling in the world, what can disturb our tranqui lity?"

She shed tears as she said this, distrusting the very solace that she gave; but at the same time she smiled, that she might chase away the fiend that lurked in my heart. My father, who saw in the unhappiness that was painted in my face only an exaggeration of that sorrow which I might naturally feel, thought an amusement suited to my taste would be the best means of restoring me to my wonted serenity. It was from this cause that he had removed to the country, and, induced by the same motive, he now proposed that we should all make an excursion to the valley of the Chamounix. I had been there before, but Elizabeth and Ernest never had; and both had often expressed an earnest desire to see the scenery of the place, which had been described to them as so wonderful and sublime. Accordingly we departed from Geneva on this tour about the middle of the month of August, nearly two months after the death of Justine.

The weather was uncommonly fine; and if mine had been a sorrow to be chased away by any fleeting circumstance, this excursion would certainly have had the effect intended by my father. As it was, I was somewhat interested in the scene; it sometimes lulled, although it could not extinguish my grief. During the first day we travelled in a carriage. In the morning we had seen the mountains at a distance, towards which we gradually advanced. We perceived that the valley through which we wound, and which was formed by the river Arve, whose course we followed, closed in upon us by degrees; and when the sun had set, we beheld immense mountains and precipices overhanging us on every side, and heard the sound of the river raging among rocks, and the dashing of waterfalls around.

The next day we pursued our journey upon mules; and as we ascended still higher, the valley assumed a more magnificent and astonishing character. Ruined castles hanging on the precipices of piny mountains; the impetuous Arve, and cottages every here and there peeping forth from among the trees, formed a scene of singular beauty. But it was augmented and rendered sublime by the mighty Alps, whose white and shining pyramids and domes towered above all, as belonging to another earth, the habitations of another race of beings.

We passed the bridge of Pelissier, where the ravine, which the river forms, opened before us, and we began to ascend the mountain that overhangs it. Soon after we entered the valley of Chamounix. This valley is more wonderful and sublime, but not so beautiful and picturesque as that of Servox, through which we had just passed. The high and snowy mountains were its immediate boundaries; but we saw no more ruined castles and fertile fields. Immense glaciers approached the road; we heard the rumbling thunder of the falling avalanche, and marked the smoke of its passage. Mont Blanc, the supreme and magnificent Mont Blanc, raised itself from the surrounding *aiguilles*, and its tremendous *dome* overlooked the valley.

During this journey, I sometimes joined Elizabeth, and exerted myself to point out to her the various beauties of the scene. I often suffered my mule to lag behind, and indulged in the misery of reflection. At other times I spurred on the animal before my companions, that I might forget them, the world, and, more than all, myself. When at a distance, I alighted, and threw myself on the grass, weighed down by horror and dispair. At eight in the evening I arrived at Chamounix. My father and Elizabeth were very much fatigued; Ernest, who accompanied us, was delighted, and in high spirits: the only circumstance that detracted from his pleasure was the south wind, and the rain it seemed to promise for the next day.

We retired early to our apartments, but not to sleep; at least I did not. I remained many hours at the window, watching the pallid lightning that played above Mont Blanc, and listening to the rushing of the Arve, which ran below my window.

CHAPTER IX.

THE next day, contrary to the prognostications of our guide, was fine, although clouded. We visited the source of the Arveiron, and rode about the valley until evening. These sublime and magnificent scenes afforded me the greatest consolation that I was capable of receiving. They elevated me from all littleness of feeling; and although they did not remove my grief, they subdued and tranquilized it. In some degree, also, they diverted my mind from the thoughts over which it had brooded for the last month. I returned in the evening, fatigued, but less unhappy, and conversed with my family with more cheerfulness than had been my custom for some time. My father was pleased, and Elizabeth overjoyed. "My dear cousin," said she, "you see what happiness you diffuse when you are happy; do not relapse again!"

The following morning the rain poured down in torrents, and thick mists hid the summits of the mountains. The rain depressed me; my old feelings recurred, and I was miserable. I knew how disappointed my father would be at this sudden change, and I wished to avoid him until I had recovered myself so far as to be enabled to conceal those feelings that overpowered me. I knew that they would remain that day at the inn; and as I had ever inured myself to rain, moisture, and cold, I resolved to go alone to the summit of Montanvert. I remembered the effect that the view of the tremendous and ever-moving glacier had produced upon my mind when I first saw it. It had then filled me with a sublime ecstacy that gave wings to the soul, and allowed it to soar from the obscure world to light and joy. The sight of the awful and majestic in nature had indeed always the effect of solemnizing my mind, and causing me to forget the passing cares of life. I determined to go alone, for I was well acquainted with the path, and the presence of another would destroy the solemn grandeur of the scene.

The ascent is precipitous, but the path is cut into continual and short windings, which enable you to surmount the perpendicularity of the mountain. It is a scene terrifically desolate. In a thousand spots the traces of the winter avalanche may be perceived, where trees lie broken and strewed on the ground; some entirely destroyed, others bent, leaning upon the jutting rocks of the mountain, or transversely upon other trees. The path, as you ascend higher, is intersected by ravines of snow, down which stones continually roll from above; one of them is particularly dangerous, as the slightest sound, such as even speaking in a loud voice, produces a concussion of air sufficient to draw destruction upon the head of the speaker. The pines are not tall or luxuriant, but they are sombre, and add an air of severity to the scene. I looked on the valley beneath; vast mists were rising from the rivers which ran through it, and curling in thick wreaths around the opposite mountains, whose summits were hid in the uniform clouds, while rain poured from the dark sky, and added to the melancholy impression I received from the objects around me. Alas! why does man boast of sensibilities superior to those apparent in the brute; it only renders them more necessary beings. If our impulses were confined to hunger, thirst, and desire, we might be nearly free; but now we are moved by every wind that blows, and a chance word or scene that that word may convey to us.

"We rest; a dream has power to poison sleep.
We rise; one wand'ring thought pollutes the day.
We feel, conceive, or reason; laugh, or weep,
Embrace fond woe, or cast our cares away;
It is the same: for, be it joy or sorrow,
The path of its departure still is free.
Man's yesterday may ne'er be like his morrow;
Nought may endure but mutability."

It was nearly noon when I arrived at the top of the ascent. For some time I sat upon the rock that overlooks the sea of ice. A mist covered both that and the surrounding mountains. Presently a breeze dissipated the cloud, and I descended upon the glacier. The surface is very uneven, rising like the waves of a troubled sea, descending low, and interspersed by rifts that sink deep. The field of ice is almost a league in width, but I spent nearly two hours in crossing it. The opposite mountain is a bare perpendicular rock. From the side where I now stood Mountanvert was exactly opposite, at the distance of a league; and above it rose Mont Blanc, in awful majesty. I remained in a recess of the rock, gazing on this wonderful and stupendous scene. The sea, or rather the vast river of ice, wound among its dependent mountains, whose aërial summits hung over its recesses. Their icy and glittering peaks shone in the sunlight over the clouds. My heart, which was before sorrowful, now swelled with something like joy; I exclaimed—"Wandering spirits, if ye indeed wander, and do not rest in your narrow beds, allow me this faint happiness, or take me as your companion, away from the joys of life."

As I said this, I suddenly beheld the figure of a man, at some distance, advancing towards me with superhuman speed. He bounded over the crevices of the ice, among which I had walked with caution; his stature also, as he approached, seemed to exceed that of man.

I was troubled: a mist came over my eyes, and I felt a faintness seize me; but I was quickly restored by the cold gale of the mountains. I perceived, as the shape came nearer, (sight tremendous and abhorred!) that it was the wretch whom I had created. I trembled with rage and horror, resolving to wait his approach, and then close with him in mortal combat. He approached; his countenance bespoke bitter anguish, combined with disdain and malignity, while its unearthly ugliness rendered it almost too horrible for human eyes. But I scarcely observed this; anger and hatred had at first deprived me of utterance, and I recovered only to overwhelm him with words expressive of furious detestation and contempt.

"Devil!" I exclaimed, "do you dare approach me? and do you not fear the fierce vengeance of my arm wreaked on your miserable head? Begone, vile insect! or rather stay, that I may trample you to dust! and, oh, that I could, with the extinction of your miserable existence, restore those victims whom you have so diabolically murdered!"

"I expected this reception," said the demon. "All men hate the wretched; how then must I be hated, who am miserable beyond all living things! Yet you, my creator, detest and spurn me, thy creature, to whom thou art bound by ties only dissoluble by the annihilation of one of us. You purpose to kill me. How dare you sport thus with life? Do your duty towards me, and I will do mine towards you and the rest of mankind. If you will comply with my conditions, I will leave them and you at peace; but if you refuse, I will glut the maw of death, until it be satisfied with the blood of your remaining friends."

"Abhorred monster! fiend that thou art! the tortures of hell are too mild a vengeance for thy crimes. Wretched devil! you reproach me with your creation; come on then, that I may extinguish the spark which I so negligently bestowed."

My rage was without bounds; I sprang on him, impelled by all the feelings which can arm one being against the existence of another.

He easily eluded me, and said:

"Be calm! I entreat you to hear me, before you give vent to your hatred on my devoted head. Have I not suffered enough, that you seek to increase my misery? Life, although it may only be an accumulation of anguish, is dear to me, and I will defend it. Remember, thou hast made me more powerful than thyself; my height is superior to thine; my joints more supple. But I will not be tempted to set myself in opposition to thee. I am thy creature, and I will be even mild and docile to my natural lord and king, if thou wilt also perform thy part, the which thou owest me. Oh, Frankenstein, be not equitable to every other, and trample upon me alone, to whom thy justice, and even thy clemency and affection, is most due. Remember, that I am thy creature: I ought to be thy Adam; but I am rather the fallen angel, whom thou drivest from joy for no misdeed. Everywhere I see bliss, from which I alone am irrevocably excluded. I was benevolent and good; misery made me a fiend. Make me happy, and I shall again be virtuous."

"Begone! I will not hear you. There can be no community between you and me; we are enemies. Begone, or let us try our strength in a fight, in which one must fall."

"How can I move thee? Will no entreaties cause thee to turn a favorable eye upon thy creature, who implores thy goodness and compassion? Believe me, Frankenstein: I was benevolent; my soul glowed with love and humanity: but am I not alone, miserably alone? You, my creator, abhor me; what hope can I gather from your fellow-creatures, who owe me nothing? They spurn and hate me. The desert mountains and dreary glaciers are my refuge. I have wandered here many days; the caves of ice, which I only do not fear, are a dwelling to me, and the only one which man does not grudge. These bleak skies I hail, for they are kinder to me than your fellow-beings. If the multitude of mankind knew of my existence, they would do as you do, and arm themselves for my destruction. Shall I not then hate them who abhor me? I will keep no terms with my enemies. I am miserable, and they shall share my wretchedness. Yet it is in your power to recompense me, and deliver them from an evil which it only remains for you to make so great, that not only you and your family, but thousands of others, shall be swallowed up in the whirlwinds of its rage. Let your compassion be moved, and do not disdain me. Listen to my tale: when you have heard that, abandon or commiserate me, as you shall judge that I deserve. But hear me. The guilty are allowed, by human laws, bloody as they may be, to speak in their own defence, before they are condemned. Listen to me, Frankenstein. You accuse me of murder; and yet you would, with a satisfied conscience, destroy your own creature. Oh, praise the eternal justice of man! Yet I ask you not to spare me: listen to me; and then, if you can, and if you will, destroy the work of your hands."

"Why do you call to my remembrance circumstances of which I shudder to reflect that I have been the miserable origin and author? Cursed be the day, abhorred devil, in which you first saw light! Cursed (although I curse myself) be the hands that formed you! You have made me wretched beyond expression. You have left me no power to consider whether I am just to you, or not. Begone! relieve me from the sight of your detested form."

"Thus I relieve thee, my creator," he said, and placed his hated hand before my eyes, which I flung from me with violence; "thus I take from thee a sight which you abhor. Still thou canst listen to me, and grant me thy compassion. By the virtues that I once possessed, I demand this from you. Hear my tale; it is long and strange, and the temperature of this place is not fitting to your fine sensations; come to the hut upon the mountain. The sun is yet high in the heavens; before it descends to hide itself behind yon snowy precipices, and illuminate another world, you will have heard my story, and can deciee. On you it rests, whether I quit for ever the neighborhood of man, and lead a harmless life, or become a scourge to your fellow-creatures, and the author of your own speedy ruin."

As he said this, he led the way across the ice: I followed. My heart was full, and I did not answer him; but, as I proceed, I weighed the various arguments that he had used, and determined at least to listen to his tale. I was partly urged by curiosity, and compassion confirmed my resolution. I had hitherto supposed him to be the murderer of my brother, and I eagerly sought a confirmation or denial of this opinion. For the first time, also, I felt what the duties of a creator towards his creature were, and that I ought to render him happy before I complained of his wickedness. These motives urged me to comply with his demand. We crossed the ice, therefore, and ascended the opposite rock. The air was cold, and the rain again began to descend: we entered the hut, the fiend with an air of exultation, I with a heavy heart, and depressed spirits. But I consented to listen; and, seating myself by the fire which my odious companion had lighted, he thus began his tale.

CHAPTER X.

"It is with considerable difficulty that I remember the original æra of my being: all the events of that period appear confused and indistinct. A strange multiplicity of sensations seized me, and I saw, felt, heard, and smelt, at the same time; and it was, indeed, a long time before I learned to distinguish between the operations of my various senses. By degrees, I remember, a stronger light pressed upon my nerves, so that I was obliged to shut my eyes. Darkness then came over me, and troubled me; but hardly had I felt this, when, by opening my eyes, as I now suppose, the light poured in upon me again. I walked, and, I believe, descended; but I presently found a great alteration in my sensations. Before, dark and opaque bodies had surrounded me, impervious to my touch or sight; but I now found that I could wander on at liberty, with no obstacles which I could not either surmount or avoid. The light became more and more oppressive to me; and, the heat wearying me as I walked, I sought a place where I could receive shade. This was the forest near Ingolstadt; and here I lay by the side of a brook resting from my fatigue, until I felt tormented by hunger and thirst. This roused me from my nearly dormant state, and I ate some berries which I found hanging on the trees, or lying on the ground. I slaked my thirst at the brook; and then lying down, was overcome by sleep.

"It was dark when I awoke; I felt cold also, and half-frightened as it were instinctively, finding myself so desolate. Before I had quitted your apartment, on a sensation of cold, I had covered myself with some clothes; but these were insufficient to secure me from the dews of night. I was a poor, helpless, miserable wretch; I knew and could distinguish nothing; but, feeling pain invade me on all sides, I sat down and wept.

"Soon a gentle light stole over the heavens, and gave me a sensation of pleasure. I started up, and beheld a radiant form rise from among the trees. I gazed with a kind of wonder. It moved slowly, but it enlightened my path; and I again went out in search of berries. I was still cold, when under one of the trees I found a huge cloak, with which I covered myself, and sat down upon the ground. No distinct ideas occupied my mind; all was confused. I felt light, and hunger, and thirst, and darkness; innumerable sounds rung in my ears, and on all sides various scents saluted me: the only object that I could distinguish was the bright moon, and I fixed my eyes on that with pleasure.

"Several changes of day and night passed, and the orb of night had greatly lessened, when I began to distinguish my sensations from each other. I gradually saw plainly the clear stream that supplied me with drink, and the trees that shaded me with their foliage. I was delighted when I first discovered that a pleasant sound, which often saluted my ears, proceeded from the throats of the little winged animals who had often intercepted the light from my eyes. I began also to observe, with greater accuracy, the forms that surrounded me, and to perceive the boundaries of the radiant roof of light which canopied me. Sometimes I tried to imitate the pleasant songs of the birds, but was unable. Sometimes I wished to express my sensations in my own mode, but the uncouth and inarticulate sounds which broke from me frightened me into silence again.

"The moon had disappeared from the night, and again, with a lessened form, showed itself, while I still remained in the forest. My sensations had, by this time, become distinct, and my mind received every day additional ideas. My eyes became accustomed to the light, and to perceive objects in their right forms; I distinguished the insect from the herb, and, by degrees, one herb from another. I found that the sparrow uttered none but harsh notes, while those of the blackbird and thrush were sweet and enticing.

"One day, when I was oppressed by cold, I found a fire which had been left by some wandering beggars, and was overcome with delight at the warmth I experienced from it. In my joy I thrust my hand into the live embers, but quickly drew it out again with a cry of pain. How strange, I thought, that the same cause should produce such opposite effects! I examined the materials of the fire, and to my joy found it to be composed of wood. I quickly collected some branches; but they were wet, and would not burn. I was pained at this, and sat still watching the operation of the fire. The wet wood which I had placed near the heat dried, and itself became inflamed. I reflected on this; and, by touching the various branches, I discovered the cause, and busied myself in collecting a great quantity of wood, that I might dry it, and have a plentiful supply of fire. When night came on, and brought sleep with it, I was in the greatest fear lest my fire should be extinguished. I covered it carefully with dry wood and leaves, and placed wet branches upon it; and then, spreading my cloak, I lay on the ground, and sunk into sleep.

"It was morning when I awoke, and my first care was to visit the fire. I uncovered it, and a gentle breeze quickly fanned it into a flame. I observed this also, and contrived a fan of branches, which roused the embers when they were nearly extinguished. When night came again, I found, with pleasure, that the fire gave light as well as heat; and that the discovery of this element was useful to me in my food; for I found some of the offals that the travellers had left had been roasted, and tasted much more savory than the berries I gathered from the trees. I tried, therefore, to dress my food in the same manner, placing it on the live embers. I found that the berries were spoiled by this operation, and the nuts and roots much improved.

"Food, however, became scarce; and I often spent the whole day searching in vain for a few acorns to assuage the pangs of hunger. When I found this, I resolved to quit the place that I had hitherto inhabited, to seek for one where the few wants I experienced would be more easily satisfied. In this emigration, I exceedingly lamented the loss of the fire which I had obtained through accident, and knew not how to re-produce it. I gave several hours to the serious consideration of this difficulty; but I was obliged to relinquish all attempts to supply it; and, wrapping myself up in my cloak, I struck across the wood towards the setting sun. I passed three days in these rambles, and at length discovered the open country. A great fall of snow had taken place the night before, and the fields were of one uniform white; the appearance was disconsolate, and I found my feet chilled by the cold damp substance that covered the ground.

"It was about seven in the morning, and I longed to obtain food and shelter; at length I perceived a small hut, on a rising ground, which had doubtless been built for the convenience of some shepherd. This was a new sight to me; and I examined the structure with great curiosity. Finding the door open, I entered. An old man sat in it, near a fire, over which he was preparing his breakfast. He turned on hearing a noise; and, perceiving me, shrieked loudly, and, quitting the hut, ran across the fields with a speed of which his debilitated form hardly appeared capable. His appearance, different from any I had ever before seen, and his flight, somewhat surprised me. But I was enchanted by the appearance of the hut: here the snow and rain could not penetrate; the ground was dry; and it presented to me then as exquisite and divine a retreat as Pandæmonium appeared to the dæmons of hell after their sufferings in the lake of fire. I greedily devoured the remnants of the shepherd's breakfast, which consisted of bread, cheese, milk, and wine; the latter, however, I did not like. Overcome by fatigue, I lay down among some straw, and fell asleep.

"It was noon when I awoke; and, allured by the warmth of the sun, which shone brightly on the white ground, I determined to re-commence my travels; and, depositing the remains of the peasant's breakfast in a wallet I found, I proceeded across the fields for several hours, until at sunset I arrived at a village. How miraculous did this appear! the huts, the neater cottages, and stately houses, engaged my admiration by turns. The vegetables in the gardens, the milk and cheese that I saw placed at the windows of some of the cottages, allured my appetite. One of the best of these I entered; but I had hardly placed my foot within the door, before the children shrieked, and one of the women fainted. The whole village was roused; some fled, some attacked me, until, grievously bruised by stones and many other kinds of missile weapons, I escaped to the open country, and fearfully took refuge in a low hovel, quite bare, and making a wretched appearance after the palaces I had beheld in the village. This hovel, however, joined a cottage of a neat and pleasant appearance; but, after my late dearly-bought experience, I dared not enter it. My place of refuge was constructed of wood, but so low, that I could with difficulty sit upright in it. No wood, however, was placed on the earth, which formed the floor, but it was dry; and although the wind entered it by innumerable chinks, I found it an agreeable asylum from the snow and rain.

"Here then I retreated, and lay down, happy to have found a shelter, however miserable, from the inclemency of the season, and still more from the barbarity of man.

"As soon as morning dawned, I crept from my kennel, that I might view the adjacent cottage, and discover if I could remain in the habitation I had found. It was situated against the back of the cottage, and surrounded on the sides which were exposed by a pig-stye and a clear pool of water. One part was open, and by that I had crept in; but now I covered every crevice by which I might be perceived with stones and wood, yet in such a manner that I might move them on occasion to pass out: all the light I enjoyed came through the stye, and that was sufficient for me.

"Having thus arranged my dwelling, and carpeted it with clean straw, I retired; for I saw the figure of a man at a distance, and I remembered too well my treatment the night before, to trust myself in his power. I had first, however, provided for my sustenance for that day, by a loaf of coarse bread, which I purloined, and a cup with which I could drink, more conveniently than from my hand, of the pure water which flowed by my retreat. The floor was a little raised, so that it was kept perfectly dry, and by its vicinity to the chimney of the cottage it was tolerably warm.

"Being thus provided, I resolved to reside in this hovel, until something should occur which might alter my determination. It was indeed a paradise, compared to the bleak forest, my former residence, the rain-dropping branches, and dank earth. I ate my breakfast with pleasure, and was about to remove a plank to procure myself a little water, when I heard a step, and, looking through a small clink, I beheld a young creature, with a pail on her head, passing before my hovel. The girl was young and of gentle demeanor, unlike what I have since found cottagers and farm-servants to be. Yet she was meanly dressed, a coarse blue petticoat and a linen jacket being her only garb; her fair hair was plaited, but not adorned; she looked patient, yet sad. I lost sight of her; and in about a quarter of an hour she returned, bearing the pail, which was now partly filled with milk. As she walked along, seemingly incommoded by the burden, a young man met her, whose countenance expressed a deeper despondence. Uttering a few sounds with an air of melancholy, he took the pail from her head, and bore it to the cottage himself. She followed, and they disappeared. Presently I saw the young man again, with some tools in his hand, cross the field behind the cottage; and the girl was also busied, sometimes in the house, and something in the yard.

"On examining my little dwelling, I found that one of the windows of the cottage had formerly occupied a part of it, but the panes had been filled up with wood. In one of these was a small and almost imperceptible chink, through which the eye could just penetrate. Through this crevice, a small room was visible, whitewashed and clean, but very bare of furniture. In one corner, near a small fire, sat an old man, leaning his head on his hands in a disconsolate attitude. The young girl was occupied in arranging the cottage; but presently she took something out of a drawer, which employed her hands, and she sat down beside the old man, who, taking up an instrument, began to play, and to produce sounds, sweeter than the voice of the thrush or the nightingale. It was a lovely sight, even to me, poor wretch! who had never beheld aught beautiful before. The silver hair and benevolent countenance of the aged cottager, won my reverence; while the gentle manners of the girl enticed my love. He played a sweet mournful air, which I perceived drew tears from the eyes of his amiable companion, of which the old man took no notice, until she sobbed audibly; he then pronounced a few sounds, and the fair creature, leaving her work, knelt at his feet. He raised her, and smiled with such kindness and affection, that I felt sensations of a peculiar and overpowering nature: they were a mixture of pain and pleasure, such as I had never before experienced, either from hunger or cold, warmth or food; and I withdrew from the window, unable to bear these emotions.

"Soon after this the young man returned, bearing on his shoulders a load of wood. The girl met him at the door, helped to relieve him of his burden, and, taking some of the fuel into the cottage, placed it on the fire; then she and the youth went apart into a nook of the cottage, and he showed her a large loaf and a piece of cheese. She seemed pleased; and went into the garden for some roots and plants, which she placed in water, and then upon the fire. She afterwards continued her work, while the young man went into the garden, and appeared busily employed in digging and pulling up roots. After he had been employed thus about an hour, the young woman joined him, and they entered the cottage together.

"The old man had, in the mean time, been pensive; but, on the appearance of his companions, he assumed a more cheerful air, and they sat down to eat. The meal was quickly dispatched. The young woman was again occupied in arranging the cottage; the old man walked before the cottage in the sun for a few minutes, leaning on the arm of the youth. Nothing could exceed in beauty the contrast between these two excellent creatures. One was old, with silver hairs and a countenance beaming with benevolence and love: the younger was slight and graceful in his figure, and his features were moulded with the finest symmetry; yet his eyes and attitude expressed the utmost sadness and despondency. The old man returned to the cottage; and the youth, with tools different from those he had used in the morning, directed his steps across the fields.

"Night quickly shut in; but, to my extreme wonder, I found that the cottagers had a means of prolonging light, by the use of tapers, and was delighted to find, that the setting of the sun did not put an end to the pleasure I experienced in watching my human neighbors. In the evening, the young girl and her companion were employed in various occupations which I did not understand; and the old man again took up the instrument, which produced the divine sounds that had enchanted me in the morning. So soon as he had finished, the youth began, not to play, but to utter sounds that were monotonous, and neither resembling the harmony of the old man's instrument or the songs of the birds; I since found that he read aloud, but at that time I knew nothing of the science of words or letters.

"The family, after having been thus occupied for a short time, extinguished their lights, and retired, as I conjectured, to rest.

CHAPTER XI.

"I lay on my straw, but I could not sleep. I thought of the occurrences of the day. What chiefly struck me was the gentle manners of these people; and I longed to join them, but dared not. I remembered too well the treatment I had suffered the night before from the barbarous villagers, and resolved, whatever course of conduct I might hereafter think it right to pursue, that for the present I would remain quietly in my hovel, watching, and endeavoring to discover the motives which influenced their actions.

"The cottagers arose the next morning before the sun. The young woman arranged the cottage, and prepared the food; and the youth departed after the first meal.

"This day was passed in the same routine as that which preceded it. The young man was constantly employed out of doors, and the girl in various laborious occupations within. The old man, whom I soon perceived to be blind, employed his leisure hours on his instrument, or in contemplation. Nothing could exceed the love and respect which the younger cottagers exhibited towards their venerable companion. They performed towards him every little office of affection and duty with gentleness; and he rewarded them by his benevolent smiles.

"They were not entirely happy. The young man and his companion often went apart, and appeared to weep. I saw no cause for their unhappiness; but I was deeply affected by it. If such lovely creatures were miserable, it was less strange that I, an imperfect and solitary being, should be wretched. Yet why were these gentle beings unhappy? They possessed a delightful house (for such it was in my eyes,) and every luxury; they had a fire to warm them when chill, and delicious viands when hungry; they were dressed in excellent clothes; and, still more, they enjoyed one another's company and speech, interchanging each day looks of affection and kindness. What did their tears imply? Did they really express pain? I was at first unable to solve these questions; but perpetual attention, and time, explained to me many appearances which were at first enigmatic.

"A considerable period elapsed before I discovered one of the causes of the uneasiness of this amiable family; it was poverty: and they suffered that evil in a very distressing degree. Their nourishment consisted entirely of the vegetables of their garden, and the milk of one cow, who gave very little during the winter, when its masters could scarcely procure food to support it. They often, I believe, suffered the pangs of hunger very poignantly, especially the two younger cottagers; for several times they placed food before the old man, when they reserved none for themselves.

"This trait of kindness moved me sensibly. I had been accustomed, during the night, to steal a part of their store for my own consumption: but when I found that in doing this I inflicted pain on the cottagers, I abstained, and satisfied myself with berries, nuts, and roots, which I gathered from a neighboring wood.

"I discovered also another means through which I was enabled to assist their labors. I found that the youth spent a great part of each day in collecting wood for the family fire; and during the night, I often took his tools, the use of which I quickly discovered, and brought home firing sufficient for the consumption of several days.

"I remember, that the first time I did this, the young woman, when she opened the door in the morning, appeared greatly astonished on seeing a great pile of wood on the outside. She uttered some words in a loud voice, and the youth joined her, who also expressed surprise. I observed with pleasure, that he did not go to the forest that day, but spent it in repairing the cottage, and cultivating the garden.

"By degrees I made a discovery of still greater moment. I found that these people possessed a method of communicating their experience and feelings to one another by articulate sounds. I perceived that the words they spoke produced either pleasure or pain, smiles or sadness, in the minds and countenances of the hearers. This was indeed a God-like science, and I ardently desired to become acquainted with it. But I was baffled in every attempt I made for this purpose. Their pronunciation was quick; and the words they uttered, not having any apparent connection with visible objects, I was unable to discover any clue by which I could unravel the mystery of their reference. By great application, however, and after having remained during the space of several revolutions of the moon in my hovel, I discovered the names that were given to some of the most familiar objects of discourse: I learned and applied the words *fire*, *milk*, *bread*, and *wood*. I learned also the names of the cottagers themselves. The youth and his companion had each of them several names, but the old man had only one, which was *father*. The girl was called *sister* or *Agatha*; and the youth *Felix*, *brother*, or *son*. I cannot describe the delight I felt when I learned the ideas appropriated to each of these sounds, and was able to pronounce them. I distinguished several other words, without being able as yet to understand or apply them; such as *good*, *dearest*, *unhappy*.

"I spent the winter in this manner. The gentle manners and beauty of the cottagers greatly endeared them to me: when they were unhappy I felt depressed; when they rejoiced, I sympathized in their joys. I saw few human beings beside them; and if any other happened to enter the cottage, their harsh manners and rude gait only enhanced to me the superior accomplishments of my friends. The old man, I could perceive, often endeavored to encourage his children, as sometimes I found that he called them, to cast off their melancholy. He would talk in a cheerful accent, with an expression of goodness that bestowed pleasure even upon me. Agatha listened with respect, her eyes sometimes filled with tears, which she endeavored to wipe away unperceived; but I generally found that her countenance and tone were more cheerful after having listened to the exhortations of her father. It was not thus with Felix. He was always the saddest of the group; and, even to my unpractised senses, he appeared to have suffered more deeply than his friends. But if his countenance were more sorrowful, his voice was more cheerful than that of his sister, especially when he addressed the old man.

"I could mention innumerable instances, which, although slight, marked the dispositions of these amiable cottagers. In the midst of poverty and want, Felix carried with pleasure to his sister the first little white flower that peeped out from beneath the snowy gronnd. Early in the morning, before she had risen, he cleared away the snow that obstructed her path to the milk-house, drew water from the well, and brought the wood from the out-house, where, to his perpetual astonishment, he found his store always replenished by an invisible hand. In the day, I believe, he worked sometimes for a neighboring farmer, because he often went forth, and did not return until dinner, yet brought no wood with him. At other times he worked in the garden; but as there was little to do in the frosty season, he read to the old man and Agatha.

"This reading had puzzled me extremely at first; but, by degrees, I discovered that he uttered many of the same sounds when he read as when he talked. I conjectured, therefore, that he found on the paper signs for speech which he understood, and I ardently longed to comprehend these also; but how was that possible, when I did not even understand the sounds for which they stood as signs? I improved however, sensibly in this science, but not sufficiently to follow up any kind of conversation, although I applied my whole mind to the endeavor: for I easily perceived that, although I eagerly longed to discover myself to the cottagers, I ought not to make the attempt until I had first become master of their language; which knowledge might enable me to make them overlook the deformity of my figure; for with this also the contrast perpetually presented to my eyes had made me acquainted.

"I had admired the perfect forms of my cottagers—their grace, beauty, and delicate complexions: but how was I terrified when I viewed myself in a transparent pool! At first I started back, unable to believe that it was indeed I who was reflected in the mirror; and when I became fully convinced that I was in reality the monster that I am, I was filled with the bitterest sensations of despondence and mortification. Alas! I did not yet entirely know the fatal effects of this miserable deformity.

"As the sun becaume warmer, and the light of day longer, the snow vanished, and I beheld the bare trees and the black earth. From this time Felix was more employed; and the heart-moving indications of impending famine disappeared. Their food, as I afterwards found, was coarse, but it was wholesome; and they procured a sufficiency of it. Several new kinds of plants sprung up in the garden, which they dressed; and these signs of comfort increased daily as the season advanced.

"The old man, leaning on his son, walked each day at noon, when it did not rain, as I found it was called when the heavens poured forth its waters. This frequently took place; but a high wind quickly dried the earth, and the season became far more pleasant than it had been.

"My mode of life in my hovel was uniform. During the morning I attended the motions of the cottagers; and when they were dispersed in various occupations, I slept: the remainder of the day was spent in observing my friends. When they had retired to rest, if there was any moon, or the night was star-light, I went into the woods, and collected my own food and fuel for the cottage. When I returned, as often as it was necessary, I cleared their path from the snow, and performed those offices that I had seen done by Felix. I afterwards found that these labors, performed by an invisible hand, greatly astonshed them; and once or twice I heard them, on these occasions, utter the words *good spirit, wonderful;* but I did not then understand the signification of these terms.

"My thoughts now became more active, and I longed to discover the motives and feelings of these lovely creatures; I was inquisitive to know why Felix appeared so miserable, and Agatha so sad. I thought (foolish wretch!) that it might be in my power to restore happiness to these deserving people. When I slept, or was absent, the forms of the venerable blind father, the gentle Agatha, and the excellent Felix, flitted before me. I looked upon them as superior beings, who would be the arbiters of my future destiny. I formed in my imagination a thousand pictures of presenting myself to them, and their reception of me. I imagined that they would be digusted, until by my gentle demeanor and conciliating words, I should first win their favor, and afterwards their love.

"These thoughts exhilarated me, and led me to apply with fresh ardor to the acquiring the art of language. My organs were indeed harsh, but supple; and although my voice was very unlike the soft music of their tones, yet I pronounced such words as I understood, with tolerable ease. It was as the ass and the lap-dog; yet surely the gentle ass, whose intentions were affectionate, although his manners were rude, deserved better treatment than blows and execration.

"The pleasant showers and genial warmth of spring greatly altered the aspect of the earth. Men, who before this change seemed to have been hid in caves, dispersed themselves, and were employed in various arts of cultivation. The birds sang in more cheerful notes, and the leaves began to bud forth on the trees. Happy, happy earth! fit habitation for gods, which, so short a time before, was bleak, damp, and unwholesome. My spirits were elevated by the enchanting appearance of nature; the past was blotted from my memory, the present was tranquil, and the future gilded by bright rays of hope, and anticipations of joy.

CHAPTER XII.

"I NOW hasten to the more moving part of my story. I shall relate events that impressed me with feelings which from what I was, have made me what I am.

"Spring advanced rapidly; the weather became fine, and the skies cloudless. It surprised me, that what before was desert and gloomy should now bloom with the most beautiful flowers and verdure. My senses were gratified and refreshed by a thousand scents of delight, and a thousand sights of beauty.

"It was on one of these days, when my cottagers periodically rested from labor—the old man played on his guitar, and the children listened to him—I observed that the countenance of Felix was melancholy beyond expression: he sighed frequently; and once his father paused in his music, and I conjectured by his manner that he inquired the cause of his son's sorrow. Felix replied in a cheerful accent, and the old man was recommencing his music, when some one tapped at the door.

"It was a lady on horseback, accompanied by a countryman as a guide. The lady was dressed in a dark suit, and covered with a thick black veil. Agatha asked a question; to which the stranger only replied by pronouncing, in a sweet accent, the name of Felix. Her voice was musical, but unlike that of either of my friends. On hearing this word, Felix came up hastily to the lady; who, when she saw him, threw up her veil, and I beheld a countenance of angelic beauty and expression. Her hair of a shining raven black, and curiously braided; her eyes were dark, but gentle, although animated; her features of a regular proportion, and her complexion wondrously fair, each cheek tinged with a lovely tint.

Felix seemed ravished with delight when he saw her, every trait of sorrow vanished from his face, and it instantly expressed a degree of ecstatic joy, of which I could hardly have believed it capable; his eyes sparkled, as his cheek flushed with pleasure; and at that moment I thought him as beautiful as the stranger. She appeared affected by different feelings; wiping a few tears from her lovely eyes, she held out her hand to Felix, who kissed it rapturously, and called her, as well as I could distinguish, his sweet Arabian. She did not appear to understand him, but smiled. He assisted her to dismount, and, dismissing her guide, conducted her into the cottage. Some conversation took place between him and his father; and the young stranger knelt at the old man's feet, and would have kissed his hand, but he raised her, and embraced her affectionately.

"I soon perceived, that although the stranger uttered articulate sounds, and appeared to have a language of her own, she was neither understood by, or herself understood, the cottagers. They made many signs which I did not comprehend; but I saw that her presence diffused gladness through the cottage, dispelling their sorrow as the sun dissipates the morning mists. Felix seemed peculiarly happy, and with smiles of delight welcomed his Arabian. Agatha, the ever-gentle Agatha, kissed the hands of the lovely stranger; and, pointing to her brother, made signs which appeared to me to mean that he had been sorrowful until she came. Some hours passed thus, while they, by their countenances, expressed joy, the cause of which I did not comprehend. Presently I found, by the frequent recurrence of one sound which the stranger repeated after them, that she was endeavoring to learn their language; and the idea instantly occurred to me, that I should make use of the same instructions to the same end. The stranger learned about twenty words at the first lesson, most of them indeed were those which I had before understood, but I profited by the others.

"As night came on, Agatha and the Arabian retired early. When they separated, Felix kissed the hand of the stranger, and said, 'Good night, sweet Safie.' He sat up much longer, conversing with his father; and, by the frequent repetition of her name, I conjectured that their lovely guest was the subject of their conversation. I ardently desired to understand them, and bent every faculty towards that purpose, but found it utterly impossible.

"The next morning Felix went out to his work; and, after the usual occupations of Agatha were finished, the Arabian set at the feet of the old man, and, taking his guitar, played some airs so entrancingly beautiful, that they at once drew tears of sorrow and delight from my eyes. She sang, and her voice flowed in a rich cadence, swelling or dying away, like a nightingale of the woods.

When she had finished, she gave the guitar to Agatha, who at first declined it. She played a simple air, and her voice accompanied it in sweet accents, but unlike the wondrous strain of the stranger. The old man appeared enraptured, and said some words, which Agatha endeavored to explain to Safie, and by which he appeared to wish to express that she bestowed on him the greatest delight by her music.

The days now passed as peaceably as before, with the sole alteration, that joy had taken place of sadness in the countenances of my friends. Safie was always gay and happy; she and I improved rapidly in the knowledge of language, so that in two months I began to comprehend most of the words uttered by my protectors.

In the meanwhile also the black ground was covered with herbage, and the green banks interspersed with innumerable flowers, sweet to the scent and the eyes, stars of pale radiance among the moonlight woods; the sun became warmer, the nights clear and balmy; and my nocturnal rambles were an extreme pleasure to me, although they were considerably shortened by the late setting and early rising of the sun; for I never ventured abroad during daylight, fearful of meeting with the same treatment as I had formerly endured in the first village which I entered.

"My days were spent in close attention that I might more speedily master the language; and I may boast that I improved more rapidly than the Arabian, who understood very little, and conversed in broken accents, while I comprehended and could imitate almost every word that was spoken.

While I improved in speech, I also learned the science of letters, as it was taught to the stranger; and this opened before me a wide field for wonder and delight.

"The book from which Felix instructed Safie was Volney's *Ruins of Empires*. I should not have understood the purport of this book, had not Felix, in reading it, given very minute explanations. He had chosen this work, he said, because the declamatory style was framed in imitation of the eastern authors. Through this work I obtained a cursory knowledge of history, and a view of the several empires at present existing in the world; it gave me an insight into the manners, governments, and religions of the different nations of the earth. I heard of the slothful Asiatics; of the stupendous genius and mental activity of the Grecians; of the wars and wonderful virtue of the early Romans—of their subsequent degeneration—of the decline of that mighty empire; of chivalry, christianity, and kings. I heard of the discovery of the American hemisphere, and wept with Safie over the hapless fate of its original inhabitants.

"These wonderful narrations inspired me with strange feelings. Was man, indeed, at once so powerful, so virtuous, and magnificent, yet so vicious and base? He appeared at one time a mere scion of evil principle, and at another as all that can be conceived of noble and godlike. To be a great and virtuous man appeared the highest honor that can befall a sensitive being; to be base and vicious, as many on record have been, appeared the lowest degradation, a condition more abject than that of the blind mole or harmless worm. For a long time I could not conceive how one man could go forth to murder his fellow, or even why there were laws and governments; but when I heard details of vice and bloodshed, my wonder ceased, and I hurried away with disgust and loathing.

"Every conversation of the cottagers now opened new wonders to me. While I listened to the instructions which Felix bestowed upon the Arabian, the strange system of human society was explained to me. I heard of the division of property, of immense wealth and squalid poverty; of rank, descent, and noble blood.

"The words induced me to turn towards myself. I learned that the possessions most esteemed by your fellow-creatures were, high and unsullied descent united with riches. A man might be respected with only one of these acquisitions; but without either he was considered, except in very rare instances, as a vagabond and a slave, doomed to waste his powers for the profit of the chosen few. And what was I? Of my creation and creator I was absolutely ignorant; but I knew that I possessed no money, no friends, no kind of property. I was, besides, endowed with a figure hideously deformed and loathsome; I was not even of the same nature as man. I was more agile than they, and could subsist upon coarser diet; I bore the extremes of heat and cold with less injury to my frame; my stature far exceeded theirs. When I looked around, I saw and heard of none like me. Was I then a monster, a blot upon the earth, from which all men fled, and whom all men disowned?

I cannot describe to you the agony that these reflections inflicted upon me; I tried to dispel them, but sorrow only increased with knowledge. Oh, that I had for ever remained in my native wood, nor known or felt beyond the sensations of hunger, thirst, and heat.

"Of what a strange nature is knowl dge! It clings to the minds, when it nas once seized on it, like a linchen on the rock. I wished sometimes to shake off all thought and feeling; but I learned that there was but one means to overcome the sensation of pain, and that was death—a state which I feared, yet did not understand. I admired virtue and good feelings, and loved the gentle manners and amiable qualities of my cottagers; but I was shut out from intercourse with them, except through means which I obtained by stealth, when I was unseen and unknown, and which rather increased than satisfied the desire I had of becoming one among my fellows. The gentle words of Agatha, and the animated smiles of the charming Arabian were not for me. The mild exhortations of the old man, and the lively conversation of the loved Felix, were not for me. Miserable, unhappy wretch!

"Other lessons were impressed upon me even more deeply. I heard of the difference of sexes; of the birth and growth of children; how the father doated on the smiles of the infant, and the lively sallies of the older child; how all the life and cares of the mother were wrapt up in the precious charge; how the mind of youth expanded and gained knowledge; of brother, sister, and all the various relationships which bind one human being to another in mutual bonds.

"But where were my friends and relations? No father had watched my infant days, no mother had blessed me with smiles and caresses; or if they had, all my past life was now a blot, a blind vacancy in which I distinguished nothing. From my earliest remembrance I had been as I then was in height and proportion. I had never yet seen a being resembling me, or who claimed any intercourse with me. What was I? The question again recurred, to be answered only with groans.

"I will soon explain to what these feelings tended; but allow me now to return to the cottagers, whose story excited in me such various feelings of indignation, delight, and wonder, but which all terminated in additional love and reverence for my protectors (for so I loved, in an innocent, half painful self-deceit to call them.)

CHAPTER XIII.

"Some time elapsed before I learned the history of my friends. It was one which could not fail to impress itself deeply on my mind, unfolding as it did a number of circumstances each interesting and wonderful to one so utterly inexperienced as I was.

"The name of the old man was De Lacey. He was descended from a good family in France, where he had lived for many years in affluence, respected by his superiors, and beloved by his equals. His son was bred in the service of his country; and Agatha had ranked with ladies of the highest distinction. A few months before my arrival, they had lived in a large and luxurious city, called Paris, surrounded by friends, and possessed of every enjoyment which virtue, refinement of intellect, or taste, accompanied by a moderate fortune, could afford,

"The father of Safie had been the cause of their ruin. He was a Turkish merchant, and had inhabited Paris for many years, when, for some reason which I could not learn, he became obnoxious to the government. He was seized and cast into prison the very day that Safie arrived from Constantinople to join him. He was tried, and condemned to death. The injustice of his sentence was very flagrant; all Paris was indignant; and it was judged that his religion and wealth, rather than the crime alleged against him, had been the cause of his condemnation.

"Felix had been present at the trial; his horror and indignation were uncontrollable, when he heard the decision of the court. He made, at that moment, a solemn vow to deliver him, and then looked around for the means. After many fruitless attempts to gain admittance to the prison, he found a strongly grated window in an unguarded part of the building, which lighted the dungeon of the unfortunate Mahometan; who, loaded with chains, waited in despair the execution of the barbarous sentence.

"Felix visited the grate at night, and made known to the prisoner his intentions n his favor. The Turk, amazed and delighted, endeavored to kindle the zeal of his deliverer by promises of reward and wealth. Felix rejected his offers with contempt; yet when he saw the lovely Safie, who was allowed to visit her father, and who by her gestures, expressed her lively gratitude, the youth could not help owning to his own mind, that the captive possessed a treasure which would fully reward his toil and hazard.

"The Turk quickly perceived the impression that his daughter had made on the heart of Felix, and endeavored to secure him more entirely in his interests by the promise of her hand in marriage, so soon as he should be conveyed to a place of safety. Felix was too delicate to accept this offer; yet he looked forward to the probability of that event as to the consummation of his happiness.

"During the ensuing days, while the preparations were going forward for the escape of the merchant, the zeal of Felix was warmed by several letters that he received from this lovely girl, who found means to express her thoughts in the language of her lover by the aid of an old man, a servant of her father's, who understood French. She thanked him in the most ardent terms for his intended services towards her father; and at the same time she gently deplored her own fate.

"I have copies of these letters; for I found means, during my residence in the hovel, to procure the implements of writing; and the letters were often in the hands of Felix or Agatha. Before I depart, I will give them to you, they will prove the truth of my tale; but at present, as the sun is already far declined, I shall only have time to repeat the substance of them to you.

"Safie related, that her mother was a Christian Arab, seized and made a slave by the Turks; recommended by her beauty, she had won the heart of the father of Safie, who married her. The young girl spoke in high and enthusiastic terms of her mother, who, born in freedom, spurned the bondage to which she was now reduced. She instructed her daughter in the tenets of her religion, and taught her to aspire to higher powers of intellect, and an independence of spirit, forbidden to the female followers of Mahomet. This lady died; but her lessons were indelibly impressed on the mind of Safie, who sickened at the prospect of again returning to Asia, and the being immured within the walls of a haram, allowed only to occupy herself with puerile amusements, ill suited to the temper of her soul, now accustomed to grand ideas and a noble emulation for virtue. The prospect of marrying a Christian, and remaining in a country where women were allowed to take a rank in society, was enchanting to her.

"The day for the execution of the Turk was fixed; but, the night previous to it, he had quitted prison, and before morning was distant many leagues from Paris. Felix had procured passports in the name of his father, sister, and himself. He had previously communicated his plan to the former, who aided the deceit by quitting his house, under the pretence of a journey, and concealed himself, with his daughter, in an obscure part of Paris.

"Felix conducted the fugitives through France to Lyons, and across Mont Cenis to Leghorn, where the merchant had decided to wait a favorable opportunity of passing into some part of the Turkish dominions.

"Safie resolved to remain with her father until the moment of his departure, before which time the Turk renewed his promise that she should be united to his deliverer; and Felix remained with them in expectation of that event; and in the mean time he enjoyed the society of the Arabian, who exhibited towards him the simplest and tenderest affection. They conversed with one another through the means of an interpreter, and sometimes with the interpretation of looks; and Safie sang to him the divine airs of her native country.

"The Turk allowed this intimacy to take place, and encouraged the hopes of the youthful lovers, while in his heart he had formed far other plans. He loathed the idea that his daughter should be united to a Christian; but he feared the resentment of Felix if he should appear lukewarm; for he knew that he was still in the power of his deliverer, if he should choose to betray him to the Italian state which they inhabited. He revolved a thousand plans by which he should be enabled to prolong the deceit until it might be no longer necessary, and secretly to take his daughter with him when he departed. His plans were greatly facilitated by the news which arrived from Paris.

"The goverment of France were greatly enraged at the escape of their victim, and spared no pains to detect and punish his deliverer. The plot of Felix was quickly discovered, and De Lacey and Agatha were thrown into prison. The news reached Felix, and roused him from his dream of pleasure. His blind and aged father, and his gentle sister, lay in a noisome dungeon, while he enjoyed the free air, and the society of her whom he loved. This idea was torture to him. He quickly arranged with the Turk, that if the latter should find a favorable opportunity for escape before Felix could return to Italy, Safie should remain as a boarder at a convent at Leghorn; and then, quitting the lovely Arabian, he hastened to Paris, and delivered himself up to the vengeance of the law, hoping to free De Lacey and Agatha by this proceeding.

"He did not succeed. They remained confined for five months before the trial took place; the result of which deprived them of their fortune, and condemned them to perpetual exile from their native country.

"They found a miserable asylum in the cottage in Germany, where I discovered them. Felix soon learned that the treacherous Turk, for whom he and his family endured such unheard of oppression, on discovering that his deliverer was thus reduced to poverty and impotence, became a traitor to good feeling and honor, and had quitted Italy with his daughter, insultingly sending Felix a pittance of money to aid him, as he said, in some plan of future maintenance.

"Such were the events that preyed on

the heart of Felix, and rendered him, when I first saw him, the most miserable of his family. He could have endured poverty, and when this distress had been the meed of his virtue, he would have gloried in it: but the ingratitude of the Turk, and the loss of his beloved Safie, were misfortunes more bitter and irreparable. The arrival of the Arabian now infused new life into his soul.

"When the news reached Leghorn, that Felix was deprived of his wealth and rank, the merchant commanded his daughter to think no more of her lover, but prepare to return with him to her native country. The generous nature of Safie was outraged by this command; she attempted to expostulate with her father, but he left her angrily, reiterating his tyrannical mandate.

"A few days after, the Turk entered his daughter's apartment, and told her hastily, that he had reason to believe that his residence at Leghorn had been divulged, and that he should speedily be delivered up to the French government; he had, consequently, hired a vessel to convey him to Constantinople, for which city he should sail in a few hours. He intended to leave his daughter under the care of a confidential servant, to follow at her leisure with the greater part of his property, which had not yet arrived at Leghorn.

"When alone, Safie resolved in her own mind the plan of conduct that it would become her to pursue in this emergencey. A residence in Turkey was abhorrent to her; her religion and feelings were alike adverse to it. By some papers of her father's, which fell into her hands, she heard of the spot where he then resided. She hesitated some time, but at length she formed her determination. Taking with her some jewels that belonged to her, and a small sum of money, she quitted Italy, with an attendant, a native of Leghorn, but who understood the common language of Turkey, and departed for Germany.

"She arrived in safety at a town about twenty leagues from the cottage of De Lacey, when her attendant fell dangerously ill. Safie nursed her with most devoted affection; but the poor girl died, and the Arabian was left alone, unacquainted with the language of the country, and utterly ignorant of the customs of the world. She fell, however, into good hands. The Italian had mentioned the name of the spot for which they were bound; and after her death, the woman of the house in which they had lived took care that Safie should arrive in safety at the cottage of her lover.

CHAPTER XIV.

"Such was the history of my beloved cottagers. It impressed me deeply. I learned from the views of social life which it developed, to admire their virtues, and deprecate the vices of mankind.

"As yet I looked upon crime as a distant evil; benevolence and generosity were ever present before me, inciting within me a desire to become an actor in the busy scene where so many admirable qualities were called forth and displayed, but, in giving an account of the progress of my intellect, I must not omit a circumstance which occurred in the beginning of the month of August of the same year.

"One night, during my accustomed visit to the neighboring wood, where I collected my own food, and brought home firing for my protectors, I found on the ground a leathern portmanteau, containing several articles of dress and some books. I eagerly seized the prize, and returned with it to the hovel. Fortunately the books were written in the language the elements of which I had acquired at the cottage; they consisted of *Paradise Lost*, a volume of *Plutarch's Lives*, and the *Sorrows of Werter*. The possession of these pleasures gave me extreme delight; I now continually studied and exercised my mind upon these histories, while my friends were employed in their ordinary occupations.

"I can hardly describe to you the effect of these books. They produced in me an infinity of new images and feelings, that sometimes raised me to ecstacy, but more frequently sunk me into the lowest dejection. In the *Sorrows of Werter*, besides the interest of its simple and affecting story, so many opinions are canvassed, and so many lights thrown upon what had hitherto been to me obscure subjects, that I found in it a never ending source of speculation and astonishment. The gentle and domestic manners described, combined with lofty sentiments and feelings, which had for their object something out of self, accorded well with my experience among my protectors, and with the wants which were forever alive in my own bosom. But I thought Werter himself a more divine being than I had ever beheld or imagined; his character contained no pretension, but it sunk deep. The disquisitions upon death and suicide were calculated to fill me with wonder. I did not pretend to enter into the merits of the case, yet I inclined towards the opinions of the hero, whose extinction I wept, without precisely understanding it.

"As I read, however, I applied much personally to my own feelings and condition. I found myself similar, yet at the same time strangely unlike the beings concerning whom I read, and to whose conversation I was a listener. I sympathized with, and partly understood them, but I was uninformed in mind; I was dependent on none, and related to none. 'The path of my departure was free,' and there was none to lament my annihilation. My person was hideous, and my stature gigantic: what did this mean? Who was I? What was I? Whence did I come? What was my destination? These questions continually recurred, but I was unable to solve them.

"The volume of *Plutarch's Lives* which I possessed, contained the histories of the first founders of the ancient republics. This book had a far different effect upon me from the *Sorrows of Werter*. I learned from Werter's imaginations despondency and gloom: but Plutarch taught me high thoughts; he elevated me above the wretched sphere of my own reflections, to admire and love the heroes of past ages. Many things I read surpassed my understanding and experience. I had a very confused knowledge of kingdoms, wide extents of country, mighty rivers, and boundless seas. But I was perfectly unacquainted with towns and large assemblages of men. The cottage of my protectors had been the only school in which I had studied human nature; but this book developed new and mightier scenes of action. I read of men concerned in public affairs governing or massacreeing their species. I felt the greatest ardor for virtue rise within me, and abhorrence for vice, as far as I understood the signification of those terms, relative as they were, as I applied them, to pleasure and pain alone. Induced by these feelings, I was of course led to admire peaceable law-givers, Numa, Solon and Lycurgus, in preference to Romulus and Thesus. The patriarchal lives of my protectors caused these impressions to take a firm hold on my mind; perhaps, if my first introduction to humanity had been made by a young soldier, burning for glory and slaughter, I should have been imbued with different sensations.

"But *Paradise Lost* excited different and far deeper emotions. I read it, as I had read the other volumes which had fallen into my hands, as a true history. It moved every feeling of wonder and awe, that the picture of an omnipotent God warring with his creatures was capable of exciting. I often remarked the several situations, as their similarity struck me, to my own. Like Adam, I was created, apparently united by no link to any other being in existence; but his state was far different from mine in every other respect. He had come forth from the hands of God a perfect creature, happy and prosperous, guarded by the especial care of his Creator; he was allowed to converse with, and acquire knowledge from beings of a superior nature: but I was wretched, helpless, and alone. Many times I considered Satan as the fitter emblem of my condition; for often, like him, when I viewed the bliss of my protectors, the bitter gall of envy rose within me.

"Another circumstance strengthened and confirmed these feelings. Soon after my arrival in the hovel, I discovered some papers in the pocket of the dress which I had taken from your laboratory. At first I had neglected them; but now that I was able to decipher the characters in which they were written, I began to study them with diligence. It was your journal of the four months that preceded my creation. You minutely described in these papers every step you took in the progress of your work; this history was mingled with accounts of domestic occurrences. You, doubtless, recollect these papers. Here they are. Everything is related in them which bears reference to my accursed origin; the whole detail of that series of disgusting circumstances which produced it is set in view; the minutest description of my odious and loathsome person is given, in language which painted your own horrors, and rendered mine ineffaceable. I sickened as I read. 'Hateful day when I received life!' I exclaimed in agony. 'Cursed creator! Why did you form a monster so hideous that even you turned from me in disgust? God in pity made man beautiful and alluring, after his own image; but my form is a filthy type of yours, more horrid from its very resemblance. Satan had his companions, fellow devils, to admire and encourage him; but I am solitary and detested.'

"These were the reflections of my hours of despondency and solitude; but when I contemplated the virtues of the cottagers, their amiable and benevolent dispositions, I persuaded myself that when they should become acquainted with my admiration of their virtues, they would compassionate me, and overlook my personal deformity. Could they turn from their door one, however monstrous, who solicited their compassion and friendship? I resolved, at least, not to despair, but in every way to fit myself for an interview with them which would decide my fate. I postponed this attempt for some months longer; for the importance attached to its success inspired me with a dread lest I should fail. Besides, I found that my understanding improved so much with every day's experience, that I was unwilling to commence this undertaking until a few more months should have added to my wisdom.

"Several changes, in the mean time, took place in the cottage. The presence of Safie diffused happiness among its inhabitants; and I also found that a greater degree of plenty reigned there. Felix and Agatha spent more time in amusement and conversation, and were assisted in their labors by servants. They did not appear rich, but were contented and happy; their feelings were serene and peaceful, while mine became every day more tumultuous. Increase of knowledge only discovered to me more clearly what a wretched outcast I was. I cherished hope, it is true; but it vanished, when I beheld my person reflected in water, or my shadow in the moonshine, even as that frail image and that inconstant shade.

"I endeavored to crush these fears, and to fortify myself for the trial which in a few months I resolved to undergo; and sometimes I allowed my thoughts, unchecked by reason, to ramble in the fields of Paradise, and dared to fancy amiable and lovely creatures sympathizing with my feelings and cheering my gloom; their angelic countenances breathed smiles of consolation. But it was all a dream: no Eve soothed my sorrows, or shared my thoughts; I was alone. I remembered Adam's supplication to his Creator; but where was mine? he had abandoned me, and, in the bitterness of my heart, I cursed him.

"Autumn passed thus. I saw, with surprise and grief, the leaves decay and fall, and nature again assume the barren and bleak appearance it had worn when I first beheld the woods and lovely moon. Yet I did not heed the bleakness of the weather; I was better fitted by my conformation for the endurance of cold than heat. But my chief delights were the sight of the flowers, the birds, and all the gay apparel of summer; when those deserted me, I turned with more attention towards the cottagers. Their happiness was not decreased by the absence of summer.

They loved, and sympathized with one another; and their joys, depending on each other, were not interrupted by the casualties that took place around them. The more I saw of them, the greater became my desire to claim their protection and kindness; my heart yearned to be known and loved by these amiable creatures: to see their sweet looks turned towards me with affection, was the utmost limit of my ambition. I dared not think that they would turn them from me with disdain and horror. The poor that stopped at their door were near driven away. I asked, it is true, for greater treasures then a little food or rest; I required kindness and sympathy; but I did not believe myself utterly unworthy of it.

"The winter advanced, and an entire revolution of the seasons had taken place since I awoke into life. My attention, at this time, was solely directed towards my plan of introducing myself into the cottage of my protectors. I revolved projects; but that on which I finally fixed was, to enter the dwelling when the blind old man should be alone. I had sagacity enough to discover, that the unnatural hideousness of my person was the chief object of horror with those who had formerly beheld me. My voice, although harsh, had nothing terrible in it; I thought, therefore, that if, in the absence of his children, I could gain the good-will and mediation of the old De Lacey, I might, by his means, be tolerated by my younger protectors.

"One day, when the sun shone on the red leaves that strewed the ground, and diffused cheerfulness, although it denied warmth, Safie, Agatha, and Felix, departed on a long country walk, and the old man, at his own desire, was left alone in the cottage. When his children had departed, he took up his guitar, and played several mournful, but sweet airs, more sweet and mournful than I had ever heard him play before. At first his countenance was illuminated with pleasure, but, as he continued, thoughtfulness and sadness succeeded; at length, laying aside the instrument, he sat absorbed in reflection.

"My heart beat quick; this was the hour and moment of trial, which would decide my hopes, or realize my fears. The servants were gone to a neighboring fair. All was silent in and around the cottage: it was an excellent opportunity; yet, when I proceeded to execute my plan, my limbs failed me, and I sunk to the ground. Again I rose; and, exerting all the firmness of which I was master, removed the planks which I had placed before my hovel to conceal my retreat. The fresh air revived me, and, with renewed determination, I approached the door of their cottage.

"I knocked. 'Who is there?' said the old man—'Come in.'

"I entered; 'Pardon this intrusion,' said I, 'I am a traveller in want of a little rest; you would greatly oblige me, if you would allow me to remain a few minutes before the fire.'

"'Enter,' said De Lacey; 'and I will try in what manner I can relieve your wants; but, unfortunately, my children are from home, and, as I am blind, I am afraid I shall find it difficult to procure food for you.'

"'Do not trouble yourself, my kind host, I have food; it is warmth and rest only that I need.'

"I sat down, and a silence ensued. I knew that every minute was precious to me, yet I remained irresolute in what manner to commence the interview; when the old man addressed me—

"'By your language, stranger, I suppose you are my countryman; are you French?"

"'No; but I was educated by a French family, and understand that language only. I am now going to claim the protection of some friends, whom I sincerely love, and of whose favor I have some hopes.'

"'Are these Germans?'

"'No, they are French. But let us change the subject. I am an unfortunate and deserted creature; I look around, and have no relation or friend upon earth. These amiable people to whom I go have never seen me, and know little of me. I am full of fears; for if I fail there, I am an outcast in the world for ever.'

"'Do not despair. To be friendless is indeed to be unfortunate; but the hearts of men, when unprejudiced by any obvious self-interest, are full of brotherly love and charity. Rely, therefore on your hopes; and if these friends are good and amiable, do not despair.'

"'They are kind—they are the most excellent creatures in the world; but, unfortunately, they are prejudiced against me. I have good dispositions; my life has been hitherto harmless, and, in some degree, beneficial; but a fatal prejudice clouds their eyes, and where they ought to see a feeling and kind friend, they behold only a detestable monster.'

"'That is indeed unfortunate; but if you are really blameless, cannot you undeceive them?'

"'I am about to undertake that task; and it is on that account that I feel so many overwhelming terrors. I tenderly love these friends; I have, unknown to them, been for many months in the habits of daily kindness towards them; but they believe that I wish to injure them, and it is that prejudice which I wish to overcome.'

"'Where do these friends reside?'

"'Near this spot.'

"The old man paused, and then continued, 'If you will unreservedly confide to me the particulars of your tale, I may perhaps be of use in undeceiving them. I am blind, and cannot judge of your countenance, but there is something in your words which persuades me that you are sincere. I am poor, and an exile; but it will afford me true pleasure to be in any way serviceable to a human creature.'

"'Excellent man! I thank you, and accept your generous offer. You raise me from the dust by this kindness; and I trust that, by your aid, I shall not be driven from the society and sympathy of your fellow creatures.'

"'Heaven forbid! even if you were really criminal; for that can only drive you to desperation, and not instigate you to virtue. I also am unfortunate; I and my family have been condemned, although innocent: judge, therefore, if I do not feel for your misfortunes.'

"'How can I thank you, my best and only benefactor? From your lips first have I heard the voice of kindness directed towards me; I shall be forever grateful; and your present humanity assures me of success with those friends whom I am on the point of meeting.'

"'May I know the names and residence of those friends?'

"I paused. This, I thought, was the moment of decision, which was to rob me of, or bestow happiness on me for ever. I struggled vainly for firmness sufficient to answer him, but the effort destroyed all my remaining strength; I sank on the chair, and sobbed aloud. At that moment I heard the steps of my younger protectors. I had not a moment to lose; but, seizing the hand of the old man, I cried, 'Now is the time! save and protect me! You and your family are the friends whom I seek. Do not you desert me in the hour of trial!'

"'Great God!' exclaimed the old man, 'who are you?'

"At that instant the cottage door was opened, and Felix, Safie, and Agatha entered. Who can describe their horror and consternation on beholding me? Agatha fainted; and Safie, unable to attend to her friend, rushed out of the cottage. Felix darted forward, and with supernatural force tore me from his father, to whose knees I clung: In a transport of fury, he dashed me to the ground, and struck me violently with a stick. I could have torn him limb from limb, as the lion rends the antelope. But my heart sunk within me as with bitter sickness, and I refrained. I saw him on the point of repeating his blow, when, overcome by pain and anguish, I quitted the cottage, and in the general tumult escaped unperceived to my hovel.

CHAPTER XV.

"CURSED, cursed creator! Why did I live? Why, in that instant, did I not extinguish the spark of existence which you had so wantonly bestowed? I know not; despair had not yet taken possession of me; my feelings were those of rage and revenge. I could with pleasure have destroyed the cottage and its inhabitants, and have glutted myself with their shrieks and misery.

"When night came, I quitted my retreat, and wandered in the wood; and now, no longer restrained by the fear of discovery, I gave vent to my anguish in fearful howlings. I was like a wild beast that had broken the toils; destroying the objects that obstructed me, and ranging through the wood with a stag-like swiftness. Oh! what a miserable night I passed! the cold stars shone in mockery, and the bare trees waved their branches above me: now and then the sweet voice of a bird burst forth amidst the universal stillness. All, save I, were at rest or in enjoyment: I, like the arch fiend, bore a hell within me; and, finding myself unsympathized with, wished to tear up the trees, spread havoc and destruction around me, and then to have sat down and enjoyed the ruin.

"But this was a luxury of sensation that could not endure; I became fatigued with excess of bodily exertion, and sank on the damp grass in the sick impotence of despair. There was none among the myriads of men that existed who would pity or assist me; and should I feel kindness towards my enemies? No: from that moment I declared everlasting war against the species, and, more than all, against him who had formed me and sent me forth to this insupportable misery.

"The sun rose; I heard the voices of men, and knew that it was impossible to return to my retreat during that day. Accordingly I hid myself in some thick underwood, determining to devote the ensuing hours to reflection on my situation.

The pleasant sunshine, and the pure air of day, restored me to some degree of tranquility; and when I considered what had passed at the cottage, I could not help believing that I had been too hasty in my conclusions. I had certainly acted imprudently. It was apparent that my conversation had interested the father in my behalf, and I was a fool in having exposed my person to the horror of his children. I ought to have familiarized the the old De Lacey to me, and, by degrees have discovered myself to the rest of his family, when they should have been prepared for my approach. But I did not believe my errors to be irretrieveable; and, after much consideration, I resolved to return to the cottage, seek the old man, and by my representations win him to my party.

"These thoughts calmed me, and in the afternoon I sank into a profound sleep; but the fever of my blood did not allow me to be visited by peaceful dreams. The horrible scene of the preceding day was for ever acting before my eyes; the females were flying, and the enraged Felix tearing me from his father's feet. I awoke exhausted; and, finding that it was already night, crept forth from my hiding-place, and went in search of food.

"When my hunger was appeased, I directed my steps toward the well-known path that conducted to the cottage. All there was at peace. I crept into my hovel, and remained in silent expectation of the accustomed hour when the family arose. That hour past, the sun mounted high in the heavens, but the cottagers did not appear. I trembled violently, apprehending some dreadful misfortune. The inside of the cottage was dark, and I heard no motion; I cannot describe the agony of this suspense.

"Presently two countrymen passed by; but, pausing near the cottage, they entered into conversation, using violent gesticulations; but I did not understand what they said, as they spoke the language of the country, which differed from that of my protectors. Soon after, however, Felix approached with another man: I was surprised, as I knew that he had not quitted the cottage that morning, and waited anxiously to discover, from his discourse, the meaning of these unusual appearances.

"'Do you consider,' said his companion

to him, 'that you will be obliged to pay three months' rent, and to lose the produce of your garden? I do not wish to take any unfair advantage, and I beg therefore that you will take some days to consider of your determination.'

"'It is utterly useless,' replied Felix, 'we can never again inhabit your cottage. The life of my father is in the greatest danger, owing to the dreadful circumstance that I have related. My wife and sister will never recover their horror. I entreat you not to reason with me any more. Take possession of your tenement, and let me fly from this place.'

"Felix trembled violently as he said this. He and his companion entered the cottage, in which they remained for a few minutes, and then departed. I never saw any of the family of De Lacey more.

I continued for the remainder of the day in my hovel in a state of utter and stupid despair. My protectors had departed, and had broken the only link that held me to the world. For the first time the feelings of revenge and hatred filled my bosom, and I did not strive to control them; but allowing myself to be borne away by the stream, I bent my mind towards injury and death. When I thought of my friends, of the mild voice of De Lacey, the gentle eyes of Agatha, and the exquisite beauty of the Arabian, these thoughts vanished, and a gush of tears somewhat soothed me. But again, when I reflected that they had spurned and deserted me, anger returned, a rage of anger: and, unable to injure anything human, I turned my fury towards inanimate objects. As night advanced, I placed a variety of combustibles around the cottage; and, after having destroyed every vestige of cultivation in the garden, I waited with forced impatience until the moon had sunk, to commence my operations.

"As the night advanced, a fierce wind arose from the woods, and quickly dispersed the clouds that had loitered in the heavens; the blast tore along like a mighty avalanche, and produced a kind of insanity in my spirits, that burst all bounds of reason and reflection. I lighted the dry branch of a tree, and danced with fury around the devoted cottage, my eyes still fixed on the western horizon, the edge of which the moon nearly touched. A part of its orb was at length hid, and I waived my brand; it sunk, and with a loud scream I fired the straw, and heath, and bushes, which I had collected. The wind fanned the fire, and the cottage was quickly enveloped by the flames, which clung to it, and licked it with their forked and destroying tongues.

"As soon as I was convinced that no assistance could save any part of the habitation, I quitted the scene, and sought for refuge in the woods.

"And now, with the world before me, whither should I bend my steps? I resolved to fly far from the scene of my misfortunes: but to me, hated and despised, every country must be equally horrible. At length the thought of you crossed my mind. I learned from your papers that you were my father, my creator; and to whom could I apply with more fitness than to him who had given me life? Among the lessons that Felix had bestowed upon Safie geography had not been omitted; I had learned from these the relative situations of the different countries of the earth. You had mentioned Geneva as the name of your native town; and towards this place I resolved to proceed.

"But how was I to direct myself? I knew that I must travel in a south westerly direction to reach my destination; but the sun was my only guide. I did not know the names of the towns that I was to pass through, nor could I ask information from a single human being; but I did not despair. From you only could I hope for succor, although towards you I felt no sentiment but that of hatred. Unfeeling, heartless creator! you had endowed me with perceptions and passions, and then cast me abroad an object for the scorn and horror of mankind. But on you only had I any claim for pity and redress, and from you I determined to seek that justice which I vainly attempted to gain from any other being that wore the human form.

"My travels were long, and the sufferings I endured intense. It was late in autumn when I quitted the district where I had so long resided. I travelled only at night, fearful of encountering the visage of a human being. Nature decayed around me, and the sun became heatless; rain and snow poured around me; mighty rivers were frozen; the surface of the earth was hard, and chill, and bare, and I found no shelter. Oh, earth! how often did I imprecate curses on the cause of my being! The mildness of my nature had fled, and all within me was turned to gall and bitterness. The nearer I approached to your habitation, the more deeply did I feel the spirit of revenge enkindled in my heart. Snow fell, and the waters were hardened, but I rested not. A few incidents now and then directed me, and I possessed a map of the country; but I often wandered wide from my path. The agony of my feelings allowed me no respite; no incident occurred from which my rage and misery could not extract its food; but a circumstance that happened when I arrived on the confines of Switzerland, when the sun had recovered its warmth, and the earth again began to look green, confirmed in an especial manner the bitterness and horror of my feelings.

"I generally rested during the day, and travelled only when I was secured by night from the view of man. One morning, however, finding that my path lay through a deep wood, I ventured to continue my journey after the sun had risen; the day, which was one of the first of spring, cheered even me by the loveliness of its sunshine and the balminess of the air. I felt emotions of gentleness and pleasure that had long appeared dead, revive within me. Half surprised by the novelty of these sensations, I allowed myself to be borne away by them; and, forgetting my solitude and deformity, dared to be happy. Soft tears again bedewed my cheeks, and I even raised my humid eyes with thankfulness towards the blessed sun, which bestowed such joy upon me.

"I continued to wind among the paths of the wood, until I came its boundary, which was skirted by a deep and rapid river, into which many of the trees bent their branches, now budding with the fresh spring. Here I paused, not exactly knowing what path to pursue, when I heard the sound of voices, that induced me to conceal myself under the shade of a cypress. I was scarcely hid, when a young girl came running towards the spot where I was concealed, laughing as if she ran from some one in sport. She continued her course along the precipitous sides of the river, when suddenly her foot slipt, and she fell into the rapid stream. I rushed from my hiding place, and, with extreme labor from the force of the current, saved her, and dragged her to shore. She was senseless; and I endeavored, by every means in my power, to restore animation, when I was suddenly interrupted by the approach of a rustic, who was probably the person from whom she had playfully fled. On seeing me, he darted towards me, and, tearing the girl from my arms, hastened towards the deeper parts of the wood. I followed speedily, I hardly knew why; but when the man saw me draw near, he aimed a gun, which he carried, at my body, and fired. I sunk to the ground, and my injurer, with increased swiftness, escaped into the wood.

"This was then the reward of my benevolence! I had saved a human being from destruction, and, as a recompense, I now writhed under the pain of a wound, which shattered the flesh and bone. The feelings of kindness and gentleness, which I had entertained but a few moments before, gave place to hellish rage and gnashing of teeth. Inflamed by pain, I vowed eternal hatred and vengeance to all mankind. But the agony of my wound overcame me: my pulses paused, and I fainted.

"For some weeks I led a miserable life in the woods, endeavoring to cure the wound which I had received. The ball had entered my shoulder, and I knew not whether it had remained there or passed through; at any rate I had no means of extracting it. My sufferings were augmented also by the oppressive sense of the injustice aud ingratitude of their infliction. My daily vows rose for revenge, such as would alone compensate for the outrages and anguish I had endured.

"After some weeks my wound healed, and I continued my journey. The labors I endured were no longer to be alleviated by the bright sun or gentle breezes of spring: all joy was but a mockery, which insulted my desolate state, and made me feel more painfully that I was not made for the enjoyment of pleasure.

But my toils now drew near a close; and, two months from this time I reached the environs of Geneva.

"It was evening when I arrived, and I retired to a hiding place among the fields that surround it, to meditate in what manner I should apply to you. I was oppressed by fatigue and hunger, and far too unhappy to enjoy the gentle breezes of evening, or the prospect of the sun setting behind the stupendous mountains of Jura.

"At this time a slight sleep relieved me from the pain of reflection, which was disturbed by the approach of a beautiful child, who came running into the recess I had chosen with all the sportiveness of infancy. Suddenly, as I gazed on him, an idea seized me, that this little creature was unprejudiced, and had lived too short a time to have imbibed a horror of deformity. If therefore, I could seize him, and educate him as my companion and friend, I should not be so desolate in this peopled earth.

"Urged by this impulse, I seized on the boy as he passed, and drew him towards me. As soon as he beheld my form, he placed his hands before his eyes and uttered a shrill scream: I drew his hand forcibly from his face, and said, 'Child what is the meaning of this? I do not intend to hurt you; listen to me."

"He struggled violently; 'Let me go,' he cried; 'monster! ugly wretch! you wish to eat me, and tear me to pieces—You are an ogre—Let me go, or I will tell my papa.'

"'Boy, you will never see you father again; you must come with me.'

"'Hideous monster! let me go; my papa is a Syndic—he is M. Frankenstein; he would punish you. You dare not keep me.'

"'Frankenstein! you belong then to my enemy—to him towards whom I have sworn eternal revenge; you shall be my first victim.'

"The child still struggled, and loaded me with epithets which carried despair to my heart: I grasped his throat to silence him, and in a moment he lay dead at my feet.

"I gazed on my victim, and my heart swelled with exultation and hellish triumph: clapping my hands, I exclaimed, 'I, too, can create desolation; my enemy is not impregnable; this death will carry despair to him, and a thousand other miseries shall torment and destroy him.'

"As I fixed my eyes on the child, I saw something glittering on his breast. I took it; it was a portrait of a most lovely woman. In spite of my malignity, it softened and attracted me. For a few moments I gazed with delight on her dark eyes, fringed by deep lashes, and her lovely lips; but presently my rage returned: I remembered that I was for ever deprived of the delights that such beautiful creatures could bestow; and that she whose resemblance I contemplated would, in regarding me, have changed that air of divine benignity to one expressive of disgust and affright.

"Can you wonder that such thoughts transported me with rage? I only wonder that at that moment, instead of venting my sensations in exclamations and agony, I did not rush among mankind, and perish in the attempt to destroy them.

"While I was overcome by these feelings, I left the spot where I had committed the murder, and was seeking a more secluded hiding place, when I perceived a young woman passing near me. She was young, not, indeed, so beautiful as her whose portrait I held, but of an agreeable aspect, and blooming in the loveliness of youth and health. Here, I thought, is one of those whose smiles are bestowed on all but me; she shall not escape: thanks to the lessons of Felix, and the sanguinary laws of man, I have learned how to work mischief. I approached her unperceived, and placed the portrait securely in one of the folds of her dress.

"For some days I haunted the spot where these had taken place; sometimes wishing to see you, sometimes resolved to quit the world and its miseries for ever. At length I wandered toward these mountains, and have ranged through their immense recesses, consumed by a burning passion which you alone can gratify. We may not part until you have promised to comply with my requisition. I am alone, and miserable; man will not associate with me; but one as deformed and horrible as myself would not deny herself to me. My companion must be of the same species, and have the same defects. This being you must create."

CHAPTER XVI.

The being finished speaking, and fixed his looks upon me in expectation of a reply. But I was bewildered, perplexed, and unable to arrange my ideas sufficiently to understand the full extent of his proposition. He continued—

"You must create a female for me, with whom I can live in the interchange of those sympathies necessary for my being. This you alone can do; and I demand it as a right which you must not refuse."

The latter part of his tale had kindled anew in me the anger that had died away while he narrated his peaceful life among the cottages, and, as he said this, I could no longer suppress the rage that burned within me.

"I do refuse it," I replied; "and no torture shall ever extort a consent from me. You may render me the most miserable of men, but you shall never make me base in my own eyes. Shall I create another like yourself, whose joint wickedness might desolate the world? Begone! I have answered you; you may torture me, but I will never consent."

"You are in in the wrong," replied the fied; "and, instead of threatening, I content to reason with you. I am malicious because I am miserable; am I not shunned and hated by all mankind? You, my creator, would tear me to pieces, and triumph; remember that, and tell me why I should pity man more than man pities me? You would not, certainly, call it murder, if you could precipitate me into one of those ice-rifts, and destroy my frame, the work of your own hands. Shall I respect the man, when he contemns me? Let him live with me in the interchange of kindness, and, instead of injury, I would bestow every benefit upon him, with tears of gratitude at his acceptance. But that cannot be; the human senses are insurmountable barriers to our union. Yet mine shall not be the submission of abject slavery. I will revenge my injuries: if I cannot inspire love, I will cause fear; and chiefly towards you, my arch-enemy, because my creator, do I swear inextinguishable hatred. Have a care: I will work at your destruction, nor finish until I desolate your heart, so that you curse the hour of your birth."

A fiendish rage animated him as he said this; his face was wrinkled into contortions too horrible for human eyes to behold; but presently he calmed himself, and proceeded:

"I intended to reason. This passion is detrimental to me; for you do not reflect that you are the cause of its excess. If any being felt emotions of benevolence towards me, I should return them an hundred and an hundred fold; for that one creature's sake, I would make peace with the whole kind! But I now indulge in dreams of bliss that cannot be realised. What I ask of you is reasonable and moderate; I demand a creature of another sex, but as hideous as myself: the gratification is small, but it is all that I can receive, and it shall content me. It is true, we shall be monsters, cut off from all the world; but on that account we shall be more attached to one another. Our lives will not be happy, but they will be harmless, and free from the misery I now feel. Oh! my creator, make me happy; let me feel gratitude towards you for one benefit! Let me see that I excite the sympathy of some existing thing; do not deny me my request!"

I was moved. I shuddered when I thought of the possible consequences of my consent; but I felt that there was some justice in his argument. His tale, and the feelings he now expressed, proved him to be a creature of fine sensations; and did I not, as his maker, owe him all the portion of happiness that it was in my power to bestow? He saw my change of feeling, and continued:

"If you consent, neither you nor any other human being shall ever see us again: I will go to the vast wilds of South America. My food is not that of man; I do not destroy the lamb and the kid, to glut my appetite; acorns and berries afford me sufficient nourishment. My companion will be of the same nature as myself, and will be content with the same fare. We shall make our bed of dried leaves; the sun will shine on us as on man, and will ripen our food. The picture I present to you is peaceful and human, and you must feel that you could deny it only in the wantonness of power and cruelty. Pitiless as you have been towards me, I now see compassion in your eyes; let me seize the favorable moment, and persuade you to promise what I so ardently desire."

"You propose," replied I, "to fly from the habitations of man, to dwell in those wilds where the beasts of the field will be your only companions. How can you, who long for the love and sympathy of man, persevere in this exile? You will return, and again seek their kindness, and you will meet with their detestation; your evil passions will be renewed, and you will then have a companion to aid you in the task of destruction. This may not be; cease to argue the point, for I cannot consent."

"How inconstant are your feelings! But a moment ago you were moved by my representations, and why do you again harden yourself to my complaints? I swear to you, by the earth which I inhabit, and by you that made me, that, with the companion you bestow, I will quit the neighborhood of man, and dwell, as it may chance, in the most savage of places. My evil passions will have fled, for I shall meet with sympathy; my life will flow quietly away, and, in my dying moments, I shall not curse my maker."

His words had a strange effect upon me. I compassionated him, and sometimes felt a wish to console him; but when I looked upon him, when I saw the filthy mass that moved and talked, my heart sickened, and my feelings were altered to those of horror and hatred. I tried to stifle these sensations; I thought, that as I could not sympathize with him, I had no right to withhold from him the small portion of happiness which was yet in my power to bestow.

"You swear," I said, "to be harmless; but have you not already shown a degree of malice that should reasonably make me distrust you? May not even this be a feint that will increase your triumph by affording a wider scope for your revenge?"

"How is this? I thought I had moved your compassion, and yet you still refuse to bestow on me the only benefit that can soften my heart, and render me harmless. If I have no ties and no affections, hatred and vice must be my portion; the love of another will destroy the cause of my crimes, and I shall become a thing of whose existence every one will be ignorant. My vices are the children of a forced solitude that I abhor; and my virtues will necessarily arise when I live in communion with an equal. I shall feel the affections of a sensitive being, and become linked to the chain of existence and events, from which I am now excluded."

I paused some time to reflect on all he had related, and the various arguments which he had employed. I thought of the promise of virtues which he had displayed on the opening of his existence, and the subsequent blight of all kindly feeling by the loathing and scorn which his protectors had manifested towards him. His power and threats were not omitted in my calculations: a creature who could exist in the ice-caves of the glaciers, and hide himself from pursuit among the ridges of inaccessible precipices, was a being possessing faculties it would be vain to cope with. After a long pause of reflection, I concluded, that the justice due both to him and my fellow-creatures demanded of me that I should comply with his request. Turning to him, therefore, I said:

"I consent to your demand, on your solemn oath to quit Europe for ever, and every other place in the neighborhood of man, as soon as I shall deliver into your hands a female who will accompany you in your exile."

"I swear," he cried, "by the sun, and by the blue sky of heaven, that if you grant my prayer, while they exist you shall never behold me again. Depart to your home, and commence your labors: I shall watch their progress with unutterable anxiety; and fear not but that when you are ready I shall appear."

Saying this, he suddenly quitted me, fearful, perhaps, of any change in my sentiments. I saw him descend the mountain with greater speed than the flight of an eagle, and quickly lost him among the undulations of the sea of ice.

His tale had occupied the whole day; and the sun was upon the verge of the horison when he departed. I knew that I ought to hasten my descent towards the valley, as I should soon be encompassed in darkness; but my heart was heavy and my steps slow. The labor of winding among the little paths of the mountains, and fixing my feet firmly as I advanced, perplexed me, occupied as I was by the emotions which the occurrences of the day had produced. Night was far advanced, when I came to the half-way resting-place, and seated myself beside the fountain. The stars shone at intervals, as the clouds passed from over them; the dark pines rose before me, and every here and there a broken tree lay on the ground: it was a scene of wonderful solemnity, and stirred strange thoughts within me. I wept bitterly; and clasping my hands in agony, I exclaimed, "Oh! stars, and clouds, and winds, ye are all about to mock me: if ye really pity me, crush sensation and memory; let me become as nought; but if not, depart, depart, and leave me in darkness."

These were wild and miserable thoughts; but I cannot describe to you how the eternal twinkling of the stars weighed upon me, and how I listened to every blast of wind, as if it were a dull ugly siroc on its way to consume me.

Morning dawned before I arrived at the village of Chamounix; but my presence, so haggard and strange, hardly calmed the fears of my family, who had waited the whole night in anxious expectation of my return.

The following day we returned to Geneva. The intention of my father in coming had been to divert my mind, and to restore my lost tranquillity; but the medicine had been fatal. And, unable to account for the excess of misery I appeared to suffer, he hastened to return home, hoping the quiet and monotony of a domestic life would by degrees alleviate my sufferings, from whatever cause they might spring.

For myself, I was passive in all their arrangements; and the gentle affection of my beloved Elizabeth was inadequate to draw me from the depth of my despair. The promise I had made to the dæmon weighed upon my mind, like Dante's iron cowl on the heads of the hellish hypocrites. All my pleasures of earth and sky passed before me like a dream, and that thought only had to me the reality of life. Can you wonder, that sometimes a kind of insanity possessed me, or that I saw continually about me a multitude of filthy animals inflicting on me incessant torture, that often extorted screams and bitter groans?

By degrees, however, these feelings became calmed. I entered again into the every-day scene of life, if not with interest, at least with some degree of tranquillity.

CHAPTER XVII.

Day after day, week after week, passed away on my return to Geneva; and I could not collect the courage to recommence my work. I feared the vengeance of the disappointed fiend, yet I was unable to overcome my repugnance to the task which was enjoined me. I found that I could not compose a female without again devoting several months to profound study and laborious disquisition. I had heard of some discoveries having been made by an English philosopher, the knowledge of which was material to my success, and I sometimes thought of obtaining my father's consent to visit England for this purpose; but I clung to every pretence of delay, and could not resolve to interrupt my returning tranquillity. My health, which had hitherto declined, was now much restored; and my spirits, when unchecked by the memory of my unhappy promise, rose proportionably. My father saw this change with pleasure, and he turned his thoughts towards the best method of eradicating the remains of my melancholy, which every now and then would return by fits, and with a devouring blackness overcast the approaching sunshine. At these moments I took refuge in the most perfect solitude. I passed whole days on the lake alone in a little boat, watching the clouds, and listening to the rippling of the waves, silent and listless. But the fresh air and bright sun seldom failed to restore me to some degree of composure; and, on my return, I met the salutations of my friends with a readier smile and a more cheerful heart.

It was after my return from one of these rambles that my father, calling me aside, thus addressed me:

"I am happy to remark, my dear son, that you have resumed your former pleasures, and seem to be returning to yourself. And yet you are still unhappy, and still avoid our society. For some time I was lost in conjecture as to the cause of this but yesterday an idea struck me, and if it is well founded, I conjure you to avow it. Reserve on such a point would be not only useless, but draw down treble misery on us all."

I trembled violently at this exordium, and my father continued—

"I confess, my son, that I have always looked forward to your marriage with your cousin as the tie of our domestic comfort, and the stay of my declining years. You were attached to each other from your earliest infancy; you studied together, and appeared, in dispositions and tastes, entirely suited to one another. But so blind is the experience of man, that what I conceived to be the best assistants to my plan may have entirely destroyed it. You, perhaps, regard her as your sister, without any wish that she might become your wife. Nay, you may have met with another whom you may love; and, considering yourself as bound in honor to your cousin, this struggle may occasion the poignant misery which you appear to feel."

"My dear father, re-assure yourself. I love my cousin tenderly and sincerely. I never saw any woman who excited, as Elizabeth does, my warmest admiration and affection. My future hopes and prospects are entirely bound up in the expectation of our union."

"The expression of your sentiments on this subject, my dear Victor, gives me more pleasure than I have for some time experienced. If you feel this, we shall assuredly be happy, however present events may cast a gloom over us. But it is this gloom, which appears to have taken so strong a hold of your mind, that I wish to dissipate. Tell me, therefore, whether you object to an immediate solemnization of the marriage. We have been unfortunate, and recent events have drawn us from that every-day tranquillity befitting my years and infirmities. You are younger; yet I do not suppose, possessed as you are, of a competent fortune, that an early marriage would at all interfere with any future plans of honor and utility that you may have formed. Do not suppose, however, that I wish to dictate happiness to you, or that a delay on your part would cause me any serious uneasiness. Interpret my words with candor, and answer me, I conjure you, with confidence and sincerity."

I listened to my father in silence, and remained for some time incapable of offering any reply. I revolved rapidly in my mind a multitude of thoughts, and endeavored to arrive at some conclusion. Alas! to me the idea of an immediate union with my cousin was one of horror and dismay. I was bound by a solemn promise, which I had not yet fulfilled, and dared not break; or, if I did, what manifold miseries might not impend over me and my devoted family! Could I enter into a festival with this deadly weight yet hanging round my neck, and bowing me to the ground? I must perform my engagement, and let the monster depart with his mate, before I allowed myself to enjoy the delight of an union from which I expected peace.

I remembered also the necessity imposed upon me of either journeying to England, or entering into a long correspondence with those philosophers of that country, whose knowledge and discoveries were of indispensable use to me in my present undertaking. The latter method of obtaining the desired intelligence was dilatory and unsatisfactory: besides, any variation was agreeable to me, and I was delighted with the idea of spending a year or two in change of scene and variety of occupation, in absence from my family; during which period some event might happen which would restore me to them in peace and happiness: my promise might be fulfilled, and the monster have departed; or some accident might occur to destroy him, and put an end to my slavery for ever.

These feelings dictated my answer to my father. I expressed a wish to visit England; but, concealing the true reasons of this request, I clothed my desires under the guise of wishing to travel and see the world before I sat down for life within the walls of my native town.

I urged my entreaty with earnestness, and my father was easily induced to comply; for a more indulgent and less dictatorial parent did not exist upon earth. Our plan was soon arranged. I should travel to Strasburgh, where Clerval would join me. Some short time would be spent in the towns of Holland, and our principal stay would be in England. We should return by France; and it was agreed that the tour should occupy the space of two years.

My father pleased himself with the reflection, that my union with Elizabeth should take place immediately on my return to Geneva. "These two years," said he, "will pass swiftly, and it will be the last delay that will oppose itself to your happiness. And, indeed, I earnestly desire that period to arrive, when we shall all be united, and neither hopes or fears arise to disturb our domestic calm."

"I am content," I replied, "with your arrangement. By that time we shall both have become wiser, and I hope happier, than we at present are." I sighed; but my father kindly forbore to question me further concerning the cause of my dejection. He hoped that new scenes, and the amusement of travelling, would restore my tranquillity.

I now made arrangements for my journey; but one feeling haunted me, which filled me with fear and agitation. During my absence I should leave my friends unconscious of the existence of their enemy, and unprotected from his attacks, exasperated as he might be by my departure. But he had promised to follow me wherever I might go; and would he not accompany me to England? This imagination was dreadful in itself, but soothing, inasmuch as it supposed the safety of my friends. I was agonized with the idea of the possibility that the reverse of this might happen. But through the whole period during which I was the slave of my creature, I allowed myself to be governed by the impulses of the moment; and my present sensations strongly intimated that the fiend would follow me, and exempt my family from the danger of his machinations.

It was in the latter end of August that I departed, to pass two years of exile. Elizabeth approved of the reasons of my departure, and only regretted that she had not the same opportunities of enlarging her experience, and cultivating her understanding. She wept, however, as she bade me farewell, and entreated me to return happy and tranquil. "We all," said she, "depend upon you; and if you are miserable, what must be our feelings?"

I threw myself into the carriage that was to convey me away, hardly knowing whither I was going, and careless of what was passing around. I remembered only, and it was with a bitter anguish that I reflected on it, to order that my chemical instruments should be packed to go with me; for I resolved to fulfil my promise while abroad, and return, if possible, a free man. Filled with dreary imaginations, I passed through many beautiful and majestic scenes; but my eyes were fixed and unobserving. I could only think of the bourne of my travels, and the work which was to occupy me while they endured.

After some days spent in listless indolence, during which I traversed many leagues, I arrived at Strasburgh, where I waited two days for Clerval. He came. Alas, how great was the contrast between us! He was alive to every new scene; joyful when he saw the beauties of the setting sun, and more happy when he beheld it rise, and recommence a new day. He pointed out to me the shifting colors of the landscape, and the appearances of the sky. "This is what it is to live;" he cried, "now I enjoy existence! But you, my dear Frankenstein, wherefore are you desponding and sorrowful?" In truth, I was occupied by gloomy thoughts, and neither saw the descent of the evening star, nor the golden sun-rise reflected in the Rhine. And you, my friend, would be far more amused with the journal of Clerval, who observed the scenery with an eye of feeling and delight, than to listen to my reflections. I, a miserable wretch, haunted by a cure that shut up every avenue to enjoyment.

We had agreed to descend the Rhine in a boat from Strasburgh to Rotterdam, whence we might take shipping for London. During this voyage, we wassed by many willowy islands, and saw several beautiful towns. We staid a day at Manheim, and, on the fifth from our departure from Strasburgh, arrived at Mayence. The course of the Rhine below the Mayence becomes much more picturesque. The river descends rapidly, and winds between hills, not high, but steep, and of beautiful forms. We saw many ruined castles standing on the edges of precipices, surrounded by black woods, high and inaccessible. This part of the Rhine, indeed, presents a singularly variegated landscape. In one spot you view rugged hills, ruined castles overlooking tremendous precipices, with the dark Rhine rushing beneath; and, on the sudden turn of a promontory, flourishing vineyards, with green sloping banks, and a meandering river, and populous towns, occupy the scene.

We travelled at the time of the vintage, and heard the song of the laborers, as we glided down the stream. Even I, depressed in mind, and my spirits continually agitated by gloomy feelings, even I was pleased. I lay at the bottom of the boat, and, as I gazed on the cloudless blue sky, I seemed to drink in a tranquillity to which I had long been a stranger. And if these were my sensations, who can describe those of Henry? He felt as if he had been transported to Fairy-land, and enjoyed a happiness seldom tasted by man. "I have seen," he said, "the most beautiful scenes of my own country; I have visited the lakes of Lucerne and Uri, where the snowy movntains descend almost perpendicularly to the water, casting black and impenetrable shades, which would cause a gloomy and mournful appearance, were it not for the most verdant islands that relieve the eye by their gay appearance; I have seen this lake agitated by a tempest, when the wind tore up whirlwinds of water, and gave you an idea of what the water-spout must be on the great ocean, and the waves dash with fury the base of the mountain, where the priest and his mistress were overwhelmed by an avalanche, and where their dying voices are still said to be heard amid the pauses of the nightly wind; I have seen the mountains of La Valais, and the Pays de Vaud: but this country, Victor, pleases me more than all those wonders. The mountains of Switzerland are more majestic and strange; but there is a charm in the banks of this divine river, that I never before saw equalled. Look at that castle which overhangs yon precipice; and also that on the island, almost concealed among the foliage of those lovely trees; and now that group of laborers coming from among their vines; and that village half-hid in the recess of the mountain. Oh, surely, the spirit that inhabits and guards this place has a soul more in harmony with man, than those who pile the glacier, or retire to the inaccessible peaks of the mountains of our own country."

Clerval! beloved friend! even now it delights me to record your words, and to dwell on the praise of which you are so eminently deserving. He was a being formed in the "very poetry of nature."* His wild and enthusiastic imagination was chastened by the sensibility of his heart. His soul overflowed with ardent affections, and his friendship was of that devoted and wondrous nature that the worldly-minded teach us to look for only in the imagination. But even human sympathies were not sufficient to satisfy his eager mind. The scenery of external nature, which others regard only with admiration, he loved with ardor:

> ————————" The sounding cataract
> Haunted him like a passion; the tall rock,
> The mountain, and the deep and gloomy wood,
> Their colors and their forms, were then to him
> An appetite; a feeling, and a love.
> That had no need of a remoter charm,
> By thought supplied, or any interest
> Unborrowed from the eye."†

And where does he now exist? Is this gentle and lovely being lost forever? Has this mind so replete wlth ideas, imaginations fanciful and magnificent, which formed a world, whose existence depended on the life of its creator; has this mind perished? Does it now only exist in my memory? No, it is not thus; your form so divinely wrought, and beaming with beauty, has decayed, but your spirit still visits and consoles your unhappy friend.

Pardon this gush of sorrow; these ineffectual words are but a slight tribute to the unexampled worth of Henry, but they sooth my heart, overflowing with the anguish which his remembrance creates. I will proceed with my tale.

Beyond Cologne we descended to the plains of Holland; and we resolved to post the remainder of our way; for the wind was contrary, and the stream of the river was too gentle to aid us.

Our journey here lost the interest arising from beautiful scenery; but we arrived in a few days at Rotterdam, whence we proceeded by sea to England. It was on a clear morning, in the latter days of December, that I first saw the white cliffs of Britain. The banks of the Thames presented a new scene; they were flat but fertile, and almost every town was marked by the remembrance of some story. We saw Tilbury Fort, and remembered the Spanish armada; Gravesend, Woolwich, and Greenwich, places which I had heard of even in my country.

At length we saw the numerous steeples of London, St. Paul's towering above all, and the Tower famed in English history.

CHAPTER XVIII.

LONDON was our present point of rest; we determined to remain several months in this wonderful and celebrated city. Clerval desired the intercourse of the men of genius and talent who flourished at this time; but this was with me a secondary object; I was principally occupied with the means of obtaining the information necessary for the completion of my promise, and quickly availed myself of the letters of introduction that I had brought with me, addressed to the most distinguished natural philosophers.

If this journey had taken place during my days of study and happiness, it would

*Leigh Hunt's "Rimini."
†Wadsworth's "Tintern Abbey."

have afforded me inexpressible pleasure. But a blight had come over my existence, and I only visited these people for the sake of the information they might give me on the subject in which my interest was so terribly profound. Company was irksome to me; when alone, I could fill my mind with the sights of heaven and earth; the voice of Henry soothed me, and I could thus cheat myself into a transitory peace. But busy, uninteresting, joyous faces brought back despair to my heart. I saw an insurmountable barrier placed between me and my fellow-men; this barrier was sealed with the blood of William and Justine; and to reflect on the events connected with those names, filled my soul with anguish.

But in Clerval I saw the image of my former self; he was inquisitive, and anxious to gain experience and instruction. The difference of manners which he observed was to him an inexhaustible source of instruction and amusement. He was for ever busy; and the only check to his enjoyments was my sorrowful and dejected mien. I tried to conceal this as much as possible, that I might not debar him from the pleasures natural to one who was entering on a new scene of life, undisturbed by any care or bitter reflection. I often refused to accompany him, alleging another engagement, that I might remain alone. I now also began to collect the materials necessary for my new creation, and this was to me like the torture of single drops of water continually falling on the head. Every thought that was devoted to it was an extreme anguish, and every word that I spoke in allusion to it, caused my lips to quiver, and my heart to palpitate.

After passing some months in London, we received a letter from a person in Scotland, who had formerly been our visiter at Geneva. He mentioned the beauties of his native country, and asked us if those were not sufficient allurements to induce us to prolong our journey as far north as Perth, where he resided. Clerval eagerly desired to accept this invitation; and I, although I abhorred society, wished to view again the mountains and streams, and all the wondrous works with which Nature adorns her chosen dwelling-places.

We had arrived in England at the beginning of January, and it was now February. We accordingly determined to commence our journey towards the north at the expiration of another month. In this expedition we did not intend to follow the great road to Edinburgh, but to visit Windsor, Oxford, Matlock, and the Cumberland lakes, resolving to arrive at the completion of this tour about the end of July. I packed my chemical instruments, and the materials I had collected, resolving to finish my labors in some obscure nook in the northern highlands of Scotland.

We quitted London on the 27th of March, and remained a few days at Windsor, rambling in its beautiful forest. This was a new scene to us mountaineers; the majestic oaks, the quantity of game, and the herds of stately deer, were all novelties to us.

From thence we proceeded to Oxford. As we entered this city, our minds were filled with the remembrance of the events that had been transacted there more than a century and a half before. It was here that Charles I. had collected his forces. This city had remained faithful to him, after the whole nation had forsaken his cause to join the standard of parliament and liberty. The memory of that unfortunate king, and his companions, the amiable Falkland, the insolent Gower, his queen, and son, gave a peculiar interest to every part of the city, which they might be supposed to have inhabited. The spirit of elder days found a dwelling here, and we delighted to trace its footsteps. If these feelings had not found an imaginary gratification, the appearance of the city had yet in itself sufficient beauty to obtain our admiration. The colleges are ancient and picturesque; the streets are almost magnificent; and the lovely Isis, which flows beside it through meadows of exquisite verdure, is spread forth into a placid expanse of waters, which reflects its majestic assemblage of towers, and spires, and domes, embossed among aged trees.

I enjoyed this scene; and yet my enjoyment was embittered both by the memory of the past, and the anticipation of the future. I was formed for peaceful happiness. During my youthful days, discontent never visited my mind; and if I was ever overcome by *ennui*, the sight of what is beautiful in nature, or the study of what is excellent and sublime in the productions of man, could always interest my heart, and communicate elasticity to my spirits. But I am a blasted tree; the bolt has entered my soul: and I felt then that I should survive to exhibit, what I shall soon cease to be—a miserable spectacle of wrecked humanity, pitiable to others, and abhorrent to myself.

We passed a considerable period at Oxford, rambling among its environs, and endeavoring to identify every spot which might relate to the most animating epoch of English history. Our little voyages of discovery were often prolonged by the successive objects that presented themselves. We visited the tomb of the illustrious Hampden, and the field on which that patriot fell. For a moment my soul was elevated from its debasing and miserable fears to contemplate the divine ideas of liberty and self-sacrifice, of which these sights were the monuments and the remembrances. For an instant I dared to shake off my chains, and look around me with a free and lofty spirit; but the iron had eaten into my flesh, and I sank again, trembling and hopeless, into my miserable self.

We left Oxford with regret, and proceeded to Matlock, which was our next place of rest. The country in the neighhood of this village resembled, to a greater degree, the scenery of Switzerland; but everything is on a lower scale, and the green hills want the crown of distant white Alps, which always attend on the piny mountains of my native country. We visited the wondrous cave, and the little cabinets of natural history, where the curiosities are disposed of in the same manner as in the collections at Servox and Chamounix. The latter name made me tremble, when pronounced by Henry; and I hastened to quit Matlock, with which that terrible scene was thus associated.

From Derby still journeying northward, we passed two months in Cumberland and Westmoreland. I could now almost fancy myself among the Swiss mountains. The little patches of snow which yet lingered on the northern sides of the mountains, the lakes, and the dashing of the rocky streams, were all familiar and dear sights to me. Here also we made some acquaintances, who almost contrived to cheat me into happiness. The delight of Clerval was proportionably greater than mine; his mind expanded in the company of men of talent, and he found in his own nature greater capacities and resources than he could have imagined himself to have possessed while he associated with his inferiors. "I could pass my life here," said he to me; "and among these mountains I should scarcely regret Switzerland and the Rhine."

But he found that a traveller's life is one that includes much pain amid its enjoyments. His feelings are forever on the stretch; and when he begins to sink into repose, he finds himself obliged to quit that on which he rests in pleasure for something new, which again engages his attention, and which also he forsakes for other novelties.

We had scarcely visited the various lakes of Cumberland and Westmoreland, and conceived an affection for some of the inhabitants, when the period of our appointment with our Scotch friend approached, and we left them to travel on. For my own part I was not sorry. I had now neglected my promise for sometime, and I feared the effects of the demon's disappointment. He might remain in Switzerland, and wreak his vengeance on my relatives. This idea pursued me, and tormented me at every moment from which I might otherwise have snatched repose and peace. I waited for my letters with feverish impatience: if they were delayed I was miserable, and overcome by a thousand fears; and when they arrived, and I saw the superscription of Elizabeth or my father, I hardly dared to read and ascertain my fate. Sometimes I thought that the fiend followed me, and might expedite my remissness by murdering my companion. When these thoughts possessed me, I would not quit Henry for a moment, but followed him as his shadow, to protect him from the fancied rage of his destroyer. I felt as if I had committed some great crime, the consciousness of which haunted me. I was guiltless, but I had indeed drawn a horrible curse upon my head, as mortal as that of crime.

I visited Edinburgh with languid eyes and mind; and yet that city might have interested the most unfortunate being. Clerval did not like it so well as Oxford; for the antiquity of the latter city was more pleasing to him. But the beauty and regularity of the new town of Edinburgh, its romantic castle, and its environs, the most delightful in the world, Arthur's Seat, St. Bernard's Well, and the Pentland Hills, compensated him for the change, and filled him with cheerfulness and admiration. But I was impatient to arive at the termination of my journey.

We left Edinburgh in a week, passed through Coupar, St. Andrews, and along the banks of the Tay, to Perth, where our friends expected us. But I was in no mood to laugh and talk with strangers, or enter into their feelings or plans with the good humor expected from a guest; and accordingly I told Clerval that I wished to make the tour of Scotland alone. "Do you," said I, "enjoy yourself, and let this be our rendezvous. I may be absent a month or two; but do not interfere with my motions, I entreat you: leave me to peace and solitude for a short time; and when I return, I hope it will be with a lighter heart, more congenial to your own temper."

Henry wished to dissuade me; but seeing me bent on this plan, ceased to remonstrate. He entreated me to write often. "I had rather be with you," he said, "in your solitary rambles, than wiih these Scotch people, whom I do not know: hasten, then, my dear friend, to return, that I may again feed myself somewhat at home, which I cannot do in your ab sence."

Having parted from my friend, I determined to visit some remote spot of Scotland, and finish my work in solitude. I did not doubt but that the monster followed me, and would discover himself to me when I should have finished, that he might receive his companion.

With this resolution I traversed the northern highlands, and fixed on one of the remotest Orkneys as the seene of my labors. It was a place fitted for such a work, being hardly more than a rock, whose high sides were continually beaten upon by the waves. The soil was barren, scarcely affording pasture for a few miserable cows, and oatmeal for its inhabitants, which consisted of five persons, whose gaunt and scraggy limbs gave tokens of their miserable fare. Vegetables and bread, when they indulged in such luxuries, and even fresh water, was to be procured from the main land, which was about five miles distant.

On the whole island there were but three miserable huts, and one of these was vacant when I arrived. This I hired. It contained but two rooms, and these exhibited all the squalidness of the most miserable penury. The thatch had fallen in, the walls were unplastered, and the door was off its hinges. I ordered it to be repaired, bought some furniture, and took possession; an incident which would, doubtless, have occasioned some surprise, had not all the senses of the cottagers been benumbed by want and squalid poverty. As it was, I lived ungazed at and unmolested, hardly thanked for the pittance of food and clothes which I gave; so much does suffering blunt even the coarsest sensations of men.

In this retreat I devoted the morning to labor; but in the evening, when the weather permitted, I walked on the stony beach of the sea, to listen to the waves as they roared, and dashed at my feet. It was a monotonous, yet ever-changing scene. I thought of Switzerland; it was far different from this desolate and appalling landscape. Its hills are covered with vines, and its cottages are scattered thickly in the plains. Its fair lakes reflect a blue and gentle sky; and when troubled by the winds, their tumult is but as the play of a lively infant, when compared to the roarings of the giant ocean.

In this manner I distributed my occupations when I first arrived; but, as I proceeded in my labor, it became every day more horrible and irksome to me. Sometimes I could not prevail on myself to enter my laboratory for several days; and at other times I toiled day and night in order to complete my work. It was indeed a filthy process in which I was engaged. During my first experiment, a kind of enthusiastic frenzy had blinded me to the horror of my employment; my mind was intently fixed on the sequel of my labor, and my eyes were shut to the horror of my proceedings. But now I went to it in cold blood, and my heart often sickened at the work of my hands.

Thus situated, employed in the most detestable occupation, immersed in a solitude where nothing could for an instant call my attention from the actual scene in which I was engaged, my spirits became unequal; I grew restless and nervous. Every moment I feared to meet my persecutor. Sometimes I sat with my eyes fixed on the ground, fearing to raise them lest they should encounter the object which I so much dreaded to behold. I feared to wander from the sight of my fellow-creatures, lest when alone he should come to claim his companion.

In the mean time I worked on, and my labor was already considerably advanced. I looked towards its completion with a tremulous and eager hope, which I dared not trust myself to question, but which was intermixed with obscure forebodings of evil, that made my heart sicken in my bosom.

CHAPTER XIV.

I sat one evening in my laboratory; the sun had set, and the moon was just rising from the sea; I had not sufficient light for my employment, and I remained idle in a pause of consideration of whether I should leave my labor for the night, or hasten its conclusion by an unremitting attention to it. As I sat, a train of reflection occurred to me, which led me to consider the effects of what I was now doing. Three years before I was engaged in the same manner, and had created a fiend whose unparalleled barbarity had desolated my heart, and filled it forever with the bitterest remorse. I was now about to form another being, of whose dispositions I was alike ignorant; she might become ten thousand times more malignant than her mate, and delight, for its own sake, in murder and wretchedness. He had sworn to quit the neighborhood of man, and hide himself in deserts; but she had not; and she, who in all probabiiity was to become a thinking and reasoning animal, might refuse to comply with a compact made before her creation. They might even hate each other; the creature who already lived loathed his own deformity, and might he not conceive a greater abhorrence for it when it came before his eyes in the female form? She also might turn with disgust from him to the superior beauty of man; she might quit him, and he be again alone, exasperated by the fresh provocation of being deserted by one of his own species.

Even if they were to leave Europe, and inhabit the deserts of the new world, yet one of the first results of those sympathies for which the dæmon thirsted would be children, and a race of devils would be propagated upon the earth, who might make the very existence of the species of man a condition precarious and full of terror. Had I right, for my own benefit, to inflict this curse upon everlasting generations? I had before been moved by the sophisms of the being I had created; I had been struck senseless by his fiendish threats; but now, for the first time, the wickedness of my promise burst upon me;

I shuddered to think that future ages might curse me as their pest, whose selfishness had not hesitated to buy its own peace at the price, perhaps, of the existence of the whole human race.

I trembled, and my heart failed within me; when, on looking up, I saw by the light of the moon, the dæmon at the casement. A ghastly grin wrinkled his lips as he gazed on me, where I sat fulfilling the task which he had allotted to me. Yes, he had followed me in my travels; he had loitered in forests, hid himself in caves, or taken refuge in wide and desert heaths; and he now came to mark my progress, and claim the fulfilment of my promise.

As I looked on him his countenance expressed the utmost extent of malice and treachery. I thought with a sensation of madness on my promise of creating another like to him, and, trembling with passion, tore to pieces the thing on which I was engaged. The wretch saw me destroy the creature on whose future existence he depended for happiness, and, with a howl of devilish despair and revenge withdrew.

I left the room, and locking the door, made a solemn vow in my own heart never to resume my labors; and then, with trembling steps, I sought my own apartment. I was alone; none were near me to dissipate the gloom, and relieve me from the sickening oppression of the most terrible reveries.

Several hours past, and I remained near my window gazing on the sea; it was almost motionless, for the winds were hushed, and all nature reposed under the eye of the quiet moon. A few fishing vessels alone specked the water, and now and then the gentle breeze wafted the sound of voices, as the fishermen called to one another. I felt the silence, although I was hardly conscious of its extreme profundity, until my ear was suddenly arrested by the paddling of oars near the shore, and a person landed close to my house.

In a few minutes after, I heard the creaking of my door, as if some one endeavored to open it softly. I trembled from head to foot; I felt a presentiment of who it was, and wished to rouse one of the peasants who dwelt in a cottage not far from mine; but I was overcome by the sensation of helplessness, so often felt in frightful dreams, when you in vain endeavor to fly from an impending danger, and was rooted to the spot.

Presently I heard the sound of footsteps along the passage; the door opened, and the wretch whom I dreaded appeared. Shutting the door, he approached me, and said, in a smothered voice—

"You have destroyed the work which you began; what is it you intend? Do you dare to break your promise? I have endured toil and misery; I left Switzerland with you; I crept along the shores of the Rhine, among its willow islands, and over the summits of its hills. I have dwelt many months in the heaths of England, and among the deserts of Scotland. I have endured incalculable fatigue, and cold, and hunger; do you dare destroy my hopes?"

"Begone! I do break my promise, never will I create another like yourself, equal in deformity and wickedness."

"Slave, I before reasoned with you, but you have proved yourself unworthy of my condescension. Remember that I have power; you believe yourself miserable, but I can make you so wretched that the light of day will be hateful to you. You are my creator, but I am your master; obey?"

"The hour of my weakness is past, and the period of your power is arrived. Your threats cannot move me to do an act of wickedness; but they confirm me in a resolution of not creating you a companion in vice. Shall I, in cool blood, set loose upon the earth a dæmon, whose delight is in death and wretchedness? Begone! I am firm, and your words will only exasperate my rage."

The monster saw my determination in my face, and gnashed his teeth in the impotence of anger. "Shall each man," cried he, "find a wife for his bosom, and each beast have his mate, and I be alone?

I had feelings of affection, and they were requited by detestation and scorn. Man, you may hate; but, beware! your hours will pass in dread and misery, and soon the bolt will fall which must ravish from you your happiness for ever. Are you to be happy, while I grovel in the intensity of my wretchedness? You can blast my other passions; but revenge remains—revenge, henceforth dearer than light or food! I may die; but first you, my tyrant and tormentor, shall curse the sun that gazes on your misery. Beware; for I am fearless, and therefore powerful. I will watch with the wiliness of a snake, that I may sting with its venom. Man, you shall repent of the injuries you inflict."

"Devil, cease; and do not poison the air with these sounds of malice. I have declared my resolution to you, and I am no coward to bend beneath words. Leave me; I am inexorable."

"It is well. I go; but remember, I shall be with you on your wedding-night."

I started forward, and exclaimed, "Villain! before you sign my death-warrant, be sure that you are yourself safe."

I would have seized him; but he eluded me, and quitted the house with precipitation: in a few moments I saw him in his boat, which shot across the waters with an arrowy swiftness, and was soon lost amid the waves.

All was again silent; but his words rung in my ears. I burned with rage to pursue the murderer of my peace, and precipitate him into the ocean. I walked up and down my room hastily and perturbed, while my imagination conjured up a thousand images to torment and sting me. Why had I not followed him, and closed with him in mortal strife? But I had suffered him to depart, and he had directed his course toward the main land. I shuddered to think who might be the next victim sacrificed to his insatiate revenge. And then I thought again of his words—"*I will be with you on your wedding-night.*" That then was the period for the fulfilment of my destiny. In that hour I should die, and at once satisfy and extinguish his malice. The prospect did not move me to fear; yet when I thought of my beloved Elizabeth—of her tears and endless sorrow, when she should find her lover so barbarously snatched from her—tears, the first I had shed for many months, streamed from my eyes, and I resolved not to fall before my enemy without a bitter struggle.

The night passed away, and the sun rose from the ocean; my feelings became calmer, if it may be called calmness, when the violence of rage sinks into the depth of despair. I left the house, the horrid scene of the last night's contention, and walked on the beach of the sea, which I almost regarded as an insuperable barrier between me and my fellow creatures; nay, a wish that such should prove the fact stole across me. I desired that I might pass my life on that barren rock, wearily, it is true, but uninterrupted by any sudden shock of misery. If I returned, it was to be sacrificed, or to see those whom I most loved die under the grasp of a dæmon whom I had myself created.

I walked about the isle like a restless spectre, separated from all it loved, and miserable in the separation. When it became noon, and the sun rose higher, I lay down on the grass, and was overpowered by a deep sleep. I had been awake the whole of the preceding night, my nerves were agitated, and my eyes inflamed by watching and misery. The sleep into which I now sunk refreshed me; and when I awoke, I again felt as if I belonged to a race of human beings like myself, and I began to reflect upon what had passed with greater composure; yet still the words of the fiend rung in my ears like a death-knell, they appeared like a dream, yet distinct and oppressive as a reality.

The sun had far descended, and I still sat on the shore, satisfying my appetite, which had become ravenous, with an oaten cake, when I saw a fishing boat land close to me, and one of the men brought me a packet; it contained letters from Geneva, and one from Clerval, entreating me to join him. He said that nearly a year had elapsed since we had quitted Switzerland, and France was yet unvisited. He entreated me, therefore, to leave my solitary isle, and meet him at Perth, in a week from that time, when we might arrange the plan of our future proceedings. This letter in a degree recalled me to life, and I determined to quit my island at the expiration of two days.

Yet before I departed, there was a task to perform, on which I shuddered to reflect: I must pack my chemical instruments; and for that purpose I must enter the room which had been the scene of my odious work, and I must handle those utensils, the sight of which was sickening to me. The next morning, at daybreak, I summoned sufficient courage, and unlocked the door of my laboratory. The remains of the half-finished creature, whom I had destroyed, lay scattered on the floor, and I almost felt as if I had mangled the living flesh of a human being. I paused to collect myself, and then entered the chamber. With trembling hand I conveyed the instruments out of the room; but I reflected that I ought not to leave the relics of my work to excite the horror and suspicion of the peasants, and I accordingly put them into a basket, with a great quantity of stones, and laying them up, determined to throw them into the sea that very night; and in the mean time I sat upon the beach, employed in cleaning and arranging my chemical apparatus.

Nothing could be more complete than the alteration that had taken place in my feelings since the night of the appearance of the dæmon. I had before regarded my promise with a gloomy despair, as a thing that, with whatever consequences, must be fulfilled; but I now felt as if a film had been taken from before my eyes, and that I, for the first time, saw clearly. The idea of renewing my labors did not for one instant occur to me; the threat I had heard weighed on my thoughts, but I did not reflect that a voluntary act of mine could avert it. I had resolved in my own mind, that to create another like the fiend I had first made would be an act of the basest and most atrocious selfishness; and I banished from my mind every thought that could lead to a different conclusion.

Between two and three in the morning the moon rose; and I then, putting my basket aboard a little skiff, sailed out about four miles from the shore. The scene was perfectly solitary: a few boats were returning towards land, but I sailed away from them. I felt as if I was about the commission of a dreadful crime, and avoided with shuddering anxiety any encounter with my fellow-creatures. At one time the moon, which had before been clear, was suddenly overspread by a thick cloud, and I took advantage of the moment of darkness, and cast my basket into the sea; I listened to the gurgling sound as it sunk, and then sailed away from the spot. The sky became clouded; but the air was pure, although chilled by the north-east breeze that was then rising. But it refreshed me, and filled me with such agreeable sensations, that I resolved to prolong my stay on the water, and fixing the rudder in a direct position, stretched myself at the bottom of the boat. Clouds hid the moon, every thing was obscure, and I heard only the sound of the boat as its keel cut through the waves; the murmur lulled me, and in a short time I slept soundly.

I do not know how long I remained in this situation, but when I awoke I found that the sun had already mounted considerably. The wind was high, and the waves continually threatened the safety of my little skiff. I found that the wind was northeast, and must have driven me far from the coast from which I had embarked. I endeavored to change my course, but quickly found that if I again made the attempt the boat would be instantly filled with water. Thus situated, my only resource was to drive before the wind. I confess that I felt a few sensations of terror. I had no compass with me, and was so little acquainted with the geography of this part of the world that the sun was of little benefit to me. I might be driven into the wide Atlantic, and feel all the tortures of starvation, or be swallowed up in the immeasurable waters that roared and buffeted around me. I had already been out many hours, and felt the torment of a burning thirst, a prelude to my other sufferings. I looked on the heavens, which were covered by clouds that flew before the wind only to be replaced by others: I looked upon the sea—it was to be my grave. "Fiend," I exclaimed, "your task is already fulfilled!" I thought of Elizabeth, of my father, and of Clerval; and sunk into a reverie, so despairing and frightful, that even now, when the scene is on the point of closing before me for ever, I shudder to reflect on it.

Some hours passed thus; but by degrees, as the sun declined towards the horizon, the wind died away into a gentle breeze, and the sea became free from breakers. But these gave place to a heavy swell; I felt sick, and hardly able to hold the rudder, when suddenly I saw a line of high land towards the south.

Although spent, as I was, by fatigue, and the dreadful suspense I endured for several hours, this sudden certainty of life rushed like a flood of warm joy to my heart, and tears gushed from my eyes.

How mutable are our feelings, and how strange is that clinging love we have of life, even in the excess of misery! I constructed another sail with a part of my dress, and eagerly steered my course towards the land. It had a wild and rocky appearance; but as I approached nearer, I easily perceived the traces of cultivation. I saw vessels near the shore, and found myself suddenly transported back to the neighborhood of civilized man. I eagerly traced the windings of the land, and hailed a steeple which I at length saw issuing from behind a small promontory. As I was in a state of extreme debility, I resolved to sail directly towards the town as a place where I could most easily procure nourishment. Fortunately I had money with me. As I turned the promontory, I perceived a small neat town and a good harbor, which I entered, my heart bounding with joy at my most unexpected escape. As I was occupied in fixing the boat and arranging the sails, several people crowded towards the spot. They seemed very much surprised at my appearance; but, instead of offering me any assistance, whispered together with gestures that at any other time might have produced in me a slight sensation of alarm. As it was, I merely remarked that they spoke English; and I therefore addressed them in that language: "My good friends," said I, "will you be so kind as to tell me the name of this town, and inform me where I am?"

"You will know that soon enough," replied a man with a gruff voice. "May be you are come to a place that will not prove much to your taste; but you will not be consulted as to your quarters, I promise you."

I was exceedingly surprised on receiving so rude an answer from a stranger; and I was also disconcerted on perceiving the frowning and angry countenances of his companions. "Why do you answer me so roughly?" I replied: "surely it is not the custom of Englishmen to receive strangers so inhospitably."

"I do not know," said the man "what the custom of the English may be; but it is the custom of the Irish to hate villains."

While this strange dialogue continued, I perceived the crowd rapidly increased. Their faces expressed a mixture of curiosity and anger, which annoyed, and in some degree alarmed me. I inquired the way to the inn; but no one replied. I then moved forward, and a murmuring sound arose from the crowd as they followed and surrounded me; when an ill-looking man approaching, tapped me on the shoulder, and said, "Come, Sir, you must follow me to Mr. Kirwin's to give an account of yourself."

"Who is Mr. Kirwin?" Why am I to give an account of myself? Is not this a free country?"

"Aye Sir, free enough for honest folks. Mr. Kirwin is a magistrate, and you are to give an account of the death of a gentleman who was found murdered here last night."

This answer startled me: but I presently recovered myself. I was innocent; that could easily be proved: accordingly I followed my conductor in silence, and was led to one of the best houses in the town. I was ready to sink from fatigue and hunger; but being surrounded by a crowd, I thought it politic to rouse all my strength, that no physical debility might be construed into apprehension or conscious guilt. Little did I then expect the calamity that was in a few moments to overwhelm me, and extinguish in horror and despair all fear of ignomy and death.

I must pause here; for it requires all my fortitude to recall the memory of the frightful events which I am about to relate in proper detail, to my recollection.

CHAPTER XV.

I WAS soon introduced into the presence of the magistrate, an old benevolent man, with calm and mild manners. He looked upon me, however, with some degree of severity, and then, turning towards my conductors, he asked who appeared as witnesses on this occasion.

About half a dozen men came forward; and one being selected by the magistrate, he deposed, that he had been out fishing the night before with his son and brother-in-law, Daniel Nugent, when about ten o'clock, they observed a strong northerly blast rising, and they accordingly put in for port. It was a very dark night, as the moon had not yet risen; they did not land at the harbor, but as they had been accustomed, at a creek about two miles below. He walked on first, carrying a part of the fishing tackle, and his companions followed him at some distance. As he was proceeding along the sands, he struck his foot against something, and fell all his length on the ground. His companions came up to assist him; and, by the light of their lantern they found that he had fallen on the body of a man who was to all appearance dead.

Their first supposition was, that it was the corpse of some person who had been drowned, and was thrown on shore by the waves; but, upon examination, they found that the clothes were not wet, and even that the body was not then cold. They instantly carried it to the cottage of an old woman near the spot, and endeavored, but in vain, to restore it to life. He appeared to be a handsome young man, about five and twenty years of age. He had apparently been strangled, for there was no sign of any violence, except the black mark of fingers on his neck.

The first part of this deposition did not in the least interest me, but when the mark of the fingers was mentioned, I remembered the murder of my brother, and felt myself extremely agitated; my limbs trembled, and a mist came over my eyes, which obliged me to lean on a chair for support. The magistrate observed me with a keen eye, and of course drew an unfavorable augury from my manner.

The son confirmed the father's account: but when Daniel Nugent was called, he swore positively, that, just before the fall of his companion, he saw a boat, with a single man in it, at a short distance from the shore; and, as far as he could judge by the light of a few stars, it was the same boat in which I had just landed.

A woman deposed, that she lived near the beach, and was standing at the door of her cottage, waiting for the return of the fishermen, about an hour before she heard of the discovery of the body, when she saw a boat, with only one man in it, push off from that part of the shore where the corpse was afterwards found.

Another woman confirmed the account of the fisherman having brought the body into her house; it was not cold. They put it into a bed, and rubbed it; and Daniel went to the town for an apothecary, but life was quite gone.

Several other men were examined concerning my landing; and they agreed, that with the strong north wind that had arisen during the night, it was very probable that I had beaten about for many hours, and had been obliged to return nearly to the same spot from which I had departed. Besides, they observed that it appeared that I had brought the body from another place, and it was likely, that as I did not appear to know the shore, I might have put into the harbor ignorant of the distance of the town of —— from the place where I had deposited the corpse.

Mr. Kirwin, on hearing this evidence, desired that I should be taken into the room where the body lay for interment, that it might be observed what effect the sight of it would produce upon me.

This idea was probably suggested by the extreme agitation I had exhibited when the mode of the murder had been described. I was accordingly conducted, by the magistrate and several other persons, to the inn. I could not help being struck by the strange coincidences that had taken place during this eventful night; but, knowing that I had been conversing with several persons in the island I had inhabited about the time that the body had been found, I was perfectly tranquil as to the consequences of the affair.

I entered the room where the corpse lay, and was led up to the coffin. How can I describe my sensations on beholding it? I feel yet parched with horror, nor can I reflect on that terrible moment without shuddering and agony, that faintly reminds me of the anguish of the recognition. The trial, the presence of the magistrate and witnesses, passed like a dream from my memory, when I saw the lifeless form of Henry Clerval stretched before me. I gasped for breath; and throwing myself on the body, I exclaimed, "Have my murderous machinations deprived you also, my dearest Henry, of life? Two I have already destroyed; other victims await their destiny: but you, Clerval, my friend, my benefactor,"——

The human frame could no longer support the agonizing suffering that I endured, and I was carried out of the room in strong convulsions.

A fever succeeded to this. I lay for two months on the point of death; my ravings, as I afterwards heard, were frightful; I called myself murderer of William, of Justine, and of Clerval. Sometimes I entreated my attendants to assist me in the destruction of the fiend by whom I was tormented; and, at others, I felt the fingers of the monster grasping my neck, and I screamed aloud with agony and terror. Fortunately, as I spoke, my native language, Mr. Kirwin alone understood me; but my gestures and bitter cries were sufficient to affright the other witnesses.

Why did I not die? More miserable than man ever was before, why did I not sink into forgetfulness and rest? Death snatches away many blooming children, the only hopes of their doating parents: how many brides and youthful lovers have been one day in the bloom of health and hope, and the next a prey for worms and the decay of the tomb! Of what materials was I made, that I could thus resist so many shocks, which, like the turning of the wheel, continually renewed the torture.

But I was doomed to live; and, in two months found myself as awaking from a dream in a prison, stretched on a wretched bed, surrounded by gaolers, turnkeys, bolts, and all the miserable apparatus of a dungeon. It was morning, I remember, when I thus awoke to understanding: I had forgotten the particulars of what had happened, and only felt as if some great misfortune had suddenly overwhelmed me; but when I looked around, and saw the barred windows, and the squalidness of the room in which I was, all flashed across my memory, and I groaned bitterly.

This sound disturbed an old woman who was sleeping in a chair beside me. She was a hired nurse, the wife of one of the turnkeys, and her countenance expressed all those bad qualities which often characterize that class. The lines of her face were hard and rude, like those of persons accustomed to see without sympathizing in sights of misery. Her tone expressed her entire indifference; she addressed me in English, and the voice struck me as one that I had heard during my sufferings:

"Are you better now, sir?" said she.

I replied in the same language, with a feeble voice, "I believe I am; but if it be all true, if indeed I did not dream, I am sorry that I am still alive to feel this misery and horror."

"For that matter," replied the old woman, "if you mean about the gentleman you murdered, I believe that it were better for you if you were dead, for I fancy it will go hard with you; but you will be hung when the next sessions come on. However, that's none of my business, I am sent to nurse you, and get you well; I do my duty with a safe conscience; it were well if everybody did the same."

I turned with loathing from the woman who could utter so unfeeling a speech to a person just saved, on the very edge of death; but I felt languid, and unable to reflect on all that had passed. The whole series of my life appeared to me as a dream; I sometimes doubted if indeed it were all true, for it never presented itself to my mind with the force of reality.

As the images that floated before me became more distinct, I grew feverish; a darkness pressed around me; no one was near me who soothed me with the gentle voice of love; no dear hand supported me. The physician came and prescribed medicines, and the old woman prepared them for me; but utter carelessness was visible in the first, and the expression of brutality was strongly marked in the visage of the second. Who could be interested in the fate of a murderer, but the hangman who would gain his fee?

These were my first reflections; but I soon learned that Mr. Kirwin had shown me extreme kindness. He had caused the best room in the prison to be prepared for me (wretched indeed was the best;) and it was he who had provided a physician and a nurse. It is true he seldom came to see me; for, although he ardently desired to relieve the sufferings of every human creature, he did not wish to be present at the agonies and miserable ravings of a murderer. He came, therefore, sometimes to see that I was not neglected; but his visits were short, and at long intervals.

One day, when I was gradually recovering, I was seated in a chair, my eyes half open, and my cheeks livid like those of death, I was overcome by gloom and misery, and often reflected I had better seek death than remain miserably pent up only to be let loose in a world replete with wretchedness. At one time I considered whether I should not declare myself guilty, and suffer the penalty of the law, less innocent than poor Justine had been. Such were my thoughts, when the door of my apartment was opened, and Mr. Kirwin entered. His countenance expressed sympathy and compassion; he drew a chair close to mine, and addressed me in French:

"I fear that this place is very shocking to you; can I do anything to make you more comfortable?"

"I thank you; but all that you mention is nothing to me: on the whole earth there is no comfort which I am capable of receiving."

"I know that the sympathy of a stranger can be but of little relief to one borne down as you are by so strange a misfortune. But you will, I hope, soon quit this melancholy abode; for doubtless, evidence can easily be brought to free you from the criminal charge."

"That is my least concern: I am, by a course of strange events, become the most miserable of mortals. Persecuted and tortured as I am and have been, can death be any evil to me?"

"Nothing indeed could be more unfortunate and agonizing than the strange chances that have lately occurred. You were thrown, by some surprising accident, on this shore, renowned for its hospitality; seized immediately, and charged with murder. The first sight that was presented to your eyes was the body of your friend, murdered in so unaccountable a manner, and placed, as it were, by some fiend across your path."

As Mr. Kirwin said this, notwithstanding the agitation I endured on this retrospect of my sufferings, I also felt considerable surprise at the knowledge he seemed to possess concerning me. I suppose some astonishment was exhibited in my countenance; for Mr. Kirwin hastened to say:

"It was not until a day or two after your illness, that I thought of examining your dress, that I might discover some trace by which I could send to your relations an account of your misfortune and illness. I found several letters, and, among others, once which I discovered from its commencement to be from your father. I instantly wrote to Geneva: nearly two months have elapsed since the departure of my letter. But you are ill; even now you tremble: you are unfit for agitation of any kind."

"This suspense is a thousand times worse than the most horrible event: tell me what new scene of death has been acted, and whose murder I am now to lament."

"Your family is perfectly well," said Mr. Kirwin, with gentleness; "and some one, a friend, is come to visit you."

I know not by what chain of thought the idea presented itself, but it instantly darted into my mind that the murderer had come to mock at my misery, and taunt me with the death of Clerval, as a new incitement for me to comply with his hellish desires. I put my hand before my eyes, and cried out in agony:

"Oh! take him away! I cannot see him; for God's sake, do not let him enter!"

Mr. Kirwin regarded me with a troubled countenance. He could not help regarding my exclamation as a presumption of my guilt, and said, in rather a severe tone:

"I should have thought, young man, that the presence of your father would have been welcome, instead of inspiring such violent repugnance."

"My father!" cried I, while every feature and every muscle was relaxed from anguish to pleasure. "Is my father, indeed, come? How kind, how very kind. But where is he, why does he not hasten to me?"

My change of manner surprised and pleased the magistrate; perhaps he thought that my former exclamation was a momentary return of delirium, and now he instantly resumed his former benevolence. He rose and quitted the room with my nurse, and in a moment my father entered it.

Nothing, at this moment, could have given me greater pleasure than the arrival of my father. I stretched out my hand to him, and cried:

"Are you then safe—and Elizabeth—and Ernest?"

My father calmed me with assurances of their welfare, and endeavored by dwelling on these subjects so interesting to my heart, to raise my desponding spirits; but he soon felt that a prison cannot be the abode of cheerfulness. "What a place is this that you inhabit, my son!" said he, looking mournfully at the barred windows and wretched appearance of the room. "You travelled to seek happiness, but a fatality seems to pursue you. And poor Clerval——"

The name of my unfortunate and murdered friend was an agitation too great to be endured in my weak state; I shed tears.

"Alas! yes, my father," replied I; "some destiny of the most horrid kind hangs over me, and I must live to fulfil it, or surely I should have died on the coffin of Henry."

We were not allowed to converse for any length of time, for the precarious state of my health rendered every precaution necessary that could insure tranquillity. Mr. Kirwin came in, and insisted that my strength should not be exhausted by too much exertion. But the appearance of my father was to me like that of my good angel, and I gradually recovered my health.

As my sickness quitted me, I was absorbed by a gloomy and black melancholy, that nothing could dissipate. The image of Clerval was for ever before me, ghastly and murdered. More than once the agitation into which these reflections threw me made my friends dread a dangerous relapse. Alas! why did they preserve so miserable and detested a life? It was surely that I might fulfil my destiny, which is now drawing to a close. Soon, oh, very soon, will death extinguish these throbbings, and relieve me from the mighty weight of anguish that bears me to the dust; and, in executing the award of justice, I shall sink to rest. Then the appearance of death was distant, although the wish was ever present to my thoughts; and I often sat for hours motionless and speechless, wishing for some mighty revolution that might bury me and my destroyer in its ruins.

The season of the assizes approached. I had already been three months in prison; and although I was still weak, and in continual danger of a relapse, I was obliged to travel nearly a hundred miles to the county-town, where the court was held. Mr. Kirwin charged himself with every care of collecting witnesses, and arranging my defence. I was spared the disgrace of appearing publicly as a criminal, as the case was not brought before the court that decides on life and death. The grand jury rejected the bill, on its being proved that I was on the Orkney Islands at the hour the body of my friend was found, and a fortnight after my removal I was liberated from prison.

My father was enraptured on finding me freed from the vexations of a criminal charge, that I was again allowed to breathe the fresh atmosphere, and allowed to return to my native country. I did not participate in these feelings; for to me the walls of a dungeon or a palace were alike hateful. The cup of life was poisoned for ever; and although the sun shone upon upon, as upon the happy and gay of heart, I saw around me nothing but a dense and frightful darkness, penetrated by no light but the glimmer of two eyes that glared upon me. Sometimes they were the expressive eyes of Henry, languishing in death, the dark orbs nearly covered by the lids, and the long black lashes that fringed them; sometimes it was the watery clouded eyes of the monster, as I first saw them in my chamber of Ingolstadt.

My father tried to awaken in me the feelings of affection. He talked of Geneva, which I should soon visit—of Elizabeth, and Ernest; but these words only drew deep groans me. Sometimes, indeed, I felt a wish for happiness; and thought, with melancholy delight, of my beloved cousin; or longed, with a devouring *maladie du pays*, to see once more the blue lake and rapid Rhone, that had been so dear to me in early childhood: but my general state of feeling was a torpor, in which a prison was as welcome a residence as the divinest scene in nature; and these fits were seldom interrupted, but by paroxysms of anguish and despair. At moments I often endeavored to put an end to the existence I loathed; and it required unceasing attendance and vigilance to restrain me from committing some dreadful act of violence.

I remember, as I quitted the prison, I heard one of the men say, "He may be innocent of the murder, but he has certainly a bad conscience." These words struck me. A bad conscience! yes, surely I had one. William, Justine, and Clerval, had died through my infernal machinations; "And whose death," cried I, "is to finish the tragedy? Ah! my father, do not remain in this wretched country; take me where I may forget myself, my existence, and all the world."

My father easily acceded to my desire; and, after having taken leave of Mr. Kirwin, we hastened to Dublin. I felt as if I was relieved from a heavy weight, when the packet sailed with a fair wind from Ireland, and I had quitted for ever the country which had been to me the scene of so much misery.

It was midnight. My father slept in the cabin; and I lay on the deck, looking at the stars, and listening to the dashing of the waves. I hailed the darkness that shut Ireland from my sight, and my pulse beat with a feverish joy, when I reflected I should soon see Geneva. The past appeared to me in the light of a frightful dream; yet the vessel in which I was, the wind that blew me from the detested shore of Ireland, and the sea which surrounded me, told me too forcibly that I was deceived by no vision, and that Clerval, my friend and dearest companion, had fallen a victim to me and the monster of my creation. I repassed, in my memory, my whole life; my quiet happiness while residing with my family in Geneva, the death of my mother, and my departure of Ingolstadt. I remembered shuddering at the mad enthusiasm that hurried me on to the creation of my hideous enemy, and I called to mind the night during which he first lived. I was unable to pursue the train of thought; a thousand feelings pressed upon me, and I wept bitterly.

Ever since my recovery from the fever, I had been in the custom of taking every night a small quantity of laudanum; for it was by means of this drug only that I was enabled to gain the rest necessary for the preservation of life. Oppressed by the recollection of my various misfortunes, I now took a double dose, and soon slept profoundly. But sleep did not afford me respite from thought, and misery; my dreams presented a thousand objects that scared me. Towards morning I was possessed by a kind of nightmare; I felt the fiend's grasp in my neck, and could not free myself from it; groans and cries rung in my ears. My father, who was watching over me, perceiving my restlessness, awoke me, and pointed to the port of Holyhead, which we were now entering.

CHAPTER XVI.

We had resolved not to go to London, but to cross the country to Portsmouth, and thence embark for Havre. I preferred this plan principally because I dreaded again to see those places in which I had enjoyed a few moments of tranquillity with my beloved Clerval. I thought with horror of seeing again those persons whom we had been accustomed to visit together, and who might make inquiries concerning an event, the very remembrance of which made me again feel the pang I endured when I gazed on his lifeless form in the inn at ————.

As for my father, his desires and exertions were bounded to the again seeing me restored to health and peace of mind. His tenderness and attentions were unremitting; my grief and gloom was obstinate, but he would not despair. Sometimes he thought that I felt deeply the degradation of being obliged to answer a charge of murder, and he endeavored to prove to me the futility of pride.

"Alas! my father," said I, "how little do you know me. Human beings, their feelings and passions, would indeed be degraded, if such a wretch as I felt pride. Justine, poor unhappy Justine, was as innocent as I, and she suffered the same charge; she died for it; and I am the cause of this—I murdered her. William, Justine, and Henry—they all died by my hands."

My father had often, during my imprisonment, heard me make the same assertion; when I thus accused myself, he sometimes seemed to desire an explanation, and at others he appeared to consider it as caused by delirium, and that, during my illness, some idea of this kind had presented itself to my imagination, the remembrance of which I preserved in my convalescence. I avoided explanation, and maintained a continual silence concerning the wretch I had created. I had a feeling that I should be supposed mad, and this for ever chained my tongue, when I would have given the whole world to have confided the fatal secret.

Upon this occasion my father said, with an expression of unbounded wonder, "What do you mean, Victor? are you mad? My dear son, I entreat you never to make such an assertion."

"I am not mad," I cried energetically; "the sun and the heavens, who have viewed my operations, can bear witness of my truth. I am the assassin of those most innocent victims; they died by my machinations. A thousand times would I have shed my own blood, drop by drop, to have saved their lives; but I could not, my father, indeed I could not sacrifice the whole human race."

The conclusion of this speech convinced my father that my ideas were deranged, and he instantly changed the subjection of our conversation, and endeavored to alter the course of my thoughts.

He wished as much as possible to obliterate the memory of the scenes that had taken place in Ireland, and never alluded to them, or suffered me to speak of my misfortunes.

As time passed away I became more calm: my misery had her dwelling in my heart, but I no longer talked in the same incoherent manner of my own crimes; sufficient for me was the consciousness of them. By the utmost self-violence I curbed the imperious voice of wretchedness, which sometimes desired to declare itself to the whole world; and my manners were calmer and more composed than they had ever been since my journey to the sea of ice.

We arrived at Havre on the 8th of May, and instantly proceeded to Paris, where my father had some business, which detained us a few weeks. In this city, I received the following letter from Elizabeth:

"To Victor Frankenstein.

"My dearest friend,

"It gave me the greatest pleasure to receive a letter from my uncle dated at Paris; you are no longer at a formidable distance, and I may hope to see you in less than a fortnight. My poor cousin, how much you must have suffered! I expect to see you looking even more ill than when you quitted Geneva. This winter has been passed most miserably, tortured as I have been by anxious suspense; yet I hope to see peace in your countenance, and to find that your heart is not totally devoid of comfort and tranquillity.

"Yet I fear that the same feelings now exist that made you so miserable a year ago, even perhaps augmented by time. I would not disturb you at this period, when so many misfortunes weigh upon you; but a conversation that I had with my uncle previous to his departure, renders some explanation necessary before we meet.

"Explanation! you may possibly say; what can Elizabeth have to explain? If you really say this, my questions are answered, and I have no more to do than to sign myself your affectionate cousin. But you are distant from me, and it is possible that you may dread, and yet be pleased with this explanation; and, in a probability of this being the case, I dare not any longer postpone writing what, during your absence, I have often wished to express to you, but have never had the courage to begin.

"You well know, Victor, that our union had been the favorite plan of your parents ever since our infancy. We were told this when young, and taught to look forward to it as an event that would certainly take place. We were affectionate playfellows during childhood, and, I believe, dear and valued friends to one another as we grew older. But as brother and sister often entertain a lively affection towards each other, without desiring a more intimate union, may not such also be our case? Tell me, dearest Victor. Answer me, I conjure you, by our mutual happiness, with simple truth—Do you not love another?

"You have travelled; you have spent several years of your life at Ingolstadt; and I confess to you, my friend, that when I saw you last autumn so unhappy, flying to solitude, from the society of every creature, I could not help supposing that you might regret our connection, and believe yourself bound in honor to fulfil the wishes of your parents, although they opposed themselves to your inclinations. But this is false reasoning. I confess to you, my cousin, that I love you, and that in my airy dreams of futurity you have been my constant friend and companion. But it is your happiness I desire as well as my own, when I declare to you, that our marriage would render me eternally miserable, unless it were the dictate of your own free choice. Even now I weep to think, that, borne down as you are by the cruellest misfortunes, you may stifle, by the word *honor*, all hope of that love and happiness which would alone restore you to yourself. I, who have so interested an affection for you, may increase your miseries ten-fold, by being an obstacle to your wishes. Ah, Victor, be assured that your cousin and playmate has too sincere a love for you not to be made miserable by this supposition. Be happy, my friend; and if you obey me in this one request, remain satisfied that nothing on earth will have power to interrupt my tranquillity.

"Do not let this letter disturb you; do not answer it to-morrow, or the next day, or even until you come, if it will give you pain. My uncle will send me news of your health; and if I see but one smile on your lips when we meet, occasioned by this or any other exertion of mine, I shall need no other happiness.

"ELIZABETH LAVENZA.

"Geneva, May 18th, 17—."

This letter revived in my memory what I had before forgotten, the threat of the find—"*I will be with you on your wedding night!*" Such was my sentence, and on that night would the dæmon employ every art to destroy me, and tear me from the glimpse of happiness which promised partly to console my sufferings. On that night he had determined to consummate his crimes by my death. Well, be it so; a deadly struggle would then assuredly take place, in which if he was victorious, I should be at peace, and his power over me be at an end. If he were vanquished, I should be a free man. Alas! what freedom? such as the peasant enjoys when his family have been massacred before his eyes, his cottage burnt, his lands laid waste, and he is turned adrift, homeless, pennyless, and alone, but free. Such would be my liberty, except that in my Elizabeth I possessed a treasure; alas! balanced by those horrors of remorse and guilt, which would pursue me until death.

Sweet and beloved Elizabeth! I read and re-read her letter, and some softened feelings stole into my heart, and dared to whisper paradisaical dreams of love and joy; but the apple was already eaten, and the angel's arm bared to drive me from all hope. Yet I would die to make her happy. If the monster executed his threat, death was inevitable; yet, again, I considered whether my marriage would hasten my fate. My destruction might indeed arrive a few months sooner; but if my torturer should suspect that I postponed it, influenced by his menaces, he would surely find other, and perhaps more dreadful means of revenge. He had vowed *to be with me on my wedding night*, yet he did not consider that threat as bidding him to peace in the meantime; for, as if to show me that he was not yet satiated with blood, he had murdered Clerval immediately after the enunciation of his threats. I resolved, therefore, that if my immediate union with my cousin would conduce either to her's or my father's happiness, my adversary's designs against my life should not retard it a single hour.

In this state of mind I wrote to Elizabeth. My letter was calm and affectionate. "I fear, my beloved girl," I said, "little happiness remains for us on earth; yet all that I may one day enjoy is concentered in you. Chase away your idle fears; to you alone do I consecrate my life, and my endeavors for contentment. I have one secret, Elizabeth, a dreadful one; when revealed to you, it will chill your frame with horror, and then, far from being surprised at my misery, you will only wonder that I survive what I have endured. I will confide this tale of misery and terror to you the day after our marriage shall take place; for, my sweet cousin, there must be perfect confidence between us. But until then, I conjure you, do not mention or allude to it. This I most earnestly entreat, and I know you will comply."

In about a week after the arrival of Elizabeth's letter, we returned to Geneva. My cousin welcomed me with warm affection; yet tears were in her eyes, as she beheld my emaciated frame and feverish cheeks. I saw a change in her also. She was thinner, and had lost much of that heavenly vivacity that had before charmed me; but her gentleness, and soft looks of compassion, made her a more fit companion for one blasted and miserable as I was.

The tranquillity which I now enjoyed did not endure. Memory brought madness with it; and when I thought on what had passed, a real insanity possessed me; sometimes I was furious, and burnt with rage, sometimes low and despondent. I neither spoke or looked, but sat motionless, bewildered by the multitude of miseries that overcame me.

Elizabeth alone had the power to draw me from these fits; her gentle voice would soothe me when transported by passion, and inspire me with human feelings when sunk in torpor. She wept with me, and for me. When reason returned, she would remonstrate, and endeavor to inspire me with resignation. Ah! it is well for the unfortunate to be resigned, but for the guilty there is no peace. The agonies of remorse poison the luxury there is otherwise sometimes found in indulging the excess of grief.

Soon after my arrival my father spoke of my immediate marriage with my cousin. I remained silent.

"Have you, then, some other attachment?"

"None on earth. I love Elizabeth, and look forward to our union with delight. Let the day therefore be fixed; and on it I will consecrate myself, in life or death, to the happiness of my cousin."

"My dear Victor, do not speak thus. Heavy misfortunes have befallen us; but let us only cling closer to what remains, and transfer our love for those whom we have lost to those who yet live. Our circle will be small, but bound close by the ties of affection and mutual misfortune. And when time shall have softened your despair, new and dear objects of care will be born to replace those of whom we have been so cruelly deprived."

Such were the lessons of my father. But to me the remembrance of the threat returned: nor can you wonder, that, omnipotent as the fiend had yet been in his deeds of blood, I should almost regard him as invincible; and that when he had pronounced the words, "*I shall be with you on your wedding night*," I should regard the threatened fate as unavoidable. But death was no evil to me, if the loss of Elizabeth were balanced with it; and I therefore, with a contented and even cheerful countenance, agreed with my father, that if my cousin would consent, the ceremony should take place in ten days, and thus put, as I imagined, the seal to my fate.

Great God! if for one instant I had thought of what might be the hellish intention of my fiendish adversary, I would rather have banished myself forever from my native country, and wandered a friendless outcast over the earth, than have consented to this miserable marriage. But, as if possessed of magic powers, the monster had blinded me to his real intentions; and when I thought that I prepared only my own death, I hastened that of a far dearer victim.

As the period fixed for our marriage drew nearer, whether from cowardice or a prophetic feeling, I felt my heart sink within me. But I concealed my feelings by an appearance of hilarity, that brought smiles and joy to the countenance of my father, but hardly deceived the ever-watchful and nicer eye of Elizabeth. She looked forward to our union with placid contentment, not unmingled with a little fear, which past misfortunes had impressed, that what now appeared certain and tangible happiness, might soon dissipate into an airy dream, and leave no trace but deep and everlasting regret.

Preparations were made for the event; congratulatory visits were received; and all wore a smiling appearance. I shut up, as well as I could, in my own heart the anxiety that preyed there, and entered with seeming earnestness into the plans of my father, although they might only serve as the decorations of my tragedy. A house was purchased for us near Cologny, by which we should enjoy the pleasures of the country, and yet be so near Geneva as to see my father every day; who would still reside within the walls, for the benefit of Ernest, that he might follow his studies at the schools.

In the mean time I took every precaution to defend my person, in case the fiend should openly attack me. I carried pistols and a dagger constantly about me, and was ever on the watch to prevent artifice; and by these means gained a greater degree of tranquillity. Indeed, as the period approached, the threat appeared more as a delusion, not to be regarded as worthy to disturb my peace, while the happiness I hoped for in my marriage wore a greater appearance of certainty, as the day fixed for its solemnization drew nearer, and I heard it continually spoken of as an occurrence which no accident could possibly prevent.

Elizabeth seemed happy; my tranquil demeanor contributed greatly to calm her mind. But on the day that was to fulfil my wishes and my destiny, she was melancholy, and a presentiment of evil pervaded her; and perhaps also she thought of the dreadful secret, which I had promised to reveal to her the following day. My father was in the mean time overjoyed, and, in the bustle of preparation, only observed in the melancholy of his niece the diffidence of a bride.

After the ceremony was performed, a large party assembled at my father's; but it was agreed that Elizabeth and I should pass the afternoon and night at Evian, and return to Cologny the next morning. As the day was fair, and the wind favorable, we resolved to go by water.

Those were the last moments of my life during which I enjoyed the feeling of happiness. We passed rapidly along: the sun was hot, but we were sheltered from its rays by a kind of canopy, while we enjoyed the beauty of the scene, sometimes on one side of the lake, where we saw Mont Salêve, the pleasant banks of Montalêgre, and at a distance, surmounting all, the beautiful Mont Blanc, and the assemblage of snowy mountains that in vain endeavor to emulate her; sometimes coasting the opposite banks, we saw the mighty Jura opposing its dark side to the ambition that would quit its native country, and an almost insurmountable barrier to the invader who should wish to enslave it.

I took the hand of Elizabeth: "You are sorrowful, my love. Ah! if you knew what I have suffered, and what I may yet endure, you would endeavor to let me taste the quiet, and freedom from despair, that this one day at least permits me to enjoy."

"Be happy, my dear Victor," replied Elizabeth; "there is, I hope, nothing to distress you; and be assured that if a lively joy is not painted in my face, my heart is contented. Something whispers to me not to depend too much on the prospect that is opened before us; but I will not listen to such a sinister voice. Observe how fast we move along, and how the clouds, which sometimes obscure and sometimes rise above the dome of Mont Blanc, render this scene of beauty still more interesting. Look also at the innumerable fish that are swimming in the clear waters, where we can distinguish every pebble that lies at the bottom. What a divine day! how happy and serene all nature appears!"

Thus Elizabeth endeavored to divert her thoughts and mine from all reflection upon melancholy subjects. But her temper was fluctuating; joy for a few instants shone in her eyes, but it continually gave place to distraction and reverie.

The sun sunk lower in the heavens; we passed the river Drance, and observed its path through the chasms of the higher, and the glens of the lower hills. The Alps here come closer to the lake, and we approached the amphitheatre of mountains which forms its eastern boundary. The spire of Evian shone under the woods that surrounded it, and the range of mountain above mountain by which it was overhung.

The wind, which had hitherto carried us along with amazing rapidity, sunk at sunset to a light breeze; the soft air just ruffled the water, and caused a pleasant motion among the trees as we approached the shore, from which it wafted the most delightful scent of flowers and hay. The sun sunk beneath the horizon as we landed, and as I touched the shore, I felt those cares and fears revive, which soon were to clasp me, and cling to me for ever.

CHAPTER XVII.

It was eight o'clock when we landed: we walked for a short time on the shore, enjoying the transitory light, and then retired to the inn, and contemplated the lovely scene of waters, woods, and mountains, obscured in darkness, yet still displaying their black outlines.

The wind, which had fallen in the south, now rose with great violence in the west. The moon had reached her summit in the heavens, and was beginning to descend; the clouds swept across it swifter than the flight of the vulture, and dimmed her rays, while the lake reflected the scene of the busy heavens, rendered still busier by the restless waves that were beginning to rise. Suddenly a heavy storm of rain descended.

I had been calm during the day; but so soon as night obscured the shapes of objects, a thousand fears arose in my mind. I was anxious and watchful, while my right hand grasped a pistol which was hidden in my bosom. Every sound terrified me; but I resolved that I would sell my life dearly, and not relax the impending conflict until my own life, or that of my adversary, were extinguished.

Elizabeth observed my agitation for some time in timid and fearful silence; at length she said, "What is it that agitates you, my dear Victor? What is it you fear?"

"Oh! peace, peace, my love," replied I: "this night, and all will be safe; but this night is dreadful, very dreadful."

I passed an hour in this state of mind, when suddenly I reflected how dreadful the combat which I momentarily expected would be to my wife, and I earnestly entreated her to retire, resolving not to join her until I had obtained some knowledge as to the situation of my enemy.

She left me, and I continued some time walking up and down the passages of the house, and inspecting every corner that might afford a retreat to my adversary. But I discovered no trace of him, and was beginning to conjecture that some fortunate chance had intervened to prevent the execution of his menaces; when suddenly I heard a shrill and dreadful scream. It came from the room into which Elizabeth had retired. As I heard it, the whole truth rushed into my mind, my arms dropped, the motion of every muscle and fibre was suspended; I could feel the blood trickling in my veins, and tingling in the extremities of my limbs. This state lasted but for an instant; the scream was repeated, and I rushed into the room.

Great God! why did I not then expire! Why am I here to relate the destruction of the best hope, and the purest creature of earth. She was there, lifeless and inanimate, thrown across the bed, her head hanging down, and her pale and distorted features half covered by her hair. Everywhere I turn I see the same figure—her bloodless arms and relaxed form flung by the murderer on its bridal bier. Could I behold this, and live? Alas! life is obstinate, and clings closest where it is most hated. For a moment only and I lose recollection; I fainted.

When I recovered, I found myself surrounded by the people of the inn; their countenances expressed a breathless terror: but the horror of others appeared only as a mockery, a shadow of the feelings that oppressed me. I escaped from them to the room where lay the body of Elizabeth, my love, my wife, so lately living, so dear, so worthy. She had been moved from the posture in which I had first beheld her; and now, as she lay, her head upon her arm, and a handkerchief thrown across her face and neck, I might have supposed her asleep. I rushed towards her, and embraced her with ardor; but the deathly languor and coldness of the limbs told me, that what I now held in my arms had ceased to be the Elizabeth whom I had loved and cherished. The murderous marks of the fiend's grasp was on her neck, and the breath had ceased to issue from her lips.

While I still hung over her in the agony

of despair, I happened to look up. The windows of the room had before been darkened; and I felt a kind of panic on seeing the pale yellow light of the moon illuminate the chamber. The shutters had been thrown back; and, with a sensation of horror not to be described, I saw at the open window a figure the most hideous and abhorred. A grin was on the face of the monster; he seemed to jeer, as with his fiendish finger he pointed towards the corpse of my wife. I rushed towards the window, and drawing a pistol from my bosom, shot; but he eluded me, leaped from his station, and, running with the swiftness of lightning, plunged into the lake.

The report of the pistol brought a crowd into the room. I pointed to the spot where he had disappeared, and we followed the track with boats; nets were cast, but in vain. After passing several hours, we returned hopeless, most of my companions believing it to have been a form conjured by my fancy. After having landed, they proceeded to search the country, parties going in different directions among the woods and vines.

I did not accompany them; I was exhausted: a film covered my eyes, and my skin was parched with the heat of fever. In this state I lay on a bed, hardly conscious of what had happened; my eyes wandered round the room, as if to seek something that I had lost.

At length I remembered that my father would anxiously expect the return of Elizabeth and myself, and that I must return alone. This reflection brought tears into my eyes, and I wept for a long time; but my thoughts rambled to various subjects, reflecting on my misfortunes, and their cause. I was bewildered in a cloud of wonder and horror. The death of William, the execution of Justine, the murder of Clerval, and lastly of my wife; even at that moment I knew not that my only remaining friends were safe from the malignity of the fiend; my father even now might be writhing under his grasp, and Ernest might be dead at his feet. This idea made me shudder, and recalled me to action. I started up, and resolved to return to Geneva with all possible speed.

There were no horses to be procured, and I must return by the lake; but the wind was unfavorable, and the rain fell in torrents. However, it was hardly morning, and I might reasonably hope to arrive by night. I hired men to row, and took an oar myself, for I had always experienced relief from mental torment in bodily exercise. Bnt the overflowing misery I now felt, and the excess of agitation that I endured, rendered me incapable of any exertion. I threw down the oar; and, leaning my head upon my hands, gave way to every gloomy idea that arose. If I looked up, I saw the scenes which were familiar to me in my happier time, and which I had contemplated but the day before in the company of her who was now but a shadow and a recollection. Tears streamed from my eyes. The rain had ceased for a moment, and I saw the fish play in the waters as they had done a few hours before; they had then been observed by Elizabeth. Nothing is so painful to the human mind as a great and sudden change. The sun might shine, or the clouds might lower; but nothing could appear to me as it had done the day before. A fiend had snatched from me every hope of future happiness: no creature had ever been so miserable as I was; so frightful an event was single in the history of man.

But why should I dwell upon the incidents that followed this last overwhelming event. Mine has been a tale of horrors; I have reached their *acme*, and what I must now relate can but be tedious to you. Know that, one by one, my friends were snatched away; I was left desolate. My own strength is exhausted; and I must tell in a few words, what remains of my hideous narration.

I arrived at Geneva. My father and Ernest yet lived; but the former sunk under the tidings that I bore. I see him now, cxcellent and venerable old man! his eyes wandered in vacancy, for they had lost their charm and their delight—

his niece, his more than daughter, whom he doated on with all that affection which a man feels, who, in the decline of life, having a few affections, clings more earnestly to those that remain. Cursed, cursed be the fiend that brought misery on his gray hairs, and doomed him to waste in wretchedness! He could not live under the horrors that were accumulated around him; an apoplectic fit was brought on, and in a few days he died in my arms.

What then became of me? I know not; I lost sensation, and chains and darkness were the only objects that pressed upon me. Sometimes, indeed, I dreamed that I wandered in flowery meadows and pleasant vales with the friends of my youth; but awoke, and found myself in a dungeon. Melancholy followed, but by degrees I gained a clear conception of my miseries and situation, and was then released from my prison. For they had called me mad; and during many months, as I understood, a solitary cell had been my habitation.

But liberty had been a useless gift to me had I not, as I awakened to reason, at the same time awakened to revenge. As the memory of past misfortunes pressed upon me, I began to reflect on their cause—the monster whom I had created, the miserable dæmon whom I had sent abroad into the world for my destruction. I was possessed by a maddening rage when I thought of him, and desired and ardently prayed that I might have him within my grasp, to wreak a great and signal revenge on his cursed head.

Nor did my hate long confine itself to useless wishes; I began to reflect on the best means of securing him; and for this purpose, about a month after my release, I repaired to a criminal judge in the town, and told him that I had an accusation to make; that I knew the destroyer of my family; and that I required him to exert his whole authority for the apprehension of the murderer.

The magistrate listened to me with attention and kindness: "Be assured, sir," said he, "no pains or exertions on my part shall be spared to discover the villain."

"I thank you," replied I; "listen, therefore, to the deposition that I have to make. It is indeed a tale so strange, that I should fear you would not credit it, were there not something in truth which, however wonderful, forces conviction. The story is too connected to be mistaken for a dream, and I have no motive for falsehood." My manner, as I thus addressed him, was impressive, but calm; I had formed in my heart a resolution to pursue my destroyer to death; and this purpose quieted my agony, and providentially reconciled me to life. I now related my history briefly, but with firmness and precision, marking the dates with accuracy, and never deviating into invective or exclamation.

The magistrate appeared at first perfectly incredulous, but as I continued, he became more attentive and interested; I saw him sometimes shudder with horror; at others a lively surprise, unmingled with disbelief, was painted on his countenance.

When I had concluded my narration, I said, "This is the being whom I accuse, and for whose detection and punishment I call upon you to exert your whole power. It is your duty as a magistrate, and I believe and hope that your feelings as a man will not revolt from the execution of those functions on this occasion." This address caused a considerable change in the physiognomy of my auditor. He had heard my story with that half kind of belief that is given to a tale of spirits and supernatural events; but when he was called upon to act officially in consequence, the whole tide of his incredulity returned. He however, answered mildly, "I would willingly afford you every aid in your pursuit; but the creature of whom you speak appears to have powers which would put all my exertions to defiance. Who can follow an animal which can traverse the sea of ice, and inhabit caves and dens, where no man would venture to intrude? Besides, some months have elapsed since the commission of his crimes, and no one can conjecture to what place he has wandered, or what region he may now inhabit."

"I do not doubt that he hovers near the spot which I inhabit; and if he has indeed taken refuge in the Alps, he may be hunted like the chamois, and destroyed as a beast of prey. But I perceive your thoughts: you do not credit my narrative, and do not intend to pursue my enemy with the punishment which is his desert."

As I spoke, rage sparkled in my eyes; the magistrate was intimidated; "You are mistaken," said he, "I will exert myself; and if it is in my power to seize the monster, be assured that he shall suffer punishment proportionate to his crimes. But I fear, from what you have yourself described to be his properties, that this will prove impracticable, and that, while every proper measure is pursued, you should endeavor to make up your mind to disappointment."

"That cannot be; but all that I can say will be of little avail. My revenge is of no moment to you; yet, while I allow it to be a vice, I confess that it is the devouring and only passion of my soul. My rage is unspeakable, when I reflect that the murderer, whom I have turned loose upon society, still exists. You refuse my just demand: I have but one resource; and I devote myself, either in my life or death, to his destruction."

I trembled with excess of agitation as I said this; there was a phrenzy in my manner, and something, I doubt not, of that haughty fierceness, which the martyrs of old are said to have possessed. But to a Genevan magistrate, whose mind was occupied by far other ideas than those of devotion and heroism, this elevation of mind had much the appearance of madness. He endeavored to soothe me as a nurse does a child, and reverted to my tale as the effects of delirium.

"Man," I cried, "how ignorant art thou in thy pride of wisdom! Cease; you know not what it is you say."

I broke from the house angry and disturbed, and retired to meditate on some other mode of action.

CHAPTER XVIII.

My present situation was one in which all voluntary thought was swallowed up and lost. I was hurried away by fury; revenge alone endowed me with strength and composure; it modelled my feelings, and allowed me to be calculating and calm, at periods when otherwise delirium or death would have been my portion.

My first resolution was to quit Geneva for ever; my country, which, when I was happy and beloved, was dear to me, now, in my adversity, became hateful. I provided myself with a sum of money, together with a few jewels which had belonged to my mother, and departed.

And now my wanderings began, which are to cease but with life. I have traversed a vast portion of the earth, and have endured all the hardships which travellers, in deserts and barbarous countries are wont to meet. How I have lived I hardly know; many times have I stretched my failing limbs upon the sandy plain, and prayed for death. But revenge kept me alive, I dared not die, and leave my adversary in being.

When I quitted Geneva, my first labor was to gain some clue by which I might trace the steps of my fiendish enemy. But my plan was unsettled; and I wandered many hours around the confines of the town, uncertain what path I should pursue. As night approached, I found myself at the entrance of the cemetery where William, Elizabeth, and my father, reposed. I entered it, and approached the tomb which marked their graves. Everything was silent, except the leaves of the trees, which were gently agitated by the wind; the night was nearly dark; and the scene would have been solemn and affecting even to an uninterested observer. The spirits of the departed seemed to flit around, and to cast a shadow, which was felt, but seen not, around the head of the mourner.

The deep grief which this scene had at first excited quickly gave way to rage and despair. They were dead, and I lived; their murderer also lived, and to destroy him I must drag out my weary existence. I knelt on the grass, and kissed the earth, and with quivering lips exclaimed, "By the sacred earth on which I kneel, by the shades that wander near me, by the deep and eternal grief that I feel, I swear; and by thee, O Night, and by the spirits that preside over thee, I swear to pursue the dæmon, who caused this misery, until he or I shall perish in mortal conflict. For this purpose I will preserve my life: to execute this dear revenge, will I again behold the sun, and tread the green herbage of the earth, which otherwise should vanish from my eyes for ever. And I call on you, spirits of the dead; and on you, wandering ministers of vengeance, to aid and conduct me in my work. Let the cursed and hellish monster drink deep of agony; let him feel the despair that now torments me."

I had begun my adjuration with solemnity, and an awe which almost assured me that the shades of my murdered friends heard and approved my devotion; but the furies possessed me as I concluded, and rage choaked my utterance.

I was answered through the stillness of night by a loud and fiendish laugh. It rung on my ears long and heavily; the mountains re-echoed it, and I felt as if all hell surrounded me with mockery and laughter. Surely in that moment I should have been possessed by phrenzy, and have destroyed my miserable existence, but that my vow was heard, and that I was reserved for vengeance. The laughter died away; when a well-known and abhorred voice, apparently close to my ear, addressed me in an audible whisper—"I am satisfied: miserable wretch! you have determined to live, and I am satisfied."

I darted towards the spot from which the sound proceeded; but the devil eluded my grasp. Suddenly the broad disk of the moon arose, and shone full upon his ghastly and distorted shape, as he fled with more than mortal speed.

I pursued him; and for many months this has been my task. Guided by a slight clue, I followed the windings of the Rhone, but vainly. The blue Mediterranean appeared; and, by a strange chance, I saw the fiend enter by night, and hide himself in a vessel bound for the Black Sea. I took my passage in the same ship; but he escaped, I know not how.

Amid the wilds of Tartary and Russia, although he still evaded me, I have ever followed in his track. Sometimes the peasants, scared by this horrid apparition, informed me of his path; sometimes he himself, who feared that if I lost trace I should despair and die, often left some mark to guide me. The snows descended on my head, and I saw the print of his huge step on the white plain. To you first entering on life, to whom care is new, and agony unknown, how can you understand what I have felt, and still feel? Cold, want, and fatigue, were the least pains which I was destined to endure; I was cursed by some devil, and carried about with me my eternal hell; yet still a spirit of good followed and directed my steps, and, when I most murmured, would suddenly extricate me from seemingly insurmountable difficulties. Sometimes, when nature, overcome by hunger, sunk under the exhaustion, a repast was prepared for me in the desert, that restored and inspirited me. The fare was indeed coarse, such as the peasants of the country ate; but I may not doubt that it was set there by the spirits that I had invoked to aid me. Often, when all was dry, the heavens cloudless, and I was parched by thirst, a slight cloud would bedim the sky, shed the few drops that revived me, and vanish.

I followed, when I could, the courses of the rivers; but the dæmon generally avoided these, as it was here that the population of the country chiefly collected. In other places human beings were seldom seen; and I generally subsisted on the wild animals that crossed my path. I had money with me, and gained the friendship of the villagers by distributing it, or bringing with me some food that I had killed, which, after taking a small part, I always presented to those who had provided me with fire and utensils for cooking.

My life, as it passed thus, was indeed hateful to me, and it was during sleep alone that I could taste joy. O blessed sleep! often, when most miserable, I sank to repose, and my dreams lulled me even to rapture. The spirits that guarded me had provided these moments, or rather hours, of happiness, that I might retain strength to fulfil my pilgrimage. Deprived of this respite, I should have sunk under my hardships. During the day I was sustained and inspirited by the hope of night: for in sleep I saw my friends, my wife, and my beloved country; again I saw the benevolent countenance of my father, heard the silver tones of my Elizabeth's voice, and beheld Clerval enjoying health and youth. Often, when wearied by a toilsome march, I persuaded myself that I was dreaming until night should come, and that I should then enjoy reality in the arms of my dearest friends. What agonizing fondness did I feel for them! How did I cling to their dear forms, as sometimes that haunted even my waking hours, and persuade myself that they still lived! At such moments vengeance, that burned within me, died in my heart, and I pursued my path towards the destruction of the dæmon, more as a task enjoined by Heaven, as the mechanical impulse of some power of which I was unconscious, than as the ardent desire of my soul.

What his feelings were whom I pursued, I cannot know. Sometimes, indeed, he left marks in writing on the barks of the trees, or cut in the stone, that guided me, or instigated my fury. "My reign is not yet over," (these words were legible in one of these inscriptions;) "you live, and my power is complete. Follow me; I seek the everlasting ices of the north, where you will feel the misery of cold and frost, to which I am impassive. You will find near this place if you follow not too tardily, a dead hare; eat, and be refreshed. Come on, my enemy; we have yet to wrestle for our lives; but many hard and miserable hours must you endure, until that period shall arrive."

Scoffing devil! again do I vow vengeance; again do I devote thee, miserable fiend, to torture and death. Never will I omit my search, until he or I perish; and then with what ecstacy shall I join my Elizabeth, and those who even now prepare for me the reward of my tedious toil and horrible pilgrimage.

As I still pursued my journey to the northward, the snows thickened, and the cold increased in a degree almost too severe to support. The peasants were shut up in their hovels, and only a few of the most hardy ventured forth to seize the animals whom starvation had forced from their hiding-places to seek for prey. The rivers were covered with ice, and no fish could be procured; and thus I was cut off from my chief article of maintenance.

The triumph of my enemy increased with the difficulty of my labors. One inscription that he left was in these words: "Prepare! your toils only begin: wrap yourself in furs, and provide food, for we shall soon enter upon a journey where your sufferings will satisfy my everlasting hatred."

My courage and perseverance were invigorated by these scoffing words; I resolved not to fail in my purpose; and calling on heaven to support me, I continued with unabated fervor to traverse immense deserts, until the ocean appeared at a distance, and formed the utmost boundary of the horizon. Oh! how unlike it was to the blue seas of the south! Covered with ice, it was only to be distinguished from land by its superior wildness and ruggedness. The Greeks wept for joy when they beheld the Mediterranean from the hills of Asia, and hailed with rapture the boundary of their toils. I did not weep; but I knelt down, and, with a full heart, thanked my guiding spirit for conducting me in safety to the place where I hoped, notwithstanding my adversary's gibe, to meet and grapple with him.

Some weeks before this period I had procured a sledge and dogs, and thus traversed the snows with inconceivable speed. I know not whether the fiend possessed the same advantages; but I found that, as before I had daily lost ground in the pursuit, I now gained on him; so much so, that when I first saw the ocean, he was but one day's journey in advance, and I hoped to intercept him before he should reach the beach. With new courage, therefore, I pressed on, and in two days arrived at a wretched hamlet on the seashore. I inquired of the inhabitants concerning the fiend, and gained accurate information. A gigantic monster, they said, had arrived the night before, armed with a gun and many pistols; putting to flight the inhabitants of a solitary cottage, through fear of his terrible appearance. He carried off their store of winter food, and placing it in a sledge, to draw which he had seized on a numerous drove of trained dogs, he had harnessed them, and the same night, to the joy of the horror-struck villagers, had pursued his journey across the sea in a direction that led to no land; and they conjectured that he must speedily be destroyed by the breaking ice, or frozen by the eternal frosts.

On hearing this information, I suffered a temporary access of despair. He had escaped me; and I must commence a destructive and almost endless journey across the mountainous ices of the ocean—amid cold that few of the inhabitants could long endure, and which I, the native of a genial and sunny climate, could not hope to survive. Yet at the idea that the fiend should live and be triumphant, my rage and vengeance returned, and, like a mighty tide, overwhelmed every other feeling. After a slight repose, during which the spirits of the dead hovered round, and instigated me to toil and revenge, I prepared for my journey.

I exchanged my land sledge for one fashioned for the inequalities of the frozen ocean; and, purchasing a plentiful stock of provisions, I departed from the land.

I cannot guess how many days have passed since then; but I have endured misery, which nothing but the eternal sentiment of a just retribution burning within my heart could have enabled me to support. Immense and rugged mountains of ice often barred up my passage, and I often heard the thunder of the ground sea, which threatened my destruction. But again the frost came, and made the paths of the sea secure.

By the quantity of provision which I had consumed I should guess that I had passed three weeks in this journey; and the continual protraction of hope, returning back upon the heart, often wrung bitter drops of despondency and grief from my eyes. Despair had indeed almost secured her prey, and I should soon have sunk beneath this misery; when once, after the poor animals that carried me had with incredible toil gained the summit of a sloping ice mountain, and one sinking under his fatigue died, I viewed the expanse before me with anguish, when suddenly my eye caught a dark speck upon the dusky plain. I strained my sight to discover what it could be, and uttered a wild cry of ecstacy when I distinguished a sledge, and the distorted proportions of a well-known form within. Oh! with what a burning gush did hope revisit my heart! warm tears filled my eyes, which I hastily wiped away, that they might not intercept the view I had of the dæmon; but still my sight was dimmed by the burning drops, until, giving way to the emotions that oppressed me, I wept aloud.

But this was not the time for delay; I disencumbered the dogs of their dead companion, gave them a plentiful portion of food; and, after an hour's rest, which was absolutely necessary, and yet which was bitterly irksome to me, I continued my route. The sledge was still visible; nor did I again lose sight of it, exeept at the moments when for a short time some ice rock concealed it with its intervening crags. I indeed perceptibly gained on it;

and when, after nearly two days journey, I beheld my enemy at no more than a mile distant, my heart bounded within me.

But now, when I appeared almost within grasp of my enemy, my hopes were suddenly extinguished, and I lost all trace of him more utterly than I had ever done before. A ground sea was heard; the thunder of its progress, as the waters rolled and swelled beneath me every moment more ominous and terriffic. I pressed on, but in vain. The wind arose; the sea roared; and, as with the mighty shock of an earthquake, it split, and cracked with a tremendous and overwhelming sound. The work was soon finished: in a few minutes a tumultuous sea rolled between me and my enemy, and I was left drifting on a scattered piece of ice, that was continually lessening, and thus preparing for me a hideous death.

In this manner many appalling hours passed; several of my dogs died; and I myself was about to sink under the accumulation of distress, when I saw your vessel riding at anchor, and holding forth to me hopes of succor and life. I had no conception that vessels ever came so far north, and was astounded at the sight. I quickly destroyed part of my sledge to construct oars; and by these means was enabled, with infinite fatigue, to move my ice-raft in the direction of your ship. I had determined, if you were going southward, still to trust myself to the mercy of the seas, rather than abandon my purpose. I hoped to induce you grant me a boat with which I could still pursue my enemy. But your direction was northward. You took me on board when my vigor was exhausted, and I should soon have sunk under my multiplied hardships into a death, whiich I still dread—for my task is unfulfilled.

Oh! when will my guiding spirit, in conducting me to the dæmon, allow me the rest I so much desire; or must I die, and he yet live? If I do, swear to me, Walton, that he shall not escape; that you will seek him, and satisfy my vengeance in his death. Yet, do I dare ask you to undertake my pilgrimage, to endure the hardships that I have undergone? No; I am not so selfish. Yet, when I am dead, if he should appear; if the ministers of vengeance should conduct him to you, swear that he shall not live—swear that he shall not triumph over my accumulated woes and live to make another such a wretch as I am. He is eloquent and persuasive; and once his words had even power over my heart; but trust him not. His soul is as hellish as his form, full of treachery and fiend-like malice. Hear him not; call on the manes of William, Justine, Clerval, Elizabeth, my father, and of the wretched Victor, and thrust your sword into his heart. I will hover near, and direct the steel aright.

CHAPTER XIX.

WALTON, IN CONTINUATION.

August 26th, 17—.

You have read this strange and terrific story, Margaret; and do you not feel your blood congealed with horror, like that which even now curdles mine? Sometimes, seized with sudden agony, he could not continue his tale; at others, his voice broken, yet piercing, uttered with difficulty the words so replete with agony. His fine and lovely eyes were now lighted up with indignation, now subdued to downcast sorrow, and quenched in infinite wretchedness. Sometimes he commanded his countenance and tones, and related the most horrible incidents with a tranquil voice, suppressing every mark of agitation; then, like a volcano bursting forth, his face would suddenly change to an expression of the wildest rage, as he shrieked out imprecations on his persecutor.

His tale is connected, and told with an appearance of the simplest truth; yet I own to you that the letters of Felix and Safie, which he showed me, and the apparition of the monster, seen from our ship, brought to to me a greater conviction of the truth of his narrative than his asseverations, however earnest and connected. Such a monster has then really existence; I cannot doubt it; yet I am lost in surprise and admiration. Sometimes I endeavored to gain from Frankenstein the particulars of his creature's formation ; but on this point he was impenetrable.

"Are you mad, my friend ?" said he, "or whither does your senseless curiosity lead you ? Would you also create for yourself and the world a demoniacal enemy ? Or to what do your questions tend ? Peace, peace ! learn my miseries, and do not seek to increase your own."

Frankenstein discovered that I made notes concerning his history : he asked to see them, and then himself corrected and augmented them in many places ; but principally in giving the life and spirit to the conversations he held with his enemy. "Since you have preserved my narration," said he, "I would not that a mutilated one should go down to posterity."

Thus has a week passed away, while I have listened to the strangest tale that ever imagination formed. My thoughts, and every feeling of my soul, have been drunk up by the interest for my guest, which this tale and his own elevated and gentle manners have created. I wish to sooth him ; yet can I counsel one so infinitely miserable, so destitute of every hope of consolation, to live ? Oh, no ! the only joy that he can now know will be when he composes his shattered feelings to peace and death. Yet he enjoys one comfort, the offspring of solitude and delirium : he believes, that, when in dreams he holds converse with his friends, and derives from that communion consolation for his miseries, or excitements to his vengeance, that they are not the creations of his fancy, but the real beings who visit him from the regions of a remote world. This faith gives a solemnity to his reveries that render them to me almost as imposing and interesting as truth.

Our conversations are not always confined to his own history and misfortunes. On every point of general literature he displays unbounded knowledge, and a quick and piercing apprehension. His eloquence is forcible and touching ; nor can I hear him, when he relates a pathetic incident, or endeavors to move the passions of pity or love, without tears. What a glorious creature must he have been in the days of his prosperity, when he is thus noble and god-like in ruin. He seems to feel his own worth, and the greatness of his fall.

"When younger," said he, "I felt as if I were destined for some great enterprise. My feelings are profound ; but I possessed a coolness of judgment that fitted me for illustrious achievements. This sentiment of the worth of my nature supported me, when others would have been oppressed ; for I deemed it criminal to throw away in useless grief those talents that might be useful to my fellow-creatures. When I reflected on the work I had completed, no less a one than the creation of a sensitive rational animal, I could not rank myself with the herd of common projectors. But this feeling, which supported me in the commencement of my career, now serves only to plunge me lower in the dust. All my speculations and hopes are as nothing ; and, like the archangel who aspired to omnipotence, I am chained in an eternal hell. My imagination was vivid, yet my powers of analysis and application were intense ; by the union of these qualities I conceived the idea, and executed the creation of a man. Even now I cannot recollect, without passion, my reveries while the work was incomplete. I trod heaven in my thoughts, now exulting in my powers, now burning with the idea of their effects. From my infancy I was imbued with high hopes and a lofty ambition ; but how am I sunk !

"Oh ! my friend, if you had known me as I once was, you would not recognise me in this state of degradation. Despondency rarely visited my heart ; a high destiny seemed to bear me on, until I fell, never, never again to rise."

Must I then lose this admirable being ? I have longed for a friend ; I have sought one who would sympathize with and love me. Behold, on these desert seas I have found such a one ; but I fear I have gained him only to know his value and lose

I would reconcile him to life, but he repulses the idea.

"I thank you, Walton," he said, "for your kind attentions towards so miserable a wretch; but when you speak of new ties, and fresh affections, think you that any can replace those who are gone? Can any man be to me as Clerval was; or any woman another Elizabeth? Even where the affections are not strongly moved by any superior excellence, the companions of our childhood always possess a certain power over our minds, which hardly any later friend can obtain. They know our infantine dispositions, which, however they may be afterwards modified, are never eradicated; and they can judge of our actions with more certain conclusions as to the integrity of our motives. A sister or a brother can never, unless indeed such symptoms have been shown early, suspect the other of fraud or false dealing, when another friend, however strongly he may be attached, may, in spite of himself, be invaded with suspicion. But I enjoyed friends, dear, not only through habit and association, but from their own merits; and, wherever I am, the soothing voice of my Elizabeth, and the conversation of Clerval, will be ever whispered in my ear. They are dead; and but one feeling in such a solitude can persuade me to preserve my life. If I were engaged in any high undertaking or design, fraught with extensive utility to my fellow-creatures, then could I live to fulfil it. But such is not my destiny; I must pursue and destroy the being to whom I gave existence; then my lot on earth will be fulfilled, and I may die."

September 2d.

My Beloved Sister: I write to you encompassed by peril, and ignorant whether I am ever doomed to see again dear England, and the dearer friends that inhabit it. I am surrounded by mountains of ice, which admit of no escape, and threaten every moment to crush my vessel. The brave fellows, whom I have persuaded to be my companions, look towards me for aid; but I have none to bestow. There is something terribly appalling in our situation, yet my courage and hopes do not desert me. We may survive; and if we do not I will repeat the lessons of my Seneca, and die with a good heart.

Yet, what, Margaret will be the state of your mind? You will not hear of my destruction, and you will anxiously wait my return. Years will pass, and you will have visitings of despair, and yet be tortured by hope. Oh! my beloved sister, the sickening failings of your heart-felt expectations are, in prospect, more terrible to me than my own death. But you have a husband, and lovely children; you may be happy: Heaven bless you, and make you so!

My unfortunate guest regards me with the tenderest compassion. He endeavors to fill me with hope; and talks as if life were a possession which he valued. He reminds me how often the same accidents have happened to other navigators, who have attempted this sea, and, in spite of myself, he fills me with cheerful auguries. Even the sailors feel the power of his eloquence: when he speaks, they no longer despair; he rouses their energies, and, while they hear his voice, they believe these vast mountains of ice are mole-hills, which will vanish before the resolutions of man. These feelings are transitory; each day's expectation delayed fills them with fear, and I almost dread a mutiny caused by this despair.

September 5th.

A scene has just passed of such uncommon interest, that although it is highly probable that these papers may never reach you, yet I cannot forbear recording it.

We are still surrounded by mountains of ice, still in imminent danger of being crushed in their conflict. The cold is excessive, and many of my unfortunate comrades have already found a grave amid this scene of desolation. Frankenstein has daily declined in health: a feverish fire still glimmers in his eyes; but he is exhausted, and, when suddenly roused to any exertion, he speedily sinks again into apparent lifelessness.

I mentioned in my last letter the fears I entertained of a mutiny. This morning, as I sat watching the wan countenance of my friend—his eyes half closed, and his limbs hanging listlessly—I was roused by half a dozen of the sailors, who desired admission into the cabin. They entered; and their leader addressed me. He told me that he and his companions had been chosen by the other sailors to come in deputation to me, to make me a demand, which, in justice, I could not refuse. We were immured in ice, and should probably never escape; but they feared that if, as was possible, the ice should dissipate, and a free passage be opened, I should be rash enough to continue my voyage, and lead them into fresh dangers, after they might happily have surmounted this.

They desired, therefore, that I should engage with a solemn promise, that if the vessel should be freed, I would instantly direct my course southward.

This speech troubled me. I had not despaired; nor had I yet conceived the idea of returning, if set free. Yet could I, in justice, or even in possibility, refuse this demand? I hesitated before I answered; when Frankenstein, who had at first been silent, and, indeed, appeared hardly to have force enough to attend, now roused himself; his eyes sparkled, and his cheeks flushed with momentary vigor. Turning towards the men, he said—

"What do you mean? What do you demand of your captain? Are you then so easily turned from your design? Did you not call this a glorious expedition? and wherefore was it glorious? Not because the way was smooth and placid as a southern sea, but because it was full of dangers and terror; because, at every new incident, your fortitude was to be called forth, and your courage exhibited; because danger and death surrounded, and these dangers you were to brave and overcome. For this was it a glorious, for this was it an honorable undertaking. You were hereafter to be hailed as the benefactors of your species; your names adored, as belonging to brave men who encountered death for the honor and benefit of mankind. And now, behold, with the first imagination of danger, or, if you will, the first mighty and terrific trial of your courage, you shrink away, and are content to be handed down as men who had not strength enough to endure cold and peril; and so, poor souls, they were chilly, and returned to their warm fire-sides. Why, that requires not this preparation; ye need not have come thus far, and dragged your captain to the shame of a defeat, merely to prove yourselves cowards. Oh! be men, or be more than men. Be steady to your purposes, and firm as a rock. This ice is not made of such stuff as your hearts might be; it is mutable, cannot withstand you, if you say that it shall not. Do not return to your families with the stigma of disgrace marked on your brows. Return as heroes who have fought and conquered, and who know not what it is to turn their backs on the foe."

He spoke this with a voice so modulated to the different feelings expressed in his speech, with an eye so full of lofty design and heroism, that can you wonder that these men were moved? They looked at one another, and were unable to reply. I spoke; I told them to retire, and consider of what had been said: that I would not lead them further north, if they strenuously desired the contrary; but that I hoped that, with reflection, their courage would return.

They retired, and I turned towards my friend; but he was sunk in languor, and almost deprived of life.

How all this will terminate, I know not; but I had rather die, than return shamefully—my purpose unfulfilled. Yet I fear such will be my fate; the men, unsupported by ideas of glory and honor, can never willingly continue to endure their present hardships.

September 7th.

The die is cast; I have consented to return, if we are not destroyed. Thus are my hopes blasted by cowardice and indecision; I come back ignorant and disappointed. It requires more philosophy than I possess, to bear this injustice with patience.

September 12th.

It is past; I am returning to England. I have lost my hopes of utility and glory; I have lost my friend. But I will endeavor to detail these bitter circumstances to you, my dear sister; and, while I am wafted towards England, and towards you, I will not despond.

September 10th, the ice began to move, and roarings like thunder were heard at a distance, as the islands split and cracked in every direction. We were in the most imminent peril; but, as we could only remain passive, my chief attention was occupied by my unfortunate guest, whose illness increased in such a degree, that he was entirely confined to his bed. The ice cracked behind us, and was driven with force towards the north; a breeze sprung from the west, and on the 11th the passage towards the south became perfectly free. When the sailors saw this, and that their return to their native country was apparently assured, a shout of tumultuous joy broke from them, loud and long-continued. Frankenstein, who was dozing, awoke, and asked the cause of the tumult. "They shout," I said, "because they will soon return to England."

"Do you then really return?"

"Alas! yes; I cannot withstand their demands. I cannot lead them unwillingly to danger, and I must return."

"Do so, if you will; but I will not. You may give up your purpose; but mine is assigned to me by Heaven, and I dare not. I am weak; but surely the spirits who assist my vengeance will endow me with sufficient strength." Saying this, he endeavored to spring from the bed, but the exertion was too great for him; he fell back, and fainted.

It was long before he was restored; and I often thought that life was entirely extinct. At length he opened his eyes, but he breathed with difficulty, and was unable to speak. The surgeon gave him a composing draught, and ordered us to leave him undisturbed. In the meantime he told me that my friend had certainly not many hours to live.

His sentence was pronounced; and I could only grieve, and be patient. I sat by his bed watching him; his eyes were closed, and I thought he slept; but presently he called to me in a feeble voice, and, bidding me come near, said—"Alas! the strength I relied on is gone; I feel that I shall soon die, and he, my enemy and persecutor, may still be in being. Think not, Walton, that in the last moments of my existence I feel that burning hatred, and ardent desire of revenge, I once expressed, but I feel myself justified in desiring the death of my adversary. During these last days I have been occupied in examining my past conduct; nor do I find it blameable. In a fit of enthusiastic madness I created a rational creature, and was bound towards him, to assure, as far as was in my power, his happiness and well-being. This was my duty; but there was still another, paramount to that. My duties towards my fellow creatures had greater claims to my attention, because they included a greater proportion of happiness or misery. Urged by this view, I refused, and I did right in refusing to create a companion for the first creature. He showed unparalleled malignity and selfishness in evil: he destroyed my friends; he devoted to destruction beings who possessed exquisite sensations, happiness, and wisdom; nor do I know where this thirst for vengeance may end. Miserable himself, that he may render no other wretched he ought to die. The task of his destruction was mine, but I have failed. When actuated by selfish and vicious motives, I asked you to undertake my unfinished work; and I renew this request now, when I am only induced by reason and virtue.

"Yet I cannot ask you to renounce your country and friends, to fulfil this task; and now, that you are returning to England, you will have little chance of meeting with him. But the consideration of these points, and the well-balancing of what you may esteem your duties, I leave to you; my judgment and ideas are already disturbed by the near approach of death. I dare not ask you to do what I think right, for I may still be misled by passion.

"That he should live to be an instrument of mischief disturbs me; in other respects this hour, when I momentarily expect my release, is the only happy one which I have enjoyed for several years. The forms of the beloved dead flit before me, and I hasten to their arms. Farewell, Walton! Seek happiness in tranquillity, and avoid ambition, even if it be only the apparently innocent one of distinguishing yourself in science and discoveries. Yet why do I say this? I have myself been blasted in these hopes, yet another may succeed."

His voice became fainter as he spoke; and at length, exhausted by his effort, he sunk into silence. About half an hour afterwards he attempted again to speak, but was unable; he pressed my hand feebly, and his eyes closed for ever, while the irradiation of a gentle smile passed away from his lips.

Margaret, what comment can I make on the untimely extinction of this glorious spirit? What can I say, that will enable you to understand the depth of my sorrow? All that I should express would be inadequate and feeble. My tears flow; my mind is overshadowed by a cloud of disappointment. But I journey towards England, and I may there find consolation.

I am interrupted. What do those sounds portend? It is midnight; the breeze blows fairly, and the watch on the deck scarcely stir. Again; there is a sound as of a human voice, but hoarser; it comes from the cabin where the remains of Frankenstein still lie. I must arise, and examine. Good night, my sister.

Great God! what a scene has just taken place! I am yet dizzy with the remembrance of it. I hardly know whether I shall have the power to detail it; yet the tale which I have recorded would be incomplete without this final and wonderful catastrophe.

I entered the cabin, where lay the remains of my ill-fated and admirable friend. Over him hung a form which I cannot find words to describe; gigantic in stature, yet uncouth and distorted in its preparations. As he hung over the coffin, his face was concealed by long locks of ragged hair; but one vast hand was extended, in color and apparent texture like that of a mummy. When he heard the sound of my approach, he ceased to utter exclamations of grief and horror, and sprung towards the window. Never did I behold a vision so horrible as his face, of such loathsome, yet appalling hideousness. I shut my eyes involuntarily, and endeavored to recollect what were my duties with regard to this destroyer. I called on him to stay.

He paused, looking on me with wonder; and again turning towards the lifeless form of his creator, he seemed to forget my presence, and every feature and gesture seemed instigated by the wildest rage of some uncontrollable passion.

"That is also my victim!" he exclaimed; "in his murder my crimes are consummated; the miserable series of my being is wound to its close! Oh, Frankenstein! generous and self-devoted being! what does it avail that I now ask thee to pardon me? I, who irretrievably destroyed thee by destroying all thou lovedst. Alas! he is cold; he may not answer me."

His voice seemed suffocated, and my first impulses, which had suggested to me the duty of obeying the dying request of my friend, in destroying his enemy, were now suspended by a mixture of curiosity and compassion. I approached this tremendous being: I dared not again raise my looks to his face, there was something so scaring and unearthly in his ugliness I attempted to speak, but the words died on my lips. The monster continued to utter wild and incoherent self-reproaches. At length I gathered resolution to address him, in a pause of the tempest of his passion: "Your repentance," I said, "is now superfluous. If you had listened to the voice of conscience, and heeded the stings of remorse, before you had urged your diabolical vengeance to this extremity, Frankenstein would yet have lived."

"And do you dream?" said the dæmon; "do you think that I was then dead to agony and remorse? He," he continued, pointing to the corpse, "he suffered not more in the consummation of the deed; oh! not the ten-thousandth portion of the anguish that was mine during the lingering detail of its execution. A frightful selfishness hurried me on, while my heart was poisoned with remorse. Think ye that the groans of Clerval were music to my ears? My heart was fashioned to be susceptible of love and sympathy; and, when wrenched by misery to vice and hatred, it did not endure the violence of the change without torture, such as you cannot even imagine.

"After the murder of Clerval, I returned to Switzerland, heart-broken and overcome. I pitied Frankenstein; my pity amounted to horror: I abhorred myself. But when I discovered that he, the author at once of my existence and of its unspeakable torments, dared to hope for happiness; that while he accumulated wretchedness and despair upon me, he sought his own enjoyment in feeling and passions from the indulgence of which I was forever barred, then omnipotent envy and bitter indignation filled me with an insatiable thirst for vengeance. I recollected my threat and resolved that it should be accomplished. I knew that I was preparing for myself a deadly torture; but I was the slave, not the master of an impulse, which I detested, yet could not disobey. Yet when she died!—nay, then I was not miserable. I had cast off all feeling, subdued all anguish to riot in the excess of my despair. Evil thenceforth became my good. Urged thus far, I had no choice but to adapt my nature to an element which I had willingly chosen. The completion of my demonical design became an insatiable passion. And now it is ended; there is my last victim!"

I was at first touched by the expressions of his misery; yet when I called to mind what Frankenstein had said of his powers of eloquence and persuasion, and when I again cast my eyes on the lifeless form of my friend, indignation was rekindled within me. "Wretch!" I said, "it is well that you come here to whine over the desolation that you have made. You throw a torch into a pile of buildings, and when they are consumed you sit among the ruins, and lament the fall. Hypocritical fiend? if he whom you mourn still lived, still would he be the object, again would he become the prey, of your accursed vengeance. It is not pity that you feel; you lament only because the victim of your malignity is withdrawn from your power."

"Oh, it is not thus—not thus," interrupted the being; "yet such must be the impression conveyed to you by what appears to be the purport of my actions. Yet I seek not a fellow-feeling in my misery. No sympathy may I ever find. When I first sought it, it was the love of virtue, the feelings of happiness and affection with which my whole being overflowed, that I wished to be participated. But now, that virtue has become to me a shadow, and that happiness and affection are turned into bitter and loathing despair, in what should I seek for sympathy? I am content to suffer alone, while my sufferings shall endure; when I die, I am well satisfied that abhorrence and opprobrium should load my memory. Once my fancy was soothed with dreams of virtue, of fame, and of enjoyment. Once I falsely hoped to meet with beings, who, pardoning my outward form, would love me for the excellent qualities which I was capable of bringing forth. I was nourished with high thoughts of honor and devotion. But now vice has degraded me beneath the meanest animal. No crime, no mischief, no malignity, no misery, can be found comparable to mine. When I call over the frightful catalogue of my deeds, I cannot believe that I am he whose thoughts were once filled with sublime and transcendant visions of the beauty and the majesty of goodness. But it is even so; the fallen angel becomes a malignant devil. Yet even that enemy of God and man had friends and associates in his desolation; I am quite alone.

"You, who call Frankenstein your friend, seem to have a knowledge of my crimes and his misfortunes. But in the detail which he gave you of them, he could not sum up the hours and months of misery which I endured, wasting in impotent passions. For while I destroyed his hopes, I did not satisfy my own desires. They were for ever ardent and craving; still I desired love and fellowship, and I was still spurned. Was there no injustice in this? Am I to be thought the only criminal, when all human kind sinned against me? Why do you not execrate the rustic who sought to destroy the saviour of his child? Nay, these are virtuous and immaculate beings? I, the miserable and the abandoned, am an abortion, to be spurned at, and kicked, and trampled on. Even now my blood boils at the recollection of this injustice.

"But it is true that I am a wretch. I have murdered the lovely and the helpless; I have strangled the innocent as they slept, and grasped to death his throat who never injured me or any other living thing. I have devoted my creator, the select specimen of all that is worthy of love and admiration among men, to misery; I have pursued him even to that irremediable ruin. There he lies, white and cold in death. You hate me; but your abhorrence cannot equal that with which I regard myself. I look on the hands which executed the deed; I think on the heart in which the imagination of it was conceived, and long for the moment when they will meet my eyes, when it will haunt my thoughts, no more.

Fear not that I shall be the instrument of future mischief. My work is nearly complete. Neither your's nor any man's death is needed to consummate the series of my being, and accomplish that which must be done; but it requires my own. Do not think that I shall be slow to perform this sacrifice. I shall quit your vessel on the ice-raft which brought me hither, and shall seek the most northern extremity of the globe; I shall collect my funeral pile, and consume to ashes this miserable frame, that its remains may afford no light to any curious and unhallowed wretch, who would create such another as I have been. I shall die. I shall no longer feel the agonies that consume me, or be the prey of feelings unsatisfied, yet unquenched. He is dead who called me into being; and when I shall be no more, the very remembrance of us both will speedily vanish. I shall no longer see the sun or stars, or feel the winds play on my cheeks. Light, feeling, and sense, will pass away; and in this condition must I find my happiness. Some years ago, when the images which this world affords first opened upon me when I felt the cheering warmth of summer, and heard the rustling of the leaves and the chirping of the birds, and these were all to me, I should have wept to die; now it is my only consolation. Polluted by bitter crimes, and torn by the bitterest remorse, where can I find rest but in death?

"Farewell! I leave you, and in you the last of human kind these eyes will ever behold. Farewell, Frankenstein! If thou wert yet alive, and yet cherished a desire of revenge against me, it would be better satiated in my life than in my destruction. But it was not so; thou didst seek my extinction, that I might not cause greater wretchedness; and if yet, in some mode unknown to me, thou hast not yet ceased to think and feel, thou desirest not my life for my own misery. Blasted as thou wert, my agony was still superior to thine; for the bitter stings of remorse may not cease to rankle in my wounds until death shall close them for ever.

"But soon," he cried, with sad and solemn enthusiasm, "I shall die, and what I now feel be no longer felt. Soon these burning miseries will be extinct. I shall ascend my funeral pile triumphantly, and exult in the agony of the torturing flames. The light of that conflagration will fade away; my ashes will be swept into the sea by the winds. My spirit will sleep in peace; or if it thinks, it will not surely think thus. Farewell."

He sprung from the cabin-window, as he said this, upon the ice-raft which lay close to the vessel. He was soon borne away by the waves, and lost in darkness and distance.

THE END.

CATALOGUE

OF

INTERESTING BOOKS.

Just Published and for Sale by

HENRY G. DAGGERS, No. 30 Ann-street, New-York.

Who takes this occasion to assure Agents and Dealers that no one of his publications will ever, in any case, be sold for less than the first prices mentioned in this Catalogue. There will be but one uniform retail and wholesale price.

I.

THE NUN; OR, LIFE IN A CONVENT—By one of the Sisterhood. This is a romance of great beauty and remarkable interest, being the genuine production of a young lady who witnessed the scenes she so vividly describes. It will be read with the greatest interest by both the religious and secular classes, 25 cents.

II.

LAWRIE TODD; OR, THE SETTLERS IN THE WOODS. BY JOHN GALT, ESQ. Author of the Ayrshire Legatees, Southenan, &c., with an original Preface by GRANT THORBURN, Esq., the original Lawrie Todd. This is pronounced on all sides the most excellent novel of its distinguished author. Mr. Thorburn's preface is quaint and curious. 25 cents.

III.

POOR JACK. BY CAPTAIN MARRYAT, Author of Peter Simple, Jacob Faithful, Midshipman Easy, &c., with several appropriate engravings. But a few copies are left of this popular and thrilling story of a sailor's life. It is its author's latest novel. 25 cents.

IV.

MOUNT SOREL; OR, THE HEIRESS OF THE DE VERES, by the Author of Two Old Men's Tales, Tales of the Woods and Fields, &c. A romance of the purest character, which every father should recommend to his children, and husbands to their wives. 12½ cents.

V.

THE WONDERFUL ADVENTURES OF BARON MUNCHAUSEN.—To which is added an acconnt of his veracious visit to America. This most mendacious of travelling-books—which is universally quoted, and without reading which no scholar can be considered to have completed his classical education—is running over with fun. 12½ cents

VI.

THE MYSTERIES OF PARIS, translated by HENRY C. DEMING, Esq.—This is a new edition of this correct, complete, elegant, and eloquent version of Eugene Sue's greatest romance. The price is the same as Town's incomplete, abridged, and faulty translation, published by the Harpers. 50 cents.

VII.

THE BOOK OF BRITISH BALLADS, edited by S. C. HALL, Esq., with an original introduction and preliminary remarks to each ballad by PARK BENJAMIN.—This neat and elegant collection comprises all the ballads (all the finest in the language) contained in the two large and very expensive volumes published in England. It is a book without which no library can be considered complete, since it comprises a most important department of English romantic literature. 37½ cents.

VIII.

FOREST LIFE. By Mrs. MARY CLAVERS, (C. M. Kirkland,) Author of "A New Home," &c. &c. Few writers have elicited more sincere admiration than this lady. Her sketches of Western life in all its phases are admirable. There is a quiet vein of mingled humor and simplicity pervading her books, which has seldom been surpassed. The present book was originally published at $1.25. This is an elegant though cheap edition, in two volumes. 50 cents.

IX.

A PLEA FOR WOMAN. By Mrs. HUGO REID. With an Original Introduction, by Mrs. C. M. KIRKLAND (Mary Clavers.) A more impressive and sensible exposition of the true claims of the female sex than this, has never been pub lished. Every woman, who has a heart and mind too, should possess it; and every man, who loves and respects the better and brighter half of creation, should commend this admirable work. 25 cents.

X.

THE ADVENTURES OF LITTLE MARY. By UNCLE PETER PARLEY. This is a most charming story for grown people as well as children. It is pronounced delightful by all who have read it. 12½ cents.

XI.

MESMERISM AND ITS OPPONENTS, with a Narrative of Cases. By GEORGE SANDBY, Jr., M. A. Now that the subject of Human Magnetism is attracting universal attention, a book of so high and true a character as this must be read with great interest. No fact is better established than that of the beneficial influence exercised by Mesmerism in many cases of disease. Several interesting and remarkable cures are related in this book, the authenticity of which does not admit of a doubt. 25 cents.

XII.

LIFE IN THE NEW WORLD.—This is by far the best work of the celebrated SEATSFIELD, who is spoken of in a late number of Blackwood's Magazine, as one of the greatest authors of modern Germany. 50 cts.

XIII.

PUSS IN BOOTS, versified by MRS. FRANCIS OSGOOD, with beautiful Lithographic Illustrations by GEORGE ENDICOTT; after designs by OTTO SPECKTER.—This is by far the most beautiful picture-book for the young ever published in the United States. It is pronounced on all hands quite equal, if not superior, to the English edition issued by John Murray. Neatly bound in silk and gold, and stamped. 50 cents.

XIV.

HANS OF ICELAND, translated from the French of VICTOR HUGO, Author of the Hunchback of Notre Dame, &c. &c.—A more brilliant, exciting and powerful romance than this has seldom appeared even in France. 25 cents.

XV.

THE POEMS OF SIR EDWARD BULWER LYTTON, Author of Pelham, Zanoni, The Lady of Lyons, &c. This is the only collection extant of the beautiful poetical productions of this distinguished novelist, dramatist and poet. They are eminently worthy of his genius. A very neat volume, suitable for a present to a friend or lover—neatly bound. 50 cents.

XVI.

MARTIN CHUZZLEWIT, by CHARLES DICKENS, Esq., author of the Pickwick Papers, Nicholas Nicklebv, the Christmas Carol. Complete in one volume. 25 cents.

XVII.

RICHLIEU IN LOVE, a comedy in five acts.—This comedy is very interesting: it was prohibited to be played by the Lord Chancellor in London on account of its political allusions. Printed very neatly 12½ cents.

XVIII.

FAMILIAR LETTERS ON CHEMISTRY, by JUSTIN LIEBIG, author of Animal Magnetism, &c.—This little work is replete with the most important elementary instructions, and should be read by every one who desires to possess a general acqnaintance with this most interesting science 6¼ cents.

XX.

THE BIBLE IN SPAIN, by the REV GEORGE BORROW.—A more charming book of travels than this—one more replete with good feeling, wit, and the emanations of a happy and brilliant spirit, canuot be found in the whole range of English letters. 25 cents.

XIX.

ZINCALI, by the REV. GEORGE BORROW, author of the Bible in Spain.—The interest of this work is much much greater than that of a romance, being full of the most thrilling and heart-touching stories of the gipsey race. 25 cents.

XXI.

FATHER GORIOT; OR, SCENES OF LIFE IN PARIS. By H. DE BALZAC. Translated from the French by Edward S. Gould. De Balzac is one of the greatest of modern French novelists—and there is no story of his extant, more characteristic of his strange and fascinating style. 25 cents.

XXII.

KATE IN SEARCH OF A HUSBAND. No lady should venture to accept a lover without first having read this delightful and instructive story. 12½ cents.

XXIII.

PHILIP IN SEARCH OF A WIFE.—No gentleman should dream of choosing a wife without attentively studying the adventures of Philip. 12½ cents.

XXIV.

THE EMIGRANT'S TRUE GUIDE.—This valuable little work comprises advice and instruction in every stage of the voyage to America; such as choice of a ship; provisions and clothing for the voyage; hints during the voyage; custom-house laws; what to do on landing; interesting anecdotes, &c. Also, information which the emigrant needs on arrival, &c. &c. 25 cents.

XXV.

A MEMOIR OF MRS. JUDITH S. GRANT, late Missionary to Persia, by the Hon. W. W. CAMPBELL.—This is a biography of one, whose life was beautiful, and whose death was worthy of a Christian. 25 cents.

XXVI.

WILHEM'S CELEBRATED METHOD OF TEACHING SINGING IN CLASSES. This work is a standard in Great Britain, and universally approved of by musicians. It must become a text book in our schools. 25 cents.

XXVII.

GRIMALDI, THE CLOWN, by CHARLES DICKENS, Esq. (Boz,) author of Pickwick Papers, Oliver Twist, Christmas Carol, &c. Boz never wrote a more funny and diverting book than these humors in the life of a comic actor. 25 cents.

www.ingramcontent.com/pod-product-compliance
Lightning Source LLC
LaVergne TN
LVHW021049110826
845150LV00001B/19